RUSSIA IN THE AGE OF PETER THE GREAT

LINDSEY HUGHES

YALE UNIVERSITY PRESS
NEW HAVEN AND LONDON

Set in Garamond by Fakenham Photosetting, Norfolk
Printed in Great Britain by St Edmundsbury Press

Library of Congress Cataloging-in-Publication Data

Hughes, Lindsey, 1949–
    Russia in the age of Peter the Great/Lindsey Hughes.
    Includes bibliographical references and index.
    ISBN 0-300-07539-1 (hbk.)
    ISBN 0-300-08266-5 (pbk.)
    1. Russia—History—Peter I, 1689–1725.   2. Peter I, Emperor of Russia, 1672–1725.
    I. Title.
DK131, H84   1998
947´. 05—dc21

                                                                98–18667
                                                                CIP

A catalogue record for this book is available from the British Library.

10 9 8 7 6 5 4 3 2

To the memory of my mother,
Audrey Ethel Hughes, née *Bond (1926–65)*

Contents

Illustrations

Illustrations are printed by courtesy of the individuals and institutions listed. Where no acknowledgement is given, materials are from the author's collection.

GRM: Gosudarstvennyi Russkii Muzei, St Petersburg. Buildings are in St Petersburg unless otherwise indicated.

Preface

All Russia is your statue, transformed by you with skilful craftsmanship.
(Feofan Prokopovich, 1726)[1]

The groundwork for this book was laid in 1991 in St Petersburg. Shortly before I left England in September of that year, just a few weeks after the abortive *coup* to overthrow Mikhail Gorbachev, the inhabitants of what was then Leningrad voted in a referendum to restore the city's old name. During the next two months I saw the name 'St Petersburg' reinstated on the title-pages of newspapers, in tourist brochures, on maps, and in TV weather reports. The seventh of November found me in front of the Winter Palace, where crowds had gathered to celebrate not the October Revolution but the restoration of the city's name. A series of speakers addressed the assembled crowds on such themes as the reopening of Peter the Great's 'window on Europe' and the Petrine origins of the armed forces. Across the River Neva in the Peter–Paul fortress, the site of the city's foundation, a twelve-gun salute was fired, and flares were lit, both on the ramparts and on the lighthouses on the spit of Vasil'evsky Island, recalling the waterscape of Peter's time and his love of boats, fireworks and artillery.

Yet it was not all adulation, for together with new freedoms came freedom to question and criticize the sacred cows of the past. Alongside the celebration of Peter's legacy appeared a less festive train of thought, which traced the Stalinist 'administrative command' system back to Peter, the alleged inaugurator of disastrous attempts to introduce 'happiness by coercion' for the sake of higher ideals, be they the 'good of the State' or the 'triumph of Communism'. The new criticism was embodied in a controversial statue of Peter by the sculptor Mikhail Shemiakin, set up in front of the cathedral of Sts Peter and Paul in June 1991, which portrays the tsar as an ill-formed freak, unnaturally small-headed and spindly limbed, a menacing and uncomfortable figure. Local people apparently dislike it. Muscovites, it seems, are even less enthusiastic about the unashamedly triumphalist 165 foot monument to the tsar by the sculptor Tseretelli on the banks of the Moskva River. The reaction of the citizens of Greenwich to their own statue of Peter, a gift from the Russian Embassy to mark the tercentenary of the tsar's visit to London in 1698, is still awaited.

One of the best-known contemporary images of Peter, Carlo Bartolomeo Rastrelli's 1723 bronze bust, is also the work of a sculptor. But how many people have looked below the hero's stern gaze to the plaques on the bronze armour, one of which depicts Peter as Pygmalion, putting the finishing touches to a statue of New Russia, a crowned, armed woman bearing orb and sceptre? That creation—Peter's New Russia—is the subject of this book. But it is not my intention to ignore the sculptor entirely. In early Soviet times Marxist historians tried to leave Peter out of the picture, handing the laurels instead to the common people, or 'material forces'. Under Stalin, 'forces' ceded the limelight to selected heroes from the imperial past, Peter included, whose feats of strength and courage were harnessed to the Communist cause and the war effort. Clearly, both approaches have their limitations. Peter was neither the puppet of impersonal economic interests nor some kind of superman who steered Russia 'solely by his own direction', as was claimed in a speech celebrating Russia's victory over Sweden in 1721. Any historian of Peter's reign must attempt to strike a balance—not an easy task with a tsar whom some Russian citizens, in this post-Soviet era of opinion polls, continue to nominate as their 'most admired' ruler and whom others regard as the devil incarnate.

What, apart from Peter himself, then, should be included in a book on his reign? The table of contents suggested by Peter in 1722 to the compilers of an official history reads as follows: 'Write about what was done during this past war and what regulations were made on civil and military order, statutes for both branches of the services and the ecclesiastical regulation; also about the building of fortresses, harbours, fleets of ships and galleys and various manufactures, and about construction work in St Petersburg, on Kotlin Island and in other places'.[2] This limited range of subjects is unlikely to satisfy readers today, even if it reflects Peter's own practical priorities. The present study gives due weight to the 'traditional' areas of foreign policy, army and navy, economy and government, but it also examines neglected topics such as women and the intriguing subject of pretence and disguise. It challenges half-truths and misconceptions about the Petrine era, such as the assumption that Peter attempted—and even achieved—the 'secularization' of Russian life, that foreign influence and input predominated in most spheres of activity, that Peter's concerns were more or less exclusively practical and pragmatic, and that he believed in and practised 'meritocratic' policies. The final sections include a character study of Peter (which some readers may wish to turn to first), and examine his inner circle—family, friends, and aides—without whom it is difficult to grasp the political and social dynamics of a country ruled by an absolute monarch, where personal relations exert more influence than institutions or ideologies. The book ends with a selective review of attitudes towards Peter and his legacy, from his contemporaries to the present day.

My response to a Russian friend (not a history specialist) who dismissed the idea of this book with the words 'I can't imagine what else there is to say about Peter I' was that there is plenty more to be said about Peter's Russia, especially to English-speaking readers, who still lack an accessible, detailed scholarly study of early eighteenth-century Russia. At the same time, I am aware of my debt to those predecessors—among them M. S. Anderson and B. H. Sumner—whose shorter surveys may well continue to be preferred to this weighty tome, not to mention Robert K. Massie, whose vivid, although not uniformly scholarly, life and times continues to inspire many a student to investigate the subject further. In particular, I acknowledge Reinhard Wittram's two-volume *magnum opus*, long out of print and sadly inaccessible to the vast majority of students and even many scholars in the English-speaking world by virtue of its length and language. Writing thirty years after Wittram, I have had access to much new literature, both primary and sec-ondary, but I do not claim to have superseded Wittram in those areas which were his particular forte. I acknowledge all my predecessors in the study of Petrine Russia, whose works are selectively cited throughout.

This rich scholarly heritage notwithstanding, I have returned wherever possible to primary sources, including well-used ones such as the *Complete Collection of Russian Laws* (*Polnoe sobranie zakonov*), which sometimes yielded fresh insights. The sources for Peter's reign are both voluminous and frag-mentary. Some types of record (e.g., diplomatic correspondence, government papers) are so well represented that for a survey of Peter's reign one can at best select documents to provide a flavour. Others are relatively scant: for example, private (as opposed to business and service) correspondence and Russian memoirs, especially from the non-noble and female sections of the popu-lation.[3] The disappointing dearth of private Russian writings—no Samuel Pepys or John Evelyn to provide wry insights into public events and personal *mores*—is in part compensated by the comparative wealth of accounts by the many foreigners who came to Russia as a direct result of Peter's policies, men such as Friedrich Christian Weber, Georg Grund, Charles Whitworth, Friedrich von Bergholz, and Just Juel. One must, of course, be alive to the dangers of prejudice (all tended to regard Russia as 'uncivilized'), ignorance (especially of the Russian language), and a tendency to reproduce the remarks of their predecessors, as far back as the sixteenth-century traveller Sigismund von Herberstein. Even so, foreigners were able to travel around and mix with Russians much more freely in Peter's Russia than in Muscovy. On topics as diverse as Russian women, architecture, fashions, drinking habits, and dwarfs, their observations, treated with due caution, are invaluable.

At once the most colourful and the most contentious of sources are the home-grown 'anecdotes' about Peter, of which there are three main collec-tions. Andrei Nartov, Peter's instructor in wood turnery, left 162 stories about the tsar and his associates, which he claims were collected from Peter himself, from 'trustworthy persons', and from his own observations. In fact, the stories were probably put together by Nartov's son, Andrei junior, using both his father's notes (mainly from the last four years of Peter's life, when Nartov spent much time in his company) and published sources.[4] The German scholar Jacob Stählin (1709–85), professor of eloquence and poetry at the St Petersburg Academy of Sciences, was in touch with many people who had known and worked for Peter. His collection of 117 anecdotes, 'taken from the mouths of distinguished persons in Moscow and St Petersburg', was first published in Leipzig in 1785. Stählin took pains to verify his sources and to choose suitable informants, of whom about half were foreigners. He usually wrote down their recollections as soon as he returned home, anxious to preserve the memoirs from oblivion and for posterity.[5] But he was far from neutral. Along with other German scholars who came to Russia as a result of Peter's educational policies, he praised Peter as a bringer of enlightenment, and sometimes suppressed his cruder aspects. The third collector, Ivan Ivanovich Golikov (1735–1801), son of a merchant, published a thirty-volume history of Peter's reign as well as a set of anecdotes. After falling into debtors' prison, Golikov was pardoned in a general amnesty proclaimed to celebrate the opening of the new equestrian statue to Peter in St Petersburg in 1782. He fell upon his knees before the monument, and vowed to give thanks for his salvation by devoting his life to writing about Peter. His anecdotes, like Nartov's and Stählin's, were collected from people who had known Peter or from handed-down reminiscences.[6]

The wide scope of my own work allowed only selective use of archives, although those which I visited have proved invaluable. The most important collections were the continuation of the *Letters and Papers of Peter the Great* for the years 1714–25, in *fond* 270 of the archive of the St Petersburg Institute of Russian History of the Academy of Sciences, *fond* 9 (archive of Peter's Cabinet office) in RGADA in Moscow, and selected *fondy* from the Manuscripts Department in the Russian National Library in St Petersburg. Thanks are due to staff in all these reading-rooms, especially Sergei Iskul' in the Institute of History. The British Library and the library of the School of Slavonic and East European Studies provided essential back-up at all stages of the work. Among the other institutions to which I am indebted are the British Academy, which funded a study visit to Russia in 1991, the SSEES conference fund, the Institute of Russian History in Moscow, the Summer Research Laboratory of the University of Illinois at Champaign–Urbana, and the Renval Institute in Helsinki, whose invitation to a visiting lectureship in 1992 allowed me to use the excellent resources of the Slavic Library in Helsinki.

I acknowledge the help (with the usual proviso about all remaining errors being my own) of colleagues who read all or part of the manuscript: Roger Bartlett, Paul Dukes, David Kirby, David Moon, and especially Isobel de Madariaga, whose study of the reign of Catherine the Great was an inspiration and a model for my own work. Evgeny Anisimov, the leading Russian expert on the Petrine era, gave generous advice, inspiration, and encouragement, as well as materials from his own library. My Russian friends Elena Stolbova (Russian Museum, St Petersburg) and Galina Andreeva (Tret'iakov Gallery, Moscow) allowed access behind the scenes of their respective galleries, and Elena Mozgovaia (Academy of Arts) shared her ideas about sculpture. Other Russians who were generous with their knowledge were Dmitry Serov, Iury Bespiatykh, and Pavel Sedov. This book has also benefited

in more ways than I can enumerate from discussions with friends and colleagues in the Study Group on Eighteenth-Century Russia and with my
students in SSEES, whose successors I hope will read it. Caroline Newlove,
secretary of the SSEES History Department, helped me with many practical
chores, not least printing out the voluminous manuscript. Closer to home, I
would not wish to forget the cats Sophie, Catherine, and Tablet, who often
helped calm frayed nerves, and the supportive hero of most authors' prefaces,
the spouse, Dr Jim Cutshall, who gave constant encouragement and also
helped to compile the index.

I am especially grateful to Robert Baldock at Yale University Press in
London for his unwavering support and encouragement.

Lindsey Hughes
May 1998

Note on Transliteration, Abbreviations, Weights and Measures

I have made certain assumptions in the writing of this book. One is that the majority of readers will not know Russian. Apart from certain transcribed terms, quotations from Russian sources are given in translation, in most cases my own, although reliable published translations are used, where available, to allow readers access to the whole. Full references to Russian sources are included in the notes.

Russian spellings have been transcribed using a modified Library of Congress system, with further adaptations in the interest of readability in the main text. Feminine proper names, which in Russian have alternative spellings, with a soft sign (Mar'ia) or *-iia* (Mariia), are all rendered simply as *-ia*: e.g., Maria, Natalia, Evdokia. The *-ii* and *-yi* endings of masculine proper names are rendered with *-y*: e.g., Dmitry. Names of famous individuals are given in their English equivalent. These include Peter (Petr), Catherine (Ekaterina), Sophia (Sof'ia or Sofiia), and Alexis (Aleksei). In transcribed citations and bibliographical titles, however, the original is rendered in full.

Abbreviations used in Notes and Bibliography

Bantysh-Kamensky	N. N. Bantysh-Kamensky, *Obzor vneshnikh snoshenii Rossii s derzhavami inostrannymi*, 4 vols (M, 1894–1902)		*Obshchestve Istorii i Drevnostei Rossiiskikh*
		CMRS	*Cahiers du monde russe et soviètique*
		CSP	*Canadian Slavonic Papers*
Bergholz, 1721–3	F. W. von Bergholz, *Dnevnik kammer-iunkera Berkhgol'tsa, vedennyi im v Rossii v tsarstvovanie Petra Velikogo s 1721–1725 g.* (M, 1857–60)	DPPS	*Doklady i prigovory sostoiavshiesia v pravitel'stvuiushchem Senate v tsarstvovanie Petra Velikogo*, vols 1–6 (SPb., 1880–1901)
Bergholz, 1724–5	Ibid., 3rd edn. (M, 1902–3)	DR	*Dvortsovye razriady*, 4 vols (SPb., 1852–5)
BL	British Library	Garrard	J. Garrard, ed., *The Eighteenth Century in Russia* (Oxford, 1973)
BP	*Bumagi imp. Petra I, izdannye akademikom A. Bychkovym* (SPb., 1873)	GPB OR	Gosudarstvennaia Publichnaia Biblioteka (now Rossiiskaia National'naia Biblioteka), Otdel Rukopisei
CASS	*Canadian-American Slavic Studies*		
Chteniia	*Chteniia v Imperatorskom*		

Grebeniuk — V. P. Grebeniuk, ed., *Panegiricheskaia literatura petrovskogo vremeni* (M, 1979)

Grund — Georg Grund, *Bericht über Russland in den Jahren 1705–1710. Doklad o Rossii v 1705–1710 gg.*, ed., introd., and trans. Iu. N. Bespiatykh (SPb., 1992)

IPS — *Istoriia pravitil'stvuiushego Senata za 200 let*, vols 1 and 5 (SPb., 1911)

IZ — *Istoricheskie zapiski*

JGO — *Jahrbücher für Geschichte Osteuropas*

Juel — Just Juel, 'Iz zapisok datskogo poslannika Iusta Iulia', *Russkii arkhiv*, 30 (1892), no. 1: 273–304, no. 2: 35–74, 319–33, 495–518, no. 3: 5–48, 113–50, 241–62.

Kaliazina — N. G. Kaliazina and G. N. Komelova, *Russkoe iskusstvo Petrovskoi epokhi* (L, 1990)

Korb — J.-G. Korb, *Diary of an Austrian Secretary of Legation at the Court of Czar Peter the Great*, trans. and ed. Count MacDonnell, 2 vols (London 1863/1968)

Kurakin — B. A. Kurakin, 'Gistoriia o tsare Petre Alekseeviche', in *Rossiiu podnial na dyby*, vol. I (M, 1987), 353–91

L — Leningrad

LOI — Leningradskoe Otdelenie Instituta Istorii Akademii Nauk, arkhiv (now Sankt-Peterburgskii filial Instituta Rossiiskoi Istorii Rossiiskoi Akademii Nauk)

M — Moscow

MERSH — *Modern Encyclopedia of Russian and Soviet History*, 59 vols and supplements (Gulf Breeze, Fla, 1976

MIGO — *Materialy dlia istorii Gangutskoi operatsii*, 3 vols (Petrograd, 1914)

MLC — *The Muscovite Law Code (Ulozhenie) of 1649*, part I: Text and Translation, trans. and ed. R. Hellie (Irvine, Calif., 1988)

Muller — A. Muller, ed. and trans., *The Spiritual Regulation of Peter the Great* (Seattle, 1972)

Nartov — L. N. Maikov, *Rasskazy Nartova o Petre Velikom* (SPb., 1891)

NS — New Style (Gregorian Calendar)

OS — Old Style (Julian Calendar)

PiB — *Pis'ma i bumagi Imperatora Petra Velikogo*, 1: 1689–1701 (1887); 2: 1702–3 (1889); 3: 1704–5 (1893); 4: 1706 (1900); 5: 1707, Jan.–June (1907); 6: 1707, July–Dec. (1912); 7(i): 1708, Jan.–June (1918); 7(ii): 1708, Jan.–June, notes (1946); 8(i): 1708, July–Dec. (1948); 8(ii): 1708, July–Dec., notes (1951); 9(i): 1709 (1950); 9(ii): 1709, notes (1952); 10: 1710 (1956); 11(i): 1711, Jan.–June (1962); 11(ii): 1711, July–Dec. (1964); 12(i): 1712 (1975); 12(ii): 1712 (1977); 13(i): 1713, Jan.–June (1992)

Pososhkov	Ivan Pososhkov, *The Book of Poverty and Wealth*, ed. and trans. A. Vlasto and L. Lewitter (London, 1987)		the Great. A Reign Begins 1689–1703, trans. L. A. J. Hughes (Gulf Breeze, Fla., 1994)
		SPb.	St Petersburg
PRO SP	Public Record Office, State Papers	SR	*Slavic Review*
PRP	*Pamiatniki russkogo prava*, VIII: *Zakonodatel'nye akty Petra I* (M, 1961)	SSEES	School of Slavonic and East European Studies
		Stählin	J. Stählin, *Podlinnye anekdoty o Petre Velikom* (L, 1990)
PSZ	*Polnoe sobranie zakonov rossiiskoi imperii*, vol. 2: 1649–1688; vol. 3: 1689–1699; vol. 4: 1700–1712; vol. 5: 1713–19; vol. 6: 1720–1722; vol. 7: 1723–1727 (SPb., 1830)	*Tezisy*	*Vserossiiskaia nauchnaia konferentsiia 'Kogda Rossiia molodaia muzhala s geniem Petra', posviashchennaia 300-letnemu iubileiu otechestvennogo flota. Tezisy dokladov* (Pereiaslavl'-Zalessky, 1992).
PZh	*Pokhodnye zhurnaly Petra I 1695–1726* (SPb., 1853–5) (one vol. per year, separately paginated)	Tumansky	F. O. Tumansky, ed., *Sobranie raznykh zapisok i sochinenii*, parts 8 and 10 (SPb., 1788)
RGADA	Rossiiskii (formerly Tsentral'nyi) gosudarstvennyi arkhiv drevnikh aktov		
RGIA	Rossiiskii Gosudarstvennyi Istoricheskii Arkhiv, St Petersburg	*VI*	*Voprosy istorii*
		Weber	F. C. Weber, *The Present State of Russia*, 2 vols (London, 1722–3)
RPR	*Rossiia v period reform Petra I*, ed. N. Pavlenko (M, 1973)	*WOR*	M. di Salvo and L. Hughes, eds, *A Window on Russia: Papers from the Fifth International Conference of the Study Group on Eighteenth-Century Russia, Gargnano, 1994* (Rome, 1996)
RR	*Russian Review*		
Sbornik	*Sbornik vypisok iz arkhivnykh bumag o Petre Velikom*, 2 vols (M, 1872)		
SEER	*Slavonic and East European Review*		
SGECRN	*Study Group on Eighteenth-Century Russia Newsletter*	*ZA*	A. Voskresensky, *Zakonodatel'nye akty Petra I*, vol. 1 (M&L, 1945)
SIRIO	*Sbornik imperatorskogo rossiiskogo istoricheskogo obshchestva*, 148 vols (SPb., 1867–1926)	*ZhMNP*	*Zhurnal ministerstva narodnogo prosveshcheniia*
Soloviev	S. M. Soloviev [Solov'ev], *History of Russia*, vol. 26: *Peter*	*200-letie*	*200-letie Kabineta ego imp. velichestva 1704–1904* (SPb., 1911)

Russian archival references follow Russian practice: f. = fond (collection), otd. = otdelenie (section), op. = opis' (section), d. = delo (file), kn = kniga (book), l. = list (folio) (ll. = listy)

Russian Currency

Units of Russian currency referred to in the text had the following value (expressed in copecks):

1 rouble = 100 copecks
1 poltina = 50 copecks
1 polupoltina = 25 copecks
1 grivna = 10 copecks
1 altyn = 3 copecks
1 denga = 0.5 copecks

Foreign—1 efimok (Joachimsthaler: silver coin) = about 1 rouble (the value fluctuated)
1 chervonets (ducat: gold coin) = about 3 roubles

Weights and Measures

1 chetvert (dry measure) = 126.39 pounds (about 8 bushels)
1 chetverik = 1/8th of a chetvert = 15.8 pounds
1 pud = 36.113 pounds (16.38 kilos)
1 arshin = 28 inches (72.12 cm)
1 vershok = 1.75 inches (4.445 cm)
1 verst = 0.663 miles (1.067 km)
1 sahzen = 7 feet (2.133 metres)

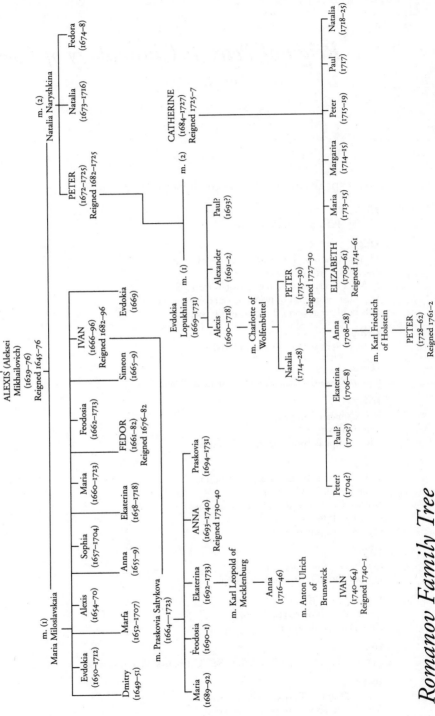

Romanov Family Tree

Reign of Peter I: Chronology of Events

Dates are given according to the Julian (OS) calendar.

1672
30 May Peter born in Moscow.

1682
27 Apr. Death of Tsar Fedor. Peter proclaimed tsar.
15–17 May Strel'tsy revolt.
29 May Declaration of regency of Tsarevna Sophia.
25 June Coronation of Ivan and Peter as joint tsars.
17 Sept. Execution of Prince Ivan Khovansky.

1684
22 May Renewal of treaty with Sweden.

1686
6 May Russo–Polish Treaty of 'Permanent Peace'.

1687
First Crimean Campaign:
June Golitsyn retreats.
July Mazepa becomes hetman of Ukraine.

1689
27 Jan. Peter marries Evdokia Lopukhina.
Second Crimean Campaign:
21 May Golitsyn withdraws from Perekop.
6–7 Aug. Peter flees from Moscow.
Sept. Overthrow of Sophia.

1690
19 Feb. Birth of Tsarevich Alexis.
17 Mar. Death of Patriarch Joachim.

1692
1 Sept. Beginning of year 7200.
Nov. Peter seriously ill.

1693
Summer Peter's first visit to White Sea. Celebrates New Year (1 Sept.) in Archangel.

1694
25 Jan. Death of Tsaritsa Natalia.
Sept. Kozhukhovo 'mock' manoeuvres.

1695

Summer First Azov campaign.
Nov. Moscow nobles ordered to register their sons for service.

1696

29 Jan. Death of Tsar Ivan.
Second Azov campaign:
May Russians besiege Azov.
18 July Azov surrenders to Russians.
Sept.–Oct. Triumphal parade in Moscow.
26 Oct. Decree on shipbuilding.
Nobles sent abroad to study shipbuilding and navigation.
Tsykler plot.

1697

Jan. Alliance with Austria and Venetian Republic.
10 Mar. Grand Embassy leaves Moscow.
Apr. Peter insulted in Riga. Accession of Charles XII to the Swedish throne.
Aug. Peter in Brandenburg and Hanover.
Spends rest of year in Holland.
Treaty of Ryswick (ends War of the League of Augsburg).

1698

10 Jan.–22 Apr. Peter in England. Returns to Holland.
June Strel'tsy revolt.
June–July Peter in Vienna.
Peter recalled to Moscow. Meets Augustus II en route.
25 Aug. Peter arrives back in Moscow.
26 Aug. Shaves off boyars' beards.
Sept. Beginning of trials and executions of strel'tsy.
25 Dec. Austro–Ottoman Peace of Carlowicz. Russia begins negotiation of separate peace.

1699

30 Jan. Chamber of Burgomasters established (1700 renamed *ratusha*).
May Evdokia forced to take the veil.
July/Oct. Peter joins anti-Swedish coalitions with Denmark and Saxony (Augustus II).
27 Oct. Petitions to tsar banned.
Nov. Enlistment of volunteers into Guards regiments.
30 Nov. Order of St Andrew instituted.
10 Dec. Decree on conscription.
19–20 Dec. Decrees on calendar reform.

1700

1 Jan. First new New Year celebrations.
4 Jan. Decrees on foreign dress.
Feb. Augustus declares war on Sweden and invades Livonia.
27 Feb. Law Code Commission established.
3 July Russia signs 30-year truce with Turkey.
19 Aug. Russia declares war on Sweden. Danish–Swedish Treaty of Travendal.
16 Oct. Death of Patriarch Adrian.
19 Nov. Swedes defeat Russians at Narva.
16 Dec. Appointment of Stefan Iavorsky as 'overseer' of patriarchate.
Grigory Talitsky denounces Peter as Antichrist.

1701

Jan. Monastery department created.

Feb. Peter meets Augustus at Birsen.
May William III offers mediation.
July Swedes occupy Courland.
Sept. Grand Alliance of Maritime Powers and Austria.
30 Dec. Russian victory at Erestfer.
School of Mathematics and Navigation founded in Moscow.

1702

Jan. Wedding of jester Filat Shansky.
3 Apr. Decree on betrothals.
May War of Spanish Succession begins.
9 July Charles XII defeats Saxons and Poles at Klistów. Occupies Cracow.
July Russian victory at Hummelshof.
25 Aug. Sheremetev takes Marienburg.
11 Oct. Russians take Nöteborg and rename it Schlüsselburg.
Künst's theatre founded in Moscow.

1703

2 Jan. First issue of Moscow *Vedomosti*.
1 May Russian victory at Nienschants.
16 May Founding of St Petersburg.
Petrovsky ironworks founded.

1704

Jan. Augustus deposed.
2 July Stanislas Leszczynski declared (Swedish-backed) king of Poland.
4 July Death of Tsarevna Sophia.
13 July Russians take Dorpat (Tartu).
Aug. Russo–Polish treaty recognizes Augustus as rightful king.
9 Aug. Russian victory at Narva.
16 Aug. Ivangorod captured.
28 Sept. Peter writes to Menshikov from his 'capital' St Petersburg.
5 Oct. Aleksei Makarov becomes Privy Cabinet secretary.
Nov. Admiralty yard founded in St Petersburg.
22 Dec. Decree on dress reissued.
Dec. Moscow Narva victory parade.
First son of Peter and Catherine born (Peter: dies in infancy).
First silver rouble and first copper copeck minted.
First general inspection of young nobles.

1705

16 Jan. Decree on beards.
19 Jan. Decree on protection of forests.
20 Feb. Conscription edict.
Peter occupies Grodno.
July/Aug. Outbreak of Astrakhan revolt.

1706

Feb. Swedes defeat Saxons at Fraustadt.
Mar. Russians evacuate Grodno. Sheremetev quells Astrakhan revolt.
May First ship made wholly in Admiralty yard launched.
Aug. Swedes take Dresden and Leipzig.
28 Sept. Peace of Altranstädt. (Augustus renounces crown.)
18 Oct. Russo–Saxon victory at Kalisz.
Nov.–Dec. Council of war at Żolkiev.

1707
Jan. Peter issues orders for scorched earth policy.
Aug. Decrees on defence of Russian borders against Swedes.
Oct. Prince Dolgoruky murdered. Bulavin revolt.

1708
Jan. Charles reaches Grodno.
27 Jan. Birth of Anna Petrovna.
Mar. Renaming of regiments by district. First book printed in civil script.
May Don Cossacks admit Bulavin to Cherkassk.
3 July Russians defeated at Holowczyn.
7 July Bulavin killed.
Russian victories at Dobroe (29 Aug.) and Raevki (10 Sept.). Charles's army turns south.
28 Sept. Russian victory at Lesnaia.
Oct. Mazepa defects to Swedes.
31 Oct. Menshikov burns Baturin.
6 Nov. Peter's manifesto to the Ukrainian people.
11 Nov. Ivan Skoropadsky elected hetman. Mazepa excommunicated.
Dec. Formation of *gubernii* (provincial reform).
Russian troops withdraw from Baltic garrisons. Dorpat burnt.

1709
Jan. Swedes freeze to death at Hadyach.
12 Apr. Swedes defeated at Sokolki.
Apr.–May Peter in Azov.
14 May Zaporozhian Sich stormed by Russians.
May Swedes besiege Poltava.
27 June Battle of Poltava.
30 June Remnant of Swedish army surrenders at Perevolochna. Charles escapes.
9 Oct. Peter meets Augustus in Torun. New Russo–Polish alliance.
10 Oct. Treaty with Prussia.
11 Oct. Treaty with Denmark.
18 Dec. Birth of Elizabeth Petrovna.

1710
Jan. Renewal of peace treaty with Turks.
2 Feb. Capture of Elbing.
Feb. Census ordered.
Capture of Baltic fortresses: 14 June, Viborg; 4 July, Riga; 8 Aug., Dünamünde; 14 Aug., Pernau; 8 Sept., Kexholm; 13 Sept., Oesel; 29 Sept., Reval.
31 Oct. Wedding of Anna Ioannovna and Duke of Courland.
9 Nov. Turks declare war.
14 Nov. Dwarf wedding.
Building in St Petersburg of Summer and Winter Palaces, Alexander Nevsky monastery, Menshikov's palace.

1711
22 Feb. Russia declares war on Turkey. Peter establishes Senate.
2 Mar. Decrees on duties of the Senate.
6 Mar. Peter declares Catherine his official consort.
Peter appeals to Orthodox subject peoples in the Balkans.
12–13 Apr. Council of war in Slutsk. Russia signs treaty with hospodar of Moldavia.
May St Petersburg press opens.
23 June Peter arrives on the River Pruth.
9 July Turks defeat Russians at Pruth.

12 July Peace treaty. Russia surrenders Azov and Taganrog.
14 Oct. Wedding of Alexis and Charlotte.
10 Dec. Statute on War Commissariat.
'History of the Swedish War' begun.

1712
19 Feb. Peter and Catherine married.
5 Apr. Iusuf–Pasha pact confirms Treaty of Pruth.
Building of Peter–Paul cathedral begun.

1713
Russian Project for Peace in the North.
Apr. Peace of Utrecht ends War of Spanish Succession.
23 Apr. Beginning of Finnish campaign.
May Russians capture Helsinki.
13 June Treaty of Adrianople with Turkey.
June Menshikov besieges Tönningen fortress.
30 Aug. Peter enters Åbo.
Sept. Menshikov takes Stettin.
Senate moves to St Petersburg.

1714
23 Mar. Law on Single Inheritance.
May Second Legislative Commission.
May Prince A. Bekovich-Cherkassy's mission to Khiva.
27 July Naval Battle of Hangö.
Kunstkamera founded. Peterhof begun.
Education for nobles made compulsory. 1,000 nobles forced to move to St Petersburg.

1715
Jan. Wedding of Prince-Pope Zotov.
28 Jan. Revision of provincial organization.
12 Oct. Birth of Peter Alekseevich.
29 Oct. Birth of Peter Petrovich.
Oct. Peter outlaws production of narrow cloth.
27 Nov. Post of General Inspector of Senate created.
Ivan Nikitin paints Peter's portrait. Naval Academy founded in St Petersburg.

1716
Feb. Peter begins major tour of Western Europe.
31 Mar. Military Statute issued.
Apr. Fall of Wismar.
8 Apr. Marriage of Ekaterina Ioannovna to Duke Karl of Mecklenburg.
May Peter meets kings of Prussia and Denmark.
26 Aug. Peter sends ultimatum to Alexis from Copenhagen. Alexis flees to Vienna.
Peter assumes temporary command of British, Danish, Dutch and Russian fleets.
Massacre of Russians at Khiva.

1717
2 Jan. Birth and death of Pavel Petrovich.
Apr.–June Peter in Paris.
10 July Peter invites Alexis to return to Russia.
4 Oct. Alexis agrees to return.
Oct. Peter returns to Russia.
11–15 Dec. Creation of collegiate boards (*kollegii*).

First edition of *Honourable Mirror of Youth*. Publication of Shafirov's *Discourse Concerning the Just Causes of the War between Sweden and Russia*.

1718
10 Jan. Installation of new prince-pope.
31 Jan. Alexis arrives in Moscow.
3 Feb. Manifesto depriving Alexis of the succession.
8 Feb. Double tax imposed on Old Believers.
13 Feb. Decree on Monsters.
Mar. 'Suzdal' affair'. Stepan Glebov and Alexander Kikin executed.
May Fick's memorandum on provincial reform.
May Åland peace congress opens.
June Trial of Alexis in St Petersburg.
24 June Alexis condemned to death.
26 June Alexis dies.
27–9 June Celebration of Poltava and Peter's name-day.
30 June Funeral of Alexis.
19 Aug. Birth of Natalia Petrovna.
Nov. Beginning of new provincial reform on Swedish model.
26 Nov. Decree on Assemblies.
30 Nov. Charles XII killed in Norway.
22 Dec. Edict on petitions.
Beginning of establishment of provincial court system.

1719
Jan.–Feb. Instructions to *voevody* and other provincial officials.
Mar. Ulrika-Eleonora crowned queen of Sweden.
25 Apr. Death of Peter Petrovich.
24 May Russians capture Swedish ships off Oesel Islands.
29 May Creation of fifty provinces.
July Russian fleet bombards Swedish mainland.
Summer Russian troops leave Mecklenburg under pressure from Hanover.
Sept. Åland congress breaks up.
9 Dec. New Law Code Commission established.
10 Dec. Privileges of the College of Mines issued.
11 Dec. Regulation of the *Kamer-kollegiia*.
New census ordered (first *reviziia*: completed 1723).

1720
13 Jan. Naval Statute issued.
28 Feb. General (*Kollegiia*) Regulation.
3 May Frederick I crowned king of Sweden.
27 July Russian naval victory at Grengham.
Publication of Prokopovich's Primer.

1721
First of four years of crop failure.
16 Jan. Chief Magistracy created.
18 Jan. Factory owners allowed to buy serfs.
25 Jan. Ecclesiastical Regulation.
14 Feb. Holy Synod founded. Printing-houses subordinated to Synod.
15 Apr. Ban on sale of individual serfs.
Apr. Russo–Swedish peace talks begin at Nystad.
30 Aug. Peace of Nystad.
Sept. Wedding of Prince-Pope Buturlin.

22 Oct. Peace celebrations in St Petersburg. Peter takes title 'emperor'.
Nov. Major flood in St Petersburg.
18 Dec. Nystad celebrations begin in Moscow.

1722

12 Jan. Non-senators appointed college presidents.
24 Jan. Table of Ranks created.
Feb. Office of chief herald created.
5 Feb. Law on Succession to the Throne. Office of *reketmeister* established.
Feb. Grand carnival in Moscow.
Mar. Ban on removal of fugitive workers from factories.
5 Apr. Admiralty Regulation. Supplement to the Naval Statute.
6 Apr. Passports required for peasants' travel. Order on wearing traditional dress with beards.
17 Apr. Edict to the Senate on obeying the laws.
27 Apr. Office of procurator-general created. Revised duties of the Senate.
11 May Office of over-procurator of Synod created.
17 May Supplement to the Ecclesiastical Regulation.
9 June Instructions to Moscow chief of police.
7 July War declared against Persia.
7 Aug. *Justice of the Monarch's Right* published.
25 Sept. Derbent captured.

1723

Financial crisis. Peasants allowed to register in urban communities.
Spring Fears of Turkish attack.
Aug. Russians capture Baku.
30 Aug. Ceremonies to greet the 'grandfather of the Russian navy'.
Sept. Carnival in St Petersburg.
12 Sept. Peace treaty with Persia.
25 Oct. Edict on crimes against the State and against the person.
5 Nov. Decree on law court procedures.
Dec. Regulation of Manufacturing College.

1724

Poll tax collected for first time.
Jan. Draft plan for Academy of Sciences. Execution of *Ober-Fiskal* Nesterov and other officials.
20 Jan. Decree on reporting breaches of regulations.
31 Jan. Protective tariff issued.
1 Feb. Funeral of dwarf Iakim.
11 Feb. Russia and Sweden sign defensive alliance.
7 May Catherine crowned as empress-consort.
June Regimental districts introduced in provinces.
30 Aug. Ceremonial interment of relics of St Alexander Nevsky.
Nov. Betrothal of Anna Petrovna and Duke Karl of Holstein.
8 Nov. Arrest of William Mons.
16 Nov. Execution of Mons.

1725

28 Jan. Death of Peter. Accession of Catherine I.
10 Mar. Peter buried in St Petersburg.

The Petrine Year

Major festivals and anniversaries publicly celebrated in Russia after the end of the Great Northern War

1 January	*New Year's Day (from 1700)
6 January	Epiphany
February/March/April	Shrovetide/Easter
3 February	*SS Simeon & Anna: name-day of Anna Petrovna
19 February	*Marriage of Peter and Catherine (1712)
5 April	*Catherine's birthday
7 May	*Catherine's coronation (1724)
30 May	*Peter's birthday (St Isaac of Dalmatia)
25 June	*Coronation of Ivan and Peter (1682)
27 June	*Battle of Poltava (1709) (St Samson)
29 June	*SS Peter and Paul: name-day of Peter and his grandson
27 July	*Battles of Hangö (1714) and Grengham (1720) (St Panteleimon)
9 August	*Battle of Narva (1704) (St Matthew)
26 August	*St Natalia: name-day of Natalia Alekseevna (Peter's sister, died 1716), Natalia Alekseevna (Peter's granddaughter, born 1714), Natalia Petrovna (Peter's daughter, born 1718)
30 August	*St Alexander Nevsky (changed from 23 Nov.); official anniversary of Peace of Nystad (1721); 'grandfather of the Russian navy' (1723)
5 September	*St Elizabeth: name-day of Elizaveta Petrovna
28 September	*Battle of Lesnaia (1708) ('the Mother of Poltava')
11 October	*Battle of Nöteborg (1702)
18 October	Battle of Kalisz (1706)
24 November	*St Catherine: name-day of Empress Catherine; institution of Order of St Catherine (1714)
30 November	*St Andrew (day of Knights of Order of St Andrew from 1699)
25 December	Christmas/Yuletide

* included in *Kalendar' ili mesiatsoslov khristianskii po staromu shtiliu ili izchisleniiu, na leto ot voploshcheniia Boga Slova 1725* (M, 1724)

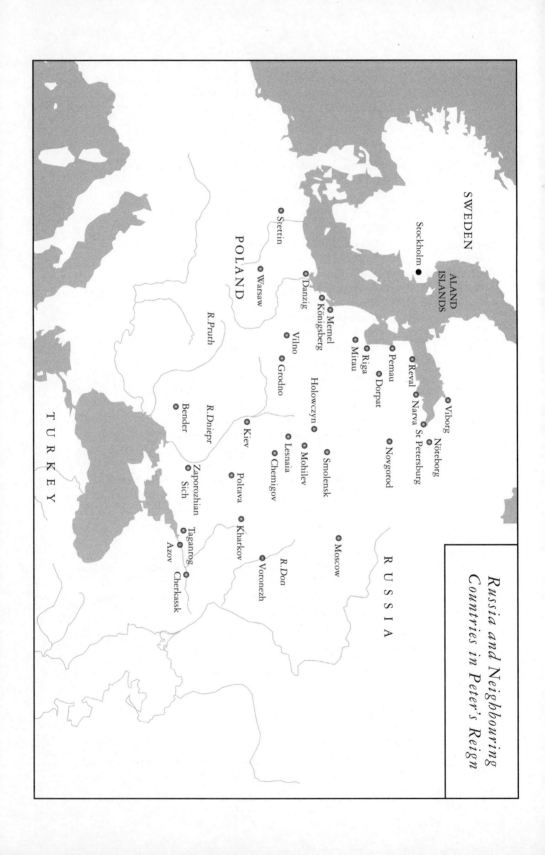

Russia and Neighbouring
Countries in Peter's Reign

SWEDEN

ALAND
ISLANDS

Stockholm

POLAND

Stettin

Warsaw

Danzig

Memel

Königsberg

Vilno

Grodno

Holowczyn

Mirau

Riga

Dorpat

Pernau

Reval

Narva

St Petersburg

Nöteborg

Viborg

Novgorod

R.Pruth

R.Dniepr

Bender

Kiev

Lesnaia

Mohilev

Chernigov

Smolensk

Zaporozhian
Sich

Poltava

Kharkov

Moscow

Taganrog

Azov

Cherkassk

Voronezh

R.Don

RUSSIA

TURKEY

I

Beginnings

I. RUSSIA IN 1672

> Russian Bethlehem, Kolomenskoe,
> You delivered Peter to the light!
> You the start and source of all our joy,
> Where Russia's greatness first burned clear and bright.[1]

Peter Alekseevich Romanov was born in or near Moscow at around one in the morning on Thursday 30 May 1672. A patron saint's 'measuring' icon of the apostle Peter made shortly after his birth showed the infant to be nineteen and a quarter inches long.[2] The future emperor's exceptional height was clearly prefigured, but the time and place of his birth, like much else in his life, have been the subject of controversy. For want of concrete evidence locating it elsewhere, the event may be placed in the Kremlin in Moscow, but legends persist, as in the verse by the poet Sumarokov above, that Peter was born in the village of Kolomenskoe to the south of Moscow, where his father had built a wooden palace, or even in Preobrazhenskoe, which later became Peter's favourite retreat and the base for his new guards regiments, formed from the 'play' troops of his boyhood.[3] As for the date, most sources accept 30 May, as did Peter himself by honouring St Isaac of Dalmatia, whose feast falls on that day. But at least one record gives 29 May, following the old Russian practice of starting the new day not at midnight but at dawn.[4] In those countries which had adopted the Gregorian calendar (which Russia did only in 1918) the date was ten days ahead of those which still followed the older, Julian calendar, and 30 May fell on 9 June. Contemporary Russian chroniclers (using not arabic numerals but Cyrillic letters with numerical equivalents) recorded the year of Peter's birth as not 1672 but 7180, following the Byzantine practice of numbering years from the notional creation of the world in 5509 BC. The year 7181 began on 1 September 1672, which, following the usage of Constantinople, marked the start of the Muscovite new year.

These peculiarities of time and record keeping provide a foretaste of the different customs observed in the Russia where Peter was born and the West into which he was later to forge a 'window'. On the eve of the new century, in December 1699, Peter himself decreed that official records would henceforth adopt calendar years from the birth of Christ in the manner of 'many

European Christian nations'. When he died on 28 January 1725, there were no arguments about how the date should be recorded.[5] It is appropriate that questions of time and chronology should arise at the outset of Peter's life, for he was to be obsessed with time and its passing, believing that 'wasted time, like death, cannot be reversed'.[6] Traditionalists denounced the tsar for tampering with 'God's time' by changing the calendar. There were even rumours that the Peter who was to adopt the title 'Emperor' in 1721 was not the Peter who had been born in 1672. We shall return to these matters later, but let us take a closer look at the Russia into which Peter was born.

Peter's parents had been married for less than eighteen months when he arrived. On 22 January 1671 nineteen-year-old Natalia Kirillovna Naryshkina married forty-two-year-old Tsar Alexis (Aleksei) Mikhailovich, whose first wife Maria Miloslavskaia had died in 1669 at the age of forty-three after giving birth to her thirteenth child, a girl who did not survive.[7] Given a more robust set of male half-siblings, Peter might never have come to the throne at all. His father's first marriage produced five sons, but in 1672 only two were still alive. The heir apparent, Fedor, born in 1661, had delicate health, while Ivan, born in 1666, was mentally and physically handicapped. There were six surviving half-sisters: Evdokia, Marfa, Sophia, Ekaterina, Maria, and Feodosia, ranging in age from twenty-two to ten. They were not regarded as direct contenders for power: no woman had ever occupied the Muscovite throne in her own right, and the policy of keeping the royal princesses unmarried minimized the complications of power-seeking in-laws and inconvenient offspring through the female line. The practice of keeping well-born women in virtual seclusion also meant that they were unknown to the public.[8]

When Tsar Alexis died at the age of forty-seven in January 1676, Fedor succeeded him without the formal appointment of a regent, even though he was only fourteen. (Rumours of attempts to place three-year-old Peter on the throne in his stead may be discounted.[9]) Twice in the next six years Peter narrowly escaped being pushed further down the ladder of succession. Fedor's first wife, Agafia Grushetskaia, and her newborn son Il'ia died in July 1681. His second wife, Marfa Matveevna Apraksina, was left a widow after only two months of marriage, by Fedor's death in April 1682. Rumours that she might be pregnant proved unfounded. But this is to leap ahead. In 1672 there was every prospect of Tsar Alexis continuing to rule for many years, and a fair chance, given infant mortality rates, that Peter would not survive for long. Modern readers will treat with scepticism the intriguing story recorded by one of Peter's early biographers to the effect that the royal tutor and court poet Simeon Polotsky predicted Peter's rule and future greatness by the stars on the supposed day of his conception, 11 August 1671.[10]

Many pages of print have been devoted to Peter's childhood and adolescence.[11] His first two decades will be considered here only briefly, in order to give a context for the changes which he later forced upon Russia—the main subject of this book. I will begin by dispelling a few misconceptions, such as that Peter's early environment was closed and stultifying, dominated solely by Orthodox ritual and concepts. In fact, seventeenth-century Romanov child-rearing practices did not exclude 'modern' elements. For example, Peter's interest in military affairs was stimulated in the nursery, where he, like his elder brothers before him, played with toy soldiers, cannon, bows and arrows, and drums. Military affairs were the right and proper concern of a tsar almost from the cradle. His father had gone to war with his troops, as Peter was well aware and was proud to recall in later life. On the other hand, Peter's prowess as a soldier, virtually from the cradle (a contemporary compared him to the young Hercules, who strangled serpents), has been greatly exaggerated. The myth that Peter was already a cadet at the age of three has been refuted: in fact, at that age, Peter still had a wet-nurse.[12] Toy weapons were supplemented by spades, hammers, and masons' tools, which no doubt fostered Peter's love of mechanical crafts. The fiercest of Peter's boyhood passions—his love of ships and the sea—is at first sight harder to explain. Why should a boy raised in a virtually land-locked country with no tradition of seafaring have developed such a passion? It is even said that as a boy Peter had a dread of water.[13] But Russia's naval inexperience should not be exaggerated. Most major Russian towns were situated on rivers, which small craft plied. Russians may not have been expert sailors on the high seas, but they knew how to navigate inland waters, and Russian peasant navigators had long sailed the northern coastline.[14] Peter did not see the open sea until he was twenty-one, but there was no lack of stimuli to the imagination closer to hand: toy boats, maps and engravings, and, what he himself identified as the spark which lit the flame, the old English sailing dinghy, the 'grandfather of the Russian fleet', which he discovered in the outhouse of a country estate.[15] The fact that it should have found its way to Moscow is not so surprising when one considers that English sea-going vessels had been docking on the White Sea since the 1550s, and that Tsar Alexis had commissioned Dutch shipwrights to build a small fleet on the Caspian Sea in the 1660s.

In some respects, however, Peter's introduction to the wider world actually lagged behind that of his half-siblings. His brothers Fedor and Alexis (who died in 1670), and even his half-sister Sophia, were taught by the Polish-educated monk Simeon Polotsky, who gave instruction in Latin, Polish, versification, and other elements of the classical syllabus. Polotsky died in 1680, before he had the chance, had it been offered, to tutor Peter. His protégé, Silvester Medvedev, was at daggers drawn with the conservative patriarch, Joachim, who, as adviser to Peter's mother, would scarcely have recommended a suspect 'Latinizer' as the tsarevich's tutor. Peter thus received indifferent tuition from Russians seconded from government chancelleries; they included Nikita Zotov and Afanasy Nesterov, an official in the Armoury, whose names first appear in records as teachers round about 1683.[16] Not only did Peter's education lack scholarly content; it also seems to have been deficient in basic discipline. His prose style, spelling, and handwriting bore signs of lax methods for the rest of his life.[17] It should be added that there was no question of Peter receiving his education from a Muscovite university graduate or even from the product of a local grammar school or its equivalent. There were no universities in Muscovite Russia and no public schools, apart from some training establishments for chancellery staff in the Kremlin. In fact, clerks (*d'iaki* and *pod'iachie*) and clerics were the only two orders of Muscovite society who were normally literate, many parish priests being only barely so.

The inadequacies of Peter's primary education were later offset by practical skills learned from foreigners, whom he was able to encounter in Moscow thanks to the policies of his predecessors. Foreigner-specialists first started arriving in Muscovy in significant numbers during the reign of Ivan IV (1533–84). Their numbers increased when Peter's grandfather, Tsar Michael (1613–45), reorganized certain Russian infantry regiments along foreign lines. In 1652 Tsar Alexis set aside a separate area of Moscow called the 'New Foreign' or 'German' Quarter to accommodate military, commercial, and diplomatic personnel. It was here that Peter encountered officers such as Patrick Gordon, Franz Lefort, and Franz Timmerman, his teachers and companions in the 1680s and 1690s. Residents of the Foreign Quarter also made their mark on Russian élite culture. From the 1650s several foreign painters were employed in the royal Armoury workshops. Alexis is the first Russian ruler of whom we have a reliable likeness, his daughter Sophia the first Russian woman to be the subject of secular portraiture.[18] It was the Foreign Quarter which in 1672 supplied the director and actors for Russia's first theatrical performance. Unlike portraiture, however, which quickly became more widespread, theatricals were discontinued after Alexis's death.[19] During Sophia's regency (1682–9) Huguenots were offered sanctuary in Russia, Jesuits were admitted to serve Moscow's foreign Catholic parish, and invitations were issued to foreign industrialists and craftsmen. In the 1670s and 1680s foreigners were no longer a rarity on the streets of Moscow, and were also well represented in commercial towns on the route from the White Sea port of Archangel.

Of course, Moscow was not the whole of Russia, any more than a few relatively outward-looking individuals in the Kremlin were representative of Moscow society as a whole. Most Muscovites, from the conservative boyars who rubbed shoulders with them to the peasants who rarely encountered one, regarded foreigners as dangerous heretics, and viewed foreign 'novelties' and fashions with intense suspicion and even terror. During the reign of Peter's immediate predecessors, foreigners were still in Russia on sufferance, tolerated as a necessary evil. The building of the new Foreign Quarter in 1652 was actually an attempt to concentrate foreigners and their churches in a restricted locality, away from the city centre, where they had lived previously. Patriarch Joachim urged that mercenaries, the most indispensable of foreign personnel, be expelled, and non-Orthodox churches demolished. Russian culture was prevented from falling further under foreign influence by strict controls. For example, publishing and printing remained firmly in the hands of the Church. It is a striking statistic that in the whole of the seventeenth century fewer than ten secular titles came off Muscovite presses, which were devoted mainly to the production of liturgical and devotional texts. There were no Russian printed news-sheets, journals or almanacs; no plays, poetry or philosophy in print, although this lack was partly compensated by popular literature in manuscript, a flourishing oral tradition, news-sheets from abroad (albeit restricted to the use of personnel in the Foreign Office), and foreign books in the libraries of a few leading nobles and clerics. Presses in Kiev, Chernigov, Vilna, and other centres of Orthodoxy supplemented the meagre output of Moscow printers. Russians were still clearly differentiated from Western Europeans by their dress, although a number were tempted by Polish influence to don Western fashions in private. According to Tsar Alexis's decree of 1675, 'Courtiers are forbidden to adopt foreign, German (*inozemskikh i nemetskikh*) and other customs, to cut the hair on their heads and to wear robes, tunics and hats of foreign design, and they are to forbid their servants to do so.'[20]

The 'courtiers' to whom this warning was addressed formed the upper echelons of Russia's service class. Sometimes loosely referred to as 'boyars', roughly the equivalent of the Western aristocracy,[21] they belonged to noble clans residing in and around Moscow. The upper crust were the 'men of the council' (*dumnye liudi*), the so-called boyar duma, which in the seventeenth century varied in number from 28 to 153 members.[22] Those in the top rank were the boyars proper (*boiare*), next the 'lords in waiting' (*okol'nichie*), followed by a smaller group dubbed 'gentlemen of the council' (*dumnye dvoriane*), and a handful of 'clerks of the council' (*dumnye d'iaki*). All enjoyed the privilege of attending and advising the tsar. Membership of the two top groups was largely hereditary. Unless there were contrary indicators (e.g., serious incapacity or disgrace) men from leading families generally became boyars in order of seniority within their clan. Their numbers were swelled by royal in-laws (marrying a daughter to the tsar or one of his sons usually boosted a family's fortunes) and by a handful of men of lower status who were raised by royal favour. The council's participation in decision making is indicated by the formula for ratifying edicts: 'the tsar has decreed and the boyars have affirmed' (*tsar' ukazal i boiare prigovorili*). Nobles immediately below the 'men of the council' (often younger aspirants to the grade) bore the title 'table attendant' (*stol'nik*), a reference to duties which they had once performed and in some cases still did. Below them were 'attendants' (*striapchie*), Moscow nobles (*dvoriane moskovskie*), and 'junior attendants' (*zhil'tsy*). In peacetime Moscow nobles performed a variety of chancellery and ceremonial duties. In wartime they went on campaign as cavalry officers. On duty, be it military or civil, they bore their court ranks: *boiarin, okol'nichii, stol'nik* and so on; there was no differentiation by office.

In 1672 commissions, appointments, and other placings, such as seating at important banquets, were still in theory governed by the code of precedence, or 'place' system (*mestnichestvo*), which determined an individual's position in the hierarchy of command by calculations based on his own and his clan's service record and his seniority within his clan. It was considered a great dishonour to be placed below someone who, regardless of ability, was deemed to merit a lower 'place'. Such an insult gave grounds for an appeal to the tsar. Increasingly, *mestnichestvo* was suspended in order to allow the Crown a freer hand in appointing officers. For some campaigns it was ordered that military rolls be drawn up 'without places' (*bez mest*).

With the exception of members of the élite sent to serve as provincial governors (*voevody*), outside Moscow the ruler relied on a larger group of the 'middle servicemen', provincial gentry (*gorodovye dvoriane*), and 'junior servicemen' (*deti boiarskie*, literally and misleadingly 'children of boyars') to perform policing duties and swell the ranks of the army in wartime. All the categories described above, it should be repeated, were counted among the élite and enjoyed certain privileges, the first of which was exemption from tax and labour burdens (*tiaglo*). The second was the right to land and serfs. Most of the Moscow élite owned both inherited estates (*votchiny*) and service lands (*pomest'ia*), the latter, in theory, granted and held on condition of service, but increasingly passed from generation to generation. The peasants living on both *votchina* and *pomest'e* holdings were serfs, the property of their landlords, who could freely exploit their labour (in the form of agricultural work and other duties) and collect dues (in money and kind). It should be noted, however, that nobles were not automatically supplied with serfs. Some of the top families owned tens of thousands of peasants distributed over dozens of estates, whereas many in the provincial *deti boiarskie* category owned only one or two peasant households, and in some cases worked their own plots.[23] The Muscovite Crown also deployed non-noble servicemen (*sluzhilye liudi po priboru*). Men in this category were subject to a service, not a tax requirement, but they could not own serfs. They included the strel'tsy ('musketeers'), who formed army units in wartime and did escort and guard duty in peacetime, carrying on small businesses and trades when off duty; artillerymen (*pushkari*), and postal drivers (*iamshchiki*).[24] Civilian personnel in the non-noble service category included secretaries and clerks (*d'iaki, pod'iachie*), the backbone personnel of the government chancelleries.

Most of the non-noble residents of Russia's towns were bound to their communities by tax obligations, apart from a handful of chief merchants (*gosti*), who dealt in foreign trade. Including merchants of the second and third grades (*gostinnye* and *sukonnye sotni*) and the mass of clerks, artisans, and traders, or 'men of the *posad*' (*posadskie liudi*), the total registered male urban population in the 1670s has been estimated at 185,000.[25] In addition, substantial numbers of peasants resided temporarily in towns, which also had shifting populations of foreigners and vagrants, but lacked many of the native professional categories—bankers, scholars, scientists, doctors, schoolteachers, lawyers, and actors—to be found in most contemporary Western European towns of any size.

If townspeople were less numerous and played a less prominent role in

Muscovy than they did in Western European countries, the opposite was probably true of church personnel. The Russian clerical estate was divided into 'white' (secular) and 'black' (monastic) clergy, the former group, consisting of parish priests and deacons, who were obliged to marry. The prelates—the patriarch, metropolitans, bishops, and abbots of monasteries—were drawn from the celibate black clergy, who also formed the monastic rank and file. The ecclesiastical estate enjoyed considerable privileges. Apart from the royal family and the nobles, only they could own serfs (although, strictly speaking, peasants were attached to monasteries and churches, not individuals). They were exempt from taxation. They had access to church courts. But the rural clergy, like the lesser rural gentry, were often barely differentiated in wealth and education from the mass of the population.

This brings us to the masses themselves: rural dwellers engaged in working the land—*pashennye liudi*. Roughly 50 per cent were serfs or bonded peasants, living on lands owned by the royal family (*dvortsovye*), nobles (*pomeshchichie*), or the Church (*tserkovnye*). The rest were 'State' peasants (*gosudarsvennye*), not bound to any one landlord, but obliged to pay taxes to the State and perform labour duties as required—for example, by providing transport and carrying out forestry and road work. All were eligible for military service, which freed them from obligations to their former owners. Another group of 'unfree' persons were slaves, who entered into contracts of bondage with richer people (usually, but not invariably, nobles) in return for loans and support. It has been calculated that as much as 10 per cent of the population may have fallen into this category.[26]

Thus, in 1672, it was possible to divide the great majority of people in Muscovy into those who performed service (*sluzhilye liudi*), those who paid taxes (*tiaglye liudi*), and those who served the Church (*tserkovnye liudi*). They included the tsar's non-Russian subjects: various tribespeople who rendered taxes in the form of tribute (*iasak*, often in furs) or did occasional military service. Some of the tsar's subjects fell outside these estates: these included so-called wandering people (*guliashchie liudi*) unattached to any locality or category, who were either incapable of performing service or paying taxes—for example, cripples and 'fools in Christ'—or who wilfully escaped obligations—runaway serfs, deserters, and religious dissidents, of which the biggest category were the Old Believers, protesters against Nikon's church reform of the 1650s. A number set up communities in remote localities out of reach of the government. Cossack communities, consisting originally of refugees from the long arm of government, maintained a variety of links with Moscow, being either bound in service, like the registered Cossacks of Ukraine, intermittently loyal, like the Cossacks of the Don, or persistently hostile, like the Host of the Zaporozhian Sich.

This, then, was the Russia into which Peter was born, a country, on the one hand, deeply rooted in tradition and in many ways very distinct from Western Europe, where Russia was still regarded as a 'rude and barbarous' kingdom, on the other, increasingly open to the influence of Western people and ideas. In the year 1672 the birth of a Russian prince went more or less unnoticed in the rest of Europe, of which Russia was at best a fringe member. There would have been scarcely any speculation about the new prince's eligibility as a marriage partner, since the Muscovite royal family was known to be uninterested in such foreign involvements, although this had not always been the case. The concept of the European community as 'a single, integral system of mutually interdependent states', which came into being after the 1648 Treaty of Westphalia, rested on a Protestant–Catholic balance of power in which Orthodox countries barely figured.[27] But Russia was poised to play an increasingly active role in world affairs. In the reign of Alexis, during the so-called First Northern War (1654–60), it entered the wider sphere of international relations when it was pitted against its old enemies Poland and Sweden. War with Poland began in 1654, as a result of Moscow's provocative acceptance of the allegiance of Ukrainian (Little Russian) Cossacks under their leader Bogdan Khmel'nitsky, who were formerly Polish subjects, and ended in 1667 to Russia's advantage, with Left Bank Ukraine (to the east of the River Dnieper) and Kiev brought under the tsar's rule. But there was no progress during the shorter conflict of 1656–61 with Sweden, which had blocked the way to the Baltic since the 1617 Treaty of Stolbovo removed Moscow's narrow foothold on that sea. At the time Sweden's King Gustav II Adolph boasted that Russia could not even launch a rowing boat on to the sea without Sweden's permission.[28] When Peter was born, Russia's only seaport was Archangel, on the White Sea. In the south, Russia and Poland vied for possession and domination of the steppes with the Turks and the Crimean Tatars, who barred Russia from the Black Sea. Direct conflict was usually with the Tatars, who exacted a heavy toll of prisoners and livestock, as well as demanding and receiving annual tribute, known as 'gifts'. In 1672 the Turks and the Tatars seized parts of Polish (Right Bank) Ukraine, and threatened incursions across the Dnieper into Muscovite territory. It was this crisis which prompted Tsar Alexis to send envoys all over Europe seeking aid for an anti-Turkish league. In 1676 his son Fedor found himself at war with the Turks and the Tatars. After losing the fort at Chigirin on the Dnieper, and fearing a Turkish attack on Kiev, Moscow made an uneasy twenty-year truce with the Tatars at Bakhchisarai, in January 1681.

II.   SOPHIA: THE 1680s

On 27 April 1682 Fedor died childless.[29] The same day, Peter, a month short of his tenth birthday, was declared tsar, on the grounds that his elder half-brother Ivan was 'weak-minded'. Matters might have rested there. Ivan's afflictions evidently precluded him from taking an active role in civil or military affairs. There was no written law of succession to rule out the accession of a younger brother under these circumstances. Observance of primogeniture was a matter of custom rather than constitution. Peter's accession had the support of the patriarch, who intervened in such matters in the absence of mature royal males. But Peter's maternal relatives, the Naryshkins, and their hangers-on, who could expect to enjoy considerable power in Peter's minority and to retain key government posts when he came of age, had not reckoned on a lethal combination of unrest among Moscow's armed guard, the strel'tsy, and the fury of the affronted Miloslavskys, kinsmen of Tsar Alexis's first wife, led by Ivan's sister Sophia, that 'ambitious and power-hungry princess', as a contemporary described her.[30]

The Miloslavskys succeeded in harnessing the strel'tsy, who were ultra-sensitive to rumours of abuses in high places as a result of a series of disputes over management, pay, and conditions dating from Fedor's reign. After two weeks of negotiations, during which the new Naryshkin government made concessions, to the extent of handing over unpopular officers to strel'tsy mobs, a rumour that Tsarevich Ivan had been strangled by his 'ill-wishers' brought rebel regiments to the Kremlin. There on 15–17 May, the strel'tsy settled personal grudges by butchering commanding officers and unpopular officials, and, at the instigation of the Naryshkins' rivals, singled out members of the Naryshkin clan and their associates as 'traitors', and slaughtered them. The victims included Peter's uncle, Ivan Naryshkin (who was accused of trying on the crown), and his mother's guardian, the former foreign minister Artamon Matveev, who was accused of plotting to murder Ivan. In all, about forty persons fell victim to axe and pike. The role in all this of Sophia, Peter's twenty-five-year-old half-sister, has been widely debated.[31] Although there is little hard evidence that she had the 'Machiavellian' tendencies attributed to her by some writers, still less that she plotted to kill Peter and his mother (who remained unharmed, despite being the easiest of targets), the events of April–May 1682 undoubtedly allowed her to champion the legitimate claim to the throne of her brother Ivan and to emerge as regent over a joint tsardom, with Ivan as senior tsar and Peter as junior.

No attempt will be made here to chart the further outbreaks of strel'tsy unrest after the dynastic question had apparently been settled, or to examine the role of Prince Ivan Khovansky in the events of May–September 1682, sometimes referred to as the 'Khovanshchina', which were complicated by the activities of Old Believers, who enjoyed some support from the strel'tsy. We shall be concerned only with those events and features of Sophia's regency which had relevance for Peter's future policies and reforms. The most immediate consequence of the seven-year regency on Peter's own circum-stances was that he was by and large relieved of ceremonial duties, which Sophia was happy to have performed at first by Ivan, who was thus given a prominent, active role in the public eye, and later by herself.[32] It is difficult to overestimate the significance of these seven years for Peter's development. They may be regarded as a sort of 'sabbatical' from the routine burdens of rulership, which allowed him to pursue his own interests (military games and sailing) and to build up a circle of friends and assistants at a slight distance from traditional clan networks. Members of the boyar élite predominated in

Peter's circle, but foreigners and men of lower rank appeared in greater numbers than in the past. Ivan's role as Orthodox figure-head meant that Peter had less contact with the church hierarchy. It should be emphasized that Peter was neither banished nor persecuted. As for the charge that Sophia 'stifled Peter's natural light', rather the opposite was true,[33] although some contemporaries believed that lax supervision and too much contact with foreigners and 'low' types ruined the tsar's character. On occasion he was still required to do ceremonial duty—for example, at ambassadorial receptions and important family anniversaries—but by and large his being out of Moscow suited him as much as it did Sophia. If it had one unfortunate effect, it is that it further alienated Peter from Sophia's chief minister and reputed lover, Prince Vasily Vasil'evich Golitsyn (1643–1714), a man with the sort of talent and vision that Peter could have used, had not hostility towards his sister made it impossible later to employ someone so close to her. Under Golitsyn's direction, the Foreign Office pursued policies which provided both foundations and lessons for Peter's future programme. The major achievement was the 1686 treaty of permanent peace with Poland, which ratified the secession of Kiev and its Right Bank hinterland to Moscow (which had been in dispute since the 1667 Treaty of Andrusovo), and Russian rule over Smolensk, Dorogobuzh, Roslavl', and Zaporozh'e. In return, Russia was to pay the Poles 146,000 roubles indemnity 'out of friendship', to sever relations with Turkey and Crimea 'on account of the many wrongs committed by the Muslims, in the name of Christianity and to save many Christians held in servitude', and to wage war on Crimea. Other clauses included a ban on the persecution of Orthodox Christians in Poland by Catholics and Uniates (thus allowing the tsar a pretext for intervention), permission for Catholics in Russia to hold divine worship (but only in private houses), recognition of royal titles, encouragement of trade, and a pledge to seek the aid of 'other Christian monarchs'.[34] Russian suspicion of Catholics was exploited by Prussian envoys in Moscow, who induced Golitsyn and Sophia to offer sanctuary to Protestant exiles from France. In 1689 commercial treaties were signed allowing Prussia trading rights in Archangel, Smolensk, and Pskov, thereby laying the foundations for future Russo–Prussian co-operation during the 1710s.[35]

Thus Russia joined the Holy League against the Turks, formed in 1684 with papal backing, between Austria and Poland, both of which had lands bordering on the Ottoman Empire, and Venice, Russia's rival at sea, following the relief of the Turkish siege of Vienna in 1683. Russian ambassadors were dispatched all over Europe with appeals for assistance and closer alliance—to Holland, England, Sweden, Denmark, Prussia, France, Spain, Florence, Austria, and Venice.[36] In 1687 and 1689 Vasily Golitsyn led huge armies south to Crimea. On both occasions logistical problems forced the Russian armies to withdraw, on the second occasion with huge losses of men and horses, from thirst and epidemics. Golitsyn's return to Moscow in the summer of 1689, where he was fêted as a hero on Sophia's instructions, gave his opponents an opportunity to undermine both him and Sophia, whose public appearances Peter (prompted by his maternal relatives) had begun to criticize. Peter was well into his majority (Fedor, it will be recalled, was tsar without a regent at the age of fourteen); he was married (in January 1689), and his wife, Evdokia Lopukhina, was pregnant; he had troops at his disposal, notably his own 'play' regiments and foreign officers; and he had the support of the patriarch. In fact, Sophia's rule was doomed from the start, because it could be perpetuated indefinitely only by disposing of Peter. This she seems never seriously to have contemplated, despite ample opportunities. Even the crisis of August 1689, when Peter believed that the strel'tsy were coming to kill him and fled to the Trinity monastery, may have been engineered by Peter's own supporters in order to force a confrontation between Peter and Sophia which they knew she was unlikely to win, given dissatisfaction with the Crimean campaigns, and which Peter, too wrapped up in his own interests, could not be relied upon to precipitate. August–September saw a stand-off between Sophia and her fast-dwindling forces in the Kremlin and Peter's supporters, massed at the Trinity–St Sergius monastery. The brief clash ended in late September, when Vasily Golitsyn was exiled to the north of Russia, and Sophia was locked up in the Novodevichy convent, were she remained until her death in 1704.

For the rest of his life Peter associated Sophia with the dark forces of opposition, even if he blamed most of the active wickedness on her male supporters. The perpetrators of the so-called Tsykler plot to kill Peter in 1696–7 were executed over the exhumed coffin of Ivan Miloslavsky, identified by several contemporaries as the master-mind behind the 1682 rebellion. 'The seed of Ivan Miloslavsky is sprouting,' wrote Peter, when called back to Russia to deal with another strel'tsy revolt in 1698.[37] He apparently recognized Sophia's 'great intelligence', but thought it was overshadowed by 'great malice and cunning'.[38] Engraved portraits depicting her wearing a crown and carrying royal regalia were sought out and destroyed, but many copies survived, along with painted portraits set against the background of the double-headed eagle bearing the seven Virtues on its wings, eloquent testimony both to Sophia's political aspirations and to the new cultural trends which she encouraged. At least one of Peter's successors did not share his view. Catherine the Great wrote of Sophia: 'Much has been said about this princess, but I believe that she has not been given the credit she deserves ... she conducted the affairs of the Empire for a number of years with all the sagacity one could hope for. When one considers the business that passed through her hands, one cannot but concede that she was capable of ruling.'[39]

III.   THE MAKING OF A SOVEREIGN: THE 1690s

There are good reasons for devoting some space to the period between the overthrow of Sophia and Golitsyn and the declaration of war against Sweden in August 1700. The fact that these years have generally been regarded as merely a 'prelude' to reform has condemned the 1690s to neglect in general histories, which tend to confine themselves to such selected highlights as the Grand Embassy and the Azov campaigns.[40] Yet this decade is vital for understanding both the man and his Russia, the moulding of Peter's priorities and the clarification of the options open to him, both at home and abroad. For a start, a closer examination of the early 1690s reveals the error of assuming an unbroken line of developing 'Westernization' from the 1680s into the new century. The 1690s were not merely a bridge between the cautious modernization of the Sophia–Golitsyn regime and Peter's full-blooded post-1700 variant. Some new trends—in art and architecture, for example—continued and flourished, while others were suspended. The 1690s saw a continuing struggle, to use a cliché, between the 'old' and the 'new', personified in the figures of the two ruling monarchs: 'pious' Ivan making stately progress in his heavy brocade robes and 'impious' Peter clad in German dress dashing from shipyard to military parade.

In a letter to Tsar Ivan, written between 8 and 12 September 1689, Peter wrote: 'And now, brother sovereign, the time has come for us to rule the realm entrusted to us by God, since we are of age and we must not allow that third shameful personage, our sister the Tsarevna S.A., to share the titles and government with us two male persons.'[41] In fact, Peter showed little inclination to 'rule the realm'. His preoccupation with his own interests for the first few years, then his prolonged absences, first at Azov, then in the West, ceded the centre to others, to the extent that some of the first actions of the new regime appeared to turn back the clock, taking advantage of the removal of Vasily Golitsyn, the 'friend of foreigners', to annul concessions made during Sophia's regency and to adopt closer supervision of foreigners in general, in order to stem the spread of heresy from across the borders. Patriarch Joachim was the prime mover. On 2 October 1689 the Jesuit fathers Georgius David and Tobias Tichavsky were expelled.[42] Sanctions were imposed against Jesuits in particular, not Catholics in general, probably because there were some influential foreign Catholics close to Peter, and Russia was still allied to Catholic powers. A decree of 1690 allowed two priests to serve the foreign Catholic community, but the authorities were to take precautions to ensure that they did not try to convert Russians, visit them in their homes, carry on foreign correspondence or turn out to be Jesuits in disguise.[43] In October 1689 the Protestant mystic Quirinus Kuhlman was burned on Red Square together with his works.[44] P. I. Prozorovsky, governor of Novgorod, was warned to take care that 'such criminals should not enter the country and that foreigners who in future arrive from abroad from various countries at the border and in Novgorod the Great and claim that they have come to enter service or to visit relatives or for some other business in Moscow, should be questioned at the border and in Novgorod and detained and not allowed to proceed to Moscow until you receive our royal instructions'. All foreign travellers were to be interrogated and asked to provide certificates and passes, and transcripts of such interrogations were to be made.[45] Just before his death in 1690, Patriarch Joachim called a church council to consider the recantation of the monk Silvester Medvedev, who was accused, among other things, of propagating a Catholic view of transubstantiation. Copies of Medvedev's book *Manna* were seized and burnt, and its author was defrocked and beheaded in 1691.[46] Another whiff of Old Russia comes from a report of the uncovering in 1689 of a sorcerers' conspiracy, master-minded by Andrei Bezobrazov, who allegedly attempted to undermine the health of Peter and his mother by casting spells 'on bones, on money and on water'. The ring-leaders were beheaded or burnt, other 'conspirators' flogged and banished.[47] For a few months after Sophia's overthrow the atmosphere was so oppressive that Peter's friend, the Scottish mercenary General Patrick Gordon, contemplated leaving Russia.

But in the midst of this resurgence of the old, the new was asserting itself with unprecedented vigour. Despite the Church's dire warnings about the dangers of contamination by heretics, Peter himself was spending more and more time in the company of foreigners. The Foreign Quarter was only a few miles from the Preobrazhenskoe palace, where Peter spent much of Sophia's regency. Peter became a frequent visitor at the homes of Lefort and Gordon, and soon got to know other foreign soldiers and merchants, attending banquets, weddings, and funerals. Lefort's palace, with a splendidly appointed ballroom added, was turned into a semi-official residence for the sort of reception which it was still difficult to hold in the Kremlin, accompanied by 'debauchery and drunkenness so great that it is impossible to describe it'.[48] At about this time Peter probably learned Dutch (from Andrei Vinius, a government official of Dutch descent), and also took lessons in dancing, fencing, and riding. In February 1690 the birth of Peter's first child, Alexis, was celebrated not only with the customary church services and bells but also with cannon-fire and drum-beats. Foreign-led infantry regiments were drawn up in the Kremlin, presented with gifts and vodka to mark the occasion, and ordered to fire off rounds of shot, 'disturbing the peace of the saints and ancient tsars of Moscow'.[49] Over the next few days there were firework displays, more gun salutes, banquets, and feasts. Conservatives took retaliatory action. On the patriarch's orders, a banquet on 28 February was held without the now customary foreign guests, who were banned; but the next day the tsar dined with Patrick Gordon.[50] Then in March Joachim died. His 'Testament', which denounced the policy of hiring foreigners and deplored toleration of other faiths, has been described as the 'last gasp' of Old Russia:

May our sovereigns never allow any Orthodox Christians in their realm to entertain any close friendly relations with heretics and dissenters—with the Latins, Lutherans, Calvinists and godless Tatars (whom our Lord abominates and the church of God damns for their God-abhorred guile); but let them be avoided as enemies of God and defamers of the Church.[51]

Joachim's successor was Adrian, consecrated on 24 August 1690. He was to be Russia's last patriarch, his office left vacant after his death in 1700, and abolished altogether in 1721.

As long as Tsar Ivan was alive, the old guard still retained a figure-head in the Kremlin. After the overthrow of Sophia and Golitsyn, the old Muscovite court life, with its liturgical emphasis, was resumed with a vengeance, cleansed of the 'unseemly' female variants introduced by Sophia. Festivals gave special prominence to the history of the Russian Orthodox Church, celebrating earlier hierarchs who had assumed a strong political role, such as Metropolitans Philip and Alexis, and paying homage to the ruling dynasty with requiems for departed royalty (such as Tsarevich Alexis Alekseevich, whose death had not been marked in previous years).[52] Old palace protocols persisted, on paper at least; for example, the practice of listing in order of rank all the nobles 'in attendance' (*za nimi Velikimi Gosudariami*) on the tsars at such occasions as summer outings (*pokhody*) to country residences and monasteries.[53] The Church continued to make its contribution to the business of warfare and government: in April 1695 General Avtamon Golovin was issued with icons of the Saviour, the Mother of God, and St Sergius and ten pounds of incense to carry in the campaign to Azov.[54] In September 1697 Prince M. Ia. Cherkassky, the new governor of Tobol'sk, received a set of instructions, the first of which was to go to the Cathedral of the Holy Wisdom and hear prayers for the tsar and his family read by Metropolitan Ignaty of Siberia.[55] A few months later Patriarch Adrian issued a long instruction to churches and monasteries on priorities and procedures.[56]

Despite the apparent vigour of tradition, the keepers of the palace records could not conceal the fact that one of the tsars was opting out of the usual rituals. Nowhere is the spirit of the new better illustrated than in an entry recorded shortly after Joachim's death. On 27 April 1690 (April was traditionally the start of the royal pilgrimage season) 'the Great Sovereign Peter Alekseevich deigned to visit Kolomenskoe'. For his trip a rowing boat was got up to look like a sailing ship; the boyars followed in two boats and strel'tsy went in front in seven, and 'as they sailed along the water there was firing from cannon and hand guns'. The 'play' regiments, Peter's private troops, went along in smaller craft. Tsar Ivan travelled by land.[57] Thus we see two tsars, one firmly rooted in old Russia, the other looking to new horizons. (Thirty-four years later, in 1724, Peter again travelled to Kolomenskoe along the river, in a small flotilla with Russian and foreign guests who had gathered in Moscow for the coronation of his second wife, Catherine. The interior of the old wooden palace, it seems, had been preserved exactly as it was in the tsar's youth. [58]) In May 1690 we find Peter making a tour of monasteries, but more often than not Ivan carried out such duties alone. This turn of events was noted by contemporaries. Boris Kurakin records: 'First the ceremonial processions to the cathedral were abandoned and Tsar Ivan Alekseevich started to go alone; also the royal robes were abandoned and Peter wore simple dress. Public audiences were mostly abandoned (such as were given to visiting prelates and envoys from the hetman, for which there were public processions,); now there were simple receptions.'[59]

Many of Peter's unofficial activities are recorded in the diary of Patrick Gordon, which provides a secular alternative to the old records which were so deeply rooted in the religious calendar. We learn that on 30 May 1690 Peter spent his birthday at Preobrazhenskoe enjoying gun salutes and target practice. On 19 January 1691 Peter visited P. V. Sheremetev, and the next day Gordon had such a dreadful hangover that he could not get out of bed until the evening. A dinner at Boris Golitysn's on 16 May had similar consequences. And so on.[60] Royal account books for 1690–1 show numerous entries for orders for 'German dress' in the royal workshops, made from materials bought from foreign merchants and intended for Peter and members of his play regiments.[61] Peter's enthusiasm for things foreign is indicated by the motley collection of foreign goods shipped to Archangel in 1692: mathematical instruments, two globes, a large organ, four large clocks, five barrels of Rhine wine, and a barrel of olive oil.[62]

The new was taking its place alongside the old. After the traditional blessing of the waters at Preobrazhenskoe on 1 August, for example, there was firing from guns.[63] Tsaritsa Natalia's name-day celebrations on 27 August 1691 combined the usual church services, visits from churchmen and receipt and dispensing of gifts on the tsaritsa's behalf, with a reception of visitors by the tsaritsa herself (from which, however, foreigners were excluded), followed by gun salutes and fireworks.[64] We must also look to the beginning of the 1690s for the origins of one of Peter's most controversial 'institutions', the All-Drunken, All-Jesting Assembly or 'Synod'. Sometimes dismissed as an adolescent aberration, in fact the Drunken Assembly flourished throughout Peter's reign. The new trends seemed to be growing inexorably, yet how easily it might all have changed. In November 1692 Peter fell ill, and for ten days was at death's door. There were rumours that many of his supporters were preparing to flee. His recovery signalled the resumption of the new life with a vengeance. In July 1693 Peter set off for Archangel to see the sea. This was an 'outing' (*pokhod*) for which the record-keepers lacked the vocabulary. The clerks compromised by listing the courtiers in attendance on Peter in the usual manner, but without reference to their destination. Yet this historic journey had much in common with the royal outings of old. The accompanying retinue was listed according to rank, from boyars to secretaries. Peter travelled with a priest, eight choristers, two dwarfs and forty strel'tsy.[65] During Peter's travels Tsar Ivan's activities were solemnly chronicled, and Peter's absences were sometimes noted—for example, at the requiem mass for the late Tsarevna Anna Mikhailovna on 24 July. Moscow was depleted of courtiers. More than ever, the life-style of the two courts diverged. For example, the Russian New Year on 1 September 1693 was celebrated in Archangel with gun salutes from both foreign and Russian ships in the harbour, while back in Moscow, Tsar Ivan, clad in robes of red velvet, 'deigned to go from his royal chambers to the cathedral' to hear the patriarch celebrate the liturgy 'according to the usual rites'.[66] On occasion, Peter assumed a traditional role, visiting his father's favourite place of pilgrimage, the St Sabbas monastery at Zvenigorod, in May 1693;[67] but after Tsar Ivan's death in January 1696, more and more rituals were enacted without any tsar at all. An old formula was adopted to cover for Peter's absence, be it on campaign or abroad, i.e., the appointment of a small group of deputies to attend services and ceremonials in his stead. An order to this effect was issued: from 2 April to 1 September 1697 'the tsarevichy, boyars, okol'nichie and gentlemen of the duma shall follow behind the holy icons in parades and services',[68] although entries in the palace records reveal that the escort usually comprised only token representatives of these ranks. So, for example, the 1697 Epiphany ceremony was attended by Tsarevich Vasily of Siberia, boyar Prince P. I. Khovansky, okol'nichii S. F. Tolochanov, and Secretary Avatamon Ivanov.[69]

If the early 1690s were a time of exploration and game playing, they also saw the beginnings of serious activity. Peter's first chance to try out his strength came in 1694 when his mother died. The demise of Natalia Naryshkina, a useful figure-head for the leading men, whose power rested upon their relationship to the royal mother, threatened a new configuration of forces which could have worked to Peter's disadvantage. But any thoughts of, for example, using the strel'tsy again against Peter were discouraged by Peter's own forces, based upon the 'play' (poteshnye) troops. The two regiments took their names from the adjacent royal villages at Preobrazhenskoe and Semenovskoe to the north of Moscow. Their organization—foreign ranks, training, uniforms—was modelled on the new-formation infantry regiments introduced in the 1630s. The story goes that in the 1680s Peter discovered about 300 men idle at a former royal hunting-lodge, and signed them up to play military games. Others were requisitioned from regular units: for example, a drummer and fifteen troopers from the Butyrsky infantry regiment in 1687. Young nobles who might once have served as gentlemen of the bedchamber and in other junior court posts were recruited alongside local lads from a variety of backgrounds. The Semenovsky regiment was formed from the overflow from the Preobrazhensky regiment. Officers and men were all said to be known to the tsar personally.[70] By 1685 the embryonic guards had a scaled-down wooden fortress which Peter named Presburg, with barracks and stables adjacent to the Preobrazhenskoe palace. In deference to foreign expertise, Russians, including the tsar himself, served in the ranks or as non-commissioned officers. A list of officers (nachal'nye liudi) of both regiments for 1695 shows that they were all foreigners,[71] although Russian names appear in the next year or so, mostly in the lower officer ranks.[72]

In September 1694 Peter staged the so-called Kozhukhovo manoeuvres, mock exercises which were 'partly political in nature', in which some 30,000 men participated.[73] The 'campaign' presented Muscovites with a show of strength, as armies commanded by Fedor Romodanovsky, the 'king of Presburg', and Ivan Buturlin, the 'king of Poland', paraded through the city.[74] The mock battle included an assault with explosives on a specially constructed fortress, which left twenty-four dead and fifteen wounded. Members of both the Lopukhin and the Naryshkin families were placed on the losing side, perhaps to make the point that Peter did not intend to be beholden to *any* of his relatives unless they proved their worth.

Soon there were to be opportunities for real service. In the wake of the disastrous Crimean campaigns of 1687 and 1689, which attracted little allied support, Russia began to lose confidence in the Holy League, fearing exclusion from any future peace negotiations with the Turks.[75] Even so, Peter was determined to continue the war in the hope of real gain and in 1695 he reopened hostilities in a campaign against the Turkish coastal fort of Azov at the mouth of the River Don, in an attempt to recover Russian prestige, gain a stronger bargaining position with his allies and ward off Turkish attacks on Ukraine. It was widely believed in 1694–5 that Peter was planning to make another assault on the Crimea, 'march with a mighty army against the Crim Tartar, having an Artillery of 80 great guns and 150 Mortars', to bring relief to hard-pressed Poland,[76] rumours which Peter was happy to encourage. In the event, he marched not to Perekop, but to Azov, a plan which may have been suggested by Patrick Gordon.[77] Two armies were dispatched: the joint force of B. P. Sheremetev and the Ukrainian hetman Ivan Mazepa to the Dnieper, to deflect the Tatars from the mouth of the Don, and a smaller unit consisting of the Preobrazhensky and Semenovsky guards and strel'tsy on river craft down the Don.

Peter wrote to Fedor Apraksin: 'In the autumn we were engaged in martial games at Kozhukhovo. They weren't intended to be anything more than games. But that play was the herald of real activity.'[78] In this, as in some subsequent campaigns, Peter ceded nominal command to others. The commander-in-chief was A. S. Shein, while the tsar marched as a bombardier in the Preobrazhensky regiment.[79] The first Azov campaign was a failure, and the fortress remained in Turkish hands. Peter blamed this on multiple command, tactical errors, and technical deficiencies. Foreign engineering specialists were hired for the next campaign, in an effort to avoid such fiascos as mines planted on ramparts far away from the enemy blowing up 130 Russians without doing any damage to the Turks. The Turks, meanwhile, were able to replenish supplies from the sea, with no Russian ships to hinder them.

This set-back has often been identified as the real beginning of Peter's career, when he was forced to 'grow up' and discover 'astonishing reserves of energy'.[80] Such formulae should not simply be dismissed as part of a Petrine myth propagated by both tsarist and Soviet writers. Failure did indeed stimulate the implementation of a number of measures, characterized by what was to become the typically 'Petrine' use of speed, mass recruitment, and command from above. The prime example was the preparation of galleys at Voronezh on the Don for a renewed campaign in 1696, a huge effort in which thousands of the tsar's subjects were expected to do their bit, from the leading churchmen and merchants, who reluctantly supplied the cash, to the hapless labourers drafted in to hack wood in terrible conditions. Both river craft and seagoing vessels were to support an army of some 46,000 Russian troops, 15,000 Ukrainian Cossacks, 5,000 Don Cossacks, and 3,000 Kalmyks.[81] At the end of May 1696, Peter's land and sea forces laid siege to Azov. By 7 June a Russian flotilla was able to take to the sea and cut off access to Turkish reinforcements.[82] Apart from the use of sea power, Russian success was aided by General Gordon's plan of a rolling rampart ('the throwing up a wall of earth and driveing it on the Towne wall') and the services of Austrian engineers.[83] On 18 July the fortress surrendered.

This victory prompted some striking manifestations of the new culture. In the past, military triumphs had been largely religious affairs, celebrated by parades of crosses and icons headed by chanting priests. Such displays of thanksgiving continued right to the end of Peter's reign—in Russia, as in every other European country, military victory and defeat were interpreted as inextricably linked with God's will—but from now on the religious processions were supplemented, and usually eclipsed, by secular parades bristling with 'pagan' symbols. After Azov, triumphal gates of Classical design bearing the legend in Russian 'I came. I saw. I conquered' gave a preview of the imperial Roman references and imagery which culminated in the festivities of 1721, when Russia became an empire. There were references to Christian Rome, too, and comparisons of Peter to the Emperor Constantine. In addition to the customary prayers, verses were chanted through a megaphone by State Secretary Andrei Vinius. Peter, wearing German uniform, marched in the parade behind the official heroes Admiral Lefort and General Shein, while the religious authority was parodied by 'prince-pope' Nikita Zotov in a carriage.[84] It is said that Peter had in mind not only Roman precedents but also the example of Ivan IV, who organized a similar parade after the conquest of Kazan in 1552.[85] This was the first public display of the new manners, which until then had by and large been confined to semi-private indulgence at Preobrazhenskoe or in the Foreign Quarter. This new openness fanned growing popular disapproval of Peter's foreign ways, which expressed itself in full force in 1698, when the strel'tsy revolted.

The 1690s saw interesting developments in art and culture. The semi-Westernized Moscow baroque style of the 1680s matured and spread beyond the capital, where masonry churches and civic buildings displayed decorative features such as Classical columns and carved stone and brick ornament inspired by Western Renaissance and baroque originals. Peter's maternal relatives commissioned so many churches in this style that it is often referred to as 'Naryshkin baroque'. One of the finest examples, the Church of the Intercession at Fili, built for Lev Naryshkin in 1690–3, had icons which reflected family history—images of SS Peter and Paul, John the Baptist, Alexis Man of God, and St Stephen, the latter bearing a striking resemblance to the young Peter, who often visited the church. An even more remarkable church, commissioned by Prince Boris Golitsyn on his estate at Dubrovitsy in 1690, dispensed with the traditional cupolas (the tower is capped by an open-work crown) and had statues of saints over the parapets and Latin inscriptions inside.[86]

The painting of the 1690s also exhibits interesting 'transitional' features. In January 1692 the Armoury received an order for eleven large pictures for Peter's residence at Pereiaslavl'-Zalessky (where he was experimenting with sailing), the subjects of which were the Saviour, the Mother of God, the martyr Natalia, Alexis Man of God, Alexander Nevsky, Peter and the martyr Evdokia. The family references (Alexander Nevsky, for example, was the patron saint of Peter's second son Alexander, born in October 1691[87]) were almost certainly chosen by Peter's mother rather than Peter himself. But the commission reflected 'modern' trends in so far as these were not traditional icon panels but paintings on canvas in frames.[88] There are even more revealing indications of Peter's emerging individual taste: for example, his order in July 1691 for twelve German portraits (*person nemetskikh*) in gilt frames, to be taken to his apartments from the confiscated property of Prince Vasily Golitsyn.[89] In August 1694 a team of painters in the Armoury received orders for twenty-three battle paintings for Peter's apartments, 'after the German model', with frames also of German design. Four painters were to take four subjects each, and the rest were to be done by apprentices, 'painting different subjects, making use of German pictures [as models]'.[90] In June 1697, when Peter was abroad, the same team of Armoury painters was instructed to paint eight pictures on canvas depicting 'troops going by sea, making use of foreign German pictures or engravings, employing the best workmanship'. Again, these were large canvases, evidently executed in some haste, given that the same painters were all dispatched to work in Voronezh in July, and the frames were ordered in August.[91] Painters were called upon to do other jobs to meet new demands: for example, to decorate the new ships built at Voronezh in 1696–7.[92] These few examples indicate clearly the emergence of a distinct secular culture from within the walls of the Moscow Armoury, that early 'academy of arts' which housed a secular painting studio separate from the icon-painting workshops only since the 1680s.[93]

It is very difficult to assess the art of the 1690s because, like the 1696 triumphal gates, so few examples have survived. Accurate likenesses of Peter pre-dating the Grand Embassy are notable by their absence. Earlier engravings, such as Larmessen's double portrait of Peter and Ivan (ca.1687), are mostly imaginative reconstructions. Evidently others existed but have disappeared; thus, in July 1695 an order was given for a printed 'persona' of Peter to be stuck on to canvas and framed.[94] Perhaps Peter's restless activity in the 1690s precluded sitting for portraits. Yet it is with portraits that we shall conclude our examination of the 1690s. The first is the most famous (once thought to be the only) image of the young tsar, painted by Sir Godfrey Kneller in London in 1698, now hanging in Kensington Palace in London. The startling contrast between this wholly Western depiction of a monarch and the few surviving images of Peter's father has often been pointed out, but is worth drawing attention to here: the bearded Orthodox tsar of the 1660s with traditional robes and pectoral and crown crosses gives way to the warrior in armour with a warship in the background. For Kneller, Peter was just another European monarch. All traces of Russian 'exoticism' were expunged. Indeed, Kneller used the same set formula—column and crown to the left, warship in the background to the right, royal ermine, and armour—as in his 1680s portrait of James II.[95] Yet there are other portraits of Peter from this period which remind us that the break with Old Russia was far from complete. One by the Dutch artist Pieter Van der Werff shows Peter dressed in the Polish style, while in an anonymous portrait now in the Rijksmuseum he wears Russian dress.[96] A similar contrast may be observed in two much smaller images, produced a year later in an entirely different medium. In 1699 two experimental half-roubles were minted. The first, by Vasily Andreev of the Armoury, shows Peter full face, in icon style, wearing the Crown of Monomach. The second is wholly Western, showing the tsar as a Roman emperor in profile, with laurel wreath and mantle. On the reverse is a collar of St Andrew and a coat of arms.[97] On the eve of the new century and the outbreak of the Northern War, the designers had, albeit unconsciously, expressed the contrast between old and new. Which of the two would prevail? In Peter's mind, at least, the contest was already decided, as were the means for augmenting national prestige and prosperity. The focus would shift from the Black Sea to the Baltic and the country which barred Russia's way, Sweden.

2

Russia and the World: 1696–1725

For patriotic Russians, from Peter's contemporaries to the post-Soviet generation, the most valuable service that Peter performed for his country was to transform it from a maligned nation on the fringe of European affairs, engaged mainly in fending off the attacks of its neighbours, to a world power with a pro-active role in international politics. 'From now all European nations are convinced that they were wrong about Russia's rulers, about the strength of Russia and the good sense of the Russian people. Now Denmark, Holland, the Hanseatic towns and Gaul itself, famed of old, Saxony, too, and almost all the German empire, who once spoke and thought ill of the Russian realm, have changed their bad opinions for the better,' wrote one of Peter's admirers in 1718.[1] Such a reversal was not easily achieved. Soviet historians infused Petrine foreign policy with a strong heroic element by referring constantly to Russia's 'struggle' (*bor'ba*) to achieve various aims: access to the Baltic and Black Seas, a share in world trade, and international recognition.[2] The reform of the army, the creation of the navy, the establishment of new administrative institutions, the opening of factories and mines, were all regarded as means to a highly desirable end: the attainment and maintenance of world power status. Associated hardships and sacrifices could be forgiven and forgotten. There were dissident voices: those who, like Nikolai Karamzin, argued that Russia's new prominence in European affairs was achieved at the expense of national institutions and traditions, or, like Pushkin, in his poem 'The Bronze Horseman', (1833), highlighted the fate of the 'little man', forced to sacrifice his small private happiness for the greater good.[3] But mostly such scruples were drowned out by patriotic cheers, especially during and immediately after the Second World War, when Peter's exploits, along with those of other heroes of the past, were harnessed to the war effort. In the words of a history of the Northern War published in 1946: 'The Russian people—the elder brother among the other peoples of our country—has on numerous occasions had to wage war for its national independence against foreign invaders.'[4] In recent times, modern Russian rulers' loss of an empire has been compared unfavourably with Peter's conquests, their 'vacillations' contrasted with Peter's firm resolution and clear aims.[5] In the belief, following V. O. Kliuchevsky, that war was the 'central feature' of Peter's reign, and that military success provided the impetus for the great majority of Peter's reforms, this chapter will endeavour to provide a dispassionate guide to Russian foreign policy from the close of the seventeenth century to the immediate post-Petrine period.[6]

I.   FROM AZOV TO THE GRAND EMBASSY: 1696–1698

The success at Azov in 1696 was a stepping-stone for more ambitious policies, its significance appreciated far afield. In September 1696 the *London Gazette* reported: 'The loss of this Place is like to be of very ill Consequence both to the Turks and the Tartars, It giving the Moscovites passage into the Country of the latter, who will be thereby hindered from sending any Assistance to the Turkish Army in Hungary.'[7] In Moscow more grandiloquent tributes were forthcoming. The Likhud brothers, teachers at the Moscow Academy, predicted the restoration of Greece and the banishing of the Turks: 'Is not Constantine's town your inheritance? Are not the sceptres, crowns and thrones of Honorius and Arcadius befitting your royal majesty?'[8]

In future, especially after Azov was lost again to the Turks in 1711, the 1696 victory and Peter's southern policy in general were to be overshadowed by successes in the north and regarded as a poor second to the 'window on the West' policy. In the 1690s priorities may not have been so clear-cut. It is possible to argue that Peter continued to regard the Don and the Dnieper as equally vital outlets to the rest of the world, for both trade and war. Peter's south-oriented policies included projects for the Volga–Don and Oka–Don canals and attempts to force Ukrainian trade through Azov. He set about building a harbour at Taganrog thirty miles to the west of Azov, and over the next few years, foreign technical specialists, seamen and peasant labourers were drafted in to man the new base.[9] But Azov, as a glance at the map will confirm, allowed entry only to the Sea of Azov. Kerch, which guarded the straits into the Black Sea, remained in Ottoman hands.

The victory at Azov led to a renewed Russian alliance with Austria and Venice against the Turks early in 1697.[10] In October 1697 Russians went into action at Tavani fortress (when the Turks again besieged Azov) and in December near Kazykermen, both incidents ending with Russian victories.[11] Soon after, however, Austrian successes prompted the Turks to offer peace without reference to Russia. The Austrians, contemplating a struggle with France over the succession to the Spanish throne, to which both countries laid claim, were in no mood to refuse. Not for the first or last time, Russia felt let down by its allies. Azov also provided the background for one of the key diplomatic missions of Peter's reign, the so-called Grand Embassy, by which he hoped to exploit his recent success to seek aid for the alliance against the Turks and to pay courtesy calls on friendly European rulers, 'for the confirmation of ancient friendship and love, and the weakening of the Turkish sultan, the Crimean khan and all their Muslim hordes, the enemies of the Cross of Our Lord'.[12] In March 1697 the Swiss soldier Franz Lefort, appointed chief ambassador, left Moscow with his fellow ambassadors Fedor Golovin and Prokopy Voznitsyn at the head of a 250-strong contingent. Lefort wrote to his brother: 'Never has there been such a big embassy from here ... I have six pages, four dwarfs, about twenty liveried servants, who will all be splendidly dressed, five trumpeters, musicians, a pastor, surgeons, physicians and a company of well-equipped soldiers.'[13] Apart from its impressive size and trio of plenipotentiaries, there was on the face of it little to distinguish this delegation from recent Russian missions, like the ones dispatched by Sophia to European courts in the late 1680s. But Peter may even then have been on the verge of formulating a grander design, which signalled a change of policy: the creation of a 'mighty anti-Swedish league', drawing in those countries and principalities—Courland, Prussia, Poland, Saxony, Denmark, possibly England, and the Dutch Republic—which had scores to settle and territory to dispute with Sweden.[14]

The embassy was a landmark in Peter's personal career. Lefort's retinue was accompanied by thirty-five Russian 'volunteers' bound for the Dutch Republic to study shipbuilding and navigation, among them one Peter Mikhailov. 'I am a student and I require teachers' was written on the seal that he carried. This was a voyage of discovery for the tsar, in his quest not only for practical knowledge but also for ideas. It was significant that the first major destination was the Dutch Republic, home of a thriving merchantry, a free press, and a cosmopolitan atmosphere. Similar impressions of institutions and social relations very different from Russia's were to be gained in England.[15] In the course of his journey, Peter was to see with his own eyes the extent to which Russia lagged behind the countries of Western Europe in its economic and technological development. Here was stark confirmation, already sensed in Moscow's Foreign Quarter, that Russia faced the danger of falling into economic dependence on more advanced countries, turning into a colony or even being conquered by its neighbours.[16]

Peter's decision to travel incognito has usually been attributed to his loathing of diplomatic protocol and his desire to retain the freedom to work and observe without getting bogged down in official duties, although he dropped his disguise when it suited him, notably in Vienna in June–July 1698, when he took over negotiations from his 'figure-head' ambassadors.[17] There may also have been a security aspect to the subterfuge, an attempt to hide for as long as possible the fact that the tsar had left Russia, not only from the Turks, who might stage an attack in his absence, but also from Russians, who would be both worried and in some cases outraged by their sovereign venturing abroad. Muscovite politics were an intensely personal affair, revolving around the ruler's physical presence. An absent tsar left an uncomfortable vacuum. As was the custom, edicts issued in Moscow during the embassy retained such familiar formulae as 'The great sovereign decreed', giving no hint of Peter's absence.[18]

This deception may have fooled the wider public in the vast expanses of Russia, but in the places which he visited, Peter's incognito was less effective, which is hardly surprising in view of his great height. Peter Lefort, Franz's nephew, writing to relatives in Switzerland in the middle of August 1697, found it impossible to keep the secret:

> I want to tell you, without subjecting myself to the risk of actually writing it, that the person whom you mentioned is with us. And everyone knows. We did all we could to hide the fact but it was impossible ... The rumour is so widespread that people run after every Muscovite thinking that it's His Majesty. All the ambassadors are fearful on his account, which puts them in an awkward position. They would have preferred him to stay at home but that wasn't possible. He is too interested in foreign countries for anyone to mention the possibility of his returning home. In the Dutch Republic an order was issued on threat of a huge fine forbidding the printing of any information or mention of His Majesty's name in the papers.

In early September he wrote: 'We are no longer hiding the fact of the tsar's presence as it would be pointless.'[19]

One incident exacerbated by the tsar's ineffective disguise was to have long-term repercussions. In Riga in April 1697 Peter asked to inspect, and even sketch, the fortifications, and understandably aroused the suspicions of the Swedish governor Erik Dahlberg, who at the same time made no special arrangement to receive or honour Mr Mikhailov.[20] Permission was refused. Peter felt insulted, and left for Courland three days before the main embassy left Riga. On 8 April 1697 he wrote to Andrei Vinius: 'Today we departed hence for Mitau [in Courland]. Here [in Riga] we lived in servile fashion and feasted only with our eyes. The merchants here go about in cloaks and seem very upright, but they haggle with our coachmen over a copeck, they curse and swear, but charge three times the normal price.'[21] Later he referred to his reception as 'barbaric and Tatar-like'.[22] He had, however, learnt that the town was well fortified, though the defences were incomplete and the garrison force was small, as was the case with a number of Swedish strongholds on the south-east shore of the Baltic. Bad memories of Riga and information about its defences were stored up for future use. For the time being, relations with Sweden remained officially cordial. Early in 1697 'in token of his neighbourly friendship to Russia', King Charles XI offered to make Russia a gift of 300 iron cannon, following an enquiry about the purchase of brass cannon. In December 1697 Peter congratulated the new King Charles XII on his accession, promised to 'keep the established treaties in perpetuity', and thanked him for his late father's gift (which was received early in 1698). Peter asked to hire captains, skippers, steersmen, and other naval personnel for his new fleet.[23] In August 1698 Charles announced his intention of sending ambassadors to Moscow to renew the 1661 Kardis peace treaties with Russia, to which Peter responded that this would be 'highly pleasing to him'. In October 1699 Peter received the Swedish ambassadors in Moscow and swore to observe all the treaties. A return visit to Stockholm scheduled for 1700 was overtaken by events.[24]

Another significant incident occurred during the Grand Embassy, when Peter met Augustus, elector of Saxony and the new king of Poland, in Rawa in Galicia, on his way back to Moscow in July 1698. Augustus's election in 1697 had been supported by Moscow and Denmark against the French candidate for the elective Polish throne, the Prince de Conti.[25] In Rawa the tsar and the king discussed mutual aid, and Peter expressed his wish to avenge the 'insult' suffered in Riga. Peter learned that Augustus had designs on Swedish Livonia, which offered his new kingdom outlets to the sea. Denmark was eager to limit Sweden's possessions in Germany and to discourage the ties of the dukes of the adjoining lands of Holstein-Gottorp with the Swedish Crown. Thus the outline of an alliance against Sweden was already taking shape, although no formal agreement was signed at the time. There was an element of reckless opportunism in Augustus, one of the most colourful characters of his era, who pursued titles, wealth, and women with equal energy.[26] Peter was captivated by this enthusiastic drinker and entertainer (when the tsar returned to Moscow, he went around in Augustus's tunic and with his sword and praised his new friend[27]), but his approval did not extend to Poland itself. At this stage the link was with Augustus in his capacity as elector of Saxony.

The *rapprochement* with Brandenburg-Prussia, initiated by the signing of trade agreements in 1689, was ratified during the Grand Embassy, when Lefort signed agreements on friendship, trade, and training opportunities for Russians, although assurances of mutual aid in the case of attack were expressed only orally.[28] Friendship with Protestant Prussia and Russia's 1697 treaty with Austria (France's arch-enemy) further cooled relations between Russia and France. Russia was still smarting from the allegedly hostile reception given to its ambassadors to France in 1687, and the two countries were in dispute over guardianship of the holy places in Palestine.[29] These antagonisms in turn helped to bring Peter closer to the Dutch stadtholder William of Orange, king of England since 1688, a tireless campaigner against the French.[30] After spending four and a half months in the Dutch Republic, much of it devoted to studying shipbuilding in the East India docks, with William's encouragement, Peter sailed across the Channel to England, where he stayed from 10 January to 22 April 1698 to continue his studies.[31] His activities included tours of the Mint, the Royal Observatory and the Arsenal; visits to the Royal Society, Anglican services, and Quaker meetings; and excursions to Oxford, Windsor, and Portsmouth, where he reviewed the fleet, and to the theatre and Parliament (neither of which much impressed him). English motives in welcoming Peter were chiefly economic. The Russia Company pursued its long-term policy of trying to recover commercial privileges lost in 1649, although in the end the contract to sell tobacco to Russia, signed in April 1698, was won not by the company but by Peregrine Osborne, marquis of Carmarthen, with the backing of city merchants. (Carmarthen was able to tempt the tsar with the gift of the frigate *Royal Transport*.[32]) Russia's role was still seen mainly as a remote, eastern one. A contemporary poem portrayed Peter and William of Nassau as 'the Twins of Fate':

> [Peter's] Glist'ning Sabre on proud *Asia* Gleams,
> Dazling the Frighted *Tarters* by its Beams;
> Its Conquering Steel shall to the *East* give Law,
> Whilst NASSAW's Scepter keeps the *West* in Awe.[33]

In April 1698 Peter returned briefly to the Dutch Republic before heading south-east for his next major engagement, in Vienna. In June he was forced to cancel the next stage of his journey to Venice, and return to Moscow to deal with a revolt of the strel'tsy.[34] In terms of its stated diplomatic aims, the Embassy was a failure—indeed, was rendered redundant while it was still in progress, although it produced practical results in the form of personnel hired for service in Russia.[35] In September 1697 a decisive Austrian victory over the Turks at Zenta had allowed Austria to press for peace with Turkey on the basis of *uti possidetis*, which resulted in the Treaty of Karlowitz late in 1698. Meanwhile, the Peace of Ryswick (autumn 1697) had freed Austria, the maritime powers, and Spain from the Nine Years' War with France. This allowed the Dutch to refuse the aid against Turkey requested by the Russian delegation in The Hague, on the grounds that they had just concluded peace with France, the sultan's protector. Lefort, in a letter of December 1697, wrote of trying to persuade the Dutch to give money for the war against the Turks, if not war supplies or some ships. Their refusal was blamed on the newspapers reporting 'with the mouth of France'.[36] Perhaps the main lesson that Peter learned was the importance of 'lateral thinking' when it came to coalitions for the pursuit of Russia's goals. By the time he reached Moscow in August 1698, a new configuration of powers was indeed in the making. The 'insult' at Riga, cordial relations with Sweden's rival Prussia, personal friendship with King Augustus, the realization that immediate further gains in the south were unlikely in view of the collapse of the Holy League, all pointed to a new phase in Peter's foreign programme.

II. THE GREAT NORTHERN WAR: FROM NARVA TO POLTAVA 1700–1709

Surveys of the Great Northern War are usually obliged to telescope events, reducing the extended hostilities to a few crucial battles. The bare bones of the story from the Russian point of view are condensed into defeat (1700) then victory (1704) at Narva, the founding of St Petersburg (1703), the decisive battle of Poltava (1709), the capture of ports on the south-eastern Baltic shore (1710), the Finnish campaign (1713–14), and the Treaty of Nystad (1721). Hostilities then end, and Russia's status as a major European power is confirmed. This chronology raises a number of questions: why, for example, did the 'decisive' battle of Poltava fail to 'win' the war? Why, in particular, did the war continue after 1710, when Peter had achieved his main aims—ports on the Baltic, the weakening of Sweden, and a decisive hand in Polish affairs? Simplified schemes inevitably gloss over the international dimensions: for example, the fact that at the outset of the war Russia had a limited role and limited aims (the reconquest of 'Novgorod lands' on the Baltic), the initiative coming from Augustus rather than Peter. Only later did it become a question of the partition of the Swedish empire.

Peter's declaration of war against Sweden in 1700 was not unheralded. In 1695 a British agent in Stockholm quoted a letter from Lefort to the effect that two Russian armies were to be dispatched: one against Perekop to restrain the Tatars, the other against Azov. This was deemed good news in Stockholm: 'being otherwise apprehensive it may take him in the head to make an attempt at Liefland [Livonia], where not a few of the Gentry are dis-contents, and inclined to change masters'.[37] Opportunism played a part. The accession of a fifteen-year-old to the throne of Sweden in April 1697 and the aspirations of nobles in Livonia, led by Johann von Patkul, to break free of Sweden promised to ease Peter's task. On the basis of rumours imparted by a Swedish prisoner of war, it was apparently believed that Sweden had long been planning a war against Russia to seize Novgorod, Pskov, Olonets, Kargopol', and Archangel, 'thereby entirely to cut off the Russians from the Commerce with Foreigners'.[38] Diplomacy had its own momentum. No European ruler was a free agent; each had to take account of the complex system of alliances and be alert to nuances and sudden changes. Russia had to join in the 'concert' of nations, come what may, and to that end, in the course of his reign, Peter entered into diplomatic relations with virtually all the countries of Europe and some Asian ones too. For a start, in 1699 Russia for-mally joined an anti-Swedish coalition with Christian V of Denmark (in July) and Augustus II of Poland (in October). Both, it seems, regarded Peter as very much a 'junior partner'.[39]

The catalyst for Peter's decision to attack Sweden was the end of the war with Turkey. The Austro–Ottoman Peace of Karlowitz (25 December 1698) appeared to leave Russia out in the cold, with only a two-year truce and none of the gains (notably Kerch) deemed essential for consolidating the capture of Azov.[40] (Relations with Austria remained cool for the rest of Peter's reign.) Peter's ambassador, Emel'ian Ukraintsev, travelled to Constantinople on the Russian ship *Fortress* in the autumn of 1699 to negotiate a separate peace.[41] The Russian demands appear lavish: retention of Taganrog, Azov, and fortresses on the lower Dnieper (Kazikermen, Taman, Nustrekermen, and Saginkermen) and cession to them of Kerch; free navigation of the Black Sea and the straits (a claim advanced for the first time in 1698); the return of the holy places to the Greeks and the right of pilgrimage for Russians; protection for the sultan's Orthodox subjects; no resumption of 'gifts' (tribute) to the Tatars; and Russian diplomatic representation in Constantinople. In the end, Russia kept Taganrog and Azov, and obtained rights of pilgrimage, conces-sions on gifts (the annual tribute to the khan, last paid in 1683 and renounced in 1700, was not restored even after Russia's defeat on the Pruth in 1711), and representation in Constantinople. On 3 July 1700 Ukraintsev signed a thirty-year truce with Turkey.[42] 'On 18 August we announced the peace with the Turks with a splendid firework display, on the 19th we declared war against the Swedes,' Peter wrote to Fedor Apraksin.[43]

The reasons given for Moscow's declaration of war on 19 August 1700 were the insult suffered at Riga in 1697 and the Swedish Crown's 'illegal' occupation of Russian territory. What may appear a flimsy pretext was taken very seriously, the insult to Russian honour by Charles XII's governor being inextricably linked with violations of Russian territory by Charles's predecessors. As an illustration, a rescript to the Ukrainian people in 1709 explained that Peter had broken the treaties with Sweden for good reason:

> We were avenging the insult dealt to us and our ambassadors in Riga [in 1697] for which, in response to our request to the Swedish ambassadors, the king of Sweden refused point blank to give satisfaction by making the rude governor of Riga publicly apologize, and also for the restoration of the provinces of Izhera [Ingria] and Karelia, which belonged to our ancestors, the great sovereigns of Russia, for many centuries, but which the Swedish crown in truth treacherously snatched by dishonest military means during a time of major internal upheavals and occupation by foreign foes, which were then raging in the Russian realm, after their ancient practice, as that crown did with other realms, worming its way in under the guise of good will and offering help to restore peace, then breaking its word and unjustly snatching and at first occupying them for several years as a pledge of money allegedly owed for help which was not given.[44]

Peter never forgave Riga; in November 1709 he reported from outside the walls of the besieged city that he had thrown the first three bombs into the town with his own hands, 'for which I thank God that he allowed me personally the honour of starting the vengeance against this accursed place'.[45] Charles claimed that Peter's delegation had been treated with all possible civility in 1697, greeted with ceremonial gun salutes, and given the best accommodation. He pointed out, reasonably enough, that it was not the usual practice for diplomatic personnel to look around forts with telescopes, explore the fortifications, and make sketches of walls and buttresses.[46]

Peter consistently argued that he was reclaiming what had been stolen from his ancestors. In a statement made to the British court in April 1714, he stated that 'not only Ingermanland and Karelia but also the greater part of Estonia and Livonia always belonged of old to the Russian Crown; and although for certain circumstances these provinces were ceded to the Swedes, now for the many wrongs committed by the king these ancestral lands have been reunited with Russia'.[47] A fuller exposition is provided by the first original work on international law to be published in Russia, Peter Shafirov's *A Discourse Concerning the Just Causes of the War between Sweden and Russia* (1717). The author set out to demonstrate that Russia was part of an international system, saw itself as such, and observed the 'continuity of realm'. His historical arguments included the claim that Dorpat (formerly Iur'ev) was a Russian foundation, as was Reval (Kolivan, or 'Ivan's town').[48] The Peace of Stolbovo in 1617 was 'prejudicial and forced'.[49] Contemporary arguments centred on 'which of the two Parties most observed the Rules established among Christian and polite Nations in carrying on the War'. The Swedes, he claimed, waged war 'with inhuman Cruelty and bitter Animosity against his Czarish Majesty'.[50] None of this was new. Similar arguments and recriminations had been deployed by Ivan IV in the 1550s. Russian claims could not be justified by the religion or language of the inhabitants of most of the disputed territories, who were neither Orthodox nor Russian, in contrast to the ethno-religious arguments deployed in reference to parts of Ukraine and the grand duchy of Lithuania; but then Swedish claims were also shaky in this respect.

For Peter it turned into a case of out of the frying pan into the fire. Having lost his allies in the south, he found the same thing happening in the north. He was disappointed in the initial stages of the war by his Saxon ally. Augustus invaded Livonia in February 1700, but, in the absence of anticipated support from the Livonian nobles, failed to take Riga. There was no support from Poland (of which Augustus was the elected king, but where he had no personal power base), which remained neutral at the beginning of the war because Russia refused to revise the terms of the treaty of 1686, and certain noble factions were prepared to support the Swedes. Russia's defensive alliance with Denmark collapsed when Frederick IV (who succeeded his father, Christian V, in September 1699) was forced to make peace when Sweden dispatched 10,000 troops to attack Copenhagen with Anglo–Dutch naval help at a time when most of the Danish army was in Holstein. The Treaty of Travendal (August 1700) was signed on the same day as Peter declared war against Sweden. Frederick's promise not to aid Sweden's enemies meant, among other things, the loss of Danish naval support.[51] Peter had probably been unaware of Denmark's precarious economic position and of the powerful government factions, including pro-Swedish ones, which limited the king's power.

Peter was also taking on a more formidable enemy than he imagined. Far from being an easy target, Sweden's 'boy king' proved to be even more single-mindedly devoted to war than Peter himself. The Swedish army was regarded as the best in the world, its soldiers credited with almost superhuman qualities. It is against this unpromising diplomatic and military background that Peter's army of about 40,000 faced Charles's force of fewer than 9,000 men at the port of Narva in November 1700, with weak artillery, inexperienced and disunited commanders, unreliable supplies, and little prospect of allied aid. The Russians had arrived outside the fortress in September already exhausted, and maintained a month-long siege, during which munitions and supplies ran out. In late October Charles landed at Pernau on the Gulf of Riga, and reached Narva on 19 November, shortly after Peter had abandoned his camp to fetch reinforcements from Novgorod. The fact that the Russian troops were thinly stretched out over a huge distance made it easy to break through their unclosed ranks. Many Russian troops, in poor physical and psychological shape, fled. Only the Preobrazhensky and Semenovsky guards stood firm. Between 8,000 and 10,000 Russians were killed, and thousands captured. A medal was struck in Sweden: on one side Peter was depicted warming himself by the fire of his cannon, from which bombs were flying towards Narva, with the biblical legend: 'Peter stood and warmed himself.' The reverse showed Russians fleeing from Narva with Peter at their head, his crown askew, and the legend: 'He went out and wept bitterly.'[52]

So, with Denmark neutralized, Augustus compromised, and Russia defeated, why did Charles continue the war not in the direction of Moscow but by pressing further attacks against Saxony and Poland? Why did the war continue at all? Peter sought mediation, but it seems that in the end both the Grand Alliance (formed by the maritime powers and Austria in September 1701) and France were not averse to the continuation of a Swedish/ Saxon/Russian conflict. Louis XIV's efforts as mediator in 1701–2 came to nothing, when Russia could not agree to French terms (which included a request for Cossack aid for the Hungarian revolt against Austria and a substantial loan to France). Anglo–Dutch attempts to win over Sweden also failed.[53] In the end, it seems that the Grand Allies were just as happy for Charles to be safely bogged down in Lithuania and the Baltic. Charles's personal motives were an important factor. He was determined to knock out Augustus, wanted control of Poland, despised the Russians, and had the reputation of enjoying war for its own sake.[54] 'The king dreams only of war,' wrote a French envoy; 'he has been told too many tales of the exploits and campaigns of his ancestors. His heart and mind are filled with it, and he regards himself as invincible at the head of his Swedes.'[55] Charles was 'married to the army'. Strong commitment and loyalty to his troops were matched by firm religious convictions. Given Charles's belligerence, Peter had reason to be grateful to Augustus, who 'deflected that fearsome enemy from Russia's borders and gave the tsar time to revive his troops and teach them how to beat the Swedes'.[56] The 'rebirth' of the Russian armed forces after Narva, symbolized by the melting down of church bells to make cannon, was one of the many legendary events of Peter's reign, demonstrating, as had Azov, the tsar's resolution in adversity.[57]

In the meantime, Charles moved against Augustus, with the aim of installing a pro-Swedish king in Poland and creating a buffer zone between Sweden and Russia, by taking Courland and securing Livonia. In July 1701 Swedish troops crossed the Dvina and occupied Courland, without facing a decisive engagement. Victories followed at Kliszów in summer 1702 (against the Saxons and Poles) and Torun in 1703. Still, Augustus proved a hard nut to crack, despite some support for Sweden from Polish magnates, notably the Sapiehas in Lithuania, who hoped for local autonomy, and from the Polish primate, Cardinal Radziejowski. While Swedish attention was focused on Poland, Russia scored a first victory in the Baltic when B. P. Sheremetev beat

General Schlippenbach's forces at Erestfer in Livonia on 30 December 1701. In July 1702 he secured a further victory over Schlippenbach at Hummelshof.[58] There was relief for Russia in May 1702 with the outbreak of the War of the Spanish Succession, when the British and the Dutch reconstituted the Grand Alliance and Austria declared war on France in response to the French occupation of Spanish possessions in the southern Netherlands and Italy. Peter wrote to Apraksin: 'Long may it last, God willing.'[59] Summer 1702 saw several more Russian successes: on 25 August at Marienburg and on 11 October at the fortress of Nöteborg on Lake Ladoga, captured after a two-week siege with the aid of naval support. It was renamed 'Schlüsselburg', the 'key' to the River Neva. Peter wrote, with reference to the town's old Russian name 'Oreshek': 'This nut was very hard, but, praise be to God, it has been cracked.'[60] Thus the background to the foundation of St Petersburg in May 1703, near the site of the Swedish fortress of Nyenkans (Nienschants) on the Okhta river, was the deflection of Charles's main force into Poland and steady Russian encroachment in the Baltic.

In January 1704 Augustus was deposed by the Swedes and Charles's protégé, Stanislas Leszczynski was elected king of Poland by a rump *sejm* (parliament). In a treaty signed in 1705 with Leszczynski, the Swedes agreed to help the Poles to regain territory lost to Russia in 1667 and 1686. This was a serious blow to Peter, especially with the prospect of Turkey joining an anti-Russian league. He did not abandon Augustus, however, his main aim being to keep Poland in the war. In August 1704 a Russo–Polish treaty recognized Augustus as rightful king and promised him Livonia.[61] Peter further acknowledged the importance of the Polish alliance when he sent auxiliaries to Saxony in 1704, occupied Grodno in 1705 and attempted to restore Augustus even after he officially abdicated as king of Poland in 1706.[62] Throughout 1705–6, Russian units under Commanders Sheremetev, Ronne, Ogilvie, Bauer, Repnin and Golovin raced all over Lithuania and Courland. Thus Peter was drawn into the Polish morass, because a friendly, neutral or preferably subordinated Poland was needed to maintain Russia's Baltic gains. The Baltic campaign continued to go well for Russia. On 13 July 1704 the Russians took Dorpat (Tartu), on 9 August Narva, and on 16 August Ivangorod. In 1705 Swedish troops were cleared from Courland, and a Swedish naval attack on the recently founded fortress of St Petersburg was successfully repelled. Thereafter the fortifications, which were still under construction, were not to be required against enemy action. Of the major towns on the south-east Baltic shore, only Riga, Pernau, Arensburg, and Reval remained in Swedish hands.

In the west, things were going badly for Russia's awkward ally Augustus. Rehnsköld's victory over the Saxons at Fraustadt, near Poznan, in February 1706 (where all Russian prisoners were executed) was followed by the entry of Swedish troops into Saxony.[63] In March, surprised by Charles's rapid march from Warsaw, the Russians evacuated Grodno, where they had been ensconced since 1705, and retreated from Poland to Kiev. Charles turned his army back to Saxony. In August the Swedes took Dresden and Leipzig. Augustus was forced to surrender. Under the terms of the Peace of Altranstädt (28 September 1706), Augustus renounced the Polish crown in favour of Leszczynski, broke his alliance with Russia, handed over Patkul and other Livonian rebels to the Swedes and agreed to maintain the Swedish army through the winter to the sum of 625,000 reichsthalers per month.

The Swedes looked poised to turn on Russia, but even then there were signs that Charles might hold back. On 18 October 1706 a joint force of Russian and Saxon troops at Kalisz, near Poland's western border, caused heavy Swedish losses. At this crucial point, in November–December 1706, a vital council of war was held in the town of Žolkiev, near Cracow. Peter (who had only just learnt of the terms of the Treaty of Altranstädt), Menshikov, Sheremetev, Dolgoruky, and others discussed how to respond to a likely Swedish thrust eastwards and reached the decision to avoid a general battle for as long as possible.[64] Orders issued to F. M. Apraksin in January 1707 pre-scribed guerilla tactics and a scorched earth policy in order to wear the Swedes down, with peace terms held in reserve. Peter was willing to cede Dorpat, and if the Swedes were still not satisfied, to offer them money in compensation for Narva, or even cede Narva. But St Petersburg must not be relinquished under any circumstances. But Charles wanted the 1700 Russo–Swedish border to be recognized. He declared himself ready to fight to the last Swede rather than leave St Petersburg in Russian hands. In fact, Charles wanted even more: the crushing of Russian military strength and a return to Muscovite status to safeguard Sweden's borders. The king of Prussia's envoy in Altranstädt in January 1707 reported to Berlin that the Swedes expected 'to dethrone the Czar, compelling him to discharge all his foreign officers and troops, and to pay several millions as an indemnification'.[65] This may not have been a true reflection of Swedish policy, but such rumours caused alarm in Moscow.

Disillusioned with Augustus, Peter tried to find new candidates for the Polish throne as counterweights to Leszczynski.[66] It looked as though there might even be a chance to end the war with backing from the maritime powers, who were tired of disruptions to Baltic trade, and from France, which was bidding for Charles's support in the War of the Spanish Succession. Jottings for a letter to his German aide Heinrich Huyssens show that Peter was ready to offer the duke of Marlborough (Britain's negotiator) the pick of titles to the principalities of Kiev, Vladimir, or Siberia, 50,000 reichsthalers per year for life, one of the biggest rubies in Europe and the order of St Andrew if he would facilitate peace.[67] But Marlborough refused to be bribed and the Russian ambassador A. A. Matveev's mission to London in May 1707–July 1708 failed.[68] At Altranstädt in April 1708 Marlborough (who in December 1706 had expressed the opinion that it is 'better that the King of Sweden turns his armies against the Czar rather than stay to cause trouble for the Allies'[69]) recognized Leszczynski, and persuaded Charles not to help France against Austria but to carry on the war in the east. It seems that the

Western powers were frightened of Sweden, and therefore acted against their own best interests: for example, Britain and the Dutch Republic refrained from trading through the new Russian Baltic ports, even though they needed naval supplies, and Austria cancelled an embassy to Russia in 1704 when Sweden protested.[70]

The spring and summer of 1707 brought fresh fears of a Swedish attack. In March 1707 Peter wrote to Apraksin from Poland: 'I can't tell you anything more about what's going on, as all Polish affairs here are fermenting like young ale. The Swedes are advancing, committing unspeakable atrocities in Saxony. Now the Saxon has found out for sure what sort of friends and co-religionists the Swedes are.'[71] In the middle of 1707 Moscow went on the alert and repaired the fortifications of the Kremlin.[72] A decree of August 1707 on preparing border areas for an invasion stated: 'This war is now directed against us alone.'[73] Russia appeared to be in dire straits, faced with the loss of its allies, the outbreak of the Bulavin revolt in the autumn of 1707, then at the end of 1707 the news that a Swedish army of 45,000 had crossed the Vistula. Charles reached Grodno in January 1708, and by June was at Minsk.

Peter was a worried man.[74] But he was not to succumb to defeatism. He wrote to his son Alexis on 22 January: 'Give greetings to my sister and the others from me, and tell them not to grieve, for war is war and with God's help all our men are eager to march and ready to fight. Instead of grieving let them pray, which will be more help to us.' A letter to the acting patriarch, Stefan Iavorsky, written on the same day, stated that they were ready to lay down their lives for the Church and the fatherland, and asked Stefan to pray for the assistance of the heavenly host who aided St Peter. If a saint needed such help, how much more did mere sinners require it![75]

Peter returned to St Petersburg in March 1708, only to fall ill with a fever, which required a course of treatment with mercury (the standard remedy for gonorrhoea) and confinement to quarters. He wrote to Menshikov: 'You know that I have never written like this before, but God sees when you have no strength because without one's health and strength it's impossible to do your duty.' He hoped that he would not be called up straightaway. Treatment had left him as 'weak as a baby'.[76] Anxieties were increased by the continuation of the Bulavin rebellion. Measures such as the division of the country into eight provinces indicate the concerted efforts being made to concentrate resources as 'the country was placed for all practical purposes under martial law'.[77]

In June 1708 Charles was still poised in Lithuania preparing, according to rumours, to 'march on Moscow, dethrone the tsar, divide his country into petty princedoms, summon the boyars and divide the realm between them into voevodstva'.[78] But this grandiose plan was to be frustrated by the terrain through which the Swedes were about to pass. 'The land is not so well tilled,' wrote Whitworth, 'the villages few, their wooden houses of little value, and the furniture almost nothing, so that whenever an enemy approaches, the people are warned away with what they can save, and the cozacks set fire to the rest, as they have several times already done in sight of the Swedish army, who find all desolate before them, and as they advance will run further into want and cold.' [79] Scorched earth tactics were spelled out in Peter's instructions to Major-General Nikolai Iflant: if the enemy entered Ukraine, all provisions and fodder and corn in the fields and in grain stores or threshing floors in villages (although not in towns) which were superfluous to their own needs, Polish and Russian, were to be burnt, not sparing buildings in the vicinity; bridges were to be destroyed, forests cut down. All mills were to be burnt, and all the inhabitants to be sent out into the fields with their possessions and livestock. No millstones were to be left behind: they were to be either taken away or smashed. If anyone resisted going into the forest, their villages were to be burnt. This policy was to be broadcast in advance, with the warning: 'If anyone brings the enemy food, even for cash, that person shall be hanged; also anyone who knows [of such activities] but says nothing [will be executed]. Also those villages from which the food is given will be burnt.'[80] The old Soviet reading was that these desperate measures represented a heroic united struggle of the Russian, Belorussian, and Ukrainian people against the foreign invader.[81] In reality, as in so much else during Peter's reign, the population had little choice in the matter.

On 3 July 1708 the Swedes won a victory over the troops of A. I. Repnin at Holowczyn. Charles was soon in Mogilev. This was a low point for Russian morale, but the tide was beginning to turn. On 7 July the rebel leader Bulavin was killed, allowing the recall back to the western front of some 15,000 men who had been dispatched east to deal with the rebellion.[82] In late August Charles moved his troops to Mstislavl', but minor engagements at Dobroe on the Chernaia Napa River (29 August) and Raevki (10 September) impeded his progress. The Russians were beginning to wear Charles down without engaging him in a major pitched battle. It was predicted that he might make next for Moscow or even St Petersburg. But in mid-September, discouraged from crossing the Russian border by reports of shortages of food and fodder all the way to Smolensk, some sixty miles away, and anticipating reinforcements, the main Swedish army turned south. This proved to be a serious miscalculation, for almost immediately one of the supports on which Charles was relying was knocked out. On 28 September, in an engagement near Lesnaia (about thirty miles south-east of Mogilev), General Löwenhaupt with 12,500 troops transferred from the Baltic, and a baggage train of equipment and provisions consisting of several thousand carts, was cut off from the main army and attacked by Peter's *corps-volant* composed of the 7th Dragoons, the 5th Infantry on horses and thirty field guns. Löwenhaupt escaped to join Charles with only 6,000–7,000 of his men, and had to abandon the wagons. Peter later referred to this as the 'first day of our good fortune'.[83]

What made Charles turn into Ukraine, rather than continuing eastwards? One consideration was that the terrain to the east of the border had been subjected to a scorched earth policy, whereas Ukraine was regarded as populous, rich in food supplies, and lacking in strong garrisons. Moreover, Charles had been able to make a secret agreement with Ivan Mazepa, hetman of Left Bank Ukraine, and was also counting on assistance from Devlet-Girei, the Crimean khan. The hetman apparently pledged to supply the Swedes with 20,000 Cossacks, bases at Starodub, Novgorod–Seversk and Baturin, and vital provisions. It is uncertain whether a written agreement ever existed (no original has been found), although it had long been Swedish policy to urge King Stanislas Leszczynski to win Mazepa over to their side.[84]

Mazepa's decision to turn against Peter is unremarkable in the context of Muscovite–Ukrainian relations during the period in question. He suffered the same dilemma as all previous hetmans of the Little Russian Cossack Host, who had wavered between accepting the 'protection' of their fellow Orthodox tsar and pledging allegiance to non-Orthodox sovereigns, Polish, Turkish, or Swedish, all of whom might have something to offer by way of protection and profit for Cossacks, but none of whom could be relied upon to observe traditional Cossack liberties. After Vasily Golitsyn's campaigns against the Crimea in 1687 and 1689 had failed to improve the security of the region, certain local Cossack leaders made overtures to the Tatars. In 1692, for example, the rebel Petrik attacked the fortress at Kamenny Zaton with Tatar aid.[85] Since his investiture as hetman in 1687 (which he owed partly to Golitsyn's patronage), Mazepa had remained loyal to Moscow, but he did not regard himself as permanently bound.[86] At times he enjoyed at least the illusion of independent power, governing 'with little less authority than a sovereign prince'.[87] He conducted a semi-independent foreign policy: for example, maintaining his own communications with the Poles.

Muscovites and 'Little Russians' had common interests, which included alleviating the Tatar threat and taking Right Bank Ukraine from the Poles. Indeed, in 1704 Mazepa occupied part of the Right Bank with Peter's permission. However, trouble was brewing. The Great Northern War took Cossacks beyond their own borders, often under foreign officers. Mazepa was under constant pressure from his own troops. In March 1702, for example, he wrote to Peter that his men were complaining of hardships, of loss of income at home as a result of the long campaign in Livonia, of beatings and abuse, and of confiscation of their weapons and horses, 'all complaining against me with one voice, saying that I don't defend their rights and liberties'.[88] They feared that the Cossack regiments would be reorganized along European lines, as had happened to the strel'tsy. The last straw seems to have been Peter's refusal to supply Ukraine with troops to defend it against a possible attack by Leszczynski's army. Mazepa apparently reasoned: 'If we do not have the strength to defend Ukraine and ourselves, why should we go to our doom and doom our Motherland as well?'[89] A Swedish protectorate seemed like a guarantee of 'independence' from Russia, Poland, and the Turks and Tatars. Mazepa clearly believed that his obligations to the tsar were at an end: 'We, having voluntarily acquiesced to the authority of his Tsarist Majesty for the sake of the unified Eastern Faith, now, being a free people, we wish to withdraw, with expressions of our gratitude for the Tsar's protection and not wishing to raise our hands in the shedding of Christian blood.'[90]

In October 1708 a summons from Menshikov to a council of war gave Mazepa a pretext to flee to Charles's side. Mazepa pretended to be ill, and when Menshikov tried to visit the 'mortally sick' man and found his way barred, he realized what was happening. On 31 October he stormed and burned the hetman's headquarters at Baturin, killing, according to one estimate, some 6,000 persons 'without distinction of age or sex'.[91] This drastic action proved crucial, for it deprived the Swedes of men and supplies. Peter wrote in reply to Menshikov's report: 'We received your letter about the totally unexpected wicked event of the hetman's treachery with great amazement.'[92] To Prince V. V. Dolgoruky he wrote: 'Mazepa did not wish to die with a good name: (already with one foot in the grave) he turned traitor and went over to the Swedes. However, praise be to God, he had scarcely five collaborators in this scheme and this land is as it was.'[93] Peter regarded the defection of his 'loyal subject', whom he had made a knight of St Andrew in February 1700, as a personal insult. Mazepa was 'a new Judas'.[94]

After Mazepa's defection, Peter sent huge numbers of letters to individuals and groups in Ukraine. He played upon religious sentiments—for example, by accusing Mazepa of plans to hand over Orthodox monasteries and churches to the Catholics and the Uniates.[95] The Zaporozhian Cossacks were urged to

> stand against that enemy for the sake of the Orthodox faith and for your fatherland ... And for your loyal service to us, the great sovereign, our favour will never be removed from you, although that damned traitor, former hetman Mazepa, constantly cast false aspersions upon you, claiming that you were not loyal to us. ... But now, seeing your loyal service to us, and that libels were made wrongfully against you, our loyal subjects, by that criminal and traitor Mazepa, our favour to you for your loyal and constant services will increase and you can be sure of our favour.[96]

On 6 November 1708 a lengthy statement was issued to the Little Russian people, which accused Charles of desecrating Orthodox churches in Lithuania, turning them into kirks, entering them with dogs, hurling the Sacrament on the ground, and other such violations.[97] On 12 November Ivan Staropadsky, the colonel of Starodub, was installed as hetman, and Mazepa was excommunicated. An effigy of him was stripped of the cross of the order of St Andrew and hanged, and the sentence was read out in churches all over Ukraine.[98] The new hetman was assured that Cossack rights would be respected, except 'in cases of conflict with affairs of the state, such as treason'.[99]

In fact, Peter had reason to be grateful for Mazepa's 'treachery' in so far as it helped to lure Charles into Ukraine. Captain James Jeffereys, the English envoy at Swedish field headquarters, echoed Swedish hopes when he wrote that 'the invasion of this country will not only fournish His Maj:ty provision for his army, but give him occasion of bringing Gen:ll Mazeppa ... to some reason'. He wrote of Swedish anticipation of coming into a country 'plenti-full of all necessaryes' and 'flowing with milk and honey', in stark contrast with borderlands which had been laid waste and burnt as far as Smolensk, and where there was little sustenance for man or beast.[100] In the event, Mazepa brought only 3,000–4,000 men to aid the Swedes and the huge stockpiles of provisions at Baturin were lost. Substantial aid turned out to be a 'mirage'. On the contrary, there was resistance from Ukrainians against the Swedes in the form of guerilla warfare. The prospect of a restoration of Polish Catholic rule, via Charles's puppet Leszczynski, was probably even more unappealing than the continuation of rule from Moscow.[101]

Despite these developments, in December 1708 Peter was far from confi-dent of victory. He wrote to Apraksin: 'I don't expect this winter to pass without a general battle (since to wait until spring is not without danger), but this game is in God's hands, and who knows who will have the good fortune?'[102] There was no battle, but the winter itself, one of the severest in living memory all over Europe, did its work. In early January 1709 hundreds of Swedes froze to death outside the town of Hadyach, where Charles sought winter quarters. The Lutheran pastor, Daniel Krman, travelling with the Swedes, describes how surgeons cut off frost-bitten fingers and toes. 'We experienced such cold as I shall never forget. The spittle from mouths turned to ice before hitting the ground, sparrows fell frozen from the roofs to the ground. You could see some men without hands, others without hands and feet, others deprived of fingers, face, ears and noses, others crawling like quadrupeds.'[103]

In early spring of 1709 Peter was in Voronezh, while Menshikov stayed in the south with the main army. On 12 April 1709 the Swedes were beaten at Sokolki, let down by the Zaporozhian Cossacks who accompanied them but did not enter the battle. April and May found Peter in Azov and Taganrog taking a course of strong medicine which left him feeling 'as weak as a child'.[104] Charles, meanwhile, was hoping for Crimean support, despite the fact that Turkish opposition to such an alliance had already resulted once in the overthrow of the Crimean khan Devlet-Girei in 1703. The latter's son, Khandzhi-Selim-Girei, proposed an alliance with Charles; but only in 1708, with Devlet back on the throne, was an agreement reached, to include a force of Zaporozhians and Bulavin refugees under the command of the rebel Don Cossack ataman Nekrasov. The Crimeans tried to get the Turks to throw in their support, but the sultan preferred to remain neutral. In spring 1709 Peter is said to have met a Turkish envoy in Azov, bribed him with gold, and released a group of prisoners of war. The energetic efforts of P. A. Tolstoy, Russia's ambassador in Constantinople, also helped.[105] Fears of resurgence of a Greater Poland may have made the Turks unwilling to aid the Swedes. Nevertheless, Charles continued to expect Tatar aid, perhaps not fully aware of the extent to which the khan depended on the decisions of the sultan. The threat of another unwelcome alliance, between the Zaporozhians and the

Tatars, was averted when on 14 May 1709 Russian troops stormed the Zaporozhian Sich (Camp) on the Dnieper. Peter rejoiced at the news of the destruction of 'that accursed place which was the root of evil and a hope for the enemy'. In a letter to his son Alexis, he referred to the Sich as a 'nest of traitors'.[106] Other Cossack settlements were burnt, sacked, and pillaged. This action was an important prelude to Poltava, as it not only deprived Charles of already wavering Zaporozhian support, but made the Turks even less inclined to sanction Tatar aid. Auxiliaries and supplies from the north failed to materialize, and the troops of the Swedish General Krassow (in Pomerania) and King Stanislas were hampered by the Russians. To gain time, in May the Swedes began to besiege the small Ukrainian town of Poltava on the River Vorskla.

III.   POLTAVA: 27 JUNE 1709

The ground was prepared for one of the great landmarks in Russian history, which maintained its patriotic appeal into Soviet times, when countless historians parroted Frederick Engels's remark that the defeat of Charles XII showed Russia's 'invincibility' to the world, and Vissarion Belinsky's to the effect that Poltava was a battle 'for the existence of a whole nation, for the future of a whole state'.[107] If Poltava has lost some of its gloss in the post-Soviet era, it is because both the site and the Baltic conquests which it helped to secure are no longer part of Russia. The battle has been described many times, the field plans pored over by generations of military historians.[108] The 'heroism' of Peter and his men was enhanced by the invincible reputation of the Swedish army. In the words of the Czech pastor Daniel Krman, who was at the battle, 'The whole world is witness to the fact that nowhere on earth could you see soldiers more easily bearing heat and cold, strain and hunger, who carried out orders with greater ardour, went into battle more readily at the signal, were more prepared for death, who avoided revolt for longer, lived peacefully in camp, behaved themselves so piously or, changing battle positions, were able more skilfully to form themselves into a wedge or a circle then immediately into a triangle or a square or perform scissor or saw movements.'[109]

The reality is perhaps less heroic than the legend. By the time Charles's troops arrived at Poltava, they were overstretched and exhausted after two years on the move in alien terrain, worn down by a severe winter and intense summer heat, by skirmishes, and shortages of food and fodder. Leadership played a role. Charles was forced into ineffectiveness as a result of a wounded foot, and anxiety for his safety may have distracted the attention of his already overburdened staff. The two Swedish generals Rehnsköld and Löwenhaupt were at loggerheads, with the result that the former failed to communicate the battle plan to the latter, who made a fatal error in detaching his troops from the main army. General Roos sacrificed men by a prolonged attack on a

useless redoubt in the initial stages of battle. By the time the main engagement commenced, something like a third of the Swedish troops had been lost.
Another crucial factor was the relative numbers of cannon and men. Peter
had at least 40,000 men and 5,000 irregulars, while the Swedes had a force
variously estimated at 22,000–28,000.[110] The Swedes failed to deploy their
artillery (which in any case they barely had the strength to transport), anticipating a quick breakthrough with cavalry, and they met with fire from seventy
guns in the Russian camp, which had 102 pieces, including regimental guns,
at its disposal. This thinned Swedish ranks. The Russians' artillery 'laid our
men low, as grass before a scythe', wrote an eyewitness.[111] The Russians
'destroyed the whole guard of King Charles, which was the heart and soul of
the Swedish army. These old and splendidly trained soldiers were bombarded
as though by a hail of iron. They fell before they could draw their weapons.'[112]
Even when Swedes had the chance to fire a volley, the poor quality of their
powder meant that most bullets fell short. Calculations that the Russians
would remain passive or could be cut off from a difficult escape route from
behind their camp (on the assumption that they would flee) proved
unfounded. Swedish losses on the battlefield were 6,901 dead or wounded
and 2,760 captured. Russians suffered 1,345 killed and 3,290 wounded (figures
from the official Russian war journal). On 30 June the remnant of the
Swedish army, 14,299 men and 34 cannon, surrendered at Perevolochna on
the Dnieper to Menshikov's Russian contingent of only 9,000 troops. Charles
made his escape across the Dnieper into Turkish territory, with his aides, a
handful of Cossacks, and a few hundred cavalrymen.

Daniel Krman defended the king's decision to go into battle, criticized by
many as foolhardy, on the grounds that it was taken

as a result of cruel and severe necessity. For he saw that the enemy, in its own
country, had an abundance of provisions whereas the Swedes with each day
were experiencing more and more difficulties and shortages; the few villages
which till now had supplied provisions at great cost were exhausted and were
incapable even of feeding themselves, and the bread which separate regiments
had obtained for themselves was running out and it was impossible to
replenish the stores. After the exhaustion of provisions following the long siege
of Poltava and the weakening of the soldiers' strength as a result of the Scythian
cold of the previous winter, terrible spring roads and summer famine, many,
although they hoped that fate would take a turn for the better, preferred an
honourable death to a life of disaster. ... His majesty the tsar openly admitted
that his aim was to weaken the Swedes by means of dragging out a fair fight,
wearing them out with frequent sorties of light cavalry composed of Cossacks
and Kalmyks, preventing them from obtaining provisions, increasing hunger
and leading them to the thought of making peace. I think that King Charles
pitied the lot of his men and wanted to defend his just cause in open battle.
However the inner driving force of that day is known best of all to God and
Charles.[113]

The battle has generated some powerful legends, including one about Peter's address to his men before the battle:

> Let the Russian troops know that the hour has come which has placed the fate of all the fatherland in their hands, to decide whether Russia will be lost or will be reborn in a better condition. Do not think of yourselves as armed and drawn up to fight for Peter but for the state which has been entrusted to Peter, for your kin and for the people of all Russia, which has until now been your defence and now awaits the final decision of fortune. Do not be confused by the enemy's reputation for invincibility which they themselves have shown to be false on many occasions. Keep before your eyes in this action that God and truth are fighting with us, which the Lord strong in battle has already testified by his aid in many military actions, think of this alone. Of Peter know only that he sets no value on his life if only Russia lives and Russian piety, glory and well-being.[114]

There is no original written text and no eyewitness testimony to this speech (the earliest reference is found in *The History of the Emperor Peter I*, edited by Archbishop Feofan Prokopovich), but it is not entirely implausible that Peter said something along these lines before the battle. Peter himself was mentioned in dispatches for 'bravery, magnanimity and military skill', and his image on his steed was captured in several paintings and engravings.[115]

Immediately after the victory Peter summed up its significance with the memorable phrase: 'Now with God's help the final stone has been laid in the foundation of St Petersburg.'[116] Years later in 1724 he drafted plans for celebrating what was to be the last Poltava anniversary before his death, in which he asked that in speeches and verses mention of victory should be tempered by reference to 'our lack of experience in all matters' and to the fact that 'at the beginning of the war, we started like blind men ignorant of the opposing forces and our own condition. ... We had many internal hindrances, also the affair of our son and the Turks moving to attack us. All other nations had the policy of maintaining a balance in the forces of their neighbours and refused to admit us to the light of reason in all matters, especially in military affairs, but they did not succeed in this affair.' The victory was, in the final analysis, 'a divine miracle; it reveals that all human minds are as nothing against the will of God'.[117] Foreign observers viewed the event with some foreboding. Leibniz wrote to the Russian envoy in Vienna: 'You can imagine how the great revolution in the north has astounded people. It is being said that the tsar will be formidable to the whole of Europe, that he will be a sort of Turk of the North.'[118]

In 1722, after the war had ended, a churchman would describe the victory at Poltava as 'the seed and the root of this wondrous peace, which has now been harvested';[119] but it was not sufficient to end the war in 1709, nor did Peter expect it to. In October 1709 he was giving orders for 10,000 'essential' recruits to be made ready by December.[120] Guns were moved up to the Baltic. Without fortified bases in Estonia and Latvia, the eastern Baltic acquisitions were still vulnerable. Charles for his part regarded Poltava as only a temporary set-back. He escaped to Turkish territory, to resume his campaign later. Victory gave Peter the opportunity to attempt to restore and extend the northern alliance and to push Russian influence further west. Poland was freed from Swedish occupation, and Augustus was restored to the Polish throne. A meeting between him and Peter in Toruń produced a new treaty of alliance, signed on 9 October 1709, allowing Peter to station troops in Poland. A secret clause recognized Augustus's claim to Livonia. Augustus, for his part, realized that he owed his crown to Russia. The Poltava victory determined Russia's programme of maintaining Poland's 'golden liberties' and the territorial integrity of the Republic right up to the first partition of 1772. In 1710 a conference in Warsaw ratified the Russo–Polish peace treaty of 1686 and agreed to recognize the Russian–Polish borders it had established.[121] Any signs of resistance were quickly nipped in the bud. In 1715 a confederation opposed to Augustus's reforms was checked by Russian mediation and 18,000 Russian troops. In 1717 the so-called Dumb Sejm agreed to a set of Russian conditions which limited the number of guards to be kept by the king and restricted the Polish army to 12,000 men. Russia thus assumed the role of protector which heralded its future role as ruler of a large section of the former Polish commonwealth. Under Peter, Russian ascendancy over Poland was still expressed in diplomatic terms rather than in terms of territorial expansion. Peter probably felt that his involvement in Poland was already sufficient, without stretching resources. Russia was in charge, although vigilance was needed. In 1722 fears about Augustus's health led Peter to urge that a successor be found. Other courts were searching, 'but we are sleeping and if something were to happen suddenly we would be left out, therefore we should have someone up our sleeve too'.[122] He suggested making a pact with the king of Prussia against the king of Poland if the latter tried to incline the Poles towards making the monarchy hereditary by crowning his son.[123]

IV.   BATTLE FOR THE BALTIC: 1709–1710

Poltava also affected Russia's relations with other northern states. On 10 (21) October a treaty was signed with Prussia, which had designs on Swedish possessions in Germany. Frederick I agreed to bar Swedish troops from access to Poland from Pomerania. A secret clause agreed on ceding Elbing to Prussia. A treaty of 11 (22) October bound Denmark, which now had less cause to fear Sweden, to operations in Scania on the Swedish mainland.[124] Britain expressed willingness to act as mediator between Russia and Sweden, even to draw Russia into the Northern Alliance.[125] The French, for whom 1709 had been a disastrous year, were prepared for Russia to act as mediator, together with Denmark and Poland, in the War of the Spanish Succession.[126] Such developments seem to confirm the view of Soviet historians that Peter held most of the cards in the post-Poltava period.[127] But Poltava also brought complications. The maritime powers were anxious lest Russia become too powerful. Britain in particular insisted that Sweden must not be allowed to collapse completely, and that a balance must be maintained among the northern powers.[128] Russia still had to consolidate its position in the Baltic. A unit of about 8,000 Swedish troops remained in Pomerania under the command of Major-General Krassow. Peter would have liked to eliminate them, but was prevented from doing so by various agreements between the northern allies, who did not welcome the prospect of Russian troops in Germany and were keen to neutralize the latter.[129] No wonder Peter was soon to get bogged down in northern politics.

Nor was Russia completely secure in the south. The king of Denmark had asked Peter for money to arm his fleet. In February 1710 the Danish envoy Just Juel received the following reply to his king's request: 'Now on account of the state of war and many expenses, also for fear of a sudden attack by the Turks, for which emergency preparations are being made, His Majesty cannot help, but will do what can be done in the future. Although His Majesty the tsar has no obligation to do so, he will help His Majesty the King as best he can. In the meantime His Majesty the king should himself act for the common good and arm his fleet at his own expense and go into action, which he is capable of doing as they have been at peace for a long time while we have been at war.'[130] On 6 February 1710 news reached Russia that the 1700 peace treaty with Turkey had been renewed. Peter wrote: 'For this fine deed, praise be to the all-powerful Lord: now we can turn our eyes and thoughts in one direction.'[131]

There were successes in the north: in early February Elbing was captured.[132] On 14 June Peter entered the fortress of Viborg, which was subdued with naval support. Karelia had been cleared of Swedish troops. 'By the capture of this town [Viborg] St Petersburg has finally become secure.' It was a 'firm bolster' for the city. The conquest was duly celebrated in the company of the All-Drunken Assembly, and proclamations were sent to allies and to the mock sovereigns Romodanovsky and Buturlin.[133]

On 4 July 1710 Riga capitulated to Sheremetev, after a long siege which had begun in November 1709.[134] In May plague struck: 9,800 Russians died as well as some 30,000 people inside the town.[135] Thereafter, several Swedish garrisons, many laid low by plague, fell to the Russians in quick succession: on 8 August Dünamünde, 14 August Pernau, 8 September Kexholm (Korela), 13 September the island of Oesel and the fortress at Arensburg and 29 September the Estonian port of Reval (Tallin). Peter wrote to Romodanovsky on 10 October: 'I beg to inform your majesty that the All-Highest has granted us success in this campaign almost comparable with the last, for the last town, Reval, has surrendered to Lieutenant-General Bauer. And so Livonia and Estonia are cleansed of the enemy. In a word, the enemy on the left side of this eastern sea not only has no towns but also no territory left. Now it only remains to ask the Lord God for a good peace.'[136] There was no more talk of handing over Livonia to Augustus, with whom Peter now had no compunction about breaking agreements.

Russian victories in the Baltic ports were consolidated by maintaining, and in some cases restoring, local privileges and laws. The occupation of Riga, for example, was followed by a series of guarantees of the rights of townspeople and nobles with regard to religion, municipal lands, income, charters, justice, customs, and freedoms as established under Polish and Swedish kings, and the continuation of local religious and secular officials; all debts, except those to the Swedish Crown, were to be honoured; magistrates were to be in charge of weapons; German was to remain the official language; the local currency was to remain, but Russian currency was to be accepted as legal tender, 'in order that the property and income of the town, both inside and outside, should not suffer any decrease or change, but be maintained and as far as possible increased'. There was to be no billeting except in barracks. Foreigners and refugees from Dorpat were also to enjoy the tsar's protection. Those wishing to leave or return were allowed to do so in the course of a year, but anyone with property not back within six months would forfeit it. 'On the basis of the points above, all offences which were committed at the time of the blockade and seige are discounted, forgiven and committed to oblivion, and the town and its inhabitants, also all strangers resident here, each and every one, with all his property is free from any pillage, bombardment, military requisition and all other such burdens with which they might be loaded, and enjoy the full protection of His Majesty the Tsar.'[137] The charter issued to the nobility of Livonia in 1561 by Sigismund Augustus was confirmed, thereby guaranteeing their noble rights, statutes, freedoms, status, legal possessions, and estates. Those who were still away, even in Swedish service, were allowed to return to their estates, within a time limit of one year and six weeks; if they were in enemy service, the deadline was six months after capitulation.[138]

In August 1710 Reval was promised privileges similar to Riga if it capitulated.[139] Charters were issued to Estland (Estonia) in February 1712, one to the town of Reval, the other to the nobility, 'confirming all their previous privileges, rights of legal proceedings, law codes and customs which they have enjoyed of old'.[140] On 1 March 1712 a charter to the nobility promised to defend and protect all their privileges received of old, grants, rights, justice, charters, law codes, and 'other praiseworthy Christian practices'.[141] Baltic privileges were to be further guaranteed in Peter's General Regulation of 1720 and in the 1721 Treaty of Nystad, under clauses 9 (on the privileges and rights of the 'Swedish provinces') and 10 (on the Evangelical Faith).[142]

These and other enactments formed the basis of the special status of the Baltic provinces. Peter was anxious to restore trade and enterprise to the region on the basis of laws and structures which had proved effective in the past. There could be no question of a wholesale replacement of local officials by Russians, even if skilled Russian manpower had been available. On the contrary, in Peter's reign and beyond, Russia was able to make good use of Baltic personnel, from experts to teach Russians leather tanning and how to make improved scythes[143] to educated nobles in government service. Nobles from Livonia and Estonia were to serve on the same conditions as Russians. Those with ranks were to keep them, those without, to follow the same path—guards infantry, education, and training—as Russians.[144] Estonian and Livonian laws were later used as models for new Russian legislation: for example, statutes on landed estates and laws on provision for orphans.[145] But privileges were accompanied by watchfulness on the part of the Russian authorities. Peter wrote to the governor of Riga in 1716 warning him that there were still many supporters of Sweden in the Baltic towns, and that he should act with caution, taking regular censuses of the population. All new arrivals were to be questioned and arrested on the least suspicion; a curfew was to be imposed on traders inside the city walls (only essential commodities were to be brought in); and a maximum of 300 people were to be allowed into the town each day. Carts and cargoes should be searched for weapons, and ships docking in summer were to be searched below the decks.[146] In February 1720 the magistrates and councillors of Riga were rebuked for failing to keep up with repairs of the fortifications and maintenance of the garrison and munitions stores and for irregularities in the election of magistrates and in court procedures. The governor was instructed to oversee these matters. In other words, the Russian authorities did not shrink from interfering in local affairs.[147]

Rights were a two-way deal. Religious freedom was guaranteed in the conquered provinces, but at the same time facilities for Orthodox worship had to be provided. In Riga a wooden Lutheran church and a chapel in the citadel were turned into Orthodox churches (one in the name of SS Peter and Paul). A destroyed Catholic church in the town was restored and reconsecrated as Orthodox in the name of Alexis Man of God, and in 1715 a new church was founded in honour of the Annunciation. Priests had to be imported. In April 1715 Peter wrote to the governor: 'As you are well aware, the priests (*popy*) in Riga are very bad, which shames us in the eyes of the local inhabitants. Therefore find decent and experienced priests in Smolensk and other church servitors, and send them to Riga and send away the ones who are no good.'[148]

Russian needs came first, but Peter was anxious to be seen as better (or at least not worse) than the Swedes. When in 1712 Estonian officials complained of misbehaviour by dragoons stationed on the Baltic, Peter at once ordered the latter's commander to investigate.[149] On 9 July 1720 he wrote to Repnin in Riga, following complaints against Peter Bestuzhev's behaviour in Courland: 'In Courland our men have committed many offences, including the taking of excessive contributions [for upkeep of troops], and especially interfering in local administration and collection of revenues.' They were ordered to restrict their activity to the estates allocated to the dowager duchess Anna Ioannovna, and not to keep too many carriages at post stations, as this deprived the locals of horses, and to pay the proper rate.[150]

The main effect of war on the Baltic region was devastation. Weber (in Riga in 1714) records that the land was 'so dispeopled, that not the fourth Part of it is inhabited, and the vast Number of Ruins of Gentlemens Seats, and other Houses, shew what Ravage the War has made there'. Apparently at the beginning of the war Kalmyk and Tatar troops committed 'horrid Barbarities'. But he suggests that the nobles were not entirely hostile, but were in favour of 'continuing under the Russian Government, as they entertained Hopes of being restored to their former Estates which they lost by the late Resumption during the Swedish Administration; but the Burghers and the Country People wished to return to their former Allegiance'.[151] A report from Governor Repnin in April 1721 complained of garrisons undermanned (often with old or inexperienced troops), low munitions and food supplies, and fortifications in Riga and Dünamünde in need of repair.[152]

V.   WAR WITH TURKEY. THE PRUTH CAMPAIGN AND THE TREATY OF ADRIANOPLE: 1711–1713

In 1710 Peter had only just begun to consider the longer-term implications of his new Baltic acquisitions, and in general he had good reason to be pleased rather than apprehensive. The summer campaign had been a brilliant success, with the capture of eight fortresses in a season made all the more impressive by the fact that more powder had been expended on firing victory salutes than on military operations.[153] A carnival atmosphere prevailed in St Petersburg, which witnessed a three-day victory celebration on 8–10 October, followed by the wedding of Peter's niece Anna to the duke of Courland.[154] The same good cheer might have prevailed through Christmas and New Year, but on 23 December 1710 Peter received the news that Turkey had declared war and that his ambassador, Peter Tolstoy, had been thrown into the Seven Towers in Constantinople.[155] Just Juel wrote that the Russians were so depressed by the news that they wandered around listlessly (although he attributed at least some of their limpness to the fast which preceded Christmas).[156]

Historians have paid so much attention to Peter's 'window on the West' policies that Turkish affairs are often relegated to the background, and the Russo–Turkish war of 1711 is treated as an unfortunate interlude that deflected Peter from his main purpose. As we know, however, Turkish and Crimean activities were an important consideration in the calculations of Peter's government throughout the Northern War, particularly when the theatre of operations shifted to Ukraine in 1707–9. The Turks had stopped short of intervention at the time of Poltava, but now Charles's escape to Turkish Bender tipped the scales. Charles had been pressing the Turks to declare war on Peter. The Turks were irritated by Peter's demands to hand over the king, and the rabidly anti-Russian Crimean khan Devlet-Girei offered Tatar troops to escort Charles north, and succeeded in winning the sultan's ear.[157] French diplomacy, loans to Charles XII by British bankers, Austrian neutrality, even the intervention of the sultan's doctor and mother, all influenced the Ottoman decision to go to war. The expansion of Russian influence in Ukraine was particularly unwelcome to the Ottomans.

There is reason to believe that Peter himself was not averse to the prospect of a 'short, victorious war' in the south. The switch of attention to the Baltic in 1700 had been caused by international circumstances (notably the collapse of the Holy League, as discussed earlier) as much as by any overwhelming preference for pursuing conquests in the north. Peter was almost as pleased with Azov as with St Petersburg. On 20 April 1709 he returned there for the first time since 1699, delighted to find towns in places 'where once there were open fields and water'. He wrote to Menshikov from Trinity fortress at Taganrog on 4 May: 'In this place, where ten years ago we saw just open country, with God's help now we find a fine town with a harbour (and although when the master has been away for a long time not everything is in order, still there is something to look at).'[158] He even diverted workers originally intended for St Petersburg to work there.[159] A new Turkish war offered opportunities for propaganda to Russians still basking in the glory of Poltava and the Baltic campaign. A Russian victory could change the political map of south-east Europe and speed up a solution in the north by depriving Sweden of a potential ally. There was also the religious factor. The 'Third Rome' doctrine had its strongest practical appeal not in the sixteenth century, when it was formulated as a more or less abstract ideal, but in the eighteenth, when it became plausible to act upon it. Peter was the first Russian ruler to 'don the mantle of liberator of the Balkan Christians'.[160] If we take into account the more ambitious hopes, dormant until now, of further expansion into Ottoman lands and a crusade against the infidels, then it is easy to see that although Peter may have regretted the timing of the Turkish declaration of war, he had good reasons for reviving his southern policy.

Orders were issued for a large-scale mobilization. On 5 January 1711 Peter ordered Sheremetev to march south from Riga, collecting recruits at Smolensk. 'If there is any delay, you will be held responsible,' he told him.[161] Sheremetev's appeal for more time was greeted by an order to proceed 'without delay, with all haste, setting all excuses aside' in order to reach the Moldavian border by the end of March.[162] Afraid that the Turks would invade Ukraine and Poland (10,000 janissaries set off to attack Kamieniec in December), Peter was also aggrieved at the tardiness of the governors in supplying reinforcements for the Riga garrison.[163] Preparations went slowly. Peter wrote to Menshikov: 'Don't be upset because I don't write often; really there's indescribable confusion and depression on account of the mess things are in here.'[164] The tsar's own route south had to be changed to avoid Tatar raids, away from Kiev to a more northerly road via Smolensk and Slutsk.

Routine peace proposals were made to the Swedes, in the hope of avoiding war on two fronts; but Charles refused to relinquish even one province to buy a 'shameful peace'.[165] Russian hopes of mediation by the maritime powers proved unfounded. On 22 February Peter issued a declaration of war, which depicted the 'oath-breaking' sultan as the ally of Sweden and Leszczynski, and accused him of using followers of Mazepa and Bulavin against Augustus and all Christendom. The document set out the history of Russo–Turkish relations for the past thirty years or so, itemizing offences committed by Turkish subjects against Russia during truces.[166] Peter was apprehensive. On 24 February he chided Aleksei Kurbatov, the new vice-governor of Archangel, for complaining about his posting, 'like some faint-hearted Jonah, without regard for the troubles and griefs in which your leader finds himself'.[167]

An appeal was made to the 'subject peoples' of the Balkans, in the hope of turning the campaign into a crusade by linking up with the Orthodox provinces of Moldavia and Wallachia. In a rescript addressed to the 'Christian peoples subjugated to Turkey', Peter wrote: 'I am taking upon myself a heavy burden for the sake of the love of God, for which reason I have entered into war with the Turkish realm.' He appealed to all who loved God to take on the same burden, 'because the Turks have trampled on our faith, taken our churches and lands by cunning, pillaged and destroyed many of our churches and monasteries'.[168] Standards carried in the campaign bore the image of the cross and the legend of Constantine the Great: 'Under this sign we conquer.' Peter left for Smolensk on 6 March, accompanied by his future wife Catherine, to whom he had just become formally betrothed.[169]

On 12–13 April a council of war in Slutsk produced a plan which envisaged a forced Russian march to the Danube to head off the Turks before they reached Moldavia and Poland. It was hoped that simultaneous revolts in Turkish possessions would sap Turkish morale. Sheremetev was supposed to reach the Dniester by 20 May, but protested on the grounds that his troops were worn out, recruits were needed, and supplies and guns were in the wrong places. Where was he to obtain three months' supplies for 40,000 men? A forced march meant that they could not carry heavy supplies with them. But Peter insisted upon *speed*. It was vital to reach the Danube before the Turks did and to join forces with the hospodars of Moldavia and Wallachia, who were promising support, the former on the basis of a secret defensive treaty of 1709. A treaty was signed with the hospodar Dmitry Cantemir (former friend of the Crimean khan) in Moldavia in April 1711. In return for military support, Moldavia was to become an autonomous Russian protectorate. Cantemir was to be given sanctuary in Russia if he needed it. But no further agreement could be reached with Brancovan, the hospodar of Wallachia. The Russians may not have been fully aware of dissensions within the ruling circles of the two provinces, or of the fierce rivalries between the respective hospodars. In Wallachia the pro-Russian Thomas Cantacuzene denounced Brancovan, but apparently the majority of the Wallachian élite held the view that 'it is dangerous to declare for Russia until the tsar's army crosses the Danube. Who knows whether Wallachia in the power of the Russians will be happier than under the domination of the Turks?'[170] In the meantime, poor harvests had created food shortages along the way, which were not alleviated by the hoped-for aid from Wallachia. The intense heat burned the grass, causing fodder shortages reminiscent of those during Golitsyn's 1680s campaigns against the Tatars. What little water there was was putrid. Lack of supplies and logistical failures were to prove crucial.[171]

The decision to continue the Russian march to the River Pruth was based on hopes of aid and the mistaken belief that the Turks were weaker than turned out to be the case. In the event, the Turks got there first, and 38,000 Russian troops found themselves facing a combined Turkish and Tatar force of 130,000 men. Cantemir supplied only about 5,000 men, while any lingering hope of aid from the reluctant Brancovan was dashed by the arrival of the Turkish army, to whom he had turned over his supplies. Peter arrived on the River Pruth on 23 June, and on 30 June wrote to Menshikov: 'Our march was indescribably hard on account of the heat and thirst ... I expect things to be resolved by the middle of July as to whether there will be a battle or not. May God give his grace to the righteous in this affair. People are saying that the Turks are not very enthusiastic about this war, but God alone knows if this is so. They have strong artillery, five hundred cannons.'[172]

The battle which was joined on 9 July is renowned as a major defeat. In fact, the Turks suffered huge losses in their first encounter with the Russian artillery, but the Russians were unaware of the extent of the damage inflicted. The janissaries were afraid of Russian fire power, and urged the vizier to start peace talks. Peter refused to counter-attack before digging in his supply train. The battle was thus inconclusive, but the Russians could not afford to wait for a conclusion because of impending starvation and lack of ammunition. Peter's dilemma was summed up in a letter to the Senate dated 10 July: his troops were surrounded, and he was likely to either die or be taken prisoner. In the latter event the senators were instructed to cease to regard him as their sovereign until he returned in person. In the event of his death, they were to choose 'the most worthy of my successors'.[173] In the end, total disaster, including Peter's own capture, was averted by the moderation of Turkish demands, which were probably tempered by news of the Russian General Rönne's successful raid of 7 July, on the Danube at Brailov, where Turkish powder stores were burned. There were also rumours that a huge bribe persuaded the grand vizier to allow the Russians to retreat, despite the protests of the Crimean khan.[174]

Peace negotiations began promptly. By the peace treaty of 12 July 1711, Russia surrendered Azov and its environs to Turkey. Taganrog and Kamenny Zaton (on the Dnieper above the Sich) were to be razed. (In Peter's hand-corrected version of the treaty, Azov is not mentioned by name.)[175] The Russians were to refrain from interference in Polish affairs. Merchants were to be allowed free passage across the borders. The Russians must not impede the return home of the king of Sweden, who was currently under the sultan's protection. The Russian fleet at Azov was to be destroyed, with the exception of four ships which were to be sold to the Turks.[176] There was much argument about the status of Poland, which was to be designated a free state (subject to neither Russian nor Turkish interference). Peter commented to Apraksin and others in letters dated 15 July that 'it is not without sadness to lose those places in which so much effort and losses have been invested, but this loss means a strengthening for the other side [i.e., war with Sweden], which is an incomparable gain for us'.[177] In fact, Russia got off lightly. The sultan could have pushed Swedish claims for the return of territory. (Peter was willing to give up everything except St Petersburg, but the vizier did not know this.) Anxious to turn to conquests in the Mediterranean, Turkey contented itself with 'formal signs' of Russian withdrawal from Poland, and refused to give any further guarantees to Sweden. Charles was furious. Western powers who had hoped that more radical losses would keep Russia out of North German politics were also disappointed. As for Peter, he made the best of the defeat on the Pruth. 'On the one hand,' he wrote, 'this peace represents a loss; on the other by this event we have entirely disengaged ourselves from the Turkish side and are [better] able with all our strength and with God's help to fight the Swedes.'[178] To Apraksin, who was dealing with the evacuation of Azov, he again looked on the bright side: 'Of course, it's very painful, but it's best to choose the lesser of two evils, for you yourself can judge which war is the more difficult to conclude.'[179] He pointed out the perils of being engaged on two fronts if the War of the Spanish Succession were to end and allow a third front to open against Russia.

But Peter was not entirely resigned to giving up Azov and its environs. 'The Lord God drove me out of this place, like Adam out of paradise,' he is alleged to have said, using an image more often associated with St Petersburg.[180] It was decided to delay the destruction of Taganrog until confirmation was received that Charles had left Turkey. It was specified that the foundations should be retained, 'as in time God might make things different'. Peter expected to be back![181] He hoped to get away with token demolition, and reprimanded Apraksin for being too 'desperate' to comply with Turkish demands, instructing him to make accurate sketches of the fortifications.[182] The handover had still not taken place in November, as there was no confirmation that Charles had left; but Peter made it clear that if the Turks threatened to declare war again over Azov and Taganrog, the order should be carried out immediately, even without confirmation of the king's whereabouts.[183] At the same time, Peter gave instructions to Sheremetev that, once Charles set off, his journey should be slowed down as much as possible, to prevent him from arriving in Sweden too long before the start of the next campaign. Early in 1712 the Turks responded to these delays by declaring war, but the conflict was resolved after Azov was finally handed over by the signing of a second peace treaty (the Iusuf–Pasha Pact) on 5 April 1712, which gave a deadline for the withdrawal of Russian troops from Polish territory. Further delays by the Russians in honouring this clause resulted in yet another declaration of war in October 1712. These hostilities were precipitated by the forging in September 1712 of an alliance between Sweden and France (at Bender) in the interests of the Turks: the Swedes were to guarantee Leszczynski as king of Poland and to make Poland return Kamieniec and Podolia to the Turks. The Porte was supposed to force the tsar to return Kiev and its district to Poland and to enforce the clause in the Treaty of Pruth about the tsar not interfering in Polish and Cossack–Ukrainian affairs.[184] But this agreement had no force, even though Peter took it sufficiently seriously to make emergency plans to abandon Kiev and blow up the walls of Caves Monastery after the Porte declared war.[185]

On 13 June 1713 a new treaty was finally signed at Adrianople by Peter's envoys (held as hostages) Peter Shafirov and Mikhail Sheremetev on the basis of the treaties of 1711 and 1712.[186] The first clause obliged Russia to withdraw its troops from Poland within two months. Peter was not to interfere in the government of Polish affairs, and henceforth must not send his troops into Poland on any pretext, but must 'keep his hands off' (*otnimet ruku ot onoi*), except in the case of an alliance between Sweden and Poland against Russia. (The Russian negotiators had protested that the tsar was a sovereign ruler (*samovlasten*) who went wherever he wanted. At this point the Turks accused the Russians of wasting time and of 'deceit', and threatened to tear up the whole document. ('In view of the pride of these barbarians and the savagery of the vizier', Shafirov and Sheremetev acquiesced.[187]) Clause 2 reiterated the guarantees about Charles XII's safe passage home from Turkey. Clause 3 confirmed that Cossacks on the Left Bank of the Dnieper were to remain subjects of the tsar, and that Kiev was a Russian possession. Clauses 4–6 banned the building of fortifications between Azov and Cherkassk (on the Don) and at Kamenny Zaton, and specified the return of Turkish cannons. Clause 7 for the first time attempted to mark the border between the two countries, along a line between the Samara and Orel rivers. Cossacks were to refrain from breaking the peace (clauses 8–9), as were Tatars and Cossacks on the Turkish side. Clause 10—on tribute payments (*zapros*) to the Crimean khan—was especially hotly contested. Shafirov wrote in his memorandum to Peter: 'This point was the most troublesome of all, for the Turks kept insisting that we agree to the tribute, saying that we promised orally at Pruth' (which they had). The Russian negotiators were threatened with death by the vizier, but they managed to hold out with the help of bribes. In the treaty it was simply stated that the issue would be resolved 'at another time'.[188] A clause which Shafirov did not succeed in including was the restoration of permanent diplomatic representation in Constantinople, although this appeared in the second Treaty of Constantinople (1720).[189] Few of the clauses of the Treaty of Adrianople had any lasting effect. Peter did not 'keep his hands off' Poland;[190] the Russo–Turkish border remained fluid; Cossacks and Tatars took little notice of agreements between Moscow and Constantinople; Charles XII returned to Sweden in November 1714, avoiding Russian territory; and Russia regained Azov in 1739. But peace allowed Peter once again to concentrate his efforts in the north.

VI. FROM PRUTH TO NYSTAD: 1711–1721

Peter's thoughts had turned to operations in the north immediately after the Treaty of Pruth. September 1711 found him in Germany, where he was to spend much of 1712, visiting Dresden and Carlsbad to arrange the marriage of his son Alexis to Princess Charlotte of Wolfenbüttel.[191] In his first letter of 1712, dated 1 January, Peter wrote to the Senate: 'And so, praise God, because of this victory [of the Danes over the Swedes at Wismar on 1 December] this year began here with celebrations. I consider it a piece of good fortune that I am able to write this in the first letter of the year. May God be so kind henceforth.'[192] The main task for the allies, having driven the Swedes from the south-eastern Baltic, was to evict them from their North German possessions, starting with Pomerania. Claims on Sweden's German territories were complicated: Hanover coveted Bremen and Verden, while Prussia and Denmark contested Stettin. Peter, it is fair to say, did not envisage stretching his resources to occupy Swedish possessions in North Germany, even though the politics of the eventual carve-up were of interest to Russia. Matters were complicated by difficulties with the authorities in Poland, who were slow to provide food supplies for Russian troops.[193] Peter felt frustrated by the inactivity of his northern allies. Lack of Danish naval support prevented the capture of the island of Rügen opposite Stralsund. ('What can you do when you have allies like these?', Peter wrote to Menshikov in August.[194]) Allied efforts to counter the incursion of Swedish troops into Mecklenburg resulted in a heavy defeat for a Saxon–Danish force at Gadenbusch.

The year 1713 began with attempts at reconciliation with Sweden through pressure from France and Britain. Menshikov and Boris Kurakin were appointed ambassadors to a congress to be held in Brunswick.[195] Peter wrote to Menshikov, in terms reminiscent of those in which foreigners once spoke of Muscovite diplomacy: 'Act with as much flattery and obligingness (*nizost'*) to the Danish court as possible, for even if you speak the truth, unless you are compliant they will take it ill; you know what they are like, they have more regard for the protocol than the actual business.'[196] A Russian 'Project for Peace in the North', which mentioned the possibility of ceding Riga and Livonia to Poland, indicates that Peter was ready to compromise to secure peace.[197] Instructions issued to Menshikov dated 14 February specified that the lands which Sweden had 'unlawfully annexed in the last century'— namely Ingria and Karelia—must under no circumstances be ceded; Estonia and Reval must be retained as compensation for loss of revenue from the aforementioned, and part of Finland ceded to Russia for compensation for the present war; and Livonia, except for the Dorpat district, if not secured for Peter, was to go to the king of Poland.[198] The latter concession was later withdrawn on the pretext that Russia's interests would not be served by a weak Poland in Livonia, 'for this Crown, which is unstable and subject to incessant changes, could easily lose them [the Livonians] and cede them into the hands of Sweden or some other power'.[199]

In January 1713 a Swedish force under General Magnus Stenbock, who had been cut off from his supply fleet, was put to flight at Friedrichstadt in Holstein, and was forced to take refuge in the fortress at Tönningen in Jutland. In June they were besieged by Menshikov, who forced Stenbock to surrender with 11,485 men.[200] On 13 September 1713 Stettin capitulated to Menshikov, who was left with the dilemma of whether to turn the city over to Denmark or to Prussia. Russia needed Danish naval support, but Menshikov placed Stettin under Prussian control because Russia felt let down by the Danes and the Saxons.[201] The continuing wrangles over the city's fate indicate how easy it was to get bogged down in North German affairs. Peter chided Menshikov for allowing himself to be 'tied in knots' by Flemming, the Saxon commander, who occupied the city temporarily with Saxon and Holstein troops.[202]

On 23 April 1713, independently of their allies, the Russians launched a campaign in Finland. The galley fleet (with Peter as rear-admiral) landed with 16,000 troops at Helsingfors in early May, and took the town without a battle. On 27 July Peter wrote to Menshikov: 'With God's help we hope that all the Finnish land will be in our hands by the end of this campaign.'[203] On 30 August Peter entered Åbo (Turku) on the west coast.[204] On 27 October, in numerous dispatches home, he was able to report that the Swedes had been driven out of Finland.[205]

Despite the continuing diplomatic complexities (in April 1713 the Peace of Utrecht ended the War of the Spanish Succession, thereby giving Britain and France in particular more leisure to interfere in northern affairs), Peter continued to hope for peace: 'Now it is vital to take steps for the next campaign and to reach an agreement with the Danish court to make a successful operation and compel the enemy to make the desired peace.'[206] Despite many set-backs, the Swedes still had the power to resist. At the beginning of 1714 Peter wrote to Iaguzhinsky: 'Now all the Swedish defence force consists of their fleet. It is vital, therefore, that we are well informed about it.'[207] In May a manifesto was sent to the people of Sweden expressing Russia's desire to end the 'destructive war' between the two states.[208] Peter expressed sorrow that his 'good proposals' had been unsuccessful and that the king continued to 'demand the impossible'. [209] In July the Russians staged an impressive demonstration of naval superiority in a victory over the Swedish fleet off Cape Hangö in Finland. Peter wrote:

> We beg to report the manner in which the Almighty Lord God was pleased to glorify Russia. For, after granting us many victories on land, now we have been crowned with victory at sea, for on the 27th day of this month by Hangö [Gangut] near the haven of Rilax-Figl we captured the Swedish rear-admiral Nilsson Erenschild with one frigate, six galleys and two sloops, after much and very fierce fire. It is true that till now in this war, as with our allies in the war with France, many generals and even field marshalls have been taken, but not one flag-officer. And so we send our congratulations on this our unprecedented victory.[210]

Peter set great store by Hangö, which has been described as the 'naval Poltava'. He ordered the mock sovereign Romodanovsky to go to St Petersburg and set up some wooden triumphal gates, 'however small', on the square in time for the arrival of the fleet at Kronstadt.[211]

The year 1715 saw a joint British–Dutch squadron arrive in the Baltic to protect merchant shipping (loaded mainly with naval supplies) from Swedish attacks, and a short-lived coalition formed against Sweden by Prussia and Hanover, joined later by Poland, Saxony and Denmark. Russian troops moved into northern Germany with plans to take Wismar (which fell in April 1716) and launch a landing in Scania on the Swedish mainland with Danish naval support. In February 1716 Peter set off on a major tour of Western Europe, where he was to remain until October 1717. The pretext for this journey was the wedding of his niece Ekaterina Ioannovna to Duke Karl Leopold of Mecklenburg in Carlsbad on 8 April. Peter desired a foothold in northern Germany with a Russian garrison in Mecklenburg, and hoped to acquire the port of Wismar as a base for Russian trade through the Baltic and the Elbe. The marriage contract guaranteed the right of Russian merchants to reside and trade in Mecklenburg and free passage to Russian troops. The tsar pledged to support the duke against his enemies, including members of the local gentry, with ten Russian infantry regiments.

This constituted a virtual protectorate by Russia over Mecklenburg, which particularly alarmed Mecklenburg's neighbour George of Hanover, who had designs on Mecklenburg himself and, as George I of Great Britain, also had reason to be wary of Russia's growing naval power. The Holy Roman Emperor also had cause for concern.[212] In May 1716 Peter met the king of Prussia in Stettin, then the king of Denmark in Altona. A decision was taken to move Russian troops in preparation for an invasion of Sweden. Early August witnessed a highlight of Peter's naval career and a temporary show of allied unity when he assumed command of four fleets—Danish, Dutch, British, and Russian—off Copenhagen.[213] This event, commemorated by a medal featuring Neptune riding the waves on sea-horses, turned out to be little more than messing about in boats. The Scania landing was abandoned as a result of Russo–Danish disagreements and the deflection of the Danish fleet by Charles's operations in Norway. British support was soon to turn to opposition.

After spending the autumn and winter of 1716–17 revisiting old haunts in the Dutch Republic, in April Peter set off for Paris.[214] Relations with France had taken a turn for the better after the low of the 1680s. France played little part in the Northern War as long as the War of the Spanish Succession tied its hands and Russian action was concentrated in the eastern Baltic. But France was interested in what happened in North Germany and in maintaining a Swedish presence there, especially in Pomerania, as a counterweight to the Holy Roman Empire. In October 1716 an Anglo–French defence treaty was signed (for dynastic reasons: Britain agreed to block a Spanish successor to the French throne in the event of the death of the king of France, and France pledged not to support Stuart pretenders to the British throne). In January 1717 a triple alliance was formed between Britain, France, and the

Dutch Republic, who were joined in August 1718 by Austria. During his visit to Paris, Peter sought a friendship treaty with France in order to minimize the danger of this alliance interfering in the Northern War. He hoped to detach France from its traditional Swedish connection and to form an anti-Austrian alliance. (As it turned out, Peter overestimated the Austrian involvement in a 'plot' against him following the flight of his son Alexis to Vienna in 1716.) France resisted Russian overtures and restricted itself to reducing its subsidy to Sweden. Even so, in 1719–20 the French lent support to A. I. Dashkov's negotiations to restore Russia's diplomatic representation in Constantinople, in an attempt to counteract Austrian influence.[215]

Throughout 1717 Peter was followed around Europe with peace proposals, notably from Charles XII's envoy Baron Georg Heinrich von Görtz. Offers of mediation from Spain added a new dimension, closer relations being signalled by the exchange of announcements of the birth of a princess in both royal houses in 1718. Spain backed a speedy peace between Russia and Sweden, and even proposed a Spanish–Russian alliance which would operate against Britain and Austria, but Peter was naturally reluctant to be dragged in. Philip V offered to send thirty warships against Sweden, and even thought of marrying his son to Peter's infant daughter Natalia.[216] In fact, the outbreak of war between Spain and Austria in July 1717 was to Russia's advantage, because it tied the hands of the northern powers. 'As long as Spain is armed and at war with the Emperor, then the maritime powers and also France will have their hands too tied to interfere in affairs in the north,' wrote Boris Kurakin to Peter early in 1718.[217] Sweden was experiencing a severe financial crisis, and in December 1717 agreed to a peace congress, which opened in May 1718 in the Åland Islands.[218] The Russian ministers Shafirov, Bruce, and Osterman were issued with 'General conditions for peace', according to which Ingria, Karelia, Estonia, and Livonia, including Reval and Viborg, were to be Russian in perpetuity and Finland was to be returned to Sweden. Secret clauses included compensating Sweden by helping to restore Bremen and Verden to Swedish control. Various plans were discussed, including a Russo–Swedish alliance. But no agreement was reached. In the words of one historian: 'It is not easy to disentangle the motives and objectives of the participants.'[219]

A leading figure now left the scene. On 30 November (11 December) 1718 Charles XII was killed at Frederiksten in Norway while campaigning against Denmark, officially picked off by a stray bullet.[220] Peter is said to have wept at the news, perhaps more in the realization that this was a set-back to peace than in grief for his old enemy.[221] While Western powers were making their own arrangements with the new Swedish regime and carving up territories and spheres of influence in northern Germany, Russia found itself isolated. In January 1719 Hanover, Austria and Saxony signed an alliance, which prompted strong fears of war between Russia and Austria, which was alarmed by the prospect of a Russo–Spanish alliance. The coronation of Charles's sister Ulrika-Eleonora in Uppsala in March 1719 heralded a change in Swedish diplomatic views and a new orientation towards Britain. With peace apparently as far away as ever and the prospect of all its alliances falling away, in 1719 Russia made preparations for the resumption of the campaign. Weber wrote: 'The Czar had taken the Resolution to make the ensuing Summer a powerful Descent in Sweden with twenty six thousand Men, as the only Means to force that Crown to a speedy and reasonable Peace.'[222] On 24 May the capture of three Swedish ships by the Russian fleet off the Oesel Islands fanned fears in Stockholm, which appealed for British naval support. In June 1719, despite the unpromising atmosphere, the Åland Congress reopened, with Bruce, Iaguzhinsky, and Osterman in attendance, but problems soon emerged. A manifesto from Peter to the queen was printed in German and Swedish for distribution in Sweden, stating that Sweden was to blame for the war dragging on and that Russia was interested only in a firm peace.[223] In July 1719 Apraksin and Peter Lacy bombarded factories and mills on the Swedish coast, and this prompted the queen to issue a manifesto in August denouncing continuing Russian operations along the Swedish coast, including the burning of the towns of Norrköping, Norrtälje, and Södertälje. In July a British squadron commanded by Admiral Norris arrived at Copenhagen—only a token force, as the rest of the fleet was still held up in the Mediterranean (against Spain) and in the Channel (against the Jacobites), but with orders to meet the Russian fleet and capture Peter. Britain was annoyed at plans to cut a canal through Mecklenburg territory to the Elbe, which would give Russia direct access to the North Sea. In the face of international pressures, Peter had no choice but to abandon his support of Duke Karl Leopold. In the summer of 1719 Peter's troops left Mecklenburg, and George I's arrived, allegedly in support of the claims of the local gentry against the duke. Britain concluded an alliance with Sweden in August 1719, George I obtaining the promise of Bremen and Verden in return for aiding Sweden, mainly with naval support, to regain its eastern Baltic possessions. Sweden agreed to cede Stettin to Prussia in return for Prussia abandoning its treaty with Russia. In September 1719 at Åland, 'the Russian ministers, in view of the reluctance of the Swedish side [to make] peace and receiving orders from their sovereign', broke up the session.[224] In November 1719 the Poles expressed their willingness to cooperate with George I to fight Russia in return for Kiev and Smolensk.

At the end of 1719 things looked bleak for Russia. There had been hopes that James Charles Stuart's attempted landing in Scotland with Spanish help might divert the British fleet from the Baltic. The landing was aborted, and in October 1719 Jacobite bases in Spain were stormed, and Spain made peace with the Triple Alliance. Britain was making plans for an anti-Russian coalition with the possible participation of Austria, France, Prussia, the Dutch Republic, Saxony, Poland, and Turkey. Russian diplomats had to work overtime to neutralize potential coalition members. In fact, new international tensions came to Russia's rescue. It proved impossible, for example, for France or Austria to side with Britain. There was dissent in London, with commercial interests urging peace and the South Sea Bubble crisis deflecting attention from European affairs. Russia was able to continue to put military pressure on Sweden, where on 3(14) May 1720 Ulrika's consort Frederick I was crowned king. In June 1720 a Russian detachment commanded by von Mengden penetrated Swedish territory and on 27 July Russia won a galley fleet naval battle off Grengham, near the Åland Islands, under the command of Prince M. M. Golitsyn, who captured four Swedish ships and 104 guns. In October 1720 Admiral Norris's squadron withdrew from the Baltic.

In August 1720 Rumiantsev went to Sweden with peace proposals on Russia's terms, and talks began in Nystad, Finland, in April 1721. There were disputes until the end—for example, over Sweden's demands concerning the border.[225] Russia's support of the claims against Denmark of Duke Karl of Holstein (who was in Russia paying court to Peter's daughter Anna) was also a stumbling-block. The French minister Campredon managed to persuade the Russians to withdraw their support. The Peace of Nystad was finally signed on 30 August/10 September 1721. Its twenty-four clauses established 'eternal peace' on land and sea. Sweden ceded Livonia, Estonia, Ingermanland, part of Karelia with Viborg and its district, with the towns of Riga, Dünamünde, Pernau, Reval, Dorpat, Narva, Viborg, Kexholm, and the islands of Oesel, Dagö, and Meno. Russia was to evacuate Finland and to pay Sweden two million reichsthalers as compensation. There were clauses on free trade, the rights of the former Swedish provinces, religion, landed estates, Russian troops, PoWs, ambassadors and envoys, and extradition.[226]

Peter summed up his feelings about the hard-won peace in a speech delivered in Trinity Cathedral in St Petersburg on 22 October 1721:

(1) I very much desire that all our people should be fully aware what the Lord God has done for us in the past war and by making this peace. (2) We must give thanks to God with all our strength, but while hoping for peace we must not weaken our military efforts in order to avoid suffering the same fate as the Greeks and the Greek monarchy. (3) We must strive for the common good and profit, which God sets before our eyes both in internal and external affairs, which will bring relief to the nation.[227]

Russia's new world role was summed up in a paper by one of George I's officials in Hanover: 'Germany and the entire North have never been in such grave peril as now, because the Russians should be feared more than the Turks. Unlike the latter, they do not remain in their gross ignorance and withdraw once they have completed their ravages, but, on the contrary, gain more and more science and experience in matters of war and state, surpassing many nations in calculation and dissimulation and are gradually advancing closer and closer to our lives.'[228] Russia's 'advance' into Europe is underlined in a thick memorandum drawn up on Peter's orders in 1722 on relations with all the major countries of Europe, including Spain and Portugal, showing how Russia's involvement had increased during Peter's reign.[229] Russian diplomacy now spread far beyond its borders. A notice of the posting of a consul to Cadiz stated: 'There are consuls from all European nations in Spain in the town of Cadiz and merchants trade in the products of the northern countries'; so Russia was not to be left out.[230]

VII. THE PERSIAN CAMPAIGN: 1722–1723

Scarcely was the Swedish war over than Peter embarked upon a new war, this time against Persia. It seems to have been undertaken partly to increase security against Turkey (in April 1722 Peter reported that the Turks 'want at last to declare war this summer'[231]), partly as a follow-up to Russian probes into a region which promised access to the riches of India and beyond: gold, silks, and other costly fabrics; silver, copper, lead, oil, dyes, fruit, and spices. The Christian populations of the region were under pressure from 'infidels', although Peter avoided the trap of 1711 by not placing undue reliance upon local Christian support.

Peter may have had ambitious plans for re-routing Oriental trade through Russia instead of round Africa. Tsar Alexis had sent embassies to Persia, Bukhara, and India. The last two did not reach their destinations, but they signalled Russian interest in trade, as did the Pazukhin mission to Central Asia in 1669 to seek trade routes and commercial opportunities. This mission acquired useful information about routes and hostilities in the region. In Peter's reign an embassy to India was dispatched in 1694. Interest in India may have been based on 'imperfect knowledge of geography' (belief persisted, for example, in the existence of a river route to India from the Caspian), but it also stemmed from a realistic analysis of the troubles in Central Asia which made Russian influence or domination of part of the route possible, thus fulfilling 'the dream of making Russia the major bridge in the trade between Asia and Europe'.[232]

Russia took advantage of local hostilities and rivalries. In 1700 the administrator of Khiva offered tribute in return for Russian aid against his rivals in Bukhara. Peter accepted (1703), although nothing actually happened on either side. In 1713 news arrived of the discovery of gold on the Amu-Dar'ia River. In May 1714 a mission headed by Prince Aleksandr Bekovich-Cherkassky was dispatched to Khiva via the eastern Caspian, with instructions to investigate rumours of the gold finds and to survey the east coast of the Caspian. The Caspian was charted as far as Astrabad Bay. In 1715 A. P. Volynsky was sent on a mission to Persia. He was instructed to find out about the rivers flowing into the Caspian, especially 'whether there is a river that flows from India into that sea', and to look into the prospects of trade with India through Persia. He succeeded in concluding a commercial treaty, and brought back information about local politics and geography which proved invaluable a few years later. There was a new mission to Khiva in 1716: Cherkassky was to return to the mouth of the Amu-Dar'ia, build a fort, try to divert the river(!), search for gold, and win the confidence of the ruler of Khiva. The seriousness of the venture is indicated by the resources allocated:

218,081 roubles and 5,000 men. Unfortunately, after winning an engagement against the Khivans and entering the city, most of the party, including Cherkassky, were slaughtered. Cherkassky's head was sent as a gift to the emir of Bukhara, and his body was stuffed and put on display.[233]

A concerted effort in the region required a respite from war in the north and a pretext in the south. These were provided more or less simultaneously in August 1721 by the Peace of Nystad, the overthrow of the shah of Persia in an Afghan revolt, and the protests of Russian merchants about violations suffered in Daghestan, a protectorate of the shah. Relief for Trans-Caucasian Christians living under Muslim domination, Armenians and Georgians with whom Russia had long links, provided an excuse. Prince Vakhtang of Georgia, some of whose predecessors had lived in Russia, was told: 'We hope with the help of God by the time that this messenger reaches you already to be on the Persian shores, therefore we hope that this news will be pleasing to you and that you will join us with your troops for the Christian cause in fervent fulfilment of your promise.'[234] The proclamation of the campaign on 7 July 1722 ends: 'with God's help attack them but be sure not to take unnecessary risks, lest at the start of this campaign we earn ourselves infamy and thereby give these peoples cause for pride'.[235] Peter found boyish enjoyment in this campaign. It gave him another opportunity to mess about in boats, both on the journey south along the Volga to Astrakhan and on the voyage to the 'Persian shores', when he kept navigation logs and issued orders on boat building and naval protocol. At this stage the campaign was not so dangerous or arduous as to halt a stream of orders home, on such diverse matters as fountains in Peter's new residence in Reval, house building in St Petersburg, history writing, publication of a book on Islam and the organization of the Chamber of Curiosities.[236] As Peter wrote from Derbent, captured on 25 September 1722, compared with the 'difficult and bloody' Swedish war, the present one was 'easy and profitable'.[237] In fact, the campaign proved costly in men, ships, and supplies. Peter withdrew to Astrakhan that autumn, leaving others to continue the war into the following year. On 8 September 1723 Peter received news of the taking of Baku.[238] On 12 September a treaty was signed with the new shah on the cession of Gilian, Derbent, and Baku to Russia 'in perpetuity' (*v vechnoe vladenie*) in return for Russian aid against the shah's enemies.[239]

The Persian war provides valuable insights into the colonial policies of the expanding Russian empire. The new territories were to be managed by careful handling of local peoples and some resettlement. Peter wrote to Major-General Kropotov in 1724: 'The Armenian people (*narod Armianskoi*) have asked us to take them into our protection, so order suitable places to be made available in our newly acquired Persian provinces for settlement.'[240] Non-Christian populations were to be handled firmly but tactfully. Prince Boris Kurkhistanov was instructed 'on pain of death to cause no devastation or oppression to the local inhabitants, but rather to reassure them to remain in their homes and to have no fear ... firstly, because if not they will flee and we will be left with everything empty; secondly, because we shall distress everyone and thereby lose everything of which we have a common need, therefore it is better to work for what is permanent and solid rather than for a small temporary gain.'[241] In 1723 Peter wrote to one of his commanders: 'You write that you don't dare to use real force because in the order you are commanded to treat people gently, but your instruction actually says that you should not use excessive constraint and roughness (*tesnota i grubost'*) against those who behave well, but resistance must be met with force; even so ... in all the measures that you employ try to avoid destroying this province. Also at times and as occasion demands you need to treat these peoples proudly and more severely because they aren't like European nations (*oni ne takoi narod, kak v Evrope*).'[242] Peter, it will be noted, regarded Russia as an expanding *European* nation. It is easy to imagine such sentiments coming from the mouths of British colonial agents.

In the event, it proved impossible to maintain this coastal strip. The expected commercial profits were not forthcoming, and the costs of military occupation exceeded revenues. Gilian, Mazanderan, and Astrabad were returned to Persia in 1732, and Shirvan and the area between Tarki and Derbent in 1735.[243] A temporary accommodation was reached with Turkey in the region, but Turkish and Tatar raids continued to the end of Peter's reign. In January and February 1723 orders had been issued for defence preparations along the southern borders in anticipation of Tatar attacks.[244] On 6 April 1723 Peter wrote: 'We have received news that the Turks are finally preparing to declare war this summer.'[245] There was no war: in fact, 1724 turned out to be the only war-free year of Peter's reign. Peter wrote to Kurakin and other ambassadors: 'I think that now is a good time, seeing that there is no war anywhere ... to send tapestries by sea. ... Our affairs in Persia, praise God, are going splendidly.'[246] But even now there was no real prospect of relaxation. Defence remained a priority. A long memorandum prepared in December 1724 lists Russian fortresses and their functions and the state of their defences.[247] More army reforms were being planned on the eve of Peter's death.[248]

VIII. SUMMARY: RUSSIA AND THE WORLD IN 1725

At the end of Peter's reign, Russia was on the way to transforming the Baltic from a Swedish lake into a Russian one. Not only was it in possession of the eastern Baltic, but it also had a garrison in Poland and strong influence in Courland, Mecklenburg, and Holstein through marriage alliances. The western shore of the Caspian was in Russian hands. Exploration continued in the Far East: one of Peter's last acts was to finance Vitus Bering's expedition to Kamchatka.[249] As we have seen, Russia established relations with many countries well away from her borders on a scale unthinkable in previous times. In 1723 Peter even wrote to the king of 'the famous isle of Madagascar' offering his protection, but the ship bearing the letter never reached its desti-nation.[250] Even so, compared with the conquests of Ivan the Terrible or Catherine II, in terms of square miles Peter's territorial acquisitions were modest. He was not even able to maximize and maintain the conquests he made. Not only were Azov and Taganrog lost in 1711, with no further advance made towards the Black Sea, but Peter also restored his Finnish acquisitions to Sweden (their maintenance would have overstretched Russia's resources) and the Caspian strip was abandoned in the 1730s.

Peter's death in January 1725 left his successors with a number of issues to resolve. Russia's ascendancy over Sweden seemed assured. After the Treaty of Nystad the borders between the two countries were marked out by commis-sioners, and a map was signed in March 1723. In June 1723 Frederick of Sweden recognized Peter's new title as emperor,[251] and on 11/22 February 1724 Russia and Sweden signed a twelve-year defensive alliance, which contained a secret article to persuade the king of Denmark to return Schleswig to Peter's future son-in-law the duke of Holstein. A medal struck to mark the occasion shows a dove with an olive branch flying away from Noah's ark. In the dis-tance St Petersburg and Stockholm are linked by a rainbow after the 'deluge' of the Northern War.[252] This alliance speeded up negotiations for the mar-riage between Anna Petrovna and Duke Karl Friedrich of Holstein-Gottorp, whom Peter had invited to Russia in 1720.[253] But diplomatic entanglements, the inevitable corollary of becoming a European power, tied Russia's hands. In a crisis over Holstein in 1725–7, for example, Russia did not press its support for Karl Friedrich because of the arrival of a British fleet outside Reval in support of Denmark.

Courland provides a good example of the limitations on Russian expan-sion. It had ice-free ports (unlike lands further east), but could not be annexed directly because it was not Swedish but ruled by the Kettler dynasty. The marriage of Anna to the duke of Courland in 1710 created tension between Russia and Poland, which regarded Courland traditionally as its vassal state. In 1726 Russian troops occupied Courland to counter Augustus II's plan to marry his illegitimate son Maurice of Saxony to the widowed Anna, but they were forced to withdraw. This minor humiliation inspired Andrei Osterman's idea of an Austrian alliance, spurned since Austria's 'betrayal' of Russia at Carlowitz in 1698. In a memorandum 'On France' (1725) he identified the common interests of Russia and Austria in opposing Turkey and preserving the Polish commonwealth (both benefited from a weak but intact Poland), while, it was argued, relations were not complicated by disputes over adjacent territories. In August 1726 Austria and Russia signed a defensive alliance, which remained a corner-stone of European diplomacy for most the eighteenth century.[254]

Russia's international status had grown immeasurably. When Peter came to the throne, Russia had only one permanent mission abroad, in Warsaw.[255] Peter's father and brother maintained 'residents' in a handful of capitals, but elsewhere diplomatic business was carried on by *ad hoc* missions, of which the

Grand Embassy was the last important example. The Foreign Office (*posol'skii prikaz*) had experienced, knowledgeable personnel on its payroll, but their assumptions, powers, and negotiating style generally set them apart from their Western counterparts. Within a generation, the long-robed, bearded Muscovite envoys, terrified of deviating from a rigid set of instructions, were replaced by Westernized men like Boris Kurakin and Andrei Matveev, who spoke foreign languages, sprinkled their Russian language with *bons mots*, and appreciated French wine. The new-style Petrine diplomatic corps, stationed for years on end in Russia's embassies abroad, has been described as the 'élite of the officials who served in the Russian administration'. [256] The new posts were filled mostly by nobles, with an eye to the 'rank' of the country being visited. In 1700–25, of twenty-three permanent diplomats abroad, eighteen were from old Muscovite families. Often several generations of one family served; for example, Sergei Dolgoruky succeeded his father Grigory in Warsaw. Prince Boris Ivanovich Kurakin's son Alexander trained in his father's embassy in France. Vasily Lukich Dolgoruky went to France in 1687, and studied there for twelve years. In 1700 he returned to Russia, then was sent to Warsaw and Denmark (1707). He knew several languages, and was described by Cardinal Dubois in Paris as 'a minister of good sense, discreet and very able to report to his court'.[257] Successful ambassadors built up networks of local informers and agents: for example, Peter Tolstoy in Constantinople, who relied, among others, on the patriarch of Jerusalem, the Dalmatian merchant Savva Raguzinsky, and the Dutch resident Jacobus Coljer.[258] Peter's envoys were allowed more personal initiative than their Muscovite predecessors, who had to adhere faithfully to written instructions issued for the purpose of each mission, and they had to be more versatile, ranging far beyond the limited list of courtesies and quibbles over titles and protocol which provided the brief for many a Muscovite mission. They had to handle the negotiation of dynastic marriages, for example, and supervise Russian students abroad, tasks which had not troubled their predecessors.

This brings us finally to Peter's notorious 'Testament', first published in France in 1812, which was said to contain a plan for expansion inspired by unbridled ambition.[259] This was long ago unmasked as a forgery, on the basis of the lack of contemporary manuscripts, the failure of Peter's successors to refer to it, its suspect vocabulary and factual errors and its variance with Peter's reluctance—inability even—to produce clear-cut policy statements.[260] Even so, it has been argued that the document was no less true for not being genuine. As a recent commentator writes, the text is 'littered with many absurdities, patently reflecting ignorance of the international context of the Petrine era'; but it may be considered valid in a sense because 'Russia in its actions from the eighteenth to the twentieth centuries has very often confirmed the ideas voiced by the author of the "Testament"' who 'captured many general tendencies in Russia's imperial policy in the eighteenth century and extrapolated them to the earlier history, to be precise, to the Petrine era'.[261] Peter's reign laid or consolidated the foundations of policies which were to bring Russia into conflict with other powers and give birth to the image of the aggressive Russian 'bear', brought to life by such actions as intervention on behalf of the Orthodox in the Ottoman Empire, the partitions of Poland, the conquest of the Black Sea, and the 'great game' in Central Asia. The key element in Russia's success in all these areas was its army and navy, to which we will turn in the next chapter.

3

The Russian Military Machine

'God has given him to you as a recruit'

I.   WAR AND REFORM

The inextricable link between war and reform lies at the heart of most interpretations of Peter's reign. In Vasily Kliuchevsky's classic formulation, war 'determined the order of reform, set its pace and its very methods. Reforming measures followed one another in the order dictated by the requirements imposed by the war.'[1] There was barely a year in Peter's reign when Russian troops were not deployed on campaigns, both inside Russia and beyond its borders. Domestic upheavals and disturbances, major and minor, also necessitated armed intervention. It is true that most of Peter's predecessors (and his successors, too) were also tied to the needs of the war machine; but in Peter's case the links between war, domestic policy, and the man himself were quite explicit. War and conflict even shaped the ruler's image. The few surviving portraits of Tsar Alexis mostly present a static figure, the Holy Orthodox tsar clad in cumbersome robes of state, despite the fact that in the 1650s the tsar actually went on campaign with his armies in Poland.[2] Peter, by contrast, from the time he was painted in armour by Sir Godfrey Kneller in London in 1698, was depicted most often as a soldier, surrounded by military and naval symbols. War shaped the built environment. In Moscow Peter's first major project was the new Arsenal, in St Petersburg the fortress and the Admiralty. War influenced the output of publishing houses, a significant proportion of which was devoted to military and naval topics. In the reformed scheme of government (1717–18) the colleges of War, the Admiralty, and Foreign Affairs were regarded as the senior departments, eating up a lion's share of state revenues. Military men were given precedence over civilians in the new Table of Ranks (1722). Every new-born Russian male was potentially a new soldier. 'God has given him to you as a recruit,' wrote Peter to Alexander Menshikov on the birth of the latter's second son in 1711.[3]

It is hard to refute the argument that it was foreign policy, rather than domestic needs, which shaped the course of Peter's reign. The originality and effectiveness of Peter's military reforms are, however, more controversial. The debate touches such areas as the nature and extent of innovation and modernization, the sources of influence, the costs of the army and navy when weighed against their achievements, and the nature of the Petrine military ethos. It is more or less received wisdom that Peter transformed the Russian army 'from an Asiatic horde into a professional force of the kind maintained by Sweden, France or Prussia ... Peter rebuilt the army from the ground up'.[4] When Peter was born in 1672, it is argued, Russia lacked a modern regular army. The armed forces were poorly equipped, virtually untrained, and ill disciplined, and remained so until the defeat at Narva (1700) shocked Peter into drastic action. In the latter half of the seventeenth century the Russian army had a dismal reputation. Foy de la Neuville explained Prince Vasily Golitsyn's reluctance to attack the Crimea in 1687 thus: 'While he was being given an army which was formidable in terms of the number of its troops, the latter were only a multitude of peasants, poor soldiers and not battle-hardened.'[5] 'None but the Tartars fear the armies of the Czar,' remarked the Imperial envoy Johannes Korb in 1699. 'It is an easy matter for them to call out several thousand men against the enemy; but they are a mere uncouth mob, which, overcome by its own size, loses the victory it has but just gained.'[6] Yet even as Korb wrote, dramatic changes were under way, which achieved their most spectacular success at the Battle of Poltava in 1709. In 1710 the Austrian resident Otto von Pleyer commented: 'Concerning the Russian military forces, in all fairness, one must admit that they have reached an amazing degree of proficiency, thanks to the incessant application and efforts of the tsar and to severe punishments and marks of favour and distinction, as well as to the experience of foreign officers of all ranks, drawn from many nations.'[7] When Peter died in 1725, the Empire could deploy some 200,000 men, clad in uniforms, armed with Russian-made muskets and flintlocks, supported by a much improved artillery, efficiently provisioned, and commanded by trained officers. The balance had shifted emphatically from 'old-fashioned' cavalry to 'modern' infantry. Land forces now had naval support. Army administration was centralized in the War College. A new military ethos had developed, inspired by Peter himself, one of 'the outstanding military commanders of his age'.[8]

The preceding assessment is compelling, but should not be accepted uncritically. One might begin by considering the claim that the pre-Petrine army was 'an untrained mass of gentry cavalry and regiments of refractory strel'tsy'.[9] If this were the case, it would be difficult to explain Russian military successes in the seventeenth century, especially in the Thirteen Years' War against Poland. In fact, from the 1630s onwards part of the Russian army was reorganized into 'new formation', or 'new model', regiments (*polki novogo stroia*), comprising infantry (*soldaty*), lancer, and dragoon units trained and commanded by foreign officers and organized along foreign lines. In 1632 two select (*vybornye*) infantry regiments were formed. It was these new-style units, rather than the strel'tsy (a more or less hereditary corps of 'regular' troops who ran their own businesses during peacetime), who provided a model for future reform.[10] Vasily Golitsyn's army in the Crimea in 1689 had thirty-five infantry and twenty-five cavalry regiments (lancers and dragoons) of this 'reformed' variety, with forty-five strel'tsy regiments and Cossack auxiliaries.[11] As the latter figures suggest, the numbers that Peter managed to recruit were not exceptional. In

1552 Ivan IV arrived to conquer Kazan' with 150,000 troops and 150 pieces of artillery. With regard to 'professionalism', even before its abolition in 1682, the Code of Precedence[12] was regularly suspended for individual campaigns, allowing appointments to the higher military ranks to be made on merit, and foreign officers trained and led the new-formation troops. There can be no doubt, then, that in trying to create a modern army, Peter followed in his predecessors' footsteps, as he himself acknowledged: 'Everyone is well aware of the manner in which our father of blessed memory and eternally worthy of remembrance in 1650 began to use regular troops and how a Military Statute was issued; and thus the army was established in such good order that glorious deeds were accomplished in Poland and almost all the kingdom was conquered; at the same time war was waged against the Swedes.'[13] Ivan IV he referred to as his 'forerunner and example'.[14] What, then, was Peter's unique contribution? Were his military reforms rational and co-ordinated or essentially piecemeal reactions to a series of crises? A recent study has argued that 'Peter did not win the Great Northern War by creating a regular Russian army for the simple reason that he never succeeded in creating a regular Russian army at all'.[15] What follows will throw further light on these arguments.

II. RECRUITMENT

Peter's army did not spring from a 'regular' planned scheme or a systematic course of theoretical study on the tsar's part. Some of its essential features were born of impulse rather than reflection, rooted in childhood games, a youthful sense of wounded patriotism, and, perhaps, childhood nightmares about the strel'tsy. It will be recalled that during Peter's youth the Russian army suffered some resounding defeats. As he was to remark later, 'we were unable to withstand not only nations with regular armies but (shameful to recall) even barbarians. We pass over in silence what happened at Chigirin and on the Crimean campaigns.'[16] The élite core of the new army emerged from Peter's two 'play' (*poteshnye*) regiments, the Preobrazhensky and Semenovsky guards, which gained full regimental status in 1695.[17] Mock battles were not discarded once the tsar had tasted real action, however. After the capture of Azov in 1696, a model Azov was constructed in Moscow. On Peter's name-day in June 1699 three such fortresses were stormed by infantry, while the tsar and courtiers dined in tents.[18]

The Preobrazhensky and Semenovsky guards were listed at the beginning of regimental lists, along with the even older Butyrsky and Lefort regiments, but they were only four out of more than forty infantry regiments formed by the end of Peter's reign. Recruitment required a wider base than boys and men drafted into the royal villages and the tsar's personal retinue. The basis of recruitment of noble servicemen in Muscovy was the levy into cavalry units. Service continued until the end of the current war or campaign, after which men laid down their arms and were free to return to their estates, or, in the case of the Moscow-based élite, to resume some sort of civilian service. Commissions also ended with a given campaign. There were no systematic promotion procedures. This form of recruitment applied even to the 'new formation' regiments, which were still mustered on the basis of *pomest'e* holdings. Peter's first experiments on a larger scale, for the Kozhukhovo manoeuvres in 1694, combined traditional recruiting procedures—nobles from twenty-one towns around Moscow were ordered to report for duty—with less orthodox ones. Cavalry companies were formed from conscripted secretaries and under-secretaries from Moscow government offices, to serve alongside the Preobrazhensky and Semenovsky regiments under foreign officers.[19] Records for 1694 from the Belgorod military district provide a description of an old-style muster or inspection (*smotr*) of provincial nobles. Local officials had to collect data on ages, former service record and ranks, male relatives, and weapons available (in good or bad condition). They also had to handle the process of *verstanie*, by which registration for duty was accompanied by a land (*pomest'e*) allocation. The 1694 edict reveals some of the problems of the old procedures: notably the failure of nobles to report for duty ('shirking', or *netstvo*), which was causing a shortfall of men (*maloliudstvo*) in the Belgorod regiment. Landowners were forbidden to move to other towns 'on pain of severe punishment, without mercy'. Agents were warned not to include non-noble servitors such as strel'tsy and Cossacks in the registration procedure, which could lead to their acquiring land illegally.[20] The relationship between land ownership, military obligation, and status had an inhibiting effect on flexible recruitment, and was to be eliminated by Peter's reforms, which also bade farewell to the last vestiges of *mestnichestvo*. As they reached the age of fifteen, young nobles continued to be called up for military service, which remained the nobility's *raison d'être*; but under Peter there was to be no return home at the end of a campaign—service was now for life. Nor could nobles expect automatic commissions or land allocations: they had to rise through the ranks and accept service pay.[21]

Russian nobles continued to form the bulk of the officer corps, but by no means all nobles rose to officer's rank. Foreigners predominated in the very top ranks until quite late. For example, a list of generals in 1710 shows that in the infantry there were four Russians and nine foreigners, in the cavalry three Russians and nine foreigners. All the engineer commanders were foreign.[22] The Danish commercial agent Georg Grund identified some of the problems encountered in the officer recruitment drive:

> Both in the infantry and cavalry it is always difficult to find capable officers from their own nation, for the Russian nobles are proud of themselves and quite arrogant, but in their hearts they lack real ambition and love for warfare, preferring rather to sit in their estates or to obtain a civil service post by gifts than to fight for their fatherland of their own free will. The tsar usually refers to them in terms like the ones he used in my presence to the late Golovin, Sheremetev, Golovkin and Apraksin, to the effect that from time to time an individual

member of their or some other clan distinguishes himself, but that's all; all the rest are complete idiots, of which their own brothers are an example.[23]

Grund's remarks about the problems of recruitment at the top are not just the words of a prejudiced foreigner. He was almost as disparaging about foreign officers, whom he thought were drawn to Russia by greed. Still, Peter continued to regard nobles as natural officer material, placing quotas on their entry into civil occupations. Recruiting the rank and file presented different problems, for there were many conflicting requirements from the mass of the population. Tax revenues and food production, industrial output, and excavation and construction had to be balanced against replenishing army ranks. Breaking the direct link between the landholder (*pomeshchik*) and rank-and-file recruitment meant that the government could no longer rely upon landowners reporting for duty with their complement of armed retainers. In November 1699, in anticipation of war with Sweden, an appeal was issued for volunteers 'from all free men' (*izo vsiakikh vol'nykh liudei*) to sign up in the office of the Preobrazhensky regiment for eleven roubles wages per year, with the promise of food and wine on the same basis as the Preobrazhenskys and Semenovskys.[24] The annual salary was attractive, twice the allowance received by the strel'tsy, as were the victuals, the aim being to allow regular troops to be full-time soldiers without having to supplement their income through trade and craft, as the strel'tsy did. (That Peter intended his new recruits to supplement the discredited strel'tsy is indicated in his notes for the 'History of the Swedish War' (1722): 'instead of the strel'tsy they began to gather a proper regular army (*priamoe reguliarnoe voisko*) of which Generals Golovin and Weide were ordered to form eighteen regiments of foot and two dragoons in two divisions'.[25])

Volunteering (for life) brought emancipation for the unfree, but they needed their owner's permission. A decree of 1 February 1700 puts the onus firmly on the master. Anyone who wished to free his slaves and serfs was told to issue them with warrants of manumission (*otpusknye*), and to send them to the Chancellery of Contracts (*krepostnykh del*), whence they would be sent to the Preobrazhensky office for consideration for enlistment as infantrymen. Any who proved unsuitable would be issued with a new contract of bondage to a new master. Freedom from both military service and bondage was not an option.[26] In 1701 an appeal was issued for volunteers 'of all ranks' (*liudi vsiakikh chinov*) for the bombardier company of the Preobrazhensky guards to come to the Military Appointments office (*Razriad*) and sign up.[27] The phrase 'all ranks' must be understood in a limited sense. Men of certain categories were not eligible to volunteer (without permission) for the élite guards. These included Tatars, Kalmyks, Mongols, Poles, Cherkassians (Ukrainians), Wallachians, boyars' bondslaves, peasants and peasants' children, and 'courtyard people' such as cooks and bakers.[28] Categories later added to the list included slaves (*boiarskie liudi*) whom their masters had taught to sail 'for their navigation in St Petersburg'.[29]

Given the shortage of eligible 'free' men, a volunteer force could not meet Peter's requirements. In any case, army life was scarcely an attractive option. Soldiers perceived themselves to be in a condition 'close to the position of the serfs'. It was said that 'it is better to belong to the boyars; if you belong to the sovereign you live worse.'[30] Complaints lodged against foreign officers were frequent: 'Our captains are Muselmans (*busurmany*); there's no Christianity in them, they beat us so much'.[31] Even so, takers came forward. In 1711 V. V. Dolgoruky asked what to do about 'boyars' bondslaves' who were volunteering.[32] In 1712 Major-General Günther of the Artillery school reported that 'many simple folk' were applying to join the artillery as gunners. Peter ordered that they be recruited to fill vacancies.[33] The main point, however, is that, given Russia's social composition, volunteering was never likely to produce the necessary numbers. On 10 December 1699 conscription was announced on the basis of one equipped, provisioned recruit from every fifty peasant households owned by landowners already on active service (two from a hundred and fifty for Moscow landlords on service) and one from every thirty households belonging to retired servicemen, widows, *voevody*, and chancellery officials or a payment of eleven roubles (i.e., the yearly salary for one volunteer).[34] This measure, together with volunteering, yielded twenty-nine infantry regiments and two of dragoons, a total of 32,000 men. The commanding officers were all foreigners, with junior officers drawn from Moscow nobles of non-boyar rank.[35]

Rank-and-file conscription was not invariably for life. Temporary conscripts (*datochnye*) were used alongside 'lifers' (*rekruty*), strongly reminiscent of the old Muscovite system of non-regular troop levies. In 1712, for example, the Senate called up all currently non-serving *tsartsedvortsy* (i.e., Moscow nobles below the old duma ranks) who were fit for duty and 'their men with arms', one man for every fifty households, plus a levy of men from the villages of courtiers, governors, officials, and widows (i.e., non-servitors) on the same basis, to provide a temporary emergency force in case of renewed Turkish attack. This corps was to be disbanded and released home in case of no action.[36] The basis for recruitment drives changed with circumstances. In 1705 there was an attempt to systematize call-up, enlisting men aged between fifteen and twenty on the basis of one from every twenty peasant households. The levy for the cavalry was one man per eighty households.[37] But this neat prescription did not preclude supplementary levies. Recruiting methods were often 'arbitrary, unjust, and *ad hoc* despite the law of 1705', with some villages being forced to supply more than others.[38] In May 1706 the calculation was one man per 300 households from boyar estates, one per 100 for others. Anyone owning fewer than twenty households could substitute a money payment: 2 altyn, 2 denga, per peasant household for serf owners on active military service, 6 altyn, 4 denga, for others.[39] In 1707 serf owners who were themselves unfit or ineligible for service (retired men, widows, adolescents, and girls) were asked to give one in five of their household serfs (*dvorovye*) as recruits, although later they were allowed to substitute a cash payment of 15 roubles per man.[40] In 1711, for the war against the Turks, the high demand was made of one man per ten households or a payment of 30 roubles.[41] Horses were a vital adjunct of recruitment. In 1707 priests and deacons and their parishioners were ordered to pay for dragoon horses, one per 300 households, or 15 roubles per horse.[42]

Neither the use of volunteers nor that of peasant conscripts constituted a break with Muscovite practice, although under Peter the scale and frequency of the recruiting process were much more intense than they had ever been in the past. Every year throughout the Northern War thousands of new recruits were needed to fill the gaps created as much by disease and desertion as by battle casualties. Ingenuity was needed. Another basis for call-up was the redeployment of personnel deemed superfluous to the requirements of their estate or office. In 1703, for example, debt-slaves freed by the death of their owner were forbidden to contract themselves to new masters, and were enlisted as soldiers and sailors.[43] In 1705 sons of secretaries in the Moscow chancelleries, and in 1707 excess clerks, scribes, and other 'lowly ranks', were conscripted into the dragoons.[44] In 1707 a cavalry regiment was formed of secretaries.[45] Men who normally might have expected to serve the Church, sons of priests and deacons and various categories of non-ordained church people (*tserkovniki*), found their aspirations rechannelled. In 1708 such young men were required to study in Greek and Latin schools, but if they refused, they were to be conscripted into military service. It was strictly forbidden to appoint them as priests or deacons 'in their fathers' place' or as clerks.[46] Swedish deserters were offered salaries to enlist.[47] In 1704 the remnants of a number of strel'tsy regiments were assigned to infantry regiments.[48] Some strel'tsy took part in major campaigns up to the Pruth in 1711. Moscow regiments existed until 1713, and some garrison strel'tsy were still in service after Peter's death.[49]

A sizeable auxiliary force was provided by the various Cossack armies or 'hosts' (*voiska*), notably the Ukrainian, or Little Russian, Cossacks (under the command of the hetman of Left Bank Ukraine), Cossacks of the Don and Iaik, and the fiercely independent warriors of the Zaporozhian Sich on the lower Dnieper. Only the Ukrainians were regarded as regular troops. The Kolomak Articles of August 1687, under which Ivan Mazepa was appointed hetman of Left Bank Ukraine, fixed the register of such Cossacks at 30,000. These troops were called upon to fight not only on the southern borders, but also in the Baltic. They complained bitterly about the long marches, the difficulties of supplying themselves and their horses far from home, and the fact that they tended to be regarded as 'cannon-fodder', often sustaining casualties as high as 70 per cent.[50] The English ambassador Charles Whitworth described them as 'somewhat in the nature of the Emperor's Hussars, and fitter for surprise and skirmishes, than any regular action. They are armed some with short rafted guns, and others with bows and arrows, and are oblig'd to appear, when and in what number the Czar thinks fit to summon them.'[51] Other Cossack bands were called up for local emergencies.[52] But the fickle allegiance of Cossack troops made them a mixed blessing, as Peter found in 1708.

Peter could also call upon non-Orthodox troops: for example, a unit known as the Lower Volga Cavalry, comprising recruits of Kalmyks, Tatars, Bashkirs. and others.[53] The Buddhist Kalmyks, with whom the Russian government had enjoyed an uneasy relationship since the early seventeenth century and a formal alliance since 1697, provide an interesting case-study. On the one hand, feuds with their nomadic neighbours such as the Crimean Tatars or Bashkirs (as in 1708–9, when Peter faced the advancing Swedish army) could be turned to Moscow's advantage, whereas raids on Bashkirs and Nogays could distract attention from other business. They could also be lured into aiding Moscow's internal enemies, such as the Astrakhan rebels in 1705, although in the end the Kalmyk leader Ayuki khan sided with government troops. Some 15,000 Kalmyks were ordered to the Kiev area in the spring of 1707, but only 3,000 or so turned up. A Kalmyk force dispatched to Poltava arrived a few days after the battle.[54]

The army in the field was only one part of the picture. Regiments were also maintained on garrison duty. Peter's instructions of 12 January 1709 to commandants of Ukrainian fortresses facing the Swedish advance indicate what was expected. They were told to lay in provisions for four months. 'If the enemy should attack your fortress then with the help of God, fight to the last man and on no account surrender to the enemy on pain of death. If the commandant is killed then the first officer below him must take over as commandant and so on in sequence (no matter how many are killed), one after the other.'[55]

In the ways mentioned above, as well as measures to combat desertion, Peter succeeded in keeping the numbers of his army more or less stable. Petrine recruitment methods were a case of adaptation of past practice, experiment, make do, and mend, to cope with the demands of continuous war, rather than a smooth, regular, mechanical progress. Recruits served as long as they were fit for service, the last drop of useful duty squeezed out. In 1710, for example, old, wounded, and crippled officers were assigned to train recruits in the provinces. Only if utterly decrepit were they to be sent to almshouses, which were to be inspected monthly to ensure that no men with wives, children, businesses, or houses were living there—in other words, only those with no other means of support would be looked after once they were unfit for active duty.[56]

Evasion was rife at all levels and took many forms. Most common was flight before or just after recruitment,[57] to avoid not only the horrors of battle but also the harsh conditions of camp life, which meant, according to Weber, that 'more of them perish with Hunger and Cold, during the first Years of Service, than fall before the Enemy'.[58] Severe penalties and harsh deterrents were prescribed for recaptured deserters. A decree of 1705 selected one out of every three deserters by lot to be hanged and the rest to be flogged and sent to do hard labour. On the march back from the Pruth in 1711, gallows were erected in camp each night to remind deserters of the fate that awaited them.[59] In the case of trained men, penalties were tempered with clemency. In 1711 notice was given to dragoons, infantrymen, recruits, sailors, and other servicemen who had fled since the beginning of the war—even those who had committed criminal offences such as robbery—that if they declared themselves at the War Chancellery or the governor's offices in the provinces, they could simply re-register in their former ranks.[60] A 1715 decree abolished capital punishment as a penalty for desertion (except from the field of battle), although repeat offenders were subjected to the knout and the slitting of nostrils before depor-tation to hard labour.[61]

Various systems of collective responsibility were devised. A group of twenty or more men would be punished or fined if any of their number ran off. Bail could be demanded of relatives, or of the regiment in the form of a list of fines to be extracted from colonels down to the fellow rank and file of the fugitive (from 1 rouble, 50 denga, to 1 copeck) to teach them 'to be vigilant from the highest to the lowest'.[62] An example of vigilance was the requirement in the summer of 1712 that men on the march going to relieve themselves be accom-panied by a corporal.[63] There were severe penalties for harbouring deserters, including banishment to hard labour.[64] Sometimes recruiters were held to blame for shortfalls or for signing up bad specimens.[65] In 1708 one Iury Neledinsky was accused of recruiting dragoons from the old and the poor and allowing the rich and the young to do garrison duty or live in their homes, for which he received bribes of 60 or 70 roubles.[66] Brands were used to identify recruits—a cross scratched on the left arm and rubbed with gunpowder, equated by some traditionalists with the mark of Antichrist.[67]

Thus were the ranks replenished and maintained. Peter's reign saw a total of fifty-three levies, twenty-one general and thirty-two partial, which raised about 300,000 troops.[68] Called-up men, officers and rank and file, were assigned to a regiment (*polk*), which was deployed in various configurations (army, brigade, division).[69] Figures for 1711 show forty-two field infantry regiments (62,000 men), thirty-three cavalry regiments (44,000 men), thirty garrison infantry, two dragoons (58,000), and one of artillery.[70] In 1708 the infantry reg-iments, with the exception of the Preobrazhensky and Semenovsky guards, were renamed after the towns and districts which supported them, as part of Peter's reorganization of provincial government.[71] After 1708 most regiments were composed of two battalions each consisting of four companies (one grenadier and seven fusiliers), which were divided into four platoons. Each regiment had a priest, a doctor, a fiscal inspector, a commissar, a quartermaster, an auditor, a baggage supervisor, musicians, janitors, scribes, barbers, wag-oners, and orderlies.[72]

III. SUPPLYING THE TROOPS

The importation of weapons and ammunition from abroad, like the hiring of foreign military specialists, had a long history in Muscovy, dating back to the time of Ivan III (1462–1505). Russia experienced the so-called gunpowder revolution during the reign of Ivan IV. In the seventeenth century, imported weapons were supplemented by the work of hired gunsmiths and cannon-makers. Under Peter the aim was to end dependency on foreign supplies and skills. If, initially, modern hand weapons, notably flintlock muskets (*fuzeiia*) and bayonets, were imported, by the 1710s most were being supplied by home industries. Georg Grund reported that Russia supplied its own needs in grenades, powder, bullets, and bombs, but that some weapons still had to be bought abroad, usually from Holland.[73] Peter was proud of the versatility of the new design of Russian bayonets, mentioning in several letters that they could be used in place of axes to chop wood into faggots. It was forbidden to make 'old-style' bayonets.[74] In 1709 Russian works produced 15,000 muskets, in 1711, 40,000. Self-sufficiency in gunpowder production was achieved thanks to domestic saltpetre supplies.[75]

Artillery was much improved, with home-produced siege guns and field artillery (including mounted guns for the cavalry). Peter, it will be recalled, began his army career as a bombardier at Azov, and took a personal interest in big guns. In the late 1690s cannon were purchased abroad, in Lübeck and Sweden, to supplement often very old guns dating back to the sixteenth century. The capture of as many as 150 cannon by the Swedes at Narva in 1700 dented supplies, and sparked off a big production effort—from 1704 under the direction of master of ordnance James Bruce. The numbers of field guns available never reached much more than 150. In addition, there were guns stationed in fortresses.[76] There were programmes of reinforcement and construction at Kiev, Smolensk, Velikie Luki, Pskov, and Moscow, with plans to build one major fortress in every province. Russians fought from fortified positions where possible, to avoid the Swedes in open battle. The Military Statute devotes several chapters to storming fortresses (ch. 13), taking towns (ch. 14), and terms of surrender of fortresses (ch. 15).[77]

The role of modern firearms and defences should not be exaggerated. The Russian army continued to use pikes and cold weapons suitable for steppe warfare. As W. C. Fuller writes, 'such humble instruments as the spade, the pike and the ax were at least as valuable, if not more valuable, to Peter's soldiers as the musket'.[78] Jeffereys reported in 1709 that 'we found them so deeply burryed in the earth that we have not been able to attack them without hazarding the loss of our infantry'.[79] Such tactics were effective at Poltava, but insistence on digging in could lose time, as at the Pruth, when Peter refused to counter-attack against the Turks before his supply train was dug in.

One of the most visible marks of Peter's reformed army was the use of uniforms. In Muscovy only regular forces such as the strel'tsy had uniforms, home-made and of Russian cut and style. In the 1690s uniforms were still hit and miss, even for the tsar's regiments. In 1696 the former masters of men signed up in the Preobrazhensky guards were ordered to supply them each with a winter coat, a tunic of undyed cloth, a cap, mittens, boots, foot cloths, a set of shirts, pants, and trousers.[80] After the outbreak of the Northern War Peter was more insistent on clearly differentiated, government-supplied uniforms. The style and cut followed the Western, or 'German', fashion—a basic outfit of knee-breeches, shirt, vest (waistcoat), and cloth tunic worn with a three-cornered hat.[81] The Preobrazhensky guards wore dark green tunics, the Semenovskys dark blue, and artillerymen dark red coats with blue cuffs; but general army regiments were not always colour co-ordinated. Indeed, achieving any sort of regular uniform took time. Menshikov reported in 1704 that it was a 'disgrace to the name of his Tsarist Majesty' that Russian auxil- iaries fighting in Saxony were seen dressed in rags.[82] Uniforms were a matter not just of sartorial elegance, but of life and death, and fitting out annual con- tingents of new recruits required bulk orders on a heroic scale, with which Peter often concerned himself personally. In April 1709 he wrote to Streshnev from Azov to have uniforms sent urgently 'as many regiments are going round naked'.[83] To the Senate in November 1711 he complained that the soldiers (of General Weyde's division) 'are almost all naked, and might perish as a result at this freezing time of the year'.[84] Peter could display characteristic thrift on the subject of uniforms: Romodanovsky was told to have new twelve- and eleven- button tunics made, but to send them without buttons, as the old ones were to be reused.[85] When Peter requested green uniforms for the infantry and was asked what should be done if enough green cloth could not be found, he replied: 'Make them in whatever colours can be found, whichever are the cheapest, from Russian cloth, and make all the cloaks from white Russian cloth.'[86] Foreign craftsmen were often hired initially, then home supplies took over, 'in order to clothe the army with non-foreign (nezamorskim) cloth'.[87]

Although uniforms were designed and supplied by the State, the troops were made to pay for them by substantial deductions from their wages: for cavalry uniforms half the salary was deducted; for infantry, 5 roubles, 10 altyn, 4 denga, per year. [88] In 1711, however, Peter instructed the Senate to have replacements made for what the guards had lost in the Turkish campaign out of state funds.[89] There was a rapid turnover of uniforms. After the Battle of Chernaia Napa in 1708, Peter wrote to Romodanovsky asking him to send uni- forms which had not yet arrived and replacements for items lost in battle. 'The Semenovsky soldiers are complaining a lot about clothing, so have it made and sent as quickly as possible.'[90]

The time and effort spent in actual combat were minimal compared with those expended on moving around and feeding and quartering troops. Peter's correspondence contains more references to provisioning than to tactics. Logistical factors were as crucial as tactical ones, even in the major set pieces, including Poltava and the Pruth. The same may be said of the Crimean cam- paigns of the 1680s, when actual fighting was negligible, and it was a question of how soon the army would run out of food, water, and fodder. Victory came down to which side could endure the longest. Under Russian conditions, army self-sufficiency was not a virtue but a necessity—there was no other way of supplying armies in regions with few towns and little surplus food for sale or requisition.[91] The food supply system continued to be hit and miss. Feeding the army outside Russian territory was a particular headache. In 1712 Peter wrote to V. V. Dolgoruky, in response to reports that the Poles were asking to be allowed to make money payments instead of supplying provisions: 'I am amazed that the Poles want to pay money in place of supplies—how can the soldiers eat money during the coming campaign?'[92] In general, a balance of exhortation and force was needed, as demonstrated by Peter's letter to A. I. Repnin of 3 April 1712 praising him for ignoring Polish excuses that provisioning obligations were not in the treaties and taking what was needed for the Pomeranian campaign, but warning him not to take more than was required or to give offence.[93] To the Senate, in response to a complaint from General Weyde that food supplies had failed to arrive, he wrote: 'This is very bad, for the men can't be hale and hearty on just bread and water.'[94]

The culmination of years of piecemeal legislation was the 1711 Statute on the War Commissariat, which effected a separation of the duties of combat and supply personnel, with *krigskomissary* established in the army to receive and distribute supplies. The statute included such items as paying men a month in arrears (to discourage immediate desertion) and clauses on fraudulent claims for wages and supplies and fugitives.[95] Prescribed consumption norms for troopers were 3 chetverti of rye flour (for making *sukhari* rusks) and 15 chetveriki of groats per year. Battle rations allowed an extra two pounds of bread per day and a daily pound of meat, two cups (*charki*) of alcohol, and a measure of beer. The cost of rations (figures for 1720) was calculated at 5.745 roubles per man per year and 5.70 roubles per horse.[96] Figures for 1720 show 173,844 men and 76,247 horses consuming 521,532 chetverti of flour, 32,596 of groats and 457,482 of oats. The total food and forage bill for 1720 was 1,259,717 roubles.[97] Provisioning problems did not disappear with the slow-down of the Northern War and eventual peace in 1721, when a large standing army became a burden. After 1722 regiments were billeted round the country, where locals had to support them on the basis of thirty-six souls to fund one soldier and fifty souls to fund one cavalryman, either building special barracks or providing billets. In other words, 'the soldiers were hung around the neck of the peasant'.[98]

Men on active service were supposed to receive wages, but it appears that these were rarely paid on time or in full. As much as half, as we have seen, could be deducted for uniforms. Differentials between officers and rank and file were substantial. In 1711 the highest-paid rank was general field marshal (of which there were just two) at 12,000 roubles per year. Colonels of infantry were paid 300 roubles if they were Russian, 600 if they were foreign. Garrison soldiers received just 60 copecks per month (including provisions).[99] The monthly wages of officers and men in the bombardier company of Preobrazhensky in 1708 were: captain-lieutenant, 20 roubles; lieutenant, 17; sub-lieutenant, 11; sergeant, 7; corporal, 5; and troopers, 3.[100]

IV. TRAINING, WELFARE AND ETHOS

A late Soviet study claims that wholesale Western reform was abandoned after the 1700 Narva 'fiasco', and that a 'truly Russian system of training' was introduced, based on a combination of European practice and the 'national characteristics of the home-grown soldier', which included practical, gradual training methods, proceeding from simple forms of instruction to more complex.[101] In fact, training, a much publicized feature of Peter's reforms, is bound to have been inadequate given the short time between call-up and deployment of new recruits. Fuller cites evidence to suggest that though training was given (based on the use of powder and firearms), the results were poor. He also points out that Peter's 'Instructions for Combat' of 1708 laid 'such enormous stress ... on marksmanship that one can only conclude that it was generally deficient'. He concludes, from data on the issue of shot for practice, that the troops were 'far from sharpshooters'.[102] Ivan Pososhkov (who, granted, was not an expert on military affairs) appears to confirm this: 'If the men can handle their arms expertly, maintain the hammers and flints of their muskets in proper trim (so that there is never a misfire), keep the weapon clean inside and out and the barrel true, then the musket will be very reliable, accurate in aim and effective in battle. Moreover, if they do not shoot wildly (as they do now) but at the target ... then such soldiers will be more fearsome in battle.' He especially disapproved of the practice of firing 'all at once as if from a single gun', 'in one volley in the Western manner', which he regarded as a waste of shot.[103]

The rank-and-file regiments of Peter's army, which were continually being replenished with virtually untrained personnel, must not be confused with the élite guards, who spent much of the 1680s and 1690s in training, with the result that at Narva in 1700 they were the only regiments to hold out. More training was available for officers and technical specialists, combined with attempts to provide a general education for young nobles.[104] A handful of noble youths received training abroad. General rules of conduct and command, as well as technical information, were available to the literate in military manuals and instructions. However, even officers went off to war with a minimum of training, and veterans in the higher ranks generally owed their success to experience rather than technical expertise. More systematic training was not really possible until after about 1720. Military reform did not end with the Swedish war, because Peter was always expecting war. In May 1723 he wrote to General M. Golitsyn: 'Now we have to train the dragoons in a different method of combat, not as with a regular foe, therefore command Lieutenant Weisbach to carry out this exercise with one regiment immediately, in shooting drill, as the Austrians use against the Turks.'[105] More reforms were being planned on the eve of Peter's death.[106]

Much attention has been devoted to manoeuvres in linear formation, which are said to have been 'perfected'.[107] In fact, there were relatively few set-piece battles (Poltava was a rare show-piece), and, as suggested above, there was little time to train raw recruits in sophisticated techniques. The soldiers' oath of allegiance refers comprehensively to action 'in field and fortress, on water and land, in battles, sallies, sieges and storms and other military events'. Major successes included the taking of fortresses on the Baltic in 1710 and the landing of troops backed by naval support on poorly guarded terrain during the Finnish campaign of 1713–14. In both fortress sieges and set battles it was the artillery which was the show-piece. The extent of the improvement may be gauged by comparing Korb's remark in 1698–9 that 'as the Muscovites themselves are not skilled in the proper management of artillery, scientifically used, they entertain foreigners at great cost for the purpose',[108] with reports by the British ambassador Charles Whitworth (1705) to the Secretary of State in London of a 'great Reformation'. The artillery was 'extremely well served'. General Ogilvie said that he 'never saw any Nation go better to work with their cannon and mortars, than the Russians did last year at Narva'. (The rest of the army was a different story: Ogilvie, in conversation with Whitworth at Grodno in September 1705, admitted that the Russians were still 'unskilled in the general motions of army' and suffering from lack of good officers.[109] He admired the guards, but was less enthusiastic about the newer infantry, who were 'but indifferently provided with habits and firearms, nor can they be looked upon otherwise than as new levies'. The cavalry he thought not equal to the Swedes in pitched battle.[110])

Did Peter's army have an ethos? Contemporary sources, from official accounts of battles to soldiers' songs, suggest that it did. Its exploits have been preserved in the popular memory down to the present day, Peter's glorious acquisition of empire by feats of arms contrasting sharply with losses of territory, humiliation in local disputes (e.g., Chechnya), and the run-down of the army in the post-Soviet era. Yet, as we have seen, Peter's army reform was a process of trial and error, a hotchpotch of orders issued from various campaign headquarters, adaptation and resourcefulness underpinned by a set of gut-feeling convictions about Russia's humiliation as a result of military backwardness. Peter generally had neither the time nor the inclination to elaborate clear-cut, detailed ideological statements. The clearest written expression of the ethos of the Petrine armed services is contained in the Military Statute (*Voinskii ustav*) of 1716, of which a draft with Peter's corrections survives. It was both a practical and a propaganda piece, based upon earlier edicts and manuals, including the so-called Weyde Statute (1699–1700). We need not linger on the question of whether it was a 'straight copy' of German statutes or 'completely original'.[111] Both internal and external evidence show that it was a compilation, the sources for which included foreign statutes and manuals, Swedish codes from the reigns of Gustav II Adolph and Charles XI[112] and Austrian texts (Charles V (1532), Ferdinand III, and Leopold I). There was also some input from Peter himself: in the preface, some of which was quoted at the beginning of this chapter, he gives the clearest indication of the impulses behind his reforms that can be found anywhere in his writings. For a start, he is more generous than some of his own biographers in giving credit to his predecessors. He notes Alexis's publication of a military statute,[113] and praises his achievements in training regular troops and beating the Poles, but then identifies a period (during the reign of Fedor and the regency of Sophia) when progress was allegedly 'abandoned'. The key words are 'order' and 'disorder'.

The manual proper begins, like all Peter's regulations, with the oath to the sovereign, followed by the Military Articles (*Voinskie artikuly*) of 1714 (based partly on a Swedish military manual), the first two chapters of which are devoted to 'fear of God' and the divine service. Military men must respect and heed God with greater fervour than others, since God has assigned them to a station such that they are constantly called upon to put their lives at risk in the service of their sovereign. There follows a list of penalties for black magic, blasphemy, and impious behaviour. Prayers were prescribed every morning, evening, and midday (troops were summoned by drums and trumpets), with penalties for missing or misbehaving during services.[114] Chapter 3 is on commanding officers—'It is an officer's job to command and the subordinate's to be obedient' (article 29)—but officers must not mistreat their men by cruelly beating or wounding them without proper grounds (article 33) or by forcing them to do their own work (either with or without pay: article 54) or by withholding pay, food, uniforms, and other items issued to the men ('for when a soldier is not given what is due to him, all manner of evil can easily occur': article 66); but this did not give men the right to complain about delays in receiving pay and provisions (article 68). Grounds for leave included illness, arrest, insanity, 'fear of fire or water', death of wife, children or parents, and other reasons deemed valid by judges (article 100). There were articles on spies, mutiny, anonymous letters, health, and hygiene (article 90). Chapter 20 deals with sodomy, rape, and fornication. For bestiality the punishment was corporal punishment, the same as for homosexuality. The penalty for rape of a woman was permanent exile to the galleys. For homosexual rape the penalty was death or exile. In his draft version, Peter lightened the penalties for most of these sexual crimes.[115]

The Military Statute is usually cited as evidence of Peter's desire to apply military-style discipline and order universally. On 10 April 1716 he sent an advance copy to the Senate from Danzig, with hand-written instructions:

> Lord senators, I am sending you the book of the Military Statute (which was begun in St Petersburg and finished here), which I command you to have printed in large numbers, no less than a thousand copies, of which three hundred or more should be in Slavonic and German (for foreigners in our service), and although it lays down the basis for military men, it also applies to all civil administrators, as you will see when you read it. Therefore when it is printed send a quantity to all the corps of our army and also to the governors and chancelleries, so that no one can make the excuse that he was ignorant of it. Keep the original in the Senate.[116]

Peter regarded military order as a model for other reforms. In the Ecclesiastical Regulation (1721) the section on schools begins: 'It is known to all the world how inadequate and weak was the Russian army when it did not have proper training and how incomparably its numbers increased and how it became great and formidable beyond expectation when Our Most Powerful Monarch, His Tsarist Majesty, Peter I, instructed it with most excellent regulations. The same is to be appreciated as regards architecture, medicine, political government and all other affairs.' In a later section students are described as proceeding to their lessons 'like soldiers upon a drum-beat'.[117] Yet even given the statement that the Military Statute should 'apply to all civil (*zemskii*) administrators', one should be careful not to draw sweeping conclusions about the 'explicit militarization of much of the machinery of government' in Peter's Russia.[118] A supplement to the statute issued in 1722 is worth quoting at some length:

> Since officers are to their men like a father to his children, therefore they must keep them in an equally fatherly fashion and since children obey their fathers without contradiction, placing their trust in their fathers in everything, so their fathers show unsleeping solicitude for their well-being, their education, sustenance and every necessity, so that they should suffer no hardship or insufficiency. This is what officers must do (and especially our officers since no people on earth is as obedient as the Russian), do everything for the benefit of the soldiers that is in their power (and what they cannot do, let them report to a superior) and not burden them with unnecessary ceremonial guard duty and so forth, especially during campaigns. Of course, an officer may say in his defence when he is questioned that 'I did this according to the Military Statute'; however, this cannot justify him, even if it is written, because although the drills are written down, the [exact] times and the circumstances are not. He needs therefore to use his discretion (since he is numbered not among the children but among the fathers, as written above) about the well-being of the soldiers (for all military affairs consist of that). Many in spite of a difficult march and other hardships as soon as a superior rides up order the soldiers to stand up and present arms on guard.

Officers were warned not to cling to the Military Statute, 'like a blind man clings to a wall'.[119] The statute, as a leading Soviet military historian argued, was not just a set of rules to be copied mechanically; it was also concerned with 'the personality of the soldier and officer, with inculcating a sense of military honour, competition in battle and personal bravery'. It was written in a 'soldierly, popular language'.[120]

Harshness has been emphasized—all military codes were harsh—but care for troops was regarded as vital to morale as well as for pragmatic reasons. In 1696 Prince F. L. Volkonsky in Chernigov was ordered to look after health, hygiene, and accommodation, including rebuilding old barracks, 'so that the troops should not be inconvenienced in the winter'.[121] 'Make sure that our men are contented in Pomerania, for everything depends on it,' Peter wrote to Alexis in 1712.[122] A. I. Repnin was warned not to overtax (*utrudit'*) the soldiers, to give them rest, and not to march excessive stretches at a time (but simultaneously Peter wanted them to get to Pomerania 'by the first grass').[123] Peter did not have the attachment to parade drill of most of the later Romanov emperors, notably Paul I and Alexander I. 'I saw dressed-up dolls, not soldiers' was allegedly his response to a military parade he saw in Paris in 1717.[124] Even so, the emphasis was upon obedience, to God, to the tsar, and to superiors. Even if troops did not always match up to his ideals, Peter expected a responsible, disciplined attitude towards service. Observance of rules and regulations and strict adherence to hierarchy were required at all levels and in all walks of society. In the oath of allegiance men pledged to act as 'honourable, loyal, obedient, brave and deliberate' soldiers.[125]

But just how disciplined and obedient were the Russian troops? An anecdote published by Golikov relates how Peter and the kings of Denmark and Poland all claimed that their soldiers were the bravest, but that only the Russian soldier was willing to obey his master's order to leap from a window without any protest.[126] Some foreign sources record a rather different story: General Ogilvie in February 1706 complained about the 'general disobedience and absence of any discipline' among the troops under his command in Lithuania. He frequently wrote urging Peter to improve discipline: 'Everything is fine here except that no one is obeying my orders'.[127]

Georg Grund, observing the army at Grodno in 1705, about 40,000 troops, confirmed this negative impression: 'These troops were in a very poor condition as a result of a lack of training and shortage of experienced officers, amongst whom none the less was sensed all possible indications of rivalry.'[128] The picture after Poltava was much improved:

> Now the tsar has sufficient strength as he has under arms a regular army a hundred thousand strong, which he can, without overburdening the country, annually furnish with recruits, in spite of the fact that in Russia they have not yet learnt to value a man, but often treat him worse than a horse and people fall in their thousands and perish for lack of provisions. . . . The simple soldier is not wanting in military skill. Not only is he very good and adept in the use of weapons, he also looks good even given very poor nourishment consisting of rusks and salt, he is capable of accomplishing the longest marches, whatever is demanded of him, and he is already well used to fire and it has become extremely hard to break the ranks of Russian infantrymen, whereas previously you could slaughter or tie them up like sheep.[129]

To take up Fuller's argument again, the very weaknesses indicated by Grund may, in fact, have been strengths: a huge army could be maintained *without overburdening the country* precisely because they did not 'value a man'. The ethos of the common soldier was one of endurance.

V. CENTRAL COMMAND

The supreme military commander was, of course, the tsar. Article 18 of the Military Statute of 1716 states that 'wherever His Majesty the Tsar is present in his lofty person the authority and power of all commanders are taken away, apart from those whom His Majesty has expressly ordered to execute a task'.[130] Although in practice Peter frequently chose to operate under one of his alternative personae—for example, as a simple bombardier—the choice was his. As we have seen, he had a personal hand in virtually every aspect of military organization, including direct command. His immediate subordinates included such men as B. P. Sheremetev, M. M. Golitsyn, and A. I. Repnin, whose careers are outlined in a later chapter.

The army needed considerable bureaucratic support. In the seventeenth century military affairs were overseen by a number of departments (*prikazy*), notably the *Razriad* (for military appointments), which maintained registers of noble servicemen, and departments of strel'tsy (*streletskii*), foreigners, and new army units (*inozemskii*), artillery (*pushkarskii*), gunpowder (*pushechnyi*), new-type cavalry and dragoons regiments (*reitarskii* and *dragunskii*).[131] These were all subject to name changes and amalgamation, along with other government departments, in the 1690s and 1700s. The *Pushkarskii prikaz* was renamed the Department of Artillery (*artilleriia*) in 1701. The Department of Military Affairs (*prikaz voennykh del*) gave way to the Military Chancellery (*voennaia kantseliariia*), which in 1718 was subsumed in the College of War (*voennaia kollegiia*), originally known as the *krigs-kollegiia* after the Swedish *krigskollegium*, organized along the same lines as the other new government departments. Naval affairs, to which we now turn, were separately administered by the Admiralty.

VI. THE NAVY

The Russian navy is not only one of Peter's most famous creations; it also serves as a striking metaphor for his Russia. In the formulation of Evgeny Anisimov, for Peter a ship 'was not only a means of transport for freight across the water's surface. The ship—Peter's eternal love—was for him a symbol of a structure organized and calculated to the inch, the material embodiment of human thought, complex movement by the will of rational man. Furthermore, the ship for Peter was a peculiar model of the ideal society, the best form of organization relying on knowledge of the laws of nature in man's eternal struggle with the blind elements.'[132] Peter's decision to build a navy sprang from deeply personal motives, going back to his boyhood. 'Of all the various institutions introduced by the tsar for the support and increase of his power,' observed one foreigner, 'by natural inclination he devotes most care and attention to the fleet.'[133]

When did the idea of building a fleet first come to Peter? Was it on Lake Pleshcheevo, where he took his first sailing lessons? On the White Sea, where in 1693 he saw his first seagoing vessels? Or at Azov in 1695 when he became aware of the disadvantages of Russia's inability to cut the Turks off from their sea-borne supply lines? Perhaps it was even earlier, when he was given his first toy ships and maritime prints.[134] The official prehistory of the Petrine fleet begins with the discovery at Izmailovo in 1688 of the little sailing dinghy (*botik*) *St Nicholas*, which Peter himself later elevated to the status of 'grandfather' of the Russian navy.[135] Built in the 1640s, the famous boat was almost certainly of English-type construction. As Peter admitted in his preface to the Naval Statute (*Morskoi ustav*), there were great-grandfathers in the form of the ships commissioned by his father to facilitate trade and exploration through the Caspian. One of the ship's gunners, Carsten Brandt, was still in Russia when Peter advertised for a shipwright to repair the Izmailovo dinghy. However, his father's commissioning of Dutchmen to build the three-masted *Eagle* in 1667–8 was ill-fated: the ship, transferred to Astrakhan in 1669, was burnt by Stenka Razin's rebels in 1670 before it could put out to sea.[136] Still, like the military code of 1647,[137] the *Eagle* provided a link with Tsar Alexis's endeavour when Peter re-employed some of the laid-off shipwrights in the 1690s. 'Then did the seed of Tsar Alexis Mikhailovich begin to sprout.'

Feofan Prokopovich, who revised Peter's preface to the Naval Statute, detected divine providence in the discovery of the little boat: 'Who will not say that this small dinghy was to the fleet as the seed is to the tree? From that seed there grew this great, marvellous, winged, weapon-bearing tree.'[138] The boat provided a striking emblem to illustrate the aphorism that 'great oaks from little acorns grow'. To underline the point, the 1720 edition of the Naval Statute has an engraving of a sailing ship without a steering-wheel and a naked boy sitting in it to signify inexperienced Russia. A. F. Zubov's engraving of the boat (1722) is inscribed: 'Childhood games brought mature triumph.'[139] The statute notes: 'But this Monarch was so particularly remarkable in all he did, that the very Pastimes of his Childhood are esteem'd, as Transactions momentous and weighty, and appear worthy to be recorded in History.'[140] The little boat was to the great navy as the little boy was to the great man. There are implicit parallels with Lives of the Saints: for example, the fact that Peter's mother twice tried to dissuade him from his endeavour, first from sailing on a lake, then from sailing on the White Sea. His first visit to the latter, and later to the West, is presented as a new sort of pilgrimage, not to holy shrines, but to maritime 'holy places' —harbours, shipyards, and docks.

Peter sought ever wider waters in which to sail. His first purpose-built boat was the *Fortune*, made at Pereiaslavl', and launched on 1 May 1692 with ten oars, now preserved in the museum at Pereiaslavl'-Zalessky.[141] The first Russian seagoing ship was the *St Peter*, built on the Solombasky wharf (at Archangel) and like the *Divine Predestination*, bought from the Dutch. Both ships went to sea under Dutch flags. The first Russian sailors were probably members of the Preobrazhensky and Semenovsky guards assigned to sailing duties in 1694. In order to build Russia's first war fleet for the second Azov campaign, foreign experts were summoned, and orders were placed for two ships (the 36-gun *Apostles Peter* and *Paul*), four fire-ships, and 1,300 longboats. Twenty-two galleys were constructed at Preobrazhenskoe, on the model of a Dutch three-gunner. The parts were taken to Voronezh for assembly, ready to be launched in April 1696. Peter began to devise the organizational trimmings—flag signals, use of lanterns for communication, fines for breaches of rules—in a fifteen-article document 'On the Order of Naval Service'.[142]

The new fleet scored its first success on 20 May 1696, when Cossacks drove back Turkish ships to allow a Russian flotilla of galleys and longboats out into the Sea of Azov.[143] This campaign also saw the first use of the naval emblems and imagery which are such a striking feature of the art of the Petrine era. A celebratory medal was struck, bearing an image of Neptune · uttering the words: 'I too congratulate you on the capture of Azov and myself submit.'[144] Peter chose to date the 'birth' of the Russian fleet proper from 1696.[145] Following a resolution of the boyar duma—'Let there be ships!'[146]—at the end of that year churchmen and nobles were commanded to form 'companies' (*kumpanstva*), of which some sixty-one were set up to build eighty ships at Voronezh and nearby wharves. The clergy were required to build one ship for every 8,000 peasant households, and nobles one for every 10,000. One of these, the *Predestination* (launched in 1700) was built partly by Peter's own labour. Shipbuilding continued during Peter's absence on the Grand Embassy, when the focus of his personal programme was studying the theory and practice of shipbuilding in Amsterdam and London. In 1699 Peter held manoeuvres off Azov, and later that year the 46-gun ship *Fortress* took the Russian ambassador Ukraintsev to Constantinople, the first official voyage by a Russian ship on the Black Sea. But in general results were poor because of bad workmanship, cheap materials, and high levels of desertion and absenteeism. (Teams of forced labourers were drafted.) Many of the ships were not even seaworthy. Still, 215 vessels (including 44 warships) were built for the Azov fleet before its elimination in 1711.

The focus soon shifted to the Baltic. In 1701 Peter ordered hundreds of small craft to be built on the Volkhov and Luga rivers, and in January 1702 six 18-gun ships on the River Sias' (Lake Ladoga).[147] In March 1703 at Olonets on the River Svir' the keel of the frigate *Standard* was laid, and several smaller vessels built. Olonets continued to turn out ships, including the first 50-gunners in 1710. Following the founding of St Petersburg, on land captured with the help of small craft, Kronstadt was founded as a naval base. The Admiralty wharf on the Neva, built in 1705–7, launched its first ship in 1706.[148] The first 50-gunner produced there, the *Poltava*, was launched in 1712. By the time of Peter's death the Baltic fleet consisted of 36 ships of the line, 16 frigates, 70 galleys, and 280 other vessels.[149] The complex organization of naval matters—building and equipping ships, maintaining ports and wharves, rope and canvas factories, personnel and training, naval campaigns, navigation—was placed first under the Admiralty chancellery, reformed in 1717–18 as the Admiralty College (*admiralteistv-kollegiia*), the first president of which was F. M. Apraksin. (Apraksin, like another early naval commander, Fedor Golovin, found himself involved in naval affairs as a result of closeness to the tsar rather than any specialist training or skills.[150])

Peter was concerned not just with warships and seagoing merchant vessels, but also with the smaller river and coastal craft which had always been part of the Russian scene. A veritable war was waged for many years with the owners of 'old-style' vessels. In 1718 it was decreed 'from boats built in the new manner, which are made according to instructions, charge the usual duty for a load [of goods], but from old-style take double duty in 1719, treble in 1720 and keep adding for every year'.[151] In St Petersburg the 'private wharf' (*partikul'iarnyi verf*) built craft for civilians. All public figures in St Petersburg, both laymen and clergy, were expected to maintain and staff their own river-going transport, and turn out for public occasions as required. Sometimes transport was supplied: seven persons listed in 1724 as being without barges, including the archbishops of Pskov and Tver, Ivan Musin-Pushkin and Savva Raguzhinsky, were all given barges free of charge.[152]

Of all Peter's foundations, the fleet relied most upon foreign expertise. 'Peter I built a fleet of seventy ships steered by Muscovites who didn't even have a word to express the idea of a fleet in their language,' wrote a French commentator.[153] The introduction to the Naval Statute explains that 'the word "fleet" (Russian *flot*) is French. By this word is meant a number of water-going vessels travelling along together, or standing, both military and merchant'.[154] In 1697, as the first fleet was under construction, a group of nobles was sent abroad for naval studies (*dlia ucheniia morskogo dela*), with instructions to master 'charts or sea maps, the compass and also other naval appurtenances ... to command a ship both in battle and also in normal motion and to know all the tackle or instruments as required: sails and ropes and on galleys and other craft oars and other such'.[155] In early 1698, while Peter was studying shipbuilding in England, attempts were made to set up a naval school in Azov under the direction of a Venetian master. Ten Russian apprentices were chosen from among the 'Moscow ranks', supplemented by students of Italian and Greek.[156]

Peter's visits to Holland and England in 1697–8 were crucial. The preface to the Naval Statute suggests that he acquired practical hands-on knowledge in the former and theoretical knowledge, including drawing and design, in the latter. In England he worked in the shipyards at Deptford, sailed on the Thames, reviewed the fleet at Portsmouth, had conversations with mariners, and was presented with a yacht, the *Royal Transport*.[157] He recruited shipbuilders and seamen. British influence is felt in the names of the ships of the Russian navy in the 1710s—*Britannia, London, Arundel, Marlborough, Devonshire, Portsmouth*, and *Randolph*.[158] Peter's English experience revealed the crucial importance of mathematics. Future naval personnel were trained in the Moscow School of Mathematics and Navigation, a school run by British teachers,[159] and gained practical experience aboard British ships as well as those of other friendly nations, which was normal practice in European naval training.[160]

One of Peter's longest-serving naval experts was the Norwegian Cornelius Cruys (1657–1727), recruited in Amsterdam in 1697. Cruys built ships, charted and described rivers, and hired naval experts abroad. He was arrested in 1713 for alleged malpractice, but was pardoned and went on to serve in the Admiralty as its first vice-president.[161] A memorandum sent to F. M. Apraksin in 1723 sums up his pride in the achievements of the new Russian navy: 'Not only all Europe but also the greater part of Asia has great respect for our fleet; therefore it is essential to maintain everything in the best order. ... I don't think that in the course of twenty-five years service either of us has wasted a minute's time in idleness or caused the loss of one shilling (*polushka*). I wish to serve his Imperial Majesty loyally and justly to the grave.'[162] Another foreign expert was the Dalmatian Greek rear-admiral Botsis (?–1714), known in Russia as Ivan Fedoseevich, recruited by Peter Tolstoy in 1702 for the galley fleet. After working at the Olonets wharf, he went on to command a squadron of galleys in naval operations in the Finnish gulf, capturing the town of Borgo and burning a number of Swedish merchant ships in 1708. He assisted in the capture of Viborg in 1710 and the bombardment of Helsinki in 1713.[163] Foreigners did not always see eye to eye. Cruys complained in 1712 that he could not serve with Botsis, 'either on sea or on the land'.[164] Admiral Matvei Zmaevich (1680–1735) came to Russia from Dalmatia (via Constantinople, where he was imprisoned with Peter Tolstoy) in 1712. He served with distinction at Hangö in 1714, and commanded a galley fleet that served off Denmark in 1715–17, becoming vice-admiral of the fleet in 1721 and full admiral in 1727. In 1723–4 he was employed in building a new Don flotilla at Voronezh, ending his career there in disgrace after being accused of malpractice in 1728.[165]

Despite Peter's enthusiasm for the navy, only a small number of trainees could be spared to travel abroad—hence the note of frustration in a report to Apraksin (April 1706) that only five had been assigned, and that even if they all turned out to be de Ruyters, it would be impossible to improve the fleet with just five men.[166] Heavy reliance on foreign expertise was also prompted by the apparent unwillingness of Russians to join the navy. Several of the prospective pupils allotted to the 1697 training programme ran away, setting a precedent for later reluctant recruits.[167] Peter complained from Holland in 1697 that some of the first to be sent abroad 'have learned how to use a compass and now want to return to Moscow without having been to sea. They thought that was all there was to it.'[168] Students who made poor progress were threatened with a variety of punishments, including confiscation of their estates.[169] Poor results may in part have been due to the fact, to quote Captain John Deane, a seaman in the tsar's service, that 'the Russians in general have an aversion to the sea'.[170] Naval trainee Mikhail Golitsyn wrote from abroad: 'My life here is most distressing and difficult.' He complained of poverty, loneliness, the problems of learning the language, and the technicalities. Finally, 'my nature cannot bear seafaring'.[171] The point is well illustrated by a letter from Peter to Konon Nikitich Zotov, congratulating him for applying to undergo practical naval training in England and wishing him luck in his studies abroad. 'I think I can say I have not had such a request from a single Russian. You are the first, for one hears very rarely of any young man left in the company of amusement wishing to hear the sound of the sea of his own volition.'[172] In 1715 Zotov was sent to France in order to observe and describe 'all that pertains to the fleet at sea and in port', to obtain and translate books, and to acquire practical experience.[173] He acted as supervisor of Russian naval trainees in France, saw active service in the Baltic, contributed to the Naval Statute, and was the author of several books on naval signals, exercises, and command. He eventually became a rear-admiral.[174]

Another successful naval recruit was Count Aleksandr Petrovich Apraksin (?–1725), who was attached to the British navy for seven years and made many long voyages. His uncle, Admiral F. M. Apraksin, warned him to 'practise without rest in order to fulfil the will of the tsar and if you do not, do not expect to return home until you know naval matters from keel to pennant, as behoves a skilled seaman'. He told him to get as many testimonials as possible. Aleksandr went back to Russia in 1716, later returning to England to buy ships and to recruit.[175] A few of the volunteers who travelled with Peter in 1697–8 made a naval career for themselves. Feodosy Moiseevich Skliaev received a diploma certifying that he had studied with Peter for ten years, 'and has so mastered his craft that he is able to build all variety of sea craft not only according to the general rules but can also add to or subtract from them'.[176] When it came to the rank and file, sailors were conscripted, initially from the maritime provinces and rivers, where there was already knowledge of navigation, but later from other regions as well, usually by the tsar's personal command.[177] There were also naval regiments, who did guard duty on board and formed boarding and landing parties during combat. The first ones were drawn up in 1705. One such regiment was comprised of postal drivers.[178]

Foreign expertise provided models for Peter's naval codes, the predecessor of which, Tsar Alexis's abortive naval 'articles', was translated directly from a Dutch code of 1668.[179] Peter's code of 1696 was superseded by Cruys's regulation of sixty-four articles, based on Dutch and Danish models. Over the next twenty years a number of orders were issued. Clerks drawing up manuals for use on board ship and in dock in 1718 were told to write out points, starting with the English, then listing versions from the French, Danish, Swedish, and Dutch.[180] Peter's mania for written rules and regulations, specifying precisely what each person's duties were, 'from the first to the last', perhaps reached its height in naval matters. One of the main topics covered in the Naval Statute of 1720[181] concerns the duties of all on board. Book 3 includes among the tasks of the orderly (*profos*) responsibility for ensuring that people relieve themselves in the authorized places.[182] There are templates for ships' logs, provisions allocation, complete lists of tackle, and several pages on flag and lantern signals. There were also the Admiralty Regulation of 1722, which includes provisions for medical care, and merchant navy regulations. In addition to codes and regulations, numerous translations of books on naval matters were published. Forty-five works have been identified in this category, including a book on signals (*General'nye signaly, nadziraemye vo flote*), published first in 1708 and several times thereafter. Others are a work on navigation in the Baltic, from the Swedish, and *New Dutch Shipbuilding* (*Novoe galanskoe korabelnoe stroenie*) (1709).[183]

Did Peter set too much store by his navy? The Azov fleet, which barely saw action after 1696 and had to be dismantled after the Pruth disaster (only twenty-seven warships were at Azov when war was declared), may well be dismissed as a white elephant. It failed to provide any substantial assistance in 1711, when a Turkish squadron laid siege to Azov (as a recent study remarks, the campaign consisted of 'two distant sightings, a chase with three cannon shots, and a single defensive action on land'[184]), although its very existence may have 'held the Turks and Tatars in check'.[185] Early in the Northern War Peter was not averse to using it as a bargaining counter: for example, offering to cede or sell parts to the Turks in return for rights of navigation or to ward off the threat of war in the south. Early in 1709 Peter's presence in Azov making naval preparations may have influenced the sultan in his decision to forbid the Crimean khan to assist Ivan Mazepa. The Baltic fleet was also inactive for much of the first part of the Northern War, although there were some minor operations even before St Petersburg was founded, such as support for the siege of Nöteborg in August 1702. During the campaigns of 1704–10 naval power was used sporadically, mainly because there were few direct threats from Swedish action off Kronstadt and St Petersburg. Georg Grund commented: 'The ships are generally in a poor state, for all of them, from the admiral's downwards, are built only of pine and the iron on them is of poor quality. The tsar himself admitted in 1710 that four of the older ships were not seaworthy.' He ordered more to be built, but the practice of building them at Olonets led to damage en route to the open sea.[186] On the evidence of Ivan Pososhkov, the fleet continued to suffer from a catalogue of ills, and was plagued by wastefulness, ignorance, and cheating by foreign experts (of which Pososhkov complained in other institutions and organizations). 'A good sound ship is like the defences of a fortress; one built of rotten timber is worse than a wattle palisade. A palisade is not a strong defence in itself yet if it is well manned with troops the enemy cannot take the place easily; whereas no battle is needed to cause the loss of a vessel made of unsound oak. ... A vessel made of rotten timber will not last even five years and all the work and money expended on it goes for nothing.' He recommended a new system of fines for suppliers and inspectors who gave rotten wood, and preference for properly seasoned pine over inferior oak.[187]

From 1712 the fleet, in spite of all its shortcomings, became more important to the war effort. In 1713 Peter wrote to Kurakin in Holland: 'I ask you to make every effort to buy ships, for our whole war is now centred around them.'[188] Russian sea power played a central role in the 1713–14 Finnish campaign, which was based on the use of Russian troops on land, with galleys hugging the coast and sailing ships protecting them from Swedish naval attack. The commander-in-chief of the Finnish campaign forces was an admiral, F. M. Apraksin, rather than an army commander. The high point was the Battle of Hangö, the 'naval Poltava', in July 1714. In campaigns of 1719–21 troops from Russian ships burned villages and blew up mines on the Swedish mainland. In one of the last major encounters of the war, on 27 July 1720, the Russian galley fleet beat the Swedes off Grengham in the Åland Islands. The four Swedish frigates captured in the encounter were among the last trophies of the war. Naval support was also used in the 1722–3 Persian campaign, notably in the successful attack on Derbent, transporting troops, artillery, and provisions, and in July 1723 carrying a landing force against Baku.[189] The British rated the Russian fleet quite highly, regretting their own contribution to its creation, despite the fact that the Russian and British fleets were not strictly comparable, the former relying more on shallow-draught galleys and vessels, the latter on deep-draught ocean-going ships. Jeffereys is reported as saying: 'If we don't take measures against the development of the Russian fleet we shall live to regret it. Not long ago the tsar openly stated that his fleet and the fleet of Great Britain are the two best in the world. If he now ranks his fleet higher than the fleets of France and Holland, why should we not assume that in a few years time he will pronounce his fleet to be the equal of ours or even better?'[190]

Whatever its achievements (even as a bargaining counter), it seems unlikely that the fleet, unlike the army, could have survived without the tsar's constant attention. Peter was anxious to maintain the Baltic fleet after the end of the Northern War, being only too aware that it could fall into disrepair once the pressure was off. A new point added to the Admiralty record book (handwritten by Peter) in 1722 states: 'The College must maintain a firm watch over the fleet and its staff to ensure that the fleet is always prepared and the staff do not forget their practical knowledge. Therefore every year as soon as the ice breaks the fleet must be equipped, at the very least half of it (if necessity so requires) and sometimes the whole, when it is deemed appropriate, and exercises should be carried out and the men trained around the Berezovy Islands for three weeks or so and the ships thoroughly inspected, for it is impossible to inspect so thoroughly for damage when lying in port as when the ships are under way.'[191] 'See to it that not only ships but also tackle are made not only for appearances but also in fact, that they are sound and of good workmanship,' he wrote. 'This can be achieved not only voluntarily but also by force; violators are to be punished first with fines, for a second offence with physical punishment. ... This should be published so that no one has the excuse of ignorance.'[192] On his way south to the Caspian in 1722, he wrote that all boats found in Nizhny Novgorod with rotten planks and other defects were to be reported to him, with details of who owned them and who had built them.[193] Before setting off to Moscow in 1724, he left a detailed list of instructions, mostly in his own hand, of 'what work to do in my absence' on a ship he was building in St Petersburg.[194]

The naval flavour at Peter's court was provided by, among others, shipwrights like Joseph Nye, who had a place of honour at public gatherings, and the 'court sailors' (*dvortsovye matrozy*) who performed various ceremonial duties.[195] Peter was often referred to in account books by his naval rank, as *gospodin vitse-admiral*, and so on. He was married in 1712 in naval uniform, and was attended by naval personnel as best man (Cruys) and guests of honour. Court life was embellished with symbols and ceremonies connected with the fleet, numerous references to Neptune in engravings and medals, and festivals honouring the fleet's 'grandfather'. There are few images of St Petersburg which do not include ships. See, for example, A. F. Zubov's panorama of St Petersburg (1716), in which the buildings are confined to a narrow strip in the middle ground and the foreground is filled with ships, or his 1714 view of Vasil'evsky Island where, again, ships captured at Hangö occupy the foreground.[196] It is possible to identify a complex 'semiotics' of the fleet, centred on individual construction and décor, naming (favourite ships were often given family names: for example, the yacht *Natalia*[197]), the creation of 'biographies' (starting with the anniversary of a ship's launch), and listing the peculiarities of an individual ship's 'behaviour' (speed, manoeuvrability, and so on), all of which turned the ship into a 'living person'.[198] 'Naval baroque' was a vital element in Petrine culture, another phenomenon which gives the lie to the easy assumption that Peter's was a 'utilitarian' reign.

Peter's navy provoked controversy. Pavel Miliukov expressed it thus:

> For the sake of the fleet Peter waged all his wars; but even this project remained incomplete at the time of his death and was broken up into a series of scattered and unfinished attempts abandoned in part by Peter himself, in part by his immediate successors. The paucity of the results compared with the magnitude of the wasted resources is especially striking. ... Maybe it will be argued that Peter was working for the future. Well, in 1734, just nine years after his death it was necessary to blockade Danzig from the sea, but the St Petersburg admiralty could provide at most fifteen ships and even these lacked crews and had no officers.[199]

If in the 1730s it turned out that Russia lacked a viable fleet, then 'countless human lives and endless resources had been spent in vain'.[200]

These critical views echo the thoughts of a contemporary observer who wrote that 'the Russian nation has little inclination for naval affairs but rather regards it all as an unnecessary expense. ... The fleet is regarded more as a whim of the tsar's than an essential for Russia's military strength.'[201] But what is 'essential'? Evgeny Anisimov compared the cost of building and maintaining a navy in the early modern world with that of developing a space programme in the twentieth century.[202] It is an apt analogy, especially in the Russian context, for both projects were as much for prestige as for practicality. Both generated a host of symbols above and beyond their immediate function, conveying the clear message that Russia was a major contender on the international stage, equipped with the means to conquer worlds beyond its immediate frontiers. Both attracted criticism for wasting public funds, on the grounds that much else—not least the living standards of ordinary Russians—was in desperate need of improvement. But it is no more credible to imagine that Peter might have renounced his navy in order to build more schools or improve the nutrition of peasants than that the Soviet leaders of the 1950s to 1970s would abandon the 'space race' in order to concentrate on public welfare. The actual costs were indeed high, although the fleet cost far less than the army. Using Miliukov's figures, in 1705, for example, total expenditure on the fleet was 174,469 roubles, compared with 263,274 for artillery and 99,716 for military uniforms and various regimental supplies. (In the same year education claimed just 3,786 roubles of state funds, medicine 11,335, and 'administration' (mainly salaries) 12,166.) In 1708 (the last full year in Miliukov's charts) the sum entered for the navy was only 19,281. In 1724 the Admiralty received 770,394 roubles (compared to 105,693 for the life-guard regiments, 1,237,240 for army regiments and Don Cossacks, and 135,187 for the artillery).[203]

Peter and his official publicists were not beset by doubts. 'A potentate who has only land forces has a single arm. He who also has a fleet has two arms', proclaims the preface to the Naval Statute.[204] 'See, O Russia, the usefulness of thy fleet!', wrote Feofan Prokopovich. 'Not only is it a ready and strong defence against enemy attack, which without a fleet you would not have, but also a great attacking force against the enemy for the winning of easy victories. Is it not marvellous that those same enemies were forced to testify to the truth of their predicament when on the coins, not long since issued in memory of their fallen king, they imprinted a lion bound with a rope?'[205] The creation of a fleet 'from nothing' merged with the myth of Peter's creation of Russia 'out of nothingness'.[206] 'He was your first Japhet!', declared Prokopovich in his funeral oration. 'He has accomplished a deed hitherto unheard of in Russia: the building and sailing of ships, of a new fleet that yields to none among the old ones. It was a deed beyond the whole world's expectations and admiration and it opened up to thee, Russia, the way to all corners of the earth and carried thy power and glory to the remotest oceans.'[207]

VII. CONCLUSION

Peter's success in war has conventionally been attributed to the *novelty* of his military programme, which centred on the creation of a regular army (as opposed to the allegedly 'irregular' one of his predecessors) and a navy (which his predecessors did not have at all) and the use of modern tactics and technology (firearms, linear formations, infantry rather than cavalry, and so on). But it has been argued that Russia's military success under Peter relied just as much on the ability to combine the new with the old: thus modern European infantry warfare based on linear formations backed by artillery (which, it will be recalled, Russia had developed from the 1630s) was combined with infantry fighting from defensive positions (e.g., occupying trenches, armed with pikes) and East European 'Tatar-style' cavalry, using speed, mobility, and cold steel. The replacement of 'old-fashioned' cavalry with infantry should not be exaggerated either. Far from being 'nearly worthless' before 1709,[208] cavalry or dragoons (mounted infantrymen) were used to good effect in Sheremetev's campaigns in 1702–4 and at Lesnaia in 1708, and were prominent at Poltava. Ultimately, one can endorse Fuller's thesis that Russia itself was the most effective weapon, as summed up in the formula 'The Russian State was poor but strong'.[209] Opponents could be defeated by 'negative' factors which turned to Russia's advantage: terrain (vast distances), climate (harsh winters, hot summers), demography (sparse population), economy (relatively poor villages), and social structure (serfdom and slavery allowing unlimited recruitment) could all favour the team ensconced at home over the invading enemy far from its supply bases. 'Just enough money, food, weapons and equipment were collected and distributed to make the difference between the barely tolerable and the completely unendurable.'[210] Luck played its part, a series of poor harvests occurring after the end of the war, rather than during it. Things might have turned out differently had Peter decided to invade Sweden and capture major cities. At Poltava, one of the few set-piece battles of the war, officers and men withstood the Swedes in linear formation, artillery was used to devastating effect, and cavalry were usefully deployed. But Poltava was equally a defensive battle, a response to Swedish invasion. Swedish mistakes and misfortunes (e.g., abandoned artillery and Charles's injury) were exacerbated by the 'Russia factor' (lack of supplies and back-up after a severe winter and scorched earth tactics). It was not so much what happened on the field at Poltava as the events of the preceding nine years which counted in the end.

The responsibility for the war effort and all vital decisions were Peter's. If a commander is judged by the success of the whole, especially his acquisitions, then it was a brilliant record. Failures (Azov in 1695, Narva 1700—associated with incidents of alleged cowardice as Peter left the scene before the crucial battle—and Pruth 1711) were overshadowed by successful engagements in which Peter actually participated (normally under the pseudonym of his current army or navy rank): Azov in 1696, Nienschants in 1703, the siege of Riga in 1710 (where Peter tossed the first bomb), the Finnish campaign and Hangö in 1713–14, and the first part of the Persian campaign in 1722. Foremost, of course, was Poltava, in which, according to official accounts, the tsar, 'paid no heed to any danger to his lofty person, and during it the hat he was wearing was pierced by a bullet'.[211] (This gives rise to probably fruitless speculation about whether Russia would have won the Northern War if that bullet had pierced Peter's head rather than his hat.) Fuller believes, however, that 'it was on the strategic level that Peter really defeated the Swedish monarch', rather than in individual ostentatious set pieces.[212] He regards the main strengths of Peter's method as the councils of war (especially the one at Żolkiev in 1706), which allowed genuine debate and scrutiny of alternatives; clever use of diplomacy in order to form coalitions and 'make sure that the war would be fought somewhere other than Russia' (e.g., in 1701 with Augustus, which diverted the Swedes into Poland);[213] avoidance of any attempt to occupy mainland Sweden; and, notably, managing to spend most of the war avoiding actually fighting the Swedes. We might add that Peter's main contribution consisted in neither symbolic acts of bravery nor strategic 'cowardice', but in the sheer dogged persistence with which he bullied underlings to produce uniforms, fodder, and bayonets or to train for unpopular naval service, and his stubborn refusal to relinquish St Petersburg, his 'Paradise', when he had a chance earlier in the war to reach agreement with the Swedes.

But how long could such an effort be maintained? Peter left his less energetic, unwarlike successors with a dilemma. Once the tsar's driving force was removed, there were those bold enough to argue that Russia should cut its military budget and relieve pressure on servicemen and taxpayers alike. Others, like B. C. von Münnich, one of eighteenth-century Russia's most astute statesmen, understood only too well that successful nations had to continue to pay for military success and territorial expansion long after the event. There could be no more than a breathing-space if Russia was not to revert to being a second- or third-rate power. Warning of the *danger* of cuts in the army and the military budget, von Münnich wrote in December 1725 that 'in the present condition of the Russian state, since it has increased its size in the east and the west with new conquered provinces, the number of its open and secret enemies has increased'. He called for an increase rather than a decrease in the army, and argued (as it turned out, in vain) against cutting allowances.[214]

On 28 January 1722 Feofan Prokopovich, who always managed to include at least a grain of truth in his publicity exercises on Peter's behalf, delivered a 'Sermon on the Peace between the Russian Empire and the Swedish Crown' in Moscow's Dormition Cathedral:

> What emblem did the monarch's wit invent to portray the fleet he created and the navigation introduced into Russia? It was the image of a man, in a ship, naked and unskilled in steering the ship. This emblem, the same image serves as a commentary on all Russia's military condition as it was at the beginning of these past wars. Russia was naked and defenceless indeed! Weapons are not weapons in name only, that is, skilfully made of iron and bronze to harm the infidel; one also needs to make good use of weapons. It is not enough to have a sword of good steel unless the hand which wields it is strong and skilled. Just as an educated and an uneducated writer write differently with the same pen, skilled and unskilled music entertains unequally the same organ of hearing, a strong and a weak reaper harvests unequally with the same sickle, so one weapon works differently in different hands. Where there is no strength or skill, combined with a courageous heart, a weapon is no help but rather a burden and an impediment. Even rank and file soldiers, not to mention military instructors, do not need to be told this.[215]

One may peel away the panegyric, but it is hard to deny that Peter must have done something right. The three decades immediately following his death may have been marked by fewer military exploits than the previous two, but in general Russia continued to be regarded as a major military power until the middle of the nineteenth century, when the Crimean defeat revealed that the 'Russia factor' was no longer sufficient to outweigh the empire's backwardness with regard to technology and transport. Only then were the underpinnings of the Petrine military system—recruitment and industry based upon servitude—dismantled. Consideration of their partial restoration in the Soviet period and the part played by the 'Russia factor' in 1941–5, when Peter's image was harnessed to the war effort, along with the images of other heroes of the past, is beyond the scope of the present study.

4

Government

'The orderly running of His Majesty's state affairs'

I. MONARCH AND MOCK SOVEREIGNS

The key figure in the deployment of resources for the war effort and in decision making was the monarch. If the primary meaning of the much-debated term 'autocracy' is 'self-sustained power' and an autocrat (in Russian, *samoderzhets*) is his own master, then Peter was as complete an autocrat as any in Russian history. He was a man who enjoyed unlimited power in principle, ruling without limitation by any elected or corporate bodies, and often exercised this power in practice, behaving 'autocratically', to use the term in its looser sense. The fact that Peter disdained some aspects of pomp and ceremony, enjoyed chatting with shipwrights, and tried to promote individual initiative hardly alters the picture. 'It is said that the sovereign from the beginning wielded his monarchical power more absolutely than his predecessors,' Strahlenberg observed, 'and that he had little or no respect for his old and wise state councillors, but treated them like his abject slaves, and therefore had no reason to rely upon them. And he renounced the formula in verdicts and decrees "the boyars have affirmed (*prigovorili*)" and all decrees were issued only under his own name. He often treated the Senate with suspicion, ignored their wise advice and opinions and always tried to find ways of keeping the senators hostile to one another.'[1]

Peter was not much given to the elaboration of theoretical concepts, preferring to leave theorizing to others. A succinct formula, borrowed from the Swedish, appears in both the Military and the Naval Statutes: 'His majesty is a sovereign monarch, who is not answerable to anyone in the world in his affairs, but holds the power and authority to rule his realms and his lands as a Christian monarch by his own will and good opinion.'[2] In a statement to the clergy during the trial of his son Alexis in 1718, Peter declared that 'we have a sufficient and absolute power to judge our Son for his Crimes, according to our own Pleasure'. The prelates replied that 'the absolute Power established in the Czarian Empire, which is a Monarchy, is not to be submitted to the Judgement of Subjects'.[3]

The ground for Peter's brand of absolutism was prepared by his predecessors. His grandfather Tsar Michael, despite being an elected tsar and an unassertive personality, enjoyed the same hereditary monarchical powers as

Ivan the Terrible. During the reign of Alexis, the assembly of the land (*zemskii sobor*), which had elected Michael, ceased to function. The Byzantine notion of the 'symphony' of priesthood and tsardom was struck a terminal blow by the clash between Alexis and Patriarch Nikon, which resulted in the latter's demotion. The abolition of *mestnichestvo* in 1682 under Fedor removed restrictions on the monarch's choice of appointees at the same time as the boyar duma fell into decline. From the 1690s, legislation bore the tsar's sole signature in the form of personal (*imennye*) edicts, instead of the old joint formula of the tsar decreeing and the boyars affirming.

Yet in some respects Peter was an autocrat by default, in that he tried to make others take decisions and act independently, to the extent of resorting to mock delegation and pretending on occasion that he was not tsar at all. He was sensitive to foreign charges of 'despotism', all too familiar with accusations that, for example, the Russian government was 'absolute in the last degree, not bound up by any law or custom, but depending on the breath of the prince, by which the lives and fortunes of all the subjects are decided'.[4] Peter could retort that 'English freedom is not appropriate here. . . . You have to know your people to know how to govern them. I am happy to hear anything useful from the lowest of my subjects; their hands, legs and tongues are not fettered.'[5] Although rejecting representative institutions, Peter developed bodies—from the Magistrates' Chamber of 1699 to the Senate in 1711—with a semblance of independent authority, in so far as they were not immediately reliant on the presence of the tsar, as was, for example, the old-style boyar duma. Even more ambitiously, he tried to transfer his subjects' loyalty from his own person to more abstract concepts such as the State and the fatherland (virtually synonymous), the common good, and even the law, and to discourage them from bypassing the proper machinery of state which he reformed radically with the aim of defining clear procedures and chains of command in which the sovereign was the last, not the first, port of call. An edict of 27 October 1699 stated: 'Before this decree people petitioned the great sovereign on all manner of business. Now the great sovereign has decreed that petitions be presented to the judges in the chancelleries, where and to whom as appropriate and in those chancelleries where the petitioner has business but not to the great sovereign himself.' The tsar was to intervene only in the case of a dispute between the petitioner and the chancellery officials, in order to avoid 'idle tedious requests'.[6] A decree of 1700 reiterated that the tsar was to be approached only on matters of treason and as a last resort in cases of grave injustice. Such injunctions were, in fact, reformulations of the ban on submitting petitions to the tsar in chapter 10, article 20, of Tsar Alexis's 1649 Law Code.[7]

One of the principles behind the interlocking institutions of central and local government devised in 1718–20 was the notion that the new system should work like a well-oiled machine, without any need for the intervention of its inventor. But an edict of December 1718 shows that Peter was not confident of success. In terms reminiscent of the edicts passed almost twenty years previously, each petitioner who 'pestered' the tsar was reminded 'what a multitude there is of them, whereas it is one person they petition, and he is surrounded by so much military business and other burdensome work ... and even if he did not have such a lot of work, how would it be possible for one man to look after so many? In truth it is impossible either for a man or even for an angel.'[8] But the naïve idea that justice could be obtained only from the true tsar was difficult to eradicate. Four years later petitioners were ordered to address their complaints to the newly created 'maître de requêtes' (*Reketmeister*) instead of bothering the emperor, 'giving him no peace'.[9] In fact, Peter himself did little to alter old views about royal power. Anisimov calculates that the proportion of legislation issued as a personal decree of the tsar, sometimes written by him alone, increased, rather than diminished, after the installation of the new machinery of government.[10]

Peter's preferred brand of absolutism was customized for him by loyal churchmen like Feofan Prokopovich, bishop of Novgorod. A commentary on the Ten Commandments in Prokopovich's primer for youths, first published in St Petersburg in 1720, offers a definition for popular consumption, setting out in simple terms the basic principles of governmental hierarchy within a natural patriarchal order:

Q. What is ordained by God in the Fifth Commandment ['Honour thy father and thy mother']?

A. To honour those who are as fathers and mothers to us. But it is not only parents who are referred to here, but others who exercise paternal authority over us.

Q. Who are such persons?

A. The first order of such persons are the supreme authorities instituted by God to rule the people, of whom the highest authority is the tsar. It is the duty of kings to protect their subjects and to seek what is best for them, whether in religious matters or in the things of this world; and therefore they must watch over all the ecclesiastical, military and civil authorities subject to them and conscientiously see that they discharge their respective duties. That is, under God, the highest paternal dignity; and subjects, like good sons, must honour the tsar.[11]

The context is religious, but the balance is towards the secular: kings and princes have authority over matters *both* temporal *and* spiritual; they are pro-moters of 'the public good'. Below kings and princes rank 'ecclesiastical pastors, senators, judges and all other civil and military authorities'. Inferiors must love and respect their superiors, pray for them, and cheerfully obey all their just commands. The third order of persons vested with paternal dignity and authority are natural parents, together with other relatives, masters, teachers, and so on, but if one of them orders something forbidden by the civil authorities, they must be disobeyed.

Feofan's Palm Sunday sermon 'On Royal Authority and Honour' (1718), which starts out with a description of the greeting given to Christ the King in Jerusalem and alludes to the trial of Tsarevich Alexis, was addressed to a wider public. Some people, he declares, seemed unaware 'that the highest power is established and armed with the sword of God and that to oppose it is a sin against God himself, a sin to be punished by death, not temporary but eternal'. Christ's 'freedom' does not mean freedom to disobey to the 'powers' or law of God. Freedom is freedom *from* sin, death, and 'legislation of ritual and human inventions supposedly necessary for salvation'. This includes freedom to prefer sun to rain, beauty to ugliness. He goes on to speak of natural laws 'in men's hearts', such as self-defence and loving one's parents; 'and we hold it certain that supreme authority receives its beginning and cause from Nature itself. If from Nature, then from God himself, the Creator of Nature.' Rulers are called 'gods' and 'Christs' in the Bible, anointed ones, even if they are 'perverse and faithless powers'. 'If therefore it is so, if Christians have to be subject even to perverse and faithless rulers, then how much more must they be utterly obligated to true believing and true judging lords!'[12] Sovereigns, it was argued, are fathers to their people, an idea illustrated with the image of Peter 'renewing' Russia, giving her 'a new birth'.[13] In this and other writings Feofan drew upon the ideas of Pufendorf, Hobbes and Grotius, playing down the Orthodox basis of Peter's rule (with its possible implications of the Byzantine parallelism of secular and religious powers) and the notion of a specifically Orthodox mission. *All* Christians must obey their monarchs on the basis of both divine right and natural law.[14] In other writings, Feofan warned of the dangers of division. In the preface to the Naval Statute, for example, he praises Prince Vladimir's service to Russia in baptizing his country in 988, but laments his disservice in dividing his realm among his twelve sons, thereby bringing a 'great harm' to the Russian people.[15]

Similar ideas are found in *The Justice of the Monarch's Right* (1722), the 'chief ideological manifesto of Petrine absolutism'.[16] Here is not the place to debate questions of authorship. Recent studies offer convincing evidence that it is 'of a piece with analogous works by Prokopovich', and that Peter's own contribution remains 'a matter for speculation'.[17] This work, ostensibly written to 'justify' Peter's appropriation of the right to appoint his own heir in 1722, identifies the divine basis of monarchical power, starting with divine right, with reference to Scripture and Byzantine and Classical authors. But it also uses a Western frame of reference, drawing on Grotius (*On the Law of War and Peace*, 1625) in order to stress 'affinities with European natural law theory'. The author identifies popular sources of monarchical power: 'popular will' (*vsenarodnaia volia*) delegates power to rulers for the sake of the common good (*k obshchei pol'ze nashei*). There is a 'contract' between people and ruler: once agreed, the people cannot retract their consent. Even if a monarch is (or becomes) evil, people cannot take back the power they have granted; a monarch may choose to adhere to 'man-made law', but is not obliged to do so. Rulers are subject directly to God, not to intermediaries such as the Church. The thrust of the work was to show that there is no rational or divine reason to prefer primogeniture, a mere *custom* which can be set aside for a higher purpose. Prokopovich may have been influenced by John Locke in formulating the notion of the separate spheres of Church and government, the former concerned with the salvation of souls, the latter with the protection and well-being of subjects. The Church's role is more or less restricted to ritual and dogma, while education, and even marriage, fall within the State's sphere. Such ideas were given full expression in the Ecclesiastical Regulation.[18]

Was Peter viewed as divine? Prokopovich's primer, quoted above, certainly appears to associate the father of the fatherland with the heavenly Father. In the commentary on the Lord's Prayer, the explanation of 'Give us this day our daily bread' is immediately followed by the admonition to 'bless the government' and ask God to grant health and long life to 'our Most Blessed Sovereign Peter the Great, Emperor and All-Russian Autocrat'.[19] Yet Peter himself appears consciously to have avoided such sacralization by his behaviour and life-style, adopting dress, menial occupations, and an informality calculated to make him seem more like an 'ordinary' person than a divine emperor, not to mention indulging in 'impious' activities which led some subjects to identify him with the Antichrist. But, as Cherniavsky points out, discarding the Muscovite image of the 'pious and gentle tsar' could have 'two alternative consequences'.[20] On the one hand, the tsar might appear less 'holy'; on the other, 'sacralization' of the monarch increased as a result of the loss of the 'balancing' figure of the patriarch. The tsar, pious or not, could now be regarded as head of the Church, even if technically speaking he was not.[21] Peter's propagandists, churchmen and laymen alike, employed rhetoric and imagery which likened the tsar's activities to God's, most notably in their use of creation motifs. For example, the phrase 'from nothingness into being', as used by Golovkin in 1721 or by P. N. Krekshin ('Our father, Peter the Great! you have brought us from non-being to being') comes from a liturgical prayer.[22] The Old Believer Ivan Pavlov complained that 'his name was written not only as Antichrist but also as Christ'(as, for example, when Peter's 'Christ' was contrasted with Mazepa's 'Judas').[23] Stefan Iavorsky, metropolitan of Riazan' and *locum tenens* of the patriarchal throne, wrote to Peter in 1714: 'What greater virtue can be more fitting to a royal eminence (*prevoskhodstvu*) than to forgive guilt. In this way you, earthly god (*zemnyi bozi*), are like unto God in heaven himself.' Liturgical texts were applied to the tsar as a matter of course, often in routine correspondence or in the use of Hosanna and Palm Sunday imagery to greet him: 'Blessed is he who cometh in the name of the Lord'.[24] Here it was the triumphal aspects of Christ's life which were presented for emulation rather than qualities of mercy, forgiveness, care for the poor, and so on.[25] Zhivov and Uspensky argue that even when there were attempts to create distinctly secular ceremonies, popular understanding often confused panegyric conventions about 'gods' and 'goddesses' with religious concepts. The message seemed to be that the tsar *was* a supernatural being, not simply 'like' God in his power in earthly matters, as Russo-Byzantine tradition stressed.

The sacralization of the royal image ran parallel with its 'paganization', as Old Russian Orthodox tsarist imagery was increasingly replaced by Roman imperial motifs in public displays. The identification of Peter with a Roman *imperator*, or military commander, is first seen in the Azov triumphs in 1696.[26] From the 1700s the image on the new rouble coins was consistently Roman.[27] The Roman epithet *pater patriae* (father of the fatherland) was used by Prokopovich in 1709 in a panegyric to Poltava at his first meeting with Peter.[28] More recent emperors also provided models. In 1710–14 an imperial crown emblem appears on seals, standards, engravings, coins, and medals.[29] Just Juel records a conversation with Peter Shafirov (February 1710) in which the latter noted that the English ambassador Whitworth had addressed Peter as 'Imperial Majesty' and that other crowned heads ought to do the same.[30] A letter (found by Shafirov) from the Emperor Maximilian I to Vasily III of Moscow was published in 1718 to justify Peter's proposed titles on the basis of precedent.[31] There was also a conscious link with the empire of the east, despite the fact that Peter played down the religious element of the Byzantine inheritance. Thus the ground was well prepared for the declaration in October 1721 of new titles—father of the fatherland, Emperor of All Russia, Peter the Great—with a firm Roman and Byzantine ('Greek') provenance. 'We thought it right,' pronounced the Senate in its speech, 'in the manner of the ancients, especially the Roman and Greek people ... also as was the custom of the Roman Senate in recognition of their emperors' famous deeds to pronounce such titles publicly as a gift and to inscribe them on statues for the memory of posterity.'[32] The full titles, with a complete listing of all the emperor's domains, were generally used only for foreign charters. At the beginning of edicts Peter termed himself 'We Peter the First, Emperor and Autocrat of All Russia', while the correct form of address for petitions was 'All-Illustrious, Most Sovereign, Emperor and Autocrat, Peter the Great, Father of the Fatherland, Most Gracious Lord (*gosudar*')'. New seals were made for the tsar and for government departments.[33] The new titles outraged traditionalists, some of whom continued to use the old ones. Peter had to remind the Synod that the title 'tsar' in prayers and sermons had been replaced by the word '*imperator*'. A prayer of thanks for the victory over the Swedes was printed as a model, with the correct formulae.[34] Even the designation 'First' reflected an alien tradition. Muscovite tsars were called by name and patronymic, never by their regnal number.[35]

The sacralization and Romanization of the tsar's image are just part of the story of Peter's peculiar brand of absolutism. These processes went hand in hand with deliberate and consistent debunking of the trappings of power. On one level this involved Peter behaving in an 'un-tsar-like' manner: wearing ordinary clothes, working at a lathe, and so on.[36] Such behaviour was uncommon but not unique. Charles XII, for example, was famous for living the life of a common soldier. On another, more complex level, the tsar denied his royal identity, shed titles, regalia, and office, and adopted pseudonyms or went incognito. The fact that Peter was unusually tall, with distinctive physical features, made this rejection especially provocative; maintenance of the pretence required the complicity of others. Some of these scenarios required a substitute to occupy the throne and confer honours upon 'simple' Peter and his comrades-at-arms. Until his death in 1717, this mock tsar, or 'Prince-Caesar', was Fedor Iur'evich Romodanovsky,[37] who for much of this period was aided by a 'junior sovereign' in a parody of the joint rule of Peter and his late brother Ivan. In an early example of 'substitution', an announcement about Peter's second visit to Archangel in 1694 was issued in the name of Romodanovsky from the 'capital city of Presburg', where he performed the role of king in Peter's mock battles.[38] Peter's retinue for the visit included the mock sovereigns Romodanovsky and Ivan Ivanovich Buturlin, whose role as vice-sovereign originated with his 'command' of the mock troops at Semenovskoe.[39] After the death in 1696 of Tsar Ivan, who had performed the useful function of *legitimate* 'stand-in' for Peter, decked out in full regalia at religious ceremonies and other state occasions, Romodanovsky became even more invaluable and even more powerful, when in the same year the Preobrazhensky office, which he headed, was given exclusive powers to investigate and try political crimes.[40]

The best-known and most prolonged maintenance of the 'tsar as commoner' fiction was the Grand Embassy of 1697–8 when Peter travelled as 'Peter Mikhailov' in the retinue of the plenipotentiary ambassadors Lefort and Golovin. Romodanovsky 'reigned' in Moscow, while Mikhailov pursued his studies, a logical arrangement given the real tsar's incognito, although one that fooled nobody.[41] In October 1698 Romodanovsky received the returning ambassadors Lefort and Golovin, who presented their credentials and a monkey to the prince 'with ludicrous and scenic solemnity'. Peter mingled with the rank and file, who were all clad in 'German dress' in order to irritate the traditionally minded Romodanovsky.[42] Peter's letters to Prince-Caesar, customarily addressed to 'Min Her Konich', later amended to 'Sire' or 'Siire', were formulated in the manner of correspondence between an underling and his superior, with liberal sprinklings of 'your slave' and 'your humble servant'.[43] In his turn, Romodanovsky on occasions lorded it over his 'subject', rebuking Mikhailov for arrogance and conceit when he failed to remove his hat in his sovereign's presence.[44] It was Romodanovsky who authorized the wages, 366 roubles, which 'Piter Michailof' drew from the Admiralty for his work as a shipwright.[45] He was always among the first to receive notification from his 'humble subject' of Russia's victories—for example, the capture in May 1703 of the fortress of Nienschants near what was to become St Petersburg, with a request that 'this victory be celebrated properly' with prayers and cannon-fire.[46] Romodanovsky was the first to be notified of the victory at Poltava. He was congratulated and asked to promote the bearer of the news to the rank of lieutenant.[47] In March 1711, when Peter left Moscow for the Turkish war, Romodanovsky was again appointed 'Tsar of Russia'.[48] It is worth noting that Romodanovsky held court in Moscow, thus investing the old capital with the role of 'substitute' for the new one. He even founded a royal dynasty. On 21 November 1704 Peter wrote from Narva offering congratulations (as was 'his humble duty') on the birth of a son to 'our sovereign's son', wishing the boy long life with the increase of his grandfather's reign.[49] Name-day greetings were sent to the same son, 'our sovereign tsarevich and great prince Ioann Fedorovich', in July 1706.[50] When Prince Fedor died in 1717, his son succeeded him.[51]

A particularly interesting incident dates from the Russian victory at Hangö in July 1714 when Peter, still a rear-admiral (*shaubenakht*), won promotion to vice-admiral. (The previous year, while in Finland, he had been promoted to full general.[52]) He wrote ordering Menshikov to ensure that 'our sovereign should arrive as soon as possible, by 1 September' and that triumphal arches should be erected.[53] On 13 September Peter wrote to Admiral Apraksin from St Petersburg: 'I arrived here with the captured ships on the 9th of this month and on the same day we were all received by His Majesty, where I handed over the letter from you. His Majesty deigned to ask after your health and praised your loyal service, whereupon he awarded me the rank of vice-admiral, for which I thank your honour for recommending me.'[54] Weber described the ceremony, at which the assembled company 'unanimously declared him Vice-Admiral of Russia in consideration of the faithful Service he had done to his native Country, of which Proclamation being made, the whole Room resounded with Sdrastwi Vice-Admiral, Health to the Vice-Admiral (which is the Russian Vivat)'.[55] Even official accounts of the battle of Hangö maintained Peter's incognito, referring to him as *gospodin shaubenakht*.[56]

Mock deference to a substitute tsar continued to the very end of Peter's life. Romodanovsky's successor, Ivan Fedorovich, was received with great solemnity just before Easter 1718 (during Alexis's trial), and was served with wine and brandy by Peter and his wife Catherine in person.[57] Peter was not unaware of the confusion that might arise from the existence of an alternative authority. In April 1722, preparing to leave for the Persian campaign, he instructed Prince-Caesar to deal only with matters such as murders or brigandage which occurred 'in the presence of your person', and not with any matters except the ones listed, 'in order to avoid confusion to the agreed regulation'.[58] Even so, in July Peter wrote to Romodanovsky: 'Sire. I inform Your Majesty that this day we and *gospodin* general-admiral left Astrakhan on your royal service with all the fleet and hope with God's help soon to reach the shores of Persia. Your Majesty's most humble servant, Peter.'[59] Later examples include letters of October 1723 (asking 'Sire' to deal with two arrested suspects) and January 1724 (requesting him to send some clerks to St Petersburg).[60] The name 'Peter Mikhailov' had a long life: Peter used it to sign instructions on a ballot for officer promotions in 1721 and in a petition to the mock tsar in 1723 for the promotion of fellow shipwright Dmitry Dobrynin (jointly with the promotions of Skliaev, Richard Cozens, Joseph Nye and other British master craftsmen, and Ivan Golovin, to whom Peter also deferred as 'chief surveyor'.)[61]

The Prince-Caesar was one of a number of mock offices and institutions, the best known of which was the All-Drunken Assembly. They could be confusing to foreign outsiders (and to unwary historians), but there is no evidence that Peter confused the worlds of reality and play, or that he had any doubts about the extent of his real power. Peter could discard the servile tone and subservient role in an instant. Romodanovsky, for example, was deferred to only on Peter's own terms. In the postscript to a letter of December 1697 the tsar called him a 'beast', and ordered him to 'stop consorting with Ivan Khmelnitsky' (the Russian John Barleycorn).[62] In other letters he ordered him to send shirts, trousers, and accessories for 4,000 men to Novgorod without delay, to dispatch artillery supplies to Smolensk, to have 100 mortars made.[63] The example of Romodanovsky makes the point. Peter required servitors to fulfil a multiplicity of roles. These roles were created and written for them by the tsar, who also created the structures and institutions in which they were expected to operate in their 'real' capacity. Let us now turn to the real governing apparatus that Peter reformed and created.

II. CENTRAL GOVERNMENT: FROM BOYAR COUNCIL TO SENATE

From early on, Peter imbibed modern theories of state building, notably that the 'common good' could be furthered by a state mechanism improved along rational lines to create all-encompassing legislation and run like clockwork.[64] The main reason for the failure to implement this vision immediately was Peter's preoccupation with naval and military affairs. But it was precisely military and naval affairs and the ever-pressing need to finance them which gave the impetus for radical reform once there was a breathing-space. In the interim Peter had to achieve his objectives through old institutions with some *ad hoc* additions.

The most venerable of these old bodies was the 'boyar council', with its essentially patrimonial career structure, which from 1699 had a new executive organ, the Privy Chancellery (*blizhnaia kantseliariia*), attached to its inflated body. The chancellery was established to exert financial control over the income and expenditure of government departments (*prikazy*), whose heads met, in the Kremlin or the General Court at Preobrazhenskoe, from 1704. After 1708 this body was referred to as the council (*konsiliia*) of ministers. Although it could function in the tsar's absence (and was instructed to keep minutes), on occasion Peter summoned it to attend him in the manner of the old duma—as at Belgorod in February 1709.[65] It survived, manned by trusted individuals in Moscow, when Peter was away at war, until ousted by the Senate in 1711. Personal ties provide the key to how Russia was ruled during the 1690s and 1700s. Institutional historians can be put off the scent by attributing authority only to properly constituted institutions. Claus Peterson, for example, expresses surprise at the fact that in 1697 Peter left affairs in the keeping of F. Iu. Romodanovsky, 'who was not a member of the

Duma', and that when the latter became head of the *konsiliia* in 1708, he held a lower rank than other members. He fails to point out that, as mock sovereign of Peter's substitute court, Romodanovsky ranked higher than all the rest, and as 'sovereign' could not logically be a member of the duma.[66]

The first new institution of Petrine central government which could truly claim to wield some power was the ruling (*pravitel'stvuiushchii*) Senate. Peter's hand-written *ukaz* on its creation, dated 22 February 1711 and listing the names of ten men 'to govern in our absence', was penned on the same day as the declaration of war with Turkey.[67] The senators' duties were specified in a laconic edict dated 2 March.[68] In the first draft, article 1 laid down the duty to look after state expenses and eliminate unnecessary ones—a primarily fiscal function—but in the second and third versions this article was placed after the requirement 'to pass honest (*nelitsemernyi*) judgement and to punish unjust judges by depriving them of their honour and all their property, the same to apply also to false informers'. The other requirements were (article 3) to collect as much money as possible, 'since money is the artery of war'; (article 4) to recruit young nobles to replenish the officer corps and to track down shirkers, and to take 1,000 literate men from among the boyars' bondsmen to be officers; (article 5) to regulate bills of exchange and keep them in one place; (article 6) to inspect and certify goods held in franchises or chancelleries and provincial offices; (article 7) to try to farm out salt to franchise and make a profit; (article 8) to form a good company and hand over Chinese trade to it; (article 9) to increase trade with Persia and attract more Armenians to come and trade. A footnote read: 'To appoint fiscals (*fiskaly*) in all matters, instructions to be sent on their duties.'[69] (These latter officers were supposed to uncover embezzlement, bribe taking, and serious infringements of the law. Law-breakers, regardless of high station, were to be summoned before the Senate by the fiscal and indicted. Half the resulting fine was to go to the treasury, half to the fiscal himself.[70] To whom was the fiscal answerable? The monetary incentive might be conducive to initiative, on the one hand, to abuse on the other, especially as in cases where a conviction was not secured, the fiscal was protected from punishment. Eventually there were 500 fiscals, most of whom were notoriously corrupt.)

Orders issued on 2 March defined the Senate's authority: 'We command everyone who needs to know, both churchmen and laymen, the highest and the lowest grades of military and civil administration, that we, for reason of our continual absences in these wars, have appointed a ruling (*upravitel'nyi*) Senate, to which and to whose edicts everyone must be as obedient as to us ourselves under threat of cruel punishment or death, depending on the crime.' Even if someone suspected senators of committing a crime, they were to 'remain silent' until the tsar's arrival in order not to impede other business, and were then to present proper evidence.[71] The senators had to take an oath in which they vowed, first, loyalty to their sovereign and all the realm; secondly, to dispense justice and fair judgment; thirdly, to collect revenues and recruits in the sovereign's and State's interests 'to the last drop of their strength'. In performing their duties, they vowed not to be influenced by personal gain (*vziatka*) or fear, or to show undue leniency or to take vengeance on anyone.[72] All senators had an equal voice, and their decisions must be unanimous (in 1714 this was changed to majority decision).[73] Any individual opposing a measure had to give his reasons in writing. Unlike the boyar council, the Senate could issue its own edicts (*ukazy*) independently of the sovereign, and all institutions and persons had to obey them. Peter wrote to Menshikov on 11 March 1711: 'You are probably already aware that we have appointed a ruling Senate, to which we have given full powers. Therefore write to them with all your demands, and write to us only to keep us informed in order not to waste time.'[74] Here, as elsewhere, Peter's attempts at delegation were not always successful. On 9 April he wrote to Menshikov again: 'Please write to them (the senators) on all matters, because in writing to us here and from here to the Senate in Moscow more time is wasted in writing than if you write direct to them.'[75] In other words, the institution was supposed to exercise many of the judicial, legislative, and economic powers previously vested in the person of the sovereign.

The link between the creation of the Senate and the impending war with Turkey has prompted debate over whether it was intended as a temporary measure or as a long-term one. N. I. Pavlenko, for one, believed that Peter 'did not intend to make use of [the Senate's] services for a long period'. It was created 'in a rush, without any clear idea of its rights, duties and role in the mechanism of government'.[76] A number of pronouncements in February and March 1711—for example, of Peter's betrothal to Catherine as a measure to safeguard the interests of their daughters in the event of his death—reflect a mood of pessimism about the outcome of the war.[77] Peter was afraid that he might not return from the south, and was aware that there was no one individual to whom he could entrust the country's domestic affairs (though the omission of specifically military and foreign policy tasks from the Senate's brief suggests some confidence that these would be properly conducted). There is no evidence that the Senate was created after detailed consideration of foreign models, as was to be the case with the colleges and the Table of Ranks. Adam Weyde, recently returned from Sweden, may have supplied information about the Swedish *ricksrodet*, or state council (the term 'Senate' itself was not borrowed from Sweden), but this body was frequently at loggerheads with the king and did not provide a good model.[78] The Poles had a *senat*, but it seems doubtful, given Peter's views on Poland, that he would have found it appropriate.[79] In fact, the Russian Senate may best be seen as a variation on the Muscovite practice of leaving the capital in the charge of a group of named boyars during the ruler's absence. In this case the *konsiliia* mentioned above, which superseded the boyar duma *c.* 1696, may be regarded as a transitional stage between the old duma, with its variable number of members, lack of protocols and regulations, absence of a permanent staff or headquarters, and *ad hoc* committees, to a properly constituted body of men with a secretariat. As for the name, Peter admired the spirit if not the substance of ancient imperial institutions. The term 'Senate' is one of many pieces of Roman 'window-dressing' with which the new empire was embellished, and senators were happy to see themselves in a Classical light. When conferring the imperial titles on Peter in 1721, they pointed out that they were following the example of their Roman predecessors.[80]

The Senate's brief was wide, to the point of being unmanageable. From the start, the new senators were expected to perform tasks above and beyond those set out in the 2 March edicts. They had to draft in the work-force for St Petersburg, which always fell below quota, to deal with merchants' petitions and supervise the notaries (*pod'iachie*) who drew up and witnessed contracts.[81] The Senate took on responsibility for recruiting and provisioning the army, the old *Razriad* chancellery being abolished and its functions transferred to an office attached to the Senate.[82] In 1713–20 the Estates chancellery (*pomestnyi prikaz*) was attached to the Senate, partly in an attempt to counteract the influence of the old *prikaz* staff, who tended to decide in favour of boyar landowners.[83] Senators were expected to keep an eye on other government officials. For example, in January 1714 they were ordered to carry out an interrogation of the provincial governors (one by one) immediately and call them to account for arrears in payments for the army and the navy. They were to make them hand over any ready cash and make a clear declaration of any shortfalls, rejecting 'vague excuses'. Anyone who prevaricated was to be placed under arrest immediately, and 'to be given no quarter'.[84] There were inevitably clashes with the governors, notably Menshikov (of St Petersburg) and Romodanovsky (of Moscow), both of whom outranked the early senators.

The first senators met in a building in the Kremlin behind the Annunciation cathedral. In June 1711 new glass windows, stoves, desks, tables, benches, and a huge ink-well were ordered. In 1713 the Senate moved to St Petersburg, first to a building inside the fortress, then to specially built premises (which were sometimes also used as a banqueting hall) on Trinity Square, where the original colleges were also situated, until Trezzini's building for the twelve colleges on Vasil'evsky Island was completed in 1732.[85] Working hours were specified as three days a week—Monday, Wednesday, and Friday. Anyone absent without good cause was fined fifty roubles per day. One senator was on duty on a monthly rota every day ('even after lunch') in order to deal with urgent business.[86] Peter often visited the Senate and took part in its discussions. Mementos of his presence (still extant in 1911) included an hour-glass, for timing discussions, and his personal gavel. His last attendance was on 14 December 1724.[87]

Given the weight of business and the fact that the original senators were fairly mediocre individuals,[88] it is not surprising that they at first failed to meet the tsar's expectations. On 4 May 1711 Peter wrote: 'We are amazed that since our departure from Moscow we have had no word from you about what is happening there, especially whether the new regiments have been sent to Voronezh as ordered and the recruits to Riga, which is vital. We have written to you twice and received no report as to whether it has been done or not.'[89]

On 19 May Peter reprimanded them for writing with excuses 'just like the old judges ... or has the oath which you swore not long ago already escaped your memory?'[90] In September he criticized procedures for implementing his proposals for extending the right to trade freely to 'all ranks', pointing out that it was foolish to ask the opinion of those who already made their wealth from trade, 'as they will never agree to [changes]'. The senators had acted 'in the old stupid manner' (*po starym glupostiam*).[91] If Peter had hoped that the Senate would be an agent of change and that its members would act differently from their predecessors in Muscovite government departments, he was continually disappointed. They were scolded for sending to Moscow troops which were needed for the Finnish campaign ('You should have been able to work out from our letters to you in which we always kept saying that this affair is vital to the interests of our State, therefore we commanded you to increase and strengthen the corps in St Petersburg, not to diminish it'[92]) and for backlogs of court cases ('We have been informed in reports from the fiscals that you have not resolved one major case but just keep putting everything off from one date to the next, forgetting God and your soul. Therefore I am writing for the last time to say that if five or six major cases, if you can't manage any more, ... are not completed by 1 November and the criminals (who damage state interests for their own benefit) are not put to death, showing mercy to no one, ... it will be the worse for you'[93]).

By the end of Peter's reign the original 'nonentities' had been replaced by the tsar's closest associates, such as Menshikov, Apraksin, Golovin, and D. M. Golitsyn, and the Senate had become an established institution. But Peter still felt the need for someone to guard the guardians. On 27 November 1715 he created the post of general inspector (*revizor*), or 'supervisor of edicts' (*nadziratel' ukazov*), who soon complained that the Senate had been sending him only extracts of selected documents.[94] In 1721 a guards officer was appointed to 'watch over' the Senate, to ensure that senators did their duty and put orders into practice ('not just on paper'), and to prevent quarrels or bad behaviour 'on pain of death'.[95] Finally, in April 1722, Peter formulated the duties of the procurator-general (*general-prokurator*) simultaneously with a new document on the duties of the Senate:

1. The procurator general is supposed to sit in the Senate and watch carefully to see that the Senate does its duty and acts in all matters which are subject to the Senate's scrutiny and resolution truthfully, diligently and correctly, without wasting time and in accordance with the regulations and edicts, unless some valid reason prevents them from carrying out their duties, and he must note down everything in his journal.

2. He must also see to it that business is completed not only on the desk [on paper] but also put into action according to instructions, and he must ask those who have been issued with instructions whether they have been carried out in the time which is feasible to start and complete the business.

3. If [he finds] it has not been carried out, he must find out the reason,

whether some circumstance prevented it, or some whim (*strast'*) or as a result of laziness.

4. He must immediately bring the matter to the attention of the Senate.

5. For this he must have a book in which to write on one half [of the paper] what instructions were given/edict was passed on a certain day and on the other half what was carried out and when or not, according to that instruction and why, and any other circumstances are to be noted down.

Further clauses went into more detail about procedures, including communication with the tsar, with fiscals, and under-procurators. The procurator was to act as the tsar's eye (*oko nashe*).[96]

The flurry of legislation in April–June 1722 illustrates the focusing of Peter's conception of the interlocking parts of the state apparatus, in which institutions were supervised by a hierarchy of individuals, with safety-valves installed at various levels to allow bypassing the system from below. The procurator-general had an office in the Senate, and subordinated to him were college, magistracy, and court procurators.[97] (In 1724 the procurator-general's duties were extended more directly to college offices. He was told to keep an eye on the office personnel, 'for I am sure that behind our back there are many goings-on'.[98]) This network was envisaged before the post of procurator-general was announced officially. The 1722 Admiralty Regulation (5 April) contained a clause on the duties of the Admiralty procurator, who was to ensure that board members did their duty, wasted no time, and observed the regulations. This post was to be 'the eye of the procurator-general in this college'.[99] The Synod had its own lay over-procurator (created in May–June 1722), who in turn had under-procurators subordinate to him. His instructions referred to him, too, as the sovereign's 'eye'. He was the 'assistant' of the procurator-general and his deputy.[100] The work of the fiscals, created in 1711, was extended, and the chief fiscal (*ober-fiskal*) 'a clever and good man (from any rank)', who was supposed to 'supervise all matters in secret and learn of wrong verdicts, also of the collection of revenue and so on', was subordinated to the procurator-general. In 1724 the additional post of Senate administrator (*ekzekutor*) was created, to see that decisions were implemented.[101] Everybody, it seemed, was watching or being watched by someone else.

III. FROM *PRIKAZY* TO *KOLLEGII*

'There cannot be good administration except with colleges; their mechanism is like that of watches, whose wheels mutually keep each other in movement.'[102] Muscovite tsars administered the country through forty or so chancelleries, or *prikazy*, each headed by a handful of noble servitors (boyar or lower in rank, according to the importance of the department) and a larger team of trained, mainly non-noble secretaries and scribes. The *prikazy* were overlapping and unwieldy—'even modern scholars cannot agree on their exact number and classification'[103]—but they managed to collect revenue, run wars and dispense justice more or less effectively. Some did business throughout Russia—two of the most important were the department of Military Appointments (*Razriad*), which selected and deployed higher and middle servicemen, and the Estates department (*Pomestnyi prikaz*), which administered service lands and allocated fiefs (*pomest'ia*) to serving individuals, and kept records of noble land and serf holdings.[104] Others administered a given region (the departments of Siberia, Kazan', Novgorod, and Smolensk). Some major functions were spread over many departments—for example, tax collecting—while others were concentrated in a single agency.[105]

Contrary to the impression that Peter neatly replaced the *prikazy* with a new 'streamlined' administrative structure, throughout much of his reign business continued to be conducted in these old-style offices. Altogether sixty-five *prikazy* were in existence at different times.[106] Peter himself created many new ones, including the offices of the Admiralty (1700–11), Artillery (1700–11), Military Affairs (1701–11, which merged the Cavalry and Foreign Mercenaries departments[107]), Provisioning (1700–11), Preobrazhensky (1686–1729) and Semenovsky Chancelleries (1688, 1693, 1699), Mining (1700–11), Contracts (*krepostnikh del*, 1702–11), and Moscow Police (*zemskikh del*, 1701–20, into which the Strel'tsy chancellery was incorporated).[108] Some were created for specific short-term purposes, such as the chancellery of Investigations (*rozysknykh del*) to try Fedor Shaklovity in 1689–94, and of Shipbuilding (1698–9), to build the Azov fleet. Another of Peter's offices, the Monastery chancellery, was created in 1701 as a response to the suspension of the patriarchate. Originally intended to supervise church revenues, it also oversaw printing and publishing.[109]

The most novel of Peter's new *prikazy* was the Preobrazhensky department, founded in 1686 as an administrative base for the play regiments. It was headed by the mock sovereigns Romodanovsky and Buturlin, and was designated a *prikaz* from the first Azov campaign in 1695. It grew into an office for trying cases of treason and opposition, probably as a result of being entrusted with guarding Tsarevna Sophia in the Novodevichy convent and, from 1695, for investigating cases 'deserving special attention'.[110] In 1696 Peter gave the office exclusive rights for investigating and trying crimes of opposition, with powers of arrest over all classes of people.[111] Thereafter the office had well-defined sections: the General courtyard (*general'nyi dvor*) for running the regiments, the Play Regiments courtyard (*Poteshnyi dvor*) for policing, and the Main chancellery (*glavnaia kantseliariia*) for criminal investigations. In 1697–1708 the latter pronounced 507 convictions (not including sentences on the rebels of 1698 and Astrakhan). So many accusations came in that in 1714 those reporting 'simple matters' which did not involve treason were threatened with flogging.

The number of chancelleries did not diminish until late in Peter's reign, but some of their power as all-Russian agencies did. In 1699 the Magistrates' chamber (*Ratusha*) replaced the Great Treasury for tax-collecting purposes.[112] The creation of provinces (*gubernii*) ruled by governors (see below) in 1708 took much business out of the hands of the existing chancelleries, abolishing all territorial-based departments with the exception of the Siberian one. In 1711 the Senate took over many chancellery functions, notably those of the *Razriad* and the Estates department, which had formed the 'heart of a vast patronage system extending over the entire country'.[113] Surviving chancelleries were subordinated either to the office of Moscow province (*guberniia*) or to the Senate.[114]

Still, Peter was not satisfied and wanted to achieve better co-ordination. The idea of creating collegiate boards (*kollegii*) is first mentioned in a note to the Senate dated 23 March 1715.[115] There are several possible sources for the idea, including an anonymous memorandum to Peter usually ascribed to Leibniz, expounding the theories of the German cameralists, with an emphasis upon the utility of rational, 'clockwork' organizations: 'God, as a God of order, rules everything wisely and in an orderly manner with his invisible hand. The Gods of this world, or the likenesses of God's power (I am thinking of the absolutist monarchs), have to establish their forms of government in accordance with this order if they wish to enjoy the sweet fruits of a flourishing state for their great efforts.'[116] Most influential was a memorandum, dated 9 May 1718 and attributed to one of Peter's foreign advisers, Heinrich Fick, which outlined something close to the Swedish system.[117] Fick was sent to Sweden to study and collect Swedish statutes, which he brought back to Russia early in 1717. Prince I. V. Trubetskoy was asked to send copies of all the laws of Sweden, 'from the peasant to the soldier, right up to the Senate', including ranks and grades in the *kollegii*.[118] The debt to Sweden was spelt out in an order of 28 April 1718, as was the principle that there must be no slavish imitation: 'All the *kollegii* are now to operate on the basis of the Swedish statute in all business and procedures, and any points which are inconvenient in the Swedish statute or incompatible with the situation of this country are to be included only if they see fit (*onye stavit po svoemu razsuzhdeniiu*).'[119] Information was also sought about the Danish civil service, because Peter had heard that the Swedes had borrowed from the Danes; but apparently this approach was abandoned when it became known that the converse was true.[120] Austrian, Prussian, and British practices were also consulted. Peter wrote to F. F. Veselovsky in Vienna 'to hire clerks (*shreiberov*) and other such chancellery workers who had been in the Emperor's service— Bohemians, Slovakians, Moravians [i.e., Slavs] working in his *kollegii*, one from each, except for the ecclesiastical department'.[121]

The resulting edicts on the establishment of colleges, nine to begin with, were issued on 11 and 15 December 1717.[122] The principle behind *kollegii*, apart from further centralizing government in a systematic way, was that decisions were reached collegially, by a board which operated on a majority decision, supported below by a hierarchy of trained officials. In theory, the president of the board could not create a personal power base. Voting members consisted of a president and a vice-president (initially the former was a Russian, the latter a foreigner), four or five councillors (*sovetchiki*), and four assessors (*assessory*). This decision-making board was supported by an office (*kantseliariia*) staffed by non-voting functionaries (*kollezhskie sluzhiteli*): secretary, minutes secretary (*notarius*), translators, actuary (who kept lists of letters and supplies of stationery), registrar (in charge of copying letters and documents and keeping the journal); and they in turn were serviced by a team of lower-level chancellery clerks and copyists, as well as assorted domestics and doormen. Each college was also assigned a fiscal, 'to check that everything was administered in good order according to the set regulations and edicts, with justice and good zeal'.[123] There was to be no promotion of 'relatives or personal creatures'.[124] To ensure fair appointment on merit, candidates were to be selected by ballot, as set out in a decree of 1720.[125] A systematic explanation of the function and duties of college staff was set out in the General Regulation of 1720.

The composition and duties of the Senate were adapted to the new collegiate structure. In 1718 presidents of colleges were made senators, but as several of the new college presidents were already members of the Senate, this simply concentrated more power in the hands of those who had it already. In 1722 Peter issued an edict that in view of the 'unceasing labours' required of members of the Senate, it was too much to expect them also to head colleges. The Senate was to 'watch over the colleges' independently of them, whereas now, 'being in them, how can they judge themselves?' New presidents were therefore appointed for all but the Foreign, War, and Admiralty colleges (the Mines College was added to the list later). Even the college presidents who remained Senate members were supposed to attend only in special circumstances, such as discussion of a new state edict, 'new matters demanding a resolution', or when the tsar was present.[126]

The main advantage of the new system has been identified as 'the elimination of confusion caused by some organs having competence over one activity throughout the State and others controlling many activities in a single territory'.[127] The colleges were set up simultaneously with an initiative to reform local government, also on Swedish lines. But although the new collegiate boards were more regular and rational on paper than the old *prikazy*, as well as being far fewer in number, there were still overlaps and loose ends, and they inherited most of their personnel from the old system. Peter complained in a note to the Senate in June 1718 that progress in setting up the colleges (which were supposed to be fully functional by 1 January 1719) was too slow in some cases and non-existent in others.[128] The presidents were 'very lazy about assembling to do their business', and he found not one person at work. They were without fail to be at work on Tuesdays and Thursdays, and when on duty, not to engage in unnecessary talk and gossip, only to discuss the matter in hand. 'Also, when someone has something to say, no one else should interrupt but allow him to finish, then the other may speak, as befits honest men, not all at once like some old market women.'[129] There were attempts to limit the transaction of business in people's homes or on the street by restricting it to the office (where employees worked under the watchful eye of various procurators and fiscals).[130] Peter's dissatisfaction prompted the appointment of Pavel Iaguzhinsky, subsequently procurator-general, to 'encourage' the college presidents to do their duties better and to report back to Peter every month on the progress made in each college in setting up its affairs.[131]

The first colleges were accommodated on Trinity Square, and later in Trezzini's twelve colleges (now St Petersburg University). This consisted of twelve units housing the Audience chamber, Senate, Foreign, War, Admiralty, Revenues, Justice, Commerce, Mining, Estates, and Expenses colleges and the Holy Synod. The building's design—a long façade with individual entrances—reflected Peter's intention that the staff of each college should shoulder individual responsibility, whilst offering a unified façade to the public gaze. Trezzini expressed anxiety that the colleges were to be built 'all in a row' but that construction was to be handled by individual offices, warning of delays if each college was responsible for its own construction. Peter relented by allowing all the materials to come from one place, but insisted that the principle of individual administration of buildings be retained.[132]

The rules for college administration were set out in a 'regulation of regulations', the General Regulation of 28 February 1720,[133] which opens by explaining that the colleges were founded, following the example of other 'Christian monarchs', 'for the sake of the orderly running of His Majesty's state affairs and the correct allocation and calculation of his revenues and the improvement of useful justice and police (*politsiia*) . . . also for the sake of the utmost preservation of the safety of his loyal subjects and the maintenance of his naval and land forces in good condition as well as commerce, arts and manufacture and the good establishment of his sea and land taxes and for the increase and spread of mining works and other state needs'.[134] The regulation was imbued with concern for public accountability and good order. For example, all business was to be carried on in the college, and not in private homes, except in exceptional circumstances. Petitions and cases were to be made in writing in front of witnesses. 'No one is to be provided with a chair except for those whose rank is distinguished, namely, of colonel's rank or higher, but others have to make their depositions standing up' (chapter XXI, clause 4). Even furnishings were not neglected. Audience chambers were to be equipped with good-quality carpets and chairs. The collegiate table was to be covered with a decent cloth and draped with a canopy. Each member of the board was to have an ink-well and stationery in front of him. There was to be a good clock on the wall, but no throne was provided for the tsar (XXIII, 2, 4). Every college was also to keep copies of the charters of non-Russian areas with special privileges, 'and govern every people (*narod*) according to their laws and charters as confirmed by His I.M.' (XXVII). Separate articles set out the duties of the non-voting staff, from secretary (XXIX) to trainee clerks (XXXVI) and janitors (XLVI). In 1724 supplements were issued. The General Regulation was to be adhered to strictly, and was to be read aloud like the Military Statute ('as it is read out to soldiers and sailors . . . for the proper understanding of soldierly duty') under the supervision of the procurator.[135] Minutes were to be written up on the day following a meeting, and 'other business not to be tackled until the protocols of the previous day are confirmed'.[136]

Each college had its own regulation, based on Swedish models (with inappropriate sections omitted—for example, a clause on the *reduktion* of Swedish Crown estates in the draft instructions for the College of State Revenues). The first, for the College of State Expenses, was introduced in February 1719.[137] Their proliferation accorded with the idea that maintenance of the state apparatus was 'best served, according to the absolutist cameralist teachings, by intensive legislative activities'.[138] As Peter wrote in the revised duties of the Senate in 1718: 'How can a state be governed when edicts (*ukazy*) are not implemented; contempt for edicts is in no respect different from treason.'[139]

The backbone of the Senate and collegial administration was provided by teams of clerks and scribes, drawn initially from the old *pod'iachie* class, but designated by borrowed terms. *Kantseliaristy* worked in the *kantseliariia*, dealing with *koreshpondentsiia*.[140] New working practices had come into being long before the reform of the institutions, replacing the old system in which no diaries, work books, or records of working hours were kept.[141] In January 1699 paper stamped with the double eagle crest (*gerbovaia bumaga*) was issued for drawing up contracts for sale of lands, businesses, residences, and serfs, loans and contracts in excess of 50 roubles. The State received a fee of 10 copecks per sheet for a big stamp, 1 for a medium, ½ for a small.[142] Since the turn of the century, clerks had been keeping records in books (*tetradi*) rather than on scrolls (*stol'btsy*) sometimes several hundred metres long, as had been the Muscovite practice, on the grounds that many cases went missing owing to the clerks' carelessness. For a time this reform had to be confined to the Estates chancellery in order to avoid wasting stocks of paper in the scroll format.[143] At the end of 1700 it was extended to Siberia, where, it was reported, scrolls containing a year's worth of business were rotting, being eaten by mice and generally disintegrating from constant handling. New record keeping on both sides of sheets of paper, subsequently bound into books, would economize on paper and be easier to consult. Precise instructions were given on such matters as the use of margins, making inserts, recording dates, signatures, and so on.[144] Old practices had relied mainly upon clerks' memories. In 1714 an order was issued 'for the better procedure of business' to keep proper records (*protokoly*) in all departments and for signatures to be added in the correct order.[145] A similar act of 31 January 1723 required accurate records to be kept of each day's business in the Senate, colleges, courts, and other departments.[146] It seems that modern practices were slow to catch on: for example, double bookkeeping (*shchetnye dvoinye knigi*), as recommended by a local official in 1723, together with the appointment of inspectors and regulators of accounting 'for the efficiency of the state and national interest'.[147] In 1723 the secretary of the *Kamer-kollegiia*, Stefan

Kochius, complained to the Senate that a proper registry had still not been set up, that clerks kept correspondence, and that it sometimes took two or three days to find a file.[148]

Formal working hours also pre-dated the new institutions: a 1703 act on chancellery procedures included a rota for clerks, fines for lateness and absenteeism, and dismissal 'if it is found that someone was absent not because of some urgent need but as a result of laziness'.[149] In 1708 ministers of the *Blizhnaia kantseliariia* were required to attend on Mondays, Wednesdays, and Fridays and to account for any absences.[150] The General Regulation (chapter III) specified attendance on Monday to Friday for the collegiate boards with the exception of major church festivals and royal name-days. Office staff attended every day except Sundays and holidays. When there was special urgent business, they had to be there no matter what the hour. Employees had four weeks' summer vacation 'to visit estates and amuse themselves in summer merriment', but the four weeks were staggered throughout June, July, and August. There were holidays from 25 December to 7 January, during Lent, at Shrovetide, and in Holy Week and Easter week (IX).[151]

One of the toughest problems to resolve was that of the chain of command and 'line management', and how to strike a balance between encouraging personal initiative and discouraging abuses of power. An edict of January 1724 tried to establish procedures whereby an official reported breaches of regulations to his immediate superior, but if the latter refused to listen, then to someone higher up, right up, if necessary, to the procurator-general and over-procurator of the Synod and, as a last resort, to the emperor himself (but woe betide the informer if his complaint proved false!).[152] 'If the over-procurator sees the procurator-general doing something contrary to his duty, he should point it out to him discreetly, but if he won't listen report to us. . . . If someone commits some misdemeanour against the orders as Shafirov did amongst the senators, it should be reported to the Senate and that person should be arrested.' Anyone failing to assist in the arrest or to denounce such miscreants, was to be given the same sentence as the accused. Anyone not guilty of such a misdemeanour, but who quarrelled, squabbled, or shouted, was to be told three times to stop, and if he disobeyed, to be sent out, and the matter reported to Peter.[153] Officials must 'know all the state laws (*ustavy*) and their significance as the first and chief matter, since on this depends the just and conscientious (*nezazornoe*) administration of all affairs and it is vital for everyone for the maintenance of his honour and avoidance of falling by ignorance into error and risking punishment'.[154] Several of these orders, issued in Moscow in early 1724, were written in Peter's own hand, underlining his concern to establish 'guards for the guardians'. But initiative was for ever being stifled by pulling of rank: for example, the newly appointed chief of police in Moscow was reprimanded for issuing some instructions on building regulations without asking the Senate's permission. He was let off on grounds of inexperience (*dlia novosti togo dela*), but the message was clear. Little autonomy was allowed.[155]

IV. PETER'S CABINET

Peter was forced to intervene and handle many fairly routine affairs himself, above and beyond major decisions on issues of war, peace, and legislation. In this context, one more institution of central government needs to be considered, which although attached neither to the Senate nor to a college, wielded considerable authority. This was the tsar's own private secretariat, the Cabinet (*kabinet*). No document survives of its foundation, which is usually dated 5 October 1704, when the title of privy cabinet secretary was conferred upon Aleksei Makarov.[156] The Cabinet's prototypes were Tsar Alexis's Privy Chancellery (*prikaz tainykh del*), which was established in 1655 when Alexis was at war, and ceased to function on his death in 1676, and the former Chancellery of the Royal Household (*prikaz bol'shogo dvortsa*). Peter's Cabinet had no permanent premises like the Senate and the colleges. It functioned wherever Peter happened to be, and had a fairly minimal permanent staff, requisitioning additional help *ad hoc* and drawing together 'all the threads of both foreign policy and domestic administration'.[157]

Under Makarov's supervision, it was run with the sort of rule-book efficiency (that was the intention, at least) which Peter despaired of seeing elsewhere. The 'Rules on Procedures for Cabinet Business' (1721) included regulations on bookkeeping, binding of correspondence, filing of papers, and the keeping of appointment diaries and records. 'Except in the above-described manner, business cannot be conducted without confusion (*konfuziia*), therefore these procedures must be observed correctly in all particulars and abided by, and without fail letters are to be recorded in order in the book and the register with all necessary corrections on the same day that they arrive or are sent out, and only of necessity (if it is not a postal day or some emergency arises) on the next day, and the next day or day after that these entries in the register and for previous days are to be reported to the Cabinet secretary, but if they are a matter of urgency and cannot be postponed, then they are to be reported at once, not left until the next day.'[158]

Business which came specifically under the Cabinet's control included Russians studying abroad (*pensionery*) and foreign specialists in Russia.[159] For both these purposes the Cabinet maintained agents abroad. The St Petersburg Chancellery of Building, headed by A. M. Cherkassky with his deputy, U. Siniavin, also reported to the Cabinet. The Cabinet oversaw certain state enterprises, such as the Olonets mines, Petrovskii zavod, and the Sestra river works. It ran Peter's Chamber of Curiosities (the Kunstkamera) and the gardening department, including the royal aviaries and menageries, employing several hundred staff under its director Boris Neronov. Trials of special interest and denunciations involving treason, attempts on the sovereign's life and crimes against the treasury, were reported to the Cabinet, as were petitions, anonymous letters, and projects deemed to be of special interest to the tsar, especially new inventions. The Cabinet handled items of 'petty expenditure', such as wages and clothes for palace servants, goods purchased by agents abroad for Peter and his family, the costs of Peter's turnery and personal boats, tips and gifts for name-days, carol-singers, well-wishers, and couriers, 'rewards for the declaration of monsters, for mothers and midwives at the birth of children and various other such petty items'. It also paid the tsar his military service and labourer's salaries in his various ranks as captain, colonel, and ship's carpenter.[160] Important tasks were keeping the tsar's journals (both appointments diaries and records of activities) and supervising the writing of the official history of the Swedish war (*Gistoriia sveiskoi voiny*).[161] With the Cabinet we come back full circle to the discussion of autocracy with which we began this chapter. The workings of Russian government cannot be grasped without taking account of the personal, non-institutional aspects. How different were the workings of the tsar's business away from the efficient Makarov and his neatly organized records. It is to the provinces that we now turn.

V.   PROVINCIAL AND MUNICIPAL GOVERNMENT

Of all the problems Peter inherited, governing the provinces remained one of the most intractable. The government's ability to deal with local problems was not aided by institutional structures. Muscovite towns were subordinated to various *prikazy*, for example, the Volga towns to the Kazan' department, the southern border towns (mostly military settlements) to the *Razriad*, Ukraine and the Don to the Foreign (*posol'skii*) Office, and so on. It was sometimes difficult to discern a firm geographical principle: the Vladimirsky *prikaz* collected taxes from Tula and Putivl': the Galich *prikaz* from Suzdal' and Iur'ev-Pol'sky; Novgorod from Archangel, Vologda, Pskov, and Nizhny Novgorod. To confuse matters further, different categories of person in a given town could fall under the jurisdiction of different *prikazy*: for example, higher servitors (*sluzhilye liudi po otechestvu*) came under the *Razriad* and the Siberian *prikaz*, lower servitors (*sluzhilye liudi po priboru*) under the chancelleries of the Artillery or Strel'tsy. Chief merchants and members of the merchants' association (*gostinaia sotnia*) answered to the *Bol'shoi dvorets*.[162] As late as 1708 a document lists 323 towns, of which 87 came under the Siberian and Kazan' *prikazy*, 24 border towns under the Foreign Office, and 212 under the *Razriad*, Estates, and various court departments.[163]

The main representative of Muscovite government in the provinces was the *voevoda*, a military and fiscal agent subordinate to the *prikazy*. The *voevoda's* tasks varied according to location. The most important were keeping the roll of nobles, arranging mobilization in case of war (or local troubles), and collecting direct taxes. (Indirect ones were collected by sworn officials called *tseloval'niki*.) A good example of the range of duties before the job description changed can be gauged from a forty-seven-point memorandum issued to Prince P. L. L'vov, governor of Kazan', in March 1697.[164] The Muscovite *voevody* were nobles, but not usually from the top of the boyar élite, who maintained their status by physical proximity to the tsar. The posts were often allocated to older men past active military service, or even as postings of 'honourable exile'. To the ambitious, though, they offered rich pickings. The *kormlenie*, or 'feeding' system, with its roots in earlier centuries, whereby officials maintained themselves from local resources, was still going strong at the beginning of Peter's reign. In addition to providing subsistence, the local population was expected to pay for the *voevoda*'s removal and feast-day expenses and for name-day gifts (*pominki*) and 'tokens of respect' (*pochesti*). The government mistrusted the system, as numerous investigations of abuses indicate, but failed to pay proper salaries, and was too far away to exercise much control. Even a letter from the tsar sometimes waited a year for a reply.[165] There may have been a few 'paragons of virtue', but most officials adhered to the 'conception of state service as an extension of personal interest'.[166] S. M. Solov'ev described Russia on the eve of Peter's reforms as 'a young society which was yet to impose restraints upon the strong ... who lived separate, untramelled lives and waged war among themselves'.[167] Funds siphoned off into local officials' pockets not only put a strain on the local population but also depleted government revenues. Moscow could not remain deaf to complaints such as those from the merchant Grigory Stroganov that *voevody* were setting up their own unauthorized 'customs posts' on main roads and rivers to tax merchant goods, or to news of manipulation of the lucrative liquor trade and other commercial swindles.[168]

Recognition that the *voevody* were not doing their job properly prompted the first significant reform of provincial government, heralded on 1 March 1698, when local officials were instructed to collect certain taxes 'bypassing the *voevody* (*mimo voevod*).[169] An edict of 30 January 1699 set up a new body, at first called the Chamber of Burgomasters (*burmisterskaia palata*) and from 1700 the Town Hall (*ratusha*), composed of local merchants (*gosti* and *gostinnye sotni*) and townsmen (*posadskie*), artisans of the urban tax-paying community (*chernye sotni*), tradespeople, and entrepreneurs. The *ratusha* was influenced by the system of urban self-government set out in Magdeburg law. This is a good example of early Petrine legislation, in that it spells out the *reasons* for the measure, which were to combat the 'red tape' and losses being suffered by both townspeople and the royal exchequer as a result of 'attacks and damage' by chancellery officials. Responsibility for collecting duties and taxes was taken away from the chancelleries and handed to the towns' own burgomasters (*burmistry*), who were to be elected every year, as many members as required, with presidents to hold office for one-month periods.[170]

In provincial towns the *ratusha* remained the main government revenue-collecting agency until new provinces (*gubernii*) were formed in 1708. The system did not extend to Siberia, which continued to be ruled in all matters by *voevody*, as did the strategically important southern regions of Russia. A surprising feature of the new institution was the faith it apparently placed in untrained elected officials, whose work required familiarity with the 1649 Law Code, the trade statute of 1667, and other laws. Why should they behave any

better or more efficiently than the old officials? In March 1700 the new burgomasters were already being warned (in this case with reference to peasants
illegally residing in towns) against wrong-doing and sending in false information on threat of severe punishment.[171] In 1702 local gentry were ordered
to appoint '*voevody* aides' (*voevodskie tovarishchi*) to administer the districts
(*uezdy*) in civil matters, at the same time as the old elected office of *gubnyi
starosta* was abolished. But they seem to have been ineffective, no doubt
because of the pressures created by the war.[172]

In 1708–9 a military crisis, as Russia faced the advance of Charles XII's
army, prompted a more radical provincial reform.[173] A decree of December
1708 announced the formation of eight provinces, or *gubernii*,[174] followed in
February 1709 by a ninth, each to be administered by a governor (*gubernator*):
Moscow (Romodanovsky), St Petersburg (Menshikov), Kiev (D. M.
Golitsyn), Smolensk (P. S. Saltykov), Archangel (P. A. Golitsyn), Kazan' (P.
M. Apraksin), Azov (I. A. Tolstoy), Siberia (M. P. Gagarin), Voronezh (F. M.
Apraksin).[175] (In 1710 Riga province was added, incorporating Smolensk, and
Nizhny Novgorod replaced Voronezh. In 1713–14 three more provinces were
added.) The governors were to take over the functions of the burgomasters,
voevody and other local officials, especially with reference to revenues and
accounts. Designated military units were to be supported by the *gubernii*,
which collected money and supplies for the army within their own areas,
bypassing Moscow and the main *ratusha*. Officials subordinate to the governor included the *ober-komendant* (for military matters), *ober-komissar* and
ober-proviant (for taxes in cash and in kind), and *landrikhter* (provincial
judge), although in practice the governors often combined all these functions
and appointed their own deputies. The new 'commandants' at district (*uezd*)
level were often the old *voevody* renamed.[176] In 1712 the *provintsiia* was introduced as a sub-unit of the *guberniia*, to be governed by an *ober-komendant*.
In 1713 the idea of *landraty*, elected local noble provincial councillors, between
eight and twelve per *guberniia*, was borrowed from the annexed Baltic
provinces. Apparently no elections ever took place; instead, lists of nominees
were submitted to the governors.[177] These efforts were accompanied by an
attempt to replace *kormlenie* and various forms of bribe taking with decent
salaries (which in reality were paid only intermittently, if at all). Earning extra
income through fees was forbidden.[178]

In 1715 another system was introduced: *uezdy* were replaced by *doli* (based
upon a unit of 5,536 tax-paying households), each to be administered by a
landrat, whose tasks included pursuing fugitive peasants. All provincial councillors were supposed to report to the governor every year, and did not have
jurisdiction over the townsmen.[179] The government recognized that billeting
landraty and their assistants on peasants caused 'great damage and losses'.
They ordered special accommodation to be built in crown and monastery villages in each *dolia*, with office, prison cells, and a residence, at a cost of no
more the 200 roubles per house. Others were to be accommodated in the
commandant's house.[180]

The new *gubernatory*, who were all powerful men, related to the tsar by family and personal ties, continued the fiscal and military functions of their predecessors. Recruitment was a constant task, and as fiscal agents they had to supply figures for the national budget. An examination of the duties of Peter Alekseevich Golitsyn (1660–1722), governor of Riga from 1713 to 1719, provides a picture of the work of a provincial governor, albeit in a post with its own peculiar features. We find him arranging winter quarters for troops in 1714–15; dealing with the large numbers of foreign personnel who passed through the port, such as the architects Georg Mattarnovy and Jean-Baptiste Le Blond, clothmakers from Schleswig and Poland, French craftsmen, the sculptor Rastrelli and his son, and English sea captains.[181] Valuable objects had to be transported—for example, in January 1717 Golitsyn received orders for handling ('carefully so as not to break it') and forwarding the famous amber room, a gift to Peter from the king of Prussia.[182] Transport had to be arranged for numerous dignitaries and officials, including Peter himself on his outward and homeward journeys in spring 1716 and autumn 1717.[183] From 1715 he organized the construction of a new harbour at Reval, for which timber had to be collected and 3,000 puds of iron from the inhabitants of Riga, as usual accompanied by the tsar's demands for speed. In December 1716 Golitsyn was ordered to repair storm damage to the new harbour.[184] Other tasks included handling the export of hemp and mast timber, supplying the Russian fleet, helping foreign merchants to store unsold goods, and housing officials. Golitsyn's successor, Prince Nikita Repnin (1668–1726), had to deal with a similarly wide range of tasks: planting chestnut-trees near Peter's Riga residence, sending oysters and lemons (Peter wrote to thank him, adding that they had arrived very fresh), and dispatching an English envoy in transit (taking care that he did not hob-nob with the local residents).[185] Arrangements had to be made for Peter's visit to Riga in March–May 1721, when he and Catherine met their prospective son-in-law the duke of Holstein and Peter established a garden, which in turn involved additional work for the governor.[186]

Instructions issued to Artemy Petrovich Volynsky, who became governor of Astrakhan in 1720, mentioned guarding against internal troubles and incursions from local tribesmen and against foreign invasions, and facilitating trade and enterprise. He was to keep an eye on local affairs, ensuring that co-operative tribesmen were well treated, but that hostile ones were deprived of supplies, especially firearms. News of Ottoman and Persian affairs were to be dispatched to St Petersburg. He was also supposed to encourage conversions to Orthodoxy, fight fires, and send melons, grapes, and other local produce to the tsar.[187] A further list of requests included herbs and grasses (for the Apothecary department), 'curious' beasts, exotic woods, shells, and horses.[188] Instructions to the *voevoda* in Belgorod show variations on a theme: here local concerns included relations with Tatars and Cossacks, army units, and fighting plague. The governor was to maintain good relations with Ukraine (where Ivan Skoropadsky had replaced the renegade Mazepa in 1708), 'since the Hetman and Little Russian people have been His Majesty's subjects since olden times'.[189]

In 1718–19, in parallel with the introduction of new colleges, and with advice from Heinrich Fick, Peter attempted yet another reorganization of local government, this time on the Swedish model. A project of November 1718 ordered 'Governors or *landsgevding* to function in the administration, as in Sweden'.[190] The Senate was instructed: 'In the *gubernii* all personnel in all offices are to be appointed and given instructions and other procedures after the Swedish model.' The new system was to be implemented by 1720, with a pilot project in St Petersburg province to be set up by 1 July 1719. A list of Swedish terms for various posts, in Peter's hand with Russian equivalents, was appended: for example, *landsgevding* (from Swedish *landshövding*) was described as 'glava zemskoi' (local governor). In the event, most of the Swedish terms were given Russian equivalents; for example, *landsgevding* reverted to *voevoda*, *lantsekretar* to *zemskii d'iak*.[191] In January 1719 sets of instructions were issued to various provincial officials, based on Swedish models: for example, to *voevody*, chief accountants (*kameriry*), commissaries (*zemskie komissary*), bursars (*rent-meistry*), prosecutors (*fiskaly*), and secretaries (*sekretari*).[192] The chief accountant or supervisor of revenue collection (*kamerir*), who was to manage crown revenues, draw up budgets, and supervise the distribution of pay and provisions to the army, was responsible to the *Kamer-kollegiia*. The collected monies were to be handled by the *rent-meister*, or bursar. The *zemskii komissar*, also answerable to the *Kamer-kollegiia*, had more general duties, including raising conscripts, repairing roads, and policing duties.[193] The *voevoda's* job description, set out in forty-six articles, included detecting spies, protecting the Faith, overseeing judges, maintaining military installations and defences, supervising factories, rounding up vagrants and runaways, taking inventories, supervising the census (in preparation for the poll tax), keeping order, promoting business and craft, supervising tax collections and fiscal staff, and monitoring the inheritance of estates.[194] On 29 May 1719 fifty provinces were created by dividing the old *gubernii* thus: St Petersburg (twelve), Moscow (nine), Kiev (four), Azov (six), Riga (two), Archangel (four), Siberia (five), Kazan' (four), Nizhny Novgorod (three), Astrakhan' (one).[195] One of the features of the Swedish system which Peter tried to emulate was the separation of justice from administration by subordinating judicial districts to the Justice College.

The government signalled a new active interest in the provincial economy, promoting it rather than exploiting it from afar, with an order for one member of the Senate and one person from each college to make an annual inspection tour of the provinces.[196] Town administration was reformed along with that of the provinces in 1718–19, also under the influence of Fick's memorandum of 9 May 1718, which urged Peter to install town magistrates (*magistratov gratskikh*), regarded as vital for the running of the *Kamer-kollegiia*. Peter appended a note ordering implementation of Fick's proposal on the model of Riga and Reval town councils, although Fick had recommended

Stockholm as a model.[197] The Chief Magistracy (*Glavnyi magistrat*) was a new college, its regulation (January 1721) apparently a version of Fick's memorandum amended by the Senate in an attempt to 'gather in' the scattered merchantry (*vserossiiskoe kupechestvo*), whose traditional role was that of taxpayers. The duties of the Magistracy were (1) to set up a magistracy in all towns; (2) to provide it with good statutes and defences; (3) to make sure that there is justice; (4) to establish good 'policing'. Clause 10 ('o politseiskikh delakh') sets out in some detail the concept of *politsiia* (not to be confused with the modern idea of a police force), which 'facilitates laws and justice and nurtures good order and morality'.[198] The fifth of the magistrate's duties was 'to increase commerce and manufactures. (By manufactures is understood not major ones such as textiles, fabrics, metal and copper works and so on but those essential for the market, such as tailors, cobblers, carpenters, smiths, silversmiths and others and to bring them to a good condition and to get into good order and perfection any others which belong to the purview of the Magistracy.)' The significance of commerce and manufacture for the 'usefulness of the state' is elaborated in clause 11: 'all abundance in every town with God's help and good policing, starting from maritime navigation and from the free and unoffended merchantry and skilful handicraft, has its own strength and augmenting activity'.

The magistrates' duties were varied: to collect maps and statistics, to make registers of inhabitants and their profession/status, and to expel illegal residents and restore them to their rightful abodes. Towns were listed in five categories, from major centres (St Petersburg, Moscow, Novgorod, Kazan', Riga, Reval, Archangel, Astrakhan', Iaroslavl', Vologda, Nizhny Novgorod) to small settlements. Appointments of magistrates and other local officials were to be organized by the governors and *voevody* from 'first-grade, good, prosperous and clever persons'.[199] The urban populations were assigned to two guilds, the first to comprise chief merchants, master craftsmen (including doctors and surgeons, ship's captains, icon-painters, smiths of all varieties, turners, and others), the second, artisans and petty traders. The regulation paints a negative picture of life in towns. Section 9, on courts, states that 'merchants and tradesmen in all the towns find themselves ... nearly all ruined as a result of various offences, attacks and intolerable burdens, from which their numbers have declined'. Townspeople's cases were to be heard by the burgomasters, with the magistracy in St Petersburg as the court of appeal. Local magistrates were supposed to appoint agents to perform such services as collecting customs and toll charges.

The instructions for the new Moscow chief of police, issued in June 1722, provide another glimpse of attempts at urban regulation. His duties included supervision of building regulations and fire prevention (detailed rules were included for the use of stoves and the operation of bath-houses) and maintenance of pavements and bridges. In order to prevent crime, street barriers and night watchmen were to be introduced, as in St Petersburg. Guarding public morals involved closing down gambling dens, rounding up loose women, drunks, vagrants, and beggars (who were to be found work). The police chief was to supervise health and hygiene, refuse collection, and hygienic handling of food in markets, to prevent river pollution, and to report outbreaks of infectious diseases. Paper and rags were to be recycled. Shooting on the streets was outlawed (anyone wishing to shoot 'for enter-tainment' should be sent to out-of-town firing ranges), as was horse racing on the streets, a favourite pastime with cab drivers. He was also responsible for registering all strangers in town.[200] In general, the impression remains that this Germanic structure was little more than an unfinished façade, which did little to conceal old behaviour patterns and social relations, even though only a fraction of the population of the empire was thus administered: in 1723 the taxable town population was just 230,910 males, 3.6 per cent of the total population.[201]

In 1724 further reforms were enacted in connection with the billeting of army units around the provinces in time of peace. These included the intro-duction of yet another administrative unit, the regimental district (*polkovyi distrikt*), with its own officials. A decree of 26 June 1724 prescribed the use of soldiers in the provinces to deal with fugitives, brigands, and other law-breakers.[202] It was accompanied by a decree on the duties of colonels in supervising the local police (*zemskaia politsiia*) in the district allocated for the quartering and provisioning of their regiments.[203] This led to a sort of martial law, with overlap and conflict between the old authorities (themselves barely established) and the new. The new civilian official to liaise between the locals and the military was the land commissar (*kommisar ot zemli*), who was chosen from among local landowners to collect census registers, supervise poll tax collection, hand over money to the colonels of regiments, and supervise the provisioning of men and horses in kind.[204] It is hard to say whether this was a trend towards devolution of power, involving the nobles more in local affairs, or just another layer of bureaucracy and oppression for local people. Only a few taxes were left for the 'old' officials to collect.

Peter's provincial reforms were successful in so far as they maintained the extraction of resources, in money, people, and kind, for the war effort and the peacetime army. They cannot be understood at all if they are divorced from questions of finance, the primary concern of Petrine local government, or judged from a modern standpoint with reference to their promotion of local enterprise, education, and welfare in the broadest sense, or even in the sense of 'policing' the provinces, with the exception of the magistracy created in 1721. As bearers of 'civilization', including law and order, they were singularly unsuccessful. For a start, the Swedish system on which they were partly mod-elled operated at parish level, with peasant participation and an input from local pastors, which were absent in Russia. There was no question of Russian priests aping their Swedish counterparts (although they did have a role as agents of government, as we shall see), and it was stated that 'in the provinces [in Russia] there are no qualified persons among the peasantry'.[205] One sup-poses that those same peasants saw the new officials in much the same light as the old. A major problem in implementing reforms was finding suitable personnel and persuading the old officials to hand over their duties or, in some cases, to remain in their post until their replacements arrived. A report from Moscow *guberniia*, in January 1720, complained that only a small number of the officials needed for its nine provinces had turned up, and even they had not started work.[206] Once appointed, officials were not always sure what their duties were. In December 1722 the College of Justice complained to the Senate that 'governors and assessors keep writing to the Justice College from the provinces asking us to dispatch instructions about how they are to conduct business in those provincial affairs. They say that work is at a standstill and they ask for the necessary instructions to be sent. Therefore the Justice College requests that the Senate send back the [draft] instruction sent to it from this college for dissemination in the provinces about administration in the provinces.'[207] As Duke Karl Friedrich of Holstein-Gottorp commented after Peter's death, 'The military staff cannot exist without the civil ones and for the latter educated, clever and honest people are needed; one can make a good non-commissioned officer in a short time, but a clerk, let alone a secretary, cannot be created so quickly. They must invest a great deal of money in their training and people will never begin to devote themselves to civil service as long as they are given such a poor livelihood. From this follows something else, namely that all civil positions will in future be left in the hands of dull individuals and thieves.'[208]

Not surprisingly, most of the new officials indulged in the same bad old habits as their predecessors. A notorious case was Prince M. P. Gagarin, governor of Siberia, who was executed in 1721 for bribery and corruption on a grand scale. Foreigners provide some interesting observations. Weber described local officials as 'cormorants ... who make it their sole Study how to build their Fortunes upon the Ruin of the Country People, and he that came among them having hardly Clothes to his Back, is often known in four or five Years time, to have scraped so much together, as to be able to build large Stone-Houses, where at the same Time the poor Subjects are forced to run away from their Cottages'. [209] The Swede Strahlenberg, who spent several years in the provinces as a prisoner of war, wrote that, on the recommendation of favourites, 'base' men were appointed to the most responsible jobs, as *landrichtery, kameriry* and commissars, *voevody* and vice-governors. Governors were given a free hand in appointing local agents. He claims that peasants were forced to sell their livestock and grain to pay agents or resort to flight.[210] A particularly interesting analysis was sent from Siberia in October 1723 by the inspector of mines Wilhelm Henning: 'I am heartily sorry that you yourself have not been here and do not know the state of affairs in Siberia in any detail. It's true, the governor here Cherkassky is a good man, but he lacks courage, and has few decent assistants, especially in the local courts and police work (*zemskie dela*). As a result local affairs do not flourish, and much is burdensome to the people.' Henning urged Peter to send Cherkassky support, more officials from central institutions—for example, an *ober-*

komendant for the military, an official from the Commerce College for the merchantry, and a secretary from the *Kamer-kollegiia*.

> Terrible deeds are in evidence, the poor peasants suffer ruin at the hands of officials, and in the towns much oppression is caused by the local officials sent from the local finance office [*Kamerirstvo*] and the merchantry has been so badly damaged, that an artisan with any capital is scarcely to be found, which has led to a decline in revenues. Lord, do not begrudge the administrators here a decent salary, for no one here owns villages [i.e. serfs] and everyone has to eat and even if a man is good, if he has no means of livelihood he is forced to feed himself by illegal means; at first he will take enough to satisfy his needs, but then he will try to get rich. In this way you will suffer great loss and the people will be ruined.[211]

The old *kormlenie* system was alive and well. The weak (like their counterparts in much of Europe, it should be added) were as vulnerable as ever.

VI.   LAW AND ORDER

The prime mover in efforts to promote the general good was the ruler, who stood above the law, not in the sense that he had licence to act unlawfully or immorally (although, as we saw earlier, he did not forfeit his authority if he did so), but because he presided over the dispensation of justice in the widest sense and protected his subjects and their welfare. In the words of a 1722 decree: 'The sovereign is concerned for his subjects to ensure that each case will always receive fair and swift judgement and that cases are resolved as His Majesty's edicts command, justly and in the stipulated time and that no one should be oppressed by unfair judges and red tape.'[212] Any ruling made by the tsar had the force of law. Even so, it continued to be accepted even in Peter's Russia that rulers dispensed only temporal justice, to the wicked and the good alike. 'If a judge dispenses justice inequitably he will receive from the Tsar temporal punishment, but from God eternal punishment both in body and soul.'[213] Everyone would be on trial at the Last Judgement.

It is, in fact, difficult to separate the topics of justice and law in Peter's Russia from the questions of government and administration examined in previous sections. As the editors of the English translation of Ivan Pososhkov's *The Book of Poverty and Wealth* explain in their introduction to the chapter 'Of Justice and the Law', despite Peter's 'half-hearted endeavours to separate the judicial from the administrative power, justice was dispensed by the higher officials, the subject involves the author in an examination of the manner in which the country is governed'.[214] Ruler and government strove to establish 'order' (*poriadok*), which included the concept of orderly and consistent regulations as well as lawful obedience (as in 'law and order'). In his preamble to the Military Statute, Peter wrote: 'But when (with the Almighty's help) the army was brought to order, then what great progress was made with the Almighty's help against glorious and regular nations. Anyone can see that this occurred for no other reason than the establishment of good order, for all disorderly barbarian practices are worthy of ridicule and no good can come of them.'[215] The quest for order applied equally to civil matters. The preamble to an edict on petitions issued at the end of 1718 states: 'His Majesty, in spite of all his unendurable efforts in this difficult war, has been obliged not only to wage the war but also to instruct people anew and draw up military laws and codes and he has with the help of God brought it into such good order that it is known to all what the military nowadays is like when compared with the earlier forces and what fruits have been borne. Now that this has been accomplished, His Majesty, in his mercy towards his people, does not want fair civil (*zemskoe*) administration to be neglected but is taking pains to see that this, too, is brought into as good order as military affairs.'[216] To Peter's way of thinking, good order proceeded from good statutes, ranging from short edicts (*ukazy*) to multi-claused regulations (*ustavy* and *reglamenty*). 'Laws and decrees should be written clearly so that they cannot be reinterpreted. There is little justice in people but much perfidy.'[217] Law must be unambiguous and there must be plenty of it, for wickedness is all-pervasive. As Peter stated in a famous edict to the Senate: 'Nothing is so vital to the administration of the State as the firm keeping of civil laws, for laws are written in vain if they are not adhered to or if they are played with like cards, one suit being picked up after another, something which was more common in this country than anywhere in the world and sometimes still happens when some people do their utmost to undermine the fortress of the law.'[218] There followed strict warnings against individual interpretation of laws and a firm reiteration that the tsar was the chief legislator and everything must have his approbation. This edict was to be displayed on boards on a table 'like a mirror, before the eyes of judges in all places, starting with the Senate right down to the most minor courts'. In February 1723 Peter added other notices to these display boards, one setting out penalties for 'swearing, shouting and talking' and a warning that 'he is cursed who does God's work carelessly', the other to remind people of 'state laws and their importance, as the first and chief matter'.[219]

These edicts underline the tsar's concern for the honesty and integrity of those who administered the law: in other words, the members of the Senate and the colleges and provincial officials. In his view, wilful dereliction of duty and law breaking by judges were the worst of crimes. This principle was most clearly embodied in an order of 25 October 1723 (published in February 1724) explaining the differences between crimes against the State and 'particular' crimes against the person: 'Whosoever shall commit an injustice in a court or in any matter whatsoever entrusted to him or which is a part of his job (*dolzhnost'*) and he commits that injustice out of passion (*po kakoi strasti*) knowingly (*vedeniem*) and of his own volition, that man, as an infringer of the state laws and his own duty, shall be condemned to death, either physical or political (*naturalnoiu ili politicheskoiu*) according to the severity of the crime, and deprived of all his property.'[220]

Peter's reign is remarkable for the sheer number of edicts issued. Whereas in the second half of the seventeenth century the average number of decrees issued annually was 36, in the first quarter of the eighteenth century the figure rose to 160.[221] In Muscovite Russia legislation was created in an evolutionary way (the establishment of serfdom is a good example) by bringing together precedents; eighteenth-century legislation was concerned less with fixing traditions and customs, more with 'active interference in life, often with the aim of overturning previous customs'.[222] Peter's reign also involved a quest for 'ultra-laws', based on a belief in 'correct, all-embracing legislation as a cure-all ... The law was seen as a means for the realization of general happiness.'[223] But the sheer number of laws or their comprehensiveness proved not to be synonymous with lawfulness, still less with popular concepts of justice. Ivan Pososhkov wrote: 'I believe that our most vital need is for the rule of law; once that principle can be established all will shrink from unrighteous actions. Fair and impartial dispensation of justice is the foundation of all well-being, and once that is laid it must follow that His Majesty's revenues will be doubled.'[224] Let us look at Peter's record as a maker and protector of the law.

Law Codes and Legislation

Peter inherited his father's code (*Sobornoe ulozhenie*) of 1649, a set of laws divided into 25 chapters and 967 articles, incorporating not only Muscovite codes (the *sudebniki* of 1497 and 1550) but also the Lithuanian statute of 1588 and elements of Byzantine law. Most famous for its codification of the laws on serfdom, it also claimed that 'for people of all ranks, from the highest to the lowest, of the Muscovite state the law and justice will be equal for all in all cases'.[225] Russian law was statute law: that is, individual cases were not tried with reference to previous cases (precedents) but 'judges' (government officials) applied the written law to the case in hand.[226] At the most basic level, they needed to have access to copies of the laws, but these were not readily available. Since 1649 many new edicts ('novels') had been issued, producing a confusing and inaccessible proliferation, scattered around the files of various government departments.[227]

There were several attempts to codify the existing laws and also to produce a new code (*Novoulozhennaia kniga*). A law code commission (*Palata ob Ulozhenie*), comprising representatives from the boyar and sub-boyar classes, in session in 1700–2, was charged with correcting and bringing the 1649 code up to date (incorporating and rationalizing edicts issued since 1649, particularly on landed estates). Its royal charter (27 February 1700) paints a picture of disorder, in both religious and civil life.[228] This attempt failed, according to A. N. Medushevsky, because of strong Church interference.[229] (The patriarch was still alive when the commission was formed.) The timing was also less than ideal, given foreign policy commitments. The next attempt at codification was signalled by an order of 20 May 1714, with a preamble stating that Peter was issuing it 'in his fervent concern for the law of God, in order that in all the realms given to him by God justice (*sud*) might be equal everywhere for all, without hateful-to-God hypocrisy and damned self-interests contrary to the truth'.[230] Judges of all degrees were to try all cases according to the 1649 *Ulozhenie*, not on the basis of new statutes and separate edicts except in areas not mentioned in the *Ulozhenie*. In other words, there was a return to the *Ulozhenie* on matters for which piecemeal legislation had proliferated, notably on landholding and immovable property. Many conflicting and contradictory edicts had been issued which had to be withdrawn, and the Senate was to identify the correct versions from a mass of texts, with the help of the *prikazy* officials who would sort through documents issued in their departments since 1649.[231] There is no evidence that Peter considered consulting public opinion in the manner of his father (the 1649 *Ulozhenie* was discussed by the now defunct *zemskii sobor*) or as proposed by Pososhkov ('for the establishment of a just code the opinion of all should be consulted'[232]).

A few years later Peter considered revising the law, like government institutions, on foreign models. In December 1719 the Senate was commanded to study the Swedish *Ulozhenie* and to replace any points which 'are unsuitable for our people' with those from the 1649 code or to devise new ones. Estonian and Livonian laws on landed estates were recommended as models because their system was 'closer to the Russian'. This commission had Russian and foreign members.[233] In August 1720 additional staff were appointed to the commission 'for collating the Russian law with the Swedish' (*u sochineniia Ulozheni'ia rosiiskogo s shvedtskim*).[234] Work dragged on to little effect, apparently. A memorandum to the Senate of 20 January 1724 refers to the *Ulozhenie* 'which is not yet finished'.[235] The major problem was the proliferation of edicts, often on the same subject, issued piecemeal during the war. Peter ordered the Senate to gather together all such acts and consolidate them into one law (*snest v odin*), and to 'look very carefully to make sure that there are not two edicts on one case'.[236] This work was completed only after Peter's death and remained unpublished.[237]

Given this state of affairs, it is not surprising that for criminal offences the Military Statute was often regarded as the authority, a tendency strengthened by Peter's April 1716 memorandum to the Senate on printing and distributing copies 'to all governors and chancelleries'.[238] Although the Military Statute was never intended to replace the civil law code,[239] military justice was sometimes the only variety available, especially in the provinces. Strahlenberg writes: 'No defendant, even if he were innocent, had any hope of vindicating himself, for the judicial personnel were all guards officers who knew no law but the military articles, where minor offences were subject to cruel corporal punishment and the death penalty, and also they were rewarded by the sovereign with the goods and property of the condemned.'[240] For a long time the Military Statute remained the sole printed source on certain points of law: for example, on the distinction between homicide and manslaughter. It was even used to try women. It has been argued that, far from being crude, it was informed by a number of modern concepts, such as accessory to crime, extenuating and aggravating circumstances, self-defence, and unsound mind.[241] At the same time, the statute contained more archaic precepts: for example, the statement (article 154) that murderers were to be beheaded 'to avenge the blood of the victim' (*onogo krov' paki otmstit*).[242] It also listed a large number of crimes against the State. The fact that the Military and Naval Statutes (the latter based upon the former) continued to be regarded as basic legal documents is indicated by their continued use as texts when Russian law started to be taught at Moscow University in the 1770s.[243]

Another area in which there was possible overlap and confusion was with ecclesiastical law. In Muscovy the clergy were subject to the ecclesiastical courts except in cases of treason, robbery, and murder. Under Peter this juridical privilege was by and large lost between 1700 and 1721, then restored in 1721 after the foundation of the Synod, which had its own court 'for trials of the clergy'.[244] There was no attempt to integrate the two systems of justice. In theory, clergymen were to be tried by church courts in all but 'serious affairs of state' (i.e., treason) and became subject to secular law only if they were found guilty and defrocked. In practice, as Freeze points out, state officials often arrested priests anyway, and throughout the century protests from the Synod are recorded. For their part, priests often made false 'word and deed' declarations in order to escape from local officials.[245] Conversely, laymen continued to be subject to church courts for a number of crimes, as specified in 1722, including blasphemy, heresy, dissidence, black magic, illegal marriage, divorce, forced marriage, and forced tonsure. But the sexual crimes of rape, incest, and fornication were subject to civil courts, as were cases of 'recalcitrance' in ecclesiastical crimes and 'disrespect' for the Synod. The Synod was the highest court of appeal for religious matters, but its verdicts were subject to 'highest resolution' by the tsar.[246] This was a natural extension of the requirement imposed on the clergy to report nonattendance at communion and secular crimes revealed during confession to state officials.

Courts and Trials

Before we examine the mechanics of the law, it needs to be reiterated that 'the administration of justice did not constitute an autonomous sphere of activity'.[247] The administration and the judiciary were one and the same. In Muscovy any *prikaz* could hear cases, but some specialized in law cases: for example, the *Razboiny prikaz*, renamed the Investigations (*Sysknoi*) *prikaz* in 1683, dealt with cases of robbery and murder. Nobles had recourse to special courts even for these crimes—the Vladimirskii Sudnyi *prikaz* ('higher court', its name reflecting the historical precedence of the town of Vladimir in Muscovite times, which in 1677 incorporated the court of appeal, the Chelobitnyi *prikaz*) and the Moskovskii sudnyi *prikaz* ('lower court'). In 1699 these two were amalgamated, incorporating the Moscow police authority (*Zemskii prikaz*), which was later superseded by the Magistracy.

The highest judge was the tsar. But Peter acted in this capacity only very occasionally, notably during the trial of Tsarevich Alexis. Even then he consulted representatives of civil and Church authorities. As we have seen, numerous bans were issued on direct petitions to the sovereign. But he did sometimes set up special tribunals which outranked the Senate, as in 1717, when a military tribunal was appointed to investigate corruption, including charges against Senate members. The highest of Peter's courts, in so far as it investigated crimes committed by civilians against the sovereign's person and reputation, was the Preobrazhensky *prikaz*. An order of 25 September 1702 stated that all suspected of such deeds be sent there 'without interrogation elsewhere'.[248] Procedures usually started with investigation of denunciations (*izvety*) reported to the authorities under the formula 'the sovereign's word and deed' (*gosudarevo slovo i delo*). A Senate edict of 1713 stated:

> Anyone who writes or utters the accusation of a crime against the sovereign by word or deed, such persons are ordered to write and testify only in such matters as concern the health of his tsarist majesty or the lofty monarchical honour or know of some rebellion or treason. Any other business which has no reference to the above should be reported to the proper authority and if they have accusations against anyone in their testimonies they are to write the absolute truth; they are not to write or speak about such matters as though they were the sovereign's word and deed; anyone who makes a claim of the sovereign's word and deed about any matters apart from the above reasons shall be subjected to harsh punishment and ruin and banished to hard labour.[249]

Legal procedures tended to be triggered by reports and denunciations rather than by active attempts by the authorities to bring criminals to justice. Of 772 'slovo i delo' cases examined by Golikova, only five did not begin in this fashion. The informer could express his intention to bring a 'slovo i delo' charge anywhere, street or field, as long as people were present. Both denouncer and accused were arrested.[250] Informers making false or time-wasting claims were themselves subjected to punishment, as was anyone who *failed* to denounce a 'word and deed' crime which subsequently came to light.

The wider definition of treason is most clearly formulated in chapter 2 of the 1649 *Ulozhenie* and chapter 3 of the Military Statute. The latter extended the list from attempts on the sovereign's life and revolt (article 19) to 'sinning against His Majesty's person with words, holding his activities and intentions in contempt and speaking of them in an indecent manner' (article 20). Not just poison plots and black magic, but also criticism of the government and the tsar's behaviour, misuse of titles and 'indecent utterances' (*nepristoinye rechi*), even grumbling, were listed. Revolt, suspicious gatherings, and group petitions from civilians were all investigated under this category (although not cases of treason by military personnel, which were dealt with by the

Military Statute, chapters 15, 16–17). No distinction was made between crimes committed and crimes plotted.[251]

In 1717–18 there was a move to reduce the chaotic number of jurisdictions by concentrating criminal and civil cases in the Justice College, which incorporated all departments with judicial functions except for the Preobrazhensky *prikaz* and (from 1722, when it became a separate institution) the Estates College, which handled cases of landed property.[252] The department was modelled on the Swedish Court of Appeals (*Svea hovrätt*), as specified in memoranda by Fick and amended by its first president, Andrei Matveev.[253] Peter envisaged it as presiding over courts in the towns and *gubernii*. He described its work in a memorandum of January 1723 to the Synod: 'In the Justice Department there are trials (*rozyski*) from which proceed torture and executions (*kazni*) and public punishments. If there are abuses (*ezheli ... pogreshat*) in the Justice Department, the Senate investigates them; and carries out torture and executions.'[254] In 1718–19, as part of the reorganization of local government, Peter set up courts of appeal (*nadvornye sudy*) in the provinces under the auspices of the Justice College. The forty-nine-article instruction to these courts explains that the sovereign is establishing the Justice College and the *nadvornye* courts subordinate to it in ten major (*znatnye*) towns for the benefit of the State, 'in order that true justice (*istinnoe pravosudie*) and defence be available for every person'.[255] Judges in the courts were exhorted to 'keep the laws safe with utter loyalty and with utmost diligence without any deception, with no respect for persons, no matter what a person's rank or name might be but most of all to treat the offended to just resolutions without red tape (*bezvolokitnye*) or any bias to one side or the other'. They were to temper strictness with mercy. For example, if no unanimity was reached in a case meriting the death sentence, they should err on the side of clemency, 'for it is more just and safer in dubious and unclear cases to act like this; better to let off a guilty person than to condemn an innocent man injudiciously'.[256] The judges could appeal to the Justice College for arbitration in difficult cases. They in turn acted as courts of appeal for lower provincial courts. This system envisaged a main court (*nachal'nyi sud*) in each *guberniia*, presided over by an *ober-landrikhter*, and lesser courts (*menshie sudy zemskie*) headed by a *landrikhter* in the districts. The Justice College and the Senate were the final courts of revision or 'last resort'.[257] Swedish models were used to set up higher courts of appeal (*gofgerikhty*) in St Petersburg, Moscow, Kazan', Kursk, Iaroslavl', Voronezh, Nizhny Novgorod, Smolensk, and Tobol'sk.[258] An article in the instruction to provincial governors also issued in January 1719 made the intentions clear: 'The *voevoda* shall not judge in any legal disputes between our subjects, and not obstruct the judges in their functions.' But at the same time he was expected to supervise the judges and make sure they did not 'waste time'.[259]

The new courts proved a failure, and were quickly subverted by local officials. Often governors and military officers were appointed chairmen of the courts for want of other suitable candidates. In 1722 governors and *voevody* were again put in charge, except where there were higher courts of appeal.[260] After Peter's death the courts of appeal were closed (1727) in the interests of streamlining and economy, and *voevody* resumed control in law as well as in fact. The attempt to separate the administrative and judicial systems failed.[261]

Wortman speaks of 'a judiciary faithful to statute law, whose actions were monitored by supervisory institutions intent on protecting the law'.[262] In fact, as in other areas, Peter relied upon persons as much as institutions, as indicated by the creation in 1722 of the new post of *reketmeister*, modelled on the office of *maître de requêtes* at the French court. Only he, not the emperor, was to be given petitions. If for some reason he would not or could not accept a petition, it was to go to the Senate.[263]

Regardless of the setting in which they took place, trials were conducted by two methods: inquisitorial and accusatorial. In inquisitorial trials (*rozysk*), the judge tried to establish the facts by 'weighing' the evidence, most weight being given to confession (extracted by torture), and the court itself investigated the material facts. In accusatorial or adversarial trials (*sud*), the adversaries (the plaintiff and defendant) conducted the trial, bringing evidence and witnesses before the judge. Evidence was presented in a process called *ochnaia stavka* (confrontation). Enquiry was sometimes aided by the general perquisition (*poval'nyi obysk*), which involved questioning witnesses, from immediate family and neighbours to informants within a twenty-mile radius in major criminal cases.[264] Inquisitorial procedures were set out in a section of the 1716 Military Statute under the heading 'Short presentation of trials'. Trials were held in secret. Judges consulted a list of formal proofs, with weighting, which included confession ('the best evidence in the world') and evidence of witnesses. There was no distinction between civil and criminal cases.[265] Peterson argues that *rozysk* became the norm, and links this development with the growth of absolutism. In 1697 the accusatorial trial system even appears to have been abolished, on the grounds of 'much untruth and deception from plaintiffs and defendants'.[266] However, a decree 'On the form of trials' (5 November 1723) gathered together legislation on the use of written evidence, bail, simplification of procedures, and forms of petition.[267] Based partly on Swedish statutes, it actually reintroduced the accusatorial (*sud*) type of trial, except for cases of treason, revolt, and major crime (*zlodeistvo*). This appears to be a reversal of the trend favouring inquisitorial trials observed in the 1697 law. Peterson argues for a growing distinction between crimes against the State and the existing order (including brigandage and religious dissent) and 'red-handed' acts, where there was damning evidence before the trial started, and 'particular' crimes against the person, where accusatorial procedures were more appropriate.[268] In such cases the State tended to leave the decision to prosecute to the aggrieved party.

Peter issued copious legislation to bring order into court procedures, showing the same attention to detail as elsewhere, right down to the type of notebooks to be used. The slowness of trials was always a bone of contention, and numerous decrees were issued denouncing excessive 'red tape' and foot

dragging (*volokita*). An adverb derived from this, *bezvolokitno*, could be translated 'without red tape' or 'efficiently'.[269] There were no barristers and no bar
in Russian courts, no legal training, although there was provision for defendants to use an 'advocate', defined as a stand-in or substitute if the defendant
was unable to appear in person, but by and large advocates were thought to
drag out proceedings with 'unnecessary long arguments'. They were not
allowed at all in *rozysk* trials.[270] Torture (generally consisting of beating with
the knout) was routinely used in serious cases on both defendants and witnesses, following the article in the *Ulozhenie* of 1649 that if a person gave the
same testimony three times under torture, it was to be believed. If he changed
his testimony, another three sessions of torture could be prescribed. In the
Preobrazhensky court more blows were often applied. Sessions were often
conducted several weeks or months apart because defendants were so weakened, hence trials were prolonged. Boyars, officers, and upper clergy were
subjected to torture only in extreme cases.[271] An order of 4 April 1722 ordered
the Senate to look into the use of torture, 'because even in minor cases torture
is used and on people who are only suspected (*na kotorykh tolko mnenie
imeiut*), and this should be stopped'.[272] Its use was almost totally eliminated
in the reign of Catherine II.

Punishment

Types of capital punishment listed in the Military Statute included the firing
squad (for military personnel only), beheading, hanging, the wheel, quartering, and death by fire (for arsonists, witches, and heretics). Corporal
punishment included flogging with sticks, the whip and the knout, branding
with iron, amputation of ears, hands, or fingers (e.g., for a murderer who
beats someone to death). 'Light' corporal punishments were running the
gauntlet, shackles, bread and water, thrashing with sticks (*batogi*), confinement in the stocks, and stakes (*khozhdenie po kol'iam*).[273] There was also
imprisonment under a strict regime, 'light' imprisonment, banishment to
estates, and deportation. Penalties mentioned elsewhere are confiscation of
property, loss of rights, dishonour (the criminal's name attached to the
gallows), and *shelmovanie* (from German *Schelm*, a proclamation that a man
is dishonoured).[274] Instances of impaling and drowning (not mentioned in
the statute) were also recorded. Gorlé points out that in the 1649 *Ulozhenie*,
35 crimes carried the death penalty, in the Military Statute, 122, but argues
that it would be wrong to think that Russian punishments were crueller than
those inflicted in the West. In England in 1715, 160 crimes carried the death
penalty. To give but one example, the English penalty for the murder of husbands by wives was death by burning alive.[275] The Military Statute left the
choice of penalty to the judge: for example, the penalty for theft was either
beheading or permanent banishment to hard labour.[276] And often penalties
were alleviated by law. The punishment for forgery in the *Ulozhenie* was death
by choking on molten metal. In 1723 executioners were instructed to cut off

the head of any criminal who failed to die quickly by this method, 'for a speedy death'.[277] The penalty for counterfeiting stamped paper was the same as for forging currency—death—but without pouring molten metal down the throat.[278] Murderers who confessed were given a lighter sentence, death commuted to corporal punishment and ten years' hard labour.[279] At least one old Muscovite custom officially disappeared: *pravezh*, or beating on the legs, in order to extract payment from defaulters of various kinds (on private debts and tax and customs arrears). Peter abolished it in 1718, replacing it with discharge of debts by labour in public works (at the rate of one rouble per month), but apparently *pravezh* continued to be applied.[280]

Certain 'moral' crimes were not harshly punished. Peter's response, on hearing that Emperor Charles V had prescribed the death penalty for adultery, was allegedly: 'Evidently he had more superfluous people in his state than I have in mine. Without doubt there must be punishments for disorder and crime, but also it is important to spare the life of as many subjects as possible.'[281] Such sentiment (that the death penalty was a waste of human resources) is reflected when in 1723 Peter commuted the death sentence for forgery of two smiths from Tula on the grounds that they were doing essential work in the artillery factory, but ordered that they be kept in shackles and provided with subsistence only.[282] Peter is said to have expressed his regret about Mary Hamilton, the lady-in-waiting beheaded for the infanticide of her three illegitimate children, but he said he could not save her from death without breaking the laws of God and the State.[283]

The tradition of proclaiming an amnesty to mark military victories and other state celebrations was maintained: for example, for the Nystad celebrations in October 1721 all prisoners were released (except murderers and multiple robbers), including state debtors who incurred debts up to 1718 and prisoners in galleys.[284] On the other hand, the cruelty of public executions provided retribution for the convicted and a deterrent to observers. In 1721 Peter ordered that Commandant Volkhov, convicted of robbery, be executed publicly and 'his corpse not to be buried in the ground (but to lie on the ground *visible to all*) until the spring as long as there are no warm spells'.[285] In January 1724 Bergholz witnessed the mass execution of Ober-Fiskal Nesterov, who was broken alive on the wheel for robbing the treasury of 300,000 roubles, and a dozen or so lesser officials, who were beheaded or flogged and exiled to the galleys after their nostrils had been slit. He noted: 'All the officials from the chancelleries and offices were obliged to attend the execution as a warning to them.'[286] Another notorious case was that of William Mons, in November 1724. Bergholz speaks of the calm with which Mons met his death and of his good qualities in general. Five days after the execution, Bergholz notes, Mons's body was still lying on the scaffold.[287]

Harsh penalties for seemingly trivial offences reflected Petrine priorities, although it is difficult to say how frequently these penalties were inflicted. His sliding scale of punishments for dropping litter seems particularly drastic: for a first offence of failing to keep clean the area in front of his house, a home-owner was sentenced to beating with *batogi*; for a second, beating plus a five-rouble fine, for a third, the knout and a ten-rouble fine. Passers-by caught throwing rubbish got the knout, with ten roubles added for a second offence.[288] In 1703 a ten-rouble fine was imposed for the felling of any tree more than 12 vershok in diameter. Cutting down an oak of any size whatsoever was punishable by death. (Felling saplings of lime, ash, birch, aspen, alder, fir, nut, osier, black poplar, and pine was allowed.[289]) In 1705 protection was afforded certain forests, with felling of trees allowed only for carts, sledges, and barrels, but not for buildings. The death sentence was prescribed for offenders, and hard labour even for picking up windfall oaks![290] (The shortage is highlighted by the story that a German forester ordered to mark all oaks in the forests of Ingria and the Novgorod region found none, although they were comparatively abundant in the upper Volga.[291])

In general, permutations of corporal punishment and hard labour (*katorga*[292]) were preferred. The latter—in Azov, Taganrog, Olonets, and St Petersburg—was for men only. Women were sent to spinning mills.[293] Golikova's statistics on 507 cases tried in the Preobrazhensky *prikaz* in 1697–1708 (excluding the 1698 strel'tsy and 1705 Astrakhan revolts) show that most were banished (although with different degrees of mutilation and prior flogging). Only 48 were executed. Flogging was used for a range of offences, military, civil, and criminal. Some punishments appear in line with those of other countries: for example, a recruit deserting before a year's service was made to run the gauntlet. After more than a year he was subjected to the knout, slit nostrils, and hard labour.[294] For nobles the usual penalty for 'shirking' was deportation to hard labour, accompanied by confiscation of property. A bizarre case is that of Vasily Sheremetev and his wife, who were condemned to hard labour for allowing their son to marry (thereby escaping posting abroad) without the tsar's permission.[295] 'Political death' was imposed on so-called *netchiki*, nobles who failed to report for musters. Their names were to be nailed to gallows by an executioner to the sound of drum-beats.[296]

For lesser crimes there were money fines, much favoured by Peter for careless and recalcitrant nobles and officials. Examples of such crimes include non-attendance at regattas, fifty roubles; use of oars rather than sails on the Neva when there was a wind, five roubles per oar. (The latter incident was recorded by Just Juel in November 1710. He himself was threatened with a fine, but managed to wriggle out of it.[297]) Weber noted the same in 1714, since Peter was 'resolved to force his Russians to learn Navigation, which forcible Method has actually made many an able Sailor'.[298] There were fines for talking during church services, and special boxes were installed to receive them.[299] There were fixed scales of fines for missing work. For leave without a sick-note or some other valid reason, the General Regulation prescribed a week's wages docked for every day lost, a month's for a week (article 10). If a chancellery official did not have the means to pay, the fine had to be worked off by hard labour (article 24).[300] Fines for late reports could be as much as 100 roubles for a month's delay, confiscation of property and exile for life to hard labour for more than four months![301] But lack of consistency and definition is indicated by the announcement to the Senate in April 1722 mentioned above, which laid down the death sentence for any infringement of laws by state officials 'following the example of Gagarin'.[302] This was a variant of many such decrees which Peter periodically issued to express his frustration at non-co-operation. For example, a decree of 24 December 1714 on bribery and corruption (*likhoimstvo*) was aimed at 'rogues whose only goal is to undermine all that is good and to fill their insatiability'. Offenders were to undergo corporal punishment and confiscation of property, and to be disgraced (*shelmovan*) and expelled from the company of good people, or even executed.[303]

By and large, detention and prison were used only for remand. Those remanded on *sud* cases were supposed to be maintained by the plaintiffs, while state detainees were set to hard labour or even sent out in gangs to beg. Prisoners were not supposed to be gaoled for long periods, presumably to save state funds rather than from any humanitarian impulse.[304] In fact, many languished in custody, their cases untried. Pososhkov cites cases, including his own week's imprisonment 'for no known reason'.[305]

VII. CONCLUSION

The problem of law in Russia will be appreciated by anyone who has consulted the relevant volumes of the *Complete Collection of Russian Laws* (from 1649 to 1833, started in the 1830s) and been puzzled by the odd (to Western eyes) materials contained in it, recognizably legal enactments alongside the tsar's personal one-off orders. This was typical not just of the reign of Peter, but of subsequent reigns, where no clear distinction was made between a law (*zakon*) and an administrative ruling (*razporiazhenie*). Any decree issued by the monarch (*ukaz*) had the force of law, requiring no special procedures or prescribed channels.[306] At the same time, away from the centre, the monarch's autocratic command was diluted. Nobles literally 'took the law into their own hands'. In the provinces, landowners had legal jurisdiction over their serfs. They often disregarded laws on property and inheritance. What they wanted was not a strong independent judiciary, but rather officials sympathetic to their particular needs. The average nobleman had no particular desire to deal with paperwork and procedures. This was a matter for the comparatively lowly class of clerks and scribes.[307] Expertise was associated with low status. Even the presidents of colleges were generally not 'career bureaucrats' but men who had distinguished themselves in military or other spheres. Military exploits, especially if combined with closeness to the ruler, continued to be valued more highly than exploits with the pen. Peter tried to correct this: for example, by instituting a 'fast stream' for young nobles on government service and insisting on in-house training (there was a course in jurisprudence available in Russia) and forcing local nobles into provincial government, but with little success.

Peter's reform of government overall has generally been assessed positively, with major disagreements centring on how co-ordinated his efforts were and how much the reform owed to foreign models. Did Peter succeed? If the aim was to perform the immediate tasks of tax gathering and recruitment, yes. If the grand aim of the exercise was to impose order and legality, to make Russia better governed, no. The net result was disappointing given that so much energy had been expended on producing 'super laws', rules, and regulations, in the hope that no one would sin 'out of ignorance'. The most damning indictments appear after Peter's death in a number of memoranda from top officials, including P. I. Iaguzhinsky (the procurator-general) and members of the new Supreme Privy Council, which actually led to the dismantling of much of the 1718–19 provincial reform and a further reorganization in the countryside: 'The proliferation of officials and chancelleries all over the country not only creates a great burden on the State but also is very oppressive to the people. ... Now the peasant has a dozen or more commanders instead of one—military commanders, fiscals, *voevody*, forestry commissioners (*valdmeistry*), etc., of which some are not so much shepherds as wolves attacking the flock.'[308] The preference was for a return to the 'simplicity' of the seventeenth-century system of *voevody*.[309] The decade after Peter's death saw drastic reductions in offices and personnel, both at the centre (cuts in the number of college board members, dismissal of foreign personnel, abolition of the Magistracy) and in the provinces (dismantling of regimental districts, abolition of posts such as *rentmeister* and *kamerir*, transferring duties to *voevody*, abolition of courts of appeal and *zemskie komissary*). Although some of these posts were restored in the reign of the Empress Elizabeth (1741–61), the result was the virtual disappearance for a time of Peter's local administration and its replacement by a hierarchical system of governor, provincial *voevoda*, and district *voevoda*.[310] The fiscals disappeared, as did most of the under-procurators and the Preobrazhensky *prikaz*. It is true that the Senate and the Synod survived until 1917, and the collegiate system until the early nineteenth century, but the underlying spirit and rationale of Peter's reform were lost. In some areas, such as the use of complex 'spy' networks and chains of command, this was to be welcomed; in others, such as the attempt to create a separate judiciary, it was to be regretted. The immediate post-Petrine dismantling process was destructive rather than constructive, the result not of any great vision but of immediate imperatives. Nowhere was the Petrine service ethic so challenged as in the fact that the driving force behind this dismantling consisted of the nobles, who, as we shall see in the next chapter, set about reclaiming some of the privileges lost during Peter's reign. It is evident that Peter failed to establish a 'well-regulated police state' which would function efficiently with the minimum of intervention from its ruler (and creator). One cannot but agree with Peterson's conclusion that 'instead of creating a rational and efficient administration ... the [provincial] reform led to an even greater disorder in the Russian administration'.[311] It seems that a semblance of order existed only in the tsar's immediate vicinity. The antithesis of street lighting in front of the Winter Palace and orderly rows of maples along St Petersburg streets (see below) was the state of near-lawlessness which prevailed in 'dark' provincial towns, where the strong continued to exploit the weak with impunity. Robbery and brigandage were rife. In November 1710 landlords in the districts of Klin, Volokolamsk, and Mozhaisk (near Moscow) complained that bands of armed robbers were burning their houses, killing their peasants, carrying off their women, and stealing horses and food.[312] Just Juel reported (early in 1711) that even the centre of Moscow was unsafe because of robbers. In the three months he was in Moscow, sixteen people were killed outside his house alone, one of whom, Baron von Willemovsky, died in his house.[313] Weber, who visited Moscow in 1716, reported that it was risky to go out at night because of villains on the streets. Crime was said to increase when the tsar was abroad. (*Bog vysoko. Gosudar' daleko.*[314])

Recent studies speak of organized crime and a Petrine 'mafia'. A notorious case was that of the Solov'ev brothers, former slaves of Lev Naryshkin, the tsar's uncle, who after his death in 1705 were freed and given responsible positions, Dmitry Alekseevich as *ober-kommissar* in Archangel, with access to funds from trade and customs dues, and Osip Alekseevich as commercial agent in Amsterdam. The two brothers, who made fortunes through fraud, were arrested in 1717 after tip-offs, but managed to get off. (Their accuser, Kurbatov, was arrested instead.) They were reappointed to offical posts and ended up as barons, in 1727. Apparently, the investigator appointed by Peter, Mikhail Matiushkin, married a Solov'ev daughter in 1721![315] Russia's problem was not so much excessive government as under-government and the absence of law, problems which it shared with many, perhaps—most—contemporary European states. Pososhkov summed it up: 'Whatever laws His Imperal Majesty promulgates are all set at naught and everyone continues in the bad old ways ... Until the rule of law is established in Russia and is firmly and universally rooted among us no measures applied for the remedy of the abuses as in other countries will have any effect. Likewise we shall never acquire a good name since all the nastiness and want of principle among us is due to deficiencies in the law and in the dispensation thereof and also to short-sighted government.'[316]

5

The Economy

'Money is the artery of war'

I. TAXATION AND THE STATE BUDGET

Peter's most memorable observation on economic affairs is that 'money is the artery of war'.[1] His grasp of matters fiscal may have been fairly unsophisticated: the total of two treatises on economics in his library (a German work, *The Prince's Statecraft*, and John Law's *Money and Trade Considered*) suggests that he had 'little interest or faith in economic doctrine.'[2] But he grasped the fundamentals of the Russian economy: namely, that vast resources were required to fund military ventures and that the main source of funding was the indigenous population. [3] He was able to exploit Russia's 'backwardness' by applying his absolute power to extract service, labour, and taxes. Onto a 'backward' main stem he grafted 'modern' features, such as industry and technology, reform of the coinage, and free trade, and watered it with a sprinkling of borrowed mercantilist theory. Charles Whitworth wrote:

> The maintenance of all these forces does not cost the Czar above two thirds of what other European Princes must pay for the same number, since the Russians who have estates are obliged to serve at their own charge, or for a very inconsiderable salary: so the only expense is in foreign officers and the common foot soldiers. Yet I find there is no small difficulty in raising the sums necessary for the service, which is one reason why most part of the soldiers are not equipped and armed as they might have been abroad. For the riches of these countries are in no way answerable to the extent thereof, there are no gold or silver mines yet found, and their trade tho' it daily increases is far from being on a right footing.[4]

Korb summed it up even more succinctly: 'The Czar will never want as long as he knows of his subjects having any gold and silver remaining. For their riches and private valuables are his only mines of gold and silver. This absolute master uses his subjects at his will, and their wealth in what share he pleases.'[5]

Was Peter at all concerned to maintain a balance between the needs of the State and the needs of the citizens, or sympathetic to the notion that the 'common good' could be fostered by individual wealth? (To quote Ivan

Pososhkov's Hobbesian argument, 'if the people are rich so is their country, and if the people are poor their country cannot be accounted rich'.[6]) This is a question we shall return to at the end of the chapter when considering the longer-term effects of economic policy. Let us first examine the nuts and bolts of Petrine financial management.

The Russian government's chief concern both before and after Peter's reign was collecting taxes. The bulk of revenues went into the war effort and maintaining the administrative system, which itself was largely concerned with running wars. Figures for 1704, the fourth year of the Northern War, give an indication of priorities. Military expenditure swallowed up 1,439,832 roubles (40.9 per cent); the state apparatus, 1,313,200 roubles (37.6 per cent); the royal household, 156,843 roubles (4.4 per cent); diplomacy, 75,042 roubles (2.1 per cent); the Church, 29,777 roubles (0.8 per cent); education, medicine, and postal services, a paltry 17,388 roubles (0.5 per cent).[7] Proportions varied little in subsequent years.

One approach to maximizing revenues was simplification and rationalization, following earlier trends, of Russia's bewildering range of taxes and tax-collecting agencies. These began to be reduced under Peter's immediate predecessors. In 1679 many direct taxes (land tax, postal tax, ransom money, strel'tsy money) were consolidated into the strel'tsy tax (levied mainly on townspeople and collected by the Strel'tsy chancellery) and the postal tax (*iamskaia podat'*, collected by the Postal chancellery). In 1680 a number of regional tax-collecting agencies (in Kostroma, Ustiug, Galich, Novgorod, and other towns) were merged under the Great Treasury (*Bol'shaia kazna*), with the result that the Strel'tsy and Postal chancelleries collected most direct taxes and the Great Treasury most indirect ones.[8] In Peter's reign, before the introduction of the poll tax in 1724, there were two types of direct taxes: permanent or fixed (*okladnye*: from 1710 also referred to as *tabel'nye*) and extraordinary (*zaprosnye vremennye* or *chrezvychainye*). These taxes could be designated by the end 'beneficiary' or the group of the population who paid them. Fixed taxes included *prikaznye*: for example, postal and ransom (*polonianichnye*) taxes at the rate of 5 copecks for peasants living on landlords' and crown lands and 10 copecks for church peasants, and taxes earmarked for dragoons, shipbuilding, recruits, and (from 1710) the building of St Petersburg. There were also special (but still fixed) taxes exacted from specific groups of the population for specific purposes: for example, dragoon wages were levied on church peasants (35 copecks), as was a levy for the transport of masons and bricklayers. Townspeople of the *posad* community paid various earmarked taxes, notably strel'tsy money; while in the south single householders (*odnodvortsy*, military servitors who both paid taxes and were entitled to own serfs) paid an *odnodvortsy* tax of 1–3 roubles which went to various purposes. There were regional fixed taxes: for example, Kazan' residents paid for timber transportation, and inhabitants of the St Petersburg region for Admiralty shipbuilding.

Extraordinary taxes was also levied annually, but the amount varied, so they were not regarded as 'fixed'. They included collections for fodder and provisions—*proviantskaia povinnost'*. In 1711 60 per cent of taxable urban households in Kazan' province paid 1.2 roubles for provisions for St Petersburg; 13 per cent paid 80 copecks for Iaroslavl'; and 27 per cent were supposed to send provisions in kind to Iaroslavl', but failed to do so and paid 90 copecks instead. Taxes to fund the Admiralty and provide provisions for the fleet in 1720 were 15 copecks per head; in 1721, 41.5 copecks; in 1722/3, 25 copecks. Extraordinary taxes included recruit and horse money (*rublevye*; an estimated 100 roubles per recruit was needed for uniform, supplies and transport) and labourers' money (*otrabochnye*), which paid upkeep and travel expenses for work gangs. Another 'occasional' tax was wagon or transport money (*podvodnye den'gi*). An edict of 13 January 1710 levying 2 altyns per peasant household for hiring transport for artillery and other supplies is an example of the sort of order which filled the statute books.[9] Thus the sum total of taxes paid by any particular set of taxpayers varied in its composition. Liability was calculated on the basis of the household (*dvor*), the number of which determined the sum owed collectively by a given village or community. Data from Kiev for 1714–16 indicate an annual payment per household of 4.18 roubles, made up of 1.64 roubles (39.2 per cent) in fixed and 2.54 roubles (60.8 per cent) in extraordinary taxes. Anisimov calculated the average figure per taxpayer (1720–3) as 0.57 copecks, of which 0.34 was in fixed taxes.

The first recipient of tax revenues was the military, whose demands were relentless. In the aftermath of Poltava, a detailed review (order of 27 January 1710) of expenditure on the army, fleet, garrisons, artillery, and 'other essentials' revealed expenditure of 3,834,418 roubles and income of approximately 3,133,879 roubles.[10] Measures to make good the shortfall included earmarking vital *prikazy* (Military, Admiralty, Foreign Affairs, and Artillery) for receipt of taxes direct from the provinces and a ban on private distilling.[11] Peter also ordered a census of the population in order to get more accurate estimates of tax liabilities. An edict of 12 February 1710, *ukaz o perepisi*, instructed governors to 'register all peasants and agricultural slave (*delovye*) households in your *gubernii* by heads, people of both sexes separately'.[12] This census took in not only peasants and urban taxpayers but also members of the middle and lower service classes (*deti boiarskie, odnodvortsy*, artillery men, garrison guards, and gatekeepers). The decision to conduct a census was based on the assumption that the population must have grown since the last one in 1678 and was therefore being undertaxed. In fact, the results of the count indicated an almost 20 per cent *decrease* in population, not in actual terms but as a result of peasant abandonment of homes, recruitment, concealment by landlords in order to avoid state taxes, amalgamation of several homesteads into one, and so on.[13]

New problems arose with the return of troops from campaign in the late 1710s, when the whole burden of their upkeep fell upon Russian territory. One solution, as we have seen, was provincial reform, coupled with a new way of calculating liability in order to raise money to go directly to the army. In 1715–17 the idea was conceived of quartering army units in those provinces which had direct responsibility for supplying them. This shortened substantially 'the route of the money from the pockets of the peasants into the regimental cash boxes',[14] and prompted investigations of the number of peasant taxpayers required to maintain each soldier in quarters. Officials were ordered to examine the Swedish system of levying taxes to maintain the troops, 'how they allocate them, by homestead or by unit [*Haken*] or by individual'.[15] Such thinking produced the poll tax (*podushnaia podat'*), which was imposed on each male head, or 'soul' (*dusha*), rather than on households. Collecting the data took a considerable time. Figures submitted in 1721 were regarded as unreliable, which prompted a revision (*revisiia*) of the census, carried out by military commanders in 1722–3.[16] The count identified some 5.5 million 'souls' liable to pay the tax, which was collected for the first time in 1724 at a rate of 74 copecks per head, reduced to 70 after Peter's death.[17] At this rate it was reckoned that it took forty-seven peasants to maintain one infantryman (28.5 roubles per year) and fifty-seven to maintain one cavalryman.[18] Crown and state peasants paid an additional 40 copecks (roughly equated to the serfs' dues to their masters), and urban taxpayers paid 1 rouble, 20 copecks.

The new tax had marked administrative and social implications. It centralized record keeping and clarified or changed the status of certain groups by making them taxable: for example, single householders (*odnodvortsy*), who were once classified among the non-taxpaying gentry. Some old social groups, such as slaves or bondsmen (*kholopy, delovye*, etc.), disappeared as distinct categories as they became liable to the tax on the same basis as peasants. But did the poll tax represent an increased burden on the mass of the population? In the words of Arcadius Kahan, 'One of the axioms of the Russian historiography of the fiscal system has been the assumption that the introduction of the poll tax led to an increase in the burden of the Russian serfs.'[19] Miliukov's figures indicate that direct taxes collected as a result of the poll tax rose from 1,778,533 to 4,614,638 roubles, an increase of 61 per cent.[20] Anisimov's figures also show a rise, although a much smaller one: from 3,669,000 roubles in 1721 to 4,324,000 (at 74 copecks per head) for the first poll tax year. By Gerschenkron's calculation the tax burden after Poltava amounted to 64 per cent of grains harvested from the peasant plot, 'a most shocking result'.[21] Kahan argued that taxation reached a peak at the height of the war (1705–15), followed by a devaluation of the rouble in 1718. The poll tax actually *reduced* the individual's burden after the very high rates of the Northern War. He suggested that the apparent increase in the poll tax collected was accounted for by more taxpayers being included, and tentatively concluded that 'for the total enserfed rural population, the poll tax constituted a reduction of the tax in money compared with the household tax, although this reduction may have been arrived at by simultaneously increasing the burden on the private serfs in some regions and decreasing it for the state-owned serfs'.[22] The 'myth' of the increased burden arose because the introduction of the tax coincided with famine years (the period of harsh winters sometimes referred to as the 'Little Ice Age' which affected Russia most drastically in 1721–4) and a temporary decline in money supply as a result of the payment of compensation to Sweden. In turn, the Russian historian Boris Mironov has challenged Kahan's conclusions, arguing that he failed to take account of inflation at the beginning of the eighteenth century, and that the poll tax restored the peasants' obligation in real terms.[23]

If the thinking behind the introduction of the poll tax was fairness, the idea that everyone should pay 'no more than is possible and no less than is proper', there is ample evidence of individual hardship.[24] Sums were fixed regardless of ability to work or pay, and included minors and the aged among the taxpayers. Ivan Pososhkov urged: 'Let each peasant's obligation be reckoned in proportion to the amount of land he holds.'[25] As we shall see, warnings of the 'ruin' of the peasantry were sounded after Peter's death, and the sum was reduced, although the poll tax itself turned out to be one of Peter's most enduring legacies, abolished only in 1887.

People's liability did not end with direct taxes. Just Juel was not exaggerating when he wrote that 'there is not one item of national income which the tsar does not monopolize and from which he does not receive his portion . . . Every fishing net with which a poor man scrapes a living has an annual duty laid on it.'[26] Peter is famous for taxing everything in sight, although in fact he merely added to a long list of existing duties. A 1698 list of goods liable to duty (*mytnaia poshlina*) included livestock, building materials, cheeses, barrels, tubs, troughs, cups, spoons, sleighs, cabbages, and cucumbers.[27] The list started to lengthen after the creation in 1699 of the office of 'profit-makers' (*pribyl'shchiki*), one of whose suggestions for raising revenue was stamp duty on official 'eagle crest' paper for contracts.[28] In 1704 a census of private bath-houses was conducted in order to impose a new rent tax (*obrok*) according to the rank of the owner: 3 roubles per year for boyars and chief merchants, 1 rouble for other noble servitors and churchmen, and 15 copecks for peasants. The fine for concealing a bath-house was 50 roubles.[29] In 1704 the sale of oak coffins was regulated, and a hefty duty slapped on. Anyone bringing in a body for burial in an oak coffin without the proper tax receipts was prosecuted.[30] The year 1709 saw a tax imposed on beehives, which were included in Weber's list, alongside mills, ponds, fisheries, meadows, gardens, and bath-houses.[31] Another ingenious idea for a tax, combined with a fine, was to place an eagle stamp (5 copecks per pack) on foreign-made playing cards (1720), with a 500 rouble fine for packs found without the stamp.[32]

Certain public services and facilities were farmed out under franchise (*otkup*). In 1704 franchisers collected duties on public bath-houses, fisheries, mills, horse tethers, and collars, and tolls on bridges and fords. The dues collected went to the office of the Semenovsky chancellery.[33] Such taxes brought in comparatively little revenue, and may even have been counter-productive by contributing to Peter's unpopularity and encouraging evasion. A dissident interrogated in the Preobrazhensky *prikaz* in 1705 complained that 'all Ukraine has collapsed on account of taxes and now we have such taxes which are inpenetrable to the mind, which even affect the clergy. They have started to tax us on bath-houses, beehives and cottages, such as our fathers and fore-fathers never saw nor heard of.' He concluded that Peter was the Antichrist.[34]

Liquor licences were, as in the past, a major source of revenue. According to Weber, the right to sell alcohol was reserved to the Crown in tap-houses; 'by this Method the greatest Part of the Nation's Money is drawn into the Czar's Treasury'.[35] Sales of English and home-grown tobacco were also a royal monopoly, but Turkish tobacco could be traded freely. The government had monopolies on potash, weed-ash, ising-glass, tar, and the products of Siberia, especially furs. But Weber saw much illegal trading.[36] Another profitable source of government revenue was the purchase tax on salt (gabelle). The trade was made a state monopoly in 1705 (repealed in 1727). Salt was bought from traders and entrepreneurs and was sold to the populace from state ware-houses for twice the price paid to the producers, from whom the treasury also took a 10 per cent duty.[37]

Figures for duties collected in 1720 show a total of 4,461,198 roubles 35 copecks (excluding revenues from crown lands). These included duties on customs, liquor, and tobacco (by far the most profitable) and chancellery revenues: for example, from stamped paper, printing taxes, legal fees, licences and horse sales tax. The least profitable categories were rentals and franchises (obrochnye i otkupnye), which included the famous list of beehives, mills, bath-houses, fisheries, cabs, boats, bridges, barns, stamping of brand marks on hats and boots, and tagging of horse collars, apple-trees, grapes, melons, cucumbers and nuts. Beard and clothing fines brought in the meagre sum of 297 roubles, 20 copecks, with 1,852 roubles, 20 copecks in arrears.[38]

Total state revenues from direct and indirect taxes showed a marked rise over the years—in 1680, 1.5 million roubles; in 1701, 3.6 million; in 1724, 8.7 million[39]—but Peter was always hard up. Weber gave a gloomy analysis of the state of Russian finances in a résumé of revenues between 1714 and 1717, as gathered from 'friends' and his own observations. His conclusions are worth noting, even if he was not immune to the standard foreign prejudices. 'Russia abounds in merchandise, but not in ready Money ... the War has deprived the Country of abundance of Inhabitants, and those who are left, labour under the Oppression of the Czar's Officers, and of the Nobility, to such a Degree, that they are quite disheartened from Industry, and content them-selves with making a poor Shift of living from Hand to Mouth.... All manner of Industry and Desire of Gain is extinguished among the Boors, and if by chance one happens privately to get a small Sum, he hides it out of Fear of his Lord under a Dunghill, where it lies dead to him.' Nobles locked up their money or put it in banks in London, Venice, and Amsterdam, thus depriving their country of the benefit that the circulation of their wealth could bring.[40] Weber identified another endemic problem: 'A certain Russian ... was once heard to say, that of one hundred Rubels collected in the Country, he was positively assured not thirty ever came into the Czar's Coffers, the Remainder being divided among the Officers for the Trouble of gathering them in.'[41] Thus the war, lack of capital and 'enterprise culture' and corruption conspired to keep Russia poor.

Russian sources reveal regular short-term cash shortages. For example, in 1706 F. M. Apraksin reported to Peter from Moscow that in the Postal chancellery there was a total of 220 roubles in cash, in the Armoury, 105 roubles. 'I fear that there may be a stoppage in arms production and various military supplies,' he wrote.[42] In 1720 there was no money at all in the Chancellery of Building because none had been sent from the provinces. It was unable to pay anyone's wages, including those of foreign specialists, who threatened to leave Russia.[43] On 12 May 1712 Peter promised Menshikov that he would try to get him money for the purchase of provisions from the king of Poland, but warned him not to rely on it, 'for you are well aware of our shortage of money and that money is urgently needed for the refurbishment of the army and for buying ships'.[44] Peter himself often ran out of money. On at least one occasion he apologized to Catherine for not sending a gift with the courier, because of a 'shortage of cash' (*nedostatok v kazne imeiu*).[45] Accounting methods were often rough-and-ready, with officials expected to make up the difference out of their own pockets. In correspondence with Romodanovsky in 1708, Peter points out the wastefulness of sending wages to troops in Poland, then deducting uniform money and sending it back to Moscow.[46] Romodanovsky was to have uniforms made for the Semenovsky regiment. 'If the money sent is insufficient, make it up out of your own and the sum will be deducted from the soldiers and sent to you right away.'[47]

In 1723 there was a more serious general alarm. The Senate was instructed to deduct from the salaries of 'all ranks of all the State, clergy and laypersons, a rouble per head in such a way that nobody is particularly hurt but that all should share a common deprivation in this time of need'. In the Siberian chancellery officials' salaries were to be paid in goods from the treasury rather than in money 'because of the present deficit in cash'.[48] Fears of a Turkish attack, following the Caspian campaign, and shortfalls in money and grain (these were famine years) prompted a 25 per cent salary cut for all ranks with the exception of foreigners. This also included cuts in subsistence allowances. Appeals were made for people to bring gold and silver to the Mint. Duties on liquor (including French brandy, which people were buying 'instead of vodka') and stamped paper were raised. Foreigners were allowed to import grain duty-free into St Petersburg in order to alleviate pressure on the Moscow region.[49] However, complaints of hardship—for example, from troops serving in the south, where apparently Persians gave a poor exchange rate for Russian money, and from officers without estates to supplement their incomes—led to further exemptions being made.[50] Petty economies were made even in the royal household: for example, sailors' uniforms ordered for the holiday were to be made from cheap Russian cloth.[51] Famine relief measures were announced: 'In those places where people are starving (*gde narodnyi golod iavilsia*) surplus grain shall be inventoried from local inhabitants (*postoronnye*), whoever they may be.' After the household's needs for food and seed were calculated, the rest was to be distributed to other poor (*neimushchie*) peasants. Measures were taken to prevent concealment of stocks or fraudulent claims on requisitioned grain. Merchants must be prevented from selling at a high price 'and thereby burdening the people'. The inventory of grain stocks was to be made only in those places where there was famine. 'In other places where there is no shortage of grain do not make inventories in order not to impede grain contracts and sales.'[52]

II.   FINANCIAL ADMINISTRATION AND COINAGE

Seventeenth-century Muscovy had no central financial administration, even though most of the revenues were consumed centrally. Virtually all the *prikazy* had some kind of tax-gathering function, right down to the crown stables (*Koniushennyi prikaz*), which collected taxes on horse sales throughout Russia. Some *prikazy* were primarily fiscal: notably the Great Treasury (*Bol'shaia kazna*), which had responsibility for crown enterprises and minting; the Revenues chancellery (*prikaz bol'shogo prikhoda*), which collected customs duties; and the Chancellery of the New Quarter (*prikaz novoi chetverti*), which collected duties on salt and alcohol. Various 'quarters' (Vladimir, Galich, Ustiug) administered finances in the regions. The new collegiate system consolidated the trend towards rationalization by devoting three of the nine colleges—State Revenues (*Kamer-kollegiia*), State Accounting (*Revizion-kollegiia*), and State Expenses (*Shtats-kontor-kollegiia*) —to fiscal administration, while the colleges of Commerce (*Kommerts*) and Mines and Manufacture (*Berg i manufaktur*) were concerned with promoting national wealth.[53]

The *Kamer-kollegiia* had 'supreme supervision and direction of His Majesty's and his whole realm's ordinary and extraordinary revenues'.[54] It was to be supplied with information from the provinces of revenues and from the centre of 'how much is needed for expenditure each year'.[55] The college was supposed to administer records of taxes and to ensure that the population was taxed fairly and not to the point of ruination. It supervised the maintenance of forests, and discouraged the abandonment of farming land. It also collected domestic customs duties, but not foreign ones, which came under the Commerce college. Initially it administered the Mint (transferred to the College of Mines and Manufacture in 1720). It could review expenditure, but not order payments. The *Shtats-kontor* (*shtat* from *staten* = budget) planned and supervised state expenditure on the basis of an annual budget. It also controlled the treasury, and issued payment orders for salaries (paid quarterly).[56] In fact, the complex procedures of bookkeeping, payment orders, and so on, modelled faithfully on the Swedish system, were probably not followed.[57] The *Revizion-kollegiia* was responsible for auditing accounts and punishing abuses in the hope of preventing officials from helping themselves to state funds, which meant it also had judicial duties. 'As soon as the *Kamer-kollegiia* finds that someone has been careless or unfaithful to a high degree with regard to the administration and accounting of His Majesty's revenues, word of such a crime shall be sent immediately from the *Kamer-kollegiia* to the *Revizion-kollegiia*.'[58] In 1718–19 commercial matters were centralized in the *Kommerts-kollegiia* (from the Swedish *kommerskollegium*).[59] Its instruction was based on a Swedish text of 1712, which included supervising customs, maintaining and devising customs regulations and watching over market-places and towns.[60]

All these departments suffered from serious teething troubles, above and beyond the problems discussed in the previous chapter. The president of the *Kamer-kollegiia*, Prince D. M. Golitsyn, wrote in December 1719 that the college 'still does not have full information about all the revenues and expenditures of the Russian state ... and has not been provided with enough officials and cannot, without that base, start its work'.[61] Stefan Kochius, the secretary of the college, and Fick, one of its councillors, complained that the instructions were 'impossible to implement and everything is so confused that not a single point is in its natural place'. Revenue collections were still in the hands of several colleges; they lacked trained personnel; there was a plethora of paperwork (several hundred letters daily). The *Shtats-kontor* did not draw up a state budget during Peter's reign, and the *Revizion-kollegiia* so rarely received the information it needed that it barely functioned at all, and was taken over by the Senate accounts office in 1722. Peterson attributes the lack of success of all three colleges to the inadequacy of local government and the infrastructure.[62]

Peter's interest in coins and coinage is attested by the several visits he made to the Mint during his stay in London in 1698. His reign saw the introduction of a whole new coinage. In the seventeenth century the basic units of local currency were copecks, small silver ones made from blanks of flattened wire, which were too small for large transactions but too high for small ones, which meant that people clipped them. Silver coins of larger denomination were produced by overstamping foreign coins, the so-called *efimki*, or *Joachimsthaler*. The first Russian silver roubles date from 1704. In 1700 there was an issue of a copper denga, polushka, and polupolushka (1/2, 1/4, and 1/8 copeck, respectively); in 1701–2 a silver poltina (50 copecks), polupoltinnik (25 copecks), grivennik (10 copecks), and polugrivna (5 copecks). The year 1704 saw the first copper copecks (but silver wire copecks continued to be made until 1718). In 1704–26 the silver altyn (3 copecks) was issued, and in 1724 the grosh (2 copecks).[63] In fact, the copeck was not in general use as a unit of accounting until 1721, when the decimal system (roubles and copecks) replaced the old method of calculating in units of roubles, altyns (3 copecks), and dengi (half a copeck). Thereafter, state offices were forbidden to mention altyns, although the old system remained popular.

Coins were produced in several mints. In 1711 (when Peter ordered the Senate to improve the supervision and organization of mints) there were three in Moscow: the Old Red Mint in Kitaigorod, the New Red Mint (1696), and the Kadashevsky Mint (one section for copper, one for gold and silver). The first mechanized mint (1700) was run by foreigners. The first good likeness of Peter on the coins is said to have been made in 1717 in Nuremberg and put on the coins in 1718.[64]

Weber reports that the newly coined roubles were found to be deficient in composition and weight, but could not be improved because of poor local yields of gold and silver. Russian ducats were said to be worth less than foreign ones because of the alloys used, but foreign ducats were undervalued, which was destructive to trade.[65] The metal content of the coinage was reduced, with 20 roubles' worth of copper currency struck from metal worth 6–8 roubles.[66] There were problems in maintaining the money supply. Foreign merchants were buying up gold crowns (chervonnye, each worth 2 or 3 roubles) and exporting them, and had even begun to do the same with silver, 'and we must look into this carefully for we have so little gold and silver in Russia that we must beware that what remains is not exported'.[67] In 1723 it was decreed that foreign merchants arriving in Russia with Russian coins were to be expelled, and the money confiscated.[68]

III.   WAGES AND PRICES

Wage-earners formed a small proportion of the Russian population, but comparisons of earnings are instructive. The fullest records available pertain to the royal household. The French architect Le Blond received 5,000 roubles per year, as did the Italian Michetti.[69] The German painter Dannhauer for the first half of 1715 earned 320 roubles, 16 altyns, 4 denga; a Russian painter on enamel, 30 roubles. The Russian portraitist Ivan Nikitin earned 200 roubles in 1721.[70] Clerks (d'iaki) also earned 200 roubles per annum, an extra 100 if they worked in a prikaz.[71] Peter's secretary Makarov was paid 400 roubles per annum.[72] A list of wages in the Justice college for 1719 shows differentials between foreign and Russian staff, as well as between higher and lower grades: councillors were paid 1,200 roubles per annum (foreigners) and 800 (Russian); middle-grade clerks (who were all Russian), 143 roubles; junior grades, 150 (foreign) and 62 (Russian).[73] A porter in the college received 21 roubles; a lackey, 18 roubles. The total budget for college salaries in 1720 was 111,544 roubles.[74] A governor in the provinces was paid 1,200 roubles plus 6,000 chetverti of grain; a provincial councillor, 120 roubles and 120 chetverti of grain.[75] Military salaries ranged from 7,000 for a field marshal, 3,500 for a general, 180 for a captain, and 84 for a quartermaster.[76] A foreign vice-admiral earned 2,160 roubles per annum.[77] Skilled workers at the Sestrenetsky ironworks earned 28–72 roubles per month; smiths, 20 roubles or less.[78]

At the lower end of the scale, soldiers working on the construction of the palaces at Peterhof and Dubki were paid 3 copecks per day for summer days, 2 copecks for shorter winter days (malye zemnye).[79] Soldiers and workers on building sites in Moscow in 1723 received 3 copecks (1 altyn) per day.[80] Rates for hiring peasant transport and porterage were 10 copecks per day for a man with a horse, 5 without a horse, in summer; in winter, 10 copecks with a horse, 4 without.[81] Menshikov in exile (in 1728) was given 1 rouble per day for his expenses, plus 1 for his wife and each of his children, and 10 copecks for each of his ten servants.[82] Compensation (to nobles) for serfs taken as carpenters was 20 roubles for males over ten years of age, 10 roubles for under tens. For womenfolk over ten, they received 10 roubles, under ten 5 roubles.[83]

Detailed accounts of Peter's personal expenditure survive in the records of the Cabinet. A remarkable number of tips and gifts were distributed, gifts to priests and churches, for alms, christenings, and weddings. Name-day gifts were routine: records for March–December 1719 include 110 references to gifts of this kind. For example, on 8 November 1724 (the feast of the Archangel Michael) a poltina per head was paid out for all the Michaels in the Preobrazhensky and Semenovsky guards.[84] Payments for special services rendered must have seemed like a fortune compared with day wages: a reward of 10 roubles was paid for saving someone from drowning, 10 roubles for a stone suitable for a grotto, 2 for an eagle, 200 for a strongman who performed for Peter and Catherine.[85] In April 1722 Christian Bernard, the court hairdresser, received 10 roubles for making a 'negro' wig for Peter's orderly Vasily Pospelov to wear at a party.[86]

IV.   TRADE

If trade was seen in early modern Europe as a route to national prosperity, then Peter's reign, despite the drain of war, should have laid the foundations for Russia's future wealth, with its opening of new sea and river routes, acquisition of ports, trade missions, the encouragement of commerce, strengthening of the merchantry, fostering of industry, tapping of natural resources, and commitment to free trade. Peter's views were influenced by Samuel Pufendorf's *Introduction to European History*, which praised British trade; the development of wool, linen, and shipbuilding by Elizabeth I; and, of course, the fleet.[87] Peter was also, according to anecdote, well aware that a country needed something to trade *with*: 'As long as this country makes only enough goods as is sufficient for its own use, until then it is like a little Imperial town, where one citizen works for another, one receives bread from another, but both remain poor and are unable to promote the town's wealth.'[88] It has been argued, however, that Peter's efforts on trade were less energetic than his activities in many other areas.[89]

Russia's exports were concentrated on bulky commodities with a low price per unit of weight: on the agricultural goods, forest products, and iron much in demand by Western navies, merchantmen, and manufacturers.[90] The most important exports were flax and hemp (from the central and south central regions), in which Russia dominated the European supply. Exports of these commodities through the Baltic during the 1720s ranged from 23,024 ship pounds to 101,286 (in 1725). Even so, there was felt to be room for improvement. A report on measures to increase hemp production in Russia (May 1720) declared that the quality must be raised to the level of the Polish, 'for some Russians put little care and effort into this enterprise and in their ignorance they spoil it with the result that the peasants and also merchants receive little profit from it'.[91]) For flax the five-year average was 11,258.2 ship pounds (1720–4). Some finished products were exported, notably 'Muscovy narrow' (the strip cloths which Peter tried unsuccessfully to widen), sailcloth, crash, and diaper (for towels and napkins). Tow, yarn, and cordage (very little), linseed oil, and bristles were exported, as was tallow, much in demand for British soap- and candle-makers. Russian leather (*iuft*) was sought after because it was very cheap. Producers resisted government attempts to 'improve' their product.[92] Lumber products included deals, planks, boards, balks, and masts.[93] Georg Grund's long list of exports (1710) includes (in addition to items already mentioned) wax, grain, grain spirit, oil, pitch, tar, potash, beaver skins, caviar, bast matting, salted fish and meat, pelts, rhubarb, hogs' hair, and fish glue. Imports included silver, copper, brass, tin, iron, and manufactured goods such as sealing wax, weapons, fine cloth, wine and brandy. Grund also mentions the considerable trade in fine fabrics from China, Persia, and Turkey.[94]

Iron, Russia's great success story in the later eighteenth century, began to be exported in bulk only after Peter's death. Figures for exports from the Baltic ports and St Petersburg in 1720–4 indicate a combined total of less than 5,000 ship pounds, compared with almost 450,000 in the early 1770s.[95] Grain policy under Peter was to route the trade through Archangel in order to discourage it. Only after Peter's reign did Riga become a main route for grain. In the period 1713–18 thousands of chetverti of rye were exported (260,738 in 1715), falling right off in the 1720s. Totals for wheat exports in 1715 were 17,885 cheverts.[96]

As for import figures, Kahan points out that they are 'truly terra incognita', and that the 'vast majority of Russians were not in the market for imports'.[97] Even so, it was deemed necessary to follow protectionist policies. A 1723 decree banned the import of Russian money by foreign merchants and also, apparently, foreign money. Customs officials were to check for forbidden imports, including leather, wax, bristle and caviar.[98] In 1724 a tariff was introduced to protect Russian goods in an exercise of 'import substitution': that is, the more capacity there was domestically to produce a given product, the higher the tariff on imports. Foreign imports were taxed *ad valorem*, the highest taxed items (37.5 per cent) including iron, coal, potash, silk, vodka, and sailcloth. Tax-free items included diamonds, gold and silver, trees for gardens, lemons, books, exotic birds, and tiles for stoves. There were small duties on such things as chocolate, human hair, soap, lace, and dyes. Importers sometimes falsified the value of their goods to pay lower duties, and there was also much smuggling and bribing of customs men. A new tariff was introduced in 1731.[99]

Some of the commodities which entered Russia, despite restrictions, in Peter's reign reflect a certain 'modernization' and widening of horizons for some of the population at least, a continuation of trends noted in the seventeenth century. In some cases these commodities excited protests from traditionalists: for example, tobacco, which was associated with the work of the devil and was forbidden by previous monarchs. In 1697 edicts on the tobacco trade allowed its open sale on the grounds that people had been trading secretly and depriving the treasury of revenue.[100] Some of the items imported for royal use were good pencils and ale from England,[101] wines and olive oil from a French merchant ship which docked at St Petersburg,[102] velvets and brocades from France and Italy, coarse cloths, linens, and wool from England and Holland, silks from China. But foreign goods also filtered through to a wider public. In 1723 the foreign merchant Joseph Dasser requested permission to import and sell a list of items which includes books on mechanics, architecture, and drawing, prints, mirrors, knives, fans, scissors, paints, beads, spectacles, ink-wells, teaspoons, shoe-laces, belts, tooth-brushes, combs, wood and alabaster figurines, tobacco pouches, and telescopes.[103]

Peter was anxious to escape from dependence upon other countries' flags for transporting Russian goods. An order of 31 January 1723 on the sale of rope abroad states: 'Export such goods on Russian ships and make sure that whatever the selling price of such ropes, the capital be returned to Russia.'[104] Instructions to Russia's ambassador to Spain in August 1723 expressed fears about interference from foreign merchants, especially the French, Dutch, and Italians, who would sell cheaper than the Russians, 'simply in order to impede the Russian commerce which is beginning, then later they will raise the prices of their goods'.[105] Peter was willing to sell Russian goods cheaply in order to break into markets: witness, for example, his 1723 decree on trade in cloth.[106] In 1723 an agent was sent to Paris to negotiate the sale of goods 'for our best interest', either for gold or silver or in exchange for 'good French wine'. He was to find out which Russian goods could be sold direct to France and to report back as soon as possible so that cargoes could be prepared: 'Take good care that the merchants of other nations, for example English, Dutch and any others who have trade with France, do not interfere in the undertaking of that trade by tampering with prices.' Again, the concern was to set up direct trade (*priamoe kupechestvo*).[107] Peter's preoccupation with conducting trade for cash rather than barter is indicated by a hand-written note in his papers for 1723, to the effect that 'we should buy more for money than we exchange for goods'. The published edict in which these words appear advocates increased trade with France, Spain, and Portugal in such products as oil, fruits, nuts, and saffron.[108] But barter was regularly used. In May 1722 an agent was sent to Hungary to buy wine, and was ordered to take exchange from the Siberian office: 1,000 bales of nankeen, 440 wolf (skins), 100 sheep skins, 50 puds of aniseed (*bad'iana*), and 20 pairs of sables.[109] Foreign trade interests extended eastwards, in the hope that Russia could be an intermediary between Western

Europe and Persia and China, and that trade could be diverted via the Caspian, where Peter had extra confidence because of his new sea power.[110]

The so-called window on the West policy is conventionally associated with trading interests. Yet, notwithstanding the received wisdom that St Petersburg was a key factor in advancing Russian trade (closer to Baltic routes and less ice-bound than Archangel, with its own shipyards, central government institutions, and so on), in reality, it proved difficult to get it going. In 1718, 41 foreign ships visited St Petersburg, but Riga saw 171 in 1713 and 238 in 1721, and Narva, 72 in 1721.[111] Reval and Pernau also received more shipping. But there were worries about Russian goods going through Danzig and Hamburg.[112] Attempts to promote the trade of St Petersburg at the expense of Archangel were problematic, because existing transport networks and other support services were geared towards the older port. The insistence upon St Petersburg had serious diplomatic implications, forcing Dutch and English vessels to risk possible attacks from Swedish ships in the Baltic, rather than taking the longer but safer White Sea route. In 1714 twenty English and twenty-four Dutch ships were seized by the Swedes, which prompted Britain in 1715 to send a squadron into the Baltic to protect its merchant vessels.[113] At the same time, Governor P. A. Golitsyn in Riga was instructed to maintain trade 'as it was formerly, so that the merchantry does not suffer any disadvantages in comparison with previous practice but it should be preserved in all respects as it was under Swedish rule'.[114]

Compulsion was necessary to force trade away from the old, northern Dvina route, as well as other Baltic ports. Russian leather and hemp from Smolensk *guberniia* were to be routed only through St Petersburg, not Riga or Archangel, although there were no such restrictions on other goods, such as grain.[115] Port duties at Archangel were made 25 per cent higher than at St Petersburg.[116] Weber cites complaints about the effects of re-routing on the hemp trade in 1715. Everything in St Petersburg was said to be five times more expensive than in Vologda, where hemp was customarily prepared and sent to Archangel. There were warnings that hemp in storage would spoil in the St Petersburg climate, not to mention the dangers of shipping by the Baltic.[117] Strahlenberg's list of the disadvantages of St Petersburg includes its distances from many provinces, the high costs there, and the ruin of merchants in Siberia, Perm', Viatka and Iaroslavl'.[118] Even so, Peter kept a strict eye on breaches of the rules. In 1724, for example, he ordered checks on illegal trade out of Archangel and the arrest of offenders, who were to be brought with their goods to St Petersburg.[119] There were attempts to make St Petersburg more attractive to foreign ships. In April 1722 the Senate was instructed to speed up the court cases brought by foreign or Russian skippers in the colleges during the navigation season: 'Set aside everything else and deal with their cases as quickly as possible lest you delay their sailing and thereby drive foreigners away and ruin our own people.'[120]

Russian merchants proved resistant to being remoulded, despite forced resettlement, especially in the area of foreign trade. Only a few individuals succeeded. Most maintained a 'passive' role, collecting or distributing goods on behalf of foreigners, who continued to dominate external trade. Russians had little capital and no systems of insurance or quality control. The capital (credits) for foreign trade and ancillary services (insurance, shipping, and brokerage) was supplied by foreigners. Russians' main strength was in retail and wholesale trade within Russia and on export commodities. Merchants were probably right to be cautious. Non-landed property was not protected by law. There was competition from peasants and nobles as well as foreign traders, not to mention 'the psychological impact of their own sense of economic dependency and social inferiority'.[121] The failure of the Russian merchant class to thrive under Peter has posed a problem for Soviet historians, because of the need to demonstrate that the 'national bourgeoisie' was formed at that time. Foreigners remarked on the huge state interest in trade and the impossibility of merchants getting rich. 'Not one Russian merchant, however rich he might be, will ever become a major figure,' wrote Grund, 'but will always live only in a wooden house with poor furniture in order that some boyar shouldn't take his property, for the boyar will always find a pretext and the opportunity to make his case before a judge, just as the tsar also treats the boyars if they abuse their wealth or show reluctance to carry out his commands.' The picture is of a hierarchical society with checks downwards on the amassment of power and wealth.[122]

There were attempts to reduce the State's share of trade. By 1719 only two commodities (resin and potash) were still state monopolies.[123] Despite the fact that internal trade was limited by the agricultural subsistence economy and the small non-rural population, there was a lively internal market which common sense suggests could not be state-run.[124] Traded goods included cloth, ironware and tools, salt, alcohol, hides and woollens. There was some specialization of village crafts, such as Ivanovo linens. The main mechanisms for distribution of goods, both wholesale and retail, were fairs or bazaars, the bigger ones attracting buyers and sellers from a wide area. Minor fairs fed major ones (such as the Makarevskaia at Nizhny Novgorod), and vice versa in June to September (when waterways and roads were passable). St Petersburg became a gathering point for flax, hemp, tallow, furs and forest products for export, and the main point of entry for luxury goods, foreign cloth, and dyes. Moscow was the main market for manufactured goods. There were no full-time retail stores in the country or even in small towns, because there was insufficient trade outside markets to support them. The State took a hand in regulating this internal trade: for example, through the work of the *Pomernaia izba* in Moscow on standardization, which included checking weights and measures for grain against the 'eagle' measure (state brass standard weights of *osmina, poluosmina,* and *chetverik*) and collecting duties from the sale of grain.[125] Internal duties were exacted from all traders, especially those who previously traded rent-free (*bezobrochno*) by selling from carts or river transport on unassessed squares and quays (as opposed to rented stalls). A decree of 1704 lists a wide array of goods which were sold in town markets: wax, honey/mead, canvas, sheepskins, furs, flax, hemp, potash, caviar, Russian leather, raw skins, tallow, pitch, tar, silk, cloth, brass, tin, lead, iron, tin-plate, mica, glass, foreign wines, berries, currants, grapes, prunes, walnuts and hazelnuts, olive oil, butter, foodstuffs for fast-days, dyes, dry-salter's wares (*moskotilinye*), sturgeon gristle, roots, salt, and fresh fish—all taxed at four copecks per wagon.[126]

V.   INDUSTRY AND MINING

Among Peter's achievements, the growth of industry and mining figure prominently, constituting, in the view of one study, 'an abrupt economic leap ... equal in significance to the industrialization of the Soviet period' and opening 'a new chapter in the economic history of the country'.[127] The two dozen or so factories in operation when Peter came to the throne had grown to almost two hundred by his death.[128] Of course, one must appreciate the limits of 'industrialization' in a pre-industrial age, and bear in mind the vital statistic that the vast bulk of the Russian population continued to be engaged chiefly in agriculture, a fact that held good until the 1930s.[129] The fallibility of figures must also be borne in mind; there are 'no proper statistics to measure the speed of industrial growth during Peter's reign, let alone what happened to national income during the period'.[130] What can be reiterated with some confidence is Kliuchevsky's assertion that war was the 'lever' for most Petrine activity. New industries and factories were created, and old ones given a new lease of life by the demands of the army and navy for weapons, ammunition, transport, uniforms, and other supplies. The fact of Russia's being at war for twenty-one years in a row was crucial, creating regular demands for a co-ordinated range of commodities, as opposed to the hap-hazard 'bring it yourself' philosophy of the old cavalry mobilization or the 'make it yourself' approach of the strel'tsy. At the same time, the urgent demands of war allowed little leisure for carefully planned industrial projects, still less any chance of waiting for the 'natural' growth of Russian capital or free markets. The State was the number one producer and the number one customer, and its needs were urgent.

At end of the seventeenth century Russian enterprises included ironworks at Tula (the Vinius–Marselis enterprise), Serpukhov, Tikhvin, and Ustiug. More widespread were small-scale cottage industries: for example, linen and flax in the Novgorod, Pskov, and Smolensk regions, salt and leather in Iaroslavl', Nizhny Novgorod, and Ustiug. Mining was poorly developed. Given this state of affairs, when Russia went to war with Sweden in 1700, adaptation and 'recycling' by royal decree were the order of the day—hence the renowned melting down of church bells after the failure at Narva in 1700. A lesser-known example of 'make do and mend' dates from March 1707, when Peter ordered B. P. Sheremetev to have a consignment of bayonets made in Lithuania, telling him to obtain iron, if none were available by normal channels, by demolishing the houses and other stone buildings of local residents hostile to the Russians. A few weeks later Sheremetev replied from Ostrog that orders had been issued to the regiments to look for iron struts in houses, but so far there had been no reports of finding any, 'since in the buildings here struts are mainly made of wood'.[131]

Peter tried to stimulate mining activity. Previously mines came under a number of separate *prikazy*, according to location or end use. The Mining (*rudokopnyi*) department set up in 1700 to encourage the extraction of precious metals was dismantled in 1711 and re-established in 1715.[132] In 1719 the Mines and Manufacturing college was established (in 1722 a separate *manufaktur-kollegiia* was created) to supervise mining works and all other crafts and their establishment and increase and, in addition, the artillery (of which its president Bruce was head). Its functions were set out in a charter, the *Berg-privilegii* of December 1719:

> Compared with many other lands, our Russian state is blessed with large quantities of useful metals and minerals, which have not till now been mined with much diligence; since they have not been exploited as they should have been, much benefit and many profits, which could have been obtained for us and our subjects, have been lost. We acknowledge that the main reason for this has been partly that our subjects have not understood mining and what can be done with it for the good of the State and the people and partly also that they have been unwilling to take the risk and invest money and labour for fear than once these mining works are established and making good profits they will be taken away from their owners. ... [Therefore] all are allowed and each and every one is permitted, whatever his rank or dignity, in all places, both on his own land and on that of others to excavate, smelt, found and refine all types of metals.[133]

The charter makes it clear that the mines themselves belonged to the Crown and that a tenth of profits must come back to the State. It also underlines the weakness of private property rights. Owners of land on which another person excavated ores had no redress if damage was caused, but could claim a share of the profits. Not surprisingly, there were frequent clashes between landowners and their stewards and prospectors.[134]

A prime aim of the College of Mines was 'to provide and maintain [the tsar's] Armies out of his own Stock, without any Aid or Supplies from foreign Countries'.[135] To this end, other home industries were promoted. The Manufacturing college was the main base for industrial organization of state enterprises and the supervision of individual enterprise. Its regulation (3 December 1723) sets out its main methods and ideas.[136] Georg Grund and other foreign observers painted a rather negative picture of 'artificial' new industries based on imported raw materials: hosiery from Persian silk, mirror glass from Berlin, Polish woollens, and so on.[137] Peter insisted on setting up woollen mills in Moscow, to make army uniforms, but, as John Perry recounts, home-produced fleece was of poor quality: 'Russ wool ... is very short, and as coarse almost as Dog's Hair.'[138] Sheep were imported and raised in the south. On the other hand, Russian flax, of good quality, was not fully exploited, linen cloth for shirting being produced in widths of about 20 inches, which was regarded as uneconomical. 'The Russes still obstinately persist in their own Way, and will make their Cloth to [sic] narrow for any Use.'[139] In 1715 Peter issued a decree outlawing this 'wasteful' practice, but the cure proved worse than the disease, forcing out of business many weavers without the funds to replace their looms or with insufficient room to accommodate the bigger new ones, and eventually it had to be revoked.[140] Footwear provides a good example of ideology clashing with practicality. Lighter German-style boots were unsuitable for Russian conditions; even so, boots made with nails and staples were banned, and merchants selling them were threatened with hard labour.[141]

The textile industry came under pressure from the army and the navy. Western dress reforms also created a demand for cloth to replace old clothes with new, even though some recycling took place. New wool and linen industries sprang up to supply the army, and silk manufacture for the nobility, both for dress and for furnishings. There was work for tailors, cobblers, hatters, and milliners.[142] New silk manufacturers drew on French and Italian expertise.[143] In November 1724 a proposal for a huge project for making Italian silk was submitted by Andrei Kassis to the Manufacturing college. It includes an interesting comparison between the Russian and the Italian character: the latter are described as 'economical ... when they receive wages or some other profit they hold on to it tightly and don't spend it rashly'. Russians were said to be altogether less thrifty.[144] A wide variety of foreign craftsmen were employed, such as the English tanner Thomas Humphreys, who in 1720 complained that he could not meet the targets for skins if the drying process were to be properly completed 'according to the English way of doing things'. In a letter to Makarov he said that he had been put under excessive pressure, and 'not allowed time to make suede leathers for His Majesty as they should be made'.[145] Some textile factories came under the direct patronage of the tsar: for example, the linen mill at Ekaterinhof, whose employees enjoyed special favours, including gifts for weddings (dowries of 5 roubles each).[146] The main factory for sailcloth on the Iauza River in Moscow, founded in the 1690s, employed more than a thousand workers by 1719.[147]

St Petersburg provided a new site for industries but created problems and demands of its own. For importing raw materials and technicians, the Baltic route was shorter than the Archangel route, and had a longer navigational season, but the new capital was not ideally situated in relation to internal resources: there were no ore deposits in the region and little water power; local conifers were good for masts, but not for planking; and so on. The first enterprise to get under way in St Petersburg was the Admiralty wharf, begun in 1705. By 1709 it had 900 workers, in 1713, 10,000, working in forges and workshops, sawmills and ropeworks.[148] This and other enterprises, including the artillery works, set the pattern of state-owned works operated by 'possessional' (i.e., requisitioned) labour. Other St Petersburg industries included woollen cloth (calamanco); the State Rope Factory (run privately from 1722); leather works for footwear, belts, pouches, and harnesses (1718); gunpowder factories, including a plant on the Okhta River using water power; and cartridges.[149] A number of factories—*kazennye zavody*—came under the direction of Peter's Cabinet office.

The lack of local ores prompted the development of the Olonets region on the shore of Lake Ladoga, where Peter had learned that there were copper and iron deposits during a trip to the White Sea in 1702. New factories were opened: the Alekseev works (near Lake Telekin), Povenetsky (on the River Povenchanka), Vichkovsky (at the mouth of Lake Onega), and in 1703 Petrovsky zavod (present-day Petrozavodsk), specializing in heavy cannon, shells, and anchors. In 1707 the Konchesersky smelting works was built. But the low grade of local ores and the depletion of timber supplies (it cost ten times more to process iron here than to process the pig iron of Urals) soon led to the curtailment of state operations, and many of the factories were turned over to private enterprise. In 1718 the Olonets factories had 42,244 male workers, in 1725 only 15,835.[150] The Urals had better supplies of good, easily workable ore (discovered in the 1620s), as well as abundant timber and water power. Existing small iron foundries were expanded, from the 1690s, under the direction of Andrei Vinius, head of the Siberian chancellery, starting with the ore seams at Magnitogorsk. A copper foundry was also set up. All enterprises used ascribed (forced) labour (recruited from state peasants, as many as 30,000 workers by the 1720s). They were linked to St Petersburg by the Vyshnevolotskaia water system. Metals represented by far the greatest achievement of Peter's industrial drive. By 1725 Russia was the major producer in Europe of iron, of which 60 per cent came from the Urals.[151] The problem was that the Ural factories were able to thrive only with the guarantee from the State of servile labour and access to forests and mines. There was no competition and no incentive to improve techniques. Only a tiny fraction of profits was reinvested.

Roads and transport were another significant growth area. Improvement in the Russian transport network was one of Peter's highest priorities.[152] The 450 miles of the Moscow–Pskov road were improved and supplied by peasants doing carting services, as were the Kharkov and Smolensk roads. A 1723 project called for roads to be built on the Swedish model, and canals, sluices and locks on the Dutch.[153] Canals were planned for military purposes, starting with the south (the Don–Volga canal, never completed), then the north, with the aim of linking the Volga and the Neva systems. Other canal projects included the Ivanovsky Canal (from Moscow to Voronezh, 1702). The Azov and Caspian Seas were joined. Some projects were completed by the most primitive mobilization of resources. In 1705 the authorities sought to obtain materials for paving the main streets of Moscow by ordering peasants to supply one stone an arshin in circumference per ten households (or fewer if only smaller stones could be found) and deliver them in winter with other supplies. Anyone entering Moscow before winter was ordered to bring 'three unhewn rocks no smaller than a goose egg' and to hand them over to officials at the city gates.[154] Evidently this did not produce enough materials: in 1705 serf owners and merchants were instructed to prepare a quantity of stones and sand based on the number of the serfs they owned, or on the value of their business, and store them in their Moscow yards.[155] Similar methods were later used to build the harbour at Reval. These developments were a drop in the ocean given the vast expanses of the country. As Pavlenko points out, the instructions issued to *voevody* in 1719 to 'keep all the winter and summer roads in good repair and order, also to set up milestones on the road to the sea and in the steppe to avoid all accidents and difficulties to travellers' was clearly a 'fantastic' task.[156]

One of the chief ways of acquiring new industrial technology, tried and tested by Peter's predecessors, was to hire foreign craftsmen. Getting the right men sometimes proved difficult, as a result of the reluctance of potential employees to come and of their governments to let them go. In order to attract foreign industrialists, Peter favoured the seventeenth-century pattern of granting tax-free concessions for a given period on condition that Russian craftsmen were trained. But there were a number of disasters. In 1709 William Lloyd appealed to take over glassware and pane production in the glass works on Sparrow Hills in Moscow (founded in 1705 and doing badly) at his own expense for ten years, promising to train twelve Russian apprentices. He was granted a monopoly to build other factories and to sell the wares all over Russia. But the factory burned down in 1713, and was not rebuilt.[157] Peter offered generous incentives, including 2,000 peasants and the order of St Andrew, to encourage the British banker John Law to build towns and villages on the Caspian and set up factories and a commercial company. Unfortunately Law's bank collapsed, and he fled to Brussels before the invitation was even sent.[158]

VI. RUSSIAN CAPITALISM AND MERCANTILISM

In the Soviet Marxist–Leninist scheme of Russian economic history Peter's reign was a watershed. Put simply, the capitalist process was 'speeded up' by Peter's efforts 'to flee from the frame of a backward economy'.[159] In an earlier era, Slavophiles and Westerners alike clung to the same 'tenacious myth', namely, that Peter transformed the economy by will alone, introducing large-scale industry, encouraging mining, and so on. Where they did not agree was in their estimation of whether capitalism was 'progressive' or not. Other commentators have accused Peter not only of failing to stimulate capitalism in Russia, but even of delaying its development. A. P. Spunde wrote that Peter 'so strengthened the feudal class and so weakened the inevitable growth of the bourgeoisie and bourgeois relations that the Russian nobility, which at the beginning of his reign had almost entirely exhausted its inner resources, was able to retain its monopoly of power for another 200 years'.[160] Anisimov writes: 'Coercion remained a constant component of the Petrine "New Economic Policy" ... What had happened amounted to a shift not of principles but of emphasis in commercial-industrial policy ... In the system of bondaged industry there was no room for the development of capitalism (and consequently for the formation of the bourgeoisie).' Anisimov argues that Peter *weakened* individual enterprise by increasing 'the overriding role of the State in the life of society as a whole'. He 'enslaved' merchants who were restricted by monopolies, enforced settlement in St Petersburg, high taxation, and reliance on state commissions. Although there appeared to be a change of policy after 1719 or so, with more encouragement of private enterprise, extension of mining rights, transfer of state enterprises, and the granting of loans, the State still retained its leading role by using its right of confiscation, distributing treasury orders (mainly military), and leaving little room for the open market. What was missing, Anisimov argues, was competition. The creation of serf manufactories was 'a reversion to feudal norms'.[161] Ia. Vodarsky argued similarly that Peter did not lead the country on the path of accelerated economic, political, and social development, did not force it to 'achieve a leap' through several stages. On the contrary, his actions 'put a brake on Russia's progress and created conditions for holding it back for one and a half centuries'![162] Some Western historians adopted this line even earlier, for example, Gerschenkron who wrote: 'Wage or no wage, the labour was essentially a coerced, forced labour, created as an industrial labour force by the fiat of the State.'[163] Most factories and mines actually looked like fortresses with guards. Forts had to be built to defend Siberian factories. The managers were forbidden to take on fugitives, and the poll tax was deducted from workers' notional wages.[164]

Did the State play a disproportionate role in Russian economic life? Did it promote or suffocate the Russian entrepreneurial class? There can be little doubt that it was Peter's intention to foster the spirit of individual enterprise by transferring 'his belief in the possibility of a *perpetuum mobile* (one of his pet projects) into the area of social and economic relations'.[165] He wrote: 'It is necessary both to compel and to provide aid in the form of manuals, machines and other items and thus be a good steward'.[166] The 'other items' included, crucially, the right to buy serfs for factories (from 1721), for how else were new entrepreneurs to staff their factories? The task of 'creating' a capitalist class (which could hardly be achieved in one fell swoop) was hampered by limited social mobility and the shortage of free labour. Simone Blanc traced these problems back to the 'surplus' labour problem of the sixteenth century, when a rise in the price of agricultural products led to pressure on peasants by landowners, which in turn caused peasants to flee. Many ended up in the Urals, where, together with itinerants, beggars, and other dispossessed persons, they could be assigned to factory work. The demand for rents also led to peasants selling their labour. In other words, the industrial workforce was supplied by fugitives (*beglie*) and 'free-lance' workers (*otkhodnye*), neither of whom were free. In order to meet *its* needs and the needs of the nobility, the State had to outlaw flight, as enshrined in the 1649 *Ulozhenie* and other edicts, which cut the number of surplus workers. The feudal lords won, and potential manufacturers lost. Peter believed that free labour was more productive, but it was scarce, hence the decree of 18 January 1721 giving the right to factories (although, strictly speaking, not to individual entrepreneurs) to buy villages.[167] This decree did not result in an immediate take-up, perhaps because there was a demand for labour more skilled than that of serfs, and the purchase of 'souls' required capital outlay.[168] Owners were more likely to hire seasonal workers, and benefited as much from the March 1722 ban on the removal of 'fugitive' workers from industries as from the right to purchase serfs.[169] It should be noted that state-run enterprises needed no such legislation. State peasants were routinely assigned to factories.

Sometimes Peter was exasperated by non-co-operation. He tried to farm out cloth manufacture to individuals—'if they won't do it willingly, then by force'—in order to end dependency on foreign sources for cloth for uniforms within five years. This led to merchants being transferred by decree to Moscow.[170] Apparently the measure was unsuccessful. Such companies as were formed quickly folded. An example dating from 1720 demonstrates the principles. The Moscow cloth factory was to be turned over to a company of merchants headed by Vladimir Shchegolin, 'and the maintenance of that factory is to be entirely by their own funds and they are to put effort and labour into that manufacture, in order to increase production ... in order that in a few years import of textiles from overseas might cease'. To aid them, a ban was imposed on the export of wool from Russia; an interest-free loan of 30,000 roubles was granted for three years; and orders were secured from the Uniform chancellery and the Admiralty at fixed prices (the surplus to be sold freely), together with a guarantee that the factory would not be taken away from the Shchegolins or their wives and children 'as long as they keep it in good order'. They were exempted from billeting. They could take lawsuits directly to the College of Mines. Governors and other officials were forbidden from 'hindering' the enterprise, on pain of earning the sovereign's 'wrath and punishment'. The factory was to take apprentices for seven years, 'and see to it that Russian people (*Rossiiksii narod*) study that craft with diligence', not only for the benefit of the company owners, but also for the state benefit. It was acknowledged that foreign expertise was vital, 'for in Russia manufacture has only recently been introduced but already with God's help we can see how some work-loving and assiduous Russian people have learned how to spin and weave the wool for that manufacture, although they are not yet familiar with how to dye and glaze and press and iron, to sheer the cloth and process the nap'. For the time being, some dyes would have to be imported, but it was hoped that eventually Russian dyes too could be produced without the need for imports.[171]

Kahan concluded that the Petrine period 'laid much groundwork for future economic activity', including its infrastructure (roads, canals, plant) and skills. He identified a number of areas of continuity in the post-Petrine period, including self-sufficiency in the arms industries, government encouragement of industry and commerce, and the transfer of enterprises to private ownership (the debate went on).[172] It may well be that Anisimov and Vodarsky, faced with the new post-Soviet capitalism, overestimate the 'freedom' of the so-called free market, and equate capitalism with complete lack of state control, whereas many of the problems of the new Russian capitalism stem precisely from the lack of such things as quality and safety controls, consumer legislation, and so on. Those who question Peter's achievement tend to argue that he shackled those subjects who were half way to being 'capitalists'. Peterson writes: 'The liberties previously enjoyed by merchants and manufacturists were replaced by detailed state regulation and monopoly rights granted by the State which obstructed the development of an expansive capital and commodity market. The burden of taxes on Russian businessmen increased so much during this period that no capital could be accumulated for future investments.'[173]

Even if Peter did have to 'manufacture the manufacturers', within this framework there were successes, with many Russians proving to be far from reluctant 'capitalists'. There were increased numbers of applications for manufacturing charters or 'privileges' in the 1720s, which entitled the holders variously to shares of lands and forest, exemption from taxes, liberation from other forms of service (e.g., army draft and carting), to loans and subsidies.[174] Success stories included that of Nikita Demidov, who started out as a Tula smith, established foundries in the Urals and was ennobled in 1720. The Privileges of the College of Mines (1719) and Regulations of the College of Manufactures (1723) ('all the economic policies of Peter's reign are contained in these two ... documents'[175]) recognized the autonomy of business and industry, not just as offshoots of some other activity but also for their contribution to national 'glory'. The Mining college employed a number of very able administrators, such as Wilhelm Henning and Vasily Tatishchev, who encouraged enterprise in Siberia and the Urals. The subsequent failure of 'Russian capitalism' to keep pace with its Western counterpart cannot be attributed solely to anything that Peter either did or did not do.

Another long-running debate revolves around whether Peter was a mercantilist. Soviet economists tried to prove that he was not (it was deemed inadmissible at that time to speak of direct imitation of the West in economic affairs), whereas a number of Western scholars have argued with certain reservations that he was. 'Protectionism and the setting up of a favourable monetary or commercial balance', wrote Blanc, 'were the result of a policy which, national in aim and mercantilist in method, aimed at endowing Russia with an autonomous economy and with as varied an industry as possible.'[176] Gerschenkron believed that Peter was faced with 'the standard mercantilist situation'—the task of raising the country's potential to an appropriate level.[177] This could suggest creating a unified economic area *within* the State, establishing standard weights and measures, abolishing tolls on roads, improving communications and reforming currency. 'The very magnitude of the effort, its vigour, amplitude, and persistence endow Peter's reign with unique features. Nowhere else in the mercantilist world do we encounter a comparable case of a great spurt, compressed within such a short period.' But it was 'mercantilisme sans doctrine',[178] since the basic 'building blocks' for mercantilism, as understood in the West, were missing or under-developed in Russia. Peter was a 'proto-mercantilist'.[179]

There was certainly surprisingly little borrowing of Western economic and accounting terms and concepts: of some 3,500 new foreign linguistic borrow-ings, only about 24 were remotely connected with 'economics'.[180] The first protectionist tariff was issued only in 1724. Even if one assumes an industrial growth of at most 8 per cent (based on the estimated figure for pig iron, which reached the highest rate), in Kliuchevsky's words, 'the State grew fatter and fatter and the people grew leaner and leaner'. Under Peter, the mercan-tilist system, if it existed, was created by the State as a result of the country's economic backwardness. Indeed, those elements of mercantilism which *were* adopted may actually have retarded Russia's development. Patterns designed to allow Russia to 'catch up' actually forced Russia away from the West. 'If human freedom is one criterion of civilization, then Russia was becoming less civilized as—*and because*—it was aspiring to move closer to Europe.'[181] In the end the policy paid off. Economic success, although crude and unsophisti-cated, tipped the balance, and allowed Russia to win the war against Sweden, in contrast to some earlier wars (e.g., the Smolensk campaign of the 1630s), where running out of money forced unfavourable peace terms. In Fuller's words, 'The Petrine military economy ... produced not copious abundance but rather marginal sufficiency.'[182]

6

Peter's People

The wealth of the realm

I. ORDERS OF SOCIETY

Early modern Russian society was composed of categories, or 'orders', to which virtually all persons could be assigned, although historians have often disagreed about the origin of those orders, the appropriate terminology with which to describe them, and whether Russia was a *Ständestaat* in the West European sense, in view of the lack of corporate entities enjoying inalienable rights.[1] Suffice it to say here that it proved possible for Peter to tamper with the orders of Russian society from above and to move individuals or groups from one category to another. The classic formula recognizes just three 'orders': those who fight (servicemen), those who work (taxpayers), and those who pray (churchmen); but finer distinctions can be drawn by identifying four: priestly, serving, trading, and agricultural.[2] The 'priestly' category encompasses secular and monastic clergy and 'church people' (e.g., their off-spring and non-ordained churchmen); the 'serving', all other categories of the non-tax-paying population, including not only the nobility and non-noble civil officials, but also all armed servicemen (who were removed from their previous social category by conscription); 'trading', the townspeople, including craftsmen; 'agricultural', the peasantry. Most foreign nationals belonged tem-porarily to the service class, while non-Russian subject peoples owed both tax and service. The government constantly battled to extract either service or taxes or both from fringe groups of evaders: fugitives, shirkers, dissidents, schismatics, and vagrants. When all else failed, there existed the category of *raznochintsy*, or 'people of other ranks', the most difficult to define.

No accurate population data exist for the first twenty years of Peter's reign, and the census (first *reviziia*) of 1719–23 counted only tax-paying males. These totalled 5,722,332 peasants and a taxable urban population of just 230,910 males, 3.6 per cent of the total.[3] There were no contemporary figures for nobles. Estimates suggest figures of just over 15,000 men in 1700, rising to 37,326 in 1744.[4] Kahan calculates a total male population in 1719 of 7,791,063, of which 7,126,135 were taxable citizens. Put another way, the taxable popu-lation accounted for 94.13 per cent of the whole. This barely changed throughout the century (cf. 1762, when it was 97.37 per cent).[5] Women were not counted at all, but on the assumption that as many females as males were born and that the relative perils of warfare and hard labour as against child-birth meant more or less equal populations of the sexes, this gives a total population of something under 16 million. Estimates for 1719 give a total population of 14.9 million in Russia proper, 500,000 in the Baltic, and 100,000 non-Russians in Siberia. Of these, 13 million were peasants, and 600,000 townspeople, while landowners, clergy, and military personnel accounted for 1,300,000.[6]

Although Peter's policies are famed for limiting social mobility and assigning people to categories to ensure that everyone fulfilled their obligations, one should bear in mind Elise Wirtschafter's useful thought that Russian society was 'fragmented and porous', and that 'social status ... was fundamentally indeterminate and changeable'.[7] The most 'porous' of all was the urban–rural divide. Throughout the eighteenth century, a large percentage of town-dwellers were in fact peasants, and the chief occupation of most town-dwellers was agriculture.[8] The interests of the State encouraged some social adjustment. Merchants who ran industrial enterprises were permitted to become serf owners (1721); younger sons of nobles were encouraged to take up a trade or profession (1714); and non-nobles could be ennobled by achieving a commission in the Table of Ranks (1722). The most important case of social mobility was that of serfs who exchanged tax-paying for service status as a result of conscription into the armed forces. There were also numerous cases of 'downgrading' whereby previously non-taxable persons found themselves paying the poll tax, which will be considered below.

The following analyses take as case-studies peasants and workers and nobles (with a detailed examination of the Table of Ranks). Church people will be examined in a later chapter. Townspeople were considered earlier with reference to the Chief Magistracy (1721) and economic policy.[9] Examples will be drawn mainly from the territories that Peter inherited, including Siberia and Ukraine. No attempt will be made to examine populations incorporated into the Empire in the course of Peter's reign—Baltic Germans, Latvians, and Estonians—or to look at Cossacks and tribespeople. Most women, who neither served nor were directly assessed for taxes, were classified according to their fathers' or husbands' status. In no sense did they comprise a social 'order', which may in part explain why they have been neglected in most studies of Peter's reign. The final section of this chapter is devoted to them.

II.   PEASANTS AND WORKERS

During Peter's reign the great mass of the population were the 'ploughing peasantry', a situation that continued well into the twentieth century. The 1678 census (the last one before Peter's reign) registered 906,101 peasant households, of which 435,924 belonged to noble serf owners, 148,997 to churches and monasteries, the rest to the Crown and the State. It is a moot point whether some of these peasants were serfs and others not. Kahan classifies all Russian peasants as serfs, on the grounds that all, including state peasants, were bound by obligations either to individuals or institutions and mobile only by someone else's authorization (be it a landlord's travel document or a government conscription order), but the word 'peasantry' remains a useful generic term.[10] Peter's first census (1719–23) gave a total of 5,722,332 male peasants, of whom 3,193,085 belonged to noble landlords (*pomeshchich'i*), 1,227,956 to the State (*gosudarstvennye*), 791,798 to the Church (*tserkovnye*), and 509,484 to the Crown (*dvortsovye*).[11] There were finer divisions within these categories. A general census of Moscow district (*uezd*) carried out in 1704 distinguished between peasants on hereditary and service lands (*votchinnikovy* and *pomeshchikovy*). Agricultural and household slaves and landless labourers are also mentioned.[12] By 1723 the difference between service and hereditary estates had disappeared, as had slavery as a separate status. The 'patchwork quilt' of state peasants (a term coined at this time to designate peasants who did not fit into other categories) included such diverse groups as peasants in the far north, Siberia and on the Volga, some single-homesteaders on the southern borders, and Kazan' Tatars.[13]

It can be argued further that all peasants belonged to the sovereign, regardless of their provisional owners, in the sense that the Crown had first call on their revenues and labour. 'Landowners do not own their peasants in perpetuity,' wrote Ivan Pososhkov; 'hence, being but temporary owners, they do not treat them with much care. The true owner of the peasants is our Sovereign, Autocrat of All Russia. Therefore it behoves the landowners not to ruin them but to take care of them in accordance with the Tsar's commands, so that our peasants should be proper peasants and not paupers. For the wealth of the peasantry is the wealth of the realm.'[14]

Received wisdom (underpinned by most Soviet writing) teaches that the great mass of the ploughing peasantry were impoverished and downtrodden, a view apparently confirmed by many contemporary accounts. Charles Whitworth, for example, wrote: 'The peasants are perfect slaves, subject to the arbitrary power of their lords, and transferred with goods and chattels: they can call nothing their own ... A couple of earthen pots, a wooden platter, wooden spoon and knife, are all their household goods; their drink is water; their food oatmeal, bread, mushrooms and roots, on great days a little fish or milk, but flesh very rarely.'[15] Leaving aside the true extent of Whitworth's (and other foreigners') knowledge of Russian peasants, it is probably true that most peasants had few possessions and lived on a simple diet. But it should not be assumed that the institution of serfdom meant that peasant lives were not valued. On the contrary, peasants had a high value both to their owners (as chattels to be sold or as payers of rent and agricultural producers) and to the State (as taxpayers, army recruits and labourers). The problem is that State and estate owners were often in conflict, with the interests of the former frequently taking precedence over those of the latter.[16] After Peter's death the pendulum swung back slightly towards landowners. A memorandum submitted to Catherine I in 1725 by Menshikov and a group of top administrators argued that peasants were being ruined, which was disastrous, because 'the soldier is linked to the peasant like the soul to the body, and if there is no peasant there will be no soldier'.[17] Although this may be interpreted more as an appeal by the landowners for a greater share of peasant 'wealth' (with a chance of success now that Peter's iron rule had gone) than an expression of humanitarian concern, it is still instructive.[18] That was the problem: how could all claimants to a peasant's output get their fair share while still allowing the peasant to satisfy his and his family's basic needs? This dilemma became particularly acute under an active, expansionist, demanding regime like Peter's, in a country where there was a wealth of land, but of relatively low quality, and a dearth of manpower.[19]

Peter himself was well aware of a peasant's value. In amendments to a translation of *Georgica Curiosa*, a seventeenth-century agricultural treatise by A. von Hohberg, he produced the formula that 'agriculturalists are the arteries of the state and just as the whole human body feeds through an artery, so does the state on the former, for which sake they must be conserved and not excessively overburdened, but rather protected from all attacks and ruin, and servicemen (*sluzhilye liudi*—i.e., nobles) in particular should treat them decently'.[20] The cameralist notion that the well-being of the State depends on the well-being of peasants (i.e., that the latter should be sufficiently prosperous to render their dues to the State) appears also in the law on single inheritance of 1714, which argued that constant division of estates placed excessive burdens on the serfs. Instructions to *voevody* (1719) warned them to look out for 'certain vile persons who are themselves the dissolute ravagers of their own villages, who, as a result of drunkenness or some other dissipated behaviour, do not provide for their estates or protect them but instead destroy them, imposing upon the peasants various intolerable burdens and also beating and torturing them, as a result of which ill-treatment the peasants abandon their tax obligations (*tiaglo*) and run away, which causes depopulation (*pustota*) and a growth in the shortfall of state revenues from taxes'.[21] Similar fears were expressed in the instruction (1719) to the *Kamer-kollegiia*, which was to ensure 'that between the high and the low and the poor and the rich, according to proportion, there is an appropriate likeness, and that no one is burdened, or alleviated more than another person. ... For if that happens, the hard-pressed poor will leave their farms and cultivation and the state revenues will diminish greatly in time and the lamentations of the poor will bring God's wrath upon the realm.'[22] The *Kamer-kollegiia* numbered among its tasks discouraging the abandonment of farming land, for depopulation meant loss of revenue.

It was certainly envisaged in theory that the bulk of the population should share in the 'common good'. Peter's speech at the Nystad celebrations in 1721 declared that 'it is necessary to toil for the benefit and profit of all ... to bring relief to the people'; or, in Prokopovich's formulation, among the fruits of peace must be the 'diminution of the people's burdens'.[23] Peter himself was not totally indifferent to the sufferings of individual members of the 'masses'.[24] But overall the 'common good' was an abstraction, 'not called forth by any humanitarian considerations, but . . . dictated entirely by the need for revenues with which to maintain the governmental apparatus'.[25] Only one piece of legislation, issued on 15 April 1721, attempted to limit abuses: 'It was the practice in Russia, and still is, that petty nobles sell peasants and agricultural and household serfs separately to whomever wants to buy them, like cattle, which is not done anywhere else in the world, all the more when a serf owner sells a daughter or a son apart from their family, their father or their mother, which causes much distress. His Imperial Majesty orders that such sales be stopped, and if it is impossible to stop them completely, only if necessary should whole families be sold, but not separately.'[26] This edict could not be implemented, and in practice did not end individual sales of serfs.

There has been some speculation about whether Peter might even have abolished serfdom, given different circumstances.[27] Weber made an intriguing remark: 'The Czar was once advised to abolish Slavery, and to introduce a moderate Liberty, which would both encourage his Subjects, and promote his own Interest at the same time; but the wild Temper of the Russians, who are not governed without Constraint, was a sufficient Reason for rejecting the Proposition at that Time.'[28] Perhaps Weber had in mind the report of Foy de la Neuville (the only source) that in the 1680s Prince Vasily Golitsyn had produced a scheme for limiting, if not abolishing, serfdom.[29] But for Peter serfdom was one of several institutions through which the State satisfied its demands. Far from reducing serfdom, he increased its effectiveness by further limiting mobility and drawing more people into tax-paying categories.[30] In particular, the introduction of the poll tax made it even harder for peasants to change their location or status. Many categories of person who previously had paid no taxes were made liable to pay the poll tax. *Odnodvortsy* (single-homesteaders) had to pay the same tax as the peasants, but in addition (because they did not pay rent or work for owners) had to perform duties in, or contribute to the upkeep of, hussar units.[31] Ordained priests, who were service- and tax-exempt, were distinguished from unordained members of the church estate (*tserkovniki*), who were included in the tax census returns.[32] 'Superfluous' sons of priests for whom no living was available were to be registered for poll tax and turned into serfs of the nearest landowner.[33] Itinerants (*guliashchie liudi*), children of church people, soldiers' children: all were registered for tax.[34] An edict of 23 October 1723 provided for the elderly and disabled to be accommodated in almshouses, but for stray orphans ('who don't remember who they previously belonged to') to be sent as sailors if over ten years old, or be turned over to an owner in perpetuity (*v vechnoe vladenie*) and registered for poll tax—in other words, to become serfs—if less than ten. Freed slaves (*kabal'skie liudi boiarskie*) were also to be registered for the poll tax, which in most cases led to their being reduced to the status of serfs.[35] Slavery as a separate institution disappeared, the main reason being that limited contract slaves owed no taxes or services to the State and enjoyed the right of manumission upon the death of their owner. Such loopholes were anathema to Peter.[36] Another category that Peter tried to redeploy was that of household serfs (*dvorovye liudi*), many of whom were transferred into the army or navy. But top men could sometimes get permission to maintain staff. In 1724 Pavel Iaguzhinsky was granted permission to keep one of the slaves of the disgraced *ober-fiskal* Nesterov (others had been sent to be soldiers) as he had 'a considerable need for more servants'.[37]

The issue of passes for peasants was mentioned in instructions to *voevody* in January 1719 as part of the provincial reform, and in October 1719 it was declared illegal for peasants to travel from town to town or village without a pass (*proezzhee*).[38] An edict of 6 April 1722 required peasants going to towns on business to obtain permission from their landlords or village elders in the form of 'maintenance papers'.[39] In 1724 the requirement was formalized as a passport. 'Wandering' people were a major irritant. This was an old problem. Edicts of 1691 refer to people of no fixed abode (*prishlie i guliashchie liudi*), such as wagoners, victuallers (*kharchevnye*), and kvas-sellers, living in various settlements in Moscow without proper papers (*bez poruk i bez poruchnykh zapisei*) and engaging in crime.[40] Another edict referred to those 'who bind up their arms and legs, pretend to be blind and lame ... and with deceptive cunning beg for alms, but on inspection they turn out to be well'. Such fraudsters were to be ejected from the towns and villages, and if they reappeared in Moscow, were to be flogged and transported to Siberia.[41] Peter fought an unsuccessful battle throughout his reign with able-bodied beggars. The Ecclesiastical Regulation included a long clause supporting the campaign against 'sluggards in perfect health'. Anyone feeding healthy but lazy beggars was described as an 'accomplice' in the impoverishment of the fatherland.[42] This campaign was defeated partly by circumstances (the war created many more beggars, both fake and real), and partly by Orthodox ethics, which approved of better-off believers giving alms and succour to the needy, as enjoined in the Gospels.

It is easy to present the life of the mass of the population solely in terms of exploitation and abuse. But peasants were not wholly without rights. They chose their own village elders (*starosty*) and crown officials (*tseloval'niki*); conducted lawsuits in their own names; made contracts, albeit with restrictions (e.g., in 1704 church and monastery peasants were forbidden to enter into government contracts without permission). It was very difficult for a serf legally to change his status by his own volition, but not impossible. He could volunteer for military service, although this required the lord's permission. By an edict of 4 February 1714 peasants were allowed to trade if they paid both merchant and peasant dues. In 1723 they were allowed to register in an urban community (*posad*), but had to continue paying poll tax and rents to their lords. Peasants were by no means totally mute and passive. In January 1716, for example, the peasants Sofron Obival'ny and Nikifor Teliakov petitioned the Senate: they had come to St Petersburg 'in fear of their lives' to complain against their lord, Prince Semen Semonovich Gagarin, whom they accused of harbouring two deserters and a fugitive ship's carpenter, of torturing

Obival'ny's brother, of illegally distilling liquor, and of stealing several peasants from Crown lands. They also accused the master and his brother Ivan of
evading service.[43] Occasionally a peasant might even gain the ear of the tsar,
despite laws forbidding direct appeals. In May 1722 Anton Ivanov complained
in Peter's presence that the village elder and his friends had insulted him,
demanded excess taxes, taken his son and nephew as recruits illegally, and
ruined him. Peter called for an investigation and for 'cruel punishment' if
they turned out to be guilty. The chief culprit was to be sent to St Petersburg
for hard labour.[44] Peasants sometimes sided with the authorities and took
revenge on their owners by reporting them for 'word and deed' crimes. The
case of Klim Evtifeev (1704) against his owner Chirikov resulted in the arrest
of most of Chirikov's family, although the testimony proved to be false. In
1705 peasants accused a nobleman named Pavlov of wishing Peter dead. The
accusers were forced to admit that they were taking revenge for the fact that
Pavlov had flogged them with lashes and sticks.[45] The Preobrazhensky *prikaz's*
trial records show that 47.5 per cent of cases concerned peasants expressing
discontent with the existing order, notably through complaints against their
owners, but also in general against increases of tax burdens and recruitment.
'The years have become hungry but taxes are great and now an edict has
arrived to take a rouble per household for pork fat. But we have no profitable
enterprises (*promysli*) and God knows where we are to find the means to pay.
And carpenters have been taken from us and transferred to Voronezh to permanent residence and as a result in the district some houses are empty.'[46]
Peasant grievances frequently expressed a general sense of injustice: 'If we did
not exist, he, the sovereign would not exist, either.' 'The sovereign has conquered many towns, but there are no concessions for the peasants' (1720).[47]
They also voiced religious and ideological concerns: for example, in response
to rumours about the tsar's 'German' behaviour and alleged change of faith
(variously to 'Muslim', Swedish or Latin). Tales circulated of the tsar's capture
and replacement by a German impostor.[48]

Just how badly off were the peasants under Peter? The Marxist–Leninist
view of all peasants as victims has long been suspect. Indeed, it was occasionally challenged even by Soviet historians.[49] Kahan, as we saw, questioned the
assumption that 'the introduction of the poll tax led to an increase in the
burden of the Russian serfs'. Scholars have begun to construct a more subtle
and more complex model of the relations between the State, lords, and peasants, which takes account of mutual dependency, regional variations, and
periods of greater and lesser hardship.[50]

The question of relative freedom is also complex. Tax avoidance loopholes
were cut off, passports were introduced, and recruiters and labour requisitions
could appear at any time. Many persons and institutions governed the lives
of peasants and serfs, who were the property of their lords and subjects of the
sovereign, subject to Christian laws, the customs of the commune, and the
patterns of the agricultural year. Just one area of peasant life in which lords
might take an active interest was serf reproduction: fines were imposed on

single people, compensation was demanded from those who married outside the estate, and arranged marriages were quite usual.[51] Yet one could argue that the mass of truly 'agricultural' peasants who escaped conscription into the army or forced labour actually enjoyed more freedom than many of Peter's subjects. Central government was remote—even more so when it moved to St Petersburg—and local government, as we have seen, was undermanned, rather than overmanned, and suffered from a shortage of competent officials. Peasants were relatively unaffected by cultural reforms as long as they stayed out of towns. They had more chance to flee and permanently disappear in a manner which must have been nearly impossible in Western Europe. During Peter's reign most landlords other than the very young, the very old, and shirkers were absent from their estates on service. The Church, it is true, was expected to supervise its parishioners and inform them of government decrees; but it was hardly within the power (or inclination) of the parish priest to police the activities of every peasant, and parish priests as a class do not seem to have enjoyed high status among the peasantry. Even so, the religious calendar and custom were strong determinants of the structure of peasant life and behaviour, governing such matters as dress, diet, entertainments, and rites of passage, while the village community and village élites imposed more effective moral and physical restraints than outside agencies.[52] Perhaps most influential of all was the environment. 'For the overwhelming majority in eighteenth-century Russia, the rhythm of life was not determined by wars, the reforms of Peter the Great, or by anything his successors managed to accomplish or fail in, but by the conditions affecting the agricultural cycle of plowing, planting and harvesting'.[53]

The low output–seed ratio of grains so characteristic of Russia left a narrow margin between sufficiency and starvation. Peter's reign saw a number of crises: a cold winter in 1704 killed the winter crop; there was a particularly severe winter in 1708–9; 1716 saw excessive rainfalls in the Moscow region; and in 1721–4 crops failed for four years running, leading to very high grain prices.[54] The last years of Peter's reign were particularly difficult. A memorandum written by Iaguzhinsky in 1725 records that

> the growth of bread grains has been meagre for several years and the soul tax is becoming a heavy burden since (i) runaways, the dead and those who have been taken as soldiers have not been excluded, (ii) the very old, invalids and children who cannot work have been included in the same tax, and the poll tax has been collected in cash, for which reason the peasants in such time of crop failure are not only forced to sell horses and livestock, but even their seed grain, and they themselves must suffer hunger and the greater part of them are such as have no hope of being able to feed themselves in the future and a great number of these have already died of nothing else but hunger ... and a large number flee to the Polish border and to Bashkiria, against which not even the border posts help.[55]

The peculiarities of the Russian agricultural year governed the structure of peasant existence. In the winter months peasants were busy with home crafts (making sandals, spinning, and so on), in the early spring with repairs to buildings and equipment, then ploughing and planting (oats, hemp, flax, millet, and garden vegetables in April to May, in June buckwheat and barley, in August winter rye), and harvesting and haymaking. Other seasonal tasks included gathering firewood, spinning and weaving, picking mushrooms and berries, hunting and fishing; nature provided rich pickings at the cost only of labour. Despite the fact that there were local differences, other generalizations can be made about the way of life of the Russian peasantry. Peasants lived in small villages or hamlets (which in the seventeenth century averaged just five households) in cottages made of wood, which also accommodated farm animals. The cottage was dominated by the stove, above which everyone slept. Men's outdoor clothing was a coat reaching to the knee, a shirt with a girdle, a cap, and bast (birchwood) shoes. (According to Weber, even peasants were obliged to abandon their long coats, although they were not expected to adopt Western fashions.[56]) Women wore variations on the shift (*sarafan*) and over-tunics. For special occasions festive clothing, decorated and embroidered according to regional traditions, was worn. And so on—space does not allow further detail. Indeed, information relating specifically to the Petrine era is scarce.[57]

Given the vital importance of agriculture to the mass of the population, and hence to the government, one might have expected Peter to take an interest in it. According to anecdote, he did. 'Agriculture was one of the most important objects of the wise Russian Monarch's concern,' recorded Stählin. 'Wherever he could note something serving to improve it or something in general relating to the economy, he gave all his attention to it.' Apparently on journeys through Holland and Germany he often got out of his carriage to inspect farms and talk to peasants.[58] But this concern was not reflected in legislation. In fact, agriculture and husbandry were among the weaker areas of Peter's activity, with just a 'series of rather fragmentary and disconnected government efforts to improve agricultural methods and productivity'.[59] Peter is accused of 'underestimating' the economic potential of agriculture and paying little attention to its improvement.[60] When he did take an interest, it tended to be related to industry and equipment, as, for instance, in the famous decree on scythes (1721)[61] and orders on sheep rearing in Ukraine (15 June 1724): 'for the good of our whole state we have set up cloth factories ... since God has blessed Little Russia with better air for the propagation of sheep than other regions of our state'.[62]

Can this uncharacteristic lack of interventionism be explained by the fact that Peter regarded the peasants as a hopeless case? Peter's response to the information in Heinrich Fick's memorandum of May 1718 that in Sweden peasant members played an active role in parish councils was: 'there shall be no parish bailiff nor anyone elected from among the peasants in the courts', one reason being that 'there are no clever [i.e., educated] persons among the peasants in the districts'.[63] Weber observed (as did most foreigners) that 'their

Minds seem so darkned [sic], and their Senses so stupiefied by Slavery, that though they are taught the most obvious Improvements in Husbandry, yet they do not care to depart from the old way, thinking that no body can understand it better than their Ancestors did'.[64] Yet there is something to be said for customary techniques which ensured survival from one generation to the next and in good years a little bit extra. During Peter's reign the internal market for Russian grain increased, as did flax and hemp production for export. The fact that 'none of this owed anything to the tsar and his activities'[65] indicates that agriculture operated smoothly enough of its own accord, and that Peter saw no need to interfere in age-old practices which fed the population except in crisis years. In this respect, he would have been of one mind with other contemporary rulers who left peasants and agriculture to take care of themselves.

Foreigners' reports indicated that food was plentiful in Moscow, at least. Korb (1699) describes markets 'overflowing with fresh meats. ... Everything that one could wish for was to be had.'[66] A record of foodstuffs served to Patriarch Adrian and his guests in the year 7205 (2 September 1698 to 31 August 1699) gives a taste of traditional fare: large pies (round with apples, oblong with onions), small pies in gravy, cold mushrooms with horseradish, prunes, kasha, cabbage soup, peas and kisel (thickened fruit gruel); for Christmas, fresh perch in brine.[67] Of course, it would be wrong to equate the patriarch's table with the peasant's (and both examples above relate to the period before the Great Northern War), but these items were supplied by peasants on the patriarchal estates. With the exception of some imported foreign products for the tables of the tsar and some leading nobles, eating habits seem to have changed little during the rest of Peter's reign.

There is no space to discuss Kahan's hypothesis any further. It is worth bearing in mind, however, that Western scholars have tended to be more influenced by Marxist ideas about exploitation than they care to admit. We may take for granted that Russian peasants were uniformly oppressed and *hungry*, but the evidence of population growth suggests that domestic agriculture (given little importation of food) was sufficient to sustain it. Kahan argues, too, that the large amount of non-agricultural activity engaged in by peasants was not just a response to below-subsistence levels of production, 'soil exhaustion', or huge taxes, but a reaction to the pull of the market, which encouraged peasants to produce income differentials.[68] One man's 'flight' from the intolerable was another man's move to earn extra cash. For example, money rents (*obrok*) to landlords were preferred in areas where serfs could make a wage—for instance, by working in river transport services or in the textile industry. Market forces during the early eighteenth century had an impact not only on grains (wheat) but also on flax and hemp, livestock products (tallow, hides, meat), and forest products, in all of which peasants had a share. In other words, we gain a distorted picture if we regard peasants only or even chiefly as victims.[69]

This approach may profitably be applied to the issue of peasant flight, the main way in which peasants evaded their obligations. An order from the tsar to Prince Iury Vladimirovich Dolgoruky in 1707 gives the flavour of countless such cases:

> It has come to our attention that artisans and peasants of various service and hereditary lords from Russian border towns and others of our towns, from the artisans' quarters and the rural districts, not wishing to pay the usual money dues and leaving their former trades, are fleeing to various settlements on the Don, and especially from those towns from which workmen are sent in rotation to Voronezh and other places. And having taken large sums of money on account in advance of their work, they run away with their wives and children and hide on the Don in various settlements; and now many are fleeing and committing robbery and violence. However, the Cossacks of the Don settlements do not send back these fugitives but keep them in their homes.[70]

Was this mass flight born of desperation, or was it evidence of a pioneering spirit? What were they fleeing from? Sadistic landlords and cruel bailiffs were not unknown, but neither was violence from fellow peasants. Violence among themselves was a staple ingredient of peasant life. In 1725 the landowner N. G. Stroganov sent instructions to his steward:

> It happened in the past and still happens at the present time that the wealthier and propertied peasants try to give themselves a break, to burden the poorer ones and their children with equal payments of the poll tax and rents. They base their calculations on sheer numbers rather than the volume of property they possess. Poor peasants all come in force to provide their labour either for the government's tasks or for the transportation duties, while the richer ones send only one member of their household. Therefore I order you to act as follows: all government taxes ought to be collected according to the commune's distribution of duties. The commune will assess the payments according to the revenues derived from crafts, commerce, land and from all other activities, and also according to quantity of personal possessions, not according to the number of 'souls' so that the poor will not be overburdened.[71]

In this case, the inherent injustice of the poll tax was being exploited by richer peasants at the expense of the poor. The document makes the point graphically: distribution of poll tax payments among peasants was not decided by the government but left to serf owners, who were endeavouring to correct injustice in consultation with the communes.

There was no firm distinction between peasants and 'workers' in Peter's reign, which saw an increased demand for a non-skilled, non-agricultural work-force. Shipbuilding, industry, mining, construction, transport, and services associated with the Northern War all created 'the bottomless pit' in which, to quote Weber, 'innumerable Russian subjects perish and are destroyed'.[72] Much of the work was done by labour conscripts (*prinuditel'nye*). State peasants and townspeople owed labour services as a matter of course, and, as we shall see, various sources of unfree labour could be exploited. But Peter believed that free labour was more productive. An interesting decree dating from 1720 refers to the problem of maintaining the work-force for constructing the canal at Lake Ladoga, one of Peter's pet projects. Henceforth 'no one engaged on that canal work is to be subjected to bondage (*nevolia*) or insult'. Workers were assured proper payment and the right 'to leave work by their own volition unrestrictedly'. Local officials were warned not to impede volunteers for the work (*okhochie liudi*).[73]

Carpenters, too, were needed in vast numbers. There were plenty of men with traditional Russian woodworking skills, but availability was another matter. In February 1703 Peter wrote to Fedor Golovin from Voronezh: 'I have to inform you that we have a terrible shortage of carpenters here, because by God's will men have been ill and are falling ill, and many have even died. Therefore please immediately gather 600 men from Vologda, Iaroslavl', Kostroma, Galich and other places and send them here. Otherwise, everything will be held up, *is* already being held up.'[74] A list of craftsmen required by the Admiralty drawn up in October 1714 included 1,449 carpenters, and a note to the effect that half should be recruited from Olonets, the rest from northern towns such as Vologda, Kholmogory, and Ustiug, including 500 from the sons of priests and deacons, 'and other lower orders of young literate persons'.[75] Despite such efforts, in September 1716 the Admiralty reported that there were 'considerable delays in shipbuilding works for a lack of carpenters and workers'.[76] In June 1723 Vice-Admiral Zmaevich was still complaining that not one of the 300 men required for building a flotilla of galleys and other craft on the Don near Voronezh had arrived, neither had any free carpenters been hired or soldiers assigned, although a number of bakers, tailors, and others had been assigned as carpenters. Not one plank had been cut from the list of requirements sent by the Admiralty, even though the timber had been prepared.[77]

Finding workers with even basic skills was always difficult. In 1719 a search was ordered in the Petrozavodsk area for 300 literate young men to be apprenticed in weapon making. Only two 'church people' and sixty peasants were found in Olonets, of whom nine ran away, 'and since many of the smiths are already very old and dying off and since the numbers have not been made up', guards officers were requested to round up recruits. 'Without this nothing will happen.'[78] Peasants hired themselves out, but often only on a seasonal basis. As one linen factory director stated, 'in the winter they work, but in summer they go off to their villages to their own work and as a result there is a great stoppage in our enterprise'. About fifty looms were unmanned.[79]

The bottom line in the work-force were people who could be deployed without formalities or pay, such as convicted criminals and debtors. Such people were also used to populate new towns.[80] In 1701 a priest was sentenced to death for making his spiritual son tell lies. The 'son' was flogged with the knout, and sent to Azov 'in perpetuity'. In the same year it was decreed that debtors of non-boyar noble rank (from *stol'nik* to *dvorianin*) were not to be bound over to their creditors (*golovoiu ne otdat*) but sent to Azov to do hard labour with their wives and children.[81] In 1701 the icon-painter Luka Ivanov from the Armoury and his accomplices and their families were exiled to Azov, convicted of counterfeiting stamped paper.[82] In 1703 the death sentence for criminals with multiple convictions for robbery without murder was commuted to flogging with the knout, branding, and banishment to hard labour in Azov, which also played host to army deserters who gave themselves up.[83] Peter could transfer people at will. In 1722 some 300 families were taken from Siberia (as chosen by the governor) and sent to work in the Daurian silver mines.[84] St Petersburg, as we shall see, also had to be populated by a mass transfer of population, although Peter was more reluctant to fill his 'Paradise' with criminals. A 1716 list of artisans transferred from all parts of the country included coach-builders, wheelwrights, coppersmiths, taylors, potters, goldsmiths, bookbinders, candle-makers, swordsmiths, saddle-makers, turners, carvers, joiners, locksmiths, cobblers, fishermen, painters, and icon-painters.[85]

The galleys were a favoured destination for wrongdoers. In 1705 it was specified that only traitors and murderers were to be executed. All others were to be flogged, branded, and sent to the galleys. Recidivists were to be identified by being branded on the forehead, and the wound was to be rubbed with powder, 'so that the marks are visible on those criminals until their death'.[86] In August 1707 Peter wrote to Alexander Kikin, noting that work on the curtain wall connecting the bastions of the Peter–Paul fortress had stopped for lack of labour; therefore, 'for this work use galley prisoners, since this summer has gone by quietly with no more work for the galleys; and also add some crown bondslaves (*kholopei gosudarevykh*), so that at least the foundation of the curtain, which is urgently needed, can be laid by autumn'.[87] Vagrants and beggars were another useful source: for example, 21 per cent of the work-force in the factories of Moscow, Iaroslav', and Kazan' in the 1730s formerly belonged to this category.[88]

Additional workers could be bought. In December 1711 Peter ordered the governor of Kazan', P. M. Apraksin, to buy horses from the local tribesmen, and in the next breath to buy a couple of thousand of the prisoners who had just been taken from among the Kuban Tatars, at a price of five roubles or less per head and only to take those who were fit for work, neither the very young nor the very old.[89] Just being tall could be reason enough to be taken from home and family. In May 1722 an order was issued for tall men to be conscripted from all classes except the clergy and sent to the War college, presumably for employment as bodyguards.[90]

The social welfare of workers was not entirely neglected. Ivan Timmerman, director of the Moscow sail factory, for instance, submitted plans for building workers' accommodation (to have workers living near the factory, not *in* it, where they constituted a fire risk! The same document also proposed abolishing sick pay in order to stop false claims).[91] The Admiralty Regulation (1722) made provisions for hospital care, while in 1724 the Sestroretsk armaments factory installed a physician and a pharmacy. The widows of

Sestroretsk workers received a pension. In 1725 a hospital was attached to the Ekaterinburg ironworks.[92] In general, considerations of welfare were linked with maximizing the productivity of the work-force. In 1702, for example, Demidov received charters allowing him to 'mete out punishment to his workers' and to punish the lazy with lashes, whips, and irons. However, 'so that the workers will not flee the ironworks as a result of excessive cruelty, he should not cause unnecessary insult to the injured, for every offence, particularly when inflicted upon a poor man, is an unpardonable sin'. The formula of 'lazy people' was introduced into labour legislation by Peter, as in a 1706 order to the government gunsmith works in Tula to punish workers for 'laziness, drunkenness, insubordination and low quality production'.[93] The Admiralty Regulation charged overseers to ensure 'that the workers are working honestly and not just having a good time, and to beat the lazy ones with clubs'.[94]

In non-state enterprises a major impediment to manning new industries sprang from the conflict of interests between landowners and manufacturers. (This led Peter to decide in 1721 to allow factory owners to buy serfs, who were then 'attached' to the enterprise.[95]) There were numerous attempts to balance claims between the original owners or communes of factory workers and the new employers. A long petition written in 1722 by Ivan Tames, owner of a linen factory, complained that workers trained at great expense for seven years were being taken away and returned to their original owners, with the result that looms stood idle, the work-force remained static, and ultimately the State suffered. There are numerous such petitions about lack of manpower (*maloliudstvo*) in manufacture.[96] Decrees of 1722–3 stated that workers with obligations elsewhere were not to be sent away from factories, 'in order not to abandon those works and thereby stop the enterprise', but that they should pay their taxes to the State and former owners 'as before', and that factory serfs (*rabotnye liudi*) who had been transferred from elsewhere should be registered in their home villages, 'but should not be sent away from the factories against their will in order not to hold up production'. This applied also to peasants working in shipbuilding (*na sudakh*).[97]

III. NOBLES

The status of the Russian nobility was in flux when Peter came to the throne. Important changes during the seventeenth century included the erosion of the distinction between service (*pomest'e*) and hereditary (*votchina*) landholding and the abolition of the code of precedence in 1682, which hastened a new configuration of the élite. But as the system of rewards and promotions fluctuated, service itself was more than ever the defining characteristic of being a nobleman, even though the nobles themselves may not have taken this view. For the able-bodied there was soon to be no escape from lifelong compulsory service. For most this meant military service, starting as an ordinary soldier in the infantry, or in a guards regiment if they were lucky. Restrictions were placed on recruitment from the nobility into the civil service, limited to 'no more than a third of any noble (*shliakhetskoi*) family, in order not to deplete our land and sea forces'.[98]

The career paths of young nobles were determined at the *smotry*, or reviews (major ones were held in 1704, 1706, 1711, 1712, 1713, 1714, 1716, 1718, and 1720), which Peter often attended in person to decide the fate of the youngsters inspected.[99] In 1712, for example, a group of seventy-three young men was assigned to duties in Reval, Holland or the Preobrazhensky guards. One of those inspected, Vasily Vasil'evich Golovin, left a record of the occasion, in which he expressed his sense of powerlessness.[100] In February 1714 nobles were assigned to regiments from the age of thirteen. When called up, they had to serve in the ranks before being considered for a commission.[101]

For many a young noble the prospect of allocation to a field regiment or a journey abroad was a terrifying prospect. Noble absenteeism or 'shirking', like its peasant equivalent, runs like a refrain through documents of the period.[102] In November 1695 Moscow nobles were ordered to register their grown-up sons for service 'without concealment'. Failure to declare new recruits would result in demotion of families to the ranks of the provincial nobility and postings to 'remote towns'.[103] In a letter to Tikhon Streshnev in 1703 Peter wrote: 'I suggest that all shirkers who did not appear at your inspection with Boris Petrovich [Sheremetev] should report here on the feast of the Dormition [15 August] under penalty of death.' Anyone who failed to report was to be arrested and thrown into prison in irons, pending instructions, and their hereditary and service estates, houses, and belongings confiscated.[104]

Things did not improve in the post-Poltava period. On 28 January 1716 an order was issued for 'lists of the names of those adolescents who have reported for duty to be printed and distributed around the provinces and stuck up in the towns and main villages so that it can be seen who is missing and in hiding, to give people better information for denouncing them'. Informers would be rewarded with the villages and homesteads of the shirkers.[105] Informers came forward. In April 1716 one Ivan Plotnikov in Saratov reported that 'very many nobles and nobles' children in Kazan' and Kazan' province are living concealed in their homes and have failed to report for inspection in St Petersburg for either of His Majesty's reviews'. Others were getting themselves registered for garrison duty (a safer posting, usually reserved for the elderly and disabled). Plotnikov named names. He had to be given an armed escort from Kazan', but fear of retribution must have made him change his mind because he gave his guard the slip and disappeared.[106] Late arrival for reviews was also punished. In 1723 Alexander Tovarishchev and Ermil Miasoedov were initially threatened with the confiscation of their estates for missing the deadline, but this was commuted to a fine of 50 roubles per month for lateness.[107] Ivan Pososhkov, who was particularly incensed by disobedient nobles, cites cases of men who had 'never lifted a finger to serve His Majesty in any capacity', feigning illness or madness, giving bribes, sending substitutes, or simply hiding from inspectors, not to mention others who found lucrative sinecures in government service, evading the military service which Pososhkov deemed appropriate for 'vigorous young men'.[108]

The tsar kept a personal eye on the children of his favourites. In March 1707, for example, he approved the marriage of Boris Golitsyn's son Sergei, but stressed that he should not be allowed to spend more than a year in Moscow, but should be sent away to complete his studies, 'since he still doesn't know anything apart from the language'.[109] In 1709, when Fedor Romodanovsky appealed for his new son-in-law Vasily Sheremetev to be allowed to postpone his study visit abroad on account of being newly married, Peter complained that he had not even been informed of the boy's marriage, and therefore did not recognize that Romodanovsky had a son-in-law. The same day he gave orders for young Sheremetev's father Vasily Petrovich, brother of the famous general Boris Petrovich, to be demoted and condemned to hard labour building fortifications, and his wife, Praskovia Mikhailovna, to work in the spinning mills as punishment for allowing their son to marry before he had completed his education: 'Let them work as common folk do!' Young Vasily promptly left for Europe, and his parents received a pardon two months later.[110] Peter was angered by what he regarded as an attempt to use 'clandestine' marriage as an excuse to avoid further training. Orders were given to priests to refuse to marry anyone early in the morning or late at night on pain of defrocking.[111] Noble families, in the meantime, continued to regard the marriage of their offspring as their own affair, and were not above breaking the law for the sake of financial gain and prestige. In February 1715, for example, Peter Iur'ev complained that he had been married at the age of thirteen, 'which is not allowed according to the behest of the holy apostles and the rules of the holy fathers', and forced to sign a paper making over his estates to his new in-laws.[112]

Compulsory education for nobles was one of Peter's more radical innovations. In the seventeenth century such matters had been left to the discretion of parents, only a handful of whom (mainly those who had been exposed to other cultures by travel abroad or association with foreigners) educated their sons beyond basic literacy, if that. In 1696 the first contingent was sent abroad to study navigation.[113] From 1714 all nobles were required to receive some form of education between the ages of ten and fifteen (when service began),[114] but some were then selected for further education or training. Perry reported that 'whoever in his Countrey that is Master of an Estate to the Value of 500 Rubles per Annum, and doth not teach his Son to read and write, and learn Latin, and some other foreign Language, such a Son shall not inherit his Father's Estate, but the same shall be forfeited to the next Heir of the same Family'.[115] On 16 August 1707 Peter wrote to Tikhon Streshnev: 'On receipt of this letter select by winter good young adolescents, a hundred or more, for the [mathematical] school, and announce that all adolescents are to be ready for an inspection by winter, including those I have already inspected.'[116] But education was not a substitute for service, merely a preparation for it. A decree of 1723 stated that no noble should spend more than fifteen years in formal education.

Nobles were told not only where to serve and where to go to school, but also where to live. In 1714 a thousand families were ordered to move permanently to St Petersburg. The move was resented. Nearly all those concerned had estates and business to attend to in Moscow and elsewhere, and Senate records contain numerous cases of nobles making special appeals for leave. In February 1716 Prince Ivan Nesvitsky, who had been transferred to St Petersburg but retired from active service, reported that peasants on his Kostroma estate had burnt down his house and fled, and he needed to go there to sort things out. The Senate granted him leave, but on 7 March a supplementary order was issued by Peter specifying that Nesvitsky was to report back to the Senate chancellery by 29 July on threat of a fine.[117] Numerous such entries indicate that leave was granted only under supervision, although many petitions have notes attached offering excuses (usually life-threatening illness) for staying away beyond the deadline. Living in St Petersburg was expensive, as indicated in the appeal of the nobleman Andrei Maslov, who described himself as *malokrest'iannyi*—that is, owning only a few peasants (twenty-one households). He reported that he was living in St Petersburg 'in great hardship', and had little to eat because of his straitened circumstances and the flight of many of his peasants. He begged leave to visit Azov province and other places to try to get his peasants back and also to have food supplies sent to St Petersburg for the following year. He was given permission and the same warning as Nesvitsky. Maslov missed the deadline for his return, pleading that a 'near fatal' illness had delayed him and that about eighty of his peasants had died from fever.[118] But no excuse, however good, could long delay or interrupt the transfer of the able-bodied. An even worse case was that of Semen Agdavletev who wrote that he had lost the use of his arms and legs, had only sixteen meagre peasant households (*dvorishki*), and, living in St Petersburg, had run out of supplies and had nothing to eat; thieves had burnt his house, and he had suffered great losses. Even in this case he was allowed only the standard four months' leave.[119] In March 1716 Prince Ivan Shcherbatov asked permission to stay in Moscow for as long as he remained in charge of running the estates and mills of the late Lev Naryshkin, Peter's uncle, while the latter's heirs were still studying abroad. The resolution was that 'He, Prince Ivan, is to reside in St Petersburg without fail, as stated in his majesty's order'.[120]

Prolonged leave from service was a rarity. Families spent years apart. A series of letters from the army officer Ivan Ivanovich Buturlin to his daughter Anna gives a vivid indication of how heavily such absences weighed: 'I live in unceasing cares and difficulties,' he wrote from the Dnieper in 1711 and from Åbo in Finland in April 1714: 'If I live, I hope at last to see you in September.' He should have been with his family for Christmas 1714 ('God alone knows how much I long to be with you all'), but was delayed by duties at court: 'I desperately want to spend more time with you—this delay has cost us two weeks and four days.' In June 1715 he wrote to say that he had no idea where his winter quarters would be.[121] Many nobles were absent from their estates for years: for example, Brigadier Kropotov, who in 1727 reported to the Senate that he had not seen his Moscow estate since 1700.[122] Alexander Andreianovich Iakovlev left a laconic account of his tours of foreign duty: trips to Denmark and Holland via the Baltic countries in 1716; then to Vienna, via Frankfurt and Regensburg; returning to Holland via France, back to Holland by August, then immediately to Riga, via Berlin; then on to Helsinki, Åbo, and Sweden. Early 1718 found him on a short break in Russia (when he was sent to the Staritsky district to collect some 'large ancient human bones'), then on a secret mission to Berlin, back to Moscow by March, St Petersburg in April, followed by missions along the Baltic coast. He set out on a trip to Italy, but was ordered to return when he reached Berlin, arriving back in St Petersburg in December. In January 1719 he was finally given leave to go home for two months, after which duties resumed in similar hectic fashion.[123] After the peace of 1721 things became slightly easier. Noble infantrymen were given six months' leave. After 1724 leave was granted on a more regular basis.

Ultimately what distinguished the nobleman, be he petty squire or great magnate, from the rest of the population in Muscovite Russia were his rights of ownership over landed estates (immovable property) and serfs. In this area, too, Petrine nobles found themselves worse off than their predecessors. Peter's law on single inheritance, issued on 23 March 1714, went against all tradition, not so much by abolishing the distinction between hereditary property and service estates, which had already been severely eroded, but by outlawing the ancient custom of partible inheritance (dividing landed estates among all sons).[124] In the preparations for this legislation, Peter consulted foreign examples of entail: in March 1711, for example, he ordered the Foreign Office to collect translations of French, English and, if possible, Venetian law.[125] The tsar may also have been influenced by Fedor Saltykov's memorandum of 1713, which anticipated Peter's own reasoning in declaring that 'the younger sons, not having the family's immovable [i.e., landed] property, ought to choose service to the state or study of the sciences in order to attain high rank and wealth'.[126] However, Peter did not adopt Saltykov's advocacy of primogeniture or inheritance by the first-born (based on the English model, which Saltykov knew well). The law stipulated *edinonasledie*, or 'inheritance by one' (unigeniture). Immovable property (*nedvizhimoe imenie*) was to go to one heir only, normally the first-born son, but a parent could nominate someone else if the elder son was deemed unworthy. In the absence of sons, daughters could inherit. Single inheritance applied only to real estate. 'Movable' property—money, goods, livestock—was to be divided among all the children. The main aim was to avoid the wasteful fragmentation of estates, with the desired knock-on effect that those who did not inherit would seek their fortune in state service, although it should be pointed out that during Peter's reign service was compulsory for all males, whether they inherited an estate or not.

This law increased the State's interference in nobles' lives. Nobles now had less control than before over their own property. Although historians have generally discussed the law in the context of the nobility, who had most to bequeath, it in fact applied to all classes, 'whatever their rank and title'.[127]

Peter expected resistance from the nobles, and he got it. This proved to be one of the most unpopular of his laws. On 27 March he had copies of the new law sent to governors with a covering note telling them to report at once any cases which could not be resolved on the basis of the law and ordering that its sixteen clauses be strictly adhered to 'for it is usual for accursed informers to ruin all laws with their fabrications'. There were fears that landowners would backdate wills, pass off bequests as sales and resort to other forms of evasion.[128] A related example of state interference was the ban on inheritance by the mentally impaired (the blunt term used is *durak*, or 'fool'). An edict of 6 April 1722 gave instructions for identifying *duraki*. The rather crude procedure was to ask a number of questions on everyday matters 'which a sane person would be able to answer'. If the 'mad' estate owner proved unable to answer or started to talk about something else, this was to be taken as proof of imbecility (*durachestvo*). His estates were to be transferred to someone else, unless he were already married with children, although it is specified when the children should inherit.[129]

The right of nobles to buy estates was limited, with the aim of maximizing service. Nobles who had no inherited estates and wished to buy land were allowed to do so only after completing seven years' service in the military, ten in the civil service, or fifteen in trade. Anyone who had not served was forbidden to buy villages 'even unto death'.[130] The regular granting of land by the Crown also ceased. The old system of *verstanie*, whereby service nobles were automatically granted *pomest'e* when they entered service, based on previous allocations to their relatives, was abolished and replaced by salaries in cash (which sometimes remained unpaid). There are few examples of the common pre-Petrine practice of granting *votchina* lands to individuals or families as a reward. Medushevsky argues that, on the contrary, Peter strove to maintain the stock of state lands intact. The main exception being estates granted to Russians in newly conquered territories on the Baltic.[131] Estates were also awarded from confiscated property. In 1723 Ivan Cherkasov petitioned that he had served for eleven years in Peter's Cabinet office and had accompanied the tsar on military campaigns and missions, but had no landed property and had not been rewarded 'in the same manner as your other faithful servants'. Cherkasov saw a window of opportunity, estates confiscated from two convicted clerks. So had several others, including Egor Miliukov of the Semenovsky regiment, who pleaded 'abject want and poverty' as the reason for his application for a share of the confiscated properties. The petitions were granted.[132] In 1724 Under-lieutenant Peter Iunsen complained that he had accumulated large debts on account of his small salary and constant travels in foreign lands on His Majesty's service. He had been granted an estate in Livonia, which had been restored to the former owner after the peace treaty (of Nystad). Unless Peter helped, he would 'die of poverty'.[133] ,

The powers of the tsar over individuals were extreme. Nobles could be demoted on the slightest pretext, like Andrei Ivanovich Golitsyn, who was deprived of his boyar status for 'ranting' (*neistovye slova*) and sent to be a *syn boiarskii* of lowest rank and to live in the country until further orders.[134] Certain individuals and families enjoyed considerable power and authority, but there was no corporate representation, no consultation of the nobles as an estate. (When Peter did consult, as on drafts of the Table of Ranks, it was with institutions—the Senate, the Admiralty and the War College.) On the contrary, as Korb observed: 'It is the old habit of the Czars to sow and foster discords among their very magnates, whom they find it easier to oppress each and all with more security and under a greater mask of equity, when they are divided by mutual hate, and striving in savage plots to get the better of one another in accordance with the old law—*divide et impera*.'[135] Weber writes: 'As to the Nobility, though their Subjection to the Czars has been very great at all Times, it is much greater at present, beyond all Comparison.'[136]

A recent study asks: 'Can one call this bureaucratized, regimented nobility that was obligated to study in order then to serve and to serve in unlimited military and civil service ... the ruling-class estate?'[137] Previously ideology placed the burden of exploitation firmly on noble shoulders. In Kafengauz's words: 'In Peter's time the "common good" was understood to be the defence of the interests of the nobility and meant the cruel exploitation of the labouring masses.'[138] The facts show that under Peter the position of the nobility actually deteriorated. Many nobles felt not only oppressed by compulsory service and education, forced transfer to St Petersburg and the law on single inheritance, but also humiliated. There was resentment towards 'new men' and foreigners. Serf owners often felt themselves to be the losers in the competition with the State for the peasants' services—tax and service burdens on peasants swelled the numbers of fugitives and 'empty' estates—and from 1721 they saw the entitlement to buy serfs (although not 'ploughing peasants' and household serfs) extended to merchant industrialists. The nobles still employed the old rhetoric about being the sovereign's 'slaves', even though the term 'kholop' with which their seventeenth-century predecessors had addressed themselves to the tsar was replaced with the term 'rab'. As M. M. Bogoslovsky argued (on the grounds that the new term for serf was 'subject' (*podannyi*)), 'if slaves were called subjects, then subjects could be called slaves. These expressions were not empty forms of words; they corresponded entirely to reality.' He quotes the account of the nobleman A. P. Volynsky, who, when beaten by Peter with a stick, apparently said: 'Even though I suffered, I didn't suffer as much as I should have done, slave (*rab*) that I am, from my sovereign. But he was good enough to chastise me as a kind father chastises his son with his own hand.' He quotes also the case of Anton Devier who in 1727 was banished, among other things, for failing to show servile respect (*rabskii respekt*) to Tsarevna Anna Petrovna by remaining seated in her presence. Bogoslovsky concludes from this episode that 'the feeling of personal honour, essential to any Western aristocrat, meant little to a Russian noble in the late seventeenth–early eighteenth century'.[139] Clan honour remained strong, long after the abolition of the code of precedence: in 1691, for example, Prince Grigory Kozlovsky refused to attend a dinner at the patriarch's residence because of the inferior origins of his fellow guests, who included Lev Naryshkin (the tsar's uncle). He went to extraordinary lengths to avoid the invitation. When forcibly brought to the residence in a simple cart, he pleaded that he was too ill to go upstairs, at which point he was dragged from the cart up to the patriarch's chambers. Even then, 'the boyar lay on the floor for a long time and refused to sit at the table'. He was stripped of rank and demoted to provincial service, but later pardoned.[140] Another case of disputed honour was heard in 1693 when Prince M. G. Romodanovsky insulted S. S. Shein, beat him, drew his knife, tried to stab him and insulted his ancestors, father, mother, and grandfather. Shein retaliated by calling Romodanovsky a low-born and 'shabby princeling', and his father a 'shirker' (nesluga) and hit him with a stick. Both parties were punished for dishonouring the other.[141]

Peter attempted to instil a new 'knightly' ethos into the nobility by the establishment of orders of chivalry (St Andrew, Alexander Nevsky) and the Table of Ranks, to be discussed in detail below, which specifically recognized the honour owing to birth, unless there were strong reasons for disregarding it. Noble privileges were marked in various ways: for example, only the distinguished (znatnye) could be buried inside towns.[142] The size of site and type of building allocated to residents on Vasil'evsky Island in St Petersburg were determined by the number of serfs they owned; possessors of 700–1,000 peasant households, for example, qualified for a stone mansion on a ten sazhen plot. At the same time, recognition of status was accompanied by coercion. Residents in the Moscow district of St Petersburg were to transfer, 'and if anyone has failed to move by 1725 not only will their houses be demolished but the householders themselves will be sent forcibly to live on Vasil'evsky in common huts (chernye izby)'.[143] Information on family trees and coats of arms (a new departure for Russian nobles), as well as lists of nobles from birth to death, were stored in the office of the new chief herald (gerol'dmeister), established shortly after the Table of Ranks in 1722. But it was a dual-edged sword from the nobles' point of view. On the one hand, the office recognized noble honour through genealogy; on the other, it was another government agency to ensure they did their duty, including acquiring an education, which the chief herald was to supervise. He also added newly made nobles to the list, which was not popular with the older families.[144]

IV. THE TABLE OF RANKS

For much of Peter's reign the ranks used by his predecessors were still in use. The upper echelons of the Moscow-based nobility, as we know, aspired to membership of the boyar council. In the 1680s, when membership of the council swelled in order to accommodate supporters of the Miloslavsky and Naryshkin factions, many members performed a purely ceremonial role, but the old Muscovite hierarchy were still going strong in the 1690s. In 1693, for example, it was specified that the petitions and disputes of men of boyar rank would be heard in the Golden Chamber of the Kremlin palace, those of sub-boyar grades 'on the square by the Red Porch'.[145] But boyar rank was less and less frequently awarded, and then as a token of special respect; for example, the rank of *okol'nichii* was bestowed for the last time in 1711, upon *stol'nik* Alexander Iushkov 'for his many and extraordinary services', and he was entered in the register of boyars at the request of Peter's sister-in-law Tsaritsa Praskovia.[146] Surviving ranks died out with those who still held them. The last boyar to be created was Ivan Musin-Pushkin, in 1699, and the last boyar to die was Prince Ivan Iur'evich Trubetskoy, in 1750.[147] In 1705 there were twenty-three boyars, in 1718 only six. The signatories of Tsarevich Alexis's death sentence in that year included two boyars, one *okol'nichii*, and eleven *stol'niki*.[148] Even so, the term 'boyar' continued to be used in popular parlance long after Peter's death. Ivan Nepliuev in his memoirs refers to a feast given by Peter in 1721 'for all the boyars'.[149] Holders of Moscow non-boyar ranks tended to be referred to under the generic title *tsaredvortsy* (courtiers), while provincial servitors were lumped together as *gorodovye* (town servitors).[150] *Tsaredvortsy* continued to pull rank: for example, in a dispute in 1719 between a group of them and lesser-ranking (by their criteria) personnel from the Justice college, which prompted an edict reminding people that 'the old ranks (*razriady*) have been abandoned forever and instead we have glorious service without precedence (*bezmest'e*)'.[151]

The old ranks at first coexisted with, and were then superseded by, newer military, civil, and court ranks based mostly on foreign originals. Ranks such as general, major, and colonel, designating specific military commissions, had been in use since the 1630s in the new formation regiments of infantry and dragoons, but they were held along with the older ranks which all originated in civilian rather than military offices, producing such odd hybrids as table attendant-colonel. As late as 1712 a list of persons assigned to move to Kronstadt described them as boyars, *okol'nichie*, men of the duma, and privy councillors, table attendants, and so on, immediately followed by generals, brigadiers, colonels, and other newer military ranks.[152] An informal scale recognized equivalent ranks. An edict of 1692 established that the widow of General I. D. Lukin was to receive a portion of her husband's service estate on the same basis as the wife of a *dumnyi dvorianin*.[153] New ranks made their appearance piecemeal, civilian ones after Poltava, when Grigory Dolgoruky became actual privy councillor (*deistvitel'nyi tainyi sovetnik*) and Ivan Musin-

Pushkin *tainyi sovetnik*.[154] The offices of chancellor and vice-chancellor were created for Golovkin and Shafirov respectively on 16 July 1709.[155] New court grades were introduced after Peter's marriage to Catherine for use in the tsar-itsa's court, which, in contrast to Peter's largely military retinue, had functionaries with such German-sounding names as *ober-gofmeister*, *ober-shenk*, and *shtalmeister*.[156]

In 1721 Peter jotted in his notebook the words 'o rangakh'.[157] This heralded the publication of the famous Table of Ranks (*Tabel' o rangakh vsekh chinov*), signed on 24 January 1722 and printed in Moscow on 30 January.[158] The decree was the outcome of several years of planning. In 1719 Andrei Osterman had been entrusted with the task of gathering information. Osterman started with Muscovite court ranks, matching them with new German titles: for example, *striapchii* was equated with *gofmeister*. Foreign sources consulted included Frederick I of Prussia's regulations on ranks, the Danish statute of Christian V, and the Swedish of Charles XI. (Many names of offices, as we have seen, had already been borrowed from Sweden.)[159] English, French and Spanish examples were consulted, but were regarded as less appropriate to Russian conditions. Osterman eventually came up with a fourteen-point pro-posal *Ob"iavlenie o rangakh* based on court and civil ranks, but omitting military grades. Clauses 1–5 were taken (with amendments) from the 1696 Swedish statute; 6, 8–10, and 12 from the Danish of 1699. Clause 7 (8 in the final version)—the crucial rule that only service rank gives a person eminence in society, regardless of origins—is found in the regulations of Sweden, Denmark, and Prussia.

S. M. Troitsky argues that out of this Peter 'created a new Table of Ranks, in which he set civil and court offices in dependence upon the system of mili-tary offices'.[160] For a start, he added military and naval ranks to Osterman's draft. He crossed out some offices, added or re-graded others: for example, the chief herald (*gerol'd-meister*, keeper of registers of nobles in the College of Arms) went up to rank 5. Peter wavered about the hierarchy of military and civil grades, favouring the former. Only four of Osterman's clauses were left unedited. In Osterman's clause 10 (11 in the final version), on hereditary nobility earned through service, rank 6 was set as the qualifying grade, whereas in Denmark nobility was attained only on reaching rank 3. In the final version holders of rank 8 upwards were entitled to ennoblement if they were not nobles already. Peter also added a new clause (15 in the final version) regarding the children of new nobles, which strengthened the hereditary element. He raised the status of guards and artillerymen (placed two ranks higher than other branches of the service), and correlated years spent in edu-cation for nobles with years in service grades. The revised project was presented to the Senate for discussion on 1 February 1721. Some of its rec-ommendations on the grading of various offices were accepted—in some drafts, for example, the highest civil grade (state chancellor) was relegated to rank 2, whereas the Senate argued it should be in rank 1[161]—but their pro-posal for the inclusion of old Muscovite grades was rejected.[162] Menshikov's

War College and Apraksin's Admiralty also considered the project, the latter requesting the wider inclusion of naval grades. Further revised drafts were discussed in ten sessions of the Senate in January 1722.

The published table divides the services into three columns (reading from left to right): military (*voinskie*), civil (*statskie*), and court (*privdvornye*). The military column is further divided into four: infantry, guards, artillery, and navy. The vertical columns are divided horizontally into fourteen[163] classes (*klassy*), each containing a variable number of offices (*chiny*) for the different branches of the service. There are marked variations. The guards column, set two higher than the rest, for example, contains just eight *chiny*, starting at class 4 (colonel) and ending at 12, whereas court class 14 contains a plethora of *chiny*, including court librarian, head chef (*kukhenmeister*), and barber (*barbir*)! The most crowded grades are the civilian ones, sometimes a dozen or more *chiny* packed into one in order to accommodate newly created central and provincial officials. The layout made plain that one of the purposes of the table was to correlate status and identify seniority between different branches of service. The charts were followed by nineteen explanatory points (*punkty*).

There are still many misconceptions about this most important and enduring of Peter's reforms, the most widespread being that it demonstrated a firm commitment to 'meritocracy' to the detriment of lineage, or, even more radically, raised commoners at the expense of nobles. It has been argued that from boyhood Peter championed the principle of advancement by merit, insisting upon earning his own promotion through the ranks. Foreigners were impressed. 'By taking upon himself both a Post in his Navy, and in his Army, wherein he acted and took the gradual Steps of Preferment, like another Man,' wrote John Perry, '[Peter wished] to make his Lords see that he expects they shall not think themselves nor their Sons too good to serve their Countrey, and take their Steps gradually to Preferment.'[164] Russian contemporaries reached similar conclusions. Ivan Nepliuev's account of an audience with Peter in 1721 is instructive: the tsar forbade him to bow, on the grounds that he, Peter, had been placed there by God, and it was his duty 'to see that the unworthy receive nothing and that the worthy are not deprived; if you are good you will be good not to me but more to yourself and to the fatherland'.[165] These ideas were spread further after Peter's death in numerous anecdotes about the tsar's common touch.[166]

The insistence upon qualifications runs through Peter's recruitment policy. Instructions given to ambassadors Lefort, Golovin and Voznitsyn when they set out on the Grand Embassy in March 1697 state: 'Seek to hire good captains for naval service (three or four) who themselves have been sailors and were promoted to their office (*chin*) as a result of service and not for any other reasons.'[167] The same was to apply to hired lieutenants and second lieutenants. The principle was stated even more clearly and comprehensively in the 1705 manifesto on the hiring of foreign officers. A special welcome was reserved for officers who had 'earned their good reputations and experience not as a result of recommendation, acquaintaince or payment, but from active service in the field and have made themselves known for good action and experience necessary for war'.[168] But Peter was far from consistent. In 1698, for example, he awarded posthumous recognition to a loyal and efficient governor of the Siberian town of Nerchinsk (a rarity among a species more often accused of embezzlement and corruption) by making his son governor in his place, despite the fact that the latter was still a minor of, as far as one can tell, unproven worth.[169] Peter sometimes bestowed titles upon the incompetent as a sort of joke (e.g., the title of 'chief surveyor' upon Ivan Mikhailovich Golovin[170]). Many observers commented on the tsar's propensity to surround himself with unprepossessing orderlies and servants.[171] Qualifications could be squandered: for example, in the case of Ivan Nepliuev, who was put through a long course of naval training abroad only to be sent as ambassador to Constantinople in 1721.[172]

A closer examination of the document confirms that the Table of Ranks reflected these inconsistencies. Birth and marriage continued to confer privilege. Point 1 confirmed the precedence of princes of the blood and royal sons-in-law. Women were ranked according to their husbands or fathers, depending on marital status (points 7 and 9), but ladies-in-waiting held ranks in their own right.[173] Point 8 blends both principles: it concedes 'free access' to sons of princes, counts, barons, and the aristocracy (*znatneishago dvorianstva*) to those places where the court assembled 'before others of lowly office (*chin*)', but 'we wish to see them distinguish themselves from others in all cases according to their merit', and they would not be awarded any rank (*rang*) until they had shown services to the tsar and the fatherland. Point 11 conferred nobility equal in status to old nobles on those who reached rank 8, and made it hereditary. Point 15 put a further gloss on this: in the military lists, reaching rank 14 conferred these same privileges. Military ranks took precedence over civil ones. But certain civil offices were designated as temporary (point 17 lists them), conferring rank only as long as they were held. All new nobles had the right to coats of arms, while old coats of arms and patents of nobility were to be supervised by the chief herald (point 16).

The table was strict about qualifications for actual jobs. No office (*chin*) involving duties was supposed to be allocated to any candidate who was unqualified, which in practice meant serving for an amount of time deemed necessary to gain experience, plus some element of testing, certification, and acquisition patents (points 4–6). Neither office nor rank could be inherited. There were strict penalties for demanding deference or position higher than one's rank, although certain occasions—meetings of friends and informal assemblies—were declared rank-free (reminiscent of the old *bez mest* declaration in the time of the code of precedence). One aim of the table was to lay to rest the *mestnichestvo* disputes which still flared up forty years after its abolition. It was conceded (point 13) that the proliferation of new offices in the civil service meant that top jobs often had to be filled by men who had not worked their way up, and that, from now on, a regular process of promotion of young nobles (point 14) would be observed, with equivalents for regular length of service in the military. As this indicates, the process of 'time-serving'—that is, automatic promotion after a certain length of time, was included, but fast stream promotion was possible for able candidates.

The prime beneficiary of the Table of Ranks, as of all the major reforms, was to be the State, not corporate interests or the nobility, still less the individual citizen. There is no place here for such modern concepts as equality of opportunity or help for the disadvantaged. The table was intended to encourage the nobility to perform more efficiently than hitherto. The concept of nobles as natural leaders of society was endorsed by the fact that anyone who reached a designated rank from outside the nobility should enjoy noble status, *including its heritable aspects.* The table also satisfied Peter's passion for orderly, regulated legislation, of which the General Regulation and Military and Naval Statutes already existed as examples. Contemporaries grasped the point. Bassewitz writes: 'What [Peter] had in mind was not the abasement of the noble estate. On the contrary, all tended towards instilling in the nobility a desire to distinguish themselves from common folk by merit as well as by birth.'[174] He remarks on the fact that in 1723 Peter confirmed the privileges of the Estonian nobility in order that they should not be 'swallowed up'. Deference to status was natural in a society of orders, and Peter always retained an 'innate respect' for lineage and titles.[175] Thus the General Regulation of 1720 stipulated that each government college should have two reception rooms or a suitably divided room where people of 'well-born status' (*znatnogo china*) could be separated from the lower classes (*podlye*) and 'have their own special place'.[176] During curfews in St Petersburg, only the well-born (*znatnye*) and their servants were allowed to pass the guards at night. Single *podlye* could pass if they could give a good reason and were carrying a lamp, but guards were under strict instructions not to let groups of the 'low-born' pass.[177] The final point 19 of the Table of Ranks summed it up: people were to have clothing, carriages, and livery appropriate to their office and calling.

Peter did not intend to diminish the traditional 'boyar élite' in principle, nor did he do so in practice. In 1730, of the 179 officials in the *generalitet* (ranks 1–4 of the table), nine-tenths were descended from old Muscovite nobility, and one-third from men who had recently been boyars. Seven-tenths were related to some other member of the *generalitet.* Of the fifty-four foreigners on the list, forty-two were military men (in other words, foreigners had made little inroad into civil administration), and of these most were 'one-offs'.[178] New skills meant, for example, that by the end of Peter's reign the nobility actually had replaced the more or less hereditary caste of chancellery secretaries and clerks (*d'iachestvo*) who enjoyed some power without high birth in the seventeenth-century *prikazy.*[179] *Dumnye d'iaki* (who had been members of the boyar duma, it will be recalled, and in 1692 were even given an apparent enhancement of status by having their patronymics, not just their surnames, included in the records of the boyar duma[180]) and *pod'iachie* who entered the Table of Ranks were relatively downgraded as they were given the grades of collegiate secretary (rank 10) and collegiate clerk respectively, which carried only personal (that is, not hereditary) noble status (although, as Brown points out, boyars and *okol'nichie* had been taking over from the career bureaucrats in the chancelleries from the 1680s, *de jure* if not *de facto*[181]). The lower grades of bureaucrats were almost exclusively drawn from the lower orders. An analysis of the social origins of twenty-six *pod'iachie* in the Foreign Office in 1680–1710 reveals 47 per cent as the sons of *pod'iachie*, 22 per cent as sons of priests, only 11 per cent as nobles.[182] Other jobs were upgraded. A decree of 1723 pointed out that the original *fiskaly* had been chosen 'for the sake of speed from people of the lowest kind (*samykh nizhnikh liudei*) without any testimonial'. Apart from the chief fiscal, they served without ranks, but many committed serious crimes and misdeeds. Now *fiskaly* were to be appointed 'from among the well-born (*znatnykh*) and officers' and so were to be included in the Table of Ranks'.[183] In 1722 it was decreed that anyone appointed to serve at a foreign court who did not already hold a rank was to be given the grade of *kamer-iunker* (14) but no higher, except for those sent to the most important courts, who would be given the rank of *legationsrat*.[184] A supplement of 31 January 1724 banning the promotion of non-nobles to the rank of secretary and above states: 'If someone holding the office of clerk (*pod'iacheskogo china*) distinguishes himself and shows merit, then such a person is to be promoted with the testimony of the Senate and anyone of such a rank who becomes a Secretary shall be given [hereditary] noble status (*shli-akhtestvo*).' Lower ranks in the colleges were to receive training, but supervisors must ensure 'that there is no deception, no playing about under the guise of studying'.[185]

It is worth comparing the principles set out in the Table of Ranks with the Manifesto on the succession to the throne, published on 5 February 1722, just two weeks later. In the manifesto accidents of birth and custom are firmly rejected in favour of reason and the common good. Most telling is the reference to Peter's decree 'that immovable property might be left to one son, leaving to the will of the parent which son he wished to inherit, with regard to worthiness (*usmotria dostoinogo*), even if it is the younger in preference to the elder. . . . How much more concern we need to show for the integrity of our whole realm, which with God's help is now more widespread than all can see.'[186] But even here there is no suggestion that the monarch *ought to* look beyond the imperial family, by raising a commoner, for example. Still less is there any idea of trusting the choice to popular acclaim or corporate interests. In other words, the normal expectation, as with the Table of Ranks, was that those born to high office would occupy it unless there were strong arguments to the contrary.[187] Even so, Peter's reign undoubtedly saw more power concentrated in the hands of the ruling monarch than ever before, to the detriment of the nobility. After his death nobles began to claw back some of their lost status, but there is no evidence of any significant attempt to discard Petrine cultural reform, which will be examined in detail in the next chapter.

V.   WOMEN: FROM *BOIARYNI* TO *DAMY*

If eras in Russian history were to be designated 'masculine' or 'feminine', then the Petrine age would surely qualify as one of the most virile. But it also saw some fascinating developments in the area of women's history. 'Thanks to Peter,' wrote Count Münnich in a memoir written for Catherine II, 'the fair sex began to appear in society.'[188] By the 'fair sex' he had in mind women of the upper classes, who were driven from the seclusion of the Muscovite *terem* or women's quarters and squeezed into Western corsets in order to become fit counterparts for their 'decent beardless' spouses. We still know remarkably little about these women, partly because most studies of the Petrine era have focused upon the masculine activities of war, seafaring, and diplomacy, and partly because the women themselves are for the most part silent, their lives undocumented. The census of 1719–23 counted only male 'souls'—and the non-tax-paying population was not counted at all. When females were counted at a slightly later date—for example, for parish registers in 1730—female births were consistently under-reported.[189] Even when women appear in sources, they cannot always be readily identified, like the 'maid Khitrovo' for whom Peter ordered transport to bring her to St Petersburg in 1710.[190] Sources continue to be unearthed, like the letters of A. S. Mordvintsova to her son;[191] but evidence about women's lives is likely to remain for the most part indirect, based largely on second-hand observations. We have little hope of entering into the inner lives of individual Petrine women, as we can, to a degree, with a few later eighteenth-century ones. Even artifacts are mute. It is a remarkable fact that only one example of female court dress from the period survives in Russia, and that in the form of the sumptuous gown worn by Tsaritsa Catherine at her coronation as consort in 1724.[192]

The path to a more public role for upper-class women was paved in the 1680s by Sophia Alekseevna, who made appearances in and around Moscow, and even showed her face to the wider world by having her portrait painted and engraved.[193] Sophia's example was calculated to inspire Peter to restrict women rather than liberate them. In fact, the open break between them was precipitated when Peter objected to the unseemliness of Sophia, a woman, following the crosses in a religious ceremony near the Kremlin. The prime mover of this righteous indignation was probably not Peter himself, but his mother and her relatives, who had good reason to undermine Sophia's authority at every opportunity. Despite evidence of a freer atmosphere when she arrived in the palace in the 1670s (she had been raised in the Westernized household of A. S. Matveev), Natalia Naryshkina seems to have reasserted traditional values later in life. Palace records for the 1690s mention women in such conventional contexts as name-day celebrations carried out on their behalf, although there is growing evidence of less conventional activity—for example, a feast with fireworks in February 1690 attended by both tsars and their wives and several unspecified tsarevny.[194] After Natalia's death, Tsarevna

Ekaterina Alekseevna is said to have visited a German friend, a confectioner, in the Foreign Quarter and to have pawned goods there.[195]

If the early 1690s provide few examples of new trends, it would be wrong to postpone female 'emancipation' to the other end of Peter's reign, as many historians have done by associating it with Peter's decree of 1718 on assemblies, which laid down rules for informal public gatherings.[196] Women reappeared in public long before 1718. The crucial factor here was the Grand Embassy of 1697–8 and the death of the last patriarch in 1700. Peter was far from being a New Man in the modern sense. He had no compunction, for example, about banishing his unwanted wife Evdokia to a convent. His attitude towards the female sex in general was characteristically pragmatic. He must have reasoned (although he never articulated his thoughts) that it was no use creating a new breed of men to run the reformed army, navy, and government departments and to represent Russia abroad without also reforming their wives on the model which he had observed in Europe. In addition, Peter had a bevy of royal women on his hands,[197] and in Peter's scheme of things no one, royal women included, could be allowed to be idle.

An observer unusually well placed to observe the women of the court at close quarters during the transitional period was Filippo Balatri (1684?–1756), a young castrato singer brought to Russia from Italy by Prince P. A. Golitsyn. He seems to have arrived in Moscow in December 1698 (he saw the corpses of the strel'tsy), and returned to Venice in the spring of 1701.[198] One of his first impressions when he arrived at the Russian border in Smolensk was that the women did not appear in the same room as the men (a room which struck him by its sparse furnishings and many icons), but listened in hiding to the concert which he gave.[199] In the provinces practices did not seem to have changed much since Mayerburg's observations on female 'servitude' in the 1660s: 'You keep your women locked up like slaves and make them work all day long. No man is allowed to look them in the face and you marry off your daughters without even showing them their fiancés from a distance.'[200] In Moscow, where Balatri joined the royal household as a chamberlain, segregation of the sexes was less strictly observed, but full integration had not yet arrived. Peter approached the problem in characteristic manner. Balatri recounted how some 'Muscovite ladies' were invited to a concert and ball in the Lefort palace. The tsar went out to greet them, 'like a galant cavalier', but the women were very timid and entered the hall 'in confusion, having quite lost their composure'. The tsar danced with them, but the ladies danced very badly, with convulsive movements. These were the wives of boyars, who had been ordered to bring them to the ball, and they had been 'forced to obey the tsar's will'. Guards were posted at the doors to stop the guests leaving early, a practice that Peter later employed in St Petersburg.[201] Balatri is especially informative on Prince Golitsyn's wife, Daria (née Liapunova), who later spent several years in Vienna with her husband in 1701–5.[202] At home in Moscow Daria seemed 'nun-like', pious and reserved, fearful of mixing with foreigners. Once she got used to Vienna, however, she developed a passion for social life, visiting theatres and balls even against the advice of their Russian priest.[203]

Johannes Korb's observations agree with Balatri's. At a reception in Lefort's palace in February 1699 he saw Peter's sister Natalia peeping through a curtain from an adjoining room, escorted by the *crème* of the married ladies. This was 'a great departure from Russian manners, which up to this forbade the female sex to appear at public assemblies of men, and from festive gaieties'.[204] But it was evidently still not the norm. A few months later Korb went to a reception at Lev Naryshkin's, where guests were taken to his wife's chamber to receive a sip of brandy in traditional Muscovite style.[205] Russian visitors to Europe at about the same time were struck by the relative sophistication of women there.[206] A. A. Matveev observed: 'Even the female sex in France has no shame whatsoever about associating in polite society with the male sex, just as the men themselves [socialize] with them with sweet gallantry and attentiveness.'[207]

In 1700 women living in towns were forced by decree to adopt Western dress. In 1702 Peter made a point of setting up a wedding feast which began in the 'old style', with men and women segregated in separate rooms wearing Muscovite dress, and ended with mixed company clad in 'German' fashion.[208] Female seclusion was quite gone at court by the time the artist Cornelius de Bruyn arrived in Moscow in the same year. Not only was he introduced on several occasions to the widowed tsaritsa Praskovia ('pretty bulky', but with 'a genteel manner and most engaging manners'[209]); he also painted two sets of portraits of her three daughters (intended, perhaps, for sending abroad), an inconceivable breach of female seclusion during Tsar Alexis's time. The same daughters, destined for foreign husbands, were educated by foreign tutors, the German Dietrich Osterman (brother of the more famous Andrei) and the Frenchman Rambourt.[210] Even so, there were still occasions—for example, weddings—when etiquette required separate rooms or tables. The key to Zubov's engraving of the dwarf wedding of 1710 indicates one table for the tsar, Menshikov, and courtiers and another for 'His Majesty's imperial ladies', the bride and her maids, the groom and his attendants, although an overflow table accommodated 'His Majesty's courtiers and some ladies'.[211] Bergholz's plan of the chamber in the Kremlin Palace of Facets where Catherine's coronation banquet was held shows a gallery for the imperial princesses, whence they watched the dinner unobserved.[212] But mixed company was the norm. Just Juel wrote in January 1710 of a New Year banquet at which Catherine and the other women were entertained in a separate room, 'so that on this occasion, *contrary to the normal practice*, they were apart from the men'.[213]

A good illustration of the change is provided by a comparison of Muscovite name-day ceremonies (among the rare occasions on which royal women were mentioned at all in pre-Petrine records) and their Petrine successors. In Muscovy, well into the 1690s, the entertainment of courtiers to mark such occasions was presided over by the tsars on behalf of their daughters, sisters, and wives. Women might distribute cakes and gifts only in strictly female company. But the celebration of the name-day of Peter's daughter and grand-daughter, Natalia Petrovna and Natalia Alekseevna, on 26 August 1724, took place in the gallery in the summer garden in a gathering of mixed company which included a group of foreign shipwrights. The name-day girls handed out glasses of Hungarian wine to their guests in person.[214]

One of the most acute observers of Russian women was the young German noble Bergholz, who took a keen interest in the niceties of female apparel, jewellery, dance steps, and seating at table. Bergholz thought the changes were for the better: 'The Russian woman, until recently coarse and uneducated, has changed for the better to such a degree that now she concedes little to German or French ladies in subtlety of manners and good breeding and in some respects is even superior to them.'[215] He pronounced the gowns of Peter's daughters at a coronation anniversary banquet in 1721 to be in the latest French fashion, and their elaborate bejewelled coiffures 'of an elegance which would have done credit to the best Paris hairdresser'.[216] Even so, he noted tell-tale signs of provincialism. On seeing the royal women in full evening dress on the anniversary of Poltava in 1721, he remarked he had 'never seen so many precious gems at once, except perhaps at an audience of the Turkish envoy in Paris'.[217] 'In general the ladies here adore precious gems, with which they try to outdo each other,' he remarked.[218] He thought that they were 'as skilful at painting their faces as French women; but Princess Trubetskaia is one of those who most enthusiastically follows that bad and repulsive fashion'.[219]

Peter Henry Bruce noted something similar: 'The Russian women are of a middling stature, generally well proportioned, and might pass for handsome in any part of Europe; their features far from despicable, were it not for that preposterous custom of painting their faces, which they lay on so abundantly, that it may truly be said they use it as a veil to hide their beauty.'[220] Weber noted the fashion for black teeth observed in 1714 (old Russians believed that 'white Teeth only became Blackmoors and Monkeys'), but conceded that by the end of his stay, a foreigner entering an assembly 'will hardly believe he is in Russia, but rather, as long as he enters into no Discourse, think himself in the midst of London or Paris'. Even so, he found that in conversation with strangers Russian ladies 'cannot yet conquer their in-born Bashfulness and Awkwardness'.[221] Gaucheness of manner and suspicion of things foreign lingered. At a dinner at the duke of Courland's residence in September 1710, Just Juel noted that the Russian ladies scarcely touched the well-prepared food, 'because the cuisine was not Russian'.[222] The inexperience even of younger women is indicated by their refusal to dance with foreigners (as Bergholz noted with annoyance).

Outside the court and the new capital, old customs persisted more strongly. Moscow women were less modern than their St Petersburg counterparts. Weber, visiting the Ascension convent in the Kremlin in 1716, was struck by the curiosity of the laywomen he met there, who asked him about women in Germany and 'whether they were kept so close and low as they are in Russia'. He noted that 'Russian Wives and Daughters are extremely retired, and never go abroad, unless it be to Church, or to see their nearest Relations ... they are disgraced by their old Customs, which they cannot yet leave off, the Court being too far off to break them of them. Ladies of Quality are dressed after the German Fashion, which indeed they prefer to their old antick Dress; but as to their Courtesies, still the old Custom prevails of bowing with the Head to the Ground.' Even women who accompanied their husbands abroad apparently had to resume traditional manners when they got back to Moscow.[223] Old Muscovite etiquette was especially persistent among merchant families, whose womenfolk continued to be brought in for a brief time to greet the male company with a low bow and to proffer a glass of vodka, but did not speak. Such a woman, notes Bruce with more than a hint of salacious enjoyment, eschewed Western fashion: 'Her whole body is unconfined, wearing neither stays, waistcoat or petticoat, or even garters to her stockings.'[224] Outside St Petersburg, many women preferred the old, more comfortable fashions, and who can blame them if one thinks of the Russian climate when looking at the low necklines and thin materials of court dress in portraits?

When it comes to individual female biographies, we know most about royal women. Peter's daughters were relatively well educated, at the insistence of their mother, who was illiterate.[225] One of the most interesting cases of the impact of Peter's reforms on royal women is provided by Peter's sister Natalia Alekseevna, born in 1673, and thus straddling the two contrasting worlds of the *terem* and the assembly. She just missed the generation of royal women who contracted foreign marriages, although she was asked. In 1701 a proposal arrived from Vienna for one of the Russian princesses, either Natalia or one of her nieces, to marry the Austrian archduke. Portraits were requested and sent, but nothing came of it.[226] Natalia was best known for her work in reviving her father's court theatre, which had ceased its activities after his death.[227] Evidence of her tastes and occupations is provided by the invento-ries of her St Petersburg mansion and other properties made after her death in June 1716.[228] She owned sixty-one paintings and pictures, including royal portraits and self-portraits, but she also owned nineteen icons, among which images of the Mother of God figured prominently. Among the 110 books found in her house (76 printed and 34 in manuscript), religious literature, especially lives of saints, prayerbooks, sermons, and edifying works predomi-nated, alongside panegyrics on Poltava and works on Alexander the Great and the liberation of Livonia. The house contained thirty-one mirrors, in which Natalia could have admired herself in her vast wardrobe of Western-style outfits in all the colours of the rainbow and accessories such as corsets and French-style *fontanges* (in Russian *fantanzhi*, elaborate head-dresses with ribbons and lace). It is interesting that the one set of old Russian clothes (*ruskovo starovo ubora*) was listed separately. An allegorical memorial portrait, painted by an anonymous artist in 1717 and presented to Peter I, suggests the essential duality of Natalia's existence.[229] The image in the central oval is worldly (Natalia is depicted in Western dress and royal ermine, elaborately coiffed, looking younger than her forty-three years); but the bulk of the texts and smaller images surrounding the central one are religious and icon-like, suggesting that Natalia has conquered death by piety in life. Texts and imagery point to the fleetingness of all earthly things. Fame is short-lived; all is vanity.[230]

Tsarevna Maria Alekseevna is another interesting hybrid, the only one of Tsar Alexis's daughters to go abroad. In the spring of 1716 she went to Carlsbad for the wedding of her niece Ekaterina, and insisted on travelling in the style of previous reigns, when tsarevny were accompanied by vast trains of servants and retainers. Many documents survive charting the preparations for this unprecedented journey. Peter, both by his own example of travelling with just a few retainers and by drafting the 'spare attendants' of nobles into the army, was trying to discourage the old wasteful habits.[231] He wrote to Maria on 7 February 1716: 'My wife has passed on your letter about the number of servants [to accompany you]. I bow to your will in this matter, only I advise you that the fewer you take the better, because with a large retinue people will recognize you more easily as nobody travels nowadays in such great numbers. However, do as you think best.'[232] Peter himself preferred to travel incognito in a one-horse carriage, but he allocated the tidy sum of 4,000 roubles for Maria's travelling expenses and assigned her a doctor and an interpreter.[233] Even so, Maria managed to spend more. On 25 October Peter wrote to Count Golovkin in Berlin instructing him to repay at once the sum of 1,500 chervonnye borrowed by Maria from merchants while she was in Berlin.[234] What we know of Maria's life-style in St Petersburg suggests traditional manners. Members of her household petitioning for unpaid wages in 1716 included three choristers, two priests, a deacon, a psalmist, and sexton as well as assorted servants, chambermaids, washerwomen and caretakers.[235]

In 1718 Maria fell under suspicion in the witch-hunt which followed the return of Tsarevich Alexis to Russia. The scene around her deathbed (9 March 1723) indicates that, despite her trips abroad, she was associated to the last with the old culture. 'Her bed was surrounded by priests, who in accordance with the ancient practice of comforting the souls of the dying brought her food and drink and enquired in piteous tones whether she had a sufficiency of everything required for the maintenance of life in this world.' Peter is said to have been very angry when he heard of this 'absurd custom' persisting in his own family, and to have driven the priests away.[236] Peter's sister-in-law Tsaritsa Praskovia, who maintained a residence in Moscow and preferred traditional fashions, also prepared to meet her end in Orthodoxy. In a last letter to her daughter Anna, she begged her to pray for her and not to forget to say prayers for her after her death.[237]

In the seventeenth century it had been the custom for royal women to offer shelter to an assortment of waifs and strays. This continued into the eighteenth century. Tsarevna Ekaterina Alekseevna, for example, housed one old woman and seven poor girls in her apartments. Tsarevna Marfa kept a girl without any legs.[238] In exile Tsaritsa Evdokia had a special room fitted out for a prophesying 'fool in Christ' called Mikhail Bosoi, with whom she often dined.[239] Tsaritsa Praskovia made concessions to the new times, frequently receiving foreign visitors and herself visiting the Foreign Quarter. But she was particularly devoted to her collection of widows, orphans, holy fools, and cripples. When she moved to the palace at Izmailovo outside Moscow after her husband's death in 1696, she took in even more, the most revered of whom was a half-mad former clerk by the name of Timofei Arkhipovich, who claimed a gift of prophecy. Such hangers-on had to hide when Peter came to visit. Peter once declared that his sister-in-law's house was a 'refuge for freaks, hypocrites and religious fanatics'.[240] When Bergholz visited Praskovia and her daughter Ekaterina at Izmailovo in 1722, a half-blind, filthy old bandura player, stinking of sweat and garlic, was brought out to perform 'spicy' songs. He was shown another 'ragged creature', who often danced for the princess and would display 'everything she had' if asked. 'I could not imagine,' he writes, 'how the duchess [Ekaterina], who had been so long in Germany and lived there as befits her station, could tolerate such an old hag in her presence.'[241] Even Peter's own household was far from being thoroughly 'modern' in this respect. Alongside architects, orderlies, and tutors in palace payroll records we find the elderly sister of the late jester Filat Shansky, Princess Anna's old wet-nurse, and assorted women such as 'the widow Matrena Efimova'.[242]

The royal women also spent their time in the company of ladies of the court, now styled by the new term *damy* rather than the Muscovite *boiaryni*, women such as Pavel Iaguzhinsky's second wife, née Golovina, who spoke perfect German and good French as well as being a graceful dancer.[243] Princess Cherkasskaia loved music and had her own orchestra.[244] A fascinating example is Countess Matveeva, wife of A. A. Matveev. Her husband had been raised in a comparatively Westernized household, knew foreign languages, and worked in the Foreign Office. In 1689 he introduced her to the French traveller De la Neuville, who wrote 'To do me greater honour, he called his wife and presented her to me. I greeted her in the French manner and she drank a cup of vodka to my health, passing the cup to me so that I might do likewise. She is the only woman in that country who uses no rouge and has never painted herself. She is also quite pretty.'[245] Trips abroad with her husband removed all traces of Muscovite manners. In 1710–11 we find her taking part in the negotiation of the marriage contract between Tsarevich Alexis and Charlotte of Wolfenbüttel. She was declared by one of Charlotte's ladies-in-waiting to be 'extraordinarily clever, with noble and elegant manners. No one would take her for a Muscovite.'[246] The French ambassador Campredon paid a similar compliment to her daughter (Rumiantseva), whom he described as 'extremely polished and with manners quite different from those of her country'.[247]

The Petrine noblewoman 'stood on the threshold of two eras, two moral codes—old Russian and modern European—unable to reject either one, but tending in externals in the direction of the latter, in beliefs and superstitions to the former'.[248] Girls received conflicting messages about proper behaviour. The message 'from above' was to put on low-cut dresses and socialize; yet Russian women continued to be raised as good Orthodox girls. The 1717 manual of etiquette *The Honourable Mirror of Youth*, a compilation from various Western sources, best known for its advice to young men derived from Erasmus, contained sections on 'maidenly honour or the crown of virtue': this included desire and love for the word of God and divine service, true knowledge of God, fear of God, meekness, appealing to God, gratitude, confession of faith, respect for parents, industriousness, decorum, affability, kindness, bodily cleanliness, bashfulness, restraint, chastity, thrift, generosity, righteousness, and taciturnity. 'Of all the virtues which adorn well-born ladies or maidens and are required of them, meekness is the leading and chief virtue, and contains within it much. It is not enough to wear simple clothing and bow your head and show meekness in your outward actions and pronounce sweet words. The human heart must also know, love and fear God, you must acknowledge your own weaknesses, frailties and imperfections and be humble before God and consider your fellow being more than yourself.'[249]

Peter's court may have been very different from that of his predecessors in breaking down the barriers between men and women by ending female seclusion. But in other ways—for example, by forbidding early marriages and subjecting nobles to compulsory military service for life, thereby keeping husbands away from their wives and daughters for years on end—it heightened the separation. Ivan Nepliuev, for instance, was abroad on service and naval study for four years, leaving behind a young family.[250] The military ethos of the Petrine era shifted the balance of public ceremonial from all-male religious rites to all-male military parades, in which women remained onlookers rather than participants. Most foreign observers assumed, even so, that the changes they observed were welcomed by women. Thus Peter Henry Bruce writes (of Moscow) that 'as the fair sex are allowed all manner of freedom in company, they live in a perpetual round of pleasure and diversion, spending most part of their time in balls and entertainments, inviting each other by turns to their houses, as they are left lonely by their husbands, who are for the most part employed abroad'. He notes a trend for employing Swedish prisoners of war as instructors to their children and music and dancing masters.[251] John Perry writes that 'the Russ Ladies soon reconciled themselves to the English Dress, which they found rendred [sic] them more agreeable'.[252]

Yet life in St Petersburg under the nose of the monarch, who required life-long service of all his subjects, could be as oppressive for women as for men. For many noblewomen the very move to St Petersburg was painful. Princess Maria, widow of Prince M. S. L'vov, petitioned the Senate for permission to leave St Petersburg to visit her estate for a while, 'on account of her old age and ill-health'. The entry also noted that she had been ordered to build homes for widows and girls in the capital. She was allowed leave for five months, extended at the request of Peter's sister Natalia for whom she was making a dress.[253] Women were expected to do their duty alongside men at Peter's compulsory entertainments. There was even a female section of the All-Drunken Assembly, with Daria Rzhevskaia and Anastasia Golitsyna taking leading roles.[254] Peter's later outdoor assemblies in the summer gardens had well-defined male and female activities, centring on two areas: the *damskaia*, where guests were received by the empress and ladies, and where later in the evening they were joined by the men for dancing; and the *skiperskaia*, where Peter presided over pipes of tobacco and stronger drink.[255] Bergholz recounts the chilling tale of Olsuf'eva, the German wife of an official, who in November 1721 in the last stages of pregnancy was summoned to the palace along with about thirty other women who had failed to appear at a masquerade in the Senate house, in order to drink a penalty draught of alcohol. Olsuf'eva apparently was so distressed that she gave birth to a stillborn boy on the morning of the ordeal.[256] This misfortune made no impact on Peter. In July 1724 the celebrations of the tenth anniversary of the Russian naval victory at Hangö, which were held on the newly launched ship *Derbent*, went on till three in the morning, 'and even the ladies had to drink, and many were ill the next day, even though some among them are no strangers to a good glass of wine'. On 29 July those who had failed to attend were rounded up to drink a penalty.[257]

Heavy drinking was not always forced. In a contest between Moscow and St Petersburg ladies, the former apparently had to drink a penalty for calling the latter 'drunkards' with reference to the amounts consumed at a masquerade.[258] Just Juel records a visit to Tsaritsa Praskovia and her daughters in May 1710 where he and his companions were forced to drink so many huge goblets of alcohol that they got completely drunk in less than half an hour.[259]

For élite women in Peter's Russia, emancipation thus centred on the obligation to appear in public when summoned and the privilege of receiving sufficient education, notably in foreign languages and dancing, for getting by in polite society. In the palace women continued to fulfil roles similar to those of their predecessors in 'unemancipated' times, although there was some institutional change to reflect their more public role. For example, ladies-in-waiting—*damy i devitsy pri dvore*—held ranks in their own right for the period of their office. The highest—the chief lady-in-waiting (*ober-gofnesterina*)—presided over a team of *deistvitel'nye stats-damy*, *kamer-devitsy*, *gof-damy*, and *gof-devitsy* in the households of the empress and her daughters.[260] All other women were treated according to the ranks of their husbands or fathers. Women's names, as elsewhere, also reflected their marital status. In a petition of 1715, for example, the claimaint (who had been driven out of her late husband's estate by a male relative) is referred to as 'the widow, wife of Prince Fedor Myshetsky, Princess Daria daughter of Dorofei'.[261] An example of female ranking in practice is provided by Peter's funeral, when the court ladies-in-waiting (*pridvornye shtatsdamy*) Olsuf'eva, Kampernhauzen, Villebois, Tolstaia, Devier, and Arsen'eva walked in front of the wives of men of the top eight ranks. The length of the women's mourning veils was determined by rank: two arshins (about 52 inches) for ranks 1 and 2, one and a half for ranks 3 and 4, one arshin for ranks 5 and 6. In church, ranks 1–6 were accommodated inside the wooden chapel, 4–6 standing at a lower level than the others; but ranks 7–8 stood outside in the main body of the church.[262] 'Chivalry' for women was instituted in 1714 with the creation of the order of St Catherine, in praise of female courage, to mark the escape of the Russian army from the Turks in 1711. The head of the order was the empress.[263]

Although Peter's attitude towards women was very much of his time, in some ways he was ahead of Russian public opinion. His scheme for sending young women abroad to German towns to finish their education, for example, envisaged a curriculum restricted to languages, social graces, and 'female work'; but the nobles fiercely opposed such an undertaking on the grounds that their daughters would be led into temptation and their virtue and reputations endangered. None, it seems, was sent.[264] Plans to send wives abroad with their husbands on state service were also opposed, although some women did accompany their husbands.[265] Perhaps Peter was influenced by Fedor Saltykov, who in his 'Proposition' (1713), apparently read carefully by the tsar, urged that girls' schools be established to teach reading, writing, arithmetic, French, German, painting, needlework, and dancing, 'so that our women will be equal to those of European countries'.[266] In a memorandum of 1714 Saltykov proposed that female orphans receive lessons in arithmetic, drawing, painting, sewing, weaving, carpet making, and other crafts. However, the subjects listed as appropriate for female painters—perspective drawing, flowers, landscapes, and portraits—omitted the grander, more masculine genres of history, naval, military, and 'tragic' subjects prescribed in addition for male orphans. Trained women and girls were to be sent out to earn their living by their handiwork and contribute to the 'general good'.[267] Formal education for girls had to wait for the reign of Catherine II.

Women of the street-trading, artisan, and peasant classes—*baby, zhenki,* and *devki,* as opposed to *damy* and *devitsy*—had never been confined to the *terem.* They could not afford the luxury of idleness. These women worked, most of them in the agricultural economy, others in traditional female occupations such as spinning and dress making. In the towns textile industries became and remained until modern times centres of women's work, and in some cases served as penal institutions for errant women on the model of similar institutions in the Netherlands and elsewhere. In 1719, for example, six women and girls were sent to Moscow to clean and spin flax in the linen factories.[268] A distinct category of women worked as servants at court and in noble households. The young Peter had a wet-nurse (*kormilitsa*), nurse (*mama*), and nanny (*niania*).[269] Women from the tax-paying classes, especially widows, sometimes enjoyed a degree of independence. A resolution on artillery dated 7 February 1704 contains a curious reference to a petition by the wife of Grigory Belsky, 'that she be allowed to prepare 10,000 puds of powder in her powder works from her saltpetre, sulphur etc. using her masters and workers'.[270]

Women of the lower classes were not entirely mute. Their voices can be heard in testimonies—for example, in the records of the Preobrazhensky *prikaz*: 'What sort of tsar is it who destroys the peasants' homes, takes our husbands for soldiers and leaves us orphaned with our children and forces us to weep for an age?' one woman complained. In 1701 the peasant woman Daria had her tongue cut out for spreading the rumour that Peter was the son of a German swapped at birth for a daughter.[271] In November 1707 Peter Matveevich Apraksin sent a report from Astrakhan', at the time recovering from the recent revolt, for the tsar's attention. One of the matters raised was that some wives and children of the strel'tsy had been abandoned by their husbands, who were presumed dead, but were refusing to marry soldiers, awaiting their husbands' return, and demanding allowances. Should these women remain in Astrakhan' and be married off, or should they be sent to towns on the upper Volga, 'in order that the recent wicked deeds and rebellions should not be referred to by anyone?' Peter ordered Apraksin to 'give the women (*babam*) nothing, but register their male children, send a list and await orders'. The outcome is not known.[272] In areas occupied by Russian troops, women and children were sometimes captured, sent to Russia, and in some cases sold.[273]

A reform which was potentially beneficial to all women involved marriage customs. In pre-Petrine Russia marriage contracts were made between the parents, or, in their absence, close relatives of the bride and groom, who usually did not set eyes upon each other until the contract had been sealed. The suitor at least visited his intended's home with the betrothal party, so he had some idea of her circumstances in advance; but the bride was betrothed without prior sight of husband or new home. The husband saw his bride only after the wedding ceremony, when she was unveiled. Naturally, in high society such secrecy could be maintained only under the *terem* system in which young unmarried men and women led separate lives. Once Peter's mixed parties and assemblies started to bring them together before marriage, reform was inevitable, especially as the tsar believed that marriage based on choice rather than compulsion would be conducive to higher birth rates. A law of 1702 outlawed old-style marriage contracts, stipulating a six-week period of betrothal (*obruchenie*) before the wedding (*venchanie*) during which the couple could meet and the betrothal be broken at the request of either party. A groom could refuse to marry an ugly, sick, or disfigured bride if these handicaps had been hidden at the time of the betrothal or if he had been shown a healthy girl in her place. The same condition is not specified for girls thus tricked.[274] In April 1722 forced marriages were banned. This included prohibition on guardians marrying off wards and masters their slaves (*rabov i rabyn*).[275] Provisions for dealing with illegitimate children were also amended. Earlier, the Church had compelled the father to marry the mother. An edict of 1697, issued during Patriarch Adrian's regime, urged the woman to name the father, who was then flogged and sent to a monastery for a month, where he had to prostrate himself a hundred times each day after mass. The mother was to perform the same penance forty days after the birth of the child. If the father was unmarried and deemed to be a suitable partner, he was to marry the mother. If he was a married man and had raped a virgin or a widow, he was to be punished as above and pay a fine to the girl's father or to the widow, based on his income or that of her deceased husband. If the woman refused to name the father of her child or claimed that he had gone away, she got double the above punishment in order to discourage the protection of 'fornicators'.[276] Later, men were encouraged to marry women whom they had made pregnant by being faced with maintenance payments if they refused; but they were not forced to do so unless they had promised marriage.[277]

A conviction for rape was punishable by death or hard labour in the galleys. The formulation in both the Military and the Naval Statute has some interesting ideas on evidence. Witnesses were needed to obtain a clear-cut conviction, for 'bad women, in order to expiate their shame, may claim to have been raped'. If the reported incident took place in a 'remote place far from people or alone', then the accuser must not be believed automatically. In such cases the judge needed further evidence of torn clothing, bruises, and wounds before proceeding. He must be sceptical if the charge was brought long after the event. Even so, 'rape is rape and whether it is committed against a loose woman (*bludnitsa*) or an honourable wife, the judge must not take account of the individual involved but look to the deed and actual circumstances'. However, the wording suggests that the violator of a 'blatant whore' would be less harshly punished.[278]

Russian women enjoyed some property rights, although it has been argued that these had been eroded in the Muscovite period.[279] The 1649 *Ulozhenie* stipulated that on the death of a husband a childless woman had a claim to a quarter of her husband's property. The rest reverted to his family. She could claim only purchased lands, which could be left to a wife until she remarried or took the veil. A *prozhitok*—a small piece out of *pomest'e* holdings—could be reserved for dependent mothers and daughters under the age of fifteen. Their only absolute right was to their own dowry, which could take the form of serfs.[280] Under Peter there were attempts to stop the giving of land as dowry in order to minimize the fragmentation of estates. The 1714 act on single inheritance stipulated that immovable property (i.e. land) should no longer be given as dowry,[281] but the custom was restored with the repeal of the law in 1731. In other respects, the law of 1714 improved a woman's position, Daughters had a right to a share in movable property, and when the only surviving children were daughters, one of them could inherit the land. A Senate decision of 22 February 1716, in the case of Elena Saltykova, whose male cousin tried to claim her father's estate when the latter died intestate, cites the 1714 law: 'anyone who has sons and wants to give his immovable property to one of them in his will and who has other children, the latter shall receive movable property, both sons and daughters, and if a person has no sons but has daughters, they will be allocated in the same way, and if he fails to allocate in his lifetime, then allocation is determined by the decree, the immovable property going to the eldest son and the moveable is to be divided equally, the same applying to daughters.' Therefore Elena inherited, 'because apart from her, he left no children'. It was specified that the estate went to her, and not jointly to her husband, even if that had been her father's unspoken wish.[282]

The last male in a line was encouraged to leave his property to a surviving female relative, who took his name if she did not bear it already.[283] After the death of F. I. Romodanovsky in 1717, in order to preserve the name (his only son had no children), Peter married off the late mock-tsar's two daughters to noblemen on condition that the latter adopted the name of Romodanovsky.[284] The law of 1714 also allowed a childless widow to inherit all her husband's land until her death or remarriage, when the lands reverted to the husband's line. Such cases could be complicated. In 1712 the husband of Princess Avdotia Ivanovna Cherkasskaia died, leaving sizeable estates with 746 peasant households. Her petition to the Senate underlined the dilemma of a widowed woman when there were sons from a previous marriage. She was living, she said, in her late husband's house, but there had been no resolution (*ukaza . . . ne uchineno*) 'on how she should get her livelihood and what she should own', and she had no dowry estates, so made a claim under clause 9 of the 1714 Act: that on the death of her husband a childless wife received all his property until her death, at which point it reverted to the male line. Unfortunately the clause did not cover the event of a second wife being left childless when there were children and potential heirs from a first marriage. The case provoked a debate in the Senate, at which various opinions were expressed: for example, that she should not inherit, as there was no specific mention in the law that a stepmother should inherit when there were stepchilden alive. Others said that the son could inherit only after the stepmother died or took the veil. In this case, the decision was made in favour of Avdotia (19 February 1715). In April 1715 her stepson Boris Cherkassky appealed on the grounds that he had been reduced to penury.[285] The disputes over this and many other cases indicated both the rejection of new concepts of female inheritance and confusion over the law itself, which was badly drafted. As Strahlenberg writes: 'Since this law was formulated in concise terms there were many disputes and quarrels, for no one could formulate a clear opinion and correct definition. ... The point of legislation on inheritance by daughters is unclear.'[286] Inheritance through the female line was repealed in 1731.[287]

Peter tried to amend women's status in respect of property, but made little impact, either by legislation or by personal example, on divorce customs. Grounds for a woman seeking divorce continued to be adultery or abandonment (based on the canon law). Wife beating was not grounds for divorce. If a wife was granted a divorce, she could take back her dowry property. Women who became a burden or a nuisance—for example, by standing in the way of their husbands' remarriage—were still dealt with in the time-honoured way by seclusion in a nunnery, of which Peter's treatment of his first wife Evdokia is a prime example. A sad case entails the petition for divorce in September

1722 of Pavel Iaguzhinsky against his first wife Anna Fedorovna Khitrovo, on account of his wife's 'offences against the Christian law and other outrages, most of all to ensure that my small children are not utterly ruined by such an indecent mother'. Anna was an heiress in her own right, the only child of a father of distinguished boyar rank, hence a catch for the low-born Iaguzhinsky; but he had her estates made over in his name, and left her alone for long periods. The pretext for her dispatch to a convent was a row at a wedding in April 1722, when she allegedly refused to dance with her husband; but the real reason was his wish to marry Anna Golovkina, the daughter of the chancellor, with the encouragement of Peter and the connivance of Catherine, who was Golovkina's patron. There seems to be plenty of evidence, notably in the Synod divorce papers, that Anna Khitrovo was suffering from a mental illness (described variously by witnesses as 'hypochondria' or 'melancholia'), which caused her to wander around or even go to church skimpily dressed, to break glass, to tear icons from the wall, to defecate in public, and to commit 'obscenities and acts which are too vile and shameful even to speak of'. She attributed her illness to grief and sadness caused by separation from her husband and children in St Petersburg in 1721.[288] She was sent to the convent of St Theodore in Pereiaslavl'-Zalessky, but, despite the appointment of guards, continued to be a nuisance, trying to burn down the monastery and escape. She died in 1733, having taken the veil under the name of Agafia.[289] On occasion women voluntarily sought the sanctuary of a convent: for example, the daughter of Prince Gagarin, who took the veil in order to avoid marrying the son of Prince Ivan Musin-Pushkin. 'It is frequent in those Parts for Wives to leave their Husbands, and for Daughters to run away from their Parents and to take Refuge in Convents,' wrote Weber.[290] Nunneries provided welfare relief. In a petition of February 1723 the nun Kharitina in the Moscow Resurrection convent complained that she had been left in poverty since the death of her husband. It was ordered that she be 'allocated to some convent where she would be able to receive subsistence and clothing'.[291]

Inside nunneries the abbesses enjoyed some power. In 1716 Weber was entertained by nuns in the Ascension convent in the Kremlin. The abbess asked him questions 'about the Manners of Germany and the Nunneries there, and was very attentive to the Account I gave her in answer to what she asked'. He noted that there were many young, attractive nuns of good family in the convent.[292] Sometimes old traditions came into conflict with new needs, however. There are instances of women successfully avoiding the veil, not because Peter had any particular sympathy for the individual case, but because their protests complemented his own efforts to limit monastic communities, which he regarded as bad for the Russian birth rate. In 1700 it was decreed that young women living in nunneries with female relatives who had taken the veil should be married if they so wished and not allowed to take the veil before the age of forty.[293] Perhaps Peter was influenced by an anonymous memorandum submitted in 1700 which proposed that women and girls committed to convents but with no vocation be set to work in handicrafts and manufacturing instead.[294] (A similar principle applied to rules on remarriage (formerly forbidden) of widowed priests, who were now encouraged to remarry and work as teachers, rather than taking monastic vows.[295])

In general, Peter's church reform made it more difficult for women to enter convents. A lower age limit of forty was increased to sixty in the supplement to the Ecclesiastical Regulation (1722). Convents were supposed to be supervised and enclosed, with strict limitations on trips outside the convent, and nuns and laypersons were segregated even at festivals. No one was supposed to receive nuns in their homes.[296] Inside convents, women must have useful occupations. In 1722 lay seamstresses were sent to Moscow convents to train nuns in spinning, while in 1724 nuns were sent to supervise female workers in navy hospitals in St Petersburg.[297] A unique area of female activity was the book copying carried out by the sisters of the Old Believer Vyg community.[298] Outside nunneries the highest ecclesiastical position to which women could aspire was the exclusively female profession of baker of communion loaves (*prosfirnitsa*). In order to perform this role, women had to obtain a certificate and seals for printing the sign of the cross on the dough.[299]

The law continued to take a harsh view of women who erred, especially sexually. The barbaric punishment for wives who murdered their husbands—being buried in the ground up to their necks and left to die—is supposed to have been repealed in the regency of Sophia,[300] but was still in use during Peter's reign and beyond. Filippo Balatri, Johannes Korb and Cornelius de Bruyn all reported instances of this practice in Moscow, the latter noting (in 1702) that spectators threw coins at the victims.[301] Bruce recounts the tale of three women who took revenge on their drunken husbands by drowning them in the river when their husbands had beaten them after they tried to drag them from the tavern. According to him, they were put to death by interment in the ground up to their necks, two living for ten days, the third for eleven.[302] Korb reported the case of a woman who killed both her husband and her mother, whose limbs were burnt in addition.[303] Men who killed their wives, such as Prince Alexander Krupsky in 1693, were merely flogged with the knout.[304] For the lesser crime of adultery, women were sentenced to forced labour, usually in spinning mills. Weber noted that the linen mill outside St Petersburg employed eighty 'loose Women' supervised by an elderly Dutch woman, who used the whip to teach them how to handle a spinning wheel.[305] This replaced the older penalty of taking the veil. In general, assignment to work in the spinning mills was the regular punishment for female offenders found guilty of crimes for which men would serve hard labour. A decree of 26 July 1721 stated that convicted women and girls were to be handed over to the College of Mines and Manufacture, and given over to industrialists or sent to Moscow.[306] This was also the fate of a girl who disguised herself as a man and served seven years as a dragoon before being discovered. Her punishment was assignment to the Moscow spinning mill, where Bergholz saw her during a visit in 1722.[307] Another case was the infantryman's wife Marfa Dobriachina, who was sent to the mill for deserting her husband and committing adultery.[308] Factory directors were not always happy with this free labour.[309] For crimes not differentiated by gender, women were subject to the same penalties as men, with the exception of *katorga* (hard physical labour), which was replaced by work in spinning mills. But women committed crimes less frequently. For example, out of 498 cases heard in the Preobrazhensky *prikaz* in the period 1697–1708, only 52 involved women.[310]

In Peter's reign, then, the lives of élite women were dramatically different in many respects from those of their grandmothers. They were more public, their appearance more Westernized. But what on superficial acquaintance might be identified as 'emancipation' in fact represented a female version of service to the State, albeit in ballroom and assembly hall rather than regiment or chancellery. To the modern observer, perhaps the most striking innovation is that for the first time in Russian history the images of women come alive in art. In Orthodox religious painting the Mother of God and female saints had always had a special place. On the few occasions when living women were depicted, it was in devotional attitudes according to iconographic rules.[311] The Petrine era produced a picture gallery of live images, from Louis Caravaque's highly idealized canvases of Peter's daughters to Andrei Matveev's earthier Anastasia Golitsyna.[312] By mid-century the female portrait was possibly the dominant form of Russian art. On another level, allegorical figures and Classical goddesses, almost unknown in pre-Petrine Russia, entered the repertoire. Russia itself was often depicted as a woman.[313] On the ceiling of the Summer Palace, paintings of 1719 depicted the *Triumph of Russia* (three women representing the ruler, religion, and Plenty) and the *Triumph of Catherine*, with cupids and clouds. An anonymous artist painted the *Triumph of Minerva* in Peter's Cabinet, one of the first examples in Russia of secular painting on allegorical themes.[314] In the Summer Gardens, statues such as Pietro Baratta's *Mercy* and Marino Gropelli's *Truth* provided curious Russians with their first sight of female nudes in the round, a source of outrage to traditionalists who objected even to women being shown with uncovered hair.

How did the women who experienced them respond to Peter and his reforms in general? Little evidence survives, except of opposition in the files of the Preobrazhensky *prikaz*. There are no female equivalents of Feofan Prokopovich or Gavriil Buzhinsky singing Peter's praises. One needs to turn to women of a slightly later generation for a view. For Catherine II, speaking as a fellow sovereign, Peter was a role model, her 'spiritual father'; but privately she deplored the crudity and cruelty of his court and manners. Her *gofmisterina* was the Rumiantseva mentioned earlier, daughter of Andrei Matveev, who told her many stories about Peter. Ekaterina Dashkova was also severely critical of the coarse, military ethos of Peter's reign and the heavy cost in human life. She objected to nobles being turned into 'gardeners, black-smiths, and miners' and even more to a monarch playing the artisan: 'It was not Peter's business to be climbing up masts and working on the wharves with an axe!' This woman's voice is very much in harmony with post-1785 sentimentalism, sympathy with 'suffering humanity'.[315] Dashkova's view of Peter as a despot who treated people like slaves was probably affected by her discovery in the 1780s of the two glass jars containing the heads of Mary Hamilton and William Mons, executed in 1724. She had them buried.[316]

7

St Petersburg and the Arts

I.   FROM MOSCOW TO ST PETERSBURG

There are few better places to experience the palpable differences between late
Muscovite and Petrine culture than in Russia's national art collections, the
Tret'iakov Gallery in Moscow and the Russian Museum in St Petersburg,
where the images of the saintly dead which dominated the subject-matter of
Russian art for eight centuries give way, via a few meagre examples of the late
seventeenth-century *parsuna* (half-icon, half-portrait), to pictures painted
from life or recent memory, a gallery of royal personages, ladies, and gentlemen indistinguishable in dress and hair-style, if not always in the quality of
the painting, from their European contemporaries. An English observer will
readily call to mind portraits of William and Mary, Anne, and their courtiers.
Some Western visitors experience relief at reaching familiar territory, others
disappointment at the abrupt transition from an 'exotic' Russian idiom to a
mundanely international one.

But to what extent do the selected images in the Petrine portrait gallery
reflect Russian reality? Reforming the army, the taxation system, and the
Church, creating new administrative institutions, and building a new capital
were simple and straightforward in comparison with transforming people.
This was the greatest challenge that Peter had to face, and opinions of his
success vary. Even some of his admirers doubt whether his reforms went
much more than skin-deep, while critics accuse him of sacrificing national
identity in order to create 'citizens of the world'.[1] We are dealing here with an
attempt at cultural engineering rarely attempted in so short a space of time or
on such a scale. A nobleman of Peter's time was 'like a foreigner in his own
country: even when fully grown he had to learn artificially what people
usually absorb from direct experience in infancy'. European manners, trans-
posed to Russian soil, acquired a new significance. 'One did not have to
become a foreigner, but to behave like one.' Thus, 'daily life took on the features of theater'.[2] Just as it is almost impossible for grown-ups to become fully
bilingual, so nobles had to work hard to acquire a convincing cultural accent,
with varying degrees of success.

For such a transformation even to be attempted, extensive monarchical
powers were essential, such as those set out in *The Justice of the Monarch's Right*.

A sovereign monarch can lawfully command of the people not only whatever is necessary for the obvious good of his country, but indeed whatever he pleases, provided that it is not harmful to the people and not contrary to the will of God. The foundation of his power, as stated above, is the fact that the people has renounced in his favour its right to decide the common weal, and has conferred on him all power over itself: this includes civil and ecclesiastical ordinances of every kind, changes in customs and dress, house building, procedures and ceremonies at feasts, weddings, funerals.[3]

Before embarking upon a closer examination of Petrine culture, a number of points need to be considered. Although St Petersburg is clearly the focal point of cultural reform, both materially and symbolically, before about 1710, leading artists continued to be concentrated in Moscow, particularly in the royal Armoury. Provincial craftsmen continued to erect buildings and manufacture artifacts displaying traditional stylistic features well into the eighteenth century, and religious art continued to account for a substantial proportion of their output. As a result of the ephemeral nature of collective cultural displays, decay (many buildings were flimsily constructed), and war damage (especially during the Second World War), Petrine art had a poor survival rate. Of the numerous triumphal arches erected, for example, only one, the Petrovskie entrance gates to the Peter–Paul fortress, remains. In other words, to concentrate exclusively on the extant, primarily secular monuments and artifacts of St Petersburg dating from the 1710s to the 1720s, as both Soviet and Western studies have tended to do, gives an incomplete picture, but at the same time the limited evidence obscures the broader view.

The rare spectacle of a new city rising from 'nothing' led many writers to exaggerate the revolutionary nature of Petrine culture, an attitude which Slavophile thinkers who accused Peter of destroying Old Russia did nothing to discourage. The abandonment of Moscow in favour of St Petersburg was a potent symbol of Peter's rejection of Russia's past. In 1787 Prince Mikhail Shcherbatov put words of indignation into the spurned capital's mouth:

Alas! He left me. Whether out of necessity, to build a fleet, to institute commerce, and to direct in person the war then taking place, or out of disdain for my ancient customs, he transferred his capital to the newly built city bearing his name. ... My best citizens left my walls to found their homes in a strange land and crowds of peasants were sent to cultivate a marshy and infertile soil; my buildings, which no order was given to restore, fell to ruins, and it was forbidden to erect new ones.[4]

In fact, many Moscow buildings were no less 'modern' than their St Petersburg counterparts. The Main Pharmacy and Sukharev tower (1690s) demonstrated new trends in masonry construction for civic architecture. Peter's first major project there, the Arsenal, 1702–36, by Christopher Konrad, Mikhail Choglokov et al. and their group, was of Classical design. Its construction required extensive demolition of older buildings, including a church.[5] Other notable buildings include F. A. Golovin's impressive mansion and gardens on the outskirts of the city (completed in 1702, by D. Ivanov), M. P. Gagarin's Italianate villa with grand curving flights of steps on Tverskaia (1707, by D. Fontana), and Alexander Menshikov's Church of the Archangel Gabriel, which boasted the tallest tower outside the Kremlin.[6] Both churches and civic buildings displayed strong Moscow Baroque features in their design and decoration, along with a more Westernized use of decorative orders.

Many of the rules and fines later employed to bring 'regularity' to urban life in St Petersburg were first introduced in Moscow. An order of 1699 laid responsibility on each home-owner living on the main streets to ensure that the area in front of his gates was clean. Offenders were to be beaten with the knout.[7] Insistence on masonry construction dates from well before the founding of St Petersburg in wooden Moscow, as a continuation of fire pre-vention measures instituted by Peter's predecessors. In January 1701 it was ordered that buildings which had burned down were to be replaced with stone ones.[8] In January 1704 residents of the Kremlin and neighbouring Kitaigorod were told to erect stone houses and to build along the main streets and side streets, not in the middle of their plots, 'with good quality work-manship', a foretaste of the requirements for uniform skylines and façades in St Petersburg. Those without the means to erect stone buildings were forced to sell their plots to better-off owners.[9] There were many repetitions of such orders, even after the famous 1714 decree restricting masonry construction to St Petersburg.[10] In 1722 the call for stone pavements and houses in Moscow centre was repeated. An architect was to be summoned from St Petersburg to supervise planning. On the same day the appointment of a chief of police (*ober-politseimeister*) for Moscow was announced.[11] In other words, there were concentrated attempts to turn Moscow, too, into a model city. The old capital also had its share of major celebrations. Peter was there in December 1709–January 1710 for the lavish parades to celebrate the victory at Poltava. In May 1724 the whole court and the diplomatic community were summoned to Moscow for the coronation of Peter's wife, Catherine, staged in the Kremlin Dormition Cathedral, the traditional setting for the coronations of the tsars.

There were marked elements of continuity between élite Muscovite art—for example, the Moscow or Naryshkin Baroque architecture of the 1680s to the 1690s—and Petrine art, provided by those leading exponents of the Moscow Baroque era and their pupils who continued their activity well into the Petrine age. Armoury accounts for 1701–2 list Ivan Saltanov (a leading painter in the 1680s), Mikhail Choglokov and Grigory Odol'sky, and their pupils Aleksei Zakharov and Ivan Fedorov. No foreign painters are men-tioned, but there is a foreign engraver Adrian Schoenebeck (with Russian pupils Aleksei Zubov and Peter Bunin), and assorted foreign craftsmen, some engaged on 'the big clock which is being made on the model of Amsterdam clocks'. Russians and foreigners had worked side by side in the Armoury since the 1650s.[12] Most of the artists in this transitional period worked on both sacred and secular projects, although records for 1701–2 include just two artists, Tikhon Ivanov and Kirill Ulanov, specifically designated as icon-painters. In 1702 Armoury painter Grigory Odol'sky made banners for the Preobrazhensky and Semenovsky regiments, adorned with the cross of St Andrew, swords, and ships.[13] In 1704 F. A. Golovin, director of the Armoury, forwarded to Ivan Musin-Pushkin the request of a Moldavian envoy who was having some icons painted in Moscow, but explained that 'the painter [Ivan Zherebtsov] has been consigned to work on the triumphal gates and the work of painting the icons has been interrupted; if possible, please have that painter released from the triumphal gates so that he can finish the icons; he [the envoy] is a good man and will be most obliged to your honour in this matter'.[14]

The project which kept Zherebtsov away from his icon painting, the triumphal gates, was a notable innovation of the Petrine era, visible to a wide public and utilizing the services of teams of craftsmen. These gates, copied from foreign examples, themselves derived from Roman models, sup-plemented, without entirely replacing, the parades of icons, crosses, and religious banners which had accompanied victory celebrations in the past. Indeed, triumphal arches adorned with carvings, paintings, and texts had much in common with iconostases, which in turn were influenced by the designs of the new arches.[15] The first were erected in Moscow after the capture of Azov in 1696. At the end of 1702 triumphs were organized for the capture of Nöteborg, including a tower decorated with banners of various colours and illuminated with lanterns.[16] It was mostly icon-painters who carried out this type of work. In December 1709 Prince M. P. Gagarin was ordered to build five triumphal towers along the Moskva River by the Kremlin for the Poltava celebrations. He was ordered to hire carpenters and other craftsmen for the purpose. Icon-painters were entrusted with the repainting of some thirty pictures, some of which were torn and others of which suffered from damp, having been kept in a barn in the Armoury, then set up on the city walls where they were damaged by strong winds and their frames broken. Triumphal arches by the Serpukhov gates were to be decorated with pictures painted in 'perspective'.[17] The 1709 gates represented the 'temple of deeds and valours of the Russian Hercules' on sixteen pillars, with Corinthian orders and eight pedestals depicting the virtues of the monarchy 'on which the building of state rests firm'.[18]

This prolific use of Classical imagery, often in interplay with Christian motifs, is a common thread running throughout all the arts to be considered below and a distinguishing feature of the Baroque culture which spanned the Moscow and St Petersburg periods. Seen first in Russia in comparative abun-dance in the poetry of Simeon Polotsky and in Moscow Baroque art, the Classical repertoire expanded under the direct influence of Western works and artists, until, to quote Metropolitan Dmitry of Rostov (1708), in the houses of the Russian élite Venus replaced the Virgin.[19] From the 1630s in the Kiev Mohyla Academy, then in the Moscow Academy from the 1680s, pane-gyric verses were composed and school dramas were performed, fusing

Classical mythology, medieval allegory, and contemporary politics.[20] The same characters and devices found their way into the figurative and decorative arts, often drawn from published source-books like *Simvoly i emblemata* (1705).

Peter himself appeared in stock guises in several genres—painted, printed, carved, and sculpted. He was Hercules, for his victories over the Swedish 'lion', and Samson, who forced apart the lion's jaws. A printed description of triumphal gates erected by the Moscow Academy in 1709 refers to the 'All-Russian Hercules', although the engraved frontispiece depicts St George smiting a dragon and a double eagle dropping a thunderbolt on a lion.[21] A medal issued to mark Russian victories in Livonia in 1710 has Peter wearing a laurel wreath, armour, and mantle, and on the reverse Hercules bearing a globe with the towns Narva, Reval, Dorpat, Pernau, Arensburg, and Riga marked and the legend in Latin 'I have the strength to bear such a burden'.[22] Peter was Neptune, Jupiter, the 'Orthodox Mars' (a wall-painting in Menshikov's palace *The Triumph of Mars* is said to have Peter's features), and Pygmalion.[23]

Behind all these references lay the notion of *translatio imperii*. Peter was the central figure in the re-enactment on Russian soil of heroic feats of yore, notably in the area of empire building. He was Russia's Alexander the Great to his father's Philip of Macedon,[24] although Peter actually preferred Julius Caesar ('a clever leader') to Alexander (who 'fought for his own glory alone').[25] Constantine the Great was another figure for comparison, founder of a new capital and the creator of a Christian empire, who combined both secular and sacred power.[26] Peter was likened to Numa, legendary second ruler of Rome, who reformed the calendar and religion. In his eulogy (*Panegirikos*) to Poltava, Feofan Prokopovich compares Russia's current situation with the Second Punic War (third century BC), when the Romans were in a tricky position, but Scipio Africanus managed to defeat Hannibal and make Rome great.[27]

After 1700 Peter's image on the new rouble coins settled down as recognizably Roman (laurel wreath, armour, mantle, Roman hair-style).[28] Roman historical imagery infiltrated many areas of the secular state, from the imperial titles adopted in 1721 (Imperator, Pater Patriae, Maximus) to the Latinate letters in the reformed civil script.[29] In its congratulatory speech the Senate declared: 'We thought it right, in the manner of the ancients, especially the Roman and Greek people ... as was the custom of the Roman Senate in recognition of their emperors' famous deeds to pronounce such titles publicly as a gift and to inscribe them on statues for the memory of posterity.'[30] But imperial examples also served as warnings. At the same Nystad celebrations people were reminded that 'in the past the Greeks [i.e., Byzantines] were brave men, but then by their lack of effort and weakness they fell behind in their study of military affairs'.[31] Foreigners grasped the significance of Roman imagery long before the new titles were introduced. The Dane Erebro Rasmus described the Poltava triumphal parade in Moscow in 1710 as 'undoubtedly the grandest and most magnificent triumphal procession in Europe since the time of the ancient Romans'. A portrait set up outside the Moscow residence of Fedor Romodanovsky was captioned 'The unconquerable and most fortunate Emperor'.[32]

Peter and his associates, few of whom had had much formal education, left it to experts to devise the details, but often made stock references to Classical mythology. Bacchus was a particular favourite. Peter wrote to Menshikov in November 1706: 'as we make a sacrifice to Bacchus with a sufficiency of wine and praise God with our soul'.[33] Neptune carried personal resonances. In 1711 Peter wrote to Fedor Apraksin about the fact that the ice lay on the Neva only three months that winter: 'I think that Neptune must be angry with me, as while I have been there he has never once allowed me the pleasure of such a short winter.'[34] A shipwreck off the Finnish coast prompted the remark: 'We have a shortfall, for Neptune has exacted a customs due.'[35] Peter's command in 1716 of the combined Russian, English, Danish and Dutch fleets was commemorated by a medal depicting the sea-god in a chariot drawn by four sea-horses.

Coins and medals were a rich source of imagery. The first Russian commemorative medal, issued by the Admiralty Mint in 1702, depicted Azov. A collection based on twenty-eight subjects commissioned from P. H. Müller of Nuremberg to commemorate Russian victories in the years 1702–14 featured Mars, Mercury, Hercules, Minerva and Victoria, with inscriptions based on Ovid and Virgil. Inspired by Louis XIV's medallic history by Warin, this series performed a function similar to that of icons in the religious sphere.[36] Because these medals were also intended for propaganda abroad, the inscriptions were in Latin. Medals awarded to veterans of Russian victories (some twelve battles were thus commemorated) were inscribed in Russian, but still Classical in their imagery.[37]

Classical knowledge was restricted to the élite. A description of a silver globe in the Armoury (1701) notes that on top were seated two men, 'one large one in a hat, with wings on his hat and his feet, in his right hand he holds an orb, in his left a staff with wings'. The scribe evidently did not know that he was describing Mercury.[38] A small literate audience had access to printed pamphlets describing and explaining triumphal procession, arches and firework displays, many of which emanated from the Moscow Academy. Precedents in ancient history were quoted. One describes four angels throwing flowers 'after the manner of the celebrants of old who entered the Capitol Appenine Way bearing flowers'.[39] An explanation of the New Year fireworks in 1704 stated that 'Jupiter was accepted by the ancient pagans as the first and foremost almighty power', and that Pallas Athene was 'the goddess of martial art and other honourable wisdom'.[40] Figures were set up in the Summer Garden in St Petersburg depicting characters from Aesop's fables, each with a plaque bearing a short explanation of the tale.[41] It was felt necessary not only to explain but also to justify the use of pagan imagery. In his preface to the 'pious reader', in a description of a parade held in Moscow, Iosif Turoboisky first prepared the ground with some familiar David and Goliath imagery, then expounded the principle of the use of metaphors and images, pointing out how the Bible was full of images such as the olive branch, four beasts, lambs, vines, and so on.[42]

Moscow, then, was the cradle of the new art and imagery, but the creation of a new capital from scratch required different priorities and organizational methods: foreign architects directed all major projects, Russian artists were trained abroad, and a greatly increased repertoire of Classical and allegorical motifs and new genres was imported. Moscow, with its 2,000 churches, was too indelibly stamped with the image of Old Russia to serve Peter's purposes. A famous panorama of the city (1707–8) makes this clear—the irregular skyline is dominated by the cupolas and spires of countless churches. Stone buildings alternate with wooden shacks. The impression is picturesque and disorderly.[43] Moscow provided neither the 'blank sheet' nor the combination of sea and riverscape which made St Petersburg so irresistible. So although Peter did not spurn Moscow to the extent suggested by Prince Shcherbatov, he decisively relegated it to the status of 'second capital'.

Moscow's 'relegation' was most clearly reflected in the amount of time the tsar and high nobles spent there. As early as August 1706, when St Petersburg was no more than a few huts and earthworks, Charles Whitworth wrote from Moscow:

> We have as cold rainy weather now as you have in November. We have no manner of Company, neither Courtiers Soldiers nor Merchants, the first being at the army and the others getting money at Archangel, we have neither Plays, Musick nor paintings, we have no good fruit, no good venaison, and little good wine, and the Women are ugly, silly and ill bred: my greatest diversion is to go twice a week to the little English Chappel, and there Good Lord delivers us in a hearty prayer.'[44]

During the earlier years of the Northern War Peter rarely visited Moscow except at Yuletide. He hated to be away from St Petersburg during the navigation season and when he was not sailing he was campaigning or abroad.

After the Battle of Poltava, attention shifted even more decisively from Moscow to St Petersburg. A well-wisher advised Peter in an anonymous letter of 1710: 'In St Petersburg for the common good of the people of the all-Russian state and for the profit of the nation's merchantry ... there ought to be masters of various skills and handicrafts.'[45] Peter did not need to be convinced. A transfer of Armoury-trained craftsmen had begun. In March 1710 the painter Ivan Shvertserov complained that he had been ordered to St Petersburg but allotted no travel allowance. He received five roubles.[46] In 1711 more painters were transferred from Moscow. Thereafter the new capital had first call on resources.[47]

II. PETER'S PARADISE

> What gardens are these established here
>   Planted by the great father,
> Where now his daughter is ruler,
>   Equally great, equally first,
> A goddess on earth like Minerva?
> Cry out: 'The Northern Eden!'[48]

'... this great window recently opened in the north through which
Russia looks on Europe' (Francesco Algarotti, 1739)[49]

No contemporary first-hand account survives of the events of 16 May 1703,
the traditional date of the founding of St Petersburg. There are no entries, for
example, in the court journals.[50] One of the first references appears in a letter
from Peter to Cornelius Cruys, dated 1 July 1703, reporting that the Russian
flag had been planted beside the ex-Swedish fortress, but that the 'desired spot
was still three (naval) miles off'. The account included in the official history
of Peter's reign was composed many years later: 'After the capture of
Nienschants a council of war was sent to determine whether to fortify this
spot or to find a more convenient place (since this one was small, far from the
sea and not well fortified by nature), and it was decided to look for somewhere else and after a few days' search they found a convenient island, called
Lust Eland, where on 16 May the foundations of a fortress were laid and
named Saint Petersburg.'[51] There is another version in *The Book of Mars*
(1713), according to which Peter himself made the discovery 'in a very conveniently located place', and laid the foundation of the fortress and named
it.[52] There are still more fanciful versions, such as an allegorical tale in the
style of the old chronicles. As Peter walked to the centre of the island, he saw
an eagle hovering overhead. He grabbed a bayonet, cut two strips of turf, laid
one on top of the other in the shape of a cross, then made a crucifix from
some wood which he erected on the turf, with the words: 'In the name of
Christ Jesus on this place shall be a church in the names of the apostles Peter
and Paul.' A more formal ceremony of foundation took place later, with the
digging of a trench and the placing in it of a casket with the relics of St
Alexander Nevsky. Two birch-tree trunks were driven into the ground to
suggest gates. The eagle, first mentioned hovering over the island, lands on
the birch gatepost, then on Peter's arm, and is carried in to the service. The
writer records the legends that Constantine the Great was led to Byzantium
by an eagle and that the apostle Andrew, en route from Kiev to Novgorod,
planted his staff in a spot not far from St Petersburg and blessed the region.
Thus Peter's city was placed in the context of Christian world history.[53]

In fact, it is possible that Peter was not even on the spot for the legendary
founding.[54] The notion that the city was built on 'empty' land is also
mistaken. This myth, later fuelled by the opening lines of Pushkin's poem
'The Bronze Horseman', which pictures the tsar looking out over a wilderness

dotted with an occasional fisherman's hut, was current among contemporaries, and used for rhetorical effect by Peter's publicists. A Polish observer wrote: 'Anyone wishing to describe St Petersburg properly would need to have been there before its foundation and seen what was there before on the spot where now a great stone city has arisen.'[55] In fact, in addition to the fort of Nienschants, there were many populated settlements in the area, including the fairly substantial residences of Swedish officials.[56]

The first written mention of the name St Petersburg appears to post-date the dedication of the fortress church on 29 June, the feast of SS Peter and Paul, the tsar's name-day.[57] The first friendly foreign ship, a Dutch vessel, appeared in the vicinity in November 1703, bringing salt and wine. The captain was rewarded with 500 gold crowns, and similar gifts were promised to other ships which docked there.[58] The first new buildings were hastily erected earthwork fortifications and Peter's wooden cabin, but from the start the tsar had more ambitious plans. In a letter to Menshikov dated 28 September 1704 he referred to the fortress as *stolitsa*, the capital: 'If God grants, we expect to be in the capital (Piterburkh) in three or four days.'[59] The first engraving of the town (by Pieter Picart, in 1704) features an expanse of water with ships in the middle ground and spires of the fortress and adjoining land in the far distance, a reflection of Peter's priorities.[60] Another early engraving of the fortress, with the legend 'Petropolis 1703', was included on a leaflet on the rules of mathematics published in Moscow in 1705.[61]

Early St Petersburg was to be beautiful as well as useful. In March 1704 Peter wrote to Tikhon Streshnev: 'Don't miss the opportunity to send various plants, especially ones with scent, from Izmailovo to St Petersburg with gardeners'.[62] He wrote again on 16 June, reporting almost in the same breath in which he mentioned the recent Russian victory at Narva that 'the flowers, six peony bushes, have been brought here intact; I'm amazed that they weren't shaken to pieces, but there are plenty of blooms. Only it's a great pity that the camphor, mint and other perfumed plants haven't been sent. If peonies got here, the latter should be much easier to deal with. Have some sent.'[63] Trees and plants were an early priority, not just native species but exotic flowering, medicinal, and fruit-bearing ones, for nutrition and for pleasure. In August 1708 Peter ordered orange, lemon, and other trees from Persia to be placed in boxes, imported via Astrakhan and brought up the Volga. 'And have heated huts made for them to overwinter so they don't die from frost.'[64] Oaks, scarce in the region, were planted with an eye to shipbuilding.[65] Early St Petersburg was austere, but not entirely lacking in comforts. An order sent to Archangel in September 1706 lists for dispatch to St Petersburg items of English tableware, striped taffeta, Indian printed fabrics, some 'good-quality stockings', olives, and anchovies. (Peter's mistress and wife-to-be Catherine was in residence by this date.[66]) In July 1707 Peter sent for an expert on fountains, the progress of which figures in many letters, no matter how far away Peter was—for example, to Alexander Kikin from the Ukraine in January 1709.[67]

Clearly, then, Peter had a number of things in mind when he referred to St

Petersburg as 'paradise'. On 7 April 1706 he wrote to Menshikov: 'I cannot omit to write to you from this Paradise where, with the help of the Almighty, everything is fine. .... We may be living in heaven here; only we must never forget, as you know yourself, to place our hope not in man but in the will and grace of God.'[68] Peter was no Classical scholar, but from the beginning he strove to re-create his patch of swampy wasteland after the model, albeit dimly perceived, of the 'pleasant place' (*locus amoenus*) associated in Ovid's *Metamorphoses* with the Classical imagery of paradise, of which springs, pleasant streams, trees, gardens, flowers, and birds' voices were staple ingredients. The city's watery location, of course, had contemporary and personal heavenly resonances.[69] The new-founded city of St Peter was the successor to earlier Russian versions of the New Constantinople, New Rome, and New Zion. Parallels were drawn by contemporaries between Peter, the creator of a new city, and God, the creator of Eden.[70] But Peter's Russia was successor not so much to the second Rome, the *religious* empire of Byzantium (although this idea was not abandoned entirely), as to the *first* pre-Christian Rome, the secular, military empire.

These grandiose concepts were challenged by practical realities. For most people St Petersburg was not paradise but hell, both on material grounds (its cold climate, the expense of transporting food and goods, a mosquito-infested building site on a marsh) and religious and ideological grounds (Moscow was the heart of Orthodox Christianity, seat of the patriarch, containing the tombs of the tsars and grand princes). But 'removing spiritual primacy from Moscow' was one of Peter's major aims,[71] and for this he relied on the support of a team of churchmen-publicists, mainly Ukrainians, who came up with a potent package of images and devices to praise St Petersburg. Their repertoire included Christian sea symbols, a ship representing the salvation of the soul on the sea of life and St Peter's ship—the Church. The legend of St Andrew's (the former fisherman's) visit to the north of Russia was fruitfully exploited, as was St Petersburg's identification with New Jerusalem as described in Revelations: 'and I saw the Holy City New Jerusalem, coming down out of heaven from God' (21:2), and 'he showed me a river of water of life' (22:1). Given a lengthy war which placed heavy burdens on everyone, from boyar to serf, plus a programme of modernization that earned Peter the name of Antichrist in conservative circles, it was vital to encourage national pride while relocating national priorities. Few cities in history can have borne such a heavy symbolic burden as St Petersburg.

We should not rule out the possibility that Peter also manipulated the 'paradise' image for his own private ends, adding an element of parody and private jest. Most paradise references are found in letters to Menshikov, who, as governor of Ingria, was well aware of the drawbacks of the city under construction, even if he too called it the 'promised land'.[72] Expressing his joy at receiving letters from Menshikov a few weeks after he wrote the first 'paradise' letter, Peter wrote: 'everyone was delighted; up till now although we lived in heaven, our hearts were always heavy.'[73] Reporting on departure plans delayed by a course of blood-letting, he wrote: 'Don't worry about what is going on here, because in God's heaven there can be no evil.'[74] The town was ever in his thoughts. In September 1707 he wrote to Menshikov from near Grodno that a messenger had arrived from Paradise, or Petersburg, 'and brought much consolation'.[75] In March 1708, newly returned to the city, however, he was forced to report to G. I. Golovkin that 'where God builds himself a church, there is an altar for the devil also'. He had always felt well 'in this heavenly place', but now it seemed that he had brought the fever from Poland (by implication the antithesis of 'paradise'[76]), and the Easter holiday had been ruined. References to 'paradise' often coincide with Peter's return to the city after long spells of 'exile' in various 'hell-holes'. In January 1706 he had written to Fedor Golovin from Dubrovna asking him to deal with various matters in his absence, because 'being in this *hell* I have not just enough but, alas, more troubles than I can cope with'.[77] In February 1710 he wrote to Menshikov: 'I only wish that the Lord God might sort out your affairs as quickly as possible and that we could see you here, so that you too could see the beauty of this Paradise in reward for the labours in which you participated together with us, which I wish with all my heart, for this place really is thriving like a fine infant.'[78] In May of the following year, in Poland, on the eve of war with the Turks, he wrote to Menshikov with greetings for the feast of the Trinity and in the hope that that 'this holy comforter in his justice might bring this affair to a speedy conclusion and allow us quickly to return to our own Eden'.[79]

However we interpret Peter's use of 'paradise' imagery, there is no doubt that he regarded the land as sacred *Russian* soil. He referred to it as 'this holy place' in a letter to Menshikov congratulating him on his name-day, the feast of St Alexander Nevsky, the Russian saint famous for his struggle against the Teutonic knights and named after the river which flows through St Petersburg.[80] Returning from campaigns and foreign travel after a long break away from the city in November 1709, Peter again wrote to Menshikov on the eve of St Andrew from 'this holy land'.[81] Holy Russian land was not to be relinquished lightly. Early in 1707 Peter jotted a note to the effect that 'we must find all possible means to hold on to Petersburg; its surrender is not even to be contemplated'.[82]

In the meantime a sizeable town with more mundane preoccupations was springing up. In November 1706 Peter ordered the formation of two shifts of workers for the St Petersburg summer building season, with 15,000 in each.[83] The following year the numbers were increased to 20,000 in each, the first group to arrive by late March or early April. The recruits were to be accompanied to St Petersburg by armed guards, to prevent escape en route. They were to bring only enough food for the journey, 'since to send off workmen with their bread as happened last year is a very great burden to the workmen'.[84] This order continued to be issued annually, with variations,[85] but despite attempts to regularize the draft—for example, by specifying the towns and rural districts from which workers were to be drawn—there were annual shortfalls in numbers, which were exacerbated by heavy casualties in service. Extra hands were drafted in from distant regions, including teams of Tatars, Cheremys, and Mordvinians.[86] The problem was chronic: in 1710 Peter complained that only 1,000 of a batch of 3,000 men needed to build brick factories had been sent.[87]

Even in 1708–9, the most tense period of the Northern War, Peter expected to be kept informed about current building projects. He asked for a report on the progress of the fortress, at first a simple construction of earthworks and wood, then rebuilt in stone from 1706. (The fortress bore Peter's personal stamp, its bastions named in honour of his cronies Menshikov, Zotov, Golovkin, Trubetskoy and Naryshkin.) In the same letter he regretted that some orange blossoms had been sent to him packed in olive oil (the gardener thought this was a good way of preserving them), and asked for more to be sent wrapped in tobacco leaves! He was eager to receive some tangible fruits from 'paradise'. Ulian Siniavin, master of works, was ordered to report more often: 'Keep us informed by every post.'[88] After Poltava, which laid the city's 'final foundation stone', more attention could be paid to its embellishment.[89] On 8 July 1709 Peter wrote to 'great sovereign' Fedor Romodanovsky: 'Now without any doubt your majesty's desire to have your residence in St Petersburg can be satisfied now that the enemy has met his final end.'[90] The words were written half in jest (Romodanovsky moved into his new residence in 1711), but gave a hint of things to come for those still cosily ensconced in Moscow. In action-packed 1709 Peter spent only a couple of weeks in St Petersburg, but he was there for most of 1710, when military operations were focused on the Baltic, and he was able to devote more time than hitherto to matters other than fortress building. In late 1709 to early 1710 not only did he found a church in honour of St Samson to commemorate Poltava, he also 'ordered houses of amusement to be built of stone of fine architectural design, to embellish gardens and speed the erection of fortifications, and also gave orders for more houses to be built for naval servitors and merchants, and the gentlemen ministers, generals and distinguished nobles were ordered to build stone mansions'.[91]

The first major buildings date from 1710: the Summer and Winter Palaces (the latter was replaced by another in 1725, which in turn made way for Rastrelli's creation), the palaces of Menshikov, Gavrila Golovkin, and other magnates, the Alexander Nevsky monastery (founded on the spot where the prince was said to have fought the Swedes in 1240, although in fact the battle took place some miles away), and the wooden church of St Isaac of Dalmatia, whose feast fell on Peter's birthday. In 1711 a 'perspektiva', or avenue, later Nevsky Prospect, was laid, leading from the Admiralty. In 1712 the construction of the stone cathedral of SS Peter and Paul began, although not until after Peter's death did it eclipse the Trinity Cathedral on the St Petersburg side as the city's main church.[92] Apprentice gardeners were summoned from Moscow, together with plants and seeds; architects were hired; paintings were ordered from abroad.[93] From 1710 a Gardening bureau (sadovaia kontora), headed by Boris Neronov, was attached to the Cabinet to run the tsar's gardens.[94] Modest wooden summer-houses began to spring up out of town along the Finnish gulf, including Ekaterinhof and Strel'na, to be replaced by stone palaces a few years later.[95]

After Poltava, St Petersburg came to be regarded as the capital, although no formal decree was issued. In August 1710 provincial governors were ordered to assemble to make their reports not in Moscow but in St Petersburg, where the court was to celebrate Christmas that year.[96] In 1711 choristers from the former patriarchal office were summoned from Moscow for the same reason.[97] In December 1711 Peter's sister Natalia travelled from Moscow with Peter's daughters, to be followed there by other royal women.[98] The transfer of the court and government offices to the shores of the Baltic did not take place all at once or even permanently, however. Peter himself was constantly on the move, accompanied by a travelling court. Christmas and New Year were often spent in Moscow, and some members of the royal family, such as Peter's sister-in-law, Praskovia, maintained residences in Moscow. One can distinguish several other landmarks in the transfer of the capital: for example, the wedding there of Tsarevna Anna Ioannovna to the duke of Courland in 1710 and Peter's own wedding to Catherine in February 1712, which brought together dignitaries from all over Russia. In December 1711 Peter summoned the Senate to join him in St Petersburg.[99] In early 1712 a St Petersburg Senate chancellery was established, although the Senate did not move as a body until late 1713.[100] Even then, they and other members of the court and officialdom were obliged to spend lengthy periods in Moscow when the tsar so ordered.

Mass transfers of population were an annual occurrence. In 1714 a thousand nobles on military and government service, those with a hundred or more peasant households, were ordered to build houses in St Petersburg. Pleading illness or poverty was to no avail. In 1716 the nobleman Vasily Zmeev argued that he had been bedridden for many years. A doctor's report confirmed that he could not walk and was 'incurable', being over seventy years of age. Even so, the order that he go to St Petersburg 'at once' and build a house there was repeated.[101] Weber records that families ordered to move to St Petersburg in 1716 complained that they had lost about two-thirds of their capital by the move. 'However, it is surprising to see with what Resignation and Patience those People, both high and low, submit to such Hardships.'[102] St Petersburg's role as a centre of shipbuilding, inaugurated by the foundation of the Admiralty in 1705, was boosted by the demotion of the Voronezh yards after the loss of the Azov fleet in 1711 and the transfer of shipwrights.[103] Charles Whitworth observed that the nobles moved to St Petersburg 'with no small difficulty since the climate is too cold, and the ground too marshy to furnish the conveniences of life, which are all brought from the neighbouring countries; however, the Czar is charmed with his new production and would lose the best belt of his provinces sooner than this barren corner'.[104] Peter ordered: 'Announce that people must go [to St Petersburg] with their whole families, with everyone who lives in the same household with them.' Later, though, he warned officials to show a little humanity by not forcing women who were about to give birth or the very sick to travel. They were to be given time, but not too much.[105]

Once there, reluctant immigrants were expected to become seafarers. An order to the fiscal I. S. Potemkin in June 1710 set out a table of fines for officials and officers who used oars instead of sails to cross the river when there was a wind.[106] Inhabitants were assigned to 'permanent residences' by social category; for example, in 1712, 1,000 of the 'best families' were ordered to build houses up-river from the tsar's palace, 500 merchants and 500 traders to build opposite them on the other bank, and 2,000 artisans further along.[107]

The first detailed description of the new city, an *Exact Account of the Newly Built Fortress and Town of St Petersburg,* published anonymously in German in Leipzig in 1713, is based on observations made in 1710–11.[108] Foreigners agreed that it was an uncomfortable place to live, not just because of the climate and the building-site atmosphere, but also because of the high cost of basic supplies. The Danish envoy Just Juel complained that even hay, oats, and firewood were often unavailable, and that wine and vodka were hard to find. A flood in December 1710 exacerbated the problems by spoiling provisions in cellars.[109] There had been little improvement by 1714, when Weber described St Petersburg as 'a Heap of Villages linked together, like some Plantation in the West Indies'; although he conceded that it was a 'Wonder of the World' in view of the short time it had been in existence and that the improvements which Peter had made 'were not merely calculated for Profit, but for Delight also'.[110] Weber reported that there were 50,000 houses in the city, ranging from palaces to hovels.[111] Peter changed his mind several times about where the focal point of the city should be. Attempts to persuade inhabitants to move to Vasil'evsky Island are reflected in repeated orders in June 1720 instructing any persons not employed in the Admiralty and fleet (except for magnates) and resident on the Admiralty side to move their residences across the river to Vasil'evsky Island. The said residences would be demolished if they persisted in disobeying. Residents with sites on the Neva but without the funds to construct stone residences were ordered to sell their plots to naval personnel who did have the means.[112] This peremptory command to sell up and move out was typical of the way the city was planned. The German envoy Mardefeld reported that people were 'in despair' at having to abandon houses, gardens, and greenhouses, not to mention the expense of having to build in stone. He notes the case of Baron Löwenwold, who had just paved around his house and spent 20 roubles for tree planting, only to be told to move. There was no compensation, for, as Mardefeld explained, 'this complies with the fundamental laws of the country in which everything belongs to God and the Tsar'.[113]

The idea that there was a strictly planned differentiation of dwelling design according to class (model houses for the 'lowly' (*podlykh*), 'well-off' (*zazhitochnykh*), and 'titled' (*imenitykh*)) has been challenged, however. The designs in question, by Domenico Trezzini, were intended 'for those who wish to build' on different sizes of plot, but carried no 'class' designation as such, even if the grander designs were beyond the means of the less well-off.[114] The main point is that residents in the prestigious, visible parts of the city, especially on the river banks, were required to build from architectural plans (*po arkhitek-ture*) and keep to the authorized roof line (*v odin gorizont*), submitting drawings for approval. Away from the main façade, in courtyards, residents could please themselves about such details as the design of windows or door frames.[115] The residences of top officials (virtually all gone today) sprang up along the embankment between the Summer and Winter Palaces—for example, F. M. Apraksin's house, which rivalled Menshikov's in style and size, 'all furnished splendidly and in the latest fashion'.[116]

Foreign architects and craftsmen contributed to the planning and construction of the city. They were never very many compared with the tens of thousands of Russian labourers drafted in to do the hard graft (in 1722, for example, there were sixty-five foreigners on the books of the Chancellery of Building, ranging from fully fledged architects to roofers and 'cement masters'[117]); but men such as Domenico Trezzini (Swiss Italian); Johann Friedrich Braunstein, Georg Johann Mattarnovy and Andreas Schlüter (German); Nicholas Friedrich Härbel (Austrian); Jean-Baptiste Le Blond (French); and Gaetano Chiaveri and Nicola Michetti (Italian) were responsible for designing most major buildings. Peter's own contribution to the planning of St Petersburg was substantial, not one important building being built without his participation at some stage of construction.[118] Every year, even when he was abroad for much of the time, as in 1716–17, he would produce a list of projects for the next building season, often in his own hand, from prominent public buildings to small details of embankments and garden walls.[119] Architects were often summoned to attend the tsar. Not all of Peter's pet projects were successful, notably the one to make Vasil'evsky Island the centre of the city. An anecdote tells of Peter's disappointment on returning from France in 1717 only to see that the grid-plan streets and canals on the island were of narrow proportions, only about half as wide as those in Amsterdam, which he regarded as a model. When told by Le Blond that the only remedy was to demolish everything and start from scratch, Peter lost interest.[120]

Some projects were planned as ensembles. One of the most interesting is the complex of the Summer Palace and Gardens, which provided both a residence and a site for outdoor entertainments. Zubov's 1717 engraving, taken as from an aerial view looking south towards the gardens over the Neva, demonstrates features of distinct Petrine stamp, starting with the river frontage, the palace itself being built right on the river bank, with a canal to one side for direct access to boats to sail across to the fortress and Trinity Square. The embankment walls are lined with galleries in the shape of triumphal arches; canals and trees in serried ranks, like troops, create the main lines of an orderly and rational plan; garden plots are divided by diagonals reminiscent of the St Andrew's cross; the gardens are dotted with fountains and statues, including the famous *Venus* purchased in Italy. In the grounds were orangeries and greenhouses.[121]

Special objects of attention were Peter's out-of-town palaces, Peterhof (known as Petrodvorets in Soviet times) and the lesser-known Ekaterinhof and Strel'na.[122] The latter, the last palace to be started, was to be a royal seat to 'vie with Versailles' (reflecting the influence of Peter's visit to France in 1717, when he acquired, among other things, an album of views of the palace and gardens at Versailles, which he always kept in his study).[123] The garden would be 'of a vast Extent', and a 'noble and costly Palace' was to be built on the hill, but Peter's death brought work to an end, and the site did not interest his daughter Elizabeth, as Peterhof did in the 1740s.[124] Archives are full of Peter's orders, from home and abroad, often amending the proposals of his architects. Thus in Peterhof the master of works was ordered 'to build a small grotto and ponds in front of it and fences around them from the old plan, only to build the open room in the small grotto as I ordered Braunstein to do, and not as on the model; water is to be plumbed and the weir made on the stream as in Le Blond's plan, but don't dig the ponds until I arrive. In Strel'na do everything according to Le Blond's plan, except on the hillock, where he designates a small cottage, but don't do anything until I arrive.'[125] No effort or expense was too great. In February 1723 the head gardener demanded 340 cubic sazhens of black earth and manure and peasants in the outlying districts of Kopor'e and Iamburkh were commanded to deliver this amount.[126] The work was viewed as an ensemble and a lasting monument. In a letter to the works director Peter warned: 'Most of all take care that everything is done solidly and finished off properly and cleanly so that it won't have to be done over again.'[127] Another small palace was built at Sara's homestead (Sarinina myza) by Catherine, as a gift to Peter.[128] It came to be known as Tsarskoe Selo, and in the 1750s the wooden palace was replaced by Rastrelli's vast Catherine Palace. Along the coast nobles were encouraged to build their own country estates and to plant avenues and groves.[129] On a clear day most of these palaces had a view of Kronstadt out in the gulf on Kotlin Island. The island had as much attention lavished on it as the palaces; but whereas the latter were for relaxation, Kronstadt's purpose was utilitarian, its buildings plain. It is as good an example of regular planning as anything constructed in the Petrine era, with its docks and canals, hospitals and barracks, and regular street grid (much of it surviving to this day), all embellished with trees.[130]

Peter's interest in improving his new capital went far beyond hiring foreign architects to design buildings in Western style. In 1718 plans were drawn up in the local government reform for a new subdivision of the St Petersburg *guberniia*, which envisaged the appointment of a Swedish-style governor-general (*ober-shtat-galter*) for the city. The first to hold the post was Menshikov. Heinrich Fick, who drew up the plans, remarked: 'there now lies upon the River Neva a great, commanding city, which previously did not exist, and therefore there is a great similarity with this country, and in particular it may be noted that St Petersburg is situated just as is Stockholm, for Stockholm lies on the River Mälaren [sic] between the two provinces of Uppland and Södermanland, and St Petersburg lies on the River Neva between the two provinces of Ingria and Karelia, and both residences are very similar in their situation'.[131] In effect, St Petersburg was the first Russian city to be under 'police' administration, in the eighteenth-century sense of provisions for order, cleanliness, and welfare, as well as crime prevention.[132] The first European city to enjoy such a regime, Peter's model, was Paris, the word *politsiia* entering Russian in 1718 in the decree on police administration for the capital. The first chief of police (modelled on the French Lieutenant-Général de Police) was Anton Devier. Weber wrote in 1719: 'The new Regulations of Police, a thing unheard-of in Russia before, has already produced a very good Effect, particularly as to the Safety of the publick Streets.'[133] With admirable resourcefulness learned from his master, Devier supplemented the small work-force allocated to him with the efforts of the population at large. On 20 March 1720, for example, 'St Petersburg inhabitants of all ranks possessing horses' were ordered to bring a cart-load of manure for each horse they owned to a place on Vasil'evsky Island to be designated by the bureau of the Chief of Police; 'if people fail to carry out this order they will be fined the sum of one rouble for each [undelivered] cart-load. Let this be announced in St Petersburg to the beat of drums.'[134] On 20 October 1721 Devier received an order for the construction of abattoirs at the mouth of the Moika 'to be built to resemble residences with false windows, and to improve their appearance painted with paints obtained from the *Kamer-kollegiia,* since when His Majesty was travelling along that river past the paper mills he had a good look at the abattoirs which the butchers have built and found them to be very poor, scattered all over the place, and the surrounding area was dirty'.[135] On 20 April 1722 Devier received another order for distribution: 'Anyone who has to construct wooden buildings should boil moss well in boiling water before using it [for stuffing cracks], because cockroaches hatch out in raw moss, which contains flies and other vermin and they will subsequently grow and multiply.'[136] Public hygiene measures involved setting up model stalls made of canvas to replace the ramshackle premises used by street food-traders, 'for better appearance and cleanliness'. Earlier decrees had apparently resulted in people making tents from dirty, smelly rags sewn together and 'disgusting to the human sight'.[137] In April 1721 there was an attempt to set up a regular refuse collection service, with a team of horses and drivers and vagrants to collect rubbish from outside houses.[138] Live detritus was not allowed to litter the streets, either. Beggars were banned (especially any on the streets 'out of laziness and young people who are not being employed in work and for hire, from whom no good can come, only robbery'). There was a five-rouble fine for anyone caught giving alms to beggars. They were advised to dispense charity by giving their money to hospitals or other such institutions.[139]

Residents were expected to improve the environment at their own expense.

An edict of 17 August 1721 states: 'All St Petersburg residents who were required by edict to plant maples on the streets and have already planted some are ordered by the end of this month, in order to protect them from passers-by and to guard them from cattle, to fence them off with boxes of the type which has been made on Admiralty island opposite the newly built stone market. Also, anyone who in the future plants maples along the streets must be sure to make boxes as described above. Anyone contravening this order will be fined, and a notice to this effect is to be published in St Petersburg.'[140] Anyone with property on the river was expected to build their portion of embankment and piles, but regular repetitions of the order indicate that response was poor.[141] In general, exhortation was supplemented with a system of harsh penalties—knout, exile, and hard labour—for offences such as polluting the waterways, selling rotten meat, and building double walls between adjoining properties (a waste of brick!)[142] According to one anecdote, Devier himself felt the tsar's cudgel on his back when, during an inspection tour of the city, Peter noticed that planks were missing from a bridge across one of the canals.[143]

The better parts of town were provided with street lights based on a design by Ivan Petling, master of mechanics. Characteristically, the project started with a model lantern set up outside the Winter Palace, with glass panels made in the Iamburkh glass factories under Menshikov's supervision. In September 1721 Devier wrote to Menshikov that the tsar had now ordered a further 595 lamps, and asked the prince to have glass for a hundred by the end of autumn.[144] By October 1724, according to a memorandum from Devier on money for the upkeep of the lamps (which he insisted should be fuelled from public funds), they were installed 'on the main squares, thoroughfares and around the Admiralty and his royal majesty's courtyards and other places'.[145] The purpose of such measures was more to do with law and order than aesthetics, to ensure that the life of citizens was constantly under the authorities' 'spotlight'. In 1720 there was an order to build swing-beam barriers (shlagbaumy) to close off main streets in the city at night and to post guards. Only authorized persons (military patrols, doctors) were allowed to pass (with lanterns), thus introducing a sort of curfew.[146] Other measures included laying drainage pipes and street paving (by forced labour and Swedish prisoners of war) 'according to the prescribed models'.[147]

Fire-fighting services in the city benefited from the tsar's personal interest. Devier organized watch points and local fire-fighting teams, and introduced new fire-hoses from Holland.[148] Candles in front of icons in shops and market stalls had to be protected with holders.[149] In Weber's view the regulations were admirable, 'the like of which are hardly to be met with anywhere else in the World'.[150] But new regulations went only some way towards preventing fires, because, despite measures to encourage the use of brick and stone, many houses and outdwellings were still made of wood. In this respect life in St Petersburg resembled that in Moscow, which suffered from frequent fires. But in other respects, life was more hazardous than in the old capital.

There was always a danger of flooding. The first flood during the city's existence, in August 1703, was regarded as a bad omen, and was welcomed by Peter's opponents who interpreted it as a sign of God's displeasure.[151] In September 1706 a flash-flood brought the water to a height of 21 inches in the tsar's apartments, but the royal spirits were not downcast. 'It was very amusing,' he wrote to Menshikov, 'to see people sitting on roofs and up trees, not only men but women, too.'[152] Peter rose to the challenge of the elements. There was a particularly severe flood in November 1721, which damaged many houses and structures, including the temple of Janus used for the Nystad celebrations the previous month, which crushed several people. 'If, without being superstitious, one can give any credence to a certain prophecy, this city is at risk of being destroyed by water one day,' wrote the French envoy Lavie, who saw the water in his apartment rise to a height of three feet.[153]

Land communications between St Petersburg and the outside world improved. Just Juel travelled the 717 versts to Moscow in February 1711 in six days.[154] He calculated that it was possible to do a verst in three minutes in a sleigh, although four was more usual.[155] Weber did the journey in four days in February 1716, although apparently it took very much longer in spring or summer, as he discovered in April 1718, when a journey from Moscow to St Petersburg by a less direct route took three weeks. He counted twenty-four post-stages between the capitals with twenty or more horses. After 1718 a 'Germanic' system was introduced, with the post-boys blowing horns and wearing grey coats.[156] Travel costs were half a copeck per horse per verst (according to region and road), usually with two horses. In September 1719 it cost 14 roubles, 11 altyn, 2 denga, for the transport of a servant from the Cabinet in St Petersburg to Moscow.[157] Juel complained about the lack of a properly organized foreign postal service from St Petersburg except by Russian messenger via Memel, which was infrequent and erratic.[158] In his memorandum of 1718 Heinrich Fick noted that the colleges could not do their work properly without a postal service once or twice a week linking all the main towns and provinces. Peter ordered a service to be established between St Petersburg and towns with governors and the governors were told to determine which other towns should be included.[159]

Despite the hazards of the climate, life in the city probably was an improvement for many residents. The Holstein envoy Bergholz arrived in St Petersburg in June 1721 and found that 'the city has changed so much since the time of my [last] visit that I simply did not recognize it'. He was impressed by Nevsky Prospekt. 'Despite the fact that the trees planted on both sides in rows of three or four are still small, the street is unusually fine with its great length and the clean state in which it is kept. ... It makes a splendid sight such as I have encountered nowhere else.'[160] Work continued right up to Peter's death. In the autumn of 1724, 33 officers and 1,590 men were engaged in hauling earth, laying stones, digging roads and paths, cutting trees, and excavating fountains.[161] Still, like much else created by Peter, the city was far from complete when he died. Even the cathedral of SS Peter and Paul had to be fitted with a temporary chapel for his funeral.[162] Bergholz visited Vasil'evsky Island on 11 March 1725, and commented:

> A large number of splendid stone houses have been erected, notably along the bank of the Neva, and this row of houses makes an extraordinarily picturesque impression when you go up-river from Kronstadt. But the majority of these houses have not been decorated inside. Each of the local magnates who received orders to build there was given a plan by which to construct the façade of his house; interior design was according to choice. Although the streets have been laid out, at present few of them, except the main ones running along the embankment, have many buildings on them. Individual houses stand here and there, but most of those will be knocked down in time. Apart from Prince Menshikov and a few others, not many of the local magnates live on this island, because almost all of the owners here have homes in other parts of town.[163]

The reality was a sort of ribbon development, with splendid buildings jostling for space on the embankments (as in Aleksei Zubov's famous engraved panorama of the city made in 1716), but not far behind them 'miserable cabins', a predominance of log buildings and general squalor.[164] Rural disorder forever threatened to disrupt the symmetry of Peter's city. A series of edicts issued during the tsar's lifetime warned residents not to allow cows, goats, pigs and other livestock to wander around the streets unless accompanied by herdsmen, in order to prevent damage to roads and trees. Owners were supposed to apply to the police for grazing places. Unsupervised animals would be confiscated and sent to the hospital (presumably to provide food for the inmates). Repetitions of this order indicate that little attention was paid to it.[165]

It is hard to reconstruct Peter's St Petersburg today, not only because it was unfinished when he died and because so few early eighteenth-century buildings have survived, but also because so much of the city's cultural trappings was ephemeral. The city centre was at its most impressive when decorated for festivals, with temporary installations such as triumphal gates, pedestals, pyramids, obelisks, and columns. These were liberally decorated with painting, sculpture, carving, cartouches, trophies, towers, and arbours, framed with insets of pictures, monograms, heraldic devices, emblems, garlands of greenery, and wreaths, and illuminated by torches and fireworks.[166] From 1709 the Town chancellery of St Petersburg and its successor, the Chancellery of Building, had on their staff architects, painters, sculptors, draughtsmen, gilders, and other craftsmen. But their work is nearly all lost to us.

The symbolic association of St Petersburg with Peter's New Russia and of Moscow with Old Russia is not a modern invention. The new city became such a symbol during the lifetime of its creator. In 1716, in a speech to mark the birthday of the infant Tsarevich Peter Petrovich, Feofan Prokopovich declared:

> And you, new and newly ruling city of Peter, is not the glory of your founder great indeed? ... What strangers, arriving here and not knowing the truth of

the matter, would not, upon seeing the magnificence and splendour of the city, think that it had already existed for two or three hundred years? The efforts of our monarch bring to mind that ancient Sarmatian proverb: 'Cracow was built more than once' . . . or Augustus the Roman emperor who, when he was dying, said in his own praise: 'I found a Rome built of brick but left it in marble.' Our illustrious monarch would consider it vain, not praiseworthy, to say such a thing, but in truth he ought to say that he found a Russia made of wood but created her out of gold; he has adorned her outside and within, with buildings and fortresses, laws and administrators and the benefit of various useful sciences.[167]

In 1717 Gavriil Buzhinsky, bishop of Riazan' and chaplain to the fleet, delivered a speech 'in praise of St Petersburg and its founder', which was presented to the tsar with Zubov's engraved panorama of 'this city called St Petersburg . . . embellished with fine buildings, perfect in its beauty'. Buzhinsky referred to Peter as its 'most wise and first architect'.[168] There can be no doubt that Tsarevich Alexis's statement (according to the testimony of his mistress) that 'when I become sovereign I shall live in Moscow, and leave St Petersburg simply as any other town' was particularly offensive to his father.[169] The city remained firmly associated with the New in the immediate post-Petrine period, when, for a time during the reign of his grandson, Peter II, it seemed possible that it would be demoted. There was even some debate about burying Peter I in the Kremlin Dormition Cathedral in Moscow, the traditional resting-place of the Muscovite grand princes and tsars; but Prokopovich, among others, argued successfully for St Petersburg.[170] When the court remained in Moscow after Peter II's coronation in 1728, foreigners interpreted this as a return to the 'old' ways. The duc de Liria, the Spanish ambassador, wrote that

> the main reason why Peter I . . . established his residence here [in St Petersburg] was in order always to keep in view Russia's growing sea power, which gave him great pleasure, and to keep neighbouring countries, especially Sweden, respectful. The young monarch is different: he hates naval matters and is surrounded by Russians who are tired of their separation from their home territory and constantly tell him to move back to Moscow, where his ancestors lived. They praise the Moscow climate and the limitless game in its vicinity, and say that here not only is the climate unhealthy but also the weather is gloomy and there is nowhere to hunt.[171]

According to the duke, the young tsar himself wished to return to St Petersburg (where he had been brought up) because he wanted to escape from his grandmother (Evdokia Lopukhina) and from 'the old Russians whose ideas and rules he hates because they only want his majesty to remain here without regard for the fact that this might lead to bad consequences for the tranquillity and preservation of the monarchy. The tsar wants to live in St Petersburg and follow the rules of his grandfather.'[172] The attempts to turn back the clock were doomed to failure. In 1732 the Empress Anna and her court were back in St Petersburg, and there the court remained until its demise in 1917. In 1756 a poet wrote: 'You are a blessed country, where Peter's daughter [Elizabeth] lives, where the temple of science is open and its entrance is vast. The golden ages have come again, the fields are splendid, the trees are bearing fruit. What a great city you are. You have become like Rome.'[173] Subsequent rulers took care to acknowledge their ancestor's achievement, usually with a tribute to that special Petrine naval flavour. On 16 May 1803, for example, Alexander I marched past the statue of the 'Bronze Horseman' erected by his grandmother Catherine II, and had the 'little grandfather of the Russian navy' displayed on the deck of the 110-gun *Gabriel* with four 100-year-old men in attendance.[174] There were lavish festivities for the two-hundredth anniversary.[175] One awaits the celebrations of the city's tercentenary in 2003.

III.   ARCHITECTURE

Architecture and architects provide apt metaphors for the Petrine reforms and their creator. 'This is a good architect who began a war to create a pillar to reinforce his state,' wrote Feofilakt Lopatinsky in 1722, 'and was able not only to lay a good foundation by strife but also to complete it with a good peace. No one can say of him: this man started to build but was unable to finish.'[176] Where the tsar led, magnates followed. Buildings in the setting of a brand new city stimulated other branches of the fine and applied arts. Peter relied upon foreign architects to bring his vision to life. The most energetic and compliant was the Swiss-Italian Domenico Trezzini, who came to Russia in 1703 and died there in 1734. He was master of works, 'lieutenant-colonel of fortification and architect' for much of Peter's reign, in charge of much of the work in the Peter–Paul fortress, including the cathedral, Peter's Summer Palace, the Alexander Nevsky monastery, and countless administrative buildings, and drew up plans for whole districts and squares. He was also in charge of the first architectural training brigade.[177] Others enjoyed rather briefer careers in Russia—for example, Jean-Baptiste Le Blond, who died in 1719 after only three years there. (According to a Stählin anecdote, Le Blond's death was precipitated by an outburst of Peter's anger after Menshikov informed on him.[178]) The Russian career of Andreas Schlüter (1665–1714) was even shorter.[179] After working in France, Holland, Italy, and Poland, he went to Berlin to build a royal palace and arsenal (1698) for Frederick I; but after a spell as director of the Berlin Academy of Fine Arts, he was 'disgraced' on account of allegations of technical faults in some of his buildings. Despite this, Peter saw and admired some of Schlüter's work in Berlin and Potsdam in 1712, and hired him as his *Oberbaudirektor*, with a salary of 5,000 roubles, many times the average Russian master mason's pay. Schlüter arrived in Russia in 1713, but died a year later. The most prolific of St Petersburg's German architects was Johann Friedrich Braunstein, in Russia from 1714 to

1728, who was hired on the recommendation of Schlüter. His major project was at Peterhof, St Petersburg's 'Versailles', started in 1714 on the basis of some of the tsar's rough sketches. When it came to planning the Grand Palace, with its terraces of fountains, Braunstein was ousted by Le Blond, but the Frenchman's death left Braunstein in charge again. He was the designer of Peter's favourite retreat, the small Mon Plaisir palace (the end pavilion bears the German name *Lusthaus*), the Marly (1721–3) and Hermitage (1721–4) pavilions, as well as the upper and lower parks and grotto. Braunstein is said to have beaten his Russian pupils, deprived them of firewood in winter and set them to work on household tasks. Many such stories circulated about foreign masters, who were frequently resented by their Russian charges.[180]

A third architect hired at the same time as Schlüter was Gottfried Johann Schädel (1680–1752) from Hamburg. He worked mainly for Alexander Menshikov, supervising work on the prince's palaces in the centre of St Petersburg (1713–27) and at Oranienbaum (1713–25) on the Finnish gulf. A fourth was Georg Johann Mattarnovy, who arrived in St Petersburg on Schlüter's recommendation in February 1714, and died in 1719. He described himself as 'a master of the construction of grottos and fountains'. Mattarnovy's first known Russian project was a grotto and gallery for the Summer Palace. He also designed the second Winter Palace (1716–21) and the first stone cathedral of St Isaac (1717–27), both predecessors of more famous surviving buildings on the same sites. His only extant building is the Kunstkamera (Chamber of Curiosities, 1718–34, completed by N. Härbel). Mattarnovy's son Christian (known as Ivan Ivanovich, born 1705) also worked in St Petersburg, teaching drawing in the Cadet Corps.[181] Other foreigners included Gaetano Chiaveri, in St Petersburg in 1718–26; Nicolo Michetti, formerly a papal architect, builder of the cathedral of St Michael (in Rome); and Nicholas Friedrich Härbel, who arrived in 1719 and died in 1724.

The sources for the designs of major Petrine buildings were as diverse as the origins and talents of the architects listed above, who themselves had trained in an international environment. Foreigners had to adapt to the requirements and resources of their patrons, taking account of the Russian climate and conditions and the demands of an exacting client, both practical and aesthetic. Peter's tastes and experiences, especially what he saw abroad, were crucial.[182] He even supplied rough sketches for some of his creations, such as the Mon Plaisir pavilion.[183] No major Dutch architects are known to have worked in Russia, but Dutch principles, which Peter admired, are clearly reflected in the intersection of the city by canals, the construction of embankments, and the use of brick and tiles. A Dutch engineer, Harman van Boles, was responsible for constructing the tall slim spires on the Peter–Paul cathedral and the Admiralty, although it has recently been argued that the idea may not only have come from the Netherlands. The first such spire which Peter saw was in Riga. But the London churches of Sir Christopher Wren, such as St Martin-within-Ludgate, may also have inspired him. Wren-type devices are visible in unexecuted designs for the Peter–Paul cathedral and the Trinity cathedral in the Alexander Nevsky monastery.[184] There are no records of British architects working in Russia during Peter's reign; but Peter was interested in English building. In 1724 he wrote to a British contact asking whether there might not be another book about English architecture in addition to *Vitruvius Britannicus*, which he already had.[185] Among Peter's papers for April 1724 is a list of drawings of English palaces, country houses, and gardens, including St James's Palace and menagerie (*polaty i zverinets korolevskie nazyvaemy Sv. Iakov*), the Duke of Kent's residence in Bedfordshire, Ragley in Warwickshire, Badminton, Longleat house and gardens, Wollaton Hall in the county of Nottingham, and Hampton Court.[186]

A Russian architectural profession along Western lines developed only slowly. Peter's experience told him that although it was perfectly feasible to study Western painting and engraving techniques without travelling abroad, for the apprentice architect there was no substitute for seeing the real thing. In 1723 the apprentices Ivan Mordvinov, Afanasy Grek, Ivan Michurin, and Ivan Korobov were directed to gather in Holland 'in order to study the manner of Dutch architecture. ... They should learn all there is to know. Send them for practice to whichever place in Holland [*Gollandiia*] there is suitable work.'[187] To Ivan Korobov, who had complained that there were no major works going on and nowhere to see building in practice, and who had expressed a wish to travel to France and Italy to study, he wrote:

I myself have been to France, where there is no architecture and they don't like it, but only build flat and simple and very thickly, and all from stone, not brick (since there is stone everywhere). I have heard a fair bit about Italy from three Russians who studied there and know it specifically, but in both these places the building is the opposite to the situation here. Holland is more similar and therefore you should live in Holland and not in [French] Brabant and learn the manner of Dutch architecture, especially foundations which are needed here, for we have the same conditions with regard to the lowness of the land and also the thinness of the walls; also learn how to measure the proportions of gardens and to decorate them with trees and figures, which none in the world are so fine as in Holland, and I need nothing as much as I need that; and also [study] the building of sluices, which is very vital here. Put all else aside and study those things.[188]

In the Chancellery of Building in St Petersburg, only two Russian-trained architects were on the books: Ivan Ustinov (who worked in Moscow, then on premises for the Senate chancellery) and Mikhail Zemtsov, the latter confirmed in the title of architect in September 1724, after training with Trezzini and a spell in Sweden in 1723, 'to inspect masonry work for a cold climate'.[189] His request that Peter certify his qualifications 'by virtue of his merit and expertise ... for the glory of the Russian nation' underlines his awareness of his unusual status.[190] Zemtsov's major works, the Anichkov palace and the Church of SS Simeon and Anna in St Petersburg, were completed after Peter's death. Peter Eropkin and Timofei Usov, who studied abroad, returned to

Russia only in 1723. In the provinces, routine construction work continued to be handled by Russians apprenticed in the traditional fashion. A rare example of a successful home-grown architect was Fedor Vasil'ev (?–1737), who trained as a painter in the Moscow Armoury in the 1680s, working on Kremlin projects and royal palaces. Later he worked in Voronezh, then in St Petersburg (on the Summer Palace and Iaguzhinsky's mansion) and at Narva. His name appears quite often in Cabinet papers: for example, in May 1722 he was paid ten roubles for delivering to Peter two books of drawings, two drawings, and a plan of a house (*palatnyi chertezh*).[191]

The stylistic blanket 'Petrine Baroque', which appears in many surveys as a description of the work of Peter's architects, has little to recommend it except convenience. The composite nature of architectural practice produced a hybrid style, of which Menshikov's palace on Vasil'evsky Island provides a good example. Started in 1710, it was designed by a series of architects, including Mario Fontana, Gottfried Schädel, and Gottfried Mattarnovy. By the time its owner fell from power in 1727, it had several wings and courtyards. To Friedrich Weber, the main façade appeared to be 'after the Italian Manner',[192] stuccoed and painted in the two tone favoured in a climate more often gloomy than sunny and topped with a steep Dutch roof line. Behind was a formal garden with trees in the Dutch style. Inside the palace Dutch influence was even more evident in the blue and white Delft tiles, which covered not only the walls of its living quarters but also some of the ceilings. The vaulted ceilings of the cellars recall Muscovite designs. The Menshikovs were *nouveaux riches*, and the illustrious prince was not too proud to flaunt his royal connections: witness the entwined letters P and M (Peter and Menshikov) in the metal bannisters of the main staircase, ceilings decorated with the cross of St Andrew, and a fresco of a warrior bearing the tsar's features. The Grand Hall, often 'borrowed' by the tsar for receptions, was decorated with mirrors, Classical statues alluding to military victories, and pilaster capitals bearing reliefs of Menshikov's knightly orders and coronets. These grand political touches contrast sharply with the homeliness of his sister-in-law Varvara's apartments, the wall tiles featuring cupids and household objects such as cups, brushes, and chairs.[193] The household Chapel of the Resurrection had a basilical design with spire, reminiscent of the Peter—Paul cathedral. The palace was built right on the water's edge, its main entrance immediately opposite a landing-stage. In Zubov's engraving of 1717 it appears to float on the water.[194]

Another rare surviving domestic structure of early St Petersburg is the royal Summer Palace, begun in 1710–12 by Trezzini to replace a wooden building. The building is the antithesis of the Moscow Kremlin palaces in the simplicity and clarity of its design and almost total absence of religious accoutrements, more like a Dutch or Scandinavian burgher's house than a royal palace. This was where Peter and his family spent most summers from 1712. The interiors were comfortable, with wood panelling, parquet flooring, and painted ceilings, Chinese silks, tapestries, and Delft tiles. There was a portrait gallery. But for all Peter's preference for simplicity, there are ample indications that this was a royal residence: the bas-reliefs on the walls show allegorical scenes celebrating Russian victories designed by Schlüter, Le Blond, Mattarnovy, Braunstein, and Morberg. And as we have seen, the palace was set in a Dutch-style formal garden. Peter oversaw the construction of palaces and gardens simultaneously, paying attention to landscaping, and to the erection of pavilions, fountains, statues, and other garden furniture. Foreign expertise was essential here, too. Foreign gardeners in Peter's employ included the Frenchman Denis Broquet and the Dutchmen Leonal Gernifeld, Jan Roosen, and Cornelius Schreider.[195]

Some of the most radical innovations were in church design. Trezzini's Cathedral of SS Peter and Paul (1712–33) is dominated by its tall spire and bell-tower, which overshadows the modest Orthodox dome at the east end. The basilica design, large windows, and three-dimensional sculpted iconostasis all depart from older Muscovite traditions, although there is a clear line of descent from Moscow churches of the early 1700s. But let it not be forgotten that as the building of the cathedral began, unknown Russian architects were building the fantastic wooden Church of the Transfiguration at Kizhi (1714), with its multiple shingled cupolas and barely a hint of Western influence. All over Russia, wood remained the standard building material for churches and domestic structures alike, while provincial builders with funds for masonry continued to favour a modified Moscow Baroque style well after Peter's reign. With leading nobles more or less permanently absent from their estates on service, it was to be several decades before the impact of the Petrine 'revolution' in architecture was felt in the countryside.

IV.   THE FIGURATIVE ARTS

At first sight, sculpture seems to be the poor cousin among the Petrine arts. The native tradition of sculpture in the round was weak, because of the Church's disapproval of 'graven images'. Wooden statues of religious subjects were made (and provided prototypes for a number of subjects later favoured in more secular form by Peter—for example, mounted warriors[196]), and in the later seventeenth century high-relief decorative carving in wood and stone (so-called Belorussian ornament) became widespread, but the techniques of deep chiselling in stone and casting in metal (with the exception of bells) were unknown in Muscovite Russia. The claim that knowledge of wood-carving techniques 'prepared the ground for quick assimilation of new types and genres of the plastic arts'[197] is patently exaggerated, for the early eighteenth century saw no Russian school of sculpture and only one sculptor of any note, Carlo Bartolomeo Rastrelli, working in St Petersburg. This was probably due not only to a shortage of skills but also to the fact that in the eyes of the public, not to mention the Church, nude figures in marble and bronze looked indecent and 'pagan'.

Despite such barriers to assimilation, Petrine sculpture was less of a rarity than might appear. Wood was the material from which most of the new-style images were fashioned. It was plentiful (unlike marble, which had to be imported), and did not take as long to work as bronze and stone, but it was perishable. Among the first secular sculptures in the round produced in Russia were wooden figures depicting Mars and Hercules set up on the triumphal gates to honour the victory at Azov in 1696. They perished, like much of the occasional art of the Petrine era.[198] Major palaces were decorated with sculptures long since lost—see, for example, Zubov's engraving of the Menshikov palace showing a row of figures on the pediment over the main façade, or the statues in the grotto (by Mattarnovy and Zemtsov) in the Summer Gardens.[199] Religious sculpture was also quite plentiful, but was largely ignored by Soviet art historians, as it does not fit in with the ideologically approved version of the 'secularization' of Russian art. Early examples of religious free-standing sculptures can still be seen at the Church of the Sign at Dubrovitsy, commissioned by Prince Boris Golitsyn in the 1690s, and at Menshikov's Moscow Church of the Archangel Gabriel. A spectacular example is the iconostasis of the Peter–Paul cathedral, designed in 1722–6 by Ivan Zarudny and a team of Russian wood-carvers.[200] Here some of the traditional rows of icons were replaced by three-dimensional wooden gilded figures. The whole structure was influenced by the design of triumphal arches. (Zarudny built these too—for example, for the Nystad celebrations in Moscow in December 1721.) The military theme is continued in the figures of War and Peace.[201] Similar iconostases were built in new churches in Riga and Reval. Menshikov commissioned sculptures for his private Church of the Resurrection next to his St Petersburg palace. The Church remained suspicious of such 'pagan' images. In 1743–4, when the church was being refurbished, the Synod ordered workmen to add wings to the surviving wooden cupids, turning them into angels, and to destroy the rest![202]

The best known of Peter's sculptors was Carlo Bartolomeo Rastrelli (1675?–1744), father of the famous architect. He met Peter in Königsberg in February 1716, came to Russia, and immediately set to work on an equestrian statue of the tsar, based on the statue of Marcus Aurelius on the Capitol in Rome. It was also reminiscent of statues of Louis XIV (by François Girardin, which Peter saw in 1717, in the Place Vendôme) and the Great Elector Friedrich Wilhelm by Schlüter. (The bronze was not actually cast until the 1740s. Today it stands in front of the Mikhailovsky fortress.) Rastrelli's masterpiece is considered to be the bronze bust of Peter in armour (1723–30), which, with its flowing metal draperies and swirling lines, succeeds in capturing something of Peter's dynamism and stern determination. Rastrelli also made wax models, a speciality of Florence, his home town. The most famous Russian example was his full-figure model of Peter, based on a death mask, and casts of hands and feet taken on the night of Peter's death, and a wooden body made to his measurements. It is dressed in the outfit which Peter wore for Catherine's coronation.[203] Rastrelli also made a portrait bust in 1719, taken from a wax mask (which did not survive), which found its way to Italy in return for the Tauride *Venus*, and was returned to Russia in 1861. An iron casting of his bust of the tsar, 'as was made in ancient times for the Roman emperor' (1724), was sent as a gift to Frederick IV of Denmark. Only about thirty works survive from Rastrelli's thirty years of activity in Russia.[204] Lost works include busts of Natalia Alekseevna and Menshikov (later done in marble by Vitali) and heads of Peter and seven of his companions on the Grand Embassy.[205] Bergholz reported that Rastrelli was working on two statues, one on foot, the other mounted, towards the end of Peter's life.[206]

Russian exponents of wood carving, both in relief and in the round, some of whom trained with foreigners such as Nicholas Pineau, appear in documents as *figuristy*.[207] Foreign craftsmen described in histories as architects also carried out sculptural commissions. For example, in 1722 Michetti prepared designs for 'marble figures' for Peterhof which were commissioned in Rome.[208] The projects of Konrad Osner the Elder (1669–1739/47) from Nuremberg, who came to Russia in 1703 via Berlin, included carving, sculpture, and plasterwork. He worked on the Peter–Paul fortress and on cascades and grottos at Peterhof. The bas-relief of the overthrow of Simon Magus (an allegory of the triumph of Peter over Charles XII) on the Petrovsky gates (1717–18) has been attributed to him.[209] Unfulfilled projects include a lighthouse in triumphal gate form in Kronstadt, designed by Pineau and Michetti, with figures of Russian naval victories and a triumphal column by Rastrelli and Pineau. After Poltava Peter conceived a scheme for a stone pyramid on the battle site, topped by an equestrian statue of himself in front of a church of SS Peter and Paul and a lower chapel dedicated to St Samson, on whose day the victory fell.[210] Nartov relates that he planned to erect statues of leading generals, including Lefort, Sheremetev, Shein, and Gordon, in the Alexander Nevsky monastery, but never did.[211]

The training of Russian sculptors lagged behind that of architects and painters. In his project for a Russian academy of arts, Iury Kologrivov proposed that a stone-carver, someone who knew relief carving but had difficulty understanding the 'life-likeness of depiction' (*zhivosti izobrazhenila*), be sent to Italy to train as a sculptor. In 1724 four apprentice sculptors and four stone-carvers were sent there.[212] In the absence of trained sculptors, the solution was to import artwork. Just Juel saw busts of King John Sobieski of Poland and his wife along with thirty other marbles statues in the Summer Gardens, a section of which contained fountains modelled on characters in Aesop's fables.[213] Extensive correspondence survives between Peter and his agents in Italy on the import of sculpture, both antique and modern works on Classical themes, some from the Venice workshops of Giovanni Bonnacca and Marino Gropelli. About ninety of the Summer Gardens purchases survive today, including *Truth* and *Sincerity*, Bonnacca's models on the themes of *Dawn*, *Midday*, *Dusk* and *Night*; Pietro Baratta's *Peace and Plenty*

(1722) and *Mercy* (1719) (Baratta taught Russian pupils in Venice).[214] Iury Kologrivov travelled to Rome, Genoa, and Florence, collecting statues, fountains, urns, and architectural fittings, including the groups *Venus, Mars* and *Diana with Satyr*, purchased with the help of the Pope's nephew, Cardinal Spinola.[215] In 1719 in Rome he snapped up a statue of Venus which, he said, bore comparison with the famous Florentine *Venus*—in fact, was superior because the latter was broken in several places. The statue was confiscated by the Pope's agent, and retrieved only after long negotiations, when Peter proposed to exchange it for relics of St Brigitte captured at Reval. Elaborate arrangements were made to transport the work overland via Innsbrück, then by the Danube to Vienna, where Iaguzhinsky was ordered to have a special transport made to send it on via Cracow. The Tauride *Venus* (so named because for many years it stood in the Tauride palace) survives in the Hermitage.[216]

Prints and engravings were the essential figurative art-form of Petrine Russia.[217] In the seventeenth century wood-block engravings were used as frontispieces in religious publications, but secular subjects were rare. In the 1680s official circles began to exploit the political usefulness of prints—for example, in the engraved portraits of Tsarevna Sophia and Vasily Golitsyn, both commissioned from Ukrainian artists and in the case of Sophia also printed with Latin captions in Amsterdam. The Moscow Academy drew upon Ukrainian expertise to produce *conclusiones* (engraved pamphlets) and prints on religious and allegorical subjects.[218] From the 1690s the demand grew for speedily produced illustrations to depict subjects virtually unknown in Muscovite art except in foreign originals: triumphal scenes, battle panoramas, naval scenes, maps and plans of newly captured towns and territories. Armoury lists of subjects commissioned in 1703 include plans of Schlüsselburg, charts of the White Sea, pictures of ships, French fashions (*frantsuzskikh mod*), 'one engraving of a victory' (unspecified), fireworks, triumphal arches, an atlas, and scenes from the wedding of the jester Filat Shansky. The Dutch artist Pieter Picart and his assistant were summoned to Schlüsselburg, rather in the manner of official press photographers today, 'to engrave various subjects during the visit of the great sovereign'.[219]

Peter's demand for engraving and printing, comparatively quick and cheap methods of producing images with an end product that could be distributed in multiple copies, arose from his need to publicize and justify Russia's achievements at home and abroad. About a hundred engravings on thirty-four subjects were devoted to the Great Northern War alone. Some were accompanied by long captions so that the literate could not miss the message—for example, the inscription on a print of the siege of Nöteborg 1702 reads: 'In such a manner, by God's help, was our patrimonial fortress returned, which had been in the hands of the enemy unrighfully for ninety years.'[220] The new fleet was a favourite subject. (See, for example, Schoenebeck's *Ship St. Peter* (1701), with the figure of the tsar identified by the initials P. M. (Peter Mikhailov) and the 1710 engraving of the sailing of the fleet from St Petersburg to Viborg, featuring 250 vessels.[221]) Prints could be made separately or be incorporated into books. The first work to be printed in the new civic type-face in St Petersburg, *The Book of Mars*, contained plans, engravings, and maps designed by leading engravers. Archaic features—a high horizon, allowing bands of actions, as in old Russian painting—combined with real perspective and Baroque allegorical figures.[222] There was a big demand for heroic portraits in imitation of standard Western European compositions. The first mounted portrait of Peter, for example, of 1699, showed him taking Azov, accompanied by his generals. A 1710 print by Picart of Menshikov and Peter on horseback follows another stereotypical European design: military commanders in armour, bearing batons, the taking of a city on one side, the retinue on the other.[223]

Prints and engravings did not enter the public domain to the extent that they did in the West. (The exceptions to this were popular woodcut prints (*lubki*), to be considered below.) In Peter's reign cultural affairs were in the hands of the State, which disposed of all Russia's resources, both animate and inanimate. In Western Europe engraving and printing were produced for profit by private firms and individuals, and were widely distributed; whereas in Russia they were at the disposal of the tsar and his inner circle, and official production was confined to three main centres: the Armoury and the Moscow and St Petersburg printing-houses, which responded first and foremost to official commissions. The engraver was a servant of the State, no less than a soldier or an administrator. Pieter Picart, who came to Russia in 1702, wrote: 'I worked on his Imperial Majesty's service in many campaigns and attacks, as a result of which I suffered many difficulties and losses, grew old and decrepit.'[224] Adrian Schoenebeck in a project for a frontispiece presented to Peter in 1698 depicted the tsar 'graciously extending his hand to an artist on bended knee'.[225] Artists in the West also sought royal and aristocratic patronage, but they were not totally dependent on it. A characteristic example of Peter's promotion of prints appears in a letter of 18 October 1708 to Tsarevich Alexis: 'I enclose a sketch with an inscription of the battle at the village of Lesnaia. Give it to Picart to engrave, without delay and print it; also print the inscription in Russian and Dutch, as we have Latin type-faces and Dutch printers, and send them to us.'[226] Peter later gave orders for this print to be sold 'everywhere in Moscow and in the provinces'.[227] In March 1710 he ordered a large print of the triumphal entry into Moscow celebrating Poltava to be improved and sent as a gift to the king of Poland.[228] An engraver accompanied the tsar on his Persian campaign in 1722.[229]

The most prolific and talented of Petrine engravers were Ivan (1677–1743) and Aleksei Fedorovich Zubov (1682–1751). Sons of a royal icon-painter, they started their careers as apprentice icon-painters in the Armoury, then became pupils of Schoenebeck, engraving coats of arms. Ivan worked and studied with Picart, mainly in the Moscow Press, where eventually he organized almost single-handedly the production of book illlustrations, creating 'a virtually new Russian religious art'.[230] Here much of his work was on *conclusiones* for the Moscow Academy and religious books—for example, John Chrysostom's *Sermon on the 14 Epistles of the Apostle Paul* (1709). In the 1720s he was involved in producing large prints of victories, firework displays and other spectacles. Aleksei's first known works are all copies of Western engravings, then maps and charts of the south (in connection with the peace with Turkey—a characteristically practical commission).[231] In 1710 he was among the first craftsmen to be transferred to St Petersburg, where he headed the engraving workshop of the new St Petersburg Press. Some of his first works were illustrations for prints of ships' signals to accompany a booklet.

To these artists we owe a good share of our visual impression of the Petrine era and its St Petersburg setting. Aleksei Zubov's most striking and most reproduced work is his panorama of St Petersburg (1716), presented to Peter on his return from abroad in 1717. Like many views of the city, it focuses not on the buildings, which are confined to a narrow strip in the middle ground, but on the ships—warships, yachts, barges, and a sloop bearing Peter and Catherine—in the foreground. The sky takes up more than half the sheet, with hosts of heaven bearing a ribbon with the city's name. It shows St Petersburg from an 'impossible' angle, ignoring the rules of aerial perspective, while at the same time showing buildings in their correct order as a strip of façades. Unfinished projects (e.g., the spire of the Peter–Paul cathedral) are shown completed.[232] Another famous engraving is of Peter's wedding feast in 1712, which again distorts true perspective and dimensions in order to accommodate the assembled wedding guests.[233] Zubov commemorated Russian victories—for example, Hangö, dynamically capturing the thick of battle, with galleys swarming around the Swedish ship *Elephant* and details of the rigging, and the victory parade for Grengham (1720), with a line of captured ships and Russian galleys sailing in front of Trinity Square and gun salutes from the fortress in the background.[234] He also provided the vignette of Mercury on the first editions of the newspaper *St Petersburg News* (1711). Aleksei Zubov was able to capture the 'spirit of the age' as well as its concrete image. What is striking is that in the last years of his career, back in Moscow, he reverted to a 'primitive' style in the manner of *lubki* and religious engravings. Ivan's art, more Moscow-based, is even more indicative of the hybrid culture of Petrine Russia, with its mixture of Christian, mythological, and realistic imagery. His *conclusio* to mark the coronation of Catherine in 1724 has portraits of the emperor and empress based on true likenesses, dressed in the fashion of the period. Saints mingle with antique gods and goddesses, including Pallas Athene, allegorical figures of Glory, Truth, Piety, and Foresight, and putti in clouds.[235] Other talented engravers included V. O. Kiprianov, who made intricate, highly decorative prints for educational publications; A. I. Rostovtsev (a member of his team); and S. Korovin, who trained in Paris.

After Peter's death the halt in propaganda activity was marked by a sharp decrease in official print production. The production of woodcuts, or *lubki*, on the other hand, continued to flourish. The first dated print, of the

Archangel Michael (1668), underscores the religious origins of this popular art-form, as does the set of thirty-six prints on biblical subjects produced by the engraver Vasily Koren' (probably in the upper Volga region) in the 1690s.[236] Many prints originated in northern Russia, in towns which in the seventeenth century exhibited vigorous local schools of icon and fresco painting and architecture. Folk-tales and fables supplied themes. Occasionally this 'provincial' art gave a hint of popular attitudes to government activity— for example, the famous image of the barber (often erroneously identified as Peter himself) cutting the Old Believer's beard, the 'Cat of Kazan'' (with 'Petrine' moustache), or the many variations on the theme of 'The Mice Bury the Cat', a seventeenth-century subject which later came to be associated with popular rejoicing at Peter's death.

In painting, home-grown achievements were much less visible and more modest than in buildings or prints. The background to developments in the figurative arts during Peter's reign is an almost complete absence of secular art in the reigns of his predecessors. The first Russian portraits made from life, nearly all royal, date from the 1650s. (Few Russian aristocrats can claim ancestral portraits painted before the eighteenth century.) In the second half of the seventeenth century, against a background of modest Western influences at court, a small contingent of foreign artists worked in the royal workshops, but their impact was limited.[237] Court art remained under the auspices of the icon-painting workshops of the Armoury, and hence subject to a degree of church control, until well into Peter's reign. Peter was less interested in painting than in architecture, and among the figurative arts he favoured engraving and printing.

Russian painters fully trained in Western techniques, like architects, remained in short supply during Peter's lifetime and information about them tends to be fragmentary. The biography of even the most successful Russian painter of the Petrine era, 'the founder of Russian portraiture' Ivan Nikitich Nikitin (ca.1680–after 1742), is 'full of mysteries', including possible confusion with other similarly named artists.[238] An anecdote attributed to the architect Mikhail Zemtsov recounts that Peter discovered young Nikitin's talent by chance, and apprenticed him to a painter in Amsterdam, where Nikitin was at the time with his father. The anecdote mentions paintings in churches, including a crucifixion.[239] In fact, Nikitin received his early training in the Armoury. There is strong evidence, mainly stylistic in nature, that he was then apprenticed to the German painter Dannhauer (see below) and possibly the engraver Schoenebeck.[240] In 1716–19 he found himself in Italy as a royal *pensioner*, studying at the Venice Academy and in Florence under Tommaso Redi, with a generous annual allowance of 300 roubles from Cabinet funds.[241] In 1720 he returned with his certificates to become 'master portraitist to the tsar's court'. After Peter's death he fell into disfavour—in 1737 he was 'whipped and sent to Siberia' under somewhat mysterious circumstances; he was subsequenly pardoned, but died on his way home.

Nikitin's main achievements were in portraiture. The subject of his first signed portrait (1714), of the tsar's niece Praskovia Ivanovna (his only other signed portrait, of S. G. Stroganov, dates from 1726), shows that he enjoyed royal patronage quite early, which was confirmed when he painted Peter's portrait in 1715.[242] A list of his paintings, completed but not paid for between 1721 and 1725, submitted to Catherine I includes two of Peter, two of Catherine, four of Anna Petrovna, three of Elizaveta Petrovna, two of Natalia Petrovna, one of the priest Ioann Khisanfov, and four of 'long-lived' peasants.[243] Thanks to Nikitin, we have likenesses of royal women and court dignitaries (Gavrila Golovkin), not to mention Peter himself, whom he painted (according to documentary evidence) at least twice from life, in 1715 and again in 1721, when the court journal records that 'on Kotlin island before mass the painter Ivan Nikitin painted his majesty's portrait (*persona*) and then his majesty attended mass'.[244] The identification of these portraits with surviving works is disputed.[245] Another portrait of Peter usually attributed to Nikitin shows him on his deathbed. His most strikingly original work, in so far as it strays from the categories of royal or aristocratic portraits, is what was once known erroneously as the 'Field Hetman', a realistic psychological study. Recent research has suggested that this may actually be a self-portrait.[246]

The other major Russian painter of the Petrine era, Andrei Matveev (1701/4–39), was, like Nikitin, a beneficiary of Peter's *pensioner* programme, but his long period of training abroad, in the Netherlands and at the Antwerp Academy of Arts, kept him away from Russia until 1727. His contribution to the immediately post-Petrine period is worth considering, nevertheless, since it indicates the directions which Russian art was to take as a result of Peter's reforms and priorities. Matveev is credited with the first Russian easel painting of an allegorical subject and also one of the first nudes (amazing 'firsts' when one bears in mind how utterly commonplace such works were in the West). In his *Allegory of Painting* (painted in Amsterdam in 1725) a woman at an easel, naked from the waist up, personifies Painting. Minerva presides in the clouds.[247] His best-known work is usually referred to as *Self-Portrait with Wife* (ca.1729), although its history is disputed. Some identify it as a portrait of Anna Leopol'dovna (granddaughter of Tsar Ivan V) and her husband Anton Ulrich of Brunswick.[248] Similar differences of opinion exist over Matveev's authorship (in Antwerp in 1724–5) of an oval portrait of Peter the Great, alternatively attributed to the artist Karl Moor.[249] Problems of attribution are not peculiar to Russian art, of course; but apart from a handful of signed paintings, nearly all the major Petrine paintings have a chequered history of authorship. Take, for example, the portrait of Peter the Great against the background of a naval battle, identified as Hangö, displayed in the Catherine palace at Tsarskoe Selo. In its time it has been credited to Jan Kupetsky, to Dannhauer, then in Soviet times (on documentary, stylistic, and technical analysis) to Ivan Nikitin.[250]

Several foreign artists worked for Peter. Louis Caravaque (1684–1754) was hired in 1716 'to paint various historical works'.[251] He spent the rest of his life in St Petersburg, ever at the royal beck and call. In 1722 he went on the

Persian campaign, and painted Peter and Catherine's portrait.[252] His grandest historical composition, painted in 1718 for the palace at Peterhof, was the Battle of Poltava, with Peter on horseback in the right foreground pointing to fleeing Swedes.[253] This image was reproduced on a tapestry, one of the first from the St Petersburg tapestry (*shpalernaia*) factory (1722).[254] Caravaque also introduced a new element into Russian art, almost totally absent in the Muscovite period—the feminine-erotic, of which the best-known example is his double portrait of Peter's daughters, painted in 1717. Clearly intended as a celebration of marriageable princesses (in the 1710s to 1720s numerous foreign princes showed an interest), the portrait depicts two little nymphs, personifications of youth, beauty, wealth, and fruitfulness. The flowers and garden behind suggest summer. A striking feature is the exposed right nipple of Anna, peeping out above the drapery of the low-cut gown, based on allegorical dress rather than the actual court fashion of the period.[255] Caravaque went even further in his reclining nude portrait of the young Elizabeth. He also specialized in decorative art—for example, a *Diana* (1721) on the ceiling in the Vol'er pavilion at Peterhof, rather similar in style and dress to the twin portrait of the tsarevny mentioned above.

The longest-serving court painter was a German, Johann Gottfried Dannhauer (Tannhauer, Donouer, 1680–1733/7), who worked in St Petersburg for twenty-six years. He was of South German extraction, Bavarian or Swabian, and had worked under Sebastiano Bombelli in Venice, earning something of a reputation as a copyist of Rubens.[256] Peter first met him in Holland in 1697, but he was hired only in 1710. In his contract Dannhauer specified: 'I am skilled in the making of both large-scale portraits in oils and smaller ones, in miniature.' He could turn his hand to making clocks, musical instruments, and sculptures. He was expected, like all foreign artists under contract, to 'teach painting to Russian pupils', and probably later acted as tutor to Ivan Nikitin. In 1712 (after being forced to accompany the royal party on the Pruth campaign against the Turks, where he lost all his belongings) he became *gofmaler* (from *Hofmaler*—court painter—one of many German loan-words in Russian), painting portraits of members of the royal family and their circle, including Menshikov, his wife and daughters, F. M. Apraksin, and Peter Tolstoy. Dannhauer's best-known works are a profile portrait of Peter, made in the 1710s, a full-length portrait in armour, and a deathbed portrait of the tsar. He also played a prominent role in the artistic preparations for Peter's funeral.[257] After Peter's death he requested leave to go home, but in 1728 returned ill to Russia and died there.

Dannhauer enjoys a mixed reputation, earning praise for his 'excellent placing of light and shade'[258] and censure for his 'pedestrian and uninspired portraits.[259] His work is ripe for reassessment. It may well be that the number of foreign painters working in Russia in Peter's reign has been underestimated. One of the most prolific turns out to have been the hitherto almost unknown Johann Heinrich Wedekind (1674–1736) from Reval, who started work for the Russian court after the capture of Reval in 1710 and continued to work for Peter's successors, although he was known less as an original por-traitist than as a copyist, 'who filled almost all the walls in St Petersburg homes with his copies of portraits of the imperial family and distinguished persons'. His copies include portraits of Catherine I from Nattier.[260]

There was a steady demand for artists to decorate the interiors of new palaces, a few of which survive. In February 1721, for example, Peter ordered that ceilings at Peterhof be painted 'with decorative or historical subjects'.[261] One of the most successful decorative artists was the Swiss artist Georg Gsell (1673–1740), who worked in Vienna and Amsterdam before coming to Russia in 1717. From 1726 he taught drawing in the Academy of Sciences.[262] His sur-viving works include 1719 *plafonds* for the green study of the Summer Palace: *The Triumph of Russia* and *The Triumph of Catherine*. The study has painted panels with flower subjects (rare examples of still life) and a series of medal-lions of allegorical continents.[263] An anonymous artist painted the *Triumph of Minerva* in Peter's study, possibly the first example in Russia of secular painting on allegorical themes.[264] Philippe Pillement from Lyons (1684/1700–?), in Russia from 1717 to 1723, painted the ceilings in Mon Plaisir (1718–22) and the Grand Palace at Peterhof. The domed ceiling of the central hall at the former has a painting of Apollo in the centre, with the four Elements below and sculpted alabaster figures representing the four seasons in the corners. The paintings incorporate depictions of exotic birds, flowers, and fruits. The latter subjects reappear in the pale greens and golds of the Lusthaus pavilion ceiling.[265] Pillement trained a team of Russian pupils. S. Bushuev, M. Negrubov, and L. Fedorov received a testimonial that 'they have studied with me the art of painting and ornament for the decoration of ceil-ings, interior walls and others and they are capable of carrying out all such painting work without any problems'.[266]

The bulk of the easel pictures which adorned Petrine residences were imported from abroad, in some cases specially commissioned. In Paris in 1717, for example, Peter and Catherine were painted by several artists, including Jean-Marc Nattier.[267] The choice of subjects depended very much on Peter's tastes, which ran to townscapes, marine and battle pictures by the lesser Dutch and Flemish artists, as well as the work of masters such as Rembrandt, Van Dyck, Stein, and Brueghel.[268] He was especially fond of Adam Silo, formerly a ship's captain, and his precise depictions of ship's tackle, and of the seascapes of Abraham and Jacob Storck. These were the sort of canvases which adorned his private apartments at Peterhof, especially Mon Plaisir palace on the shore of the Finnish gulf, described as 'the first picture gallery in Russia'.[269] A typical order for a royal job lot was sent in 1711 to the agent Christopher Brandt in Holland: 'about four dozen pictures of good workmanship, on which are depicted sea battles and seafaring vessels of various kinds, perspectives of Dutch towns and villages with canals and boats. If such cannot be found, then landscapes and others, whatever is best.'[270] In 1716 another agent, Kologrivov, bought 117 pic-tures in Brussels and Antwerp, and in 1717 he hired an artist in Amsterdam who agreed to paint both large and small canvases for a set sum, and had already started a picture of the Battle of Poltava. 'A painter who can paint various battle scenes also townscapes and landscapes' was sought.[271]

Religious art was purchased, too. The subjects of paintings by Juvenet bought in Paris in 1717 included St Peter fishing, the raising of Lazarus, the healing of the man with palsy, and the driving of the money-lenders from the temple.[272] Russian painters working in the Western idiom assimilated the conventions of Western religious art, contributing to the further decline of the Russo-Byzantine tradition. At the same time, the public demand for icons far outweighed that for secular works, and both Church and State monitored quality and correctness. In 1707 Ivan Zarudny became superintendent of religious painting, based in the Armoury, and later presided over a team of provincial icon inspectors. Icon-painters were to be examined and awarded certificates after a period of study with a qualified master. In 1723 a decree reiterated ancient rules, based on the resolutions of the church council of 1551.[273] Ivan Pososhkov, for one, deplored the proliferation of icons 'terrible to behold', with figures depicted 'in such a way that living men with these proportions would be monsters', even though he conceded that 'the holiness of the icon does not reside in the quality of the painting'.[274] One should not conclude from such complaints that standards had fallen as a result of the shift in priorities (although the siphoning-off of painters for secular work may have taken its toll). Complaints about badly painted icons were commonplace in sixteenth- and seventeenth-century writings.

The dividing line between secular and sacred art was by no means clear-cut. In January 1723 Peter complained about painted portraits (*zhivopisnye persony*) of the emperor and empress, sold around Moscow and displayed in people's homes, which were 'painted unskilfully by ignorant persons'. What is interesting is that this order was sent to Zarudny, who was told to gather up the offending paintings in the Synod, and see to it that no more were painted or sold, and 'to order such portraits to be painted skilfully by artists with certificates of good workmanship, with all care and fitting assiduity'. The Church's authority in the matter of images was still strong.[275]

Plans for a secular academy of the arts were not realized in Peter's lifetime, although various projects were put forward. In 1716, for example, Kologrivov proposed establishing a school for Russian art students in Rome:

For painting (*piktura*) find a young painter who already paints well and teach him, first how to mix paints, which our painters are very bad at; secondly, to paint battles and assaults on towns, in order to make a most precious ornament for your majesty's home for the eternal glory of Russia with your illustrious victories. Learning the language in two years, in the third he can learn history and fable (*fabuly*), which is most useful in their profession for thinking up new [subjects?] and the proper depiction of persons in action, in order not to paint a cavalryman as an infantryman.[276]

A curious illustration of the state of the figurative arts at the end of Peter's reign, especially the relative contributions of native and foreign craftsmen, is provided by documents regarding the preparations for Peter's funeral, which took place on 10 March 1725. Under the direction of James Bruce, the carver Nicholas Pineau produced designs and oversaw work for the lying-in-state in the Grand Hall of the Winter Palace, assisted by Louis Caravaque (who among other things made painted banners and coats of arms) and the wood-carvers and joiners Simon and Jean Michel. Rastrelli produced a death mask. M. G. Zemtsov, S. M. Korovin, and A. I. Rostovtsev made engravings of the lying-in-state. Ivan Nikitin and Dannhauer both painted deathbed portraits. Konrad Osner made the carved chandeliers. Bartolomeo Tarsia and Georg Gsell did paintings, Grigory Musikiisky and Andrei Ovsov enamel work, and Domenico Trezzini supervised the construction of a temporary wooden chapel in the unfinished Peter–Paul cathedral.[277] The list of dozens of craftsmen who took part bears witness to the large numbers of Russians trained in new skills, many of them with their own teams of students. Among the names of the trainee painters (*zhivopisnogo dela podmaster'ia*, or in some cases *moliary*), twelve in all, who helped in the work were Ivan and Gavrila Vishniakov, Mikhail Zakharov, and Nikita Cherkasov.[278] In St Petersburg, at least, firm foundations had been laid for propagating new skills, techniques, and styles. But the Synod refused permission for the publication of Pineau's detailed description of the decorations, on the grounds that they were 'pagan'.[279]

The Petrine era is generally regarded as a period of apprenticeship in the figurative arts. The comparative modesty of native achievement has been attributed, among other things, to the inexperience of artists, the practical priorities of the State, the weakness of noble and middle-class patronage, and the poor development of urban life. Low survival rates distort the picture, but can hardly account for the apparent absence of whole subject areas. There was very little still life or landscape, plenty of individual portraits but few group subjects. O. S. Evangulova argues that genres such as still life were too 'frivo-lous' for the needs of the age, and that the lack of double or group portraits reflects social priorities as well as immature technical skills.[280] Especially striking is the scarcity of personal, informal images and genre-painting. With few exceptions, all the art of the Petrine era seems to have been created for public purposes. This is why something like Fedor Vasil'ev's sketches of Berezovy Island, with cows lying in the foreground, or of a corner of the Peter–Paul fortress, with wooden shacks and a rowing boat,[281] seem almost shocking in their informality, and why Ivan Nikitin's 'hetman' painting stands out by not trumpeting an allegorical advertisement for the glory of emperor, State, and aristocracy.

Soviet historians tended to regard the predominant triumphalist Classical imagery of the age as 'progressive' in so far as it allegedly replaced religious motifs. Its foreign origins could be forgiven. According to this line of reasoning, Zarudny's iconostasis for the Peter–Paul cathedral, in which tri-umphal gates and allegorical figures replaced or overshadowed icons, was preferable to its Muscovite predecessors, in which sacred images predominated. Less easy to accommodate was the fact that so much of the élite art and architecture of eighteenth-century Russia was produced by foreigners. There are to date no monographs devoted specifically to Petrine foreign painters (architects have been better served[282]), and general surveys of the period tend to contain only the sketchiest information about foreign artists. Peter attracted criticism both from nineteenth-century Slavophiles, who condemned him for spurning native genius and placing too heavy a reliance on foreign models, and from Soviet art historians, especially in the aftermath of the Second World War. The remark on Dannhauer in the multi-volumed Soviet *History of Russian Art* is characteristic: he was, it seems, 'incapable of conveying all the complexity of Peter's image [in his portraits], something which was achieved only by Ivan Nikitin'.[283] A possible way out of the dilemma posed to national pride was to emphasize the fact that Peter chose only the best, most appropriate elements of foreign art. It was also argued that certain foreigners chose to work in Russia rather than elsewhere, thus distancing themselves from their origins and becoming 'one's own' foreigners (*svoi nemtsy*). Such specialists were said to have assimilated Russian tastes, adapted their designs to Russian conditions, and in some cases become 'Russified', better artists than they had been in their native environment, so that the recipients rather than the bearers of new cultural trends took the credit for their achievements. The main point, of course, is that the eighteenth century was a period of considerable artistic mobility and interchange, in which artists, regardless of their country of origin, looked to ideal models drawn from earlier times and civilizations. In a modern State, national art could advance only in an international context, as Peter observed during his European tours.

V.   THEATRE AND MUSIC

The official history of the Russian theatre began a few months after Peter's birth, in October 1672, when Tsar Alexis sat down to watch a company of German amateur actors perform *The Play of Ahasuerus and Esther*. The tsar had expressed an interest in theatre a few years earlier, when he instructed the agent John Hebdon to bring thespians to Moscow.[284] He was well aware that 'theatrical presentations were often given for European monarchs', from information available in the news sheets (*kuranty*) of foreign events, as well as from foreign visitors and Russians returning from abroad. Artamon Matveev (guardian of Peter's mother), who was denounced by conservatives for staging home theatricals, also influenced the tsar, staging a production of a ballet, *Orfeo*, at Shrovetide 1672, several months before the legendary first performance.[285] Alexis's theatre was in operation until the tsar's death, after which it was closed down.[286] This was a pity, since the young Peter would probably have enjoyed plays such as *The Comedy of Bacchus*, which featured drunkards, maidens, and performing bears. Peter's own theatrical initiation took place during the Grand Embassy, probably in The Hague, where on 17 August 1697 he saw a 'play about Cupid', which he mentioned in a letter to Andrei Vinius,[287] and in England, where his experience extended to a brief affair with the actress and singer Letitia Cross.[288]

For various reasons Peter did not give the theatre high priority. Bassewitz, for one, considered that the considerable progress made by Russia on the road to enlightenment and moral development did not extend to the theatre. He noted the existence of a 'barbaric' theatre in Moscow, attended only by the lower orders, and a theatre built by Peter for a German company where standards were also low.[289] The modesty of the achievements may be blamed in part on Peter's indifference to the dramatic arts as confined behind the proscenium arch. Weber wrote that 'Operas and Plays will also be in Fashion in Process of Time, and they are now looking out for a Fund for those Diversions, though the Czar himself has as little Inclinations that Way as he has for Hunting, or the like. His Subjects indeed have made some Attempts for acting on the Stage, but with very indifferent Success, for want of proper Rules.'[290] Peter preferred to be a player in the theatre of court life, his restless energy preventing him from sitting still for more than short periods. In his youth he treated even warfare as theatre, in a 'spirit of masquerade and jest'.[291] If the role of spectator was unavoidable, then Peter preferred to watch performing dwarfs, strongmen, acrobats, or the Italian 'comedian' who twice came to His Majesty's apartments in Spa in July 1717 to do a turn, and also cleaned the tsar's teeth.[292]

Notwithstanding his personal apathy towards it, Peter was well aware that theatre was part of the Western cultural package, although he may have noted that in Britain, for example, the royal family did not maintain a theatre at court. In 1701 an agent was sent to Danzig to negotiate with an itinerant German theatrical troupe.[293] Despite hearing horror stories of conditions in Russia, they eventually signed a contract, and Johann-Christian Kunst (Director von Ihro Zarischen Majestät Hof-Komödianten), his wife, and seven players arrived in Moscow in June 1702. It was decided to build a playhouse (*komedial'noi dom*) in the Kremlin by the Nikolsky Gates, with large windows with shutters ('since no light is needed for plays'). This work and the company of players were placed under the direction of F. A. Golovin in the Foreign Office.[294] Chancellery officials were unhappy with the task: 'We are not accustomed to such business and don't know how to deal with it. We beg that this theatrical business (*komediinoe delo*) be transferred from us to the Armoury because in that chancellery there are craftsmen who are used to dealing with such things and the work will be speeded up.'[295] They complained that the site chosen was unsuitable, because it was piled up with rubble and earth in 'a great mound' from the old houses. Golovin urged his underlings to get on with the project if they did not wish to incur the sovereign's wrath. They complained that Kunst was badgering them for money for costumes, which they suspected him of diverting for personal expenses. They doubted whether he was a 'competent master'. The translators (scripts were to be rendered from German into Latin into Russian!) were saying that the plays were 'of little merit'. 'If the premises are built in such a famous place and at great expense and the performance turns out to be poor, we fear your wrath, my lord.'[296]

Regular performances began in September 1703. The actors were Germans, and the first plays were all performed in German, but Kunst had to take on ten Russian pupils from sons of government clerks, and from 1705 plays in Russian (all translations) were put on. The first Russian actors were all male. The leading player Fedor Buslaev was supposed to receive 40 roubles per annum, others from 20 to 30, but judging by a petition of 1704 wages were not paid on time.[297] Women's parts in the German plays were performed by Miss von Willich and Mrs Paggenkampf. Kunst was paid a huge salary, 3,500 roubles, but did not live long to enjoy it, dying in 1703. His replacement, another German, Otto (Artemy) Fürst, a goldsmith by profession, demanded 4,000. In winter 1704 only three productions were mounted. Russian trainees complained that Fürst was hardly ever in the theatre, and that they were not taught their parts properly, mainly because he was unable to take rehearsals in Russian. Audiences were treated to impressive scenery, machinery, and costumes, but were deterred by the fact that in addition to paying for a seat (for 10, 6, 5, or 3 copecks), they also had to pay a toll for entering and leaving the Kremlin.[298] The theatre fell into disrepair, and ceased functioning altogether in 1713.[299]

The repertoire of the Moscow playhouse during its short existence seems to have consisted mainly of low-brow material, chosen for comic or sensationalist effect, adapted from German and Dutch texts based on old histories, chronicles (plays about Hercules and Tamerlane), courtly tales, and bowdlerized versions of other plays, such as Molière's *Le Médecin malgré lui.* German offerings included *Prince Pickled Herring or Jodelet,* adaptations of Andreas Gryphius and Daniel Casper. It has been suggested that these German comedies 'were quite alien to Russian life at that time and had no points of contact with our customs and concepts, hence the failure'.[300] Whatever the reason, it was 'the most unmitigated disaster in the history of Russian theatre'.[301]

Kunst's theatre was open to the public, and in this regard had no Russian precedents. The private theatre organized by Peter's sister Natalia, however, may be regarded as a revival of her father's experiment. The first plays were produced in 1707–10 at Preobrazhenskoe, where Alexis's theatre had been based, and in 1711 the scenery, props, and costumes were transferred to St Petersburg, where the tsarevna organized an all-Russian troupe of ten actors, male and female. Peter occasionally attended.[302] The Hanoverian ambassador, F. C. Weber, saw one of Tsarevna Natalia's productions in 1716 just before her death, a *Compound of Sacred and Profane History,* written by Natalia herself, on the subjects of 'the late Rebellions in Russia'. (Weber was not impressed by the performance.[303]) The Lives of Saints published by Dmitry of Rostov (well represented in Natalia's library) provided material for such dramas as the

Play about the Holy Martyr Evdokia, a life of St Catherine, and *The Comedy of the Prophet Daniel*. Texts were borrowed from adventure tales, school dramas, and scripts from Kunst's theatre, from which in 1713 twenty painted scenery flats were taken.[304] An inventory of Natalia's belongings compiled after her death in 1716 includes details of costumes, props, and books of plays, some of them copied in Natalia's own hand: twenty curtains on canvas, stage lights, tights and cloaks with spangles, Turkish and Persians costumes, angels' dresses, a jester's costume, military uniforms, a king's crown, a silver sceptre, eleven hats with feathers, beards, wigs, armour and painted backdrops, 'a hat for Peter of the Golden Keys'.[305] In 1713–23 Tsaritsa Praskovia sponsored a theatre at Izmailovo, in which her daughter Ekaterina Ivanovna (the future duchess of Mecklenburg), young ladies, and servants took parts. Bergholz's attendance in November 1722 (he reported that there were lights only on-stage and that pickpockets operated) shows that the theatre was open to a wider public.[306]

Apart from these royal ventures, home-grown theatre did not progress much beyond the Latin-based school drama, imported to the Moscow Academy from Ukraine in the 1680s to 1690s. It was no doubt this sort of drama and 'comedies' which were recommended for students in the educational sections of the 1721 Ecclesiastical Regulation, on the grounds that it was 'exceedingly beneficial for instruction and motivation, that is toward the honest courage that preaching the word of God and diplomatic work require'.[307] Seminary theatres existed in Rostov (founded in 1702 by Bishop Dmitry), Tver', and Novgorod. Metropolitan Filofei Leshchinsky set up a theatre in Tobol'sk in 1702 attached to the archbishop's school.[308] The Moscow Academy's repertoire set the standards for other theatres, featuring characters personifying virtues and vices, Time and Death, mixed with figures from Classical mythology. Humankind tended to be represented by an Everyman-type figure, the Sinner, often without gender, nationality, or class. Abstract figures appeared at the beginning to announce what was about to happen and at the end to explain what had happened. But contemporary events also featured, notably Russian victories against Sweden, in such plays as *The Realm of Peace*, *Triumph of Peace* and *Russian Glory*, composed by churchmen and performed in the Moscow Academy and other schools.[309] In 1702 a 'triumphal comedy' about the taking of Schlüsselburg was commissioned in German and Russian and the same thing for Dorpat and Narva in 1704. *The Fervour of Orthodoxy* (*Revnost' pravoslaviia* (1704)) dealt with military victors personified by the biblical Joshua. There were also plays with more subtle contemporary resonances, such as the ever-popular *Play about Esther and Artaxerxes*, staged on the eve of Catherine's coronation in 1724, in which proud Astine is rejected in favour of the foreign woman Esther. Plays preached the usefulness of foreign travel—for example, *The Comedy of Count Farson* and *Comedy of Xenofont and Maria*. Secular topics, such as Peter of the Golden Keys and Beautiful Melusine, had been well known in Russia for some time in Polish translations.[310] In 1724 the duke of Holstein attended a 'mean Latin comedy' in the Moscow Academy, and was much annoyed to find, having arrived at four, that the performance did not end until eleven and he was forced to linger in order to take wine and sweets.[311] School plays were also staged at the Medical School under Dr Bidloo, where pupils were rewarded for performing a comedy in the tsar's presence in December 1722.[312]

Home-grown playwrights were mostly churchmen, and the theatrical repertoires in both the capital and the provinces drew heavily on biblical subjects; but this did not preclude entertainment and spectacle. The most successful works, by Bishop Dmitry of Rostov, were *The Drama of the Dormition of the Virgin* (*Uspenskaia drama*) and *The Nativity Play* (*Rozhdestvenskaia drama*). The latter, first staged in December 1702, opens with the appearance of Human Nature (*Natura liudskaia*), who meets an assortment of virtues and vices. There are dialogues between Heaven and Earth and interludes with rustic shepherds Boris and Avram, the Magi, and Herod slaughtering the innocents. Herod ends up in the bowels of Hell suffering horribly.[313] Feofan Prokopovich's only play, *Vladimir* (1705), based on the Christianization of Rus' by Prince Vladimir of Kiev in the tenth century, features a group of stubborn, ignorant pagan priests, whose resistance to the new religion readily brought to mind Peter's unenlightened opponents.

The new capital remained without a permanent public theatre. Peter is said to have visited theatres in Carlsbad in 1711 and 1712, and to have had further thoughts after he returned from Paris in 1717. In 1720 he instructed Iaguzhinsky to hire a company in Prague 'who can speak Slavonic or Czech', no doubt to avoid unpalatable German plays; but it proved impossible to find an all-Czech company, as Germans predominated, and Peter regarded the salary demanded as 'exorbitant'.[314] A troupe with some actors from Bohemia does seem to have played in St Petersburg in 1723–4, headed by Johann Eckermann, or Mann, although information about the repertoire is scanty.[315] The first public theatre in St Petersburg dates from 1756. In the meantime, the lack of 'serious' theatre was compensated for by various entertainments, such as juggling and feats of strength. In 1719 the strongman Samson performed in St Petersburg, and members of the clergy were invited on to the stage to assure themselves that there was nothing supernatural about his tricks.[316]

It is unlikely that anyone assessing the musical achievements of the Petrine era would have predicted the triumphs of Russian composers in the nineteenth and twentieth centuries. In the seventeenth century Russian music fell into two main categories: sacred vocal music and folk-song. The introduction of linear (five-line) notation and increased polyphonic composition bear witness to Western influence on choral music, but the development of instrumental music was hampered by the disapproval of the Church, which did battle with wandering minstrels, who were associated with sorcery and drunken 'debauchery', a campaign spearheaded early in Alexis's reign by the Zealots of Piety, a group of clergymen with a mission to purify Orthodoxy. An edict of 1645 stated: 'Take great care that nowhere should there be shameful spectacles and games, and no wandering minstrels with tambourines and flutes either in the towns or the villages.' Tambourines, flutes, and horns were to be smashed 'without exception'. Instruments were also confiscated from private persons. Olearius reported that about five cart-loads were burnt.[317] On the other hand, 'seemly' musical entertainment at court functions and diplomatic receptions was tolerated. Alexis employed a Polish organist Simeon Gutkovski. Organs, pipes, and drums were played at his wedding to Natalia Naryshkina in 1671.[318] The tsar was at first hesitant about instrumental music for his new theatre, 'as being new and in some ways pagan, but when the players pleaded with him that without music it was impossible to put together a chorus, just as it was impossible for dancers to dance without legs, then he, a little unwillingly, left everything to the discretion of the actors themselves'.[319] The ballet *Orfeo* was accompanied by music played by foreigners. For later performances musicians were hired from Courland, Danzig, and Saxony.[320] The entry of the Dutch embassy of Konraad van Klenk into Moscow in 1676 was accompanied by 'the continual and unceasing sounds of trumpets and percussion', as well as pipes and flutes.[321] Evidently music in Muscovy was not confined to the human voice, as is sometimes claimed.

As court life changed and became diversified, to include mixed company and free access for foreigners, so more music was needed. Lingering objections to secular music were dropped, although tradition still precluded the use of musical instruments, including the organ, during the liturgy. Musical entertainment and instruction on a small scale were envisaged in the seminaries projected in the Ecclesiastical Regulation: 'On great holydays it is well that, at the table of those seminarians, there be the sound of musical instruments.' One musician would be hired, and seminarians would take lessons and teach others in turn.[322] Peter (whose toys included musical instruments) probably heard his first Western-style music in the Foreign Quarter, then abroad, where he attended ballets in Vienna and Amsterdam and heard chamber music in Königsberg. In Vienna Italian singers performed serenades for Peter's name-day.[323] In the last decade of Peter's life, when there was more leisure for entertainments, court functions were invariably accompanied by music. With the move to St Petersburg, Western-style music, like paintings and foreign chefs, became an élite fashion accessory, especially after the act on Assemblies of 1718 encouraged home entertainment.[324] Cornelius de Bruyn said that the orchestra heard in Menshikov's Moscow residence sounded 'just like in our countries: violins, basses, trumpets, oboes, flutes'.[325] Inventories of Menshikov's houses list clavichords, harps, organs (including a 'self-playing organ'), and tune-playing clocks (one of which still survives). His resident musicians included Swedish prisoners of war, the German singer Elizabeth Blesendorf, an organist, and Ukrainian bandura-players.[326] He also kept a considerable choir of Russian and Ukrainian singers, augmented in 1716 by the transfer of Tsarevna Natalia's choir, along with a number of vocal scores for between four and forty voices, mostly but not exclusively religious.

Apparently the scores were 'well worn', evidence of frequent use. Natalia herself may have written songs.[327] Menshikov's musicians played at the wedding feast of Anna Ioannovna, at the dwarfs' wedding in 1710, and at the masquerade after Nystad. For special occasions musicians would be sent to play a greeting, as in 1719, when Menshikov gave six roubles to the tsar's musicians, who came to play for the name-day of his wife.[328] Peter paid Johann Pomorsky and his eleven assistants to play for his daughter Elizabeth's birthday in December 1721.[329] Catherine in turn sent her German trumpeters to play for Peter's birthday.[330]

Peter was fond of trumpet music, which he had heard in German towns during the Grand Embassy. He also liked church bells, and 'simple Polish music', but not French or Italian music, and especially not opera, which he had experienced in Paris. (The first operas were seen in Russia only in the 1730s.[331]) His first and enduring love was for military music, especially drums. 'The sound of Russian music is in general so displeasing to the ear that it is more calculated to sadden than to rouse valour to martial daring,' wrote Korb. 'It is more like the moan of a funeral wail; and they possess not the art of inflaming martial ardour with nobler stimulants. The chief instruments are fifes and kettledrums.'[332] Musical education was imparted according to the rules of military discipline:

> They are taught Musick, as well as other Sciences, by the Help of the *Batogs* [canes], without which Discipline nothing goes down with them. ... If a General pitches upon some spare Fellow in a Regiment, whom he will have learn Musick, notwithstanding he has not the least Notion of it, nor any Talent that Way, he is put out to a Master, who gives him a certain Time for learning his task; as, first, the handling of the Instrument, then to play some Lutheran Hymn, which are their Airs, or some Menuet, and so on; if the Scholar has not learnt his Lesson during the Term prescribed, the *Batogs* are applied, and repeated till such Time as he is Master of the Tune.[333]

Military music was required, not only for campaigns, but also for triumphal parades. The first Western-style parade, in 1696, featured trumpeters and kettledrummers.

It would be wrong, however, to associate the Petrine era chiefly with martial music. Parades featured not only fanfares, but also choirs singing panegyric verses and *Kanty* (composed by teachers of the Moscow Academy).[334] A notable example were *Kanty* in honour of the victory at Poltava, commissioned by Peter, himself an enthusiastic singer. In other words, the seventeenth-century choral tradition was harnessed to the needs of the secular State, 'an evolutionary process of both spiritual and secular lineage continuously unfolding side by side'.[335] The compositions of Vasily Titov, who set Polotsky's *Psalter in Verse* to music, remained popular. Institutions such as the Moscow Academy and the Alexander Nevsky monastery had great choirs. Russian instrumental players may still have been learning the ropes, but Russian vocalists were second to none. Bergholz declared Russian basses to be superior to any in the world. In Italy they would have 'earned considerable sums of money'.[336] Thus the music of the Westernized élite remained organically linked to older traditions. The rich expansiveness of the Russian unaccompanied choral music in church lived on into the new age, under the influence of both Russian native composers and foreigners, as did folk-song. All three strands were to continue into the great age of Russian music more than a century later.

8

The Petrine Court

I. INTRODUCTION

It has been suggested that, as a result of being constantly on the move, Peter did not maintain a court in the sense then current in Europe.[1] The tsar's unpretentious tastes and thrifty attitudes and his frequent appearances in the guise of a commoner persuaded many that Peter had no time for pomp and ceremony. But to take this view is to miss a vital aspect of the Petrine era. Hard work created the need for play; painfully won achievements provided the stimulus for celebration. The last five years of Peter's reign saw not only a substantial increase in legislative activity but also a seemingly never-ending succession of feasts, masquerades, and balls. Peter's court was not so different in spirit from that of Louis XIV, which provided the model for much of the rest of Europe. Peter did not hunt, it is true; there were no *levée* and *coucher*, no carousels, no grand titles for courtiers; but Peter's court featured a striking element of theatrical performance, in which Peter himself sometimes played a leading role, at other times ceded the limelight to others. The figure at the centre was not so important as the ideological focus, which shifted from God to the State. In Peter's Russia entertainments and celebrations were reformed along with institutions; new ones were introduced, and old ones were updated.[2] An added perspective is provided by the fact that many 'serious' institutions and endeavours had their own mock counterparts. The ceremonial aspects of the Petrine era cannot be understood without attempting to reconcile the apparent conflict between, on the one hand, the elevation of monarchical power through lavish triumphal parades, panegyric literature, and engravings, and on the other hand, its debunking through mock rituals and play offices and institutions.[3]

The picture is also distorted by the misconception that Peter 'secularized' court ritual. There is no doubt that Peter's hatred of the stuffy, restrictive ritual of Muscovite court life, with its interminable religious observances, was a motivating force in his pursuit of change, symbolized by the removal of the court to a new city. The physical appearance of the courtiers changed, and foreigners and men of low birth rubbed shoulders with the old boyars. But the Church and churchmen continued, as we shall see, to play a vital, albeit different, role in ceremonial activity. The changes in festive life were 'two-faced and contradictory', reflecting a 'dualism' in state policy.[4]

An innovation which reflected this inherent dualism was the replacement of the old method of counting the years from the notional creation of the world or the birth of Adam with numbering from the birth of Christ. In addition, the New Year was to begin on 1 January, rather than 1 September. Like a number of traditional festivals, the September New Year celebrations had been dropped in the 1690s, especially during Peter's absence in Europe, and were 'left unrevived as things worn out and obsolete. It was considered that the worship of by-gone generations was needlessly superstitious in allowing majesty to be wrapped up with so many sacred rites'.[5] Decrees of 19 and 20 December 1699 noted that not only many European Christian nations, but also Orthodox Slavic people, had adopted the new calendar.[6] The Muscovite New Year was a strictly religious occasion: the tsars and the patriarch walked in a procession of crosses and icons in the Kremlin, and pious speeches were delivered.[7] Peter's new prescription for the celebration of this 'goodly undertaking and the new century' had markedly secular elements. This is an early example of 'enjoyment by decree': details were specified, right down to the type of festive greenery to be set up in public places. People of humble means were asked to display at least one branch. A public firework display on Red Square on 1 January 1700 was to be complemented by better-off citizens firing celebratory salvos from guns and muskets and letting off rockets, while poorer residents were instructed to pool resources to provide a few flares and beacons. (The decree contained no warnings about fire risks.) Protests from traditionalists that the Almighty created the world in autumn, when there was an abundance of produce and clement weather for the first man and woman, were brushed aside. Such die-hards continued to gather in secret to celebrate on 1 September.[8] As for counting the years from the birth of Christ, even clerks in government departments continued to use the old creation-based calendar for many years to come, as there were no sanctions against using both versions. Moreover, the decree had no retrospective effect. In official documents, years preceding 1700 were expressed according to the creation calendar.[9] Like a number of his contemporaries, Peter did not go all the way to modernity by adopting the Gregorian calendar, which had been introduced by Pope Gregory XIII in 1582, in order to adjust discrepancies with the solar year. Instead, he stuck to the Julian system, which by the eighteenth century had fallen eleven days behind. (The change was not made until 1918, when thirteen days had to be lopped from the 'Old Style' calendar.)

II. THE ALL-DRUNKEN ASSEMBLY AND THE MOCK COURT

The new New Year fell in the middle of the winter Yuletide festivities, another reason why traditionalists disapproved of the change of date. Yule (*sviatki*) was a sacred–secular hybrid, mingling *slavlenie* (from the verb *slavit'*, 'to praise'), or 'carol singing', unaccompanied singing of sacred music by members of the clergy, with older pagan rituals, involving mummers (*riazhenye*) in fancy dress. These old customs continued, and were attached to the new New Year. Johannes Korb described the 'sumptuous comedy' with which, in January 1699, sham ecclesiastical dignitaries visited the houses of richer Muscovites and foreign officers, singing the praises of the 'new-born Deity' and collecting money for their efforts.[10] Weber records that at New Year 1715 the tsar and priests visited the magnates' houses to sing a Te Deum, receiving hospitality and gifts, 'which was very profitable to the Clergy on account of the Czar's being with them'.[11]

These occasions involved the All-Mad, All-Jesting, All-Drunken Assembly (*sumasbrodneishii, vseshuteishii, vsep'ianeishii sobor*), one of the most noto-rious phenomena of the Petrine era.[12] Soviet scholars used to handle this potentially embarrassing phenomenon gingerly—to quote an example, 'the indecency [of the ceremonies] was in keeping with the spirit of the times so that now it is difficult to bring oneself to describe them in detail'[13]—cen-soring the lewder details and declaring the assembly's antics to be 'educational', an ingenious way of poking fun at religion and opponents of reform and promoting new attitudes and manners. A few Western scholars have been equally puritanical, referring darkly, like B. F. Sumner, to 'ghastly entertainments' and 'disgusting ritual', but providing the curious reader with no details.[14] Most have declared the Drunken Assembly an 'enigma'. It still awaits a thorough examination.[15] The impression was sometimes given that the assembly's activities were most vigorous in the 1690s, when Peter was still immature and impressionable, so foreigners could be blamed for leading the tsar astray. But far from being an adolescent aberration, not only did the assembly remain in existence to the end of the reign, it was also an integral part of court life, involving a wide variety of participants and overlapping with other mock institutions. To investigate the rationale behind the Drunken Assembly, it is necessary to return to the circumstances of its foun-dation. Peter may well have gleaned inspiration from the election and installation of Patriarch Adrian in August 1690, the last such ceremony before Peter suspended the patriarchate in 1700, and the only one at which he assisted.[16] He was obliged to attend, wearing the heavy robes and regalia which he so disliked; he had to beg Adrian (who had not been his personal choice) to accept the nomination and make a speech in unison with his brother, addressed to their mentor and guide, 'the Great Lord, Your Holiness, our father and pastor', and then sit through a speech from the patriarch appealing for deliverance from 'all crafty shamefulness and from Latinism, Lutheranism and Calvinism and all other heresies'.[17] As we have seen, immediately after the overthrow of Sophia and Golitsyn in September 1689, the Church initiated a number of measures against foreigners. Patriarch Joachim denounced the hiring of foreign specialists in his testa-ment. It would seem to be no coincidence, therefore, that Peter and his friends elected their own mock 'arch-pastor' not long after Adrian's installation. They may have stopped short of calling him 'Patriarch', but his titles mimicked those of the real one.[18] No details are available of the first mock election, but the Orthodox procedures of election (*chin izbraniia*) and installation (*chin postanovleniia*), spread over two days, which Peter observed in 1690, were mimicked in the election of a new mock patriarch in 1717–18.

The second circumstance is that the mock church assembly and its prelates were inseparable from the mock court and sovereigns, 'Prince-Caesar', and his deputy. After 1689 Peter spent less and less time attending traditional Kremlin ceremonies, leaving these to his brother Ivan. As he abandoned the old court, he began to construct a parallel one of his own. Pavlenko argues that the personnel centred around the 'Prince-Caesar' and the 'Prince-Pope' were separate, the former consisting of Peter's close associates, the latter selected on the grounds of their gluttony, ugliness, advanced old age and, above all, the ability to drink prodigious quantities of alcohol.[19] But the two groups frequently mingled on festive occasions, and clearly complemented each other in a parody of the Byzantine 'diarchy' of tsardom and priesthood.[20]

The third notable circumstance of the beginnings of the Drunken Assembly is Peter's close relations with foreigners.[21] Franz Lefort's palace and 'King' Fedor Romodanovsky's residence at 'Presburg' across the Iauza River provided venues for many of the assembly's proceedings. One of the prince-pope's titles was 'patriarch of all Iauza and Kukui'.[22] Specific foreign influences included the 'British Monastery'[23] and possibly freemasonry, in the form of the 'Neptune Society'. Based later at the Moscow School of Mathematics and Navigation, the latter is said to have had Peter as supervisor and Prokopovich as orator. Farquharson, Menshikov and Bruce were all linked with black magic, like a 'virtuosi' or alchemists' club. There are stories that Peter was initiated into a masonic lodge by Sir Christopher Wren in 1698 and established a lodge in Moscow, with Lefort as grand master and Patrick Gordon as warden.[24] Charles Whitworth mentioned the activities of a 'Brotherhood ... as true as pleasant, and a great glass of wine sanctified the occasion, I have several other gallantrys no less diverting but they are more proper for conversation than Letter'.[25] This subject requires further investigation, but evidently there existed a number of overlapping groupings and activities which may have influenced the young Peter.

It is difficult to reconstruct the membership of the assembly. Strahlenberg, who devoted several pages to its noxious influence on public morals, gives a figure of 300 members, but without any indication of what period he is writing about.[26] Tradition links a group of portraits, the so-called Preobrazhenskoe Palace series, with the early members, in an inventory made in 1739, which describes a 'portrait gallery' in the assembly hall of persons belonging to both the mock 'synod' and the mock court. Portraits of the 'sovereigns' Fedor Romodanovsky and Ivan Buturlin were prominent. From 1694, when they commanded the two armies in the Kozhukhovo manoeuvres, Preobrazhenskoe was (under the name Presburg) to all intents and purposes Romodanovsky's court, a status further emphasized when Romodanovsky 'ruled' Russia in Peter's absence in 1697–8.[27] This mock court was all built of wood, even the palace Church of the Resurrection, as if to emphasize its transitory nature.[28] According to tradition, the first 'prince-pope' was Matvei F. Naryshkin, who is identified with the Preobrazhenskoe portrait of 'Patriarch Milaka'; but the best-known incumbent was Nikita Zotov, who rode in the 1694 Kozhukhovo parade as prince-pope, and is referred to in some sources as 'Patriarch Bacchus'.[29] There were mock metropolitans of Kazan' (M. F. Zhirovoi-Zasekin, whose portrait hung at Preobrazhenskoe) and, later, of Izhora and St Petersburg (Peter Ivanovich Buturlin, whose activity probably dates from 1706), and Archdeacon Gedeon (Iu. Shakhovskoy). Peter was a proto-deacon. The subject of another famous portrait of the Preobrazhenskoe series, Iakov Turgenev, was a secretary in the office of Peter's mock, or 'play', regiments. His wedding in January 1695, in which the bride and groom rode in the tsar's 'best carriage' with a retinue of boyars and courtiers in fancy dress decorated with animals' tails and pulled by bullocks, goats, pigs, and dogs, is generally regarded as an early example of the Drunken Assembly's activity.[30] There were also portraits of A. Besiashchii (actually A. M. Apraksin, brother-in-law of Tsar Fedor) in a monk's habit[31] and a fool who bore the title 'cardinal and prince Vymeni, king of the Samoeyeds', a mad Frenchman whom Peter acquired from the king of Poland.[32]

A letter to Peter from Zotov, who signed himself the Reverend (*smirennyi*) Anikita, dated 23 February 1697 (the eve of Peter's departure for the West), gives a flavour of the bantering tone and cryptic language adopted by members of the assembly in their correspondence. Zotov expressed his dismay that Peter had befriended his 'banished slave' Maslenitsa (Shrovetide) without asking his permission. He warned Peter to beware of her if she was accompanied by 'Ivashka' (Ivan Khmel'nitsky, the Russian John Barleycorn) and Eremka (Dissipation).[33] This sequence of events confirms, incidentally, that Peter's indulgence in such play pre-dated his first trip abroad, although his experience in Vienna, famed for lavish court spectacle, may have given him some fresh ideas for Russian court carnivals. Peter attended a masquerade there in July 1698 dressed as a Friesian peasant, and was toasted by the emperor with the words: 'I know that you are acquainted with the great Russian monarch, so let's drink to his health', a gesture which must have appealed to Peter's love of disguise.[34]

After the execution of the strel'tsy in 1698–9 and the outbreak of the war with Sweden, the company of assembly members apparently became even more vital to Peter. Johannes Korb recorded a session in February 1699 at which a stark naked Bacchus sported a bishop's mitre and the insignia of Cupid and Venus. The mock bishop blessed proceedings with two crossed tobacco pipes.[35] Many references survive from the early years of the Northern War, when Peter was constantly on the move. The tsar's entourage in Voronezh at Easter 1705 included Zotov, Zhirovoi-Zasekin, Shakhovskoi, Musin-Pushkin, Stroganov, and Rzhevsky.[36] A letter sent to Menshikov from St Petersburg in March 1706 was signed by Peter's 'drunken' companions, the dog Lizetka, who affixed her paw, and the royal dwarf Iakim Volkov, who added that he had been given permission to be drunk for three days. The tsar signed himself 'Archdeacon Peter'.[37] In March 1708, returning from Lithuania, Peter summoned listed members to St Petersburg: the two 'sovereigns' Fedor Romodanovsky and Ivan Buturlin, the 'first sovereign lady' Avdotia Vasil'evna Romodanovskaia, the metropolitans of Kiev, Novgorod, and Vologda, the British deacon, the merchants Semen Ivanovich Ponkrat'ev and Aleksei Astaf'evich Filat'ev, Prince Mikhail Cherkassky, P. I. Prozorovsky, Avtamon Ivanov, and the mock abbess.[38]

The original mock abbess was Daria Gavrilovna Rzhevskaia, wife of Ivan Ivanovich Rzhevsky. In 1708 she was granted the St Petersburg mansion of the late Fedor Golovin; in 1712 she received the title of 'princess-abbess' (*kniaz'-igumen'ia*), and in 1717 was promoted to the office of 'arch-abbess' (*arkhi-igumeniia*) by the newly elected prince-pope Peter Buturlin, who wrote that he had lauded her 'exploits' (in drinking) before the assembly.[39] In 1716 a habit was purchased for her with Cabinet funds.[40] She enjoyed Peter's confidence, being instructed to supervise his daughter-in-law Princess Charlotte when Peter heard of 'irregularities' in his son's household.[41] After her death in March 1720 (Peter attended the funeral), Rzhevskaia's place was taken by Princess Anastasia Petrovna Golitsyna (née Prozorovskaia), 'a nun from the far-off wilderness'.[42] Golitsyna had performed the duties of 'jester' to Tsaritsa Catherine, which probably accounts for Peter's remark in 1711 that she had 'served instead of her husband', Prince Ivan Alekseevich, who was excused from service in the Turkish campaign.[43] Peter sent her a joking letter informing her that the Turks were on the march, and that she should prepare to meet the enemy with her weapons and shield at the ready in the autumn.[44] Golitsyna accompanied the royal party on its foreign travels in 1716–17, and was rewarded in Schwerin 'for howling', and similarly in Persia in September 1722 for 'crying in front of Their Majesties'.[45] In June 1723 she received a new habit from the treasury, to replace the one she gave away to a Kalmyk.[46]

A landmark in the history of the Drunken Assembly was Zotov's wedding.[47] In September 1714 guests were instructed to appear in groups of three in matching costumes, and to report their choice of outfit by 29 September in order to avoid duplicating the fancy dress. There was an inspection in December: masks included Menshikov as a Hamburg burgher, Gavrila Golovkin in Chinese dress, Ivan Musin-Pushkin in Venetian costume and Peter Tolstoy in Turkish. Each matching group was assigned musical instruments—drums, pipes, and horns.[48] Weber, among others, describes the wedding, which took place in Moscow in January 1715, as a 'world turned upside down'. The 'young' groom was over eighty, invitations to guests were delivered by stammerers, the bridesmen were cripples, the runners were fat men with gout, the priest was allegedly almost 100 years old. The mock tsar was carried in a sledge drawn by bears.[49]

One of the assembly's regular activities was to go 'carol-singing'. The following gives a flavour:

Our intemperance dictates that we are sometimes so incapacitated that we cannot move from the spot and it may happen that we are unable to visit all the houses that we have promised to visit on a given day, and the hosts may be out of pocket as a result of the preparations they have made. Therefore we declare and firmly confess, on threat of punishment of the great eagle cup, that nobody should prepare any food. And if we should deign to have a meal from someone, we shall advise our orders in advance, and for confirmation we have signed this *ukaz* with our own hand and ordered it sealed with the great seal of Gabriel.

Announcement of what each should have at home when we arrive:

bread, salt, rolls, caviar, hams, dried chicken or hares, cheese if there is any, butter, sausages, tongues, cucumbers, cabbage, eggs and tobacco. What we like best of all are wines, beer and mead. The more there is, the more pleased we shall be.[50]

Sometimes the revellers demanded money for their songs, in the manner of modern carol-singers. For well-to-do people this was tantamount to having to pay a New Year tax.[51] Palace account books include many payments for such occasions: to the prince-pope in January 1715 'for regular carol-singing'.[52] Just Juel provides a description of *slavlenie* in St Petersburg in October 1710, when the tsar visited houses accompanied by more than 400 completely drunk people.[53] The tradition was carried on abroad. On 25 December 1716 in Germany the chaplain Bitka was paid three chervonnye and the choristers ten efimki.[54] But mock *slavlenie* coexisted with the traditional variety. There are numerous records of gifts made to priests and deacons of the Kremlin cathedrals and chapels for singing.[55]

The Drunken Assembly was subordinated to the mock court, just as the Holy Synod was to be subordinated to the secular power. In December 1717, when Zotov's death necessitated the election of a new prince-pope, Peter asked permission of Prince-Caesar Romodanovsky: 'Our All-Mad Assembly has been left without a head; therefore we beg Your Majesty to see to the election of a Bacchus-like (*Bakhusopodrazhatel'nogo*) father for the vacant throne.'[56] The new pontiff was the former 'Metropolitan of St Petersburg' Peter Ivanovich Buturlin, who was chosen in a spoof election on 28 December 1717, based on a ballot using eggs, followed by installation on 10 January 1718. As the new 'pope' wrote, he had been elected 'by the will of the universal Prince-Caesar and the whole of the All-Jesting Assembly'.[57]

In the last years of Peter's reign such gatherings remained an integral part of court life. Officials were even sometimes required to forsake their regular duties in order to attend. In 1720 Anikita Repnin, governor of Riga, received a personal invitation from Peter to the all-jesting prince-pope's 'entertainment' starting on 15 October and lasting three days, and in the following year he received a summons to come to the pope's house-warming party.[58] In September 1721 about a thousand masked revellers turned out to celebrate the prince-pope's wedding. The tsar attended in his favourite guise of a ship's drummer, as did Menshikov; Catherine came as a Friesian peasant, mingling with Roman soldiers, Turks, Indians, abbots, monks and nuns, shepherdesses, nymphs and satyrs, artisans and peasants. There was Bacchus in a tiger skin draped with vine leaves, Neptune and giants dressed as babies. The fattest courtiers—P. P. Shafirov, I. F. Buturlin, and I. S. Sobakin—were chosen as runners (*skorokhody*) to announce the wedding. Bears, dogs and pigs, 'so well trained that they walked very obediently in harness', pulled carts.[59] After the feast, the bride and groom were led to an improvised bedchamber inside a wooden pyramid on Trinity Square, with holes drilled in the walls for spectators. The second day of the wedding feast included a ceremonial crossing of the river by the prince-pope and his 'cardinals' on a bridge of linked barrels led by Neptune on a sea-monster. The prince-pope floated in a wooden bowl in a great vat of beer, into which he was tipped when he reached the other side. It is worth recalling that this ceremony and the masquerade which followed took place just a week after the announcement of the peace with Sweden, celebrated on 4 September with church services and gun salutes.[60] Ratification on 23 September was followed by a masquerade with a naval flavour, when the Nevsky fleet sailed to Kronstadt and back, all in fancy dress.[61] The carnival parade of February 1722 in Moscow (a continuation of the Nystad celebrations) took the form of floats in the shape of ships mounted on sledges. Peter's was a 36-gunner in full sail, followed by a huge whale containing revellers dressed as animals or in various national costumes. The prince-pope was drawn along in a huge shell, followed by his 'cardinals' mounted on bulls or in sledges drawn by pigs, bears, and dogs.[62] The court was back in Moscow for Christmas and Carnival in 1723, again using the ship floats, sixty-four of them, even though the snow had melted. The procession visited, among other sites, triumphal arches set up on Red Square for the peace celebration the previous year. The master of ceremonies was Bruce. The third day of the carnival coincided with Peter's and Catherine's wedding anniversary, and on the final day there was a festive burning of 'the old house' at Preobrazhenskoe.[63] The empress and her ladies rode in a barge, all dressed as Amazons. In September 1723 there was a carnival with almost a thousand masks, at which the tsar appeared as a sailor and the empress and her ladies were again dressed as Amazons, the duke of Holstein's party as Romans.[64] There was another masquerade in 1724, at which Peter and Catherine appeared in matching Dutch costumes.[65] Bergholz records a gathering of the 'merry company' in February 1724, which featured a table of commoners, 'who try to amuse the emperor with various affectations and funny antics when he is in a bad mood'. A sailor did acrobatics.[66] Peter spent his last Yuletide in the customary manner (as observed by Campredon, who was annoyed that there was no opportunity to catch the tsar's attention), visiting the homes of courtiers with carol-singers.[67] On the night of 8–9 January 1725 there was a 'conclave' to elect a new prince-pope.[68]

Historians have debated whether the intended butt of the assembly's ridicule was Catholicism or Orthodoxy.[69] The Prussian envoy Vockerodt believed that Peter wished to ridicule the Roman Catholic hierarchy, and 'also indirectly his own clergy'.[70] Campredon wrote that the aim was to 'make the old clergy look ridiculous' (*pour tourner son ancien clergé en ridicule*).[71] Bergholz reasoned: 'Of course, he may have some other, hidden aim because, as a wise sovereign he looks after the welfare of his people and tries by all means at his disposal to eradicate its old crude superstitions.'[72] Certainly, Russian Orthodox elements mingled with Catholic (e.g., inspecting the nether regions to verify that candidates for the 'papacy' were male), but there was no attempt at a systematic pastiche. The early costumes were not modelled on Russian prelates' robes; for example, the prince-pope wore a tin mitre.[73] According to Lotman, 'For the people of Peter's entourage mockery directed against Catholic Rome inevitably progressed to the discrediting of the Russian Patriarchate, and the ridiculing of the Patriarch of All Russia merged with the parodying of the power of the Pope at Rome.'[74] But, as Cracraft points out, the assembly began some time before Peter instituted any church reform, and continued long after there was any patriarch left to mock and when the church reform was completed, with the hierarchs firmly harnessed to state service.[75] It is a mistake to look for a consistent political or religious purpose. Commentators have been reluctant to admit that 'such a wise ruler could have given such a shameful title to an institution he had founded without some ulterior motive or some secret higher aim'. It was more convenient to believe that it was a 'mask under which was concealed the great ruler's lofty aim to hide his country's political strength from his powerful neighbours: generals and ministers apparently drunk by day, at night turned out to be sober and working on "patriotic business" '![76]

The Drunken Assembly was not an isolated phenomenon, either in the Russian or in an international context. There were elements reminiscent of the common culture of Saturnalia, the Feast of Fools, Lords of Misrule, and mystery plays (Russia had its own version, the Furnace play (*peshchnie deistvie*)). There were also links with Yuletide mummer customs. As Kurakin wrote, 'There is an old custom among the Russian people before Christmas and after to play at *sviatki*, that is friends gather together at someone's house in the evening and dress up in masquerade costume and the servants of distinguished people act out all sorts of funny stories. According to this custom His Majesty the tsar in his court also played at *sviatki* with his courtiers.'[77] All over Europe at carnival time laymen and women donned the habits of priests, monks, and nuns, even impersonating the pope in *parodia sacra*. There were cross-dressing and erotic undertones.[78] Within Russia, too, far from existing in isolation, the Drunken Assembly coexisted and overlapped with other cases of 'elaborate parody'. To describe it as an 'influential social institution' is to misunderstand its essence, which was rooted in personal relationships and private jokes, and seemed more often than not to satisfy a need for letting off steam in male cameraderie rather than teaching the Russian people a lesson about the evils of overpowerful organized religion. Weber favoured a similar explanation: 'the Czar among all the heavy Cares of Government knows how to set apart some Days for the Relaxation of his Mind, and how ingenious he is in the Contrivance of those Diversions'.[79]

This was Peter's version of 'rebellious ritual' and 'group abdication from the structures of the social order itself',[80] but it was subversion with rules, which took established models (in this case religious rites, dress, and formulae), then undermined them. Rather than being subverted from below, however, with paupers becoming princes, in this case it was the 'prince' himself who effected the swap, but the iron hand of the autocrat was never very effectively disguised in the person of Archdeacon Peter, Peter Mikhailov, or whoever. The prince-pope was expected to discipline his subordinates. A document of 23 April 1723 lists those members who had been 'disobedient' and were living 'in unruly fashion' in Moscow. The fact that it was drawn up and annotated by the tsar indicates that Archdeacon Peter kept a firm hold on proceedings. Peter was also responsible for a list of the prince-pope's 'servitors', on which all were given rude names based on the Russian for 'prick' (*khui*).[81] An English merchant, who observed the company's antics at Archangel in 1702, summed up the situation succinctly: 'None of them can complain of his [Peter's] frolics since he is always the first man.'[82] An account by the French ambassador Campredon of the carnival in St Petersburg in September 1723 contains some telling details. For much of the proceedings Peter dressed in a sailor's costume, but one day he appeared dressed as a cardinal and proceeded to ordain four 'priests', then changed back into his sailor's outfit.[83] The mock-religious interlude was clearly not intended as a lesson concerning the Church, any more than Catherine's changes of costume, an Amazon one day, a grape-seller the next, were a comment on the role of women or an exercise in promoting private enterprise. That particular carnival, incidentally, ended at the house of the mock tsar Ivan Romodanovsky, in a massive drinking session.

How were such activities viewed by contemporaries? Some evidence of popular protest survives in the papers of the Preobrazhensky *prikaz*. In his 1700 tract identifying Peter as Antichrist, Grigory Talitsky cites Prince Ivan Ivanovich Khovansky's complaint that he had been installed as a 'metropolitan' at Preobrazhenskoe by Nikita Zotov, who had asked him 'Do you believe? Do you drink?', which blasphemy caused him, he feared, to 'forfeit his heavenly crown'. He also complained about being forcibly shaved.[84] The Astrakhan rebels, in letters sent out to the Iaik Cossacks in 1705, complained that 'instead of God-respecting carol singing they use masquerades and games, in which one of his courtiers, a jester, was given the title of patriarch and others—archbishops'.[85]

III. DWARFS AND GIANTS

Readers may have difficulty appreciating the offence caused by Peter's ceremonies to his contemporaries' religious sensibilities. More uncongenial to the modern West European taste, but less so in early modern society, was Peter's treatment of the disabled and disadvantaged, starting with what political correctness might term the 'vertically challenged'. Peter's mock court and assembly numbered among their participants dwarfs, a vital component at the court of the six-foot seven-inch tall tsar. The wedding of the royal dwarf Iakim Volkov on 14 November 1710 provides a striking example of how 'real' and 'mock' court life intermingled, for it followed closely the wedding of Anna Ioannovna and the duke of Courland, who were themselves guests at the dwarfs' wedding feast, which was held in the same room in Menshikov's palace as their own.[86] Peter planned both weddings simultaneously. On 7 August he ordered Prince-Caesar Romodanovsky to round up the dwarfs listed in an attached document and send them to St Petersburg; the day after he wrote to Boris Golitsyn asking him to send a pair of diamond ear-rings as a gift for his niece.[87] He sent an order that 'dwarfs of male and female sex now residing in Moscow in the homes of boyars and other courtiers are all to be collected and sent from Moscow to St Petersburg this 25th day of August', and 'German' clothes were ordered.[88] On arrival in St Petersburg they were shut up 'like cattle' for several days, then allocated to the lords and ladies who were to dress them up for the nuptials.[89] On the day of the wedding the dwarfs, about seventy in number,[90] were taken across the river in barges to the fortress. In the church the ceremony followed the usual religious offices, but was accompanied by the stifled giggles of the congregation and even the priest.[91] The tsar in person held the wedding crown over the head of the bride. At the feast the dwarfs sat at miniature tables in the centre of the room, and were served by a dwarf marshal and his assistants, while full-sized guests looked on from the sides of the room. 'Some of the dwarfs had huge hunchbacks and short little legs, others great big bellies, others short crooked legs like dachsunds;[92] some had a big fat head or a crooked mouth and large ears, or little tiny eyes and chubby cheeks and much else funny.'[93] There were roars of laughter as dwarfs, especially the older, uglier ones, whose short legs made it difficult for them to dance, fell down drunk.[94] Miniature cannons were standing at the ready, and the groom had prepared his own fireworks, but they were not fired, as Menshikov's only son was seriously ill, and, indeed, died the same evening.[95] The occasion was immortalized in an engraving made by Aleksei Zubov in 1711.[96]

There was nothing remarkable about the taste of Peter and his courtiers for dwarfs, who had long been a standard feature in the apartments of Russian royal children. The brothers Petrushka and Nikita Komar formed part of the retinue of the infant Peter, who sometimes travelled in a miniature sledge accompanied by dwarfs on horseback.[97] Twenty-five dwarfs in cloaks and plumed hats marched in the parade before the Kozhukhovo manoeuvres in 1694.[98] The groom at the dwarf wedding was with Peter at Poltava.[99] In 1716, two dwarfs went to Germany for the wedding of Peter's niece Ekaterina Ioannovna. Iakim was allowed to choose some clothes 'in any colour he likes', and ordered a green suit with gold buttons which, with all the trimmings, cost 23 roubles, 91 copecks.[100] Several instances are recorded of dwarfs leaping from pies—for example, during the celebrations for the birth of Tsarevich Peter Petrovich in 1715, when a naked female was served up at the men's table and a naked man at the women's, and at the wedding of Anna and the duke of Courland, when two female dwarfs dressed in the height of French fashion popped out, read some poems, and performed a minuet.[101] Peter Henry Bruce records the wedding of dwarfs belonging to Tsarevna Natalia Alekseevna, in which Shetland ponies featured and a feast was held, attended by the princesses Anna and Elizabeth.[102] The first of February 1724 saw Iakim's funeral (his bride had died the year after their wedding as a result of a difficult labour), to which all the male and female dwarfs resident in St Petersburg were summoned, to follow the coffin in pairs, the smallest at the front, the tallest bringing up the rear, the men in black, the women in long black veils.[103] Six tiny horses pulled the coffin, and the smallest priest in the city was enlisted to officiate. The procession included giants and the tallest guardsmen, including the tsar himself, who walked part of the way and funded the wake.[104] Weber records another funeral in 1715 which included 'She-dwarfs . . . ranged according to their several Sizes like Organ-pipes'.[105]

At the other end of the scale, 1720 saw the wedding of the giant Nicolas Bourgeois (sometimes referred to in documents as Nikolai Zhigant) and a 'giantess' from the Finnish tundra. Giants were in shorter supply than dwarfs, and Bergholz records that Peter gave his permission for the couple to marry only when the bride-to-be became pregnant, in the hope of obtaining additional tall recruits. Bourgeois, it seemed, had no duties, as his obesity made him incapable of doing anything. He was paid the considerable salary of 300 roubles per year.[106] After his death in 1724, a stuffed effigy in his skin went on show in Peter's Cabinet of Curiosities.[107] His skeleton is still displayed in the Kunstkamera. The dimensions confirm Bergholz's remark that Bourgeois was not so much excessively tall as unnaturally fat.

Close in spirit to amusement with dwarfs was the keeping of young Kalmyks and other natives of the Russian East, who were prized for their amusingly grotesque (by European standards) features. In September 1709 Peter ordered ten pairs of boys and girls to be sent to Moscow.[108] In 1722 four Kalmyks were sent from Astrakhan and fitted out in 'simple garb'.[109] They were treated (and neglected) rather like household pets: in 1723 Catherine wrote to Moscow asking for food (*korm*) for the little Kalmyks who are left in Preobrazhenskoe, 'as they are dying of hunger and keep drinking water and are now all lying down'. A couple of days later a servant was warned to travel carefully with the Kalmyks and dogs.[110] Black servants were also popular throughout Europe, and there were several black men (referred to as *arapy*) at Peter's court, including Peter and Abraham, the latter an ancestor of the poet Pushkin (Peter purchased several black slaves in London in 1698).[111] There was nothing peculiarly Russian about this passion for the 'exotic', the miniature, the grotesque, and the afflicted. Fools or jesters, too, were a familiar feature of royal courts. Several people performed the role in Peter's court, including Shakhovskoi, the Frenchman called Vymeni, Taras the Fool (*durak*), Stefan 'Medved', also known as 'Vytashchi' (Vittaschy or Witaschy in foreign sources), and a Portuguese called La Costa, who was declared king of the Samoyeds, an honorary title borne by several jesters.[112] Menshikov had his own jester, Prokopy Ushakov, also known as Chok.[113] Regular court personnel were sometimes called upon to play the fool. Peter's Danish cook Johann Velten so hated the Swedes that he was often asked to impersonate a Swede at ceremonies—for example, to put on a display of weeping at the opening of the celebrations of Russia's successful 1710 Baltic campaign.[114] Peter's love of 'turning the world upside down' was reflected in many other 'amusing' rites, such as the wedding in July 1710 of Prince Cherkassky, so old and feeble that he had to be held up,[115] and the cook's funeral in February 1724, at which mourners dressed in cook's hats and aprons.[116] One of the last festivities that Peter ever attended, the wedding of Mishka, the manservant of Peter's orderly Vasily Pospelov, to gudok-player Nastasia, was attended by all the gudok-players and lords and ladies of the court.[117]

IV.   WEDDINGS, CORONATIONS, AND FUNERALS

Not all Petrine ceremonies were jocular. Serious festivities, too, reflected the spirit of the age. Wedding rituals, as set out in the sixteenth-century *Domostroi*, had not changed much in Russia for centuries. Such customs as displaying the bride's blood-stained nightdress were easily rejected by nobles, merchants, and better-off townspeople, but persisted among common folk.[118] No description of Peter's own wedding to Evdokia in 1689 has come down to us, but there is every reason to believe that it was thoroughly traditional. This assumption is endorsed by a special presentation book on the 'honourable state of marriage' hand-made for the occasion with verses by Karion Istomin.[119] The frontispiece shows Peter and his bride in traditional garb, with the earthly plane linked to the heavenly one, as in icons, by depicting the saintly patrons Evdokia and Peter in heaven. This first wedding, and traditional nuptials in general, were parodied in the arrangements for the wedding of Peter's jester Filat (Feofilakt) Shansky in January 1702.[120] The festivities, held in the mansion of the late Franz Lefort, lasted three days, of which the first two were celebrated in Old Russian style, men and women in separate rooms presided over by the mock sovereigns Fedor Romodanovsky and Ivan Buturlin, with 'Patriarch' Nikita Zotov in one and 'Tsaritsa' Buturlina in the other. The Dutch artist Adrian Schoenebeck engraved the two scenes, which were inscribed with captions identifying the guests.[121] The painter Cornelius de Bruyn was in Moscow at the time. 'All that were invited were ordered to dress after the ancient manner of the country, more or less richly, according to the regulation in that case prescribed.'[122] John Perry also described the scene: 'The Victuals and the way of serving it to the Table, was, on purpose for Mirth made irregular and disagreeable ... their Liquor also was as unacceptable, the best of which (as in the Days of old) was made of Brandy and Honey.'[123] Bruyn continues: 'The third and last day it was resolved to appear in the German dress, and everybody did so, except some of the Russian Ladies. The men and the women sat at table together, as the custom is with us; and there was dancing and skipping about, after the entertainment, to the great satisfaction of the Czar himself, as all his guests.'[124] A similar old/new wedding was held in February 1704 for Ivan Kokoshkin and his bride, a woman from the artisan community. The long robes and caftans already looked so old-fashioned that a Russian contemporary described them as 'masquerade' costumes.[125]

The wedding of Anna and the duke of Courland, held in St Petersburg in October 1710, confirmed the new pattern.[126] But the most famous wedding of the reign was that of Peter and Catherine on 19 February 1712, immortalized in an engraving by Aleksei Zubov and described in some detail in the court records and foreigners' accounts.[127] The religious ceremony took place privately in the morning,[128] after which the couple paid a visit to Menshikov's house, then drove in sledges to the newly built Winter Palace. Menshikov supervised proceedings as marshal, with a diamond-studded cane. Peter's choice of dress and attendants emphasized a naval theme.[129] He wore the uniform of a rear-admiral, and the 'adopted' fathers were Vice-Admiral Cruys and Rear-Admiral Botsis. Cruys's wife played one of the 'adopted' mothers at Catherine's table. Many of the attendants were dressed as naval officers. Foreigners were well represented—Charles Whitworth, the Polish ambassador Fitztum, Just Juel—as were members of the Drunken Assembly—Zotov, Peter Buturlin and Iury Shakhovskoi—who sat at their own small table in the middle of a huge circle of tables, while others, such as Abbess Rzhevskaia and Anastasia Golitsyna, sat at the women's table. The couple's daughters Anna and Elizabeth appeared for a short while as bridesmaids.[130] In addition there were six other rooms in use for various categories of guest, including real clergy, vice-governors, and officers. There were toasts and dancing from six till eleven, at which time there were exploding shells and a firework tableau of the word 'Vivat'. Fireworks depicted two entwined columns with monograms. Peter was represented by Hymen, the god of marriage, with a torch and an eagle at his feet. The bride carried a burning heart and kissing doves. Above was a crown with the device: 'United in your love'.[131] The following day the guests reassembled for fruit and sweets and more dancing. The contrasts between this occasion and Peter's first wedding in 1689 are evident: the naval theme, the gun salutes, bewigged and *décolleté* ladies and foppish gentlemen in the setting of the newly built Baroque Winter Palace. But in Zubov's engraving, icons can be observed in the corners of the room; men and women, including the bride and groom, sit in the same room but at separate tables (a custom which continued to be observed until the end of the reign, as indicated by Bergholz's descriptions[132]). Members of the clergy were invited. Moreover, the old wedding custom persisted of appointing adopted (*posazhennye*) fathers, brothers, mothers, and sisters, who were the guests of honour at the tables of bride and groom respectively (apparently never their natural parents or siblings, even if they were alive). The 'best man' (*druzhka*) was the only male to sit at the women's table on the first day. On the second day the groom joined his wife at the women's table, where he symbolically tore down the wreath which had hung over his wife's head the day before.

A state occasion for which Peter had a fairly free hand in devising new ceremony and symbolism was the coronation of Catherine as empress-consort on 7 May 1724. Plans were made well in advance; an order to the Synod in December 1723 to erect triumphal gates set the tone.[133] In April amnesties and remissions on certain tax arrears were granted, uniforms were purchased.[134] Although there was no precedent for the coronation of a tsaritsa (except perhaps the unwelcome one of Marina Mniszek in 1605), the association of coronations with Moscow was strong enough to stage the event in the traditional location of the Cathedral of the Dormition in the Kremlin. But there was much from the new era: regimental music mingled with church bells as Peter and Catherine entered the cathedral, escorted by the newly formed life-guards (*kavalergardy*); guests needed tickets to get into the church; women participated in the procession, as did numerous foreign dignitaries, notably the duke of Holstein and his attendants. The crown was also new, made by a St Petersburg jeweller, 'quite differently from the others, just like an imperial crown should be'. Among the gems was a ruby 'bigger than a pigeon's egg'.[135] Page-boys in green velvet tunics, white wigs, and hats with feathers were in attendance. Older precedents were followed in the allocation of ceremonial duties to the favoured few—the marshal of ceremonies was P. A. Tolstoy; Peter was escorted by Menshikov and Repnin, Catherine by F. M. Apraksin and I. I. Buturlin. Prince Dmitry Golitsyn and Osterman held the mantle, the orb was held by Prince Vasily Dolgoruky, the sceptre by Ivan Musin-Pushkin, the crown by James Bruce. Golovkin threw medallions, traditional good luck tokens. Women were also honoured—Princess Menshikova, Countess Golovkina, Buturlina, Trubetskaia.[136] There were some traditional touches—for example, a second ceremony in the Archangel cathedral where the earlier tsars were buried, and also a visit to the Convent of the Ascension, to the tombs of former tsaritsy and princesses. Gold and silver medals were thrown to the crowd. Two fountains were set up, one spouting red, the other white wine, pumped through pipes from the bell-tower of Ivan the Great.[137] On 10 May an official edict ordered prayers of thanksgiving and three-gun salutes to be fired.[138] The coronation, in Wortman's words, 'laid claim to Muscovite ceremonies, but changed them freely to give religious sanction to the principle of utility, Western ways, and the unchallenged supremacy of secular power'.[139]

Perhaps no state occasion of the Petrine era was more suggestive of cultural change than the one which closed it: the double funeral of Peter and his youngest daughter Natalia in 1725, which was organized by General James Bruce 'after the manner of other European states'.[140] One of Bruce's major tasks was to arrange the decoration of the Hall of Mourning. This in itself was a break with Muscovite tradition, which did not include lying-in-state. Burial normally took place on the day or day after decease. Beneath a canopy draped with the imperial mantle and skeleton devices, Peter's body lay clad in breeches and a shirt of silver brocade with lace cuffs and cravat and military accessories: boots with spurs, a sword, and the order of St Andrew. (Military trophies were absent from Muscovite funerals.[141]) The coffin was surrounded by nine tables with Peter's orders and regalia and four bronze statues depicting Russia weeping (with a cloth in one hand wiping her eyes and a shield with the Russian coat of arms in the other), Europe mourning, Mars grieving (bearing a shield with the arms of Moscow), and Hercules.[142] Among the most striking features were the four pyramids of white marble on pedestals, draped with genies in sad poses and allegorical representations of Death, Time and Glory, bearing the legends 'Solicitude for the Church', 'Reform of the Citizenry', 'Instruction of the Military', and 'Building of the Fleet', with verses extolling Peter's feats:

From teaching military art
He failed in body but not in spirit.
The Russian Samson has fallen asleep after his labours.

A sheet of cloth spread between the pyramids capped by a medallion portrait exhorted Russia 'to grieve and weep, your father PETER THE GREAT has left you'. Pedestals bore statues of seven virtues: Wisdom, Bravery, Piety, Mercy, Peace, Love of the Fatherland, and Justice.[143] The whole room, illuminated by candles, was swathed in black, with festoons of black and white flowers and funereal drapes scattered with tears of silver satin. A nightly vigil was kept by senators and a military guard, with a single priest reading continuously from the gospels. Much of the imagery was strongly Catholic, a mixture of religious and secular statuary extolling the monarch's feats in life, rather than grieving for his end and heralding his life hereafter. Publications of descriptions and illustrations of the proceedings imitated the funeral books which had been produced at both Catholic and Protestant courts since the sixteenth century.

Secular aspects were to the fore in the procession on 10 March, which was announced two days before with trumpets and drums, and carefully orchestrated with a list 'of who should walk in the parade, both male and female'.[144] Unlike the funerals of seventeenth-century Russian monarchs, women walked alongside men. The parade was markedly military, with trumpeters and drummers and naval standards. Lining the route, which including an avenue (*prospekt*) marked across the ice on the Neva from the Winter Palace to the fortress, were 10,638 troops from various regiments. The procession was led by drummers and trumpeters in black cloaks, merchants (including foreigners) and deputies from the towns, and the nobility of Estonia and Livonia. Thirty-two horses, among them Peter's favourite, clad in black cloths and plumes, carried the coats of arms of the towns and provinces. There was a religious component to the cortège, with choristers, deacons, priests, archimandrites, and members of the Synod preceding the coffins; but Peter's distinguished associates formed the centre-piece, some holding the ends of his coffin drape, others, including the British ship's master Joseph Nye, holding the strings of the canopy, followed by Catherine, supported by Menshikov. Cannon-fire from the fortress at one-minute intervals mingled with church bells.

By comparison with the detailed description of the lying-in-state and procession, the official description of the funeral devotes just one line to the religious service, which was conducted in the still unfinished Cathedral of SS Peter and Paul: 'And then the funeral service was conducted according to the church statute.'[145] This was followed by Feofan Prokopovich's funeral oration. The last farewells were made 'with indescribably sad wailing', especially from Catherine.[146]

This new-age ritual, conducted against the backdrop of St Petersburg, can be contrasted with the interment of Tsar Ivan V on 30 January 1696, the last of the old-style royal funerals in the Kremlin Cathedral of the Archangel Michael, the mausoleum of the Muscovite great princes and tsars since the early sixteenth century. Ivan was buried on the day after he died, and the ceremonies followed a time-honoured pattern. The coffin was borne out of the palace and into the adjoining cathedral to the solemn toll of a funeral bell. The patriarch officiated, walking in front of the coffin at the rear of a long procession of priests, deacons, archimandrites, archbishops, and metropolitans; behind came secular persons, led by Peter and prominent leading boyars, followed by Ivan's wife, Praskovia, and various female members of her household (but not, according to official records, Ivan's sisters). In the cathedral, mass was celebrated, then the funeral service was sung over the open coffin, after which Peter took leave of his brother, followed by courtiers, who went up to kiss his hand 'with great tears and wails'. Finally Ivan was laid to rest in the cathedral next to his brother, Tsar Fedor. On the following days requiem masses were sung at prescribed intervals, culminating on 7 March, the fortieth day after the tsar's death. Throughout this period courtiers kept a twenty-four-hour vigil in groups of ten.[147] The funeral of Tsarevna Tat'iana Mikhailovna, the last surviving child of Tsar Michail, on 24 August 1706, also followed tradition, with a procession of secular and religious persons, crosses, icons, and incense, with solemn peals of bells and divine liturgy. Women carried out the vigil in the Ascension convent where royal women were traditionally interred. But it was noted that members of the duma were dressed in black French and Saxon coats, as were, one may assume, other government officials.[148]

V. DRINKING, ASSEMBLIES AND POPULAR ENTERTAINMENTS

While even the most solemn of ancient rites bore the imprint of the new era, others sprang from new requirements and Peter's own passions. Prominent among the new secular ceremonies of Peter's reign were laying the keel and launching ships. Even these involved prayers and sprinkling with holy water, but a secular mood prevailed, with the beating of drums and the firing of salutes, followed by a feast, often on board the new ship. Campredon attended one such banquet on 5 March 1721 (a Sunday) for the launching of the 86-gun *Friedmacher*. The tables set out in the cabins included one for the prince-pope and his cardinals, who indulged in prodigious drinking and singing, noise and smoking. Guards prevented the guests from leaving.[149] Another new form of Petrine entertainment 'by decree' was the regatta, or 'marine assembly' (*vodiannaia asambleia*) aboard the craft of the so-called Nevsky fleet. No doubt for Russians less enamoured of the sea than Peter, one of the new capital's most disagreeable features was the amount of time one was expected to spend in boats. Dignitaries were required to maintain one yacht, one barge, and two launches, and to join the royal sailing parties to Strel'na, Ekaterinhof, Kronstadt and beyond. On these occasions the royal daughters and nieces were dressed in canvas jackets, skirts of red material, and small hats, rather like the contemporary style of the wives of Saandam shipwrights.[150] The idea for the St Petersburg regattas probably came from Peter's travels, especially in Holland, but the big difference was that in the West attendance was voluntary. Peter took personal umbrage at any lack of enthusiasm for nautical jaunts. Non-attendance met with the same sort of penalties as dereliction of military or naval duty. On 30 July 1723, for example, Peter issued an order to Devier: 'There has been constant disobedience to attend the marine assemblies, and today attendance was poor, especially for our return. Therefore those who were not in their barges, except for legitimate reasons, are to be fined fifty roubles tomorrow, and not allowed until the next day to pay. If they say that they have no money then take goods instead and at the same time inform them in their homes that if they do the same again the fine will be doubled, and for a third offence they will be banished to the spinning mills.'[151] On 1 September it was reported that fifty-rouble fines had been collected from Admiral Apraksin, James Bruce, Cornelius Cruys, and Peter Apraksin, but Archbishop Feodosy of Novgorod had his fifty returned.[152] In June 1723 a lesser fine of fifteen roubles was charged to nine people who failed to turn up to greet the arrival of the 'grandfather of the Russian navy' in St Petersburg.[153]

Peter would sometimes go in person to root out shirkers. An entry in the court diary for 19 January 1724 reads: 'In the morning it froze over and there was a hard frost all day. In the morning His Majesty attended the Foreign College, then heard mass in the Trinity church, after which he was pleased to visit the coffee-house, and those present who had not been to Prince Prozorovsky's funeral on the previous day were made to drink an eagle cup of wine as a penalty.'[154] In February of that year, when all courtiers and officials were required to take part in the masquerade, senators were ordered to continue to wear their costumes even during the morning session of the Senate, as were officials from the government colleges, which struck Bergholz as 'rather inappropriate, especially as many of them were fitted out in a manner most unbecoming to elderly men, judges and councillors; but in this case everything was done in accordance with the old Russian saying: may the tsar's will be done'.[155]

These and similar incidents confirm the suspicion that Peter's masquerades were not true carnival at all, in the sense that 'people are liberated from authority, behavior is unfettered and hierarchy is suspended'. On the contrary, Peter's 'courtly carnival' celebrated authority as sacred.[156] Courtiers, officials and foreign diplomats were obliged to move between St Petersburg and Moscow at the tsar's command, regardless of their own convenience. In 1724, for example, everyone was uprooted to attend Catherine's coronation in Moscow in May (the exact date was a matter of speculation for weeks), then peremptorily ordered to return to the new capital in time for the tsar's name-day on 29 June.[157] In 1704 it is recorded that the nobleman Grigory Grigor'evich Kamynin was whipped, because although he was on the list of those to go carolling, he did not go.[158] At virtually every court gathering there were instances of reluctant guests being cajoled into participation, often *en masse*. Peter took a personal delight in forcing guests to drink more than they wanted, sometimes preventing them from leaving parties by means of an armed guard. No one was allowed to leave unless he or she was drunk to the point of vomiting. Just Juel recounts many such incidents. During a party on board ship he tried to hide in the ship's rigging, but the tsar climbed up with a huge glass of vodka for him. On another occasion the Dane decided to feign illness in order to escape a 'life-threatening' three-day victory celebration at the end of the summer campaign, but later he was collected by the tsar in person as he was preparing for bed, and had to go back to the party in his nightshirt and slippers. He had already been in bed for a few hours when he was forced to return to a St Andrew's day party.[159] 'For the foreign envoy these drinking sessions are a dreadful ordeal: he either participates in them and ruins his health or misses them and earns the tsar's disfavour.' Juel tried to negotiate a fixed measure, after which he would be 'left in peace', but Peter thought his suggested one litre of Hungarian wine too little and insisted on two litres.[160] The Hanoverian minister Weber was somewhat bemused after waking up with a hangover in the grounds of Peterhof in 1715 to be marched off with other foreign guests by the tsar to cut down trees in the grounds, after which 'we received such another Dose of Liquor, as sent us senseless to Bed', only to be wakened an hour later to drink more. Breakfast next morning consisted of large cups of brandy instead of tea or coffee. The guests were then required to ride round the grounds on horses without saddles or stirrups. The excursion was rounded off by a storm at sea on their way to Kronstadt, which sobered everyone up.[161] Bergholz records the entry of the grenadier guards into the Summer Gardens bearing a vat of evil-smelling grain spirit in which guests were obliged to drink the health of the regimental colonel—in other words, the tsar, in whose temporary absence no guest was allowed to leave the garden, even though many were soaked to the skin after a heavy shower.[162] A yellow flag was raised over the fortress as a sign that a party was on in the gardens, and the signal for the start was given by gun-fire. Guests would be greeted by the empress with a glass of vodka or wine and by Peter at a table with tobacco, pipes, and bottles. During the dinner to celebrate the Treaty of Nystad in October 1721 the tsar ordered that no one should leave while he retired to his yacht for an after-dinner nap. Bassewitz regretted that he had forgotten to take some cards along to ease the tedium, and Bergholz managed to escape to the Four Frigates coffee-house for a breath of air.[163] Campredon records several such incidents—for example, an assembly in March 1721 at which Menshikov handed round enormous glasses of Hungarian wine 'without mercy', and all were required to drink to the health of the fleet ('the tsar's principal delight'). Campredon, on the point of 'expiring', was saved by the start of the fireworks, which allowed him to sneak away unobserved.[164] In May 1723 a party was held for Peter's birthday at the Senate building, from 12 noon to 3 in the morning, during which time no one was allowed to leave. Simple grain vodka was served by force from wooden scoops dipped into a barrel by guards officers. Campredon, who confessed that never in his life had he so feared anything as he feared the approach of these 'cups of sorrow', was in no fit state to write his regular dispatch to the king.[165]

Heavy drinking was not a Petrine innovation, of course. Boris Kurakin dates the beginning of excessive drunkenness at court to the 'reign' of Franz Lefort, who encouraged drinking and debauchery, which came into fashion among the great houses and never went out again.[166] But with the exception of a few attempts at temperance, under the influence of the Zealots of Piety in the 1640s, Russians were famed for drinking, as foreigners, starting with Herberstein, were quick to point out.[167] Peter's reign seems to have been a high point in this respect, with such special refinements as the great eagle cup, an oversized goblet for drinking forfeits. No one was exempt. In August 1721 at a party to celebrate the launch of a new ship, Peter ordered that only Hungarian wine would be drunk, but Menshikov was caught with a glass of Rhine wine, for which he had to drink a penalty of two bottles of strong wine, after which he collapsed in a drunken stupor.[168] Drinking often had unfortunate consequences. In October 1722 Peter Shafirov wrote to the Senate about a quarrel he had had with the over-procurator of the Synod, Pisarev, at Iaguzhinsky's house, where they had been celebrating the news of Peter's entry into Derbent. As Shafirov admitted, he was already well loaded (*otiagchen*) with wine and 'barely conscious', but was forced to defend himself, as he was told later by others, 'as I don't remember what happened myself'. (Pisarev, he wrote, had behaved in a similar fashion at the name-day party of Tsarevna Natalia Petrovna.[169])

In 1718, inspired by what he had seen in France in 1717, Peter issued his Act on Assemblies in an attempt to encourage his subjects to entertain and extend polite society beyond the court. The decree of 26 November, signed by police chief Anton Devier, explained that 'assembly (*assemblei*) is a French word, which cannot be expressed in Russian in one word, but means a free meeting or gathering in someone's house not only for amusement but also for business'.[170] Like much Petrine legislation, the 1718 edict formalized already-existing practice. The assemblies were remarkable for their level of informality. So 'free' were the social gatherings envisaged by Peter that not only was access to be granted to a wide social range, from nobles to craftsmen, but the host was not obliged to greet or entertain his guests or even to be at home! This was in marked contrast to traditional Russian receptions, which involved elaborate rituals of meeting and farewell. Assemblies challenged the last vestiges of Muscovite ranking protocol (*mestnicheskii etiket*), allowing, in theory, participants to mix across barriers of service class and family circle. Intending hosts were to hang up a sign advertising the time and place of their assembly, which was not to start earlier than 4 p.m. or continue beyond 10 p.m. Guests could arrive and leave at any time within these limits. Access was open to any decently dressed persons except servants and peasants. No guest, not even the tsar himself, was to be met by the hosts, whose only responsibility was to provide furniture, lighting, and other necessities. Guests were also specifically encouraged to indulge in activities once denounced by the Church (and still abhorred by traditionalists) as 'foreign devilishness'— smoking, dancing, cards, chess, draughts, and instrumental music.[171] Weber mentions various games such as forfeits, 'questions and commands', and 'cross-purposes'.[172] A gentleman could invite any lady to dance, even the empress. The host of the ball could give flowers to any lady of his choice (except for his wife!), and at the end the lady gave the bouquet to the man she wished to be her partner next time.

The first assembly under the new regulations was held in the house of the reigning prince-pope Peter Buturlin in St Petersburg on 27 November 1718, thus establishing a firm association with Peter's mock court.[173] Sixty-five assemblies were documented between the edict and Peter's death, although a recent study argues that there must have been more, perhaps sixteen to eighteen balls in a season.[174] Peter attended many—in 1720, for example, Dolgoruky's on 14 January, Golitsyn's on the 19th, Tolstoy's on the 21st.[175] In 1722 assemblies were introduced into Moscow, but Moscow had fewer houses with the capacity to provide separate rooms for guests, and often everyone was packed into one room.[176] Bergholz records a Moscow assembly at which 'in the room where the ladies sit and dancing is held people were smoking and playing draughts, which caused a stink and clatter which was inappropriate in the presence of ladies and music'.[177] Even the clergy were encouraged to hold assemblies on the initiative of Feodosy Ianovsky, vice-president of the Holy Synod. The first took place on 23 December 1723 in the Donskoy monastery.[178]

Despite the alleged 'freedom' of the assemblies, there was a characteristic degree of compulsion in both the manner of their introduction and their subsequent supervision. Before the start, homes were visited by the police to check that everything was in order, and lists of guests were sometimes demanded by the authorities.[179] Perhaps these gatherings are best viewed as another attempt to limit and control, rather than extend choice, to *discourage* individual initiative, fix rules, eliminate unsupervised gatherings. This was the view of one Slavophile commentator, who wrote that 'above all the apparent jollity and revelry of life there reigned the iron will of the head pedagogue (*pervovospitatel'*), which knew no bounds—everyone made merry by decree and even to the sound of drum-beats, they got drunk and made merry under compulsion'.[180] Prince M. M. Shcherbatov regarded assemblies as harmful encouragement to lavish spending, at the cost of the elimination of 'simpler', indigenous traditions of hospitality.[181] In fact, Peter's 'democratic' assemblies did not last long after his death, soon being replaced by gatherings of the nobility (*sobranie*) with strictly limited access. After Peter's death, although Catherine and the tsar's old associates maintained many of his customs, there was evidently a sense of relief that an iron hand had been lifted. As Bergholz reported on a ship-launch in April 1725, 'they drank not nearly as much as had been the custom in the time of the late emperor; everything was over by nine'.[182]

The authorities had less control over how members of the wider public spent their free time and less interest in the niceties. The Petrine era is associated more with harnessing the whole population for hard toil than for providing leisure opportunities. Even so, open-air public entertainments were encouraged by decree. Indeed, providing recreational facilities could be regarded as serving enlightened self-interest. Wine fountains, roasted oxen, and public firework displays were routinely provided for victory celebrations. Stählin recounts how Peter insisted that the Katarinental 'pleasure palace' at Reval be built not just for his own use but for everyone. When he discovered that guards had been keeping the local people out of the grounds, a very ostentatious show was made of summoning the public by drum-beat.[183] In 1723 inhabitants of St Petersburg with estates out of town and on the coast were invited to make room on their plots for strolling (*gulian'ia*) by clearing the forest.[184] Popular entertainments included ice-hills (for tobogganing) and boxing matches. Alexander Nevsky monastery records mention workers' summer entertainments in 1720, with dancing and singing around a fire. The monastery would not tolerate such entertainments on church premises, however. In 1719 musical instruments, pipes, gusli, and balalaikas, in possession of monastery work-people were confiscated, a measure reminiscent more of the era of Tsar Alexis than that of his son.[185] Restraints were common: a decree of 27 September 1722, banned the sale of liquor on monastery premises before the end of services, but sanctioned 'folk entertainments'.[186] Traditional festivities and entertainers were popular. Just Juel observed strolling players (*skomorokhi*) who 'piped, whistled, sang and cuckooed, each one on his own note, in the manner of singing birds in the forest'.[187] In 1699 a lottery 'in the foreign manner' was set up at ten copecks a ticket, the draw to be made by two babies. The organizer, one Jacob Gasenius (Hasenius?) took one copeck per ticket 'for his pains'. 'And in this affair there will be an equal chance for the grand gentleman and the slave and the baby, without any deception.'[188] The public at large was sometimes subjected to the tsar's practical jokes. On 1 April 1719, for example, an audience was invited to see a performance by Samson the strongman, only to be dismissed after an inscription was let down from the scenery with the word APRIL on it. Apparently the year before Peter had staged a mock fire and summoned the brigade who were then rewarded with beer and brandy.[189]

The flavour of royal leisure pursuits can be captured from entries in the engagements calendar for the summer of 1720. On 30 July, having spent the last week or so cruising the Baltic as far as Viborg, Peter sailed from Kotlin to Peterhof with Admiral Apraksin, naval officers, I. M. Golovin, and an assortment of shipwrights. After Peter docked near Mon Plaisir palace, Catherine, who had travelled by land from neighbouring Strel'na palace, joined him by the statue of Adam, where wine was served. That evening the company took a turn round the gardens and dined in Mon Plaisir. The next day Peter acted as godfather at the christening of the son of Major Khotiantsov. 'After lunch they walked around Mon Plaisir in the garden avenues and towards evening, having crossed the canal across the new bridge which had just been finished, they drank wine and from there went to the groves where the hay had been mown. They stacked it up into ricks. At dusk His Majesty paid a visit to the major in his quarters. They spent the night at Mon Plaisir.' On 1 August they drove out to inspect the reservoir for the cascades and fountains, and that evening 'made merry with various invented games'.[190]

VI. THE COURT CALENDAR

Days in the calendar set aside for special celebrations bore the stamp of Peter's reforms and achievements, as well as marking family anniversaries. Some thirty special anniversaries were added to the court calendar, although not all were celebrated with the same pomp or regularity.[191] The anniversaries most closely associated with Peter's reforms and military programme were victory days (*viktorial'nye dni*). By the end of his reign just seven were listed in the official calendar: Poltava (27 June), Hangö and Grengham (both 27 July), Narva (9 August), Lesnaia (28 September), Schlüsselburg (11 October), and Kalisz (18 October). These triumphal anniversaries invariably included both religious and secular elements, an Orthodox service (*ordin dukhovny*) followed by *ordin politicheskii*, a variety of parades, assemblies, balls, and fireworks.[192] The nearest Muscovite equivalents were festivals for miracle-working icons, notably the annual processions of crosses and icons from the Kremlin Dormition cathedral to the Donskoy monastery (19 August, to celebrate Moscow's victory over the Tatar khan Murat Girei in 1591) and to the cathedral of the Icon of Our Lady of Kazan' on Red Square (22 October, marking the liberation of Moscow in 1612), and the feasts of the icons of Our Lady of Vladimir (23 June: Ivan III's stand-off against Tatars in 1480) and Our Lady of Smolensk (28 July: the capture of Smolensk from the

Poles in 1514, commemorated by the founding of the Novodevichy convent). Despite their association with military victories, these occasions were religious in their symbolism and emphasis. Vasily Golitsyn's return from the Crimean campaigns in 1687 and 1689 had been celebrated with parades, but Petrine solemnities differed in form and content. They were intended as much for foreign consumption as domestic, a demonstration to the greatly extended diplomatic community that Russia was a worthy partner in alliances and coalitions.[193] The emphasis was upon the achievement of the monarch and his troops, rather than on God's grace, as previously.[194] The new tone of military parades was reflected in various new details, such as the introduction of new regimental banners. The 'impersonal' saints, crosses, and other religious symbols of Muscovite standards were replaced first by the tsars' special patron saints (John and Peter), then from the 1690s by the double-headed eagle of State, often with a horseman resembling Peter himself.[195] New symbols were devised based upon old legends, notably St Andrew and his diagonal cross, which appeared (in blue) on regimental standards from 1700 and on naval flags.[196]

The first such parade in the new style was organized to celebrate the capture of Azov in 1696.[197] Buildings along the route were decorated with garlands, shields, and paintings. Each of the triumphal gates was dedicated to some aspect of victory, such as the Triumph of Peace, and each site had a programme of speeches, verses, and music, devised largely in the Moscow Academy. Later triumphal processions acquired a rhythm, with marching troops carefully timed and co-ordinated and use of music, drum-beats, and gun-fire. At each point there was a musical interlude, chants (*kanty*) composed in the Moscow Academy and sung by choirs, then speeches by leading orators from the Academy.[198]

Descriptions of arches, published for both propaganda and didactic purposes, provide details of these ephemeral art-forms. The triumphal scenery for Peter's entry into Moscow in November 1703 after the successful Baltic campaign included depictions of Neptune, Vulcan, Ulysses, Agamemnon (Peter's conquest of 'Troy' was deemed greater, because it was accomplished not by cunning but by open battle), Perseus (saving Andromeda, who represented Izhora), Jason, Hercules, Mars, Zeus (hurling thunderbolts at Kanets), and other Classical gods and heroes with whom Peter came to be associated. Tsars Michael and Alexis as military victors were also included alongside various allegorical females. The Swedish lion, in one case with an inscription 'Do not steal what is not yours', was shown being beaten by the Russian eagle, in one case hurling three thunderbolts to signify the three main towns captured from the Swedes. Villains included a three-headed dog and a seven-headed serpent.[199] A 1704 description of triumphal gates underlines their secular purpose: 'I think, Orthodox reader, you will marvel at these triumphal gates (as in past years) which are based not on divine scripture but on secular stories, not based upon holy icons but on secular historians, or from versifiers. . . . You should know that this is not a temple or a church created in the name of one of the saints but political (*politichnaia*), this is civic praise by those who toil with their labour for the security of the fatherland.'[200]

The greatest celebrations were held in 1709–10 for Poltava.[201] Peter drew up plans for a firework display, with orders that nothing should be fixed permanently before he arrived, 'because sometimes things have to be added or subtracted'.[202] The parade entered Moscow on 18 December (the day that Peter's daughter Elizabeth was born), but the formal march past began on 21 December. Peter's own role was, as usual, that of an officer with his regiment, the Preobrazhensky guards, but this time riding rather than marching, followed by a battalion of the Semenovsky guards with trophies and prisoners from the Battle of Lesnaia. Between the two regiments was a carriage drawn by reindeer bearing the fool Vimeni.[203] On 22 December Peter and other officers submitted formal reports of the victories at Lesnaia and Poltava to His Imperial Majesty Fedor Romodanovsky, who was enthroned in state to receive the captured Swedes.[204] Celebrations continued until 1 January. The New Year was marked by a huge firework display, the centre-piece of which was a fiery Russian eagle shooting an arrow into the Swedish lion. Just Juel wrote: 'In the display were to be seen beautiful blue and green lights, invented by the tsar himself, and also numerous fiery globes and rains, which turned night into daylight.'[205]

In June 1710 Poltava was celebrated in St Petersburg, with the customary combination of a church service, then gun salutes from the fortress and ships, a mini-regatta and fireworks, followed by a feast.[206] Another major victory parade in St Petersburg in September 1714 marked the Russian naval victory at Hangö on 27 July. Celebrations included an escort of captured Swedish ships from Kronstadt, a parade of prisoners, triumphal gates on the quay, and gun salutes, presided over by the mock tsar Romodanovsky. Engravings immortalized the occasion.[207] It continued to be marked. On 27 July 1716 Menshikov wrote to Apraksin: 'The day after tomorrow we shall celebrate the anniversary of the naval battle at Hangö, with which I congratulate your excellency. May God grant you a new victory, which I wish with all my heart.'[208]

Some of the most extended, best-recorded celebrations marked the signing of the Peace of Nystad in August 1721. Peter had begun to plan the celebrations even before the document was signed, well aware of their importance for both domestic and foreign consumption. In a letter to Menshikov he mentioned hearing that some monarchs sent out cuirassiers with white sashes and trumpets, and asked him to make preparations, but to take care that news did not leak out prematurely, 'to avoid shame if peace is not signed'.[209] Once peace was official, letters were sent out: 'We wish to report that the all-merciful God has been pleased to bless this cruel and dangerous war of twenty-one years' duration with a good and desirable peace, which was concluded on 30 August at Nystad and with which we congratulate you. For such divine mercy we must give threefold thanks: the first as soon as this news is received, the second on 22 October, the third on 28

January, the latter two to be carried out simultaneously all over the realm. All three to be marked with three rounds of cannon-fire.'[210]

In St Petersburg itself the first celebration was a more or less spontaneous reaction to the news, with mass in Trinity Cathedral and short speeches and gun salutes from the fortress. Beer and wine were supplied for the public. More formal celebrations were held on 22 October, starting with a service in the cathedral, followed by a sermon by Prokopovich and a speech by Golovkin (representing the two arms of Church and State), at which the latter asked Peter to take the imperial titles.[211] 'Then from all the people both inside the church and outside there went up three great joyful cries of Vivat, accompanied by a simultaneous thunderous blast of noise from trumpets and cymbals and drums and a round of fire from numerous cannons and guns from the guards and a hundred and twenty-five galleys and thirty-three field regiments.' Peter delivered a speech, and prayers of thanks were said, during which the tsar 'with great devotion and genuflections offered up the prayers to the Almighty'.[212] There was a feast for a thousand people in the Senate house, 'all distinguished servitors in the ranks of Church and State'. That evening the city was illuminated by candles in windows and braziers of tar and firewood on the streets. Fireworks depicted the temple of Janus with open gates, and in the middle Janus illuminated in blue, with a laurel wreath in his right hand and an olive branch in his left. The illuminations were ignited by Peter releasing an eagle which flew along a rope from the Senate building. Screens depicted Justice fighting two Furies and a boat coming into harbour. Pyramids gave out a bright white light. The doors were closed by two warriors, representing Russia and Sweden, who joined hands in a sign of peace, then from the fortress and boats in the harbour about a thousand guns fired simultaneously, 'and from this great round of gun-fire it seemed as if the whole fortress and the river Neva were covered in flame'.[213]

An even bigger Janus temple was erected for the Nystad celebrations held in Moscow. Lavish triumphal gates were built for Peter's arrival on 18 December 1721, at a cost of 4,000 roubles. Peter was greeted by Metropolitan Stefan Iavorsky, president of the Synod, and teachers of the Moscow Academy. The duke of Holstein sent musicians and tables with food and drink were set up. Feofilakt Lopatinsky and Feofan Prokopovich delivered victory sermons in the Cathedral of the Dormition on 1 and 28 January respectively. Thereafter, Peter ordered that the peace be celebrated every year 'both in religious and civil manner' on 30 August, the feast of St Alexander Nevsky. Gates were erected by the Synod in December 1722 to celebrate the capture of Derbent. This time Peter was greeted by a choir from the Latin schools dressed in hired wigs and crowned with greenery.[214]

Despite the emphasis upon the new, some older traditions proved remarkably resilient, albeit with an update. One such was the blessing of the waters of the 'Jordan' at Epiphany (6 January), which seventeenth-century tsars had celebrated on the banks of the Moskva River below the Kremlin. This continued to be celebrated annually in the 1690s, although often without Peter and with some novel additions. In January 1693, for example, foreign officers, including Gordon, and their men marched to the Kremlin. The next day Peter organized a firework display.[215] Foreign officers and their regiments were also in attendance at the 1699 celebrations, as witnessed by Johannes Korb, with Peter leading the Preobrazhensky regiment in their new green uniforms amid hundreds of priests and 'an incredible multitude of people'.[216] Cornelius de Bruyn witnessed the event in 1702. A hole thirteen feet in diameter was cut in the ice and enclosed by wooden panels with representations of evangelists and saints. A stockade and ballustrades were erected around this, 'all painted, but sadly enough, and like the rest, represented sacred things'. (Bruyn, a painter himself, shared the common Western contempt for Russian religious art.) A huge procession of clergy performed the ritual, which culminated in dipping a cross in the water to the words 'Lord save thy people and bless thine inheritance'. Later a priest soused a great broom with the water and washed the spectators with it. Bruyn saw 'something ridiculous in this part of the solemnity'. He remarked that previously the festival had been celebrated 'with much more pomp and solemnity than at present, it having been customary for their Majesties and the Grandees of state to be present thereat'.[217] It was repeated the following year, but there were 'not so many churchmen as before, nor so great a number of the fine caps and mitres'. Changes were predicted.[218] The ceremony was transferred to St Petersburg and was still going strong in the last years of Peter's reign, but was partially hijacked by the secular authorities. The German traveller N.G. witnessed the ceremony in 1711, when several thousand people attended. A regiment of infantry was drawn up in attendance, and a salute was fired from the fortress. After the royal and aristocratic spectators had been sprinkled with holy water and had dispersed, ordinary folk collected pails of water from the hole in the ice (to be drunk or used for washing at home), and others stripped off and bathed in the freezing water.[219] Weber recorded the 1715 ceremony, which Peter attended as colonel of his regiment.[220] Court records preserve a detailed account of the ceremonial of 6 January 1724: after matins in St Isaac's cathedral, the Preobrazhensky and Semenovsky guards were drawn up and marched to the Trinity quay near the Winter Palace, where Catherine watched from a window. Peter marched at the head of the Preobrazhensky guards in his colonel's uniform. The tsar, tsaritsa, and their daughters attended mass in Trinity Cathedral, 'and after mass there was a procession of the Cross to Jordan. When the divine service at Jordan was over the standards of all the battalions were taken to the Jordan and sprinkled with [holy] water and there was a gun salute from the fortress, then the soldiers fired a round of rifle shot.'[221] The same ceremony was enacted a year later, just a few weeks before Peter fell ill and died.[222]

Another Muscovite ritual, the Palm Sunday procession (said to have been instituted by Constantine the Great), in which the tsar on foot led the patriarch's donkey, had already fallen into abeyance when the patriarchate lapsed in 1700. It was still going strong in the early 1690s when, as we have seen, the

Church reasserted itself, while Peter pursued his own interests.[223] The last recorded observance was in 1696, the year of Tsar Ivan's death.[224] Thereafter, in the years 1697–1700 Peter was away from Moscow at Easter. Entries in the palace records for 1699 and 1700 to the effect that there 'was no palm ceremony' suggest that the ceremony was simply abandoned, rather than abolished. No edict to that effect is known to have been issued.[225]

The symbolic subservience of the secular power to the sacred was unacceptable to Peter. At the same time, echoes of the events of Palm Sunday appear in Hosanna-type greetings ('Blessed is he that cometh in the name of the Lord') made to Peter by eminent churchmen on various occasions later in his reign. The honour previously given to the patriarch was thus appropriated by the tsar, while the demoted patriarch was ridiculed in mock ceremonies involving the prince-pope, with pigs, bears or goats—even a camel— substituted for the biblical ass.[226] Holy Week as a whole, the high point of the Muscovite Church calendar, was a casualty of the Petrine reform, probably because the intensity of the religious ceremonies which had kept his predecessors occupied in a week of processions, night and day, was alien to Peter. He celebrated Easter, but on a reduced, more private scale.

In general, the number of Church festivals celebrated *publicly* was reduced to about twenty. Lesser religious feasts, including most Russian and Byzantine saints' days, disappeared from the public calendar, although these saints continued to be honoured in churches and monasteries by appropriate liturgies. Those thus demoted included Russian saintly prelates such as Metropolitans Philip, Peter, Alexis, and Job, who perhaps provided unwelcome reminders (to Peter) of the Church's once powerful political role.[227] Certain largely devotional (although politically and ideologically coloured) court rituals, which had occupied a substantial part of the royal timetable right up to the death of Tsar Ivan in 1696, disappeared completely: notably the royal family's 'secret outings' (*tainye vykhody*) to almshouses and prisons, formal royal processions (*shestviia*) to church (when several churches in the vicinity of the Kremlin might be visited), and the lengthy *pokhody* to monasteries (e.g., around the time of the September feast of St Sergius).[228] Peter avoided such rituals, especially if they involved wearing traditional heavy robes and regalia. Likewise, regular services of remembrance (*panikhidy*) on the anniversaries of the deaths and the name-days of deceased Romanovs, including Tsars Michael, Alexis, and Fedor, lapsed. Peter had already begun to neglect such observances in the 1680s; in 1689, for example, he missed the services in memory of his brother Tsar Fedor on 27 April (requiem mass) and 8 June (feast of Fedor Stratilat).[229]

Peter's reign witnessed a marked decrease in the number of icons in public places and a decline in the number of fast days, at least in part to meet the practical demands of an army marching.[230] But as a number of saints' days and other festivals more or less disappeared from public view, others were added. A good example of the use of personalized religious symbolism for political purposes is the introduction in 1699 of the Order of St Andrew, which combined commemoration of a saint associated by legend with the Russian land and a personal connection: Andrew was the brother of Peter, and was hence regarded as one of the tsar's patrons. Apart from his legendary local link with the St Petersburg region (an early chronicle account has him reach Novgorod), Andrew had the advantage of not being so directly associated with the Vatican as St Peter.[231] His cult may also have been suggested to Peter by Scottish associates such as Bruce and Gordon.

Peter also extended the cult of Prince Alexander Iaroslavich of Novgorod (1220–63), who beat the Swedes on 15 July 1240, on the Neva River (site of future St Petersburg), for which he received the title 'Nevsky', and in 1242 defeated the Teutonic knights in the famous battle on the ice on Lake Peipus. He also had to contend with the Mongol invasion. Alexander was canonized in the fourteenth century. The usefulness of such a figure to Peter is immediately clear. The revival and enhancement of Alexander's cult was inaugurated in 1704 by Peter in person planting wooden crosses at the spot not far from the Neva River where Alexander was supposed to have scored his victory over the Swedes. (In fact, the battle took place farther off, at the confluence of the River Neva with the Izhora.[232]) In July 1710 the Alexander Nevsky monastery was founded, the only monastery in St Petersburg in Peter's time.

On 23 November 1718 (Alexander's feast-day) Feofan Prokopovich delivered a sermon in which he preached that the prince 'bore the burden of state affairs with fortitude. ... He held firm the tiller of his fatherland in those difficult times. Russia was internally and externally enfeebled and poor, very like a ship in distress (*otchainny korabl'*).' Feofan likened the Mongols on one side and the Swedes on the other to 'winds' buffeting the ship, and Russia's internal dynastic struggles and disputes were like 'holes' or 'cracks' in the hull. But helmsman Alexander saved his 'ship' and earned the title 'Nevsky'—and 'to this day the Neva is a Russian (*rossiiskaia*) river'. The sermon ended by describing Peter as 'a living mirror' of Alexander, completing tasks which Alexander had started. 'Where Alexander planted a small seed, Peter has cultivated a great meadow.'[233]

Thus the analogies between Peter and Alexander were drawn with little doubt as to who was the greater. In 1723 Peter ordered an armed guard to transport the saint's relics from Vladimir to St Petersburg. On 30 August 1724 the relics were laid to rest in the monastery Church of the Annunciation, the upper storey of which was dedicated to the saint.[234] The gilded silver casket was borne to the monastery on a barge beneath a rich canopy, the royal family following behind on boats. In addition to the 1,000 priests, monks and pilgrims said to be in attendance, an estimated 6,000 spectators turned up to witness the procession, and at night bonfires were lit, and gun salutes and illuminations set off. The political motivation is clear: the analogies between Alexander's and Peter's victories over the Swedes, the confirmation of the ancestral right to the land on the Neva which Peter's ancestors had fought to preserve, not to mention the *translatio imperii* as St Petersburg, the New Rome, received the baton from its illustrious predecessors—Kiev, Vladimir, and Moscow. The transfer of Alexander's relics was also a public relations exercise, an injection of patriotic spirit in the wake of the victory over the Swedes, celebrated three years earlier. That astute observer Bassewitz suggests another reason: 'By the respect paid to the memory of this saint, who had served God and his country with such distinction, the emperor cleared himself from the suspicion that he intended to eliminate altogether the worship paid by the Greek church to its patrons in heaven.'[235]

In practice, Alexander's military feats, not his piety, were emphasized. In 1724 the Synod ruled that the iconographic depiction of St Alexander as a monk was to be discontinued. Only the model of the warrior-prince was to be used. In other words, Nevsky's retirement from active service and his taking of monastic vows were played down, his dynamic military character-istics highlighted to the extent of moving his feast-day from 23 November (the date of his burial) to 30 August, the anniversary of the Treaty of Nystad.[236] Thus, the prince was 'put to work not for the salvation of Russian souls but for the glory of the imperial state and its new capital, St Petersburg'.[237] Peter's successor, Catherine I, added to the cult by instituting the order of St Alexander Nevsky, to be issued to all holders of the order of St Andrew from the rank of major-general on up, to be worn only on St Alexander's day, 30 August.[238] This also happened to be the saint's day of Alexander Menshikov, Peter's right-hand man and virtual ruler of Russia for a few years after Peter's death.

If the ceremonies associated with Alexander Nevsky and St Andrew adapted sacred symbols for mainly secular purposes, another set of cere-monies took a wholly secular relic and imbued it with religious significance. The pre-history of the Petrine fleet began with the discovery at Izmailovo of the little sailing dinghy (*botik*) which came to be known as the 'grandfather' of the Russian navy.[239] Prokopovich drove home the point in a sermon in praise of the Russian fleet, delivered in 1720. 'Who will deny that this small dinghy was to the fleet as the seed is to the tree? From that seed there grew this great, marvellous, winged, weapon-bearing tree. O little boat, worthy of being clad in gold. Some seek the planks of Noah's Ark on Mount Ararat; my advice would be to keep this boat and preserve it as an unforgettable mem-orial.' (Prokopovich also pointed out that God created seas as a means of communication between countries. Anyone disliking the fleet was displaying ingratitude to God.[240])

In 1722, Peter, just back from his successful campaign on the Caspian, made elaborate arrangements for the transport of the dinghy from Moscow, where it had been displayed in front of the Dormition cathedral in the Kremlin, to St Petersburg.[241] On 30 May 1723, for his birthday, Peter orga-nized a grand regatta in honour of the navy in which the 'grandfather' had a place of honour, receiving gun salutes from the Peter–Paul fortress. To under-line the theme first elaborated in the Naval Statute, a plinth was made, carved with the inscription 'The amusement of the child brought the triumph of the man'.[242] On 30 August 1723 an even grander regatta for the entire navy was organized outside Kronstadt.[243] The small craft, steered by Peter, was rowed between the warships of the Russian navy, 'in order that the good grandfather could receive due honour from all his spendid grandsons',[244] as the navy fired guns in honour of the boat and the creator of the navy. The festivities finished with a service in the Alexander Nevsky monastery.[245] After this the boat was replaced on its plinth in the Peter–Paul fortress, but in 1724 Peter ordered that it be brought out on the water and taken to the monastery every year on 30 August.[246] It made the journey in August 1724, flying the flag of St Andrew, to coincide with the transfer of the relics described earlier.[247]

The name-days and birthdays of the imperial family provided suitable occasions for parties.[248] Name-days were celebrated more lavishly than birthdays. In 1721, for example, guests were invited to a modest reception for Anna Petrovna's birthday on 27 January, but for her name-day on 3 February, the feast of Saints Simeon and Anna, there was a mass, a dinner, the launch of a ship, and a party at the Post Office, 'where there were fireworks and a lot of rockets'.[249] From 1721 Peter and Catherine's wedding anniversary (19 February) was included in the court calendar, as was the coronation of Ivan and Peter (25 June).[250] On 19 February 1721 there was a ball at the Post Office and a firework display, with one panel lighting up the word 'Vivat' and a monogram of P and C in Latin letters under a crown. On coronation day guests walked in the gardens, and there was a gun salute from the fortress and galleys.[251] Together with the imperial birthdays, these occasions extended the cult of monarchy, belying Peter's 'plain man' myth or the idea that loyalty was redirected towards an impersonal State. May and June, the period of 'white nights' when the sun hardly sets in St Petersburg, were crammed with such anniversaries: Peter's birthday on 30 May and his name-day on 29 June, the anniversaries of the coronation on 25 June, Poltava on 27 June. Festivities took place outside, often in the gardens of the Summer Palace. On these occasions, reports Bassewitz, a large table was set aside for members of the clergy, with whom the tsar conversed on matters of scripture. Anyone who misquoted had to drink a large glass of vodka as a fine.[252]

As we have seen, many festivities, both public victories and family celebrations, were accompanied by fireworks.[253] Fireworks were not unknown in Russia before Peter's time. Some church festivals used fire, explosives, and lighting effects, notably the Fiery Furnace play and the play of the Last Judgement. Fireworks, including rockets (*letaiushchie poteshnye ogni*) were set off for Tsar Alexis at Shrovetide in 1672.[254] To Peter, pyrotechnics were closely linked with a love of shells and explosions, adolescent passions which stayed with him throughout his life. He is also said to have told a Prussian ambassador that one reason for staging firework displays was to get his subjects used to gun-fire and make them keener in battle.[255] 'It would be better to spend those millions on fireworks, on something wondrous and memorable in which the people can take great pleasure.'[256] From an early age Peter liked to make his own fireworks. (At the celebrations of the birth of Tsarevich Alexis in February 1690, a courtier was killed by a five-pound rocket falling on his head.[257]) In 1693 two displays were lit at Voskresenskoe, one for foreigners and one for Russians, featuring a pavilion of white fire with the monogram of the mock tsar Fedor Romodanovsky and a transparency with Hercules opening the lion's mouth.[258] In Moscow in February 1697 traditional strolling (*gulian'ia*) was combined with victory celebrations for Azov, in which 'His Majesty the Tsar was highly delighted to be among the engineers and himself took part in working the biggest [firework] machine which stood in the midst of the others', a two-headed eagle with open wings, its left leg hurling rockets at a crescent moon.[259] Peter's enthusiasm was fuelled by the displays he saw abroad in 1697–8. Frederick III of Prussia, for example, put on a display with emblems of Russia's victory at Azov, and in Amsterdam in August 1697 Peter's name appeared in lights: 'Many great fireworks which burned very harmoniously and properly and gave out many different coloured lights; and the rockets (*verkhovye rakety*) were very good and flew high.'[260]

From 1700 onwards, New Year provided the opportunity for firework displays, as did successes in the Northern War from 1702. To mark Russia's first victory over the Swedes, at Erestfer, transparencies were produced showing Fortune and Time, a broken oak with a growing branch and a beaver gnawing a tree trunk, to give the message that Russian persistence had prevailed after set-backs.[261] Fireworks in 1704 featured a twenty-metre-high double eagle holding a shield depicting the White, Azov, and Caspian Seas, to which Neptune in a chariot handed a shield depicting the Baltic.[262] For the wedding of Anna and Frederick of Courland in 1710, fireworks on rafts on the Neva illuminated crowns over the letters A and F and two palm-trees with entwined tops with the inscription 'Love unites'. Cupid with his hammer and anvil welded together two hearts under the inscription 'Two joined together as one'.[263] To enlighten a possibly bemused public, brochures were produced with explanations and engravings. In 1704 the *Book of Triumph* (*Triumfal'naia kniga*) contained a 'complete description of fireworks which were skilfully and splendidly set off after the successful campaign of 1703'.[264]

Any lingering illusions that Peter was indifferent to celebration and display should by now have been dispelled. On the contrary, Peter's court (in the widest sense of the word) was a complex, often bemusing phenomenon, with Peter himself and other leading figures sometimes playing several roles at once. In Peter's case these included sovereign emperor, skipper, shipwright, archdeacon, and captain of the guards. Peter had an amazing capacity to combine work and play, but there were times when the latter predominated. In January 1722 the French ambassador Campredon reported that the emperor had no time to arrange an audience with him because 'he is so busy with his new regulations and with the arrangements for the great masquarade'. January 1722, it will be recalled, saw the publication of new rules on the Senate, edicts on provincial courts, and, most notably, the Table of Ranks. Edicts on the procurator-general and over-procurator of the Holy Synod were in the pipeline. Yet Peter seems to have given equal attention to planning a week-long carnival during which, to quote Campredon again, all other business stopped. At the same time, Peter brought to the planning of the masquerade the same precision that he brought to regulations. All the floats in the parade were numbered, to prevent 'disorder and confusion'.[265] One can agree with Wortman, that in the Petrine era the 'theatre of power ... was a play performed principally for the participants. It is the various strata of the élite who gather to celebrate their collective domination, justifying it.'[266] Peter's associates were even more sharply separated from the rest of the population than their counterparts in other European countries, not physically (parades were public affairs) but through their assumed 'foreignness'.

We have examined the various theatres in which the drama of Peter's cultural changes were enacted, notably St Petersburg, with its backdrop of Classical buildings and watery vistas. The star actor, the emperor himself, was a versatile player, an actor-manager, who could take on supporting and even walk-on roles, as well as doing the star turn. Let us turn finally to the supporting company who donned the costumes devised for them by their director and learned their parts as best they could.

VII. DRESS AND HAIR CODES

A German tunic worn by a German means nothing, but a German tunic worn by a Russian turns into a symbol of his adherence to European culture.[267]

Those dramatic and visible signs of cultural reform—changes in dress and hair-style forced upon urban dwellers—were not unheralded. Peter's father's ban on Western fashion issued in 1675, aimed primarily at distinguishing Russians from foreigners, in order to prevent the latter from entering churches undetected, showed that some Russians were flouting the dress codes.[268] In 1680 Tsar Fedor issued a further decree, banning heavy, expensive court dress, at the same time outlawing specifically foreign styles.[269] The need to repeat the ban on foreign fashion indicates that Alexis's decree had been ineffective, and so, apparently, was Fedor's. A Polish observer in Moscow in 1682 writes in error that Fedor was persuaded by his wife, a woman of Polish extraction, to *allow* 'the cutting of hair, shaving of beards and wearing of Polish tunics', no doubt because he saw examples of such fashions at court despite the tsar's disapproval.[270] Even so, this was a minority trend. Until well into the 1690s court dress for public display remained traditional: a costume made for Peter in 1682 comprised an over-caftan with wide sleeves, in gold satin on a crimson background, with patterns and plant motifs in gold and silver, lace of spun gold, lined with crimson taffeta.[271] Tsar Ivan wore such costumes until his death in 1696. Peter's own private sartorial habits were influenced early on by his friends in the Foreign Quarter, whose numerous tailors probably supplied the court in the period 1672–5 with costumes for court plays.[272] From 1690 or so court account books are full of orders for 'German' dress, an outfit including buttons, silk, and wig, obtained from

General Lefort; boots, swords, and belts from Thomas Knipper; a silk-lined tunic with gold buttons, trimmed with lace at the neck and cuffs, a hat with a feather and shoes with silver buckles.[273] But Russian dress was still *de rigueur* for ceremonial occasions, even for members of the Grand Embassy, who wore high fur hats and brocade robes at receptions in Europe.[274]

The Grand Embassy was crucial for crystallizing further Peter's image of Europeans, hitherto confined to his observations of foreigners out of context in Russia. It was no accident, either, that Peter's notorious orders regarding beards and Western dress were issued soon after his premature recall to Russia in 1698 to do battle with some of the more conservative elements in society. Vasily Surikov's famous painting *The Morning of the Strel'tsy Execution* (1881) made the point graphically, contrasting the traditional clothing of the bearded strel'tsy and their families with the Western uniforms of the clean-shaven guardsmen and the tsar himself in the plain tunic of a Preobrazhensky guard. Peter made his initial onslaught on beards on 26 August 1698, the day after his return from abroad. Johannes Korb, on the spot in Moscow, recorded the details:

> The report of the Czar's arrival had spread through the city. The Boyars and principal Muscovites flocked in numbers at an early hour to the place where it had become known he had spent the night, to pay their court.... Those who, according to the fashion of that country, would cast themselves upon the ground to worship majesty, he lifted up graciously from their grovelling posture, and embraced with a kiss, such as is only due among private friends. If the razor, that plied promiscuously among the beards of those present, can be forgiven the injury it did, the Muscovites may truly reckon that day among the happiest of their lives.[275]

In Korb's account the razor appears out of the blue, with no direct reference to Peter actually wielding it, but the imperial envoy Ignatius von Guarient reported that the tsar 'clipped the long beards with his own hand'.[276] The first to be shorn was Aleksei Semenovich Shein; next came Fedor Romodanovsky; then 'all the rest had to conform to the guise of foreign nations, and the razor eliminated the ancient fashion'.[277] Apart from the patriarch (exempted by 'superstitious awe for his office'), only Prince Mikhail Alegukovich Cherkassky[278] and Tikhon Streshnev were let off, the former on account of his extreme old age, the latter because of his close ties with the royal family.

The campaign continued on 1 September, when the court jester went around the guests at a banquet held at Shein's house shaving those who still had beards. 'It was of evil omen to make show of reluctance as the razor approached the chin, and was to be forthwith punished with a boxing on the ears. In this way, between mirth and the wine cup, many were admonished by this insane ridicule to abandon the olden guise.'[279] On this occasion forced shaving was combined with another offence to tradition: failure to observe the traditional old New Year ceremonies in which tsar and patriarch presided jointly. Instead, 'common sailors' were allowed to mix with guests, and toasts were accompanied by gun salvos. The attack on beards was thus part of a wider package of cultural reform.

Peter may have thought about taxing beards at this time,[280] but a decree was not issued until 16 January 1705, when men of all ranks, including merchants and artisans, were ordered to shave, but anyone who wished to keep beard and whiskers was given the option to pay a fine, 60 roubles for nobles, military officers, and chancellery officials, 100 roubles from merchants of the first guild, 60 roubles from middle guild merchants and artisans, 30 roubles for members of the third guild, boyars' bondslaves, postal drivers, coachmen, junior deacons (but not priests and deacons), and 'Moscow residents of all ranks'. Bearded residents of other towns (except in Siberia and around the White Sea) had to come to Moscow to get a permit in the form of a disc (*znak*) from the Police Office (*prikaz zemskikh del*) and to display their discs at all times. Peasants had to pay a copeck (two denga) every time they entered the city gates.[281]

According to Cornelius de Bruyn, who first visited Moscow in 1702 (the first edition of his illustrated account of his travels came out in 1711), the tsar's orders were executed by men who went around the street shaving 'all manner of persons without distinction', many of whom 'would not be comforted for the loss of their beards'.[282] According to John Perry, the tsar 'to reform this foolish Custom [of growing long beards], and to make them look like other Europeans, ordered a Tax to be laid, on all Gentlemen, Merchants and others of his Subjects (excepting the Priests and common Peasants, or Slaves)'.[283] He attributed opposition to the fact that 'the holy Men of old had worn their Beards according to the Model of the Picture of their Saints', and recounts the tale of an old Russian carpenter at Voronezh who hid his shaved-off beard under his shirt with the intention of taking it with him to the grave.[284] Charles Whitworth spoke of the reluctance with which the nation 'submitted to the Razor ... their fore fathers lived unshaven, their priests saints and martyrs were venerable for their beards, then they were bid to imitate, and the ignorant thought part of the devotion lay in the beard, as Samson's strength did in his hair, nay even the Ladies themselves joyned in the faction, and could at first be scarce brought to suffer the Reformation in their husbands'.[285]

Dress reform quickly followed. Korb records that in February 1699 Peter cut off the long sleeves of some of his officers' garments, and that some returning envoys were required to wear 'German dress', a point confirmed at the end of the account of Boris Sheremetev's visit to Europe, which records that the boyar arrived at Lefort's mansion 'clad in German dress on his majesty's orders'.[286] Printed instructions on approved fashions were issued on 4 January 1700, immediately after another cultural innovation, the celebration of the New Year on 1 January.[287] This first decree was addressed to Moscow nobles and to 'all ranks of service and chancellery and tradespeople, and boyars' bondslaves, in Moscow and in the provinces'. It dealt specifically only with male attire: 'Hungarian' coats down to the garter (just below the knee) were to be worn over a shorter undercoat, or 'vest'. Those who could were asked to appear in such garments by Epiphany (two days away), the rest by Shrovetide.[288] Evidently too few took heed. On 20 August new deadlines were set: 1 December 1700 for men and 1 January 1701 for women to acquire new wardrobes.[289] Dummies wearing examples of 'French and Hungarian' dress were displayed at the city gates.[290] These measures were followed up by a decree of 1701: classes of person not mentioned in the January 1700 edict were now specified: chief merchants, dragoons, infantrymen, strel'tsy, and even peasants living and working in Moscow. All with the exception only of the clergy and 'ploughing peasantry' were to wear 'German' dress, French and Saxon topcoats, and German vests, breeches, boots, shoes, and hats, and to ride on German saddles. Women of all classes, even the wives of the clergy and of dragoons, infantrymen and strel'tsy, and their children, were to wear dresses, hats, and coats (*kuntyshi*), German jackets, petticoats, and shoes. Henceforth no one was to wear Russian and Cherkassian (Ukrainian) caftans, sheepskin coats, long caftans (*aziamy*), trousers, boots, shoes, and hats or ride on Russian saddles. Craftsmen were forbidden to make them or sell them. Fines were imposed on anyone wearing the old fashions: forty copecks for people on foot, two roubles for those on horseback.[291]

Foreign visitors to Russia commented on these visible signs of change. Filippo Balatri noted that it was not difficult for hard-up Russians to transform their capacious, Muscovite robes into 'French' garments, 'just as it is easy to make a handkerchief from a sheet'.[292] Cornelius de Bruyn commented: 'Time has wrought great changes in this Empire, and especially since the Czar's return from his travels. He immediately altered the fashion of dress, as well with regard to the men as to the women, and particularly with regard to those who have dependence on the Court, or enjoyed any office there, not excepting one soul, not even children; and the Russian merchants and others dress so as not to be distinguished from the people of our country.' Bruyn included engravings of traditional female costume in his book, 'as this great alteration may in time blot out the remembrance of the ancient dress'.[293]

Peter's own clean-shaven visage and 'German' attire and his imposition of these fashions were seen as evidence of his ungodliness. The complaint by an artisan in 1704 that Peter was destroying the Christian faith by forcing people to shave off their beards, wear German dress, and smoke tobacco provides a characteristic list of offences.[294] There were various strands to the Orthodox tradition on beards. One was that a natural growth of beard hair conformed with the image of God, although the notion that the Christian God was bearded may be fairly late. Early Christians, still influenced by Roman ideals of youth and beauty, often depicted Christ as a beardless youth. There are no references to beards in the New Testament, and Old Testament rulings are ambiguous. But by the time of the Stoglav council in 1551, it was clearly stated that 'the sacred rules to all Orthodox Christians warn them not to shave their beards or moustaches or to cut their hair. Such is not an Orthodox practice but a Latin and heretical bequest of the Greek Emperor Constantine V.'[295]

The key was clearly the difference between Orthodox clergy and monks and Catholics: in 1073 Pope Gregory actually forbade priests to wear beards. Patriarch Adrian warned: 'Latin Jesuits, Dominicans, Bernardines and others not only shave their beards but also their moustaches and look like apes or monkeys.'[296]

The importance of the Orthodox beard was reflected in the great attention paid to variants in icon pattern books, differences in the beard being one of the main distinguishing features of saints, from a few beardless ones (denoting their extreme youth) to ascetics and 'holy fools' with beards down to their ankles, a sign of great piety. The beard marked out men from women, underlining the superiority of the former to the latter: 'He made man and woman, providing a visible difference between them. ... The man, as the leader, he allowed to grow a beard as an adornment, but he did not give this adornment to the woman, as an imperfect and subordinate being, so that seeing her husband's beauty and being herself deprived of that beauty and perfection she will be humble and always submissive.' It followed, therefore, that by shaving a man made himself effeminate, or worse, came to resemble 'dumb beasts or dogs' which, as the treatise pointed out, could grow whiskers but not beards.[297] One treatise warned: 'Look often at the icon of the Second Coming of Christ, and observe the righteous standing at the right side of Christ, all with beards. At the left stand the Muselmen and heretics, Lutherans and Poles and other shavers of their ilk, with just whiskers, such as cats and dogs have. Take heed whom to imitate and which side you will be on.'[298] In iconographic traditions demons were depicted beardless; hence Peter 'dressed people like demons'.[299]

It is hardly surprising in view of threats of eternal damnation for those who shaved that the decree on beards met with fierce resistance. The authorities tried punishment and persuasion, enlisting the aid of churchmen such as Dmitry of Rostov, whose *Treatise on the Image of God and his Likeness in Man*, published in three editions in 1707, 1714, and 1717, disputed the necessity of beards for laymen.[300] The task was made all the more difficult by the fact that in the popular mind beards were associated not only with Orthodoxy but also with nationality, which at this date was inextricably linked with religious identity.[301] Peter was killing two birds with one stone, by removing personal appearance, along with many other matters, from the Church's traditional sphere of influence and undermining national pride in an area which was at odds with his Western-oriented reforms. As one of Nartov's stories asserts, Peter believed that God was willing to admit anyone to heaven as long as they were honest, regardless of whether they were shaved or bearded, wearing wigs or long-haired, in long or short coats.[302] At the same time, Peter could not tolerate opposition.

The new dress and hair codes caught on quickly at court, where it was difficult to evade the tsar's eagle eye, as well as in Moscow as a whole, where inspectors went around collecting fines and chopping off the bottom of robes which exceeded the mandated length. A decree of 28 February 1702 laid down formal dress rules for feast-days and ceremonies such as receptions for ambassadors, when all courtiers and servitors were to appear in French tunics with cloth-of-gold vests (*kamzoly*). Lesser ranks were allowed vests of coloured cloth.[303] Gone were the tall-hatted bearded boyars in flowing robes who featured in many a sketch by seventeenth-century foreign visitors. When the court transferred to St Petersburg, the new style was already well established. The only beards allowed at court were false ones. An order issued for masquerade costume includes instructions 'to take the false beard (*mashkaratnuiu borodu*) of Neliubokhtin of the guards and have it sent here'.[304] To Vockerodt, secretary to the Prussian Embassy towards the end of Peter's reign, it appeared that the reform of dress had cost Peter little effort, 'except for the disadvantage that the German frock coat, especially in such a cold climate, does not cover so well but requires just as much cloth'.[305]

But away from the court and government offices many retained or reverted to the old style. In December 1704 it proved necessary to reissue the dress decree of 1701.[306] In 1705–6 inhabitants of Siberia petitioned Moscow to be allowed to keep their former clothes and saddles because they could not afford new ones, and the government had little choice but to withdraw its order.[307] In 1707 Peter ordered that the handiwork of tailors and hatters be checked and stamped, 'as many are making clothes and hats which are not of the [approved] German model'. Items without the stamp of approval were to be returned to the makers and remade to the approved pattern.[308] In the town of Belev an official attempted to close shops selling Russian dress, but they were open again the next day. He reported that the governor and officials were all bearded and dressed in Russian fashion.[309] In January 1713 Aleksei Kurbatov, vice-governor of Archangel, wrote complaining about problems in his province, including the fact that almost all people of all ranks were wearing old-style dress and not shaving, and, 'as I hear, previous governors have not used compulsion ... and so the laws which are passed are not kept; and people who come to the markets from other provinces nearly all wear Russian dress and beards, even young people. Truly, lord, such boorishness must be stopped and these heathen customs of dress rooted out.' Peter advised Kurbatov to 'try to correct this problem by degrees'.[310] Even in Moscow, Weber noted in 1716, 'they wear the German Dress; but it is easy to observe on many, that they have not been long used to it'.[311] Further evidence that Muscovites were flouting the rules is contained in an anonymous letter received in the Preobrazhensky *prikaz* in 1708 pointing out that when the tsar was in Moscow everyone went around in German dress, but in his absence the boyars' wives put on Russian dress and wore old-fashioned gowns to church, even though they put skirts over them. 'On their heads they don't wear Polish hats but some sort of *kamilavki* [priests' headgear] and they all curse your decree ... and if they see anyone wearing [foreign] hats and headdresses they mock them, laugh at them and call them bad women for obeying your orders.' The wives of such leading figures as Peter Dolgoruky, Ivan Musin-Pushkin, Ivan Buturlin, and Tikhon Streshnev were named.[312]

Periodic repetitions and amendments to the rule on beards indicate that it, too, was flouted. Fines remained unpaid. Figures show that in 1720 beard and clothing fines brought in meagre revenues.[313] In June 1723 an order specified that bearded men (*borodachi*) who would not or could not pay the fine were to be arrested, shaved by force, and released on bail. However, peasants coming to town with useful commodities, such as grain or firewood, were not to be charged.[314] An alternative punishment for those who refused to shave or pay was banishment to the port of Rogervik near Reval to work off their fines. If they agreed to shave and gave written confirmation, they would be released without a fine. Siberian offenders were to be sent to work in the nearest factories or mines.[315] In the case of Old Believers and any others who retained their beards, legislation *required* them to dress in the old style only. In addition, Old Believers had to wear an identifying stripe of red cloth. A decree of 6 April 1722 warned that bearded men and Old Believers who came to government offices to make an application *not* dressed in traditional garments would be charged an additional fine, even if they had already paid the annual beard tax. Anyone witnessing such breaches of the dress code and reporting them to the authorities would receive half the fine and the man's clothes(!) as a reward. The law applied 'to all ranks of laymen without exception, except peasants truly agricultural, but not to industrialists'.[316] On 10 November 1724 Peter wrote in a list of instructions to the Senate: 'Take good care to issue stricter orders that all those with beards should also wear old-style garments; apprehend those without; don't give a hearing or accept appeals but place them under guard.' The wives of Old Believers had to wear old-fashioned (*starinnye*) gowns and hats.[317]

Resistance did not abate after Peter's death. Decrees on dress were issued by the empresses Catherine in 1726 and Elizabeth in 1743.[318] An order issued in July 1726 stated that it had come to the attention of the authorities that officers and non-commissioned officers on leave or retirement 'are going around with beards and in old-fashioned Russian dress'. The order on German dress, swords, and shaving was reiterated, with the concession that in the absence of a barber the beard could be trimmed with scissors. Infringements met with fines, beatings for non-commissioned officers, money fines and deprivation of their patents of nobility for a fourth offence for officers.[319] Even some leading nobles hung on to their old clothes. An inventory of the belongings of Princes A. G and I. A. Dolgoruky made as a result of their banishment in 1730 contained large quantities of 'pre-reform' clothing, both male and female, easily recognized by the different vocabulary used to describe it.[320]

At court, however, Western norms were firmly established. Peter's daughter Elizabeth was later famed for the thousands of dresses in her wardrobes. Courtiers were required to maintain lavish wardrobes to keep up with an endless round of balls and masquerades, to which an estimated half of Elizabeth's time was devoted in the first decade of her reign. Decrees specified details of hair-style and accessories.[321] In the reign of Catherine the Great, however, Old Russian dress in stylized form began to make a come-back for ladies at court for special occasions (partly because the stout empress preferred loose gowns), and remained popular to the end of the empire. In 1826, an observer at Nicholas I's coronation ball commented approvingly on women in Russian dress, which he described as patriotic attire (*otechestvennyi nariad*), recalling a time 'when Russians were not ashamed of their splendid dress, proper for the climate, which had a national character and was incomparably more beautiful than foreign dress'.[322] Russian style still remained a sort of fancy dress reserved for grand special occasions. From the early 1700s Western fashion remained the accepted norm for the Russian upper classes for both everyday and evening wear.[323]

Peter probably never intended Western fashion to extend to the whole population—the clergy (although not their wives) and village peasantry were excluded—only that dress and beard style should be consistent and clearly reflect a person's status and function in society, as in sumptuary laws and dress codes in other countries, an idea that is clearly stated in the final point of the Table of Ranks.[324] At least one supporter of Peter's felt that the tsar had not gone far enough, however. Ivan Pososhkov wrote: 'At present there is no way of telling from his dress to what station a person belongs, whether he is a townsman, an official, a gentleman or a bondman. ... It would surely be a good thing if one could tell the station of one civilian from another by his dress. ... There are many people nowadays who have two or three thousand roubles yet go about in a grey cloth coat, and conversely some with less than a hundred roubles who dress as if they had a thousand.' Merchants should be allowed brocade, but not gold and silver braid and piping or silk breeches. Monks must on no account wear silk garments.[325] These demands were to some extent met by Peter's immediate successors—for example, in specification of the quality and cost of fabrics with reference to rank, by Anna Ioannovna in 1740 (only ranks 1–3 could wear satins with gold and silver thread) and Elizabeth in 1742 (limiting the use of certain foreign fabrics and lace to ranks 1–5).[326]

Russian ladies and gentlemen of fashion adhered as far as possible to Western style, but even foreign commentators were far from unanimous about the approved model for the new fashions. Decrees mention Hungarian and French styles.[327] John Perry wrote that Peter ordered his courtiers 'to equip themselves with handsome Cloaths made after the English Fashion ... and that a Pattern of Cloaths of the English Fashion should be hung up at all the Gates of the City of Mosco';[328] while according to Bruyn, people were ordered to wear coats of Polish cut.[329] Such indecision simply underlines the blurring of national identities in fashion as in other spheres. The male dress of collarless topcoat, long under-vest or waistcoat, and breeches reaching just below the knee had originated in Restoration England, been adopted by the French ('who pretended it was their idea') and spread over most of Europe.[330] The general outline of what Peter (who got his sartorial ideas generally from northern Europe) required was clear, the precise origin unimportant. Male clothing, including many samples from Peter's own wardrobe, has survived in greater quantities than female dress, notably the 300 items in the 'Wardrobe of Peter I' collection, as well as descriptions in inventories—for example, of Menshikov's wardrobe, compiled in 1726. (The latter includes four sets of masquerade costume, including cloaks with a big hat and masks and a Polish costume.[331]) One of the most influential changes in male dress was the introduction of military and naval uniforms, court dress being seen infrequently until the ending of the war with Sweden. Most of Peter's portraits show him in uniform.

The changes were perhaps even greater for women. Cornelius de Bruyn considered that 'alterations in dress ... have not been so very extraordinary among the women, excepting among the higher sort, who dress just as the women do with us'.[332] Royal women were expected to be leaders of fashion from childhood. Bruyn records that in his portraits of Princesses Ekaterina, Anna, and Paraskeva, aged twelve, ten, and eight respectively, he portrayed their costume 'after the German mode, in which they commonly appear in public'.[333] An exception was made for their mother, dowager Tsaritsa Praskovia. According to Bassewitz, Praskovia was the only woman (at court) who was allowed to keep traditional Russian dress.[334] Surviving portraits of Praskovia confirm that she indeed maintained the old style, but no doubt was let off only because the tsar 'respected her immensely'. Bergholz, as we have seen, pronounced the gowns of Peter's daughters Princess Anna and Elizabeth on the 1721 coronation anniversary to be in the latest French fashion, and their elaborate bejewelled coiffures 'of an elegance which would have done credit to the best Paris hairdresser',[335] but noted signs of inexperience. On occasion he criticized standards, agreeing with Duchess Anna Ioannovna that 'Russian women are too lazy and cannot be bothered to dress their hair properly'.[336] A few years later the duc de Liria commented on the lavishness of court dress—'The local magnates dress up in a different outfit on every feast-day'[337]—but clearly such spending was confined to narrow court circles. A new industry and profession appeared in Russia: the *parikhmakher*, or 'wig-maker' (still the modern Russian term for hairdresser). An *ukaz* of 1711 offered up to three roubles for suitable long female hair, especially grey hair. But in January 1712 a local official from Iaroslavl' district wrote to Menshikov to report that there had been no takers.[338] Wigs were expensive: 15 roubles for a woman's, 3–5 for men's everyday wigs, 9 roubles if made from natural hair.[339]

VIII. MANNERS AND BEHAVIOUR

In his magisterial *History of Russia* S. M. Solov'ev frequently employs the term 'young society' to characterize Russia in the early modern period. This term is interchangeable with 'primitive society', as evidenced by the numerous examples of violent, uncivilized, and 'childish' behaviour which he quotes in order to underline the scale of the task which Peter I faced. The essence of 'young society' was domination of the weak by the strong (the 'law of the jungle') and the feeble development of social restraints upon selfish behaviour. Peter may have succeeded in dressing his nobles up as Europeans and forcing men and women into each other's company. The next step was to inculcate Western manners, the minimum requirements for which were to abandon rustic or boorish behaviour (in the seventeenth century there was little to distinguish the manners of the upper and lower classes) or, in the case of women, undue bashfulness, then to acquire accomplishments such as foreign languages and dancing. Further refinements might include collecting Western books, and even reading them. The highly educated Russian was able to pepper his speech with Classical references.

The transformation of a select few was aided by trips abroad, of others by observing foreign behaviour at home or from etiquette books such as *The Honourable Mirror of Youth*, first published (twice) in 1717, with further editions not only in Peter's reign (1719 and 1723) but also in 1740, 1745, and 1767.[340] What is not often noted about this publication, however, is that in most editions the sections on etiquette are preceded by a primer (*azbuka*) of moral admonitions ('Love God and the Tsar, and oppose neither one of them'; 'Honour priests, respect your elders'; 'Don't be quick with your tongue and lazy and feeble in your actions'; 'Wide is the path leading to ruin and many are they that enter on it'), along with handy charts of the new civic type-faces and arabic and roman numerals. The etiquette manual was 'collected from various authors', unspecified in the text,[341] but including Erasmus, whose *De civilitate morum puerilium* (1530), widely circulated all over Europe, provided the sections on how to behave at table and make polite conversation.[342] The source of the title may be found in such publications as *Miroir de la jeunesse pour former à bonnes moeurs et civilité de vie* and *Spiegel für der Bildung*.[343] Some of the topics chosen reflect traditional values in the West as well as the East: the book opens with admonitions to honour and respect your parents. 'Young men should always speak foreign languages amongst themselves, in order to become proficient, especially when they have something secret to tell, so that the servants don't find out.'[344] The second half of the manual was devoted to advice to young ladies, but Russian women seeking guidance on new modes of Western behaviour consulted the *Mirror* in vain.[345] To get the *Mirror's* likely influence into perspective, the first edition had a print run of only 100 copies, subsequent editions 600, 1,200, and 578 respectively. Even so, it was a comparative best-seller, selling over 300 copies in the first two years, over 1,500 of the first three editions.[346]

The *Mirror*, published in the new civic script,[347] was supplemented by publications by the Church, which had traditionally guided the education of youth. The good Christian's duty to his sovereign and country was emphasized. In his own preface to a pamphlet on the Beatitudes, Peter disapproved of those who sought salvation by attending large numbers of services and making many genuflections, or who insisted that the only means of salvation was tonsure, thereby neglecting their earthly duties. The message was clear:

good works in the secular life were to be preferred.[348] The preface of *A Youth's First Lesson*, a primer in the old Cyrillic script edited by Prokopovich and first published in 1720,[349] was wholly in the new Petrine spirit, written not in 'high Slavonic dialect' but in simple language.[350] Peter (father of the fatherland) had given thought to 'how to establish in Russia an effective and essential rule of education for youth and had been inspired by God to order this booklet with a clear explanation of the law of God'. There were commentaries on the Ten Commandments, the Lord's Prayer, the Creed, and the Beatitudes. Traditional psalms and prayers were omitted. The primer was infused with exhortations to obey the supreme authorities, to 'bless the government' and grant health to the emperor.[351] The underlying message was that the tsar's subjects, especially young ones, were sinful and ignorant and in need of firm guidance: 'Childhood is as it were the root whence both good and evil grow throughout the whole of life. The reason for which is this: because of the sin of our first parents, we are inclined from birth to evil. . . . Thus what good can be expected where there is no good instruction for children?'[352] As many as 16,000 copies of the primer were printed during Peter's lifetime. It saw its last edition in 1859.[353] Copies were sent out as basic textbooks for all episcopal schools in 1722, and in 1723 a Synod *ukaz* ordered readings from the primer to replace readings from Ephrem of Syria in churches at Lent, 'in order for the people to prepare themselves for genuine repentance'.[354]

The extent to which Peter succeeded in creating 'new men' is best assessed by looking at a few cases. Some Russians immediately took to a Western life-style, like Prince Peter Alekseevich Golitsyn (1660–1722), who received a thorough grounding in the ways of the West, having been sent to study in Venice in 1697 and to Vienna in 1701. The Italian singer Balatri, whom he brought back from his first trip, found Golitsyn quite civilized for a Russian. His Moscow home, built by an Italian architect, was fitted with European furniture and Persian and Chinese carpets.[355] On the other hand, Gavrila Golovkin, whom an authoritative survey of Petrine art describes as 'an extremely impressive embodiment of the new type of personality which was formed during the Petrine era',[356] looks thoroughly at home in his Western clothes in Ivan Nikitin's formal portrait. But Bergholz's account of a visit to the chancellor's home in 1721 raises doubts. In one room Bergholz saw a fine white wig displayed on a stand, but 'our host, because of his immeasurable meanness [worse than Molière's *Avare*] never wears it. It must have been a gift, since he would never have agreed to acquire such an item, still less to wear it. . . . He is always very badly dressed, in an old-fashioned brown caftan.'[357] The duc de Liria writes of Golovkin: 'He loved his fatherland and although he was attached to the old ways, he did not reject new customs if he saw that they were useful.'[358] Apparently Golovkin wished to end his days as a monk, but was refused permission.[359] It was said of Fedor Romodanovsky that 'although he loved the old ways, all the same he always carried out all his monarch's commands with zeal and honour'.[360] Korb reported that Romodanovsky's reaction to the information that Fedor Golovin had worn

1. Detail from bronze bust of Peter I by C.B. Rastrelli,
1723, depicting Peter as Pygmalion carving the image of
New Russia as Galatea.

2. (*right*) Tsar Alexis. Portrait in oils by unknown artist, 1670s.

3. Tsaritsa Natalia. Portrait in oils by unknown artist, 1680s.

4. (*left*) Peter I by Sir Godfrey Kneller, 1698.

5. Peter I at Poltava by J.G. Dannhauer, 1710s.

6. (*right*) Officer, bombardier and rifleman of artillery regiment in the 1710s, from a nineteenth-century lithograph.

7. Tsarevna Natalia Alekseevna in an allegorical memorial portrait by unknown artist, 1717.

8. Summer Palace designed by Domenico Trezzini, 1710-14.
(Photo: William Brumfield)

9. Summer Gardens from an engraving by Aleksei Zubov, 1716.

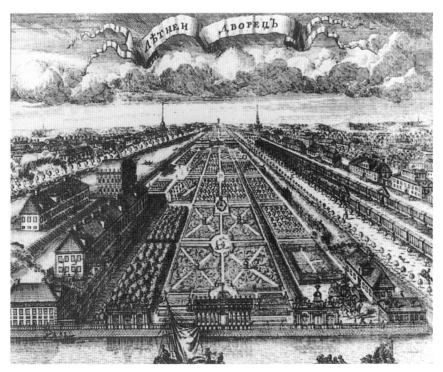

10. Peterhof Palace, designed by J.F. Braunstein, J.B. LeBlond *et al.*, 1714-52.
(Photo: William Brumfield)

11. Kunstkamera, designed by G.J. Mattarnovy, 1718-34. (Photo: William Brumfield)

12. (*above*) Menshikov's Palace, designed by Gottfried Schädel *et al.*, 1710s-1720s. (Photo: William Brumfield)

13. Cathedral of SS Peter and Paul by Domenico Trezzini, 1712-32. (Photo: William Brumfield)

14. Church of the Transfiguration at Kizhi, 1714.
(Photo: William Brumfield)

15 a and b. Portraits of Peter I attributed to Ivan Nikitin (*above*) and Louis Caravaque (*below*), 1720s.

16. Detail from portrait of Peter's daughters Anna and
Elizabeth by Louis Caravaque, 1717.

17. (*left*) Tsarevich Alexis by J.G. Dannhauer, before 1718.

18. Portrait of the 'giant' Nicholas Bourgeois by Georg Gsell, 1720s.

19. Details from views of St Petersburg by Aleksei Zubov: (*above*) Peter and Catherine sailing on the Neva, from *Panorama*, 1716, and (*left*) the Neva embankment, 1727.

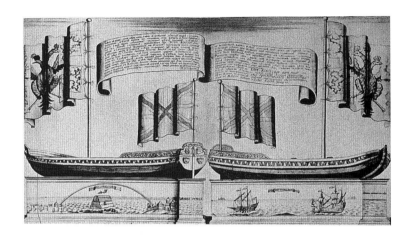

20. (*above*) Split perspective view of
Peter's sailing boat from an engraving
by Ivan Zubov, 1722.

21. Frontispiece by P. Picart to
Uchenie i praktika artillerii, 1711.

22. Engraved portrait of Catherine I with black slave by
Aleksei Zubov and I. Odol'sky, 1726.

23. (*above*) Tsarevna Natalia
Petrovna by Louis Caravaque,
before 1725?

24. Engraving of Alexander
Menshikov by unknown artist,
c. 1720.

25 a and b. Plaster head of Peter I by C.B. Rastrelli (E.V. Anisimar).

26. Deathbed portrait of Peter I by Ivan Nikitin, 1725.

foreign dress in Vienna in 1698 was disbelief that Golovin would have been 'such a brainless ass as to despise the garb of his fatherland'.[361]

Given that Golovkin was born in 1660 and Romodanovsky in 1640, some reservations are to be expected. Yet well into Peter's reign Russians who spent time abroad found themselves subject to ridicule and suspicion at home. Ivan Nepliuev records his and his companions' return in 1720 from three years' training in the West; their absence made them 'detested (*voznenavideny*) not only by our peers but also by our relatives who at the first opportunity mocked us with laughter and oaths for the European manners which we had acquired'.[362] Some foreigners claimed that it was virtually impossible to reform the Russians, since most 'have not only thrown off again that Politeness they had acquired in foreign Parts, and shew an intolerable Pride on account of what they may have learned there of bodily Exercises (for to cultivate the Mind was not their Design); but also are returned again to their former Way of Life'.[363] Once in retirement and out of the public eye, preferably on a Moscow estate, nobles reverted to comfortable old life-styles. 'In all matters such as food, drink and decoration of rooms,' a Prussian ambassador commented, 'the Russian is even now an old-fashioned Muscovite.'[364] Descriptions of Moscow estates suggest a cosy old-fashioned style with few Western trimmings: for example, the Lopukhin estate at Iasenevo (described in 1718 when it was confiscated) had a two-storeyed wooden mansion roofed in turf, with mica windows, benches, and wooden tables, icons, and about thirty foreign prints. There was a single-domed wooden church, bath-house, cook-house, orchards, and ponds.[365]

Princess Anastasia Petrovna Golitsyna, née Prozorovskaia, as painted by the artist Andrei Matveev in 1728, offers a female variation on the theme.[366] She is dressed in a gown with a very low neckline, not concealed by the velvet cloak which the artist has draped around her. Her head and neck are bare. A miniature portrait of Peter the Great dangles below her left breast. The downward droop of the mouth may reflect Golitsyna's age—sixty-three years old when the portrait was painted, a year before her death—but also hints at trials and disappointments. She was already a mature woman when Peter's reforms were launched, born into an old boyar family and married into another. In 1718 she was implicated in the Tsarevich Alexis affair and sentenced to be flogged, events which linked her with the traditionalist camp. A few years later she was restored to favour. Like all women of her class and generation, she was required to don unfamiliar, perhaps unnervingly revealing clothes, and appear in public in the company of foreigners. Golitsyna suffered even worse indignities: she was appointed 'jester' to Catherine, and from 1717 served as mock abbess of the female section of the All-Drunken Assembly. All this was a sharp break with the life of the *terem*.

Early Petrine travel literature provides some good examples of the feelings of Russians forced to confront another world. The account of B. P. Sheremetev's Western journey starts with the words 'In the year of the creation of the world 7205' and prayers to the Almighty, the Mother of God, and all the saints for protection, 'for although we are not worthy, do not abandon us on this our most difficult journey but prepare for us a peaceful and serene road and success in all things, like Moses going down into Egypt'.[367] The route took them through Cracow and Vienna, where the party was exposed to court culture in the form of two ladies instructed by the empress to converse with them in Czech, music, and gifts of expensive paintings, food, drink, and sweets.[368] Most of the entries are either laconic (notes on where they stayed and whom they met) or long transcripts of speeches delivered at various audiences. The writer's interest was captured most of all by religious paraphernalia: for example, in Loretta he describes the house of the Virgin Mary brought by angels from Nazareth, which contained the plates from which Jesus ate and the stove on which Mary cooked.[369] Once in Rome the list of relics becomes voluminous—the spear from the crucifixion, Veronica's veil, the garments of the slaughtered Innocents, the icon of Mary painted by St Luke, or, more ambitious, the staircase on which Christ was taken from Caiaphas to Pilate, still spattered with traces of his blood. In Naples the group witnessed the liquefaction to boiling point of the blood of St Januarius. Even more detailed attention is paid to the tomb of St Nicholas at Bari—not surprising, given the veneration he enjoyed in Russia.[370] (Such lack of scepticism was not, of course, exclusive to Russian pilgrims.) The writer was impressed by the hospitals (the 'soft beds' and 'great pharmacies' in Rome, 'an abundance of every supply, building, painting, bedding and everything for the needs of the patients' in Malta), terrified by the sight of Vesuvius with its 'great column of smoke' and noise 'which strikes great fear into a man'.[371] He was almost ready to believe that another volcano, Stromboli, was the abode of the devil who sent demons to lure sailors to their deaths.[372] Peter Tolstoy's travel diary shows very similar attitudes.[373]

Much Soviet writing on the Petrine era was based on the formula 'religious = bad and backward' and 'secular = good and progressive'. Because the Petrine era as a whole was deemed progressive, therefore it had to be demonstrated that it was more secular than what preceded it.[374] But did individuals really have to make a stark choice between secular and sacred, between the traditional and the new culture, 'a sort of religious decision, binding a man for his whole life'?[375] For the mass of the population, from the lowest to the highest, the culture of seventeenth-century Russia, in the widest sense of the word, had been primarily religious and traditional, little influenced by fashion. From the middle of the century elements of Western art and manners filtered in to affect a few people in court circles. By the 1680s a hybrid 'baroque' style could be identified in architecture and painting. From the late 1690s these random, spontaneous phenomena became the focus of government policy, with decrees on dress and hair-style. The new architecture, painting and engraving, music and theatre, and some areas of publishing relied overwhelmingly on foreign models and usually foreign exponents. Yet there was ample room for religious culture, which maintained a firm grip upon everyday life and behaviour at all levels throughout Peter's reign and beyond, and not just among the peasants. Several foreign witnesses recorded the deeply engrained habit of bowing to the icons when entering a room. The painter Cornelius de Bruyn wrote: 'This is a custom they observe even when they go to see foreigners, addressing themselves to the first picture they see, for fear they should not pay the first honours to God, as they ought.'[376] Peter Henry Bruce recounts a significant incident: 'A Russian once came running to me with a message, looked round about the room for an image, and seeing none, asked me, Where is thy God? I answered, in heaven: upon which he immediately went away without delivering his message. I told the general this circumstance, and he directly ordered a saint's picture to be hung up in my room, to prevent giving any further offence of that kind.'[377]

The fact that contemporaries believed that Peter had demoted icons tells us much about perceptions of the radical nature of his reform.[378] In fact, decrees reiterated the ancient rules, based on the resolutions of the church council of 1551.[379] A dissident priest who chopped up icons with an axe was duly burnt alive 'as a Heretick and Violator of Images'.[380] Icons were found among the possessions of even the most 'worldly' Russians, including, of course, the tsar himself. In a letter to Fedor Apraksin, Boris Sheremetev invites him to visit him on his Moscow estate and to take the opportunity of praying to a miracle-working icon of the Virgin on the way. In 1712 Sheremetev, exhausted by his duties, begged leave to retire and take monastic vows, but was refused.[381] Accounts of the libraries of Petrine nobles indicate the tenacity of religious traditions. The Moscow house inventory of M. P. Gagarin, disgraced former governor of Siberia, listed just six books, of which five were devotional.[382] The best evidence is provided by Peter's own library, of which an estimated 28 per cent was religious in content.[383] Women in particular maintained their devotions. Inventories of the contents of the palace of Tsarevna Natalia Alekseevna compiled just after her death in 1716 make the point.

In general, Peter and his supporters had no problem combining the sacred with the profane. Peter Shafirov (a converted Jew) wrote to Admiral Apraksin in March 1716 asking why he had failed to remind Menshikov about a residence in Reval promised to Shafirov by the tsar. In a postscript he writes: 'I greet your excellency with the imminent feast of the resurrection of Christ and say: Christ has risen.'[384] Ivan Nepliuev records in his memoirs how in 1713, at the age of twenty and recently married, he 'went off to a monastery to fulfil a promise', where he spent more than a year. Nepliuev later served as an officer in the marines, but he records how a fellow student in Venice ran away to Mount Athos to become a monk.[385] It was natural for Menshikov to call in at the Trinity–St Sergius monastery to pray on his way from Moscow to St Petersburg in 1703 and at the same time to give the monks some plans of Schlüsselburg,[386] or to write to his wife in March 1709 on her name-day that 'after the divine liturgy was over we each drank a cup of vodka to your health', and that before posting the letter they were all going to drink again to her health in Hungarian wine, 'committing your health and that of our dearest son into God's most gracious protection'.[387] Menshikov is said to have consulted Abbot Dosifei, who had a reputation for second sight, when he fell out with the tsar. Dosifei predicted that God would release him from his troubles. Princess Menshikova later helped Dosifei to become bishop of Rostov.[388]

On Christmas Day 1716 Menshikov rose at 5 a.m. and heard morning prayers, later attended mass in Trinity Cathedral, then visited the mock 'bishop of St Petersburg' Ivan Buturlin and the house of the prince-pope, where bawdy carols were sung.[389] In similar fashion, on New Year's day 1719 Menshikov was up at 5 a.m. to hear the singing of vigils, thence to the palace, then to mass and in the evening to a firework display, at which 'various rockets and fireworks on the ground were let off'.[390] On 6 January, the feast of the Epiphany, he again rose at five to hear vigils, went to St Isaac's Cathedral, where the tsar was attending matins, after which mass was celebrated, then to the headquarters of the Preobrazhensky regiment, where prayers were held and the proceedings were rounded off with a gun salute.[391] When Menshikov was on military service in the Ukraine, religious observance was even more regular, hardly a day without a service.[392]

If even Prince Menshikov maintained a 'hybrid' life-style, it is hardly surprising that lesser officials sometimes failed to grasp the new ways completely. Mistakes of vocabulary give interesting insights. For example, a compiler of the court diary, probably a clerk for the fleet in St Petersburg, several years running states that during firework celebrations for Menshikov's name-day on 23 November 'on the streets they burned problems' (*problemy*) instead of 'emblems' (*emblemy*).[393] Yet there were examples of greater sophistication, especially among those who went abroad, proving that with enough exposure it was possible to make the leap to new ways of thinking. Kologrivov, for example, Peter's agent in Holland and Italy, in 1718 warned against hiring a relative of the famous architect Michetti to paint a picture of Poltava, as the artist had depicted the tsar on horseback trampling on Turks (in the approved manner for such subjects), whereas, as Kologrivov pointed out, the Battle of Poltava had nothing to do with the Turks, and it would be out of character for the tsar, who, rather than trampling on his enemies, saved many from death.[394] Prince G. F. Dolgoruky appealed to Peter: 'Your Majesty, be merciful to the people of your state, continue to labour unceasingly that they may be delivered from their old Asiatic customs and taught to behave like the Christian peoples of Europe.'[395] Things could change in a couple of generations. Thus F. A. Golovin had a traditional Muscovite education, but his son (born in 1695) attended the School of Mathematics, then went to Holland, served on an English ship, knew French and English, and his children attended courses at Leipzig University.[396]

A key issue is whether 'new men and women' exchanged one form of slavery (submission to custom) for another (submission to the State). In the conventional form of writing petitions in seventeenth-century Russia, even the highest magnates referred to themselves as the sovereign's 'slaves' (*kholopy*), wrote their names in their diminutive form, and prostrated themselves at the ruler's feet. Peter outlawed these practices, but without changing the fundamental relationship of ruler and nobles. As Perry expressed it, with characteristic contempt for his hosts: 'although there is no real Advantage to them in it, (for they are but Slaves still) yet the very Sound or Change of the Word has pleased them.'[397] There were no limitations on the sovereign's power. Nobles were more than ever vulnerable to death or disgrace at the sovereign's whim. They were the full-time servants of the State, appointed at random while still in their teens to a branch of the service. Small wonder, then, that none but a privileged handful dared to approach the ruler, even 'carpenter' Peter, with less than awe. The following letter was written not to Peter but to his daughter Elizabeth in 1724 by Artemy Petrovich Volynsky, governor of Kazan', who was related to the royal family by marriage to Aleksandra Naryshkina, Peter's cousin: 'My lady, I do not wish to trouble your highness any further, I only humbly beg you graciously to keep me your lowest slave in your maternal grace amongst your sincere, pure-hearted and loyal servants, as I am and shall remain with my due servantly humble respect and loyalty, most gracious sovereign lady, your highness's most humble servant.'[398]

Peter recognized that he faced a stiff challenge in attempting to make Russians into Europeans. 'I have ordered the governors to collect monsters and send them to you. Have show-cases made. If I wished to send you humans who are monsters not on account of the deformity of their bodies but because of their freakish manners, you would not have space to put them all.'[399] Foreigners tended to share his view of the magnitude of the task. In the words of the British chaplain Thomas Consett, Peter encountered 'all over his Dominions Superstition and Ignorance universally prevailing, a general Corruption of Manners, and his People grown almost savage and barbrous'.[400] Consett, who witnessed the confusion of the years immediately after Peter's death, feared that his efforts would have been in vain, as many of the magnates were 'thought to be so enamoured with their old Customs and Manners that they wish for nothing more than a Restitution of them'.[401] The Prussian secretary Vockerodt made similar observations: 'The young Russian nobleman no matter how long he has lived abroad and managed to acquire decent and polite manners, once he returns to his fatherland and the bosom of his family reverts to his former animal existence, to such an extent that if you had seen him a year previously in a different place, you wouldn't recognize him.'[402]

It should be recalled that Vockerodt witnessed the period after the deaths of Peter and Catherine I and before the reign of Peter's daughter Elizabeth, when Peter's name was not held in such high regard. The attitude of foreigners by and large remained as it had been, as expressed by generations of Western travellers from the time of Richard Chancellor onwards, one of disdain. John Perry, for example, embittered by the experience of unpaid wages and non-co-operation, continually contrasts English 'Honesty and Integrity' with Russian vices. His comment towards the end of his account is significant: 'I believe I have said enough to let the Reader see the Happiness of living in a free Countrey.'[403] Perry's account of Peter's Russia is one of the earliest to be published; its author was not an 'armchair compiler', but spent time in Russia. Even so, he drew on earlier accounts, thereby mingling Petrine and pre-Petrine times. For example, he recounts the anecdote found in Olearius decades earlier of a surgeon being condemned to death as a sorcerer for keeping a skeleton in his house, a scholar condemned for predicting an eclipse of the sun, and a monkey for throwing down icons. It remains a moot point whether the world-view of the average Russian was significantly more conservative and traditionalist than that of contemporaries elsewhere. All over Europe the mass of the population continued to be ruled by custom rather than reason. To give one example, it is easy to mock the fact that in 1699 the Russians were still counting years from the birth of Adam, and that there were protests about the theft of God's time as a result of the decree on the new calendar. But the smile fades when it is recalled that in England the replacement of the Julian calendar by the Gregorian in 1752, which required cutting eleven days from September (Chesterfield's Act), was greeted with riots and cries of 'Give us back our eleven days!'

Perhaps the best indication of Peter's relative success in imposing Western manners is that at court, which is where the world judged Russia, there was no going back. Some contemporary foreign observers considered even 'superficial' reform a remarkable achievement. Campredon wrote: 'One has to admit that this great prince has truly worked wonders. If internally the majority of his subjects have remained the same as they always were, at least externally there has been such a considerable change (*une métamorphose si considérable*) that those who knew Russia thirty years ago and see what is going on now are bound to admit that it needed just such a courageous, enlightened (*éclairé*) and hard-working monarch to bring about such a happy and general transformation (*révolution*).'[404] Foreigners' accounts of the period immediately after Peter's death record that the life-style introduced under Peter did not change: fireworks, balls, mixed company, were the order of the day. There was talk of a return to Moscow by those higher aristocrats who might benefit by the restoration of Muscovite modes of royal marriage and hereditary progression into the boyar duma, but they had no quarrel with the new life-style. In order to be 'an adequate Russian at Peter's court', one had to be a 'pseudo-European',[405] like Princess Kurakina, whose conversation was mainly 'praise of French fashions and free behaviour'. She mocked pious women and tried to prove 'that amorous adventures are possible in Moscow no less than in Paris or London'.[406] Some were content with mimicking Westerners, but for a few, 'becoming Europeans' had implications beyond what Peter intended. Did becoming more like an Englishman or a Frenchman, or even a Pole, mean demanding a parliament, or corporate rights? When the Senate in its address to Peter in 1721 boasted that Russia had 'joined the community of political nations', it had in mind not 'political' in the modern sense, with implications of institutions and constitutions, still less popular participation, but nations with status in the international arena.

When in 1730 Prince D. M. Golitsyn demanded that the nobles be treated like the nobles in other Western countries, he went further than many of his peers were prepared to go. His demands were not so much a result of Peter's government reforms as a response to cultural change: access to foreign travel, languages, and books. To these areas we now turn.

9

Education and Learning

I am a student and I seek teachers

I. RUSSIA AND THE WEST

Of all the chasms which separated Russia not only from Western countries but also from some of its Eastern neighbours at the beginning of Peter's reign, the learning gap was perhaps the widest. Comparisons make bleak reading. At the end of the seventeenth century all major European countries had universities, many of them medieval foundations, the oldest, at Bologna and Paris, dating from the twelfth century. Central and Eastern Europe could boast of universities at Cracow, Vilna, Torun, and elsewhere. Russia had none. It had no equivalent of the Académie des Sciences (founded in 1666) or the Royal Society (1660). The seventeenth century is associated with the discoveries and inventions of the 'scientific revolution', a more or less random list of which might include Harvey on the circulation of the blood (1628), Boyle's experiments with gases, Leibniz's differential and integral calculus (1684), Pascal's invention of a calculating machine, Newton's *Principia* (1687), Galileo's and Johann Kepler's astronomical theories and observations, not to mention the rational underpinnings to scientific thought elaborated by thinkers such as Bacon and Descartes. Nicholas Copernicus, born at Torun in Poland, produced his heliocentric theory in the early sixteenth century. No Russian names can be added to this list, hardly surprising when one considers that not only did Muscovy lack universities or academies, but for most of the seventeenth century it also lacked schools.

In the world of books and publishing, the statistics are equally bleak. In the whole of the seventeenth century the single, Church-run press in Moscow published fewer than ten books which were not wholly religious in content, and even liturgical and devotional works amounted to only a few hundred titles. (There was no vernacular Russian version of the New Testament, for example, until 1820.) Some foreign books found their way into private and institutional libraries, but they were mainly of curiosity value, as few Russians were capable of reading them. When the French traveller De la Neuville claimed in 1689 that only one Russian knew French and only four Latin, he was probably not exaggerating very much.[1] I am not suggesting that Russia's European neighbours enjoyed universal literacy or had an abundance of intellectuals. In most countries the rural masses remained illiterate. In towns boys received their primary education in religious foundations until well into the nineteenth century, and most girls received none at all. But however hard one tries to avoid cultural relativism and find compensating factors in the greater spirituality of Russians, their closeness to nature, or refined aesthetic sense, the 'intellectual silence' of Old Russia was deafening indeed.[2] The silence was deepened by an active cultivation and celebration of 'ignorance' by some leading Orthodox churchmen. Foreign learning was still equated with 'guile' and 'deception' even during Peter's childhood. Russian reverence for the holy fool has often been cited as suggesting how the national psyche associated goodness with simple-mindedness.

Foreign authors of accounts of Russia were usually more than averagely educated, with a tendency to treat with *Schadenfreude* the 'gross ignorance' they observed all around them, especially when they themselves became the objects of denunciation or 'barbaric' treatment. The British engineer John Perry, for example, bemoaned the opposition he encountered to hydraulics work from certain boyars, who argued 'that God had made the Rivers to go one way, and that it was Presumption in Man to think to turn them another'.[3] A vital fact in Peter's career is that, despite his own inadequate education, he early on understood that education was a key that could unlock Russian potential, and that there was no place for wounded national pride. This idea runs like a refrain, from the device 'I am a student and I seek teachers'[4] on Peter's personal seal to the sections devoted to education in the Ecclesiastical Regulation of 1721, the fullest expression of state policy on the subject: 'When the light of learning is extinguished there cannot be good order in the Church; there cannot be but disorder and superstitions deserving of much ridicule, in addition to dissension and most senseless heresies. ... Learning is beneficial and basic for every good, as of the fatherland, so also of the Church, just like the root and the seed and the foundation.'[5]

It has been said that Peter viewed education as 'simply a matter of preparation for state service'.[6] But for Peter state service was not 'simply' anything: it was the highest calling. It is true that there was no room for twentieth-century ideas of 'personal development' or of individuals fulfilling their potential, still less for learning purely for its own sake. Even so, this 'simple' notion gave rise to ambitious schemes. A new type of Russian citizen was to be produced, carved out, like Galatea under Pygmalion's chisel, from rough stone: literate and numerate, in possession of skills appropriate to his office— military, naval, architectural, administrative—and with wider horizons than his predecessors: a better knowledge of geography and a smattering of Classical history and languages. Educating this 'new man' (and the occasional 'new woman') turned out to be no easy task.

II. SCHOOLS

Although he inherited little on which to base his educational programme,

Peter did not start with a completely blank sheet. Within his realm were two institutions of higher learning, albeit both Church foundations: the Slavonic–Greek–Latin Academy in Moscow, established in 1687, and the Kiev Academy, on which it was modelled. The latter originated in the 1630s during the struggle of Orthodox schools in the Polish Republic to compete with the Catholic schools founded by Jesuits during the Counter-Reformation, at a time when Orthodox Poles were coming under ever greater pressure to convert to Catholicism or the Uniate faith. They competed by imitating. The curriculum, administrative procedures, and rules for Ukrainian schools, be they Jesuit or Orthodox, were 'virtually identical'.[7] Their curricula were very similar to those of classical grammar schools, based on a vertical structure of forms, which started with basic Latin vocabulary followed by grammar classes, poetics, and rhetoric, then philosophy (logic, physics, metaphysics) and theology, based on Aristotle and Aquinas respectively. There were no age limits for pupils, no set time for completion of any section, no textbooks. Courses were studied from manuals prepared by tutors based on their own training, to which elements could be added. (Feofan Prokopovich's, when he was a teacher in the Kiev Academy, included arithmetic and geometry.)

Peter began to take an interest in the Moscow Academy in the 1690s, when he is said to have considered reforming its curriculum to include mathematics and navigation.[8] The school went into decline after the expulsion of its founding teachers, Ioanniky and Sofrony Likhud, in 1693. In the 'conservative' 1690s, only Greek was allowed; there was no Latin or theology. Even so, Peter's intention underlines the fact that he was willing to exploit this ecclesiastical base. After the death of Patriarch Adrian in 1700 the Moscow Academy was revived under the initiative of Stefan Iavorsky, as 'a duplicate of the Latin Academy in Kiev'.[9] When Just Juel visited the Moscow Academy in 1711, it had about 145 pupils from different backgrounds.[10] In 1716 Weber estimated between 200 and 300 students. He was treated to a speech delivered in Latin.[11] There is evidence, however, that the academy still suffered from neglect and ill-prepared entrants. In a memorandum (1713) to Peter, Fedor Saltykov wrote: 'The school must be totally reorganized. The ceilings have fallen down and the walls are crumbling. The 150 students are among the least gifted youths and some are plainly unteachable.'[12] Saltykov proposed schools, or 'academies', in the provinces offering Latin, English, French, history, geometry, and dancing, a more ambitious proposal that Peter's edict on local schools issued the following year. He also urged education for girls.[13]

The Moscow Academy could not supply all the education that Peter deemed necessary, but notwithstanding a commonly held misapprehension that Peter 'secularized' education, common sense shows that he needed the Church, indeed may have wished to forge an 'alliance between religious and scientific-technological values'.[14] There was no hope of educating even a select band of nobles' and townspeople's children without harnessing ecclesiastical resources. This included the experiment with 'cipher' schools (considered below), which were under the control of the Admiralty but housed locally in church premises. Figures for 1706 suggest that a quarter of the Church revenues administered through the Monastery department went on education, including funding some students abroad.[15]

The prime example of the 'alliance' between State and Church (with the former laying down the terms, needless to say) was the new academy envisaged in the Ecclesiastical Regulation, which was to offer a course of study based on grammar, geography and history, arithmetic and geometry, logic and dialectics, rhetoric and poetics, physics and metaphysics, the *Politia brevis* of Pufendorf and theology, with Latin as the language of instruction. Laymen training for government service would be admitted alongside intending higher clergy on the basis of an entrance test.[16] The proposed regulations demonstrate modern attitudes towards education. Time was to be allowed for excursions to places of interest (including the royal palaces), games, sailing, and constructing regular forts (all strongly reminiscent of Peter's own favourite pastimes as a youth), as well as amateur drama and debates. Accounts of the lives of great men and passages from history were to be read aloud at mealtimes.[17] This new academy, in St Petersburg, did not open during Peter's lifetime, but several of the seminaries envisaged in the Ecclesiastical Regulation did, in St Petersburg (1724, in the Alexander Nevsky monastery) and in Moscow and Kiev, where they were attached to the existing academies.[18] Forty-five diocesan clerical schools were also opened between 1721 and 1724.[19] After Peter's death some seventeen ecclesiastical academies were created, which, along with older religious establishments, in turn prepared most of the staff and students for secular higher schools, including the Academy of Sciences gymnasium and university.[20]

The first new schools to attract Peter's personal attention were military and technical schools. The Preobrazhensky guards school (1698) taught arithmetic, geometry, fortification, and artillery. There was also a naval training school at Azov.[21] An Artillery school opened in 1699, and by 1703 had 300 students, mainly destined to serve as non-commissioned officers. In 1712 this spawned the Moscow School of Engineering, which in 1719 moved to St Petersburg as the higher engineering school.[22] The Moscow military hospital school, under the direction of Dr Nicholas Bidloo, dates from 1706-7 (ten students graduated in 1712), the St Petersburg medical school from 1716. Mining institutes were attached to state ironworks at Olonets (1716) and Ekaterinburg in the Urals (1721).

Peter's best-known technical establishment was the Moscow School of Mathematics and Navigation, which started life as an offshoot of the Armoury. It was modelled on the Royal Mathematical School at Christ's Hospital, the 1673 founding charter of which specified that boys were to study 'until their proficiency in arithmetic and navigation should have fitted them for public service'. Peter must have learned about the school during his time in England. Just before he left, he gave instructions to hire teaching assistants, who arrived in Moscow in August 1699, whereupon they were apparently forgotten until the publication of the following order:

In 1701 on the great sovereign's personal orders mathematical and navigational sciences were established and the following teachers of English nationality were appointed: in mathematics: Andrei Danilov Farkhvarson [Henry Farquharson, ca.1675–1739], in navigation: Stepan Gvyn and Ritser Grys [Stephen Gwyn and Richard Grice, graduates of Christ's Hospital]. As students volunteers are to be enrolled, and others in addition by compulsion (*po prinuzhdeniiu*), and those without means are to be allotted a daily ration (*podennoyi korm*), depending on whether someone is found suited to study arithmetic or geometry, 5 altyns per day, others a grivna or less per day, depending on their degree of competence, and these studies are to be run in the Armoury by the boyar F. A. Golovin and his assistants.

Leonty Magnitsky, a graduate of the Moscow Academy, was appointed to work with the British teachers and to produce a book on mathematics, geometry, and navigation 'in the Slavonic dialect'.[23]

Premises were found in workshops in the Kadashevy district of Moscow, but Farquharson objected that the location was unsuitable for taking measurements of the horizon, so they were given rooms in the Sukharev tower, which was appropriately decorated and equipped. Teachers and pupils were fitted out with 'French outfits'.[24] By 1702 the school had 200 students, divided between the preparatory department (of Russian and 'ciphering') and the naval division.[25] Advanced students studied arithmetic, geometry, trigonometry, plane navigation, Mercatorian navigation, diurnals (astrolabe), spherics, astronomy (celestial navigation), geography (naval cartography), and Great Circle navigation.[26]

John Perry, who knew the teachers well, provides details of some of the problems they had, some no doubt as a reaction to the initial language of instruction being English![27] Richard Grice was murdered one night on the street. Farquharson was 'long and unjustly kept out of his Pay', not receiving the 100 roubles promised upon the graduation of each scholar.[28] Sectors, quadrants, drawing instruments, and books of charts, as well as more mundane slates and slate pencils, were in short supply.[29] In 1714–15 it was reported that no stipends had been paid for months, and students were destitute.[30] Things may have improved somewhat after the higher classes moved to St Petersburg in 1715, and with them Farquharson and Gwyn, by now on decent salaries. The new director was Baron Saint-Hilaire (formerly of French naval schools in Toulon, Brest, and Rochfort). In 1716 the Senate allocated 5,000 roubles, to include the salary of the director, 1,200 roubles per annum for the first year, and 600 roubles to be added in years 1 and 2 'if he demonstrates his skill'. A dancing master and fencing coach (at 300 roubles per year) were to be hired, as were masters of Latin, French, and German, and allowances were to be paid to the students.[31] Drawing and painting also appeared on the curriculum.[32] French influence is reflected in the designation of students of the academy as *garde-mariny* (*gardes de la marine*). Saint-Hilaire was dismissed in 1717 after a quarrel with Farquharson, who continued in his post until his death in 1739.[33]

The basics of the training programme for marines were set out in part 2 of the Naval Statute. No promotion was allowed unless examinations had been passed in artillery, navigation, and fortification. In addition, there were lessons in shipbuilding, infantry exercises, and shooting and rigging (on which students were to 'work with their hands'). Marines who lacked basic schooling had to attend general classes, with armed guards posted outside the schoolroom to deter truancy.[34]

Weber reported that the Naval Academy contained the 'Flower of the Russian Nobility' and was kept under strict discipline,[35] as confirmed by the following instruction: 'In order to prevent shouting and unruliness choose from the guards good retired infantrymen and let one be in each classroom during lessons and hold a whip; and if any of the pupils starts to misbehave, let him be beaten, without regard to which family he comes from, under penalty of punishment for anyone who shows indulgence.'[36] Harsh discipline may explain in part why in 1722 127 students were registered as absent and given an amnesty to induce them to return.[37]

The School of Mathematics and its successor, the Naval Academy, had a profound influence, not only by producing the first generation of Russian explorers, surveyors, cartographers, astronomers, and the like,[38] but also in the area of secondary education. Graduates of the Mathematical school (by 1716 there were 200 of them) were expected to teach in the provinces in the so-called cipher schools, first mentioned in decrees of 1714: 'In all the provinces children of the nobility and chancellery rank, of secretaries and clerks (but not the children of single homesteaders (*odnodvortsy*)) aged from ten to fifteen are to study numbers (*tsifiri*) and some part of geometry.' After completion of their studies they would receive a diploma, 'and without such diplomas they are not to be allowed to marry or to give pledges of betrothal'. These schools were to be housed in monasteries and parish church annexes.[39] There were never enough trainee teachers to meet the government's demands. In 1715 it was specified that two graduates in geometry and geography should be sent to each province 'to teach young boys from people of all ranks'.[40] In January 1716 a further call was issued for teachers for 'children of secretaries, clerks and people of other rank' by taking two pupils for each province 'from Apraksin's school' (i.e., the School of Mathematics).[41]

If the first hurdle in setting up cipher schools was a shortage of teachers, by the beginning of the 1720s it was lack of pupils. Grigory Skorniakov-Pisarev, put in charge of the schools, reported in 1720 that the Moscow cipher school had seventy pupils, but little progress had been made in the provinces. Cipher schools in Pskov, Novgorod, and other major towns had no pupils at all. The local authorities were ordered to round up pupils and herd them into classrooms 'without delay, lest the teachers assigned to work in the *gubernii* are left idle and take their wages for doing nothing'.[42] Poor enrolment stemmed partly from the clash of interests between education and service. For the nobles these decrees went hand in glove with the act on single inheritance (23 March 1714), which sought in even more radical form to bind the nobles to state service by interfering in traditional inheritance patterns. Initially Peter's idea seems to have been to educate the nobles alongside other ranks, but soon nobles appear to have been excluded from cipher schools. This may have been in response to their hostility. Richer nobles preferred to educate their sons at home (which from 1716 they were allowed to do). Poorer ones either resorted to the village priest or failed to provide schooling altogether. By 1726 nobles accounted for less than 3 per cent of the 2,000 students in twelve cipher schools.[43]

In the meantime, nobles tightened their grip on higher establishments such as the Naval Academy. (Their wish for exclusive, superior schooling was finally consolidated by the creation in 1730 of the Noble Cadet Corps, which was exclusively for the children of nobles, and gave accelerated promotion to officers' rank in the guards.) In 1721 a Senate-organized school for junior college staff was set up, as 'this training had not gained a foothold when it comes to civil matters'.[44] Provisions for special training for entrants into the civil service were included in the instructions for the new office of chief herald (February 1722): 'Since learning has not yet taken root here, especially in civil affairs, and is especially lacking in economic affairs, therefore until academies are set up, he should set up a temporary school.'[45] Some training was provided on the spot in apprenticeships based on the Swedish system, by which so-called junkers, 'sons of the nobility', were to be instructed in copying and other skills. This provision was set out in the General Regulation[46] and also in the Table of Ranks: each college was to recruit six or seven young nobles, to serve from the lowest grade. Just as in the military ranks, no one, however illustrious his origins, could proceed higher without training.[47]

Members of urban communities had their own axes to grind. In 1721 they petitioned for the exemption of merchant children from the cipher schools on the grounds that this damaged the family business. Their sons, it was argued, were needed for minding shops and going on trade trips. 'If it is ordered to take the children of merchants into those schools they will be completely detached from their trades and enterprises and in the future it will be impossible to train them in commercial affairs.' This would adversely affect the community's ability to pay its state taxes and duties. It was no doubt the latter argument which led to the merchants' request being granted.[48] When in 1721–2 sons of clergy too were removed from the rolls of cipher schools and transferred to the episcopal schools, set up by the Ecclesiastical Regulation for the training of clergy, the cipher schools lost most of their pupils. In May 1722 it was specified that churchmen's children be released 'from Arithmetical schools and other secular studies' and transferred to episcopal schools in the expectation of creating a 'better and reformed clergy'. Any who proved 'lazy' were threatened with the poll tax. Teachers were expected to teach good grammar, spelling, and rules of punctuation, using as textbooks the primer and a Slavonic grammar.[49] Eventually it was proposed that remaining cipher schools be merged with episcopal schools, starting in Novgorod.

Of course, no country in the world educated all its citizens during this period. In Russia, as elsewhere, children in rural communities remained uneducated not just because of a shortage of teachers or the fear of educating peasants 'above their station', but because child labour was no less vital to the rural economy than to the trading community.[50] There is no corroboration of Weber's report that Peter, having established schools in towns, was 'resolved to do the like in the Villages, and to banish the former Ignorance from among his Subjects'.[51] A few landowners made provision for educating selected village youths, but even they probably believed that only a handful of literate peasants was needed in any given village. Ivan Pososhkov deplored this situation, believing that, 'like the blind, none of them [the peasants] sees or understands anything'.[52] He proposed that peasants be obliged to send their children to the sacristan for lessons: 'It seems to me that it would be no bad thing to ensure that even in the smallest village all are able to read and write.' Apart from the usefulness to their masters and the tsar, he argued, this would make the peasants less easy to fool with subversive faked orders and letters.

Some educational initiatives operated outside the official programme. There was even a Jesuit school in Moscow from 1701, after Jesuit priests (expelled in 1689) were readmitted. It offered more than thirty pupils, mostly Russians, a curriculum which included Latin, mathematics, German, and military science. Peter rejected complaints from Orthodox churchmen about the spiritual dangers of such an enterprise.[53] The success of the Jesuits was surpassed by another foreign school, the Glück gymnasium or 'German school', established in Moscow by Pastor Ernst Glück, who was hired by Peter after the capture of Marienburg in Livonia in 1703. The ambitious-looking programme included geography, philosophy, ethics, politics, Latin rhetoric, poetics, Cartesian philosophy, Greek, Hebrew, Chaldean, French, German, Swedish, arithmetic, dance, equestrianism, and dressage.[54] The school continued to function after Glück's death in 1705, with seventy-seven pupils in 1711, but was closed in 1715.[55] The Likhud brothers, formerly teachers in the Moscow Academy, ran their own schools. The most successful was in Novgorod. Some Swedish prisoners of war offered tuition, both for the children of fellow prisoners and for Russians, providing a curriculum which included Latin, German, French, mathematics, morality, and 'divers bodily Exercises'.[56] A school said to have attracted pupils from far afield was von Brech's Pietist school in Tobol'sk, which in 1720 had 139 pupils. Its curriculum included Bible reading, psalms, and prayers.[57] In some cases foreigners acted as tutors. Young Peter Shafirov, for example, was taken into the house of Just Juel for six months to be taught by his secretary.[58]

One of Peter's most famed methods of educating his subjects was sending them abroad. (He was not the first Russian ruler to do so: Boris Godunov dispatched a contingent in the late sixteenth century, but none of them returned.) Peter's first order of this variety dates to 1696. Franz Lefort wrote to his brother, describing an inspection of the sixty 'chamberlains' destined for foreign education, to be dispatched in March 1697, forty to Italy and the rest to the Netherlands.[59] The following year Peter undertook his own visit to Europe with fellow 'volunteers'. It is not surprising that the first 'study trip' students (*pensionery*, as they were called in Russian) were ill-prepared. Strahlenberg writes: 'They barely knew their own language (not to mention foreign ones) and so much time was wasted before they could begin their training. And since they lacked proper supervision, many of them fell into various excesses.'[60] Peter Tolstoy's account of his experiences with this group gives a graphic picture of the problems as well as the rewards, although his age—fifty-two—made him atypical. Practical training was the usual way of learning seamanship. (The 1697 *pensionery* were expected to 'try to be at sea in time of combat'.[61]) Groups were assigned to a captain or a shipbuilder as assistants. Instruction included types of ship, the compass, winds and currents, geometry, and navigation. It is a remarkable fact that none of the original naval apprentices actually entered the navy later, although their experiences no doubt stood them in good stead for other occupations.[62]

By the 1710s training was established on a more regular basis, with agents abroad supervising the students, Prince L'vov in Holland, Konon Zotov in France, Fedor Saltykov in England, and Iury Kologrivov in Italy. Funds were dispensed by the Cabinet. Training abroad was not just military and naval, especially after 1716 or so, when Peter's concepts of education began to broaden. Nor was it reserved for nobles. On his way home to Russia via Amsterdam, Ivan Nepliuev met young Russians studying metalwork, copperwork, and joinery.[63] On 12 February 1712 instructions were issued 'to choose thirty persons, from captains to ensigns, good and young men, without regard for their families or whether they are rich or poor, only that they have a good heart and inclination and diligence in their duties and send them to study on service in France'.[64] Young men from Latin schools were selected to be sent to Persia to learn Turkish, Arabic, and Persian, and 'it would be best if such lads were good and had at least learned grammar and also were willing to go there to study of their own accord'.[65] In March 1716 forty clerks, including five from the Cabinet, were ordered to go to Königsberg for training,[66] and in June 1716 sons of Moscow merchants were sent to Holland to study commerce and language.[67] In 1716 Aleksei and Lev Semennikov, sons of a chief merchant, were sent to Italy to study, their expenses being met by a charge of 200 efimki per head on the Moscow *gosti* and members of the second merchants' guild (*gostinnaia sotnia*).[68] There were art and architecture students in Italy and students of philosophy in Paris, the latter appointed as clerks to the Senate in 1723.[69] By then Peter was beginning to summon most of his *pensionery* back to Russia, where they were assured of 'profit and wealth'.[70]

Pensionerstvo has received mixed reviews. Okenfuss concludes that study abroad 'paid valuable dividends'. He points out, too, that Petrine travel fiction featuring young men studying abroad provides evidence of a broader cultural impact.[71] Successes included Peter's cousin Alexander L'vovich Naryshkin, who together with Grigory Grigorievich Skorniakov-Pisarev, transformed the Naval Academy in the 1720s after study abroad.[72] But for many *pensionery* life abroad was torment. Many complained of penury and ill treatment. In 1721 the architectural students Eropkin and Usov reported from Rome that they had received only ten of their fifteen Reichsthaler monthly allowance because the rest was pocketed by an agent in Holland.[73] Another complained from London: 'I am really suffering great hardship, more or less naked and barefoot and my creditors won't give me more time and want to throw me into prison.' Meanwhile, those in charge of them complained that the students often wasted their time in the 'pursuit of Bacchus and Venus', gambling and brawling.[74] In 1722 a group of trainee craftsmen in England complained that their stipend was insufficient to live on; they were in debt and could not afford to keep company with their English colleagues, as a result of which their studies were suffering and they felt ashamed.[75] Architectural student Kolychev in Rome aroused local hostility by making false promises of marriage to three girls.[76] The account of Ivan Nepliuev, sent abroad to study in 1717–18, offers many details. He describes various mishaps suffered by fellow students: one ran off to Mount Athos to become a monk, another was stabbed during a brawl in a tavern, and another went mad in Spain and had to to be detained. He describes study with the French *garde de la marine* (he visited France in 1718), who taught navigation, engineering, artillery, drawing, shipbuilding, dancing, fencing, and horse riding. Punishment for bad behaviour involved a spell in gaol. He also did a stint in Cadiz, where he received training in dancing and fencing, but found classes in mathematics useless, because 'we sat around with nothing to do because it was impossible to learn anything as we didn't know the language'. In a complaint to St Petersburg he wrote that 'there is no point in our life here since lessons in sword-play and dancing cannot be suitable for preparing us for His Majesty's service'.[77]

By the end of his reign Peter, although still inspired mainly by practical concrete goals, had come to appreciate the wider appeal of science and the acclaim due to its patrons. The Academy of Sciences is generally regarded as the crowning glory of his education programme.[78] The impulses behind it were both internal (the failure of existing facilities to produce top administrators) and external (the need to 'civilize' Russia in the eyes of the world). Peter was strongly influenced by the ideas of Leibniz, by discussions with French scholars during his visit to the Académie des Sciences in 1717, and latterly by Christian Wolff (professor of philosophy and physics at Halle), who corresponded with Lavrenty Blumentrost, the future president of the new academy. Peter chose to ignore Wolff's advice to start with a university. In February 1721 he sent his librarian J. D. Schumacher to tour Europe to recruit personnel 'for the creation of a society (*sotsietet*) of sciences, like the ones in Paris, London, Berlin and other places'.[79] The founding of an academy was mentioned, as we have seen, in the 1722 instruction to the chief herald. This scheme, devised in parallel with plans for religious education, set out in the Ecclesiastical Regulation, has been described as 'the political marriage of religion and science ... performed under the canopy of the so-called Leibniz–Wolff cosmology', encouraging change within a stable order.[80] Peter was familiar with Leibniz's view that knowledge glorified God and that Russia was ripe to be opened up for scientific research, initially to geographical exploration, which would further enrich Western knowledge. The national-istic notion of the 'glory' of scientific endeavour is found in Peter's famous speech in which he imagined the 'transmigration of sciences' from ancient Greece, via England, France, and Germany, to Russia, which had the poten-tial to 'put other civilized nations to the blush, and to carry the glory of the Russian name to the highest pitch'.[81]

The recommendations of Schumacher and Blumentrost (Peter's annotated copy survives) were published in January 1724, exactly a year before Peter's death, opening with the words: 'For the spread of arts and sciences two types of establishment are generally used: the first type is called a university, the second an academy or society of arts and sciences.' Nine points follow. In the section on personnel Peter noted: 'Two more men should be added from the Slav nation (*slovenskogo naroda*) in order the better to teach Russians.'[82] The initial cost was estimated at 20,000 roubles, the money to be gathered from Narva, Dorpat, Pernau, and Arensburg customs and licence fees.[83] The academy was to combine scientific research with teaching in a university (fac-ulties of law, medicine, and philosophy, but not theology) and a gymnasium. It was opened in Catherine I's reign (formally only in August 1726), with an all-foreign staff, mostly Germans, with the exception of the president, Lavrenty Blumentrost. The first full Russian member (1741) was Mikhail Lomonosov.[84]

The received opinion that Peter's concept of science and learning was 'narrowly utilitarian, highly specialized, and closely tied to military require-ments' has rightly been challenged—the academy is a case in point—as has the notion of 'secularization'. The Church played a central role in running schools, although it too had to concede ground. So-called church schools were more like European Classical colleges or grammar schools, whose prime aim was not to train clergy.[85] Petrine education was a typical compromise, with native and foreign, religious, and secular elements. It was closely super-vised, usually selectively élitist and frequently imposed by the State in the interests of the State—prosperity and glory, not the enlightenment of the individual—but it was also underfunded. This was not so very different from the situation in many other countries, but in Russia apathy and hostility among all classes of a population that was burdened with so many other obligations often frustrated the government's best efforts.[86]

The nobles' education suffered from both inadequate provision and lack of enthusiasm. In Peter's reign the norm for the young provincial nobleman, unless he was selected for special training or study abroad, was some basic reading (sometimes not even writing) acquired from a parish priest.[87] Only civil servants had need of much more. In 1767 an estimated 60 per cent of the nobility in Orenburg province were still illiterate, and even in Moscow *guberniia* the figure was 18 per cent.[88] By 1725 there were only about 2,000 pupils in secular schools and 2,500 in diocesan schools, together with a few hundred in special schools.[89] The Naval Academy reached a peak of 394 students in 1724. Numbers for the Moscow and Kiev academies in 1725 were 505 and 654 students respectively. In 1724 the bishop of Nizhny Novgorod reported that 132 students had completed the elementary course in schools in his diocese and that 295 were enrolled, but not all the new episcopal schools did so well. Statistics provided by bishops for the period 1727–8 indicate that about 3,100 students, nearly all sons of priests, enrolled in episcopal schools, but in some towns (e.g., Voronezh, Pereiaslavl', Astrakhan) no schools were founded for lack of funds, while a school in Suzdal' closed as a result of famine.[90] The Kazan' church school opened in 1723 with fifty-two students. Of these, nine were sent home because they were too poor, eleven were too young, and two too stupid, fourteen ran away, and six died almost at once! More were recruited, and by the 1730s things had improved, mainly as a result of employing teachers from Kiev.[91] Another striking statistic is that in 1719–22 only 93 of the 1,389 pupils registered (often by force) in cipher schools were awarded diplomas.[92] The 'university' attached to the academy initially failed to attract Russian students because they lacked adequate secondary training, especially linguistic skills, to cope with the course, so that even the first students had to be imported from abroad.[93] Prokopovich therefore stretched the truth somewhat when he declared in his funeral oration that Peter was Russia's Solomon, as proved by 'the manifold philosophic disciplines introduced by him and by his showing and imparting to many of his subjects the knowledge of a variety of inventions and crafts unknown to us before his time'.[94] In fact, as Prokopovich sensed, admiration for Peter abroad was inspired not so much by his concrete achievements in establishing schools or training civil servants as by his aspirations to civilize a 'savage' nation. The image is captured in a well-known engraving in which the tsar presents two globes, scientific books, and mathematical instruments to a maiden representing Russia.[95] The fact that Peter had to borrow all the objects depicted from the West in his 'crash campaign of technical transfer'[96] was naturally a pleasant thought for the guardians of wisdom abroad. Imitation has always been the best form of flattery.

III.   SCIENCE AND LEARNING

In science, as in schools, Peter more or less had to start from scratch. Byzantine scholars pursued scientific enquiry, but their work, like other Byzantine writings of a speculative nature, failed to reach Russia, where rational modes of thought remained alien to all but a select handful.[97] One may detect the beginnings of scientific curiosity in Muscovy in the seventeenth century in a few individuals with the desire and awareness to look beyond immediate day-to-day existence and religious explanations to a wider world. The royal palace housed globes (presents to Tsar Alexis from Sweden and the United Provinces) and telescopes, the first recorded one sold to Tsar Michael in 1614.[98] The inventory of Prince Vasily Golitsyn's property made in 1689 included a telescope, a magnifying glass, a thermometer, and maps of the world and Europe.[99] Archbishop Afanasy of Kholmogory, who was close to Peter in the 1690s, also owned globes and telescopes, and wrote a handbook on folk medicine. Foreign specialists such as doctors and apothecaries, merchants and weapons-makers, brought with them books and ideas, as did churchmen from Ukraine and the grand duchy of Lithuania, in the form of such works as Vesalius's *De humani corporis fabrica* and the compilation *Hortulus regime* translated by Epifany Slavinetsky and Arseny Satanovsky respectively, albeit in single manuscript copies. But in Muscovite Orthodox circles philosophy, in the literal sense, by and large was 'tolerated only to the extent that it generates piety'.[100] Knowledge of the inductive method was limited, and there was little sympathy with the notion of the pursuit of scientific enquiry as a religious duty in order better to comprehend God's ordered universe.

Under Peter scientific curiosity—knowledge for its own sake—was overshadowed by practical aims, in line with the thinking of the time about expanding resources, which in turn prompted the collection of knowledge of more general interest. Stories from Peter's youth—his questions about an astrolabe[101] or sailing against the wind—were concerned with how things worked and how they could be usefully applied. This was the focus of his shipbuilding training in 1697–8, but his travels also brought him into contact with observatories, museums, hospitals, botanical gardens, and cabinets of curiosities, which in turn brought dawning awareness, which he had sensed already in the Moscow Foreign Quarter, of the immense gap that separated Russia and Western countries.

Mathematics was an area of particular concern. As we saw earlier, numeracy was the core curriculum of the cipher schools, which were manned by graduates of the Moscow Mathematical school. In this respect a major role was played by Farquharson and Gwyn; but Soviet textbooks underplayed their contribution, while raising to the level of genius the native Russian mathematician Leonty Magnitsky (1669–1739).[102] The latter's famous *Arifmetika* (1703), although remarkable in the Russian context, was in fact a compilation from various foreign works. Little of the more advanced mathematics filtered through to the population. According to John Perry, Russians did not know the 'use of figures', but calculated on an abacus, a method which apparently continued in use in government offices, 'excepting some very few persons, who now reckon by Figures'.[103] Progress was aided by the publication of textbooks, virtually unknown in the seventeenth century, apart from multiplication tables (1682) and some manuscript works. Twelve works on mathematics and geometry were published between 1703 and 1724, the first being Magnitsky's *Arifmetika*, followed in the same year by logarithm tables.[104] These books were distinguished by the use of arabic numerals (as distinct from the Cyrillic literal system), which were first used in print in a book published in Russia in *Journal of the Siege of Nöteborg* (*Iurnal ob osade Notenburga*) (Moscow, 1702). They were also used in Amsterdam editions in Russian and found in fragments in a few earlier works—for example, on tables and plans in the military manual *Uchenie i khitrost' ratnogo stroeniia* (1647–9) and in Karion Istomin's 1692 primer.[105]

Not surprisingly in an age of shifting borders and expanding horizons, geography was a subject which claimed considerable attention. Peter's new Russians were encouraged to take a wider view of the world. The section on seminaries in the Ecclesiastical Regulation (1721) recommended that a teacher use a map or a globe, to which students would be asked to point in response to the questions 'Where is Asia? Where is Africa? Where is Europe? In what direction does America lie?'[106] 'Spatial considerations' informed much of Peter's activity and policies, creating 'a willingness to face the challenges and opportunities presented by space' in order to gain greater control over a stronger (and bigger) state.[107] Many developments—acquisition of new territories and coastlines, the building of a navy, busy foreign relations, attempts to exploit natural resources—called for better geographical knowledge and modern methods of measuring and charting. A nautical atlas of the Baltic and a general atlas of the Baltic Sea were just two products of these trends.[108] The fact that the tsar enjoyed surveying (a hobby that had got him into trouble in Riga in 1697) and looking at globes also helped, as did the fact that geography was perhaps also the first field of Russian scientific endeavour to attract foreign interest, with reference to exploration and charting of 'exotic' locations. An allegorical engraving published to celebrate the coronation of Catherine in 1724 shows the emperor pointing with a cane to Russia on a globe.[109] In 1715 the famous globe of Gottorp, made by Adam Olearius with seating inside for twelve people, was brought to St Petersburg at great expense as a gift from the duke of Holstein.[110] Peter was quite knowledgeable—see, for example, his conversation with French cartographer Guillaume Delisle in Paris in 1717 when he pointed out that St Petersburg had the wrong latitude on Delisle's 1706 map of Russia.[111]

Publications on geography included Bernhard Varenius's *Geographia generalis*, translated and published in 1718 as *Geografiia general'naia*, Johann Hübner's *Kurtze Fragen aus der neuen und alten Geographie* (which mentions Tycho Brahe's geocentric theory of the universe), and P.-A. Ferrarius's *Lexicon geographicum*.[112] The heavens were not neglected. The study of astronomy was promoted by James Bruce. Christian Huygens's *Cosmotheros*, translated by Bruce as *Kniga mirozreniia ili mnenie o nebesnykh globusakh* (1717), contains references to the Copernican system (regarded as 'heretical' in conservative Orthodox circles). Copernicus also features in the engraved figures on Kiprianov's arithmetical chart (1705) and in his *Depiction of the Globe of the Heavens* (1707), which features a graphic demonstration of the heliocentric system.[113]

Maps and map making were far from unknown in pre-Petrine Russia, but the weak development of native cartography is indicated by an order of 1696 for the making of two large canvas maps of the towns, villages, and roads of Siberia 'of the finest workmanship ... since there are no maps (*chertezhi*) of the Siberian towns in the Siberian chancellery, and no way of getting the information'.[114] In 1720 the General Regulation (article 48) again acknowledged the need for maps to describe 'all the borders, rivers, towns, villages, churches, hamlets, forests and so on'. Every college was to have up-to-date maps (*lant'karty ili chertezhi*) 'in order to obtain proper knowledge and information about the state of the realm and the provinces which belong to it'.[115] Maps had propaganda as well as commercial value; in 1724, 500 maps were printed showing the new Russian–Swedish borders.[116] They were routinely embellished with royal portraits surrounded by appropriate Classical allegories and baroque flourishes. Developments included the first maps with lines of longitude and latitude (unknown in Russia at the beginning of the century), maps of the Caspian (a map of the entire sea was presented to great acclaim in Paris in 1720) and Derbent, and plans of St Petersburg and Siberia. Improved maps of rivers became available—for example, Cornelius Cruys's atlas of the Don, Azov, and the Black Sea (1703–4). The Dnieper and its tributaries were surveyed, in the hope of solving the problem of the rapids which hampered navigation.[117] In 1715 the first comprehensive map of Russia was begun, work on which continued into the 1730s.[118]

Map making was stimulated by exploration—expeditions to Novaia Zemlia in 1705 (on the ship *Mercurius* belonging to Menshikov), to the far north and east, and to the Caspian and Central Asia, the latter prompted by commercial interests rather than scientific curiosity. Peter was interested in finding routes to China and India via the Arctic Ocean or through rivers running into the Caspian.[119] In 1720 Daniel Messerschmidt, a physician from Danzig, was sent on a mission to collect 'all possible information' about Siberia, including artifacts.[120] The Bering (First Kamchatka) expedition of 1727–30 was ordered by Peter just before his death.

Throughout his reign Peter collected information about Russia, ranging from surveys of forests to records of births and deaths. *The Flourishing Condition of the All-Russian State*, published in 1727 by I. K. Kirilov, was the first attempt at a comprehensive description of Russia based on local information collected by the Senate a few years earlier. The result was that by Peter's death both Russians and foreigners were better informed than ever before about the empire—itself a geographical construct—although vast tracts remained unexplored and uncharted. In the broader sense, Russians began to redefine their country's 'place on the map'. Vasily Tatishchev's new geographical description of Russia was to take the Urals as the boundary between Europe and Asia, thus pushing European Russia much further eastwards than the river boundaries used in Classical times. In future, Russians were to regard themselves as Europeans with a civilizing mission in Asia, but it was Peter's reign which firmly identified Western civilization as the desirable standard and attempted to make Russia measure up to it.[121]

In the area of medicine Peter built on slightly firmer foundations. In the

1650s the needs of the army prompted Tsar Alexis to begin training Russian doctors (mainly surgeons—*lekari*) in the Apothecaries chancellery (founded in 1620), which started life as a court pharmacy. The training was given by foreign doctors, who also served as royal physicians—for example, Samuel Collins and his successors. Reliance upon foreigners continued. In 1698, for example, Fedor Golovin hired a number of Dutch, Danish, Austrian, German, Italian, and French *lekari* to serve as military and naval surgeons.[122]

Peter's interest in medicine was both pragmatic and personal. He was fascinated by diseases and deformities and enjoyed conducting autopsies. Abroad he loved to visit operating theatres. A famous story recounts how members of his retinue were forced to assist at a dissection. In Paris in 1717 he watched a cataract operation being performed by the British doctor Woolhouse, and asked the latter to take a Russian apprentice.[123] Peter himself continued to hire foreign personal physicians. Robert Erskine (Areskin), an Oxford-educated Scot and member of the Royal Society, was invited to Russia in 1704, initially as physician to Menshikov.[124] In 1707 he was appointed president of the Apothecaries chancellery, and in 1713 he became Peter's personal physician. He reorganized medical schools, improved the pharmacy, oversaw the hiring of foreign medical personnel, and studied spas. In 1714 he became head of Peter's *Kunstkamera*, exhibits for which included anatomical models and specimens.[125] In April 1716 he was named 'arkhiator', chief supervisor of medicine in Russia, with the rank of state councillor and a salary of 5,000 roubles per annum. He accompanied Peter to Holland, Germany, and France in 1716–17.[126] When Erskine died in 1718,[127] he was replaced by Lavrenty Blumentrost (1692–1755), the future president of the Russian Academy of Sciences.

Modern medical facilities for the mass of the population were another matter, in Russia as elsewhere, although foreigners found Russia lacking by their own standards. A story recorded by Just Juel 'for the sake of future visitors to Russia' relates that in February 1711 a servant travelling from St Petersburg to Moscow with the Danish envoy broke a leg, but Juel could not leave him in Novgorod, the first major town on their route, because there was not one qualified doctor in the town.[128] For most people (including the nobility) folk medicine and home remedies continued to be the order of the day. In 1700, for example, a servant of Peter Petrovich Saltykov was sentenced to hard labour in Azov for inadvertently killing his master by administering a strong sleeping draught of hemp.[129]

The first military hospital was established in Moscow in 1707 by Dr Nicholas Bidloo (1670–1735) from Leiden. Bidloo trained several young men who already knew Dutch and Latin as surgeons, using practical methods based on the study of anatomy through dissection of corpses. Just Juel was impressed when he visited the hospital in February 1710, noting that it owned a large library of medical books, 'in every possible language'.[130] Bidloo reported in 1712: 'I accomplished things unheard of in all this land in promoting this enterprise, for the good of the patients and the education of the students, on many occasions not hesitating to remove shot and to set bones with my own hands.' His pupils, he boasted, not only had 'specialist knowledge of one or other illness ... but also a general knowledge of all illnesses from the head to the feet with a genuine and practical training in how to cure them, and also know how to bind up sores and to change the dressings on a hundred to two hundred patients a day'. However, of the fifty pupils originally enrolled, only thirty-three remained, six having died, eight run away, two being sent to another school, and one into the army for intemperance.[131] A medical school was founded in St Petersburg in 1716, and a medical college in 1721.[132] Stählin has a report from Villebois about a general hospital in St Petersburg for sick and old soldiers and sailors, staffed by 'the most skilled doctors and surgeons and to train young Russian doctors to study Latin, anatomy, physiology, surgery, knowledge and use of medical preparations'.[133] Other public medical institutions included the Pharmacy (Apteka) in Moscow, the descendant of the Apothecaries' department, and the *Aptekarskaia kantseliariia* in St Petersburg (founded in 1714).

An interesting glimpse of Petrine medicine in action is provided by measures to fight bubonic plague, of which there were two major cycles, in 1709–13 in the Baltic, Novgorod, and (to a lesser extent) Ukraine and 1718–19 in the south (Kiev, Belgorod, and Azov).[134] In a series of letters sent to commanders in 1710 (a year in which many more died from the plague than in battle), Peter mentions quarantine (in Mitau and other towns) to stop infected persons getting closer to the army, and road-blocks to keep away the mobile population, especially traders and food vendors.[135] Letters were to be unsealed, kept in the air for two to three hours, then smoked in juniper fumes to kill infection.[136] Regiments were stationed away from towns and far apart from each other. Fires of juniper were lit to produce smoke, or, in the absence of juniper, horse manure 'or something else which smells bad, as smoke is very effective against these diseases'.[137] Medicine for plague was sent from Moscow.[138] For those not already sick, wine with camphor was prescribed.[139] Riga was stricken. In July infection spread to Narva, and there were fears for Reval.[140] In September there were reports from Valdai and Torzhok, which led to fears of the spread of pestilence along the road to Moscow.[141] This outbreak died down, but struck again in the summers of 1711 and 1712.

Military medical services were regularized in the Military Statute of 1716, which specified that one doctor and one staff surgeon be assigned to each division and a field surgeon to each regiment. They were to be supported by paramedics (*feldshery*) and travelling pharmacies. Medical staff were enjoined to treat all 'from the highest to the lowest' without taking any payment.[142] A more systematic attempt to set up a medical service was put forward in the 1722 Admiralty Regulation, which gave details of provisions for a hospital for the navy on shore and for shipbuilding workers.[143] 'At ports everywhere there shall be hospitals, with Commissars in charge of them, under the direction of the Commissar-General for War' (chapter 47, article i). Each was to be staffed by one doctor, one senior surgeon (*starshii lekar'*) plus other surgeons (one per

200 patients), several apothecary's assistants (*gezeli lekarskie*), and trainees. Female assistants supervised by nuns were hired to wash linen and do other menial tasks: one per twenty patients in cases of severe diarrhoea, one per thirty for milder diarrhoea, one per forty for severe illness without diarrhoea, and one per fifty for moderate illness. Male orderlies were employed to deal with stoves, cleaning, and general duties. A church and a priest were attached to each hospital. Treatment was not free: half the money wages and all the rations of hospital patients were retained, and 'the duration of his stay in hospital will be recorded so that deductions can be made from his wage'.

On paper the hospital looks well provided for: linen was to be changed daily for patients with diarrhoea (who were entitled to three changes of clothes). The kitchen is described in some detail, from cutlery (one knife between two) to napkins.[144] Meals for the sick consisted of oatmeal or barley porridge (in winter), cabbage and greens with porridge (in summer), meat (a pound or half a pound per day), one tankard of beer, and a glass of wine. Cows were kept to provide milk, and there were a vegetable garden and ice-houses. The regulation shows the preoccupation with record keeping common to all Peter's statutes: information had to be entered into the clerk's book (mainly to make sure of the dates of admission and release for wages). Concern was shown for cleanliness (the clerk was to 'take diligent steps to ensure that all is kept very clean, and that the patients do not lie in filth') and working hours ('the Physician will be at the hospital at seven o'clock in the morning and at five o'clock in the afternoon, and he will order the bell to be rung, when all employees must assemble at their places'[145]). Dissections were to be carried out for educational purposes. The document is, in fact, closely based on the section on hospitals in *Ordonnance de Louis XIV pour les armées navales et arsénaux de marine* (Paris, 1689). The 1735 General Regulation for Hospitals drew heavily on this 1722 document.[146]

One of the many scientific 'firsts' credited to Peter was the founding of a museum, although in fact his father, and perhaps earlier Russian rulers, owned small collections of 'curiosities'. In this respect Peter's own taste for the bizarre and for freaks of nature coincided with a 'typical manifestation of Baroque culture'. Monsters were eagerly sought after all over Europe.[147] No doubt he was also encouraged by Leibniz's recommendation 'Concerning the Museum and the cabinets and *Kunstkammern* ... [which] should serve not only as objects of general curiosity, but also as a means to the perfection of the arts and sciences'.[148] Peter's own collection started in the Netherlands in 1697, when he acquired preserved birds, fish, and insects, which were initially stored with other specimens in the Pharmacy. He visited the cabinets of curiosities of Frederick Ruysch and Nicholas Chevalier in Holland and the Elector of Saxony's Kunstkammer in Dresden in June 1698. These acquisitions formed the basis of his own new Kunstkamera, which from 1714 was housed in the Summer Palace in St Petersburg. The collection included exotic and freakish natural specimens and ethnographic rarities, as well as weapons and diplomatic gifts. It grew significantly after Peter's 1716–17 visit to Europe, when Ruysch's anatomical cabinet was purchased, as were the zoological specimens of the apothecary Albert Seba and the cabinet of the physician Gottwald of Danzig, which included minerals, shells, and rare stones.[149] In 1718 a new building was started, according to legend on the spot where a misshapen pine-tree grew. The idea was to establish a *public* museum which people would visit to look and learn, encouraged to do so by free coffee, wine, or vodka.[150] For the official opening, in 1719, exhibits were on show in the Kikin mansion. The first directors were Lavrenty Blumentrost and the librarian Johann Schumacher.[151]

Peter extended his collections energetically. Most famously, in 1718 he issued a decree on 'monsters' and rarities: 'It is well known that in the human species, as in that of animals and birds, monsters are born, that is freaks (*monstry, to est' urody*), which are collected in all countries as objects of wonder.' The decree points out that in parts of Russia, as a result of ignorance, some people might regard such freaks as works of the devil, whereas in fact they are products of nature. Specimens were to be delivered to commandants in towns for a scale of payments: for dead specimens, 10 roubles for humans, 5 for animals, 3 for birds; for live exhibits, 100, 15, and 7 roubles respectively. More was offered if they were 'very strange' (*ochen' chudnoe*), less if only slightly deformed. People concealing such freaks were to be fined and the sum given to informers. Archaeological specimens were sought also. Dead specimens were to be preserved in spirits, or, in case of necessity, in double-distilled *vino*.[152] Peter was disappointed by the poor response, and wrote to Makarov urging him to take measures to get more specimens.[153] 'Monsters' handed in included an eight-legged lamb, a three-legged baby, a two-headed baby, a baby with its eyes under its nose and its ears below its neck, Siamese twins joined at the chest ('arms, legs, and heads normal'), a baby with a fish's tail, two dogs born to a sixty-year old virgin, and a baby with two heads, four arms, and three legs.[154] In April 1722 a search was ordered to be made in monasteries, especially the Trinity–St Sergius monastery, for old coins, stones, anything 'old and curious' (*staroe i kurioznoe*).[155] English merchants were told to purchase 'for our library and *Kunstkamera* instruments, books and other curious things' (*kurioznykh*).[156] Cabinet papers record that on 11 May 1722 'His Majesty ordered the payment of 30 roubles to Semen Shikov, peasant of the village of Senikov, for declaring a live female monster, by the name of Natalia Antonova, and to the peasant Mikhail Piskurin ... from whom that monster was taken, 20 roubles'.[157] Bergholz reported seeing live freaks by the names of Yakov, Stepan, and Foma in the museum. In 1724, however, Dr Blumentrost refused to accept another live monster on the grounds that 'in the *Kunstkamera* we keep only dead freaks'.[158]

IV. BOOKS AND READERS

Peter's reign has been associated with a printing 'revolution'. In the words of S. P. Luppov, the major Soviet specialist, 'The basic feature of publishing in the Petrine era was that it was completely devoted to the service of reforming the country. From here flows the clearly marked secular character of Petrine publications, the marked expansion of subject-matter and the appearance of new types of printed material ... and new genres.'[159] It is indeed a remarkable fact that in the last twenty-five years of Peter's reign 100 times more books, pamphlets, prints, maps, plans, and drawings were produced in Russia than in the whole of the previous century. Perhaps even more striking is the statistic that when Peter came to the throne, only three books 'not specifically religious' in character had been published by the Moscow press since its establishment in the 1560s: Melety Smotritsky's Slavonic grammar (1648), Tsar Alexis's Law Code of 1649, and the military manual *Kriegs-Kunst zu Fuss* by Jacobi, published in Russian in 1649 under the title that translates as *The Training and Art of Infantry*.[160] Some writers extend the list of pre-Petrine 'secular' works to include Pseudo-Basil I's *Exhortations to his Son Leo* (1661–3 and 1680), although it contains sections on faith and humility, and various alphabet primers (Burtsov's of 1634 and 1637, an anonymous one published in 1657, 1664, 1667, and 1669, Polotsky's of 1679, and Istomin's of 1696), even although they too had a dual purpose.[161] Multiplication tables (1682), customs tariffs and service regulations (1654), and a set of military instructions (1699) hardly affect the conclusion that publishing remained firmly in the service of the Church until the very end of the seventeenth century.[162] Even religious literature was not produced in great quantities; in the seventeenth century, Muscovite presses published fewer than 500 titles (supplemented by Slavonic titles published by presses in Kiev, Chernigov, Vilna, and elsewhere).[163] Manuscript literature covered a wider range of topics and reached a wider audience.

As in many other areas, the Grand Embassy was a turning point. Peter observed for himself the variety of materials printed in the West, and began to appreciate more clearly the usefulness of the printed word and of images, essential features of the 'paper' or 'pamphlet' war in seventeenth- and early eighteenth-century Europe, with which rulers and others won over public opinion or blackened the reputation of enemies. Russia had particular need of the modern media as a counterweight to European disparagement.[164] In 1698 a commission was issued to the translator Ilia Kopievich (Kopievsky) to prepare twenty-one titles by December 1699 for publication by the Amsterdam printer Johann van Thessing (Jan Tessing).[165] Peter's instructions of February 1700 give a clear indication of his purpose and priorities: 'in the town of Amsterdam [you are] to print European, Asian and American land and sea maps and charts and all manner of prints and portraits and books in the Slavonic and Dutch languages on land and naval troops, mathematics, arithmetic, architecture and townbuilding and other crafts.' These works were to be produced 'for the glory of the great sovereign and his tsardom ... for the general usefulness and profit of the nation and instruction in various crafts'.[166] Kopievich obtained a separate charter for printing books in Latin and Russian, which resulted in twelve titles, including panegyric verses and engravings relating to the Azov victory and a copy of the 1700 treaty with Turkey.[167] These arrangements, made while the patriarch was still alive, may represent an attempt on Peter's part to bypass the normal channels and church censorship at home in order to define clearly a secular publishing sphere. Magnitsky's book on mathematics, geometry, and navigation in 2,400 copies came out by this route.[168]

In publishing, as in other areas, public enthusiasm often lagged behind royal decree. Most of the books printed by Thessing and Kopievich had a poor circulation in Russia.[169] Even so, Peter was determined to expand publishing even further, and harnessed the resources of the Moscow Printing House (*pechatny dvor*, subsequently renamed *Moskovskaia tipografiia*), which in 1701 had twelve working printing-presses, three spare ones, and about fifty-eight titles (70,000 volumes) in store.[170] This he did in tandem with his reform of church administration following the death of Patriarch Adrian in October 1700. The Monastery department, a civil office created in 1701, took over the printing-house and placed all publishing under civil control.[171] Under the direction of F. P. Polikarpov the press began to produce secular books: logarithm tables (1703), lexicons, and official documents (1702).[172] The activities of the Moscow press were later augmented by the attachment to it of Pieter Pickart's engraving workshops.

The Moscow press was initially responsible for producing Russia's first 'newspaper', *Vedomosti*, created on 16 December 1702 to carry 'news about military and other affairs, which need to be made known to the people of the Muscovite realm and neighbouring states'. Suitable reports were to be sent from the government *prikazy* to the Monastery chancellery, and from there collated and sent to the printers.[173] The first issue was dated 2 January 1703. As a recent study demonstrates, *Vedomosti* was not exactly either a periodical or a newspaper: it appeared erratically, the title kept changing, and the size and number of pages varied (from 1 to 48), as did the type-setting. Up to February 1710 it was set in Church (Slavonic) type-face, in both Church and civil type from 1710 to 1715, thereafter only in civil script. Print runs varied from 30 to 4,000. It was probably influenced more by Polish 'flysheets' than by the Western periodical press, in its first three years averaging about three to four issues per month (whereas most Western newpapers came out in one or two issues per week), sometimes falling to one per year, or, conversely (in December 1722), appearing almost daily.[174] It was 'more a perpetual celebration of governmental authority and military glory than a newspaper in the modern sense'.[175] There was some correlation between content and popularity. For example, issues containing reports of the Battle of Poltava sold well, but by and large the paper mirrored official concerns rather than popular ones. The fact that about a third of the issues were distributed free indicates a shortage of voluntary subscribers. By the end of the reign, print runs were under a hundred. It is hard to imagine that even Peter's most devoted followers were much interested in, say, reports about the arrival and departure of merchant shipping; but to the outside world flourishing foreign trade signalled Russia's new status, just as translated news of foreign events signalled that Russia was part of a wider world. Needless to say, with high illiteracy rates among the population at large, the target audience consisted of government officials and army and navy officers.

Printing was one of a number of design areas—architecture, gardens, hydraulics—in which Peter took a personal interest. His orders for the new Military Statute (1716), for example, specified a type-face which would not make the volume too big for a man's pocket. The chapter headings and index were to be printed at the back, 'after the model of the book of French military rules or some other that the printer knows better'.[176] A landmark in secular publishing was the devising, with the tsar's active participation, of a new type-face for non-religious works, the so-called civil script (*grazhdanskii shrift*). The first version, ordered to be made in both Amsterdam and Moscow in 1707, consisted of thirty-three letters (with 'redundant' ones from church script excluded) in upper, middle, and lower case, based upon modern designs for Latin letters (a choice with clear cultural intentions). A team of printers came from Amsterdam to train Russian apprentices. Various type-faces were tried out and samples printed, and a revised *azbuka* (alphabet primer) was prepared for press in 1708. This new type was in use from March 1708 (the first book printed in it was A.-G. Burckhard von Pürkenstein's *Geometria slavenski zemlemerie* in Bruce's translation) until 1710.[177] On 29 January of that year a decree was published, the draft of which had Peter's own amendments (notably the reintroduction of a number of letters to increase the total to thirty-eight), accompanied by a hand-written instruction to print 'historical and manufactory books (*istoricheskiei manifakturnye knigi*) in this print'.[178] The first schedule of new books (1710) included works on the etiquette of letter-writing, geometry, locks, storming warfare, fortification, artillery, engineering, geography, history (Alexander the Great, the capture of Troy), calendars, descriptions of triumphal gates, and manifestos of the kings of Poland and Denmark.[179] The first books actually to be printed in the revised script were *Poverennye voinskie pravila* and *Pobezhdaiushchaia krepost'*, translations from Ernst-Friedrich Borgsdorf's works on siege warfare and fortification.

It is hard to agree that the two 'opposing' scripts were 'linked with the opposition of two cultures, Petrine and anti-Petrine' in an entirely consistent way, even though the effect of the reform was to 'clericalize' certain letters and to give civil publications a Latin orientation corresponding with a wider package of imperial Roman images and reflections which embellished the Petrine 'secular' state.[180] Civil script did not replace church script (*kirillitsa*). In fact, a third of the titles printed in the old script during Peter's reign were actually secular in content, such as laws and manifestos.[181] Ecclesiastical printing not only continued, notably of liturgical and devotional works, but was also considerably augmented. Moreover, the Church regained guardianship of the printed word. On 22 February 1721 a decree ordered that 'the St Petersburg, Moscow, Kiev, Chernigov and other typographies of the All-

Russian realm are to be under the direction of the holy ruling Synod'. In July 1721 Gavriil Buzhinsky, archimandrite of the Ipat'ev monastery, was appointed inspector of presses, 'for their better supervision'.[182] At least part of the reasoning behind the apparent restoration of secular publishing to the Church was Peter's determination that the Church should play an active educational role (as set out in the Ecclesiastical Regulation), as well as recognition that the most educated men in his country were churchmen, whose learning was to be harnessed to state service. The Synod was concerned not with restricting 'secular' works,[183] but with controlling unauthorized religious works, such as privately printed or manuscript prayers and paper icons, as well as Old Believer and other dissident literature. Inspections were made of bookshops and stalls.[184]

The first St Petersburg press was established in 1711 as a result of the transfer of machinery and staff from Moscow, at a time when many government personnel were beginning to make the move to the new capital. Its first publication (May 1711) was the St Petersburg *Vedomosti*. Subsequently, more presses and a team of engravers were transferred. Even in St Petersburg a Church press worked alongside two civil ones.[185] In turn, equipment from the St Petersburg press was transferred to the Senate (from 1719, printing mainly decrees, manifestos, and reports), the Alexander Nevsky monastery (operating from 1720, with strong input from Feofan Prokopovich, and producing textbooks, primers, grammars, and the second edition of the Ecclesiastical Regulation), and the Naval Academy (from 1721, issuing edicts of the Admiralty college, textbooks, and naval books).[186] By the end of Peter's reign there were eleven active official printing-houses. Outside the capitals, the presses in Kiev and Chernigov continued to be important. There were also presses in Riga and Reval, and even a travelling press which Peter took to Persia in 1722.[187] V. A. Kiprianov's press, established in May 1705 for the production of schoolbooks and graphics, was the sole 'private' publisher, but it, too, worked solely on government commissions, printing maps, tables, and drawings.[188] These included the 'New Globe of the World', a mathematical primer, and the so-called Bruce calendar. In other words, this was not private publishing in the Western sense, and there was no outlet for individual authors outside the state publishing service.

Despite all this effort, publishing output remained modest, private purchase was insignificant, and the actual reading of books may have been even less. Luppov's analysis of the output of presses between 1701 and 1724 lists 1,877 items, but this includes separate issues of *Vedomosti* and government decrees and manifestos often one or two sheets in length (the largest categories, 636 and 584 items). Some books were published in tiny print runs: a Russian–Dutch lexicon (1717) in forty-two copies and a German alphabet in just ten, although 1,200 copies remained the norm, as in the seventeenth century. The biggest print runs were for calendars and primers, for which there was genuine public demand (over 14,000 primers per year in 1722–4). Prokopovich's *First Lesson to Youths* (1720) was reprinted twelve times within four years (and continued to be reissued into the nineteenth century).[189] It seems unlikely that long print runs of political and propagandist literature, such as Shafirov's treatise on the causes of the Northern War (20,000 copies of the 1722 edition) or the Nystad peace treaty (5,000 copies in 1721, 20,000 in 1723), were much read. Some government announcements were distributed free—for example, the manifesto depriving Tsarevich Alexis of the throne.[190]

Analysis of the subject composition of 1,312 publications in 1700–25 indicates that laws and regulations accounted for 44 per cent (581 titles), official notices 14.6 per cent (192), religion 23.5 per cent (308), military affairs 7.9 per cent (104), calendars 1.8 per cent (24), *Vedomosti* 1.8 per cent (24), primers and language 1.7 per cent (22), history and geography 1.5 per cent (18), technology and science 1.1 per cent (14), secular philosophy 0.5 per cent (7), and *belles-lettres* 0.2 per cent (3). This list does not tell us what people actually read, nor does it indicate large print runs or repeat publications. Although religious literature accounted for 23.5 per cent of titles, it represented over 40 per cent of actual books and a large proportion of works purchased, notwithstanding received wisdom about the 'secularization' of culture. In fact, more religious books were published in Peter's reign than in the seventeenth century.[191]

Luppov placed just 208 titles in his religious category, and identified a further forty-six works of 'religious literature with secular motifs'.[192] In the light of Marker's figures, Luppov's claim that religious works accounted for only 14 per cent looks dubious. In fact, Luppov's own tables indicate that religious literature sold better than secular. In charts of sales for 1714–16 (the Moscow press bookshop) the best-sellers were primers at 3 copecks, followed by calendars, then by the schoolbook psalter (*Psaltyr' uchebnaia*), with more than 1,700 copies sold in one year compared with just one copy of Blondel's book on fortification (*Novaia manera ukrepleniia gorodov*) over the whole period. Price does not seem to have been the determining factor. A textbook on geography (*Geografiia ili kratkoe zemnogo kruga opisanie*) at 30 copecks attracted only 20 buyers, whereas the Prologue, despite the high cost of 4 roubles, 50 copecks, sold 197.[193]

Luppov remained unconvinced that books sold badly, especially when they came out in several editions, arguing that the main sales of practical manuals were in fact not through bookshops but direct to institutions. Figures for the St Petersburg bookshop certainly indicate rather better sales for foreign translations, but confirm the popularity of calendars, primers and religious literature, alongside the military and Naval Statutes (which were required reading for army and navy personnel) and other official manifestos and edicts, reflecting the different composition of the population in the old and new capitals. The discrepancy between distribution in St Petersburg and Moscow is underlined by figures for big print runs distributed free—for example, 1,950 of the 2,350 copies of the *Manifesto Depriving Alexis Petrovich of the Throne* were shifted in St Petersburg, but only half of the Moscow press's 11,000. Of *Justice of the Monarch's Right*, 5,100 of the St Petersburg copies were distributed, but only 3,000 of Moscow's 17,000 copies.[194] Outside these two centres, given lack of bookshops, low literacy rates, and low spending power, secular literature made little impact.

Marker's charts for books distributed 'fail to reveal a clear secularist or modernist trend'.[195] By and large, the popularity of calendars, alphabet books, and psalters shows continuity with sales in the seventeenth century. It is, of course, misleading to make a sharp distinction between the secular ('progressive') printed word and the sacred ('unprogressive'). Religious literature and writers also served the State. Sermons, prayers of thanksgiving for victories, and allegorical engravings (often with a mixture of biblical and mythological motifs) provided the essential theological underpinnings of autocracy in both sophisticated and simple form. Respect for authority was a constant message, even in such famed 'secular' works as the *Honourable Mirror of Youth*,[196] not to mention in the alphabet primers, in which faith, piety, and obedience were inculcated in young minds.

The verdict of the market was ultimately negative. The Moscow and St Petersburg presses were earning less combined in the 1720s than the Moscow press alone had in 1702.[197] In 1726 there was just 16 roubles in the coffers of the St Petersburg press and almost 21,000 roubles' worth of unsold stock. In Moscow in 1724 press wages were paid in books. In January 1725 the Synod proposed reducing the press's activity from fourteen presses to four ecclesiastical, two civil, and one for engravings.[198] In fact, in 1727 the St Petersburg and Alexander Nevsky presses were closed and the equipment was transferred to Moscow, for the printing of church books under Synod supervision. All civil publishing was concentrated in the Senate press and the Typography of the Academy of Sciences.[199] By 1728, as a result of huge deficits and unsold stock, Peter's publishing operation was all but dismantled. The late 1720s were a sort of publishing 'doldrums', when only about twenty books were published each year.[200]

The facts suggest that publishing was yet another area of Petrine activity where everything had to be done from above: policy was shaped by the tsar's priorities, with a strong input from the Church. With that in mind, let us look at some specific areas of publication. A subject in which the State showed an active interest was history. It would be wrong to say that there was no history of Russia before Peter, but earlier works, including Gizel's *Synopsis*, published in Kiev in 1674 and reissued well into the nineteenth century, tended to concentrate on ancient, legendary history and the medieval period. The use of *contemporary* national history as an aid to international publicity was well understood in Peter's reign. In the words of Fedor Saltykov, it was necessary to gather information about battles won, towns captured, treaties signed, and countries visited, to be translated into foreign languages 'for His Majesty's eternal praise for posterity'.[201] The first attempt to chronicle Peter's reign more or less as it unfolded, the 'History of the Swedish War' (*Gistoriia Sveiskoi voiny*), was started in 1711. This was a collective work with several editors—Makarov, Huyssen, Shafirov, Polikarpov, Prokopovich, and the tsar himself. After 1721 Peter set aside a morning each week, usually a Saturday, to complete the compilation.[202] Eight drafts survive, mostly with the tsar's corrections.[203] Weber reported that Huyssen finished a version ('a great Historical Work') in 1715, but it was not published.[204] Prokopovich at least attempted to write a history which went beyond military matters (post-1722), but only succeeded in producing a shortened version of the *Gistoriia*.[205] Both he and Peter were aware of the need to collect material more or less as it came into being. In August 1722 he wrote asking the tsar to have a proper account kept of the current Persian campaign, 'in order that your majesty's present campaign is described in detail and that where something distinguished occurs worthy to be included in the history it should not be overlooked but be all written down with necessary circumstances'. He recommended that the writing up be entrusted to Archimandrite Lavrenty of the Resurrection monastery, who was on the campaign, and would write 'without any ornamentation, in simple style'.[206] In 1724 Peter ordered the inclusion of all the greetings and congratulations received during his triumphal entry into Moscow in 1722.[207]

A number of works with a political purpose adopted a historical approach. Notable among them was Peter Shafirov's *Discourse Concerning the Just Causes of the War between Sweden and Russia* (1717), which delved into both recent history (Peter's visit to Riga in 1697) and more distant events (the history of Baltic towns from the Middle Ages) to establish the 'justness' of the war.[208] *The Book of Mars* (1713), a collection of materials (accounts and plans) on Russian victories published in several sections, had an equally clear political purpose,[209] as did F. I. Soimonov's unpublished 'History of Peter the Great'.[210]

A remarkable uncompleted project was I. Iu. Iur'ev's 'Book of Degrees' (*Iur'evskaia stepennaia kniga*), compiled in the Foreign chancellery in 1716–18. Three hundred and sixty-nine chapters set out Russian history from Riurik to Ivan IV (to 1563), the basis for which was the old sixteenth-century *Book of Degrees*, or royal genealogy. But Peter was dissatisfied and the book was never published.[211] The work of the 'new Chronicler', begun in the Monastery chancellery in 1703, tracing Russian history from its beginning to the 1700s, also came to nothing. The most far-ranging work, A. I. Mankiev's *Core of Russian History*, was not published until 1770, maybe because it devoted only a few pages to Peter's reign.[212] In 1712 Musin-Pushkin instructed Polikarpov to write 'a history of the Russian state ... but not from the beginning of the world and other states, as much has been written about this already'.[213] Even so, the old chronicle approach, in which current rulers and events were placed in the context of divine providence and their ancestral rights to rulership were underlined, prevailed. In 1717, for example, Feofan Prokopovich published a table of Russian rulers from Vladimir I to Peter, *Rodoslovnaia rospis' velikikh kniazei i tsarei rossiiskikh do gosudaria Petra I*. In 1720 Peter ordered Old Russian chronicles, documents, and 'historical books' to be collected from monasteries and preserved.[214] The first private collections of historical documents also date from Peter's reign (e.g., the collation of the future historian V. N. Tatishchev), as do archives. The *Razriad* (1711) and *Posol'skii prikaz*

(1720) papers formed the kernel of the archive of the College of Foreign Affairs.[215]

The vast majority of secular titles published in Peter's reign were not original Russian works but translations, a trend set in the seventeenth century, when most remained in manuscript. It may be an exaggeration to suggest that Peter himself translated whole books,[216] but he certainly took an interest in translation, seeing books through the press—for example, the Russian version of Vignola's *Five Orders of Architecture*.[217] He had a definite view of the translator's art:

> For the translation of books we urgently need translators, especially for crafts. Since no translator can translate unless he is familiar with the craft about which he is translating, therefore it is desirable to do things in the following way: those who know languages but not crafts should be given over to study the crafts; and those who know the crafts but not the language should be sent to study the language and they should be Russians or foreigners who either were born here or came here when very young and know our language like natives, because it is always easier to translate into your own language than from one's own into a foreign one.[218]

The 'crafts' mentioned were mathematics, mechanics, surgery, civil architecture, anatomy, botany, military science, and hydraulics.[219] In 1709 Peter rebuked Konon Zotov for his translation of Blondel's book on fortification: 'You need to translate more clearly, especially those passages which tell people how to do something, you mustn't keep the text word for word in the translation but having understood the sense (*sens*) write it as clearly as possible in your own language.'[220] In 1717 Musin-Pushkin wrote to F. Polikarpov, translator of Varenius's *Geographia generalis*, forwarding Peter's complaint that he had done it 'very badly' and demanding that he 'make thorough corrections not in high-flown Slavonic words but in simple Russian language'.[221] Stählin records an anecdote, supplied by Iaguzhinsky, about the tsar's anger with the translator of Pufendorf's *Introduction to the History of European States* because of the omission of some passages of criticism of Russia, which he ordered restored for the 'correction and instruction of his subjects'.[222] Competent translators were not always easy to find. In 1716 the Senate reported that it had been impossible to find a translator for the German version of the Military Statute in the Foreign Office or in St Petersburg as a whole, and they had sent it to Baron Huyssen, who replied that 'he didn't know Russian very well, but would do his best to translate it'.[223]

The contents of libraries and private collections echo the patterns already observed. In the seventeenth century libraries in the Kremlin, *prikazy*, monasteries, and private hands contained an overwhelming predominance of religious books, some with a proportion of foreign, even secular items—for example, in the collections of the Foreign Office and Prince Vasily Golitsyn. Peter's establishment of the 'first public library' in Russia, which formed the basis of the Academy of Sciences library, had a firmly secular emphasis, with almost 12,000 volumes by 1725. It was the result of a haphazard process, made up from collections of deceased associates such as Andrei Vinius and James Bruce, the dukes of Courland (died 1714, 2,500 books) and of Holstein, Archibald Pitcairn (1,906 books of a British writer, bought by Dr Erskine), and Erskine's own library (1718, 2,322 titles).[224] Weber wrote: 'If they continue to augment the pretious [sic] Library at Petersbourg, it may in a few Years be reckoned one of the best in Europe, if not for the Number of Books, at least on account of their Value.'[225] But in 1724 only five readers borrowed books.[226] Another large institutional library was the Typography collection, comprising more than 3,000 items (in the 1727 catalogue), of which the majority were in foreign languages. A landmark in Russian publishing was the issue in 1723 of a catalogue of Greek manuscripts in the libraries of the Synod and Typography, published in Russian and Latin and in Leipzig in Latin in 1724. In his introduction, the compiler compared the Synod library to famous libraries in Rome, Paris, Oxford, and Vienna.[227]

Some of the more impressive private collections belonged to 'reformed' nobles who had worked abroad, including D. M. Golitsyn's estimated 3,000 volumes (inventories dating from Golitsyn's exile and death after 1737), of which 75 per cent were foreign, a third in French, and a considerable number in Latin. Subjects included works on parliaments and constitutions, political thinkers, history (especially the history of Poland), Classical authors, and law. Even in this sophisticated collection 50 per cent of the Russian titles were religious.[228] Andrei Matveev owned more than 1,300 books, some 80 per cent of them foreign.[229] Leading churchmen also owned books in foreign languages and some secular works: for example, Dmitry of Rostov's collection included a sizeable number of books on history, Stefan Iavorsky owned many Latin books (more than 73 per cent of his collection, as one would expect of an academy-educated man). Feodosy Ianovsky's included many on jurisprudence and politics (probably translated for him, as he did not know foreign languages). Gavriil Buzhinsky's library was 80 per cent foreign, mainly Latin, including works on politics, philosophy, and history. Feofil Krolik likewise owned mainly foreign books.[230] Not surprisingly, the prize collection belonged to Feofan Prokopovich, which after his death went to the Novgorod seminary. Listed in the catalogue are 3,192 titles, the vast majority in foreign languages, mainly Latin, German, and Polish, of which some 948 were theological, another 500 'historical', 360 'philosophical' (including mathematics, astronomy, geography, physics, medicine, astrology, and anatomy), 500 juridical, and 600 'scholastic' (works by Calvin, Erasmus, Homer, Cicero, Ovid, and other classical authors). Only 44 were in Slavonic.[231] The tsar's own library gives graphic evidence of how the fairly limited output of Russian presses also had to be supplemented by foreign imports. It contained as many as 50 per cent foreign titles.[232]

V.   LITERATURE AND LANGUAGE

The American author of a study of eighteenth-century Russian literature records the response of one colleague to the project: 'Why, is there any?'[233] Certainly literary genres are more conspicuously absent from Petrine publication statistics (accounting for just 0.2 per cent of titles[234]), than from those for the eighteenth century as a whole, which accords well with received wisdom about the 'utilitarian' atmosphere of Petrine Russia, with its impatience with trifles and 'mere' entertainment. In the words of one writer, 'Peter and poetry is a completely contradictory concept'.[235] Peter tried his hand at other arts, including architecture, garden design, and engraving, but he does not seem to have attempted versification (unlike his predecessor Tsar Fedor, who is said to have composed Latin verse under Polotsky's guidance) or writing plays (a pastime enjoyed by his 'spiritual daughter' Catherine II). To concentrate on printed books, of course, gives a distorted picture of what was written and read in early eighteenth-century Russia. Petrine publications hardly catered at all for readers of tales and stories, chronicles, saints' lives, and other such religious works, not to mention dissident religious literature. Copyists stepped in to meet demand, sometimes even transcribing printed books into cheaper manuscripts. Stories popular in the seventeenth century or earlier were re-copied, such as the tales of Frol Skobeev, Bova Korolevich, Uruslan Lazarevich, Varlaam and Josaphat, 'The Tale of the White Cowl' and 'The Tale of the Seven Wise Men'. Even the tsar's library contained almost 300 Russian titles in manuscript.[236] Peter apparently enjoyed tales from history and adventures, although little evidence of his lighter reading habits survives. He is said to have taken the tale of Peter and Fevronia (about the love of a prince for a peasant) with him on his Persian campaign.[237] The two best-known examples of Petrine prose tales are the 'History of the Russian Sailor Vasily Koriotsky and the Beautiful Queen Iraklia of the Land of Florence' and the much longer 'History of the Valiant Russian Cavalier Alexander and his Mistresses Tira and Eleonora'. Both are unsophisticated pieces (Brown describes the latter as 'an artistic failure of catastrophic proportions'[238]) which fuse travellers' tales, love interest, and exotic detail with some contemporary elements. Young sailors are sent to Holland to study 'arithmetical sciences and various languages'; valiant Alexander wishes 'to enjoy foreign states with his own eyes' and to study their 'polite manners'; but in the end both heroes found themselves distracted from 'science' by amazing adventures and love affairs.[239]

Panegyric, celebratory verse was the dominant poetic genre of the Petrine era—poetry harnessed to the service of the State, much of it occasional. Commonly the Petrine era has been included in an extended 'age of the Baroque', from the seventeenth to the mid-eighteenth century. Not only was its literary style heavy with emblems and allusions, but the 'Baroque' notions of life in flux and of transitoriness were particularly appropriate to an age of war and reform.[240] The trend began with syllabic verse borrowed from Poland

and developed at the Muscovite court by Simeon Polotsky and his successors Silvester Medvedev and Karion Istomin. Polotsky's *Rifmologion* collection (1679), which contained the eulogy 'The Russian Eagle', and his 'Vertograd mnogotsvetnii', an anthology of poetic subjects (neither was published), set the tone and provided models for declamatory verse, odes, epigrams, and narrative poems.[241] It is verses of this kind which Andrei Vinius, organizer of the celebrations for the 1696 Azov victory, proclaimed through a megaphone from the top of the triumphal gates, and which Feofan Prokopovich and other churchmen penned to suit the occasion.

Virtually all the known exponents of 'high' literature in Peter's reign were churchmen, not surprisingly, given the still low level of education and the lack of time for versifying of the only other generally literate classes, nobles and 'bureaucratic specialists'. Dmitry Tuptalo, bishop of Rostov, was famed for his sermons and poetry as well as drama. But it is significant that his most enduring work was the *Reading Menaea* (*Cheti Minei*), a religious anthology. Stefan Iavorsky wrote poems in both Slavonic and Latin and a textbook on rhetoric. The major writer of the Petrine era was Feofan Prokopovich. A typical piece of Petrine poetry is his *Epinikion* (1709) in praise of Poltava, a poem in the epic style. It includes Classical allusions ('Already the war was entering its tenth year / (The time of the Trojan war)') and references to Peter as the 'Russian Mars' and some striking images ('A terrible glimmer, terrible and great / Hail of iron is falling').[242]

The activity of Russia's first successful secular author, Antiokh Kantemir (1708–44), post-dated Peter's death, although it is significant that he, like many of Russia's major eighteenth-century writers, penned his own tribute to the emperor, *Petrida*, which affirmed allegiance to the principle of absolute monarchy. Other writers of the next generation, such as Vasily Trediakovsky (1703–69) and Mikhail Lomonosov (1711–65), were likewise products of Peter's reforms and avid admirers of the emperor.

Thus, although Peter's reign undoubtedly represented a new chapter in Russian secular publishing, there was still no publishing on a Western scale (no private presses, no catering for the market, whole genres missing). The output of, and demand for, religious books did not diminish, while nearly all the secular works published, and some of the religious ones, were linked to the needs of the State. The readership for printed books was far outweighed by that for manuscript books. In fact, the reading public for printed books of the type pushed through the press by Peter was minimal. Serious doubt must be cast on Luppov's hypothesis about the 'democratization' of readership through ever wider social strata, a trend which he identifies from the seventeenth century onwards.[243] Why did secular printing face near-collapse when Peter died? Clearly because a large number of the books published reflected the tsar's view of what was important, regardless of potential readership. A case in point is the numerous editions of *General Signals* for the fleet, the proliferation of which can hardly be justified by actual need. Papers in Peter's own hand confirm that Peter loved playing around with signals. His own library contained no fewer than eighteen versions, for both galley and ship fleets.[244] Similarly, works such as Minno von Koehorn's *Novoe krepostnoe stroenie*, 1,000 copies of which were published (2nd edition), were perhaps never really intended to be widely read. But the very fact of the existence of such books in Russia signified new priorities and values; they were *symbols* of modernity. This is why someone like Menshikov who could not even read required a large library. Books on technology and science had a semiotic value, like Western dress and buildings. Marker, too, concluded that the impact of the reform was 'far more muted' than that suggested by Luppov and others.[245] Whether people actually read materials is not always the point. Thus the very scale of production and dissemination of government decrees and notices (negligible in the previous century) 'engendered in the populace a clearer vision of the connection between the (mostly disagreeable) changes that they were experiencing and the will of the tsar', even when the parish priest, not to mention the mass of villagers, was incapable of interpreting the decrees. These pieces of paper brought the 'voice of the state' into the provinces, thereby constituting a 'powerful instrument of secularization'.[246]

The influx of foreigners into Russia and Russian trips abroad, and the need to translate manuals and textbooks on new skills, had an impact on the Russian language to an extent matched only in recent times, when the language of twentieth-century technology, commerce, and popular culture almost threatens to swamp native expression.[247] Then, as now, Western influence was not unheralded: examples of earlier borrowings include military vocabulary—the *reitari* and *draguny* of the new infantry (*soldatskie*) regiments (dating from 1630s) led by *kapitany*, *generaly*, and so on. Architectural terms like *baza* and *kaptel'* make their appearance from the 1650s. Under Peter, words were suddenly needed where none had been before, notably the word for 'fleet'.[248] The Naval Statute explains that the word (*flot* in Russian) was French: 'By this word is meant a lot of water-going vessels travelling along together, or standing, both military and merchant.' The titles of naval crew included *shkiper*, *shtiurman*, *botsman*, *michman*, *kvartir meister*, *kupor*. Long lists of tackle, ropes, and sails indicate that in many cases terms were simply transcribed direct—'oit en in galder', 'for-mars-zeil', and so on.[249] Italian, Dutch, and English were the main sources for the language of navigation (*navigatsiia ili moreplavanie*, as a manuscript attributed to Farquharson explains).[250] Of some 3,500 new foreign borrowings, roughly 25 per cent were shipping and naval terms, 25 per cent administrative, and 25 per cent military.[251] Swedish provided many words for administrative affairs, as one would expect, given the extensive borrowing from Swedish texts and practice for the reorganization of both central and local government in 1718–19, although, as Peterson points out, many Swedish terms themselves had German roots. Examples include the names of the colleges—*berg- i manufaktur*, *kammer-revizion*, and so on—and officials (*landgevding* from *landhövding*). The *shtats-kontor-kollegiia* (from Swedish *statskontoret*) was manned by officials with more or less the same titles as their Swedish equivalents: *sekretar'*, *kamerir, aktuar, notar, bukhgalter, kamornyi shreiber, kantslist* and *kopist.* [252] Foreign medical terms made their appearance. Alongside the Russian *lekar'* (from *lechit'*, 'to cure') we find *dokhturstvo, dokhtur,* and *shpital'* (field hospital).[253] Russian and foreign terms coexisted until one or other prevailed. The Russian for 'spinning mill' is normally *priadel'nyi dom,* but in the 1722 instruction to the Moscow police superintendent, *shpingaus* (from the Dutch) is used.[254] This sort of change must have caused confusion. There are also striking gaps: for example, economic and business terminology provides few examples, such as *bankir, ekonom,* and *ekonomiia.*[255]

The unfamiliarity—not to say incomprehensibility—of many of the new terms is underlined by the inclusion of glossaries in some official publications. The General Regulation ends with an explanatory list of foreign words, including *interes, publichnyi, rezoliutsiia, direktsiia, report, respekt, kharakter,* and *instruktsiia.*[256] To the modern-day speaker of English these are all comprehensible without translation, but not to the average Russian official ca.1720. Although all had Slavonic equivalents, as listed (e.g., *interes = pribytok i pol'za*), clearly a change of language signified a change of practice. It may be going too far to claim that Russian was 'too poor and clumsy for the richness and subtlety of thought which [Western] philosophy [*filosofiia,* another loan-word] had attained', but there was certainly a lot of catching up to do.[257] In many cases the foreign word used preceded comprehension of the object or concept it signified. Old practices were 'dressed up' and 'disguised' in new terms, in much the same way as the post-reform government officials bore new names and wore Western dress. Even the regulation itself bore two titles, a foreign one followed by a Slavonic one: *reglament ili ustav.*

Many Petrine borrowings, especially Latin-based abstract nouns, remain in the vocabulary today. Others came into and went out of fashion, or were peculiar to individuals. Curious examples can be found in the works of Prince Boris Kurakin, who spent many years abroad. His writings (from the 1720s) are full of French loans: *uvrazh, proklemavat', konsideratsiia, opiniia, povoir, domestik,* to name but a few.[258] Princess Kurakina is said to have used 'so many French and Italian words with Russian endings, that the native Russians had a harder time understanding her than foreigners'.[259] Isolated examples catch the eye in letters of the period. In 1716 V. L. Dolgoruky, who had once lived in France, wrote to Catherine asking her to intervene on behalf of his uncle B. P. Sheremetev, who was in disgrace with Peter. He refers to the *afront* suffered by Boris Petrovich, who was 'in despair' (*v takoi on desperatsii*).[260] In 1711 G. I. Golovkin wished for 'good success' (*dobrogo suktsesu*) in the forthcoming clash with Turkey.[261] Peter himself was not immune: in a letter of 10 September 1722 he wrote: 'when the enemy is weak it is natural good sense to stop and get on with the business' (*natural'nyi rezon est' ostanovittsa i dela delat*).[262] In February 1720 he wrote to senators about the drafts of the Ecclesiastical Regulation. If something seemed wrong, they were to append remarks (*remarki*) and to each remark add an explanation (*eksplikatsiia*).[263] His favourite foreign terms were to do with ships and navigation.

In March 1721 he reminded Apraksin to dispatch ships to Riga as soon as the ice began to break, 'by the first wind, for you are well aware of this channel (*farvater* from the Dutch), if you miss the wind then much is lost'.[264]

Many Russians made great strides in learning foreign languages, notably those sent abroad on diplomatic missions and for study. The course of foreign relations and contacts meant that German was more current than French (in 1733 the Noble Cadet Corps had 51 pupils studying French, but 237 taking German),[265] although Russian remained firmly the language of the court, not least because the tsar himself was not a fluent speaker of any foreign language. De la Neuville's claim that only one person knew French and four Latin in the whole of Russia[266] was no longer valid by the 1720s, but the French-speaking nobleman who had all but forgotten his native tongue, a phenomenon of the late eighteenth and early nineteenth centuries (epitomized in Tolstoy's *War and Peace*) was rare during Peter's reign.

V.   CONCLUSION

Disagreement continues about Petrine educational, scientific, and publishing achievements. It is hard to accept Luppov's conclusion that 'in the Petrine era the level of knowledge of leading Russians [whom he called, in true Soviet fashion, the "secular intelligentsia"] reached the level of advanced learning in the West', any more than the sweeping statements about Russians keeping up with the latest in foreign publication and having an excellent knowledge of languages.[267] Such Russians were the exception rather than the rule, and even some of the better educated, as we have seen, were far from being 'secularized'. Peter's reign was understandably lacking in thinkers or scholars of international repute. The more notable writers nearly all turn out to have foreign elements in their background—Bruce and Shafirov, Prokopovich and Dmitry of Rostov, and Kantemir. And notwithstanding attempts to turn Peter himself into a thinker and inventor (see, e.g., the claim that Peter thoroughly deserved the honour of his election to the French Academy of Sciences in 1717[268]), he has no claim to any truly original inventions or theories. In matters scientific, as in so much else, Peter was an enthusiastic amateur. But in science and learning, again as in other areas, backwardness could be turned to some advantage by the issue of imperial decrees. In the words of the French geographer Guillaume Delisle, Peter was 'a prince renowned for his love of science as much as for his great talent in the art of government'.[269] He was recognized as 'an indefatigable investigator and unsparing disseminator of all arts and sciences beneficial to mankind'.[270] Petrine science and learning, like Petrine art and architecture, were a public, propagandist exercise. The idea that Russia was a 'blank sheet' before Peter came along made even modest achievements seem remarkable. The state loudly publicized its role in the civilizing process. To take but one example, in the print *A New or Visual Aid to Arithmetical Theory* (V. O. Kiprianov's press, 1705) what strikes the viewer first of all are not the sections on addition and subtraction in the centre but the double-headed eagle, baroque cartouches, and architectural framework above and plans of the Moscow and St Petersburg fortresses below. The impression is of a triumphal arch rather than an educational aid, which is perhaps what was intended.[271]

These reservations aside, the seeds of a future native 'intelligentsia' were surely sown in Peter's reign. A 'scholarly band' (*uchenaia druzhina*) has been identified among Petrine supporters, who came into their own in the immediate post-Petrine period.[272] This includes Antiokh Kantemir, Vasily Tatishchev, A. M. Cherkassky, I. Iu. Trubetskoy, A. F. Khrushchev and Vasily Trediakovsky, as well as Gavriil Buzhinsky and Feofan Prokopovich. The latter's plea for the reconciliation of modern scientific theories with the Scriptures, which needed to be taken 'not literally but allegorically', has a modern ring.[273] Several of these men were associated with 'firsts' in Russian cultural history—Kantemir with poetry, Tatishchev with history, Trediakovsky with the reform of versification. One might add to this list Mikhail Lomonosov, who in 1731 entered the Moscow Academy. His achievements ranged over chemistry, physics, history, poetry, mosaics, and philology. Although he may not have been Peter's natural son (a legend which is easily discounted[274]), he was undoubtedly Peter's spiritual offspring.

10

Religion

There is a straight path to salvation—through faith, hope and charity —but people know very little, or wrongly, about the first and the last, and haven't even heard of the middle one, since they place all their hope in singing in church, fasting and bowing and so forth, in the building of churches, candles and incense. They believe that the suffering of Christ was caused only by original sin; in fact, they will obtain salvation as a result of their own deeds.[1]

I.   THE RELIGIOUS INHERITANCE

The Russian Orthodox Church at the end of the seventeenth century presents a contradictory picture. On the one hand, it had been weakened by the schism which resulted from Patriarch Nikon's reforms in the 1650s. Valuable resources had to be deployed to check dissidents, and Nikon's personal humiliation at the hands of the secular authorities demonstrated where the real power lay when patriarch tried to compete with tsar. On the other hand, the old notion of the 'parallelism' or 'symphony' of the State and the Church had not been revoked officially. The statement made at the church council of 1667 that 'the tsar has pre-eminence in secular matters, the patriarch in eccle-siastical' held good.[2] The office of patriarch still had sufficient authority to allow the holder to intervene in a national crisis, as when Joachim helped to engineer Peter's election to the throne in April 1682 and supported him in 1689. Despite some limitations on its ability to acquire land, the Church remained a substantial proprietor, owning about a fifth of all peasants in the realm. The 1678 census showed that 148,997 peasant households—on a rough calculation, about 525,000 souls—were owned by the patriarch, higher clergy, monasteries, and cathedrals.[3] Under Peter, as we shall see, this figure was to rise rather than fall: by the time of the first census of 1719–21 the number of the Church's male souls had grown to 791,085. The 'ecclesiastical order' of monastic and secular clergy numbered about 86,300 persons. During Peter's reign there was a total of twenty-six bishoprics, including four in Left Bank Ukraine, although not all survived.[4] Perhaps most important, to be Russian was to be Orthodox. (The tsar's non-Orthodox subjects were classified as *inovertsy*—'people of other faiths'.) In the last decades of the seventeenth century the Church continued to exert a strong, decisive influence over the everyday lives of all Russians, from the tsars down to their humblest subjects, not only in matters of devotion and morals but also in appearance, eating habits, and customs. But the strength and nature of this influence were already being redefined.

No one reading Patriarch Adrian's long set of instructions to provincial clergy issued in 1697 would have suspected the storm that was about to buffet the Church. Intended to be read out to priests, deacons, and junior deacons, it dealt with diverse matters: services should be conducted from the revised (Nikonian) books, with the correct number of properly baked communion loaves of good wheat flour; the sanctuary must be swept of dust and cobwebs; oil for baptisms must be kept in clean containers, and baptism must be by full immersion. Parishioners must attend church to make their confession at the very least before the major fasts, 'and stand in church decently and quietly, with awe, and listen to the divine service attentively, and pray to the Lord God to forgive their sins'. Persistent absentees were to be reported. Suicides and people killed while committing murder or robbery were not to be buried in sanctified ground. Priests were admonished to observe the ban on close degrees of consanguinity in marriage, and to ensure that people asking to be married were not deserters or fugitive peasants. The document ended: 'See to it that town and village priests and deacons do not go to the tavern and drink liquor and misbehave with the result that laymen are led into temptation, and that priests and deacons don't keep drink in their houses or vessels for drinking.' Violators of these rules were to be fined and sent to work in a monastery for a month.[5] Adrian's list included issues which church authorities had been addressing for centuries. It also contained measures which Peter himself later reinforced in his own fight against dissidents, such as the systematic reporting on those who failed to attend church. Peter was to endorse the Church's policing role among the population at large, and encourage measures aimed at improving the quality of the clergy. There was little here to suggest a clash of interests.

Patriarchal invectives against foreigners were quite a different matter. In his testament Joachim (patriarch from 1674 to 1690) wrote: 'May our sovereigns never allow any Orthodox Christians in their realm to entertain any close friendly relations with heretics and dissenters—with the Latins, Lutherans, Calvinists and godless Tatars (whom our Lord abominates and the Church of God damns for their God-abhorred guile); but let them be avoided as enemies of God and defamers of the Church.'[6] These words were written at a time when Peter was employing foreign officers to train his own 'play' regiments and had several close foreign friends. They signalled an inevitable clash between a ruler who sought to open Russia up to useful influences from outside and a Church which lived in fear of foreign 'guile'. Joachim's successor Adrian ranted against shaving just as beardless Peter was about to embark on his campaign to introduce Western fashions. The Church's objection to shaving rested on two main arguments: the word and example of God and tradition. As Adrian wrote, the practices observed by his predecessors were taken from the Church Fathers, 'and I am obliged to follow them in everything and proclaim their teachings'. Elsewhere he echoed Joachim in warnings to reject and repudiate all 'newly introduced foreign customs' and to protect the Orthodox faith from 'Latin and Lutheran heretics'. Orthodox Russians must resist all the tempting, corrupting teachings and customs of the Latins, Lutherans, and Calvinists, and not associate with them, but abhor and shun them as wicked men.[7] In the same missive, Adrian reiterated the Byzantine concept of the symphony of the spiritual and the temporal power: 'God has established two higher authorities on earth: the priesthood and the tsardom.' If faith demanded, the temporal power could be censured: 'True pastors do not subordinate themselves to strong men nor do they show shame before rich men, but must denounce, beseech and censure those who live badly.' All Orthodox Christians must respect, love, and fear the tsar; but they carried his sword for the sake of salvation, not destruction, and must fear God and do his holy will. Adrian's formulation was close to that of Nikon: although the royal authority had power on earth, the priesthood had power on earth *and* in heaven. All Orthodox Christians were the patriarch's 'spiritual sons', including the monarch himself: 'All Orthodox Christians are my sheep and know me and obey my voice.'[8]

Peter was to do battle with the Church's claims to wield power over men's lives as well as their souls, for the Church thereby challenged the State's need for a free hand in deploying resources, both human and material, native and foreign. The results were to be radical. It is hard to disagree with James Cracraft's conclusion that 'of all the achievements of Peter's reign his church reform constituted the most decisive break with the past'.[9] Even so, Peter did not 'secularize' Russia in the way that the Soviet Communists later tried to secularize it, declaring religion to be the 'opium of the people', demolishing churches, imprisoning priests, and persecuting believers. Rather, Peter firmly subordinated the priesthood to the tsardom, a process which had already gained momentum under his predecessors. He also, by his actions and priorities, if not always by unambiguous ideological statements, subordinated spiritual goals to secular ones. The tsar's main function was no longer primarily to facilitate the salvation of souls and to advance the coming of God's kingdom by maintaining a pious, well-ordered earthly realm, but actively to pursue worldly goals for their own sake: winning wars and glory, promoting both the 'common good' and personal fame. Peter looked to the more distant past for examples of the danger to the national welfare posed by Byzantine-style theocracy, which allegedly placed too much emphasis on the saving of souls, too little on armies. The result for Byzantium, he warned, was the fall of Constantinople in 1453.[10]

This readjustment of public values was facilitated by the curtailment of the Church's near monopoly in such spheres as publishing and the arts and a redefinition of its role in others, such as education and charity. To take some cases in point, religious publishing was not diminished, nor were church building and icon painting discontinued—on the contrary, both flourished—but secular books, civic buildings, and non-religious art received a greater share of attention and resources than in the past. In areas which it had once dominated, such as public ceremonial, the Church was obliged to cede centre-stage or at least share the limelight with secular rites. Church bells competed with ceremonial cannon-fire; processions of priests were escorted by columns of soldiers. The Church was also expected to keep its nose out of areas where once it had wielded moral authority. In an anecdote about the negotiation of tobacco contracts in London in 1698, Peter declared that the patriarch would do well not to interfere: 'He is only the guardian of the faith, not a customs inspector.'[11] The same source underlines that Peter was ever conscious of the troubles his father had by allowing Nikon too much power at the beginning of his patriarchate: 'The bearded ones, monks and priests, are the root of much evil. My father had to deal with just one of them, but I with thousands.'[12] These fears are confirmed by Georg Grund, who linked the alleged attempts of Nikon to 'become pope' with Peter's decision in 1700 to suspend the patriarchate, 'in order to rid himself of any dependence on the clergy'.[13] Let us begin by investigating the background behind that decision.

II. THE 1690s: PRELUDE TO REFORM

Peter's policies towards the Church were not formulated, still less implemented, all at once. Churchmen may have noticed the adolescent Peter's impatience with some of the more tedious trappings of Orthodox piety, especially by comparison with his devout co-ruler Ivan, who was apparently happy to attend interminable services; but they had little cause to anticipate the onslaught to come. Peter did not intervene in 1689–90 when Joachim increased restrictions on foreigners, and took no action when his preferred candidate was not made patriarch in 1690, although he no doubt bore in mind (given the centrality of educated clergymen to his later church reform) that one of the reasons for the rejection of Metropolitan Markell of Pskov, according to Patrick Gordon, was that 'he had too much learning, and so they feared and said he would favour the Catholick and other religions'.[14] Cracks began to appear during and immediately after the 1695–6 Azov campaigns, which revealed potential conflict between the claims of Church and State to vital resources. Church hierarchs were forbidden to collect taxes, and monasteries to carry out new building projects: 'No superfluous buildings are to be constructed and no expenditure made without the great sovereign's orders.' Monasteries were required to supply annual returns on their revenues, in both money and grain, to the department of the Royal Household.[15] Priests were obliged to contribute funds to building the fleet at Voronezh, the so-called ship tax (*korabel'naia povinnost*) introduced in 1696, as well as to supply recruits for the army under the provisions of a decree of November 1699.[16]

The Church also lost various exemptions and privileges: for example, its share of the income from trade duties collected from markets and fairs on church land was restricted, as was the right to distil spirits, already curtailed in the 1680s. Duty on stamped paper, introduced in 1699, was applied to the Church too.[17] Peter personally facilitated the transfer of funds from Church to State by borrowing money from churchmen and not paying it back. In 1694–9 the wealthy Trinity–St Sergius monastery 'lent' Peter sums amounting to 127,500 roubles, including loans earmarked for troops and shipbuilding.[18]

These moves probably provoked annoyance rather than fear of radical change. The Church was used to rulers encroaching on its funds and disputing its proprietorial rights. To quote but one example, the 1551 Council of a Hundred Chapters (on the eve of Ivan IV's campaign against Kazan') ordered, among other things, the return of some church lands to secular ownership, a reduction in the financial privileges of monasteries, and restrictions on gifts of land to monasteries.[19] The Church was much less prepared for the turn of events in autumn 1698, when the tsar, who had already offended his devout subjects by going abroad and consorting openly with foreigners, began to introduce innovations which seriously violated religious sensibilities —cutting off beards, imposing a foreign dress code, and tampering with the calendar. The impact of these changes, on the eve of the Great Northern War, is summed up in Johannes Korb's observation: 'Nor has the authority of the clergy remained intact; for formerly they occupied without dispute the first places of honour in all public assemblies, but now their dignity has grown so vile that they are seldom, or at least only like laymen, admitted to table. . . . They are in dread, and not without reason, of being shaken from the axis of their fortune, and lest they shall reign no longer than they can succeed in keeping the populace and nation, by means of superstitious doctrine or contempt for science, in ignorance and benighted error.'[20]

Korb and other foreign observers (who tended to be dismissive of Orthodoxy) regarded Peter's willingness to borrow from other religions, especially their own, as 'enlightened'. His exposure to Protestants and Catholics, despite dire warnings from the patriarchs, started with contacts in the Foreign Quarter, and continued on travels abroad. There were meetings with Quakers in London in 1698,[21] conversations with Bishop Gilbert Burnet, who touched upon monarchical supremacy over the Church, the disposal of church lands, the appointment of bishops, and a king's duty to look after the interests of the nation and subjects, which no doubt struck a welcome chord.[22] Peter was impressed by Lutheran services and sermons. Some Protestant observers even interpreted the abolition of the patriarchate and the accompanying elevation of Peter as 'head of the Church' as a move towards Protestantism. An anonymous German tract published in 1725 stated: 'We know that His Tsarist Majesty in the depths of his heart is completely convinced of the truth of the Evangelical-Lutheran church and religion. . . . In the manner of Protestant princes he has declared himself as the highest bishop of his country.'[23] The notion of results (and ultimately salvation) by works as well as by divine grace or miracle also permeates much of Peter's thinking. Individual morality (and the Church's duty to foster it) was valued more highly than the mysteries of religion. A French representative in St Petersburg reported a gathering for the feast of St Catherine in 1719 at which Peter spent time discussing various issues with churchmen. 'He was convinced that the great number of fasts and ceremonies which they observed were not as agreeable to God as a contrite and humble heart. Finally he exhorted them to preach morality to the people above all else and then little by little superstition would be banished from his realms and God would be better served by his subjects and he more loyally.'[24]

Catholics, too, harboured hopes for the future. Proposals for uniting the Orthodox and Catholic Churches were discussed in the Sorbonne in 1717.[25] Weber thought it improbable that Peter, having suppressed the patriarchate, would subordinate himself to 'a far greater Dependency' on the Pope, not to mention stumbling-blocks to union such as married Orthodox clergy.[26] (He might also have pointed to Russians' deep-seated antipathy to Uniates (Catholics of the Byzantine Rite) in the Polish Commonwealth.) In the event, a non-committal reply was sent back to Paris in 1718, referring to ties with other Orthodox nations and the 'temporary' vacancy of the patriarchal throne in Russia as reasons for inaction. By this time, a major reform was in progress which was to sweep away the patriarchate for the next 200 years.

III.   CHURCH ADMINISTRATION, 1700–1725

On 16 October 1700 Patriarch Adrian died, and a *locum tenens* was appointed to the patriarchal throne. It was quite usual to make an interim appointment while an election was organized. The recent declaration (in August) of war against Sweden gave ample grounds for delaying a decision. Peter was preparing for the seige of Narva when he received the news of the patriarch's death.[27] But there was a hint of things to come when instead of the metropolitan of Krutitsky, who usually held the fort when a patriarch died, Peter chose his own man, Stefan Iavorsky, who early in 1700 was still a 'simple abbot' in Ukraine, and was promoted to the metropolitanate of Riazan' only in March. It is unlikely that anyone familiar with Peter's views was surprised at his reluctance to fill the vacancy. Stählin recounts an anecdote: Peter, tired of being pestered with requests to make an appointment, beat his breast and yelled (according to another version, flinging a dagger on the table) 'Here's your patriarch'.[28] No discussion about the abolition of the patriarchate was recorded at the time, but there were pressing reasons why both Peter and members of his circle were anxious to divert some of the wealth of the Church into State hands and to curtail some of its powers. In November 1700 the Russians were humiliatingly defeated by the Swedes at Narva. This was a time to consolidate resources for the war effort. Peter's thinking on the patriarchate may have been influenced by the future 'profiteer' Aleksei Kurabatov, who wrote to the tsar on 25 October 1700 advising him to appoint a stopgap and take the opportunity to review and list all church lands without patriarchal interference and hand them over to a 'special *prikaz*'.[29]

Sure enough, January 1701 saw the abolition of the patriarchal court (*patriarshii razriad*) and the creation of a Monastery department (*monastryrskii prikaz*) to supervise church courts and run church lands under the supervision of a secular official, the tsar's close friend and relation Ivan Musin-Pushkin. The new department was to act, except in spiritual matters, as the 'sole master' of all the church estates and their population.[30] It was to collect revenues 'not with the aim of ruining the monasteries' but 'to aid the fulfilment of monastic vows'. In the past, a decree noted, monks were 'industrious and made their bread by their own labour and fed many beggars by their own labour, but the present-day monks not only do not feed beggars with their labours but themselves live off the work of others'. Income was separated into two categories, one 'assigned' portion (*opredelennye*) to be used for the upkeep of the monks, the other (*neopredelennye* or *zaopredelennye*) to go straight into state coffers for the upkeep of almshouses or for redistribution to poorer monasteries. The allocation per head, regardless of status, was ten roubles and ten chetverts of grain per annum.[31] In the words of Weber, 'when the unfortunate War against Sweden required vast Sums of Money, all the Church Lands were taken from the Bishops and the Monasteries by the Advice of the Privy-Counsellor Count Mussin Puschkin, and united to the Czar's Demesnes'.[32] The Soviet scholar Bulygin concluded that in 1701 a 'complete secularization' of church lands and property was effected, arguing that although the Church formally continued to own the lands, this right had become a 'pure fiction'.[33] In fact, Peter stopped short of secularization (started by his daughter Empress Elizabeth, continued by Peter III, and implemented by Catherine II in 1764), and subsequently restored some of the Church's rights over its property. But he had no compunction about exacting taxes from the clergy, including levies for dragoon horses and bath-houses.[34] By the end of the Northern War considerable arrears had accumulated. As the bishop of Rostov complained, 'the rural clergy are worse off than beggars, because many are subjected to the beatings of the tax collectors and cannot pay'.[35]

Legislation in 1700–1 also dealt with such matters as when and where monks could write (in the refectory or in specially allocated places, 'openly, not secretly', not in their cells); only monks and nuns were to live in monasteries (to deter 'shirkers' from finding refuge); building work was restricted, as was the number of cellarers per cell, in order to cut down on superfluous staff in bigger establishments; the minimum age for women to take the veil was forty. The Monastery department took over the running of the patriarchal almshouses and also the printing-house.[36] The department was closed down temporarily in 1720, when its business was transferred to other government offices. Administration of its lands was restored to the hands of the Church, even though part of the Church's income continued to be allocated to the State.[37] These concessions were made to Peter's new hand-picked team of churchmen in order to prepare the Church for a more radical reform of its administration: the creation of the Holy Synod.

The idea of the abolition of the patriarchate was first mentioned specifically in writing in a memorandum to Stefan Iavorsky dated November 1718: 'For better administration henceforth I think it would be convenient to have a spiritual college.'[38] Clearly this remark was made in the context of the new system of collegiate boards (*kollegii*), which were to provide a model for church administration within a well-regulated state apparatus. The Ecclesiastical Regulation, setting out the rationale and structure of such a college, was commissioned in 1718. Church hierarchs and the Senate discussed and approved a draft in February 1720, and appended their signatures in March.[39] The regulation—*Dukhovnyi Reglament ili Ustav*—was published on 25 January 1721.[40] On 14 February the Spiritual College was inaugurated. The first item on the agenda at its first session changed the new body's title from 'college' to 'Most Holy Governing (*pravitel'stvuiushchii*) Synod'; in other words, the Synod was to enjoy 'equal dignity' with the Senate rather than being a 'mere' college. In church services where the word 'patriarch' had been used, the name 'Holy Synod' was now to be substituted.[41] Even so, the new Synod board was modelled on the colleges rather than the Senate, whose members were all equal: it was manned by a president, two vice-presidents, four councillors, four assessors and a twelfth man, 'an honest, right-thinking person of secular rank'. The president acted as chairman, with 'an equal voice with other members'.[42] The revised status of the 'service church' is captured in the title Archbishop President (*arkhierei prezident*) given to the first head of the Synod, Stefan Iavorsky.[43] The congruity of church and state organizations was further emphasized by the creation in 1722 of the post of over-procurator of the Holy Synod. 'In the Synod select from the [military] officers a good man who is bold and should be familiar with the administration of Synod affairs, and let him be *ober prokuror* and give him instructions using as a model the Instruction to the procurator-general.'[44] Now the Synod had its equivalent of the Senate's procurator-general, a post created just two weeks previously, thereby satisfying Peter's passion for regularity and his reluctance to allow the higher organs of State and Church to operate without supervision. A list of duties issued in June 1722 specified that the new official was to 'sit in the Synod and make quite sure that the Synod does its duty and acts in all matters which pertain to the Synod's consideration and decision truly, fervently and honestly without time-wasting, in accordance with the regulations and decrees. ... Also to ensure that in the Synod cases are not decided simply on paper but also carried out in reality according to instructions.'[45]

The Church was made to conform to the secular pattern of government by being equipped with a network of spiritual inspectors. In 1721 'inquisitors', from the arch-inquisitor (*protoinkvizitor*) in Moscow to provincial ones in all bishoprics, were appointed to watch over the behaviour of churchmen, bishops in particular. The main task of the arch-inquisitor and his underlings was to initiate proceedings against insubordinate churchmen by acting as the 'Synod's spies'.[46] Bishops, who in earlier times had ruled their dioceses more or less unchecked, became 'agents of the Synod'.[47]

Strictly speaking, the Synod 'was not an organ of the state but an organ of the clergy', in so far as all its personnel bar one were drawn from ecclesiastical ranks.[48] But both the Ecclesiastical Regulation and the subsequent actions and attitude of the tsar made clear that the Synod was firmly subordinated to the state apparatus, personified by the ruler himself. In the words of the manifesto of 15 January: 'This college may supplement its Regulation with new rules in the future, such as different occasions may require for different cases. However, the Spiritual College must not do this without our consent.' The members of the Synod were 'individuals assembled for the general welfare by the command of the Autocrat and under his scrutiny, jointly with others'.[49] Many foreigners, and perhaps most Russians, were under the impression that Peter *was* the head of the Church, although he never actually used such a title.[50] A decade *before* the establishment of the Synod, Georg Grund wrote: 'The tsar is the highest ecclesiastical figure (*summus Pontifex*) in his land and controls all matters in which the secular power ought to aid the spiritual in the realm.'[51] The French envoy, Campredon, believed that Peter's practice of singing in church together with the officiating priests was aimed at showing them that 'his person represents the patriarch',[52] an idea shared by many devout oppositionists, who, ignorant of its Classical Roman derivation, were convinced that the title 'father of the fatherland', adopted in October 1721, indicated a further blatant usurpation of patriarchal authority. Their fears must have been confirmed by such actions as the placing of the tsar's throne and canopy in the former patriarchal palace in Moscow and by the fact that at Catherine's coronation in May 1724 Peter placed the crown on his wife's head.[53]

The Synod was left in no doubt as to who its master was. Long gone were the days when a patriarch could assert that 'the tsar must be lower than the prelate and obedient to him, for I also say that the clergy are chosen people and are annointed by the Holy Ghost'.[54] The clergy had no more power to resist the tsar's commands than did secular officials. A decree of 10 February 1724 ordering all Synod members to go to Moscow is fairly typical.[55] More significant, perhaps, was imperial intervention in top appointments. It was established in February 1721 that in appointing bishops the Synod was to submit two names for the tsar to choose from.[56] In fact, Peter tended to adopt his own *ad hoc* procedures. In 1722, for example, he accepted only four of twelve names submitted to him, choosing a nomination of his own for one vacancy and leaving another vacant. After 1721 'no one could hope to become a bishop without having first attracted the tsar's attention or that of his agents or favourites'.[57] There are numerous examples of direct royal intervention in religious affairs, always with state interests in mind. For example, in 1723 Peter ordered the composition of special prayers for victories and 'other state celebrations', to replace old prayers, and commissioned new verses to hymns for St Catherine's day, his wife's name-day (24 October).[58] In 1723 he ordered the printing of a shortened wedding service.[59] In September Peter ordered a sermon which had been delivered on his name-day by Archbishop Feofan in Trinity Cathedral to be printed as a pamphlet immediately.[60] He allowed archimandrites to wear mitres.[61] Catherine, a convert from Lutheranism, also saw fit sometimes to exert her authority—as when she criticized the appointment of an abbess: 'We would consider it a good thing for her to be abbess in an almshouse, but not in a convent.'[62]

The Synod was frequently admonished by the tsar to uphold moral standards—for example, to deal with the case of a widowed priest who was keeping a liquor store and had set up house with a Finnish girl by whom he had children, 'contrary to the canons'.[63] It was expected to do battle with dissidence of all kinds, including such vestiges of paganism as the popular rituals associated with the summer festival of Kupalo, when people were drenched with water and thrown into rivers and ponds. In olden times, a decree stated, people had still not totally accepted Christianity. Now, however, 'by God's grace the people shines in piety'. There was no excuse for tolerating rituals which were 'repulsive to God' and which also posed (a touch of Petrine good sense) 'a threat to human life'.[64]

Synod salaries were generous, comparing favourably with those of civil officials. The president received 3,000 roubles, vice-presidents 2,500, councillors 1,000, assessors 600.[65] But, like state servitors, Synod members were subject to deductions and fines. An order of 1723 stated that until certain arrears were paid, they would receive no pay. If a third of the arrears were paid off, they would receive a third of their pay, if a half, one half, and so on. Payment of salaries was restored after the upper clergy made a collective appeal with reference to Catherine's coronation in May 1724, 'for without our salary we are suffering great hardship'.[66] Thrift was expected, and waste discouraged. Bishop Feofilakt of Tver' must have had Peter's economical attitudes in mind (notably his wish that the clergy should not spend money on 'superfluous' vestments) when he requested permission to issue dalmatics (*sakkosy*, vestments usually reserved for the higher clergy) to priests, in order not to waste money replacing their threadbare chasubles (*rizy*).[67] An edict of July 1722 forbade church hierarchs to build churches without permission of the Synod, 'for you know yourselves what neglect of God's glory there is in superfluous churches and a multitude of priests'.[68]

After the establishment of the Synod, Peter turned his attention again to monasteries and monks, in part 10 of the Ecclesiastical Regulation. An anecdote pithily summarizes the tsar's attitude: 'Monasteries must use the revenue from their lands for deeds pleasing to God and for the good of the state, not for parasites. A monk needs to be fed and clothed and a prelate needs enough to maintain himself decently as befits his rank. But our monks have grown fat. The gates to heaven are faith, fasting and prayer. I'll clear them a path to paradise with bread and water, not with sturgeon and wine.'[69] Peter was guided by two principles: (i) monks must do useful service, and (ii) their numbers must be restricted. In 1719 retired soldiers began to be billeted in monasteries, a policy which continued, albeit with some opposition from the Synod, which complained that the requirement imposed an excessive burden.[70] On 19 March 1722 all monasteries with populated estates were ordered to set up hospices (*lazarety*). Those monasteries which 'supported themselves with their own labour' (i.e., did not own serfs) could accommodate fewer patients. Monks were 'to tend the sick and keep the hospices clean and tidy (taking their example from the Naval Statute').[71] These provisions were included in the supplement to the Ecclesiastical Regulation, which also contained clauses on age limits for entering a convent (now thirty for men and fifty for women), educational qualifications (peasant entrants must be literate, as well as have permission from their lords), and restrictions on admitting fugitives (no debtors and escaped convicts, not to mention army deserters and runaway serfs). Civil servants needed the permission of their superiors, married men required a bishop's dispensation, and so on. Novices were to undergo a three-year probation. Severe restrictions were placed on transfers from one convent to another. Full registers were ordered of all communities. Underpopulated monasteries were amalgamated with bigger ones. In other words, a concerted effort was made to limit the spread of monasticism.[72]

Peter disliked monasteries, not only because they provided a refuge from state obligations, but also because he suspected them of harbouring opposition. Monks were dangerous because most were literate and capable of writing the notorious 'anonymous letters' by which rebels sometimes disseminated subversive sentiments. Monasteries also attracted delinquent elements; recorded abuses of the monastic calling ranged from drunkenness and debauchery to brigandage. In 1722 a retired soldier complained that the monastery to which he had been assigned had failed to feed and accommodate him, and had tried to charge him a fee. He accused it of harbouring deserters and fugitives, administering monastic vows illegally, selecting old, sick specimens for the quota of army recruits and ruining serfs.[73] In 1724 the Synod was ordered to review cases of retired soliders sent to monasteries. 'Those who are capable of carrying out some sort of task should be allocated jobs; any that are very old or sick and decrepit should remain being looked after in the monasteries.'[74]

A collection of Peter's jottings, dated late 1723–early 1724, shows that he continued to devise useful occupations for monks. One was to educate beggars and foundlings, with a basic curriculum of reading and writing, plus some grammar, arithmetic, and geometry. Girls should study 'women's crafts' instead of geometry or, in one monastery, languages. Other notes read: 'Must explain that everyone can earn salvation by carrying on his profession (*zvanie*), not only through the monastic life, as is written in the Ecclesiastical Regulation ... Church hierarchs should make most effort of all in the teaching of priests and schools.'[75] On 31 January 1724, in a personal hand-written memorandum entitled 'On Monasteries and Monks', Peter reminded the Synod of the original purpose of monasticism, arguing that the current state of affairs was a distortion. He contrasted the meaning 'isolation/cut off from secular life' with the enormous communities which later grew up. Early monks had done useful work, but where they stopped working, problems were multiplied, as in Constantinople, where the huge numbers of men taking monastic vows depleted the capacity of the army. The Russian climate was unsuitable for hermitages, Peter claimed. Monks were bringing landed estates to ruin. 'Much evil is caused as the greater majority are parasites (*tuneiadtsy*) and since the root of all evil is idleness the number of superstition-mongers, schismatics and also rebels created in the past is well known.'

Even so, monasticism could not be banned entirely. Peter acknowledged two justifications for a man becoming a monk: first, personal conviction according to conscience; second, to meet the needs of the Church, which drew its prelates from the 'black', monastic clergy. But recruitment should be reduced, and all monks provided with useful work, running hospitals, refuges for retired soldiers, orphanages, and so on. Monks not thus engaged were to 'produce their own bread'; nuns were to engage in handicrafts. All must be confined to monastery premises.[76] On 25 April 1724 Peter announced his intention of ordering monks' allowances according to grades (*po chinam*), along army lines.[77] This plan was interrupted by his death, but measures limiting recruitment to monasteries (unlike to the secular priesthood) were effective to the extent that between 1724 and 1738 the number of monks and nuns was almost halved.[78]

IV. THE SERVICE CLERGY

The Church as opponent of the State or even as passive subordinate could not be tolerated. It must be transformed into an active supporter and integrated, where possible, with reformed state structures. Clerics of a new type were as necessary as 'new' nobles. Peter was impressed by what he saw of ecclesiastical life abroad. A priest he encountered in France working his own plot and making a small profit from the sale of produce prompted the comment: 'I must try to make our own country priests work in this way, to obtain their bread, beer and kvas by work in the fields and garden, then they could live better than they now live in idleness.'[79]

Education was the key. John Perry provides a characteristically low opinion of standards: 'It was a very rare thing in Russia before this present Czar's time to have found any Man, even among the highest and most learned of the Clergy, to have understood any Language but their own; and as they were themselves void of Learning, so they were wary and cautious to keep out all Means that might bring it in, lest their Ignorance should be discovered. To which End they insinuated to former Emperors, that the Introduction of foreign Languages might be a Means of introducing foreign Customs and Innovations, which might in time prove not only dangerous to the Church, but to the State too.' He noted with approval that Peter, by contrast, obliged priests to learn Latin.[80] A 1705 order to Dmitry of Rostov to ordain only literate priests indicates the extent of the problem.[81] Early measures tended to be aimed at the sons of clergy, but more in the hope that they would swell the service ranks than in the interests of producing better-qualified priests. In 1708 education in schools offering Greek and Latin was made compulsory for the sons of priests and deacons. Those who failed to complete the course would be drafted into the army.[82] Eventually, at the end of Peter's reign, a system for training priests was established: parish priests could not be ordained unless they had attended episcopal schools ('whence a better and reformed clergy is to be hoped for'), which bishops were required to set up by the Ecclesiastical Regulation, using funds from monasteries and church lands and if necessary by making economies in their own households, cutting down on new buildings and vestments.[83] At its most basic, the course was to include grammar, mathematics, and study of a religious primer. Theology, philosophy, and more esoteric subjects would rarely be available. In 1722 Peter wrote to the Synod challenging the appointment of a new archimandrite in the Khoytn monastery, on the grounds that the man chosen was uneducated: 'Do as you see fit, he is a man of good life, ... but it would be better to send a man who was learned in order to convert the local peoples.'[84]

In order to perform a new moral and pedagogical role, Peter's priests were expected to learn how to preach and read sermons. ('Of preaching they all know nothing, consequently the People are but indifferently instructed, and live in gross Ignorance,' observed Weber.[85]) Peter's admiration for sermons is sometimes ascribed to his visit to Lutheran churches,[86] although sermons had already made a limited appearance in Moscow in the 1670s–1680s under the influence of Simeon Polotsky. Preaching was further encouraged by members of Peter's higher clergy, mostly trained in Kiev, whose works were often published in pamphlet form. The Ecclesiastical Regulation contained advice on effective speaking and body language (no rocking back and forth, jumping up and down, laughing, or weeping), and recommended the books of John Chrysostom as models. Approved topics included 'respect for the authorities, especially the supreme authority of the tsar, and the obligations of all classes'.[87] Menshikov, for one, took the hint. His private church in St Petersburg had a pulpit in which sermons were sometimes preached, 'a thing very extraordinary, and entirely new in this Country; for the Russian Priests never preached before, but contented themselves with performing Mass'.[88] It seems unlikely, however, that sermons spread much beyond Moscow and St Petersburg.

Literate members of congregations, too, were encouraged to undertake individual devotions more in the Protestant manner. Pre-Petrine practice, dented only a little in the later seventeenth century by the publication of some small-format books, did not encourage laymen to read devotional material. Church books were expensive and bulky, designed for liturgical use in churches and monasteries rather than by individuals. As the Ecclesiastical

Regulation notes, there was a need for 'some short booklets, clear and comprehensible to ordinary people'.[89] Now religious publishing for lay persons, including children, was encouraged, notably in primers and catechisms, of which Prokopovich's *Youth's First Lesson* was a Petrine best-seller.[90] In January 1723 Peter ordered copies of Catholic, Lutheran, and Calvinist catechisms to be collected, translated, and published.[91] A catechism (identified as Martin Luther's *Catechismus Maior*) was ordered to be brought from Riga for translation into the Slavonic language, 'in full, not in an abridged version as in the manual for youths'.[92] A new edition of the Bible was commissioned in Holland (in Dutch and Church Slavonic), as Bibles printed in 1663 were sold out. But apparently the project was not completed: only the Dutch text of the New Testament was printed.[93]

The mass of the population, of course, remained illiterate.[94] Churchmen were expected to act as disseminators of public information. In October 1721 orders were given for copies of the ratification of the Treaty of Nystad to be sent in sealed packets to churches all over Russia, in preparation for official victory celebrations on 22 October, when the packets would be dramatically opened up and read out to the people before the commencement of prayers.[95] A more novel idea was the requirement that on all feast-days and Sundays priests should proclaim edicts on taxes (*o sborakh*) 'for the information of parishioners so that everyone is fully informed of the tax collections and nobody can add or subtract anything'.[96] Priests were charged with reporting tax-evaders to the authorities[97] and keeping registers of births, deaths, and marriages (*metricheskie knigi*).[98] People who failed to attend church on Sundays and feast-days were denounced on the grounds that not only did they fail to hear the word of God, but also missed 'the monarch's commands'. Such people, on suspicion of being religious dissidents, were to be arrested and interrogated.[99] In other words, priests were supposed to act as agents of the secular authorities and as gatherers and promulgators of information within the local communities, where it was often difficult for the State to penetrate.

In 1722 the supplement to the Ecclesiastical Regulation made a new and sinister addition to the clergy's policing duties:

> If someone in confession informs his spiritual father of some illegality that has not been committed, but that he yet intends to commit, especially treason or mutiny against the Sovereign or against the State, or evil designs upon the honour or well-being of the Sovereign or upon His Majesty's family, and in informing of such a great intended evil he reveals himself as not repenting but considers himself in the right, does not lay aside his intentions and does not confess it as though it were a sin but rather so that with his confessor's assent or silence he might become confirmed in his intention, what can be concluded therefrom is this: when the spiritual father, in God's name, enjoins him to abandon completely his evil intention, and he, silently, as though undecided or justifying himself, does not appear to have changed his mind, then the con-

fessor must not only not honour as valid the forgiveness and remission of the confessed sins, for it is not a regular confession if someone does not repent of all his transgressions, but he must expeditiously report concerning them ... and ... bring such malefactors to designated places.[100]

This 'announcement to the Clergy' made reference to the cases of Grigory Talitsky, Tsarevich Alexis, and Varlaam Levin, all of whom had apparently confessed their evil intentions to priests who failed to reveal them.[101] According to canon law, confession was supposed to be strictly confidential, but the supplement somehow contrived to argue that 'treasonable' utterances were not part of a true confession. In addition, upon ordination a priest had to take an oath of allegiance modelled on that for civil servants, in which he swore to be an obedient servant of the emperor and not to spare his life in service and usefulness to State and Church. The supplement contained sections on candidates for the priesthood, with stipulations about education, training and character. Priests must 'curse the name of all schismatic groups', and swear to denounce and unmask them.[102]

For its part, the State undertook to uphold order and seemliness in church, as it had done in the past, as well as to aid the Church against its enemies.[103] For example, instructions to provincial governors, issued in conjunction with the local government reform in 1719, indicated that the governor must firmly uphold the Faith and report 'such people who secretly preach with enthusiasm to people about other faiths and sow discord'.[104] The supplement included rules on priestly decorum, proper dress, and behaviour at table. Stählin reports that guards were posted in palace churches to stop 'idle chatter'. There was a box for rouble fines for anyone caught talking during the service. 'Simple folk' (presumably those who were unwilling or unable to pay) were beaten with sticks outside the church. Outside the Alexander Nevsky cathedral there was a collar on a chain to punish persistent offenders.[105] Offerings were to be collected in an orderly manner in two purses, one for church needs, the other for the poor. Income and expenditure were to be recorded in books, following the example of the new bookkeeping procedures in government offices.[106]

The attempt to extend good fiscal and bureaucratic practices to church administration right down to parish level brings us back to one of the original impulses of Peter's reforms of the Church—the need to maximize revenues and the fulfilment of service obligations to the State. As far as the secular clergy were concerned, this involved various attempts both to reduce the number of ordained priests and to reassign 'superfluous' church people, notably the sons of priests and non-ordained sacristans, to more useful occupations and status—as taxpayers, army recruits, or bureaucrats. The Ecclesiastical Regulation stated: 'Superfluous clergy are not to be ordained for any reason; since many who are ordained and accepted into the clergy are fleeing state service, the number of clergy is to be promptly specified by decree.' There were supplementary measures on counting the clergy and identifying redundant or inactive churches, with a view to establishing quotas.[107] A register of the establishment of parish and other priests (*dukhovnyi shtat*) on the model of registers of state officials was drawn up, with quotas of clergy in a given parish related to the population. New churches could be constructed only with special permission.[108] Private chapels and priests were banned, except for those belonging to the imperial family and a few selected magnates.[109] Thus Peter sought both to restrict the numbers of clerics and to impose new burdens on those who remained. The latter change in particular has been described as 'revolutionary', as Peter drew the clerical estate into the service of 'his secular state', although he did not emulate Swedish models by employing priests in collecting taxes and recruiting.[110] Even so, priests who conscientiously carried out their duties were burdened with considerable paperwork as well as possible pangs of conscience about violating the confessional and denouncing their own parishioners.

Improving the quality of the parish priesthood, not to mention the religious knowledge of laymen, was a longer-term project. In the shorter term Peter's first target was to harness the support and energies of the higher monastic clergy, and for this he turned to the best-educated section of the Orthodox churchmen, many of whom came not from Russia but from the borderlands of the empire. The first president of the Synod, Bishop Stefan Iavorsky of Riazan', was, as we have seen, a graduate of the Kiev Academy, as were vice-presidents Feofan Prokopovich, whose career is dealt with below, and Feodosy Ianovsky, bishop of Novgorod.[111] The latter had been archimandrite of the Alexander Nevsky monastery in St Petersburg since 1712 and was close to the royal family, having travelled abroad with them to Germany in 1716.[112] Of the first councillors of the Synod, Gavriil Buzhinsky, another Kiev graduate, was archimandrite of the Ipat'ev monastery in Moscow, but in 1722 he took over the Trinity–St Sergius monastery. His posts included that of head chaplain to the fleet, and he was a skilful writer of sermons. The other three councillors were Peter Smelich, archimandrite of the Simonov monastery, a Serb by origin; Archimandrite Leonid of the Petrovsky monastery in Rostov; and Ierofei Prilutsky, archimandrite of the Moscow Donskoy monastery. The assessors were Ioann Semenov, archpriest of Trinity Cathedral (the main St Petersburg cathedral for much of Peter's reign); Peter Grigor'ev, priest of the Church of St Samson and later in the Peter–Paul cathedral; Anastasios Kontoeides (Condoidi), a Greek who came to Russia with the hospodar of Moldavia, Dmitry Kantemir; and the priest-monk Varlaam Ovsiannikov. In August 1721 Timofei Palekhin, a secular chancellery official, became the Synod's chief secretary. There was quite a rapid turnover in the short period before Peter's death. In 1722 Iavorsky died, and Ovsiannikov was dismissed and arrested for 'considerable crimes', and in 1723 Semenov was transferred to another post. In 1722–3 Feofilakt Lopatinsky, by then archimandrite of the Moscow Chudov monastery, was included, and soon after was made bishop of Tver', with Peter's support. Other new appointments included Feofil Krolik, who succeeded Lopatinsky in the Chudov monastery; Anastasius Mikhailov, a Greek who apparently knew no Russian; and Raphael Zuborovsky, from Kiev. Cracraft points out that the group (which, as constituted just before Peter's death, had only three Russian members) was 'hardly representative of the church they purported to rule', but that this stemmed from the lack of learned candidates among non-monastic priests.[113] Of 127 prelates active in the period to 1762, 70 were from Ukraine and Belorussia, only 47 Russian.[114]

A visitor to Russia, Michael Schend von der Bech, writing from St Petersburg in August 1725, described the members of the Synod as 'models of living erudition and a fund of the most complete education'. Prokopovich was 'the brightest ornament of the Russian church ... so skilled in eloquence that everyone calls him the Russian Demosthenes'. Lopatinsky and Kontoeides were also singled out for praise.[115] Bergholz, too, conceded that some of the members of the Synod who dined with the duke of Holstein at Christmas 1724 were quite learned, including Krolik, who knew several languages, including good German.[116] But even erudite higher clergymen were expected to know their place. The Ecclesiastical Regulation has sections decrying 'self-glorification', which accords with Peter's measures to restrict undue pomp and ceremony in everyday dealings with his own person. Bishops were not to be supported by the elbows, and their subordinates were not to prostrate themselves. Their dignity must not be regarded as 'almost equal to that of the Tsar'. Frugality was to be observed in visits around the dioceses: for example, summer visits were preferred, when less firewood and hay were needed, food was cheaper, and it was possible to stay in a tent in a field so as not to overburden the local clergy!'[117] New-style prelates were expected to perform social duties. An ecclesiastical 'assembly', held on 29 December 1722 in the Donskoy monastery, was attended by Feodosy Ianovsky, Archbishop Leonid of Krutitsky, other prelates, and lay officials. Such goings-on were condemned by Metropolitan Silvester of Kazan', who complained that Feodosy had 'abandoned church services and monastic rules to organize assemblies (*samlei*!) with music and had indulged in cards and chess and immoderate amusement'. He was disgusted that Moscow prelates and archimandrites of Moscow monasteries had been ordered to hold assemblies 'with various entertainments'.[118]

V.   RELIGIOUS LIFE AND CULTURE

As we saw earlier, religious publishing and religious art flourished. Legislation outlawed the construction of 'superfluous' churches and monasteries, but there was selective support for new buildings for State purposes. Almost all the new churches built in the capitals reflected military victories or marked some royal anniversary: churches dedicated to Ivan the Warrior in Moscow, in St Petersburg to St Samson (1709–10; Poltava, 27 June), St Panteleimon

(1722; Hangö and Grengham, 27 July 1714 and 1720), St Matthew (Narva, 9 August), and a chapel in Trinity Cathedral in honour of St Khariton Ispovednik (Lesnaia, 28 September). Generous funds were expended on the new Alexander Nevsky monastery in St Petersburg, 30 August being declared the joint feast of St Alexander Nevsky and the Peace of Nystad. There was a project for a new cathedral (1723) dedicated to St Andrew, patron saint of Peter's new military order.[119] The St Petersburg cathedrals of St Isaac of Dalmatia and SS Peter and Paul marked Peter's birthday and name-day respectively.[120] At the same time, 'superfluous' religious festivals without contemporary resonances were cut or amended in an attempt to diminish the Church's role in Russian history by playing down the notion of divine providence. In a telling example of censorship, Ivan Iur'ev, the compiler of the Book of Orders, was instructed to cut out episodes in which early Russian princes deferred to priests, consulted with church hierarchs, or gave generous gifts to churches and monasteries, although many episodes on miracles were kept in.[121]

Peter's army, navy, and civil service all had a use for religion in its proper place. Chaplains were appointed to all army units.[122] The first two chapters of the military articles (*Voinskie artikuly*) of 1714, based partly on a Swedish model, deal with 'fear of God' and the divine service. Article 13 states: 'All officers and men must love and respect priests.... Anyone who offends against one of them is to be punished doubly than if he had offended against an ordinary person (*nad prostoliudinom*).'[123] The rules for conduct on board ship included provision for morning prayers (combined with drill) and readings from the psalms and the gospels.[124] The Naval Statute contains several sections on chaplains, who were expected to conduct services on board ship on Sundays and feast-days ('if bad weather does not prevent it'), preach sermons, minister to the sick and dying, and generally supervise moral standards. Penalties were listed for various categories of blasphemy, from the practice of sorcery and black magic (punishable by death by burning) and interrupting the service by blasphemous utterances (death by choking on molten metal) to mild impiety and missing church, deliberately or accidentally (flogging with the cat-o'-nine-tails and fines).[125] A separate order (March 1721), setting out in more detail the duties of 'hieromonks' in the fleet, hints at certain restrictions, however. Chaplains were expected to ensure that no one died 'without fulfilling his Christian duty', but during services they should set up just two or three icons, not large folding iconostases; nor should they light superfluous candles, 'in order to protect the ship from damage'. The chaplain was to read the offices quietly in his own cabin, without inviting ship's personnel to join in, 'lest private reading should cause interruption and hindrance to the general ship's business'.[126] Religion had its role to play in the civil service, too. All officials took an oath of loyalty on assuming office, in which they swore to serve the sovereign, his family, and heirs by kissing the gospels and the cross.[127]

Icons and relics continued to be revered. It is interesting to read Just Juel's description of the Kremlin Cathedral of the Dormition in 1711, with its icons (no sculptures, as he pointed out) and impressive set of relics, including the head of John Chrysostom, the right hand of the apostle Andrew, a finger of Basil the Great, part of a leg of John the Baptist, and relics of assorted Russian saints. Juel heard the proclamation of war with Turkey read out in the cathedral, accompanied by prayers for victory, the sprinkling of holy water, and a sermon by the metropolitan of Moscow. Thus did the old and the new mingle.[128] A long list of priests and deacons serving in and around the Kremlin confirms that numerous churches continued to operate in the centre of the city.[129] Shrines were visited. Religious processions took place. At the same time, Peter was energetic in his battle with superstition: 'Peter exhorted them to preach morality above all else, so that little by little superstition should be banished from his country and both God and himself better served by his subjects.'[130] He did not much care for pilgrimages to the relics of saints or the use of icons for 'magical' purposes—for example, to make trade or crops prosper or protect buildings from fire—as he believed that reliance upon divine intervention discouraged human endeavour. Better to introduce superior farm implements or improve fire-fighting procedures. Juel records news that an icon of the Virgin had wept real tears and requested that a church be dedicated to her in St Petersburg. Peter went to have a look, but 'did not express an opinion on the matter'.[131] Stählin records a similar anecdote. The tears were interpreted as a sign of the Virgin's displeasure with Peter's reforms and St Petersburg. Peter went to the church, ordered the icon to be removed, and discovered how the deception had been perpetrated through a hidden receptacle in the back of the icon. He placed it in his Cabinet of Curiosities.[132] In 1723 Peter ordered false relics of saints made from ivory to be displayed in the Synod's own cabinet of curiosities as examples of the spread of superstition (superstitsiia).[133] The Ecclesiastical Regulation condemned 'everything which can be described as superstitious'. It contained prohibitions on 'blatantly false tales', paganism (e.g., praying in front of oaks), dubious relics, and miraculous icons and springs. The supplement required priests to report 'false miracles' without delay.[134] There were numerous prosecutions of people reporting visions and miracles. The recommended penalty for such acts was the slitting of nostrils and hard labour for life.[135] Manifestations of religious hysteria, such as 'shrieking' and self-mutilation, were outlawed.[136] Such practices were said to bring Orthodoxy into disrepute with foreigners.

Peter tried to reduce the number of fasts, 'considering this sort of Devotion has proved pernicious to an infinite Number of his Soldiers, Seamen and Labourers', a policy regarded favourably by foreign commentators.[137] 'Since the war, and frequent voyages of their young gentry,' writes Whitworth, 'they begin to be less strict in their fasts; the Czar himself eats flesh on all of them in private houses, but refrains from giving any scandal in publick.'[138] But devout people continued to seek dispensation from fasts (e.g., on grounds of illness) from the patriarch of Constantinople, not relying on royal opinion in such matters. 'The inhabitants of St Petersburg daily have cause to wonder when they compare the present time with the past,' wrote Mardefeld. 'At the beginning of this reign fasts were observed so religiously that anyone breaking or rejecting them was burnt. Now they write and preach publicly that fasts are nothing more than rituals established by men. All those surrounding the emperor, wishing to distinguish themselves from the common folk, hardly keep any fasts, apart from a few stubborn old men who refuse to renounce the faith of their fathers.' He pointed out that assemblies and balls continued during fast periods.[139]

VI.   RELIGION AND EMPIRE

'We are in Amsterdam to learn navigation in order to be victors over the enemies of Jesus Christ and liberators of the Christians who live under them, which I shall not cease to wish for until my last breath,' wrote Peter to Patriarch Adrian in September 1697.[140] Years later, on the eve of the Caspian campaign, prayers were ordered for the victory of Christian troops over the infidels and the liberation of Christians from the heathen yoke.[141] Orthodoxy remained on the agenda of Petrine foreign policy, be it safeguarding the rights of Orthodox Christians in Poland and Sweden, supporting the cause of Orthodox rulers subjugated by the Turks (or, more often, requesting their aid), or converting the heathen. Palace account books for 1721 show donations to Orthodox monasteries in Polish territory—100 roubles for the maintenance of monks in the Annunciation monastery in Druje and for finishing an iconostasis; the same for monks of the Descent of the Holy Spirit in Lithuania.[142] Peter championed Orthodox unity when it suited him, as in relations with Ukraine, where he reiterated the basis of the relationship between Moscow and Kiev since the Pereiaslavl' agreement of 1654: 'through the Orthodox faith of Great Rus' we are all members of one Church whose head is Jesus Christ'.[143] Such statements cost nothing. It was a different matter when it came to foreign appeals for Russian aid against oppressors. The 1686 Russo–Polish treaty set a precedent by making the tsar the guarantor of Orthodox rights of worship in Polish territory, but this role could be actively pursued only intermittently. It was even more difficult to respond actively to appeals against the forced conversion of Orthodox believers by Austrian Catholics in south Hungary or to Orthodox fears in the wake of Austrian successes against the Turks in the 1690s. 'We all pray with tears for the sovereign monarch to save us from the Papists and Jesuits, who rage against the Orthodox more than against the Turks and Jews. ... The secular war may finish some time, but the Jesuit war never will,' wrote the hospodar of Wallachia in January 1698.[144] Peter was in no position to heed this appeal at a time when he was asking both Protestant and Catholic rulers for aid against the Turks. In general, respect for religion was part of war etiquette. In 1714 Major-General Schtaff was instructed: 'When you receive this order destroy as many as possible of the fortifications in the Pomeranian towns of Anklam, Demin, Harz, Wohlgast. Also burn the houses, apart from the churches, all, without sparing any.'[145]

The 'crusade element' was subordinated to more immediate practical concerns in relations with Turkey and the Crimea, where eliminating raids, slave-taking and tribute payments were regarded as more important than 'more far-reaching projects'.[146] Guarantees of freedom of worship and religion for the Orthodox in the Ottoman Empire, although raised in negotiations, were not included in Russia's 1700 treaty with Turkey. (This had to wait until the treaty of Kuchuk–Kainardji in 1774.) In instructions issued to Peter Tolstoy, the new ambassador to Constantinople, in 1702, the emphasis was on such matters as politics, trade, fortifications, and borders. There was no mention of Balkan Christians.[147] In 1711, however, a new element crept in with Russia's first appeal to Orthodox Christians in the Balkans to rise against their Muslim oppressors. The anticipated support from Wallachia and Moldavia did not materialize.[148] In 1711 Prince-Bishop Daniel Petrovich staged a revolt in Montenegro, but it was too far from the Pruth to be more than a diversion.[149] In any case, Orthodox clergy under Turkish rule were not necessarily to be relied upon, nor were they regarded with particular respect. As Peter Shafirov, in Turkish captivity in 1711, declared: 'for money they are ready to sell their God, their faith, their soul and their sovereign'.[150]

A related issue was that of the holy places and Russian pilgrims in the Holy Land.[151] The question became acute in the 1690s when the Catholics gained guardianship of the shrines, which sparked off a series of appeals to Moscow from Greek churchmen such as Patriarch Dositheus of Jerusalem for Moscow to go to war over Jerusalem: 'Destroy the Tatars, and Jerusalem will be yours. Alexander the Great went to the war with the Persians not for God's sake but for the sake of his fellow tribesmen. All the more reason that you should be vigilant and make every effort to drive off your wicked neighbors for the sake of the holy places and our Orthodox faith.'[152] A reference to the return of the holy places was included in the instructions of a Russian envoy to the Crimea in 1692, but the point was never pushed, because Peter had 'no personal interest'.[153] Only free passage for pilgrims (which also featured in the 1681 Russo–Tatar treaty of Bakhchisarai) was included in the 1700 Treaty of Constantinople, a minor concession in view of the small numbers of Russian pilgrims, and one which was withdrawn in 1713 and restored in 1720.[154]

Thus the doctrine of the 'Third Rome', with its hint of the eventual liberation of the Second Rome by its successor, remained what it had always been, an acknowledgement of Russian superiority over its predecessor, but more a religious abstraction than an active policy. In addition, radical changes to a Church–State structure which had hitherto adhered to the Byzantine model were bound to affect relations with Constantinople, which had already been offended by the subordination in 1685 of the metropolitanate of Kiev to the patriarchate of Moscow. That act was presented to Constantinople as a *fait accompli*. Was Peter now defecting from the body of ecumenical patriarchs, of which Constantinople was the senior member, by abolishing the Moscow patriarchate and creating his own structure? Thomas Consett, the well-informed British chaplain in St Petersburg, believed that Peter 'design'd to exempt himself and his Country from a Dependence on the Patriarchs of Constantinople, and to dignify his own Church with the Character of a *Glavnoj Tserkove* or Capital Church'.[155] Even so, it was felt necessary to formulate a justification for the new structure. On 20 September 1721 Peter sent a missive to the eastern patriarchs, whose reply, not surprisingly, given their need for Russian support, was favourable: Russian Orthodox Christians were told to submit to the authority of the Synod, although it was taken for granted that the Russian Church would adhere unswervingly to the 'divine dogmas of the holy and Orthodox faith'.[156] The patriarchs continued to receive a polite mention in prayers for long life at major church festivals.[157] But Prokopovich was careful to argue in his writings that the Russian Church was independent, and that the other patriarchs had no power over it.

Converting 'heathen' subjects inside the empire posed another set of problems. Weber reported that Peter had already made a start on such conversions, and 'was resolved to continue in his Zeal for propagating the Christian Religion all over his Dominions'.[158] There were plans to send missionaries to the Tatars, Mordvinians, and Cheremiss, and to Buddhist Kalmyks.[159] In a letter to Patriarch Dositheus of Jerusalem (September 1701) Peter wrote that Azov was to be used as a base to 'guide the border peoples to the Holy Orthodox faith'.[160] Siberia saw missions to the Iakuts, Ostiaks, Tungus, and Voguls under the direction of Metropolitan Filofei Leshchinsky of Tobol'sk, who by an edict of 1714 was commanded to 'seek out their seductive false gods and idols and burn them and destroy their heathen temples and build churches instead'.[161] There were claims that 40,000 pagans in Siberia had been baptized.[162] The need for incentives was also appreciated. In 1722 Peter ordered that new converts should not be taken as recruits, as the threat of conscription was 'an impediment to their conversion into the Christian faith, therefore these newly baptized foreigners should be allowed to go back home so that seeing them other non-believers will be baptized'.[163]

Interest in China continued, always linked to trade.[164] In 1715 Archimandrite Ilarion Lezhaisky and eight priests were sent to Peking, and in 1721 Innokenty Kulchitsky was appointed bishop, but was refused entry. The 1722–3 Persian campaign offered prospects of proselytizing activity, as hinted at by the foundation of the Holy Cross (*Sviatoi Krest*) fortress between the Sulan and Agrakhan Rivers.[165] The declaration of war issued in spring 1722 mentioned saving Christians from Muslim domination.

As far as foreign nationals working in Russia were concerned, free exercise of their faith was guaranteed in Peter's manifesto of 1702, in which it was stated that 'deriving our power from the All-Highest, we do not pretend to compel any human conscience but readily allow each Christian to work for his own salvation at his own risk'.[166] Major denominations had their own churches and chapels in St Petersburg. Even so, the option remained to convert to Orthodoxy, whereby one also became the tsar's subject. In addition, a civil oath of loyalty was introduced for foreign personnel, which did not include an undertaking to convert. Attempts to make the oath of allegiance in the General Regulation (which included a pledge to be 'in eternal service' as a 'subject' (*podannyi*)) compulsory for all foreigners failed.[167]

VII. DISSIDENCE

Little leniency was shown to home-grown schismatics and dissidents, particularly the Old Believers, whose struggle was intensified by opposition not just to many of Peter's reforms, but also to the person of the 'impious' tsar.[168] In some areas, numbers were huge, an estimated 200,000 in the diocese of Nizhny Novgorod, perhaps as many as 20 per cent of the Russian population as a whole.[169] Peter was far less concerned with the niceties of the number of fingers used for making the sign of the cross than with mass evasion of obligations. The harsh penalties imposed by Tsarevna Sophia's twelve articles of 1685, which included burning at the stake and knouting, were regarded as counter-productive, but discrimination continued, with a distinctly Petrine flavour.[170] On 8 February 1716 a double tax was imposed on Old Believers. It was in this context that archbishops and governors were warned to ensure that all parishioners went to confession. 'If someone does not go to confession during the year, lists of their names are to be submitted.'[171] A decree of 16 March 1718 required all priests and other clergy to make statements swearing that they had declared all dissidents to the authorities. The penalty for concealment was defrocking, trial in civil courts, and hard labour. Anyone declaring previously hidden names would be pardoned.[172] The general principles were confirmed in the Ecclesiastical Regulation, which stated that there is 'no better sign' than repeated absence from holy communion for identifying schismatics.[173] The regular clergy neglected their new policing role at their own peril. Dissidents had to wear distinguishing clothing (red and yellow stripes on their backs to subject them to ridicule) and medallions as receipts for paying the beard tax.[174]

Bans and fines apparently had little effect. Dissidents found Peter's measures 'more of a nuisance than a threat to their continued existence'.[175] Attempts to persuade and reason with them were no more effective.[176] The official view was that most schismatics acted from 'stubborn ignorance and blindness' (rather than wickedness), and that moral persuasion should be attempted to restore them to 'the straight path of salvation' and turn them away from superstition, from all that is 'not according to the word of God but to thoughtless stories and old wives' tales'.[177] Bishop Pitirim of Nizhny Novgorod provoked local Old Believers into entering into discussion on a prepared list of questions on doctrine and ritual.[178] In 1722 the Synod issued a more general invitation to debate, in the hope that the dissidents would renounce their opposition, but with assurances of safety if they remained obdurate (in fact, a time limit, after which they would be subject to arrest and execution).[179] Missionaries were sent to dissident communities, as were armed units to collect fines. In general, Old Believers crossed the authorities when they made indiscreet pronouncements about the clean-shaven tsar being Antichrist or referred to the new capital as 'Sodom or Gomorrah'. But the days of mass suicides were past. Known Old Believers who desisted from public criticism of the tsar and his government, did not set themselves up as teachers or operate as priests,[180] refrained from luring or harbouring fugitives, paid their taxes, and did useful work were left in peace. In 1705 concessions were made to the Vyg community, allowing members to worship without persecution and run their own affairs in return for contributing to the development of ironworks in the Olonets region. The value of this contribution was recognized by the attempts of the director of mines, Wilhelm Henning, to release the Old Believer Semen Denisov from the custody of the metropolitan of Novgorod in 1714 on the grounds that the factory work was being hindered. The double tax was even paid on the community's behalf by the Admiralty, which regarded them as its employees.[181] Communities at Vetka and Starodub and the Grebensky Cossacks were awarded similar concessions. A Stählin anecdote confirms this grudging tolerance. On asking whether some Old Believers were honest and being assured that they were, Peter allegedly said: 'Fine, let them believe what they want and wear their stripes. If I can't dissuade them from their superstition either by rational proofs or by shame, then fire and sword also wouldn't do any good. They should not be made martyrs for their stupidity; it would be too great an honour for them and harmful for the State.'[182] But there were limits to toleration. In 1724 Peter ordered a stop to Old Believers moving to Siberia, saying that they would be punished as fugitives, as they already enjoyed 'all sorts of freedom' (*vsiakaia svoboda*).[183] Manifestations of schism appeared all over the place, even in the chancellery for the investigation of schismatic affairs itself, where in 1724 an icon of the seventeenth-century dissident leader Avvakum was on display![184]

VIII. CONCLUSION

Peter's church reforms combined political, ideological, and practical goals, aimed not at destroying the Church but at 'improving' and subordinating it. Peter was no 'godless Bolshevik' with thoughts of abolishing religion or even allowing it to wither away. He was highly suspicious of any alternative to state service, especially the monastic way of life, where individuals chose a path in which they communicated directly with God through prayer rather than being channelled and monitored through state obligations, be they taxes or labour duties. But he was equally suspicious of the godless. Peter and his contemporaries did not discard the deeply ingrained religious beliefs of the early modern period. For them life without religion was inconceivable. The same man who denounced lazy monks was equally capable of ordering the Synod to add commentaries from Christian writings to a book about pagan gods, to point out how mistaken the pagans were in their ignorance 'before knowledge of Christianity'. Paganism and atheism were not viable alternatives.[185]

Peter's religious opponents were not impressed by arguments about the 'common good'. A contemporary tract states:

> This false Christ began to elevate himself above all called by God as his annointed ones and began to name himself and praise himself above everybody, persecuting and tormenting Orthodox Christians, exterminating their memory from the earth, spreading his new Jewish faith (*zhidovskuiu veru*) and in 1700 brought to the church throughout Russia, in a full show of his wickedness, Janus's new year and ordered that years be counted like that and in 1721 he took upon himself the title of Patriarch, calling himself father of the fatherland ... and Head of the Russian church, and was sole ruler, having no one equal to him, having stolen for himself not only the Tsar's power but also the power of the prelate and of God, to be the autocratic pastor, single head-less head over all, the opponent of Christ, Antichrist.[186]

Less partial observers saw a power struggle, in which the tsar emerged the clear winner. 'It is notorious, how much the power of the Clergy has been limited and clipped,' wrote Weber.[187] Anisimov believes that Peter destroyed 'a spiritual alternative to the regime',[188] while Freeze likens him to 'the seventeenth-century German prince, who asserts new power over the church but does so in the name of faith'.[189] In fact, as with much else attempted by Peter, some of the impact of his church reform diminished after his death. Although the synodal structure survived until 1918, the clergy, like the nobles, were gradually 'emancipated' from taxes and from state service.[190] At the same time, the heart of the Church's activity—liturgy, texts, ritual—survives more or less unchanged to the present day.

II

Peter: Man, Mind and Methods

I. A MAN OF SIMPLE TASTES

Anyone who has read this book in strict order will constantly have been aware of Peter's looming presence. The time has come to examine more explicitly the driving force behind the reforms, policies, decrees, and campaigns which make up the 'Petrine' era by offering a short study of the man himself, and there are worse places to begin than with his physical appearance.[1] At six feet seven inches tall, Peter literally stood head and shoulders above his contemporaries. The fact that this unusual height was accompanied by small hands and feet and narrow shoulders made him something of a freak of nature. Add to this some disturbing facial ticks and bizarre behavioural traits, and one already has an alarming image. 'Tsar Peter was tall, thin rather than stout,' wrote a young Italian observer, 'his hair was thick, short, dark brown; he had large eyes, black with long lashes, a well-shaped mouth, but the lower lip was slightly disfigured.... For his great height, his feet seemed very narrow. His head was sometimes tugged to the right by convulsions.'[2] The artist Valery Serov, who produced several paintings on Petrine themes in the 1910s, was less flattering: 'He was frightful: long, on weak, spindly little legs and with a head so small in relation to the rest of his body that he must have looked more like a sort of dummy with a badly stuck-on head than a live person. He suffered from a constant tic and he was always making faces: winking, screwing up his mouth, twitching his nose, wagging his chin.'[3] These alarming twitches have been attributed to the horrors he endured in 1682 and 1689.[4] Jacob Lefort, who saw Peter in Holland in 1698, reported that he suffered from convulsions in his eyes, hands, and whole body. 'Sometimes his eyes roll right back until only the whites are visible.... He even has a twitch of the legs and can't stand in the same place for long.'[5]

Official contemporary portraits, naturally, eschewed anything unduly grotesque. Likenesses by Nikitin, Dannhauer, Caravaque, and Kneller suggest a handsome visage, with just a hint of fiercely staring eyes. One of the best impressions of Peter's appearance may be provided by the life-size model made in wax and wood by Carlo Bartholomeo Rastrelli in 1725 from a death mask and exact measurements, which is still on view in a glass cabinet in the former Winter Palace (built by Rastrelli's son). Today the model excites curiosity. In the past it must have evoked something approaching awe. It gives no hint of the facial tics and convulsions described by many foreign observers, or of the tsar's extraordinary gait, although it gives a measure of the length of his legs. It wore a wig of the tsar's own hair, cut in 1722 when Peter went to Persia, and the clothes he wore at Catherine's coronation in 1724. But it is undoubtedly 'an uncomfortable image ... of a more than uncomfortable companion'.[6] There were stories about the model being fitted with a mechanism which allowed it to stand to its full height, but these have been discounted.[7] Oleg Beliaev, who reverentially guarded the figure when it was still kept in the Kunstkamera along with other relics of the tsar and his era, pronounced the image lifelike, except for the fact that the cheeks were slightly sunken, 'because a dead body has no elasticity'.[8] He went on to provide a portrait that owed much to other representations: Peter's face was full and slightly dark-complexioned; his eyes were dark, full of fire and animation; his brow, nose, and lips were well-proportioned; his hair was dark, almost black, and not powdered, allowed to grow long or curled, but done in a simple style; his small moustache gave him a martial, courageous air; in general, his face combined a look of 'importance, severity, mercy and concern'.[9]

Beliaev's description of the artifacts in Peter's museum aimed at stressing the simplicity of the tsar's tastes and life-style—the worn boots, 'whose decrepitude demonstrates this monarch's great thrift', which were said to have been bought out of wages earned on a shift at Müller's ironworks;[10] the accompanying stockings, darned by the monarch himself; the famous battered hat from Poltava, with a bullet hole the size of a walnut, at the sight of which Emperor Joseph II of Austria was said to have been overcome by emotion;[11] the unadorned 'throne' on which the monarch sat. Peter's famous cudgel used to be kept in the museum, but had vanished by the time Beliaev wrote his book at the end of the eighteenth century. Some of the visitors who demanded to be shown the venerable relic 'would gladly have agreed to feel it on their backs if only they might see it'.[12] Beliaev described in loving detail Peter's private turnery, his lathes, and some of the handiwork produced on them, including a simple wooden mug. 'Drink tastes just as good out of a wooden vessel as from gold or silver,' Peter is alleged to have said.[13]

The simple tastes of the carpenter-tsar, that 'great contemner of all pomp and ostentation about his own person',[14] are legendary. 'The tsar sets no store by rich garments, fine furniture, carriages and residences. . . . Indeed, he gets most satisfaction from contact with simple people, especially since he loves such occupations as turning, carpentry, clockmaking, engraving, pyrotechnics and other such,' wrote Georg Grund.[15] 'It would be impossible to praise this ruler too much,' enthused Franz Lefort, 'because all his plans are so good, his undertakings so commendable and his inclinations so elevated that there is no doubt that his country will derive great benefit. He is an example for his subjects for he works like a simple man. He built a ship here with his own hands.'[16] To some contemporaries the tsar's 'simplicity' reflected admirable thrift: 'He did everything for his subjects and nothing for himself,' wrote

Baron Münnich; 'he dressed simply, and the expenses of his court did not exceed 60,000 roubles per year. He had neither chamberlains nor gentlemen of the bedchamber, nor pages; there was not even any silver tableware.'[17] (The fact that Münnich underestimated both the expenses and the number of servants shows how quickly the legend took root.) For others the tsar's frugal habits smacked of miserliness; for example, Just Juel complained of Peter's refusal to provide funds for a permanent residence for Danish envoys.[18] Peter's court is said to have had a 'Spartan, rather stern and gloomy atmosphere'.[19]

It is true that Peter cut down on 'oriental' pomp and ceremony with reference to his own person, discouraging low bows by his subjects and banning the use of time-wasting lists of titles in practical correspondence. ('Write simply, please, in letters, without "great",' he wrote to Fedor Apraksin in 1702.[20]) Anecdotes abound about his love of informality—for example, Nartov's aphorism about bans on obsequious grovelling and the use of diminutives to address subordinates: 'Less humility, more zeal for service and loyalty to me and to the State,' Peter is supposed to have advised.[21] Such developments were influenced no doubt by Peter's experience of the protocol of other European courts. Practical necessity, not to mention security, also required a new approach. The public appearances of Peter's predecessors had been strictly rationed and controlled. By and large (with the exception of Tsar Alexis's campaigns in Lithuania and the Baltic in the 1650s) they kept to the Kremlin and a handful of monasteries and residences in the Moscow region, their movements governed by the church calendar. Peter was here, there, and everywhere, in Russia and abroad. In 1722 a memo in Peter's hand stipulated that 'ceremonies for [the tsar's] arrival and departure from towns, firing from cannon, drum-beat in towns and camps when he passes by and drilling of soldiers with weapons in formation is not always necessary, for sometimes he doesn't want his movements publicized. Sometimes he even gets fed up with this sort of frequent ceremony.' It was pointed out that loud advertisement of the tsar's presence during military action was dangerous.[22]

That modesty was part of the tsar's official image during Peter's lifetime is indicated by an entry in the authorized account of the Nystad celebrations in 1721: when asked by the Senate and Synod to accept the new imperial titles, 'the tsar for a long time refused to accept with his customary and praiseworthy modesty (*modestii ili umerennosti*)'.[23] Such 'modesty' had its negative side. At times Peter's famed informality could be more inconvenient than the rigid but dependable ceremonial it replaced, especially in view of Peter's unpredictability and tendency to act on whim. He regularly ignored formal seating plans, grabbing whichever seat he fancied, as during his name-day party in 1723 when he went and sat with the foreign skippers. Often he preferred to eat standing up or walking around.[24] Informality extended to dropping in uninvited at other people's celebrations, to a German baker's wedding in 1724, for instance, at which he stayed for three hours and was 'exceedingly cheerful'.[25] On a notorious occasion in France in 1717 he strode in unannounced to inspect the aged Madame de Maintenon in her bed.[26]

One of the most striking examples of Peter's 'modesty' was his preference for small wooden houses and similarly unprepossessing accommodation. This has been attributed to his dislike of the old Kremlin palace, with its warren of vaulted chambers and chapels, richly painted and carved with religious images and full of bloody associations. 'When at Mosco,' observed Charles Whitworth, 'he never lodges in the palace, but in a little wooden house built for him in the suburbs [at Preobrazhenskoe] as Colonel of his guards.'[27] A number of such little houses survive all over Russia, the most renowned being the cabin in which the tsar resided during the first years of the construction of St Petersburg. Already in Peter's lifetime this house was something of a symbol, as evidenced by the construction of a protective stone casing in 1723.[28] It had its effect on posterity. The author of one of the first guides to St Petersburg devoted several pages to an exposition of the theme of 'Why such a Great Monarch should have chosen to dwell in such a small and wretched little house ... which, however, little though it was, was more exalted than the splendid palace of Emperor Cyrus, the many-chambered mansion of Solomon and as worthy of honour as splendid Versailles'.[29] An anonymous work of 1759 boasted that just as Romulus's little town became the sovereign of the world, Peter's little hut had become the 'Northern Rome'.[30] The tone had hardly changed in 1891 when Father Bulgakovsky opined that 'for all its simplicity the little house gleamed brighter than gold with the Great Monarch's glory'. He quotes the German academician Bielfinger who on returning home in 1731 is supposed to have said: 'O, how I marvelled at its great inhabitant as I walked round that hut! In that little cottage, I thought, were born all those schemes which spread life over such an extensive Empire. Yes, that cottage contained his body, but his soul knew no bounds.'[31] The little house at Saandam in Holland has also been preserved, even though Peter spent only a week there in 1697. (Napoleon, incidentally, expressed disapproval of the simplicity of this dwelling and of Peter's sailor habits.[32]) At Peterhof the tsar preferred the relatively small Mon Plaisir pavilion, which was right by the sea, to the grand palace on the hill.[33]

When travelling abroad, Peter usually declined the suites offered by his hosts, preferring to lodge in ordinary rooms. In Paris in 1717, for example, he rejected apartments in the Louvre, making instead for a private house where he immediately went to bed in a small room intended for the servants.[34] Best of all, Peter enjoyed sleeping in the snug, enclosed wooden space on board ship, both after lunch and at night, regarding the combination of sea air and motion of the waves as beneficial to his health. In October 1720 during a visit to Menshikov's new residence on the coast at Schlüsselburg, everyone else slept in the house, but Peter retired to his yacht.[35] When he was ill during a visit to Riga in 1721, he stayed on board ship for a week.[36]

The question of the tsar's tastes in food is an interesting example of how the 'plain man' image has edged out the more complex reality. Legend has it that Peter preferred to eat simple fare, and lots of it. According to one of Nartov's anecdotes, he favoured cabbage soup, porridge (kasha), roast meat with pickled cucumbers and salted lemons, ham and cheese, washed down with kvas (a drink made from fermented black bread).[37] Nepliuev records receiving some vodka and a slice of pie from the tsar's own hand, accompanied by the words: 'This is our own native food, not Italian.'[38] But it is clear from countless orders sent to agents abroad that Peter was not indifferent to good foreign food, and imported favourite items, including anchovies, German herring, lemons, and other fruit.[39] Even Nartov mentions Peter's love of French and Hungarian wine. On 13 March 1724 he wrote to Kurakin: 'Buy us two hundred bottles of good Hermitage and send it to St Petersburg this spring.'[40]

Peter's informality and simple tastes could be interpreted as rude bad manners in foreign court circles. Apparently Peter's behaviour did not improve much after his first encounters with Western high society, as described by the electresses of Hanover and Brandenburg in 1697, or his notorious wrecking of John Evelyn's house in Deptford in 1698. Sophia Charlotte of Brandenburg wrote: 'It is evident that he has not been taught how to eat properly,' but added that she liked his 'natural manner and informality'.[41] Wilhelmina of Bayreuth pronounced Peter and his retinue 'barbaric' when, in Berlin in 1719, Peter is said to have demanded a very expensive cupboard as a gift and wrecked the newly decorated Mon Bijou palace, which looked like 'Jerusalem after its collapse'.[42] In Copenhagen in 1716 King Frederick found Peter 'ill-mannered and importunate'. He offended the king by giving a vague response to an invitation to the court theatre. The performance was cancelled, but Peter turned up and demanded to see the king. On being told that he had gone to bed, Peter went to look for him anyway, and caught him still up with some of his ministers.[43]

Peter's preference for going on foot rather than in an official carriage could be disconcerting. Once in Berlin he is said to have slipped out of a back entrance rather than climb into the splendid carriage sent by the king and to have arrived at the royal palace with a couple of attendants on foot.[44] On another occasion, in Paris in 1717, for a trip to the Bois de Boulogne he requisitioned the carriage of a lady who had come to catch a glimpse of him, leaving her to go home on foot.[45] In France he offended his hosts on several occasions by refusing the accommodation and transport offered and suddenly departing from the arranged programme. His escort De Libois complained that he was 'assez difficile à servir'.[46] Peter's diary of activities bears witness to a neurotic restlessness. The entries for the last months of his life, when he was already seriously ill, record that he spent several months in Schlüsselburg and Ladoga, returned to St Petersburg in late October, then two days later left again for Sestroretska.[47] Many witnesses remarked upon Peter's fast walk, which left everyone else behind. Juel records an abortive audience as the tsar strode round the Admiralty wharf and he scurried after him in an attempt to have a few words in private.[48]

Peter's clothing excited comment. 'Usually one sees His Majesty so badly dressed that anyone who did not know him would never take him to be the great monarch that he is,' wrote a German observer.[49] Peter's clothes aroused particularly unfavourable criticism in fashion-conscious Paris, where they were described as 'habit de farouche'.[50] Some Frenchmen commented disparagingly on the tsar's shabby clothing. Peter, in retaliation, described a Frenchman who wears a different outfit every day as 'a man who is dissatisfied with his tailor'.[51] Other anecdotes tell of stockings darned by Catherine or the tsar himself and down-at-heel boots, of Peter's disdain for a sumptuous outfit sewn for him by Catherine and her ladies, a few silver threads from which would pay a soldier's daily wage, he remarked.[52] But this did not mean that Peter was indifferent to dress, just as he was far from indifferent to his surroundings. He might don the costume of a simple sailor or Dutch rustic for a masquerade, but, as Cornelius de Bruyn observed at the wedding of Filat Shansky in 1702, he could appear dressed in magnificent cloth of gold, in a robe 'intermixed with many figures of several colours' and a 'great red fur cap' on his head.[53] For the wedding of his niece Anna in 1710, he wore a scarlet tunic with sable trimmings, a silver sword with a silver shoulder belt, his order of St Andrew on a blue ribbon, and a powdered wig.[54] Peter bought many clothes on his foreign trips. A list of items purchased for 'Mr Vice-Admiral' in Danzig in 1716 included two pairs of lace-up boots, a pair of high boots and three pairs of shoes, lengths of red cloth for a coat and yellow fabric for a shirt, silver buttons and braid, and bright blue cloth with grey Turkish silk lining for another coat.[55] He had a taste for fine fabrics and an eye for colour ('Send the finest calamanco cloths, cornflower blue, blue, crimson, scarlet, pink,' he wrote to agent Brandt in Amsterdam[56]). In Moscow in 1724 before Catherine's coronation, he proudly showed off a pair of cuffs with wide lace trimmings which he regarded as fashionable.[57] Peter's costume for the coronation ceremony was light blue silk with rich silver embroidery —Münnich was wrong when he declared that embroidery was unknown on Russian male clothing,[58] with red silk stockings and a hat with a white feather,[59] although Bergholz, with his characteristic eye for detail, noted elsewhere that Peter retained a small (unfashionable) 'Swedish' collar on his jackets.[60] Anecdotes tell of Peter grabbing a wig from the head of the person next to him when he felt cold,[61] but in 1722 he was accompanied to Astrakhan by his personal hairdresser Christian Bernard, who made him wigs of natural hair, one of which, as we have seen, ended up on Rastrelli's wax model.[62]

Peter's costumes were chosen to make a statement. It is notable that in official portraits he was depicted not as the 'carpenter-tsar', still less in shabby disarray, but with all the conventional attributes of kingship—royal ermine and warrior's armour, martial symbols, maps, and plans of conquests. Peter's favourite portrait of himself is said to be the one produced by Carl Moor in Amsterdam in 1717.[63] Peter is shown in ordinary dress only in a few unofficial portraits. Even Ivan Nikitin's simple oval portrait shows the tsar in the uniform of a Preobrazhensky guard. Peter favoured imperial Roman symbols on the coinage and medals, and encouraged Classical mythological images at victory parades. This practical man was well aware of the importance of symbols and emblems, perhaps to the extent that he even 'thought in baroque images'.[64]

II. DISGUISES AND PSEUDONYMS

The question of clothes and portraits raises the subject of disguises and masks. Peter's spontaneous, informal behaviour and tastes were remarkable enough, but even more remarkable was the *formalized* pretence that he was not the tsar at all, but a ship's carpenter or bombardier.[65] Like his interest in the navy, Peter's alternative career has its roots in childhood games, when he progressed from playing with toy soldiers, guns, and drums in the 1670s to forming his own units of play troops in the 1680s. He began to climb the ladder of military ranks in 1695 when he served as a bombardier at Azov. For capturing two Swedish ships off Nienschants not far from the site of the future St Petersburg in May 1703, Captain Peter of the bombardiers and Governor-General Menshikov were awarded the order of St Andrew by their commanding officers Admiral Count Fedor Golovin, the first recipient of the award, and General Sheremetev.[66] After Poltava, Peter was promoted to rear-admiral of the fleet and senior lieutenant-general in the army, 'for great bravery and skill'. 'Although I have not deserved this much, it is granted to me only thanks to your beneficence, so I pray to God for the strength to be worthy of such kindness in future,' he wrote to Fedor Romodanovsky, the mock tsar who conferred his award.[67] In August 1713 during the Finnish naval campaign he wrote to inform Catherine that he had been made a full general, congratulating her on becoming a 'general's wife', adding 'like the rank of rear-admiral, this one was also awarded under strange circumstances, for I was made a *flagman* on the steppe and a general on the sea'.[68] On the day after Catherine's coronation in May 1724, Peter came to congratulate her along with other army officers in his capacity as colonel-general of the guards.[69] Peter regarded only his service salary as his own money, from which he bought personal items such as clothing; state funds had to be accounted for to God.[70]

Peter's alternative personae were no short-lived adolescent craze. The elaborate charade was maintained on occasion to the end of his life and in various ways. He even had different names for different roles. An early reference appears in a letter to F. M. Apraksin in December 1693, in which Peter, signing himself Dutch-style *Piter*, complained about being addressed with the full royal titles, 'which I hate'.[71] After the capture of Azov in 1696, the prince-pope Nikita Zotov and Kirill Alekseevich Naryshkin headed the triumphal procession into Moscow in carriages, followed by Generalissimus Franz Lefort, while naval officer Peter Alekseev, 'in German dress', followed on foot with the marching troops. The gun salute and greetings through a loud-hailer were directed not at the tsar but at the nominal commander-in-chief, General Aleksei Shein, at the rear of the procession.[72] Peter travelled to the West in

1697 under the name Peter Mikhailov. It was military ranks, rather than royal titles, which often appeared in the Cabinet office account books—for example, the various items of clothing for Mr (*gospodin*), captain (1705), colonel (1709), general (1710), rear-admiral (1713), vice-admiral (1716).[73] In 1715 he even specifically commissioned a portrait of Mr Vice-Admiral.[74]

Apparent disdain for his own God-given rank was reflected in the company he kept. Those seeking rational explanations of Peter's behaviour have suggested that he was a champion of meritocracy, always searching out the best man (and occasionally woman) for the job, regardless of rank.[75] He was 'democratic' in his choice of companions, be it his second wife (a Livonian peasant), his favourite (reputedly the son of a pie-seller), or the motley crew of foreign officers, sailors, lesser officials, and artisans whose weddings and funerals he attended, not to mention the odd assortment that made up the Drunken Assembly.[76] He especially enjoyed acting as godfather to the infants of shipwrights and orderlies, and rarely did he forget to send greetings to 'all our comrades gentlemen master shipwrights'.[77] Ivan Nepliuev recorded one of Peter's most famous utterances in 1720, at an examination of naval trainees recently returned from abroad: 'You see, lad, even though I'm the tsar I have callouses on my hands, all in order to show you an example so that I may see fitting helpers and servants of the fatherland, even if I have to wait until I am old.'[78]

But Peter was perfectly capable of mocking his own cherished principle of employing the best man to serve the State, regardless of origins. Often he seems to have made a point of choosing the *unqualified*: for example, Franz Lefort and Aleksei Shein were appointed to command the troops going to Azov in 1695 as admiral and general respectively, when neither had any experience of the navy or the army whatsoever.[79] A notorious example was Peter's deference to Ivan Mikhailovich Golovin as chief shipwright, or *baas* (from the Dutch), from 1717 *ober-sarviir* (chief surveyor). The joke is that Golovin had no talent for shipbuilding and had failed miserably at his trade when forced to study abroad. (Campredon called him 'chef de l'amirauté par dérision'.[80]) Still, Golovin was happy to play Peter's game. In November 1713 he wrote to the tsar, addressing him as 'Peter Mikhailov, foremost of all shipwrights', and ordering him, in the name of Admiral Apraksin, to have a ship built and asking him to report any problems without delay.[81] In January 1714 Peter and several foreign shipwrights wrote to Golovin with New Year greetings, hoping that 'this enterprise [i.e., shipbuilding] will increase and grow to your immortal glory as the leader of that enterprise in Russia or our second Noah'. They signed themselves 'your excellency's pupils and servants'.[82] In a letter of 23 June 1716, Peter wrote from Schwerin to 'Your Excellency Lord Prince *baas* from your pupil and servant', sending a present of 'several new instruments, which are appropriate to your trade'.[83] A new toast was even introduced to the repertoire at feasts: 'for the health of the family (or sons) of Ivan Mikhailovich'—that is, the ships of the Russian fleet.[84] The joke was kept up relentlessly, Golovin appearing at masquerades in a skipper's outfit. There is an engraved oval portrait commissioned by the tsar and depicting the *baas* against a background of wooden sections of ship and shipwright's instruments.[85] Peter seems to have enjoyed elaborating and implementing the intricacies of extended role play, of which, of course, the Drunken Assembly, with its extensive personnel, statutes, and rituals, was the most complex. James Cracraft, for one, detects a 'darker significance', evidence of 'a sense of disillusionment, of disgust, or even despair', a 'possible tragic flaw'. He believes that Peter may have been only 'dimly conscious of what he was doing', and that at the heart of his 'frolics' lay a profound lack of respect for the feelings of others.[86] One might add the cliché that Peter was a split personality, who found it hard to 'be himself', but, unlike lesser mortals faced with the same dilemma, could indulge himself in being whatever he liked. Peter had many names, many disguises, many roles, and, as tsar, was able to command whatever supporting players he required whenever he wanted.

Peter's non-conformity to the standard image of a tsar, his deliberate neglect, ridicule, and pastiche of royal and religious protocol, gave rise to a number of rumours and legends to the effect that the tsar *was* a commoner. Some claimed that his true father was a foreign barber (hence Peter's interest in autopsies and dentistry, not to mention the notorious beard shaving), that he had been substituted for the tsar's real child in 1672, or later kidnapped in the West and replaced by an impostor.[87] Those close to the tsar and loyal to him, and who had no reason to believe such rumours, were able to turn his idiosyncrasies to their own advantage. Perhaps Peter's 'simple man' image may usefully be compared with the images of his later admirers Lenin and Stalin, both of whom were said to have plain tastes, the former preferring modest surroundings and simple food, the latter clad always in an unadorned uniform tunic, but both ranking in most people's estimation alongside the most powerful rulers of history. (Lenin also had a taste for Rolls-Royces.) Like them, Peter received praise and acclamation for his man-of-the-people image *during his own lifetime*. Un-tsar-like behaviour was legitimized and declared to be the ideal rather than an aberration. In the words of Feofan Prokopovich, the chief architect of the reformed image, 'a tsar's majesty is found not in bright [imperial] purple, not in a golden diadem, but in strength, firmness, valour, in bold deeds worthy of amazement'.[88]

A predecessor springs to mind: Ivan IV, who prefigured the antics of the Drunken Assembly with members of his *oprichnina* and even appointed a baptized Tatar, Simon Bekbulatovich, to sit on the throne while he assumed the role of a 'simple boyar'.[89] Peter's contemporary and rival, Charles XII of Sweden, was also memorably unkingly, even more neglectful of dress, comfort, and hygiene than Peter. Perhaps only the really powerful can allow themselves the luxury of such frugality. Peter, this man of simple tastes, built a whole city from scratch, and had a fleet of vessels and whole armies under his command. He showed little thrift when it came to squeezing every last drop of manpower, effort, and taxes out of the Russian population. Peter's penchant for sleeping in wooden huts did not prevent him from spending considerable time and resources on several grand residences on the Gulf of Finland, including Peterhof and Strel'na, both of which have been described as Russian Versailles. He expected members of his own family and circle to live in a manner befitting their station: Catherine maintained a staff of courtiers. His daughters wore expensive jewels. Bassewitz records a telling anecdote. After Menshikov's indictment for embezzlement, Peter visited the prince's palace and found it decorated with moth-eaten old wall-hangings. When Menshikov complained that he had had to sell the good ones to settle his debts, Peter ordered him to decorate his home in keeping with his rank, saying that he expected to find proper hangings when he came to the next party.[90]

Peter's love of disguise was far from unusual in the Europe of his day. Donning fancy dress had long been a common diversion for crowned heads, whether in the exclusive court masques of the seventeenth century or the masked crowds on the streets, where a king of England might mingle with his people incognito. Royalty and aristocrats dressed up as maids, shepherds, sailors, and chimney-sweeps, while ordinary folk went about as kings and queens. The eighteenth century was an 'age of disguise', the main point being to appear 'in some sense, as one's opposite' and to seek 'a personal abdication from the responsibilities of identity and a group abdication from the strictures of the social order itself'. Hierarchies were made explicit by being suspended.[91] Even so, there can be few examples of royal subterfuge so sustained and varied as that practised by Peter I.

III. HOBBIES AND INTERESTS

One of the best explanations for Peter's 'bizarre' behaviour is the simplest: he needed to relax, to step aside from the exhausting business of state, in which he often felt alone and unaided. This is reflected in his practical, plain man's taste in hobbies. Soviet tour guides never tired of the statistic that the tsar mastered fourteen trades. Of these the favourite was wood-turning, which he practised wherever he happened to be, ordering machines, tools, materials, and manuals to be sent.[92] One minute in a letter he could refer to the trials of rebels at Astrakhan, in the next line ask for his lathe and pieces of suitable timber.[93] In December 1706 he asked the English merchant Andrew Styles to send for some bone for making snuff-boxes, a few weeks later he requested rhinoceros horns.[94] Just Juel caught him at his lathe one day, clad in a workman's leather overall and working 'as though he had to earn his living from this particular form of labour'.[95] In March 1711, on the eve of war with Turkey, amid diplomatic correspondence and orders regarding troop movements and provisions, we find a letter asking Fedor Apraksin to send a lathe which had been left in Voronezh in 1709, 'to our regiment, wherever we may be'.[96] One was ordered from Boris Kurakin in London, another purchased in July 1717 in Spa, where the turner received a tip for allowing Peter to work at his lathe.[97] Peter's turnery instructor, Nartov, was sent to France in 1718 for a period of training.[98] Various items said to have been made by Peter himself survived into the nineteenth century and even into the twentieth, such as a church chandelier in bone,[99] a birchwood armchair, a bench in his St Petersburg cabin and a rowing boat outside it.

Peter was fond of fire fighting, as noted by several foreign observers, starting with the Frenchman De la Neuville in 1689, who wrote that 'his dominant passion is to see houses burn, which is a very common occurrence in Moscow since no one bothers to put one out unless there are 400 or 500 alight'. He would arrive with fire-fighting equipment, direct operations, encourage others, and go to the most dangerous places.[100] Such behaviour may have been prompted by the wish to set a good example to less public-spirited citizens,[101] but one of the features of fires which appealed to Peter was no doubt the noise and commotion. He had a passion for explosions, cannon-fire, fireworks, and drum-beats. Not only did he love to be entertained by drummers, such as the ten who visited him in Mecklenburg on his name-day;[102] he was a dab hand with drumsticks himself. In Dresden in June 1698 Peter took a drum and in the presence of ladies beat it so expertly that he outdid all the other drummers.[103] At masquerades he often carried a drum, as at the carnival in September 1723, when he walked around drumming, preceded by a man dressed up as the sun.[104] His tastes in music may have been loud rather than subtle (drums and trumpets), but he also enjoyed religious part-singing, as in Petrozavodsk in 1720, when he sang with the choristers, who accompanied him. He is said to have had a light baritone voice.[105] He loved dancing, setting an exhausting pace for the rest of the company at balls,[106] and enjoyed such games as lotto and dice.[107] Chess was a favourite, as were billiards, spillikins (*biriulki*), and shove-ha'penny (*trukt-tafel*);[108] but he disapproved of cards, except for a Dutch game called Gravias. Only very small stakes were allowed.[109]

Peter was fascinated by mathematical instruments, as exemplified by the famous childhood story about the astrolabe brought back for him by Prince Dolgoruky from France. He usually carried a telescope, and owned a number of mathematical and navigational instruments, which were purchased and repaired at considerable expense.[110] He liked globes, the largest of which, the famous Gotthorp globe, had a planetarium in an inner cabinet which could hold several people. He was knowledgeable about fortifications and defences, and took part in the surveying of Azov and Kronstadt. (In Riga in 1697, it will be recalled, this 'hobby' sparked off a diplomatic incident.[111]) Peter's interest in architecture is well known. Simple architectural drawings in his own hand, of bastions, fountains and garden architecture, survive. He dabbled in engraving (he made an allegorical etching of 'The Triumph of Christianity over Islam' in Amsterdam in 1698, under the tutorship of Adrian Schoenebeck),[112] and could turn his hand to making charts and plans. While in Venice, Boris Sheremetev is said to have been shown a map of the Black Sea 'made with the tsar's own hands'.[113]

Despite such accomplishments, Peter had little formal education and little inclination for intense intellectual effort. Empress Elizabeth is said to have recounted how Peter often visited his daughters at their lessons, and told them to be grateful that they were receiving a good education. 'I was deprived of all that in my youth.'[114] His hand-writing and spelling were atrocious and many original autographs are barely decipherable even by specialists. There is no evidence that he ever read, annotated, or commented in any detail on 'difficult' works of philosophy, theology, or history, although the odd remark about all these topics survives. The working section of his library was concerned mainly with such matters as fortification, artillery, hydraulics, navigation, and shipbuilding. He also took a connoisseur's interest in books, discussing the finer points of type-faces, bindings, and print runs, and had a firm belief in the propaganda and educational value of the printed word. Translation was a particular interest. A report published in Paris in 1710 declared that not only was the tsar promoting science and learning and publishing books, but also 'himself did not consider it shameful to translate some of them'. It is claimed that Peter actually translated Vignola's *Rules of the Five Orders of Architecture*, first published in 1708, although generally his contribution to translation was limited to comments on individual terms.[115]

Peter enjoys the reputation of being the founding father of modern Russian science, a member of the French Academy of Sciences, and creator of the Russian Academy and the first museum, he corresponded with scientists and men of letters. Was there a serious side to Peter's scientific curiosity? Platonov thought so. When Peter was in Paris, his 'attitude to the cultural and technical wonders of Paris was indeed not superficial but serious'. The tsar observed arsenals, mints, factories, presses, botanical and pharmaceutical gardens, an anatomical theatre, observatory, mathematical, physics, and mechanics laboratories, chemical experiments, and operations.[116] He took an interest in eclipses of the sun and other natural phenomena of light.[117] Even so, his scientific interests suggest a love of practice rather than theory, a search for sensation rather than rational reflection. To a man of Peter's nationality and generation, who, it should be reiterated, had no real formal education, the world was full of puzzles. Like most people of his time, Peter dabbled in fortune telling and recreational 'black magic'. He and Catherine kept notes on dreams, and were interested in their interpretation.[118] He was delighted at the discovery of mineral waters to the north of the ironworks at Olonets (near Petrozavodsk), where he tried to set up a spa along the lines of those at Pyrmont, Carlsbad, and Spa, in the hope of bringing trade to the town.[119] After a trip to the Olonets waters in June 1724, he told Catherine that he had 'regained his old health' and was feeling much better, 'with God's help'.[120] Belief in the curative properties of spa waters was common throughout the royal courts of Europe, as was the use of folk medicine and blood-letting. Peter's and Catherine's appointments diary records, for example, that on 14 May 1720 'their majesties were bled through a vein then dined'; on 19 June they 'attended mass, were bled with cups, dined at Mon Plaisir and took a walk'.[121]

To the educated modern taste one of Peter's most unattractive traits was his unflinching fascination with freaks. At one of his first encounters with the tsar in 1702, Cornelius de Bruyn was shown a man whose intestines protruded from a wound. Peter seemed fascinated, ordering 'the poor man's excrescence to be squeezed, that I might be the more sensible of the nature of his case, and everything came out half digested'.[122] As Bruyn noted, Peter was not alone in such tastes: '[The Russians] take a great delight in being with mad people, or such as are deformed, or deep in liquor, when they happen to be so to excess.'[123] Nor were such tastes confined to Russia, he might have added. When in January 1717 Peter wrote to the vice-governor of Archangel, Lodyzhensky, ordering him to find 'two young Samoyeds, between 15 and 18 years old, with the ugliest and funniest mugs you can find, dressed in their usual costume and ornaments', as a gift for the duke of Florence, he evidently expected his generosity to be appreciated.[124] Peter's love of dwarfs had been fostered from the cradle. His elder half-brothers and sisters and his own father and his forebears, not to mention Peter's immediate successors, were all attended by dwarfs, as were Peter's own children. Fascination with giants, such as the Frenchman Nicholas Bourgeois, was a variation on the theme.[125] Peter's *Kunstkamera* contained not only preserved oddities, such as the skeleton of a child wiping its tears with a piece of brain membrane, but also live exhibits: the peasant Foma, who had only two digits on hands and feet, and the two 'monsters' Iakov and Stepan.[126] Such freak shows were not Peter's invention. People all over Europe loved to gawp at the exotic, the bizarre, and the deformed. Judging by the crowds which still mill around the two-headed calves and bottled babies in what remains of Peter's Cabinet of Curiosities in St Petersburg, fascination with such objects has not diminished. Peter himself, it should be added, was freakish by the standards of his day—a giant of a man, who drew crowds wherever he went. There was more than a hint of turning the tables on the objects of his own curiosity.

A taste for the bizarre was combined with a morbid streak. Peter was fascinated by death. Just Juel recounts a conversation with the tsar in 1711 when the latter described how the corpse of a *strelets* newly beheaded in 1698/9 remained on its hands and knees for a minute.[127] There are numerous instances of Peter's delaying funerals, either to prepare fitting solemnities or in order for post-mortems to be carried out, often on people close to him. For example, when Ivan Buturlin died in 1710, Peter ordered that his body be stored and the moisture drained off.[128] Similar orders were given regarding the corpses of Dr Erskine and Tsarevna Ekaterina Alekseevna. In November 1701 he ordered a death mask to be taken from Fedor Pleshcheev.[129] In France in 1717 Peter bought the Dutch anatomist Ruysch's secret recipe for preserving corpses, refusing to reveal it to French anatomists who were working on models of human organs.[130] He had the naturally mummified corpses of two young women, buried in 1632, brought to his camp on the Baltic for inspection.[131] According to his cook, Felten, Peter usually carried around a variety of surgical and dental instruments with which to perform a blood-letting, do a dissection or pull a tooth.[132] It should be added that Peter also loved to operate on the living. He regarded himself as an excellent surgeon, which terrified potential guinea-pigs—for example, his niece Ekaterina, who received the tsar's unwelcome attention for a bad leg.[133] There is a less macabre, almost childlike side to Peter's interest in nature. In 1721 he sent Menshikov some willow branches from Riga, and asked him to send some branches cut for Palm Sunday to find out which town, Riga or St Petersburg, had an earlier spring. A week or so later he asked Menshikov to send him buds and leaves from the gardens of the palaces at Peterhof and Dubki every week, marked with the date when they were picked.[134]

All the pastimes mentioned above were eclipsed by the greatest passion of Peter's life: ships and the sea. A much-quoted, telling anecdote about Peter's visit to England in 1698 (from Nartov) is that if he had not been a Russian tsar, he would have liked to be a British admiral.[135] A recent biographer regards a ship as the ideal symbol of Peter's reign: 'Why a ship? I think that to Peter it was not only a means of transport for freight across the water's surface. The ship—Peter's eternal love—was for him a symbol of a structure organized and calculated to the inch, the material embodiment of human thought, complex movement by the will of rational man. Furthermore, the ship for Peter was a peculiar model of the ideal society, the best form of organization relying on knowledge of the laws of nature in man's eternal struggle with the blind elements.'[136] His personal papers and library contain countless examples of naval logs, sketches of parts of ships, schemes for signals, flags, and fleet manoeuvres, books on shipbuilding and navigation. His favourite painter was the marine artist, former sea captain Adam Silo, whose detailed studies of ships decorated the walls at Mon Plaisir palace.[137]

Evidence of Peter's simple tastes and practical bent has led some commentators to the conclusion that he had no time for aesthetics. Yet there is much evidence to the contrary, especially in the case of ships. Peter's enthusiasm was tinged with aesthetic appreciation: for him a ship was a thing of beauty. In July 1717 he wrote to Captain Skliaev regarding details of a new ship which was being built, suggesting the addition of a third row of windows 'for beauty as well as for comfort'. Five years later he was writing to the same man about carved decorations, a lion and two men on horseback with sabres, for the ships *Laferme* and *Gallion*. Several craftsmen were sent to Holland and England to study ships' carved décor.[138] In 1723 Peter ordered a new yacht to be equipped with an English dinner service and Dutch table linen, 'so that when it is necessary to transport dignitaries everything will be in readiness'.[139] The unnamed craftsmen who fashioned some of the first silver to be extracted from Russia's Transbaikal mine into a miniature sailing ship complete with sailors clearly knew the tsar's tastes well.[140]

An appreciation of fine things extended to his personal supervision of books through the press, which aimed not simply at getting as many practical manuals into print as possible, but also at producing fine editions which were pleasing to the eye. On receipt of some samples in 1709 (he was stationed with the army in the Ukraine), Peter wrote: 'The print in these books is much worse than before, not clean and too thick. See to it that they are printed as well as previous ones.' He also criticized the quality of the bindings and engravings.[141] The books in question had come out in quarto in 1708, but the second editions were in more lavish folio. Unlike many men of action— Charles XII, for example—Peter was not indifferent to his surroundings. How many other busy monarchs would have written to their commissar to send three apprentices to Düsseldorf to study under an 'urn master', Carl Bakaveri,[142] or have compiled colour schemes for matching sets of soft fur-nishings, wall-hangings, and curtains, or sent hand-written instructions to his agent in Riga to plant lines of limes, maples, and hazels along paths in his new park and to put up wire trellises along narrow paths 'as in the summer garden in Petersburg'?[143] A hand-written note to Dr Bidloo in Moscow in December 1723 regarding a garden project provides evidence of Peter's eye for detail: 'On the big pond on the two islands and on the octagonal island you are to build summer houses (*liust'gosy* or *cherdochki*), also places for doves and small birds near the wood and other embellishments suitable for a garden, and across the canals bridges, little humped-backed ones, with railings on one side with just enough room for one person to cross (like they do in Holland); also send a drawing or ground plan of both residences and the garden.'[144] Peter was particularly fond of trees and plants. Dozens of letters survive with orders to agents all over Russia and Europe, some of them displaying an expert knowl-edge of such horticultural matters as the best time of year for digging and replanting. He had an eye for a bargain, ordering cheap fruit-trees from Sweden after a tip-off from a Swedish gardener,[145] and collected books and prints on gardens and horticulture.[146] Almost the first thing Peter did on returning to Moscow after the Persian campaign in 1722 was to send a messenger to St Petersburg to find out about the chestnut-trees planted at Dubki two years earlier, 'whether they had survived the frosts and how they had done in the past summer'.[147] In July 1723 he wrote to Catherine from Reval, 'The garden which was planted here two years ago has grown so much that you would scarcely believe it: for the single big trees which you saw in some places have grown together with their branches across the road, and aunty's favourite tree, which has twigs like an index finger without a nail, has really come along well. The chestnuts also all have splendid crowns.'[148]

IV. CRUELTY AND COMPASSION

Peter is famed less for green fingers, however, than for bloody hands, the most notorious example being the public executions of the strel'tsy in 1698 and 1699 at which the tsar is said personally to have wielded the axe. Johannes Korb's graphic descriptions of the horrors prompted Peter to ban Korb's book in Russia, but age and experience did not lessen Peter's belief in such public spectacles. One of the most grisly was the impalement of Stepan Glebov in Moscow in March 1718, when every effort was made, down to dressing him

in a fur coat and hat, to keep the victim alive and suffering for as long as possible.[149] Bergholz recorded a mass execution in January 1724, to which the
public was alerted by heralds beating drums, summoning them to watch the
breaking of one official on the wheel, beheadings, and slitting of nostrils.
This, like all previous executions, had a didactic aspect. As Bergholz wrote,
'All the officials from the chancelleries and offices were obliged to attend the
execution as a warning to them.'[150]

How cruel *was* Peter? I have in mind here not moral arguments about the
cruelty of rulers who send their subjects to perish in their thousands in war
or sacrifice them in vast state projects, but the propensity to inflict pain in
person or to pile on tortures beyond what was required to deter criminals.
Early modern Christian rulers were expected to administer just retribution,
showing compassion and charity on a selective basis. In Peter's case it is
significant that he earned a reputation for being cruel quite early in his reign,
which Georg Grund saw fit to refute by arguing that he had seen no evidence
of the tsar's 'renowned cruelty' during his four years in Russia, and that the
tsar always handed rebels and criminals over to the proper authorities.[151] This
is to some extent confirmed by the absence of references to Peter's presence at
torture sessions in the protocols of the Preobrazhensky *prikaz*,[152] as well as by
lack of such entries in palace journals, not to mention Peter's own correspondence. Corrections to drafts of the Military Statute show that Peter often
mitigated punishments—for example, in a clause on bestiality Peter crossed
out the punishment that the offender must be beheaded along with the beast
with which he had copulated, and replaced it with corporal punishment
(*zhestoko na tele nakazat'*). The automatic death penalty for adultery was
replaced by the formula that 'both be punished according to the circumstances and their guilt'.[153] The overall number of offences incurring the death
penalty and the approved methods of putting people to death increased
during Peter's reign, but capital punishment was not implemented indiscrim-
inately. Of eight death sentences recommended to Peter in 1700 for false
denunciations, the tsar confirmed only one, commuting the rest to flogging
and exile.[154] Some reports of Peter personally putting people to death turn out
to be legends – for example, the story that in 1697 Peter in person had
beheaded the German traitor Jacob Jansen (who betrayed Russia at Azov)
probably originated among the strel'tsy.[155] A report by a diplomat in 1721 that
Peter hit a soldier who was stealing copper from a church so hard with his
club that the man perished on the spot is hard to verify.[156]

He was least likely to show mercy when treason and revolt were involved.
He did not take part personally in the execution of the Astrakhan rebels, but
in 1706, 320 were executed, and dozens died under torture at his instigation.
Orders for the treatment of the Bulavin rebels were particularly harsh. V. V.
Dolgoruky was commanded to burn villages which joined the rebellion, massacre the villagers, and put the ringleaders on wheels and spikes to deter
others. Whole communities were to be wiped out.[157] The cruel execution of
a number of people involved in the Alexis affair, especially the so-called

Suzdal' victims (the associates of Tsaritsa Evdokia), showed a vindictive streak. Peter could be very insensitive, alternating funerals, weddings, and executions with apparent nonchalance, and expecting his court to do likewise. Notable examples are the interspersing of the death and funeral of Tsarevich Alexis in July 1718 with noisy celebrations for the anniversary of the Battle of Poltava and Peter's name-day, and following the execution of William Mons in November 1724 by festivities for the betrothal of Peter's daughter Anna and the name-day of Empress Catherine, whom he suspected of having had an affair with Mons.[158]

But there is also evidence of a more compassionate nature. In 1717 Peter wrote to Ivan Fedorovich Romodanovsky: 'I received your letter of 21 September upon arrival in which you inform me of the death of your father, for which I offer deepest condolences that he did not lose his life as a result of old age but from an attack of gangrene; still, there goes everyone one way or another by God's will, bear this in mind and don't give in to grief. And please don't imagine that I have abandoned you, or forgotten your father's good deeds. I shall write to you anon about the time and place of the burial.'[159] Writing to Apraksin in 1724, 'I heard that you want to travel to Moscow. Of course you must not. You'll do yourself in. Your phlegm has been diluted by the medicine so when you go out in the wind you will catch a sudden chill and will be worse off than you were before, and death will very likely soon follow as a result, so give yourself a rest and travel only when the doctor says it's quite safe.'[160] He could also show concern for lesser individuals, as when he offered advice to a captain who had been prescribed a spa cure, telling him that although the doctor has prescribed a summer cure, he should go in winter, 'as the waters are just as effective as in summer; so since the journey is easier in winter, you had better go now';[161] or when he scolded Ivan Orlov (a junior officer in his own regiment) in a hand-written note for not looking after his health, taking unsuitable medicines, and failing to consult a good doctor.[162] In a letter written in 1724 from the Martsialnye spa near Petrozavodsk he wrote: 'A peasant from these parts called Faddei is old and seems simple-minded, lives in the forest and comes into the village, where they regard him as a marvel. There are no reports of malice or dissidence, so in order to prevent any temptation, I have ordered him to be brought to you in the factory and fed there until his death.'[163] Just Juel records that on hearing news of storm damage to the Danish fleet in 1710, Peter hurried to find him on foot in the dark and rain to express his sympathy.[164]

Peter's softer side is illustrated by his fondness for animals, especially dogs. Stuck in Vilna towards the end of 1707 after a tiring, inconclusive campaign, he jotted down names for the puppies of his bitch Lenta—Pirois, Eois, Aeton, Flegon (males), Pallas, Nymph, and Venus (females).[165] He asked Apraksin to have a foreigner train the dogs to do tricks: taking off a hat, jumping over a stick, sitting and begging.[166] In November 1708 he had Pirois and Eois sent to him in Ukraine, together with a list of the skills they had learned.[167] Letters were sometimes 'signed' by his favourite dog Lizetka.[168] In August 1708, in the midst of a tense campaign, he sent the deceased Lizetka by messenger to Dr Bidloo for embalming.[169] On his trip to Persia in 1722 he was accompanied by dogs, including Prince, who got lost and was returned by a man who was rewarded with a rouble and fifty copecks.[170] An orderly was in charge of feeding the dogs and buying equipment, such as beds and three sheepskin coats to keep them warm on the road from Tsaritsyn to Moscow in December.[171]

Peter's concern for animals is illustrated by his detailed instructions for the welfare of some birds and monkeys being transported by ship from the Netherlands to St Petersburg. If wind and frosts delayed the ship, their keeper was instructed to take them ashore and carry them overland. 'Have them well looked after and take care that they don't die!'[172] Care and money were lavished on the imperial menageries and aviaries, which were run from the Cabinet office.[173] He hated hunting and bear-baiting, and cruelty to animals in general, although concern did not stretch to cockroaches, which he feared.[174] In a well-known anecdote, Peter halted an experiment with a lark in a vacuum which was being conducted by his physician Dr Erskine, with the words: 'Enough! Don't take the life of the harmless creature; she isn't a robber.'[175] Peter could be sentimental about objects, too. Letters on the transport of his first boat from Moscow to St Petersburg betray a nostalgic streak, as he warns the commander of the team to 'take very good care of it on the journey so that it doesn't get damaged as it is an old boat, therefore travel by day and stop at night and set it down very gently. And don't leave it in yards and streets in towns and villages where there is any danger of fires ... but set it down in fields away from buildings and post sentries.' In this case, of course, sentimentality was combined with a strong sense of personal destiny and awareness of the little boat's propaganda value.[176]

It will doubtless be pointed out that dog-loving despots who enjoyed messing around in boats are not unknown in history, but Peter may at least be distinguished in this respect from his predecessor Ivan IV, who as a child is said to have enjoyed hurling dogs and cats from towers. But Peter's heroes from Russian history included that same Ivan IV, and his attitude towards him throws light on the subject of cruelty raised earlier. Triumphal gates in Moscow celebrating the Nystad peace featured a composition with Peter on one side and Ivan IV on the other, each represented with the coats of arms of their conquests. Peter is said to have liked this particular juxtaposition, because 'this sovereign is my forerunner and example (*predshestvennik i primer*). I have always taken him as a model of prudence and courage, but until now I could not compare with him. Only stupid people who do not know the circumstances of his time, the nature of his people and his great services call him a tyrant.'[177] A foreign observer made the same comparison less positively: 'The present government is in many respects similar to that of Tsar Ivan Vasil'evich, with the difference that under the latter the clergy were raised up and rewarded, whereas under this regime they are under a heavy yoke, which must be regarded as a dangerous fire smouldering under the ashes.'[178]

V.   RELIGIOUS BELIEFS

Consideration of Peter's temperament invites reflection on his inner beliefs and religious convictions. Much contradictory evidence has come down to us on this subject—Peter singing heartily in church and reading the lesson one minute,[179] abusing monks as 'parasites' and breaking bishops on the wheel the next, pious devotions at regular Orthodox services alternating with the blasphemous anti-liturgy of the Drunken Assembly. By and large, historians have tended to assume that the impious tsar was the true Peter, rejecting as official propaganda Prokopovich's claim, in his funeral oration, that Peter's strove 'to promote the improvement of the priesthood and true religion among the people'.[180] Peter's fundamental religious beliefs were those imbibed in childhood, based on the Orthodox liturgy, prayers, catechism, better-known passages from the New Testament ('the Bible is the wisest of all books'[181]), and Psalms. His personal library, like nearly all Russian private collections at the time, contained a substantial number of religious books, ranging from standard liturgical texts (ten copies each of the *Sluzhebnik* and *Triod' tsvetnaia* in various editions, eleven copies of the Psalter, and so on) to modern theological works by such Orthodox clerics as Dmitry Rostovsky, Feofan Prokopovich, and Gavriil Buzhinsky.[182] Vespers on Saturday and mass on Sunday, usually in Trinity Cathedral if he was in St Petersburg, were a regular part of the royal calendar. During Holy Week he attended church daily and took communion.[183] But piety, business, and play were often inter-mingled. In 1693 Peter preceded his landmark trip to Archangel (his first sight of the sea) with a visit to the monastery of St Sabbas at Zvenigorod, one of his father's favourite places of pilgrimage.[184] But in the summer of 1694 he abandoned Moscow and the court during the pilgrimage season to return to Archangel and pursue the thoroughly secular passions of shipbuilding and seafaring. Yet he did not omit to visit the relics of saints on the Solovki Islands, where he founded a chapel and erected a cross to commemorate his visit.[185] On 16 April 1720 Peter attended mass, then took a walk around town and launched two boats. The following day after mass he visited Prince-Caesar and Golovin.[186]

Even the few examples given above cast doubt on the allegation that Peter had 'no feeling whatever for traditional Orthodox piety'.[187] Stählin's collec-tion includes anecdotes which challenge popular conceptions of Peter's ungodliness – for example, one which denies that he put work before God. On the contrary, he is said to have opposed work on Sundays except in extreme emergencies, on the grounds that 'he who forgets God and his com-mandments will never have any success and little benefit however hard he works'. 'From his earliest years this sovereign had a sincere reverence for God, which he preserved inviolate throughout his life and expressed at every opportunity, especially by a deep reverence for the name of God and the divine laws and respect for the essentials of the Christian religion.' He was especially critical of blasphemers and atheists.[188] (Stählin appears to draw a veil over the area of sexual morality!) On the other hand, Peter opposed superstition and extreme forms of asceticism, especially with reference to natural phenomena with scientific explanations, such as eclipses or fake icons and relics.[189] Most of all, Peter disapproved of the 'overstaffing' of the Church and ecclesiastical time-wasting. He had no understanding of the contemplative life of prayer. Put bluntly, Peter could appreciate that a certain number of priests were needed to officiate at church services, baptize babies, conduct weddings, and so on—these could be justified as a well-defined part of the priestly job, or *dolzhnost'*—but he could not see the necessity for thousands of monks and nuns 'merely' to pray. Such waste was intolerable when monks were being supported by peasant labour, the fruits of which were thus diverted from more pressing public needs. The solution was to cut down on the precious resources used up by monks (by reducing the number of monks and/or their rations) and increase the useful labour of the remaining monks (and other superfluous church people), by diverting their efforts into aiding the sick and the destitute, teaching, and other useful occupations.

That divine providence played a part in determining human fate was never questioned. In this sense, Peter's was a 'simple soldier's faith'.[190] Letters written in July 1696 to announce the surrender of Azov give a flavour: 'Now with St Paul rejoice in the Lord, and again I say, rejoice! Now our joy has been fulfilled as the Lord God has rewarded our labours of these past two years and the blood that was spilt by bestowing his grace.'[191] Accidents and set-backs were viewed equally fatalistically. In April 1703 Peter wrote to Fedor Apraksin from Schlüsselburg as he awaited an engagement with the Swedes: 'Here everything is fine, by God's grace; only for my sins there was an unfortunate incident: first Doctor Klemm, then Königseck and Petelin drowned. Grief instead of joy, but may the All-Highest's will and his judgement be done.'[192] In his reply, Apraksin (who had received a traditional Orthodox education) urged Peter: 'May His Holy will be done. May He grant you His grace to comfort you and give you hope.'[193] In July 1709 Peter wrote to the British merchant Andrew Styles, thanking him for his congratulations on the victory at Poltava, but reminding him that 'to God alone belong the glory and honour (for this is a divine deed: he raises up the humble and subdues the mighty)'.[194] This view of Poltava was reiterated in 1724 when Peter was planning the anniversary celebrations. The victory was indeed 'a divine miracle; it reveals that all human minds are as nothing against the will of God'.[195] A couple of years after Poltava, Peter was writing to Styles's widow, begging her not to abandon herself to excessive grief, 'but comfort yourself with the immortal glory which he had and will have'.[196] Writing to Apraksin in May 1711 on the death in captivity of Prince Alexander of Georgia: 'I am very sorry to hear about the death of that fine prince, but it is better to let go the irretrievable rather than recall it; we have a path laid before us which is unknown to us but known only to God.'[197] He wrote to the prince's father, advising magnanimity, good sense, and endurance, as the death of his only son and heir was caused not by human agency (therefore no revenge or recompense was to be sought) but by God's will. He could comfort himself with the thought that his son was in heaven, 'disdaining this inconstant life, in that place where we all wish to be in our own time'.[198] A number of anecdotes dwell on Peter's acknowledgement of divine purpose in nature. In the Paris observatory, for example, he is said to have looked into a telescope and exclaimed: 'See what a book of God's marvels opens up before our eyes, clearly showing the Creator's great wisdom.'[199] Peter took a more or less traditional view of his relationship to God as ruler, never setting himself higher. 'What difference is there between God and the tsar if both are given the same deference?'[200] This attitude did not preclude setting himself higher than the clergy, however.

Icons were part of Peter's environment, as of every Orthodox Christian's. An image of the 'Saviour Not Made by Hands', in a gold case studded with precious gems, is said to have been particularly venerated and carried on Peter's campaigns, including Poltava. He demanded it on his sick-bed, and it was carried in his funeral procession.[201] The fact that in the time of Empress Elizabeth the chapel in which the icon was housed had become a place of pilgrimage, especially on 16 August, the festival of the icon, shows that Peter's popular image was not entirely at odds with such associations. According to the author of a late nineteenth-century guidebook, crowds of pilgrims lined up to visit Peter's house and pray to the icon, a dual purpose in which apparently, unlike Peter's Old Believer opponents, no one saw any contradiction. 'Hundreds of candles flicker before the miraculous image and indeed a marvel worthy of the Great Peter is accomplished: it is as if his humble dwelling were transformed into a holy church for all those grieving, embittered and seeking God's mercy.'[202] But Peter cracked down hard on hoaxes associated with icons, as in the case of a priest who tricked people out of their money with a 'miraculous' image; he was challenged to get the icon to perform miracles in Peter's presence, and defrocked when he confessed to fraud.[203]

Peter's religion was quite free of all ideas of the unquestioned superiority of Orthodoxy and the heresy of other faiths, although he could not tolerate Jews or Jesuits. He visited the house of Martin Luther in Wittenberg, where he declared Luther to have been 'of great use' to his sovereign and laughed at the old tale of the devil and the ink-pot.[204] He valued Luther's good sense and reasonableness. In the final analysis, Peter too was a child of the age of rationalism, which trusted in empirical knowledge and man's own ability to forge his destiny and achieve happiness on earth in preparation for heaven.[205] 'Reasoning is the highest of all virtues,' he wrote, 'for any virtue without reason is hollow.'[206] He wrote to the Synod from Astrakhan in 1722: 'I have read the book about the Beatitudes, which is very fine and [shows] the straight path of Christianity, only a foreword needs to be written in which your various commentaries on hypocritical untruths are all explained in order that the reader will first recognize his sin and then gain real and direct usefulness.'[207] Even so, recognition of the validity of other Christian denominations and willingness to borrow elements from them did not shake his conviction that for historical reasons Orthodoxy was the faith of the Russian people, and that it was the Russian tsar's duty not only to defend and preserve Orthodoxy but also to reform and improve it, without touching its essential doctrines or basic rituals. Peter turned to God at the end of his life. He is said to have taken communion three times in preparation for death, and to have asked for prayers to be said in church; but in view of the severity of his illness it is impossible to say whether this was of his own volition or by the decision of others.[208]

VI.   RULING RUSSIA: THE COMMON GOOD

Let us turn finally to Peter as statesman. Did he have a philosophy? To this question there is no straightforward answer. Anyone who has read this far will know that Peter was no philosopher, and will not be surprised to learn that he left no political or philosophical treatises or manifestos, no equivalent of *Mein Kampf* or *What is to be Done?* Few rulers have. It hardly needs to be pointed out, in any case, that ideological tracts often conceal more than they reveal about their authors' 'real' motives. For the most part Peter's correspondence is very concrete and lacking in sustained metaphysical musings. Perhaps there would have been more stock-taking if Peter had lived longer. In his preface to the 1724 decree on monasticism he wrote: 'Now that I have some free time for the correct organization of all affairs in the state, including this class [of monks] and for informing people widely, it is necessary to set out and arrange things for people's permanent and temporary use and for the improvement (*izradstvo*) of society.'[209] A few months later he was dead.

A number of leitmotifs run throughout Peter's instructions, of which one of the most striking refers to the passage of time. For centuries the way of life in Russia, as in all medieval Western societies, changed very little. Time was regarded as more or less static, and change as cyclical, geared to the seasons and the recurring events of the church calendar.[210] Many of Peter's reforms challenged such concepts. The very notion of 'catching up', for example, implies that nations progress through linear time at differing rates. Peter hinted at this when he compared Russia with Holland in an edict on trade: 'If compulsion has to be used sometimes in that old and experienced country which has not only thrived on commerce by long practice but has it as its sole means of support, how much more is compulsion needed in our country, where our people are novices in everything.'[211] One of Peter's first reforms, it will be recalled, was to bring the calendar into line with the one used in much of Europe. He was an impatient man, and this influenced his awareness of the time factor in his struggle to reform a 'backward' country. Peter wrote to Andrei Vinius on 16 April 1701: 'I received your letters in which you write of the readiness of the artillery and of the efforts you have expended; this is a highly good and necessary matter, for time is like death.'[212] To the newly formed Senate on 8 June 1711 he wrote: 'Thank you for your letter of 16 May and for the improvements you have made; in the future you need to work and to have everything prepared ahead of time, because wasted time, like death, cannot be reversed.'[213] Similar impatience was expressed in numerous decrees on speeding up legal procedures, 'where many superfluous things are said and many unnecessary things written'.[214] Peter's correspondence is sprinkled with the Russian words for 'quick', 'fast', 'without delay' and countless variations on the formula 'Write to us at once about what is going on where you are, without wasting any time'.[215] Peter wasted little time in his own personal life. He rose early, often before 4 a.m., sometimes arriving at the Senate early to humiliate those who came later. In his timetable for 1721 he allocated Mondays to Thursdays to working on the Admiralty Regulation, Friday to visiting the Senate, Saturday morning to working on the History of the Swedish War, and Sunday morning (after church) to foreign affairs. After the river froze over, and if there was business, he would spend Thursday in the Senate.[216] He is said to have scolded King Frederick IV of Denmark, a late riser who kept him waiting for hours one morning: 'We can't get our business done properly in this manner; every day we have much of importance of which we need to inform each other, but it is impossible sometimes to get access to your majesty. I also have my business. Let us fix on a definite time in the day when we can meet.'[217]

Anxiety about time was probably aggravated by experience of ships and the sea in the Baltic, awareness of the calculations needed to catch tides and winds, to respond to freezes and thaws. He reminded Apraksin to dispatch ships to Riga as soon as the ice began to break, 'by the first wind, for you are well aware of this channel, if you miss the wind then much is lost'.[218] Peter was a Russian, and this was bound to be reflected in his attitude towards the seasons and tasks associated with them—for example, the need to seize the opportunity to plant trees and flowers in northerly St Petersburg to maximize the growing season. 'Spring is really here,' Peter wrote to Apraksin on 2 April 1721, 'warm with showers; an *arshin* of earth can be seen in the field. Trees can be planted.'[219]

In Peter's view, the best way to minimize time wasting was to create a regular framework of rules and regulations: 'The chief thing is to know your duties and our edicts by heart and not put things off until tomorrow, for how can a state be governed if edicts are not put into effect, since scorn of edicts is no different from treason.'[220] It was vital to spell everything out to the last detail and publicize it as widely as possible. The opening of the Naval Statute provides a characteristic example, with its appeal to reason and threat of punishment: 'Since this matter is of vital necessity to the State ... therefore this Naval Statute has been devised in order that everyone knows his duties and no one excuses himself on the grounds of ignorance.'[221] Even the fountains in the Summer Gardens in St Petersburg modelled on figures from Aesop's fables had explanatory plaques for the edification of strollers.[222] In June 1721 Peter wrote to Devier, blaming misunderstandings by local people of some of Devier's orders on the fact that many were delivered orally; henceforth all orders must be sent out in writing.[223] An example of this eye for detail in printed rules appears in the regulation of the Admiralty college, which includes in the duties of the college orderly ensuring 'that nobody defecates except in the appointed places. If anyone defecates in other than the appointed places, he is to be beaten with a cat-of-nine-tails and ordered to clean it up.'[224] Printed orders were distributed widely. In 1722 printed versions of one of His Imperial Majesty's personal edicts were distributed 'in Moscow in the Kremlin, Kitaigorod, Belygorod, on all gates, also in the chancelleries and offices, the trading rows and on all the main streets, at crossroads and other such places on the 12th (January) at 7 a.m. In the province and districts couriers were dispatched with the same orders on the 13th at 7 a.m.' In all, 2,566 copies were sent out for the public, also in the provinces and districts, in the colleges and the Synod.[225]

Peter did not believe in wasting words any more than he tolerated wasting time. On 16 October 1724 he sent a message to the Synod addressed to translators of books on economics: 'Since the Germans tend to fill their books with many useless stories, just in order to make them seem bigger, don't translate these passages except for the business itself and a short [introductory] passage before every item. Words shouldn't be included just for the sake of idle embellishment but for the better understanding and edification of the reader, therefore I have corrected the treatise on grain growing (crossing out the unnecessary) and send you it as an example so that these books can be translated without superfluous stories which only waste time and take away the reader's desire to read.'[226]

Concrete examples spoke even louder than words in a country where most of the population was illiterate. It will be recalled that Peter had samples of New Year decorations and Western dress set up on major thoroughfares. On 19 March 1705 he wrote to Aleksei Kurbatov: 'I'm sending you samples of knife blades. When you get them, immediately make copies and send them to Solvychegodsk and other places and have them make three hundred thousand, and without fail finish them and send them to Smolensk by the middle of April.'[227] On 7 July 1707 Matvei Gagarin received orders in a similar vein: 'With this letter I send an example of a bayonet. Make a copy of it and keep it there, only add slightly longer tubes, about an inch or slightly less. Then order that a number be made and contracted after that model; and give the sample I have sent you back to the messenger.'[228] On 19 November 1707 a personal edict was issued to soldiers and sailors working in the Admiralty. No one should wear Cossack-style caps, but all were to wear hats after the approved model, an example of which was set up on the gates of the Admiralty. Anyone caught wearing an old-style hat would have it removed by the guards.[229]

There are numerous illustrations of Peter's efforts to ensure that people got the point: 'Set up a model canvas tent, as described, on the Admiralty island near the Petrovsky tavern,' he wrote, 'and announce in St Petersburg by written orders that everyone who trades in foodstuffs in the assigned places must make tents [as stalls] after the model described, within one and a half or at the most two months from the date when the order is published.'[230] 'When the local governor from here sends you a model of a wheel for a cart to carry earth, have 2,000 wheels of dry oak made in Kazan' from the model during the winter ... and a thousand sent to Astrakhan'.'[231] Instructions for making bundles of sticks for defences were issued to peasants on the Don: 'Using strong binding and sticks of equal length means that when the sticks lie closely packed and tightly bound then one such faggot will serve better against gun-fire than three weak ones.'[232] The Synod received the following order: 'Throughout the Russian State wax candles are to be made in such a fashion that every candle has a thickness at its base twice that of its top, and the upper thickness is half that of the lower. The length should be five times the thickness at the base.'[233] Uneven tombstones in churchyards were another target of Peter's passion for orderliness. Any not flush with the ground were to be taken up and relaid, 'since stones which are untidily and improperly laid inflict ugliness on holy churches and get in people's way'. Pieces of stone chipped off during repairs were to be used for church building. Peter recalls the case of the funeral of Fedor Romodanovsky (in 1717), when unevenly strewn stones held up the military procession, which had great difficulty getting to the grave.[234]

Measuring and counting were regular features of Peter's legislation (inherited in part from Muscovite predecessors whose chancelleries were also addicted to list making). An inventory (of February 1721) of the barges belonging to St Petersburg nobles detailed the number of oars and material (oak or pine). Fifty-three oak and ninety-five pine boats were registered, with from four to twelve oars.[235] The introduction in 1724 of registers of births, deaths and marriages was accompanied by model entries: death registers were to include information about sex, age, cause of death, and who administered confession and communion.[236] The censuses preparing for the poll tax were the most extensive operation of this kind.

A particularly informative example of Petrine legislation is his decree of October 1721 ordering that sickles be replaced by scythes, for which the initial drafts in his own hand have survived, with crucial statements underlined.[237] The issue of orders was followed by the complicated operation, directed by the governor of Riga, of selecting and dispatching suitably trained peasants to Moscow, Kazan', Nizhny Novgorod, Pskov, Tver', and Riazan', especially 'Russians who have lived in Courland and know how to harvest with scythes'. Lists had to be drawn up (with such information as how long the peasant concerned had lived in the Baltic), armed guards had to be detailed, transport and food supplied.[238] There were follow-up orders: in April 1722 a thousand peasants were to be rounded up to cut hay in Astrakhan (in anticipation of the campaign in Persia), and each was to be issued with one good scythe.[239] This exercise shows how much time and effort Peter was willing to put into a practical project with limited aims. A comparable operation was the decree of 5 May 1723 on the cleaning of hemp by the method used in Riga. Precise instructions were issued in all places where hemp was grown about how to process and package it—in bundles, not bales. Agents were to travel round giving instructions in the new procedures, and a chief *brakovshchik*, Jacob Viedman from Riga, was appointed. In December 1723, however, the Riga process was declared 'burdensome', and producers were ordered to change to the Narva method.[240]

Tight schedules and clear, laconic instructions on limited projects, delivered in writing and/or by agents, went hand in hand with a faith in plans. St Petersburg became a symbol of Petrine 'regularity' (*reguliarnost'*), the parallel lines of Vasil'evsky Island's grid plan of streets and canals and the arrow projectory of Nevsky Prospekt a planner's ideal within a planned city. The rest of Russia was to be brought literally into line. Buildings in Novgorod destroyed by a fire were to be restored 'regularly, as in St Petersburg ... according to an approved plan'.[241] But unruly Russia often refused to fall into line. A decree of 1724 complained:

An edict was published in all the *gubernii* and provinces on [re]building burnt-out villages and hamlets according to drawings, and drawings were sent out with the edicts, but now His Imperial Majesty has been made aware that in the *gubernii* and provinces, in villages and hamlets, peasants' houses on burnt-out sites are being rebuilt not in accordance with this specification but after the previous practice without leaving any cottage gardens and hemp-fields between the houses. Therefore His Imperial Majesty has decreed that confirmatory edicts be sent out to all the *gubernii* and provinces that from now on peasants in the villages and hamlets without fail build according to the specification of his earlier edict. ... Wherever a village or hamlet has burned down or people want to resettle a site, then the landlords themselves, or, in the absence of landlords, bailiffs and elders should immediately mark out the site according to the published edict and drawings and compel the peasants to build in accordance with the edict and completely ban the building of houses as was done previously.[242]

Instructions issued to troops in Astrakhan in 1722 on how to behave in hot climes combine a number of Peter's concerns. Men were not to eat salted fish and meat and fruits, and 'nobody between the hours of 9 a.m. and 5 p.m. is to go out without a hat or to sit where there is no cover; and during the day it is forbidden to sleep in the open air, or to sleep on the bare earth; a bed must be made up of grass or reeds or anything that can be found to a thickness of no less than five inches (thicker if possible). When drinking water take good care not to drink too much and not to fill yourself up, especially not when on the march. All this must be observed by the officers (as an example to the men), who must see to it that the men obey these rules; and anyone who offends will be deprived of his rank or be given some worse punishment.'[243]

The examples of *reguliarnost'* of which Peter was most proud were his many lengthy statutes (*reglamenty*, or *ustavy*). In a note in his own hand in 1722 (for inclusion in the ongoing History of the Northern War) he recalled that the Military Statute was started in St Petersburg in 1715 and finished in Danzig. The Naval Statute was started in 1720 and finished in 1722, and 'done all by hard work, not just by orders [to someone else] but by his own labour, not only in the morning but in the evening, twice daily, it was done at various times'.[244] It should be emphasized that the first of the regulations to be devised was the military one, and it was to military (and naval) success that Peter always gave precedence. Military activity was 'the foremost of worldly activities'.[245] 'Tell all the nobles that every nobleman in all cases (whatever his family name) must show honour and precedence to every commissioned officer (*ober-ofitser*) and show respect for his service.'[246] Peter also believed that civilian life should be informed by military life—''tis impossible to govern well without knowing the Rules of Military Discipline'[247]—and that defence of the realm was a monarch's prime duty. The description of new-born sons as 'recruits', as well as Peter's insistence on holding ranks in the army and navy (although, not, it will be noted, the civil service), graphically underlines the idea that the whole of life from cradle to grave was military service. 'Nothing leads men to do evil so much as weak command,' states the Naval Statute.[248]

Peter's concern for punctuality and military precision must be seen not just within the context of a personal schedule and private goals (although this element is not entirely lacking, witness Peter's assiduous application of it to his hobbies), but as a timetable for the reform of a whole nation. Only then can one begin to appreciate the frustration he must constantly have experienced when his goals were thwarted by individual and collective lethargy and resistance. The problem was expressed graphically by Ivan Pososhkov with the image of Peter pulling uphill with the strength of ten men and millions pulling downhill.[249] Peter had to 'force his Subjects to take Instructions from Foreigners', wrote Weber. 'They obey, but with such inveterate Pride that it hinders them from penetrating what they are taught.'[250] Peter summed up the problems in a passage hidden away in a manifesto on the encouragement of factories in Russia in November 1723:

It's true that there are too few who are willing to participate, for our people are like children who, out of ignorance, will never get down to learning their alphabet unless the master forces them to do so. At first they find it tedious, but when they learn their lesson they are grateful. This is evident in the current state of affairs, where everything has to be done forcibly, but already thanks can be heard and fruit has been borne. It is the same with manufacturing: it is not enough to make proposals. ... This may happen in places where there is already a firm tradition, but here an enterprise is sometimes set up but remains unfinished ... it is necessary both to compel and to provide aid in the form of manuals, machines and other items and thus be a good steward (*ekonom*).[251]

Under these circumstances, when appeals to reason in the form of instructions and models failed, it is not surprising that a man of Peter's temperament resorted to 'the pedagogy of the cudgel', although, as discussed above, examples of blows struck by the tsar in person are probably fewer than anecdotes suggest. Peter was sensitive to accusations of cruelty. One of Stählin's anecdotes records Peter's reaction upon asking a returning envoy what people abroad were saying about him: 'They call me a savage ruler and a tyrant. ... But who says this? People who do not know the circumstances in which I found myself a few years ago, do not know that many of my subjects placed the most foul hindrances to carrying out my best plans for the benefit of the fatherland, and therefore it was essential for me to treat them with great severity; but I never behaved savagely or tyrannically. I also had clever and brave sons of the fatherland who perceived the benefit of my plans and promoted them with loyalty and constancy and for that they received my thanks and blessings.'[252] According to Nartov, Peter is said to have complained that foreigners did not appreciate Russian reality: 'Ignorance, stubbornness, perfidy, have always conspired against me, ever since I took the decision to introduce useful reform into the state and to transform savage manners. They, not I, are the tyrants.'[253] 'If all my stubborn subjects were as obedient as my dog Lizetka, I wouldn't have to stroke them with a club.'[254]

The great shortcoming of this approach to rulership is evident: it relied too heavily on the centre and gave little scope for personal initiative, although this is just what Peter claimed to be trying to inculcate in his subjects. If the tsar 'threw himself into everything whole-heartedly, sometimes making no distinction between the important and the secondary',[255] how could he expect his subjects to direct their energies to best effect? It seems that Peter was even 'speaking a different language' from the people he was addressing, among whom the old frame of mind persisted, including the notion of 'handing oneself over' (*vruchenie sebia*) to a 'strong' individual, as opposed to relying upon the sort of contractual relations common in the West.[256] Peter's efforts to diminish his own status as a 'strong man', be it by cutting down on deferential ceremonies or dressing like a commoner, clearly failed to convince his subjects, who always saw the tsar behind the disguise. Peter failed to carry the implications of his policy of stripping down the trappings of power to its logical conclusion, which was actually to allow others to have real power. He was never quite ready to take the reins off even his most trusted assistants and let them go their own way.

Progress must be achieved through coercion. A very telling message dates from early 1719, a period of strenuous efforts to reform both the central and the provincial administration, which saw a plethora of edicts and instructions regarding details of rational, efficient organization, often with explanations of the rationale behind them. Vasily Karabanov, sub-lieutenant of the life-guards, was ordered to go to Kiev province to extract information on finances needed by the central finance *kollegii*; if the officials charged with doing the job had not done it, 'you are to bind their legs in irons and put chains round their necks ... and not to free them until they have completed the work'.[257] An order of April 1722 warned that presidents of colleges who failed to submit the required accounts 'are to be taken to the Senate and held there until they fulfil these demands, and above and beyond that they are to be punished for not doing so'.[258]

Peter kept officials tied to his apron strings. On 9 May 1705 he wrote to Prince Nikita Repnin: 'Today I received news of your disgraceful action [allowing timber supplies to be taken into Riga], for which you can pay with your neck, for I gave strictest orders via the governor that nothing should be allowed into Riga on pain of death. You write that Ogilvie told you to do it, but I tell you, even if it was an angel that told you rather than that impudent and vexing person, you should not have done it. If one wood chip gets through after this I swear to God you'll lose your head.'[259] Peter did not stop chiding and cajoling until a few days before his death. A hand-written letter to Saltykov dated 3 January 1725 states: 'I don't know whether you are alive or dead or have forgotten your duty and become an outright criminal, for since we left Moscow I haven't had any reports from you. If you don't finish your job and get here by 10 February, you will be responsible for your own ruin.'[260] A whole series of letters dated early January 1725 deal with troops and winter quarters, and orders commanders to come to St Petersburg. If Saltykov or any of them did get to St Petersburg by the deadline, they would have found Peter in his coffin. Peter's associates, in turn, suffered from 'a sense of helplessness and despair when they did not have Peter's precise instructions or, weighed down under the terrible burden of responsibility, did not get his approval'.[261] Apraksin displayed characteristic *angst* when he wrote : 'I beg you not to leave us without news; for God's sake, come and see us; truly in all affairs we are wandering around like blind men and don't know what to do. Everywhere is in great disorder (*rastroika*), but where to turn and what to do next we don't know; we can't get any money from anywhere. All work is at a standstill.'[262]

What motivated Peter in his tireless efforts to goad his subjects into useful, directed, rational activity? Was he driven by a quest for national glory, God's glory, or personal gratification? He identified the goal of his activities as the interest of the State, sometimes expressed in the formula 'the common good'.[263] Although there are no records of Peter using the formula 'I am the servant of the State', this is the general drift of a variety of formulations. As Prokopovich declared in his speech after Poltava: 'If only your subjects and servants served you, tsar, as loyally and diligently as you, tsar, serve your servants and subjects.'[264] The very concept of an entity called the 'State' was new in Russia, although not in the West, where Church and State were already viewed as two separate institutions with separate goals.[265] 'The idea of the State as a power which takes upon itself the administration of all aspects of human activity for the aims of the common good and completely subjugates the individual,' writes Platonov, 'this idea was current during Peter's time and Peter assimilated it. He devoted himself to serving the State and demanded the same of his subjects. In his state there were neither privileged persons nor privileged groups; all were equal in a single equality of possessing no rights with regard to the State.'[266] Gerschenkron sums up: 'the never-ending cogitations of Marxian historians in Russia about the class nature of the Petrine State—was it a gentry State or was it a merchants' State?—miss the essential fact that the State was not the State of this or that class. It was the State's State.'[267]

Peter presented himself as an 'ordinary' person who had to serve this state on the same terms as everyone else (hence his carefully devised service career), but at the same time he was the embodiment, the symbol of the idea of state power, and its ultimate defender. In drafts of the Military Statute of 1716, when Peter was incorporating various texts, he always replaced the phrase 'the interest of His Majesty the Tsar' (*interes tsarskogo velichestva*) with 'state interest' (*interes gosudarstvennyi*).[268] In other texts sovereign and State are inextricably linked, as they are linguistically: 'All must protect the interests of the sovereign and the State' (*interes Gosudarev i Gosudarstvennyi*).[269] In a letter to his nephew the duke of Mecklenburg, he wrote that he could not promise to help him until the duke's affairs were in better order, 'for if I did so now I would be obliged to do so against the will and interests of my fatherland, which means more to me than my life'.[270] This driving force helps to explain Peter's apparent sacrifice of personal feelings in the affair of Tsarevich Alexis, who was disinherited for the good of the State (*dlia pol'zy gosudarstvennoi*).[271] Individuals sometimes had to be reminded to subordinate their own interests: thus General Weyde, in Swedish captivity awaiting release negotiations, was asked to be patient 'for the interest of the State'.[272]

Those who serve the interests of the State also promote the common good. The first explicit statement of this essentially collective, secular ideal appears in the manifesto inviting foreigners to work in Russia (16 April 1702):

> It is well known in all the lands which the Almighty has placed under our rule that since our accession to this throne all our efforts and intentions have been aimed at ruling this State in such a manner that as a result of our concern for the common good (*vseobshchee blago*) all our subjects should attain an ever greater degree of well-being. To this end we have striven to preserve internal tranquillity, to defend the State from enemy attack and to improve and increase trade as much as possible. For the same aim we were impelled to introduce into government some necessary changes serving the welfare of our land in order that our subjects might have more opportunity to study areas of knowledge so far unknown to them and become all the more skilled in all affairs of commerce.[273]

Thereafter the concept appears in many pieces of legislation. On 24 April 1713 Peter sent a hand-written order to the Senate: 'Let it be made known throughout the realm (in order that no one can excuse themselves on grounds of ignorance) that all criminals and harmers of the state interests (*interesov gosudarstvennykh*) with intent, except those who act out of simple-mindedness, will be executed without mercy and their villages and property confiscated. And if anyone shows mercy, he himself will be executed with the same sentence. And it is necessary to explain what the interests of the State are for people's better understanding.'[274] The interests of the State in this particular instance appear to be mainly fiscal, the maximizing of collection of taxes, recruits, duties, and services. In 1722, in another memorandum to the Senate, Peter deplored the practice of nobles marrying off 'idiots' (offspring with mental handicaps) to rich women for their property, 'from [which idiots] it is impossible to hope for any good legacy for the usefulness of the State', as they were good 'neither for education, nor for service'.[275] Elsewhere, the emphasis falls upon international prestige, flourishing trade and industry, and the preservation of internal 'peace and tranquillity' (against rebels and dissidents).

The mechanism for achieving the common good was linked with the idea of *politsiia*, or well-ordered government, a Western concept most fully expounded in clause 10 (*o politseiskikh delakh*) of the Chief Magistracy Regulation of 1721 as that which

facilitates laws and justice, nurtures good order and morality, gives to all security from robbers, thieves, violators and cheats and other such, dispels disorderly and indecent living and compels everyone to labour and to honest enterprise, makes good inspectors, careful and good servitors, creates regular towns and streets, impedes expensiveness, and brings sufficiency in all that is necessary to human life, takes precautions against all illnesses, brings cleanliness to the streets and buildings, forbids over-indulgence in domestic expenditure and all blatant transgressions, takes care of beggars, the poor, sick, crippled and other indigents, protects widows, orphans and strangers, according to God's commandments, educates youth in chaste purity and honest skills; in short, over all these matters policing is the soul of citizenship and all good order and the fundamental support of human safety and comfort.[276]

In other words, 'police' was understood not just in the modern sense of law and order (although that came into it too) but in a wider context of public welfare—even morality—including a number of areas in which previously the Church would have had a monopoly. In this sense, most of Peter's domestic policy, with its wide-ranging coverage (dress, beards, architectural planning, hygiene) and reliance upon detailed regulation, may be equated with 'policing'.

Despite references to subjects enjoying 'well-being', the common good always had higher claims than the individual good in Peter's view. In a crucial edict of 25 October 1723 he set out the differences between crimes against the State and other crimes: 'In cases of offences against one's calling [*zvanie*: crimes committed in the course of duty], wilfully and knowingly, the culprit must be punished like someone who transgresses in his duty in the midst of battle or like a traitor, for this crime is worse than treason, for once treason is discovered, precautions can be taken against it, but not everyone can take precautions against this crime, which can lurk under cover very easily for a long time and end in evil.' If someone commits a 'particular' crime, however, 'transgresses individually against another person with such an offence and under such concealment that it is impossible to bring it to court and to detect it and the judge makes this hidden wrong a right, unaware of the concealed deception, then the loss is only to the person who has suffered the deprivation (*u kogo otniato*) but not to other people'.[277] There was no place in Peter's thinking for the individual separated from his or her social station.

If the 'common good' seems a rather impersonal concept, at times it acquired more concrete features in the guise of 'Russia' or the fatherland (*otechestvo*), of which Peter was declared the father (*otets*). Peter's admiration for things foreign was tempered with patriotism, although some of his best-known and most vehement statements on this theme may have had more than a little input from others—for example, the speech before Poltava, which Prokopovich edited: 'About Peter know only that he set no value on his own life if only Russia might live together with Russian piety, glory and well-being.'[278] Another famous speech was made at the launch of a ship: 'Brethren, who is the Man among you, who thirty Years ago could have had only the Thought of being employed with me in Ship Carpenter's Work here in the Baltick?' Peter asked, before going on to imagine the 'transmigration of sciences' from ancient Greece, via England, France and Germany to Russia, which would be able to 'put other civilized nations to the blush, and carry the glory of the Russian name to the highest pitch'.[279] There is no reason to doubt the authenticity of the following outburst to his son Alexis: 'For my fatherland and people I have never spared my life and do not spare it now, so how can I spare a vile creature like you?'[280] To Peter, service to the fatherland came before flesh and blood. Officials and military commanders, in their turn, were expected to act like 'fathers' to their underlings, to be both caring and strict, 'for children raised at liberty, without chastisement or fear, generally fall into misfortune and then can also bring ruin to their parents'.[281]

To sum up, the assumptions that underlay Peter's actions as a ruler include the following: a notion that change is not only possible but also desirable, and that there is such a thing as forward, linear movement; belief in the efficacy of reason, which implies that subjects could be influenced by explanation and example (traditions, on the other hand, did not have to be explained—they just *were*); the existence of sometimes interchangeable entities known as the 'common good' and the 'interests of the State' (the Petrine State worked not for the Divine Purpose but for itself); and the close interaction of civilian and military life, the former informed by the latter. Does this add up to the well-ordered 'police state' which Raeff sees in early modern Russia? Is Peter best regarded as a representative of early Enlightened Absolutism? Virtually all of his maxims involved a break with the past, reflected also in the unconventional modes of behaviour and activities examined earlier in this chapter.

Peter deliberately broke with the past by making himself an outsider, not subject to traditional restraints.[282] In a society in which tradition and custom were revered and change was feared, this made Peter a lonely man, as did the many uncomfortable traits of his personality examined above. But no one is completely unlovable, as the next chapter will show.

12

Family Factors

I. MOTHER AND SISTERS

It has sometimes been maintained that family relationships played a small part in Peter's life. Indeed, some historians have set so little store by 'private' factors that it is a matter of indifference precisely when he married or how many children he had.[1] But a study of Peter's Russia is clearly incomplete without an examination of family relations and household politics. Accidents of fertility and infant mortality could make or break a royal dynasty, with international repercussions, and Peter suffered more than his fair share of accidents and bad luck in this area, not to mention elements of self-inflicted tragedy. Why did Peter banish one wife to a convent and crown another? Why did he subject his eldest son to torture and condemn him to death? Why did he devote time and effort to arranging foreign marriages for his children and nieces? The answers to these and other questions touch upon both personal factors and state interests.

From the moment of his birth, Peter, the first child of his father's second wife, posed a potential threat to the ambitions of the relatives of the first wife. He, in turn, was to be haunted by the 'seed of Ivan Miloslavsky'. Peter's mother, Natalia Naryshkina, was twenty-one years old when he was born. She produced sisters Natalia and Fedora (who died in infancy) in 1673 and 1674 respectively, and seemed on course to match her predecessor's, Maria Miloslavskaia's, tally of thirteen live births had not Tsar Alexis's death in 1676 made her a widow. It has often been assumed that the palace crises of the 1680s, especially the massacre in the Kremlin in May 1682, when Natalia feared for her son's life, brought mother and son closer together. In fact, it may have made Natalia over-protective. Despite a girlhood spent in the household of the 'Westernized' official Artamon Matveev, and reports that she occasionally broke the rules of seclusion,[2] Natalia in later life reverted to the 'pious tsaritsa' type. The only known portraits show her in nun-like widow's garb with head modestly covered. Clashes seemed inevitable with a son determined to extend the relative freedom and independence which he enjoyed for much of Sophia's regency. In 1689, when his mother summoned him back to Moscow to attend a requiem mass for his late brother Fedor, Peter made it clear that boat building had priority. In an exchange of letters between mother in Moscow and son in Archangel in 1693, Natalia urged him to return, and Peter found excuses to stay. Natalia's final letter reads: 'As a favour to me, my light, come home without delay. I'm so very sad that I can't see you, my light and joy. You wrote that you intend to await the arrival of all the ships, but you have seen the ones that have arrived already, so why do you have to wait for the rest to come in? Don't scorn my request. You write in your letter that you have been to sea even though you promised me that you wouldn't.'[3] Natalia died on 25 January 1694, and was laid to rest in the Ascension convent in the Kremlin next to her predecessor, Maria Miloslavskaia. 'Before the bearing out of the body of the sovereign lady from her apartment a funeral knell was tolled in the bell-tower of St John in the ancient manner, with a muffled peal.' Peter did not walk behind the coffin; in fact, he did not return to Moscow until the day after the funeral, when he visited his mother's tomb. He had been with his mother on the day before she died, but had left, even though she was clearly at death's door, more an indication of an impatient, restless nature than of callous indifference.[4] He revealed his feelings in a letter to Fedor Apraksin: 'It is hard for me to tell you how bereft and sad I feel; my hand is incapable of describing it fully or my heart of expressing it. So, like Noah, a little rested from my misfortune and leaving behind what cannot be restored, I write of what is alive.'[5] In 1706, consoling Gavrila Golovkin on the death of his mother, Peter wrote that if his own mother had lived to such a great old age as Golovkin's, he would have been grateful that God had granted her such a long life.[6]

The second woman in Peter's life was his sister Natalia, who successfully adapted to her brother's new cultural demands.[7] Relations were warm, judging by numerous surviving letters, in which Peter often used the jocular tone which he reserved for the closest of his associates. In one he jested about paying court to Queen Anne of England now that Prince George was dead. In another he asked Natalia to act as matchmaker for one of his officers.[8] Natalia was entrusted with Peter and Catherine's children during their parents' frequent absences.[9] Peter was upset by her death in 1716. The death of his half-sister Sophia in 1704, on the other hand, must have been greeted with relief rather than grief. In Peter's mind, Sophia was associated with unrest and disorder. She was a threat not so much in her own person, especially once she was securely locked away in a convent, but as a figure-head for the disaffected. We know much less about Peter's other Miloslavsky half-sisters, the youngest of whom was born in 1662. These were the faceless women of Peter's court (no portraits of them survive, probably because none was painted), too steeped in the old ways to act as role models for the new Westernized generation, too old to be married off by the time the practice of keeping the tsarevny unmarried was abandoned, and too closely associated with Sophia to be altogether trusted. People were even unsure just how many of them there were. Just Juel recorded incorrectly in 1710 that Peter had just two half-sisters (four were alive at the time), 'but as he does not especially value them, you rarely see them in his company'.[10] Even so, they were expected to take part in some public functions, albeit with a low profile. When Peter went to Voronezh to resume shipbuilding early in 1699, the tsarevny went too, with boyars' wives to attend them.[11] In 1708 all the tsarevny were ordered to visit St Petersburg with the rest of the court under the supervision of Natalia Alekseevna, in a huge convoy which arrived in St Petersburg at the end of April by ship (at Peter's insistence) from Schlüsselburg.[12] An anecdote recounts that Peter wished to 'accustom his family to water so that they were not afraid of the sea and got to like the situation of St Petersburg, which is surrounded by water', adding that 'anyone who wishes to live with me must often be on the sea'. Dutch sailing costumes were made for the women.[13] Fairly substantial sums were allocated for their upkeep and their households.[14] In 1711 the Senate was ordered to provide grooms, horses, and tackle for their households, and in 1714 they were granted allowances of 2,500 roubles each to build new houses.[15] Even so, they seem to have contrived to spend as much time as possible in Moscow. In January 1714 Peter wrote to Natalia about the alleged inability of his sisters Maria and Ekaterina to come to St Petersburg because of illness: 'If they don't want to come here when they are better, I won't force them. Let them do as they wish.' But he added that they were not to be allowed to take the veil without first coming to St Petersburg for consultation.[16] Apparently, Tsarevna Ekaterina Alekseevna (Catherine), 'a Lady of Excellent Sense and of an heroick Spirit', continued to live in her own palace in Moscow and died there in May 1718.[17]

Peter's sister-in-law Praskovia Fedorovna Saltykova (1664–1723), who was married to Tsar Ivan in 1684, and produced five daughters between 1689 and 1694, was another notable character.[18] Praskovia was traditional, pious, and uneducated. Yet, despite the fact that Peter once declared his sister-in-law's house to be a 'hospital for freaks, hypocrites, and fanatics',[19] he treated her with deference, even affection. In May 1722 he wrote to her daughter Anna urging her to heed her mother's summons to her sick-bed. 'She very much wants to see you in her illness and has written to you herself.'[20] He even paid off a 2,000 rouble debt on her behalf.[21] Good relations may also have something to do with the fact that Tsaritsa Praskovia was sufficiently astute to make concessions to the new times, not to mention the fact that her daughters were useful marriage fodder.

A more shadowy figure is Tsaritsa Marfa Matveevna Apraksina, who married Peter's half-brother Fedor just two and a half months before his death in 1682. It is said that Peter generally avoided the company of the dowager tsaritsa, preferring not to be reminded that she might have been instrumental in barring his way to the throne; but the fact that her clan connections (like Peter's mother, she was a god-daughter of Artamon Matveev) made her as close to Peter's camp as to Sophia's, and her brother Fedor's friendship with the tsar, assured her a comfortable, if not prominent, life at court, where, like Tsaritsa Praskovia, she retained certain old fashions. Portraits said to be of her show her in richly embroidered, pearl-trimmed tunic and traditional head-dress. Even so, she moved to St Petersburg towards the end of her life, and set up an extensive household there.[22] When she died on 31 December 1715 (of a surfeit of pickled mushrooms, it seems[23]), prayers were ordered for the repose of the soul of the 'sovereign lady tsaritsa' in Moscow and the towns of the patriarchal region and all the bishoprics 'in the old manner'. The funeral procession, as described by Weber, appears to have been entirely in the old style. There is no mention of gun salutes or escorts of guards.[24]

II.   PETER'S TWO WIVES: EVDOKIA AND CATHERINE

On 27 January 1689 Peter married Evdokia Lopukhina.[25] Like all Muscovite royal marriages, Peter's was determined primarily by dynastic calculations. It was arranged by Peter's mother and her relatives to emphasize the fact that Peter was now a man, and in the hope of getting a male heir before his half-brother Ivan did. As was the custom, the tsar's bride was selected from a lesser noble clan, thereby (it was hoped) minimizing rivalries among more prominent families. At the same time, the new tsaritsa's male relatives and their clientele would add weight to the Naryshkin ranks in the duma. Little is known about the preliminaries leading to the choice, just the bare fact that the groom and bride, aged seventeen and twenty respectively, were married in a Kremlin palace chapel in a 'simple, quiet ceremony, without any special festivity'.[26]

Prince Boris Kurakin, who was married to Evdokia's sister, wrote that the tsar's bride was 'fair of face, but of mediocre intellect and no match for her husband in character, which led to the loss of her happiness and the downfall of her clan'.[27] Evdokia's conventional upbringing is reflected in a handful of letters written to Peter in the early years of their marriage, formulaic texts dotted with conventional and virtually untranslatable terms of endearment expressed in the submissive tone required of a royal bride: 'Your wretched little wife Dunka greets you.'[28] 'Be so good as to write to me, my light, about your health, so that wretched me may be happy in my sadness.... You have not written a single line about your royal health.'[29] It is not known whether Peter was 'so good' as to write about his health. No letters survive from Peter to Evdokia, probably because he was too busy drilling troops, sailing and boat building to have much time for a wife who had been foisted upon him. There was a further distraction. On 22 October 1691 Peter attended a feast in the Foreign Quarter at the house of Mr Mons the vintner, which is probably when he first met the vintner's daughter Anna, his future mistress.[30] The affair was in full swing by the time Peter went to Europe in 1697, where he had further dalliances. Despite Peter's apparent indifference to his wife, the first few years of marriage produced two children: Alexis, born 18 February 1690 (to whom we shall return later), and Alexander, born in October 1691, who died the following May.[31] His funeral, when he was laid to rest beside Tsarevich Il'ia, the infant son of Tsar Fedor, was attended by the patriarch, duma members, and Tsar Ivan 'in deep mourning', but not by Peter.[32]

Evdokia may have been less of a doormat than her early letters suggest. Georg Grund recounts an interesting tale, not found in any other source, about a blazing row after Peter tried to appease his wife with gifts of trinkets bought from merchants in the Foreign Quarter, where he had just spent the night with Anna Mons. Evdokia flung them to the floor and trampled on them, cursing 'that German whore'. Peter thereupon vowed to have nothing more to do with his wife.[33] He wrote to close associates from abroad in 1697, proposing that Evdokia take the veil,[34] but this turned out to be more difficult than he anticipated. After his return to Moscow in August 1698, Peter talked to Evdokia for about four hours, trying to persuade her. She apparently refused, and was dispatched to the Intercession convent in Suzdal', where she lived under guard, although not as a nun. Not until May 1699 was an agent, Semeon Iazykov, sent from Moscow to Suzdal' to oversee in secret a ceremony in which Evdokia was forced to take the veil under the name Elena. So secret and irregular was the ceremony that not long afterwards Evdokia abandoned her nun's habit and resumed a secular life, taking a young army officer as a lover, entertaining visitors, and travelling around the district in some style.[35] Just Juel may have missed a note of irony when he records that the tsar told him outside Viborg in 1710 that he had divorced Evdokia in order to allow her 'to live a life of piety'.[36] Despite Juel's impression that by sending his wife to a convent Peter automatically got a divorce,[37] Evdokia's refusal to comply presented a real problem, especially in the light of popular discontent with Peter's impious behaviour. Grund was nearer the truth when he wrote that Evdokia was still refusing to agree to a divorce, and that 'the tsar, according to Russian laws, cannot remarry'.[38] When Evdokia's circle was interrogated in 1718, much hinged on the question of whether Evdokia did in fact take the veil (or, as in Russian, was 'shorn') in 1698–9. We shall return to this later when we consider Alexis's fate.

Failed marriage and acrimonious divorce formed the background, then, to the arrival of the future Empress Catherine I in Peter's household and her progression through the roles of camp-follower, mistress, official companion, wife, empress-consort, and, from 1725 to 1727, empress in her own right. As Bergholz commented after attending her coronation in 1724, 'One could not help but marvel at Divine Providence which has raised the empress from the lowly station in which she was born and which she previously occupied to the pinnacle of human honours.'[39] Catherine (and its foreign variants) is the name given her by non-Russian writers. Her Russian Orthodox name, Ekaterina Alekseevna (from her patron St Catherine and the patronymic borrowed from her godfather, her stepson Tsarevich Alexis), came into regular use only in 1711–12. Earlier she is sometimes referred to as Katerina Trubachova (the name of a dragoon she is supposed to have married in 1703) and Katerina Vasil'evskaia.[40] Peter used a number of pet names in letters—in the early days of their relationship the rather crude, virtually untranslatable 'matka' (old girl) and 'Muder',[41] later the affectionate Katerinushka. The name she was given at birth with was probably Martha.

Like her name, Catherine's background, nationality, and religious affiliation are still subject to debate.[42] Whether she was the illegitimate daughter of a serf or the orphaned daughter of a Swedish officer,[43] her 'lowly' origins were notorious. Princess Wilhelmina of Bayreuth, who saw her in 1719, remarked that 'you only had to take one look at her to see that she was of low origin ... From her clothes you could have mistaken her for some German strolling player.'[44] There are oblique references to Baltic origins—for example, in Peter's letter referring to the anniversary of the capture of Schlüsselburg and the 'happy day on which Russian feet occupied a piece of your lands'.[45] The story of her courtship and marriage is likewise incomplete. Martha seems to have fallen into Russian hands in the summer of 1702, when Field Marshal Sheremetev took the Livonian town of Marienburg, where she was then a servant in the family of Pastor Ernst Glück. From Sheremetev's camp she is said to have passed to Menshikov, and from Menshikov to Peter, probably at the end of 1703 or the beginning of 1704. Menshikov no doubt had his own reasons for giving the tsar such a 'gift'. Catherine often interceded on his behalf, and he on hers.[46] By 1706 she was an established fixture in the royal household, but lacked official status, to the extent that foreign observers, who listed the rest of Peter's family, including his first wife, in some detail, did not mention her at all.[47]

Catherine had to invent her own identity. Unlike Muscovite royal brides, she came to court without the usual contingent of male relatives,[48] which meant that her marriage had little impact on patronage networks. In the absence of supportive kinsmen, she had to make alliances of her own. With the years Catherine's contingent of female companions—Anna Tolstaia and the sisters Arsen'ev (one of whom married Menshikov)—expanded into a substantial court served by male and female courtiers, very different from the *terem* of the seventeenth century, in which royal brides had been restricted to the limited sphere of the Kremlin palace women's quarters, out-of-town residences, and convents. After the birth, in December 1706, of her first daughter, Catherine and her female retinue followed Peter round the battlefields of Lithuania and Belarus.[49] In November 1707 Catherine, heavily pregnant again, was in St Petersburg,[50] then travelled to Moscow. In this period of military tension, as Charles XII's army headed for Russia, Peter's letters are full of concern: 'If something happens to me by God's will,' he wrote in January 1708, 'then give the 3,000 roubles which are now in Prince Menshikov's house to Katerina Vasil'evskaia and the girl.'[51] 'I am missing you,' he wrote to Catherine on 29 January, and sent gifts of some fabric and a ring.[52] Soon after, Catherine evidently reciprocated by complaining that she had no one to comb her hair, to which Peter quipped: 'Get here as quickly as you can and we'll find that old comb.'[53]

Peter shared campaign news with Catherine. After a skirmish with the Swedes in August 1708 he wrote: 'We did a fine dance right under the nose of the fiery Charles. Our regiment sweated more than all the rest.'[54] At Poltava Catherine was in the baggage train. Peter wrote her a note immediately after the battle, telling her to join him, 'to congratulate me in person'.[55] After Poltava, Peter's letters to Catherine became longer and more intimate: 'Since I left you I have had no news of you, which I very much want, especially to know how quickly you can be in Vilna. I am lonely without you, and I imagine you feel the same.' He reports that they and the Poles are having continual conferences about the 'business of Ivan Khmel'nitsky',— that is, drinking sessions.[56] In September there were several letters as Peter prepared for a meeting with King Augustus in Torun. He sent Catherine some lemons, and included an anecdote which appealed to their shared sense of humour about a member of Peter's retinue who fell off a roof while drunk.[57]

It is possible that Peter and Catherine were married secretly in November 1707,[58] but their union was not made public until 6 March 1711, the day of their departure for the Turkish front, when 'it was publicly announced that the sovereign lady Tsaritsa Ekaterina Alekseevna is the true and legal sovereign lady'.[59] Peter gave the reason for this step in a letter to Menshikov written from Poland on 12 May 1711: 'Thank you for your congratulations about keeping my word, which I am obliged to do on account of this hazardous journey, so that if they [i.e., his daughters] are left orphans, they can have more security; if God brings this affair [i.e., the war] to a happy conclusion, we shall complete [the formalities] in St Petersburg.'[60] This letter and the palace records clearly indicate that a formal undertaking, if not a ceremony, had already taken place before Peter's departure, one which allowed Catherine to be referred to as 'true and legal', and made it less likely that she would be ousted and his orphan daughters declared illegitimate in the event of his death. Peter had every reason to fear the reaction of friends and relatives of his son and heir and of his ex-wife. This theory is strengthened by information supplied by foreigners. During a visit to Tsaritsa Praskovia's residence at Izmailovo on 10 March 1711, Just Juel learned from Peter's nieces that just before his departure Peter had summoned them and his sister Natalia to Preobrazhenskoe and told them that in the future they were to regard Catherine as his legal spouse and as *tsaritsa*. If he were to die in the forthcoming campaign before he was able to marry her, they were still to regard her as his wife.[61] Peter asked his relatives in the event of his death to allow Catherine 'the same rank, privileges and revenues, as was usual to the other dowagers, for she was his real wife, though he had not the time to perform the ceremonies according to the custom of his country, which should be done at the first opportunity'.[62]

Thus Catherine accompanied Peter as his wife-to-be to the south, where her endurance during the Battle of the Pruth was to provide the basis for future honours.[63] On 19 February 1712 in the Church of St Isaac of Dalmatia, in the words of Peter's secretary Makarov, 'their majesties' nuptials were happily concluded'.[64] There were no official announcements to foreign rulers, and Peter was married not in his coronation robes (as in 1689) but in naval uniform, adding an air of masquerade to a ceremony of dubious legal status, given doubts about Peter's divorce and the fact that Catherine's first husband Johann seems to have died only in 1718.[65] Boris Uspensky makes the interesting point that marriage to Catherine was bound to be viewed negatively by ordinary folk, not just because Evdokia was still alive and because Catherine was a foreigner, but also because Tsarevich Alexis was Catherine's godfather, hence she was Peter's spiritual granddaughter, making the union incestuous.[66] In court circles Catherine was accepted as Peter's consort. Her birthday (5 April) and name-day (24 November) were included in the official court calendar. Printed greetings produced for her name-day in 1717 included a speech by Feofan Prokopovich, in which Catherine's courage at the Pruth was recalled and her worthiness to be the first recipient of the order of St Catherine (instituted in 1714) was emphasized.[67]

The first known portraits of her post-date 1711 and depict a full-figured, pleasant-looking woman, of whom a foreign observer wrote: 'She has a pleasing plumpness; the colour of her face is very white with traces of natural, quite high colour, her eyes are dark and small, her hair the same colour, long and thick, fine neck and hands, a mild and very pleasant expression.'[68] In character and tastes Catherine was a match for Peter. She was strong (Bergholz records how she lifted up a heavy mace with one hand after Peter's orderly had failed to budge it)[69] and unshockable, sharing Peter's crude sense of humour and his fondness for practical jokes (even after his death when, for example, she had the alarms sounded on 1 April 1725 and imposed penalty cups of wine for gentlemen who appeared at a reception in the wrong dress).[70] They could even joke about extra-marital relationships. Peter wrote from Carlsbad in September 1711, where he was having a dreary time taking the waters: 'You write that I shouldn't hurry back to join you on account of my cure, but I think it's because you have found someone taller than me. Please write and let me know if he is one of us or from Torun? I rather think it must be a man from Torun as you want to get your revenge for what I did two years ago. That's just the sort of thing you daughters of Eve do to us old men!'[71] On 3 July 1717 Catherine wrote to Peter in Spa, where he was again taking the waters, joking that he had sent away his mistress (*matresishka*) because she was sick. 'I hope that that mistress's admirer (from which God preserve us!) will not arrive in the same state of health as she did'—evidently a reference to venereal disease. She informs Peter that they had all had a good time and drunk to his health on 29 June, and jokes that if the 'old man' had been there with her, there would probably have been another little 'nipper' (*shishechka*) on the way next year.[72] It seems that Catherine tolerated Peter's extra-marital affairs, as did the wives of many, if not most, rulers of the period.[73]

Catherine rarely seems to have been intimidated by Peter. Bergholz records a trivial but telling detail: in September 1724 Peter was celebrating the launch of a frigate in customary drunken fashion in the cabin, but late in the afternoon Catherine sailed past in her own launch and shouted in through the window: 'Time to go home, old man,' and Peter broke up the party.[74] The story of how she had the ability to soothe him when he was in a rage appears in all biographies. Did she love him? Peter's most recent Russian biographer believes that Peter was 'too dreadful' for anyone to love;[75] but there is plenty of evidence that he loved her, at least until 1724 and the Mons affair (of which more later). In a letter written in March 1723, Peter reported arriving in St Petersburg and finding the family in good health, 'only although I was pleased to see them it's very boring without you'.[76] In June 1724 he wrote from St Petersburg to the 'friend of his heart': 'All is well. Only I go into the palace and want to run out again ... it's all so empty without you. ... If it weren't for the festivals [Poltava, name-day, etc.] I would leave for Kronstadt or Peterhof.'[77] Did he intend her to be his successor? In the manifesto of 15 November 1723, on his intention to crown Catherine, Peter quoted Byzantine precedent for such a ceremony and his wife's personal courage, especially at the Pruth, where she behaved 'in a manner more male than female', but nowhere, either here or elsewhere, did he hint at nominating her as his heir. In fact, he died without making any pronouncement on the succession.[78] As the emperor's consort, in 1721 Catherine automatically received the title empress (*imperatritsa*), so the ceremony of 1724 is best regarded as a public display of recognition, and a challenge to anyone who continued to mutter about Catherine's humble origins. Thus we can only speculate on what Peter's reactions would have been to his wife's elevation after his death. He had no illusions about her capabilities as a stateswoman, but at least she blocked the accession of Peter's grandson, whose supporters, as we shall see, Peter feared.

If Peter was considering Catherine as a potential successor, the Mons affair surely would have made him pause for thought. In November 1724 thirty-year-old William Mons, brother of Peter's former mistress Anna and Catherine's chamberlain and head of her estates office, was suddenly arrested. His stated crime was abuse of the empress's trust by embezzling funds and taking bribes from petitioners. The real reason was probably rumours of an affair between him and Catherine, which, according to foreign accounts, sent Peter into a mad rage and convulsions.[79] On 16 November Mons was executed; on 22 November the court celebrated the betrothal of Peter's daughter Anna to the duke of Holstein, and on 24 November fêted Catherine's name-day.[80] The French minister Campredon remarked: 'Her relations with M. Mons were public knowledge and although she conceals her grief it is possible to see it painted on her face and in her behaviour.'[81] Just a little more than two months after these dramatic events, Peter himself was dead, and the combined efforts of Menshikov, Peter Tolstoy, and others who had an interest in preventing the accession of Alexis's son, placed Catherine on the throne. At Peter's funeral, Catherine took her leave with 'such great and indescribable grief that all those present were reduced to floods of tears and sobbing and feared lest her Majesty's health be severely damaged by such bitter grief'. The empress was led away 'beside herself'.[82] It is hard to know whether to doubt the sincerity of the new empress's emotion.

III. SONS AND DAUGHTERS

The precise number of Peter's children by Catherine remains in doubt. Massie's 'melancholy list' of twelve names starts with sons Peter and Paul, born in 1704 and 1705 respectively and dead by 1707, their existence conjectured from sparse references in a handful of letters.[83] The first mention of 'Petrushka' occurs in a letter to Daria and Varvara Arsen'eva, Catherine's companions, asking them not to 'abandon my Petrushka . . . please have some clothes made for my son, and when you decide to travel make sure he has enough to drink and eat'.[84] This must have been the 'little son' referred to by Catherine in a letter of 27 November 1704 that Peter was supposed to 'release from his prison' when he came to Moscow, a jocular reference, according to Semevsky, to Catherine's pregnancy nearing its end.[85] This means he was conceived in St Petersburg when Peter was there early in 1704. In October 1705 the women sent Peter congratulations on the capture of Mitau castle 'as a result of your labours', adding 'and we too have been amusing ourselves thanks to your labours, and we thank you most graciously for your favour, which we hope to enjoy again, and congratulate you on this new-born [boy] . . . Peter and Paul beg your blessing and greet you.'[86] This means that Paul, unless he was very premature, must have been conceived when Peter was in Moscow early in 1705, immediately after Peter junior's birth. Neither boy appears in the list of members of the imperial family buried in the Cathedral of SS Peter and Paul in St Petersburg, the first child listed there being Catherine (Ekaterina), born 27 December 1706, died 27 July (June?) 1708.[87] In a letter dated 29 December, 'Mr Colonel' was informed of the happy arrival in St Petersburg of the 'new-born girl Catherine', and asked not to grieve at the birth of a daughter.[88]

Another daughter, Anna, was born on 27 January 1708.[89] On 3 February Tsarevich Alexis wrote to Peter from Moscow reporting that he and his aunt Natalia had acted as godparents for the 'new arrival'.[90] Anna and Elizabeth (born 18 December 1709) were the only children to survive beyond childhood. Two more daughters, Maria (born 3 March 1713) and Margarita (born 8 September 1714), died within two months of each other in 1715.[91] About the first, Peter joked in a letter to Menshikov that he had heard from his wife that she had given birth to a son (sic!) called Maria,[92] but his letters contain no more specific expressions of disappointment at the birth of so many girls. Their last daughter, another Natalia, was born on 19/20 August 1718.[93] She was to receive marriage proposals while still a toddler (from the son of King Philip V of Spain in 1721),[94] but she died not long after her father, on 4 March 1725. Peter was very fond of her, referring to her in letters to his elder daughters as 'our big girl' (*velikaia devitsa*).[95] One of his last letters to her, hand-written and dated 10 May 1724, informs her of her mother's coronation, adding 'God willing, we hope to be with you soon. PS. Today there will be fireworks.'[96]

The birth of Tsarevich Peter Petrovich on 28/29 October 1715, just two weeks after Peter's grandson, also Peter, was celebrated enthusiastically.[97]

Allegorical engravings praised 'the illustrious royal union joined by God', and for the tsarevich's first birthday in 1716 Feofan Prokopovich delivered a speech in praise of hereditary monarchy.[98] Peter was his parents' pride and joy. On 28 June 1717 Peter wrote from abroad: 'Petrushenka, how are you? Greetings on our joint name-day tomorrow. God grant that I see you happy. I was unable to read your letter, but I'll put it away until I get home and then you can tell me what it says. Give regards and a kiss to your sisters from me.'[99] When Peter returned from Europe in 1717, he was presented with printed greetings from his children, including a text from Peter ('ghost-written' by Prokopovich) expatiating on 'the benefit of the whole nation' and 'the common good of the whole state', and complaining that Nature 'has not yet had time to supply me with the corporal organs with which to proclaim my heart-felt enthusiasm'.[100] All this prepared the ground for the proclamation, in February 1718, of Peter Petrovich as heir in Alexis's stead. Thereafter the boy's development was monitored with even greater anxiety. In July 1718 Catherine wrote to Peter that their son had been ailing because of teething, but now, with God's help, was in good health and had cut three eye-teeth. 'And please take care, Dad, because he has a bone to pick with you; when I remind him that papa has gone away he doesn't like it; he likes it much better and is pleased when you say that papa is here.'[101] In August Catherine reported that Peter Petrovich was 'constantly amusing himself drilling his soldiers and firing [toy] cannon'.[102] In view of all this tender concern, the laconic report of the boy's death, on 25 April 1719, in the daily journal kept in Alexander Menshikov's household, makes painful reading: 'His Excellency [Menshikov] visited the palace and spent about an hour in the apartments of His Royal Highness the tsarevich, then left for his home. At four in the afternoon General Apraksin sent an orderly with the news that the tsarevich had died, at which His Excellency left at once for the palace, went to the apartments and made the necessary arrangements for the funeral.' The scribe adds the information that at the time of his death Peter Petrovich was three feet four inches tall.[103] The loss was not altogether unexpected. Weber reports that the boy had always been 'weakly and puny', lagging far behind his cousin.[104]

Catherine was too distraught to attend the funeral, and Peter is said to have locked himself in his room for several days,[105] but I have discovered little written response to the loss. Surviving letters for April and May do not mention it, and it is oddly missing from diplomatic correspondence, as though Peter was reluctant to advertise the event too widely, for Peter Petrovich's death once again left him with no male heir other than his grandson Peter. On 2 January 1717, another son, Paul, had been born in the Netherlands. Peter had written to Catherine on 4 January, rejoicing at the birth of 'another recruit'.[106] The following day celebratory letters were dispatched to dignitaries at home and abroad (including the king of France and the emperor of Austria): 'I inform you that on the second day of this month in Wesel my wife (*khoziaka*) gave birth to little soldier Paul. ... Please inform the officers and men. I recommend him to the officers to be under their command and to the men as their comrade. Give all of them regards from me and the newborn.'[107] The stadtholder of the Netherlands was invited to be godfather, as the birth had taken place within his borders.[108] To Anna and Elizabeth, Peter wrote: 'Congratulations on the birth of a second brother; give the first one a kiss from me and his brother',[109] and to his niece Ekaterina, who was married to the duke of Mecklenburg in April 1716, he boasted: 'You are probably envious that we old folk are more productive than you young ones.'[110]

Sadly, as Peter was dispatching these celebratory letters, his son was already dead. As Catherine wrote to Boris Kurakin on 8 January, 'It is with deep sorrow that I inform you that almighty God saw fit to transpose our new-born son Tsarevich Paul from this world four hours after his birth. Truly, this sadness is very painful, but what's done is done and so we bow to the will of God.'[111] In a letter of 11 January Peter wrote of 'the sudden turn of events which changed joy to sorrow, but all I can respond is with Job, that man of many sorrows, that the Lord giveth and the Lord taketh away'.[112]

Catherine apparently suffered a miscarriage in September 1721. (Bergholz attributed her absence from the wedding of Count Pushkin on 29 September to the fact that she was recovering from this event.[113]) Some writers mention another boy named Peter, said to have been buried on 24 October 1723.[114] On closer inspection, this turns out to be the reburial of Peter Petrovich, whose remains were transferred from the Church of the Resurrection of Lazarus to the Church of the Annunciation in the Alexander Nevsky monastery on that date.[115] Massie's list ends with another Paul, who allegedly was born and died in 1724, but who left no trace in existing sources. Thus, of the children born to Catherine, only two, both girls, lived to adulthood.[116] Such a high infant mortality rate was by no means uncommon, even in the palaces of kings and emperors (British schoolchildren used to learn about the fifteen(?) prematurely deceased children of Queen Anne, Peter's contemporary), but the medical reasons differed. Peter may have inherited his own father's propensity for producing more, and relatively more robust, girl children. Venereal disease may have taken its toll. Whatever the case, for Peter, as for any monarch in a similar position, private grief was aggravated by an agonizing dilemma over succession to the throne.

As a result of his treatment of Alexis (see below), Peter has gone down in history as an uncaring father, but he seems genuinely to have loved his children by Catherine. Letters exude tender concern: 'Annushka and Lizenka, greetings!', he wrote in 1722. 'Your mother and I are well, thank God, and at this moment are on our way to Persia, God grant that we see you again safe and happy. When you are in St Petersburg kiss your big sister Nataliushka and our grandchildren for us.'[117] 'Anna, kiss Lizetka for me and the big noisy girl Natalishcha.... Thanks for the pencils in the case, which I needed as you can't get them here. God's grace be with you.'[118] 'My dear hearts, Tsarevny Anna Petrovna and Elizaveta Petrovna, I report that with God's help we are in good health; we received your letter of 4 February and thank you. With this letter we have sent you with Director of Works Siniavin a packet of China tea, which you should use for your health. Committing you to God's keeping, we remain, etc. etc.'[119] No such tenderness is shown in Peter's correspondence with his first-born, the only male in his family to grow to full manhood, to whom we now turn.

IV. ALEXIS

Alexis's birth on 19 February 1690 was greeted with celebrations, but there were inauspicious signs.[120] Peter's growing estrangement from Evdokia was bound to influence relations with his son. In August 1693 a letter written in the name of his 'little son' was enclosed with one from Peter's mother, who was anxious about her son's dangerous seafaring activities in Archangel. 'Please come back to us without delay, I beg you, our dear lord, as I see my grandmother grieving. Don't be angry, my dear lord, at this poor letter; I haven't yet learnt how to write properly.'[121] Thus the infant Alexis was recruited to the camp of Peter's critics. Who knows what mumblings of disapproval he subconsciously absorbed? Muted disapproval became more explicit in 1697–8 while Peter was abroad, and an opposition of sorts formed around Patriarch Adrian and Alexis's maternal relatives, the Lopukhins.[122] The distance between father and son widened further after Evdokia's banishment to Suzdal'.

It was not unusual for a prince to grow up with relatively little contact with his father. More surprising is the fact that Peter, who a few years later insisted that every nobleman educate his son on pain of severe penalties, appears not to have intervened until quite late in the education of his own heir, apparently leaving such matters to Tsaritsa Evdokia and his mother's relatives, none of whom was likely to inculcate the sort of skills and qualities which Peter valued. In a statement made during his trial in 1718, the tsarevich blamed his 'bad character' on his 'having been brought up from my Infancy with a Governess and her Maids, from whom I learn'd nothing but Amusements, and Diversions, and Bigotry, to which I had naturally an Inclination', and on the poor instruction given by Nikifor Viazemsky (his first tutor), Alexis Vasil'ev, and his grandmother's Naryshkin relatives, who allegedly encouraged him to drink and keep company with priests and monks.[123] Menshikov supervised Alexis's household and studies.[124] Peter thought about sending his son to Europe in 1698–9, but decided against it, engaging a German tutor, Martin Neugebauer, in the summer of 1701.[125] Neugebauer soon fell from favour. A fight over the tsarevich's manners resulted in his dismissal only a year later, 'for cursing the attendants who live with the tsarevich and calling them barbarians'.[126] As Alexis admitted in 1718, he was averse to German and sciences, so may have connived in the dismissal.

In 1702 Alexis visited Archangel, Solovki, and Novgorod with his father, stopping just short of the actual scenes of battle on the Baltic coast. In 1703 he was summoned to observe the fleet, and in 1704 he witnessed the siege of Narva. This occasioned the following intimidating letter from Peter: 'I may die tomorrow, but be sure that you will have little pleasure if you fail to follow my example. You must love everything which contributes to the glory and honour of the fatherland; you must love loyal advisers and servants, whether foreigners or our own people, and spare no effort to serve the common good. If my advice is lost in the wind and you do not do as I wish, I do not recognize you as my son.'[127]

Alexis appeared to some outsiders to show promise. Cornelius de Bruyn's observation of preparations for a victory parade in Moscow in 1702 caused him to muse on Peter's achievements, and to add that 'the young heir treads already in the footsteps of his father, and gives great signs of understanding and genius; he takes notice of everything, is very inquisitive and is of a fine disposition'.[128] After Neugebauer's departure, a more systematic programme of study was devised by Heinrich Huyssen, who declared that Alexis was 'blessed with all the qualities needed to acquire royal virtues'. According to Huyssen's report (for the journal *Europäische Fama* in 1705), Alexis devoted three hours per day to his lessons; he had to read the Bible five times in Slavonic and once in German, enjoyed reading the Greek Church Fathers and religious and secular books, had a good clear hand, spoke good German and French, learned something by heart every day, studied the biographies of emperors, kings and generals and took the feats of these persons as examples, had a real fear of God, was very obedient to his father, and was kind to his servants and subjects. He was also studying dancing, riding, and 'mechanical occupations'.[129] This glowing report was in part a propaganda exercise by Huyssen, who was hired to 'improve Russia's image abroad'.[130] An inventory of Alexis's books transferred to the Academy of Sciences in 1728 listed 269 foreign works, mainly purchased abroad, both religious and secular, but it is impossible to reconstruct the Russian titles fully. Religious literature predominated, but there were also secular books on such topics as history, philology, military science, and mathematics.[131]

Much was expected of Peter's heir. In 1705 the archbishop of Chernigov, Ioann Maksimovich, dedicated verses to Alexis, 'who has displayed greatness since his earliest years', setting out all Peter's virtues, achievements, and plans (including destroying his enemies in Africa, America, and Asia!) and encouraging his son to emulate him: 'Peter is the rock, Alexis was born from the rock.'[132] Alexis was admonished: 'When your royal highness sees the works of this most great father, he himself will do likewise, like a true fledgling of the high soaring eagle.'[133] Peter's was a hard act to follow, but Alexis tried to share some of his father's interests. A foreign instructor in turnery reported that the tsarevich had visited his home on several occasions, and 'is already a very fine turner and seems to have a great enthusiasm for it'.[134] Alexis fell in with some of his father's more eccentric enthusiasms, too. For example, he colluded in the mock tsar pretence, referring in letters to Fedor Romodanovsky as the 'big sovereign' (*bol'shoi gosudar'*) and his son Ivan Romodanovsky as the 'little sovereign'.[135] (The fact that the said Ivan was allowed the title 'sovereign tsarevich and great prince' may have reminded Alexis of his own vulnerability.) He was a heavy drinker, and even set up his own 'drunken assembly'. Later he was to emulate his father in taking as his mistress an illiterate foreign peasant girl.

Letters written during Alexis's first period of active service in 1707–8 indicate that the tsarevich understood his father's aims and methods, and that Peter was willing to entrust him with responsibilities, to the extent of having him preside over the council of ministers.[136] Letters from the Smolensk region, where Alexis was collecting provisions for the army, demonstrate that he tried to work systematically—for example, by obtaining oats and rusks from the more distant towns, hay from the closer ones. In late October 1707 seventeen-year-old Alexis was in Moscow, inspecting the fortifications and supervising the installation of cannons on the Kremlin walls in anticipation of a Swedish invasion. He inspected the garrison, which consisted of only 2,500 men, reporting that 'until now fortification work has been bad (because the people supervising the workers were bad)'.[137] He dealt with the call-up of young nobles, assuring his father that 'anyone who fails to appear will have his villages confiscated', but also asking for advice about what to do with young men without estates or villages who requested a subsistence allowance. 'But I have nowhere to get food from; I'm afraid that they may run away. Where do you wish me to obtain food for them? Also, the five regiments which are to be formed, where shall I get pay and provisions?'[138] He was also entrusted with dealing with subversive leaflets being produced by the Swedes on a Cyrillic printing-press captured in Danzig 'to raise up the people in the towns of the Russian realm'.[139]

The fact that Alexis was working on the home front rather than in a military command may reflect his lack of enthusiasm for front line service. Georg Grund recounts that Peter took Alexis with him on campaign, but the prince could not bear the pressures and was often ill, so he was sent behind the lines. According to Grund, Alexis, influenced by certain priests, viewed things 'with different eyes than some might wish and hope', disagreeing with his father on the need for expansion, a fleet, and foreign influence.[140] Peter for his part, during this period, treated his son like any other servitor, but with considerably less affection than trusted associates such as Menshikov. In March 1708 the royal women were summoned to St Petersburg, but Alexis was not invited: 'I am very sad to be left here and that I shan't see your honour,' he wrote, to which Peter responded: 'You write in your letter about being sad and bored about not being summoned here, but you should be able to work out for yourself that time requires it thus.'[141] Peter's letters to his son are curt and business-like: 'As I said in my first letter to you, send the wagons, which the French colonel is making with their fittings, here immediately, also order the recruits to be dispatched to the designated places without delay.'[142] On 17 August 1708 he ordered him to go to Moscow to discover why the work on fortification was going so slowly.[143] In the autumn of 1708 Alexis's jobs included investigating the treatment of foreign diplomatic staff in Moscow in the context of the arrest of Andrei Matveev in London, supplying more horses for the cavalry, reporting on the progress of work in the Mint, and making arrangements for a public parade of Swedish prisoners of war.[144] At the same time he was expected to continue his studies. Heinrich Huyssen returned from abroad in 1708, and Alexis was ordered to 'be obedient' to him.[145]

Peter was still displeased with his son's efforts. On 27 November he wrote complaining about the quality of the recruits whom Alexis was sending him: 'I see that you are spending more of your time in idleness than taking care of business at this crucial time.' Alexis replied on 8 December that someone must have slandered him: 'I do the tasks entrusted to me conscientiously, to the best of my strength and ability.' He wrote to Peter's secretary Makarov and to Catherine asking why his father was so angry with him.[146] A few weeks later Peter relented, saying he would not have been angry if Alexis had made it clearer that there were no good recruits available.[147] In January 1709 we find him signing papers in Peter's absence.[148] He was not at Poltava, but in August 1709 he was ordered to join Menshikov's unit in Kiev, whence he was sent to Dresden to study German, French, geometry, fortifications, and 'political affairs'.[149] His escort was Huyssen, who lauded the usefulness of foreign travel. Alexis later wrote a letter in German: to 'Allergnädigster Herr Papa' from his 'gehorsamster Diener und Sohn Alexiuss'.[150]

In the meantime Peter had set his sights on a foreign wife for Alexis— Princess Charlotte-Christina-Sophia of Wolfenbüttel.[151] The Brunswick-Wolfenbüttels were related by marriage to many of the royal and princely families of Europe. Charlotte's grandfather was Duke Anton Ulrich of Holstein-Gottorp, her sister was married to the Habsburg Emperor Charles VI.[152] There are rumours that Alexis had fallen in love with a daughter of Prince Gagarin, who was quickly married off in order to thwart any liaison. In theory, Alexis could have refused the German match, and he was encouraged to meet his intended. 'Why haven't you written to tell me what you thought of her and whether you are inclined to marry her?', wrote Peter on 13 August 1710.[153] Alexis gave his consent at the end of September (the letter has not survived), and a contract was signed in April 1711.[154] Under its terms Charlotte was allowed to retain her Protestant faith and received gifts of 25,000 reichsthaler, tableware, and carriages from Peter. Children were to be raised in the Orthodox faith.[155] There was much haggling about the upkeep of the princess's household. A memorandum sent to Peter in September 1711, reminding him about the promised gifts, received the reply that the tsar, having arrived in Germany straight from the war, could hardly have tableware and carriages about his person, but would arrange to buy them in Danzig and Elbing.[156] The wedding took place in the palace of the queen of Poland in Torgau on 14 October 1711. Peter wrote to Catherine: 'I report that on this day the wedding of my son took place, at which many distinguished persons were present ... I beg you to notify the all-jesting prince-pope and the others of this and ask him to bless the newly-weds dressed in all his robes together with all those who are there with you.' Menshikov sent a water-melon as a gift.[157]

As far as Peter was concerned, his son's marriage was just one in a series of duties. A few days after the wedding it was made clear that Alexis must continue his studies and war work. His new duties included organizing food supply depots and river transport for the troops going to Pomerania in Menshikov's regiment.[158] In 1713 Alexis returned to Russia from Germany. To this year dates the incident (reported at his trial) in which Alexis allegedly injured his hand in order to avoid an examination in drawing, one of several arranged by Peter to test the knowledge he had acquired abroad.[159] There are frequent references in Alexis's letters to his poor health, a topic which aroused in Peter annoyance rather than sympathy.[160] About this time tuberculosis was diagnosed. His physical weakness was used against him in his trial in 1718, when Peter compared his son unfavourably with his brother Ivan, who was unable to manage a rough horse and hardly even able to mount one, but loved horses; in other words, moral fibre compensated for physical disability.[161] In 1714 Alexis went to Carlsbad to take the waters. According to Weber, Peter ordered him to return to St Petersburg promptly: 'It was said, he shewed but little Inclination upon the Receipt of the Letter, and in his Answer; and that he resented his being still continued a Serjeant.'[162] Weber, incidentally, contributed to Alexis's bad reputation by alleging that he frequented 'vicious Company and contracted such corrupt Habits, as could not fail producing an Aversion to him in all honest Minds'.[163]

The marriage of Alexis and Charlotte was unhappy. Rumour had it that Alexis found his bride too thin and pock-marked, but the fact that Alexis's conservative friends disapproved of this foreign Protestant bride was probably more crucial. According to Weber, Alexis avoided Charlotte in public, and they had separate apartments. Not long after the birth of the couple's daughter Natalia in July 1714, Alexis installed his mistress Afrosinia, an illiterate Finnish peasant girl, in the palace. Alexis's treatment of his wife and his relations with his mistress precipitated a break with his father, who had other bones to pick with his son. On 19 January 1715 Peter wrote: 'Have you assisted [me] since you came to Maturity of Years in [my] Labours and Pains? No, certainly, the World knows you have not. On the other Hand you blame and abhor whatever Good I have been able to do, at the Expense of my Health, for the Love I have borne to my People, and for their Advantage; and I have all imaginable Reason to believe, that you will destroy it all, in case you should Survive me.'[164] On 11 October 1715, in what he referred to as a 'last testament', Peter wrote again to Alexis, setting out the enormous efforts he and 'other true sons of Russia' had expended since the outbreak of the war to overcome the disadvantages with which Russia embarked. He was aggrieved when he saw his unworthy heir's indifference to military affairs, rejecting all excuses about ill health, and despairing that all his attempts to reform his son had been in vain. He would cut him off 'like a gangrenous limb'. 'I have not spared and do not spare my own life for my country and my people, so why should I spare you who are so unworthy? Better a worthy stranger than my own unworthy son.'[165]

The following day Charlotte gave birth to a son, Peter, and died soon after from complications.[166] On 29 October, Peter's own son, also named Peter, was born. This sudden abundance of male heirs and his wife's death provides the background for Alexis's reply (31 October) to his father's letter, in which he expressed his willingness to relinquish his claim to the throne, in view of the fact that he was 'unqualified and unfit for the task', his memory gone, and his health undermined 'by many illnesses'.[167] On 19 January 1716, the eve of his departure for a major trip abroad, Peter wrote a belated reply in which he berated Alexis for failing to answer the charges of deliberate neglect of his duties, referring darkly to the 'long beards' whom he believed were manipulating Alexis for their own ends. Alexis was given six months to make up his mind.[168] Alexis was later to write to the Senate and others from Austria: 'There was a design to throw me into a Convent in the Beginning of the Year 1716, without my having done any Thing which may deserve it.'[169] On 26 August 1716 Alexis received another ultimatum—the succession or a monastery—and a summons to join Peter in Copenhagen, where an invasion of Sweden was about to be launched, a last chance to vindicate himself. It seems unlikely that Peter took the monastery option seriously, given his well-known disdain of the contemplative life.

Instead of going to Copenhagen, Alexis turned south at Danzig (sending a fraudulent letter postmarked Königsberg to suggest he was on his way) and headed for Vienna. In the view of the Russian historian Gordin, Alexis had decided on a course of opposition (with the hope of support from leading courtiers), and fled in order to find safety and await a convenient opportunity to return to Russia, in the event of either Peter's death or a rebellion.[170] He arrived in Vienna on 21 November 1716 in the expectation of help from his late wife's brother-in-law, Charles VI, but the Viennese court was reluctant to get too involved too quickly, and gave him sanctuary first in Tyrol, then in the fortress of St Elmo, near Naples. Hopes of further aid from the emperor were dashed when in July 1717 the troops of Philip V of Spain invaded Sardinia, which Austria had acquired by the Treaty of Utrecht in 1713. Austria was also involved in war with Turkey, and was eager to avoid complications. Spain, for its part, was worried about Russia and Austria doing some sort of deal over Alexis which might aid Charles in his dispute with Spain. To Peter, Alexis's defection was an embarrassment at a time when he was meeting foreign rulers face to face, as well as a potential danger as a bargaining counter abroad and an incentive to opposition at home. (Whether he really believed in a plot spearheaded by Alexis is unknown.) Peter had been suspicious of Austria's intentions ever since its 'betrayal' of their alliance in the late 1690s. Austria, for its part, did not want to provoke a Russian attack on its possessions in Silesia or even Bohemia. Thus 'the family drama of the Romanovs virtually gained the status of an all-European political problem'.[171]

Peter instructed his agents A. I. Rumiantsev and Peter Tolstoy to offer Alexis a pardon and bring him back to Russia. In a letter dated 10 July 1717 he wrote that although Alexis had acted 'like a traitor' in seeking refuge abroad and had inflicted insult and grief upon his father and shame upon his native land, he would inflict no punishment and show his 'best love' if he returned to Russia. If he refused, he would be eternally damned and pursued like a traitor.[172] Tolstoy, having tracked Alexis down to his refuge, explained the weakness of Austrian promises and the inevitability of his being intercepted, possibly by Peter in person. Alexis agreed to return on condition that he be allowed to marry the pregnant Afrosinia and live quietly away from the capital. He signalled his consent in a letter dated 4 October 1717, signed 'your most humble and worthless slave, unworthy of the name of son'.[173] On 31 January 1718 Alexis arrived back in Moscow, and on 3 February Peter issued a manifesto depriving his elder son of the throne and declaring Peter Petrovich as his new heir, to whom Alexis now swore allegiance.[174] Alexis now learned that to earn his pardon (previously promised unconditionally) he must disclose all his 'accomplices'. 'It is impossible to express the Consternation which has seized the Russians of the old Stamp, who look with Abhorrence on Petersbourg, Shipping and Sea Affairs, foreign Customs and Languages,' wrote Weber.[175] At the same time, members of Peter's close circle had good reason to want Alexis neutralized for good, especially in view of fears about the tsar's health, which was already beginning to arouse anxiety. Thus began a witch-hunt for Alexis's accomplices.[176]

A prelude to Alexis's trial was the so-called Suzdal' affair, the chief suspects in which were his mother Evdokia (now a nun in the Intercession convent in Suzdal', it will be recalled), her associates, and Tsarevna Maria, although, as a recent study makes clear, there were no links between Evdokia's 'party' and the Alexis affair.[177] Even so, many people suffered on flimsy charges only indirectly linked to Alexis's flight abroad. In a public spectacle in March 1718 the guards officer Stepan Glebov was executed by impalement after prolonged torture sessions, convicted of having committed adultery with Evdokia, and having written 'coded letters' (although no political content was revealed). Alexander Kikin, formerly a secretary in the Admiralty, was broken on the wheel, as was Bishop Dosifei of Rostov. 'You will be tsaritsa again,' Dosifei had allegedy told Evdokia and foretold Peter's death.[178] The abbess of the Intercession convent and the nun Kaptelina, Evdokia's confidante, were knouted and banished. Evdokia's brother Avraamy Lopukhin was executed later in the year. Tsarevna Marfa Alekseevna was charged with questioning Peter's choice of the younger son over the elder. Tsarevna Maria Alekseevna was locked up in Schlüsselburg fortress on the grounds that she acted as a go-between for Alexis and his mother, with whom she corresponded. Maria had met Alexis in Libau in October 1716, and had told him that Evdokia expected Peter to take her back as his wife. In turn, Maria tried to send Evdokia news of Alexis's escape abroad.[179] As for Evdokia, she was banished to a convent near Lake Ladoga with just one female dwarf for a servant. A guard was posted around the convent with strict orders (recalling those issued after Sophia's deposition in 1689) not to admit anyone, either male or female, of any rank, or to allow anyone to leave, including the nuns and priests. No letters were to be taken in or out.[180]

A special tribunal, the Chancellery for Secret Inquisitorial Affairs, was created to try Alexis. It conducted its initial investigations in Moscow, then in June 1718 moved to St Petersburg for the trial. In the case against Alexis, his alleged intention of reversing Peter's reforms was emphasized. When obliged to attend Peter's entertainments or watch the launch of a ship, 'he would rather chuse to go to the Gallies, or have a Fever, than to be present upon those Occasions'.[181] Afrosinia betrayed Alexis by reporting his words: 'I shall bring back the old people and choose myself new ones according to my will; when I become sovereign I shall live in Moscow, and leave St Petersburg simply as any other town; I won't launch any ships; I shall maintain troops only for defence, and won't wage war against anyone; I shall be content with the old domains. In winter I shall live in Moscow, in summer in Iaroslavl'.'[182] Afrosinia was eventually released for co-operating with the prosecution. Other charges concerned Alexis's moral and physical failings: he was accused of laziness, shirking, and attempting to escape the succession (he had, for example, feigned illness rather than accompany Peter). But the crucial charge was that he had sought Austrian aid to overthrow and assassinate Peter. ('He hop'd for his Father's Death with Expressions of Joy and told his confessor [Ignat'ev] : "I wish for my Father's death".') Although Alexis confessed to these charges under torture a few days before he died, there was no hard evidence of a plot. Nearly all the evidence was based on confession and hearsay, written evidence being confined to two letters from Alexis to the Senate from Naples, a report from the imperial envoy Otto von Pleyer of a plot to kill Peter and proclaim Alexis tsar (although without any indication that Alexis was the instigator), and some of the tsarevich's notes on Baronius's *Ecclesiastical Annals*, which indicated disapproval of some of Peter's reforms relating to dress and church property.

In June 1718 Alexis was transferred from Moscow and locked up in the Trubetskoy bastion of the Peter–Paul fortress in St Petersburg. His may be regarded as the first Russian show trial, conducted with every semblance of openness by the standards of the day. Both church and lay officials were consulted, and accounts of the proceedings were published in Russia and abroad.[183] Interrogation under torture (the normal Russian procedure) began on the morning of 19 June, when Alexis was questioned on twelve points, accompanied by twenty-five blows with the knout. This procedure was repeated in the evening, this time in the presence of the tsarevich's confessor, Iakov Ignat'ev, who also received twenty-five blows.[184] A second torture session took place on 24 June, this time with only fifteen blows, probably because of Alexis's deteriorating condition. Leading churchmen were invited to give their opinion on the case. In their summary of Alexis's crimes, they said that he had 'placed his Confidence in those who loved the ancient Customs, and that he had become acquainted with them by the Discourses they had held, wherein they had constantly praised the ancient Manners, and spoke with Distaste of the Novelties his Father had introduced'.[185] However, they declined to reach a decision on the grounds that this was a civil case and subject to the tsar's absolute power, and although tending to the side of punishment for an errant son (which they supported with copious biblical texts), they left open the option of mercy ('The Heart of the Czar is in the Hands of God').[186] The 126 members of the Senate and civil officials who constituted the court delivered a verdict of guilty and a sentence of death at noon on 24 June, but the interrogation by torture continued into the afternoon, for Peter was desperate to extract more information. On 25 June Alexis was confronted with letters found in his house. The next day he was tortured again. The same evening he was dead.

In official reports abroad, Alexis's death was attributed to a seizure. 'The next Day ... early in the Morning,' writes Weber, 'the News was brought to the Czar, that the violent Passions of the Mind, and the Terrors of Death, had thrown the Czarewitz into an apoplectick Fit.' Other versions include death by poison or beating, and there were even rumours that Peter had strangled Alexis with his own hands.[187] A story attributed to Rumiantsev, who, it will be recalled, had helped bring Alexis back to Russia, allegedly written a month after the tsarevich's death but thought to be a later forgery, claims that Alexis was suffocated with pillows in his bed, on Peter's orders.[188] The most likely cause of death is still the most obvious: Alexis, already weakened by long imprisonment and illness (tuberculosis), was subjected to a further series of floggings, the final two sessions (24 and 26 June) following each other too closely.[189] An entry in the record book of the Peter–Paul fortress garrison states: 'On June 26 [1718] at 8 a.m. there gathered in the garrison his majesty, the illustrious prince [Menshikov], Prince Iakov Fedorovich Dolgoruky, Gavrila Ivanovich Golovkin, Fedor Matveevich Apraksin, Ivan Alekseevich Musin-Pushkin, Tikhon Nikitich Streshnev, Peter Andreevich Tolstoy, Peter Shafirov and General Buturlin for a session in the torture chamber, after which, having been in the garrison until 11 a.m. they dispersed. On the same day at six in the evening, being under guard in the Trubetskoy bastion of the garrison, Tsarevich Alexis Petrovich expired.'[190]

Peter attended vespers in Trinity Cathedral on the evening of his son's death. According to Weber, Peter had had a tearful last meeting earlier that day with Alexis, when he forgave and blessed him. People present at the funeral on 30 June reported that the tsar was 'bathed in Tears', and that the priest chose the text from David: 'O my son Absalom, my son, my son Absalom'. Even so, three days before the funeral, Peter had been celebrating the anniversary of Poltava, and on 29 June his name-day. The day after the funeral Peter toasted the launch of a man-of-war in the company of Vice-Tsar Romodanovsky and English shipwrights.[191]

The incident had lasting repercussions.[192] The Chancellery for Secret Inquisitorial Affairs continued to function after Alexis's death. Between 1718 and 1725 it investigated 370 'grave matters' (including expressions of sympathy for Alexis and complaints against Catherine).[193] Its further investigations included one in 1720 when further information about Evdokia's 'scandalous' activities in Suzdal' came out, and over 150 people were arrested.[194] On 5 February 1722 Peter promulgated a new law of succession. Its opening clause referred to the 'Absalom-like wickedness' of Alexis. It ended: 'We deem it good to issue this edict in order that it will always be subject to the will of the ruling monarch to appoint whom he wishes to the succession or to remove the one he has appointed in the case of unseemly behaviour, so that his children and descendants should not fall into such wicked ways as those described above, having this restraint upon them.'[195] At that time Peter's only male heir was Alexis's son Peter. But the trial poisoned Peter against his grandson, who might provide a rallying point for the opponents of reform whose existence Peter suspected but had been unable to uncover during the trial of Alexis. Although Peter Alekseevich was not ill-treated, he was not given the prominence of an heir presumptive. For example, the name-days and birthdays of Peter Alekseevich and his sister Natalia were not included in the court calendar. In December 1721 Peter's daughters were given the title *tsesarevny*, but his grandson continued to be known simply as *velikii kniaz'*, although Peter could have named him *tsesarevich* if he had wished.[196] In a terse letter Peter wrote that 'the time has come to teach our grandson'.[197] Otherwise, he rarely paid him any attention.

In the case of Alexis, Peter claimed initially to be driven by 'fatherly affection', but parental concern had its limitations.[198] Peter's understanding of the rights of fatherhood were far from the child-centred modern-day concepts of the right of the individual, however young, to challenge, even 'divorce' his or her parents. Peter was echoing the beliefs of his day when he wrote that 'Private parents and with much more Reason those who are beside invested with a Sovereign Authority, as we are, have an unlimited Power over their Children, independently of any other Judge'.[199] Peter was first and foremost a monarch, a father only second. He could not separate Alexis's fate from the fate of Russia. 'We have seen,' he wrote, 'that all our care and attention for the education and instruction of our son were in vain, for he was always disobedient to us, showing no inclination for what was becoming of a worthy successor and ignoring the teachers we had given him.'[200] The affair was a dreadful warning to any other children of Peter's who felt inclined to be 'disobedient'. Perhaps it is just as well for Peter's other sons that they all died in infancy. We can only speculate about the impact that the terrible events of 1718 had upon the rest of Peter's family.

V.   THE YOUNGER GENERATION MARRIES

As daughters of a tsar forging new links with the outside world, Catherine's daughters were not destined for the quiet life of spinsterhood enjoyed by their Muscovite predecessors. Tsar Michael made one abortive attempt to marry his eldest daughter Irina to a Danish prince in the 1640s, while Alexis seems quite deliberately to have kept his six surviving daughters unmarried. When he died, the eldest was twenty-five, the youngest fourteen, but no discussion of matches for any of them has come to light. Foreigners surmised that this was because non-Orthodox foreigners were deemed unsuitable and Russian suitors too lowly. Certainly restrictions of consanguity in marriage (to the fourth degree) limited the number of eligible Russian bridegrooms; there were serious obstacles to marriage outside Orthodoxy and few, if any, eligible husbands in subjugated Orthodox territories such as Moldavia and Wallachia. The main aim may well have been to limit inconvenient claims to preferment at court and complications regarding precedence codes which so many sons-in-law would inevitably have created.

In Peter's reign restrictions on marriage to foreigners were swept away, along with the *terem*, in the interests of the State. The marriages of his children and nieces were no longer just a factor in court politics, but potential bargaining chips in foreign policy. The first to be put on the international marriage market was Peter's niece Anna, married in 1710 at the age of seventeen to Friedrich Wilhelm, duke of Courland, also aged seventeen. Russian military successes in the duchy prompted Peter to initiate negotiations through the king of Prussia, the duke's uncle, whom he visited in October 1709. It was hoped that a marriage alliance with his nephew would keep the Prussian king from attacking Russia or otherwise harming Russian interests. Initially the envoys from Courland brought proposals for their duke to marry 'one of their royal highnesses', and asked for portraits of all three of Tsar Ivan's daughters.[201] Any one would have done, and it is possible that Anna was married off before her elder sister Ekaterina because the latter was her mother's and uncle's favourite, and they hoped to find her a better match. The marriage contract stipulated a dowry of 200,000 roubles, which would allow the duke to pay off his debts and redeem mortgaged estates, and included clauses on religious faith.[202] Peter agreed to pay 40,000 as a straight dowry and 160,000 as a 'loan' (50,000 to be paid in advance) from which Anna would earn 5 per cent interest per year. For his part, Peter gained a useful channel of influence in Courland, which was a nominal vassal of Poland-Lithuania. Peter wrote to his niece: 'Preserve the faith and law in which you were born, to the end of your days unswervingly. Don't forget your own nation, but love and respect it above all others. Love and respect your husband as the head [of the family] and obey him in all things except the aforementioned.'[203]

The priest originally summoned to perform the ceremony, which took place on 31 October 1710, objected on the grounds that marriage between persons of different faiths was forbidden by Church Law, and Peter had to find a last-minute substitute, who used cribs of the Latin responses in his prayer-book.[204] The tone was set for weddings to come, with mixed company in Western dress, gun salutes, a firework display, and dancing, all against the backdrop of St Petersburg.[205] The newly-weds set off for Courland at the beginning of January, but when they were less than fifty miles from St

Petersburg, Friedrich died, by all accounts from the effects of 'immoderate feasting'.[206] Anna returned to St Petersburg forthwith, collected her widow's pension of 40,000 roubles, and began the nomadic existence which was to last until she became empress of Russia in 1730. No doubt she would have preferred to remain at home, but the presence of a Russian retinue in Courland was too valuable to allow her to return permanently. A scheme for her mother and sisters to move to Courland was not carried through.[207] Over the years proposals were made by various suitors, from Saxony (through Augustus) and Prussia, but nothing came of any of them.[208] So Anna alternated periods in Russia with lonely intervals in Mitau, from where she kept in touch by regular formal correspondence.[209] In Courland Anna was ruler only in name, with her household expenses controlled by Peter down to the last detail. Closer acquaintance with Anna's life as duchess of Courland puts criticism of Anna the empress into perspective. It is sometimes claimed, for example, that she was cut off from Russia and things Russian, whereas in fact she spent much time there. Bergholz, a keen observer of female character, found her 'lively and pleasant, with a good figure, not bad-looking and behaves in a manner which inspires respect'.[210]

In 1716 Anna's elder sister Ekaterina was married to Karl Leopold of Mecklenburg-Schwerin, 'the coarse, uneducated, wilful and highly eccentric owner of a scrap of German soil', who was in constant dispute with the nobility of his principality.[211] His initial proposal was to the widowed Anna when divorce proceedings from his first wife, Sophia-Hedwig of Nassau Frieland, were still in progress. The duke's bad character and insecure circumstances were public knowledge, but Peter was keen to acquire a base in north Germany and better security for Russian garrisons in Mecklenburg, as well as having his eyes on the port of Wismar, then in Swedish hands, as a base for Russian trade via the Baltic and the Elbe. These aims overrode any concern for his niece's welfare. The marriage contract, which included the right of Russian merchants to reside and trade in Mecklenburg, free passage for Russian troops, and the tsar's pledge to support the duke against his enemies, was signed before the couple met for the first time in March 1716.[212] They were married in Danzig on 8 April 1716, and their first child, Anna, was born in December 1718. In 1719 Karl was driven out of Mecklenburg by troops of George I of England (who supported the local gentry), and in August 1722 mother and daughter went for a visit to Moscow, where they continued to reside for the most part. Anna Leopoldovna's baby son was to occupy the Russian throne for just six months in 1740–1 as Ivan VI. Of Peter's nieces, only the youngest daughter, Praskovia, who was frail and in poor health, escaped a foreign marriage. She married secretly the Russian nobleman Ivan Il'ich Mamonov, by whom, according to at least one account, she had a son in 1724.[213]

In November 1724 Peter's eldest daughter Anna, then aged sixteen, was betrothed to Karl Friedrich, duke of Holstein, heir to the Swedish throne, with a dowry of 30,000 roubles. The celebratory firework display featured

Venus in a carriage drawn by swans with the legend 'Happy Concord'.[214] It had taken two and a half years to reach this stage. Anna was only fourteen when in March 1721 Karl arrived in Riga for an initial inspection by his prospective parents-in-law. The wedding did not take place until after Peter's death, on 21 May 1725.[215] In the question of his children's marriages, Peter, like fellow monarchs of his age, was motivated more by reasons of state than those of conjugal happiness. Even so, he opposed forced marriage: Bassewitz notes on several occasions that Peter 'although he was [Anna's] father, deemed her consent essential'.[216] However, the apparent non-consent of a prospective spouse could itself be a bargaining point in diplomatic negotiations, and in general children were expected to put duty before personal desires. The failure to specify which girl was the intended (the duke did not know whether he was to marry Anna or Elizabeth until the very eve of his betrothal[217]) confirms how little individuals mattered. Karl Friedrich was an eligible bachelor despite the fact that he was short, plain, 'indifferent to all intellectual interests', and a heavy drinker. (Both Anna and Elizabeth were regarded as beauties.) Moreover, if we can believe Bergholz's testimony, the duke preferred Elizabeth to Anna. In August 1724, he writes, the duke sailed past the royal palace several times in hopes of catching a glimpse of Elizabeth, but was disappointed when on each occasion it was Anna who came out on the balcony.[218] Once the engagement was official, however, the duke claimed to be 'passionately in love'.[219]

Somehow Elizabeth escaped marriage. A number of candidates were considered, among them Duke Ferdinand of Courland, Manuel of Portugal and the son of Margrave Albert (uncle of the king of Poland). In 1721 there were negotiations with a view to a match with the eleven-year-old Louis XV of France, but they fell through.[220] Campredon found Elizabeth attractive, but her faults 'if she has any, are mostly on the side of education and manners'.[221] In 1724 Peter wrote to Boris Kurakin of rumours that the duke of Bourbon was planning to seek the hand of his daughter, and asked him to make every effort to secure the match.[222] After Peter's death, Elizabeth was betrothed to a prince of Holstein who died, and even found herself being considered as a match for her nephew Peter Alekseevich. In the end she evaded all suitors, and eventually brought to Russia as her heir the future Peter III, the son of her sister Anna and Duke Karl.

Peter's granddaughter Natalia Alekseevna (born July 1714) was too young to be married while Peter was still alive, but plans were already in hand in Catherine's reign and the reign of Natalia's brother Peter II (1727–30). Hopes of a match with the Infante Don Carlos of Spain show how wide the Russian net was thrown, but Natalia Alekseevna died in November 1728 at the age of fifteen, one of the many 'faceless' royal women.[223] Marriage to foreigners had become the norm, and the efforts of Peter II's advisers to marry him to a Russian girl were regarded as a retrograde step by supporters of reform, 'for with this is linked the question of the return of this monarchy to its original state, which all old Russians desire', and it would signal a return to Russia's 'former barbarism'.[224]

Thus Peter's family life transcended personal feelings and domestic settings. Royal marriages reflected Russia's changed international status. Members of the royal family played their role as they had done in Muscovite times at the heart of patronage networks, but they also reflected breaks with tradition, none more so than when Peter himself chose to marry a low-born foreigner. Some, like Peter's sister Natalia, were beacons of cultural reform, whereas others did their best to preserve older customs. In particular, the clash between Peter and his eldest son became a metaphor for the struggle within Russia itself, between a patriarchal, traditional society and a new society in which centuries-old traditions could be discarded in favour of a greater good, focusing 'the people's consciousness of the struggle between old and new'.[225] At the same time as Peter rejected his eldest son's hereditary claims, he also provided rapid advancement for a number of people outside traditional power networks, the 'fledglings of Peter's nest' who form the subject of the next chapter.

13

Friends and Helpers

I. 'HIS OWN UNAIDED RULE'

> I am well, thank God, only life is hard, for I can't use my left hand, so I am obliged to hold the sword and the pen in my right hand alone. And you know how few helpers I have.[1]

Few rulers appear so single-minded and single-handed as Peter I, as was acknowledged in speeches made in October 1721 which credited Peter with promoting Russia's interests 'by his own unaided rule'.[2] Foreigners were under less obligation to offer eulogies, but to many of them, too, Peter seemed to work alone. The tsar, wrote the English minister Charles Whitworth, improved his empire 'without any education, without any foreign help, contrary to the intention of his people, clergy, and chief ministers, but merely by the strength of his own genius, observation and example'.[3] Another foreign observer wrote: 'I pity with all my heart the monarch who cannot find a single loyal subject apart from the two foreigners who hold the reins of the empire.'[4] But even a giant like Peter had to delegate some of his work, for 'God had given the Tsar twenty times more business than other people, but not twenty times more force and capacity to go through with it'.[5] Earlier we examined institutional reform. In this chapter we look at the people at the top, the men whom Peter used to command his armies, implement his policies, publicize his work, and, in a few cases, share his burdens as friends and confidants.

Before spot-lighting individuals, let us consider the principles by which Peter assembled his 'team'. Earlier we dispelled the common misapprehension that Peter operated a consistently 'meritocratic' policy. His most dramatic challenge to old-style patrimonial clan politics came when he declared that he would rather hand the country 'to a worthy stranger than to my own unworthy son'.[6] Even allowing for an element of rhetoric in this statement, if blood ties could be disregarded when choosing the successor to the throne, why not make talent the sole criterion for filling lesser positions? There are plenty of examples of neglect of traditional hierarchies and the elevation of foreigners or commoners. But such were far from being the rule. Peter picked and promoted his 'helpers' from a range of backgrounds, from princes to paupers, but the pool of available aides was still determined largely by custom and tradition, as was the case elsewhere in Europe. Politics in Petrine Russia remained, as they has done in much of the world up to and including the twentieth century, patriarchal and personal. There was little decline in the clan loyalties and inter-clan rivalries which characterized Muscovite politics, which also drew fresh blood from the occasional promotion of men of lower rank and foreign birth. The essentially personal character of Muscovite politics, which measured power in proportion to closeness to the sovereign, proved remarkably tenacious, even though Peter's peripatetic existence meant that 'closeness' often had to be measured by frequency and intimacy of correspondence rather than physical proximity. There is little evidence that loyalty was transferred from the person of the sovereign to more abstract concepts, although some of Peter's associates learned to ape his own formulae and pay lip-service to such notions as 'the common good' and 'the interests of the State'. Nor, despite the proliferation of new institutions, was there much evidence of clearly delineated rule by institutions or offices, still less of devolution of power to (non-existent) corporate bodies. Of necessity, Peter continued to bypass even those institutions which he himself created, such as the Senate, by having his orders executed by trusted envoys such as guards officers and orderlies, much in the same way as his father and half-brother had relied on gentlemen of the bedchamber and other favoured individuals. It goes without saying that Peter's reign did not see even the beginnings of a modicum of 'democratic processes' (despite attempts to introduce appointments by ballot). None of the men whose careers will be considered below represented anything or anyone except the tsar's and sometimes their own interests.

II. OLD NETWORKS

When Peter ousted Sophia in 1689, a ruling circle based on the younger tsar's 'party' already existed. Many members owed their positions to marriage links with the royal family: Naryshkins and Lopukhins (the relatives respectively of Peter's mother and his first wife), Streshnevs (through a long-standing link via Tsar Michael's wife), Saltykovs (Tsar Ivan's wife), and Apraksins (Tsar Fedor's wife). The inflated membership of the boyar duma in 1689 (153 compared with 66 in 1676) was determined by the need to accommodate the proliferation of royal relatives of both tsars and their associated clientele.[7] Others owed their elevation to the convention of selecting young men of leading families to serve as gentlemen of the bedchamber or chamberlains in preparation for high office later in life.[8]

Some individuals who owed their status to marriage links quickly lost their power in the early years of Peter's rule. Peter took care to limit the influence of his own in-laws even before his wife's banishment in 1698. After the Kozhukhovo campaign in 1694, Peter Abramovich Lopukhin the Elder, the tsaritsa's uncle, died at Preobrazhenskoe after being tortured on Peter's orders. The precise nature of the charges against him is not known. His younger brother, Peter Abramovich also, met a similar fate in 1699.[9] Before Peter's departure for the West in 1697, Tsaritsa Evdokia's father Fedor was banished to Tot'ma, and her uncles Vasily and Sergei to Saransk and Viazma, probably to prevent them from causing trouble in the tsar's absence.[10] The Naryshkin clan (already depleted by the massacre of 1682) failed to capitalize on its success. Only Peter's uncle Lev Kirillovich (1664–1705) enjoyed any real prominence, and he seems to have lost some ground after the death of his sister Tsaritsa Natalia in 1694, although he was nominally entrusted with foreign affairs during the Grand Embassy. Prince Boris Kurakin, a valuable source for the 1690s, was scathing about both Naryshkin ('a stupid man' and a drunkard) and the Lopukhins ('wicked, mean, scandalmongers, of little brain, knowing nothing of how to behave at court or in politics').[11]

Other royal relatives retained their influence longer. A prime example was Tikhon Nikitich Streshnev (1649–1719), sometimes referred to as Peter's 'adoptive father' (he was related to Peter's great-grandmother on his father's side) and 'the leading figure of the Naryshkin group'.[12] Johannes Korb records that Tikhon Nikitich was one of only two boyars exempted from shaving in 1698, and that his office corresponded to that of lord high steward.[13] The year 1700 found him in charge of the new grouping of military chancelleries, a crucial post at the outbreak of the Northern War. He was a founder-member of the Senate. But if we take Kurakin's acerbic comments at face value, a talent for palace intrigue and cunning were Streshnev's chief qualifications.[14] Ivan Musin-Pushkin (1661–1729) was also a member of the boyar duma (*okol'nichii* in 1682, boyar in 1698), governor in Smolensk and Astrakhan, and from 1701 head of the Monastery chancellery. He distinguished himself at Poltava, where he was apparently 'from the beginning to the end at the emperor's side inseparable from him'.[15] He continued to serve in the Senate until his death, and was awarded estates in 1722 'for his many services'.[16] The tsar was fond of him, addressing him as 'Her Bruder' in letters, which may be explained by the fact that he was Tsar Alexis's illegitimate son, hence Peter's half-brother.[17] In his turn, Ivan's son Platon was included in the tsar's party travelling to Germany and France in 1716 and sent by Peter to Prince B. I. Kurakin to study politics as 'our nephew (*plemiannika nashego*), whom I recommend to you as a relative to a relative'.[18]

Several other leading figures in Peter's regime came up by the traditional route of family networks. One such was Fedor Matveevich Apraksin (1661–1728), brother of Tsaritsa Marfa. Apraksin served with his brothers Peter and Andrei as chamberlains to Tsar Fedor, then to Peter. In the 1690s he served in the Semenovsky guards, gaining the rank of sub-lieutenant in 1696. In 1698 he was attached to Peter's new Admiralty. Peter addressed him as 'M[e]in Her Admiral' in letters.[19] A brief study of Apraksin's character confounds the meritocracy theory. Apraksin was an affable companion, rather than an expert on anything. He was not particularly well educated, and did not speak foreign languages. This early luminary of the Russian fleet was initially mainly an armchair admiral. When in February 1707 he was promoted from Admiralty secretary to full admiral, he had never actually been to sea. In 1705, charged with finding a place to build new docks at Voronezh, he picked a site dismissed as unsuitable by the English engineer John Perry. Perry's advice was ignored, with the result that when ships were required for action against Turkey in 1711, there was not enough water to launch them. Still, Peter preferred to blame Apraksin's subordinates and 'God's will', rather than the admiral himself.[20] Apraksin was also a staunch supporter of the old nobility. A well-known anecdote has him rolling up his sleeves and helping some sons of nobles who had been forced to hammer in piles on the embankments in St Petersburg as a punishment for dereliction of duty. Peter comes along and asks: 'Fedor Matveevich, you are an admiral and a knight [of the order of St Andrew]. Why are you hammering?' Apraksin replies: 'My nephews and grandsons are hammering piles, so why not me, too? Am I superior to them by birth? I have not dishonoured my order and uniform. They are hanging on a tree.' Peter pardoned the young men and sent them abroad to study.[21]

Apraksin learned on the job. Georg Grund recounts how in 1708 Apraksin won his military spurs by capturing a unit of Saxon prisoners deserted by the Swedes near Kopor'e, after an abortive campaign against St Petersburg.[22] He was awarded the order of St Andrew and a gold sword for action at Viborg in 1710. In 1713–14, as admiral in charge of operations, he helped to clear Finland of Swedish forces.[23] In 1718 he became president of the Admiralty college, but continued active service in 1719 (attacking the Swedes at Stockholm) and 1722 (the capture of Derbent during the Persian campaign).[24] Throughout these years Apraksin remained one of Peter's favourite drinking companions, although even the heavy-drinking Peter advised the admiral to drink more moderately, pronouncing himself to be 'sorry and ashamed' that he had already lost two admirals (Lefort and F. A. Golovin) to that 'disease'.[25] Apraksin took little notice. Bergholz recounts a scene at the admiral's house in July 1721, when Apraksin personally forced a reluctant drinker to down his portion. 'We never again drank so much in St Petersburg as we drank here,' noted Bergholz, in a diary awash with boozing stories.[26] For all his faults, Apraksin remained one of Peter's favourites, perhaps the only one for whom Peter's feelings remained consistently warm.[27] He was also on good terms with Catherine, who addressed him as *Kum* ('Godfather').[28]

The bottle was a common factor in Peter's relationship with another early favourite, Prince Boris Alekseevich Golitsyn (1654-1714), who won the tsar's favour despite the hostility of the Naryshkins. A member of a leading princely clan, he drew close to Peter by serving as his attendant (*d'iadka*, or *komnatnyi stol'nik*) and staunch supporter in the crises of 1682 and 1689. In the 1680s, when he directed the important Kazan' chancellery, he survived the disgrace of his cousin Vasily Vasil'evich, and overcame suspicions that for the sake of family honour he had doctored Vasily's confession in September 1689 before it was submitted to Peter.[29] There are several anecdotes about his relationship with Peter. One, mentioned in several sources, is that Golitsyn taught Peter to drink. Another is that he cured him of a fear of water, which Peter acquired after being terrified by a rushing stream when he was a young boy.[30] Golitsyn was also quite well educated for a Russian of his age and background (Kurakin described him as highly intelligent and astute,[31]) and enjoyed the company of foreigners. But his influence did not survive much beyond the 1690s, perhaps as a result of heavy drinking. He lost Peter's confidence during the Astrakhan revolt. Peter wrote to Fedor Golovin in 1705: 'Prince Boris has raised doubts in our mind with his crazy letter; he doesn't even know what he's writing himself.'[32] Evidently, towards the end of his life, Boris Alekseevich became increasingly deaf and ill. He sent a rather touching letter in June 1709, saying that in spite of his illness he was 'ready to work not only until he sweated but also to the last drop of his blood'.[33] In the year before his death he entered a monastery.

Golitsyn was friendly with another member of the Naryshkin party, Andrei Artamonovich Matveev (1666–1728), the son of Artamon Sergeevich, Tsaritsa Natalia's guardian. Matveev's bitter hostility towards Tsarevna Sophia[34] and her circle, on account of his family's exile by the Miloslavskys in 1676 and his father's murder at the hands of the strel'tsy in 1682, also brought him closer to the tsar, whom he served as an attendant in his youth. Matveev's mastery of foreign languages, unusual for a Russian of his generation, made him especially useful to Peter. He served as envoy to the Dutch Republic (1699–1712) and Austria (1712–15), on missions to France and England, returning to Russia as count of the Holy Roman Empire in February 1715. From 1719 he was president of the Justice College and senator.[35] Another close associate of Peter's who gained prominence in foreign affairs was General-Admiral Fedor Alekseevich Golovin (1650–1706). Already a seasoned diplomat when Peter ousted Sophia (he negotiated the Treaty of Nerchinsk with China in 1689), he was Lefort's second-in-command on the Grand Embassy, and in 1699 became the first knight of the order of St Andrew. His short but crucial period of office as head of foreign affairs (1699–1706) saw the formation of Russia's coalition against Sweden and the first successes of the Northern War. Whitworth declared him to be the most honest and intelligent man in all Russia.[36] His death in August 1706, en route from Moscow to Kiev, was precipitated by drink, another thread linking him with Peter.

The ancestors of Gavrila Ivanovich Golovkin (1660–1734) had been boyars since the early sixteenth century. His father served as gentleman of the bedchamber to Tsar Fedor Alekseevich, as, in his turn, did Golovkin to Peter, who entrusted him with routine household matters.[37] He headed the Foreign Office from 1706, and was made state chancellor (a new post) in 1709 and awarded the Russian title of count in 1710.[38] In his turn, Golovkin's son accompanied Tsarevich Alexis to Poland and Germany in 1709–10.[39] Yet Golovkin does not seem to have had any particular qualifications. Although he headed the Foreign Office, he apparently did not know any language apart from Russian.[40]

From the mid-1690s a group of men enhanced their positions by partici-
pating in military action with Peter. Most notable among them were Golovin,
Gordon, Lefort, Shein, Sheremetev, and Tolstoy, who conveniently appear in
an equestrian portrait of Peter at Azov, painted in 1699.[41] Avtamon
Mikhailovich Golovin, an attendant of Peter's in the 1680s, was a key figure
in the reformed army and a pioneer officer in the Preobrazhensky guards.
Capture at the Battle of Narva in 1700 (he was not released until 1718) interrupted a promising career. The story of Peter Andreevich Tolstoy (1645–1729)
proves that even initial disloyalty and comparatively advanced years did not
necessarily blight the career of a wily servitor. His allegiance to the
Miloslavsky cause in 1682 was forgiven. After serving at Azov in 1696, Tolstoy
was sent in 1697 to study abroad with a group of much younger men.[42] In
1701 he went to Constantinople as Russia's first permanent ambassador,
serving for thirteen years, including a period of incarceration in the Seven
Towers. Any lingering suspicions of disloyalty were dispelled by Tolstoy's role
in luring Tsarevich Alexis back to Russia in 1718. From 1717 to 1722 he was
president of the Commerce college, and at the age of seventy-seven went on
the Persian campaign. As stated in the charter awarding him the order of St
Andrew in 1722, 'he has shown great and important service not only to us but
also to the whole fatherland'.[43] Tolstoy's success may be attributable in part
to his being related by marriage to Apraksin and to his forging an alliance
with Catherine. But this was insufficient to save him when he fell out with
Menshikov in 1727. His long life ended in exile in the Solovetsky monastery.

Boris Petrovich Sheremetev (1652–1719), Peter's outstanding military
commander, was a member of a distinguished boyar family, and served as a
palace attendant in the 1670s. A veteran of military campaigns and diplomatic
missions, he was one of the first to join Peter's camp in August 1689, possibly
because of a feud with Prince Vasily Golitsyn.[44] In 1697–9 he headed a
delegation which visited Poland, Austria, Italy, and Malta (where he was made
a knight).[45] In 1700 he was promoted to field marshal, in 1705 he was made
a count, and in 1706 general field marshal. Loyalty and titles did not shield
him from the tsar's displeasure. In January 1708 Peter attacked him for mis-
routing troops ('Either the devil told you to do it, or you have gone mad'),
which prompted an aggrieved letter from Sheremetev to Menshikov
claiming that the tsar's angry letter had reduced him to a state of 'melancholy' (*melenkholiiu*). 'May God forbid that such anger make my illness worse
and grant that I'm not killed by palsy.'[46] In March 1709, when Sheremetev
was sent to tackle the Swedes in Ukraine, Peter was displeased with his efforts.
Sheremetev wrote: 'I beseech your majesty, my most gracious sovereign, with
tears not to make me die of grief before my time of my old age.'[47]

The demands on him were so heavy that Sheremetev had no time to visit
his Moscow estates or to settle into his residence in St Petersburg. In July 1710,
having scarcely drawn breath after the siege of Riga, he was ordered to hand
over the garrison to General Repnin and go to Poland 'without delay', as there
was news of the gathering of Turkish–Tatar forces.[48] The year 1711 found him

on a forced march from the Baltic to head off the Turks in the south. 'My God and creator,' he wrote, 'deliver us from this and allow us a little peace to live on this earth, just to live a little.'[49] Campaigns in Mecklenburg and Pomerania followed. When in 1716 Peter broke off relations with him altogether, Sheremetev wrote to the tsar's secretary Makarov complaining that his grief had left him with 'one foot in the grave' and had made his illness worse. When relations were restored through the mediation of Catherine, Sheremetev spoke of being revived 'like a corpse from the grave'.[50] Yet he would not compromise, declining to participate in the trial of Tsarevich Alexis, and harbouring doubts about the more extreme manifestations of modernization. It has been argued that Peter needed men like Sheremetev to head an army in which old *mestnichestvo* values, although officially abolished, still prevailed. Sheremetev's distinguished pedigree and family service record meant that any noble could serve under his command without compromising his clan's honour. His aristocratic background and traditional views made him a useful compromise figure, as when Peter needed someone to put down the rebellion in Astrakhan in 1705. He was respected not only by the gentry but also by the rank and file. Sheremetev's case also shows that it was possible, although sometimes uncomfortable, to have a distinguished career without enjoying friendly personal ties with the tsar.

The Swiss mercenary Franz Lefort (1655/6–99) came to Moscow in 1676, fought in the Crimean campaigns in the 1680s, and became the first admiral of the Russian fleet.[51] Lefort was so powerful that he was entrusted with both military command (at Azov) and diplomatic posts (as leader of the Grand Embassy), despite his lack of expertise in both areas. Views vary as to his talents. Boris Kurakin (who was scathing about most members of the younger Peter's circle) wrote that Lefort 'spent day and night in pleasure, dinners, balls and banquets', encouraged Peter in debauches with women and continual drinking bouts, and died of drink.[52] A recent reassessment credits him with some vision—for example, on trade ('the abundance of products of all kinds in Russia, vitally needed by all countries, will attract all trading nations to your quays')—and describes him as 'a fierce enemy of slavery'.[53] But the main point is that Peter admired and trusted him, especially as his first guide and mentor in the Foreign Quarter. On receiving news of his friend's death, Peter is said to have complained that he was left 'without one trusty man'.[54] The Scottish soldier Patrick (Peter Ivanovich) Gordon (1635–99) entered Russian service in 1661, and was a veteran of the Chigirin and Crimean campaigns (on which he served as quartermaster-general), of Azov, and of the 1698 strel'tsy revolt, which he helped to suppress. He, too, was a valued drinking companion, although somewhat less resilient than the younger Lefort.[55]

After the deaths of Lefort and Gordon within a few weeks of each other in 1699 (Peter attended both funerals),[56] no foreigners seem ever again to have enjoyed Peter's personal confidence and friendship to such a degree, although a number occupied prominent advisory posts. There is no evidence that Peter had close personal ties with any of his other foreign generals, such as Rönne or Ogilvie. He enjoyed drinking with foreign shipwrights like Richard Cozens and Joseph Nye, but such men were not given important posts. An exception was James Bruce (Iakov Vilimovich Brius) (1670–1733), who was in fact born in Moscow, the son of a Scottish soldier of fortune William Bruce, whose family came to Russia during the English Civil War. James and his brother Roman joined Peter's play troops in 1683, and later served in the Crimea and Azov and on the Grand Embassy.[57] James remained in England to study under the astronomers John Flamsteed and Edmund Halley before returning to Russia, and subsequently became Russia's 'first Newtonian'. He devised the first Russian almanac (the so-called Bruce calendar, which bore his name well into the nineteenth century). He also directed Kiprianov's press, which was devoted mainly to cartographical material, and helped to set up the Mathematical school and an observatory in Moscow, as well as being famed as a magician. Then he was needed for military service, so science had to take a back seat. He served as commander of the artillery (*general-fel'd-tseikhmeistr*), winning the order of St Andrew for service at Poltava, then as supervisor of fortress construction, and in 1717 he became president of the Mines and Manufacture college. His last service to Peter was to arrange his funeral. After the tsar's death he retired and devoted himself to science. Bruce's career underlines how widely Peter's most able supporters were forced to spread their talents.

Lefort, Gordon, and Bruce were all associated with those notorious 'nests' of Peter's 'fledglings', the All-Drunken Assembly and its various mock adjuncts, which transcended traditional sources of power around the throne in much the same way as Ivan IV's *oprichnina* had broken ancient boyar and princely power bases.[58] Just as the residence at Preobrazhenskoe served as headquarters both for Peter's premier guards regiment and for the All-Drunken company, so too, in Peter's mind, there was apparently no clear distinction between the personnel of the interlocking worlds of play acting and real activity. Thus it was possible for Nikita Moiseevich Zotov (?–1717), who started his career as a clerk in government departments, to combine the roles of prince-pope and responsible functionary, running Peter's travelling office during the Azov campaigns and later supervising financial affairs in the Accounts Office.[59] In 1683 or thereabouts Zotov became the young Peter's tutor. In 1710–11 he was made a Russian count, and given the titles privy councillor and general-president of the Privy Chancellery, as well as being appointed a fiscal.[60] Zotov was feared by other highly positioned men on account of his closeness to the tsar, to whom, in true jester fashion, he was not frightened to air his views. Just Juel records an incident in 1710 at a feast in Menshikov's residence in Schlüsselburg at which Zotov accused Menshikov of 'robbing his master, like a thief, enjoying his share of all his revenues and still remaining a cheat'.[61]

The Drunken Assembly was closely linked with the mock court, of which some of Peter's chief aides were members, foremost among them Fedor Iur'evich Romodanovsky (1640–1717). His Muscovite pedigree (his father was a leading general) paved the way for a remarkable career, from the 1690s until his death, as 'Prince-Caesar' (*kniaz'-kezar'*) or mock tsar.[62] Boris Kurakin wrote that Romodanovsky had 'the appearance of a monster and the character of a wicked tyrant; he was the greatest of ill-wishers, drunk day in day out; but he was more faithful to His Majesty than anyone'.[63] Foreigners found him crude, even hostile to some of Peter's cherished schemes. Johannes Korb, for example, reported that Romodanovsky's reaction to the information that Fedor Golovin had worn foreign dress in Vienna in 1698 was disbelief that Golovin would have been 'such a brainless ass as to despise the garb of his fatherland'.[64] Weber records that on his first meeting with Romodanovsky, the 'Vice-Czar' gave him a quart of brandy. Visitors to Romodanovsky's home were greeted by a bear with a glass of vodka which ripped off the hat or wig of anyone who refused a drink.[65] Just Juel, reporting that Peter consulted Romodanovsky in March on the eve of departure for the war with Turkey in 1711 and listened to him 'attentively, like a son to his father', assumed that this was all an elaborate charade, a 'comedy', in which Peter tried to 'reassure old Russians that he valued their stupid advice'.[66] But Romodanovsky's duties were not confined to buffoonery, nor did Peter regard him as a joke. He was head of the Preobrazhensky *prikaz*, Peter's 'secret chancellery', in which office he enjoyed considerable powers, dealing with the most sensitive of crimes: allegations of *lèse-majesté* (*gosudarevo slovo i delo*).[67] Weber referred to him as lord chief justice of Moscow, notorious for his severe and rigorous executions, with looks 'enough to make People tremble'. In Weber's view, 'it is absolutely necessary in this Country, that Justice be executed in the severest manner, for otherwise no Person of what Rank and Degree soever, would be safe'.[68] He also handled such important practical tasks as co-ordinating the production and dispatch of uniforms and munitions from Moscow to the front.[69] Romodanovsky was loyal. An anecdote tells how he guarded royal treasure saved during Tsar Alexis's time and handed it over to Peter after the Narva defeat in 1700.[70] He could not be bought, and no charges of embezzlement were ever brought against him.

Despite some overlap between real and mock posts, many members of the Drunken Assembly and mock court seem to have been exempted altogether from responsible tasks, performing instead the roles of jester and 'holy fool', with permission to speak quite freely without ceremony in front of the tsar and his councillors. Georg Grund referred to the tsar's practice of keeping three or four 'witless' people at court, including 'fools' who only pretended to be mad, and goaded and irritated the boyars, often at the tsar's bidding.[71] One such was Prince Iu. F. Shakhovskoy, known as 'Archdeacon Gedeon' and feared greatly by top officials. Kurakin described him as 'a man of some wit and reader of books, only the most evil vessel and drunkard who made mischief from the first to the last' by prying into the business of ministers. Shakhovskoy and others like him were used to punish 'distinguished persons', with a free hand to 'get them drunk, beat and insult them, without any means of defence'.[72] He was a paid member of the royal household, receiving substantial annual sums in the state budget for his upkeep.[73] Another in this category was Stefan 'Medved' (the Bear), also known as 'Vytashchi', whose ceremonial duty in the Drunken Assembly was carrying the prince-pope's crook (a sausage). He played chess with Peter, and accompanied him abroad. After his death in 1722 as the result of a fall, he was replaced by another 'Vytashchi'.[74]

Alongside those men who enjoyed Peter's special confidence in some way was a much larger group who carried out his commands in high military, civil, or diplomatic office without enjoying close personal ties. Unlike their seventeenth-century Muscovite predecessors in the higher echelons, who could expect to spend the times between wars in or near Moscow, these men ended up spending most of their careers away from home. One such was Prince Mikhail Mikhailovich Golitsyn the Elder (1675–1730), a member of the traditional boyar élite who in 1687 entered the Semenovsky regiment as an ordinary soldier. Mock battles gave way to the real thing: Nöteborg, Mitau and Grodno, Lesnaia, Poltava, Viborg, the Pruth. In 1714 he became commander-in-chief in Finland, and presided over its subjugation. In 1723 he became commander in the Ukraine.[75] His elder brother Dmitry Mikhailovich Golitsyn (1665–1737) was among the first young men to be sent abroad to study shipbuilding and navigation, in 1697. He served as governor of Kiev from 1708 to 1721 (when he had close contacts with members of the Kiev clergy and the academy), and as head of the *Kamer-kollegiia* from 1722 to 1725. One of the few Russians who went deeper into Western thought, he was to be the master-mind behind the failed 1730 constitutional project.

Diplomatic posts also kept men away from the court for many years. A notable example was Prince Boris Ivanovich Kurakin (1676–1727), a veteran of the Azov campaigns and the Northern War, and the tsar's brother-in-law through his marriage to Kseniia Lopukhina. This circumstance, together with his criticism of Peter's raising of 'new men', may have resulted in a sort of honourable exile in a series of posts in The Hague, Amsterdam, and Paris, where he found his true niche.[76]

III.   'NEW MEN'

The motley collection of aristocrats, foreigners, and fools who mingled in Peter's circle were supplemented, and to some extent eventually superseded, by 'new men' of various types. The main bases for their advancement were the Preobrazhensky and Semenovsky guards regiments. A number of Peter's most trusted aides, many of humble origins, came up by this route, several in the mixed bunch of young nobles and stable boys assembled in the 1680s to form an alternative to the more conventional court around Sophia and Tsar Ivan in Moscow. To quote Boris Kurakin again, 'Many young lads, simple folk, won His Majesty's favour. From that time common folk took on all the tasks of personal servants.'[77] The most brilliant of the stars who rose through this route was Alexander Menshikov, whose career is reviewed in detail in the next section, but many others besides him started in the guards. One such was Pavel Ivanovich Iaguzhinsky (1683–1736), who combined lowly origins (his father was organist at the Lutheran church in Moscow) with foreign birth (Poland).[78] As with others from unpromising backgrounds, luck was crucial: apparently his 'handsome appearance' was noticed by F. A. Golovin, and soon he found himself in the palace, then, in 1701, serving as an orderly (*denshchik*) in the Preobrazhensky guards and becoming one of the tsar's permanent attendants.[79] Distinction at the battle of the Pruth in 1711 brought him promotion to general adjutant (an office borrowed from foreign practice, perhaps suggested to Peter because Augustus II had one) and an annual salary of 600 roubles. From then on he was rarely out of the tsar's company, travelling to Torgau for Tsarevich Alexis's wedding in 1711, and in 1716–17 accompanying Peter to the Netherlands and France, travelling in the same carriage. It is not surprising, given the close relationship, that in 1718 Iaguzhinsky was acting as the tsar's 'eye', supervising the newly established colleges.[80] But it is characteristic of Peter's exploitation of his best personnel that scarcely had Iaguzhinsky proved his worth on domestic duties than he was dispatched on a series of diplomatic missions, which kept him in Sweden and Austria from spring 1719 until 1721. Iaguzhinsky's supervisory duties were extended on the eve of Peter's departure for Persia in 1722, when he was made procurator-general. Peter told the Senate: 'Here is my eye, with which I shall see everything. He knows my intentions and wishes; what he deems necessary, that do; and even if you feel that he is acting against my interests and those of the State, even so, do what he says, inform me and await my orders.'[81] This was no easy task. As Iaguzhinsky complained, the Senate was riven by discord. He doubted his ability to keep order amid such passions, especially given his lack of any reliable aides. In fact, just a few days after Peter's departure a quarrel flared up between Menshikov and Peter Shafirov. In a letter (probably to Makarov) Iaguzhinsky had some interesting things to say on the question of origins. One of Shafirov's complaints had to do with an insulting reference to him and his brother Mikhail as 'of Yiddish origin and their father a slave'. Iaguzhinsky disapproved of this insult on the grounds that 'when the sovereign's favour is conferred upon a person his former baseness and low birth are thereby concealed'.[82] In a letter to the tsar in 1722 he suggested that the Senate ought, on principle, to be composed of men of middling rank (*srednikh liudei*) so that there would be fewer quarrels between high-ranking individuals.[83]

Iaguzhinsky combined efficiency and honesty in carrying out his official duties with a reputation as the 'life and soul of the party'. He was an attendant at Peter and Catherine's wedding in 1712, and master of ceremonies for the assemblies instituted from 1718. Like most of Peter's associates, he was a hard drinker. Bergholz records that in March 1725, after Peter's death, he even visited the empress while very drunk: 'He is in all respects a noble and respected man, but when inebriated he forgets himself.'[84] The overall impression is of a thoroughly loyal, energetic (essential, given the range of tasks demanded), impulsive man, self-indulgent but basically honest, by the standards of the day, who 'despaired of achieving anything in the sea of perfidious and cunning men who will not forsake their own particular interests for the sake of the sovereign's'.[85] Bassewitz described him as 'very talented and astute'.[86] He is said to have dissuaded the tsar from implementing an order to execute anyone who stole as much as the price of a piece of rope, 'unless your majesty wishes to be left alone without servitors or subjects. We all steal, only some more and more visibly than others.'[87]

Another man who rose through the guards was Alexander Ivanovich Rumiantsev (1680–1749), son of an impoverished noble who entered the Preobrazhensky regiment as a private and rose through non-commissioned ranks to become an officer. From the 1710s he was one of the tsar's trusted minions, accompanying him abroad in 1716–17, and in 1717 he went with Peter Tolstoy to bring Tsarevich Alexis back to Russia, for which he was rewarded with the ranks of guards major and general adjutant.[88] He married the daughter of Andrei Matveev (who was said to be pregnant at the time with Peter's child), thus consolidating his promising career by a good marriage.[89] Andrei Ivanovich Ushakov (?–1747) followed a similar career pattern. The son of a poor noble and a Preobrazhensky officer from 1707, he appears frequently in documents carrying out missions for the tsar: investigating abuses of the peasantry, fugitive peasants, forestry, and shipbuilding. He became a senator in 1724.[90] Another former orderly was Alexander Vasil'evich Kikin, whose fate in 1718 was discussed earlier.[91]

As one orderly rose to higher things, another arrived to fill his place. Peter always had several orderlies on hand, to sleep in his room (sometimes serving him as a pillow), eat with him, accompany his carriage, and in general perform the duties which in other courts were carried out by a bevy of courtiers.[92] In return, Peter attended their weddings and christenings. During Peter's foreign travels in 1716–17 his orderlies included Afanasy Tatishchev, Iury Kologrivov, and Semen Baklanovsky, whose main task was to run errands, make purchases, and hand out tips.[93] Orderlies' wages were meagre (75 roubles per annum in 1723[94]), but their perks and sometimes their authority were considerable. In May 1724, for example, Andrei Drevnin was ordered to ride ahead of Peter's party to Ladoga and to make arrangements for transport stations with horses and carriages. 'When he collects and sets up the transport, the governors of those provinces and post drivers and other inhabitants of those places are to act in obedience to him, Drevnin, in all matters without any contradiction.'[95] Campredon observed: 'The tsar has servants called *denshchiki* who are actually nothing other than his pages, selected for the most part from among the common people; these *denshchiki* inform him about everything that goes on, especially in the private life of his subjects.'[96] Bergholz remarked on the power of the orderlies in 1721, mentioning four: Golovin, Drevnin, Tatishchev, and Vasily Petrovich Pospelov, the last described as 'of very unprepossessing appearance and in general, as far as one can tell, simple and even stupid'.[97] Strahlenberg confirms that Pospelov was a boy of 'little brain', but adds that he was good-hearted, Peter's 'greatest favourite'. It appears that a huge capacity for drink was one of his attributes. Peter commissioned Pospelov's portrait from the court artist Dannhauer.[98] After Peter's death, he was appointed chamberlain (*kamer-iunker*) to Catherine, but is said to have preferred the title 'tsar's orderly'.[99] The rise of men like Pospelov again illustrates the fact that a man's worth for Peter was not necessarily measured in brains, beauty, or even conspicuous talent. Bergholz's comment that all the magnates were expected to kow-tow to Vasily hints at the fact that this was another example of Peter's message to the nobility—that they had no God-given right to membership of the inner circle. Peter expected high ranking nobles to serve their country in leading posts, but with sufficient uncertainty to keep them on their toes. Strahlenberg, too, emphasizes the displeasure of the old nobility about Peter's preference for 'young, ill-disciplined favourites, many of humble origins', even though key posts in the administration continued to be open to men of distinguished birth. Of course, all kings had valets and personal attendants, many of whom enjoyed influence and privileges, but there seems to have been a perception that Peter went too far in blurring social boundaries.

Alongside the orderlies were other assorted people who enjoyed influence because of their closeness to the tsar. One such was Peter's cook, *kukhmistr* Johann (Jan) Felten, who prepared the tsar's favourite dishes, travelled with him everywhere, and was one of the few attendants allowed to serve at the tsar's table.[100] During Peter's visit to Germany and France in 1716–17 we find Felten running errands and dipping into his own pocket to pay the oarsmen who rowed the tsar, a peasant who brought milk and butter, another who delivered some oysters. Often he was left to pay the bill for lodgings when they were on the move, reclaiming the money later.[101] Just Juel made a point of giving Felten a gift when he came to his lodgings in Moscow to prepare a meal for Peter, as a person 'who could facilitate my access to the tsar when I had business to discuss'.[102] Felten's daughter married the orderly Andrei Drevnin.[103] Peter acted as godfather to Felten's son, granting him a village with six peasant households. But he was also liable to be beaten with the notorious cudgel, on one occasion for neglecting the tsar's orders about hiding a Limburger cheese.[104] Another essentially private attendant was the chaplain Ivan Khristanfovich Bitka (?–1720), who accompanied the tsar on his journey abroad in 1716, and was often his opponent at chess.[105] A man called Ivan Kobyliakov seems to have performed the role of personal manservant, washing the tsar's linen. In 1722 we find him in Astrakhan buying Peter a wig and materials to make cushions for his barge, canvas for dog beds, and assorted stockings. On another shopping expedition he purchased hats, fabric for cravats, and hides.[106] Generally Peter liked to be surrounded by familiar faces while abroad. An entry in an account book for June 1716 shows him sitting down to a game of lotto with Bitka, Count Golovkin, Secretary Makarov, Adjutant Iaguzhinsky, Captain Rumiantsev and the dwarf Luke.[107]

Abram *arap* (negro), otherwise Abram Petrovich Gannibal, son of an Ethiopian prince, was often included in the party.[108] Other key personnel in Peter's household included Ul'ian Siniavin, who ran his Building office, and Boris Neronov, the head gardener and supervisor of the royal aviaries and menageries.[109]

The key figure in Peter's household, Aleksei Vasil'evich Makarov (1674/5?–1750), secretary of the Cabinet, was not a military man at all.[110] His career followed the pattern of such predecessors as Fedor Shaklovity and Emel'ian Ukraintsev, bureaucrats during Sophia's regime whose literacy skills were at a premium and whom luck and ambition raised above their fellow pen-pushers. Makarov's father was a clerk (*pod'iachii*) in the governor's office in Vologda. Legend has it that Peter spotted the promising young scribe, who, unlike the tsar himself, had a fine hand and an excellent grasp of spelling and grammar, on a visit to Vologda in 1693, but it is equally likely that he came to Peter's notice when working in Menshikov's Izhora chancellery.[111] In 1704 he was appointed to run the Cabinet. Makarov never quite forgot his origins, signing himself 'your humble servant', to magnates with whom he corresponded, while they usually addressed him using the familiar 'ty' form. Neither did he accumulate great wealth; his annual salary of 400 roubles compared poorly with the salaries of top army officers and foreign architects, and he received only two royal grants of estates—in 1709 and 1723—amounting to about 130 peasant households. Working in close proximity to the tsar, Makarov accompanied him on his travels on campaign and abroad, and acting as his right-hand man. He was his 'shadow, his memory, his eyes and ears'.[112] A petitioner wrote: 'Makarov speaks and writes only on behalf of the sovereign, but his influence is felt by everyone.'[113] He was 'the irreplaceable link between the emperor and the state machine', and business which should have been channelled through the machine, to college presidents or the Senate, was actually sent to the Cabinet on the assumption that the tsar continued to decide all important matters.[114] Makarov handled much of Peter's correspondence during the Great Northern War, writing on his behalf even on matters of prime importance. In their turn, correspondents often addressed Makarov rather than the tsar. Petitioners relied on him to find the 'right moment' to put a request to the tsar, about preference for a relative, intervention in a lawsuit, matters of landed estates, or unpaid wages.[115] He also dealt with everyday domestic matters, running the private zoo, spas, the *Kunstkamera*, sending trainees abroad, and helping to compile the official history of the Northern War.

Peter Shafirov (1669–1739), son of a converted Jew, was another 'social climber' of uncertain origins. Shafirov and the tsar are said to have met just before the Grand Embassy. Peter visited a store where Shafirov was working and was impressed by his excellent knowledge of languages. Young Shafirov then took the name Peter in the tsar's honour.[116] According to another story, Shafirov was taken into the Foreign Office, where his father worked as a translator, by F. I. Golovin.[117] Recent research indicates that Shafirov senior was, in fact, a prisoner of war and subsequently a bondslave in the household of Bogdan Khitrovo, a leading boyar during the reign of Tsar Alexis, and who went into trade after his master's death.[118] Shafirov junior accompanied Golovin on the Grand Embassy. In 1709 he became a privy councillor, and in 1710 received the title of baron, an honour usually reserved for foreign servitors. In 1711–13 he negotiated peace with Turkey, but ended up going to Constantinople as a hostage and spending some time locked up in the Seven Towers as the Turks wavered between peace and war. He succeeded in thwarting Charles XII's and Devlet-Girei's plans for getting Turkey back in the war and negotiated the 1713 Treaty of Adrianople. In 1717 he became a senator. Life at the top could be dangerous. He fell out with Golovkin, Golovin's successor in the Foreign Office, whom he suspected of sabotaging his efforts in Turkey. In 1722 Menshikov (with whom he had a joint venture in fish oil production) succeeded in bringing corruption charges against Shafirov. The latter was condemned to death by beheading, but was reprieved at the last moment by the arrival of a messenger as he bowed his head, and was exiled to Novgorod. Peter was much struck by this example of 'treachery'.[119] Shafirov was recalled when Catherine, who had engineered his reprieve, became empress, but from then on he was at the mercy of changes in court factions. In Moscow at the beginning of Peter II's reign, he allied himself with the new emperor's grandmother, Evdokia, in the hope of ousting Osterman if Evdokia, who hated foreigners, gained any power.[120] He eventually resumed his position in Anna's reign.

Another case of a poor boy who made good, and a foreigner to boot, was the Portuguese, Anton Manuilovich Devier (Antonio De Vieira),[121] who was signed up by Peter in Holland when serving as a cabin-boy during a mock naval battle. He followed the familiar route of tsar's orderly to become major-general and general adjutant, and in 1718 St Petersburg chief of police (*general-politseimeister*). Peter seems to have valued Devier for his loyalty and willingness to carry out orders unquestioningly; but, like many of Peter's 'upstart' favourites, he was resented by his subordinates. 'Strict and quick in carrying out the tsar's orders, he instills in the common folk in general and all the inhabitants of the town such fear that they tremble at the very mention of his name': that was the impression gained by Bergholz.[122] Perhaps this was because Devier himself was in fear of Peter's chastisement.[123]

Non-Orthodox foreigners, who otherwise had no place within the Muscovite hierarchy, played a comparatively minor role, but there were major exceptions. The most successful was perhaps Andrei Ivanovich (Heinrich Johann) Osterman (1686–1747), a German from Westphalia who entered Russian service in 1703. Osterman reached the pinnacle of his power after Peter's death, during the reign of Anna. He ended his days in exile when Elizabeth came to the throne in 1741.

Heinrich van Huyssen (1666–1739), educated at the universities of Duisburg, Cologne, Halle, and Leipzig, arrived in Russia in 1703 after a series of teaching and clerical jobs at princely courts to tutor Tsarevich Alexis.[124] He later worked on reports on fiscal administration, primogeniture, and the official history of Peter's reign.[125] Huyssen's biographer believes that 'his superficial and narrow approach to most tasks limited his chance of becoming an effective aide to Peter'; he was a man of 'intellectual pettiness and amazingly narrow vision'.[126] After Alexis's execution he is said to have become 'embittered' towards Russia. He was dismissed in 1732, apparently suffering from dementia. Other foreign advisers included Heinrich Fick, who played a prominent role in Peter's administrative reforms, and Baron Ananias Christian Pott von Luberas, whom met Peter in June 1717 and was employed to hire personnel for the colleges, later becoming vice-president of the *Berg-kollegiia*. Among the first college vice-presidents were Magnus Wilhelm von Nieroth (provincial councillor in Reval) and Hermann von Brevern (vice-governor of Livonia).[127]

One of Peter's most able assistants was Wilhelm Henning (Gennin), who was sent on a tour of Germany, France, and Italy in 1719 to make sketches of 'curious and useful Machines', inspect foreign mines and works, and hire workmen.[128] Later he travelled all over Russia inspecting mines and factories (latterly for the *Berg-kollegiia*). His letters, quoted earlier, give useful insights into conditions of service. The rewards of the job were meagre. In a letter to Peter from Siberia in 1723 he wrote that 'without having any extra income and not having received my salary, what am I supposed to buy food with? They seem to think that it is possible to live here without wages in the manner of a military governor (*po voevodski*), but I don't know how to.'[129] The old way of doing things—officials living off the land, feeding themselves through bribes and requisitions—was still deemed to be the norm in the countryside. In another letter written on the same day he goes into more detail, complaining that so far he has received no villages, although they were promised:

> I sought my fortune through labours and endeavour in the sovereign's interest. I am already tired, and I lack the strength to defend the sovereign's interests because my supports have been undermined and I have already pestered you and the sovereign too much and if you, my lord, my last support forsake me … then the slightest breeze will bow me beneath the feet of my enemies, whoever they are. … I know already that my enemies wish me dead or pushed out, living outside Russia. But I love the sovereign; I do not want to desert him, because I know that for the work which the sovereign needs most … you will have to go a long way to find a man like me who has worked on such difficult tasks and has practice in building and knows the sovereign's intentions so well and can be of such use to him.[130]

Peter relied on a number of Orthodox churchmen, notably the Ukrainian-born Feofan Prokopovich (1681–1736), described as 'the first authentic voice in Russia of the early Enlightenment', and 'after Peter himself the most important figure of early modern Russian history'.[131] As the chief ideologist of Peter's reign, he articulated concepts and gave polished form to the tsar's often roughly formulated ideas. An orphan of well-to-do background, he graduated from the Kiev Academy, then was forced by the lack of provision for higher theological education in Muscovy to study at Jesuit colleges in Vladimir-in-Volhynia, and perhaps Vitebsk, L'vov, and Cracow, which required taking Uniate orders, then at the Greek college of St Athanasius in Rome until 1701. He returned to Kiev to teach poetics, rhetoric, and philosophy at the academy. Lectures in Latin, 'De arte poetica' and 'De arte rhetorica', survive from this period, as does the play *Vladimir*, first performed in Kiev in 1705. From 1707 he taught arithmetic, geometry and physics. Feofan, whom Peter first heard preach in 1706, made his allegiance to Moscow plain. In 1708 he took Peter's side against Mazepa, and in 1709 he delivered a panegyric on Poltava. He was recommended to Peter by Menshikov, and in 1711 preached a sermon at military headquarters in Moldavia on the Poltava anniversary. He was appointed abbot of the Kiev Brotherhood monastery, rector of the Kiev Academy, and professor of theology.

In 1716 Peter summoned him to St Petersburg, where Prokopovich made himself invaluable by offering commentaries on contemporary events from various pulpits. In 1717, for example, he delivered an oration to welcome the tsar home from abroad which included a homily on the value of foreign travel and a diatribe against the conservative opposition, which still regarded travel as dangerous to the soul. The voyager sees 'in foreign nations, as in a mirror, himself and his own people, both their good points and their bad'. The usefulness of Peter's travels for education, industry, and military affairs was all underlined.[132] In a sermon on Palm Sunday 1718, against the background of the trial of Tsarevich Alexis, he preached loyalty and obedience to the monarch.[133] Thereafter he composed odes to the Russian fleet and the Ladoga canal, wrote part of an official history, primers for the guidance of youth, and had a leading hand in the treatise *Justice of the Monarch's Right*.[134] His academy lectures displayed considerable Protestant influence, especially the principle that interpretation of dogma must be based on close reading of Scripture, the Church Fathers, and church history. His knowledge of such writers as Bacon, Spinoza, Descartes, Leibniz, and Pufendorf was unsurpassed among Peter's helpers. Despite his many rivals, notably Stefan Iavorsky, who tried to block his appointment to Pskov in 1718, by accusing him of heterodoxy, he was to survive the reigns of three more monarchs.

IV. MENSHIKOV

Of all the 'fledglings of Peter's nest' the most successful was Alexander Danilovich Menshikov (1673–1729). Menshikov's origins are obscure, as are the circumstances of his first meeting with Peter.[135] Menshikov kicked over his own traces: in Petrine Russia humble beginnings were nothing to boast about once a man had transcended them. As his star rose, Menshikov acquired a genealogy which traced his ancestors back through the grand dukes of Lithuania to the ninth-century warrior band of Prince Riurik the Viking. He added an impressive coat of arms and a string of titles as resounding, in their own way, as Peter's. The formulation in 1726 read: 'Illustrious prince of the Holy Roman Empire and Russian realm and duke of Izhora, reichsmarshal of Her Imperial Majesty of all Russia and commanding general field marshal of the armies, actual privy councillor, president of the State War College, governor-general of the province of St Petersburg, vice-admiral of the white flag of the fleet of all Russia, knight of the orders of St Andrew, the Elephant, the White and Black Eagles and St Alexander Nevsky and lieutenant-colonel of the Preobrazhensky life-guard, and colonel over three regiments, captain of the company of bombardiers.'[136] These glittering titles did not conceal what most of Peter's circle knew or suspected: that Menshikov was 'of low birth, lower than the gentry', and that his was a 'rags to riches' tale, of a poor boy raised above boyars and princes of ancient lineage to become the most titled man in the realm after the tsar himself.[137] A popular version was that Menshikov's father was a stable lad turned pastry cook, and that young Alexander met the tsar while peddling his wares. This story features in one of Nartov's anecdotes, in which Peter reminds Menshikov that he has the power to return him to his pie-selling origins whenever he wishes, and Menshikov appears with a tray of pies as a joke.[138] In fact, Menshikov's father seems to have served as a non-commissioned officer in the Semenovsky guards regiment.[139] Before that, he may have been brought to Russia as a prisoner of war from Lithuania and converted to Orthodoxy.[140]

As regards the circumstances of Menshikov's first meeting with Peter, Thomas Consett tells a story about his being arrested in 1691 for challenging the tsar while on sentry duty, then being rewarded for duty well done.[141] In 1693 his name appears in the second rank of bombardiers of the Preobrazhensky regiment, an indication that he was already close to 'bombardier Piter'.[142] They were together at Azov, sharing a tent. By the time of the Grand Embassy, Peter and Alexander, or 'Aleksasha', as he called him, were 'inseparable'.[143] Menshikov visited Germany, Holland, England, and Austria with Peter, studying shipbuilding at his side. In 1698 the two hurried back to Russia to deal with the rebellious strel'tsy, when Alexander was apparently happy to wield the executioner's axe at his master's behest. (There was a violent side to the relationship. Korb cites numerous occasions on which Menshikov felt the tsar's fists, including an incident in Voronezh when Peter knocked him out, 'so that he lay stretched at full length, quite like a dying man at the feet of irate Majesty'.[144])

As we have seen, special skills and talents were not a prerequisite for winning Peter's favour. Menshikov, for example, was, and remained, to all intents and purposes illiterate.[145] His biographer N. I. Pavlenko confirms that not one letter, or even a corrected draft, has ever been found in the prince's hand (in contrast to the volumes of paper covered with Peter's scrawl).[146] Only Menshikov's clear signature, invariable in its form, has been found on documents, and even this basic accomplishment seems to have been acquired fairly late. A memorandum of 30 November 1699 records that when Menshikov received some money from the Resurrection monastery, the clerk S. Viazemnikov signed the receipt on his behalf.[147] Why was Peter, who withheld permission to marry from young nobles who failed to complete their studies, so lenient with Menshikov in this respect? Charles Whitworth may have come close to the truth when he wrote of Menshikov: 'His parts are not extraordinary, his education low, *for the Czar would never let him learn to read and write*, and his advancement too quick to give him time for observation or experience.'[148] Peter laid so many responsibilities on Menshikov's shoulders that he had no time for systematic study. It is not inconceivable either that it suited Peter to have an illiterate favourite, just as it pleased him to crown an illiterate foreign peasant woman as his empress and to surround himself with jesters and fools. The key to advancement within the inner circle lay more in 'personal chemistry' than in formal qualifications, and loyalty was prized above technical specialization. Menshikov, for example, evidently failed to learn very much about shipbuilding in 1697–8, but this did nothing to harm their friendship. Peter was not blind to Menshikov's shortcomings, any more than he was to Catherine's. Throughout the 'honeymoon' of their friendship in the 1690s, Peter stopped short of awarding his friend officer's rank, which he earned only after the Battle of Narva in November 1700, and then only to ensign (*poruchik*).[149] Korb records the story that Peter refused to award him the Muscovite noble rank of *stol'nik* because 'already without that he takes undue honours to himself: it is better to lessen ambition than add to it'.[150]

Menshikov had a number of positive qualities which recommended him to Peter. He was versatile, energetic, even conscientious. Bergholz supplies a telling detail: in May 1725, with Peter's iron hand removed, Menshikov slept in the special pavilion being erected for Tsarevna Anna Petrovna's wedding, to keep an eye on the builders and ensure that it was finished in time.[151] He was loyal, but, unlike many, he was capable of acting on his own initiative. He shared the tsar's crude sense of humour and capacity for alcohol. It has been hinted that there was an additional element to a friendship 'so close that one would hesitate to maintain that it was altogether entirely chaste'.[152] Accusations survive in the records of the Preobrazhensky *prikaz* (where the rumour-mongers were tortured), that Peter and Menshikov 'lived in sin'.[153] A recent article quotes the case of the merchant Gavrila Romanovich Nikitin, who was arrested in August 1698 for blurting out while drunk that Peter took Menshikov to his bed 'like a whore' (*kak zhonku*).[154] The correspondence between the two men in their youth may be read as supporting such a view. The first extant letter from Peter to Menshikov, dated February 1700, begins 'Mein gertsenkin'.[155] A slightly later letter captures the tone of their friendship: 'Be here tomorrow by midday; I really need to see you, and I need to see you here, and tomorrow is a day off [Sunday]. So I ask you to be here tomorrow without fail. I write again, for God's sake, don't put off coming because you think it's unhealthy here. It's really healthy, and I only want to see you.'[156] Menshikov usually addressed Peter formally, but occasionally a 'dear heart' crept into his letters too, as in one addressed 1 October 1704 to 'mein gerts kaptein'.[157] Postscripts often included affectionate details: for example, on 4 March 1705, Menshikov sent Peter a puppy from Polotsk, to replace one which had been killed, and in return Peter sent Menshikov some examples of his turnery work.[158] On 7 April Menshikov wrote from Vitebsk: 'We are now all very bored here without your honour, especially on feast-days like this [Easter]. I trust your health to the keeping of our risen Lord Jesus Christ and pray that his victory of this present holy week may be with you all joyful, during which we shall drink to your health, although we are alone, and tomorrow we shall fire from cannons.'[159] Peter for his part wrote from Voronezh that 'everything here is fine, thank God, there's only one thing that grieves me, as you yourself are aware, especially as I was never apart from you during this holiday'.[160] When Peter finally left Voronezh, frustration at not seeing his friend was exacerbated by a delay to his travel plans caused by a fever. He wrote: 'This illness has increased the pain of separation from you, which I have suffered many times, but now I can bear it no longer. Come and see me as soon as you can, to cheer me up. And bring the English doctor with you.'[161] In March 1706 Peter wrote from Menshikov's house in Narva, where he had been celebrating with a group of the jolly company, 'Indeed we're merry, thank God, but our merriment when you are not with us and we are separated from you is like food without salt.'[162]

As the two grew older, the exchange became more business-like, terms of endearment fewer, but Menshikov continued to be the recipient of personal news and favours. On Peter's birthday in 1708 he was given the rank of sea captain *in absentia*.[163] In a letter of 26 January 1709 from Sumy, Peter expressed impatience to see his friend, and sent him a present which he had made himself 'because I was bored'.[164] Other gifts included a village belonging to Hetman Mazepa (for storming Baturin in 1708), the towns of Pochep and Iampol (for Poltava and Perevolochna),[165] instruments ('the identity of the person who made them you can work out from the signatures on them'), two jars of sherbet, a tunic ('God grant you may wear it in good health'), and wigs made from the tsar's hair trimmings.[166] Peter was godfather to Alexander's children, who received appropriate names: Luke-Peter (born February 1709) and Samson-Paul (born January 1711, named in honour of Poltava, on the feast of St Samson).[167] Gifts to the boys, neither of whom survived much beyond infancy, included a hundred-household village and commissions in the Preobrazhensky guards.[168] Peter sent Samson-Paul some fabric for making a nightshirt, but told Menshikov to make one for himself 'as he is still small'.[169] The tender, jocular tone is also found in letters, allegedly from Peter's infant daughters Anna and Elizabeth, to the infant Samson-Paul, asking him to write with news of his mother, father, and aunt.[170] In turn, Menshikov looked after Peter's children, acting as supervisor of Alexis's household, and assuming responsibility for overseeing the heir's further education in 1705. He visited the children's quarters in their parents' absence, as when Peter went abroad in 1716–17, when he sent Peter and Catherine a portrait of Tsarevich Peter Petrovich, 'our dearest Cupid', depicted as a cherub.[171]

The height of the men's friendship coincided with the courtship of their future wives. Menshikov met Daria Mikhailovna Arsen'eva (1682–1727) in about 1698 in the house of Peter's sister Natalia, and married her in 1706. During this period the two men's love lives were so closely intertwined that it is not always clear who was involved with whom. Daria and her sister Varvara were close friends of Menshikov's sister Anna, to whom the tsar may at one time have been attracted.[172] According to an old woman from Menshikov's household, interrogated in 1718, Peter may even have considered marrying Daria, but she was ousted by the arrival of Catherine in the Menshikov household. Perhaps this is why Peter urged Menshikov to 'keep his word' and marry Daria, more or less ordering him to Kiev for the ceremony in August 1706.[173] These four women, together with their companion Anisa (Anna) Tolstaia, were virtual camp-followers of the tsar and his favourites in the first decade of the Northern War, travelling between Moscow, St Petersburg, and various billets.

However one interprets the complex chemistry of their relationship, it should be emphasized that Menshikov was invaluable to Peter because of his loyalty, his commitment to reform, and his personal bravery. The latter quality was demonstrated in the attack on Schlüsselburg in 1702, after which he was appointed commandant of the fortress, and in May 1703, when he participated in Russia's first 'naval battle' on the Baltic coast, which earned him the order of St Andrew. In a letter to Daria and her friends of 10 May, he signed himself 'Alexander Menshikov, governor of Schlüsselburg and Schlotburg and knight' (*kavaler*).[174] At Kalisz in 1706 Menshikov went into the thick of battle. At this point Peter's earlier reluctance to make his friend into a public figure evaporated, and Menshikov was richly rewarded. To mark the victory, verses were composed in Menshikov's honour, likening him to the faithful servant of Alexander the Great. He is accorded honours equal to King Augustus, and rich rewards and laurels are predicted.[175] Peter presented Menshikov with a diamond- and emerald-studded cane based on his own design worth more than 3,000 roubles.[176] In May 1707 Menshikov was created prince of Russia and Izhora, the first example of the hitherto hereditary title of prince (*kniaz'*) being bestowed on a commoner. This Russian title was added to distinctions of count (1702) and prince (December 1706) obtained from the Holy Roman Emperor. The years 1708–9 were a high point for Menshikov, especially his exploits at Perevolochna, where he rounded up the remnants of the Swedish army. 'The Victory Wreath', a poem presented by the citizens of L'vov, declared: 'You are the equal of the great Alexander.'[177] In 1709 Feofan Prokopovich delivered and published a speech in honour of Menshikov's visit to the Kiev Academy based on the text 'Let us praise famous men', comparing the prince's service to Peter to Joseph's services to Pharaoh, David's to

Jonathan, and Epherstion's to Alexander. The brutal massacre at Baturin was justified by reference to the treachery of the inhabitants, who followed the 'serpent' Mazepa. Menshikov was compared with Alexander Nevsky.[178]

The more Menshikov was seen publicly to enjoy the tsar's favour, and the more he built up his own power base, the more temptations came his way, and the more enemies he made. Just Juel records a telling clash with Nikita Zotov in August 1710. Menshikov was angry because the old man asked for a small piece of land in Ingermanland, which Menshikov regarded as his personal domain.[179] Juel wrote a few months later: 'In his desire to have a complete hold on the tsar's affections, Prince Menshikov is vexed and angry with anyone to whom the tsar shows the slightest favour.'[180] Stählin prints the unedifying tale of how Menshikov encouraged the French architect Le Blond (to whom Peter had showed particular favour) to formulate plans to cut down trees at Peterhof, and then informed on him in the knowledge that Peter would be furious.[181] In 1711 Peter learned of Menshikov's acquisition of lands and titles in Lithuania by dishonest means, and of complaints against him from local people. After Poltava, Menshikov received gifts of land from both Peter and King Augustus of Poland. The giving of the land may have passed without protest, but the granting of Cossacks in Pochep and Iampol 'into the power and possession' of the prince created a storm. Peter referred to it in a letter of 11 March: 'Take care that you don't lose your reputation and credit for the sake of such paltry gains.'[182] But Catherine effected a reconciliation, which Menshikov sealed by making Peter a gift of the frigate *Samson* for his name-day.[183] In the autumn Peter appeared as concerned as ever about his friend: 'I beg you for God's sake don't come to meet me, don't do yourself damage after such a severe illness; stay in St Petersburg.' But Menshikov left anyway, and they met in Riga at the end of November.[184] Peter was well aware that Menshikov's misdemeanours in Ukraine were but the tip of an iceberg, but he failed to take a firm line. Just Juel, in most respects an admirer of the tsar, considers this a major weakness, even going so far as to suggest that Peter used Menshikov as a scapegoat when he himself was reluctant to settle legitimate claims for wages or other resources, referring petitioners to the prince. Menshikov in the mean time snatched other people's property with impunity, and decided fates on the basis of the size of the bribes which victims were able to offer, then shared the profits with the tsar.[185] Georg Grund also suggests that Peter used Menshikov to carry out unpopular measures, such as removing governors and obtaining funds. Grund disapproved both of Menshikov and of his palace, 'as different from the homes of Russian princes and boyars as are theirs from the homes of simple Russian gentry'.[186]

In February 1712 Menshikov acted as master of ceremonies at Peter's wedding to Catherine, but shortly afterwards Peter issued a stern warning: 'You represent rogues to me as honest men and honest men as rogues. I tell you for the last time, change your ways if you don't want a great misfortune to occur. Now you will go to Pomerania, but don't imagine that you will be able to behave there as you did in Poland; you will pay with your life if there is the slightest complaint against you.'[187] Peter was aware that in sending Menshikov to direct general military operations in Pomerania, he might also be encouraging the prince's aspirations to add the duchy of Courland to his acquisitions. By and large, the tour of duty was successful. In June 1713 Menshikov besieged Tönningen fortress in Jutland, and in September entered Stettin.[188] In the panegyric 'The Laurel or Crown of Immortal Glory' (1714) Menshikov was likened to the sun and (again) to Alexander the Great and Alexander Nevsky. The verses referred to his 'noble' origins in the grand duchy of Lithuania and to his father as 'a glorious warrior of the guards'.[189] The legendary biography was taking shape.

In 1714 Menshikov again managed to evade serious charges of corruption brought against him by government officials. That year found him carrying out his duties as governor of St Petersburg, directing shipbuilding and building work at Kronstadt, and organizing victory celebrations for the naval victory at Hangö. In November 1716 a great storm breached the new Reval harbour, and thirty ships were badly damaged, but Menshikov succeeded in making excuses. In February–March 1718 the old 'mein Freunt' reappeared in Peter's letters to Menshikov.[190] Menshikov does not seem to have played a prominent role in Alexis's trial, but he had every reason to welcome the eventual outcome. The 'upstart' Menshikov (mentioned unfavourably in Alexis's testimony and accused of cruelty to the tsarevich when he was a boy) could expect little joy if Peter were to die and Alexis and his supporters were to come to power. He was responsible for arranging the signing of the death sentence in the Senate while Alexis was being tortured for the last time in the Peter–Paul fortress, and his name appears first on the long list of signatures on the sentence.[191] At the end of 1718, after the execution of the last conspirators in the affair, Menshikov himself was brought before a tribunal on charges of embezzlement. The investigating commission estimated losses to the treasury from Menshikov's stealing (including 'insider dealing' on grain contracts for the army in the 1710s) at 1,581,519 roubles. Once again, friendship prevailed, and Menshikov was restored to favour upon payment of a stiff fine. Stählin records Peter's refusal to consider a list of Menshikov's crimes presented by the Senate and his remark, 'Menshikov will always remain Menshikov'.[192]

At the Nystad celebrations in October 1721 Menshikov sat at Peter's left hand, the duke of Holstein on his right. Yet new stars were rising, notably Pavel Iaguzhinsky. A clash between the two in the Senate in 1722 ended in a formal 'victory' for Menshikov over the 'new favourite', but in the process he lost his posts as senator and head of the War college. Despite this, the old friendship proved remarkably resilient, as a letter from Peter in July 1722 addressed to 'Mein Frint' indicates.[193] In 1723 Peter expressed regrets in a hand-written note that Menshikov was ill, and wished him a speedy recovery and reunion in St Petersburg: 'We drank to your health.'[194] Then in 1724 another investigation into malpractice by Menshikov got under way, conducted by Aleksei Miakinin, the general fiscal. Fears of Catherine's estrangement from the tsar following the Mons affair in November 1724 must have troubled Menshikov, who often relied on Catherine to intercede on his behalf. Two months later Peter was dead, and the alliance between the two 'upstarts' entered a new phase as Catherine became empress.

Our understanding of Alexander Menshikov's character is hampered by the lack of impartial, insider evidence, although there are plenty of outsider views. Despite the existence of at least thirteen portraits made during his lifetime, including Rastrelli's bronze bust (1716–17), even his features—big nose, thinnish lips, high forehead, rounded chin—are not as immediately recognizable as Peter's.[195] His life-style was a characteristically Petrine hybrid: devout observation of Orthodox ritual interspersed with rowdy, impious entertainments. Here was an illiterate patron of the new arts, who built splendid palaces and collected pictures and statues. By the late 1690s the humble sergeant had built a stone mansion and was acquiring an extensive clientele and ample opportunities for bribes, loans and shady deals. In 1700–1 he began to acquire property—villages at Lukino in the Moscow region and a sawmill on the Moskva River. In 1702 he received the late Franz Lefort's Moscow mansion, the biggest residence outside the Kremlin.[196] The church he built in Moscow dedicated to the Archangel Gabriel (by Ivan Zarudny, 1701–7), for a long time the highest building in Moscow outside the Kremlin, and one of the most fashionable in its day, became known as the Menshikov tower. His St Petersburg mansion, built on a more lavish scale than the royal Winter Palace or the Summer Palace across the river, was often used for state occasions. The French ambassador observed, in 1723, that the hospitality was on a grander scale than elsewhere, and that the prince, 'wishing to display all his magnificence', dressed up in the costume and regalia of the Danish order of the Elephant, all covered with diamonds.[197] (He amassed a lavish wardrobe of Western suits, wigs and accessories.)

By the end of his career he had built up a sort of state within a state, 3,000 villages and seven towns spread over forty-two districts, in Russia, the Baltic, Ukraine, and Poland, with more than 300,000 serfs. (The richest man in Russia in 1700, Prince M. Ia. Cherkassky, had only 33,000.) He owned crystal and glass factories, salt and iron mines.[198] (It is claimed, incidentally, that Menshikov managed to transfer much of his fortune into Dutch banks through his agent Osip Solov'ev in Amsterdam, and that Russia's first international loan (1769) was repaid from this money.[199]) Despite his great wealth, some of it ill-gotten, Menshikov strongly disapproved of profligacy in the young. In 1720 he wrote to his nephew, Prince Alexander Andreevich Cherkassky, to whom he had given 10,000 roubles and 1,000 gold crowns as a wedding present, warning him to desist from gambling, cut down on servants, and live within his means. 'You should live as befits a gentleman, honestly and frugally, so that your food and money and other supplies are sufficient (there's an old saying: cut your coat according to your cloth: *po odezhda protiagivai i nozhki*). . . . It wouldn't be a bad thing to have your food made by a Russian cook, because your father and grandfather, as you know, didn't keep a foreign chef (*kukhmistr*); they lived honestly and frugally and within their means.'[200]

Menshikov owned an impressive library—13,000 volumes according to one unconfirmed source[201]—but unfortunately no catalogue survives. Details remain only of his very large working collections of maps and charts (including plans of his own estates), architectural and engineering drawings and engravings, about 600 items in all. The map collection, probably the largest of its kind in early eighteenth-century Russia, concentrated on the area of operations of the Northern War.[202] Menshikov's illiteracy did not prevent him from using this sort of material; neither did inability to use a pen prevent him from having a literary style of his own, evident especially in his letters to Peter and to his own wife. Secretaries and scribes (notably his right-hand man Aleksei Volkov, and Franz Witt, who handled foreign correspondence) put pen to paper. His dictated letters suggest that he was familiar with the new Latinate vocabulary with which Petrine correspondence was liberally peppered. He even spoke some rough-and-ready Dutch and German.[203] It was recognition of Menshikov's influence rather than his erudition, however, which in 1714 secured him election to the Royal Society in London.[204]

Menshikov's collection of 143 pictures was impressive by Russian standards. The French traveller De Mottray described one gallery in 1732: 'along both sides of the room hung various pictures which connoisseurs admired. Among them were pictures depicting Poltava and other victories gained over Sweden.' Portraits included Peter Petrovich as Cupid by Caravaque, Peter's grandchildren Peter and Natalia as Apollo and Diana, a double portrait of Anna and Elizabeth (1717), and two full-length portraits of them, since lost. There were portraits of his daughters Maria and Alexandra (now in the Menshikov palace) and of European monarchs (Augustus and Charles XII), some decorative compositions, still lifes, allegories (the four seasons), and townscapes, together with religious subjects—the crucifixion, the evangelists, Esther, Peter and Paul.[205] Living in his house was a woman miniaturist and musician, Elisabeth Blesendorf. Menshikov employed both singers and instrumentalists in what must have been one of the most musical Russian households of his day.[206]

As long as Peter was alive, Menshikov would always play second fiddle. But Peter's successors, Catherine I and Peter II, did not impose the same restraints. There is a grim description of Menshikov just before his fall: 'Lust for power, arrogance, greed for wealth, neglect of friends and relations not only alienated all those close to him, but also provoked general hatred and a desire to get rid of a man with whom it had become intolerable to live. ... Everyone conspired against him.'[207] Neglect of relatives is suggested by the appeal from priests in the church in the village of Semenovskoe in 1724 complaining that they had not been paid for singing requiem masses for Menshikov's late daughter Ekaterina, and reminding him that his parents were also buried in the church.[208] Menshikov preserved his power during Catherine's reign, but finally overstepped the mark when he tried to marry his daughter Maria to the young Peter II, who was persuaded by Menshikov's aristocratic enemies to sign an order for his arrest on 8 September 1727. He was tried, and exiled to remote Berezov in Siberia. 'This colossus of a pygmy, raised almost to royal status by the hand of your parents, this arrogant man has shown us an example of his ingratitude of spirit', was Feofan Prokopovich's opinion, expressed to Tsarevna Anna Petrovna.[209] Menshikov died in exile on 12 November 1729 and was buried in a wooden church in Berezov which he had himself built.[210]

V.   POWER NETWORKS AND PECKING ORDERS

One of Peter's great problems was that although the longest-serving of his favourites was each devoted to Peter after their own fashion, they were often at daggers drawn with each other. Jealousy was rife. The 'fledglings' of the tsar's nest may have been quiet and submissive when 'father' was at home, but they lost no time in pecking each other and trying to expel the weaker as soon as Peter was out of sight. This was no straightforward split between old families and newcomers. For example, Menshikov hated Devier, an even more recent newcomer than himself, who had had the effrontery to marry Menshikov's sister Anna (some years his senior and 'on the shelf'), applying directly to the tsar for permission after Menshikov objected to the match and had had Devier flogged. Menshikov got his own back in 1727 when he managed to have Devier banished to Siberia, along with the latter's ally Peter Tolstoy.[211] Menshikov and Apraksin were on bad terms. They often quarrelled in public, even brawling at the wedding feast of Anna and Friedrich of Courland in 1710. A few days later Apraksin hit the Admiralty secretary Kikin over the head with a wine bottle at Menshikov's birthday party.[212] In November 1724 a quarrel broke out between Menshikov and Nikita Repnin at a christening party at Iaguzhinsky's, when 'they accused each other of the seven deadly sins'.[213] In turn, Menshikov and Iaguzhinsky were rivals. Just Juel commented in 1710, the beginning of the latter's rise to power, that 'the tsar's favour towards him is so great that Prince Menshikov hates him vehemently and with good reason; his majesty is so accustomed to Iaguzhinsky and so well disposed towards him that in time the latter may well succeed in depriving Menshikov of the tsar's love and favour, especially as the prince already has so many other enemies'.[214] No doubt Menshikov recognized elements of his own career in the younger man's rise, a cause for jealousy rather than solidarity. In turn, Iaguzhinsky's prominence in foreign negotiations in the 1710s aroused the envy of the diplomatic specialist Andrei Osterman, who apparently managed to exclude Iaguzhinsky from the Nystad peace talks in 1721 by bribing an associate in Viborg to delay his journey. When Iaguzhinsky arrived, the treaty had already been signed, and he missed out on the honours.[215] Menshikov engineered the downfall of Peter Shafirov, after they had fallen out over a joint venture. In 1722 the two quarrelled in the Senate, and Menshikov was able to trump up a corruption charge. Shafirov's family connections through the marriage of his five daughters into the Russian nobility did not help him. Earlier in his career, he came into conflict with Gavrila Golovkin, who was his superior in the Foreign Office (later the College of Foreign Affairs).[216] And so it went on.

The inner circle as a whole was a target for the hatred of traditionalists, who suspected its members of 'debauching' the tsar. 'Indecent words' uttered by Astrakhan rebels in 1705 included the accusation that 'all the [tsar's] heresies came from the heretic Alexander Menshikov'.[217] The granting of Menshikov's princely title had to be reinforced with orders that it be used in all public and private correspondence 'on pain of severe punishment and disfavour'.[218] More rarely, leading men made alliances with each other. For example, Menshikov was on good terms with B. P. Sheremetev, who addressed him in letters as 'my benefactor and brother', perhaps because it was useful to have an alliance with a member of the old aristocracy who was not one of the court inner circle and not a direct rival for Peter's favours.[219] Sheremetev was particularly close to Fedor Apraksin, even though the latter was often at daggers drawn with Menshikov.

Further insight into the criteria by which Peter selected his aides may be gained by looking at the careers of individuals in the context of the history of institutions. A landmark in Peter's administrative reforms was the Senate; but for all the power apparently invested in it, the members of the original Senate were neither particularly talented nor particularly favoured. Only three were from old noble families, and even they had never been duma members. Of these, M. Dologoruky was probably illiterate, and fellow senator G. A. Plemiannikov (president of the Admiralty chancellery, who died in 1713) signed on his behalf. P. A. Golitsyn (1682–1722) was a junior member of his clan, and the youngest of the original senators by more than a decade. Several of the original members soon lost their posts: Prince G. I. Volkonsky (1670–?) and V. A. Apukhtin (1661–1715) were arrested in 1714, and in 1715 had their tongues burnt for 'taking out contracts for provisioning under false names, taking a high price and thereby burdening the people'. Peter called Volkonsky a 'Judas'.[220] The oldest and the most obscure of the first senators was N. P. Mel'nitsky (1645–1712?), who survived to serve only a year. Two had close personal ties with the tsar. The boyars T. N. Streshnev and Ivan Musin-Pushkin, as we have seen, were members of Peter's circle in the 1680s. Perhaps the most eminent man to join the early Senate (from 1712) was Iakov Fedorovich Dolgoruky (1639–1720), who had spent ten years as a prisoner of war in Stockholm. The patchiness of the talent is not surprising when one recalls that the Senate was created in a military crisis, when many senior men were needed at the front. The roll of honour looks much more distinguished from December 1718, when the inclusion of the presidents of the newly formed colleges brought in such names as Menshikov, F. M. Apraksin, G. A. Golovkin, A. A. Matveev, and D. M. Golitsyn.[221] Even so, as we saw earlier, the Senate was frequently the scene of undignified brawling.

Peter had good reason to feel disappointed in his helpers, whatever their origins.[222] His leading men, in their turn, led a precarious existence. In 1715 Apraksin, Menshikov, and Bruce all managed to exonerate themselves of charges of fraud over provision contracts, but Senators Aputchin and Volkonsky were cruelly punished.[223] Many of the fledglings were expelled from the nest either for failing to make sufficient effort or for blatant abuse of their positions. Those who remained constantly appealed to the tsar for protection.

Many failed because too much was asked of them. The following letter from Fedor Apraksin to the tsar shows how many tasks one individual might be expected to handle simultaneously:

> This is how things are here, lord: work on the ships is progressing as far as possible, and other work, too; only there is a great shortage of carpenters. For my sins, very many have died, and there are many sick. We have managed to set up the ironworks in Beloozero district, but we can't get craftsmen. Without your authorization I daren't summon volunteers from Lev Kirillovich [Naryshkin]'s and Vakhromei Miller's old factories; I know that you'll be fed up with my pestering, but they have plenty to spare. The sawmill on the river Belokolodez' has been built and should be working by autumn. Also the other one, at Stupino, has been started but isn't finished yet. I am going to the Romanov factories myself to see about the cannon founding, but with great difficulty: I am so sick that I can't walk across the room; still I shall live there until things are settled and have the siege guns cast while I am there.

In a postscript he appealed for the release from duty of his brother, who had been ordered to defend Iami and Kopor'ie with two dragoon regiments but without any infantry. 'With what is he to defend such a huge frontier? Nothing can come of this except his utter ruin.'[224] In his reply, Peter authorized the transfer of ironworkers, offered condolences on Apraksin's illness, and accused his brother of being a liar, advising Apraksin to confront him with the tsar's letter: 'Then you will see the truth: no one wants to make any effort.'[225] Time and time again, even the more efficient of Peter's officials and agents were prevented from fulfilling their duties by the inefficiency not only of their subordinates, but also of their superiors. 'I await your instructions as soon as possible,' wrote Vice-Admiral Zmaevich from Voronezh in June 1723, 'since this work requires a considerable amount of time and I don't want to be held to blame for the delay.' Governor Izmailov received an official reprimand for not aiding Zmaevich 'in a matter of great importance', and was threatened with prosecution.[226]

Boris Sheremetev also had little time to rest. 'I don't know what to do,' he wrote to Fedor Apraksin. 'I'm no angel ... but I am asked to do the work of an angel rather than a human being.'[227] After his death in 1719, his wife Anna Petrovna wrote that 'during all the time he was away with the army without leave he never had the chance to reside in his home and in his absence his houses and the ancient estates of his father were run and administered by our servants', with the result that his affairs were in disarray and there had been much illegal movement of peasants both away from and on to his lands.[228]

Peter abused his underlings in plain language if they failed. He told Ivan Musin-Pushkin in June 1707: 'I am very surprised at you, as I thought you had a brain but now I see that you are more stupid than a dumb beast.'[229] But Peter could on occasion be tolerant, perhaps because he understood that his 'new Europeans' (and he himself) were still only one step removed from a primitive society, where the strong abused the weak, and clan loyalties remained stronger than devotion to State and sovereign. There was an unwritten law that almost any crime could be forgiven if the culprit confessed publicly. Writing to Fedor Apraksin in June 1704, Peter referred to the negligence of the latter's brother Peter, an army officer, who had failed to prevent a Swedish squadron from landing at Narva. 'If he makes his lack of effort and error known publicly then I shall not prosecute him, but if he doesn't then ask yourself: how can I show favour when a man errs but refuses to confess his guilt?'[230]

Andrei Matveev, one of Peter's most articulate helpers, complained about the burdens of running the Justice College:

> The [Justice] college, despatching everything correctly, according to its oath and obligation before Your Majesty, and not catering for the wishes of others, has gained many foes who are always seeking to do harm, both secretly and openly. And there are distinguished persons who have cases brought against them by the fiscal officers, or against their relatives and friends who, seeing that I, without deceit and self-interest, refuse to cater to them in their cases, they, with their friends and relatives, plot against me and threaten to do me irreparable harm both in the eyes of your Majesty and the Senate. As a result I, a mere orphan, am always in peril from them. For Hercules himself could hardly withstand two of them.[231]

The reference to Hercules recalls Pososhkov's famous remark about the tsar pulling uphill with the strength of ten men.

14

Responses

I.   DEATH

Peter the Great died between four and five in the morning on 28 January 1725 in his study in the upper apartments of the Winter Palace. Shortly before losing consciousness, he is said to have scrawled an unfinished note: 'Leave all to …' and summoned his daughter Anna.[1] He was fifty-two years, seven months and twenty-nine days old, in the forty-second year, seventh month, and third day of his reign, and had been ill for thirteen days. In winter 1723 Peter was struck down by a disease of the urinary tract and bladder. He tried various remedies, but by the summer of 1724 was suffering severe pain as a result of urine retention. Dr Blumentrost sent for Dr Bidloo from Moscow, and Dr Horn performed an operation to release the urine. Peter was bed-bound for four months that summer.[2] Thinking he was cured, he went out on his yacht in the first week of October to inspect work on the Ladoga canal, accompanied by Doctors Blumentrost and Paulson and a portable pharmacy. He returned in early November, and made a visit to Lakhta on the Finnish Gulf en route to inspect some ironworks. There follows the well-known story about a boatload of soldiers and sailors in peril in a storm, and how Peter helped to save them by wading into the water.[3] From then on, his health went downhill, although clearly the interval between this legendary incident and death precludes any direct link. In early January uremia developed again, linked (according to a Soviet analysis) with nitric poisoning. The autopsy revealed that gangrene had set in around the bladder.[4] There are several contemporary accounts of Peter's last illness, by some who were present, such as Prokopovich, and some who were not, like the French minister Campredon, who in a letter of 10 February (NS) attributed Peter's condition to 'the recurrence of an old case of venereal disease, poorly treated'. He recounts gruesome details of the release by lancing of four pounds of infected urine and the onset of gangrene, and blames Blumentrost for failing to take decisive action.[5] On 5 January a letter was dispatched to the king of Prussia, written as if by Peter in the first person and signed by Golovkin, asking the king to send his personal physician Von Stahl at once: 'Following a slight chill, I have been suffering from a severe attack of illness (*aktsidentsiia*).'[6] Stählin's account adds that Peter's doctors also consulted Professor Boerhaave in Leiden, who is said to have exclaimed that Peter could have been cured with medicine costing five copecks if treatment had started in time.[7] It seems that Peter was killed by the lethal combination of his doctors' indecision (not uncommon in physicians treating world leaders), his own obstinacy, and the accumulated effects of half a century of tireless activity, both in public and in private.

Immediate responses to Peter's demise may be divided into three broad categories. The first were stylized expressions of grief, drawing on literary conventions readily associated with a man who was a legend in his own lifetime. The best-known example is Feofan Prokopovich's funeral oration, delivered in the Peter–Paul cathedral on 10 March 1725, which exploits the notion that the dead monarch 'gave birth' to Russia, and names him Samson (strong defender of the fatherland), Japhet (creator of the fleet), Moses (law-giver), Solomon (bringer of reason and wisdom), David, and Constantine (reformers of religion). The oration ends with a eulogy to Peter's successor Catherine I, 'mother of all Russians', the embodiment of her husband's 'spirit'.[8] A medal by an unknown Russian artist bears on the back an image of Peter borne aloft by Eternity, looking down from the heavens at a seated woman personifying Russia with attributes of the arts and sciences at her feet and the legend 'See in what condition I leave you'.[9] Vasily Trediakovsky's *Elegy on the Death of Peter the Great* has Pallas Athene, Mars, Neptune, and Politika all lamenting their loss. The poem ends with thoughts of Peter in heaven.[10] Gavriil Buzhinsky's sermon on the first anniversary of Peter's death went a step further: 'Peter the Great is alive: I am the resurrection and the life ... and whoever believes in me will live forever.'[11]

There is evidence also of more straightforward mourning. Andrei Matveev wrote to Makarov from Moscow that news of the 'tragedy' of Peter's death was greeted with 'such howls, cries and tearful wailing, that women could not have howled and sobbed more bitterly. I have never in my life seen or heard such horror from the populace as was heard in all the parishes and streets when the announcement was made.' This was not the ritual wailing of women, but the grief of men.[12] Ivan Nepliuev recalls that he sobbed and was in a kind of 'delirium' (*bespamiatstvo*) for a whole day.[13] The French and Prussian ministers in St Petersburg sent back identical reports to their respective governments: 'It is easy to understand the desolation and sadness this has caused to the imperial family and to those especially attached to them, and on the other hand what dread it has struck in the inhabitants, who fear some disturbances, above all as nothing has been settled concerning the succession.'[14]

The third type of response, the rarest because it could not be expressed openly, was relief, even rejoicing. In the words of a recent study:

We could enthuse forever about the greatness of Peter's actions and still not depict in all its fullness, brilliance and worth everything that he accomplished ... But in creating, he destroyed. He caused pain to all with whom he came into contact. He disturbed the safety, peace, prosperity, interests, strength, well-being, rights and dignity of everyone he touched. He made things unpleasant for everyone. He did harm to everyone. He touched intellectual, political, social, financial, family, moral and spiritual interests. Is it possible to love such a statesman? In no way. Such men are hated.[15]

Let us examine the history of opposition during Peter's lifetime before returning to the posthumous legacy and a consideration of his reputation in Russia today.

II.   OPPOSITION

Opposition to Peter took many forms. The most widespread was sullen resistance to the sheer burden of his demands and the incomprehensibility of his goals. 'The Czar will always find the Obstinacy of his Subjects, and their natural bent to Injustice and Extortion, an insurmountable Obstacle to the wise Ends he has proposed to himself,' wrote Weber.[16] Popular displeasure was exhibited in the evading of responsibilities, ranging from dereliction of duty to wholesale flight. Well-articulated ideological protest was comparatively rare, active armed resistance rarer still. In many cases one fuelled the other; resistance was justified with arguments about principles, as when the strel'tsy in 1698 articulated their objection to heavy duties and long postings away from home with protests about foreigners, beards, and threats to the Faith. Acts of disobedience were transformed into patriotic defence of the national heritage. Whitworth observed one such inflammable combination when in 1705 he reported fears of 'some great rebellion at home from the nobility, who are all incensed now against his favourite [Menshikov] or from the clergy, who have all their revenues, holydays and ceremonies retrenched, and from the people, who are generally discontented at the forcible bringing in of foreign customs and new heavy impositions'.[17]

The simplest expression of sullen opposition was to ignore orders. Peter fought for years, for example, without total success, to change the design of river craft, issuing endless decrees banning 'old-style vessels' (*staromanernye suda*). As late as 1723, strong patrols were posted at Schlüsselburg 'in order to prevent such craft from entering the River Neva'.[18] As we have seen, there were pockets of resistance to dress and land reform, new-style entertainments, and compulsory education. There is even evidence that Peter failed to instil his cherished military ethos. The Prussian minister Vockerodt recorded the antipathy felt by the average nobleman for lifelong military service, for St Petersburg (which was associated with service), and the navy: 'However tiny his estate, even if he has to follow the plough himself, he still prefers it to being a soldier!'[19]

A common reaction to irksome duties and taxes was flight. Running away was an elemental response, born sometimes of desperation, sometimes of the desire for fresh pastures. Many fugitives made for the lower and middle Volga, Ukraine, and the Urals, attractive venues because of access to land and work and the low-key state presence. Sometimes whole illegal communities formed, living off pillage and theft. This extract from a petition of 1715 on runaways gives an idea of the sort of conditions which forced peasants to leave home: 'They fled from penury and poor harvests, from the loss of horses and livestock and from inability to pay unfair requisitions and from various communal taxes and from unjust collectors and the extortions of informers and additional levies.'[20] Such problems were not unique to Peter's reign. The 1649 Law Code has numerous clauses on flight. Indeed, its famous provisions on serfdom centred on ending the limitations on retrieving runaways. From the 1650s the numbers fleeing were boosted by the persecution of Old Believers, whose remote communities became magnets for further dissidents. Under Peter the scale of flight was increased by new burdens. Forced labour gangs, the proliferation of officials in the countryside, armed detachments in villages to procure provisions and fodder, billeting, were all expressive of an element of force. Peasants who escaped the military draft found themselves saddled with the duty of maintaining the army even in peacetime. The wholesale billeting of troops in the central *gubernii* from the late 1710s entailed the whole population being 'assigned' to the army and maintaining regiments though taxes and billeting obligation or payment for building quarters.[21] A critic of Peter's regime many years later wrote: 'The whole of Russia was turned into a sort of factory working to fulfil various plans and schemes.' This was someone writing not with the hindsight of the Stalin era, but in 1864![22]

The perception that too much was being demanded affected all levels of society. There are dozens of edicts threatening noble defectors and fugitives with harsh punishments.[23] A common reason for flight was to avoid the draft. As many as 10 per cent of marching parties may have escaped in the period 1703–6. Of 15,000 Russian auxiliaries sent to Saxony in 1704, more than a third fled.[24] Flight to avoid forced labour was also widespread. In September 1702 Peter wrote to Tikhon Streshnev on the subject of runaway carters: 'When you receive this letter be so good as to pursue those damned fugitives immediately and when you catch them, beat them all with the knout and cut off their ears, and also banish every fifth man to Taganrog by drawing lots, to stop them running off to Poland.'[25] A memorandum to the Senate in 1716 reported that of sixty-two carters transferring from Nizhny Novgorod province to St Petersburg only five arrived in the capital, the rest having run off, died, or been left ill along the route.[26]

The estimated volume of runaway peasants for the period 1719–27 was 200,000, more than the number of men in regular units of the army![27] From the middle of the seventeenth century the burden of recovery had shifted from the individual to the State, which dispatched 'bounty hunters' (*syshchiki*) and set ever higher penalties for harbouring fugitives. A decree of 1721 increased fines for harbourers (100 roubles per year for hiding males, 50 for females), and prescribed flogging and hard labour for bailiffs and stewards who aided and abetted them, and rewards for those who informed on them. Returned fugitives were to be knouted. Penalties for hiding people ranged from confiscation of estates and exile to the galleys for deliberate concealment on a large scale, to fines of from one to ten roubles for clerical errors and other minor infringements.[28] By the end of Peter's reign flight across the borders, especially into Poland, was so widespread that manned pickets (*krepkie zastavy*) were set up. Any fugitives apprehended were to be interrogated, knouted, and sent back whence they came. A repeat order a year later called for yet more pickets. Russia was being 'emptied' (*chinitsia pustota*) by illegal emigration, much of which was actively encouraged by the Poles. Anyone resisting arrest was to be shot.[29]

Opposition to Peter went deeper than indignation about heavy burdens. Ivan IV, a predecessor with whom he is often compared, imposed similar strains and engaged (allegedly) in more gratuitous personal acts of cruelty than Peter ever did, but he retained the reputation among the peasantry of being a 'good' tsar.[30] One reason for this may have been that his violence was apparently directed against the boyars, the 'wall' between tsar and his people. Peter's first violent acts, on the other hand, were aimed at the conservative, bearded strel'tsy, many of whom were Old Believers. One did not have to be an Old Believer to disapprove of many of the tsar's actions, because, unlike Ivan, Peter offended tradition; moreover, he did so during an age of 'apocalyptic expectations'.[31] Peter could have been in no doubt about the strength of conservative opposition even before he embarked on his reforms. Documents like Patriarch Joachim's testament (1690) and the tract 'Against the Latins and Lutherans', both of which denounced foreign worship in Russia and harmful foreign influences, or Patriarch Adrian's diatribe against shaving, vocalized conservative feelings. In the latter part of the 1690s there were protests against ship taxes, the sending of students abroad, measures on shaving and dress, and the neglect of fasts, culminating in the protest against the replacement of the creation-based calendar. In the words of one denunciation recorded in the Preobrazhensky *prikaz*: 'Now the counting of years in Moscow has been changed, and the great sovereign has ordered Hungarian dress to be worn, and the great fast [Lent] in Moscow has been shortened, and after Easter Sunday it is said that they will begin to eat meat on Wednesdays and Fridays.'[32]

Although not confined to members of the clergy, protests were most eloquently articulated by this group, who were also largely responsible for composing or copying tracts circulated in manuscript on such topics as the evils of shaving and tobacco. According to N. B. Golikova, something like 20 per cent of all 'political' cases tried in Peter's reign involved members of the clergy.[33] One of first recorded diatribes was the missive written and handed personally to the tsar by Father Avraamy of St Andrew's monastery in Moscow in 1696–7. Avraamy heard rumours about Peter from nobles who visited his monastery, as well as from acquaintances among clerks in government departments. He decided to give the young tsar some good advice before it was too late, beginning his tract with the story of the Creation and the reminder that 'good tsars give right judgement, bad ones forget the fear of God'. He appealed to Peter to resume the straight and narrow path, and to heed the advice of churchmen rather than laymen. Good men had hoped that after his marriage Peter would abandon childish games, but they were disappointed. Peter still spent his time indulging in 'jests and japes (*v slovakh smekhotvornykh*) and activities unpleasing to God'. War games and sailing were distracting him from his duties. Ignoring the good advice of his mother, wife, and confessor, he had left the State in the hands of intriguers and embezzlers. Scribes and clerks in certain *prikazy* had grown richer than tradesmen or even chief merchants, and their wives had more jewellery on their heads, arms, and shoulders than even the wives of chief merchants or *stol'niky*. And so on. The letter was formulated in traditional terms, expressing alarm that the tsar had abrogated his responsibility to 'wicked' power-seeking boyars. Such fears could only be endorsed when Peter disappeared not just to sail ships but off abroad in 1697, leaving others in charge. Avraamy's fate was to end up in the Preobrazhensky *prikaz*, then in a monastery in Kolomna (a mild punishment), whence he continued to write to the tsar.[34]

Avraamy's tract was unusually detailed. More common were short anonymous letters (*podmetnye pis'ma*). A typical example, found in a church in Moscow, warned that the tsar had been 'seduced by Germans and German women into the Latin faith', and was even being poisoned by them. The author railed against the lowering of moral standards and smoking, and advised the tsar to attend church services to avert a Turkish attack. Another letter described Peter's entourage as 'a swarm of demons'.[35] Such denunciations, fuelled by the Grand Embassy and the attack on tradition when Peter returned, were numerous. One tract listed seventy 'innovations' regarded as harmful to the soul, including smoking, drinking tea and coffee, German dress, Italian singing and painting, shaving, and embalming corpses.[36] Specific charges against Peter himself concerned his deviation from the traditional image of the holy Orthodox tsar. He consorted with foreigners, married one, looked like one (being beardless and wearing foreign clothes), perhaps even *was* one. There were various theories about Peter's origins, such as the story that Tsaritsa Natalia gave birth to a daughter, who was exchanged for a baby boy from the Foreign Quarter. The details are often confused: for example, it was said that Natalia had already given birth to several daughters.[37] A popular version among peasants was that the 'Germans' had put the real Peter in prison and sent a fake tsar.[38] Even the true facts of his ancestry were interpreted negatively: he was the product of the blood of slaves (the Naryshkins!), royalty, and priests (his great grandfather Filaret), a lethal combination apparently, and, as the son of a second wife, he was born in sin.[39]

Peter's irregular family relations aroused the disapproval of traditionalists, starting with the banishment of Evdokia. If this were not bad enough, he was said to have married his own granddaughter and niece, on the grounds that Tsarevich Alexis and Natalia Alekseevna were Catherine's godparents.[40] The monk Aleksei of the Alexander monastery at Svir refused to celebrate

Catherine's name-day on the grounds that her marriage to the tsar was illegal. Peter, he claimed, was spiritually related (*imel dukhovnoe srodstvo*) to the tsaritsa since her godmother at her baptism had been Peter's sister. (He added that Peter and his assistants failed to keep the fasts, a habit allegedly acquired from the 'fallen Western Church of Rome'.) Menshikov, he claimed, had been seen smoking in church, and Aleksei Petrovich Saltykov had taken out his tobacco pouch and lit up right in front of the altar during mass. The monk was defrocked, tortured, and broken on the wheel in 1720.[41] On Easter day 1718 an old man handed Peter a note objecting to the treatment of Alexis Petrovich and the new oath of loyalty to Peter Petrovich, and complaining that Catherine 'consorted with foreigners and there would be harm done to Christians because she was not of local origins (*ne zdeshnei prirody*)'.[42] Many cases were recorded of priests refusing to say prayers for Peter or to mark royal anniversaries.

Many of the complaints about Peter centred on his preference for 'German' dress and hair-style and the forcing of these fashions upon the population. In 1700 a peasant woman from Vologda was tortured in the Preobrazhensky *prikaz* for repeating the rumour that the supposed tsar in a black velvet German coat and wig was in Voronezh building ships with two Germans. 'The sovereign isn't in Moscow. The sovereign who is now in Moscow, who is he?'[43] A monk was knouted, had his tongue cut out, and was sent to hard labour in Azov for suggesting that Peter was the son of Franz Lefort (*Lefortov syn*) and was forcing Christians into the Muslim (*busurmanskaia*) faith by making them wear German dress. 'The tsar loves Germans, shares their belief and dresses his soldiers in German coats.' One Mikhail Bolshakov was arrested, and later died under torture, when he expressed disgust at a new 'Saxon' fur coat, and said that he would like to hang the person who introduced the fashion.[44] In 1701 Evtifei Nikonov, a stoker, was arrested for complaining that Peter had introduced 'German stockings and boots into the Muscovite realm'.[45]

Peter's decrees were given a sinister interpretation. According to the old Orthodox calendar, the new century, 7200, had begun on 1 September 1692; thus by announcing another new century in 1700 he had 'stolen' eight years. The accusations piled up: he had recruits stamped with the seal of Antichrist; he did not observe the fasts; he abolished the patriarchate; he killed his own son, the true heir, then, with his 1722 law of succession, set about building the royal house of Antichrist.[46] Even new taxes, such as those on bath-houses and beehives, were linked with the coming of Antichrist, as were changes in the status of the priesthood, especially the inclusion of certain categories such as sacristans in the poll tax registers.[47]

The belief that Peter was the Antichrist was particularly persistent. One of the most detailed 'proofs' was offered by the copyist Grigory Talitsky in 1700.[48] The behaviour of Peter and his circle was denounced, Moscow was likened to Babylon, Peter was said to be the eighth tsar (counting from Ivan IV): 'and now is the last time come and the Antichrist has been born and by their reckoning Antichrist is the eighth tsar Peter Alekseevich'.[49] Good Christians were admonished to resist evil by refusing to pay taxes or perform service and, ultimately, by rebelling, with the aid of the strel'tsy. Such teaching was considered so dangerous, especially as copies had been circulated quite widely and such church hierarchs as Bishop Ignaty of Tambov had been implicated, that a special tract, *Signs of the Coming of Antichrist*, was commissioned from Stefan Iavorsky. Talitsky and two of his confederates were quartered. When Peter issued orders to the clergy in 1708 during the Bulavin uprising to look out for treason, he mentioned the Talitsky case,[50] which also featured in an appeal to dissidents, published by the Synod with Peter's corrections in January 1722—'It is easy to see how such foolish and unthinking people, out of ill-grounded zeal, hold their own opinions, oppose the truth, succumb to falsehood, and blindly condemn themselves to physical and spiritual misfortune'—and again in the order to priests to report confessions.[51] All sorts of dissidents spread rumours about Antichrist. Members of the 'God's people' cult, later known as 'flagellants', were interrogated in the Preobrazhensky *prikaz* in 1717. One of them reported that the Antichrist was living in St Petersburg, and that the city would be destroyed 'like Sodom and Gomorrah'.[52] There were clues in Peter's titles: the number of the Beast (666) could be computed from the numerical values of the letters in IMPERATOR by removing the M, which Peter allegedly used to conceal his true identity.[53] Calculations based on other Petrine neologisms, with a little fiddling, produced 666—for example, *senatri* and H[G]olstein. Portraits of Peter with Minerva were identified as the icons of Antichrist, and the 70 grivna poll tax as the seven-headed serpent.[54] Peter's true identity was debated: he was said to take the shape of an animal (his German boots were identified with the 'cow's feet' of Antichrist[55]), and to be Simon Petrov the magician (Simon Magus?).[56] This was fully consistent with popular beliefs about the devil and demons, who were believed to be capable of changing their shape at will and appearing in various disguises, even as holy angels.

Boris Uspensky argues that Peter's deeds were bound to be viewed negatively because of different values attached to certain words by adherents of the old and the new, hence the title 'father of the fatherland', an honorary secular title of the Roman Empire, to Orthodox Russians sounded like a claim of priestly status, even a usurping of the role of the true father or pastor, the patriarch.[57] In December 1709 Peter was welcomed with the words usually addressed to Christ on Palm Sunday: 'Blessed is he who cometh in the name of the Lord.' (In fact, borrowings of biblical terminology are commonplace in the letters of Peter's associates, without any intention of blasphemy.) Youths in white robes cast branches and garlands beneath his feet.[58] In 1721 Golovkin declared that Peter created Russia from the void (like God in Genesis), and raised Russia as from the dead (like Christ).[59] All this corresponded to notions of the Antichrist, who 'aped Christ'. The Bible prophecy states: 'The man of lawlessness sets himself up in God's temple, proclaiming himself to be God.'[60] Uspensky points out that even something as apparently innocuous as the title

Peter the *First* was Western in style (previous tsars were known by their name and patronymic—e.g., Ivan Vasil'evich, never Ivan IV), suggestive of a blasphemous claim to be the 'beginning'.

The upper clergy, including Iavorsky, had no truck with the idea of Antichrist, but some were not averse to opposing Peter by employing the 'Catholic notion of two powers' and the 'two swords'.[61] In 1712 Iavorsky referred obliquely to Peter as the 'destroyer of the law of God', and in his book *The Rock of Faith* argued, using well-tried formulas, that 'all men must obey the monarch in civil affairs and the supreme pastor in matters of faith'. The temporal authority's duty was to protect. Although it is difficult to detect any firm assertion that the spiritual power was superior to the secular, Iavorsky's notion of power sharing was sharply out of line with Petrine politics. Publication of his book was prohibited until 1728.[62]

The major plots, uprisings, and rebellions in Peter's reign in nearly all cases combined material and ideological protest. One of the first (we shall not deal here with the strel'tsy revolts of the 1680s) was the 1696–7 Ivan Tsykler affair, an alleged plot to kill the tsar, which provided a foretaste of the revolt of the strel'tsy in 1698. The participants voiced dark fears about Peter's fate abroad. There was talk of bringing back Sophia and Golitsyn. Tsykler's 'accomplices' included the nobles Fedor Pushkin and Aleksei Prokof'evich Sokovnin, whose sisters had been imprisoned as Old Believers. Sokovnin was particularly horrified by the inclusion of two of his sons in the list of nobles to be sent abroad to study. According to Patrick Gordon, 'they all confessed that they had an intention to have murdered his Matie and to that purpose had tried to draw the streltsees to their party'.[63] Association of this incident with the Miloslavsky 'plots' of 1682 led Peter to order the exhumation of the corpse of Ivan Miloslavsky, who had died in his bed in 1685. The open coffin was placed under the executioner's block so that blood 'sprinkled on the dead carcass which in some places was rotteen & consumed'.[64] This served as a grim warning to noble dissidents. There is no evidence of other plots by nobles, although the Preobrazhensky *prikaz* dealt with a small number of cases (5.5 per cent of the total) of grumblings, mainly from provincial servitors, such as Iaroslavl' landowners Grigory and Andrei Briamin, who complained about war service and the breaking of fasts: 'We don't have a sovereign but a substitute German.'[65]

In fact, there is little evidence of threats to Peter in person, despite his habit of mixing with ordinary folk. Stählin records an attempt on the tsar's life, allegedly by an Old Believer who was mistaken for a courier in the palace and tried to stab the tsar. When questioned by Peter about his motives, he replied that he was avenging the 'evil done to our brethren and our faith'. This incident was said to have prompted the special clothing laws for Old Believers.[66] But for every dissident who wished to murder the tsar (a rarity), there seem to have been many more willing to defend legitimate authority. In 1722 a man in Penza publicly shouted out 'many wicked words' about the sovereign, and was reported by a loyal townsman, who was rewarded with 300 roubles and tax-free trading concessions until his death. This example was published in order to encourage others to denounce malcontents.[67]

The strel'tsy continued to be a thorn in Peter's flesh. The loss of Sophia, their perceived protector, in 1689, their relegation to the losing side in Peter's mock battles of the early 1690s, then hardships suffered during the two Azov campaigns were followed not by rewards or even respite, but by new postings early in 1697.[68] In June 1698 four regiments mutinied, thereby prematurely ending Peter's stay abroad. Government troops suppressed the revolt. In their petitions to the authorities, vows to kill the 'Germans' who were 'destroying Orthodoxy' mingled with threats to wipe out the new infantry regiments, their perceived rivals. During investigations it became clear that the strel'tsy had vague notions of driving out 'traitors' and foreigners, establishing leaders sympathetic to them, and restoring the 'old order' under which they, the strel'tsy, had enjoyed a privileged position. Peter was dissatisfied by the investigation and penalties imposed on the rebels before his return. A new trial, which began on 17 September 1698 and ended only in February 1700, resulted in the execution of 1,182 strel'tsy and the flogging and banishment of 601 others. The aim of the trial was not to establish guilt, but to elicit information about 'accomplices' and motives. No hard evidence was found to implicate any boyars, but the widespread opposition among the strel'tsy themselves, given their past record, was enough to ensure a harsh sentence as a warning to others. Men were broken on the wheel, heads were displayed on poles, and corpses strung up for months in full view of Sophia's windows in the convent. The execution of the strel'tsy became a symbol of Peter's cruelty and ruthless determination to root out opposition. (It is no coincidence that one of Peter's first actions upon returning to Moscow in August 1698 and preparing to deal with the strel'tsy was to cut off the long beards, symbol of antiquity, of leading boyars and officials.) Cruel retribution was not enough to suppress strel'tsy disaffection. If anything, it exacerbated it, especially as, after 1698, they were banned from Moscow and spread discontent all over Russia. There were numerous cases of strel'tsy being arrested for criticizing the tsar's treatment of their fellows. For example, Peter Krivoy admitted under torture in the Preobrazhensky *prikaz* in autumn 1699 that he and others had talked of assassinating Peter.[69]

On 30 July 1705 strel'tsy stationed at Astrakhan ambushed the guards and began a massacre of officers and government officials. The elected leaders were Iakov Nosov, an Old Believer merchant from Iaroslavl', and the local official (*burgomeistr*) Gavrilo Ganchikov. The pretext was the enforcement of rules on beards and dress. A gunner interrogated in the Preobrazhensky *prikaz* claimed that he had heard rumours in Moscow that the real tsar had gone missing and that the current one was a fake.[70] In letters sent to the Iaik Cossacks the rebels mentioned the antics of the Drunken Assembly: 'instead of God-respecting carol singing they use masquerades and games, in which one of his courtiers, a jester, was given the title of patriarch, and others made archbishops'.[71]

Letters to the Don Cossacks and others dated late July/early August declared:

> We stood up in Astrakhan for the Christian faith and against shaving and German dress and tobacco and because we and our wives and children were not admitted into God's church in old Russian dress. And those who went to church, of both male and female sex, had their garments chopped up and were pushed out of God's churches and sent packing and the governors and officers hurled all manner of abuse at us, our wives and children, and they, the governors and officers, bowed down to pagan idols and forced us to bow down too. And we rose up to defend the Christian faith and refused to bow to the idols and they, the governors and officers, tried to take away the guns of the servicemen on guard and took some away and tried to beat us to death and we removed the pagan idols from the homes of the officers.[72]

The fact that the 'pagan idols' were in fact wig blocks indicates the cultural gulf between the handful of semi-Westernized officials and the mass of the population.[73] The Astrakhan rebels' plan of action echoed the plans of the strel'tsy in 1682 and 1698: to go to Moscow and kill any German, male or female, they chanced upon, to find the sovereign and appeal for the Old Belief to be restored and for permission not to have to wear German dress or to shave. A refusal would mean that he was not the real tsar and could be killed.[74] Like their predecessors, the strel'tsy had no truck with direct anti-tsarist sentiments. In another version it was said that Peter was a prisoner in Sweden, that the boyars had taken over Moscow, and that the rebels must march against them for the sake of the Christian faith and the tsar. Others claimed that the tsar was dead.[75] Royal letters received in Astrakhan in October were treated with respect. Prayers were even sung for the tsar's health, and the citizens responded with a petition setting out their grievances.

The impetus for the Astrakhan revolt was not purely ideological. The city had long been a place of exile for unreliable elements. The authorities turned a blind eye to the vagrants and fugitives who flooded into the town to seek work in the fisheries and saltpetre works. Trade duties and indirect taxes (e.g., on bath-houses and cellars) had recently been raised, and food allowances to servicemen reduced. Labour burdens were also increased. For example, each strelets had to collect 58 cubic meters of firewood for the saltpetre works, despite a shortage of trees.[76] Charles Whitworth grasped the two sides of the argument when he mentioned heavy taxes and monopolies on salt and fish and 'the sudden change of Cloathes and Customes added new fewel to their discontent, But the specious pretence for all, was here as in other Countreys the zeal for their Religion ... they are strangely tenacious of their old Ignorance and ceremonies, some where of are represented to be so impious, that I cannot scarce believe any society of men was ever so guilty of such villanies under the notion of Religion.'[77] Peter regarded the revolt as a continuation of stubborn strel'tsy resistance. He wrote to Fedor Apraksin: 'I deduce that the all-gracious Lord has not yet finished pouring out his wrath and for twenty-five years now it has pleased him to give those destructive curs their way and solace in innocent blood, and in a miraculous way he has deigned to quench fire with fire in order that we might see all these things happened not by the will of man but by His will.'[78]

The rebels tried, but failed, to enlist the support of the Don Cossacks. Their attempts to take Tsaritsyn also failed, but their capture of Cherny Iar and Krasny Iar and the spread of the rebellion to the Terek alarmed the authorities, who were forced to divert troops from the Baltic. In early September B. P. Sheremetev was transferred from Courland with two squadrons of dragoons and a battalion of infantry, arriving in Kazan' in mid-December. Even so, Peter had written to the rebels on 30 August 1705 in conciliatory tones, advising them to send him a petition. The new governor was ordered to treat the inhabitants 'kindly and not act cruelly and to make no further mention of the current unrest'. A pardon was issued, and concessions were made.[79] But the opinion of hard-liners prevailed. Sheremetev took the town on 13 March 1706. The trials continued for the next two years. Six men were broken on the wheel, 42 beheaded, 30 executed on Red Square and 242 in other parts of Moscow, and 45 died during interrogation.[80]

The most dangerous rebellion of Peter's reign, led by the Don Cossack ataman Kondraty Afanas'evich Bulavin (ca.1660–1708), flared up in autumn 1707, just as Charles XII's army was advancing eastwards. The rebellion was a classic case of tension between central government and Cossack fringe. A census of the Don region in May 1703 specified that any fugitives who had arrived since 1695 be returned to their former place of residence, a challenge to the traditional Cossack welcome for renegades. There was also resentment of landowners who encroached upon Cossack enterprises (fishing, trapping, grazing livestock, extracting salt). It was the seizure of the Bakhmut saltworks on the North Donets by registered Cossacks from local Cossacks in 1704 which first provoked Bulavin.[81] Rumours that the authorities intended to cut off beards also caused outrage. The catalyst came in July 1707, when Peter sent Prince Iu. V. Dolgoruky to enforce the new rules on returning fugitives. The Don Cossack ataman Lukian Maksimov in Cherkassk reluctantly agreed to co-operate in rounding up illegal immigrants.[82] In October 1707 Prince Dolgoruky was ambushed and slaughtered by Bulavin near Bakhmut. Bulavin was then defeated by Maksimov, and escaped to Zaporozhie, whence he sent out letters on the defence of 'the True Faith', reassuring 'all top officials, good men and all common people who also stand firm with them … but we cannot be silent on account of the evil deeds of wicked men and princes and boyars and profitmakers and Germans and cannot let them off for leading everyone into the Hellenistic pagan faith and diverting them away from the true Christian faith with their signs and cunning tricks'.[83]

Bulavin won support. As well as enlisting Zaporozhian aid, he made common cause with workers in the Voronezh shipyards and forced labourers in Azov and Taganrog. There were negotiations with Nogays, Kalmyks, and Tatars. Peasants, Old Believers, and workmen joined in, often in protests not directly connected with Bulavin's rebellion. There were outbreaks in Tambov and Penza. In April 1708 Bulavin defeated Maksimov, and on 1 May his army was admitted to Cherkassk by Cossack sympathizers, and Bulavin was elected ataman.

Peter was desperately worried. On 2 April 1708 he had written to Tsarevich Alexis ordering him to deal with the rebellion, 'and quench that fire as quickly as possible'.[84] Punishments were to be harsh, as a warning to others. F. M. Apraksin was ordered to execute Bulavin's 'thieves' in Voronezh, and 'hang them along the roads closer to the towns where they lived and thieved'.[85] Prince Vasily Dolgoruky was dispatched with a force of 32,000 men.

Internal Cossack politics intervened when, in July, Bulavin was killed after failing to capture Azov. Peter's response to the news was jubilant. 'So this affair, thank God, had ended happily. ... Here, thank God, all is going well and today there was a celebration (*triumfovanie*) about this good occasion.'[86] He sent thanks to I. A. Tolstoy for 'the ruinous end of that nefarious criminal Bulavin', and three months' salary for officers and soldiers who participated in putting down the rebellion.[87] There were pockets of stiff resistance until early 1709, at Panshin (razed in August 1708), and a raid by Nikita Goly and Nikolai Kolychev on the Don in October, when Tsaritsyn fell to rebels. In September all new Cossack settlements on the Don and the North Donets were destroyed, and a ban was imposed on boat building. Later, the Cossack ataman had to be elected from Moscow. The Bulavin rebellion has been described as a 'virtual replica' of the Razin rebellion of 1670–1.[88] Both were copied in the even more serious Pugachev rebellion in the 1770s. The main difference is perhaps that Bulavin never directly denounced Peter as a false tsar, still less put forward a pretender.

There were numerous localized outbreaks during Peter's reign, from Kungur in the Urals (1703) to Kamchatka (1711) and Siberia (early 1720s). In 1705–11 the Bashkirs were in ferment. Whitworth (1708) reported resistance caused by the forced baptism of about 12,000 into 'the Muscovite religion'.[89] As Muslims, they were subject to Turkish influence (they spoke of the Volga as a Muslim river), but their envoys apparently received little active encouragement from the Turks.[90] In 1720 they were still proving troublesome. A *gramota* was sent to their base at Ufa, appealing to them to desist from burning the villages of Mordvins, Cheremys, and other local tribes, and to send back fugitives who had taken refuge with them. Governor Golovin was ordered to bring them to order. 'If they continue to be disobedient and contrary, tell them that they will invoke His Majesty's great wrath.'[91]

Ukraine continued to be troublesome, although the official line was adamant: the hetman and Little Russian people had been His Majesty's subjects 'since olden times'.[92] Peter wrote to the hetman in April 1722: 'Many complaints are reaching us from the Little Russian people about impositions and disorders (*neporiadki*) being committed by the chief justice and the [Cossack] officers and by the regimental colonels. In particular they complain that in the courts there are many cases of bribe-taking and great impositions and many injustices.' As a result of complaints (against local officials, it will be noted, rather than St Petersburg), in 1722 Ukraine was placed under the jurisdiction of the Senate, and shortly afterwards Peter ordered a thorough investigation into 'which taxes are tolerable to the Little Russian people, which are burdensome'.[93] That this action was prompted by considerations of state security rather than charity is indicated by a later order 'to look out for suspicious persons and for any correspondence with the Tatars and Poles and anything else which concerns good caution and economy'.[94] Ukrainian leaders continued to be regarded with deep suspicion. An edict of June 1723 on the election of a new hetman stated bluntly that 'it is well known to all that since the time of the first hetman Bogdan Khmel'nitsky right up to Skoropadsky all the hetmans have been traitors and our state has suffered calamity as a consequence, most of all in Little Russia'.[95] Peter's correspondence in the final years of his reign was littered with references to the activities of 'rebels and scoundrels' in Ukraine.[96]

Peter's response to revolts and protests by the likes of the strel'tsy, Cossacks, Old Believers and Bashkirs was unambiguous. He *expected* such people to be troublesome. By and large, they also operated on the periphery, which made them less dangerous, even if dealing with them used up valuable resources. Much more worrying was the affair of Tsarevich Alexis. It involved no open manifestation of armed revolt—in fact, there was little hard evidence that a rebellion had even been planned—but there were hints of a web of subversion that reached into inner circles. For Peter this had disturbing resonances of the past; he is said to have referred to Alexis as 'a second Sophia'.[97]

There are a number of aspects of the 'Alexis affair' which must have given Peter cause for concern. One was the tsarevich's close contacts with priests. In a letter to his confessor Iakov Ignat'ev, archpriest of the upper Cathedral of the Saviour in the Kremlin palace, Alexis wrote: 'In this life I have no other friend like your reverence, as God is my witness.'[98] Alexis corresponded with other priests, such as Abbot Ioanniky of the Monastery of St Michael in Kiev, later archimandrite of the Kiev Monastery of the Caves, who in turn sent him icons and relics. But in fact his connection with priests and 'long beards' has been exaggerated. [99]

More disturbing for Peter was the possibility that Alexis enjoyed support from the old nobility, including members of the Golitsyn and Dolgoruky clans, B. P. Sheremetev, B. I. Kurakin, A. Lopukhin, and Princess Troekurova (these last his mother's brother and sister respectively).[100] Vasily Vladimirovich Dolgoruky makes an interesting case. Suppressor of the Bulavin rebellion in 1708, veteran of Poltava and the Pruth, godfather of Elizabeth Petrovna, knight of the order of St Andrew, Dolgoruky hardly looked like a traitor. But he did try to act as a mediator between father and son. He misled Alexis about his father's intentions after the exchange of letters in 1715 and Alexis's expression of his wish to retire to a quiet life. According to Alexis, in Stettin in 1713 Dolgoruky told him: 'If it were not for the tsaritsa's [Catherine's] influence on the sovereign's cruel character (*zhestokii nrav*), our life would be impossible.'[101]

A less ambiguous supporter of Alexis was Alexander Vasil'evich Kikin, former 'play' soldier, bombardier, and volunteer on the Grand Embassy, later director of the St Petersburg wharf, whom the tsar addressed as 'dedushka' (grand-dad). However, his career was interrupted by charges of embezzlement and corruption, which led to a short period of disfavour. A clue to the reasons for Kikin's change of allegiance was given while he was being tortured in 1718, when Peter asked: 'How could a clever man like you go against me?' and Kikin replied: 'The mind needs space, but you restrict it.'[102]

What united these men—by no means die-hard traditionalists—seems to have been fears about Peter's growing despotism. The Alexis affair may be seen as a prelude to the constitutional project of 1730, in which a group of nobles attempted, unsuccessfully, to persuade the new empress Anna Ioannovna to renounce some of her powers. It had less to do with restoring Muscovite traditions than with extending the process of Westernization to the political sphere. Alexis was merely a figure-head for such aspirations, which were quite devoid of any republican tendency.[103] There is also evidence of palpable unease in the very heart of Peter's circle. Kikin's correspondents, for example, included Peter's admiral F. M. Apraksin and his general B. P. Sheremetev. (The latter apparently advised Alexis to be sure to cultivate confidants in Peter's court.) During his trial Alexis recalled conversations between himself and Pavel Iaguzhinsky, the future procurator-general, and Aleksei Makarov, Peter's secretary, who had warned him to take care lest Peter pass the throne to his younger brother.[104] Iakov Dolgoruky liked Alexis, and discussed 'the people's burdens' with him, but was cautious about being seen with him. Prince Dmitry Mikhailovich Golitsyn sent Alexis books from Kiev.[105] It is likely that these top men deemed it prudent to cultivate Alexis's patronage in the event of Peter's death, given the latter's poor health. Such men could hardly avoid having contact with Alexis before he fled Russia in 1716.

Sympathy (or at least lack of antipathy) from such people fuelled Alexis's hopes of support, as shown by the scenario that he outlined at his trial in which he anticipated support from General Bauer, Dmitry Golitsyn, Tsarevna Maria, M. M. and P. A. Golitsyn, and B. P. Sheremetev, adding, 'And many people have told me that the common folk love me.'[106]

The sentence of Alexis and a selection of 'accomplices' was a dire warning to those in high circles who had reservations about Peter's reforms, even if they queried the pace and methods of change rather than the substance. To the anonymous passive nation-wide opposition the affair simply gave additional evidence of Peter's ungodliness and 'unnatural' behaviour, and provided fertile ground for the emergence of pretenders. Even before he was killed, people claiming to be Alexis appeared. Grigory Grigor'ev, a priest from Kazan', was sent to the Preobrazhensky *prikaz* early in 1715 to be investigated for the claim that 'Tsarevich Alexis' was hiding on the estate of the Georgian prince Archill. The workman who had reported the rumour was hauled in and interrogated. He testified that in the bath-house an acquaintance of his had been shown marks on the claimant's body which identified him as the tsarevich. The impostor turned out to be the nobleman Andrei Ivanovich Krekshin, who had been thrown out by his father for drinking and gambling, and had adopted the pseudonym in expectation that local peasants would feed and clothe him out of respect for the tsarevich. He was sentenced to the knout and fifteen years' exile. The main point about the Krekshin affair is that he expected Alexis's name to win him support in the Nizhny region, and that as early as 1715 it could seem credible that the heir to the throne was living in exile.[107]

The faintly articulated, uncoordinated disaffection in high court circles revealed by the Alexis affair continued to grow during the final years of Peter's reign. Poor harvests in 1721–4 caused famine in some areas. Salaries were reduced or left unpaid. In 1724 the poll tax was collected for the first time, bringing protests. The atmosphere at court was darkened by the affair of William Mons. 'Everything is going wrong,' wrote the Saxon envoy in September 1724. 'Trade is coming to an end, there is neither navy nor paid troops, and everyone is dissatisfied and discontented.'[108] This mood is reflected in one of the most damning written indictments of Peter's reign (although it contains not a word of direct criticism of Peter himself), a 'Memorandum on the Needs of the State, Presented to Empress Catherine I' (18 November 1726), signed by Menshikov, Osterman, Makarov, and others.[109] The following are extracts and a summary.

'An examination of the present state of the all-Russian realm reveals that nearly all affairs—both spiritual and temporal—are in disarray and require speedy correction.... Not only the peasantry, on which the maintenance of the army is laid, are in dire need and are being reduced to final and utter ruin by large taxes and continual punitive expeditions and other irregularities, but other areas such as commerce, justice and the mints are also in a state of ruin. So, how can the peasants be relieved without damaging the army and fleet?'

It was recommended that 'since the army is so vital that the State cannot prevail without it, therefore we must look to the welfare of the peasant, for the soldier is linked to the peasant like the soul to the body, and if there is no peasant there will be no soldier'. The petitioners called for concessions on poll tax payments and reorganization in the countryside, where 'now the peasant has a dozen or more commanders instead of one—military officers, fiscals, *voevody*, forest supervisors and so on, some of which are not so much pastors as wolves attacking the flock'. There were bailiffs who did as they liked in the absence of the landlords. Too many people were making too many demands, forcing the peasants to sell their last livestock and belongings, mortgage their children, and take flight, so that the remainder had to pay on their behalf. They were fleeing not to new owners, but abroad—to Poland, Bashkiria, Zaporozhie, and Old Believer communities.

Landowners should be made to pay arrears. Officers and soldiers were to be relieved of tax-collecting duties, and replaced by *voevody* ('good and irreproachable men') with the rank of colonel and subordinated to the governors. Menshikov and his colleagues proposed a partial demobilization of the army, two-thirds of officers and men to be sent home, foreigners and men without estates who needed the salary to remain, 'which will give a dual advantage: firstly the wages [of the men sent home] will stay in the treasury and secondly they will see to their villages and begin to restore them to order'. The memorandum criticized a number of cherished reforms which had brought poverty rather than prosperity. One such was the decree on wide cloth, which ignored the peasants' inability to buy wider looms or even to accommodate them in their homes.[110] The favouring of St Petersburg as against Archangel had had a knock-on effect in the towns along the Dvina and Volga, destroying livelihoods.

'The proliferation of officials and chancelleries all over the country not only creates a great burden on the State but also is very oppressive to the people,' the memorandum continued.

> Moreover, in the article on poll tax it has already been shown what intolerable oppression and ruin are inflicted on the poor peasants by various commanders, and anyone can easily see the oppression that the people has to bear as a result, in that instead of having to address themselves to one official for all matters as previously, now they have to apply to ten or even more. . . . All of these officials have their own separate chancelleries and clerical staff and their own separate courts and everyone fleeces (*volochit*) the poor people for their own particular ends. And all these officials and their chancelleries and their clerical staff all want to make their living, hushing up other disorders which are caused daily by unscrupulous men to the greater oppression of the people or which might occur.

The writers looked forward to a time when (1) there would be enough money for the treasury *and* the people; (2) the army and the navy would be in good repair; (3) all the arsenals and powder stores would be full and (4) fortifications repaired and mended; (5) the merchantry and peasantry would gain relief from taxes; (6) manufactures and factories would multiply; (7) a decent amount of state capital would be amassed in silver coinage, and the perpetual worry over shortage of coin alleviated. 'Most of all, it is hoped that the wretched peasantry, by which all the army and in part the fleet are maintained, may enjoy some respite and order and that many, when they hear of these concessions, will return from flight.'[111] Of course, the authors of this memorandum had their own personal agenda, the major item on which was to redress the balance between the conflicting claims on the peasants' labour of the State and the landowners, in favour of the latter. It is no coincidence that the decade following Peter's death also saw a reduction in the nobility's service requirements. Even so, this grim analysis written by some of the late tsar's closest associates should be borne in mind as we begin to assess Peter's posthumous reputation and legacy.

III.   THE LEGACY

Few would deny that in a number of respects Russia was a very different place in 1725 when Peter died from what it had been in 1682 when he came to the throne, and that Peter himself was the initiator of much that occurred in between, even if the 'single-handedness' of his efforts has sometimes been exaggerated.[112] Many at the time and since sensed something remarkable about the period. Prokopovich's declaration that people who once thought the Russians barbarians 'now have changed their previous stories about us, have erased their ancient histories and begin to speak and write differently'[113] might be dismissed as mere rhetoric were it not for the fact that authors of diverse persuasions expressed similar thoughts. The opening lines of Weber's book on Russia read: 'It must be owned not only by all who have been in Russia themselves, but also by those who have any Notion of the Affairs of the North, that for about these twenty Years past Russia has been entirely reformed and changed.'[114] 'Thanks to [Peter], Russia, the name of which was unknown not long ago,' wrote Campredon, 'now has become the object of attention of the greater part of European powers who seek her friendship, some for fear of seeing her hostile to their interests, others for the sake of the benefits which they hope to obtain through an alliance.'[115] Ivan Nepliuev, looking back on Peter's reign in old age, wrote: 'This monarch brought our fatherland to a level with others; he taught us to recognize that we are people too; in a word, whatever you look at in Russia, all has its beginnings with him and whatever is done henceforth will also derive its source from that beginning.'[116] The notion of metamorphosis, embodied in the epithet 'tsar-transformer' (*Preobrazovatel'*), became a historiographic commonplace. 'Not one nation has ever achieved such a heroic feat as the one achieved by the Russian nation under the leadership of Peter,' wrote Kliuchevsky.[117]

But did change mean 'progress', and did progress mean improvement? Was Russia better or worse off as a result of Peter's reforms? This debate, as we have just seen, began long before Peter's death, and certainly long before the nineteenth-century Westerners and Slavophiles formulated their pro- and anti-Peter agendas. One of the earliest summaries of Russian views was provided by F. J. Strahlenberg, who wrote that 'about the reign of Peter the First there is much difference of opinion'. He first sets out twelve points in Peter's favour, interesting because they purport to be the views of 'reliable Russians' (Strahlenberg did not name his informants): (1) Peter thought out and planned all undertakings; (2) he was brave; (3) he was successful in war and built up the army, the fleet, and fortresses; (4) he propagated the arts and learning; (5) he cleansed religion of superstition; he reformed the law (6), commerce (7), and mining and manufacturing (8); (9) he rewarded his faithful servants, including those of lowly birth, and punished the unworthy; (10) he was steadfast in friendship—for example, with the king of Poland; (11) he was modest and loved hard work (simple dress, working at the lathe, and so on); (12) he issued a new law of inheritance. But Strahlenberg's list of arguments in favour, all expressed very concisely, are outweighed by his arguments against, which are bolstered by specific evidence of misdeeds, corruption of morals, waste of lives and resources, neglect of tradition, alienation of good men and cultivation of the unworthy. The list refers to Peter's childhood, when he was subjected to bad influences (such as Lefort), bad teachers (e.g., Nikita Zotov), isolation from 'good people' at Preobrazhenskoe, 'amusements' and indecent masquerades at Yuletide, the cruelty of Romodanovsky and the Preobrazhensky *prikaz*, Peter's love-affairs, the dismissal of old advisers and the appointment of bad new ones, and so on.[118]

Few members of the Russian élite could afford to be so frank about the shortcomings of Peter's programme in public, even long after his death. The official view was memorably formulated by Mikhail Lomonosov in 1755, in a laudatory speech in which he imagines a man leaving Russia at the beginning of Peter's reign and returning much later. On seeing new buildings and customs, the fleet, the arts, knowledge, even rivers altered in their courses, he would conclude 'that he had been on his travels many centuries, or that all this had been achieved in so short a time by the common efforts of the whole human race or by the creative hand of the Almighty, or, finally, that it was all a vision seen in a dream'.[119] All subsequent Russian monarchs associated themselves in some way with the Petrine legacy. His daughter Elizabeth (in whom 'lived the soul of Peter the Great, who astounded all the world with his victories and triumphs'[120]) exploited it shamelessly, while Catherine II, Peter's 'spiritual daughter', used it selectively—for example, to underline the fact that Russia was part of Europe. As stated in her *Instruction* of 1768: 'The alterations which *Peter the Great* undertook in Russia succeeded with the greater Ease, because the Manners, which prevailed at that Time, and which had been introduced among us by the Conquest of foreign Territories, were quite unsuitable to the Climate. *Peter the First*, by introducing the Manners and Customs of Europe among the European people in his Dominions, found at that Time such Means as even he himself was not sanguine enough to expect.'[121] (This formulation, in fact, rather downplays Peter's achievement. Catherine privately deplored Peter's coarseness and brutality.) The emperor Paul, whose education is said to have embodied Peter's 'ambivalent legacy' of devotion to the common good and authoritarian rule, celebrated his great-grandfather by retrieving Rastrelli's equestrian statue from a shed and setting it up in front of the fortress-like Mikhailovsky palace.[122] Nineteenth-century rulers, too, selected appropriate Petrine attributes. Nicholas I liked to wear his ancestor's dressing-gown. The bicentenary of Peter's death in 1872 allowed another 'great reformer', Alexander II, to cast some of his own activities in the Petrine mould—for example, by bringing Peter's little boat, the 'grandfather of the navy', to Moscow. Perhaps only the slightly built Nicholas II was thoroughly uncomfortable with Peter as a role model, preferring the more 'pious', cautious image of Peter's father and grandfather.[123]

Most of the eighteenth-century Russian élite genuinely admired Peter's achievements, and had no wish to discard the benefits of Westernization, but few wished for a return to the hardships and discomforts of Peter's reign or a resurrection of Peter's terrifying presence.[124] The first serious thinker of noble birth to 'desert the cult of Peter' was Prince Mikhail Shcherbatov (1733–90), who knew the Petrine era better than any of his contemporaries as a result of his work in Peter's archive.[125] Shcherbatov conceded that without Peter Russia would have needed another 200 years to reach its current level of development. There would have been no factories, he alleged, few consumer goods, no trade, no order or regulations in government departments, no proper army, and people would still be sunk in superstition, the boyars proud and arrogant. He praised Peter's promotion of science and rejection of ignorance, his attack on xenophobia, his conquest of coasts, his ports and fleet. But he attacked his cruelty, his subordination of the nobility, his treatment of Alexis and the succession, and his attack on religion, as well as his neglect of Moscow.[126] Russia's first major historian, Nikolai Karamzin (1766–1826), assessed the impact of Peter's reforms even more radically than Shcherbatov. In his view, Russia would have needed 600 years to catch up! But he too believed that 'progress' had been bought at a high price: 'We became citizens of the world but ceased in certain respects to be citizens of Russia. The fault is Peter's.'[127] (His *Memoir* (1810), like Shcherbatov's, could not be published during his lifetime.)

The belief of Shcherbatov and Karamzin (heralded by Lomonosov) that Peter's reforms had caused Russia to 'leap ahead' by several centuries was shared by an unlikely successor to their essentially Enlightenment way of thinking. '[Russia's] backwardness was perceived as an evil even earlier, in the pre-revolutionary period and later,' wrote Stalin in 1928. 'When Peter the Great, who had to deal with more developed countries in the West, feverishly built works and factories for supplying the army and strengthening the country's defences, this was an original attempt to leap out of the framework of backwardness.'[128] It was a commonplace of Marxist–Leninist thinking that Russia had to 'catch up' (and eventually overtake) the West, whatever the cost. In his introductory speech to the Twenty-Second Congress of the Communist Party in 1961 Nikita Khrushchev even boasted that the USSR's standard of living would be higher than the USA's by 1970. But there were dissident views. A. P. Spunde (who died in 1962) described Peter's achievement as 'reactionary, setting back Russia's development by a whole historical epoch'![129] He quotes Prince Viazemsky's alleged remark to Pushkin, while walking past Falconet's *Bronze Horseman* statue, that 'Peter didn't lead Russia forward at all; he only forced it to rear up'.[130]

In the post-Soviet period such views have been voiced openly. The historian Ia. Vodarsky wrote in 1993: 'It has to be admitted that [Peter] did not lead the country on the path of accelerated economic, political and social development, did not force it to "achieve a leap" through several stages. ... On the contrary, these actions to the greatest degree put a brake on Russia's progress and created conditions for holding it back for one and a half centuries!'[131] Anatoly Lanshchikov pursues the 'Peter and progress' theme further, arguing that pre-Petrine Russians were by no means as 'backward' as usually depicted: they were clever (e.g., at trade), resilient, resourceful (as indicated by their building a nation under adverse climatic conditions), and eager to learn, but needed the *freedom* to do so. This was denied by Peter, 'the Bolshevik emperor', who imposed heavier burdens, regulations, and restrictions than hitherto. Thus Peter did not speed up, but rather decelerated, Russia's development, by exacerbating features—tyranny and servitude—that separated it from Europe. 'In the reign of the "Bronze horseman" the whole country turned into one huge hierarchical GULAG and in this way the internal market was destroyed and if there is no internal market industry cannot develop.'[132]

The St Petersburg historian Evgeny Anisimov has elaborated the idea of Peter as 'the creator of the administrative command system and the true ancestor of Stalin', who laid the foundations of the totalitarian state, treating subjects like children with 'the pedagogy of the cudgel', in order to achieve progress in the name of the 'common good'. He argues that Peter destroyed alternatives ('civil society'), notably the Church, and created the 'well-regulated police state' with its reliance on regulations, spying mechanisms, and controls. The crux of the debate is whether Peter promoted and nurtured capitalism in Russia or delayed or even destroyed what there was of it. Anisimov argues that Peter weakened individual enterprise by increasing 'the overriding role of the State in the life of society as a whole'. He 'enslaved' merchants. What was missing was competition, not to mention freedom. The creation of serf manufactories signalled 'a reversion to feudal norms'.[133]

Soviet rulers used Peter and his methods (carefully pruned of unwanted features such as acknowledged reliance upon foreign aid) as models for achieving transformation not only of the material substructure but also of the human resources. This involved creating 'new' men and women and getting rid of the 'old' ones. The sacrifice of individuals, in their thousands or even millions, could be justified in the name of the greater good of the many, especially those who would come after. Peter the Great and Lenin, writes Anisimov, 'combine two different historical periods in their fanatical belief that society must have only one goal—the universal good; a goal, the achievement of which they thought could, and even must, suppress and destroy one part of society in order that the other prosper'.[134] Another historian, Ia. Gordin, writes: 'Peter conceived of himself not simply as a monarch but as a demiurge. He was not simply building a state. He was building a world. In Russian history there is only one analogy to Peter the theomachist (*bogoborets*) and that is Lenin.'[135] But what is notably absent from the Petrine balance sheet, as formulated by Peter himself, is any firm belief that those who survived were the 'chosen', those who perished the 'damned' (enemies of the people), whose extermination was justified on ideological grounds even if the ideological taint was only by association. It should be added that in world history Peter was not unique. The 'charismatic' model of reform carried out by a prophet or leader often included, for non-European nations, 'opening a window into Europe' and exchanging traditional forms (e.g., of administration) for rational ones, often to the accompaniment of great protest from conservative forces.[136] Peter occasionally mentioned his debt to his predecessors, but without ever acknowledging a 'role model'.

A special target for Peter's critics was the financial cost of reform, the wastefulness of conspicuous consumption on prestige projects while the mass of the population languished in poverty and servitude (a charge levelled also at Soviet leaders). Pavel Miliukov, perhaps the first to consider comprehensively the balance sheet of reform, argues that before 1714 there were no reforms not designed to increase income. In the first part of his reign Peter knew only one thing for sure: he had to beat the enemy, no matter what it cost. In a nutshell, 'Russia achieved the status of a European power at the cost of ruining the country.'[137] Building the fleet at Voronezh, for a start, might be condemned as the irresponsible whim of a sea-struck boy. Ships swallowed up a huge portion of the budget, something like 12,000 roubles per ship, and were built of green wood, with wooden rather than iron struts and with odd proportions, not to mention the fact that ships built on a river required modifications of the hull before they could sail on the sea. Even if the workmanship had been of better quality, where were the sailors, the navigators? St Petersburg has attracted even greater wrath. New ports and fortifications were needed on the Baltic, but was it really necessary to build a new *capital* on the periphery, when there was a perfectly decent old one in Russia's heartland? Another of Peter's wasteful projects was his grand design for a system of inland waterways, linking St Petersburg with the Volga and the Volga with the Don at a time when canal building was still in its infancy even in the West. The main section of the project was completed only in the nineteenth century, just when railways were taking over.[138]

Another controversy concerns foreign borrowing. In pre-Petrine Russia the outside world was almost universally perceived as hostile; what with 'Latin guile' and 'Lutheran heresy' to the west, Turks and Tatar 'infidels' to the east, Russia was surrounded by a sea of wickedness.[139] Under Peter borrowing became official policy. 'Firearms were in use among other nations before us; but if they had not reached us to this day, what would have become of Russia and where would she be now?', wrote Prokopovich. 'The same is true of printing, architecture, and the other liberal arts. Wise is the man and the nation which is not ashamed to adopt what is good from strangers and foreigners; foolish and ridiculous is he who will not leave off his bad ways and accept what is good from others.'[140] Stählin published a telling 'anecdote', which is worth quoting at length:

> It would be wrong to say that Peter the Great had a blind love of foreigners and foreign customs and their way of life; but it is evident from all circumstances that he loved foreigners and treated them graciously only for the benefit of his State. . . . Once he said in the presence of a number of Russian gentlemen: 'I know that the marked preference that I give to foreigners is not

pleasing to all my subjects. But I have a variety of subjects: some are intelligent and reasonable and observe that I treat foreigners well and try to get them to stay here in order that they [my subjects] can learn from them and adopt their sciences and arts, for the good of the State and for the evident benefit of my subjects. I also have foolhardy and wicked subjects who do not appreciate or acknowledge my good intentions and wish to remain in the old mire of their ignorance. In their stupidity they despise anything good which is new to them and would willingly hinder it if only they could. They do not reflect on what it was like in our country before I travelled in foreign lands and invited foreigners to Russia and how little I would have achieved without their aid in all my undertakings against our formidable enemies.'[141]

Peter, as we have seen, was neither an iconoclast nor a blind worshipper of things foreign. To quote his own words, 'It is good to build anew, but the old which is good should not be thrown away.'[142] He encouraged the awareness that it was important to become self-sufficient. A petition from the merchants Osip and Fedor Bazhenny stated that they had built a water-powered sawmill on their estate 'on the German model, by themselves, without the help of foreign masters'.[143] A decree of 1723 boasts: 'This paper was made here in a mill and we can make as much of it as we need in this country and not only commission it in France.'[144] As recent studies have shown, reliance upon foreigners during Peter's reign and those of his immediate successors—in government, army, the arts—has been exaggerated, except perhaps in the case of the fleet, which was largely dependent on foreign expertise. To quote Wilhelm Henning, one of Peter's most energetic foreign aides: 'I thank God that the Russian nation in such a short time with such a small number of foreigners has studied and learned with the result that I can run great works, factories and mines with them, although not yet as many as there ought to be, even so with good profit. But without increasing the number of good foreign masters it will be impossible to prosper and it would be to the benefit of the State to increase mining and manufacturing through their teaching of expertise.'[145]

The debate about 'foreign borrowing' is linked with the controversy over cultural change in the wider sense. Much condemnation of Peter is based on admiration for what preceded him, most forcefully expressed by Slavophiles in the 1830s–1850s. In the words of Konstantin Aksakov, the government 'must understand the spirit of Russia and embrace Russian principles, which have been rejected since Peter's day'.[146] He and his fellow thinkers paint a rosy picture of Muscovite Russia, with its harmonious relationship between tsar and people and its indigenous religious culture. Latter-day Westerners have taken a different view. Far from being a 'Slavophile Utopia', N. I. Ulianov argued, Muscovite development was 'scarcely superior to that of Khiva or Bukhara in the nineteenth century . . . Russia could not delay reform if it did not want to perish and be turned into a colony.' Peter was right. European culture had to be 'captured in battle'.[147] Ulianov selects examples of Russia's 'backwardness' before Peter: use of letters for numbers, feeble knowledge of fractions and geometry, ignorance of the theories of Copernicus and Newton, of botany and biology. He describes the impact of the Petrine reforms as the beginning of the liberation of his country from the 'medieval theocratic world-view'.[148]

Neither assessment is entirely satisfactory. Peter's methods succeeded in creating Westernized pockets in Russia, notably St Petersburg, that giant the-atrical set where Russian 'actors' mimicked foreigners, but lost no time in fleeing the public eye, shedding the restricting 'German' costumes, and relaxing in capacious garments and comfortable old traditions. In this respect, the charge made against Peter by Slavophiles, that he created a 'split' in Russian society, is ill-aimed. On the contrary, it could be argued that he *failed* sufficiently to remodel the culture and the aspirations of the élite. In Peter Chaadaev's famous words, Russians picked up the 'cloak of civilization' thrown to them by Peter, but not civilization itself.[149] Even the more 'advanced' nobles took what they fancied from 'Westernization' (fashions, houses, French, foreign travel, wine, and so on), but discarded what they dis-liked (the entail law, greater social mobility, scientific training, and so on).[150] They spurned the Church as a career (it was in the hands of a hereditary ecclesiastical caste) and the legal profession (a branch of the administration run by clerks). They failed to develop a strong corporate identity. Only a handful yearned for Western political institutions. The consequences of Peter's 'incomplete' reform, some might argue, are evident right down to the present day.

The Petrine legacy has always been subject to reassessment in periods of upheaval and reform, especially with reference to the redrawing of boundaries between state and private activity. Consider, for example, the terms in which, in 1864, the editors of the journal *Den'* discussed the *zemstvo* Act, which intro-duced an element of elected self-government into the provinces: 'Society right up to the present is still unable to free itself from Petrine tutelage and right up to the present remains, in spite of all the government's efforts, the same kind of state-society (*shtats-obshchestvo*) as was created in Peter's reign.... In order that state and society should find an appropriate balance it is vital to renounce the traditions of Petrine reform.'[151] S. M. Solov'ev, also writing in the 1860s, acknowledged the dangers of periods of reform:

> The moral condition of Old Russian society was highly unsatisfactory, as we have seen. Yet the movement which had begun in the latter half of the seven-teenth century and the struggle which ensued could only make matters worse. However feeble the moral condition of a given society, if it is alive and does not collapse altogether it means that at least some moral restraints and ties survive in order to prevent it from disintegrating completely. But if that society is set in motion and is convulsed in a violent revolution, the old ties are bound to slacken and sometimes may snap completely. Society is then subjected to powerful moral vacillation, insecurity and upheaval until the moral restraints

are made fast again or replaced by new ones. There is some truth in the saying that a period of transition is the worst time of all from the point of view of social morality.[152]

These statements strike strong contemporary chords. In the Petrine era the old monolithic Orthodox medieval world-view, valid for boyar and peasant alike, according to which behaviour was determined by authority and custom, was challenged by the dissidence and questioning of individuals, of which Peter represented the most powerful example in his challenge to the traditional image of the Orthodox ruler. The walls of the citadel of medieval Muscovy, whereby subjects were locked in and women were locked up, were breached, both by foreigners coming in and Russians going out. Peter's own example in 1697–8 was vital here. Peter, unable to stay long in one place, increased the mobility of the Russian nation, for good and for ill, sending young men abroad, uprooting nobles and their families from Moscow to St Petersburg, transferring whole villages of peasants *en masse* to work on major projects, and causing people to flee from ever-increasing burdens. The superiority of Old Russia, once upheld unquestioningly by guardians of the true faith, was challenged by the need to learn from 'heretics'. Peter's device 'I am a student and seek teachers' summed it up. But what gave the reform its impetus—the example of the tsar himself—also set its limits, for this was reform from above. Pluralism, the glimmerings, however feeble, of civil society, were killed at birth, because Peter could not break with authoritarian rule, and found no strong desire among his subjects to do so: they went from being 'worthless slaves' to being numbers in the Table of Ranks.

Some of the above may bring to mind Russia in the 1980s and Mikhail Gorbachev, a reformer in the 'Petrine' mould who challenged old orthodoxies, broke down walls, changed his titles, acknowledged the need to learn from the West, and travelled there himself, creating a new image for Soviet leaders. But whereas Peter presided over the consolidation and expansion of empire, Gorbachev precipitated its collapse. In turn, frustrated, disappointed Russians quote Peter's example to criticize the incompetence and feebleness of post-Soviet rulers. In the early 1990s the journal *Dialog*, in a series of 'think-pieces' on the lessons of history, painted a bleak picture of 'Russia humiliated and robbed, cut off from seas and without her own fleet ... history repeats itself. Our dramatic experience again calls to life the vitally necessary figure of a reformer. Whoever this contemporary figure may be, he will find Peter's experience useful.'[153]

Military circles offered their own slant. An article in the journal *Armiia* declared that Peter helped to create the 'military-patriotic consciousness of the Russian people and shaped their attitude towards service, honour and dignity ... It is useful to remember this Petrine lesson today. Our period of "self-criticism", of "wandering among the ruins" has dragged on too long, weakening people's will and sapping their energy'.[154] Interviews with 'ordinary' people reveal analogous views. Maxim, aged seventeen, told an

American sociologist: 'Peter had enormous strength of will; he slept only four hours a day, the rest of the time he gave over to work. Peter brought about a strengthening of the Russian fleet, won back some lands which belonged to Russia. It was a prosperous country then.'[155] The tercentenary of the founding of the Russian navy in 1996 provided much scope for contrasting the naval glories of the Petrine era with the sorry spectacle of the decaying Soviet fleet and the loss of Black Sea bases and vessels.[156] Today's rulers can take a hint. In a TV interview in 1993, when asked to name a hero from Russian history, Boris Yeltsin selected Peter. 'But you know, that Peter I himself cut off heads?', asked the interviewer. 'Yes, of course I know that. But on the other hand he did a lot for Russia. This also must be borne in mind,' Yeltsin replied.[157]

Peter is utilized by various organizations in Russia today both as a forward-looking symbol of progress—as logo for various firms selling modern technology, advertisements for the Menatep Bank ('a strong bank for a strong country'), or the 'Peter the Great' skyscraper on the outskirts of St Petersburg—and also, perversely, as a symbol of Russianness. Petrine images embellish Russian products in an often unequal competition with Western rivals. For example, 'Petrovskoe' beer, made at the Stenka Razin factory in St Petersburg, bears a Bronze Horseman design. The pack of 'Peter I' cigarettes bears a double eagle and the legend: 'These unique cigarettes of highest quality have been created using superior types of tobacco which were purveyed to the court of Peter I from Europe and are capable of satisfying the most discriminating connoisseur who believes in the revival of the traditions and greatness of the Russian land.'[158]

How would Peter himself react to all this? Frenetically active right up to his last illness, which struck him down well before old age forced him to sit back and contemplate his achievements, Peter had neither the time nor the temperament to indulge in self-assessments. In this respect it is instructive to return to the image with which this book opened, of Peter (Pygmalion) fashioning a statue of the new Russia (Galatea). This was an image adopted, if not designed, by Peter himself, used on his personal seal in the 1710s, proposed for the summit of a triumphal column (not completed), included on Rastrelli's bronze bust, and finally depicted on one of the banners carried in his funeral cortège.[159] This allegorical composition was evidently regarded as Peter's emblem, the symbol of his reform. But there is a variation, of a sculptor carving a statue of Peter: Peter himself (appropriately, the rock) was identified with Russia. In departing the scene, Peter left a challenging model for his successors, not least because their offspring no longer had the hereditary right to rule, but in theory were supposed to earn the honour. Peter's was a tough act to follow, and one which Russia's rulers despair of emulating. One could add that the day when Peter the Great and his reforms cease to be a live issue in Russia will be the day when Russia finally resolves the 'cursed question' of its true identity and its relationship with the outside world.

Notes

PREFACE

1. 'Slovo na pokhvalu blazhennye i vernodostoinye pamiati Petra Velikogo' (1726), in Grebeniuk, 298.
2. Peter's note, probably early 1722, in *ZA*, 115.
3. See, e.g., A. N. Medushevsky, 'Petrovskaia reforma gosudarstvennogo apparata', in F. Shelov-Kovediaev, ed., *Reformy vtoroi poloviny XVII–XX v.: podgotovka, provedenie, rezul'taty* (M, 1989), 76, where he mentions the absence of memoirs or archives of Petrine civil servants.
4. Nartov, pp. xiv–xviii.
5. Stählin, 8.
6. I. I. Golikov, *Anekdoty, kasaiushchiesia do gosudaria imperatora Petra Velikogo*, quoted in E. V. Anisimov, ed., *Petr Velikii. Vospominaniia. Dnevnikovye zapisi. Anekdoty* (SPb., 1993), 370.

CHAPTER 1: BEGINNINGS

1. A. P. Sumarokov, 'Rossiiskii Vifleem', in *Polnoe sobranie vsekh sochinenii* (M, 1787), 6:303.
2. *Sbornik*, I:1; length = 11 vershok, dated 29 June 1672.
3. See N. Aristov, 'Pervonachal'noe obrazovanie Petra Velikogo', *Russkii arkhiv*, 1318 (1875), 471. On the 'play' troops, see p. 3 below.
4. R. A. Simonov, 'Kogda rodilsia Petr I?', *Vspomogatel'nye istoricheskie distsipliny*, 21 (1990), 158–69. Palace records were published as *Dvortsovye razriady*, see 3: 889; and *Dopolneniia k tomu III dvortsovykh razriadov* (SPb., 1854), 463, 469.
5. On calendar reform, see below, p. 249.
6. *PiB*. 11: 281.
7. For more information on Peter's mother and other relatives, see pp. 390–1.
8. For more on royal women, see L. A. J. Hughes, *Sophia Regent of Russia 1657–1704* (New Haven, 1990), 16–22.
9. On the Polish source for this story (*Diariusz zaboystwa tyranskiego senatorow moskiewskich*) see L. Hughes, '"Ambitious and Daring above her Sex": Tsarevna Sophia Alekseevna (1657– 1704) in Foreigners' Accounts', *Oxford Slavonic Papers*, 21 (1988), 65–89.
10. P. Krekshin, 'Kratkoe opisanie blazhenykh del velikogo gosudaria, imperatora Petra Velikogo, Samoderzhtsa Vserossiiskogo', in N. Sakharov, ed., *Zapiski russkikh liudei* (SPb., 1841), 8–9.
11. The best studies, based on archival sources, include M. M. Bogoslovsky's *Petr I. Materialy dlia biografii*, 5 vols (M, 1940–8), and N. Pogodin's *Semnadtsat' pervykh let v zhizni imp. Petra Velikogo 1672–1689* (M, 1875).
12. Aristov, 'Pervonachal'noe obrazovanie', 478.
13. See below, pp. 419–20.
14. See S. Baron, 'Shipbuilding and Seafaring in 16th-Century Russia', in D. C. Waugh, ed., *Essays in Honor of A. A. Zimin* (Columbus, Oh., 1983), pp. 102–29.
15. See below, p. 420.

16. Aristov, 'Pervonachal'noe obrazovanie', pp. 480–1. On Zotov, see below, p. 423.

17. Aristov points out that alphabet books belonging to Peter are mentioned as late as 1683 (ibid., 480). In 1683 an *azbuka* was sent to the binders.

18. See L. A. J. Hughes, 'The Moscow Armoury and Innovations in 17th-Century Muscovite Art', *CASS*, 13 (1979), 204–23; *idem.*, *Sophia*, 138–41.

19. See below, pp. 240–1.

20. *PSZ*, 1, no. 607 (6 Aug. 1675). On dress, see below, pp. 280–8.

21. In the words of I. de Madariaga, 'The Russian Nobility in the Seventeenth and Eighteenth Centuries', in H. M. Scott, ed. *The European Nobilities 1600–1800, Eastern Europe* (London, 1995), 22: 'no Russian word precisely expressed the Western concept of nobility'.

22. R. O. Crummey, *Aristocrats and Servitors: The Boyar Elite in Russia, 1613–1689* (Princeton, 1983).

23. See C. B. Stevens, *Soldiers on the Steppe. Army Reform and Social Change in Early Modern Russia* (De Kalb, Ill., 1995).

24. See L. A. J. Hughes, 'Strel'tsy', *MERSH*, 37 (1984), 205–10.

25. Figures for 1678 from Ia. E. Vodarsky, in J. M. Hittle, *The Service City. State and Townsmen in Russia, 1600–1800* (Cambridge, Mass., 1979), 32.

26. R. Hellie, *Slavery in Russia, 1450–1725* (Chicago, 1982), 688–9.

27. E. V. Anisimov, 'The Imperial Heritage of Peter the Great in the Foreign Policy of his Early Successors', in H. Ragsdale, ed., *Imperial Russian Foreign Policy* (Cambridge, 1993), 22.

28. L. A. Nikiforov, 'Rossiia v sisteme evropeiskikh derzhav v pervoi chetverti XVIII v.', in *RPR*, 11.

29. The material in this section is condensed from my book *Sophia Regent of Russia*, which contains full documentation and further discussion of all the events and issues surveyed here.

30. F. de la Neuville, *A Curious and New Account of Muscovy in the Year 1689*, ed. L. Hughes (London, 1994), 15.

31. See Hughes, *Sophia*, 52–88, and *idem*, 'Sofia Alekseevna and the Moscow Rebellion of 1682', *SEER*, 63 (1985), 518–39. See discussion in Neuville, *Curious and New Account*, p. xxxii.

32. See L. A. J. Hughes, 'Sophia, "Autocrat of All the Russias": Titles, Ritual and Eulogy in the Regency of Sophia Alekseevna (1682–89)', *CSP*, 28 (1986), 266–86.

33. J. Banks, *A New History of the Life and Reign of Czar Peter the Great, Emperor of All Russia, and Father of his Country* (London, 1740), 48.

34. Treaty printed in *PSZ*, 2: no. 1186, pp. 770–86. See L. R. Lewitter, 'The Russo–Polish Treaty of 1686 and its Implications', *Polish Review*, 9 (1964), no. 3, 5–29; no. 4, 21–37. The Polish *sejm* ratified the treaty only in 1710. For a more detailed examination of foreign affairs in the 1680s, see Hughes, *Sophia*, 179–217.

35. *PSZ*, 3: no. 1330, pp. 7–8, no. 1332, pp. 9–10.

36. For background, see L. A. J. Hughes, 'V. T. Postnikov's 1687 Mission to London', *SEER*, 68 (1990), 447–60.

37. See Soloviev, 142–8 (Tsykler), 173–4 (1698 rebellion).

38. Nartov, 100–1.

39. *The Antidote, or an Enquiry into the Merits of a Book, Entitled a Journey into Siberia . . ., by a Lover of Truth* (London, 1772), 10.

40. There are some exceptions: e.g., Bogoslovsky, *Petr I*, covers the years 1672–99.

41. *PiB*, I: 13–14. (It seems likely that this letter was 'ghost-written' by one or more of Peter's advisers.)

42. *PSZ*, 3, no. 1351, pp. 39–40.

43. Ibid., no. 1388, pp. 86–7 (no date, 1690).

44. J. Billington, *The Icon and the Axe* (New York, 1970), 173.

45. *PSZ*, 3, no. 1358, pp. 46–7 (29 Oct. 1689).

46. On Medvedev, see A. P. Bogdanov, 'Sil'vestr Medvedev', *VI*, 1988, no. 2, pp. 84–98.

47. *PSZ*, 3, no. 1362, pp. 49–52 (23 Dec. 1689).

48. Kurakin, 379.

49. N. Pogodin, 'Petr Pervyi; Pervye gody edinoderzhaviia, 1689–1694', *Russkii arkhiv*, 1879, vol. 1, p. 9.

50. Ibid., 10.

51. Ibid., 11: excerpt from the testament of Patriarch Joachim, 17 Mar. 1690.

52. *DR*, 4: 526–7. Alexis Alekseevich, then the heir apparent, died in 1670, aged sixteen.

53. *PSZ*, 3: no. 1472, p. 160 (7 July 1693).

54. *Sbornik*, 1: 149.

55. *PSZ*, 3: no. 1594, pp. 336–75 (1 Sept. 1697).

56. See below, p. 333.

57. *DR*, 4: 552–5. *Sbornik Mukhanova*, 2nd edn. (SPb., 1866), 555–6, dates it, incorrectly, as 1689.

58. Bergholz, 1724, 43.

59. Kurakin, 381–2.

60. The original of the diary is in the Rossiiskii Gosudarstvennyi Voenno-Istoricheskii Arkhiv, f. 846, op. 15, ed. khr. 1–7. I am indebted to Paul Dukes and Graeme Herd for making available transcripts and photocopies. See also G. Herd, 'General Patrick Gordon of Auchleuchries—a Scot in Seventeenth-Century Russian Service' (Ph.D. thesis, Aberdeen, 1994), and Pogodin, 'Petr Pervyi', 11–12.

61. *Sbornik*, 1: 116–17 ('good English cloth, dark grey ... chamberlain Gavrila Ivanovich Golovkin ordered this cloth to be purchased for German dress and the money to be paid (75 R.)' (p. 117)), and many other entries. See also E. Iu. Moiseenko, 'Plat'e rubezha XVII i XVIII vekov iz "Garderoba Petra I"', in *Kul'tura i iskusstvo Rossii XVIII veka. Novye materialy i issledovaniia. Sbornik statei* (L, 1981), 60–1.

62. *Sbornik*, 1: 133–5.

63. *DR*, 4: 1 Aug. commemorated the baptism of Rus in the tenth century.

64. Pogodin, 'Petr Pervyi', 13–14.

65. Ibid., 36.

66. Ibid., 43; *DR*, 4: 821–2.

67. *DR*, 4: 794–5.

68. Ibid., 1049. The Siberian *tsarevichi* (princes) were descendants of Tatar khans conquered by Moscow in the sixteenth century. They performed ceremonial duties at the tsars' court.

69. Ibid., 1033; same format 6 Jan. 1698: ibid., 1090–1.

70. A. Kartsov, *Istoriia leib-gvardii Semenovskogo polka. 1685–1852*, vol. 1 (SPb., 1852), 3–5, and 17, appendix, p. 3. On the 'playmate regiments', see entry by D. Schlafly under that heading in *MERSH*, 28 (1982), 119–22.

71. *Sbornik*, 1: 148.

72. Kartsov, *Istoriia*, 18–20 (including Princes Vasily and Grigory Dolgoruky, Mikhail Golitsyn).

73. Kurakin, 379; see R. Warner, 'The Kožuchovo Campaign of 1697', *JGO*, 13/4 (1965), 487–96.

74. On the role of these two men in Peter's 'mock court', see below, pp. 98–100. In some sources they are referred to as the 'tsars' of Preobrazhenskoe and Semenovskoe.

75. See, e.g., correspondence with Austria, in which this is the main theme: Bantysh-Kamensky, 1: 35–6 (letters of 1691–2).

76. Sir Paul Rycant, 22 Mar. 1695: PRO SP Hamburg 82/19, f. 33.

77. See N. I. Pavlenko, *Petr Velikii* (M, 1990), 48; Herd, 'General Patrick Gordon'.

78. *PiB*, 1: 36 (16 Apr. 1695, letter to F. M. Apraksin.)

79. Kartsov, p. 25. On Peter's military career, see below, p. 363.

80. Soloviev, 123; Pavlenko, *Petr Velikii*, 39.

81. Pavlenko, *Petr Velikii*, 53. For an account of the campaign by Charles Whitworth (1708), based on Gordon, see BL, Add. MS37356, ff. 425–52. On Kalmyks, see pp. 69–70.

82. N. Novikov, 'Sozdanie voenno-morskogo flota v Rossii pri Petre I', *Partiino-politicheskaia rabota v VMF*, 1941, no. 7, 45–6.

83. Herd, 'General Patrick Gordon', 185.

84. See details in R. Wortman, *Scenarios of Power. Myth and Ceremony in Russian Monarchy* (Princeton, 1995), vol. 1, 42–4.

85. E. Mozgovaia, 'Obraz Petra I-imperatora v proizvedeniiakh tvorchestva Bartolomeo Karlo Rastrelli', in *Monarkhiia i narodovlastie v kul'ture prosveshcheniia* (M, 1995), 4. See below, pp. 271–3.

86. On sculpture in the round (frowned on by the Church), see below pp. 228–31.

87. He died in May 1692. See below, p. 393.

88. *Sbornik*, 1: 127. See also J. Cracraft, *The Petrine Revolution in Russian Imagery* (Chicago, 1997), which appeared after this book had gone to press.

89. *Sbornik*, 1: 119.

90. Ibid., 143–4.

91. Ibid., 161–2.

92. Ibid., 154.

93. See Hughes, 'Moscow Armoury'.

94. *Sbornik*, 1: 152.

95. Portrait of 1683–4, National Portrait Gallery, London.

96. Described in A. Vasil'chikov, 'O novom portrete Petra Velikogo', *Drevniaia i novaia Rossiia*, 3 (1877), 325–6.

97. I. G. Spassky and E. Shchukina, *Medals and Coins of the Age of Peter the Great* (L, 1974), illustrations 5 and 6.

CHAPTER 2: RUSSIA AND THE WORLD: 1696–1725

1. Gavriil Buzhinsky, in foreword to a translation of Pufendorf's *Introduction to European History* (1718) in Grebeniuk, 85.

    There is a vast bibliography on early modern European foreign policy. The following have been particularly useful for the background to this chapter: R. Hatton, *Charles XII of Sweden* (London, 1968); D. McKay and H. M. Scott, *The Rise of the Great Powers, 1648–1815* (London, 1983); M. S. Anderson, *Europe in the Eighteenth Century*, 3rd edn. (London, 1987); D. Kirby, *Northern Europe in the Early Modern Period. The Baltic World 1492–1772* (London, 1990); *The New Cambridge Modern History*, vol. 6: *The Rise of Great Britain and Russia 1688–1725*, (Cambridge, 1970).

2. See E. V. Anisimov, 'The Imperial Heritage of Peter the Great in the Foreign Policy of his Early Successors', in H. Ragsdale, ed., *Imperial Russian Foreign Policy* (Cambridge, 1993), 21.

3. N. Karamzin 'Zapiska o drevnei i novoi Rossii' (1811). In Pushkin's poem Evgeny confronts Falconet's equestrian statue of Peter in protest at the death of his fiancée in a flood.

4. B. S. Tel'pukhovsky, *Severnaia voina* (M, 1946), 15.

5. See, e.g., M. Iasiukov, ' "Nel'zia dolgo khodit' mezhdu razvalinami". Rasskaz o tom, kak Petr I reformiroval rossiiskuiu armiiu', *Armiia*, 1992, nos 11/12, 70–2. (This issue had an introduction by Defence Minister P. S. Grachev entitled 'A Strong Army Raises a Country's Self-Respect'.)

6. See arguments in vol. 4 of Kliuchevsky's *Kurs russkoi istorii* (various editions), the Petrine sections of which were published in English as *Peter the Great* (New York, 1956). Modern historians tend to agree: see R. Hellie, 'The Petrine Army: Continuity, Change, Impact', *CASS*, 8 (1974), 237–53; W. C. Fuller, *Strategy and Power in Russia 1600–1914* (New York, 1992); and others.

7. *London Gazette*, no. 3217 (7–10 Sep. 1696).

8. P. Pekarsky, *Nauka i literatura pri Petre Velikom* (M, 1862), 1: 364.

9. See, e.g., R. E. Jones, 'Opening a Window on the South: Russia and the Black Sea 1695–1792', in *WOR*, 123–9.

10. *PSZ*, 3: no. 1569, pp. 274–6 (29 Jan./8 Feb. 1697).

11. Bantysh-Kamensky, 1: 38. See letter from Lefort in Amsterdam, with reports of 4,000 or 5,000 janissaries killed: A. Babkin, 'Pis'ma Frantsa i Petra Lefortov o "Velikom posol'stve" ', *VI*, 1976, no. 4, 129.

12. Soloviev, 137.

13. Babkin, 'Pis'ma Frantsa', 124–5. On Lefort, see below, p. 422.

14. See analysis in V. E. Vozgrin, *Rossiia i evropeiskie strany v gody Severnoi voiny* (L, 1986), 280.

15. See discussion in A. M. Panchenko, 'Nachalo petrovskoi reformy: ideinaia podelka', in *XVIII vek*, vol. 16 (L, 1989), 15.

16. Ia. E. Vodarsky, 'Petr I', *VI*, 1993, no. 6, 65.

17. Bantysh-Kamensky, 1: 38–9.

18. 'On 16 January 1698 the great sovereign [titles] Peter Alekseevich commanded the boyar Fedor Alekseevich Golovin to serve in the Postal Drivers' chancellery', *DR*, 4: 1066, is a typical entry.

19. Babkin, 'Pis'ma Frantsa', 126–7.

20. Vozgrin, *Rossiia*, 63–5. A detailed contemporary account of the incident, from the Russian point of view, is found in P. P. Shafirov, *A Discourse Concerning the Just Causes of the War between Sweden and Russia: 1700–1721* ed. and introd. W. E. Butler (Dobbs Ferry, NY, 1973).

21. *PiB*, 1: no. 151. The reference is to the high price allegedly charged for exchanging winter sledges for wagons.

22. Bantysh-Kamensky, 4: 208.

23. Ibid., 205–6.

24. Ibid., 207.

25. On Peter's attitude to, and role in, the Polish election, see A. Kaminski, *Republic vs Autocracy. Poland-Lithuania and Russia 1686–1697* (Cambridge, Mass., 1993), 256–75; L. Lewitter, 'Russia, Poland and the Baltic, 1697–1721', *Historical Journal*, 11 (1968), 3–34.

26. Vozgrin, *Rossiia*, 75.

27. Korb, 1:1.

28. *PSZ*, 3: no. 1586, pp. 322–5 (24 May 1697), no. 1598, p. 328 (22 June 1697).

29. See L. A. J. Hughes, *Sophia Regent of Russia 1657–1704* (New Haven, 1990), 196–7.

30. In a dispatch of June 1692 the Dutch ambassador in Moscow, Johann van Keller, had written of Peter's support for King William's campaign against the French: N. Pogodin, 'Petr Pervyi: Pervye gody edinoderzhaviia, 1689–1694', *Russkii arkhiv*, 1879, vol. 1, p. 30.

31. See M. M. Bogoslovsky, 'Petr I v Anglii v 1698', *Institut istorii. Moskva. Trudy*, 1 (1926), 393–432.

32. See J. Hartley, 'England Enjoys the "Spectacle of a Northern Barbarian". The Reception of Peter I and Alexander I in England', in *WOR*,

11–18. As she points out, profits on sales of tobacco were never realized. On the immediate background to Anglo–Russian relations, see L. A. J. Hughes, 'V. T. Postnikov's 1687 Mission to London', *SEER*, 68 (1990), 447–60.

33. Quoted in L. Loewenson, 'People Peter the Great Met in England. Moses Stringer, Chymist and Physician', *SEER*, 37 (1959), 459.

34. See below, p. 454. For the theory that Peter may have visited Venice, see S. O. Androsov, 'Petr I v Venetsii', *VI*, 1995, no. 3, 129–35. The visit would have had to take place on 19–20 July, allowing Peter just one day in Venice.

35. In June 1698, 672 persons—Dutch, Danes, Swedes—arrived at Archangel, among them 345 sailors and 51 apothecaries. In Britain Peter hired John Perry, Joseph Nye, and Henry Farquharson, among others. On their careers, see A. G. Cross, *'By the Banks of the Neva.' Chapters from the Lives and Careers of the British in Eighteenth-Century Russia* (Cambridge, 1996).

36. Babkin, 'Pis'ma Frantsa', 129.

37. PRO SP 95/14, f. 276 (6 Apr. 1695, Robinson to duke of Shrewsbury). Lefort's letter dated 16 Feb.

38. Shafirov, *Discourse*, 348. See also Peter's declaration to his son Alexis in 1715 that the Swedes had 'cut off from us all Commerce with the Rest of the World': *The Tryal of the Czarewitz Alexis Petrowitz, who was Condemn'd at Petersbourg, on the 25th of June, 1718* (London, 1725), 4.

39. McKay and Scott, *Rise of the Great Powers*, 79–80. Bantysh-Kamensky, 1: 236–7.

40. *PSZ*, 3: no. 1660, pp. 562–8. On Voznitsyn's negotiation of the truce, see M. M. Bogoslovsky, *Petr I. Materialy dlia biografii*, vol. 3 (M, 1946), 345–454.

41. On Ukraintsev's mission, see Bogoslovsky, *Petr I*, vol. 5 (M, 1948). Peter accompanied the Russian flotilla, a show of strength to impress the Turks, as far as Kerch.

42. *PSZ*, 4: 66–72.

43. *PiB*, 1: 390.

44. *PiB*, 9: 69 (3 Feb. 1709). (On Mazepa, see pp. 35–7 below.) The 'internal upheavals' were the Time of Troubles at the beginning of the century. In 1608 Tsar Vasily Shuisky, fearing for his precarious crown, accepted Swedish help against Poland in return for ceding the province of Kexholm and renouncing claims to Livonia. In 1611 the Swedes took Novgorod. By the 1617 Treaty of Stolbovo the Swedes evacuated Novgorod, but retained Kexholm and Ingria.

45. *PiB*, 87: 460 (13–14 Nov. 1709, to Menshikov). Same to G. F. Dolgoruky, ibid., 462.

46. Bantysh-Kamensky, 4: 208.

47. Ibid., 213: 'nasledstvennyia onye zemli paki k Rossii prisoedineny'.

48. Shafirov, *Discourse*, 242.

49. Ibid., 10.

50. Ibid., 236, 240.

51. Vozgrin, *Rossiia*, 85–6, believes that the treaty was not particularly advantageous to Sweden.

52. Soloviev, 250.

53. See Hatton, *Charles XII*, 155–7; A. Rothstein, *Peter the Great and Marlborough. Politics and Diplomacy in Converging Wars* (Basingstoke, 1986), 39–40, 59.

54. Soloviev, 249.

55. Ibid., 242. See Hatton, *Charles XII*, and Kirby, *Northern Europe*, for a different view.

56. Soloviev, 259.

57. See above, p. 17.

58. Bantysh-Kamensky, 4: 209. (*Kniga Marsova, ili voinskikh del* (SPb. 1713/ 1766), starts with Nöteborg in 1702.)

59. *PiB*, 2: 65 (5 June 1702).

60. Ibid., 52 (letter of 13 Oct.). In Swedish, Nöteborg also means new fortress.

61. *PSZ*, 4: no. 1991, pp. 267–8 (19/30 Aug. 1704).

62. See arguments in Fuller, *Strategy*, 75–6; V. A. Artamonov, *Rossiia i Rech' Pospolitaia posle Poltavskoi pobedy (1709–1714)* (M, 1990), 188: 'the Russo–Polish alliance prevented the Swedes from uniting the Poles under the slogan imposed on them of reconquering the duchies of Smolensk and Kiev.'

63. On the campaign from the Swedish point of view, see P. Englund, *The Battle of Poltava. The Birth of the Russian Empire* (London, 1992), trans. from Swedish.

64. Fuller, *Strategy*, 72.

65. Quoted in Rothstein, *Peter the Great*, 72.

66. See Bantysh-Kamensky, 1: 43.

67. *PiB*, 5: 60 (Jan. 1707). On Huyssen, see below, pp. 430–1.

68. See detailed account in Rothstein, *Peter the Great*, 79–94. Matveev's incarceration in a debtor's prison in London in July 1708 and the subsequent Russian protest led to Queen Anne's Diplomatic Privileges Act of 1708, an act of international importance.

69. To Count Westerloo, 10 Dec., quoted in Rothstein, *Peter the Great*, 67

70. Nikiforov, 'Rossiia', 18.

71. V. N. Berkh, *Zhizneopisanie gen.-adm. F. M. Apraksina* (SPb., 1825), 8–9.

72. *PSZ*, 4: no. 2149, pp. 380–1 (6 May 1707).

73. Ibid., no. 2155, p. 383 (13 Aug. 1707).

74. Letter in *ZA*, 196.

75. *PiB*, 7(i): 28.

76. Ibid., 138 (14 Apr. 1708), 166 (14 May).

77. J. P. LeDonne, *Absolutism and Ruling Class. The Formation of the Russian Political Order 1700–1825* (Oxford, 1991), 69. See below, pp. 113–16.

78. V. S. Bobylev, *Vneshniaia politika Rossii epokhi Petra I* (M, 1990), 51.

79. C. Whitworth, Dispatches, 1704–8, in *SIRIO*, 50: 61–2.

80. *PiB*, 8: 72–3 (9 Aug. 1708).

81. See, e.g., V. E. Shutoy, *Bor'ba narodnykh mass protiv nashestviia armii Karla XII 1700–1709* (M, 1958).

82. See Whitworth, *SIRIO*, 50: 30–1. Rebel action continued, and Dolgoruky entered Cherkassk only on 27 July. See below, pp. 456–7.

83. *PiB*, 11(ii): 154, 155 (28 Sept. 1711).

84. T. Mackiv, *English Reports on Mazepa 1687–1709* (New York, Munich and Toronto, 1983), 2, 41; the agreement could have been made in either Feb./ Mar. 1708 or May/June 1708; Bantysh-Kamensky, 4: 209. (Advice from Swedish chancellor Piper in Sept. 1705.)

85. V. E. Vozgrin, *Istoricheskie sud'by krymskikh tatar* (M, 1992), 234–7.

86. See O. Subtelny, 'Mazepa, Peter I, and the Question of Treason', *Harvard Ukrainian Studies*, 2 (1978), 158–84.
87. Quoted in Mackiv, *English Reports*, 8.
88. Soloviev, 14.
89. Subtelny, 'Mazepa', 166–8, 169. Mazepa's motives are derived from an account sent by Pylyp Orlyk, chancellor of the Host, to Archbishop Stefan Iavorsky in June 1721.
90. Subtelny notes the reference to a contractual principle based on custom: 'We should serve our sovereigns because they protect us, but if they will no longer defend us, then we owe them no more service', on which he believed Mazepa based his relationship with Moscow (ibid., 170–1, 175).
91. C. Whitworth, *An Account of Russia as it was in the Year 1710. Rossiia v nachale XVIII veka. Sochineniia Ch. Uitvorta* (M-L, 1988), 14. A longer account in a dispatch to Henry Boyle, PRO SP 91/5, is found in Mackiv, *English Reports*, 152–3.
92. *PiB*, 8: 237 (27 Oct. 1708).
93. Ibid., 254 (30 Oct. 1708).
94. Ibid., 253 (30 Oct. 1708, to F. M. Apraksin).
95. See Subtelny's argument, 'Mazepa', 177, that the 'patrimonially oriented Muscovite conception of *izmena* (treason) had little impact in Ukraine', and that therefore Mazepa's betrayal of Orthodoxy was cited instead.
96. *PiB*, 8: 257–9 (30 Oct. 1708).
97. Ibid., 276–84.
98. *PSZ*, 4: no. 2213, p. 431 (12 Nov. 1708). See also nos 2210, 2211, 2212, 2224. On excommunication for treason as an example of the assertion of secular power, see discussion in V. M. Zhivov, 'Kul'turnye reformy v sisteme preobrazovaniia Petra I', in *Iz istorii russkoi kul'tury. Tom III. (XVII–nachalo XVIII veka)* (M, 1996) 539–40, and Subtelny, 'Mazepa', 174–5. The anathematization was read out in churches in Ukraine on the first Sunday of Lent until 1869.
99. Subtelny, 'Mazepa', 180; *PiB*, 9: 321.
100. Dispatches of 18 and 27 Oct. to Henry Boyle (PRO SPF, Sweden, SP 95, vol. 17), quoted in Mackiv, *English Reports*, 129–30.
101. See above, pp. 35–6.
102. *PiB*, 8: 334.
103. 'Maloizvestnyi istochnik po istorii severnoi voiny [Daniel Krman]', *VI*, 1976, no. 12, p. 98.
104. *PiB*, 9: 174 (9 May 1709, to Menshikov).
105. Vozgrin, *Istoricheskie sud'by*, 240.
106. *PiB*, 9: 191 (23 May 1709, to Menshikov), 192 (to Alexis).
107. V. G. Belinskii, *Sochineniia*, vol. 2, (SPb., 1913), 341.
108. For the most vivid account, see Englund, *Battle of Poltava*.
109. 'Maloizvestnyi istochnik', 107. On the Swedish army, see S. P. Oakley *The Story of Sweden* (London, 1966).
110. See A. A. Vasil'ev's estimates, 'O sostave russkoi i shvedskoi armii v Poltavskom srazhenii', *Voenno-istoricheskii zhurnal*, 1989, no. 7, 59–67.
111. Quoted in Englund, *Battle of Poltava*, 155.
112. 'Maloizvestnyi istochnik', 108.
113. Ibid., 106–7.
114. *PiB*, 9: 226.
115. See below, p. 236. *Kniga Marsova*, 71. For an account of the battle, see ibid., 67–80. Versions, including 'Obstoiatel'naia reliatsiia o glavnoi batalii mezh voisk ego tsarskogo velichestva Rossiiskogo i korolevskogo velichestva Sveiskogo, uchinivsheisia nepodaleku ot Poltavy', in *PiB*, 9: 258–62.
116. *PiB*, 9: 231 (27 June 1709, to F. M. Apraksin).
117. LOI, f. 270, d. 107, ll. 254–5. (RGADA, f. 9, kn. 64, l. 649.) 16 Aug. 1724.
118. Letter to Urbich, 27 Aug. 1709, in V. Ger'e, *Sbornik pisem i memorialov Leibnitsa, otnosiashchikhsia k Rossii i Petru Velikomy* (SPb., 1873), 177–80.
119. 'Slovo o bogodarovannom mire', 1 Jan. 1722, in Grebeniuk 256.
120. *PiB*, 9: 397 (5 Oct., 1709, A. I. Ivanov).
121. See Artamonov, *Rossiia*, 188; N. Davies, *God's Playground. A History of Poland*, vol. 1 (Oxford, 1981), 447–500.
122. LOI, f. 270, d. 101, l. 480 (16 Oct. 1722).

123. Ibid., l. 597 (17 Nov. 1722).
124. On these three treaties, see *PiB*, 9: 400–7; *PSZ*, 4: no. 2237; *PiB*, 9: 420–5.
125. See letter of Lord Sutherland, *SIRIO*, 50: 260, 265.
126. On French negotiations, see *SIRIO*, 34: 430 (1710).
127. See, e.g, the patriotic piece by Nikiforov, 'Rossiia v sisteme evropeiskikh derzhav', 24.
128. See analysis in Vozgrin, *Rossiia*, 284–5.
129. See Rothstein, *Peter the Great*, 143–5.
130. *PiB*, 10: 32 (5 Feb. 1710).
131. Ibid., 35 (7 Feb. 1710, to Kikin).
132. Ibid., 59 (Peter's letter congratulating Nostiz).
133. Ibid., 188–9, 190–1 (to Romodanovsky and Menshikov), 193 (to Catherine). On the Drunken Assembly, see below, pp. 249–57.
134. See letters dated 9 July to all and sundry that 'this famed and strong town was taken from the enemy with little loss with God's help': *PiB*, 10: 223.
135. Juel, 3: 13, gives a figure of 70,000 dead.
136. *PiB*, 10: 361.
137. *PSZ*, 4: no. 2278, pp. 515–19 (4 July 1710). See also no. 2298, pp. 560–7 (29 Sept.), no. 2299, pp. 567–75 (29 Sept.), no. 2301, pp. 575–7 (30 Sept.); no. 2302, p. 577 (charter to Riga).
138. Charter to the nobles and townspeople of Livonia, *PiB*, 10: 376–7 (17 Oct. 1710).
139. *PSZ*, 4: no. 2287, pp. 54–5 (16 Aug. 1710).
140. Bantysh-Kamensky, 4: 212.
141. *PiB*, 12(i): 100–2.
142. 'Since in addition to the Russian states and lands various other distinguished provinces and regions which have special charters (*privilegii*) are subject to the Russian sceptre and find themselves under His I. M.'s praiseworthy rule, therefore it is proper that every College be aware of this and take copies of those charters and govern every people (*narod*) according to their laws and charters confirmed by His I. M.': *ZA*, 496–7. On the General Regulation, see below, pp. 109–11;

143. *DPPS*, 6 (i): no. 563, pp. 497–8. On scythes, see below.
144. *PSZ*, 7: no. 4309, p. 119 (23 Sept. 1723).
145. *ZA*, 73–4, 84. See below, p. 124.
146. 'Reskripty i ukazy Petra I k lifl…andskim general-gubernatoram: Polonskomu, kn. Golitsynu i kn. Repninu', in *Osmnadtsatyi vek. Istoricheskii sbornik izdannyi P. Bartenevym*, vol. 4 (1869), 34–5 (7 Feb. 1716).
147. Ibid., 52–3 (23 Feb.). See Repnin's report to Peter of Aug.1721 in which he refers to the 'governing of this province' (*upravlenie zdeshnei provintsii*) by Baron Löwenwolde and asks for a copy of the *instruktsiia* which were given to Löwenwolde: ibid., 64.
148. Ibid., 25.
149. *PiB*, 12(i): 110 (5 Mar. 1712).
150. 'Reskripty i ukazy', 58–9. On Anna, see below, pp. 412–13.
151. Weber, 1: 98, 3.
152. 'Reskripty i ukazy', 63–5.
153. Juel, 3: 29.
154. On this wedding and the dwarf wedding, see below, pp. 257–9.
155. *PiB*, 9: 442. The declaration had been made on 9 Nov., but Tolstoy's letter was received in St Petersburg only on 20 Dec.
156. Juel, 3: 113.
157. See Vozgrin, *Istoricheskie sud'by*, 243: 'The war began at the initiative of Girei, as all contemporaries were convinced.'
158. *PiB*, 9: 167, 168.
159. *PiB*, 10: 398–9 (14 Sept. 1710).
160. B. Sumner, *Peter the Great and the Emergence of Russia* (London, 1958), 77. On religious motives, see below, p. 352.
161. *PiB*, 11: 18.
162. Ibid., 47–8 (31 Jan. 1711).
163. See letter to Menshikov, 6 Feb: ibid., 58.
164. Ibid., 60 (13 Feb. 1711).
165. Letter to the Crown Council early in 1711. Quoted in Fuller, *Strategy*, 42, n. 15.
166. *PiB*, 11: 74–83.
167. Ibid., 84.

168. Ibid., 151–2 (23 Mar. 1711). An appeal (3 Mar.) was also issued to Christians in Serbia, Slavonia, Macedonia and Herzegovina to rise up and help the Russians. See B. Sumner, *Peter the Great and the Ottoman Empire* (Oxford, 1949) 45–7.

169. See below, p. 396.

170. Quoted in Sumner, *Ottoman Empire*, 44.

171. See N. I. Pavlenko, *Petr Velikii*, 345.

172. *PiB*, 11: 305.

173. Stählin, 45–6. This document was first published in 1785 by Stählin, allegedly supplied by Prince M. M. Shcherbatov from Peter's archive, but no original has survived. Pavlenko, *Petr Velikii*, 347, concludes that it is a forgery, probably based on a letter from A. A. Nartov, son of Peter's mechanic.

174. Vozgrin, *Istoricheskie sud'by*, 243. On the debate over the rumours about the bribe, including the possible use of Catherine's jewels, see Sumner, *Ottoman Empire*, 40–1. These stories appear to post-date the events, and may have Swedish and/or Ukrainian origins.

175. *PiB*, 11(i): 325.

176. Ibid., 322–4.

177. *PiB*, 11(ii): 12.

178. Ibid., 41 (8 July, to G. F. Dologoruky).

179. Ibid., 137 (19 Sept. 1711).

180. Münnich memoir, quoted in Sumner, *Ottoman Empire*, 40. See below, pp. 210–2.

181. *PiB*, 11(ii): 138.

182. Ibid., 151 (28 Sept. 1711).

183. Ibid., 242–3 (6 Nov. 1711, to F. M. Apraksin).

184. Bantysh-Kamensky, 4: 212–13.

185. Artamonov, *Rossiia*, 191.

186. For text, see *PiB*, 13 (i): 180–6.

187. Ibid., 441–2: memorandum from Shafirov to Peter.

188. Ibid., 446. Normally 15,000–18,000 roubles per year. For the period 1684–99, 237,020 roubles were owed. Sumner, *Ottoman Empire*, 77.

189. See below.

190. In April 1714 the sultan recognized Augustus II's possession of Polish Ukraine, which in effect ratified Russian influence. Leszczynski had to abandon his claim. See analysis in Sumner, *Ottoman Empire*, 53. Orlyk turned up again as an adviser to the Turks in the Russo–Turkish war of 1735–9.

191. On the marriage, see below, pp. 405–6.

192. *PiB*, 12(i): 9. But they did not manage to capture Wismar that year.

193. Artamonov, *Rossiia*, 190: 'The prolonged story of Peter I's army in Poland [12,000 auxillaries] and the routine ... breaches of discipline in food collection sharply exacerbated Russo–Polish relations in 1712.'

194. *PiB*, 12(ii): 64 (19 Aug. 1712).

195. Bantysh-Kamensky, 1: 45.

196. 14 Feb. 1713: Pavlenko, *Petr Velikii*, 167.

197. *PiB*, 13 (i): nos 5868, 5869, 5870, etc. and pp. 275–8 ('Project for peace in the North').

198. *PiB*, 8 (i),: no. 5874, pp. 78–9.

199. E. V. Anisimov, *Vremia petrovskikh reform* (L, 1989), 395.

200. N. I. Pavlenko, *Poluderzhavnyi vlastelin* (M, 1991), 165.

201. *MIGO*, 1 (i): 47–8: on 19 Sept. Peter wrote to Menshikov about the desirability of taking Stettin to stop the king of Prussia taking it.

202. Ibid., 58–60; p. 67 (30 Sept.).

203. Ibid., 16.

204. 'Reskripty i ukazy', 9.

205. *MIGO*, 1 (i): 70–4.

206. Ibid., 31–2. (20 Aug. to V. L. Dolgoruky).

207. *MIGO*, 1 (ii): 1 (1 Jan. 1714).

208. Bantysh-Kamensky, 4: 213.

209. *MIGO*, 1 (ii): 19 (10 Feb. 1714, to Iaguzhinsky).

210. 'Reskripty i ukazy', 22 (29 June 1714, to Prince Golitsyn in Reval).

211. *MIGO*, 1 (ii): 209 (12 Aug. 1714, to Menshikov).

212. See W. Mediger, *Mecklenburg, Russland und England-Hannover, 1706–21*, 2 vols (Hildesheim, 1967); H. Bagger, 'The Role of the Baltic in Russian Foreign Policy 1721–1773', in H. Ragsdale, ed., *Imperial Russian Foreign Policy* (Cambridge, 1993), 44–6; Bobylev, *Vneshniaia*, 97.

213. See 'Sobstvennoruchnyi imp. Petra zhurnal v kalendare 1716 g.', diary of naval manoeuvres in July–Aug. 1716: LOI, f. 270, d. 81, ll. 661–76.

214. The route followed was: 26 May–14 June in Piermont (taking the waters), Copenhagen (July), Amsterdam (Oct.– 23 Feb. 1717). On 27 Feb. Peter revisited Saandam. March: The Hague, Leiden, Rotterdam. April: Antwerp, Dunkirk. 26 April–9 June in Paris. 16 June–16 July in Spa. 22 July–22 Aug. back in Amsterdam. 8 Sept.: Berlin; 18 Sept.: Danzig; 27 Sept.: Mitau; 28 Sept.: Riga. Peter arrived back in St Petersburg on 10 Oct., having been away one year and eight months. See *PZh*, vols for 1716–17.

215. See Sumner, *Ottoman Empire*, 71–2. On Alexis, see below, pp. 407–8.

216. Bantysh-Kamensky, 1: 165–6.

217. Bobylev, *Vneshniaia*, 107.

218. Bantysh-Kamensky, 4: 214–15.

219. Kirby, *Northern Europe*, 311.

220. There were rumours, unlikely, that he was the victim of a plot to sabotage peace talks.

221. Stählin, no. 74, p. 122.

222. Weber, 1: 255.

223. T. A. Bykova and M. M. Gurevich, eds, *Opisanie izdanii grazhdanskoi pechati, 1708–ianv. 1725 gg. Dopolnenie i prilozheniia* (L, 1972), 77.

224. Bantysh-Kamensky, 4: 215–16.

225. LOI, f. 270, d. 98, l. 96 (24 Aug., to Bruce and Osterman from Peterhof).

226. Bantysh-Kamensky, 4: 219–20. Full text: *PSZ*, 6: no. 3819, pp. 420–31 (30 Aug. 1721).

227. *ZA*, 156. For the Senate's speech to Peter of 1721:, see *IPS*, 1: 93–4.

228. Mediger, *Mecklenburg*, 744–9, quoted in Bagger, 'Role of the Baltic', 38–9.

229. LOI, f. 270, d. 100, l. 455–8 (21 Apr. 1722).

230. Ibid., d. 103, l. 654; *PSZ*, 7: no. 4286.

231. Ibid., d. 100, l. 349 (6 Apr. 1722).

232. See A. Donnelly, 'Peter the Great and Central Asia', *CSP*, 17 (1975), 214. Orders to envoys in *PSZ*, 5: nos 2993, 2994 (14 Feb. 1716).

233. See Donnelly, 'Peter the Great', 210–11. In 1718 Peter sent Florio Beneveni to Bukhara, where he arrived in Nov. 1721. He did not return until after Peter's death.

234. LOI, f. 270, d. 101, l. 232 (2 July 1722). See May 1724 for many letters about

arrangements for an escort for the prince to Russia: LOI, f. 270, d. 107, l. 62.

235. Ibid., d. 101, l. 253^{r-v}.

236. See various letters in ibid., d. 101.

237. Ibid., l. 428^r. (25 Sept. 1722). See account of main campaign as sent in letters to Senate, Synod, his family, Romodanovsky, et al., *BP*, 375 (30 Aug).

238. LOI, f. 270, d. 104, l. 24: 'We had much [celebratory] bombardment on that evening when the news was received.'

239. *PSZ*, 7: no. 4298, pp. 110–12.

240. LOI, f. 270, d. 107, l. 417 (10 Nov. 1724). Lands were made available near Holy Cross fortress.

241. Ibid., d. 101, l. 244^{r-v} (2 July 1722). There are several drafts of this.

242. Ibid., d. 104, l. 32^{r-v} (to Levashev, 9 Sept. 1723); *PSZ*, 7: no. 4301.

243. Pososhkov, 128–9.

244. *PSZ*, 7: no. 4137, pp. 1–2; no. 4171, p. 26.

245. LOI, f. 270, d. 103, ll. 382, 384. On the crisis in money and grain supplies in the 1720s, see below, pp. 141–2.

246. Ibid., d. 106, l. 97^{r-v} (15 Jan. 1724).

247. Ibid., d. 107, ll. 489–92 (6 Dec.).

248. See V. V. Gavrishchik, *Voennye reformy Petra I v otechestvennoi istoriografii (1917–1991 gg.)*, diss. abstract. (M, 1993), 12.

249. Bagger, 'Role of the Baltic', 41–2, analysis based of Osterman's report of Feb.–Mar. 1725, '*General'noe sostoianie del i interesov vserossiiskikh so svemi sosedami i drugimi instrannimi Gosudarstvami.*' Bagger points out that greater weight was given to European countries.

250. *PSZ*, 7: no. 4356, p. 157 (9 Nov. 1723).

251. Ibid., no. 4189, pp. 33–40 (19 Mar.); no. 4255, pp. 85–6 (28 June/8 July).

252. Bantysh-Kamensky, 4: 223–4; *PSZ*, 7: no. 4465, pp. 254–9; I. G. Spassky and E. Shchukina, *Medals and Coins of the Age of Peter the Great* (L, 1974), no. 55.

253. See below, pp. 413–14.

254. See Anisimov, 'Imperial Heritage', 30.

255. See Kaminski, *Republic vs Autocracy*, 113–44.

256. D. Altbauer, 'The Diplomats of Peter the Great', *JGO*, 28 (1980), 11, 14.

257. Ibid., 16.
258. See analysis in Sumner, *Ottoman Empire*, 63–4.
259. See text and summary in L. R. Lewitter, 'The Apocryphal Testament of Peter the Great', *Polish Review*, 63 (1966), 27–44.
260. The author was General Michal Sokolnicki (1760–1815), a Polish officer, who in turn was influenced by the anonymous work 'The Danger to the Political Balance of Europe' (1791). Subtelny finds prototypes for the 'Testament' in Peter's reign, e.g., in the diary of Pylyp and Hryhor Orlyk, Cossack chancellor of the Zaporozhian Host, linked with Mazepa. See O. Subtelny, 'Peter I's Testament: A Reassessment', *SR*, 33 (1974), 663–78.
261. E. Anisimov, *The Reforms of Peter the Great. Progress through Coercion*, trans. J. Alexander (New York, 1993), 254.

CHAPTER 3: THE RUSSIAN MILITARY MACHINE

1. V. O. Kliuchevsky, *Kurs russkoi istorii*, 2nd edn, vol. 4, (M, 1923), 77. See M. S. Anderson, *Peter the Great* (London, 1978), 82: 'war and the demands it generated were the mainspring of much of Peter's innovating and creative activity in Russia'. Useful surveys on the army in English include R. Hellie, 'The Petrine Army: Continuity, Change, Impact', *CASS*, 8 (1974), 237–53; C. Duffy, *Russia's Way to the West: The Origins and Nature of Russian Military Power* (London, 1981); J. Keep, *Soldiers of the Tsar. Army and Society in Russia 1462–1874* (Oxford, 1985). See also the illustrated reference works by A. Konstam and D. Rickman, *Peter the Great's Army*, vol. 1: *Infantry*, and vol. 2: *Cavalry*, Men-at-Arms Series, 260 and 264 (London, 1993); A. Borodulin and Iu. Kashtanov, *Armiia Petra I* (M, 1994).
2. See, however, the equestrian portraits of Tsar Alexis and Michael.

3. *PiB*, 1: 58
4. R. R. Palmer, *A History of the Modern World* (New York, 1965), 214.
5. F. de la Neuville, *A Curious and New Account of Muscovy in the Year 1689*, ed. L. Hughes (London, 1994), 24.
6. Korb, 2: 134.
7. Otto von Pleyer, 'Report on the Present State of Russia' (1710), in G. Vernadsky, ed., *A Source Book on Russian History* (New Haven, 1972), 2: 332.
8. Hellie, 'Petrine Army', 251.
9. E. V. Anisimov, *The Reforms of Peter the Great. Progress through Coercion*, trans. J. Alexander (New York, 1993), 57.
10. But see Hellie's argument that they had declined between the end of Alexis's reign and 1689.
11. Hellie's figures for Crimea 1689 were 17,206 gentry cavalry, but 78,652 'new formation', including 50,000 *soldaty* and 30,000 *reitari*. Anisimov (*Reforms*, 58) calculates that from the mid-seventeenth century three-quarters of the army comprised new-formation troops.
12. See above, pp. 5–6.
13. *PSZ*, 5: no. 3006: preface to the Military Statute, 31 Mar. 1716.
14. Stählin, no. 89, pp. 137–85.
15. W. C. Fuller, *Strategy and Power in Russia 1600–1914* (New York, 1992), 44.
16. Preface to Military Statute. The Russians were beaten by the Turks and Tatars in 1676–8 and were forced to abandon the Ukrainian border post at Chigirin. On the 1687 and 1689 Crimean campaigns, see above.
17. A. Kartsov, *Istoriia leib-gvardii Semenovskogo polka, 1683–1852*, vol. 1 (SPb., 1852), 16–7. See above, p. 16.
18. I. A. Zheliabuzhsky, 'Zapiski', in A. B. Bogdanov. ed., *Rossiia pri tsarevne Sof'e i Petre I* (M, 1990), 275.
19. R. Warner, 'The Kožuchovo Campaign of 1694', *JGO*, 13/4 (1965), 489–90.
20. *PSZ*, 3: no. 1502, pp. 186–95 (19 Dec. 1694). See also C. B. Stevens, *Soldiers on the Steppe. Army Reform and Social Change in Early Modern Russia* (De Kalb, Ill., 1995).
21. See below, pp. 172ff.
22. Grund, 23–7.
23. Ibid., 31–2.

24. Zheliabuzhsky, 'Zapiski', 277–8.
25. *ZA*, 116. On the *History*, see below, pp. 322–3. Golovin and Weyde recruited mainly in the Moscow region.
26. *PSZ*, 3: no. 1747, p. 3.
27. *PSZ*, 4: no. 1873, p. 175 (31 Oct. 1701).
28. Ibid., no. 1912, pp. 196–7 (24 Apr. 1702).
29. LOI, f. 270, d. 97, l. 267 (4 Mar. 1721).
30. N. B. Golikova, *Politicheskie protsessy pri Petre I* (M, 1957), 200. Depositions in the Preobrazhensky *prikaz* (secret investigations department).
31. Ibid., 206.
32. *PiB*, 11: 90 (28 Feb. 1711).
33. *PiB*, 12(i): 112, 382.
34. Zheliabuzhsky, 'Zapiski', 283–5
35. N. I. Pavlenko, *Petr Velikii* (M, 1990), 102.
36. *PiB*, 12(i): 162 (3 Apr. 1712).
37. *PSZ*, 4: no. 2036, pp. 291–5 (20 Feb. 1705); no. 2050 (4 May 1705, deadline extended); no. 2065 (14 July 1705).
38. Fuller, *Strategy*, 46.
39. One of a series of recruitment *ukazy* for 1706. See *PSZ*, 4: no. 1095, pp. 342–3 (2 Mar. 1706); no. 2104, pp. 348–9 (6 May 1706). See also nos 1504, 1506, 1507, on money payments in lieu for those who could not serve because of illness or service in *prikazy* or as *voevody*).
40. *PSZ*, 4: no. 2138, p. 369 (4 Feb. 1707); no. 2143, p. 375 (19 Mar. 1707).
41. Ibid., nos 2326, 2355, 2384, etc. (Mar.–June 1711).
42. Ibid., no. 2142, p. 373 (17 Mar. 1707); no. 2166, p. 393 (31 Oct. 1707).
43. Ibid., no. 1923, pp. 209–10 (14 Jan. 1703).
44. Ibid., no. 2023, p. 285 (1 Feb. 1705).
45. Ibid., no. 2151, p. 382 (9 June 1707).
46. Ibid., no. 2186, p. 401 (15 Jan. 1708). On policy towards and redeployment of the secular clergy, see below, pp. 347–8.
47. *PiB*, 9: 49 (25 Jan. 1709).
48. *PSZ*, 4: no. 1979, p. 257 (11 Apr. 1704). On the strel'tsy revolt of 1698 and the disappearance of the corps, see below, p. 454.
49. V. V. Gavrishchik, *Voennye reformy Petra I v otechestvennoi istoriografii (1917–1991 gg.)*, diss. abstract (M, 1993), 16. See also Keep, *Soldiers of the Tsar*, 101–2.
50. See T. Mackiv, *English Reports on Mazepa 1687–1709* (New York, Munich and Toronto, 1983), and Weber, 1: 50–1, on the Cossacks after Poltava.
51. Quoted in Mackiv, *English Reports*; PRO SP 91, vol. 4 (1705).
52. See Peter's letter to the Don Cossacks (9 Jan. 1711) asking them to defend Azov against the Turks. *PiB*, 11: 28
53. M. Khodarkovsky, *Where Two Worlds Met. The Russian State and the Kalmyk Nomads, 1600–1772* (Ithaca, NY, and London, 1992), 138.
54. *PiB*, 5: 397. Rewards were offered, from 1,000 roubles for murzas (chieftains) to 3 roubles for regular warriors: Khodarkovsky, *Where Two Worlds Met*, 142–3; *PiB*, 9: 133 (24 Mar. 1709).
55. *PiB*, 9: 20–1.
56. *PSZ*, 4: no. 2249, p. 476 (9 Feb. 1710). A list of 122 soldiers retired from the Preobrazhensky guards in Oct. 1708 includes as grounds for retirement old age, drunkenness, and drunkenness combined with idiocy, stupidity, incompetence, idleness, and decrepitude: *PiB*, 8: 199–207.
57. See below, pp. 447–9.
58. Weber, 1: 53.
59. Fuller, *Strategy*, 47–8.
60. *PiB*, 11: 69 (18 Feb. 1711).
61. Fuller, *Strategy*, 48, n. 35.
62. See letters to Tsarevich Alexis, 8 Jan. 1709 (*PiB*, 9: 19); to A. I. Ivanov, 13 Jan. (ibid., 23), after Ivanov complained that many were fleeing; also *PiB*, 12(i): 17 (order to Senate, 28 Feb. 1711).
63. Fuller, *Strategy*, 48, n. 34.
64. *PiB*, 12(i): 19
65. *PiB*, 8: 330 (30 Nov. 1708).
66. G. V. Esipov, *Raskol'nich'i dela XVIII stoletiia* (SPb., 1861), 2: 127–8.
67. Anisimov, *Reforms*, 61.
68. Keep, *Soldiers of the Tsar*, 107.
69. A. Vasil'ev, 'O sostave russkoi i shvedskoi armii v Poltavskom srazhenii', *Voenno-istoricheskii zhurnal*, 1989, no. 7, pp. 64–5, estimates 37,000 men in the Swedish army and 60,000 in the Russian army, which comprised 40

infantry regiments, including 2 guards and 4 grenadiers, 27 dragoon regiments and 3 cavalry squadrons, and artillery of 32 field guns, 57 regimental guns, and 13 dragoon cannon.

70. Anderson, *Peter the Great*, 85.
71. *PiB*, 7(i): 104–7 (10 Mar. 1708).
72. For the composition of the army in the middle of the Northern War (regiments, officers, men, salaries), see *PSZ*, 4: no. 2319 (19 Feb. 1711).
73. Grund, 36.
74. *PiB*, 5: 131 (14 Mar. 1707).
75. Fuller, *Strategy*, 60.
76. Figures for 1713: 3,486 cannon, 492 mortars, 37 howitzers in 18 major fortresses. Borodulin and Kashtanov, *Armiia Petra I*, 34; Anderson, *Peter the Great*, 86.
77. *PRP*, 343–8
78. Fuller, *Strategy*, 67.
79. Quoted in ibid., 66–7.
80. *PSZ*, 3: no. 1560, p. 268 (11 Dec. 1696).
81. See descriptions and illustrations in Borodulin and Kashtanov, *Armiia Petra I*. Grund (11–13) describes them as 'clothed and trained after the German manner'.
82. Fuller, *Strategy*, 50 (41).
83. *PiB*, 9: 160 (22 Apr.).
84. *PiB*, 11(ii): 263 (28 Nov. 1711). This letter has a list of uniforms and weapons appended and Weyde's letter (dated 26 Sept.) warning that 'it is already autumn and we are in great difficulties from cold and wet but when hard frosts begin they will be in a bad way as they are as naked and barefoot as it is possible to be' (ibid., 265).
85. *PiB*, 7(I): 74. (20 Feb. 1708).
86. *PiB*, 8(ii): 66–7 (5 Aug. 1708 to Mikhail Samarin).
87. 'Zapiski o vazhneishikh vnutrennikh proisshestviiakh i uchrezhdeniiakh v Rossii s 1707 po 1712 god', *Severnyi arkhiv*, 20(5) (1826), 36.
88. *PiB*, 8(ii): 65 (5 Aug. 1708); ibid., 10: 49 (20 Jan. 1710).
89. *PiB*, 11(ii): 256 (20 Nov. 1711).
90. *PiB*, 8(ii): 156 (22 Sept. 1708), 191–2 (13 Oct. 1708).
91. Fuller, *Strategy*, 50–1.

92. *PiB*, 12(i): 42 (25 Jan. 1712).
93. Ibid., 156.
94. Ibid., 172 (15 Apr. 1712).
95. *PiB*, 11(ii): 288–98 (10 Dec. 1711).
96. A. Kahan, *The Plow, the Hammer and the Knout. An Economic History of Eighteenth-Century Russia* (Chicago, 1985), 53 (4.5 roubles for flour, 0.375 roubles for groats, 0.72 roubles for meat, 0.15 roubles for salt). For horses, 6 chetverts of oats (3 roubles) and 90 poods hay (2.7 roubles) per year, allowing for free grazing in summer.
97. Ibid., 53. In 1712, 174,757 men and 77,980 horses consumed 524,271 chetverts of flour, 32,767 of groats, and 467,880 of oats. On budgets, see below, pp. 136–7.
98. N. D. Beliaev, 'Russkoe obshchestvo pri Petre Velikom', *Den'* (1864), no. 2, p. 6.
99. *PiB*, 10: 390 (1711).
100. *PiB*, 8: 226 (19 Oct. 1708).
101. Gavrishchik, *Voennye reformy*, 21.
102. Fuller, *Strategy*, 55.
103. Pososhkov, 186
104. See below, pp. 174–5, 303–4.
105. LOI, f. 270, d. 103, l. 512 (17 May 1723).
106. Gavrishchik, *Voennye reformy*, 12.
107. Hellie, 'Petrine Army', 250–1. Anisimov (*Reforms*, 63) also argues that Peter adopted a more offensive, active approach to warfare: 'For Peter the main aim of military operations was not to capture the opponent's fortresses (as it had been earlier), but to defeat him in direct, fast-moving contact-battle engagement.'
108. Korb, 2: 144.
109. *SIRIO*, 39: 161–3 (13/24 Sept.) to Harley. The 'great want of experienced officers' was mentioned again in a dispatch of 12 Jan. 1707 and again in Dec. 1707 and 9 May 1708.
110. *SIRIO*, 39: 52–5, dispatch of 14/25 March, 1705.
111. See discussion in P. P. Epifanov, 'Voinskii ustav Petra Velikogo', in A. I. Andreev, ed., *Petr Velikii. Sbornik statei* (M & L, 1947), 167–9.
112. See C. Peterson, *Peter the Great's Administrative and Judicial Reforms* (Stockholm, 1979), 337–8.

113. *Uchenie i khitrost' pekhotnykh liudei* (M, 1647–9) (translation of Jacobi's *Kriegs-Kunst zu Fuss*, 1647).

114. See *Voennye ustavy Petra Velikogo* (M, 1946), 66–79; *PRP*, 321–4. The Naval Statute has the same clauses.

115. *Voennye ustavy*, 77–8.

116. *DPPS*, 6(i): no. 388, pp. 326–8; emphasis added.

117. Muller, 30, 40; J. Cracraft, *The Church Reform of Peter the Great* (London, 1971), 263, 267; P. V. Verkhovskoy, *Uchrezhdenie Dukhovnoi Kollegii i Dukhovnyi reglament*, vol. 2 (Rostov/Don, 1916), 51.

118. See, e.g., Anderson, *Peter the Great*, 83. On courts, see below, pp. 124–5.

119. LOI, f. 270, d. 101, l. 705^{r-v} (1722).

120. Epifanov, 'Voinskii ustav', 201–2.

121. *PSZ*, 3: no. 1540, p. 233 (8 Feb. 1696).

122. *PiB*, 12(i): 120 (9 Mar. 1712).

123. Ibid., 88 (23 Feb. 1712).

124. S. F. Platonov, *Petr Velikii. Lichnost' i deiatel'nost'* (Paris, 1927), 112. But see the argument that only arms drill existed in early modern armies and that foot drill (cadenced step) arrived only with the development of modern surfaces in the later eighteenth century, in J. Keegan, 'Keeping in Time', review of W. H. McNeill, *Keeping Together in Time. Dance and Drill in Human History* (London, 1996), in *Times Literary Supplement*, 12 July 1996, pp. 3–4.

125. Oath of allegiance for military ranks: *PSZ*, 5: no. 3006, pp. 319–20.

126. I. I. Golikov, *Anekdoty, kasaiushchiesia do gosudaria imperatora Petra Velikogo*, in E. V. Anisimov, ed. *Petr Velikii. Vospominaniia. Dnevnikovye zapisi. Anekdoty* (SPb., 1993), 381–2.

127. Fuller, *Strategy*, 53–4 (57).

128. Grund, 11–13.

129. Ibid., 104.

130. *PRP*, 324.

131. See Peterson, *Peter*, 395 ff.

132. Anisimov, *Reforms*, 24–5.

133. Campredon to Louis XV, 13 June 1723(NS) *SIRIO*, 49: 345.

134. Gavrishchik, *Voennye reformy*, 19. For information on Peter's first boats (*korabliki*), see *Tezisy*.

135. See below, pp. 277–8.

136. See N. V. Novikov, ed., *Boevaia letopis' russkogo flota* (M, 1948), 24–6.

137. The 1647 statute was supposed to be supplemented with a book on 'naval military science': ibid., 22.

138. 'Slovo pokhvalnoe o flote rossiiskom' (1720), in Grebeniuk, 236; Prokopovich, *Sochineniia*, ed. I. P. Eremin (M & L, 1961), 103–12. This work was written to celebrate the Russian naval victory at Grengham.

139. Kaliazina, illustration 165.

140. 'The Story of the Ship's Boat which gave his Majesty the Thought of Building Ships of War' (preface to the Naval Statute of 1720), in J. Cracraft, ed., *For God and Peter the Great. The Works of Thomas Consett, 1723–1729* (Boulder, Colo., 1982), 210.

141. I. V. Bogotyrev, 'Petrovskie suda botovogo tipa', *Sudostroenie*, 1988, no. 6, 56–8; F. F. Veselago, 'Dedushka russkogo flota', *Russkaia starina*, 4 (1871), 463–82.

142. N. Novikov, 'Sozdanie voenno-morskogo flota v Rossii pri Petre I', *Partiino-politicheskaia rabota v VMF*, 1941, no. 7, p. 43; E. J. Phillips, *The Founding of Russia's Navy. Peter the Great and the Azov Fleet 1688–1714* (Westport, Conn., 1995), 39–42.

143. Novikov, ed., *Boevaia*, 41.

144. Ibid., 46.

145. *MIGO*, vol. 3, printed calendar for 1714: 'ot zachatiia flota rossiiskogo, 17 let'.

146. 20. Oct. 1696: *morskim sudam byt'*. On the organization of the new enterprises, see Phillips, *Founding*, 61–70.

147. See ibid., 114–15

148. I. M. Matley, 'Defence Manufactures of St Petersburg 1703–1730', *Geographical Review*, 71 (1981), 414.

149. N. Iu. Berezovsky et al., *Rossiiskii imperatorskii flot, 1696–1917. Voenno-istoricheskii spravochnik* (M, 1993), 36.

150. See below pp. 418–19.

151. *PSZ*, 5: no. 3229 (25 Sept. 1718).

152. LOI, f. 270, d. 106, ll. 127–9 (17 Jan. 1724). On naval assemblies, see below, pp. 265–6.

153. [I. Kopievsky], *Mémoires pour l'histoire des sciences et des beaux arts*, Sept. 1711,

quoted in N. A. Kopanev, 'Petr I—perevodchik', *XVIII vek.*, 16 (1989), 182.

154. *PSZ*, 6: no. 3485, p. 3.

155. *PiB*, 1: no. 129. The document on study abroad is included in the first entry in the diary of Peter Tolstoy. See M. Okenfuss (trans. and ed.), *The Travel Diary of Peter Tolstoy* (De Kalb, Ill., 1987), 6.

156. A. E. Suknovalov, 'Pervaia v Rossii voenno-morskaia shkola', *IZ*, 42 (1953), 301–6. In 1707–11 two of the former students, Stepan Neronov and Ivan Tel'nov, were sent to England to train.

157. See above, pp. 25–6.

158. *Sbornik Mukhanova*, 2nd ed. (SPb., 1866), 258–60: lists for 1718–19.

159. See below, pp. 301–3.

160. See below, pp. 305–7, on conditions of service; A. G. Cross, '*By the Banks of the Thames'. Russians in 18th-Century Britain* (Cambridge, 1980), 148–51.

161. See V. N. Berkh, *Zhizneopisanie adm. K. I. Kriuisa* (SPb., 1825).

162. Ibid., 75 (11 Nov. 1723).

163. Berezovsky et al., *Rossiiskii imperatorskii flot*, 54–5.

164. Berkh, *Zhizneopisanie*, 26.

165. See *Russkii biograficheskii slovar'*, vol. 32 (Petrograd, 1916); *Materialy dlia istorii russkogo flota*, 6 (1877), 5–6; Berezovsky, et al., *Rossiiskii imperatorskii flot*, 107.

166. *PiB*, 5: 221–2 (28 Apr. 1707).

167. Suknovalov, 'Pervaia', 303–4.

168. *PiB*, 1: p. 186.

169. See, e.g., Peter's letter to I. B. L'vov (who was supervising naval students in Holland and Denmark) on the threat of confiscation of their Moscow estates made to some students: *PiB*, 12(i): 111–12.

170. J. Deane, *History of the Russian Fleet during the Reign of Peter the Great* (London, 1899), 102.

171. Quoted in N. I. Pavlenko, 'Petr I. K izucheniiu sotsian'no-politicheskikh vzgliadov', in *RPR*, 75: 'Natura moia ne mozhet snest' morekhodstvo'. This was Prince Mikhail Mikhailovich the younger (1681–1764), who at the end of his life became general-admiral.

172. *PiB*, 6: 86 (10 Sept. 1707). Zotov died

173. *ZA*, 43.

174. Cross, '*By the Banks of the Thames'*, 155. More on Zotov in Berezovsky et al., *Rossiiskii imperatorskii flot*, 107.

175. Cross, '*By the Banks of the Thames'*, 152–3.

176. *PiB*, 6: 166–7 (23 Nov. 1707).

177. Weber, 1: 54.

178. *PiB*, 9: 130 (23 Mar. 1709).

179. B. Haigh, 'Design for a Medical Service: Peter the Great's Admiralty Regulations (1722)', *Medical History*, 19 (1975), 130.

180. *ZA*, 57, 59 (4 Apr. 1718).

181. The statute 'on all which pertains to the good organization while the fleet is at sea' drew on translations from the French, British, Danish, Swedish and Dutch. The introduction states that the code was 'selected from five maritime regulations, with a substantial part added': *PSZ*, 6: no. 3485, p. 1. See *Svod reglamentov Admiralteiskikh: frantsuzkoi, anglinskoi, datskoi, gollandskoi, shvedskoi*, in RGADA, f. 9, otd. I, kn. 45 and 46, and translations of Louis XIV's edicts on the fleet and maritime regulation from the Cabinet papers (ibid., kn. 48 and 49). K. Zotov translated *Ordonnance de Louis XIV-me. Pour les armées Navalles et arcenaux de marine 1689*. Prince B. I. Kurakin was ordered to send English naval legislation: *ZA*, 42, 44. Part 2 was published in April 1722 as a supplement to the Admiralty Regulation: *PSZ*, 6: no. 3937, pp. 608–37.

182. *PSZ*, 6: no. 3937, pp. 526–637.

183. Johann Mansson, *Een Nyttig Siö-Book* (Stockholm, 1677) in T. A. Bykova and M. M. Gurevich, eds, *Opisanie izdanii grazhdanskoi pechati, 1708–ianv. 1725 gg.*, no. 576 (M & L, 1955); S. P. Luppov, *Kniga v Rossi v pervoi chetverti XVIII v.* (L, 1973), 91–2.

184. Phillips, *Founding*, 109. See also letter from the Jesuit Ioannis Milan (Aug. 1712), describing the naval action, in *Pis'ma i doneseniia iezuitov o Rossii* (SPb., 1904; repr. 1965), 374–5. The Turks were deterred by the arrival of Kalmyk and Cossack cavalry.

185. See arguments in B. Sumner, *Peter the Great and the Ottoman Empire* (Oxford, 1949), 24–5.
186. Grund, 35.
187. Pososhkov, 351–3.
188. LOI, f. 270, d. 73, l. 177 (19 Sept. 1713).
189. For detailed descriptions of both campaigns, see Novikov, ed., *Boevaia*, 67ff.
190. Quoted in V. S. Bobylev, *Vneshniaia politika Rossii epokhi Petra I* (M, 1990), 121.
191. LOI, f. 270, d. 100, l. 296 (19 Mar. 1722). This point appeared in the Admiralty Regulation: *PSZ*, 6: no. 3937, p. 543
192. LOI, f. 270, d. 101, l. 169 (30 May 1722).
193. Ibid., l. 174 (30 May 1722).
194. Ibid., d. 106, ll. 468–9 (15 Feb. 1724).
195. *Sbornik*, 2: 96. They also took part in a masquerade on the ship *Friedemacher* on 17 Feb. 1722.
196. Reproduced in M. A. Alekseeva, *Graviura petrovskogo vremeni* (L, 1990), 140–2, and Kaliazina, illustration 164. See G. Kaganov, 'As in the Ship of Peter', *SR*, 50 (1991), 754–67, for an interesting analysis.
197. LOI, f. 270, d. 107, l. 122 (29 May 1724).
198. I. D. Chechot, 'Korabl' i flot v portretakh Petra I. Ritoricheskaia kul'tura i osobennosti estetiki russkogo korablia pervoi chetverti XVIII veka', in *Otechestvennoe i zarubezhnoe iskusstvo XVIII veka* (L, 1986), 78.
199. P. Miliukov, *Ocherki po istorii russkoi kul'tury*, pt 3 (SPb., 1903), 165–6.
200. Ia. Gordin, 'Delo tsarevicha Alekseia ili tiazhba o tsene reform', *Zvezda*, 1991, no. 11, p. 127.
201. Grund, 36.
202. Anisimov, *Reforms*, 66.
203. P. Miliukov, *Gosudarstvennoe khoziaistvo Rossii v pervoi chet. XVIII st. i reforma Petra Velikogo* (SPb., 1905), 98–107, 148–9.
204. *PSZ*, 6: no. 3485, p. 2 (13 Jan. 1720): 'Vsiakii Potentant, kotoryi edino voisko sukhoputnoe imeet, odnu ruku imeet, a kotoryi i flot imeet, obe ruki imeet.' Also *ZA*, 74.
205. Prokopovich, 'Slovo pokhvalnoe', in *Sochineniia*, 110. The reference is to the death of Charles XII in 1718. The lion represented Sweden.
206. Novikov, ed., *Boevaia*, not surprisingly for a work of its vintage, traces the first Russian naval campaign to the year 860, via the feats of Novgorod, Ivan IV's river flotilla, Baltic conquests, Cossack voyages and projects for merchant fleets.
207. Prokopovich, *Sochineniia*, 126.
208. Hellie, 251.
209. See A. Gerschenkron, 'Russian mercantilism', in *Europe in the Russian Mirror* (Cambridge, 1970), 73.
210. Fuller, *Strategy*, 64. See arguments, ibid., 82–3
211. *Kniga Marsova ili Voinskikh del* (SPb., 1713/1766), 71. Account of the battle, ibid., 67–80. Versions including 'Obstoiatel'naia reliatsiia o glavnoi batalii mezh voisk ego tsarskogo velichestva Rossiiskogo i korolevskogo velichestva Sveiskogo, uchinivsheisia nepodaleku ot Poltavy', in *PiB*, 9: 258–62.
212. Fuller, *Strategy*, 71.
213. Ibid., 75.
214. S. G. Nelipovich, 'Pozitsiia B. Kh. fon Miunnikha v diskussii 1725 goda o sokrashchenii armii i voennogo biudzheta Rossii', *Voenno-istoricheskii zhurnal*, 1990, no. 8, pp. 3–7.
215. Prokopovich, *Sochineniia*, 112–26.

CHAPTER 4: GOVERNMENT

1. F. J. Strahlenberg, *Zapiski kapitana Filippa Ioganna Stralenberga ob istorii i geografii Rossiiskoi imperii Petra Velikogo*, trans. and ed. Iu. Bespiatykh et al. (M & L, 1985), 1: 124.
2. Clause 20 of the Military Statute (1716), *PSZ*, 5: no. 3006, p. 325, and *PRP*, 325; Naval Statute (1720): *PSZ*, 6: no. 3485, p. 3; *PRP*, 467–525. The formulae are identical and are, in fact, a direct translation from Swedish into Russian of a Riksdag decision of 1693, quoted in Muller, p. xxvii.
3. *The Tryal of the Czarewitz Alexis Petrowitz, who was Condemn'd at*

Petersbourg, on the 25th of June, 1718 (London, 1725), 67, 83.

4. C. Whitworth, *An Account of Russia as it was in the Year 1710. Rossiia v nachale XVIII veka. Sochineniia Ch. Uitvorta* (M & L, 1988), 21.

5. Nartov, 82.

6. I. A. Zheliabuzhsky, 'Zapiski', A. B. Bogdanov, ed. in *Rossiia pri tsarevne Sof'e i Petre I* (M, 1990), 276–7.

7. *PSZ*, 4: no. 1748, p. 3 (2 Feb. 1700); *MLC*, 27.

8. *ZA*, 377; *PSZ*, 5: no. 3261 (22 Dec. 1718).

9. *PSZ*, 6: no. 3947, p. 643 (6 Apr. 1722). On the *Reketmeister*, see below.

10. E. V. Anisimov, *The Reforms of Peter the Great. Progress through Coercion*, trans. J. Alexander (New York, 1993), 165. Anisimov's *Gosudarstvennye preobrazovaniia i samoderzhavie Petra Velikogo v pervoi chetverti XVIII veka* (SPb., 1997) appeared too late to be extensively utilized in preparing this chapter. See his tables on the annual number and subject-matter of Peter's decrees, pp. 278, 280–1.

11. From F. Prokopovich, *Bukvar' ili pervoe uchenie otrokam*, trans. in J. Cracraft, *The Church Reform of Peter the Great* (London, 1971), 284–5. Cf. the early seventeenth-century *Orthodox Confession* of Metropolitan Peter Mohila of Kiev, which first discussed duties towards natural parents before extrapolating to attitudes towards the authorities and concluding that first obedience was to God.

12. F. Prokopovich, 'Sermon on Royal Authority and Honour' (1718), in M. Raeff, ed., *Russian Intellectual History. An Anthology* (New York, 1966), 25.

13. Ibid., 28.

14. Ibid., 15.

15. 'Predislovie k Morskomu ustava', in N. Marchenko, ed., *Petr Velikii. Mysli gosudaria o sozdanii voennoga porta na Baltiiskom beregu* (SPb., 1899), 197. In the MS Peter himself added the word great (*prevelikii*) to the word 'harm' (*vred*).

16. R. Wortman, *The Development of a Russian Legal Consciousness* (Chicago, 1976), 9.

17. See translation and introduction by A. Lentin, *Peter the Great: his Law on the Imperial Succession. The Official Commentary* (Oxford, 1996), 60–1; J. Cracraft, 'Did Feofan Prokopovich Really Write *Pravda Voli Monarshei?*', *SR*, 40 (1981), 173–93. *Pravda* was first printed 7 Aug. 1722 (in civil and Cyrillic type). See *PSZ*, 7: no. 4870.

18. See discussion in A. M. Panchenko, 'Nachalo petrovskoi reformy: ideinaia podelka', in *XVIII vek*, 16 (1989), 13–14. Translation of Locke's *Treatises of Civil Government* (1690) in papers of D. M. Golitsyn. On the Ecclesiastical Regulation, see below.

19. Primer, quoted in Cracraft, *Church Reform*, 283.

20. M. Cherniavsky, *Tsar and People: Studies in Russian Myths* (New York, 1961), 75.

21. See below, p. 340.

22. 'Bozhe sviatyi … Izhe ot nebytiia vo ezhe byti privedyi vsiacheskaia': V. M. Zhivov, 'Kul'turnye reformy v sisteme preobrazovaniia Petra I', in *Iz istorii russkoi kul'tury. Tom III (XVII–nachalo XVIII veka)* (M, 1996), 550. P. Krekshin, 'Kratkoe opisanie blazhenykh del velikogo gosudaria, imperatora Petra Velikogo, Samoderzhtsa Vserossiiskogo', in N. Sakharov, ed., *Zapiski russkikh liudei* (SPb., 1841), 4: 'S vozdykhaniem serdets vozglagolem: "otche nash, Petr Velikii! Ty nas ot nebytiia v bytie privel."'

23. V. M. Zhivov and B. A. Uspensky, 'Tsar' i Bog: Semioticheskie aspekty sakralizatsii monarkha v Rossii', in Uspensky, ed., *Iazyky kultury i problemy perevodimosti* (M, 1987), 81.

24. Ibid., 85, 89–90, 107.

25. See comment in Lentin, *Peter the Great*, 40.

26. There is a detailed study of the origins of the title and its interpretation in I. de Madariaga, 'Tsar into Emperor: The Title of Peter the Great', in R. Oresko et al., eds, *Royalty and Republican Sovereignty in Early Modern Europe* (Cambridge, 1996), 351–81. See analysis in Cherniavsky, *Tsar and People*, 79–82.

27. I. G. Spassky and E. Shchukina, *Medals and Coins of the Age of Peter the Great* (L, 1974), illustrations 5 and 6.

28. See B. A. Uspensky on the folk understanding of this, usurping the spiritual authority of the patriarch-father: 'Historia sub specie Semioticae', in H. K. Baran, ed., *Semiotics and Structuralism. Readings from the Soviet Union* (New York, 1976), 67.

29. See examples in G. V. Vilinbakhov, 'Otrazhenie idei absoliutizma v simvolike Petrovskikh znamen', in *Kul'tura i iskusstvo Rossii XVIII veka* (L, 1981), 18–20. He argues that in this period Peter stopped 'hiding' behind the symbol of St Andrew and personalized his power with imperial symbols and his monogram. On St Andrew, see below, pp. 275–6.

30. Juel 2: 55. De Madariaga, 'Tsar into Emperor', 368–9, points out that England, lacking allegiance to the Holy Roman Emperor, had less difficulty in addressing the tsar as 'emperor' as long as Russia was regarded as on a par with Eastern empires (Ottoman, Chinese, etc.). Once it entered Europe, there was more reluctance.

31. De Madariaga, 'Tsar into Emperor', 374. In Nov. 1721, in order to influence negotiations with the French on this topic, the French consul Campredon was shown Maximilian's letter and more recent examples of foreign monarchs addressing Peter with imperial titles, *SIRIO*, 40: 316–17.

32. *ZA*, 155; *PSZ*, 6: no. 3840, pp. 444–6. 'Otets Otechestviia, Imperator Vserossiiskii, Petr Velikii.' In Dec. 1721 a decree was issued on the titles for the rest of the royal family.

33. See documents in *PSZ*, 6: no. 3850, p. 454 (11 Nov. 1721), no. 3865, p. 464 (6 Dec. 1721).

34. LOI, f. 270, d. 107, l. 175 (15 June 1724.) This repeats the decree of 18 Jan. 1722: *PSZ*, 6: no. 3882, pp. 481–3. 'His Majesty the tsar' (*Ego tsarskoe velichestvo*) remained in some formulations.

35. Uspensky, 'Historia', 71: 'That Peter began to call himself "the Great" was

in the eyes of his contemporaries a good deal less immodest than calling himself "the First" '.

36. See below, pp. 363–6.

37. On Romodanovsky, see below, pp. 423–4.

38. PiB, 1: 18–19 (Mar. 1694).

39. Zheliabuzhsky, 'Zapiski', 215–16; Kurakin, 1: 378–9.

40. See N. B. Golikova, *Politicheskie protsessy pri Petre I* (M, 1957), 14–16.

41. See letter to Romodanovsky, 31 Aug. 1697, from Amsterdam, on the allocation of Russian students abroad: *ZA*, 180.

42. Korb, 1: 195–6.

43. *PiB*, 1: 162.

44. Nartov, 94.

45. *PiB*, 1: 424 (29 Jan. 1701). The tsar's pseudonym often appears written in Latin script.

46. *PiB*, 2: 159 (2 May 1703).

47. *PiB*, 9: (i): 227–8, 242–3, 983.

48. Juel, 3: 130. Apparently unaware of the long history of this substitution, Juel wrote that this was a 'joke' at Romodanovsky's expense.

49. *PiB*, 3: 195.

50. *PiB*, 4: 305.

51. In 1720 Ivan reported that the Prince-Caesar's robes and regalia had been lost. RGIA, f. 468, Kabinet e. i. v., op. 43, no. 12, l. 41$^{\text{I–v}}$.

52. *MIGO*, 1: 36 (30 Aug. 1713, letter to Romodanovsky).

53. LOI, f. 270, d. 76, l. 87; *MIGO*, 1(ii): 209.

54. LOI, f. 270, d. 76, l. 119; *MIGO*, 1(ii): 227.

55. Weber, 1: 36.

56. *Kniga Marsova ili Voinskikh del* (1713/1766), 189–90.

57. Weber, 1: 225.

58. LOI, f. 270, d. 100, l. 527 (29 Apr. 1722); A. Bychkov ed., *Pis'ma Petra Velikogo, khraniashchiesia v imp Publ. biblioteke* (SPb., 1872), 384.

59. LOI, f. 270, d. 101, l. 321 (19 July 1722); printed in *ZA*, 182.

60. LOI, f. 270, d. 104, l. 177; d. 106, l. 77 (14 Jan. 1724). See copies of letter of 17 Jan. to 'Sire' in d. 107, l. 343 (dated 17 Oct. 1724, but should be 1723): 's nizhaishim moim podanneishim

respektom'. Same letter in *ZA*, 182, also dated 1724.

61. LOI, f. 270, d. 97, l. 138; d. 104, ll. 198, 201, 209.

62. *PiB*, 1: 227.

63. *PiB*, 2: 248 (20 Sept. 1703); 3: 321 (19 Apr. 1705); 4: 18 (before 6 Jan. 1706).

64. See, e.g., Anisimov, *Reforms*, 145. For discussion of use of the concept 'common good', see below, pp. 385–8.

65. *ZA*, 196 (1707); *PiB*, 9: 77 (5 Feb. 1709, to N. M. Zotov).

66. C. Peterson, *Peter the Great's Administrative and Judicial Reforms* (Stockholm, 1979), 53, 55.

67. *PiB*, 11(i): 72. The public announcement was made on 25 Feb. The first senators were V. A. Apukhtin, M. Dologoruky, P. A. Golitsyn, N. P. Mel'nitsky, Ivan Musin-Pushkin, G. A. Plemianníkov, M. M. Samarin, T. N. Streshnev and G. I. Volkonsky. See below, p. 442.

68. *PSZ*, 4: no. 2330, p. 635. For three versions, see *ZA*, 198–200; *PiB*, 11(i): 100–3.

69. *PiB*, 11(i): 102–3. 'Bills of exchange' in (5) were receipts for goods and money received by individuals from government offices.

70. *PiB*, 11(i): 125 (5 Mar. 1711); *ZA*, 204–5.

71. *PSZ*, 4: no. 2328, pp. 634–5; *PiB*, 11(i): 99–100.

72. *PSZ*, 4: no. 2329, p. 635; *PiB*, 11(i): 98–9.

73. *PiB*, 11(i): 125; *PSZ*, 4: no. 2331, pp. 635–6 (5 Mar. 1711); *ZA*, 203–4; *PSZ*, 5: no. 2791 (4 Apr. 1714)

74. *PiB*, 11(i): 144.

75. Ibid., 166.

76. N. I. Pavlenko, *Petr Velikii* (M, 1990), 333.

77. See below, pp. 396–7.

78. For a summary of arguments, see *IPS*, 48 ff. Oddly, there is no discussion of this question in Peterson, *Peter*.

79. The full Polish senate had 140 members, with a smaller subcommittee of sixteen 'resident' senators: N. Davies, *God's Playground. A History of Poland*, vol. 1 (Oxford, 1981), 329–30.

80. *IPS*, 1: 93–4.

81. *PiB*, 11(ii): 157 (29 Sept. 1711), 229 (31 Oct. 1711).

82. *PiB*, 11(i): 71 (22 Feb. 1711): *razriadnyi stol.* This order was not repeated in the 2 March edict.

83. See A. N. Medushevsky, *Utverzhdenie absoliutizma v Rossii* (M, 1994), 131–2.

84. *PSZ*, 5: no. 2758 (10 Jan. 1714); LOI, f. 270, d. 75, l. 10.

85. *IPS*, 5: 3–7.

86. *PSZ*, 5: no. 2872 (27 Dec. 1714).

87. *IPS*, 5: 54–5; 1: 102. (See references in *PZh*, 1724.)

88. See below, p. 442.

89. *PiB*, 11(i): 218, 489.

90. Ibid., 237.

91. *PiB*, 11(ii): 112 (1 Sept. 1711).

92. *PiB*, 13(i): 93 (28 Feb. 1713).

93. *ZA*, 206–7 (2 July 1713).

94. Ibid., 216.

95. *PSZ*, 6: no. 3721 (28 Jan. 1721); *ZA*, 238.

96. Point 11, 27 Apr. 1722: LOI, f. 270, d. 100, ll. 478 ff; *PSZ*, 6: no. 3979, pp. 662–4; *ZA*, 308–11. There are six drafts of the document on the procurator's duties, all with Peter's corrections. See the earlier no. 3895, p. 497 (5 Feb. 1722): 'the Senate is to sit without fail three days per week, and more if necessary when the procurator-general requires it'.

97. *PSZ*, 6: no. 3981, p. 664 (27 Apr. 1722). On the procurator system in the Church, see below, p. 339.

98. 'Za glazami, chaiu, mnogo dikovnikov est': *PSZ*, 7: no. 4507, pp. 285–6 (20 May).

99. *PSZ*, 6: no. 3937, p. 544 (5 Apr. 1722).

100. Ibid., no. 4001, p. 676 (11 May 1722); no. 4036, p. 721 (13 June). See clause 12 of no. 3979, p. 664 (27 Apr. 1722).

101. *PSZ*, 7: no. 4484, pp. 268–9 (16 Mar. 1724).

102. Memorandum attributed to Leibniz, quoted by B. Sumner, *Peter the Great and the Emergence of Russia* (London, 1958), 126. See Peterson, *Peter*, 59–60. The text is in *ZA*, 269–70.

103. J. P. LeDonne, *Absolutism and Ruling Class. The Formation of the Russian Political Order 1700–1825* (Oxford, 1991), 65.

104. There is a good summary in Peterson, *Peter*, 36 ff.

105. See below, p. 136.

106. P. B. Brown, 'Early Modern Russian Bureaucracy. The Evolution of the Chancellery System from Ivan III to Peter the Great, 1478–1717' (Ph.D. thesis, University of Chicago, 1978), 508.

107. These two offices were incorporated into the short-lived General Commissariat, formed in 1700 but made redundant by the capture of its head, Prince Ia. Dolgoruky, by the Swedes. *PSZ*, 6: no. 1766, pp. 14–15 (18 Feb. 1700: 'generals and colonels and lieutenant colonels and other lower officer ranks, foreigners and converts and Russians and lancers and cavalry and infantrymen and all ranks of troops of land forces'); ibid., no. 1859, p. 170 (23 June, 1701).

108. Information from Brown, 'Early Modern', 508; *PSZ*, 6: no. 1859, p. 170 (23 June 1701).

109. *PSZ*, 4: no. 1829, p. 133. See below, pp. 338–9.

110. Golikova, *Politicheskie protsessy*, 9–12. See also J. Cracraft, 'Opposition to Peter the Great', in *Imperial Russia 1700–1917. State. Society. Opposition. Essays in Honor of Marc Raeff* (De Kalb, Ill., 1988), 22–36.

111. Golikova, *Politicheskie protsessy*, 14.

112. Brown, 'Early Modern', 543. See below.

113. LeDonne, *Absolutism*, 65. See Medushevsky, *Utverzhdenie*, 131–3, on Peter's struggle with the *Pomestnyi prikaz*. In 1721 it was replaced by the *Votchinnaia kollegiia*.

114. Brown, 'Early Modern', 557.

115. *ZA*, 213: six are mentioned. Peter consulted Adam Weyde on the possibility of hiring experts abroad.

116. *ZA*, 270. Also proposals from the Saxon engineer J. F. Blüher.

117. See discussion in Peterson, *Peter*, 64–6. A report from F. C. Weber to the elector of Brunswick confirms the connection.

118. *ZA*, 46, 50. As Peterson points out (*Peter*, 70), there is no evidence that Trubetskoy received this letter or acted on it. See Fick's memorandum, 9 May 1718: *ZA*, 223–5.

119. *ZA*, 60.

120. Ibid., 44–5, 45–6; Peterson, *Peter*, 124.

121. *ZA*, 47–8 (2 Sept. 1715).

122. *PSZ*, 5: no. 3129 (11 Dec.), 'o shtate kollegii i o vremeni otkrytiia onikh'; no. 3133, pp. 527–8 (15 Dec.).; *ZA*, 216–17, 219–20. The colleges, with their first presidents and vice-presidents (if appointed) in brackets, were: (i) Foreign Affairs (*Inostrannykh del*: G. Golovkin/P. P. Shafirov) [originally referred to as the *politicheskaia kollegiia*. Peterson (*Peter*, 85–6) argues that it was based on the Swedish *kanslikollegium*]; (ii) State Revenues (*Kamer-kollegiia*: D. M. Golitsyn/ Baron M. W. Nieroth); (iii) Justice (*Iustits-kollegiia*: A. A. Matveev/ Hermann von Brevern); (iv) State Accounting (*Revizion-kollegiia*: Ia. F. Dolgoruky/—); (v) War (*Voinskaia*: A. D. Menshikov/A. A. Weyde); (vi) Admiralty (*Admiralteiskaia*: F. M. Apraksin/C. Cruys); (vii) Commerce (*Kommerts-kollegiia*: P. A. Tolstoy/ Schmidt [Peterson cannot identify him,) *Peter*, 89], but see ibid., 215, Johann von Schmiden, vice-president of the *Revizion-kollegiia* in 1720); (viii) State Expenses (*Shtats-kontor-kollegiia*: I. A. Musin-Pushkin /—); (ix) Mines and Manufacture (*Berg i manufaktur*: J. Bruce/—).

123. General Regulation, *ZA*, 505.

124. On the appointment of presidents and assistants, see *ZA*, 218. Peterson, *Peter*, 87.

125. *PSZ*, 6: no. 3528: 'o balotirovanii' (19 Feb. 1720). See also LOI, f. 270, d. 100, l. 288 (17 Mar. 1722).

126. *PSZ*, 6: no. 3877, pp. 469–80 (12 Jan. 1722).

127. Brown, 'Early Modern', 581.

128. 2 June 1718: *PSZ*, 5: no. 3205; *ZA*, 226.

129. 2 Oct. 1718: *PSZ*, 5: no. 3232; *ZA*, 226.

130. See order of 11 Dec. 1717: *ZA*, 217.

131. A. A. Golombievsky, *Sotrudniki Petra Velikogo* (M, 1903), 11–12.

132. LOI, f. 270, d. 106, ll. 83–4 (14 Jan. 1724).

133. ('. . . what one will not understand, another will'). Texts in *PSZ*, 6: no. 3534, pp. 141–60 (28 Feb. 1720). Drafts and variants (12 of them) in *ZA*, 413–510. Peterson writes that 'another book' would be needed to analyze the

sources (*Peter*, 118). The original project was based on a Swedish source: *Cantselie Ordningh* of 1661. (*ZA*, 411–12), but Peterson found no close textual similarity, and believes that the Russian regulation was based on current Swedish practices as formulated by Fick. Anisimov believes that the idea of 'creating a whole hierarchy of regulations' was Peter's own (*Reforms*, 149).

134. The terms *iustitsiia* and *politsiia*, foreign words unfamiliar to most Russians, are explained as *rosprava sudnaia* and *grazhdanstvo*: *ZA*, 482. On 'police', see below, p. 387.

135. *PSZ*, 7: no. 4422, p. 205 (20 Jan. 1724).

136. Ibid., p. 206.

137. Peterson, *Peter*, 116, points out that Peter noted the unsuitability of this; *PSZ*, 5: no. 3303 (13 Feb. 1719).

138. Peterson, *Peter*, 115.

139. *ZA*, 290.

140. Ibid., 491 (General Regulation).

141. Peterson, *Peter*, 41.

142. *PSZ*, 3: no. 1673, pp. 597–8, nos. 1703, 1717, etc.; Zheliabuzhsky, 'Zapiski', 269–70.

143. *PSZ*, 4: no. 1797, p. 59 (12 June 1700); no. 1803, p. 66 (2 July 1700).

144. Ibid., no. 1817, pp. 86–7 (11 Dec. 1700).

145. 4 Apr. 1714: *PSZ*, 5: no. 2791; *ZA*, 208–9.

146. LOI, f. 270, d. 103, l. 134.

147. Ibid., ll. 576–9 (June 1723).

148. Peterson, *Peter*, 108. See Pesoshkovs 103.

149. *PSZ*, 4: no. 1953, p. 229 (15 Dec. 1703).

150. Ibid., no. 2188, p. 402 (26 Jan. 1708).

151. *ZA*, 489.

152. *PSZ*, 7: no. 4423, pp. 205–6 (20 Jan. 1724).

153. LOI, f. 270, d. 103, l. 128^{r-v} (30 Jan. 1723). See *PSZ*, 7: no. 4337, pp. 142–3 (24 Oct. 1723).

154. *PSZ*, 7: no. 4436, p. 216 (22 Jan. 1724). See also no. 4431, p. 215 (21 Jan. 1724).

155. *PSZ*, 6: no. 4113, p. 780 (5 Oct. 1722).

156. *200-letie*, pp. xiii, 11.

157. Ibid., 58.

158. Ibid., appendix II, p. 5 (RGADA, f. 9, otd. II, bk 94, ll. 1–5; also printed in *ZA*, 170–3.)

159. Famous examples include Le Blond and Rastrelli.

160. *200-letie*, 36–7 (as described by Makarov after Peter's death in 1725).

161. The first thirteen books in sec. I of the Cabinet archive (RGADA, f. 9) are devoted to the History. See below, pp. 322–3.

162. V. R. Tarlovskaia, 'Iz istorii gorodskoi reformy v Rossii kontsa XVII-nach. XVIII v.', in *Gosudarstvennye uchrezhdeniia Rossii XVI–XVIII vv* (M, 1991), 101–2.

163. LeDonne, *Absolutism*, 67.

164. *PSZ*, 3: no. 1579, pp. 284–301 (31 Mar. 1697).

165. H. J. Torke, 'Crime and Punishment in the Pre-Petrine Civil Service', in E. Mendelsohn and M. Shatz, eds, *Imperial Russia 1700–1917. State. Society. Opposition. Essays in Honor of Marc Raeff* (De Kalb, Ill., 1988), 9.

166. Ibid., 6.

167. S. M. Soloviev, *History of Russia*, vol. 25: *Rebellion and Reform. Fedor and Sophia 1682–1689*, trans. L. Hughes (Gulf Breeze, Fla., 1989), 218.

168. Peterson, *Peter*, 234.

169. Tarlovskaia, 'Iz istorii', 98.

170. *PSZ*, 3: no. 1674, pp. 598–600 (30 Jan. 1699); no. 1675, pp. 600–1 (30 Jan. 1699); no. 1685, pp. 613–14 (17 Apr. 1699); no. 1708, p. 654 (27 Oct. 1699). The term *burmistr* is sometimes translated as 'magistrate', which is misleading if it suggests the very different English office of the same name.

171. *PSZ*, 4: no. 1775, p. 19 (11 Mar. 1700).

172. Peterson, *Peter*, 235–6, fails to mention the pressure upon nobles from the war.

173. See LeDonne, *Absolutism*, 69: 'the country was placed for all practical purposes under martial law'.

174. *PSZ*, 4: no. 2218 (18 Dec. 1708).

175. *PiB*, 9: 91–6. See letters to governors dated 18 Feb. 1709. Peterson, *Peter*, 237–8, mentions only eight.

176. See Peterson, *Peter*, 239.

177. M. M. Bogoslovsky, *Oblastnaia reforma Petra Velikogo, Provintsiia 1719–27* (M, 1902), 84–5.

178. *ZA*, 212 (23 Dec. 1714).

179. Ibid., 365 (28 Jan. 1715).

180. *PSZ*, 5: no. 3025, pp. 471–2 (1 June

1716); *DPPS*, 6(i) (SPb., 1901), no. 535, p. 482 (May 1716).

181. 'Reskripty i ukazy Petra I k lifliand-skim general-gubernatoram: Polon-skomu, kn. Golitsynu i kn. Rep-ninu', in *Osmnadtsatyi vek. Istoricheskii sbornik izdannyi P. Bartenevym*, vol. 4 (M, 1869), 7 ff.

182. Ibid., 42.

183. Ibid., 37, 43.

184. Ibid., 29–31, 42.

185. Ibid., 54 (Mar. 1720; apparently two of the trees were still there in the 1860s), 54 (May 1720), 55–6 (June 1720).

186. Ibid., 62–3, 67

187. *PSZ*, 6: no. 3622, pp. 223–9 (July 1720).

188. Ibid., no. 3668, p. 251 (26 Oct. 1720).

189. Ibid., no. 3686, pp. 267–72 (14 Dec. 1720).

190. *ZA*, 61–2. For a summary of Swedish provincial government, see Peterson, *Peter*, 224–9. On Fick's memoranda (9 May 1718), ibid., 248–52. These included lists of duties and wages.

191. *ZA*, 63; *PSZ*, 5: no. 3244 (26 Nov. 1718).

192. *PSZ*, 5: nos 3294, 3295, 3296, 3304 (Jan. 1719), 3479 (Dec. 1719), 3571 (Apr. 1720). Peterson, *Peter*, 268 ff., gives details of the various Swedish originals: e.g., the instruction for *land-shövdingar* of 1687, of which Peter's instruction is a 'conscious revision' (p. 281). See also *PSZ*, 5: no. 3381 (29 May 1719).

193. Pososhkov, 101–2.

194. *PSZ*, 5: no. 3294.

195. Ibid., no. 3380. St Petersburg province was to be ruled by a governor-general (in the city), three governors outside it, a commandant, and nine provincial governors.

196. *PSZ*, 6: no. 3932; *ZA*, 101 (4 Apr. 1722).

197. *ZA*, 223 (11 June 1718). Peterson, *Peter*, 265–8, believes that Fick may have used the ordinances of Stockholm.

198. *PSZ*, 6: no. 3708, pp. 291–309 (16 Jan. 1721); also in *PRP*, 135–6. See below, p. 387.

199. *PSZ*, 6: no. 3708, pp. 291–309. (16 Jan. 1721); also in *PRP*, 126–50.

200. *PSZ*, 6: no. 4047, pp. 726–36 (9 June 1722).

201. I. A. Bulygin, *Monastyrskie krest'iane*

Rossii v pervoi chet. XVIII v. (M, 1977), 58; V. M. Kabuzan, *Izmeneniia v razmeshchenii naseleniia Rossii v XVIII-pervoi pol. XIX v.* (M, 1971), 63–5. See also Pososhkov, 108–9, introduction.

202. *PSZ*, 7: no. 4533, pp. 316–18.

203. Ibid., no. 4535, pp. 324–7.

204. Ibid., no. 4536, pp. 327–9 (26 June 1724): instruction to the land com-missar.

205. *ZA*, 61.

206. Bogoslovsky, *Oblastnaia reforma* 71; Peterson, *Peter*, 282–4.

207. Bogoslovsky, *Oblastnaia reforma, prilo-zhenie*, p. 3.

208. *SIRIO*, 55: 189.

209. Weber, 1: 72.

210. Strahlenberg, *Zapiski*, 120–1.

211. V. N. Berkh, 'Zhizneopisanie gen.-leit. V. I. Gennina', *Gornyi zhurnal*, 1826, bk 4, p. 128.

212. See edict on the *reketmeister*, *PSZ*, 6: no. 3947, pp. 642–3 (6 Apr. 1722).

213. Pososhkov, 205.

214. Ibid., 192.

215. *PSZ*, 5: no. 3006 (preface to Military Statute, 31 Mar. 1716).

216. Peterson, *Peter*, 324; *ZA*, 377–9; *PSZ*, 5: no. 3261 (22 Dec. 1718).

217. Nartov, 44.

218. *PSZ*, 6: no. 3970, pp. 656–7 (17 Apr. 1722); *ZA*, 104–8; LOI, f. 270, d. 100, l. 409 (14 Apr. 1722) and ll. 417–18, 419–21^{-v}, etc.

219. *ZA*, 124.

220. LOI, f. 270, d. 104, ll. 163–4; *ZA*, 131–2. See also *PSZ*, 7: no. 4337, pp. 142–3 (on Shafirov); LOI, f. 270, d. 104, l. 169.

221. D. Serov, 'Rossiiskaia mafiia: nachalo puti', *Russkaia Aziia*, 38/8 (1994), 14.

222. Medushevsky, *Utverzhdenie*, 91.

223. E. V. Anisimov, 'Progress through Violence from Peter the Great to Lenin and Stalin', *Russian History*, 17(1990), 413–14.

224. Pososhkov, 222.

225. *MLC*, 1. See also Torke, 'Crime and Punishment', 17.

226. See Pososhkov's proposal for abstracts of all judgments delivered in previous cases, 'so that similar cases can in future be decided out of hand and not sent up to Senate': 223.

227. See Peterson, *Peter*, 305.

228. *PSZ*, 4: no. 1765; *ZA*, 30–3; Peterson, *Peter*, 306–7.

229. Medushevsky, *Utverzhdenie*, 109–10.

230. *ZA*, 40–1. See *ukaz* of 15 June 1714: *PSZ*, 5: no. 2804, pp. 103–4.

231. See Senate *ukaz* of 3 June 1714: *PSZ*, 5: no. 2819.

232. Pososhkov, 224. Catherine II was reverting to seventeenth-century practice when she convoked her Legislative Commission in 1766.

233. *ZA*, 73–4. Earlier James Bruce was sent sixteen books of Swedish laws in German for translation (LOI, f. 270, d. 75, l. 448 (14 June 1714)).

234. *ZA*, 85–6 (8 Aug. 1720); *PSZ*, 6: no. 3626, p. 230; no. 3661 (17 Oct.): *O sochinenii novogo ulozheniia*.

235. *ZA*, 140.

236. Ibid., 132–3 (6 Nov. 1723).

237. See A. Man'kov, 'Pro"ekt Ulozheniia rossiiskogo gosudarstva 1720–25 gg.', in S. L. Peshtich et al., eds, *Problemy istorii feodal'noi Rossii* (L, 1971), 157–67.

238. *ZA*, 52–3. (10 Apr. 1716).

239. But see Peterson's argument (*Peter*, 339–40), based on the Soviet historian P. S. Romashkin, that the *Ulozhenie*, with supplements, continued to provide the basis for judgments in the Justice College and other departments. 'Vopros o primenenii voinskikh artikulov Petra I v obshchikh sudakh', *Vestnik Moskovskogo Universiteta*, 1948, no. 2, 3–12.

240. Strahlenberg, *Zapiski*, 123.

241. F. Gorlé, 'Quelques Aspects du droit pénal russe sous Pierre le Grand', *Slavica Gandensia*, 12 (1985), 100, points out that Alexander Radishchev's conviction was based on articles of the statute.

242. F. Gorlé, 'Les Sanctions en droit pénal russe sous Pierre le Grand', *Slavica Gandensia*, 13 (1986), 355.

243. Wortman, *Development*, 25.

244. *ZA*, 125 (8 Feb. 1723).

245. *PSZ*, 6: no. 3761 (1721); G. L. Freeze, *The Russian Levites: Parish Clergy in the Eighteenth Century* (Cambridge, Mass., 1977), 22–4. On 'word and deed', see below, p. 126.

246. *PSZ*, 6: no. 3963, pp. 650–2 (12 Apr. 1722); no. 4081, pp. 764–7.

247. Peterson, *Peter*, 304.

248. *PSZ*, 4: no. 1918. This right was reconfirmed in 1722.

249. *PSZ*, 5: no. 2756 (23 Dec. 1713).

250. Golikova, *Politicheskie*, 58.

251. Ibid., 24–6.

252. Peterson, *Peter*, 307. The Preobrazhensky *prikaz* was supposed to confine itself to cases of treason, but see the complaint of the Justice College, July 1719, that it was dealing with land-holding cases: ibid., 329.

253. Ibid., 313–16.

254. *ZA*, 122.

255. Bogoslovsky, *Oblastnaia reforma*, 4; No date is given.

256. Ibid., 15.

257. Peterson, *Peter*, 326.

258. Ibid., 328; *PSZ*, 5: no. 3269 (8 Jan. 1719).

259. *PSZ*, 5: no. 3294, art. 5.

260. *PSZ*, 6: no. 3935 (4 Apr. 1722).

261. Wortman, *Development*, 13. The major study of these courts is Bogoslovsky, *Oblastnaia reforma*.

262. Wortman, *Development*, 16.

263. *PSZ*, 6: no. 3900, p. 500 (5 Feb. 1722); no. 3947, pp. 642–3 (16 Apr., 1722).

264. See R. Wortman, 'Peter the Great and Court Procedure', *CASS*, 8 (1974), 303–11; Pososhkov, 194.

265. *PSZ*, 5: no. 3006: 'Kratkoe izobrazhenie protsessov ili sudebnykh tiazhb', ch. 1.

266. *PSZ*, 3: no. 1572, pp. 278–80 (15 Feb., 1697).

267. *PSZ*, 7: no. 4344, pp. 147–50; *ZA*, 400.

268. Peterson, *Peter*, 350–1.

269. See, e.g., an order of 5 Apr. 1720 that the cases of detainees in the court of appeals be decided *bezvolokitno* and swiftly: *PSZ*, 6: no. 3560, p. 177.

270. See, e.g., 'Kratkoe izobrazhenie protsessov', 1716, ch. 5; *PRP*, 586. (This provision appears in the *Ulozhenie*, ch. 10).

271. Golikova, *Politicheskie*, 66–8.

272. *ZA*, 101; *PSZ*, 6: no. 3933, p. 524.

273. Gorlé, 'Les Sanctions', 357.

274. For certain forms of desertion, loss of rights and access to law, and no one to communicate with him.

275. Gorlé, 'Les Sanctions', 360; I. de Madariaga, 'Penal Policy in the Age of Catherine the Great', in L. Berlinguer and F. Colao, eds, *La 'Leopoldina'. Criminalità e Giustizia Criminale nelle Riforme del Settecento Europeo* (Milan, 1990), 2: 499.

276. Gorlé, 'Les Sanctions', 356.

277. *PSZ*, 7: no. 4157, p. 20 (5 Feb. 1723).

278. Ibid., no. 4270, p. 94 (16 July 1723).

279. *PSZ*, 6: no. 3755, p. 368 (7 Mar. 1721).

280. Pososhkov, 202. *PSZ*, 5: no. 3140 (15 Jan. 1718); 6: no. 3950, p. 644 (6 Apr. 1722); no. 4091 (13 Sept. 1722).

281. Stählin, no. 103, pp. 158–9; also in I. I. Golikov, *Deianiia Petra Velikogo*, vol. 5 (M, 1788), 97.

282. LOI, f. 270, d. 103, ll. 178–9 (8 Feb. 1723).

283. Stählin, no. 87, p. 135; same in Golikov, *Deianiia*. Reported to Stählin by Voetsius, the court joiner.

284. *ZA*, 157.

285. LOI, f. 270, d. 97, l. 233 (24 Feb. 1721, to Romodanovsky).

286. Bergholz, 1724, pp. 10–11.

287. Ibid., 75ʳ–6ᵛ.

288. *PSZ*, 4: no. 2225, pp. 448–9 (22 Feb. 1709).

289. Ibid., no. 1950, p. 228 (19 Nov. 1703). See Stählin's anecdote about revellers being flogged with the knout for pulling branches from oaks in a grove planted by the tsar: 89–90.

290. *PSZ*, 4: no. 2017, pp. 283–4 (19 Jan. 1705).

291. I. M. Matley, 'Defence Manufactures of St Petersburg 1703–1730', *Geographical Review*, 71 (1981), 411–26.

292. This category of punishment fixed in edicts of 1703–4: e.g., *PSZ*, 4: no. 1957.

293. See below, pp. 200–1.

294. V. N. Berkh, *Zhizneopisanie gen.-adm. F. M. Apraksina* (SPb., 1825), 53 (from Prince Ia. Dolgoruky to Apraksin, 16 Dec. 1717).

295. On this case and shirking, see below, p. 174.

296. *PSZ*, 6: no. 3897, pp. 499–500 (5 Feb. 1722).

297. Juel, 3: 38

298. Weber 1: 9.

299. *PSZ*, 7: no. 4140, p. 6.

300. *ZA*, 489, 501.

301. *SIRIO*, 11: 413.

302. *ZA*, 107.

303. *PSZ*, 5: no. 2871.

304. Pososhkov, 204. *PSZ*, 6: no. 3928, p. 522 (4 Apr. 1722); 7: no. 4530, p. 303 (June 1724).

305. Pososhkov, 206–7.

306. Wortman, *Development*, 16.

307. Ibid., 21–2. For a new interpretation of the relationship of the local gentry to the centre in the seventeenth century, see V. Kivelson, *Autocracy in the Provinces, The Muscovite Gentry and Political Culture in the Seventeenth Century* (Stanford, Calif., 1996).

308. *Memorandum on the Needs of the State, Presented to Empress Catherine I* (18 Nov. 1726), in *200-letie*, appendix II, pp. 45–58 (RGADA, f. 9, op. I, kn. 33, ll. 179–93).

309. *SIRIO*, 55: 363.

310. Manifesto of 9 Jan. and 24 Jan. 1727: *PSZ*, 7: no. 5017, pp. 745–6; discussion in Peterson, *Peter*, 290–4; Pososhkov, 127–34.

311. Peterson, *Peter*, 302.

312. *PSZ*, 4: no. 2310, pp. 582–8 (30 Nov. 1710).

313. Juel, 3: 118.

314. Weber, 1: 128.

315. Serov, 'Rossiiskaia mafiia', 14.

316. Pososhkov, 230.

CHAPTER 5: THE ECONOMY

1. *PiB*, 10: 434 (11 Dec. 1710 Peter to Vasily Zotov). A more famous formulation of the same idea was included in Peter's instructions to the new Senate (2 Mar. 1711): *ZA*, 199. Variations include 'Money works in a state like blood in a man': to Golovkin, *PiB*, 6: 199 (26 Dec. 1707) and 'Money is the lifeblood of war': *PiB*, 11: 237 (19 May 1711, also to the Senate). See also, the biblical quotation 'the love of money is the root of all evil', Naval Statute (1720): *PSZ*, 6: no. 3485, p. 6.

2. L. Lewitter, 'Peter the Great and the Modern World', in P. Dukes, ed., *Russia and Europe* (London, 1991),

104–5. See E. I. Bobrova, comp. *Biblioteka Petra I. Ukazatel'-spravochnik* (L, 1978), 133, 949.

3. 'The economic policies of Peter the Great were of significance because they allowed him to expand Russia's military potential, thus making possible a protracted war': W. C. Fuller, *Strategy and Power in Russia 1600–1914* (New York, 1992), 57.

4. *SIRIO*, 39: 52–5 (14/25 Mar. 1705). A. Rothstein, *Peter the Great and Marlborough. Politics and Diplomacy in Converging Wars* (Basingstoke, 1986), 56–7.

5. Korb, 2: 153.

6. Pososhkov, 221. Cf. 'The riches, power and honour of the monarch arise only from the riches, strength and reputation of his subjects': Hobbes.

7. Analysis in A. P. Spunde, 'Ocherk ekonomicheskoi istorii russkoi burzhuazii', *Nauka i zhizn'*, 1988, no. 1, 81, based on P. Miliukov, *Gosudarstvennoe khoziaistvo Rossii v pervoi chet. XVIII st. i reforma Petra Velikogo* (SPb., 1905), 98–107.

8. Much of the discussion which follows is based upon E. V. Anisimov, *Podatnaia reforma Petra I* (L, 1982), ch. 1.

9. *PiB*, 10: 17.

10. Ibid., 24, 476–7.

11. Order to governors, ibid., 42 (9 Feb. 1710).

12. Ibid., 46. There was no census in Left Bank Ukraine.

13. Miliukov, *Gosudarstvennoe*, 201–2; M. Klochkov, *Naselenie Rossii pri Petre Velikom po perepisiam togo vremeni. I. 1678–1721* (SPb., 1911), 252–6.

14. E. V. Anisimov, *The Reforms of Peter the Great. Progress through Coercion*, trans. J. Alexander (New York, 1993), 161.

15. C. Peterson, *Peter the Great's Administrative and Judicial Reforms* (Stockholm, 1979), 280; *ZA*, 45.

16. See preparations for the new *reviziia* in early 1723, including letters to governors: 'You must carry out the registration and certification of souls and complete it by next December', (LOI, f. 270, d. 103, l. 274 (Feb. 1723)).

17. *PSZ*, 7: no. 4650, p. 413. See Miliukov, *Gosudarstvennoe*, 727.

18. Anisimov, *Reforms*, 162.

19. A. Kahan, *The Plow, the Hammer and the Knout. An Economic History of Eighteenth-Century Russia* (Chicago, 1985), 330–1.

20. Miliukov, *Gosudarstvennoe*, 727–8.

21. A. Gerschenkron, 'Russian Mercantilism', in *Europe in the Russian Mirror* (Cambridge, 1970), 75.

22. Kahan, *Plow*, 331–2.

23. See B. Mironov, review of Kahan, *Plow*, in *RR*, 46 (1987), 220; *idem*, 'The Consequences of the Price Revolution in 18th-Century Russia', *Economic History Review*, 45 (1992), 496.

24. Pososhkov, 104.

25. Ibid., 319. See calculations by eds, 304–5, which find all sorts of discrepancies.

26. Juel, 3: 15.

27. *PSZ*, 3: no. 1646, pp. 478–9 (1 Sept. 1698).

28. See below, pp. 171, 336.

29. *PSZ*, 4: no. 1968, p. 247 (9 Feb. 1704). In 1705 the peasant rate was lowered to 3 altyn, 3 denga. One person was to be responsible for paying the tax on communal baths (nos 2058 (12 June) and 2060 (13 June)).

30. Ibid., no. 2014, p. 282 (15 Jan. 1705).

31. Ibid., no. 2222, pp. 442–3 (25 Jan. 1709); Weber, 1: 63–4.

32. GPB OR, f. 1003 (Voskresensky), no. 11, ll. 95–6.

33. *PSZ*, 4: nos 1954, 1955, pp. 229–32; no. 1956, pp. 232–40 (Jan. 1704).

34. N. B. Golikova, *Politicheskie protsessy pri Petre I* (M, 1957), 146.

35. Weber, 1: 74.

36. Ibid., 77.

37. *PiB*, 11: 411. Figures for salt trade profits: 1705: 172,100 roubles; 1706: 359,100 roubles; 1707: 386,500 roubles; 1708: 396,000 roubles; 1709: 400, 400 roubles; 1710: 450,000 roubles.

38. *PSZ*, 7: no. 4220, pp. 59–60 (10 May). See below, pp. 281–2.

39. Fuller, *Strategy*, 57. These figures do not seem to take account of inflation.

40. Weber, 1: 47–9. (Peter installed a 'grand Inquisition at the End of the Year'.)

41. Ibid., 72.

42. V. N. Berkh, *Zhizneopisanie gen.-adm. F. M. Apraksina* (SPb., 1825), 127 (25 Apr. 1706).

43. L. N. Semenova, 'Inostrannye mastera v Peterburge v pervoi treti XVIII v.', in *Nauka i kul'tura Rossii XVIII v. Sbornik statei* (L, 1984), 215.

44. *PiB*, 12(i): 200.

45. LOI, f. 270, d. 104, l. 83 (letter no. 186, 24 Sept. 1723).

46. *PiB*, 7(i): 2 (4 Jan. 1708).

47. *PiB*, 8(ii): 48 (30 July 1708).

48. *PSZ*, 7: nos 4161, 4163, pp. 21–2 (9 Feb. 1723).

49. LOI, f. 270, d. 103, ll. 384–7^{r-v} (7 Apr. 1723); *PSZ*, 7: no. 4193, pp. 44–6. A decree of 13 Jan. 1723 seems to impose half the usual tariff on foreign grain imports: *PSZ*, 7: no. 4411, p. 201.

50. LOI, f. 270, d. 104, l. 51^{r-v}; *PSZ*, 7: no. 4299.

51. LOI, f. 270, d. 103, l. 395 (8 Apr. 1723).

52. *PSZ*, 7: no. 4168, pp. 24–5 (16 Feb. 1723).

53. See Peterson, *Peter*, 140–6, on Swedish practice. His chapter 'The Central Fiscal Administration', 140–220, gives much detail.

54. *ZA*, 559: instruction to the *Kamer-kollegiia*.

55. *ZA*, 560.

56. See instruction in ibid. 559–61.

57. Peterson, *Peter*, 208.

58. Ibid., 209, 217; *ZA*, 563.

59. See chapter in Peterson, *Peter*, 356 ff. There were attempts to set up a 'college for commercial affairs' in 1712.

60. *PSZ*, 5: no. 3318, pp. 671–6; 7: no. 4453, pp. 241–9 (1724, revised version).

61. *ZA*, 570.

62. Peterson, *Peter*, 175–9.

63. The standard catalogue of the coins of the Petrine era was compiled by Grand Duke Georgy Mikhailovich in 1914. See J. Perkowski, 'Peter the Great—a Catalogue of Coins and Medals in the Smithsonian Collection', *Numismatist*, 95 (1982), 1188–1204; I. G. Spassky, *The Russian Monetary System* (Amsterdam, 1967); I. G. Spassky and E. Shchukina, *Medals and Coins of the Age of Peter the Great* (L, 1974); I. Rylov and B. Sobolin, *Monety Rossii i SSSR. Katalog. 1700–1993* (M, 1994).

64. Stählin, 82.

65. Weber, 1: 252.

66. M. S. Anderson, *Peter the Great* (London, 1978), 95.

67. *IPS*, 1: 81 (20 Aug. 1717, A. Ia. Shchukin to Makarov, from Amsterdam). See Senate edict: *PSZ*, 6: no. 3441.

68. *PSZ*, 7: no. 4185, pp. 31–3 (10 Mar. 1723).

69. *200-letie*, 258.

70. Ibid., 222, 223, 259.

71. *PiB*, 11: 437.

72. *200-letie*, 222.

73. A. N. Medushevsky, 'Petrovskaia reforma gosudarstvennogo apparata', in F. Shelov-Kovediaev, ed., *Reformy vtoroi poloviny XVII–XX v.: podgotovka, provedenie, rezul'taty* (M, 1989), 78–9.

74. Peterson, *Peter*, 99, 103.

75. Ibid., 241.

76. Ibid., 101.

77. LOI, f. 270, d. 104, l. 470 (21 Dec. 1723).

78. Ibid., d. 106, ll. 248–51^{r-v} (Jan. 1724).

79. Ibid., l. 149 (19 Jan. 1724). These may be compared with Hellie's figure of 4 copecks as the median day wage in the seventeenth century, in 'Material Culture and Identity in Late Medieval and Early Modern Russia,' (unpubl. seminar paper, UCLA, 1994), 10.

80. LOI, f. 270, d. 103, l. 251 (22 Feb. 1723).

81. Ibid., d. 106, l. 57 (13 Jan. 1724).

82. N. I. Pavlenko, *Poluderzhavnyi vlastelin* (M, 1991), 367.

83. *PSZ*, 6: no. 3938, p. 637 (5 Apr. 1722).

84. *200-letie*, 237.

85. Ibid., 245 (all examples from 1719).

86. Ibid., 254, 257.

87. Rothstein, *Peter the Great*, 13–14.

88. Stählin, 157–8.

89. Gerschenkron, 'Russian Mercantilism', 82.

90. See Kahan, *Plow*, 163 and *passim*.

91. GPB OR, f. 1003 (Voskresensky), no. 11, l. 57.

92. Kahan, *Plow*, 174, 178. See Grund's remarks, 41.

93. Kahan, *Plow*, 190.

94. Grund, 37–8.

95. Kahan, *Plow*, 186.

96. Ibid., 170–3.

97. Ibid., 192.

98. *PSZ*, 7: no. 4185, pp. 31–3 (10 Mar. 1723).

99. Discussion in Kahan, *Plow*, 236–7. The document (31 Jan. 1724) was consulted in GPB OR, f. 1003 (Voskresensky), bk 10, ll. 304–79.

100. *PSZ*, 3: no. 1570, pp. 276–8 (1 Feb. 1697), and no. 1581, p. 303 (16 Apr. 1697).

101. *PiB*, 9: 96–7 (19 Feb. 1709, letter to Styles).

102. *MIGO*, 1(ii): 104 (26 May 1714). Peter instructed Menshikov to send several flagons to him in Reval.

103. LOI, f. 270, d. 104, ll. 183–6 (30 Oct. 1723); petition granted.

104. *PSZ*, 7: no. 4155, pp. 19–20: 'Chtob tot kapital paki obrashchalsia v Rossiiu.'

105. Ibid., no. 4286, pp. 102–4 (20 Aug. 1723).

106. Ibid., no. 4368, p. 163 (16 Nov. 1723).

107. Ibid., no. 4341, pp. 144–5; LOI, f. 270, d. 104, ll. 212–14^{r-v} (1 Nov. 1723).

108. LOI, f. 270, 104, l. 525 (Dec. 1723); *ZA*, p. 118; *PSZ*, 7: no. 4348, pp. 152–3 (8 Nov. 1723). On setting up a whaling company at Archangel, see no. 4349, p. 153 (8 Nov. 1723).

109. LOI, f. 270, d. 101, l. 56 (11 May 1722).

110. See A. Donnelly, 'Peter the Great and Central Asia', *CSP*, 17 (1975), 216–17.

111. G. A. Nekrasov, *Russko-shvedskie otnosheniia i politika velikikh derzhav v 1721–26 gg.* (M, 1964), 49–50.

112. LOI, f. 270, d. 101, l. 287 (letter from Peter to the *Kommerts-kollegiia*, 13 July 1722).

113. V. S. Bobylev, *Vneshniaia politika Rossii epokhi Petra I* (M, 1990), 93.

114. 'Reskripty i ukazy Petra I lifliandskim general-gubernatoram Polonskomu, kn.-Golitsynu; kn. Repninu', in *Osmnadtsatyi vek*, 4 (1869), 42–3, *ukaz* of 16 Mar. 1717.

115. Ibid., 10–11 (5 Nov. 1713).

116. *PSZ*, 7: no. 4475, pp. 264–5 (15 Feb. 1724).

117. Weber, 1: 102.

118. F. J. Strahlenberg, *Zapiski kapitana Filippa Ioganna Stralenberga ob istorii i geografii Rossiiskoi imperii Petra Velikogo*, trans. and ed. Iu. Bespiatykh et al. (M & L, 1985), 1: 129.

119. LOI, f. 270, d. 107, l. 143 (3 June 1724).

120. Ibid., d. 100, l. 370 (11 Apr. 1722); *PSZ*, 6: no. 3956.

121. Kahan, *Plow*, 264.

122. Grund, 40.

123. Anderson, *Peter the Great*, 99.

124. Kahan, *Plow*, 268.

125. *PSZ*, 3: no. 1592 (20 Aug. 1697).

126. *PSZ*, 4: no. 1972, p. 249 (1 Mar. 1704).

127. Anisimov, *Reforms*, 70; Gerschenkron, 'Russian Mercantilism', 69.

128. Anderson, *Peter the Great*, 100.

129. See, e.g., Fuller, *Strategy*, 61; Spunde, 'Ocherk', 81: 'Cannons and guns increased. But people continued as before to till the soil with the wooden plough.'

130. Gerschenkron, 'Russian Mercantilism', 85.

131. *PiB*, 5: 122 (11 Mar. 1707); 538 (24 Mar. 1707).

132. Peterson, *Peter*, 370–1.

133. *PSZ*, V, no. 3464 (10 Dec.)

134. See, e.g., *PSZ*, 6: no. 3974, pp. 653–4 (19 Apr. 1722).

135. Weber, 1: 183–4.

136. *PSZ*, 7: no. 4378, pp. 167–81.

137. Grund, 41

138. J. Perry, *The State of Russia* (1716) (London, 1967), 268.

139. Ibid., 269–70.

140. *PSZ*, 5: no. 2943 (21 Oct. 1715); 7: no. 4259 (28 June 1723).

141. *PSZ*, 4: no. 2929 (1 Sept. 1715); G. V. Esipov, *Raskol'nich'i dela XVIII stoletiia* (SPb., 1861), 2:178 (1715).

142. E. Iu. Moiseenko, comp., *Kostium v Rossii pervoi chetverti XVIII v.* (L, 1984), 18–19.

143. See LOI, f. 270, d. 107, l. 172. 15 June 1724 on studying the process of silk manufacture in Gilian and Mazendron.

144. *PSZ*, 7: no. 4600, pp. 369–72 (19 Nov. 1724).

145. GPB OR, f. 1003 (Voskresensky), no. 11, vol. 3, pt 3, ll. 38–41.

146. *200-letie*, 240–1.

147. See report by Cruys in GPB OR, f. 1003 (Voskresensky), no. 11, ll. 61–3. In 1720 the factory was placed under the direction of Ivan Timmerman.

148. I. M. Matley, 'Defence Manufactures of St Petersburg 1703–1730', *Geographical Review*, 71 (1981), 414.
149. Ibid., 421.
150. Ibid., 420.
151. Ibid., 422–3.
152. Fuller, *Strategy*, 62–3.
153. *ZA*, 129.
154. *PSZ*, 4: no. 2052, pp. 307–8 (25 May 1705); no. 2072, pp. 315–16 (15 Sept. 1705).
155. Ibid., no. 2074, pp. 315–16 (15 Sept. 1705).
156. N. I. Pavlenko, 'Petr I. K izucheniiu sotsial'no-politicheskikh vzgliadov', in *RPR*, 90. *PSZ*, 5: no. 3294, p. 627 (Jan. 1719).
157. *PiB*, 9: 347–8, 1187–8.
158. E. A. Kniazhetskaia, 'Petr I—organizator issledovanii kaspiiskogo moria', in M. I. Belov, ed., *Voprosy geografii petrovskogo vremeni. Sb. statei* (L, 1975), 35–6.
159. Joseph Stalin, 19 Nov. 1928, speech to the plenum of the Central Committee on 'the industrialization of the country and right tendencies in the CP'.
160. Spunde, 'Ocherk', 80.
161. See E. V. Anisimov, 'Petr Velikii: rozhdenie imperii', *VI*, 1989, no. 7, 3–21.
162. Ia. E. Vodarsky, 'Petr I', *VI*, 1993, no. 6, 77.
163. Gerschenkron, 'Russian Mercantilism', 79.
164. *PSZ*, 7: no. 4518, p. 291 (20 May 1724): 'te podushnye den'gi na tekh zavodakh im zarabatyvat'.
165. Kahan, *Plow*, 263.
166. From 5 Nov. 1723 (supplement to the Regulation of the College of Manufactures, July 1722): *PSZ*, 7: no. 4345, pp. 150–1.
167. *PSZ*, 5: no. 3711, pp. 311–12. The Demidovs had already bought villages in 1720, a year before the Act. On other sources of labour, see below, pp. 169–72.
168. Kahan, *Plow*, 138.
169. *PSZ*, 6: no. 3919.
170. *PSZ*, 5: no. 2876, p. 137 (18 Jan. 1715): 'bude voleiu ne pokhotiat, khotia v nevoliu'.
171. *PSZ*, 6: no. 3526, pp. 137–8 (13 Feb. 1720).
172. See Kahan, *Plow*, 157–62, and 'Continuity in Economic Activity and Policy during the Post-Petrine period in Russia', *Journal of Economic History*, 25 (1965) 61–85.
173. Peterson, *Peter*, 356. But he applies this only to the first decade, detecting a new enlightened policy in the second.
174. S. Blanc, 'The Economic Policy of Peter the Great' (1962), repr. in W. L. Blackwell, ed., *Russian Economic Development from Peter the Great to Stalin* (New York, 1974), 36–7. Copies of some of the charters (*privilegii*) can be seen in GPB OR, f. 1003 (Voskresensky), no. 11, ll. 104–5, 113–17: e.g. a St Petersburg leather factory to M. Pavlov.
175. Blanc, 'Economic Policy', 34.
176. Ibid., 31.
177. Gerschenkron, 'Russian Mercantilism', 65, 70.
178. Ibid., 72, 83.
179. Kahan, *Plow*, 235–6.
180. Gerschenkron, 'Russian Mercantilism', 81.
181. Ibid., 95.
182. Fuller, *Strategy*, 64.

CHAPTER 6: PETER'S PEOPLE

1. See more recent discussion in E. K. Wirtschafter, *Structures of Society. Imperial Russia's 'People of Various Ranks'* (De Kalb, Ill., 1994). Isabel de Madariaga (*Russia in the Age of Catherine the Great* (London, 1981)), argues that it was Catherine II who created the *Ständestaat*, or rather the *Ständegesellschaft*.
2. See, e.g., analysis in Pososhkov, 110. The first Russian formulation of orders on the basis of occupation dates from 1658. See V. Kivelson, *Autocracy in the Provinces. The Muscovite Gentry and Political Culture in the Seventeenth Century* (Stanford, Calif., 1996), 264–5.
3. I. A. Bulygin, *Monastyrskie krest'iane Rossii v pervoi chet. XVIII v.* (M, 1977), 58; V. M. Kabuzan, *Izmeneniia v razmeshchenii naseleniia Rossii v*

XVIII–pervoi pol. XIX v. (M, 1971), 63–5.

4. I. de Madariaga, 'The Russian Nobility in the Seventeenth and Eighteenth Centuries', in H. M. Scott, ed., *The European Nobilities 1600–1800: Eastern Europe* (London, 1995), 249; A. Kahan, *The Plow, the Hammer and the Knout. An Economic History of Eighteenth-Century Russia* (Chicago, 1985), 25. Kahan's otherwise useful demographic profile of Russia actually has little reference to our period.

5. Kahan, *Plow*, 8, 346.

6. Pososhkov, 104: according to 'most recent researches'.

7. Wirtschafter, *Structures*, xiii.

8. See arguments in B. N. Mironov, *Russkii gorod v 1740–1860e gody* (L, 1990). His figures start with 1737.

9. See above, pp. 117–18.

10. Kahan, *Plow*, 65. I am indebted to David Moon for useful advice on this topic. See his 'Reassessing Russian Serfdom', *European History Quarterly*, 26 (1996), 483–526.

11. Bulygin, *Monastyrskie*, 58; Kabuzan, *Izmeneniia*, 63–5. See above, p. 7.

12. *PSZ*, 4: no. 1990, p. 265 (17 Aug. 1704): *dvorovye* (household serfs), *zadvornye* and *delovye* (agricultural slaves), *kabalnye* (bondsmen), *krestianskie* and *bobylskie* (landless peasants) households.

13. See E. V. Anisimov's analysis, *The Reforms of Peter the Great. Progress Through Coercion* trans. J. Alexander (New York, 1993), 195–6.

14. Pososhkov, 317.

15. Quoted in A. Rothstein, *Peter the Great and Marlborough. Politics and Diplomacy in Converging Wars* (Basingstoke, 1986), 26.

16. See Iu. A. Tikhonov, *Pomeshchich'i krest'iane v Rossii. Feodol'naia renta v XVII–nachale XVIII v.* (M, 1974), 303, quoted in C. Peterson, *Peter the Great's Administrative and Judicial Reforms* (Stockholm, 1979), 278.

17. *200-letie*, appendix II, pp. 45 ff. See below, pp. 460–1.

18. N. I. Pavlenko, 'Petr I (K izucheniiu sotsial'no-politicheskikh vzgliadov)', in *RPR*, 68.

19. Kahan, *Plow*, 45.

20. 'O berezhenii zemledel'tsev' (1724), quoted in Pavlenko, 'Petr I', 66, and commentary in Pososhkov, 307. See reference to 1701 edn. of Hohberg's book in E. I. Bobrova, comp., *Biblioteka Petra I. Ukazatel'-spravochnik* (L, 1978), no. 1185, p. 128.

21. Quoted in Pavlenko, 'Petr I', 67. *PSZ*, 5: no. 3294, pp. 628–9. On provincial reform, see above, p. 117. See discussion in Peterson, *Peter*, 277–8.

22. *ZA*, 562.

23. Ibid., 175. 'ot chego budet oblegchen narod'. F. Prokopovich, *Sochineniia*, ed. I. P. Eremin (M, 1961), 125. See discussion of value of labour in Iu. M. Lotman, *Besedy o russkoi kul'ture. Byt i traditsii russkogo dvorianstva (XVIII–nach. XIX veka)* (SPb., 1994), 19–20 ('Work was Peter's prayer').

24. See below, p. 373.

25. Peterson, *Peter*, 277.

26. *PSZ*, 6: no. 3770, p. 377. *ZA*, 92.

27. See, e.g., N. Ogarev, 'What would Peter the Great do?', *Literaturnoe nasledstvo*, 39–40 (1941), 317.

28. Weber, 1: 49.

29. See F. de la Neuville, *A Curious and New Account of Muscovy in the Year 1689*, ed. L. Hughes (London, 1994), 67.

30. See A. Gerschenkron, 'Russian Mercantilism', in *Europe in the Russian Mirror* (Cambridge, 1970), 91; E. V. Anisimov, *Podatnaia reforma Petra I* (L, 1982), 134

31. *PSZ*, 7: no. 4138, p. 2 (11 Jan. 1723).

32. *PSZ*, 6: no. 3481 (5 Jan. 1720). See G. L. Freeze, *The Russian Levites: Parish Clergy in the Eighteenth Century* (Cambridge, Mass., 1977), 21–2, on the Synod's arguments against this policy.

33. *PSZ*, 6: no. 3932, p. 524 (4 Apr. 1722): 'a tomu votchinniku imi vladet''.

34. *PSZ*, 7: no. 4145, pp. 11–12 (19 Jan. 1723); no. 4186, pp. 32–3 (11 Mar.).

35. Ibid., no. 4335, pp. 139–40.

36. See Anisimov, *Reforms*, 197–8.

37. LOI, f. 270, d. 106, l. 386 (7 Feb. 1724): 'ibo v liudekh nuzhdu ne maluiu imeiu'.

38. Peterson, *Peter*, 275, but not in *PSZ*.
39. *PSZ*, 6: no. 3939, p. 639.
40. *PSZ*, 3: no. 1420, p. 117 (22 Nov. 1691); no. 1427, pp. 120–1 (16 Dec. 1691); no. 1454, pp. 145–7 (16 Nov. 1692).
41. Ibid., no. 1424, pp. 119–20 (30 Nov. 1691)
42. Muller, 54–5.
43. *DPPS*, 6: 120–1.
44. LOI, f. 270, d. 101, l. 136 (24 May 1722).
45. N. B. Golikova, *Politicheskie protsessy pri Petre I* (M, 1957), p. 197.
46. Ibid., 167–8, .
47. Ibid., 172–3.
48. For further examples of opposition to Peter, see below, pp. 447ff.
49. See A. Shapiro in *Ezhegodnik po agrarnoi istorii vostochnoi Evropy 1958 g.* (Tallinn, 1959), 221: 'Peasants' living standards are elastic and can decline, but surely they cannot do so indefinitely. How did they exist?'
50. Kahan, *Plow*, 330. See Moon, 'Reassessing Russian Serfdom'.
51. Kahan, *Plow*, 66–7.
52. See Moon, 'Reassessing Russian Serfdom', for recent literature on the early nineteenth century on this topic.
53. Kahan, *Plow*, 11 and 45.
54. Ibid., 48–9. On 1708–9, see above, pp. 113–16.
55. *Chteniia*, 1860, IV, smes', 269–70; quoted in Peterson, *Peter*, 288.
56. Weber, 2: 119–20.
57. See M. Confino, *Systèmes agraires et progrès agricole* (Paris, 1969).
58. Stählin, 43–4.
59. M. S. Anderson, *Peter the Great* (London, 1978), p. 103.
60. Pososhkov, 102, claims that only when famine struck in 1723 did Peter consider such measures.
61. See below, pp. 381–2.
62. LOI, f. 270, d. 107, ll. 159–60ʳ⁻ᵛ.
63. *ZA*, 61. See Peterson, *Peter*, 252.
64. Weber, 1: 70.
65. Anderson, *Peter the Great*, 103.
66. Korb, 1: 217.
67. *Sbornik Mukhanova*, 2nd edn. (SPb., 1866), 556–8.
68. Kahan, *Plow*, 79.
69. See arguments for later in the century in I. Blanchard, 'Eighteenth-century

Russian Economic Growth: State Enterprise or Peasant Endeavour?', in *Studies in Economic and Social History: Discussion Papers*, no. 95–1 (Edinburgh, 1995).
70. *PiB*, 6: 13–14 (6 July 1707).
71. Ustiugov; quoted in Kahan, *Plow*, 71–2.
72. Weber, 1: 56.
73. *PSZ*, 6: no. 3506, p. 125 (5 Feb. 1720).
74. *PiB*, 2: 129.
75. *BP*, 283–4.
76. Ibid., 331.
77. *Materialy dlia istorii russkogo flota*, 6 (1877), 5–6.
78. GPB OR, f. 1003 (Voskresensky), no. 11, ll. 84–5 (letter from W. Henning, 21 July 1720).
79. Ibid., ll. 286–7 (7 Dec. 1722).
80. *PiB*, 9: 891.
81. *PSZ*, 6: no. 1860, pp. 170–1; no. 1863, p. 171 (both 4 July 1701).
82. A. Viktorov, *Opisanie zapisnykh knig i bumag starinnykh dvortsovykh prikazov, 1613–1725* (M, 1883), 2: 474.
83. *PSZ*, 6: no. 1924, p. 210 (19 Jan. 1703); no. 2031, p. 289 (10 Feb. 1705).
84. Ibid., no. 3955, p. 648 (10 Apr. 1722).
85. *DPPS*, 6(i): no. 388, pp. 375–8.
86. *PSZ*, 6: no. 2026, pp. 286–7 (5 Feb. 1705).
87. *PiB*, 6: 53 (18 Aug. 1707).
88. Gerschenkron, 'Russian Mercantilism', 76.
89. *PiB*, 11(ii): 303–4 (16 Dec. 1711).
90. *PSZ*, 6: no. 4041, p. 693 (21 May 1722).
91. GPB OR, f. 1003 (Voskresensky), no. 11, ll. 299–300 (1722).
92. According to Kahan, *Plow*, 155, this was not so much 'enlightenment' as the 'mechanical transplanting into the armaments industry [of] some of the institutions of the armed forces'. See below, p. 342.
93. Quoted in Kahan, *Plow*, 156.
94. *PSZ*, 6: no. 3937, p. 744 (5 Apr. 1722).
95. See above, p. 156.
96. GPB OR, f. 1003 (Voskresensky), no. 11, ll. 264–5.
97. *PSZ*, 6: no. 3919, p. 516 (15 Mar. 1722); 7: no. 4145, p. 11 (19 Jan. 1723).
98. V. N. Bochkarev, 'Dvorianstvo i krest'ianstvo pri Petre Velikom', *Tri veka*, (M, 1912) 3: 198–219.

99. See Pososhkov, 200.
100. *PiB*, 12(i): 240–4 (10 June 1712); V. V. Golovin, 'Zapiski bednoi i suetnoi zhizni chelovecheskoi', in *Rodoslovnaia Golovinykh vladel'tsev sela Novospaskogo* (M, 1847), 44–57.
101. *PSZ*, 5: no. 2779; no. 3265 44–55 (1 Jan. 1719): 'O proizvodstve v voinskie chiny'.
102. This was not a new phenomenon; see an edict of 15 Feb. 1671 threatening confiscation of estates for non-appearance or desertion from service; *PSZ*, 2: 489, p. 855.
103. *PSZ*, 3: no. 1521, pp. 210–11 (27 Nov. 1695).
104. *PiB*, 2: 182 (24 June 1703).
105. *DPPS*, 6(i): 58–67, including the list of names. (Printed on 20 Mar. 1716: *PSZ*, 5: no. 2988, p. 195.)
106. *DPPS*, 6(i): no. 426, pp. 355–6; no. 460, p. 397.
107. *PSZ*, 7: no. 4295, pp. 109–10 (3 Sept. 1723).
108. Pososhkov, 232–3.
109. *PiB*, 5: 167 (30 Mar. 1707).
110. *PiB*, 9: 343–4, 1181–4 (13 Aug. 1709).
111. Ibid., 344 (13 Aug. 1709, to I. A. Musin-Pushkin).
112. *DPPS*, 5: no. 182, pp. 125–6.
113. *PiB*, 1: no. 129. The document on study is included in the first entry in the diary of Peter Tolstoy. See M. Okenfuss, ed. and trans., *The Travel Diary of Peter Tolstoy* (De Kalb, Ill., 1987), 6
114. See below, pp. 303–4.
115. J. Perry, *The State of Russia* (1716), (London, 1967), 220.
116. *PiB*, 6: 50.
117. *DPPS*, 6(i): no. 261, p. 228. See similar orders to Nazary Melnitsky (to track down fugitive serfs), no. 273, p. 238; Prince Ivan Cherkassky (needed to go to Moscow on business), no. 262, p. 228; Mikhail Rtishchev (to sort out disputes over land boundaries), no. 296, p. 258.
118. Ibid., no. 300, p. 265.
119. Ibid., no. 314, p. 270.
120. Ibid., no. 325, p. 277.
121. 'Pis'ma generala-anshefa I. I. Buturlina [1661–1738]', *Russkaia starina*, 1878, no. 10, 161–86; 1879, no. 5, 151–8.

122. M. M. Bogoslovsky, *Byt i nravy russkogo dvorianstva v pervoi pol. XVIII v.* (SPb., 1918), 34.
123. A. A. Iakovlev, 'Karmannyi zhurnal Iakovleva', *Otechestvennye zapiski*, 20/54 (1824), 74–91.
124. *PSZ*, 5: no. 2789.
125. *PiB*, 11: 149 (17 Mar. 1711); *ZA*, 37.
126. M. O. Blamberg, 'The Publicists of Peter the Great' (Ph.D. thesis, Indiana University, 1974), 178–80.
127. See discussion in A. N. Medushevsky, *Utverzhdenie absoliutizma v Rossii* (M, 1994), 92 (in which he refers to the law as *Zakon o maiorate* and discusses it in terms of primogeniture); de Madariaga, 'Russian Nobility', 253–4. Kivelson, *Autocracy*, 110–12, argues that in the seventeenth century nobles were forever augmenting their estates through purchase, marriage and exchange, and that the idea of destructive 'fragmentation' is something of a myth.
128. *ZA*, 40. See also Jan. 1719 order to governors: *PSZ*, 5: no. 3294.
129. *PSZ*, 7: no. 4385, pp. 183–4.
130. *PSZ*, 5: no. 2796, p. 97 (14 Apr. 1714).
131. See J. Paaskoski, 'Noble Land-Holding and Serfdom in Old Finland', in *WOR*, 83–90, which argues that local customs prevailed.
132. LOI, f. 270, d. 104, ll. 351–2^{r-v}.
133. Ibid., d. 106, ll. 284–6 (30 Jan. 1724).
134. I. A. Zheliabuzhsky, 'Zapiski', in A. B. Bogdanov, ed. *Rossiia pri tsarevne Sof'e i Petre I* (M, (1990), 213.
135. Korb, 1: 166.
136. Weber, 1: 221.
137. See Anisimov's chapter 'The All-Russian Subject People', in *Reforms*, 184–202.
138. B. B. Kafengauz, 'Voprosy istoriografii epokhi Petra Velikogo', *IZ* 9 (1944), 29.
139. Bogoslovsky, *Byt i nravy*, 45–6. On Devier, see below, p. 430. A forthcoming book by N. S. Kollmann on *Honor and Society in Early Modern Russia* gives a rather different view.
140. *Sbornik*, 2: 406–78, 415; *PSZ*, 3: no. 1401, pp. 100–2 (15 Apr. 1691).
141. *PSZ*, 3: no. 1460, pp. 149–50 (10 Jan. 1692).

142. *PSZ*, 7: no. 4322, p. 130 (10 Oct. 1723).

143. Ibid., no. 4405, pp. 196–7.

144. *PSZ*, 6: no. 3896: *ZA*, 353–5. See below, p. 183, for details. The first holder of the office was Stepan Kolychov.

145. *PSZ*, 3: no. 1469, pp. 177–8 (17 Mar. 1693).

146. *PiB*, 11: 236 (4 Nov. 1711).

147. Peterson, *Peter*, p. 53. Musin-Pushkin was Peter's illegitimate half-brother. See below, p. 418. According to V. V. Kvadri, *Svita Petra Velikogo* (SPb., 1902), 4, the last boyar was Stepan Petrovich Neledinsky-Meletsky, created by Catherine I in Sept. 1725. See also P. B. Brown, 'Early Modern Russian Bureaucracy. The Evolution of the Chancellery System from Ivan III to Peter the Great, 1478–1717' (Ph.D. thesis, University of Chicago, 1978), 516.

148. Kvadri, *Svita*, 3.

149. *Zapiski Ivana Ivanovicha Nepliueva (1693–1773)* (SPb., 1893), 108.

150. See, e.g. *PiB*, 11: 9 (2 Jan. 1711) and note on p. 333.

151. *PSZ*, 5: no. 3384, pp. 713–14 (4 June 1719).

152. *PSZ*, 4: no. 2563, pp. 854–5 (4 Aug. 1712, Senate).

153. Ibid., no. 1453, p. 145 (13 Nov. 1692).

154. Kvadri, *Svita*, 10.

155. *PiB*, 9: 295.

156. Kvadri, *Svita*, 39.

157. *ZA*, 68–9.

158. Texts: *PSZ*, 6: no. 3890, pp. 486–93 (24 Jan. 1722); *PRP*, 179–90.

159. S. M. Troitsky, 'Iz istorii sozdaniia Tabeli o rangakh', *Istoriia SSSR*, 1974, no. 1, pp. 98–1. More than 90 per cent of offices included by Osterman in 'Ob"iavlenie o rangakh' could be found in use already. The Byzantine Empire had fourteen civil service ranks.

160. Ibid., 104.

161. LOI, f. 270, d. 97, ll. 97, 98 (20 Jan. 1721); l. 204 (draft for review by Senate, 22 Feb. 1721).

162. Troitsky, 'Iz istorii', 106. (Mention of princes, boyars, etc. in prayers was replaced by reference to 'ruling council and military commanders', Sept. 1722: *PSZ*, 6: no. 3829, p. 436.

163. The original thirteen, an unlucky number, were swelled to fourteen by the inclusion of 'ship's secretary', the only office in class 13. See *PR*, 192 n.

164. Perry, *State of Russia*, 271, 274.

165. *Zapiski ... Nepliueva*, 110.

166. e.g., I. I. Golikov, *Anekdoty, kasaiushchiesia do gosudaria imperatora Petra Velikogo*, in E. V. Anisimov, ed., *Petr Velikii. Vospominaniia. Dnevnikovye zapisi. Anekdoty* (SPb., 1993), anecdotes 73, 74, 75.

167. *PiB*, 1: 149.

168. *PiB*, 3: 263 (10 Feb. 1705).

169. Soloviev, 209–10.

170. See below, pp. 364–5.

171. See below, pp. 427–8.

172. See *Zapiski ... Nepliueva*. B. Sumner, *Peter the Great and the Ottoman Empire* (Oxford, 1949), 74: 'It remains difficult to explain why Peter should thus have wasted so much naval training and appointed a man without any diplomatic experience to so important a centre.'

173. See below, pp. 194–5.

174. H. F. de Bassewitz, 'Zapiski grafa Bassevicha, sluzhashchie k poiasneniiu nekotorykh sobytii iz vremeni tsarstvovaniia Petra Velikogo (1713–1725)', *Russkii arkhiv*, 3 (1865), 212–13.

175. De Madariaga, 'Russian Nobility', 245.

176. *PSZ*, 6: no. 3534, p. 157.

177. Ibid., 6: no. 3676, p. 264 (16 Nov. 1720).

178. B. Meehan-Waters, *Autocracy and Aristocracy. The Russian Service Elite of 1730* (New Brunswick, NJ, 1982), 2. Peter 'reinforced the traditional status of old families by forcing on them new skills, thus blending ascription with achievement'.

179. Ibid., 10.

180. *PSZ*, 3: no. 1436, pp. 125–6 (1 Mar. 1692).

181. Brown, 'Early Modern Russian Bureaucracy', 511.

182. D. Serov, *Stepennaia kniga redaktsii Ivana Iur'eva (1716–1718 gg.)*, dissertation abstract (L, 1991), 11. (Iur'ev himself started life as a humble scribe, and died in 1751 with the rank of privy councillor and the order of Alexander Nevsky.)

183. LOI, f. 270, d. 103, l. 253 (22 Feb. 1723); *PSZ*, 7: no. 4170, pp. 25–6; *BP*, p. 391.

184. LOI, f. 270, d. 100, l. 425 (17 Apr. 1722). *Legionsrat* does not appear in the original table.

185. *PSZ*, 7: no. 4449, p. 226: 'pod vidom uchen'ia, gulian'ia'.

186. *ZA*, 175; *PSZ*, no. 3893, pp. 496–7.

187. M. Cherniavsky's argument that with the new law of succession Peter reverted to an older type of monarchical power, rejecting the principle of primogeniture, established by the grand princes of Moscow, with an act of personal will similar to that of the Mongol khan, who chose the leading prince according to his own will, does not quite stand up (*Tsar and People: Studies in Russian Myths* (New York, 1961), 89).

188. B. C. Münnich, 'Ocherk daiushchii predstavlenie ob obraze pravleniia Rossiiskoi Imperii', in *Bezvremen'e i vremenshchik. Vospominaniia ob epokhe dvortsovykh perevorotov (1720e–1760e gody)* (L, 1991), 37.

189. Kahan, *Plow*, 35: 'The reporting bias affecting the female population, regardless of whether its origin was with the family or with the parish, persisted for a very long time and affected the data throughout the eighteenth century and into the beginning of the nineteenth.'

190. *PiB*, 10: 420 (28 Nov. 1710).

191. P. A. Krotov, 'Russkaia zhenshchina Petrovskoi epokhi: A. S. Mordvitsova i ee pis'ma k synu', *Rossiiskie zhenshchiny i evropeiskaia kul'tura. Tezisy dokladov II nauchnoi konferentsi:* (SPb., 1994), 51–2.

192. Kaliazina, illustration 214. See below, p. 262.

193. See L. A. J. Hughes, *Sophia Regent of Russia 1657–1704* (New Haven, 1990); on portraits, pp. 139–44.

194. Gordon (26 Feb.), quoted in N. Pogodin, 'Petr Pervyi: Pervye gody edinoderzhaviia, 1689–1694', *Russkii arkhiv*, 1879, no. 1, 10.

195. G. V. Esipov, 'Zhizneopisanie kniazia A.D. Menshikova', *Russkii arkhiv*, 1875, no. 7, 237.

196. See below, pp. 267–9.

197. See below, pp. 391–3.

198. His works were 'Vita e viaggi di F B, nativo di Pisa', written 1725–32; see Iu. U. Gerasimova, 'Vospominaniia Filippo Balatri. Novyi inostrannyi istochnik po istorii Petrovskoi Rossii (1698–1701)', *Zapiski otdela rukopisei*, 27 (1965), 164–90) and *Frutti del mondo. Autobiografia di Filippo Balatri da Pisa 1676–1756* (Milan, 1924).

199. Gerasimova, 'Vospominaniia', 175.

200. K. Vossler, ' "Russische Zustände am Ende des 18 Jahrhunderts" nach dem Zeugniseines italienischen Sangers', *Arkhiv für Slavische Philologie*, 39 (1925), 151.

201. Gerasimova, 'Vospominaniia', 178.

202. Bantysh-Kamensky, 1: 40.

203. Gerasimova, 'Vospominaniia', 187.

204. Korb, 1: 264–5.

205. Ibid., 2: 37.

206. See, e.g., observations in Okenfuss *Travel Diary*, (De Kalb, 1987), 75–6, 154.

207. Bogoslovsky, *Byt i nravy*, 13.

208. Segregation of the sexes continued to be practised among the most conservative groups in society: e.g., Old Believers. See R. O. Crummey, *The Old Believers and the World of Antichrist. The Vyg Community and the Russian State 1694–1855* (Madison, 1970), 64–5, 111–2, on the separate men's and women's quarters in the Vyg community.

209. Cornelius de Bruyn, *Travels into Muscovy, Persia, and Part of the East Indies; Containing an Accurate Description of what is most Remarkable in those Countries*, 2 vols (London, 1737), 1: 30.

210. Bogoslovsky, *Byt i nravy*, 6–7.

211. *Pridvornaia zhizn': 1613–1913 Koronatsii, feierverki, dvortsy* (SPb., 1913), 56–7.

212. Bergholz, 1724, p. 34.

213. Juel, 2: 35; emphasis added.

214. Bergholz, 1724, p. 58.

215. Ibid., 1721, p. 101.

216. Ibid., p. 54.

217. Ibid., p. 69.

218. Ibid., 1724, p. 193.

219. Ibid., p. 99.
220. P. H. Bruce, *Memoirs of Peter Henry Bruce Esq. A Military Officer in the Service of Prussia, Russia and Great Britain* (London, 1782), 85.
221. Weber, 1: 27, 149.
222. Juel, 3: 23.
223. Weber, 1: 147–8.
224. Bruce, *Memoirs*, 86
225. See below, p. 368.
226. Bantysh-Kamensky, 1: 40–1.
227. See below, pp. 242–3.
228. *Kniga perepisnaia, chto po konchine blazhennye pamiati blagorodnyia velikiia Gosudaryni Tsarevny i Velikiia Kniazhny Natalii Alekseevny, iunia 19-go 1716-go goda, sviatykh ikon, knig, person, kartin, almaznykh veshei, deneg, posudy serebrianoi, plat'ia i posudy-zh, mednoi, oloviannoi, farforovoi i tseninnoi, khoromnogo uboru i protchego iavilos', i to pisano nizhe sego.* Two printed versions: *DPPS*, 6(i): no. 600, pp. 534–58, and *Delo o pozhitkakh gosudaryni Natalii Alekseevny* (M, 1914). Details in L. A. J. Hughes, 'Between Two Worlds: Tsarevna Natal'ia Alekseevna and the "Emancipation" of Petrine Women', in *WOR*, 29–36.
229. E. D. Kukushkina, 'Tekst i izobrazhenie v konkliuzii Petrovskogo vremeni (na primere portreta tsarevny Natalii Alekseevny)', *XVIII vek*, 15 (1986), 21–36. The painting is in the Russian Museum.
230. Peter had the Church of the Resurrection of Lazarus (not extant) built for her tomb in the Alexander Nevsky monastery. The church was completed, and her remains transferred there on 17 Oct. 1717 (Feast of Lazarus). On 24 October 1724 they were transferred to the Church of the Annunciation along with the coffin of Peter Petrovich (died 1719).
231. See Perry, *State of Russia*, 202–3.
232. LOI, f. 270., d. 81, l. 164.
233. Ibid., l. 166 (8 Feb.); *DPPS*, 6(i): 136–7 (10 Feb. 1710).
234. LOI, f. 270, d. 82, l. 279. She was a big spender. Armoury account books for 1710 contain entries on payments for making a gold chalice and for cutting

and faceting eight sapphires for her: RGADA, f. 396, op. 2, ed. khr. 1008, ll. 188, 484.
235. *DPPS*, 6(i): 144–5, 156, 162–3 (Feb. 1716).
236. Bassewitz, 'Zapiski', 222. See notices of her death in *PZh*, 1723, pp. 8, 32.
237. LOI, f. 270, d. 105, ll. 46ʳ⁻ᵛ (11 Oct. 1723). She signed it.
238. See N. Aristov, 'Pervonachal'noe obrazovanie Petra Velikogo', *Russkii arkhiv*, 13/8 (1875), 475.
239. G. Esipov, *Tsaritsa Evdokia Feodorovna* (M, 1862), 19.
240. Semevsky, *Tsaritsa Praskov'ia 1664–1724* (M, 1989), 34.
241. Bergholz, 1722, p. 212.
242. LOI, f. 270, d. 103, ll. 339–40 (Mar. 1723).
243. Bergholz, 1725, p. 100.
244. A. S-tskii, 'Russkaia preobrazovannaia zhenshchina v epokhu Petra Velikogo', *Russkii mir*, 1859, nos 29–32, 687.
245. Neuville, *Curious and New Account*, 12.
246. V. Ger'e, 'Kronprintsessa Sharlotta, nevestka Petra Velikogo. 1707–1715, po eia neizdannym pis'mam', *Vestnik Evropy*, 3/5 (1872), 37, 40–1.
247. *SIRIO*, 40: 390 (12 Dec. 1721 (NS)): 'fort polie et a des manières toutes différentes de celles de son pays'.
248. S-tskii, 'Russkaia', no. 30, p. 675.
249. *Iunosti chestnoe zertsalo* (SPb., 1717, facs. edn., M, 1990), 73–4. See below, pp. 289, 321.
250. See *Zapiski . . . Nepliueva*.
251. Bruce, *Memoirs*, 85.
252. Perry, *State of Russia*, 199–200.
253. *DPPS*, 6 (i): no. 272, p. 238.
254. Golitsyna seems to have been quite powerful. See the petition from her son Aleksei Golitsyn asking for help to pay off debts inherited from his father. She put in a word on his behalf, and he was let off the quite considerable sum of almost 5,000 roubles: LOI, f. 270, d. 103, l. 309 (Feb. 1723).
255. S. N. Shubinsky, *Letnii sad i letnie peterburgskie uveseleniia pri Petre Velikom* (SPb., 1864), 2, 10.
256. Bergholz, 1721, p. 210
257. Ibid., 1724, p. 53.
258. S-tskii, 'Russkaia', no. 32, p. 698.

259. Juel, 2: 497.
260. See points 7, 9, and 10 of the Table of Ranks: *PRP*, 186–7. Meehan-Waters, *Autocracy*, 21; See also Troitsky, 'Iz istorii', 102.
261. *DPPS*, 5: no. 199, p. 136: 'kniazia Fedorovskoi zheny Myshetskogo, kniagini Dar'i Dorofeevoi docheri'.
262. *Opisanie poriadka derzhannogo pri progrebenii blazhennyia vysokoslavnyia i vernodostoineishiia pamiati vsepresvetleishago derzhavneishago Petra Velikago* (SPb., 1725, M, 1726), 30.
263. T. A. Bykova and M. M. Gurevich ed., *Opisanie izdanii grazhdanskoi pechati. 1708-ianv. 1725 gg. Dopolnenie i prilozheniia* (L, 1972), 17–18.
264. Weber, 1: 1149.
265. Semenova, *Ocherki*, 141.
266. Quoted in Blamberg, 'Publicists', 175.
267. F. Saltykov, 'Iz"iavelniia pribytochnye gosudarstvu' (1714), in N. Pavlov-Sil'vansky ed., *Proekty reform v zapiskakh sovremennikov Petra Velikogo* (SPb., 1897), 9.
268. *200-letie*, 263.
269. Aristov, 'Pervonachal'noe', 486. In the royal household nurses and nannies were noblewomen.
270. *PiB*, 3: 9. There is no further information; unlike the men, she does not make it to the index!
271. Golikova, *Politicheskie*, 174, 181.
272. *PiB*, 6: 174.
273. Juel, 3: 8.
274. *PSZ*, 4: no. 1907, pp. 191–2 (3 Apr. 1702).
275. *ZA*, 103. Repeated (?) 5 Jan. 1723: this one includes an oath to be taken by parents or guardians to swear that the couple were marrying by their own, 'uncoerced free will': *PSZ*, 7: no. 4406, pp. 197–8.
276. *PSZ*, 3: no. 1612, p. 418 (Dec. 1697).
277. *PSZ*, 5: no. 3006.
278. *PSZ*, 6: no. 3485, p. 78; *PRP*, 360 (Military Statute, 1716, article 167).
279. See A. Kleimola, ' "In Accordance with the Holy Apostles": Muscovite Dowries and Women's Property Rights', *RR*, 51 (1992), 204–29.
280. Fedosia Fedorovna Tatishcheva brought a dowry of twenty souls when she married Ivan Nepliuev in 1711: *Zapiski … Nepliueva*, 1. Nepliuev remarks that he was married (at the age of eighteen) 'by my mother's will'.
281. *PSZ*, 5: no. 2789 (23 Mar. 1714).
282. *DPPS*, 6 (i): no. 228, pp. 191–2. See also the more straightforward case of Maria Polevoi, May 1715: ibid., (i): no. 646, p. 513.
283. *PSZ*, 5: no. 2789 (23 Mar. 1714).
284. Weber, 1: 200.
285. *DPPS*, 5(i): no. 240, pp. 177–80.
286. F. J. Strahlenberg, *Zapiski kapitana Filippa Ioganna Stralenberga ob istorii i geografii Rossiiskoi imperii Petra Velikogo*, trans. and ed. Iu. Bespiatykh et al. (M & L, 1985), 129–30.
287. *PSZ*, 8: no. 5717 (17 Mar. 1731).
288. A. A. Golombievsky, *Sotrudniki Petra Velikogo* (M, 1903), 41–6.
289. Ibid., 45–6.
290. Weber, 1: 44.
291. LOI, f. 270, d. 103, l. 307 (28 Feb. 1723).
292. Weber, 1: 135. He in error calls the convent the Miracles (*Tchude*).
293. *PSZ*, 4: no. 1856, p. 168 (8 June 1700).
294. Blamberg, 'Publicists', 73.
295. *PSZ*, 7: no. 4499 (30 Apr. 1723).
296. See Muller, 79–80; the age limit says 'sixty, or at least fifty': J. Cracraft, *The Church Reform of Peter the Great* (London, 1971), 256–7, and below, p. 343.
297. Cracraft, *Church Reform*, 254, 257.
298. See Crummey, *Old Believers*, 98.
299. *PSZ*, 3: no. 1612, pp. 415–16 (Dec. 1697).
300. See ibid., no. 1335 (1689).
301. Gerasimova, 'Vospominaniia', 188; Korb, 1: 212–13, 214; Bruyn, *Travels*, 1: 25.
302. Bruyn, *Travels*, 1: 88.
303. Korb, 1: 219. It is worth recalling that in England the penalty for the same crime was death by burning alive. See I. de Madariaga, 'Penal Policy in the Age of Catherine the Great', in L. Berlinguer and F. Colao, eds, *La "Leopoldina". Criminalità e Giustizia Criminale nelle Riforme del Settecento Europeo* (Milan, 1990), 499.
304. Zheliabuzhsky, 'Zapiski', 214. See the Military Statute on this and related crimes.

305. Weber, 1: 181.
306. *PSZ*, 6: no. 3808, pp. 410–11.
307. Bergholz, 1722, p. 65. There are many such stories, notably of Nadezhda Durova, who served in the Napoleonic Wars.
308. GPB OR, f. 1003 (Voskresensky), no. 11, ll. 97–8 (13 Oct. 1720).
309. See, e.g., the complaint that a very old sick woman and a blind girl were unfit for work and 'no use for anything': GPB OR, f. 1003 (Voskresensky), no. 11, l. 122 (16 Jan. 1721). Also, ll. 251–2, a letter from Bishop Leonid asking what to do with women convicted of adultery who were rejected by mill directors (25 May 1722).
310. Golikova, *Politicheskie*, 56.
311. See, e.g., the image of Maria Miloslavskaia proffering a scroll with a religious text to the Mother of God in Simon Ushakov's icon *Tree of the Muscovite State.*
312. See below, pp. 235–6.
313. See R. Wortman, *Scenarios of Power. Myth and Ceremony in Russian Monarchy*, vol. 1 (Princeton, 1995), 55–6.
314. G. Bolotova, *Letnii sad. Leningrad* (L, 1981), 121.
315. Dashkova, *Histoire de ma vie*, quoted in Shmurlo, *Petr Velikii v otsenke sovremennikov i potomstva* (SPb,. 1912), *Prilozhenie*, 83.
316. O. Neverov, '"His Majesty's Cabinet" and Peter I's Kunstkammer', in O. Impey and A. McGregor, eds, *The Origins of Museums. The Cabinet of Curiosities in 16th–17th-Century Europe* (Oxford, 1985), 58.

CHAPTER 7: ST PETERSBURG AND THE ARTS

1. See, e.g., an early twentieth-century author's heart-felt regret at the abandonment of 'profound, autonomous Russian tradition in favour of the great god of world culture, triumphantly striding across the centuries and wrathfully destroying anything which dared to place any feeble, timid obstacles in its path'; *Pridvornaia zhizn': 1613–1913* (SPb., 1913), 15.
2. Iu. Lotman, 'The Poetics of Everyday Behaviour in Russian Eighteenth-Century Culture', in *The Semiotics of Russian Culture* (Ann Arbor, 1984), 232–4.
3. *Justice of the Monarch's Right* (1722), in A. Lentin, trans. and ed., *Peter the Great: His Law on the Imperial Succession. The Official Commentary* (Oxford, 1996), 56–7.
4. Prince M. Shcherbatov, 'Petition of the City of Moscow on being relegated to Oblivion', in M. Raeff, ed., *Russian Intellectual History: An Anthology* (New York, 1966), 52.
5. A. Viktorov, *Opisanie zapisnykh knig i bumag starinnykh dvortsovykh prikazov, 1613–1725* (M, 1883), 2: 469–70. On Petrine Moscow, see James Cracraft, *The Petrine Revolution in Russian Architecture* (Chicago, 1988), 111–31, 141–5.
6. Readers are referred in notes to plates in Kaliazina, illustrations 152–3, 160.
7. *PSZ*, 3: no. 1684, p. 613 (29 Apr. 1699). See also *PSZ*, 4: no. 2225, pp. 448–9.
8. *PSZ*, 4: no. 1825, p. 131 (17 Jan. 1701).
9. Ibid., no. 1963, p. 243 (28 Jan. 1704)—just one of many such decrees on stone building publicized in a similar manner—e.g., no. 2232, p. 452 (12 May 1709).
10. *PSZ*, 5: no. 2848 (9 Oct. 1714).
11. *PSZ*, 6: no. 3883, 3885, pp. 483–4 (19 Jan.). See also *PSZ*, 7: no. 4224, p. 64 (14 May 1723). For his instructions (June 1722), see above.
12. Viktorov, *Opisanie*, 2: 465–6, 476.
13. Ibid., 475.
14. *Sbornik Mukhanova*, 2nd edn. (SPb., 1866), 249–50 (13 Oct. 1704).
15. See E. B. Mozgovaia. 'Sintez iskusstv v triumfakh pervoi chetverti XVIII veka', in *Problemy sinteza iskusstv i arkhitektury*, 21 (L, 1985), 58–67, and below, pp. 271–2.
16. Viktorov, *Opisanie*, 476.
17. RGADA, f. 396, op. 2, ed. khr. 1008, ll. 57–8.
18. Mozgovaia, 'Sintez iskusstv', 64. See contemporary descriptions of gates and triumphal parades: e.g., *Sostoianie*

vrat torzhestvennykh, kotorym byt' u Ego Siiatel'stva kniazia Aleksandra Danilovicha Ego Milosti Menshikova (M, 1709).

19. L. Lewitter, 'Peter the Great's Attitude towards Religion', in R. Bartlett, ed., *Russia and the World of the Eighteenth Century*, (Columbus, Oh., 1988), 68.

20. S. Baehr, *The Paradise Myth in Eighteenth-Century Russia* (Stanford, Calif., 1991). See also V. M. Zhivov, 'Kul'turnye reformy v sisteme preobrazovaniia Petra I', in *Iz istorii russkoi kul'tury. Tom III (XVII–nachalo XVIII veka)* (M, 1996), 529–83.

21. *Politikolepnaia apofeosis dostokhval'naia khrabrosti vserossiiskogo Gerkulesa*, in M. A. Alekseeva, *Graviura petrovskogo vremeni* (L, 1990), 69. Grebeniuk, 62–5.

22. I. G. Spassky and E. Shchukina, *Medals and Coins of the Age of Peter the Great* (L, 1974), no. 46. The quotation is from Ovid's *Metamorphoses*: 'Sunt mihi quae valeant in talia pondera vires.'

23. Baehr, *Paradise Myth*, 34; N. V. Kaliazina, L. P. Dorofeeva, G. V. Mikhailov, *Dvorets Menshikova* (M, 1986), 89. Kaliazina describes it as 'voin-pobeditel'', a conventional warrior in antique dress. See V. Iu. Matveev, 'K istorii vozniknoveniia i razvitiia siuzheta "Petr I, vysekaiushchii statuiu Rossii"', *Kul'tura i iskusstvo Rossii XVIII veka. Novye materialy i issledovaniia* (L, 1981), 26–43.

24. R. Wortman, *Scenarios of Power. Myth and Ceremony in Russian Monarchy*, vol. 1 (Princeton, 1995), 48.

25. Nartov, 68.

26. Zhivov, 'Kul'turnye reformy', 545–7.

27. Grebeniuk, 189–90; 'Slovo pokhvalnoe o preslavnom nad voiskami sveiskimi pobede': F. Prokopovich, *Sochineniia*, ed. I. P. Eremin (M & L, 1961), 29.

28. See Spassky and Shchukina, *Medals and Coins*.

29. See, e.g., S. Baehr, 'From History to National Myth: *Translatio imperii* in 18th-Century Russia', *RR*, 37 (1978), 1–13; idem *Paradise Myth*, 2–3. V. M. Zhivov, 'Azbuchnaia reforma Petra I kak semioticheskoe preobrazovanie', *Uch-*

enye zapiski Tartuskogo gos. universiteta, 720 (1986), 60–1: 'the change of the shape of the letters in the civic alphabet was linked with the concept of Russia as the continuer of imperial Rome, its military glory and universal power'.

30. *ZA*, 155.

31. Ibid., 159.

32. Quoted in E. B. Mozgovaia, 'Obraz Petra I-imperatora v proizvedeniiakh tvorchestva Bartolomeo Karlo Rastrelli', in *Monarkhiia i narodovlastie v kul'ture prosveshcheniia* (M, 1995), 3–4.

33. *PiB*, 4: 438 (17 Nov.).

34. *PiB*, 9: 230 (12 May 1711).

35. *MIGO*, 1: 27 (12 Aug. 1713).

36. J. Perkowski, 'Peter the Great—A Catalogue of Coins and Medals in the Smithsonian Collection', *Numismatist*, 95 (1982), 1202.

37. Ibid., 1203; Spassky and Shchukina, *Medals and Coins*, 15. See, e.g., the medal struck for Poltava.

38. Viktorov, *Opisanie*, 2: 474.

39. 'Torzhestvannaia vrata, vvodiashchaia v khram bezsmertnyia slavy, nepobedimomu imeni' (1704), in Grebeniuk, 142, 148.

40. M. A. Alekseeva, *Feierverki i illiuminatsii v grafike XVIII veke. Katalog vystavki* (L, 1978), 5.

41. Stählin, no. 75, pp. 122–3, apparently destroyed by a flood in 1777.

42. 'Preslavnoe torzhestvo svoboditelia Livonii' (1704), in Grebeniuk, 150–80.

43. Kaliazina, illustration 155.

44. BL, Stafford Papers, Add. MS 31128, ff. 50–1 (25 Aug. 1706).

45. Alekseeva, *Graviura*, 111.

46. RGADA, f. 396, op. 2, ed. khr. 1008, l. 262.

47. *DPPS*, 6(i): no. 388, p. 377.

48. From 'Veshnee teplo' ('Spring warmth') (1756), by V. K. Trediakovsky, in *Izbrannye proizvedeniia* (M & L, 1963), 261–2 (with acknowledgements to S. Baehr).

49. *Lettres du comte Algarotti sur la Russie* (London and Paris, 1769), 64.

50. See *PZh*, 1703, p. 4.

51. *Zhurnal ili podennaia zapiska Blazhennyia i vechnodostoinnyia pamiati gos. imp. Petra Velikago s 1698 goda, dazhe*

do zakliuchenia neishtatskogo mira, (SPb., 1770–2), 1: 69. According to Weber, 1: 42, the small town of Nienschants, on the river, was demolished to the foundations and the rubble used for buildings in the new city. See Cracraft, *The Petrine Revolution*.

52. *Kniga Marsova ili Voinskikh del* (SPb., 1713/66), 22.

53. 'O zachatii i zdanii tsarstvuiushchego grada Sanktpeterburga', in Iu. Bespiatykh, ed., *Peterburg Petra I v inostrannykh opisaniiakh* (L, 1991), 258–62.

54. A. Sharymov, 'Byl li Petr I osnovatelem Sankt-Peterburga?', *Avrora*, 1992, nos 7/8, 106–65.

55. 'Kratkoe opisanie goroda Petersburga i prebyvaniia v nem pol'skogo posol'stva v 1720 godu', in Bespiatykh, ed., *Peterburg*, 139. See Pushkin's opening lines in *Mednyi vsadnik* (1833): 'Na beregu pustynnykh voln. . .'.

56. N. A. Sindalovsky, *Legendy i mify Sankt-Peterburga* (SPb., 1994), 11–13. For seventeenth-century maps of the area, showing settlements and churches, see S. Kepsu, *Pietari ennen Pietaria. Nevansuun vaiheita ennen Pietarin kaupungin perustamista* (Helsinki, 1995).

57. *PiB*, 2: 173, 560–1.

58. N. I. Pavlenko, *Aleksandr Danilovich Menshikov* (M, 1981), 27; N. Bozherianov, *Sankt-Peterburg v Petrovo vremia* (SPb., 1903), 52; *Vedomosti vremeni Petra Velikogo* vol. 1: (1703–1707) (M, 1903), 15 Dec. 1703. The story that Peter acted as pilot to the boat is apocryphal. He was not there.

59. *PiB*, 3: 162.

60. See G. Kaganov, 'As in the Ship of Peter', *SR*, 50 (1991), 754–67.

61. Alekseeva, *Graviura*, 100; P. P. Pekarsky, *Nauka i literatura v Rossii pri Petre Velikom* (SPb., 1862), 1: 273–4.

62. *PiB*, 3: 42.

63. Ibid., 93.

64. *PiB*, 8: 91 (to P. M. Apraksin).

65. Several of Nartov's anecdotes feature Peter's concern for oaks: e.g., Nartov, 48.

66. *PiB*, 4: 370–1. (The tableware was unavailable, as the agent reported that no English ships were in port: p. 1047.)

67. *PiB*, 6: 27; 9: 24.

68. *PiB*, 4: 209.

69. See Baehr, *Paradise Myth*, 2, 16. He quotes one of the earliest examples from the *Primary Chronicle* of the idea that heaven and earth form a single world. He argues that what had been a religious idea was more and more usurped by the State, symbolized by the tsar's golden orb or 'apple' (*iabloko*) and centring on notions of *translatio imperii*, the Russian tsar as earthly God.

70. Ibid. Cf. Golovkin's reference to Peter giving birth to Russia from 'nothingness into being'.

71. Kaganov, 'Ship of Peter', 764.

72. Baehr, *Paradise Myth*, 69.

73. *PiB*, 4: 231 (29 Apr. 1706): 'na serdste skreblo'.

74. Ibid., 249 (10 May. 1706).

75. *PiB*, 6: 92 (12 Sept. 1707).

76. As Baehr points out, *Paradise Myth*, 31, the oppositions 'there' (= hell) and 'here' (= heaven) are commonplaces in paradise mythology.

77. *PiB*, 4: 27 (21 Jan. 1706); emphasis added.

78. *PiB*, 10: 57 (26 Feb. 1710), to Menshikov: ('cie mesto istinno, kak izraidnoi mladenets, chto den', preimushchestvuet').

79. *PiB*, 11: 242 (21 May 1711).

80. *PiB* 6: 168 (23–26 Nov. 1707).

81. *PiB*, 8: 469 (29 Nov. 1709).

82. *PiB*, 5: 61 (Jan.–Feb. 1707).

83. *PiB*, 4: 445 (19 Nov.). See for subsequent years: *PiB*, 9: 55 (27 Jan. 1709), 472 (29 Nov. 1709: two shifts of 20,000).

84. *PiB*, 6: 160–1 (20 Nov. 1707).

85. *PSZ*, 4: no. 2240, pp. 466–7 (31 Dec. 1709).

86. *PiB*, 9: 371 (10 Sept. 1709), 503 (Dec. 1709).

87. *PiB*, 10: 75 (21 Mar. 1710).

88. *PiB*, 8: 78–9 (14 Aug. 1708, to Kikin).

89. *PiB*, 9: 231 (27 June 1709, to F. M. Apraksin).

90. Ibid., 246.

91. *Zhurnal ili podennaia zapiska*, 1: 251–2.
92. Trinity Cathedral, reconstructed many times, was demolished in 1927. Its disappearance distorted perceptions of the religious configuration of Peter's city.
93. *PiB*, 10: 251 (23 July, to M. P. Gagarin), 11(ii): 158 (1 Oct. 1711, to Bruce), 200 (19 Oct. 1711, to Christopher Brandt in Holland).
94. *200-letie*, 72–3.
95. See *PiB*, 11: 34 (13 Jan. 1711, to Menshikov, when Peter was in the midst of preparations for the Turkish war).
96. *PiB*, 10: 287–92 (18 Aug., edicts to governors).
97. *PiB*, 11(ii): 235 (4 Nov. 1711).
98. Ibid., 234 (3 Nov.), 269 (2 Dec.).
99. Ibid., 299–300, 302–3 (11 and 15 Dec.); *PiB*, 12(ii): 549; *Zhurnal ili podennaia zapiska*, 1: 333–4.
100. See discussion in N. I. Pavlenko, *Petr Velikii* (M, 1990), 525: 'in our view, the town on the Neva must be regarded as the capital from that date [late 1713]'.
101. *DPPS*, 6(i): no. 359, pp. 306–7.
102. Weber, 1: 191.
103. *PiB*, 11(ii): 276 (4 Dec. 1711).
104. C. Whitworth, *An Account of Russia as it was in the Year 1710* (M & L, 1988), 44.
105. LOI, f. 270, d. 107, l. 158 (15 June); l. 189 (9 July 1724, to Devier).
106. *PiB*, 10: 218–19 (4 July 1710).
107. *PiB*, 12(i): 462; Charles Whitworth in a dispatch of 26 May 1712, *SIRIO*, 61: 205–6.
108. *Exacter Relation von der von Sr. Czaarschen Majestät Petro Alexiowitz, an dem grossen Newa Strohm und der Ost-See neu erbauten Festung und Stadt St. Petersburg, wie auch von dem Castel Cron Schloss, und derselben umliegenden Gegend, Ferner Relation von den uhralten rußischen Gebrauch der Wasser Weyh und Heiligung, Nebst einigen besonderern Anmerkungen ausgezeichnet von H.G.* (Leipzig, 1713). References are to a new Russian translation, 'Tochnoe izvestie o kreposti i gorode Sankt-Peterburg, o kreposttse Kronshlot, i ikh okrestnostiakh', in Bespiatykh, ed., *Peterburg*, 47–80.
109. Juel, 3: 45.
110. Weber, 1: 4, 185.
111. Ibid., 177.
112. *BP*, 404–5 (21 June 1721), 405–6 (28 June 1721).
113. Mardefeld to the king, 12 May 1721 (NS) *SIRIO*, 40: 185.
114. M. A. Alekseeva, 'Graviury "khoromnogo stroeniia" pervoi chetverti XVIII veka: sotsiologicheskii mif i sotsial'naia real'nost'', in *Problemy russkoi khudozhestvennoi kul'tury XVIII veka* (M, 1991), 53–5.
115. See decree of 24 June 1721, which threatens with punishment those who disobeyed. Offending buildings would be demolished: *PSZ*, 6: no. 3799, pp. 402–3.
116. See Kaliazina, illustrations 47–8.
117. L. N. Semenova, 'Inostrannye mastera v Peterburge v pervoi treti XVIII v.', in *Nauka i kul'tura Rossii XVIII v. Sbornik statei* (L, 1984), 201, 223–4.
118. See I. Grabar', *Istoriia russkogo iskusstva*, vol. 5 (M, 1960), 81–2.
119. In archives, in particular see RGADA, f. 9, otd. I, kn. 57 (letters relating to building matters, 1710–30).
120. Stählin, 102–4.
121. Kaliazina, illustrations 24–5. See elsewhere descriptions of Menshikov's house.
122. The former was restored from the rubble left by the Nazis, and remains a tourist attraction. Neighbouring Strel'na, hardly ever seen by tourists, is in disrepair. Ekaterinof was on the site of the later Tsarskoe Selo.
123. Stählin, 42.
124. Weber, 1: 352.
125. RGADA, f. 9, otd. I, kn. 57, l. 39.
126. LOI, f. 270, d. 103, l. 159ʳ⁻ᵛ (6 Feb. 1723). *BP*, 388.
127. LOI, f. 270, d. 106, l. 50 (11 Jan. 1724).
128. Stählin, 105–6.
129. *PSZ*, 7: no. 4253, p. 85 (23 June 1723).
130. See documents on building work in autumn 1723: LOI, f. 270, d. 104, ll. 87, 88, 89, 92, etc.
131. Quoted in C. Peterson, *Peter the Great's Administrative and Judicial Reforms* (Stockholm, 1979), 255. Decree on

gubernii, PSZ, 5: no. 3380 (29 May 1719). Menshikov did not officially have jurisdiction over the province.

132. See S. Monas, 'Anton Divier and the Police of St Petersburg', in M. Halle et al., eds, *For Roman Jakobson. Essays on the Occasion of his Sixtieth Birthday* (The Hague, 1956), 361.
133. Weber, 1: 278.
134. *BP*, 401–2.
135. *BP*, 432–3.
136. *BP*, 467.
137. *BP*, 458–9 (6 Apr. 1722).
138. *PSZ*, 6: no. 3777, p. 382 (29 Apr. 1721).
139. Ibid., no. 3676, p. 264 (16 Nov. 1720).
140. *BP*, 427.
141. *PSZ*, 6: no. 3585, pp. 193–4 (20 May 1720; repeat of 13 June 1718); no. 3799, pp. 402–3 (24 June 1721).
142. Ibid., no. 3799, pp. 402–3.
143. Stählin, 65.
144. *Russkii arkhiv*, 3 (1865), 292–3.
145. Ibid., 311. See decrees of 1 July and 13 Dec. 1723 (*PSZ*, 7: no. 4261, p. 88; no. 4391, pp. 186–7).
146. *PSZ*, 6: no. 3494, p. 121. The names of the streets or locality are not specified. No. 3676, p. 264 (16 Nov. 1720) repeats the order.
147. *BP*, 425–6 (28 June, 1721).
148. See *PSZ*, 6: no. 3777, p. 382. Examples are illustrated in *Peter de Grote en Holland* (Amsterdam, 1996) 223 (Catalogue of the Amsterdam Historical Museum's 1996–7 exhibition).
149. *PSZ*, 7: no. 4538, p. 334 (29 July 1724).
150. Weber, 1: 238.
151. Sindalovsky, *Legendy*, 128.
152. *PiB*, 4: 369
153. See report of La Vie and his criticism of the St Petersburg terrain and climate, *SIRIO*, 40; 348–9. On the temple, see below, p. 273.
154. Juel, 3: 117–18.
155. Ibid., 132.
156. Weber, 1: 114–16, 224. See the story about the English mathematician who plotted a new straight route for the road.
157. *200-letie*, 261.
158. Juel, 3: 33. Postal services were not new. In Apr. 1691 a weekly service was established from Moscow to Vilna: *PSZ*, 3: no. 1402, pp. 102–7.

159. *ZA*, 223.
160. Bergholz, 1721, pp. 45–6.
161. LOI, f. 270, d. 107, l. 334. Five were engaged in mixing paints for painters.
162. The cathedral was completed in 1733. On 10 Sept. 1723, payment was made for gilding the boards for roofing the cupolas and steeple: LOI, f. 270, d. 104, l. 37.
163. Bergholz, 1725, 87.
164. See Kaganov, 'Ship of Peter', 756.
165. *PSZ*, 6: no. 3589, pp. 195–6 (24 May 1720; repeat of 8 June 1719).
166. O. V. Nemiro, 'Dekorativno-ofor-mitel'skoe iskusstvo i prazdnichnyi Peterburg pervoi poloviny XVIII v.', in *Otechestvennoe i zarubezhnoe iskusstvo XVIII veka* (L, 1986), 84.
167. 'Slovo pokhval'noe v den' rozhdestva blagorodneishago gosudaria tsarevicha i velikogo kniazia Petra Petrovicha' (1716), in Prokopovich, *Sochineniia*, 45; Grebeniuk, 74–7.
168. Grebeniuk, 79–80. On the panorama, see Kaganov, 'Ship of Peter', 757–9.
169. N. Ustrialov, *Istoriia tsarstvovaniia Petra Velikogo*, vol. 6 (SPb., 1869), *prilozhenie*, 240.
170. See, e.g., account by the French minister, Campredon, *SIRIO*, 52: 431–2.
171. Duc de Liria, 'Pis'ma o Rossii v Ispaniiu', in *Osmnadtatyi vek*, vol. 2 (M, 1869), 32–3.
172. Ibid., 46.
173. A. Naryshkin, 'Pokhvala Peterburgu' (1756), quoted in Baehr, 'From History', 8.
174. Bozherianov, *Sankt-Peterburg*, p. vi. In 1836 Nicholas I took the 'grandfather' out for a review of the Baltic fleet.
175. See M. Sarantola-Weiss, 'Peter the Great's First Boat, "Grandfather of the Russian Navy"', in *WOR*, 37–41.
176. The reference is to Luke 28:30. Feofilakt Lopatinsky, 'Slovo o bogo-darovannom mire', 1 Jan. 1722, in Grebeniuk, 262–3.
177. See Cracraft, *Petrine Revolution*, 155–60, and my entry in *Macmillan Dictionary of Art*.
178. Stählin, 151–2.
179. H. Hallström, *Der Baumeister Andreas Schlüter und seine Nachfolge in St. Petersburg* (Stockholm, 1964); R.

Kroll, *Andreas Schlüter und der Sommerpalast Peters I* (Berlin, 1976). See also my article 'German Specialists in Petrine Russia', forthcoming.

180. Semenova, 'Inostrannye mastera', 213.

181. On Mattarnovy senior, see my entry in the *Macmillan Dictionary of Art.*

182. See L. A. J. Hughes, 'Russia's First Architectural Books: a Chapter in Peter the Great's Cultural Revolution', in C. Cooke, ed., *Russian Avant-Garde Art & Architecture* (London, 1983), 4–13.

183. Kaliazina, 20.

184. A. L. Punin, 'Petr I i Kristofer Ren. K voprosu o stilevykh istokakh petrovskogo barokko', in *Iskusstvo arkhitektury. Sbornik nauchnykh statei* (SPb., 1995), 34–41.

185. LOI, f. 270, d. 106, ll. 540^v–541^v (11 Apr. 1724).

186. 'Reestr chertezham domov i ogorodov kotorye u ego velichestva nyne imeetsia': LOI, f. 270, d. 106, ll. 571–2.

187. RGADA, f. 9,otd. I, kn. 53, l. 637. In LOI, f. 270, d. 107, ll. 404–5, dated 7 Nov. 1724. Similar wording to the Korobov letter.

188. RGADA, f. 9, otd. I, kn. 53, l. 635 (7 Nov. 1724).

189. LOI, f. 270, d. 103, ll. 625, 626 (20 July 1723).

190. Semenova, 'Inostrannye mastera', 216.

191. *200-letie*, 247.

192. Weber, 1:323.

193. See Kaliazina et al., *Dvorets Menshikova.*

194. Kaliazina, illustration 32.

195. List of wages paid, Cabinet funds, 1711–12, in *200-letie*, 192; Semenova, 'Inostrannye mastera', 202.

196. See Mozgovaia, 'Obraz Petra I' (1995), 5. For recent research on the figurative arts, see J. Cracraft, *The Petrine Revolution in Russian Imagery* (Chicago, 1997), which sadly appeared too late to be used in the preparation of this section.

197. Kaliazina, illustration 64, 92.

198. Ibid.

199. Ibid., illustrations 32 and 144. There are many examples of sculpture and carving inside: e.g., medallions of Justice and Plenty, possibly by Mattarnovy.

200. See payment of 3,000 roubles to Zarudny, 3 May 1722: LOI, f. 270, d. 101, l. 8. Kaliazina, illustration 31.

201. I am obliged to Dr Elena Mozgovaia of St Petersburg for discussions of the iconostasis and of her difficulties earlier in her career in publishing her conclusions regarding religious sculpture. On the 1721 gates and statues, see V. I. Vasil'ev, *Starinnye feierverki v Rossii (XVII–perv. ch. XVIII v.)* (L, 1960), 49.

202. Kaliazina, illustration 79.

203. N. M. Sharaia, *Voskovaia persona* (L, 1963).

204. Mozgovaia, 'Obraz Petra I' (1985) 33; N. I. Arkhipov and A. G. Raskin, *Bartolomeo Karlo Rastrelli* (L & M, 1964); V. Iu. Matveev and E. A. Tarasova, *Bartolomeo Karlo Rastrelli (1675–1744). K 300 letiiu s dnia rozhdeniia. Katalog vremennoi vystavki* (L, 1975).

205. O. Neverov, ' "His Majesty's Cabinet and Peter I's Kunstkammer', in O. Impey and A. McGregor, eds, *The Origins of Museums. The Cabinet of Curiosities in 16th–17th-Century Europe* (Oxford, 1985), 58.

206. Bergholz, 1724, 20.

207. V. Iu. Matveev, 'Raznykh zhudozhestv mastera', in *Nauka i kul'tura Rossii XVIII. Sbornik statei* (L, 1984), 156 (on Peter's funeral).

208. LOI, f. 270, d. 101, ll. 259, 260, 264 (9 July 1722, Peter from Astrakhan).

209. Kaliazina, illustration 27.

210. *PiB*, 9: 284–5 (11–13 July 1709). See Mozgovaia, 'Obraz Petra I' (1995), 4–5.

211. Nartov, 72. The monastery was never built.

212. *200-letie, prilozhenie*, 29; LOI, f. 270, d. 107, l. 257 (19 Aug. 1724).

213. Juel, 1: 303; Stählin, no. 75, pp. 122–3.

214. See G. Bolotova, *Letnii sad. Leningrad* (L, 1981).

215. *200-letie*, 113.

216. Ibid., 114–15. He also bought Cupid sleeping with Psyche and Venus sleeping with Cupid by Bernini.

217. Basic bibliography includes V. V. Makarov, *Russkaia svetskaia graviura I*

chet. XVIII veka. Annotirovannyi svodnyi katalog (L, 1973).

218. M. Alekseeva, 'Zhanr konkliuzii v russkom iskusstve kontsa XVII– nachala XVIII v.', in T. V. Alekseeva, ed., *Russkoe iskusstvo barokko* (M, 1977), 7–29.

219. Viktorov, *Opisanie*, 2: 477. On the Shansky wedding, see below, p. 260.

220. O. G. Ageeva, 'Severnaia voina i iskusstvo graviury v Rossii petro- vskogo vremeni', in *Russkaia kul'tura v usloviiakh inozemnykh nashestvii i voin X–nach.XX vv*, pt 2 (M, 1990), 156.

221. Ibid., 155.

222. Ibid., 164–5; M. N. Murzanova, 'Kniga Marsa—pervaia kniga grazh- danskoi pechati, napechatannaia v Peterburge', *Trudy Biblioteki Akademii Nauk, SSSR*, 1948, vol. 1.

223. Ageeva, 'Severnaia', 172.

224. Alekseeva, *Graviura*, 171.

225. Ibid., 172.

226. *PiB*, 8: 213.

227. Ibid., 837.

228. *PiB*, 10: 62. (10 Mar. 1710, to I. A. Musin-Pushkin).

229. *Sbornik*, 2: 111.

230. Alekseeva, *Graviura*, 93–4.

231. Biographical information from M. A. Alekseeva, comp., *Aleksei Fedorovich Zubov. Katalog vystavki* (L, 1988).

232. Reproduced in Alekseeva, *Graviura*, 140–2. See Kaganov 'Ship of Peter', for an interesting analysis.

233. See L. A. J. Hughes, 'Peter the Great's Two Weddings: Changing Images of Women in a Transitional Age', in R. Marsh, ed., *Women in Russia and Ukraine* (Cambridge, 1996), 31–44.

234. Kaliazina, illustrations 167 and 173.

235. Alekseeva, *Graviura*, 96–7.

236. See D. E. Farrell, 'Some Early Russian Woodcuts in the Context of the Schism', in *WOR*, 185–96. The *lubki* mentioned below are illustrated in *The Lubok. Russian Folk Pictures. 17th to 18th Century* (L, 1984).

237. See L. A. J. Hughes, 'The Moscow Armoury and Innovations in 17th- Century Muscovite Art', *CASS*, 13 (1979), 204–23.

238. I. M. Zharkova, *Tezisy*, 74–6.

239. Stählin, 111.

240. Zharkova, in *Tezisy*, 75; S. O. Androsov, 'Ivan Nikitin i Iogann Gotfrid Tannauer', *Voprosy iskusstvoz- naniia*, 10 (1997), 510–15.

241. *200-letie*, 61, 224. (His pupils each received 200 roubles.)

242. S. O. Androsov, 'O portrete Petra I raboty Ivana Nikitina iz Ekaterininskogo dvortsa-muzeia', in *Kuchumovskie chteniia. Sbornik materi- alov nauchnoi konferentsii, posvias- hchennoi pamiati A. M. Kuchumova (1913–1994)* (SPb, 1996) 9–14, cites a document (Jan. 1715) in which Nikitin is referred to as 'zhivopisets'.

243. V. Iu. Matveev, 'Raznykh zhudozhestv mastera', 161.

244. *PZh*, 1721, p. 73 (3 Sept.).

245. Zharkova, in *Tezisy*, 76, identifies these two works as portraits of Peter in an oval frame and of Peter with a sea- battle in the background, but Androsov, 'O portrete Petra I', 9–14, questions her conclusions. N. P. Sharandak, *Russkaia portretnaia zhivopis' petrovskogo vremeni* (L, 1987), 60, 63, attributes the oval portrait to Louis Caravaque, on the basis of 'tech- nological' studies made in the Russian Museum.

246. S. O. Androsov, 'Painting and Sculpture in the Petrine Era', in A. G. Cross, ed., *Russia in the Reign of Peter the Great. Old and New Perspective.* (Cambridge, 1998), 161–71.

247. See Kaliazina, illustration 105.

248. Ibid., illustration 106, accepts the self- portrait attribution.

249. Ibid., illustration 111. Her suggestion that it was painted 'from memory of a meeting with the emperor' is rather unconvincing, given the likeness. It is more likely that well-known portraits, including Moor's, were used as models.

250. Androsov, 'O portrete Petra I', 9– 14.

251. Peter to Menshikov, 22 May 1717: LOI, f. 270, d. 84, ll. 443$^{r–v}$.

252. *Sbornik*, 2: 112.

253. Kaliazina, illustration 118. Bergholz saw the painting and thought it 'not badly done': 1721, p. 135.

254. Kaliazina, illustration 217. There is a

fascinating exchange of letters about designs for tapestries. A Brussels tapestry-maker sent to inspect the designs reported that all the pictures were unsuitable, because the designs were too small in scale and there would be 'confusion'. GPB, f. 1003 (Voskresensky), no. 11, ll. 153–4 (Peter to Dolgoruky, 20 Nov. 1720).

255. Kaliazina, illustration 118.

256. Sharandak, *Russkaia*, 35; *Istoriia russkogo iskusstva*, ed. I. Grabar, vol. 5 (M, 1960), 303–6.

257. Matveev, 'Raznykh zhudozhestv mastera', 146–57.

258. Stählin, 67.

259. G. H. Hamilton, *The Art and Architecture of Russia* (London, 1983), 343.

260. I. M. Zharkova, 'Zhivopisets petrovskogo vremeni Iogann Genrikh Vedekind', in *Soobshcheniia Gosudarstvennoi Tret'iakovskoi Galerei. Drevnerusskoe iskusstvo. Iskusstvo XVIII–pervoi poloviny XIX veka* (M, 1995), 64–78, also quoting ed. K. V. Malinovsky, *Zapiski Iakoba Shtelina ob iziashchnykh iskusstvakh v Rossii*, (M, 1991), 1: 53.

261. LOI, f. 270, d. 97, l. 184 (11 Feb. 1721).

262. See Stählin, 46–7.

263. Kaliazina, illustrations 21–3.

264. Bolotova, *Letnii*, 121.

265. Kaliazina, illustrations 58–62.

266. Ibid., illustration 64.

267. *Sbornik*, 2: 71.

268. Canvases purchased in the Dutch Republic, including Rembrandt's *David and Jonathan* (1642) are illustrated in *Peter de Grote en Holland*, 275–62. An example of Rembrandt's influence can be seen in the ceiling painting *Diana and Acteon* (1720s) in the Ekaterinental palace in Tallinn. See Kaliazina, illustration 74.

269. Ibid., illustration 27. See the account of Peter's taste by the Swiss artist Gsell in Stählin, 46–7.

270. *PiB*, 11(ii): 200 (19 Oct.).

271. *200-letie*, 110–11.

272. Stählin, 42.

273. See decrees, *PSZ*, 6: no. 4079 (31 Aug. 1722); 7: no. 4154 (31 Jan. 1723). See ch. 43 of the 1551 Stoglav Council of a Hundred Chapters.

274. Pososhkov, 282–3. He advocated the production of a manual of engravings of nude figures, in order to teach icon-painters correct proportions.

275. *PSZ*, 7: no. 4148, pp. 16–17.

276. *200-letie, prilozhenie*, 29–30.

277. Kaliazina, illustration 172; Matveev, 'Raznykh zhudozhestv mastera', 146–57.

278. Matveev, 'Raznykh', 149–51. Document in RGIA, f. 468, op. 45, d. 449. Mikhail Zakharov's works for his attestation included both secular and religious subjects: drawings of historical, architectural, academic, and geometric subjects and 'perspectives' jostle with an icon of the Virgin and two standard subjects from the Western religious repertoire: the martyr St Sebastian and Judith beheading Holofernes.: Matveev, 'Raznykh', 158. See also N. M. Moleva and E. M. Beliutin, *Zhivopisnykh del mastera. Kantseliariia ot stroeniia i russkaia zhivopis' pervoi poloviny XVIII veka* (M, 1965). There is also an Aleksandr Zakharov (ca. 1670–after 1742), who worked with Odol'sky, in Menshikov's palace and Peterhof, mainly on wall-painting: Kaliazina, 258.

279. Kaliazina, illustration 172.

280. See discussion in O. S. Evangulova, 'Portret petrovskogo vremeni i problemy skhodstva', *Vestnik MGU. seriia 8. Istoriia*, 1979, no. 5, 69–82; *idem*, 'K probleme stilia v iskusstve petrovskogo vremeni', ibid., 1974, no. 3, 67–84.

281. Kaliazina, 163 and illustration 139.

282. See, e.g., Iu. Ovsiannikov, *Dominiko Trezzini* (L, 1987.)

283. *Istoriia russkogo iskusstva*, vol. 6 (M, 1961), 304.

284. C. R. Jensen, 'Music for the Tsar: A Preliminary Study of the Music of the Muscovite Court Theatre', *Musical Quarterly*, 79/2(1995), 372, also records private performances by foreigners: e.g., in the suite of ambassador Charles Howard in 1664. Documents on this topic are published in S. K. Bogoiavlensky, *Moskovskii teatr pri tsariakh Aleksee i Petre* (M, 1914).

285. Jensen, 'Music for the Tsar', 374–5.

286. See L. A. J. Hughes, *Sophia Regent of*

Russia 1657–1704 (New Haven, 1990), 173–5.

287. *PiB*, 1:186; *Pamiatniki diplomatich-eskikh snoshenii dvevnei Rossii s derzhavami inostrannymi* (SPb., 1851–7), 8: 917

288. Nartov, 9; Ustrialov, *Istoriia*, 3: 142.

289. H.-F. de Bassewitz, 'Zapiski grafa Bassevicha, sluzhashchie k poiasneniiu nekotorykh sobytii iz vremeni tsarstvovaniia Petra Velikogo (1713–1725)', *Russkii arkhiv*, 3 (1865), 239–40.

290. Weber, 1: 188–9.

291. D. Schlafly, ' "Playmate" Regiments of Peter the Great,' *MERSH*, 28 (1982), 121.

292. *Sbornik*, 2: 72: *Komediant*. Peter also visited a theatre in Spa. On Peter's love of boxing (which he saw in England) and strongmen, see Nartov, 11–12.

293. Information from P. O. Morozov, 'Russkii teatr pri Petre Velikom', in *Ezhegodnik imperatorskikh teatrov. 1893–1894* (SPb., 1894), bk 1, pp. 52–80; Pekarsky, *Nauka*, 1: 422ff.

294. The following from documents in *Sbornik*, 2: 311–19, memoranda from clerks of the Foreign Office and Golovin.

295. Ibid., 312.

296. Ibid., 314.

297. Ibid., 318.

298. Ibid., 317.

299. Ibid. In 1704 a Swedish servant of Fürst's was sentenced to a beating with sticks for misbehaviour, 'to deter others from behaving improperly and impolitely in the theatre'.

300. *P'esy stolichnykh i provintsail'nykh teatrov pervoi poloviny XVIII v.*, ed. A. S. Eleonskaia (M, 1975), 13; Morozov, 'Russkii teatr', 65.

301. S. Karlinsky, *Russian Drama from its Beginnings to the Age of Pushkin* (Berkeley, Calif., 1985), 47.

302. *P'esy*, 12 (26 Feb. 1715).

303. Weber, 1: 188–9.

304. *Sbornik*, 2: 319.

305. *Delo o pozhitkakh gosudaryni Natalii Alekseevny* (M, 1914), 113–15; *DPPS*, 6(i): no. 600, pp. 553–5. See L. A. J. Hughes, 'Between Two Worlds:

Tsarevna Natal'ia Alekseevna and the "Emancipation" of Petrine Women', in *WOR*, 29–36.

306. Bergholz, 1722, pp. 316–18.

307. Muller, 41.

308. *P'esy*, 9.

309. *Tsarstvo mira*, *Torzhestvo mira* and *Slava Rossiiskaia*: in *P'esy*, 8; *P'esy shkol'nykh teatrov Moskvy* (M, 1974), and descriptions in Grebeniuk.

310. *P'esy*, 13.

311. Bergholz, 1724, p. 46 (24 May).

312. *Sbornik*, 2: 121 (31 Dec.); Morozov, 'Russkii teatr', 72.

313. *Russkaia dramaturgiia poslednei chetverti XVII i nachala XVIII v.*, ed. O. A. Derzhavina (M, 1972), 220–74.

314. L. Titova, 'Iz istorii teatral'noi zhizni v epokhu Petra I', *Sovetskoe slavianove-denie*, 1972, no. 5, 53–9.

315. Includes Bergholz and entries in Tsaritsa Ekaterina's account books: ibid., 59.

316. Weber, 1: 264–5.

317. Adam Olearius, *The Travels of Olearius in Seventeenth-Century Russia*, ed. and trans. S. Baron (Stanford, Calif., 1967), 262–3.

318. Quoted in Jensen, 'Music for the Tsar', 371–2.

319. Reutenfels, quoted in ibid., 368–401.

320. Ibid., 375, 377. See also inventories of V. V. Golitsyn's possessions, which included an organ, clavichord, and flutes: R. Hellie, unpubl. paper 'Material Culture and Identity in Late Medieval and Early Modern Russia' (UCLA, Mar. 1994), 64.

321. Jensen, 'Music for the Tsar', 382.

322. Muller, 24.

323. *Sbornik*, 2: 90.

324. See below, pp. 267–9.

325. I. V. Saverkina and Iu. N. Semenov, 'Orkestr i khor A.D. Menshikova', *Pamiatniki kul'tury*, 1989 (1990), 161.

326. Listed ibid., 165–6.

327. Ibid., 162–3; O. Dolskaya, 'From Titov to Teplov: The Origins of the Russian Art Song', in *WOR*, 197–213.

328. Saverkina and Semenov, 'Orkestr', 161.

329. *Sbornik*, 2: 94.

330. Ibid., 93 (May 1721). See list of rewards for playing on the tsar's name-day 1722

and to celebrate the taking of Derbent 26 Aug: ibid., 110, 114.

331. Stählin, no. 101, pp. 155–7; S. F. Platonov, *Petr Velikii. Lichnost' i deiatel'nost'* (Paris, 1927), 112.

332. Korb, 2: 145.

333. Weber, 1: 190–2.

334. Mozgovaia, 'Sintez iskusstv', 62–3. Musicians appear in Zubov's engraving of the Poltava parade.

335. Dolskaya, 'From Titov to Teplov', 207, points out that Soviet musical historians were obliged to stress the importance of *secular* music in the Petrine era and to underplay sacred works.

336. Bergholz, 1723, p. 186.

CHAPTER 8: THE PETRINE COURT

1. M.S. Anderson, 'Peter the Great: Imperial Revolutionary?', in A. G. Dickens, ed., *The Courts of Europe: Politics, Patronage and Royalty, 1400–1800* (London, 1977), 276. Because of this view, very little of the article deals with the court as such. See, by contrast, R. Hatton on the court of Louis XIV in the same collection. The British historian David Starkey remarked at a meeting of the Court Studies Society that Peter's court was unlike any other of his acquaintance.

2. See, e.g., O. V. Nemiro, 'Dekorativno-oformitel'skoe iskusstvo i prazdnichnyi Peterburg pervoi poloviny XVIII v.', in *Otechestvennoe i zarubezhnoe iskusstvo XVIII veka* (L, 1986), pp. 82–94.

3. R. Wortman, *Scenarios of Power, Myth and Ceremony in Russian Monarchy*, vol. 1 (Princeton, 1995), by virtually ignoring pretence and mock ceremonies, paints only a partial picture.

4. O. G. Ageeva, *Obshchestvennaia i kul'turnaia zhizn' Peterburga I chetverti XVIII v.* (M, 1991, AN SSSR Institut istorii), 2.

5. Korb, 1. 159. Korb was present for the celebration in Sept. 1698.

6. *PSZ*, 3 no. 1735, pp. 680–1; no. 1736, pp. 681–2; I. A. Zheliabuzhsky,

'Zapiski', in A. B. Bogdanov, ed., *Rossiia pri tsarevne Sof'e i Petre I*, (M, 1990), 281–3. A foretaste of these edicts appears in a personal *ukaz* of 17 Nov. 1699 which includes among other business the instruction 'The year to be written from the birth of Christ in all business matters' (*PSZ*, 3: no. 1718, p. 671).

7. See, e.g., the description of the *deistvo novogo leta* for Sept. 1693 in *DR*, 4: 821–3. Only Ivan attended, in a red velvet robe.

8. H. F. de Bassewitz, 'Zapiski grafa Bassevicha sluzhashchie k poiasneniiu nekotorykh sobytii iz vremeni tsarstvovaniia Petra Velikogo (1713–1725)', *Russkii arkhiv*, 3 (1865), 237.

9. See *PSZ*, 4: no. 1746, p. 3 (17 Jan. 1700) (on the expulsion of the strel'tsy from Moscow): 'in the years 207 and 208 and in the present year of 1700'.

10. Korb, 1: 222–3.

11. Weber, 1: 84–5.

12. A *sobor* is a council or assembly of the Orthodox Church. The common translation as 'Drunken *Synod*' is misleading, as it associates the phenomenon with the reformed Church rather than the pre-Petrine one. The doctoral work of US scholar Ernest Zitser of Columbia University recently came to my attention, focusing on the institutionalization of parodic spectacles and the ritualization of blasphemy at Peter's court in the context of baroque court culture of late seventeenth-century European absolutist regimes.

13. L. N. Semenova, *Ocherki istorii byta i kul'turnoi zhizni Rossii: pervaia polovina XVIII v.* (L, 1982), 188–9.

14. B. F. Sumner, *Peter the Great and the Emergence of Russia* (London, 1958), 29.

15. See, e.g., Anderson, 'Peter the Great', 274; *idem, Peter the Great* (London, 1978), 107.

16. *DR*, 4: 577–9, 590 (23–4 Aug.). On the politics of the election, see below, p. 335.

17. *PSZ*, 3: no. 1381, pp. 71–3 (22–4 Aug. 1690).

18. The first reference to the mock 'His

Holiness the Patriarch' may be in a letter to F. M. Apraksin of 11 Oct. 1693. See N. Pogodin, 'Petr Pervyi: Pervye gody edinoderzhaviia, 1689–1694', *Russkii arkhiv*, 1879, 1: 47.

19. N. I. Pavlenko, *Petr Velikii* (M, 1990), 97–8.

20. See V. M. Zhivov and B. A. Uspensky, 'Tsar' i Bog: Semioticheskie aspekty sakralizatsii monarkha v Rossii', in Uspensky, ed., *Iazyki kul'tury i problemy perevodimosti* (M, 1987), 95.

21. See S. F. Platonov, *Petr Velikii. Lichnost' i deiatel'nost'* (Paris, 1927), 76.

22. *PiB*, 1: 31–2. 'Kukui' was a popular name for the Foreign Quarter, which also sounds like *khui* ('penis').

23. See S. F. Platonov, 'Iz bytovoi istorii Petrovskoi epokhi', *Izvestiia AN SSSR* (1926), 8. L. N. Semenova, 'Obshchestvennye razvlecheniia v Rossii v pervoi polovine XVIII v.', in *Staryi Peterburg* (L, 1982), 155, and *idem, Ocherki istorii byta*, 188, claims that the British Monastery was an 'imitation' of Peter's assembly.

24. N. Hans, 'The Moscow School of Mathematics and Navigation (1701)', *SEER*, 29 (1951), 535.

25. Letter of 4 Feb./24 Jan. 1706: BL, Stafford Papers, Add. MS 31128, f. 34.

26. F. J. Strahlenberg, *Zapiski kapitana Filippa Ioganna Strahlenberga ob istorii i geografii Rossiiskoi imperii Petra Velikogo*, trans. and ed. Iu. Bespiatykh et al. (M&L, 1985), 1: 114.

27. N. M. Moleva, ' "Persony" vse-shuteishego sobora', *VI*, 1974, no. 10, 208, dates the appearance of the Assembly from the mid-1690s on the basis of this coincidence, and names the Kozhukhovo campaign as the pretext for commissioning the portraits. See above, pp. 16–17.

28. *Sbornik*, 2: 183 (a description of the court villages made in 1701). There were six boyars' residences for meetings with the tsar.

29. Moleva, ' "Persony" ', 209, mentions a small copy in a private collection in Paris. The information on Naryshkin comes from Kurakin, 1: 384, who describes him as 'stupid, old and drunk'. See *PSZ*, 3: no. 1381, p. 79, and

R. Warner, 'The Kožuchovo Campaign of 1697', *JGO*, 13/4 (1965), 491. Zotov was one of the attendants of the real patriarch at the enthronement in 1690. Strahlenberg, *Zapiski*, 1: 115.

30. Zheliabuzhsky, 'Zapiski', 221; Moleva, ' "Persony" ', 208. The stick in his hand is not a jester's cane but a regimental baton.

31. Said to have been co-opted as a punishment for beating up Zheliabuzhsky in 1695: Moleva, ' "Persony" ', 209.

32. *PiB*, 9: 1297. The name 'Vymeni' recalls the Russian 'Vy menia' (you . . . me), but also sounds like the Russian for 'udder'. See his correspondence with Peter, *PiB*, 5: 561–2. See a list of jesters (*shuty*) in Strahlenberg, *Zapiski*, 1: 118.

33. M. I. Semevsky, 'Petr I kak iumorist', in *Slovo i delo, 1700–1735. Ocherki i rasskazy iz russkoi istorii XVIII veka.* (SPb., 1885), 285. I. Nosovich, 'Vsep'ianeishii sobor, uchrezhdennyi Petra Velikogo', *Russkaia starina*, 2/12, (1874), 737, identifies Shrovetide as Poland, Ivashka as the 'Zaporozhian hetman', and Eremka as the Tatar khan in an unconvincing attempt to read a political warning on the eve of Peter's departure for the West.

34. O. Beliaev, *Dukh Petra Velikogo* (SPb., 1798), 22–3; N. Ustrialov, *Istoriia tsarstvovaniia Petra Velikogo*, 6 vols (SPb., 1858–69), 3: 142.

35. Korb, 1: 255–6.

36. *PZh*, 1705, p. 2.

37. *PiB*, 4: 184, 751.

38. *PiB*, 7(i): 90–1 (to Zotov). The 'British deacon' is identified as merchant William Lloyd.

39. Semevsky, 'Petr I kak iumorist', 314–15; *PiB*, 6: 301–2.

40. *200-letie*, 223.

41. Semenova, 'Obshchestvennye razvlecheniia', 156.

42. See *PZh*, 1720, pp. 13, 48 (27 Mar.); Semevsky, 'Petr I kak iumorist', 314.

43. *PiB*, 11: 141 (10 Mar. 1711, edict to Senate).

44. Ibid., 167 (9 Apr. 1711). He informs her that the vizier has raised his flag, called

a *tui* (suspiciously close to the vulgar *khui*, 'prick') as the standard of their campaign, and that she is to march against his 'weapon'.

45. *Sbornik*, 2: 19 (entry for 9 Nov.)—*za vyt'e*, 116 (28 Sept.). In Nov. 1722 she was given 100 roubles 'for the present campaign' (p. 117).

46. LOI, f. 270, d. 103, l. 541 (10 June 1723).

47. '. . . uchinit' obrazom drevniago var-varsk'ogo obychaia': *MIGO*, 1: 67 (21 Oct. 1713).

48. Semevsky, *Slovo i delo*, 319–20.

49. Weber, 1: 89–90.

50. A. F. Bychkov, *Pis'ma Petra Velikogo, khraniashchiesia v imp. Publ. biblioteke* (SPb., 1872), 78–9.

51. Recorded by Korb, 1: 222–3 (Jan. 1699); Semenova, *Ocherki*, 191.

52. *Sbornik*, 2: 4, 90 (6 Jan. 1721, 'with all his assembly'). See also tips to various musicians, including seven of Prince Menshikov's trumpeters.

53. Juel, 3: 30–1.

54. *Sbornik*, 2: 23. On Bitka, see below, p. 428.

55. e.g. *Sbornik*, 2: 94–5 (1721).

56. Semevsky, *Slovo i delo*, 297.

57. Ibid., 310. Buturlin died in 1723. His funeral in Sept. was mentioned by Campredon.

58. 'Reskripty i ukazy', *Osmnadtsatyi vek*, 4 (1869), 62 (5 Oct.), 68 (26 July 1721, to begin 16 Aug.).

59. *PZh*, 1721, p. 75. There was a rehearsal for the wedding on 12 Feb., with a procession of about fifty sledges: ibid., 22.

60. Ibid., 59.

61. Ibid., 75 (3 Oct.).

62. Campredon, 15 Feb. (NS), *SIRIO*, 40: 47–8. The French party took part on its own float, as did other foreigners.

63. *SIRIO*, 49: 321–3.

64. *SIRIO*, 40: 281 ff. An Amazon costume, apparently the only Russian masquerade outfit to survive from this period, is in the Moscow Armoury. See *Treasures of the Czars from the State Museums of the Moscow Kremlin. Presented by Florida International Museum St Petersburg* (London, 1995), 186.

65. See order for costumes in LOI, f. 270, d. 104, l. 495 (24 Dec. 1723): 'Make in Friesland three Friesland jackets after the pattern on the sheet, one in black velvet, another in blue cloth, a third in blue serge, and trousers in the same materials and colours.' In a letter of 11 Feb. Peter mentioned that the original order had omitted the female costumes: ibid., d. 108, l. 3.

66. Bergholz, 1724, p. 18.

67. *SIRIO*, 52: 386. (9 Jan. 1725 (NS)).

68. Platonov, *Petr Velikii*, 123. But see report by Campredon that the conclave of eight 'cardinals' was usually locked away in a house on a small island near Preobrazhenskoe for 24 hours with a prodigious quantity of alcohol and not allowed to sleep until they made their nomination.

69. See Semenova, 'Obshchestvennye razvlecheniia', 155: 'The Drunken Assembly arose as a parody on the papacy. Lefort and other Protestants in the Foreign Quarter spared no effort to limit the influence of Catholics in Russia.'

70. J. G. Vockerodt, *Rossiia pri Petre Velikom po rukopisnomu izvestiiu Ioanna Gottgil'fa Fokkerodta* (SPb., 1874) (*Chteniia*, 1874, bk 2, pt 4), 19.

71. 10 Sept. 1723 (NS), *SIRIO*, 49: 379–80. Also 52: 168-9 (14 Mar. 1721 (NS)).

72. Bergholz, 1721, pp. 170–1.

73. Kurakin, 1: 384–5.

74. Iu. M. Lotman and B. A. Uspensky, 'Echoes of the Notion of "Moscow as the Third Rome" in Peter the Great's Ideology', in A. Shukman, ed., *The Semiotics of Russian Culture* (Ann Arbor, 1984), 60.

75. J. Cracraft, *The Church Reform of Peter the Great* (London, 1971), 13. He also challenges (p. 14) the interpretation of Wittram that Peter wished to 'discredit the patriarchal dignity and all ecclesiastical titles'. See R. Wittram, *Peter I. Czar and Kaiser* (Göttingen, 1964), 1: 106–11.

76. Nosovich, 'Vsep'ianeishii', 735, 739.

77. Kurakin, 386. Kurakin goes on to describe disapprovingly how fat people were dragged through chairs, how people's clothes were torn right

off leaving them naked, how candles were shoved up their backsides, how people were thrown with bare bottoms on to ice and had air blown up their backsides with bellows (from which one died). 'All this continued right up to the journey to Holland.'

78. See Terry Castle, *Masquerade and Civilization: The Carnivalesque in Eighteenth-Century English Culture and Fiction* (Stanford, Calif., 1986), 17, 62.

79. Weber, 1: 90–1. This is also quoted in Cracraft, *Church Reform*, 18, who believes that the assembly is 'best understood in the context of the often elaborate entertainments arranged by the tsar and his company' (p. 17).

80. See Castle, *Masquerade*.

81. Both lists are printed in Semevsky, *Slovo i delo*, 313–14, but in censored form, with the 'prick' references expunged. Fuller versions may be seen in eighteenth-century copies of the originals: GPB OR, Ermitazhnoe, 450. The virtually untranslatable names include Archdeacons *pakhom pukhai khui* Mikhailov and *idi na khui* Stroev. (See Bychkov, *Pis'ma*, 78–9.) It is presumably this document to which Pavlenko refers when he comments that not only could the nicknames not be printed; 'also not be spoken aloud in a public place without the risk of arrest' (*Petr Velikii*, 99).

82. Thomas Hale, quoted in Cracraft, *Church Reform*, 10.

83. *SIRIO*, 40: 383–4.

84. G. V. Esipov, *Raskol'nich'i dela XVIII stoletiia* (SPb., 1861), 1: 68–9.

85. Strahlenberg, *Zapiski*, 1: 117, 138. The terminology of the Assembly's revels was made more explicitly Catholic after the revolt in 1705, probably in response to popular protest.

86. *PZh*, 1710, p. 23

87. *PiB*, 10: 270–1.

88. A. O. Kornilovich, *Nravy russkikh pri Petre Velikom* (SPb., 1901), 50.

89. There are three main descriptions of the wedding: *Exacter Relation von der . . . neu erbauten Festung und Stadt St. Petersburg . . . von H.G.* (Leipzig, 1713), which includes a seating plan of the banquet; that of the Danish envoy Just Juel, 3: 39–41; and the court record *Pokhodny Zhurnal.* Weber's much-quoted account (1: 285–9) is, in fact, borrowed, with amendments, from the Leipzig account (but Weber may be the author of both).

90. Juel (3: 39) counted sixty-two, but was told there were more. Weber 1: 286, has seventy-two.

91. Juel, 3: 39.

92. In Weber, 1: 289: badgers.

93. *Exacter Relation*, 78.

94. Juel, 3: 41.

95. Ibid. *Exacter Relation*, 78. (This was Luke-Peter, born in Feb. 1709. A second son was born in Jan. 1711.)

96. See *Pridvornaia zhizn'*, 56–8, for the key. This work was based on eye-witness accounts rather than life, as was Zubov's later engraving of Peter and Catherine's wedding.

97. N. Aristov, 'Pervonachal' noe obrazo-vanie Petra Velikogo', *Russkii arkhiv*, 13/8 (1875), 473. Chief dwarf Nikita died in 1689.

98. R. Warner, 'The Kožuchovo Campaign of 1694', *JGO*, 13/4 (1965), 491.

99. Juel, 3: 41.

100. *Sbornik*, 2: 38–9. Palace records include many entries on clothes of dwarfs: e.g., in Mar. 1722 a red cloth suit with gold vest with velvet trimmings was made for the dwarf Luka Chestikin, at a total cost of 23 roubles, 54 copecks: *Sbornik*, 2: 97.

101. Weber, 1: 109; Juel, 3: 37. Bergholz, 1725, p. 106, records a male dwarf with bottle and glass and a female dressed as a shepherdess popping out of pies at the wedding of Anna Petrovna in May 1725.

102. P. H. Bruce, *Memoirs of Peter Henry Bruce Esq. A Military Officer in the Service of Prussia, Russia and Great Britain* (London, 1782), 87–8.

103. *PZh*, 1724, pp. 37–8.

104. Bassewitz, 'Zapiski', 243–4, and Bergholz, 1724, pp. 13–14, both left accounts.

105. Weber, 1: 84.

106. Bergholz, 1721, pp. 52–3.

107. For a description of his death, evidently from a stroke, see *Russkii*

arkhiv, 3 (1865), 309–10 (11 May 1724, letter from Devier to Menshikov); 200-letie, 76–7.

108. PiB, 9: 371 (10 Sept. 1709, to P. M. Apraksin). Entries in Cabinet account books list clothing purchased for Kalmyks in 1718: 200-letie, 252.

109. Sbornik, 2: 96. The limit for each outfit was 9 roubles (cf. the 24 roubles allowed for a dwarf's costume, above).

110. LOI, f. 270, d. 105, ll. 15, 16, 17. (19, 22 and 28 Mar. 1723).

111. Sbornik, 2: 96: an outfit made for Peter Sundukov (sent from Astrakhan). See the Zubov engraving (1726) of Catherine I accompanied by a black servant.

112. Kurakin, 385–6; Weber, 1: 256 (1719). Also mentioned in Bergholz, 1721, 37–8, as 'a broker of Jewish origin from Hamburg', known as the 'philosopher'. Cabinet account book for 1718, 200-letie, 252; Platonov, Petr Velikii, 123–4. For other examples, see below, pp. 424–5.

113. PiB, 9: 90 (17 Feb. 1709).

114. Juel, 3: 30.

115. Ibid., 11. (The wedding coincided with the taking of Riga.)

116. Bergholz, 1724, p. 17.

117. PZh, 1725, 9 Jan. p. 1.

118. Vockerodt, Rossiia, 104. See above, p. 188.

119. K. Istomin, Kniga liubvi znak v chesten brak (facs.) (M, 1989). See L. A. J. Hughes, 'Peter the Great's Two Weddings: Changing Images of Women in a Transitional Age', in R. Marsh, ed., Women in Russia and Ukraine (Cambridge, 1996), 31–44.

120. A. A. Golombievsky, Sotrudniki Petra Velikogo (M, 1903), 58. Shansky was on the royal payroll. See account book entries for elaborate costumes ordered for him, e.g., Nov. 1698, with gold buttons and braid: Sbornik, 2: 166–7.

121. For captions, see Pridvornaia zhizn', 57–8. The third print has not survived. See M. A. Alekseeva, Graviura petrovskogo vremeni (L, 1990), 34–5. Schoenebeck was employed by the Armoury at the time. See entries on the engraving in A. Viktorov, Opisanie zapisnykh knig i bumag starinnykh

dvortsovykh prikazov, 1613–1722, 2 vols (M, 1883), 4712:, 475.

122. Cornelius de Bruyn, Travels into Muscovy, Persia, and Part of the East Indies; Containing an Accurate Description of what is most Remarkable in those Countries, 2 vols (London, 1737), 1: 25–6. Zheliabuzhsky also mentions it, but only the old-fashioned dress, 'Zapiski', 306.

123. J. Perry, The State of Russia (1716) (London, 1967), 40. (He mistakenly dates the event 1701.)

124. Bruyn, Travels, 1: 28.

125. Zheliabuzhsky, 'Zapiski', 307.

126. See Juel, 3: 33–7.

127. PZh, 1712, 1–6. The relevant passage is reprinted in A. Bychkov, 'O svad'be imp. Petra Velikogo s Ekaterinoi Alekseevnoi', Drevniaia i Novaia Rossiia, 1877, no. 3, 323–4. Charles Whitworth, dispatch of 20 Feb./2 Mar. (SIRIO, 61: 142–4). See Hughes 'Peter the Great's Two Weddings'.

128. On the status of this marriage, see above, pp. 396–7.

129. PiB, 12(i): 83. On the wedding feast and Zubov's engraving of it, see below.

130. This detail from Whitworth, SIRIO, 61: 144–5.

131. V. I. Vasil'ev, Starinnye feierverki v Rossii (XVII–perv. ch. XVIII v.) (L, 1960), 51.

132. See Bergholz's detailed description of the wedding of Count Pushkin: 1721, pp. 179–81. Tables were mixed after the wedding night.

133. See hand-written draft in papers in Nov. 1723: LOI, f. 270, d. 104, l. 340 (RGADA, f. 9, kn. 33, ll. 30–1). LOI, f. 270, d. 104, l. 489 (24 Dec. 1723, signed by Feofan).

134. LOI, f. 270, d. 106, l. 553: pardon for Bishop Varlaam; l. 567: costumes ordered for Synod choristers; d. 107, l. 66: 150 new uniforms for all grooms and stable lads, including tunics of English cloth; PSZ, 7: no. 4496, p. 279 (28 Apr. 1724, on tax arrears). See also no. 4502, p. 281 (18 May), on extended deadlines for repaying loans to treasury.

135. See description in Bergholz, 1724, pp. 32–42. Wortman (Scenarios of Power,

72) links the new crown with Peter's desire to 'purge the ceremony of symbols of descent' connected with the cap of Monomach. It is hard to see what choice he had, given that the existing coronation caps (the original and the one made for Peter in 1682) were intended for the heads of ruling male monarchs. In 1724 Catherine was not being crowned as ruler.

136. LOI, f. 270, d. 107, ll. 26–8.
137. Bergholz, 1724, p. 42.
138. *PSZ*, 7: no. 4501, p. 281.
139. Wortman, *Scenarios of Power*, 69. Note the replacement of the old Russian word *venchanie* by a Western borrowing, *koronatsiia*. Wortman points out that the description of the coronation was intended for foreigners. If so, it is odd that it appeared only in Russian, whereas other pieces of Petrine publicity – e.g., the manifestos on the trial of Tsarevich Alexis – were published in foreign languages. Explanations suggest a foreign author, perhaps. See *Opisanie koronatsii e.v. Ekateriny Alekseevny* (SPb., 1724; M, 1725). Wortman, *Scenarios of Power*, 72–3, provides a description of the coronation based on this account. See LOI, f. 270, d. 107, ll. 43, 46, 47. Gun salutes were to be organized, and notices issued for 'publikatsiia v narod'.
140. F. Prokopovich, *Kratkaia povest' o smerti Petra Velikogo Imperatora i Samoderzhtsa Vserossiiskogo* (SPb., 1831), 22.
141. See illustrations in Alekseeva, *Graviura*, 164–5, by A. I. Rostovtsev and S. M. Korovin. *Opisanie poriadka derzhannogo pri pogrebenii blazhennyia vysokoslavnyia i vernodostoineishiia pamiati vsepresvetleishago derzhavneishago Petra Velikago* (SPb., 1725; M, 1726). An earlier example of military honours was the funeral of F. A. Golovin in 1706, when armour was borrowed from the props of the theatre in the Kremlin! *Sbornik*, 2: 319 (complaint by the impresario Fürst that the armour had not been returned).
142. F. Prokopovich, *Kratkaia povest'*, 49; *Opisanie poriadka*, 5.

143. *Opisanie*, 8–10.
144. Ibid., 13.
145. Ibid., 30.
146. Ibid., 31.
147. *PSZ*, 3: no. 1536, pp. 220–3 (29 Jan.–7 Mar. 1696). In 1724 Peter's daughters ordered a velvet cover for their uncle's tomb: LOI, f. 270, d. 109, l. 13.
148. *PSZ*, 4: no. 2118, pp. 354–6 (24 Aug. 1706). Tsaritsa Marfa Matveevna, widow of the late Tsar Fedor, likewise was interred in traditional style in 1715: Weber, 1: 111.
149. *SIRIO*, 60: 191–2 (22 Mar. (NS). Campredon commented that he had never had such a terrible experience, although at least he had a conversation with the tsar.
150. Kornilovich, *Nravy*, 41.
151. *BP*, 519; GPB OR, f. 1003, d. 11, l. 373.
152. *BP*, 520–1.
153. LOI, f. 270, d. 103, l. 535 (2 June 1723).
154. *PZh*, 1724, p. 35. An eagle ('double' or 'great' eagle) was a very large goblet with the double-headed eagle motif.
155. Bergholz, 1724, pp. 16–17.
156. S. Baehr, *The Paradise Myth in Eighteenth-Century Russia* (Stanford, Calif., 1991), 59.
157. Bergholz, 1724, p. 49.
158. Zheliabuzhsky, 'Zapiski', 313.
159. Juel, 3: 30 (7/18 Oct. 1710), 32 (5 Nov. 1710), 42 (30 Nov./11 Dec.).
160. Ibid., 43–4.
161. Weber, 1: 93–5.
162. Bergholz, 1721, pp. 50–62.
163. Ibid., pp. 196–7.
164. *SIRIO*, 40: 168–9 (letter of 14 Mar. 1721 (NS)). See above Campredon's explanation of the Drunken Assembly.
165. *SIRIO*, 49: 344. (to Dubois, 11 June 1723 (NS)). A fuller account for the king is dated 13 June: see p. 349.
166. Kurakin, 379.
167. Heavy drinking was a feature of many European courts. The Holsteiners, a large party of whom were in Russia during the last few years of Peter's life, were especially notorious in this respect.
168. Mardefeld, *SIRIO*, 52: 195 (11 Aug. (NS)).
169. RGADA, f. 9, otd. I, kn. 58, ll. 229–230ᵛ.

170. *PSZ,* 5: no. 3241, pp. 597–8. For a review of literature on the topic, see O. G. Ageeva, 'Assamblei petrovskogo vremeni v russkoi dorevoliutsionnoi istoriografii', in *Istoriograficheskie i istoricheskie problemy russkoi kul'tury* (M, 1983), 47–66.

171. Ageeva, *Obshchestvennaia,* 15–16.

172. Weber, 1: 188.

173. Semenova, *Ocherki istorii byta,* 199.

174. Ageeva, *Obshchestvennaia,* 15.

175. *PZh,* 1720, pp. 3–4.

176. E. P. Karnovich, 'Assamblei pri Petre Velikom', in *Istoricheskie rasskazy i bytovye ocherki* (SPb., 1884), 238–50.

177. Bergholz, 1722, p. 71; Semenova, *Ocherki istorii byta,* 203.

178. N. Bozherianov, *Sankt-Peterburg v Petrovo vremia* (SPb., 1903), p. xii. On protests, see below, p. 348.

179. Semenova, *Ocherki istorii byta,* 202. Bergholz, 1723, p. 16.

180. N. D. Beliaev, 'Russkoe obshchestvo pri Petre Velikom', *Den'* (1864), no. 2, 5–6.

181. See Prince M. Shcherbatov, *On the Corruption of Morals in Russia,* ed. and trans. A. Lentin (Cambridge, 1969).

182. Bergholz, 1725, p. 98.

183. Stählin, 49–50.

184. LOI, f. 270, d. 103, l. 553 (23 June 1723). *PSZ,* 6: no. 4253.

185. Semenova, 'Obshchestvennye razvlecheniia', 148, 149.

186. *PSZ,* 6: no. 4099, p. 776 (27 Sept. 1722). Semenova, 'Obshchestvennye razvlecheniia', 151.

187. Juel, 3: 113–14.

188. Zheliabuzhsky, 'Zapiski', 279.

189. Weber, 1: 265.

190. *PZh,* 1720, pp. 29–30.

191. See *Kalendar' ili mesiatsoslov khristianskii po staromu shtiliu ili izchisleniiu, na leto ot voploshcheniia Boga Slova 1725* (M, 1724) (in P. Pekarsky, *Nauka, i literatura v Rossii pri Petre Velikom,* 2 vols (M, 1862), 2: 625–6. This has a list of 'torzhestvennye, prazdnichnye i viktorial'nye dni, kotorye povsegodno prazdnuemy byvaiut', apparently the first time that such a list was appended to a calendar. See above, p. xxviii.

192. Ageeva, *Obshchestvennaia,* 11.

193. Ibid., 13.

194. V. M. Zhivov, 'Kul'turnye reformy v sisteme preobrazovaniia Petra I', in *Iz istorii russkoi kul'tury. Tom III (XVII–nachalo XVIII veka)* (M, 1996), 541.

195. G. V. Vilinbakhov, 'Otrazhenie idei absoliutizma v simvolike Petrovskikh znamen', in *Kul'tura i iskusstvo Rossii XVIII veka* (L, 1981), 17–21.

196. Ibid., 15–17; *idem,* 'K istorii uchrezhdeniia ordena Andreia Pervozvannogo', in *Kul'tura i iskusstvo petrovskogo vremeni* (L, 1977), 144–8.

197. E. B. Mozgovaia, 'Obraz Petra I – imperatora v proizvedeniiakh tvorchestva, Bartolomeo Karlo Rastrelli', in *Monarkhiia i narodovlastie v kul'ture prosveshcheniia* (M, 1995), 4.

198. E. B. Mozgovaia, 'Sintez iskusstv v triumfakh pervoi chetverti XVIII veka', in *Problemy razvitiia russkogo iskusstva,* vol. 18 (L, 1985), 60.

199. Grebeniuk, 135–49.

200. V. I. Vasil'ev, *Starinnye feierverki,* 25: 'siia ne sut' khram ili tserkov' v imia nekoego ot sviatykh sozdannaia, no politichnaia, sei est' grazhdanskaia pokhvala truzhdaiushchimsia o tselosti otechestva i trudy svoimi'. Variation of text in Grebeniuk, 154.

201. See *PiB,* 8: 446–7.

202. *PiB,* ibid., 473–4 (before 11 Dec.), 475 (3 Dec., to M. P. Gagarin).

203. See above and descriptions in *SIRIO,* 50: 291, and Juel.

204. *PiB,* 8: 495–6.

205. Juel, 2: 34–5.

206. Ibid., 3: 9 (8 July).

207. By Zubov and Picart. See Alekseeva, *Graviura,* 135–7; V. N. Berkh, *Zhizneopisanie gen.-adm. F. M. Apraksina* (SPb., 1825), 14–17. On the mock tsar, see above pp. 98–100.

208. Berkh, *Zhizneopisanie,* 89.

209. LOI, f. 270, d. 98, l. 119 (29 Aug. 1721).

210. 'Reskripty i ukazy', 68 (9 Sept. 1721, letter to governor of Riga).

211. This and the following description from 'Opisannoe samovidtsem torzhestvo, proiskhodivshee v S-Peterburge 22 okt. 1721 goda', in *Syn otechestva,* 1849, bk 2, pp. 1–4 (an eyewitness account) written 'for posterity'. 'Reliatsiia o zakliuchenii mira so

Shvetsiei', in *ZA*, 157–61. This official text (with corrections in Peter's hand) looks to be the same as the so-called eye-witness account. See also Campredon, *SIRIO*, 50: 297–300. Translations of Peter's speech were handed out to foreign diplomats.

212. *ZA*, 159.

213. *200-letie*, 268. The engineer responsible for setting up the Janus temple was apparently an Englishman. He asked for 570 roubles to cover the cost of materials. According to V. I. Vasil'ev, *Starinnye feierverki*, 47–8, the engineers responsible for the fireworks were Skorniakov-Pisarev and Kormchin. The temple was designed by Pineau. It was destroyed in a storm on 5 Nov. 1721.

214. S. G. Runkevich, *Uchrezhdenie i pervonachalnoe ustroistvo sviateishago pravitel'stvuiushchego sinoda (1721–1725 gg.* (SPb., 1900), 428–9. In 1722 Peter ordered the 'congratulations and greeting' pronounced by Iavorsky et al. to be written in the History, but had to repeat the order in 1724: *ZA*, 149.

215. *DR*, 4: 746.

216. Korb, 1: 224–8. See also Zheliabuzhsky, 'Zapiski', 267.

217. Bruyn, 1: *Travels*, 22–4.

218. Ibid.

219. *Exacter Relation*, 78–9.

220. Weber, 1: 85.

221. *PZh*, 1724, pp. 30–1. Bergholz was there, and counted almost 10,000 troops (1724, p. 5).

222. *PZh*, 1725, p. 1. Another 'Jordan' (Erdan) ceremony was celebrated on 1 Aug., the feast of the Wood of the True Cross, associated with the blessing of the waters and also the official anniversary of the baptism of Rus' in 988. See, e.g., *Sbornik*, 1: 119 (1691).

223. See entries in *DR* for 5 Apr. 1691 (pp. 398–401), 20 Mar. 1692 (pp. 659–63), 9 Apr. 1693 (pp. 775–9): Peter attended the last one. See M. Flier, 'Breaking the Code. The Image of the Tsar in the Muscovite Palm Sunday Ritual', in M. Flier and D. Rowland, eds, *Medieval Russian Culture*, vol. 2 (Berkeley, Los Angeles and London, 1994), 213–42.

224. Lotman and Uspensky, 'Notions', 60.

But Golikov records that Peter led a horse on which the prince-pope Zotov was seated. (*VI*, 1838, p. 277). See also Zhivov, 'Kul'turnye reformy', 535, on the 'Donation of Constantine' legend in the 'Tale of the White Cowl', still quoted in the *Kormchaia kniga* of 1653.

225. *DR*, 4: entries for Palm Sunday 1699 (2 Apr., p. 1097) and 1700 (24 Mar., p. 1127): 'iz sobornye i apostolskie tserkvi Uspeniia presviatye Bogoroditsy na lobnoe mesto krestnago khodu i deistva Vaii, protiv prezhniago obyknoveniia, ne bylo.' See L. A. J. Hughes, 'Did Peter I Abolish the Palm Sunday Ceremony?', *SGECRN*, 24 (1996), 62–5.

226. See Zhivov and Uspensky, 'Tsar' i Bog', 112–15. Kurakin (385) records the use of a camel.

227. See *DR*, 4: entries for 1694, when Tsar Ivan attended liturgies for Metropolitans Philip (8 Jan.) and Alexis (12 Feb.).

228. See Ageeva, *Obshchestvennaia*, 16–17. On the political underpinnings of sixteenth-century *pokhody*, see N. S. Kollmann, 'Pilgrimage, Procession and Symbolic Space in Sixteenth-Century Russia', in Flier and Rowland, eds, *Medieval Russian Culture*, 163–81.

229. *DR*, 4: 433.

230. See below, pp. 350–1.

231. Vilinbakhov, 'Otrazhenie idei', 15–17, and *idem*, 'K istorii', 144–8.

232. N. A. Sindalovsky, *Legendy i mifi Sankt-Peterburga* (SPb., 1994), 24–5.

233. 'Slovo v den' sviatogo blagovernago kniazia Aleksandra Nevskago' (1718), in F. Prokopovich, *Sochineniia*, ed., I. P. Eremin (M&L, 1961), 94–103; Grebeniuk, 85–6. ('on kormu derzhal otechestva svoego'). The sermon was subsequently published in a pamphlet by the Alexander Nevsky monastery press, Mar. 1720: *Sochineniia*, 468.

234. *PSZ*, 7: no. 4241, pp. 74–5 (4 June). According to Bassewitz, 'Zapiski', 251–2. See LOI, f. 270, d. 104, l. 63 (16 Sept. 1723), on the transport of the relics: instructions for them to be placed at Schlüsselburg. See also Peter's letters (28–9 Aug. 1724) to

Menshikov, on bringing the relics to the ceremony and where to stand before the ceremony, so as not to be visible from the monastery: LOI, f. 270, d. 107, ll. 271, 272, 273.

235. Bassewitz, 'Zapiski', 252.

236. Grebeniuk, 87. See also Wortman, *Scenarios of Power*, 62.

237. M. Cherniavsky, *Tsar and People: Studies in Russian Myths* (New York, 1961), 84–5. The cult was kept up after Peter's death. In 1725 almost 12,000 copies of the liturgy for Alexander Nevsky were distributed round the bishoprics: S. P. Luppov, *Kniga v Rossii v pervoi chetverti XVIII v.* (L, 1973), 121.

238. Bergholz, 1725, p. 87.

239. See above, pp. 80–1.

240. 'Slovo pokhvalnoe o flote rossiiskom' (1720), in Grebeniuk, 236; Prokopovich, *Sochineniia*, 103–112. This work was written to celebrate the Russian naval victory at Grengham, July 1720.

241. On carts via Tver' and Novgorod, with a temporary halt at Schlüsselburg, where it was to be placed on the square in front of the church and guarded day and night: letter from Peter, 29 Jan. 1723: LOI, f. 270, d. 103, ll. 115–17. See engravings of the boat made in Moscow by Zarudny and Ivan Zubov, in Alekseeva, *Graviura*, 86–7.

242. *PZh*, 1723, p. 15; N. Iu. Berezovsky et al., *Rossiiskii Imperatorskii flot, 1696–1917* (M, 1993), 54. Campredon described the regatta in a letter to Louis XV, 13 June (NS), *SIRIO*, 49: 345 ff.

243. Rules were drawn up for salutations from the 'grandchildren' as it passed: LOI, f. 270, d. 103, l. 644 (7 Aug. 1723).

244. Bassewitz, 'Zapiski', 233.

245. *PZh*, 1723, pp. 18–19.

246. *PSZ*, 7: no. 4562, p. 345 (2 Sept. 1724). For the boat's subsequent political role up to the present day, see M. Sarantola-Weiss, 'Peter the Great's First Boat, "Grandfather of the Russian Navy"', in *WOR*, 37–42.

247. There were plans to honour another of Peter's early boats, the yacht in which he made his first sea voyage in 1693. In

1723 Iaguzhinsky wrote to Archangel: 'if even a few remnants of the yacht are found, have them put in a convenient place and guarded': LOI, f. 270, d. 105, l. 30 (28 May 1723).

248. Ageeva, *Obshchestvennaia*, 13. The celebration of birthdays was a fairly recent phenomenon, first noted in the reign of Fedor Alekseevich.

249. *PZh*, 1720, pp. 19–21.

250. See Senate order of 16 May 1721 on celebrating coronation day throughout the country in the same way as the tsar's birthday and name-day. This date had been allowed to lapse. *PSZ*, 6: no. 3783, p. 389.

251. Ageeva, *Obshchestvennaia*, 14. *PZh*, 1721, pp. 24, 49.

252. Bassewitz, 'Zapiski', 198.

253. See M. A. Alekseeva, *Feierverki i illiuminatsii v grafike XVIII veke. Katalog vystavki* (L, 1978); V. I. Vasil'ev, *Starinnye feierverki.*

254. V. I. Vasil'ev, *Starinnye feierverki*, 8–10.

255. Stählin, no. 99, pp. 152–3 (Baron von Mardefeld).

256. Note by Peter for the History of the Swedish War, quoted in T. S. Maikov, 'Petr I i "Gistoriia Sveiskoi voiny"', in *RPR*, 117.

257. Pogodin, 'Petr Pervyi', 10 (from Gordon?).

258. V. I. Vasil'ev, *Starinnye feierverki*, 15.

259. Ibid., 17; Alekseeva, *Feierverki*, 1.

260. V. I. Vasil'ev, *Starinnye feierverki*, 18–19; *Pridvornaia zhizn'*, 59 (29 Aug.).

261. Alekseeva, *Feierverki*, 50–1. In 1722 Peter asked for the three designs.

262. Ibid., 5.

263. Juel, 3: 37. Peter himself explained the meaning of each allegorical picture as it burned.

264. Alekseeva, *Feierverki*, 5.

265. *SIRIO*, 40: 25 (30 Jan. (NS)), 48 (16 Feb. (NS)).

266. Wortman, *Scenarios of Power*, 5.

267. Zhivov and Uspensky, 'Tsar' i Bog', 72.

268. Edict of 6 Aug. 1675: *PSZ*, 1: no. 607.

269. P. V. Sedov, 'Reforma sluzhilogo plat'ia pri Fedore Alekseeviche', in *Tezisy*, 77–83.

270. *Diariusz zaboystwa tyranskiego senatorow moskiewskich w stolicy roku 1682* (SPb., 1901), 397.

271. *Sbornik*, 1: 233 ('Sewing book of Tsar Peter Alekseevich for 7190 [1682]').

272. See V. A. Kovrigina, 'Remeslenniki Moskovskoi Nemetskoi Slobody v kontse XVII–pervoi chetverti XVIII veka', *Russkii gorod*, 9 (1990), 185.

273. *Sbornik*, 1: 112, 121.

274. A. A. Vasil'chikov, 'O novom portrete Petra Velikogo', *Drevniaia i novaia Rossiia*, 3 (1877), 325.

275. Korb, 1: 155–6.

276. '... die lange barthe mit aigner handt gestützetetter': von Guarient to Emperor Leopold I, 12 Sept. 1698, in Ustrialov, *Istoriia*, 3: 621–3.

277. Korb, 1: 156.

278. Cherkassky was apparently regarded as a champion by conservatives: e.g., he was named as a possible candidate to replace Peter by Grigory Talitsky. See N. B. Golikova, *Politicheskie protsessy pri Petre I* (M, 1957), 137.

279. Korb, 1: 159–60.

280. But note an order to the silver workshops for 15,903 copper *chekhi* stamped with the year 7207 (1698), and on the other side *borodianye priznaki*, to be sent to the Preobrazhensky *prikaz*: *Sbornik*, 1: 166 (Oct. 1698).

281. *PSZ*, 4: no. 2015, pp. 282–3 (16 Jan. 1705).

282. Bruyn *Travels*, 1: 46

283. John Perry, *The State of Russia* (1716), (London, 1967), 195.

284. Ibid., 196–7. See also the story of Timofei Arkhipov in E. Shmurlo, *Petr Velikii v otsenke sovremennikov i potomstva* (SPb., 1912), 15.

285. PRO SP 91/4, pt II, ff. 112–13 (20 Feb./3 Mar. 1706 to Secretary of State).

286. Korb, 1: 257; B. P. Sheremetev, *Zapiski puteshestviia generala feldmarshala ... grafa B. P. Sheremeteva ... v evropeiskie gosudarstva* (M, 1773), 89.

287. On New Year, see above, p. 249.

288. *PSZ*, 4: no. 1741, p. 1 (4 Jan. 1700).

289. Semenova, *Ocherki istorii byta*, 127–8; not in *PSZ*.

290. Zheliabuzhsky, 'Zapiski' 286 (26 Aug. 1700).

291. *PSZ*, 4: no. 1887, p. 182 (1701, unfortunately undated); P. N. Petrov, 'Korennoe izmenenie russkogo byta pri Petre Velikom', *Severnoe siianie*, 2/78 (1863), 441–3.

292. Iu. U. Gerasimova, 'Vospominaniia Filippo Balatri', *Zapiski otdela rukopisei*, 27 (1965), 189.

293. Bruyn, *Travels*, 1: 46.

294. Esipov, *Raskol'nich'i dela*, 2: 171–2. For more examples, see below, pp. 251–3.

295. *Stoglav*, ch. 40 , text in *Russkoe zakonodatel'stvo X–XX vekov*, vol. 2 (M, 1985), 301–2. The hundred chapters issued by the council set out norms for the life of the Russian Church.

296. Adrian's 24-point tract on matters of faith, point 15: Esipov, *Raskol'nich'i dela*, 2: 87.

297. 'Treatise on shaving' (*Slovo o bradobritii*), attributed to Patriarch Adrian, quoted in F. Buslaev, 'Drevnerusskaia boroda', in *Drevne-russkaia literatura i iskusstvo*, vol. 2 (SPb., 1861), 228.

298. Buslaev, 'Drevne-russkaia boroda', 235.

299. B. A. Uspensky, 'Historia sub specie Semioticae', in H. K. Baran, ed., *Semiotics and Structuralism. Readings from the Soviet Union* (New York, 1976), 71.

300. Pekarsky, *Nauka*, 2: 159–60.

301. As Shmurlo, *Petr Velikii*, primechaniia, 20, points out, beards could be regarded as a sign of political unreliability as late as the reign of Nicholas I, who forbade them in the army and at court.

302. Nartov, 22.

303. *PSZ*, 4: no. 1898, p. 189.

304. LOI, f. 270, d. 105, l. 7 (to Peter Moshkov, attributed to Catherine, although original is in Kabinet, bk 63/35, 20 Jan. 1723).

305. Vockerodt, *Rossiia*, 104.

306. *PSZ*, 4: no. 1999, pp. 272–3 (22 Dec. 1704). Follows no. 1887 except for a few refinements.

307. *PSZ*, 4: no. 2132, p. 363 (1706, n.d.).

308. Ibid., no. 2175, p. 397 (17 Dec. 1707). The official stamps (*kleimy*) brought in revenue.

309. Esipov, *Raskol'nich'i dela*, 2: 177.

310. *200-letie*, 9–10; LOI, f. 270, d. 72, l. 173.

311. Weber, 1: 150.

312. Esipov, *Raskol'nich'i dela*, 2: 176.

313. *PSZ*, 7: no. 4220, pp. 59–60 (10 May).

314. Ibid., no. 4245, p. 77 (14 June).

315. Ibid., no. 4256, pp. 86–7 (28 June).
316. *PSZ*, 6: no. 3944, pp. 641–2, printed on 25 Apr. See also Bychkov *Pis'ma*, 384 (12 Apr.). On the assassination attempt which allegedly prompted this decree, see Stählin, 83–4.
317. *BP*, 557; *ZA*, 149; LOI, f. 270, d. 107, l. 427 (the latter a hand-written note).
318. See *PSZ*, 6: no. 4944 (1726).
319. Semenova, *Ocherki istorii byta*, 130.
320. D. A. Korsakov, *Iz zhizni russkikh deiatelei XVIII veka* (Kazan', 1981), 114–15.
321. Wortman, *Scenarios of Power*, 107–8.
322. Ibid., 136, 293.
323. See, e.g., Helena Goscilo, 'Keeping A-Breast of the Waist-Land: Women's Fashion in Early-Nineteenth-Century Russia', in H. Goscilo and B. Holmgren, eds, *Russia. Women. Culture* (Bloomington: Indiana, 1996), 31–63.
324. See above, p. 184.
325. Pososhkov, 262–3.
326. *PSZ*, 11: nos 8301 and 8680. See also Wortman, *Scenarios of Power*, 107–8.
327. *PiB*, 2: 115.
328. Perry, *State of Russia*, 197–8.
329. Bruyn, *Travels*, 1: 46.
330. D. de Marly, *Fashion for Men. An Illustrated History* (London, 1989), 58.
331. T. T. Korshunova, *Kostium v Rossii XVIII–nachalo XX veka* (L, 1979). E. Iu. Moiseenko, 'Opis' garderoba A. D. Menshikova', in G. I. Komelova, ed., *Kul'tura i iskusstvo petrovskogo vremeni*, (L, 1977), 88–110.
332. Bruyn, *Travels*, 1: 47.
333. Ibid., 30.
334. Bassewitz, 'Zapiski', 237.
335. See above, p. 189.
336. Bergholz, 1724, p. 26.
337. Liria, 'Pis'ma', 59 (writing in 1728).
338. *Russkaia starina*, 1880, pp. 766–7.
339. Kovrigina, 'Remeslenniki', 198.
340. *Iunosti chestnoe zertsalo* (SPb., 1717; facs. edn., M, 1990). See T. A. Bykova, *Opisanie izdanii napechatannykh kirillisei* (M, 1958), 226, 237, 378, 753. G. Marker, *Publishing, Printing, and the Origins of Intellectual Life in Russia, 1700–1800* (Princeton, 1985), 30, refers to it as one of Peter's 'attempts to create modern citizens'.
341. E. A. Savel'eva, 'Biblioteka Ia. V. Briusa v sobranii BAN SSSR', in

Russkie biblioteki i ikh chitateli (L, 1983), 126; E. I. Bobrova, comp., *Biblioteka Petra I. Ukazatel'-spravochnik* (L, 1978), 63. See reference to Bruce, Gavriil Buzhinsky and Pause as author-translators.
342. Bykova earlier insisted that most of *Mirror* was written for a specifically Russian audience, on the basis of references to young men returning from abroad, but I. A. Bykova and M. M. Gurevich, eds, *Opisanie izdanii grazhdanskoi pechati. 1708-ianv. 1725 gg. Dopolnenie i prilozheniia* (L, 1972), 33, identify Erasmus. See M. Okenfuss, 'Popular Educational Tracts in Enlightenment Russia', *CASS*, 14 (1980), 309.
343. Pekarsky, *Nauka*, 2: 382.
344. *Iunosti chestnoe zertsalo*, 18–19.
345. See above, p. 193.
346. Luppov, *Kniga v Rossii v pervoi chetverti xviii v.* (L, 1973), 103, 137, 143.
347. See below, pp. 319–20.
348. *ZA*, 119. Preface to Synod book *O blazhenstvakh* (F. Prokopovich, *Khristovo o blazhenstvakh propovedi tolkovanie* (SPb., 1722)).
349. *Pervoe uchenie otrokom*: Bykova, *Opisanie*, no. 133, pp. 121, 259. Printed at the press of the Alexander Nevsky monastery. A full description with extensive quotations is given in Cracraft, *Church Reform*, 277 ff.
350. He had in mind in particular the *Orthodox Confession* of Peter Mohila, which he described elsewhere as 'completely incomprehensible' for uneducated people. See Cracraft, *Church Reform*, 277 ff., which explains why Prokopovich wished to discard Mohila's authoritative work.
351. See J. Cracraft, 'Feofan Prokopovich', in Garrard, 99.
352. Quoted in Cracraft, *Church Reform*, 281.
353. Pekarsky, *Nauka*, 2: 548–50. The English translation by J. T. Philipps, *The Russian Catechism* (London, 1723), from the German, is inaccurate in many ways.
354. *PSZ*, 7: no. 4172, p. 26 (26 Feb. 1723).
355. Iu. U. Gerasimova, 'Vospominaniia Filippo Balatri. Novyi inostrannyi

istochnik po istorii Petrovskoi Rossii (1698–1701)', *Zapiski otdela rukopisei*, 27 (1965), 164–90, *passim*.

356. Kaliazina, 117.

357. Bergholz, 1721, p. 85

358. Duc de Liria, 'Zapiski diuka Liriiskogo i Bervikskogo vo vremia prebyvaniia ego pri Imperatorskom Rossiiskom dvore', *Russkii arkhiv*, 1909, bk 1, pt 3, 399.

359. Duc de Liria, 'Pis'ma o Rossii v Ispaniia', in *Osmnadtsatyi vek*, vol. 2 (M, 1869), 176

360. *Petr Veliki, ego polkovodtsy i ministry* (M, 1848), 10.

361. Korb, 1: 196.

362. *Zapiski Ivana Ivanovicha Nepliueva (1693–1773)* (SPb., 1893), 96.

363. Weber, 1: 19.

364. Vockerodt, *Rossiia*, 105.

365. M. M. Bogoslovsky, *Byt i nravy russkogo dvorianstva v pervoi pol. XVIII v.* (SPb., 1918), 29–30.

366. On Matveev, see T. V. Il'ina and S. V. Rimskaia-Korsakova, *Andrei Matveev* (M, 1984), 111–15. The portrait is in Kaliazina, no. 109.

367. Sheremetev, *Zapiski*, 1–2.

368. Ibid., 26, 32.

369. Ibid., 40.

370. Ibid., 78–80.

371. Ibid., 48, 54, 69.

372. Ibid., 56.

373. See excellent analysis in introduction to M. Okenfuss, ed. and trans., *The Travel Diary of Peter Tolstoy* (De Kalb, Ill., 1987).

374. Luppov, *Kniga v Rossii* (1973), 275, 283.

375. V. M. Zhivov, 'Azbuchnaia reforma Petra I kak semioticheskoe preobrazovaniiea', *Uchenye zapiski Tartuskogo gos. universiteta*, 720 (1986), 55.

376. Bruyn, *Travels*, 2: 36.

377. Bruce, *Memoirs*, 103.

378. See Bassewitz, 'Zapiski', 213.

379. See decrees, *PSZ*, 6: no. 4079 (31 Aug. 1722); 7: no. 4154 (31 Jan. 1723). See ch. 43 of the 1551 *Stoglav*.

380. Weber, 1: 82.

381. A. I. Zaozersky, 'Fel'dmarshal Sheremetev i pravitel'stvennaia sreda Petrovskogo vremeni', in *RPR*, 190, 195.

382. Luppov, *Kniga v Rossii*, (1973), 158.

383. Ibid., 170. But he tries to minimize the figure by reference to books belonging to Natalia Alekseevna, which only were there 'by chance'.

384. Berkh, *Zhizneopisanie*, 87.

385. *Zapiski I . . . Nepliueva*, 21–2.

386. G. V. Esipov, 'Zhizneopisanie kniazia A. D. Menshikova', *Russkii arkhiv*, 7 (1875), 240. (They had to pay 300 roubles for the charts!)

387. *Shchukinskii sbornik*, vol. 9 (M, 1910), 152–3. This letter, sent from Voronezh on 19 Mar. was signed at the bottom by all sorts of people, including Tsarevich Alexis, Tsarevna Natalia Alekseevna, and large numbers of Naryshkins.

388. G. V. Esipov, *Tsaritsa Evdokia Feodorovna* (M, 1862), 6. On his fate, see below, p. 408.

389. *Podennye zapiski*, in S. Elagin, *Materialy dlia istorii russkogo flota* (SPb., 1866), 181–2.

390. GPB OR, f. 480, ed. kh. 2, l.1.

391. Ibid., l. 2^{r–v}.

392. Ibid., ll. 156^{r–v}.

393. *PZh*, 1704, p. 11; 1706, p. 20; 1707, p. 14.

394. *200-letie*, 113.

395. Bogoslovsky, *Byt i nravy*, 17.

396. Ibid., 19.

397. Perry, *State of Russia*, 237.

398. *Russkii arkhiv*, 3 (1865), 337–8.

399. 'Let them lie around in the national chamber of curiosities; among people they are conspicuous,' allegedly to Dr Erskine, in Nartov, 70.

400. J. Cracraft, ed., *For God and Peter the Great. The Works of Thomas Consett, 1723–1729* (Boulder, Colo., 1982), p. xiv.

401. Ibid., p. xlvii.

402. Vockerodt, *Rossiia*, 105.

403. Perry, *State of Russia*, 267.

404. Campredon, letter to Louis XV, 13 Mar. 1723 (NS), pp. 309–10.

405. H. Ragsdale, *The Russian Tragedy. The Burden of History* (New York and London, 1996), 61.

406. H. Rogger, *National Consciousness in Eighteenth-Century Russia* (Cambridge, Mass., 1960), 50.

CHAPTER 9: EDUCATION AND LEARNING

1. F. de la Neuville, *A Curious and New Account of Muscovy in the Year 1689*, ed. L. Hughes (London, 1994), 24.

2. For the debate, see G. Florovsky, 'The Problem of Old Russian Culture', *SR*, 21 (1962), 1–15.

3. J. Perry, *The State of Russia* (1716), (London, 1967), 6–7.

4. Inscription on seal of ship's carpenter with instruments, earliest dating from 1695.

5. Muller, 30, 31–2.

6. J. L. Black *Citizens for the Fatherland. Education, Educators and Pedagogical Ideals in 18th-Century Russia* (Boulder, Colo., and London, 1979), 23.

7. See M. Okenfuss, 'The Jesuit Origins of Petrine Education', in Garrard, 110.

8. A. E. Suknovalov, 'Pervaia v Rossii voenno-morskaia shkola', *IZ*, 42 (1953), 301.

9. Okenfuss, 'Jesuit Origins', 116.

10. Juel, 3: 143. Provision for students' upkeep was four copecks per day for the top classes, three for the rest.

11. Weber, 1: 128–9.

12. Quoted in M. O. Blamberg, 'The Publicists of Peter the Great' (Ph.D. thesis, Indiana University, 1974), 169.

13. See above, p. 195.

14. See G. Bissonnette, 'Peter the Great and the Church as an Educational Institution', in J. S. Curtiss, ed., *Essays in Russian and Soviet History in Honor of G. T. Robinson* (Leiden, 1963), 7–8; A. J. Rieber, 'Politics and Technology in Eighteenth-Century Russia', *Science in Context*, 8 (1995), 352.

15. P. N. Miliukov, *Gosudarstvennoe khoziaistvo Rossii v pervoi chet. XVIII st. i reforma Petra Velikogo* (SPb., 1905), 614–78. *PSZ*, no. 2389, pp. 706–7.

16. Muller, 36–7. 'Citizenship' books included Pufendorf, *De Officio hominis et civis Juxta legem naturalem libri duo* (1673), which actually appeared in part in *O dolzhnosti cheloveka i grazhdanina* (1726): Black, *Citizens*, 29.

17. Muller, 41.

18. J. Cracraft, *The Church Reform of Peter the Great* (London, 1971), 270. See *Opisanie dokumentov i del, khraniashchikhsia v arkhive sviateishego prav. Sinoda*, vol. 1 (SPb., 1868), e.g. 714–17.

19. Black, *Citizens*, 29.

20. Rieber, 'Politics', 355.

21. L. G. Beskrovny, 'Voennye shkoly v pervoi polovine XVIII v.', *IZ*, 42 (1953), 289; Suknovalov, 'Pervaia', 301–6; W. Ryan, 'Navigation and the Modernization of Russia', in *Russia in the Age of Enlightenment: Essays for Isabel de Madariaga* (London, 1990), 76–80.

22. Pososhkov, 82.

23. N. Hans, 'The Moscow School of Mathematics and Navigation (1701)', *SEER*, 29 (1951), 532–6. As Hans points out, there were many schools of this type in Britain, training teachers of mathematics as well as naval officers.

24. A. Viktorov, *Opisanie zapisnykh knig i bumag starinnykh dvortsovykh prikazov, 1613–1725* (M, 1883), 2: 467–8, 469.

25. Ibid., 471; Hans, 'Moscow School', 534.

26. Class lists for 1711–12, in M. Okenfuss, 'Russian Students in Europe in the Age of Peter the Great', in Garrard, 137.

27. Perry, *State of Russia*, 212–13. Black, *Citizens*, 24.

28. Perry, *State of Russia*, 214.

29. Ryan, 'Navigation' 75–105.

30. Ibid., 78.

31. *DPPS*, 6(i): 18 (11 Jan. 1716).

32. Pososhkov, 83. See Okenfuss, 'Russian Students', 140, that in general the old curriculum was simply transferred from Moscow, with few embellishments.

33. Hans, 'Moscow School'.

34. *PSZ*, 6, no. 3937, pp. 632–3 (5 Apr., 1722).

35. Weber, 1: 180.

36. *PSZ*, 5: no. 2937, p. 176 (1 Oct. 1715).

37. Ryan, 'Navigation', 78.

38. Ibid., 75–105.

39. *PSZ*, 5: no. 2762, p. 76 (20 Jan. 1714); no. 2778, p. 86 (28 Feb. 1714).

40. Ibid., no. 2971 (28 Dec. 1715).
41. Ibid., no. 2979 (18 Jan. 1716); *DPPS*, 6(i): 34–5. See also P. P. Pekarsky, *Nauka i literatura v. Rossii pri Petre Velikom* (SPb., 1862), 1: 122–6.
42. *PSZ*, 6: no. 3575, p. 187 (30 Apr. 1720).
43. Black, *Citizens*, 24–5.
44. *PSZ*, 6: no. 3896, p. 499 (5 Feb. 1722).
45. *ZA*, 355.
46. Article 36, in *ZA*, 501–2.
47. See C. Peterson, *Peter the Great's Administrative and Judicial Reforms* (Stockholm, 1979), 111, and above, pp. 180–5.
48. *PSZ*, 6: no. 3575, pp. 188–9 (30 Apr., 1721).
49. Ibid., no. 4021, p. 697 (31 May 1722). See also no. 3854, pp. 168–9 (19 Nov.). In fact, it proved difficult to remove sons of clergy from cipher schools, partly at least because it took time to set up episcopal schools.
50. A. Kahan, *The Plow, the Hammer and the Knout. An Economic History of Eighteenth-Century Russia* (Chicago, 1985), 152.
51. Weber, 1: 121.
52. Pososhkov, 307 on A. P. Volynsky's instructions to his steward, and 313 for his ideas on schools.
53. Ibid., 80.
54. See Ernst Glück's programme and invitation to prospective pupils: a catalogue of teachers and their specialities, in Pekarsky, *Nauka*, 1: 128–31.
55. Pososhkov, 81–2.
56. Weber, 1: 165.
57. Pekarsky, *Nauka*, 1: 134.
58. Juel, 3: 11 (17 July 1710).
59. A. Babkin, 'Pis'ma Frantsa i Petra Lefortov o "Velikom posol'stve"', *VI*, 1976, no. 4, 123 (11 Dec.).
60. F. J. Strahlenberg, *Zapiski kapitana Filippa Ioganna Stralenberga ob istorii i geografii Rossiiskoi imperii Petra Velikogo*, trans. and ed. Iu. Bespiatykh et al. (M&L, 1985), 1: 126. He adds that they were taught 'ignoble sciences' such as shipbuilding and nautical duties, which they were too ashamed to study properly. Much of his analysis derives from the opinions of disgruntled old nobles.
61. M. Okenfuss, ed., *The Travel Diary of Peter Tolstoy* (De Kalb, Ill., 1987), 6.
62. Okenfuss, 'Russian Students', 136.
63. *Zapiski Ivana Ivanovicha Nepliueva (1693–1773)* (SPb., 1893), 88–9.
64. 'Zapiski o vazhneishikh vnutrennikh proisshestviiakh i uchrezhdeniiakh v Rossii s 1707 po 1712 god', *Severnyi arkhiv*, 20/5 (1826), 27–8.
65. *DPPS*, 6(i): 37 (18 Jan. 1716). Similar in *PSZ*, 5: no. 2978, p. 189.
66. *DPPS*, 6(i): no. 313, p. 269.
67. *200-letie*, 61.
68. *DPPS*, 6(i): 129.
69. *200-letie*, 61; LOI, f. 270, d. 103, l. 85 (20 Jan. 1723).
70. See documents in GPB OR, f. 1003 (Voskresensky), no. 11, ll. 344 ff.
71. Okenfuss, 'Russian Students', 131–45. See below, p. 326.
72. Ibid., 143–4.
73. *200-letie*, 118.
74. Ibid., 58–61.
75. GPB OR, f. 1003 (Voskresensky), no. 11, ll. 256–7 (6 June).
76. *200-letie*, 113.
77. *Zapiski . . . Nepliueva*, 56–7, 73–4.
78. See A. Vucinich, *Science in Russian Culture. A History to 1860* (London, 1963), 66–72; P. P. Pekarsky, *Istoriia Imp. Akademii Nauk*, vol. 1 (SPb., 1870).
79. Pekarsky, *Istoriia*, pp. xxviii–xxix. The first concrete plans for an Academy of Sciences date from 1720, as reported by Christian Wolff in a letter of Jan. 1721.
80. Rieber, 'Politics', 351.
81. Weber, 1: 15–16. On Leibniz's views on Russia and contacts with Peter see Vucinich, 45–8. L. Richter, *Leibniz und sein Russlandbild* (Berlin, 1946).
82. LOI, f. 270, d. 106, ll. 197–207 (here, 205ᵛ). (Peter's annotated copy, dated 22 Jan. 1724): *PSZ*, 7: no. 4443, pp. 220–4 (28 Jan. 1724).
83. But see LOI, f. 270, d. 106, ll. 209–23, the same document as above, except 16,000 roubles are quoted (l. 223).
84. Stählin, no. 108, pp. 166–8.
85. See Okenfuss, 'Jesuit Origins'.
86. See, e.g., Kahan, *Plow*, 153–4.
87. Pososhkov, 80.
88. A. P. Spunde, 'Ocherk ekonomich-

eskoi istorii russkoi burzhuazii', *Nauka i zhizn'*, 1988, no. 1, 81.

89. Black, *Citizens*, 35.

90. Cracraft, *Church Reform*, 273, 275, based on Pekarsky, *Nauka*, 1: 109–21.

91. Okenfuss, 'Jesuit Origins', 122.

92. Pososhkov, 84.

93. Vucinich, *Science*, 72.

94. Prokopovich, 'Sermon on Royal Authority and Honour' (1718), in M. Raeff, ed., *Russian Intellectual History. An Anthology* (New York, 1966), 41.

95. Frontispiece to Ivan Nestouranoi [G. Rousset de Missy], *Mémoires du règne de Pierre le Grand* (Amsterdam, 1729–37); W. Ryan, 'Scientific Instruments in Russia from the Middle Ages to Peter the Great', *Annals of Science*, 48 (1991), 384; reproduction in J. Cracraft, *The Petrine Revolution in Russian Architecture* (Chicago, 1988), fig. 141.

96. Rieber, 'Politics', 342.

97. See Vucinich, *Science*, ch. 1.

98. Ryan, 'Scientific Instruments', 377–8.

99. See R. Hellie, 'Material Culture and Identity in Late Mediaeval and Early Modern Russia' (unpubl. conference paper, UCLA, 1994).

100. Vucinich, *Science*, 5.

101. Ryan, 'Scientific Instruments', 379, argues that the famous astrolabe was in fact a circumferentor, used for measuring distance.

102. See discussion in Ryan, 'Navigation', 82–3.

103. Perry, *State of Russia*, 211. The abacus remains in use in some shops and offices in Russia today.

104. *Tablitsy logarifmov i sinusov, tangensov, sekansov k naucheniiu mudroliubivykh.* (Amsterdam, 1703). See S. P. Luppov, *Kniga v Rossii v pervoi chetverti XVIII v.* (L, 1973), 92.

105. Pekarsky, *Nauka*, 1: 263 ff. See Juel's remarks, 3: 48.

106. Muller, 36.

107. D. Shaw, 'Geographical Practice and its Significance in Peter the Great's Russia', *Journal of Historical Geography*, 22 (1996), 160–76.

108. Ibid., 164.

109. See M. A. Alekseeva, *Graviura petrovskogo vremeni* (L, 1990), 97.

110. Weber, 1: 83.

111. C. Urness, 'Rybakov on the Delisle Map of 1706', in L. Hughes, ed., *New Perspectives on Muscovite History. Selected Papers from the Fourth World Congress for Soviet and East European Studies, Harrogate 1990* (London, 1993), 24–34.

112. *Zemnevodnogo kruga kratkoe opisanie* (M, 1719); *Geografiia, ili kratkoe zemnogo kruga opisanie* (SPb., 1710): Luppov, *Kniga v Rossii* (1973), 92–3; Shaw, 'Geographical Practice', 166.

113. See Kaliazina, illustrations 149 and 151.

114. *PSZ*, 3: no. 1532, p. 217 (10 Jan., 1696).

115. *ZA*, 506; *PSZ*, 6: no. 3534 (28 Feb. 1720).

116. O. G. Ageeva, 'Severnaia voina i iskusstvo graviury v Rossii petrovskogo vremeni', *Russkaia kul'tura v usloviiakh inozemnykh nashestvii i voin X–nach. XX vv*, p 2 (M, 1990), 158.

117. LOI, f. 270, d. 104, l. 7 (1 Sept. 1723); M. I. Belov, ed., *Voprosy geografii petrovskogo vremeni. Sb. statei* (L, 1975), 6.

118. Belov, ed., *Voprosy*, 20.

119. Ibid., 10–12.

120. Shaw, 'Geographical Practice', 167. Findings published as *Forschungsreise durch Siberien, 1720–1727*, 4 vols (Berlin, 1962–8) (Quellen und Studien zur Geschichte Osteuropas, vol. 8).

121. Thanks to Mark Bassin and his lecture 'Between Europe and Asia: The Geography of Russian National Identity' (SSEES, Nov. 1996). On Tatishchev's work, see Shaw, 'Geographical Practice', 167 and *Izbrannye trudy po geografii Rossii* (M, 1950).

122. M. Lakhtin, *Materialy k istorii meditsiny v Rossii* (M, 1907), 18–34.

123. M. B. Mirskii, 'Doktor Robert Erskin —pervyi rossiiskii arkhiatr', *Otechestvennaia istoriia*, 1995, no. 2, 141.

124. On his career, see ibid., 135–45.

125. See below, pp. 315–16.

126. I. N. Lebedeva, 'Leib-medik Petra I Robert Areskin i ego biblioteka', in *Russkie biblioteki i ikh chitateli* (L, 1983), 98–105.

127. See account of his funeral in Weber, 1: 246–7.

128. Juel, 3: 117.

129. *PSZ*, 6: no. 1756, pp. 10–11 (14 Feb. 1700).
130. Juel, 166–7.
131. *200-letie*, 51–2. This hospital was run by Peter's Cabinet. See LOI, f. 270, d. 100, l. 265 (6 Mar. 1722).
132. *PSZ*, 6: no. 3811, p. 412 (Aug. 1721).
133. Stählin, no. 77, pp. 124–5.
134. Kahan, *Plow*, 15.
135. *PiB*, 10: 138–9 (to B. P. Sheremetev dated 21 May 1710). See also letter to P. S. Saltykov on the plague in Kiev: 'give orders that Cherkessians with goods and other travelling people are not admitted to the towns of Smolensk province' (ibid., 211).
136. *PiB*, 10: 212 (26 June 1710).
137. Ibid., 278 (11 Aug. 1710, to A. I. Repnin).
138. Ibid., 14 (22 May 1710, to T. N. Streshnev).
139. Ibid., 173 (3 June 1710).
140. Ibid., 262.
141. Ibid., 322.
142. *PSZ*, 5: no. 3006 (Mar. 1716).
143. *PSZ*, 6: no. 3937 (5 Apr. 1722). B. Haigh, 'Design for a Medical Service: Peter the Great's Admiralty Regulations (1722)', *Medical History*, 19 (1975), 129–46.
144. *PSZ*, 6: no. 3937 (5 Apr. 1722); Haigh, 'Design', 135.
145. Ibid., 139, 141.
146. See above, p. 172 on factory hospitals.
147. O. Neverov, ' "His Majesty's Cabinet" and Peter I's Kunstkammer', in O. Impey and A. McGregor, eds, *The Origins of Museums. The Cabinet of Curiosities in 16th–17th-Century Europe* (Oxford, 1985), 54.
148. Ibid., 56.
149. Description, see Pekarsky, *Nauka*, 1: 558–61.
150. Stählin, 58. Peter rejected Iaguzhinsky's suggestion of imposing an entrance fee.
151. See letters from Peter to Siniavin from Astrakhan: LOI, f. 270, d. 101, l. 508 (22 Oct. 1722). There is a 1741 catalogue of the exhibits and many drawings and engravings: *Musei Imperialis Petropolitani*, 2 vols (1741) (in Latin), which unfortunately lacks illustrations.

152. *PSZ*, 5: no. 3159 (13 Feb.); Pekarsky, *Nauka*, 1: 54.
153. *200-letie*, 76.
154. Pekarsky, *Nauka*, 1: 57 (1725).
155. *ZA*, 108 (to the Synod).
156. LOI, f. 270, d. 106, l. 148 (19 Jan. 1724).
157. *200-letie*, 247.
158. Pekarsky, *Nauka*, 1: 56.
159. Luppov, *Kniga v Rossii* (1973), 55.
160. F. Thomson, 'The Corpus of Slavonic Translations Available in Muscovy. The cause of Old Russia's Intellectual Silence …', *California Slavic Studies*, 16 (1993), 195; Ageeva, 'Severnaia voina', 152.
161. Thomson, 'Corpus', 213.
162. See Pekarsky, *Nauka*, 2. The first titles, from the 1690s, are all religious. The major modern catalogues of Petrine publications are T. A. Bykova and M. M. Gurevich eds., *Opisanie izdanii grazhdanskoi pechati 1708–ianv. 1725 gg.* (M&L, 1955); idem, *Dopolnenie i prilozheniia* (L, 1972); idem, *Opisanie izdanii, napechatannykh kirillitsei (1689–ianvar' 1725)* (M, 1958); A. S. Zernova, *Svodnyi katalog russkoi knigi kirillovskoi pechati XVIII veka* (M, 1968). See remarks on problems and omissions in G. Marker, *Publishing, Printing, and the Origins of Intellectual Life in Russia, 1700–1800* (Princeton, 1985), 241–2.
163. S. P. Luppov, *Kniga v Rossii XVII veka* (L, 1970), 29.
164. N. A. Kopanev, *Frantsuzskaia kniga i russkaia kul'tura v seredine XVIII v.* (L, 1988), 11.
165. Pekarsky, *Nauka*, 2: 14–15.
166. *PSZ*, 4: no. 1751, pp. 6–8. (Charter (*zhalovannaia gramota*) to Tessing).
167. Pekarsky, *Nauka*, 2: 523–6; Grebeniuk, 43–7.
168. Viktorov, *Opisanie*, 2: 468.
169. Luppov, *Kniga v Rossii* (1973), 58.
170. Ibid.
171. See *PSZ*, 4: no. 1839, pp. 159–60; no. 1856, p. 168 (1701). See below pp. 338–9. Marker, *Publishing*, 22.
172. See listings in Bykova and Gurevich, eds, *Opisanie izdanii, napechatannykh kirillitsei*. See also Bissonnette, 'Peter the Great', 5–10.

173. *PSZ*, 4: no. 1921, p. 201 (16 Dec. 1702). Republished in *Vedomosti vremeni Petra Velikogo*, vol. 1 (M, 1903) and vol. 2 (M, 1906).

174. A. I. Toshchev, 'Petrovskie "Vedomosti" kak tip izdaniia', *XVIII vek*, 16 (1989), pp. 184–99.

175. Marker, *Publishing*, 27–8. Comparative figures for English newspapers were about 44,000 sales per *week* (1704), whereas for 1708 *Vedomosti* figures—14 issues per year and an average print run of 407—indicate only about 250 of each print run sold (ibid., 29).

176. *DPPS*, 6(i): no. 388, pp. 326–7. The first print run was 1,200 copies.

177. A. G. Shitsgal, ed., *Grazhdanskii shrift pervoi chetverti XVIII veka: 1708–1725* (M, 1981), 18. V. M. Zhivov, 'Azbuchnaia reforma Petra I kak semioticheskoe preobrazovanie', *Uchenye zapiski Tartuskogo gos. universiteta*, 720 (1986), 55–66.

178. Shitsgal, ed., *Grazhdanskii shrift*, plate vi.

179. *PiB*, 10: 27, 476–7.

180. Zhivov, 'Azbuchnaia reforma', 56, 60–1, suggests that Peter's original intention may have been to publish everything in the new script.

181. Marker, *Publishing*, 21–2.

182. *Polnoe sobranie postanovlenii i rasporiazhenii po vedomstvu pravoslavnogo ispovedeniia Rossiiskoi imperii*, 1: 34; Luppov, *Kniga v Rossii* (1973), 69. See also *PSZ*, 6: no. 3741, p. 358, which refers only to the Moscow and St Petersburg presses, and also to schools. The Navigation school press was exempted from Church control. Cracraft, *Church Reform*, 301–2, does not make clear whether both religious and secular works were censored.

183. See Synod order on translation of books from Latin and Greek on the deeds of Julius Caesar into the 'Slavonic dialect': LOI, f. 270, d. 104, l. 413 (4 Dec. 1723).

184. See *PSZ*, 6: no. 3765, p. 373 (1721), on unauthorized works sold in Moscow.

185. Luppov, *Kniga v Rossii* (1973), 62.

186. Ibid., 65–6.

187. Black, *Citizens*, 26.

188. Luppov, *Kniga v Rossii* (1973), 62, but only two actual books.

189. Cracraft, *Church Reform*, 286.

190. Luppov, *Kniga v Rossii* (1973), 102–4. Other figures include Gizel's *Sinopsis* (1714, 1718): 300 copies; Pufendorf (1718): 600; Buchner, *Uchenie i praktika artillerii* (1711): 240.

191. Figures taken from Marker, *Publishing*, 30–1.

192. Luppov, *Kniga v Rossii* (1973), 98.

193. Ibid., 132–3.

194. Ibid., 132–3, 135–9, 143–4. Marker, *Publishing*, 36–8 has amended tables.

195. Marker, *Publishing*, 35.

196. See above, p. 289.

197. Marker, *Publishing*, 34.

198. Luppov, *Kniga v Rossii* (1973), 73, 75.

199. Ibid., 77.

200. Marker, *Publishing*, 41–3.

201. F. Saltykov, 'Iz"iavlenniia pribytochnye gosudarstvu', in N. Pavlov-Sil'vansky, ed., *Proekty reform v zapiskakh sovremennikov Petra Velikogo* (SPb., 1897), 15–16.

202. E. Shmurlo, *Petr Velikii v otsenke sovremennikov i potomstva* (SPb., 1912), 10. E. P. Pod"iapol'skaia, 'Ob istorii i nauchnom znachenii izdanii "Pis'ma i bumagi imperatora Petra Velikogo"', in *Arkheograficheskii ezhegodnik za 1972* (M, 1974), 56.

203. The first thirteen files of RGADA, f. 9, otd. I, op. 2, ch. 1, contain drafts of the History.

204. Weber, 1: 222. This version was later printed under the heading 'Zhurnal gos. Petra I s 1695 po 1710 god' in Tumansky.

205. Published by M. M. Shcherbatov as *Istoriia imperatora Petra Velikogo ot rozhdeniia ego do Poltavskoi batalii* (SPb., 1773).

206. *ZA*, 113.

207. LOI, f. 270, d. 107, l. 325 (2 Oct. 1724).

208. *Rassuzhdenie o prichinakh Shvedskoi voiny*. See P. Shafirov, *A Discourse Concerning the Just Causes of the War between Sweden and Russia: 1700–1721*,

introduced by W. E. Butler (Dobbs Ferry, NY, 1973).

209. *Kniga Marsova ili Voinskikh del ot voisk tsarskogo velichestva rossiiskikh vo vziatii preslavnykh fortifikatsiei i na raznykh mestakh khrabrykh batalii uchinennykh nad voiski ego Korolevskogo velichestva sveiskogo. S pervogo S-Peterburgskogo 1713 goda izdaniia vtorym tisneniem napechatannaia v S-Peterburge 1766.*

210. Pod"iapol'skaia, 'Ob istorii', 56–70.

211. See D. Serov, *Stepennaia kniga redaktsii Ivan Iur'eva (1716–1718 gg.)* dissertation abstract (L, 1991).

212. *Iadro rossiiskoi istorii.* See Vucinich, *Science,* 63–4.

213. Pekarsky, *Nauka,* 1: 317.

214. *ZA,* 86–7, (order of 16 Oct. 1720); Stählin, 88. See also *PSZ,* 6: no. 3908, pp. 511–12 (16 Feb. 1722), on the copying by the Synod of *kurioznye knigi* from monasteries.

215. A. B. Kamensky, *Arkhivnoe delo v Rossii XVIII veka: Istoriko-kul'turnyi aspekt* (M, 1991), 44–5.

216. See Kopanev, *Frantsuzskaia kniga,* 18, n. 38: 'Peter ordered the translation and printing of many remarkable books and did not regard it as beneath him to translate some of them for himself.'

217. See L. A. J. Hughes, 'Russia's First Architectural Books: A Chapter in Peter the Great's Cultural Revolution', in C. Cooke, ed., *Russian Avant-Garde Art and Architecture* (London, 1983), 4–13.

218. *ZA,* 139 (23 Jan. 1724).

219. *PSZ,* 7: no. 4438, p. 217.

220. *ZA,* 35.

221. Luppov, *Kniga v Rossii* (1973), 101.

222. Stählin, no. 94, pp. 145–6.

223. *DPPS,* 6(i): no. 388, p. 327 (6 July 1716).

224. See Luppov, *Kniga v Rossii* (1973), 319–58; Lebedeva, 'Leib-medik', 98–105.

225. Weber, 1: 185.

226. Vucinich, *Science,* 58.

227. *Catalogi duo codicum manuscriptorum graecorum, qui in bibliotheca Synodali moscovensi asservantur ...* (M, 1723), by Afanasy Skaida, head of Greek

school. Luppov, *Kniga v Rossii* (1973), 298–9; *Opisanie dokumentov,* 1: no. 752.

228. Luppov, *Kniga v Rossii* (1973), 204–23, fails to review the religious books, dubbing them 'malointeresny' (p. 222). See I. de Madariaga, 'Portrait of an Eighteenth-Century Russian Statesman: Prince Dmitry Mikhaylovich Golitsyn', *SEER,* 62 (1984), 36–60.

229. Luppov, *Kniga v Rossii* (1973) 223–6. See also Neuville, *Curious and New Account,* 227–9, 236–8.

230. Luppov, *Kniga v Rossii* (1973), 247–64. It is odd that he omits Prokopovich from this chapter.

231. P. V. Verkhovskoy, *Uchrezhdenie Dukhovnoi Kollegii i Dukhovnyi reglament,* vol. 2 (Rostov/Don, 1916), pt 5, pp. 9–71. Luppov does not include this information.

232. Luppov, *Kniga v Rossii* (1973), 175–6. E. I. Bobrova, comp., *Biblioteka Petra I. Ukazatel'-spravochnik,* (L, 1978). Luppov estimated 1,600 volumes, but Bobrova thinks as many as 2,000. Listed in the mini-catalogue are 1,663 titles.

233. W. E. Brown, *A History of Eighteenth-Century Russian Literature* (Ann Arbor, 1980), foreword.

234. Marker, *Publishing.* This includes a collection of fables, *Zrelishche zhitiia chelovecheskago, razlichykh zhivotnikh pritcham* (1712).

235. K. V. Sivkov, 'Petr-pisatel', in *Tri veka,* vol. 3 (M, 1917), 56.

236. *Biblioteka Petra I.* See above, p. 190, on Tsarevna Natalia's library.

237. L. Lewitter, 'Peter the Great and the Modern World', in P. Dukes, ed., *Russia and Europe* (London, 1991), 104.

238. Brown, *History,* 21.

239. Texts in G. Moiseeva, comp., *Russkie povesti pervoi treti XVIII veka* (M&L, 1965), 191–210, 211–94.

240. See, e.g., M. Burgess in R. Auty and D. Obolensky, eds, *An Introduction to Russian Language and Literature,* (Cambridge, 1977), 111–12.

241. See A. Hippisley, *The Poetic Style of Simeon Polotsky* (Birmingham, n.d.), and *Vertograd mnogocvetnyj,* ed. A.

Hippisley and L. I. Sazonova (Cologne, 1996), vol. 1 of the first publication of this work.

242. F. Prokopovich, *Sochineniia*, ed. I. P. Eremin (M&L, 1961), 209–14.

243. See Luppov, *Kniga v Rossii* (1970).

244. *Biblioteka Petra I*, 63–4.

245. Marker, *Publishing*, 19.

246. Ibid., 24.

247. See N. A. Smirnov, *Zapadnoe vlianie na russkii iazyk v petrovskuiu epokhu* (SPb., 1910).

248. [I. Kopievsky], *Mémoires pour l'histoire des sciences et des beaux arts*, Sept. 1711, p. 1657; (Paris), quoted in N. A. Kopanev, 'Petr I – perevodchik', *XVIII vek.*, 16 (1989), 182.

249. *PSZ*, 6: no. 3485, pp. 86–7.

250. See Ryan, 'Navigation', 90–5.

251. *PSZ*, 6: no. 4010, p. 683 (11 May 1722).

252. See Peterson, *Peter*, 189, 412–13.

253. Lakhtin, *Materialy*, 34.

254. *PSZ*, 6: no. 4047, p. 733 (9 June 1722).

255. See A. Gerschenkron, 'Russian Mercantilism', in *Europe in the Russian Mirror* (Cambridge, 1970), 81. *Bankir* ('who gives money for bills of exchange'), and *ekonomiia*, appear in the Chief Magistracy Act: *PSZ*, 6: no. 3708, p. 295 and clause 12 (16 Jan. 1721); *ekonom* (in the sense of 'good steward'), in *PSZ*, 7: no. 4345, pp. 150–1 (5 Nov. 1723).

256. *PSZ*, 6: no. 3534, p. 160.

257. M. M. Bogoslovsky, *Byt i nravy russkogo dvorianstva v pervoi pol. XVIII v.* (Spb., 1918), 21.

258. From the French *ouvrage, proclamer, considération, opiner, pouvoir, domestique*. The fact that such words did not enter the language is indicated by explanatory notes in the modern Russian edition: see Kurakin.

259. H. Rogger, *National Consciousness in Eighteenth-Century Russia* (Cambridge, Mass., 1960), 51.

260. A. I. Zaozersky, 'Fel'dmarshal Sheremetev i pravitel'stvennaia sreda Petrovskogo vremeni', in *RPR*, 176.

261. V. S. Bobylev, *Vneshniaia politika Rossii epokhi Petra I* (M, 1990), 83. The author provides the translation *uspekh* for modern readers.

262. LOI, f. 270, d. 101, l. 415.

263. *ZA*, 81.

264. LOI, f. 270, d. 97, l. 317^{r–v} (22 Mar. 1721). A whole series of letters survives on a similar theme: e.g., to Menshikov on same date, all about the weather, l. 318. See also hand-written journal entries for 28 Mar.–14 May, ll. 329–40.

265. Bogoslovsky, *Byt i nravy*, 20.

266. Neuville, *Curious and New Account*, 24.

267. Luppov, *Kniga v Rossii* (1973), 275.

268. Belov, ed., *Voprosy*, 36.

269. Quoted in Vucinich, *Science*, 62.

270. Ibid., 66: 1717 dedication to the doctoral dissertation of Arnold van der Hulst.

271. Kaliazina, illustration 149: *Novyi sposob arifmetiki feoriki ili zritel'naia*.

272. A. V. Chernysheva, 'K voprosu o sushchestvovanii "uchenoi druzhiny"', *Vestnik Moskovskovo universiteta. Seriia 7. Filosofiia*, 1989, no. 6, 40–3.

273. Vucinich, *Science*, 57.

274. See A. Portnov, 'Byl li Lomonosov vnebrachnym synom Petra I?', *Trud*, no. 65 (13 Apr. 1995), 6.

CHAPTER 10: RELIGION

1. Peter to the Synod, 19 Apr. 1724, on the production of a short manual (*kratkoe pouchenie*) to explain the main points of religion: *ZA*, 144.

2. See Muller, pp. xi, xvii.

3. Of these, 9,084 belonged to the patriarch. The next biggest individual ecclesiastical serf owner was the metropolitan of Rostov, with 4,376. The 395 monasteries listed owned 116,137 households altogether, although there were huge variations, from the Trinity–St Sergius monastery with 20,131 households to several small monasteries in the provinces with only two or three each. Sixty-nine monasteries owned fewer than nine, while in and around Moscow the Kremlin Miracles, Novospassky, Novodevichy, Resurrection at Istra and St Sabbas at Zvenigorod all owned more than 2,000. The 200 churches and

cathedrals listed owned only 3,475 between them. (The average parish priest was not a serf owner.) The richest were, predictably, the Kremlin cathedrals. See I. A. Bulygin, *Monastyrskie krest'iane Rossii v pervoi chet. XVIII v.* (M, 1977), 43–52; A. I. Kommissarenko, 'Russkii absoliutizm i dukhovenstvo v usloviiakh podgotovki i provedeniia sekuliarizatsionnoi reformy XVIII v.', in *Pravoslavnaia tserkov' v istorii Rossii* (M, 1991), 121.

4. J. Cracraft, *The Church Reform of Peter the Great* (London, 1971), 219. The secular clergy included ordained priests (archpriests, priests, and deacons) and non-ordained (sacristans). See G. L. Freeze, *The Russian Levites: Parish Clergy in the Eighteenth Century* (Cambridge, Mass., 1977), 3–4.

5. To Archimandrite Joseph of the Nativity monastery in Vladimir, for *starosty popovskie* and *blagochinnye smotriteli*: *PSZ*, 3, no. 1612, pp. 413–25 (26 Dec. 1697).

6. Testament of Patriarch Joachim, 17 Mar. 1690, in G. Vernadsky, *A Source Book for Russian History*, vol. 2 (New Haven, 1972), 361–3.

7. G. V. Esipov, *Raskol'nich'i dela XVIII stoletiia*, (SPb., 1861), 2: appendix, 72, 78, 82. Patriarch Adrian's tracts, one on shaving, the other a 24-point list of advice to priests and monks, are undated. See above, p. 250.

8. Ibid., 77.

9. Cracraft, *Church Reform*, 306.

10. See remarks to Alexis in 1715, speech at the Poltava celebration in October 1721, and tract on monks and monasteries. On the latter, see below.

11. Nartov, 16–17.

12. Ibid., 154.

13. Grund, 52–3.

14. Gordon was barred from a banquet by Patriarch Joachim, who protested against the presence of foreigners.

15. *PSZ*, 3: no. 1613, p. 425 Bulygin, *Monastyrskie*, 67.

16. See above, p. 81.

17. Bulygin, *Monastyrskie*, 65–6. See *PSZ*, 3: no. 1721, p. 672 (1699, to the Pesnoshsky monastery in Dmitriev district, telling the monks 'to be content with the peasants which are attached to that monastery').

18. Bulygin, *Monastyrskie*, 65.

19. See J. Martin, *Medieval Russia 980–1584* (Cambridge, 1995), 362.

20. Korb, 2: 162–3.

21. See *The Journal of the Life of Thomas Story* (London, 1747), 123–4; R. C. Scott, *Quakers in Russia* (London, 1964); S. M. Janney, *The Life of William Penn* (Philadelphia, 1852).

22. See Cracraft's reconstruction of the subject-matter: *Church Reform*, 28–37.

23. *Curieuse Nachricht von der itzigen Religion Ihro Käyserlichen Majestät in Russland Petri Alexiewiz* (1725), in P. V. Verkhovskoy, *Uchrezhdenie Dukhovnoi Kollegii i Dukhovnyi reglament*, vol. 1 (Rostov/Don, 1916), p. ix.

24. Dispatch by Henri La Vie, 8 Dec. (NS), *SIRIO*, 40: 66–7.

25. See account in Cracraft, *Church Reform*, 37–49.

26. Weber, 1: 282.

27. See Cracraft, *Church Reform*, 113 ff. for the sequence of events.

28. Stählin, no. 88, pp. 136–7.

29. Bulygin, *Monastyrskie*, 70. On Kurbatov, see below, p. 380.

30. Ibid., 75. See *PSZ*, 4: no. 1829, p. 133 (24 Jan. 1701) and no. 1834, pp. 139–40 (24 Jan. 1701).

31. *PSZ*, 4: no. 1886, pp. 181–2 (30 Dec. 1701).

32. Weber, 1: 66.

33. Bulygin, *Monastyrskie*, 78–9; Komissarenko, 'Russkii', 121.

34. See Freeze, *Russian Levites*, 27–8; *PSZ*, 4: nos 2011, 2130, 2263.

35. Freeze, *Russian Levites*, 28.

36. See *PSZ*, 4: no. 1839, pp. 159–60 (11 Mar. 1701); no. 1856, p. 168. The ban on keeping paper and ink in cells was repeated in the supplement to the Ecclesiastical Regulation and in a separate edict of 19 Jan. 1723. They were to be issued only to those who needed them 'for the common spiritual good': *PSZ*, 7: no. 4146, p. 16.

37. See *PSZ*, 6: no. 3659, p. 248 (16 Oct.): 'Monastery estates which were taken from monasteries and placed under

the administration of the Monastery department ... to be restored to those monasteries and be administered by the archimandrites and abbots as previously.' See also Bulygin, *Monastyrskie*, 132. In 1721 a new Monastery department was established as an adjunct to the Synod.

38. On various problems of church administration, quoted in Verkhovskoy, *Uchrezhdenie*, 155.

39. *ZA*, 81, 83 (pt I: 'What is the spiritual college') and ordinances (pts II and III on business and duties of officials) of the new structure.

40. Texts in *PSZ*, 6: no. 3718, pp. 314–46; LOI, f. 270, d. 97, l. 111 (25 Jan. 1721). English translation, Muller.

41. *PSZ*, 6: no. 3734, pp. 355–6 (14 Feb. 1721). The name change took a few days to register. See decrees of 16 Feb. (nos 3741 and 3742), which refer to the *dukhovnaia kollegiia*.

42. S. G. Runkevich, *Uchrezhdenie i pervonachalnoe ustroistvo sviateishago pravitel'stvuiushchego sinoda (1721–1725 gg.)* (SPb., 1900), 165–7.

43. *PSZ*, 6: no. 3718, pp. 314–46; LOI, f. 270, d. 97, l. 111 (25 Jan. 1721). The secular official was not in fact appointed. Iavorsky had a chequered career. In 1710 he apparently abandoned church business and left Moscow for Riazan' (because of bad relations with Musin-Pushkin, head of the Monastery *prikaz*). But Peter recalled him, in quite pleading terms. 'I want to see you and discuss in person everything which happened in our absence' (*PiB*, 11: 46 (28 Jan. 1711)). He returned to administer oaths to the new Senate (*PiB*, 11: 364). He made little impact in his new post, dying in Nov. 1722.

44. *ZA*, 109 (11 May 1722, to the Senate).

45. LOI, f. 270, d. 101, ll. 204–7 (6 June 1722).

46. See Cracraft, *Church Reform*, 193–4. Instructions (undated) in *PSZ*, 6: no. 3870, pp. 467–76. The arch-inquisitor, Hieromonk Pafnuty of the Danilov monastery, was based in Moscow.

47. Freeze, *Russian Levites*, 52.

48. Bulygin, *Monastyrskie*, 131.

49. Muller, 3–4, 9.

50. See discussion in V. M. Zhivov and B. A. Uspensky, 'Tsar' i Bog: Semioticheskie aspekty sakralizatsii monarkha v Rossii', in Uspensky, ed. *Iazyky kul'tury i problemy perevodimosti* (M, 1987), 96–7, an idea passed down, among others, by Karamzin.

51. Grund, 50.

52. 13 June (NS), *SIRIO*, 49: 348 ('marquer ... en sa personne la fonction de patriarche').

53. *Polnoe sobranie postanovlenii i rasporiazhenii po vedomstvu pravoslavnogo ispovedaniia*, vol. 2 (SPb., 1869), no. 348, p. 17; *Opisanie koronatsii*, 42. See R. Wortman, *Scenarios of Power, Myth and Ceremony in Russian Monarchy*, vol. 1 (Princeton, 1995), 73.

54. Nikon, quoted in Vernadsky, *Source Book*, 1: 256.

55. LOI, f. 270, d. 106, l. 409.

56. *PSZ*, 6: no. 3734, pp. 355–6.

57. Cracraft, *Church Reform*, 232. Other examples include episcopal transfers.

58. LOI, f. 270, d. 103, ll. 45–7 (16 Jan. 1723); d. 104, l. 123 (19 Oct. 1723).

59. Ibid., d. 103, l. 201 (14 Feb. 1723); *ZA*, 125.

60. LOI, f. 270, d. 104, l. 28 (Sept. 1723).

61. V. M. Zhivov, 'Kul'turnye reformy v sisteme preobrazovaniia Petra I', in *Iz istorii russkoi kul'tury. Tom III (XVII–nachalo XVIII veka)* (M, 1996), 10.

62. LOI, f. 270, d. 105, ll. 38–9 (30 July 1723, letter to Natalia Zimkova in the Fedorovsky convent).

63. Ibid., d. 104, l. 492^v (24 Dec. 1723).

64. *PSZ*, 6: no. 3771, p. 377 (17 Apr. 1721).

65. Runkevich, *Uchrezhdenie*, 219 (salary list published 18 Jan. 1721: *PSZ*, 6: no. 3712, p. 312).

66. LOI, f. 270, d. 104, l. 487 (21 Dec. 1723); d. 107, ll. 98$^{r–v}$ (24 May 1724); *PSZ*, 7: no. 4152, p. 18. The latter signed by Feofan, Feofilakt, Gavriil, Feodosy, Feofil, Ierofei, Peter, Raphael. Peter's resolution on the restoration of wages: l. 133 (1 June).

67. LOI, f. 270, d. 106, l. 247 (1 Feb. 1724).

68. *ZA*, 110–11.

69. Nartov, 57–8.

70. See *PSZ*, 6: no. 3962, pp. 649–50; Cracraft, *Church Reform*, 259–60.
71. LOI, f. 270, d. 100, l. 297; *ZA*, 121.
72. Muller, supplement, 72–9; *PSZ*, 7: no. 4456, p. 249 (5 Feb. 1724).
73. LOI, f. 270, d. 101, ll. 158–60 (30 May 1722).
74. Ibid., d. 106, l. 532 (27 Mar. 1724).
75. *ZA*, 137–8.
76. Published as 'O zvanii monashestvom', *PSZ*, 7: no. 4450, pp. 226–33; *ZA*, 142; Komissarenko, 'Russkii absoliutizm', 126–7. See P. V. Verkhovskoy's arguments for regarding this document as 'an example of Peter's literary work', almost all his own: *Uchrezhdenie*, 2: 128–30. In fact, it elaborates the section on monks and nuns in the supplement to the Ecclesiastical Regulation. See Muller, 72–84.
77. Komissarenko, 'Russkii absoliutizm', 127.
78. Figures in Cracraft, *Church Reform*, 252, from 25,207 to 14,282.
79. Stählin, 44.
80. J. Perry, *The State of Russia* (1716), (London, 1967), 209, 220–1.
81. Freeze, *Russian Levites*, 82.
82. *PSZ*, 4: no. 2186, p. 401 (1708).
83. Muller, 20–1.
84. LOI, f. 270, d. 101, l. 141 (30 May 1722).
85. Weber, 1: 280. See also remarks by Grund (51) about the lack of sermons or any interpretation by parish priests, who at most might read out a sermon by John Chrysostom, but not their own.
86. See, e.g., anecdotes in Stählin, no. 80, pp. 126–7.
87. Muller, 43.
88. Weber, 1: 324.
89. Muller, 16–17. The three booklets specifically recommended in the regulation were not produced.
90. On the political dimensions of the primer, see above, p. 290.
91. *ZA*, 122; *PSZ*, 7: no. 4143, p. 9 (16 Jan. 1723).
92. LOI, f. 270, d. 104, l. 78 (18 Sept. 1723); *ZA*, 127; Cracraft, *Church Reform*, 288.
93. Stählin, no. 100, pp. 154–5. See letter to Synod of 3 Feb. 1724, on the

printing of the 'newly corrected Bible': *ZA*, 142–3.
94. See, e.g., a note about devising a short catechism (*malen'kii regul*) for reading out to peasants in church: *ZA*, 67.
95. *PSZ*, 6: no. 3834 (10 Oct. 1721).
96. Ibid., no. 3515; *ZA*, 80 (10 Feb. 1720).
97. May 1721: Freeze, *Russian Levites*, 30.
98. Muller, 71; *PSZ*, 7: no. 4480, pp. 266–7 (20 Feb. 1724).
99. *PSZ*, 5: no. 3169 (17 Feb. 1719). Priests were fined for failing to declare dissidents.
100. Muller, 60–1.
101. *PSZ*, 7: no. 4012, pp. 685–9 (17 May 1722). Quoted in J. Cracraft, 'Opposition to Peter the Great', in *Imperial Russia 1700–1917. State. Society. Opposition. Essays in Honor of Marc Raeff* (De Kalb, Ill., 1988), 26–8. On Talitsky, see below, pp. 451–2. On the publishing history of the supplement, see Cracraft, *Church Reform*, 233 ff. The supplement was written by Prokopovich in 1720, but not included in the original version of the regulation. It was subsequently much amended by Peter, issued as an edict (17 May 1722), published in its final form in June 1722, and issued with the second edition of the regulation.
102. Issued before the supplement in Feb. 1722: *PSZ*, 7: no. 3911, pp. 512–13.
103. See, e.g., clause 1 of the *Ulozhenie* of 1649.
104. *PSZ*, 5: no. 3294, p. 626 (Jan. 1719).
105. Stählin, no. 81, pp. 127–8.
106. *PSZ*, 7: no. 4277, p. 96 (29 July 1723).
107. Muller, 69.
108. Quoted in Cracraft, *Church Reform*, 247; *PSZ*, 6: no. 3991 (30 Apr. 1722); no. 4035 (12 June 1722).
109. *PSZ*, 5: no. 3171 (19 Feb. 1718); Freeze, *Russian Levites*, 111; Muller, 50.
110. Freeze, *Russian Levites*, 28.
111. Most of this information, except where specifically footnoted, comes from Cracraft, *Church Reform*, 165–73.
112. Runkevich, *Uchrezhdenie*, 200.
113. Cracraft, *Church Reform*, 174.
114. Komissarenko, 'Russkii absoliutizm', 123.
115. J. Cracraft 'Did Feofan Prokopovich

Really Write *Pravda Voli Monarshei?*', *SR*, 40 (1981), 178–9.

116. Bergholz, 1724, p. 80. See above, p. 325.

117. Muller, 22–3, 27.

118. M. M. Bogoslovsky, *Byt i nravy russkogo dvorianstva v pervoi pol. XVIII v.* (Spb., 1918), 26–7.

119. O. G. Ageeva, 'Kul'tovye pamiatniki Moskvy i Peterburga Petrovskogo vremeni', in *Problemy russkoi khudozhestvennoi kul'tury XVIII veka. Tesizy dokladov* (M, 1991), 21–3.

120. See above, p. 214.

121. See D. Serov, *Stepennaia kniga redaktsii Ivana Iur'eva (1716–1718 gg.)*, dissertation abstract (L, 1991), 15–16.

122. *ZA*, 68 (1718).

123. *Voennye ustavy Petra Velikogo* (M, 1946), 66–79.

124. *MIGO*, 1(ii): 75–82 (9 May 1714).

125. *PSZ* no. 3485, pp. 42–4 (on priests), pp. 49–50 (on good behaviour on board ship).

126. Ibid., no. 3759, pp. 370–1 (15 Mar. 1721).

127. See, e.g., General Regulation, ch. 1 (ibid., no. 3534, p. 141); instruction to judges in provincial courts (M. Bogoslovsky, *Oblastnaia reforma Petra Velikogo. Provintsiia 1719–27* (M, 1902), 5).

128. Juel, 3: 125–8.

129. *Sbornik*, 2: 94–6 (Dec. 1721).

130. *SIRIO*, 40: 66–7. For a discussion of this aspect of Church reform, see Cracraft, *Church Reform*, 290–4.

131. Juel, 116.

132. Stählin, 68–70. There is a similar story about a weeping icon in Poland: ibid, 85–6.

133. LOI, f. 270, d. 103, l. 1 (1 Jan. 1723); *ZA*, 121.

134. *PSZ*, 6: no. 4012 (17 May 1722); Muller, 14–15, 29.

135. *PSZ*, 6: no. 3963, pp. 650–2 (12 Apr. 1722).

136. See decree in ibid., no. 4053, pp. 742–6. (16 June 1722).

137. Weber, 1: 238.

138. C. Whitworth, *An Account of Russia as it was in the Year 1710* (M&L, 1988), 43. See *PSZ*, 5: nos. 3020, 3178, on dispensations.

139. *SIRIO*, 15: 204–5 (20 Mar. 1722 (NS)).

140. *PiB*, 1: 194 (10 Sept. 1697, letter to Patriarch Adrian).

141. *PSZ*, 6: no. 4029, p. 718 (6 June 1722).

142. *Sbornik*, 2: 91 (29 Mar. 1721).

143. Quoted in O. Subtelny, 'Mazepa, Peter I, and the Question of Treason', *Harvard Ukrainian Studies*, 2 (1978), 174.

144. Letter quoted in B. Sumner, *Peter the Great and the Ottoman Empire* (Oxford, 1949), 34.

145. *PiB*, 13(i): 98 (28 Feb. 1713).

146. See arguments in Sumner, *Ottoman Empire*, 27–8.

147. *PiB*, 2: 30–4 (12 Apr. 1702).

148. See above, pp. 47–8.

149. See Sumner, *Ottoman Empire*, 47–8.

150. Ibid., 65. A later Russian ambassador referred to the Greeks as 'without faith or law or honour, serving only their own interests, our enemies, worse than the Turks themselves'.

151. See *PiB*, 9: no. 3249, pp. 223–5.

152. Letter of 18 Mar. 1691, quoted in Soloviev, 116–19.

153. Sumner, *Ottoman Empire*, 30–1.

154. Extracts from pilgrim accounts, ibid., 28.

155. J. Cracraft, ed., *For God and Peter the Great. The Works of Thomas Consett, 1723–1729.* (Boulder, Colo., 1982), p. xvii.

156. Verkhovskoy, *Uchrezhdenie*, 2: 152–7. *PSZ*, 7: no. 4310, pp. 119–20, (23 Sept. 1723): the patriarchs of Antioch and Constantinople bless the Synod. See Cracraft, *Church Reform*, 224–5.

157. See *PSZ*, 6: no. 3882, p. 483 (18 Jan. 1722).

158. Weber, 1: 173. See Peter's order to the clergy, Mar. 1717: ibid., 174–6.

159. *PSZ*, 7: 4492, p. 278 (19 Apr. 1724).

160. *PiB*, 1: no. 394, pp. 472–3.

161. *PSZ*, 5: no. 2863. See also *PSZ*, 4: no. 1800 (June 1700).

162. Cracraft, *Church Reform*, 69.

163. LOI, f. 270, d. 101, l. 533 (2 Nov. 1722, to the metropolitan of Kazan').

164. See E. Widmer, *The Russian Ecclesiastical Mission in Peking during the Eighteenth Century* (Cambridge, Mass., 1976).

165. See documents in LOI, f. 270, d. 104 (1723).

166. *PSZ*, 4: no. 1910, pp. 192–5. It is hard to agree with R. O. Crummey that this decree was intended or regarded as a proclamation of 'general religious toleration': *The Old Believers and the World of Antichrist. The Vyg Community and the Russian State 1694–1855* (Madison, 1970), 62–3.

167. See Peterson, *Peter*, 136–7.

168. Not all dissidents were Old Believers or followed the teachings of the leaders. See the new interpretation in C. Potter, 'The Russian Church and the Politics of Reform in the Second Half of the Sevententh Century' (Ph.D. thesis, Yale, 1993). On opposition, see below, pp. 453–6.

169. Cracraft, *Church Reform*, 298–9. The estimate is in M. Cherniavsky, 'The Old Believers and the New Religion', *SR*, 25 (1966), 4.

170. *Akty, sobrannye . . . Arkheograficheskoiu ekspeditsieiu*, vol. 4 (SPb., 1836), no. 284, p. 419; see Verkhovskoy, *Uchrezhdenie*, 2: 114–23.

171. *PSZ*, 5: no. 2991. Repeated 17 Feb. 1718: no. 3169. In May 1724 proceeds from Old Believer fines were allocated to the building of monasteries and teaching orphans. Repeated 4 June 1724: *PSZ*, 7: no. 4526, p. 300 (also mentions a ban on holding office or serving as a witness in court). Also 25 Sept. 1724, which imposed tax upon women, too, at half the male rate: ibid., no. 4575, pp. 351–2. The double tax on Old Believers was abolished by Catherine II in 1782. See *PSZ*, 21: nos 15,473 and 15,581, pp. 634 and 745.

172. *PSZ*, 5: no. 3183, p. 155.

173. Muller, 48–50.

174. *PSZ*, 6: no. 3944, pp. 641–2 (6 Apr. 1722); 7: no. 4596, p. 368 (Nov. 1724). See above, pp. 281–2. Also Crummey, *Old Believers*, 81–2.

175. Crummey, *Old Believers*, 82.

176. See, e.g., Metropolitan Dmitry of Rostov's book on the topic of shaving (*Rassuzhdenie o obraze bozii i podobii v chelovetse*), which was aimed not at convinced Old Believers, who were actually forbidden to shave (the point being to identify them clearly by their beards and old-style clothes), but at any who might be tempted to join them.

177. See admonition of the Synod, Jan. 1722: *PSZ*, 6: no. 3891, pp. 493–4 (*po babym basniam*).

178. See Crummey, *Old Believers*, 84–5.

179. *PSZ*, 6: no. 3925, pp. 518–20 (3 Apr. 1722). The response, predictably, was negative. A Senate statement in 1725 mentions that no one came forward: Cracraft, *Church Reform*, 297; *PSZ*, 7: no. 4635, pp. 404–6. The authorities specifically set up a debate with the Vyg community, which ended inconclusively. See Crummey, *Old Believers*, 86–8 on Andrei Denisov's *Pomorskie otvety*, subsequently the standard defence of the Old Belief.

180. See decrees of 1722 banning Old Believer priests and monk: *PSZ*, 6: no. 4009, pp. 678–81 (15 May) and no. 4052, pp. 738–42 (16 July).

181. Crummey, *Old Believers*, 69–70, 76–8, 90. The increasing importance of the Ural ironworks meant that after Peter's death they were released from factory service, and a compromise was reached on the double tax.

182. Stählin, 92.

183. *ZA*, 143 (8 Feb.).

184. Cracraft, *Church Reform*, 300, argues that 'by rejecting the policies either of physical persecution or of complete toleration . . . Peter's government only ensured that the schismatics would survive as a distinct group in Russian society'.

185. LOI, f. 270, d. 103, l. 240 (19 Feb. 1723); *ZA*, 126.

186. 'Sobranie ot sviatogo pisaniia o antikhriste', in *Chteniia*, Jan.–Mar. 1863, bk 1, 53.

187. Weber, 1: 221.

188. E. V. Anisimov, *The Reforms of Peter the Great. Progress through Coercion*, trans. J. Alexander (New York, 1993), 216.

189. Freeze, *Russian Levites*, 14.

190. Ibid., 32–3, on this process.

CHAPTER 11: PETER: MAN, MIND AND METHODS

1. Part of this chapter has appeared in Swedish: L. A. J. Hughes, 'Peter den store—ett karaktärsporträtt', *Historisk Tidskrift för Finland*, 81 (1996), 378–508.
2. Filippo Balatri, quoted in Iu. Gerasimova, 'Aria dlia Petra Velikogo', *Nedelia*, 1966, no. 16. On him, see above, pp. 187–8. Few contemporaries commented on Peter's great height, which is odd. For an exception, see Aaron Hill's 1718 verses on 'this *giant-genius* sent; / Divinely siz'd—to suit his crown's extent!' (A. G. Cross, *The Russian Theme in English Literature from the Sixteenth Century to 1980: An Introductory Survey and a Bibliography* (Oxford, 1985), 9–10). Stählin, no. 112, p. 117, records that there was a mark on the wall of Peter's study in the *Kunstkamera* 3 arshin minus 2 vershok (= 84 inches minus 3.5) from the floor, and that the place for his hands on a lectern was 5.5 feet above the ground. He also comments on the long stirrups on Peter's horse. His shoes are said to be size 39–40, about the size of the average European woman's foot today.
3. From I. Grabar', *V. A. Serov. Zhizn' i tvorchestvo* (M, 1913), 248–9; quoted in S. F. Platonov, *Petr Velikii. Lichnost' i deiatel'nost'*, (Paris, 1927), 126–7.
4. Stählin, 63–4. According to this anecdote, the attacks could be alleviated by the sight of a pretty face.
5. A. Babkin, 'Pis'ma Frantsa i Petra Lefortov o "Velikom posol'stve"', *VI*, 1976, no. 4, 122–3.
6. V. and E. Kennett, *The Palaces of Leningrad* (London, 1973), 11.
7. See N. M. Sharaia, *Voskovaia persona* (L, 1963). The Soviet writer Iury Tynianov based the story 'Voskovaia persona' (1929) on this idea, in which the model comes to life amidst the other freakish exhibits in the Cabinet of Curiosities.
8. O. Beliaev, *Kabinet Petra Velikogo* (SPb., 1800), 1: 4.
9. Ibid.
10. Ibid., 15, 47–8. The anecdote about the boots appears in Nartov, 54–5.
11. Beliaev, *Kabinet*, 40.
12. Ibid., 67–70.
13. Ibid., 123–4.
14. Korb, 155. See also Weber, 1: 210: 'the Czar himself loves a plain Dress and a small Retinue'.
15. Grund, 126.
16. Babkin, 'Pis'ma Frantsa', 130: letter dated 20 Jan. 1698.
17. B. C. Münnich, 'Ocherk daiushchii predstavlenie ob obraze pravleniia Rossiiskoi Imperii', in *Bezvremen'e i vremenshchik. Vospominaniia ob epokhe dvortsovykh perevorotov. 1720e–1760s gody* (L, 1991), 37.
18. Juel, 3: 42.
19. *Pridvornaia zhizn': 1613–1913* (SPb., 1913), 16.
20. *PiB*, 2: 97. (Peter had in mind various long royal titles involving the adjective 'great'; he addressed Apraksin as 'Min Her Admiral'.) On the ban on subjects falling on their knees, enforced with threat of the knout, see Stählin, 60.
21. Nartov, 17.
22. *ZA*, 178.
23. *ZA*, 158.
24. Platonov, *Petr Velikii*, 119.
25. Bergholz, 1724, p. 72.
26. Stählin, 41.
27. C. Whitworth, *An Account of Russia as it was in the Year 1710. Rossiia v nachale XVIII veka. Sochineniia Ch. Uitvorta* (M&L, 1988), 60.
28. The gallery was rebuilt in 1846. It and the cottage survive to this day as a museum.
29. G. Bogdanov, *Istoricheskoe, geograficheskoe i topograficheskoe opisanie Sanktpeterburga, ot nachala zavedeniia ego s 1703 po 1751 god.* (SPb., 1779), 54–5.
30. 'Slovo pokhval'noe o gosudare imperatore Petre Velikom'; quoted in S. Baehr, 'From History to National Myth: *Translatio imperii* in 18th-Century Russia', *RR*, 37 (1978), 1–13; idem, *The Paradise Myth in Eighteenth-Century Russia* (Stanford, Calif. 1991), 9.
31. D. G. Bulgakovsky, *Domik Petra*

Velikogo i ego sviatynia v S. Peterburge (SPb., 1891), 6, 7.

32. E. Shmurlo, *Petr Velikii v otsenke sovremennikov i potomstva* (SPb., 1912), *prilozhenie*, 93.

33. H-F. de Bassewitz, 'Zapiski grafa Bassevicha, sluzhashchie k poiasneniiu nekotorykh sobytii iz vremeni tsarstvovaniia Petra Velikogo (1713–1725)', *Russkii arkhiv*, 3 (1865), 197.

34. Platonov, *Petr Velikii*, 115.

35. *PZh*, 1720, p. 40.

36. Bassewitz, 'Zapiski', 197.

37. Nartov, 52–3. See similar list in Stählin, no. 109, pp. 168–9.

38. *Zapiski Ivana Ivanovicha Nepliueva (1693–1773)* (SPb., 1893), 107.

39. *PiB*, 10: 388–9 (27 Oct. 1710).

40. LOI, f. 270, d. 106, l. 516.

41. Quoted in L. Oliva, *Peter the Great. Great Lives Observed* (Englewood Cliffs, NJ, 1970), 108.

42. E. V. Anisimov, ed., *Petr Velikii. Vospominaniia. Dnevnikovye zapisi. Anekdoty* (SPb., 1993), 158.

43. Stählin, 107–8. On another clash with Frederick, see below, p. 379.

44. Ibid.

45. Platonov, *Petr Velikii*, 116.

46. Ibid., 113–14.

47. Ibid., 112.

48. Juel, 3: 18 (23 Aug. 1710).

49. *Exacter Relation von der ... neu erbauten Festung und Stadt St. Petersburg ... von H.G.* (Leipzig, 1713), 66–7.

50. Platonov, *Petr Velikii*, 116.

51. O. Beliaev, *Dukh Petra Velikogo* (SPb., 1798), 36–7.

52. Stählin, no. 102, pp. 157–8 (on stockings); Nartov, 45.

53. Cornelius de Bruyn, *Travels into Muscovy, Persia, and Part of the East Indies; Containing an Accurate Description of what is most Remarkable in those Countries* (London, 1737), 1: 26.

54. M. I. Semevsky, *Tsaritsa Praskov'ia 1664–1724* (M, 1989), 42.

55. *Sbornik*, 2: 32–3, 37.

56. LOI, f. 270, d. 106, l. 426 (11 Feb. 1724, letter to agent Brandt in Amsterdam). The cloth was to be packed with young trees ordered for Peterhof and two elephant tusks.

57. Bergholz, 1724, p. 24 (who notes that normally Peter was not in the least foppish).

58. Münnich, 'Ocherk', 37.

59. Bergholz, 1724, p. 37.

60. Ibid., 44. See E. Iu. Moiseenko, 'Plat'e rubezha XVII i XVIII vekov iz "Garderoba Petra I"', in *Kul'tura i iskusstvo Rossii XVIII veka. Novye materialy i issledovaniia. Sbornik statei* (L, 1981), 68–9, on examples of such coats in Peter's wardrobe.

61. E.g. Bergholz, 1724, p. 63 (31 Aug. 1724); Stählin, 37–9 (an incident in a church in Danzig in 1716).

62. *Sbornik*, 2: 110, 112, 115, etc.

63. E. Schuyler, *Peter the Great* (New York, 1984), 1: p. vii.

64. M. A. Alekseeva, *Graviura petrovskogo vremeni* (L, 1990), 188.

65. See above, pp. 97–100 and Stählin, 60–2, on how Peter approved the promotion of another to the post of counter-admiral which he had applied for, as the other candidate had a longer service record. In this sense, Peter was the antithesis of another 'pretender', the first False Dmitry, whose unconventional behaviour (adoption of Western dress, criticism of boyars, plans to send Russians abroad, neglect of Orthodoxy) was unacceptable because he was not the true tsar but pretending to be it. See M. Perrie, *Pretenders and Popular Monarchism in Early Modern Russia. The False Tsars of the Time of Troubles* (Cambridge, 1995), 86–7.

66. *PiB*, 2: 550; *PSZ*, 4: no. 1931, p. 216 (10 May 1703). Peter often sent congratulations to Menshikov on the anniversary of the award. See, e.g., letter in *MIGO*, 1(ii): 85 (10 May 1714).

67. *PiB*, 9: 292–3 (15 July 1709, to Romodanovsky and Buturlin). On promotions, see Whitworth, *SIRIO*, 39: 58. On Romodanovsky as Prince-Caesar, see above, pp. 98–100.

68. 'Tsaritsa Ekaterina Alekseevna', *Russkaia starina*, 28/8 (1880), 766 (from Helsinki, 12 Aug. 1713).

69. Bergholz, 1724, p. 42.

70. This appears in both Nartov, 92, and I. I. Golikov, *Anekdoty, kasaiushchiesia*

do gosudaria imperatora Petra Velikogo, reprinted in E. V. Anisimov, ed., *Petr Velikii. Vospominaniia. Dnevnikovye zapisi. Anekdoty* (SPb., 1993), 460–1.

71. N. Pogodin, 'Petr Pervyi: Pervye gody edinoderzhaviia, 1689–1694', *Russkii arkhiv*, 1879, 1: 47.

72. I. A. Zheliabuzhsky, 'Zapiski', in A. B. Bogdanov, ed., *Rossiia pri tsarevne Sof'e i Petre I*, (M, 1990), 248–9; Soloviev, 133.

73. *200-letie*, 185–6; *Sbornik*, 2: 7–24.

74. See S. O. Androsov, 'O portrete Petra I raboty Ivana Nikitina iz Ekaterininskogo dvortsa-muzeiia', in *Kuchumovskie chteniia. Sbornik materialov nauchnoi konferentsii, posviashchennoi pamiati A.M. Kuchumova (1913–1994)*, (SPb., 1996), 11: 'pay the painter Ivan Nikitin for painting the portrait of Mr Vice-Admiral, 60 roubles'.

75. See above, pp. 182–3.

76. For a list of gifts to new-born children and baptisms, see *200-letie*, 138–9, and above, p. 113.

77. Stählin, 53–4; hand-written letter to Joseph Nye: LOI, f. 270, d. 101, l. 110 (16 May 1722). On the same day, on the eve of departure for Persia, he also wrote to Admiral Cruys and the flagmen.

78. *Zapiski . . . Nepliueva*, 102–3.

79. See N. I. Pavlenko, *Petr Velikii* (M, 1990), 51. Shein's career had been confined to posts in the chancelleries. Perhaps appointing a Swiss admiral was a joke?

80. Campredon in *SIRIO*, 40: 381 (Sept. 1723). See also Weber, 1: 242–3: 'His Majesty to punish him, though without any Mark of Disgrace, declared him, for Jest-sake, Surveyor of his Ships by the Titles Knees Baas.'

81. *MIGO*, 2: 112 (5 Nov. 1713). The letter is signed 'Iogan Bas Golovin'.

82. *Sbornik Mukhanova*, 2nd ed. (SPb., 1866), 251.

83. LOI, f. 270, d. 81, l. 647. Bassewitz comments on this 'joke': 'Zapiski', 198–9. Catherine also wrote to *baas* in a bantering tone, e.g., from Copenhagen, 27 Aug. 1716: *Sbornik Mukhanova*, 254.

84. Bergholz, 1721, p. 205, records such a toast, at the wedding of Prince Repnin, but did not understand what it meant.

85. Kaliazina, illustration 161 (A. F. Zubov, 1717–20).

86. J. Cracraft, *The Church Reform of Peter the Great* (London, 1971), 18–19.

87. See below, p. 450.

88. Prokopovich (1706, on Peter's visit to Kiev), *Slova i rechi*, vol. 1 (SPb., 1760), 9.

89. See B. A. Uspensky, 'Tsar and Pretender: *Samozvancestvo* or Royal Imposture in Russia as a Cultural-Historical Phenomenon', in Iu. Lotman and B. A. Uspensky, *The Semiotics of Russian Culture* (Ann Arbor, 1984), 269–71, and above, pp. 97–100.

90. Bassewitz, 'Zapiski', 220–1.

91. Terry Castle, *Masquerade and Civilization: The Carnivalesque in Eighteenth-Century English Culture and Fiction* (Stanford, Calif., 1986), 5, 73, 75, 87. George II enjoyed masked balls.

92. See V. N. Vasil'ev, 'Sochinenie A. K. Nartova "Teatrum makhinarium" (K istorii peterburgskoi tokarni Petra I)', *Trudy Gosudarstvennogo Ermitazha*, 3 (1959), 70–78; *L'Art de tourner de Char. de Plumier* was purchased in Piedmont in 1716.

93. *PiB*, 3: 454–5 (8 Oct., 1705, to Romodanovsky).

94. *PiB*, 4: 476 (8 Dec.); 5: 20 (11 Jan.).

95. Juel, 3: 45–6.

96. *PiB*, 11: 120 (3 Mar. 1711).

97. Ibid., 246 (27 May 1711); *Sbornik*, 2: 73.

98. E. A. Kniazhetskaia, 'Nauchnye sviazi Rossii i Frantsii pri Petre I', *VI*, 1981, no. 5, 99.

99. See Kaliazina, illustration 194.

100. F. de la Neuville, *A Curious and New Account of Muscovy in the Year 1689*, ed. L. Hughes (London, 1994), 59; Juel, 3: 14–15; Weber, 1: 239; Bergholz, 1721, 1: pp. 32–3.

101. See analysis in N. I. Pavlenko, 'Petr I (K izucheniiu sotsial'no-politicheskikh vzgliadov)', in *RPR*, 47.

102. *Sbornik*, 2: 15 (June 1716).

103. Quoted Pavlenko, *Petr Velikii*, 79.

104. Campredon, *SIRIO*, 40: 382. On this occasion (at Golovkin's) a jester dressed as a cardinal read out a speech in Peter's honour.
105. *PZh*, 1720, pp. 11–12.
106. See Bergholz, 1721, pp. 129, 145, 164.
107. *Sbornik*, 2: 13 (in Germany in 1716).
108. See, e.g., calendar of Peter's visit to the medicinal springs near Petrozavodsk in Mar. 1720: *PZh*, 1720, pp. 9–12, when spillikins and billiards were interspersed with taking medicine and the waters and working on the lathe. On Peter and chess, see L. N. Semenova, *Ocherki istorii byta i kul'-turnoi zhizni Rossii: pervaia polovina XVIII v.* (L, 1982), 203.
109. Stählin, no. 76, p. 124. (Apparently this was written into the Military Statute.)
110. *Sbornik*, 2:13 (June 1716 in Germany, 4 groschen paid for the repair of his telescope). *200-letie*, 249, includes chronographs, a spirit level, a quadrant and compasses.
111. M. I. Belov, ed., *Voprosy geografii petrovskogo vremeni. Sb. statei* (L, 1975), 5. A letter from Peter to Kurakin about Dutch defences demonstrates a fair command of technical terminology: 'especially fine is the defence (*defenziia*) down below, from the even casements to the face of the main rampart'. He asked Kurakin to hire Dutch engineers: LOI, f. 270, d. 106, l. 176 (21 Jan. 1724).
112. E. I. Bobrova, comp., *Biblioteka Petra I. Ukazatel'-spravochnik* (L, 1978), 38.
113. Belov, ed., *Voprosy*, 5.
114. Stählin, no. 92, pp. 141–3.
115. N. A. Kopanev, 'Petr I—perevodchik', *XVIII vek.*, 16 (1989), 181. If he did translate *Pravilo o piati chinekh arkhitektury Iakova Barotsiia devignola*, which language was it from: surely not Italian, German, or French? See his correspondence with Konon Zotov who was translating a book on fortification in which Peter instructed him to make sure that the main practical points were rendered clearly and accurately: *PiB*, 9(i): 106.
116. Platonov, *Petr Velikii*, 112.
117. *PiB*, 9: 79 (6 Feb. 1709): request to F. M. Apraksin for predictions from the mathematical school about an eclipse due to take place later that month.
118. See M. Semevsky, *Slovo i delo. Ocherki i rasskazy iz russkoi istorii XVIII veka.* (SPb., 1885). J. Cracraft, 'Some Dreams of Peter the Great', *CASS*, 8 (1974), 173–97.
119. Weber, 1: 205.
120. LOI, f. 270, d. 107, l. 148: letters to Catherine, nos. 189–91.
121. *PZh*, 1720, pp. 21, 24.
122. Bruyn, *Travels*, 1: 28.
123. Ibid., 36.
124. LOI, f. 270, d. 84, ll. 60 (11 Jan.).
125. See *200-letie*, 252: payment for outfits for the two dwarfs in attendance on Tsarevich Peter Petrovich, 1718. See above, p. 259.
126. O. Neverov, ' "His Majesty's Cabinet" and Peter I's Kunstkammer', in O. Impey and A. McGregor, eds, *The Origins of Museums. The Cabinet of Curiosities in 16th–17th–Century Europe* (Oxford, 1985), 60.
127. Juel, 3: 116.
128. *PiB*, 10: 310 (23 Aug.).
129. *PiB*, 1: 417.
130. Kniazhetskaia, 'Nauchnye sviazi', 93.
131. Stählin, 96.
132. Ibid., 115–17.
133. Bergholz, 1724, p. 72.
134. LOI, f. 270, d. 97, l. 352 (2 Apr. 1721) and l. 360 (15 Apr.).
135. Nartov, 10, and Perry, *State of Russia*, 164.
136. E. V. Anisimov, *The Reforms of Peter the Great. Progress through Coercion*, trans. J. Alexander, (New York, 1993), 24–5.
137. E. I. Bobrova, comp., *Biblioteka Petra I. Ukazatel'-spravochnik* (L, 1978).
138. LOI, f. 270, d. 85, ll. 13–14. (*kak dlia krasoty tak i dlia uiuta*); d. 101, l. 576 (4 Nov. 1722); d. 103, ll. 473-6 (8 May 1723). For an example of carved decoration, see Kaliazina, illustration 201–3: *The Triumph of Neptune and Amphitrite*, which shows nymphs and cherubs riding dolphins.
139. LOI, f. 270, d. 103, l. 321 (8 Mar. 1723), to the Admiralty).
140. See Kaliazina, illustration 177.
141. *PiB*, 4: 12 (4 Jan. 1709, to I. A. Musin-Pushkin). The books in question were

translations of German works on fortification. On printing, see above, p.
319. In May 1709 Peter sent to
Amsterdam for a bookbinder: *PiB*, 9:
166.

142. LOI, f. 270, d. 85, l. 110.
143. Ibid., d. 100, ll. 293–4$^{r–v}$ (18 Mar.
1722).
144. Ibid., d. 104, l. 459 (16 Dec. 1723).
Another letter of 14 Jan. 1724 made
further references to Dutch models for
constructing the dovecotes and sum-
merhouses: d. 106, l. 80$^{r–v}$.
145. Ibid., l. 486$^{r–v}$ (21 Feb. 1724).
146. *Sbornik*, 2: 12, 13 (1716, on binding of
Le Blond's book on gardens (*ogorod-
naia kniga*) and gardening prints (*za
pechatnye listy ogorodnye*), a gardening
book bought by Felten.
147. LOI, f. 270, d. 101, l. 646 (21 Dec.
1722).
148. Ibid., d. 103, l. 599.
149. S. V. Efimov, 'Evdokiia Lopukhina—
posledniaia russkaia tsaritsa XVII veka',
in *Srednevekovaia Rus'. Sbornik nauchnykh statei k 65-letiiu so dnia rozhdeniia
professora R. G. Skrynnikova* (Spb.,
1995), 158–9. Descriptions in N.
Ustrialov, *Istoriia tsarstvovaniia Petra
Velikogo*, vol. 6 (SPb., 1869), 224–6.
150. Bergholz, 1724, pp. 10–11.
151. Grund, 129.
152. N. B. Golikova, *Politicheskie protsessy
pri Petra I* (M, 1957), 39.
153. 'Voinskie artikuly' (1714), in *Voennye
ustavy Petra Velikogo* (M, 1946), 76–7.
154. Golikova, *Politicheskie*, 54.
155. Ibid., 216.
156. Platonov, *Petr Velikii*, 125–6.
157. *PiB*, 7(i): 133 (Apr. 1708): 'ibo siia
saryn' krome zhestochi, ne mozhet
uniata byt'.
158. Platonov, *Petr Velikii*, 124–5.
159. LOI, f. 270, d. 84, l. 179 (21 Oct. 1717).
160. Ibid., d. 106, l. 492 (2 Feb. 1724).
161. Ibid., d. 103, l. 86 (21 Jan. 1723).
162. Ibid., d. 97, l. 376 (19 Apr. 1721).
163. Ibid., d. 107, l. 581 (not dated).
164. Juel, 3: 31–2.
165. *PiB*, 6: 110 (26–8 Sept. 1707).
166. Ibid., 117 (1 Oct.).
167. *PiB*, 8: 287 (7 Nov. 1708).
168. *PiB*, 4: 185. See also the Stählin anecdote about how Peter pardoned a man

after Catherine affixed a petition
written in Lizetka's name to the dog's
collar: no. 96, pp. 148–9.
169. *PiB*, 8: 90 (17 Aug. 1708): 'set up in dry
balsam so that it doesn't spoil and
there is no smell, as Dr Dunel wrote in
more detail. I beg you to put your best
effort into it.'
170. *Sbornik*, 2: 116.
171. Ibid., 120. Food and equipment for
dogs are often mentioned in account
books: e.g., chains and food, Jan. 1713:
200-letie, 189.
172. LOI, f. 270, d. 85, l. 186 (29 Oct. 1717).
173. *200-letie*, 73–5.
174. On Peter's dislike of hunting, see
Stählin, 65–6. But there is at least one
reference to Peter and Catherine going
hunting 'with birds and dogs': *PZh*,
1720, p. 33 (11 Aug. 1720). Stählin, no.
25, p. 54 (on cockroaches), and *PiB*, 8:
473–4 (before 11 Dec.), 475 (3 Dec.,
orders for quarters to be prepared for
him at Kolomenskoe, 'in which there
are no cockroaches').
175. Nartov, 101; M. M. Bogoslovsky, 'Petr
Velikii (opyt kharakteristiki)', in V.
Kallach, ed., *Tri veka* vol. 3 (M, 1912),
22.
176. LOI, f. 270, d. 103, ll. 115–17 (29 Jan.
1723).
177. Stählin, no. 89, pp. 137–85. Informant
was Baron Brimmer, who heard this
from the duke of Holstein, to whom
Peter told it.
178. F. W. Mardefeld, *SIRIO*, 15: 223 (30
Apr. 1723 (NS). Of course, individual
priests suffered under Ivan IV, but the
Church was not reformed.
179. This information from Juel, 3: 8–9.
Church singing was an early enthusiasm. Peter sang at church services in
Archangel when he was there
in summer 1693: N. Aristov,
'Pervonachal'noe obrazovanie Petra
Velikogo', *Russkii arkhiv*, 13/8 (1875),
480.
180. F. Prokopovich, *Sochineniia*, ed. I. P.
Eremin (M&L, 1961), 126–9; quoted
in translation in M. Raeff, ed., *Peter
the Great Changes Russia* (Lexington,
Ky, 1972), 39–43.
181. Nartov, 70. Peter had a new edition of
the Bible printed in Amsterdam in

1721 in Slavonic and Dutch: Stählin, no. 100, p. 154.

182. *Biblioteka Petra I.*
183. See, e.g., *PZh*, 1720, p. 15. There were services from 8 to 19 Apr., with communion on 14 Apr. In 1721 communion was taken on 6 Apr.
184. *DR*, 4: 794–5.
185. Pogodin, 'Petr Pervyi', 50.
186. *PZh*, 1720, p. 16.
187. Anderson, 'Peter the Great', 274.
188. Stählin, no. 54, p. 92; no. 79, p. 126; no. 100, pp. 154–5.
189. Golikov, *Anekdoty*, 378–9.
190. Cracraft, *Church Reform*, 22.
191. *PiB*, 1: 95.
192. *PiB*, 2: 152.
193. Ibid., 525.
194. *PiB*, 9: 331.
195. LOI, f. 270, d. 107, ll. 254–5 (RGADA, f. 9, kn. 64, l. 649).
196. *PiB*, 12(i): 81–2 (15 Feb. 1712).
197. *PiB*, 11: 230.
198. Ibid., 241 (20 May 1711, to Georgian tsar Archil II).
199. Nartov, 142. P. V. Verkhovskoy, *Uchrezhdenie Dukhovnoi Kollegii i Dukhovnyi reglament*, vol. 1 (Rostov/Don, 1916), 54–60, gives many examples.
200. Nartov, 17. See also Golikov, *Anekdoty*, no. 93, pp. 392–5, on the monarch's respect for the law of God.
201. Bulgakovsky, *Domik*, 19–20. The author attributes it to the workshop of Simon Ushakov. At the end of the nineteenth century the icon was kept in the little house on the Neva. Alexander III's survival from a train accident in 1888 was attributed to the icon, which survived unharmed.
202. Ibid., 30.
203. Weber, 1: 236.
204. Stählin, pp. 77–8. See hand-written note in notebook for 1711 on Luther's dates and age when he died: *ZA*, 38.
205. See E. V. Anisimov, 'Progress through Violence from Peter the Great to Lenin and Stalin', *Russian History*, 17 (1990), 410.
206. *ZA*, 168. Terminology is vital; Peter uses *razsuzhdenie* and *razum*.
207. LOI, f. 270, d. 101, l. 281 (13 July 1722): *o blazhenstvakh.*

208. See report by Campredon, *SIRIO*, 52: 437.
209. *ZA*, 142.
210. See discussion in A. B. Kamensky, *Arkhivnoe delo v Rossii XVIII veka: Istoriko-kul'turnyi aspekt* (M, 1991), 19–20.
211. *PSZ*, 7: no. 4348, p. 152 (8 Nov. 1723).
212. 'vremia iako smert'', *PiB*, 1: 444.
213. *PiB*, 11: 281.
214. LOI, f. 270, d. 103, l. 201 (14 Feb. 1723).
215. Ibid., d. 72, l. 21 (21 Jan. 1713).
216. *ZA*, 94 (31 Oct. 1721, hand-written).
217. *SIRIO*, 20: 61–2.
218. LOI, f. 270, d. 97, l. 317ʳ (22 Mar. 1721). A whole series of letters survives on a similar theme: e.g., to Menshikov of same date, all about the weather (l. 318). See also hand-written journal entries for 28 Mar.–14 May, ll. 329–40.
219. LOI, f. 270, d. 97, l. 353 (arshin = (roughly) a square yard).
220. *PSZ*, 6: no. 3970, p. 656 (17 Apr. 1722).
221. *ZA*, 74: 'Daby ... nikto nevedeniem ne otgovarivalsia'. This formula appears in many edicts.
222. Stählin, no. 75, pp. 122–3.
223. LOI, f. 270, d. 97, l. 576 (1 June 1721).
224. *PSZ*, 6: no. 3937, p. 591. Anisimov picked out this gem: *Reforms*, 150.
225. GPB OR, f. 1003, d. 7, l. 69.
226. LOI, f. 270, d. 107, l. 290; *ZA*, 148.
227. *PiB*, 3: 302. Kurbatov replied (he received the letter 24 Mar.) that he had done as instructed, 'only, sire, I cannot hope to get such a large number to Smolensk by the middle of April, because from Solvychegodsk to Moscow is 1060 versts, where there are plenty of such craftsmen' (ibid. 783–4). This proved to be the case. On 16 June Peter wrote from Polotsk that only 10,000 blades had arrived, with orders to send the others without delay as the campaign was being held up (ibid., 361).
228. *PiB*, 6: 11
229. *PiB*, 6: 467.
230. *BP*, 458–9 (6 Apr. 1722).
231. LOI, f. 270, d. 101, l. 549 (4 Nov. 1722, to Kudriavtsev in Kazan').
232. Ibid., d. 104, l. 53 (15 Sept. 1723).
233. Ibid., d. 106, l. 565 (27 Apr. 1724).

234. *PSZ*, 6: no. 3965, p. 653 (12 Apr. 1722).

235. LOI, f. 270, d. 97, ll. 175–80.

236. *PSZ*, 7: no. 4480, pp. 266–7 (20 Feb. 1724).

237. *PSZ*, 6: no. 3781, p. 388; LOI, f. 270, d. 97, l. 409 (28 Apr. 1721), notably: 'even though a thing is good'.

238. LOI, f. 270, d. 97, ll. 442 ff. (various letters, dated May 1721).

239. Ibid., d. 100, l. 303 (1 Apr. 1722).

240. *PSZ*, 7: no. 4210, pp. 55–6; no. 4386, p. 184 (6 Dec.).

241. Ibid., no. 4224, pp. 64–5 (14 May 1723).

242. *PSZ*, 7: no. 4490, p. 276 (3 Apr. 1724). Earlier one *PSZ*, 6: no. 4070 (26 July/7 Aug. 1722). The land commissars were to supervise this firmly and to report to the *Kamer-kollegiia* where such building is carried out according to His Majesty's edict; but where the edict is contravened, the college is to call the commissars to account.

243. A. F. Bychkov, *Pis'ma Petra Velikogo, khraniashchiesia v imp. Publ. biblioteke* (SPb., 1872), 81–2 (5 July 1722). There were several hand-written drafts of this order. See LOI, f. 270, d. 101, ll. 248, 249, 250.

244. LOI, f. 270, d. 101, l. 613 (29 Nov. 1722, Tsaritsyn).

245. *ZA*, 164.

246. *PiB*, 12(i): 25 (12 Feb. 1712 to Senate).

247. *The Tryal of the Czarewitz Alexis Petrowitz, who was Condemn'd at Petersbourg, on the 25th of June, 1718* (London, 1725), 95.

248. *PSZ*, 6: no. 3485, p. 6.

249. See M. Raeff, ed., *Peter the Great: Reformer or Revolutionary?* (Boston, 1963), 68.

250. Weber, 1: 17 (a letter from a Frenchman).

251. *PSZ*, 7: no. 4345, pp. 150–1. (5 Nov. 1723).

252. Stählin, no. 91, pp. 140–1, attributed to Count Osterman.

253. Nartov, 28.

254. Ibid., 43.

255. Pavlenko, 'Petr I'; 50. Pavlenko's admiration for Peter prevents him from seeing this indiscriminate display of

256. See B. A. Uspensky, 'Historia sub specie Semioticae', in H. K. Baran, ed., *Semiotics and Structuralism. Readings from the Soviet Union* (New York, 1976), 64–75. See also discussion in Kamensky, *Arkhivnoe delo*, 11–12.

257. *PSZ*, 5: no. 3341 (24 Mar. 1719).

258. C. Peterson, *Peter the Great's Administrative and Judicial Reforms* (Stockholm, 1979), 218.

259. *PiB*, 3: 346; he sent a back-up letter on 28 May in case Repnin had not received the first: 347–8.

260. LOI, f. 270, d. 109, l. 2; RGADA, f. 9, kn. 33, l. 80.

261. E. V. Anisimov, 'Otets otechestva', *Zvezda*, 1989, no. 11, 101–18.

262. Letter to Makarov about the Admiralty, 31 Dec. 1716, quoted in ibid., 116.

263. For further discussion of these terms (*obshchee blago, blago otechestva, gosudarstvennaia pol'za, gosudarstvennyi interes*), see Pavlenko, 'Petr I', 61 ff.

264. F. Prokopovich, *Slova i rechi*, vol. 1 (SPb., 1760), 9.

265. 'It was under Peter that there emerges in Russia a sense of the state as something distinct from and superior to the monarch': R. Pipes, *Russia under the Old Regime* (London, 1974), 128.

266. Platonov, *Petr Velikii*, 131.

267. A. Gerschenkron, 'Russian Mercantilism', in *Europe in the Russian Mirror* (Cambridge, 1970), 79.

268. P. P. Epifanov, 'Voinskii ustav Petra Velikogo', in A. I. Andreev, ed., *Petr Velikii. Sbornik statei* (M&L, 1947), 198.

269. Naval Statute: *PSZ*, 6: no. 3485, p. 5.

270. LOI, f. 270, d. 100, l. 428 (18 Apr. 1722): 'kotoroe mne pache zhivota moego est'.

271. *ZA*, 169.

272. *PiB*, 10: 335 (12 Sept. 1710).

273. *PSZ*, 4: no. 1910, pp. 192–5. The Russian idea of 'common good' does not originate with Peter. See edict of Tsar Fedor, 12 Jan. 1682, on the abolition of *mestnichestvo*: the tsar speaks of his duty 'to keep and preserve all Orthodox Christians of whatever rank

and age, in the best condition and to destroy and root out anything which might lead to ruin and the diminution of the general good (*obshchago dobra*)': *PSZ*, 2: no. 905, p. 372. There is a religious element here that is lacking in Peter's formulation.

274. *PiB*, 13(i): 131; *PSZ*, 5: no. 2673; *ZA*, 38. The list of crimes was published on 25 Aug.: *PSZ*, 5: no. 2707.

275. LOI, f. 270, d. 100, l. 352 (6 Apr. 1722).

276. *PSZ*, 6: no. 3708, pp. 291–309 (16 Jan. 1721); also in *PRP*, 135–6.

277. Peter's draft, in *ZA*, 132; published in *PSZ*, 7: no. 4460, pp. 250–1 (5 Feb. 1724).

278. F. Prokopovich, *Istoriia imp. Petra Velikogo ot rozhdeniia ego do Poltavskoi batalii* (SPb., 1773), 212. See above p. 40.

279. Weber, 1: 15–16, which is the sole reference.

280. Ustrialov, *Istoriia*, 6: 348.

281. Naval Statute: *PSZ*, 6: no. 3485, p. 6.

282. R. Wortman, *Scenarios of Power. Myth and Ceremony in Russian Monarchy*, vol. 1 (Princeton, 1995), 51.

CHAPTER 12: FAMILY FACTORS

1. See, e.g., M. S. Anderson, 'Peter the Great: Imperial Revolutionary?', in A. G. Dickens, ed., *The Courts of Europe: Politics, Patronage and Royalty, 1400–1800* (London, 1977), 267, 275.

2. See, e.g., Jacob Reutenfels's account of her opening a carriage window, in L. A. J. Hughes, *Sophia Regent of Russia 1657–1704* (New Haven, 1990), 37.

3. This and other letters in M. M. Bogoslovsky, *Petr I. Materialy dlia biografii*, vol. 1 (M, 1940), 161–3.

4. *DR*, 4: 853–6 (26–7 Jan. 1694). N. I. Pavlenko, *Petr Velikii* (M, 1990), 33, believes that Peter 'did not wish to reveal his weakness to others'.

5. *PiB*, 1: no. 21.

6. *PiB*, 4: 379 (22 Sept.).

7. See above, pp. 190–1. L. Vasil'eva's claim that Peter enjoyed an incestuous relationship with Natalia is not substantiated: ('Zhenskaia revoliutsiia Petra I', *Nauka i religiia*, 1997, no. 2, p. 17).

8. *PiB*, 9: 14 (4 Jan. 1709), 79 (5 Feb. 1709). The matchmaking was unsuccessful, as the prospective bride opted to enter a nunnery (ibid., 664).

9. See, e.g., her reports that 'Annushka' was in good health and would love to see her father 'if only for a short time': *PiB*, 9: 546 (28 Jan. 1709). After the Pruth campaign, Peter wrote instructing her to bring the children to St Petersburg: *PiB*, 11(ii): 54 (28 July 1711).

10. Juel, 3: 126.

11. I. A. Zheliabuzhsky, 'Zapiski', in A. B. Bogdanov, ed., *Rossiia pri tsarevne Sof'e i Petre I* (M, 1990), 272. See also an entry in the palace account book for 1701 on provisions for the trip: A. Viktorov, *Opisanie zapisnykh knig i bumag starinnykh dvortsovykh prikazov, 1613–1725* (M, 1883), 2: 552.

12. M. I. Semevsky, *Tsaritsa Praskov'ia 1664–1724* (M, 1989), 36–7. Peter's letter to Natalia, 6 Mar. 1708: in *PiB*, 7(i): 90. They left Moscow on about 20 Mar.

13. Nartov, 76–8.

14. See figures in P. Miliukov, *Gos. khoziaistvo Rossii v pervoi chet. XVIII st. i reforma Petra Velikogo* (SPb., 1905), 70–150: totals for the expenses of the tsarevny were: in 1701, 43,000 roubles; 1702, 38,000; 1703, 45,139; 1704, 35,853; 1705, 58,696; 1706, 18,000; 1707, 18,500; 1708, 36,600. In addition, some itemized sums appear —e.g., for Natalia Alekseevna, wine and precious gems, 2,421 roubles (p. 88); also small sums (less than 100 roubles annually)—e.g., 'for the tsaritsy and tsarevny for giving out as alms' (p. 109); for funerals of Tat'iana Mikhailovna and Marfa (Margarita) (p. 128).

15. *PiB*, 11(ii): 108 (before 31 Aug. 1711). LOI, f. 270, d. 76, l. 363ᵛ (14 May 1714).

16. LOI, f. 270, d. 75, l. 59 (24 Jan. 1714).

17. Weber, 1: 138, 225. He saw her there in

1716. On Tsarevna Maria, see above, p. 191.

18. Semevsky, *Tsaritsa Praskov'ia*, 14–15. Two died in infancy: Maria, born 1689, died 13 Feb. 1692 (*PSZ*, 3: no. 1434, p. 124); Feodosia, born 4 June 1690, died 12 May 1691 (no. 1378, p. 69). On Ekaterina, born 19 Oct. 1691 (no. 1477, pp. 114–15), Anna and Praskovia, see below.

19. Semevsky, *Tsaritsa Praskov'ia*, 34.

20. LOI, f. 270, d. 101, l. 41 (11 May 1722).

21. Ibid., l. 88 (16 May 1722).

22. See *DPPS*, 5(ii): no. 811, pp. 635–7 (July 1715) on household expenses in 1715. This source gives little hint of life-style, except that Marfa continues to be referred to as 'pious' (*blagovernaia*).

23. Weber, 1: 333.

24. *DPPS*, 6(i): 3. Weber, 1: 110–11, gives the date as 14 Jan. According to Vasil'eva, 'Zhenskaia revoliutsiia', p. 19, an autopsy revealed that Marfa was still a virgin.

25. For a recent study, see S. V. Efimov, 'Evdokiia Lopukhina—posledniaia russkaia tsaritsa XVII veka', in *Srednevekovaia Rus'. Sbornik nauchnykh statei k 65-letiiu so dnia rozhdeniia Professora R. G. Skrynnikova* (SPb., 1995), 136–65. On her male relatives, see below, pp. 417–18.

26. G. V. Esipov, *Tsaritsa Evdokiia Feodorovna* (M, 1862), 1; *Drevniaia rossiiskaia vivilofika*, 11 (SPb., 1891), 194; Bogoslovsky, *Petr I*, 1: 66. Royal weddings were usually held in the Annunciation cathedral. See L. A. J. Hughes, 'Peter the Great's Two Weddings: Changing Images of Women in a Transitional Age', in R. Marsh, ed., *Women in Russia and Ukraine* (Cambridge, 1996), 31–44.

27. Kurakin, 369.

28. 'Zhenishka tvoia Dun'ka chelom b'et' (1689): *Pis'ma russkikh gosudarei i drugikh osob tsarskogo semeistva*, vol. 3 (M, 1862), 68. These letters, it should be noted, were in Evdokia's own hand, whereas the illiterate Catherine's much livelier, more personal letters were all written by a secretary.

29. Ibid., 68–9 (both letters 1694, otherwise undated).

30. N. Pogodin, 'Petr Pervyi: Pervye gody edinoderzhaviia, 1689–1694', *Russkii arkhiv*, 1879, 1: 23. See M. I. Semevsky, *Tsaritsa Katerina Alekseevna, Anna i Villem Mons 1692–1724* (SPb., 1884).

31. *Sbornik*, 1: 23; *DR*, 4: 614–16; *PSZ*, 3: no. 1419, p. 116 (14 May 1692).

32. *DR*, 4: 685–7; *PSZ*, 3: no. 1438, p. 128: the latter records that 'the tsaritsy' (Evdokia, Natalia, Marfa, and Praskovia all had this title) took part in the burial service. Some reference books include a third son, Pavel, said to have died in 1693, but neither his birth nor his death is recorded in the admittedly incomplete palace records or in *PSZ*. In Jan. 1694 Alexis is the only boy mentioned in the patriarch's list of members of the royal family to be greeted at Epiphany: *DR*, 4: 842. When Just Juel (3: 26) visited the cathedral in 1711, he mentioned only the one tomb ('the tomb of the elder [clearly an error] son of the present monarch'). Perhaps Pavel was still-born?

33. Grund, 133.

34. *PiB*, 1: 700.

35. Esipov, *Tsaritsa Evdokiia*, 4–5. 'The Orthodox Russian people would never forgive Peter's forcing the tsaritsa to take the veil without a church court or sentence': Efimov, 'Evdokiia Lopukhina', 142–4.

36. Juel, 3: 6.

37. Ibid., 7.

38. Grund, 132–3.

39. Bergholz, 1724, p. 43.

40. 'Tsaritsa Ekaterina Alekseevna, supruga Petra Velikogo v 1707–1713 gg.', *Russkaia starina*, 28/8 (1880), 758.

41. Peter sent her regards to Menshikov together with those of his dog Lizetka and Iakim the dwarf, referring to her not by name but as 'matka': *PiB*, 4: 385 (2 Oct.), 410 (30 Oct.), 437 (17 Nov.).

42. See N. I. Pavlenko, 'Strasti u trona. Ekaterina I', *Rodina*, 1993, no. 10, 106–12.

43. See discussion in N. I. Kostomarov, 'Ekaterina Alekseevna, pervaia russkaia imperatritsa', *Drevniaia i*

novaia Rossiia (1872), no. 2, 129–31, and Pavlenko, 'Strasti u trona'.

44. E. V. Anisimov, ed., *Petr Velikii. Vospominaniia. Dnevnikovye zapisi. Anekdoty* (SPb., 1993), 157.

45. Pavlenko, 'Strasti u trona', 107 (11 Oct.).

46. Ibid., 106. As Esipov, 'Zhizneopisanie kniazia A. D. Menshikova', *Russkii arkhiv*, 1875, no. 7, 241, points out, Peter did not split up with Anna Mons until Dec. 1703. He also refers to a letter written by Catherine in 1717 in which she hints at 1 Mar. as the anniversary of their meeting.

47. See, e.g., Grund, 130–3.

48. In July 1710 Peter instructed A. I. Repnin to search for Catherine's relatives in Riga, but none was found: *PiB*, 10: 253. Her supposed brothers, Karl and Friedrich Skavronsky, came to St Petersburg only in 1726: ibid., 683–4. The brothers were created counts in 1727. For Count Karl Skavronsky's will of 1747 (bequeathing estates given in 1729), see *Sbornik Mukhanova*, 2nd edn. (SPb., 1866), 433–4. Some sisters also turned up— Christina, the wife of a peasant, and Anna: Kostomarov, 'Ekaterina', 131.

49. See Peter's instructions to Catherine and Anisa Tolstaia to wait for him in Dubno or Ostrog: *PiB*, 5: 79 (15 Feb.).

50. *PiB*, 6: 144 (2 Nov.).

51. *PiB*, 7(i): 22 (5 Jan.).

52. Ibid., 43–4.

53. Ibid., 88–9 (5 Mar. 1708).

54. *PiB*, 8(i): 110 (31 Aug. 1708).

55. *PiB*, 9: 236.

56. Ibid., 358 (31 Aug. 1709).

57. Ibid., 387 (20 Sept.), 388 (24 Sept.), 395 (30 Sept.). See Catherine's reply, ibid., 1251–2 (11 Oct.).

58. *PiB*, 12(i): 360–1. Cited by B. Sumner, *Peter the Great and the Emergence of Russia* (London, 1958), 68. See N. A. Sindalovsky, *Legendy i mify Sankt-Peterburga* (SPb., 1994), 125–6.

59. *PZh*, 1711, 308.

60. *PiB*, 11: 230, 496. (Menshikov's 'keeping your word' is probably a reference to Peter's insistence that he keep his, a few year's earlier, by marrying Daria Ars'eneva.)

61. Juel (3: 133) mistakenly attributes Peter's decision to marry Catherine to the death of his first wife.

62. C. Whitworth, *SIRIO*, 61: 144 (dispatch to London, 20 Feb. 1712).

63. In Sept. 1711 they were parted again— see Peter's letter from Poznan, en route to Carlsbad, telling her to give his regards to the prince-pope Zotov: *PiB*, 11(ii): 119 (3 Sept.).

64. *PiB*, 12(i): 86, 361, to Gavril Menshikov: 'my staruiu svoiu svad'bu vchera okonchili'. According to Whitworth, invitations to the wedding were to 'His Majesty's old wedding'. See above, pp. 261–2.

65. 'Reskripty i ukazy', in *Osmnadtsatyi vek*, vol. 4 (M, 1869), 14; A. F. Bychkov, 'O svad'be imp. Petra Velikogo s Ekaterinoi Alekseevnoi', *Drevniaia i Novaia Rossiia*, 1877, no. 3, 323–4.

66. B. A. Uspensky, 'Historia sub specie Semioticae', in H. K. Baran, ed., *Semiotics and Structuralism. Readings from the Soviet Union* (New York, 1976), 66–7. See below, pp. 450–1.

67. Grebeniuk, 83–4.

68. *SIRIO*, 34: 102.

69. Bergholz, 1722, pp. 126–7.

70. Ibid., 1724–5, 91, 94. (He adds that drinking was less heavy.)

71. *PiB*, 11(ii): 140 (19 Sept. 1711). In autumn 1709 Peter had been in Torun, where presumably he had a flirtation with a local woman.

72. *Pis'ma russkikh gosudarei*, 1: 166. A son had died at birth in Jan. 1717. See below.

73. There is a rich anecdotal and popular literature on the topic of Peter's relations with both women and men. The topic awaits a scholarly study. In the meantime, see S. Librovich, 'Zhenskii krug Petra Velikogo', *Smena*, 6 (1993), 80–97, and other reprinted works by the same author.

74. Bergholz, 1724, p. 67: 'Pora domoi, batiushka!'

75. E. V. Anisimov, in conversation. See also his *The Reforms of Peter the Great. Progress through Coercion*, trans. J. Alexander (New York, 1993), 280–2.

76. LOI, f. 270, d. 103, l. 308 (4 Mar. 1723, letter no. 180).

77. LOI, f. 270, d. 107, l. 184: 'drug moi serdeshninkoi'. Catherine was in Moscow. He sent wine, beer, pomegranates, lemons and cucumbers.

78. ZA, 179–80: 'kak muzheski, a ne zhenski, postupala'. PSZ, 7: no. 4366, pp. 161–2 (15 Nov. 1723). Pavlenko, 'Strasti u trona', 108, points out that Peter could come up with few concrete examples of great 'services' except Pruth, and that she was never a 'helper' in state affairs. On the law of succession of 1722, see above, p. 185.

79. See Villebois, quoted in Pavlenko, 'Strasti u trona', 109.

80. PZh, 1724, pp. 22–3. There is no mention of the Mons affair in this source, although plenty of details are given of the very cold weather in Nov. 1724.

81. SIRIO, 52: 358–9 (9 Dec. 1724 (NS)).

82. Opisanie poriadka derzhannogo pri pogrebenii blazhennyia vysokoslavnyia i vernodostoineishiia pamiati vsepresvetleishago derzhavneishago Petra Velikago (SPb., 1725; M, 1726), 31.

83. R. K. Massie, Peter the Great. His Life and World (London, 1981), 377 n.; Semevsky, Tsaritsa Katerina, 335. For a detailed discussion, see L. A. J. Hughes, 'A Note on the Children of Peter the Great', SGECRN, 21 (1993), 10–16.

84. PiB, 3: 283 (Mar. 1705). Petrushka is identified as the 'first child of Peter the Great from Ekaterina Alekseevna' (p. 770). Only the postscript is in Peter's hand.

85. Semevsky, Tsaritsa Katerina, 334.

86. PiB, 3: 954. Menshikov congratulated the women on the 'new arrival' in a letter of 27 Oct. 1705 from Lithuania: Esipov, 'Zhizneopisanie', 245.

87. G. Bogdanov, Istoricheskoe, geograficheskoe i topograficheskoe opisanie Sanktpeterburga, ot nachala zavedeniia ego s 1703 po 1751 god. (SPb., 1779), 283. Semevsky, Tsaritsa Katerina, 81.

88. Semevsky, Tsaritsa Katerina, 335. The letter is dated here 1707 in error. See his reply: PiB, 5: 13. He sent a gift for mother and daughter and instructions to make their way to Kiev, then to await further instructions from there as the roads were bad. The 'little one' is mentioned again in a letter to Menshikov, 26 Dec. 1707: PiB, 6: 200.

89. PiB, 8(i): 43–4.

90. Pis' ma tsarevicha Alekseia Petrovicha, k ego roditeliu gosudariu Petru Velikomu, gosudaryne Ekaterine Alekseevne i kabinet-sekretariu Makarovu (Odessa, 1849), 23. (The originals of these letters have been lost.) See also PiB, 8(i): 65 (8 Feb.), 71–2 (18 Feb. to Alexis), 390 (13 Feb., congratulations from Menshikov).

91. Bogdanov, Istoricheskoe, 283. Semevsky gives Natalia's birth date as 27 Mar.

92. PiB, 13(i): 114 (16 Mar. 1713). Maria (christened Natalia) died on 26 May 1715: ibid., 331. See also Weber, 1: 92.

93. Pis' ma russkikh gosudarei, 1: 82.

94. Bantysh-Kamensky, 1: 165.

95. LOI, f. 270, d. 101, l. 284 (13 July 1722, letter to Anna and Elizabeth from Astrakhan).

96. Ibid., d. 107, l. 39.

97. See letter from Peter to Stefan Iavorsky, dated 29 Oct. Peter was born at 11 p.m. 'of this night'—i.e., the 28th: ZA, 162.

98. M. A. Alekseeva, Graviura petrovskogo vremeni (L, 1990), 139; Prokopovich, 'Nadezhda dobrykh i dolgikh let rossiiskoi monarkhii', in Grebeniuk', 74–7; F. Prokopovich, Sochineniia, ed. I. P. Eremin (M&L, 1961), 38–48. A few years later, in Justice of the Monarch's Right, Prokopovich conjured up arguments for the predominance of the monarch's will over the hereditary principle.

99. LOI, f. 270, d. 84, l. 552 (included in letter to Menshikov).

100. RGADA, f. 9, kn. 53, l. 84; Grebeniuk, 77–8. There were similar greetings from Elizabeth and Anna.

101. Pis' ma russkikh gosudarei 1: 76.

102. Ibid., 80.

103. 'Podennye zapiski kn. A. D. Menshikova', GPB OR, f. 480, ed. khr. 2, l. 35r–v.

104. Weber, 1: 266.

105. Jeffreys, SIRIO, 61: 529; Stählin, no. 95, pp. 146–8.

106. *Pis' ma russkikh gosudarei*, 1: 83. See also *Sbornik*, 2: 54: various expenses for messengers, doctors, etc.

107. To Prince M. Golitsyn: LOI, f. 270, d. 84, l. 24. Peter was in Amsterdam.

108. Ibid., l. 42.

109. Ibid., ll. 19–20 (4 Jan. 1717).

110. Ibid., l. 44.

111. Ibid., d. 86, l. 1.

112. Ibid., d. 84, l. 67.

113. Bergholz, 1721, p. 180. The fact of her pregnancy is confirmed by La Vie, reporting on 8 Sept. (19 Sept. (NS)), but at that point, two months into pregnancy, she was said to be in 'perfect health': *SIRIO*, 40: 272. On 24 Oct., however, he reported that Catherine missed a trip to Kronstadt on account of ill health. He speculated: 'there is no more talk of her pregnancy. Either she thought she was pregnant or hurt herself (*s'est blessée*)': p. 274.

114. E.g. Semevsky, *Tsaritsa Katerina*, 342; Bogdanov, *Istoricheskoe*, 374 (buried in the Alexander Nevsky monastery).

115. *Petersburgskii nekropol' ili spravochnii istoricheskii ukazatel' lits ... po nadgrobnym nadpisiam Aleksandronevskoi lavry* (M, 1883), 103.

116. There were a number of claims that Peter fathered illegitimate children, notably by Countess Maria Rumiantseva (see J. Alexander, *Catherine the Great. Life and Legend* (Oxford, 1989), 29). The story told by Wilhelmina, sister of Frederick II of Prussia, about a visit by Peter to Berlin in 1719, accompanied by about 400 women, each carrying a baby fathered by the tsar, is obvious fantasy: E. V. Anisimov, ed., *Petr Velikii. Vospominaniia. Dnevnikovye zapisi. Anekdoty* (SPb., 1993), 156–7.

117. *Sbornik Mukhanova*, 616 (17 June 1722).

118. LOI, f. 270, d. 97, l. 322 (22 Mar. 1721) and l. 421 (1 May 1721).

119. Ibid., d. 103, l. 191 (9 Feb. 1723, from Moscow).

120. Announcement of birth: *PSZ*, 3: no. 1365, pp. 53–4. On celebrations, see above, p. 13.

121. Pogodin, 'Petr Pervyi', 41.

122. See P. Bushkovitch. 'Aristocratic Faction and the Opposition to Peter the Great', *Forschungen zur osteuropäischen Geschichte*, 50 (1995), 80–120.

123. *The Tryal of the Czarewitz Alexis Petrowitz, who was Condemn'd at Petersbourg, on the 25th of June, 1718* (London, 1725), 95. This work includes declarations and letters from 1714 onwards. See also the collection of documents and articles *Nepotrebnyi syn. Delo Tsarevicha Alekseia Petrovicha* (SPb., 1996).

124. F. J. Strahlenberg, *Zapiski kapitana Filippa Ioganna Stralenberga ob istorii i geografii Rossiiskoi imperii Petra Velikogo*, trans. and ed. Iu. Bespiatykh et al. (M&L, 1985), 1: 146. There were rumours that Alexis was dragged around by his hair by Menshikov: M. S. Anderson, *Peter the Great*, (London, 1978), 147.

125. P. P. Pekarsky, *Nauka i literatura v Rossii pri Petre Velikom*, (SPb., 1862), 1: 64–5. Viktorov, *Opisanie*, 2: 470–1, notes that Neugebauer had an interpreter. The tutor's salary was 50 roubles. He first came to Russia in 1699 in the retinue of General Carlowitz (from the elector of Saxony).

126. Pekarsky, *Nauka*, 1: 65. He later turned up as an aide to Charles XII in Constantinople: see B. Sumner, *Peter the Great and the Ottoman Empire* (Oxford, 1949), 38.

127. N. Ustrialov, *Istoriia tsarstvovaniia Petra Velikogo*, vol. 6. (SPb., 1869), *prilozhenie*, 304–5.

128. Cornelius de Bruyn, *Travels into Muscovy, Persia and Part of the East Indies* (London, 1737), 1: 48. Of course, one would need to know the source of Bruyn's 'briefing' on Alexis.

129. Pekarsky, *Nauka*, 1: 137–8. See *Biblioteka Petra I. Ukazatel'-spravochnik*, comp. E. I. Bobrova (L, 1978), item 811, p. 97: 'Instruction vortnach sich Seiner Hoheit des Durchläuchtigsten Tzarevitz Hofmeister in der Information richten soll' (1703–4).

130. P. Petschauer, 'In Search of Competent Aides: Heinrich von Huyssen and

Peter the Great', *JGO*, 24 (1978), 486–7.

131. S. P. Luppov, *Kniga v Rossii v pervoi chetverti XVIII v.* (L, 1973), 180–4.

132. *Alfavit sobranny, rifmami slozhenny, ot sviatykh pisanii, iz drevnikh rechenii* (1705), in Grebeniuk, 56–7.

133. 'Osm blazhenstva evangelskie' (1709), in Grebeniuk, 60–2.

134. *PiB*, 3: 990 (Ludwig de Sheper, 22 Oct. 1705).

135. *PiB*, 7(i): 24–5 (Feb. 1708).

136. C. Peterson, *Peter the Great's Administrative and Judicial Reforms* (Stockholm, 1979), 55 (in 1708).

137. *Pisma tsarevicha* , 1: 19.

138. Ibid., 22–3. Peter's letter of 17 Jan. ordering Alexis to form five new regiments from young nobles in hiding, and from gentry in towns, training them as rank and file: *PiB*, 7(i): 8.

139. *PiB*, 7(i): 77, 417.

140. Grund, 131–2.

141. *PiB*, 7(i): 451 (19 Mar.).

142. *PiB*, 8: 20 (10 July 1708).

143. Ibid., 89.

144. Ibid., 131 (14 Sept.), 275 (6 Nov.), 314 (18 Nov.).

145. Ibid., 133.

146. Ibid., 323, 991.

147. Ibid., 358 (19 Dec. 1708).

148. *PSZ*, 4: no. 2220, p. 440 (Jan. 1709).

149. *PiB*, 9: 442–3 (23 Oct. 1709).

150. Ibid., 1327 (19 Dec. 1709).

151. See Grund, 131.

152. Such connections were used: e.g. in May 1712 Peter wrote to Charlotte asking her to provide recommendations and introductions for his envoy in Vienna, *PiB*, 12(i): 221.

153. *PiB*, 10: 281.

154. Ibid., 422–3 (5 Dec. 1710, Peter to Alexis); *PiB*, 11(ii): 202–10.

155. *PiB*, 11(ii): 123 (10 Sept. 1711), plus letters on same theme to Augustus and Duke Anton-Ulrich (124–5).

156. Ibid., 133 (17 Sept. 1711).

157. Ibid., 170 (14 Oct. 1711) .

158. Ibid., 191–3 (18 Oct. 1711); *PiB*, 12(i): 92 (25 Feb. 1712).

159. M. S. Anderson, 'Peter the Great', 268.

160. 'On the topic of my illnesses, I have to report that neither is any better; it is flowing [a discharge?] more than

before, all day, and heavier': *Pisma tsarevicha*, 10 (31 May 1707). Reply in *PiB*, 9: 162.

161. *Tryal of the Czarewitz*, 5.

162. Weber, 1: 44.

163. Ibid., 105.

164. *Tryal of the Czarewitz*, 10.

165. Ustrialov, *Istoriia*, vol. 6, *prilozhenie*, 346–8: 'Luchshe bud' chuzhoi dobryi, nezhe svoi nepotrebnyi.'

166. See Weber, 1: 107–8, on Charlotte's sufferings. She died on 21 Oct. See V. Ger'e, 'Kronprintsessa Sharlotta, nevestka Petra Velikogo. 1707–1715, po eia neizdannym pis'mam', *Vestnik Evropy*, 3/5 (1872), 19–62.

167. Ustrialov, *Istoriia*, vol. 6, *prilozhenie*, 348–9.

168. Ibid., 349–50.

169. *Tryal of the Czarewitz*, 42.

170. Ia. Gordin, 'Delo tsarevicha Alekseia ili tiazhba o tsene reform', *Zvezda*, 1991, no. 11, 140.

171. V. S. Bobylev, *Vneshniaia politika Rossii epokhi Petra I* (M, 1990), 105.

172. Ustrialov, *Istoriia*, 6: 388–9.

173. Ibid., 411. On his relationship with Afrosinia, including their letters, see M. McLeod Gilchrist, 'Aleksei Petrovich and Afrosin'ia Fedorovna', *Slavonica*, 1 (1994), 47–66 and 2 (1995/6), 61–4.

174. Texts in Ustrialov, *Istoriia*, 6: 442–4, *PSZ*, 5: no. 3151; *ZA*, 164–9, 169–70.

175. Weber, 1: 201.

176. See reports by Pleyer in *SIRIO*, 34: 320.

177. Efimov, 'Evdokiia Lopukhina', 146–7.

178. Esipov, *Tsaritsa Evdokia*, 6.

179. Ibid., 20.

180. Ibid., 25–8; Efimov, 'Evdokiia Lopukhina', 148–9.

181. *Tryal of the Czarewitz*, 46, 64, 92.

182. Ustrialov, *Istoriia*, 6, *prilozhenie*, 240.

183. See *Tryal of the Czarewitz*, for the English version.

184. See discussion in K. Pereladov, 'Konchina avgusteishego kolodnika', *Rodina*, 1994, no. 9, 39–42. Cabbage leaves were prescribed for the wounds.

185. *Tryal of the Czarewitz*, 74.

186. Ibid., 91.

187. O. F. Kozlov, 'Delo tsarevicha Alekseia', *VI* (1969), no. 9, 220.

188. *Russkaia starina*, 1905, pp. 410–16; V.

Ulanov, 'Oppozitsiia Petru Velikomu', in *Tri Veka* (M, 1912), 80.

189. Quoted in Pereladov, 'Konchina', 41–2. See also the testimony of a Dutch carpenter working in the fortress that Alexis's head was partly covered and his neck bound up, suggesting blows to the head. No source is given.

190. Quoted in Kozlov, 'Delo tsarevicha Alekseia', 214.

191. Weber, 1: 229–31. See below on the new law of succession.

192. See below, pp. 458–9.

193. J. Cracraft, 'Opposition to Peter the Great', in *Imperial Russia 1700–1917. State. Society. Opposition. Essays in Honor of Marc Raeff* (De Kalb, Ill., 1988), 28.

194. Esipov, *Tsaritsa Evdokiia*, 23.

195. Clause 5: *ZA*, 176.

196. 23 Dec. 1721: *ZA*, 173–4; *PSZ*, 6: no. 3869, p. 467; no. 3882, pp. 481–3 (18 Jan. 1722).

197. LOI, f. 270, d. 101, l. 120 (17 May 1722, to the German Tseiker).

198. Manifesto depriving Alexis of the succession, 3 Feb. 1718: *ZA*, 164. See the English translation in *The Prerogative of Primogeniture ... Written on the Occasion of the Czar of Muscovy's Reasons in his late Manifesto for the Disinheritance of his Eldest Son, from the Succession to the Crown* (London, 1718), a good example of Petrine foreign publicity.

199. *Prerogative*, 9–10.

200. *ZA*, 164.

201. *PiB*, 10: 161–2 (between 2 and 10 June 1710).

202. A contract was agreed on 10 June 1710 in St Petersburg (*PSZ*, 4: no. 2272, pp. 494–7). The duke signed on 13 July (NS), and Peter and Anna ratified the contract on 29 Aug. (*PiB*, 10: 311–16).

203. *ZA*, 162 (n.d.). Conceivably these instructions could have been for Ekaterina Ioannovna.

204. Juel, 3: 33 (11 Nov.). The service was conducted by Feodosy Ianovsky, the tsar's confessor.

205. For a description of the wedding, see above, p. 279.

206. 'Reskripty i ukazy', 5. Juel, who described the duke as 'very young,

handsome, well-brought up and charming' (3: 18), notes that the duke was already ill when he left St Petersburg from the effect of excessive drinking and 'unpleasantness' suffered in St Petersburg, especially at the hands of Menshikov (114).

207. *PiB*, 12(I): 168 (12 Apr. 1712, letter from Peter to the Senate instructing them to make arrangements). See also *PiB*, 11: 243 (21 May 1711, letter from Peter to Tsaritsa Praskovia asking whether rumours that Anna is pregnant are true).

208. Duke Ernst-Ludwig of Sachsen-Meining: *PiB*, 13(i): 165–8 (19 May 1713). Margrave Karl of Brandenburg-Sweden in 1723 (a contract was even drawn up): *PSZ*, 7: no. 4403, pp. 192–4 (27 Dec. 1723); see also LOI, f. 270, d. 103, ll. 501–2. (16 May 1723).

209. See, e.g., *Pis'ma russkikh gosudarei*, 2: 30–4; 39–40 (15 May 1719).

210. Bergholz, 1724, p. 23 (he met her just before Catherine's coronation).

211. Semevsky, *Tsaritsa Praskov'ia*, 69. See *PSZ*, 5: no. 2984.

212. See analysis in H. Bagger, 'The Role of the Baltic in Russian Foreign Policy 1721–1773', in H. Ragsdale, ed., *Imperial Russian Foreign Policy* (Cambridge, 1993), 44–6.

213. He died in 1730, she in 1731. See report by Campredon of the punishment of Peter's orderly Vasily for 'facilitating' the relationship ('a favorisé le commerce amoureux de la princesse ... et M. Mamonoff'), *SIRIO*, 52: 324 (21 Oct. 1724).

214. *PZh*, 1724, p. 24. See letter to Bruce, LOI, f. 270, d. 107, l. 468 (17 Nov. 1724), with reference to a contract (*zgovor*) and exchange of rings and asking him to draw up a plan of ceremonies. There is a description in Campredon, *SIRIO*, 52: 357–9.

215. *PZh*, 1725, pp. 47–53.

216. H-F. de Bassewitz, 'Zapiski grafa Bassevicha, sluzhashchie k poiasneniiu nekotorykh sobytii iz vremeni tsarstvovaniia Petra Velikogo (1713–1725)', *Russkii arkhiv*, 3 (1865), 133.

217. Bergholz, 1724, p. 75.

218. Ibid., 56.

219. Ibid., 78.
220. LOI, f. 270, d. 97, ll. 435–6 (May 1721).
221. *SIRIO*, 40: 324 (13 Mar. 1723 (NS)).
222. LOI, f. 270, d. 106, l. 115 (16 Jan. 1724): 'zelo b my zhelaem chtob sei zhenikh nam ziatem byl'.
223. Duc de Liria, 'Pis'ma o Rossii v Ispaniiu', *Osmnadtsatyi vek*, vol. 2 (M, 1869), 39. Liria thought that Elizabeth might have poisoned her.
224. Ibid., 82, 152.
225. Ulanov, 'Oppozitsiia', 81.

CHAPTER 13: FRIENDS AND HELPERS

1. *PiB*: 12(i): 36 (2 Aug. 1712, Peter to Catherine).
2. 'cherez edinoe tokmo svoe rukovozhdenie': *ZA*, 157–8.
3. C. Whitworth, *An Account of Russia as it was in the Year 1710. Rossiia v nachale XVIII veka. Sochineniia Ch. Uitvorta* (M&L, 1988), 57–8.
4. Saxon envoy, *SIRIO*, 3: 366: (i.e., Iaguzhinsky and Osterman).
5. Peter's words, reported by Whitworth on 18 Jan. 1708: *SIRIO*, 39: 448.
6. N. Ustrialov, *Istoriia tsarstvovaniia Petra Velikogo* (SPb., 1869), vol. 6, *prilozhenie*, 346 ff.
7. See P. Bushkovitch, 'Aristocratic Faction and the Opposition to Peter the Great', *Forschungen zur Osteuropäischen Geschichte*, 50 (1995), 80–120.
8. J. P. LeDonne, *Absolutism and Ruling Class. The Formation of the Russian Political Order 1700–1825* (Oxford, 1991), 64.
9. N. B. Golikova, *Politicheskie protsessy pri Petre I* (M, 1957), 71.
10. I. A. Zheliabuzhsky, 'Zapiski', in A. B. Bogdanov, ed., *Rossiia pri tsarevne Sof'e i Petre I*, (M, 1990), 258, 381.
11. Kurakin, 375, 388, 370.
12. LeDonne, *Absolutism*, 66.
13. Korb, 1: 155, 2: 146.
14. Kurakin, 375–6.
15. LOI, f. 270, d. 101, l. 62 (11 May 1722).
16. Ibid., l. 20 (8 May 1722).
17. Juel, 3: 5. On his origins, see P. Dol-

gorukov, *Mémoires* (Geneva, 1867), 1: 6. See *PiB*, 2: no. 451, p. 91.
18. *Sbornik*, 2: 12. *Arkhiv kniazia F. A. Kurakina* (SPb., 1891), 1: 124. I am indebted to Dr Dmitry Serov for the latter reference. F. J. Strahlenberg, *Zapiski kapitana Filippa Ioganna Stralenberga ob istorii i geografii Rossiiskoi imperii Petra Velikogo*, trans. and ed. Iu. Bespiatykh et al. (M&L, 1985), 1: 92, also repeats the rumour that Alexis's mistress was married off to Musin-Pushkin, who gave the child his name.
19. V. N. Berkh, *Zhizneopisanie gen.-adm. F. M. Apraksina* (SPb., 1825).
20. *PiB*, 11: 194, 478.
21. Berkh, *Zhizneopisanie*, 42–3.
22. Grund, 136.
23. Berkh, *Zhizneopisanie*, 13 (9 Aug.).
24. *Petr Velikii, ego polkovodtsy i ministry* (M, 1848), 11–12.
25. *PiB*, 6: 3.
26. Bergholz, 1721, p. 84.
27. N. I. Pavlenko, *Petr Velikii* (M, 1990), 512.
28. Berkh, *Zhizneopisanie*, 46–8 (letters from abroad, 1717).
29. For further references, see L. A. J. Hughes, 'Russia in 1689. Court Politics in Foy de la Neuville's *Relation curieuse et nouvelle de Moscovie*', in Hughes, ed., *New Perspectives on Muscovite History* (London, 1993), 179–80.
30. See Strahlenberg, *Zapiski*, 156–7. I. I. Golikov, *Anekdoty, kasaiushchiesia do gosudaria imperatora Petra Velikogo*, in E. V. Anisimov, ed., *Petr Velikii. Vospominaniia. Dnevnikovye zapisi. Anekdoty* (SPb., 1993), 372–3. This is said to have happened when Peter was about fourteen. For a discussion, see Iu. Bespiatykh, 'Petr Velikii i more', in *Tezisy*, 11–13.
31. Kurakin, 376.
32. *PiB*, 3: 441 (10 Sept. 1705).
33. *PiB*, 9: 900.
34. His account of the rebellion of 1682 was a major contribution to the negative image of Sophia. See L. A. J. Hughes, *Sophia Regent of Russia 1657–1704* (New Haven, 1990), pp. 266–7.
35. Bantysh-Kamensky, 1: 46. R. Wortman, *The Development of a Russian*

Legal Consciousness (Chicago, 1976), 23–4, alleges quite wrongly that Peter 'raised' Matveev from a humble background. It was Matveev's father who was 'raised' by Tsar Alexis, becoming a boyar in 1671.

36. *SIRIO*, 39: 35. See Schoenebeck's engraving of his Moscow estate, with impressive gardens and pavilions: Kaliazina, illustrations 152–3.

37. Paying the bills for purchases, for example. See *Sbornik*, 1: 138 ff.

38. *PiB*, 10: 47–50.

39. Ibid., 511. On G. Golovkin and culture, see above, p. 290.

40. See Grund, 135.

41. O. G. Ageeva, 'Severnaia voina i iskusstvo graviury v Rossii petrovskogo vremeni', in *Russkaia kul'tura v usloviiakh inozemnykh nashestvii i voin X–nach. XX vv*, Pt 2 (M, 1990), 172.

42. On this trip, see M. Okenfuss, ed., *The Travel Diary of Peter Tolstoy* (De Kalb, Ill., 1987).

43. LOI, f. 270, d. 100, l. 302 (21 Mar. 1722).

44. See A. I. Zaozersky, 'Fel'dmarshal Sheremetev i pravitel'stvennaia sreda Petrovskogo vremeni', in *RPR*, 172–99.

45. B. P. Sheremetev, *Zapiski puteshestviia generala feldmarshala ... grafa B. P. Sheremeteva ... v evropeiskie gosudarstva* (M, 1773).

46. *PiB*, 8(i): 35–6, 312 (28 Jan. 1708).

47. *PiB*, 9: 770.

48. *PiB*, 10: 247 (23 July 1710).

49. *SIRIO*, 25: 329.

50. Zaozersky, 'Fel'dmarshal Sheremetev', 175.

51. S. Malinin, 'Ten' Leforta', *Moskovskii zhurnal*, 1991, no. 2, 64–70. On Lefort's papers, see A. Babkin, 'Pis'ma Frantsa i Petra Lefortov o "Velikom posol'stve"', *VI*, 1976, no. 4, 120–32.

52. Kurakin, 379. Lefort was forty-two when he died.

53. Malinin, 'Ten' Leforta', 70.

54. *Russkii Biograficheskii Slovar'*, 10 (1914), 352.

55. G. Herd, 'General Patrick Gordon of Auchleuchries—a Scot in Seventeenth-Century Russian Service' (Ph.D. thesis, Aberdeen, 1994).

56. For an account of Lefort's death and funeral and Peter's reaction, see Korb, 1: 267–8, 272.

57. E. A. Savel'eva, 'Biblioteka Ia. V. Briusa v sobranii BAN SSSR', in *Russkie biblioteki i ikh chitateli* (L, 1983), 123–34.

58. On the assembly's activities, see above, pp. 249–57.

59. *PiB*, 1: 48 (8 Sept. 1695).

60. *PiB*, 10: 221 (8 July 1710), 11(i): 243–4 (21 May 1711), *PiB*, 11(ii): 100 (22 Aug. 1711); *ZA*, 205; *PiB*, 11(ii): 10.

61. Juel, 3: 21–2 (31 Aug. 1710).

62. See above, pp. 98–100.

63. Kurakin, 378–9.

64. Korb, 1: 196.

65. Weber, 1: 5, 137.

66. Juel, 3: 130.

67. *PSZ*, 4: 1918, pp. 199–200 (25 Sept. 1702), specifies that all persons reporting such crimes were to be sent direct to the Preobrazhensky *prikaz* without preliminary questioning. See below, p. 126; Golikova, *Politicheskie*, 14–15, 20.

68. Weber, 1: 152–3.

69. *PiB*, 2: 248 (20 Sept. 1703); 3: 321 (19 Apr. 1705); 4: 18 (before 6 Jan. 1706). Co-ordination of uniform supplies was one of his special tasks: e.g., *PiB*, 9: 150 (10 Apr. 1709); 10: 419 (28 Nov. 1710).

70. Nartov, 37–41.

71. Grund, 61.

72. Kurakin, 386–7.

73. P. N. Miliukov, *Gos. khoziaistvo Rossii v pervoi chet. XVIII st. i reforma Petra Velikogo* (SPb., 1905), 100: 223 roubles in 1702, 700 in 1704.

74. S. F. Platonov, *Petr Velikii. Lichnost' i deiatel'nost'* (Paris, 1927), 123–4. See above, pp. 259–60.

75. *Petr Velikii, ego polkovodtsy i ministry*, 18.

76. D. Altbauer, 'The Diplomats of Peter the Great', *JGO*, 28 (1980), 11, 14.

77. Kurakin, 382.

78. He often signed his name '(I)egushinskoi'. A. A. Golombievsky, *Sotrudniki Petra Velikogo* (M, 1903), 3, describes Iaguzhinsky as half-Pole, half-Lithuanian.

79. Information in Juel, 3: 128.

80. See above, pp. 104–5.
81. Golombievsky, *Sotrudniki*, 15 (15 May 1722).
82. From a letter in the Senate archive, quoted by Golombievsky, *Sotrudniki*, 12. This did not stop Iaguzhinsky profiting from Shafirov's banishment. He received an island which had belonged to Shafirov and some of his servants: LOI, f. 270, d. 106, ll. 386, 389 (Feb. 1724).
83. Golombievsky, *Sotrudniki*, 17.
84. Bergholz, 1724–5, p. 91.
85. Golombievsky, *Sotrudniki*, 16.
86. H-F. de Bassewitz, 'Zapiski grafa Bassevicha, sluzhashchie k poiasneniiu nekotorykh sobytii iz vremeni tsarstvovaniia Petra Velikogo (1713–1725)', *Russkii arkhiv*, 3 (1865), 187; Golombievsky, *Sotrudniki*, 12.
87. Stählin, 84.
88. He survived to become a senator and a count in 1744—my thanks to D. O. Serov.
89. *Petr Velikii, ego polkovodtsy i ministry*, 43.
90. Ibid.
91. See above, p. 408.
92. Stählin, 114–15.
93. *Sbornik*, 2: 67. In June 1717 Tatishchev was paid back the tip he gave 'to the little girl who danced for His Majesty in Paris' and a musician who played on the harp, and the alms he gave to a Capuchin friar: ibid., 71.
94. LOI, f. 270, d. 103, l. 338.
95. Ibid., d. 107, l. 95 (23 May 1724).
96. V. V. Kvadri, *Svita Petra Velikogo* (SPb., 1902), 16–17.
97. Bergholz, 1721, pp. 56–7; 1724–5, p. 86. See also *Sbornik*, 2: 94, 111, 121: wages for 1722; *200-letie*, 253.
98. Kvadri, *Svita*, 15.
99. Strahlenberg, *Zapiski*, 118; Kvadri, *Svita*, 11.
100. Stählin, 79.
101. *Sbornik*, 2: 8 (entry for 12 Mar. 1716), 18 (1 Nov.), *et passim*.
102. Juel, 3: 128 (1/12 Mar. 1711).
103. Kvadri, *Svita, prilozhenie*, 25.
104. Stählin, no. 83, pp. 129–30; no. 86, pp. 134–5.
105. See entry on silk stockings, cravats and a hat bought for the chaplain in Piermont in June 1716: *Sbornik*, 2: 11, 12. *PZh*, 1720, p. 24.
106. *Sbornik*, 2: 22, *et passim*, 109 (24 June 1722), 111 (15 July 1722).
107. Ibid., 13.
108. Ibid., 68, *passim*. He was the great grandfather of the poet Pushkin, who wrote about him in the story 'The Negro of Peter the Great'.
109. *200-letie*, 72–3.
110. On the function of the Cabinet, see above. On Makarov's career, see N. I. Pavlenko, *Ptentsy gnezda petrova* (M, 1989), 246–325.
111. *200-letie*, 10.
112. Pavlenko, *Ptentsy*, 247.
113. *200-letie*, 14.
114. E. V. Anisimov, *The Reforms of Peter the Great. Progress through Coercion*, trans. J. Alexander (New York, 1993), 166–8.
115. Pavlenko, *Ptsentsy*, 262–80.
116. S. M. Ginsburg, 'Peter Shafiroff—Jewish Adviser to Peter the Great', *Judaism*, 22 (1973), 411. The anecdote is from Golikov, *Anekdoty*, quoted in Anisimov, ed., *Reforms*, 75.
117. Grund, 136.
118. D. Serov, 'Zametka o biografii P. P. Shafirova', *SGECRN*, 21 (1993), 57–63.
119. See numerous orders on the reallocation of Shafirov's property: e.g., his Moscow house went to Peter Tolstoy, all his wine was sent to the palace office and distributed to various officials, money invested abroad was allocated to Russian students abroad: LOI, f. 270, d. 103, ll. 292, 336–7, 517 (24 Feb., 13 Mar., 19 May 1723).
120. Duc de Liria, 'Pis'ma o Rossii v Ispaniiu', in *Osmnadtsatyi vek*, vol. 2 (M, 1869), 34.
121. S. Monas, 'Anton Divier and the Police of St Petersburg', in M. Halle et al., eds, *For Roman Jakobson. Essays on the Occasion of his Sixtieth Birthday* (The Hague, 1956), 361–6; Kvadri, *Svita, prilozhenie*, 22–4.
122. Bergholz, 94–5.
123. Stählin, 65.
124. P. Petschauer, 'In Search of Competent Aides: Heinrich von Huyssen and Peter the Great', *JGO*, 24 (1978), 481–502. See above pp. 403–5.

125. For the text of the journal, see 'Zhurnal gosudaria Petra I s 1695 po 1709' and 's 1709 po 1710', in F. Tumansky, *Sobranie raznykh vypisok.*
126. Petschauer, 'In Search', 499, 492.
127. See C. Peterson, *Peter the Great's Administrative and Judicial Reforms* (Stockholm, 1979), 70–81, 82–4, 89.
128. Weber, 1: 269.
129. V. N. Berkh, 'Zhizneopisanie gen.-leit. V. I. Gennina', *Gornyi zhurnal,* 1826, bk 4, 127 (22 Oct. 1723).
130. Ibid., 131–2, to A. V. Makarov.
131. J. Cracraft, 'Feofan Prokopovich', in Garrard, 75, and *idem, The Church Reform of Peter the Great* (London, 1971), 306.
132. Quoted in Cracraft, 'Feofan', 91. 'Slovo v nedeliu osmuiu nadesiat', skazannoe v Sankt"piterburkhe v tserkvi Zhivonachal'nyiia Troitsy, vo vremia prisutstviia ego ts. v. po dolgim stranstvii vozvrativshagosia', delivered 23 Oct. 1717, in Grebeniuk, 48–50; Prokopovich, 'Sermon on Royal Authority and Honour' (1718), in M. Raeff, ed., *Russian Intellectual History. An Anthology* (New York, 1966), 25.
133. Cracraft, 'Feofan', 93–4. Full text in Prokopovich, *Sochineniia,* and published version SPb., 1718: 'Slovo o vlasti i chesti tsarskoi'.
134. See above, pp. 95–6.
135. The year of his birth is based on information in Bergholz, who mentions that in Nov. 1723 Menshikov celebrated his fiftieth birthday. Russian studies of Menshikov include N. I. Pavlenko, *Aleksandr Danilovich Menshikov* (M, 1981), *idem, Poluderzhavnyi vlastelin* (M, 1991). There is nothing substantial in English.
136. Pavlenko, *Poluderzhavnyi vlastelin,* 23–4.
137. Ibid., 37; Kurakin, 389.
138. Nartov, 138. See also the Stählin anecdote in which Peter warns Menshikov, 'Alexander! Don't you forget who you were and how I made you what you are now': no. 97, p. 150.
139. A. Degtiarev and A. Lavrov, 'Baloven' bezrodnyi? Arkhivy raskryvaiut tainu Aleksandra Menshikova', *Nedelia* 31 (1991) 11.

140. Grund, 134.
141. J. Cracraft, ed., *For God and Peter the Great. The Works of Thomas Consett, 1723–1729* (Boulder, Colo., 1982), p. xxxiii.
142. Golombievsky, *Sotrudniki,* 53.
143. N. A. Baklanova, 'Velikoe posol'stvo za granitsei v 1697–1698 g.g.' in A. I. Andreev, ed., *Petr Velikii. Sbornik statei* (M&L, 1947), 47–8.
144. Korb, 2: 6.
145. Kurakin, 389.
146. Pavlenko, *Menshikov,* 16.
147. Golombievsky, *Sotrudniki,* 51.
148. Whitworth, *Account of Russia,* 64–5, emphasis added.
149. *Sbornik,* 1: 169 (13 Mar. 1699), refers to Menshikov as sergeant; Korb, 1: 259; Golombievsky, *Sotrudniki,* 63.
150. Quoted in ibid., 56.
151. Bergholz, 1725, p. 102.
152. *Mémoires secrets pour servir à l'histoire de la cour de Russie, sous les règnes de Pierre-le-Grand et de Catherine Ire. Rédigés et publiés pour la première fois, d'après les manuscrits originaux du Sieur de Villebois* (Paris, 1853), 149. A footnote expatiates on 'les habitudes vicieuses' among the Russians. This work, very hostile to Peter and his immediate successors, was published under the name of Villebois, but R. Minzloff (*Pierre le Grand dans la littérature étrangère* (SPb., 1872), 141–53) argues that he could not have been the author, naming instead Campredon, the first French diplomat accredited to St Petersburg (1721–8).
153. G. V. Esipov, 'Zhizneopisanie kniazia A. D. Menshikova', *Russkii arkhiv,* 1875, no. 7, 236. In both cases the reference was to 'bludnoe delo'. Esipov quotes these cases and makes no attempt to refute them.
154. D. Serov, 'Pervonachal'noe nakoplenie kapitala: tainy imperii kniazia Menshikova', *Russkaia Aziia,* 41/11 (1994), 3. Serov also points out that in the seventeenth century Russian homosexuals shaved, which could put the beard reforms in a new light.
155. *PiB,* 1: 331: German 'child of my heart'. According to Golombievsky, this letter included a hand-written note to 'miin

Sielenkind' (*Sotrudniki*, 58). Variations include (transcribed from Cyrillic) 'Mein Herz', 'Mein liebste Kamerad', 'Mein bezst frint', 'Mein gerts', 'bruder': *PiB*, 2: 126, 3: 94, 159, 321, *et passim*.

156. *PiB*, 2: 220–1 (17 July 1703).

157. *PiB*, 3: 700.

158. Ibid., 760, 772–3 (29 Mar.). See also *PiB*, 10: 105 (8–9 Apr., 1710 with Easter greetings).

159. *PiB*, 3: 789.

160. Ibid., 312 (13 Apr.): 'nikogda v rozni ne byval'.

161. Ibid., 342 (14 May 1705). Menshikov arrived in Moscow the day the letter was sent, and was able to report that 'through the mercy of Almighty God the tsar has been freed from his sickness': Esipov, 'Zhizneopisanie', 244.

162. *PiB*, 4: 184.

163. *PiB*, 7(i): 197. In June Peter sent him a copy of naval signals for his new rank (p. 212).

164. *PiB*, 9: 53.

165. Pavlenko, *Menshikov*, 48, 49, 54; Golombievsky, *Sotrudniki*, 80.

166. *PiB*, 7(i): 155 (8 May 1708), 11: 106 (2 Mar. 1711), 133 (6 Mar. 1711); Juel, 3: 10 (10 July 1710).

167. Golombievsky, *Sotrudniki*, 80, 86. Juel regards Menshikov's wish that the kings of Denmark, Prussia, and Poland act as godfathers to the boy as an example of Menshikov's pretentiousness. In the event, the king of Prussia sent a medal (Generosity) to the christening (3: 115–16, 117). A third son, Alexander, was born in 1714, surviving exile to die in 1764 (see Weber, 1: 8). There were also daughters: Maria (?–1729) and Alexandra (1712–36), the former the intended bride of Tsar Peter II.

168. *PiB*, 9: 88 (11 Feb. 1709).

169. *PiB*, 11: 61 (13 Feb. 1711).

170. *Shchukinskii sbornik*, vol. 9 (M, 1910), 154–5. The letters are dated 13 July, but there is no year; but it cannot have been earlier than 1711.

171. Golombievsky, *Sotrudniki*, 90.

172. Ibid., 61. (See remark allegedly made by Menshikov to the envoy of Hetman Mazepa, who wanted Anna for his nephew.)

173. Esipov, 'Zhizenopisanie', 247.

174. Ibid., 239. Esipov contrasts Menshikov's 'boasting' about his promotion with Peter's apparent modesty after receiving the same Order.

175. 'Tryumf Polskei muzy' by Daniil Gurchin, in Grebeniuk, 57–8.

176. *PiB*, 4: 442 (19 Nov. 1706).

177. 'Venets pobedy', in Grebeniuk, 204–7.

178. Ibid., 62–3.

179. Juel, 3: 21.

180. Ibid., 37.

181. Stählin, no. 98, pp. 150–1.

182. *PiB*, 11: 144–5.

183. Pavlenko, *Petr Velikii*, 338.

184. *PiB*, 11(ii): 232 (3 Nov. 1711).

185. Juel, 3: 135–6.

186. Grund, 128–9.

187. Golombievsky, *Sotrudniki*, 87, but not reflected in *PiB*, except in a letter to King Augustus of 2 Mar. asking him to report on Menshikov's behaviour (*PiB*, 12(i): 104).

188. Pavlenko, *Poluderzhavnyi vlastelin*, 165. See above, pp. 51–2.

189. 'Lavrea ili venets bezsmertnyia slavy', text by Ivan Kremenetsky, who lived in Menshikov's house: in Grebeniuk.

190. Golombievsky, *Sotrudniki*, 91.

191. K. Pereladov, 'Konchina avgusteishego kolodnika', *Rodina*, 1994, no. 9, 40.

192. Weber, 1: 247–8. Stählin, 53 (recounted by Osterman).

193. LOI, f. 270, d. 101, l. 283 (13 July 1722).

194. Ibid., d. 103, l. 298 (26 Feb. 1723).

195. N. V. Kaliazina, 'Materialy dlia ikonografii A. D. Menshikova (prizhiznennye portrety)', in G. I. Komelova, ed., *Kul'tura i iskusstvo petrovskogo vremeni* (L, 1977), 70–87.

196. All above, Golombievsky, *Sotrudniki*, 57–8.

197. Campredon, *SIRIO*, 40: 383.

198. D. Serov, 'Pervonachal'noe nakoplenie', 3. See the goblet produced at the Iamburkh glassworks with Menshikov's arms and the inscription 'Vivat Prince Alexander Danilovich': Kaliazina, illustration 184.

199. Serov, 'Pervonachal'noe nakoplenie', 3.

200. Berkh, *Zhizneopisanie ... Apraksina*, 107–12.

201. As S. P. Luppov points out (*Kniga v Rossii v pervoi chetverti XVIII v.* (L,

1973), 230), this figure, exceeding even Peter's library by eight times, is dubious.

202. S. Dolgova, 'O biblioteke A. D. Menshikova', in *Russkie biblioteki i ikh chitateli* (L, 1983), 87–104; *idem*, 'Knigoliub ili knigochei?', *Nedelia*, 26 (1983), 14.

203. See letter on the victory at Kalisz, with references *vivat* three times, 'this glorious victory' (*viktoriia*), 'such a battle' (*bataliia*): Golombievsky, *Sotrudniki*, 75, 52.

204. See A. Vucinich, *Science in Russian Culture. A History to 1860* (London, 1963), 66–7. Sir Isaac Newton sent the letter.

205. N. V. Kaliazina and I. V. Saverkina, 'Zhivopisnoe sobranie A. D. Menshikova', in *Russkaia kul'tura pervoi chetverti XVIII veka. Dvorets Menshikova. Sbornik nauchnykh trudov* (SPb., 1992), 54–61.

206. See above, pp. 245–6.

207. Esipov, 'Zhizneopisanie', 247.

208. Ibid., 234.

209. Golombievsky, *Sotrudniki*, 114.

210. P. V. Ovchinnikov, 'Krushenie "poluderzhavnogo vlastelina"', *VI*, 1970, no. 9, 87–104.

211. See their letters, *Russkii arkhiv*, 1865, pp. 309–12. Devier had the last laugh, albeit a brief one. After doing government service in Okhotsk, while still an exile, in 1743 his titles were restored, and he was reinstated by Elizabeth.

212. Juel, 3: 38.

213. 'Reskripty i ukazy Petra I k lifliandskim general-gubernatoram: Polonskomu, kn. Golitsynu i kn. Repninu', *Osmnadtsatyi vek. Istoricheskii sbornik izdannyi P. Bartenevym*, vol. 4 (1869), 76.

214. Juel, 2: 514.

215. Golombievsky, *Sotrudniki*, 13.

216. D. O. Serov in *Tezisy*, 48-50.

217. *PiB*, 6: 306.

218. Golombievsky, *Sotrudniki*, 76.

219. Zaozersky, 'Fel'dmarshal Sheremetev', 184–8.

220. *IPS*, 1: 123.

221. Ibid., 125.

222. See B. Sumner, *Peter the Great and the*

Emergence of Russia (London, 1958), 133.

223. Weber, 1: 58–9.

224. *PiB*, 2: 651–2. (11 Sept. 1703, from Voronezh, a reply to Peter's letter of 27 Aug.).

225. Ibid., p. 251 (26 Sept. 1703).

226. *Materialy dlia istorii russkogo flota*, vol. 6 (SPb., 1877), 6, 11.

227. *SIRIO*, 25: 340.

228. LOI, f. 270, d. 103, l. 13 (petition of 9 Jan. 1723).

229. *PiB*, 5: 313 (18 June 1707).

230. *PiB*, 3: 91.

231. In 1722 Quoted in Peterson, *Peter*, 329. See also Wortman, *Development*, 24; *ZA*, 382–4.

CHAPTER 14: RESPONSES

1. *PZh*, 1725, p. 3. *Opisanie poriadka derzhannogo pri progrebenii blazhennyia vysokoslavnyia i vernodostoineishiia pamiati vsepresvetleishago derzhavneishago Petra Velikago* (SPb., 1725, M, 1726), 33. According to A. L. Meyer, who did his research in the 1830s, the old Winter Palace and the room in which Peter died survived the various rebuildings on the site and remain incorporated in the Old Hermitage on the east bank of the Winter Canal: 'O starom zimnem dvortse i palate v koei skonchalsia gos. imperator Petr Velikii', *Vestnik Evropy*, 3/5 (1872), 1–18. See E. V. Anisimov's account of a visit to the room in *Rossiia bez Petra* (SPb., 1994), 13–14. The 'Leave all to …' story first appears in H-F. de Bassewitz, 'Zapiski grafa Bassevicha, sluzhashchie k poiasneniiu nekotorykh sobytii iz vremeni tsarstvovaniia Petra Velikogo (1713–1725)', *Russkii arkhiv*, 3 (1865), 259. (Voltaire later used it.) As Anisimov points out in *The Reforms of Peter the Great. Progress through Coercion*, trans. J. Alexander (New York, 1993) 268, Bassewitz's aim was evidently to persuade readers that Anna, the duke of Holstein's fiancée, was Peter's intended heir.

2. See letter to Menshikov, 28 Sept. 1724,

in which he mentions being ill: LOI, f. 270, d. 107, l. 271.

3. Stählin, no. 110, pp. 170–3: evidence of Dr Paulson.

4. Anisimov, *Reforms*, 267.

5. *SIRIO*, 52: 437 ff. The adjective used is *vénérien*.

6. LOI, f. 270, d. 109, l. 24. A German translation accompanied it.

7. Stählin, no. 111, pp. 174–5.

8. F. Prokopovich, *Sochineniia*, ed. I. P. Eremin (M&L, 1961), 126–9; quoted in translation in M. Raeff, ed., *Peter the Great Changes Russia* (Lexington, Ky. 1972), 39–43. This sermon appears to draw on the model of the Lutheran funeral oration. On Peter's funeral, see above, pp. 262–4. The long delay between death and burial was a result of the complex preparations for the lying in state and funeral procession.

9. I. G. Spassky and E. Shchukina, *Medals and Coins of the Age of Peter the Great* (L, 1974), no. 68.

10. V. K. Trediakovsky, *Izbrannye proizvedeniia* (M&L, 1963), 56–9.

11. Quoted in M. Cherniavsky, *Tsar and People: Studies in Russian Myths* (New York, 1961), 86.

12. E. Shmurlo, *Petr Velikii v otsenke sovremennikov i potomstva* (SPb., 1912), *primechaniia*, 39, which also quotes von der Burg's report from Amsterdam that Russian students 'wept inconsolably' at the news.

13. *Zapiski Ivana Ivanovicha Nepliueva (1693–1773)*, (SPb., 1893), 122.

14. *SIRIO*, 15: 252 (Mardefeld to Frederick I, in German); 52: 427 (Campredon to Louis XV, in French), both dated 10 Feb. The bulk of the reports detail the resolution of the succession to the throne. In a letter to the Comte de Morville, same date, Campredon gave a rather different account of the reaction to Peter's death: 'The affliction at his death is universal and one can say in truth that he is as missed in the tomb as he was feared and respected on his throne ... for the wisdom of his government and the continous care which he took to civilize (*civiliser*) his nation' (ibid., 437).

15. P. Kovalevsky, 'Petr Velikii i ego genii', *Dialog*, 1992, nos. 11–14, pp. 91–2.

16. Weber, 1: 80.

17. *SIRIO* 39: 124–6 (13/24 June).

18. *PSZ*, 7: no. 4224, pp. 64–5 (14 May 1723); no. 4228, p. 67 (20 May 1723).

19. J. G. Vockerodt, *Rossiia pri Petre Velikom po rukopisnomu izvestiiu Ioanna Gottgil'fa Fokkerodta* (SPb., 1874) (*Chteniia*, 1874, bk 2, pt 4), 107.

20. *DPPS*, 5(ii): no. 808 (July 1715).

21. Anisimov, *Reforms*, 162–3.

22. N. D. Beliaev, 'Russkoe obshchestva pri Petre Velikom', *Den'* (1864), no. 2, p. 5.

23. See *PSZ*, 4: nos 1947, 1960, 1978, 2090, 2098, etc. Oberfiscal Nesterov claimed to have tracked down more than a thousand military servitors: B. B. Kafengauz and N. I. Pavlenko, eds, *Ocherki istorii SSSR. Period feodalizma. Rossiia v pervoi chetverti XVIII v.* (M, 1954), 198.

24. W. C. Fuller, *Strategy and Power in Russia 1600–1914* (New York, 1992), 47.

25. *PSZ*, 2: 87 (22 Sept. 1702).

26. *DPPS*, 6(i): no. 552, pp. 492–3 (6 June 1716).

27. Kafengauz and Pavlenko, eds, *Ocherki*, 176–7. Pososhkov find this estimate 'conservative' (192).

28. *PSZ*, 7: no. 4343, pp. 145–7 (5 Nov.).

29. Ibid., no. 4181, pp. 29–30 (8 Mar., 1723); no. 4489, pp. 275–6 (3 Apr., 1724).

30. See M. Perrie, *The Image of Ivan the Terrible in Russian Folklore* (Cambridge, 1987); *idem*, 'The Popular Image of Ivan the Terrible', *SEER*, 56 (1978), 275–86.

31. See analysis in R. O. Crummey, *The Old Believers and the World of Antichrist. The Vyg Community and the Russian State 1694-1855* (Madison, 1970), 6–8.

32. N. B. Golikova, *Politicheskie protsessy pri Petre I* (M, 1957), p. 133.

33. Ibid., 130.

34. N. A. Baklanova, ed. 'Tetradi startsa Avramiia', *Istoricheskii arkhiv*, 7 (1951), 143–55. See also S. M. Solov'ev, *Istorii Rossii s drevneishikh vremen*, bk 7 (M, 1962); Golikova, *Politicheskie protsessy*, 78–86.

35. Golikova, *Politicheskie protsessy*, 131–2: examples from the late 1690s.

36. Shmurlo, *Petr Velikii, primechaniia*, 1.

37. M. Semevsky, *Slovo i delo, 1700–1725. Ocherki i rasskazy iz russkoi istorii XVIII veka* (SPb., 1884), 66: case of Marim'iana Polozova; Golikova, *Politicheskie protsessy*, 149–51, 181, lists several cases of monks and priests spreading this story.

38. Golikova, *Politicheskie protsessy*, 169.

39. Shmurlo, *Petr Velikii*, 25.

40. On computations of Peter's spiritual consanguinity with Catherine, see above, p. 397, and Golikova, *Politicheskie protsessy* 147.

41. G. V. Esipov, *Raskol'nich'i dela XVIII stoletiia* (SPb., 1861), 1: 134–55.

42. Ibid., 159–64.

43. Ibid., 2: 168.

44. Ibid., 169–70.

45. Golikova, *Politicheskie protsessy*, 213.

46. Shmurlo, *Petr Velikii, primechaniia*, 2; G. L. Freeze, *The Russian Levites: Parish Clergy in the Eighteenth Century* (Cambridge, Mass., 1977), 42. See the testimony of Archimandrite Alexander in 1720: Peter 'adopted the practice of the fallen Western Roman Church by eating meat during fasts and on Wednesdays and Fridays': Esipov, *Raskol'nich'i*, 1: 148.

47. Golikova, *Politicheskie protsessy*, 146–7.

48. Ibid., 135–45. See also an account of the case in F. J. Strahlenberg, attesting to its notoriety: *Zapiski kapitana Filippa Ioganna Stralenberga ob istorii i geografii Rossiiskoi imperii Petra Velikogo*, trans. and ed. Iu. Bespiatykh et al. (M&L, 1985), 1: 136–7.

49. From the notebooks of Grigory Talitsky, 1700: Esipov, *Raskol'nich'i*, 1: 59–84.

50. *Znameniia prishestviia Antikhristova i konchiny veka* (M, 1704). J. Cracraft, 'Opposition to Peter the Great', in *Imperial Russia 1700–1917. State. Society. Opposition. Essays in Honor of Marc Raeff* (De Kalb, Ill., 1988), 31.

51. J. Cracraft, *The Church Reform of Peter the Great* (London, 1971), 295; *PSZ*, 6: no. 4012, p. 686 (17 May 1722).

52. J. E. Clay, 'God's People in the Early 18th Century. The Uglich Affair of 1717', *CMRS*, 26 (1985), 107.

53. Shmurlo, *Petr Velikii, primechaniia*, 27. In 1799, when some Old Believers agreed to pray for Paul I in return for some concession, they insisted on using the title Tsar, not Emperor: Cherniavsky, *Tsar and People*, 95.

54. All above from Shmurlo, *Petr Velikii*, 24–6.

55. Testimony of P. Ivanov, 1700: Golikova, *Politicheskie protsessy*, 145–6.

56. Esipov, *Raskol'nich'i*, 2: 64.

57. B. A. Uspensky, 'Historia sub specie Semioticae', in H. K. Baran, ed., *Semiotics and Structuralism. Readings from the Soviet Union* (New York, 1976), 67–8.

58. Ibid., 69. Shmurlo, *Petr Velikii, primechaniia*, 22.

59. See Bergholz, 1724–5, 39. The annointing with holy oil, however, was performed by Prokopovich.

60. 2 Thessalonians, 2: 2–4.

61. S. Benson, 'The Role of Western Political Thought in Petrine Russia', *CASS*, 8 (1974), 254.

62. Ibid., 258, 260.

63. Gordon, 6: 96^{r-v} (4 Mar. 1697).

64. I. A. Zheliabuzhsky, 'Zapiski', in A. B. Bogdanov, ed., *Rossiia pri tsarevne Sof'e I Petre I* (M, 1990), 257. See Soloviev, 142–8; Golikova, *Politicheskie protsessy*, 87–101.

65. Golikova, *Politicheskie protsessy*, 160–1.

66. Stählin, 84; Semevsky, *Slovo i delo*, 337–8.

67. *PSZ*, 6: no. 3984, pp. 666–7 (28 Apr. 1722).

68. The most fundamental account is still M. M. Bogoslovsky, *Petr I. Materialy dlia biografii*, vol. 3 (1946) and 4 (1948), ch. 32; Golikova, *Politicheskie protsessy*, 101–22; Soloviev, 161–83, and L. A. J. Hughes, *Sophia, Regent of Russia 1657–1704* (New Haven, 1990), 249–55.

69. Golikova, *Politicheskie protsessy*, 118–19.

70. Ibid. See also *idem, Astrakhanskoe vosstanie 1705–6* (M, 1975).

71. Strahlenberg, *Zapiski*, 117, 138.

72. A. V. Chernov, 'Astrakhanskoe vosstanie 1705–1706 gg.', *IZ*, 64 (1959), 196; Golikova, *Politicheskie protsessy*, 226, 246–7.

73. Ibid., 233. 'Idols' were taken to Terek as

74. Esipov, *Raskol'nich'i*, 2: 103.

75. Chernov, 'Astrakhanskoe vosstanie', 205; Golikova, *Politicheskie protsessy*, 233.

76. Fuller, *Strategy*, 58, n. 74.

77. PRO SP 91/4 pt II, 20 Feb./3 Mar. 1706, f. 112 (Feb. 1706, to Secretary of State); *SIRIO*, 39: 248–9.

78. PiB, 3: 450 (21 Sept. 1705).

79. Chernov, 'Astrakhanskoe vosstanie', 212–13. See Peter's letter (4 Mar. 1706) telling Sheremetev not to undertake any hostilities against the town 'except in an emergency'.

80. Esipov, *Raskol'nich'i*, 2: 103; Chernov, 'Astrakhanskoe vosstanie', 216.

81. There is a useful synthesis in P. Avrich, *Russian Rebels 1600–1800* (New York, 1972), 147–77. Registered Cossacks were those who were listed in government service registers.

82. See Weber, I: 142.

83. *PiB*, 7(i): 600–2 (22 Mar. 1708). Avrich, *Russian Rebels*, 156.

84. *PiB*, 7(i): 131–2.

85. Ibid., 167 (15 May 1708).

86. *PiB*, 8: 36–7 (23 July 1708, to V. V. Dolgoruky).

87. Ibid., 41 (26 July 1708).

88. Avrich, *Russian Rebels*, 173.

89. *SIRIO*, 39: 466.

90. B. Sumner, *Peter the Great and the Ottoman Empire* (Oxford, 1949), 52–3.

91. *PSZ*, 6: no. 3565, pp. 179–81 (8 Apr.).

92. Ibid., no. 3686, pp. 267–72 (14 Dec. 1720): instructions to the *voevoda* in Belgorod.

93. LOI, f. 270, d. 100, ll. 489–90 (27 Apr. 1722). To the Senate: *PSZ*, 6: no. 3989 (29 Apr.).

94. LOI, f. 270, d. 101, l. 84^{r-v} (16 May 1722). Ukrainians were also exempted from the prescribed punishment of the knout for flight across the Polish border, and from certain taxes and duties (*miloserduia my o vernykh svoikh podannykh Malorossiiskogo naroda*): *PSZ*, 7: no. 4181, pp. 29–30 (8 Mar. 1723); no. 4196, 43–4 (16 Apr. 1723).

95. *PSZ*, 7: no. 4252, p. 85 (23 June).

96. See LOI, f. 270, d. 104, ll. 312, 322–4:

on flight into the Crimea; d. 106, ll. 135–6 (18 Jan. 1724): on the rebels Polubotok and Orlyk.

97. Nartov, 100–1, 103. On the career, trial, and death of Alexis, see above, pp. 402–11.

98. 'Tsarevich Aleksei Petrovich po svidetel'stvam vnov' otkrytim', *Chteniia*, 1861, bk 3, pt 2, p. 34. See also Ia. Gordin, 'Delo tsarevicha Alekseia ili tiazhba o tsene reform', *Zvezda*, 1991, no. 11, 131.

99. *Pis'ma russkikh gosudarei i drugikh osob tsarskogo semeistva*, vol. 3 (M, 1862), 56. In Aug. 1716 Alexis returned two books to Ioanniky because they were in Latin and he wanted them in Slavonic (p. 60). Gordin, 'Delo tsarevicha', 125, argues that Alexis's Moscow links were weakened, if not broken, after his marriage and transfer to St Petersburg.

100. O. F. Kozlov, 'Delo tsarevicha Alekseia', *VI*, 1969, no. 9, 217.

101. Gordin, 'Delo tsarevicha', 135.

102. Ibid., 130: 'Kakoi ia umnyi, um prostor liubit, a u tebia emu tesno.'

103. Ibid., 131.

104. Ibid., 134–5. In 1730 both these men supported the plan to limit the new empress's powers.

105. Ibid., 139.

106. Ibid., 140.

107. Golikova, *Politicheskie protsessy*, 177–9; A. Lushin, 'Nizhegorodskie samozvantsy', *Rossiia molodaia*, 1991, no. 7, 72–5.

108. *SIRIO*, 3: 387–8.

109. *200-letie*, appendix II, pp. 45–58 (RGADA, f. 9, op. I, kn. 33, ll. 179–93).

110. See above, p. 152.

111. *200-letie*, appendix II, p. 57.

112. I do not intend to retread the ground covered so thoroughly by N. Riasanovsky in *The Image of Peter the Great in Russian History and Thought* (Oxford, 1985). Other useful sources for the historiography of the Petrine era include C. E. Black, 'The Reforms of Peter the Great', in Black, ed., *Rewriting Russian History* (New York, 1962), 232–59. J. Cracraft, 'The Tercentenary of Peter the

Great in Russia', *CASS*, 8 (1974),
319–26; *idem*, 'More about Peter the
Great', *CASS*, 14 (1980), 535–44.
K. Rasmussen, 'Catherine II and
the Image of Peter I', *SR*, 37 (1978),
57–69; X. Gasiorowska, *The Image of
Peter the Great in Russian Fiction*
(Madison, 1979); H. Bagger, *Reformy
Petra Velikogo* (M, 1985); L. A. J.
Hughes, 'Peter I and the Fall of
Communism', *Irish Slavonic Studies*, 17
(1996), 1–18.

113. Grebeniuk, 74–7: speech on the
birthday of Peter Petrovich.

114. Weber, 1: preface.

115. *SIRIO*, 15: 313–14 (13 Mar. 1723).

116. *Zapiski . . . Nepliueva*, 122.

117. See Riasanovsky, *Image*, 166–73.

118. Strahlenberg, *Zapiski*, 104 ff.

119. Michael Lomonosov, 'Panegyric to
Peter I' (1755), in M. Raeff, ed.,
*Russian Intellectual History. An
Anthology* (New York, 1966), 42–8.

120. Speech of Archbishop Ambrosy at the
coronation in 1742, quoted in R.
Wortman, *Scenarios of Power. Myth
and Ceremony in Russian Monarchy*,
vol. 1 (Princeton, 1995), 102.

121. Catherine II, *Instruction* (London,
1768), art. 4.

122. See D. Ransel, in H. Ragsdale, ed.,
*Paul I: A Reassessment of his Life and
Reign* (Pittsburg, 1979), 4–11; Wort-
man, *Scenarios of Power*, 181.

123. See D. Lieven, *Nicholas II. Emperor of
all the Russias* (London, 1993), 113.

124. See Wortman, *Scenarios of Power*, 107.

125. S. A. Mezen, 'Osveshchenie deiatel'
nosti Petra I s pozitsii konservativnogo
dvorianstva. (M. M. Shcherbatova)',
Istoriograficheskii sbornik, 13 (1987),
40–60.

126. See Prince M. Shcherbatov, 'Petition
of the City of Moscow on being
relegated to Oblivion', in Raeff, ed.,
Russian Intellectual History, 49–60.

127. R. Pipes, ed., *Karamzin's Memoir on
Ancient and Modern Russia* (Cambridge, Mass., 1959), 124.

128. '. . .vyskochit' za ramki otstalosti': 'The
Industrialization of the Country and
Right Tendencies in the Communist
Party', speech to plenum of Central
Committee, 19 Nov. 1928.

129. A. P. Spunde, 'Ocherk ekonomicheskoi istorii russkoi burzhuazii', *Nauka
i zhizn'*, 1988, no. 1, p. 79. (Spunde's
work was suppressed during his lifetime.)

130. Ibid., 82.

131. Ia. E. Vodarsky, 'Petr I', *VI*, 1993, no. 6
77.

132. A. Lanshchikov, 'Imperator-bol'shevik',
Rodina, 1992, no. 3, 86–92.

133. This summary is based on E. V.
Anisimov, *Vremia petrovskikh reform*
(L, 1989), trans. J. Alexander as *The
Reforms of Peter the Great*, and a digest
of views in *idem*, 'Petr Velikii: rozhdenie imperii', *VI*, 1989, no. 7, pp.
3–21.

134. E. V. Anisimov, 'Progress through
Violence from Peter the Great to
Lenin and Stalin', *Russian History*, 17
(1990), 409.

135. Gordin, 'Delo tsarevicha', 122.

136. A. N. Medushevsky, *Utverzhdeniia
absoliutizma v Rossii* (M, 1994), cites
Mehmet Ali, Nasser, and Ataturk.
None of these examples, of course,
corresponds particularly closely to the
'Petrine model'. One can also find
examples of the *rejection* of Western
forms, in twentieth-century Iran or
Afghanistan.

137. See discussion in S. F. Platonov, *Petr
Velikii. Lichnost' i deiatel'nost'* (Paris,
1927), 33–4; P. Miliukov, *Gos. khoziaistvo Rossii v pervoi chet. XVIII st. i
reforma Petra Velikogo* (SPb., 1905),
and *idem*, *Ocherki po istorii russkoi
kul'tury*, pt 3 (SPb., 1903). Miliukov
takes the fleet as a glaring example of
Petrine wastefulness.

138. A. J. Rieber, 'Politics and Technology
in Eighteenth-Century Russia', *Science
in Context*, 8 (1995), 342–3.

139. A. B. Kamensky, *Arkhivnoe delo v
Rossii XVIII veka: Istoriko-kul'turnyi
aspekt* (M, 1991), 23–4.

140. *The Justice of the Monarch's Right*
(1722), trans. and ed. A. Lentin, *Peter
the Great: His Law on the Imperial
Succession. An Official Commentary*
(Oxford, 1996), 279.

141. Stählin, 47–9; related by P. I.
Iaguzhinsky.

142. *PiB*, 1: 225 (17 Dec. 1697, Peter to

Romodanovsky, referring to a boat built on Lake Pereiaslav, which Peter ordered transported to the Volga).

143. *PSZ*, 4: no. 1749, p. 4 (2 Feb. 1700).

144. LOI, f. 270, d. 104, l. 531 (Dec. 1723).

145. GPB OR, f. 1003 (Voskresensky), no. 11, ll. 560–5 (30 Aug. 1724, extract from long letter to Peter).

146. K. S. Aksakov, 'On the Present State of Russia' (1855), in L. Jay Oliva, ed., *Peter the Great. Great Lives Observed* (Englewood Cliffs, NJ, 1970), 152.

147. N. I. Ulianov, 'Petrovskie reformy (K voprosu o meste Petra I v otechestvennoi istorii)', *Sanktpeterburgskaia panorama*, 1992, no. 5, 4.

148. Ibid., 17.

149. P. Chaadaev, *First Philosophical Letter* (1829), quoted in R. McNally, ed., *The Major Works of Peter Chaadaev* (Notre Dame, Ind., 1969), 38. See also R. McNally, 'Chaadaev's Evaluation of Peter the Great', *SR*, 23(1964), 31–44.

150. See the argument in Rieber, 'Politics', 363–4.

151. Beliaev, 'Russkoe obshchestvo', no. 2, 3.

152. S. M. Soloviev, *History of Russia*, vol. 25: *Rebellion and Reform. Fedor and Sophia 1682–1689*, trans. L. Hughes (Gulf Breeze, Fla., 1989), 1.

153. *Dialog*, 1992, no. 3, 101.

154. '"Nel'zya dolgo khodit' mezhdu razvalinami". Rasskaz o tom kak Petr I reformiroval rossiiskuiu armiiu', *Armiia*, 1992, nos 11–12, 70–2.

155. Deborah Adelman, *The Children of Perestroika. Moscow Teenagers Talk about their Lives and Future* (New York, 1992), 143.

156. The anniversary edition of the journal *Rodina* (1996, nos 7–8) takes the story from Peter's time to current discussions of the old question 'Does Russia need a fleet?'

157. E. A. Riazanov, 16 Nov. I am grateful to Sir Roderic Braithwaite for sending me the text of this interview.

158. Packet in my possession.

159. F. Prokopovich, *Kratkaia povest' o smerti Petra Velikogo Imperatora i Samoderzhtsa Vserossiiskogo* (SPb., 1831), 29–30. See picture in V. Iu. Matveev, 'K istorii vozniknoveniia i razvitiia siuzheta "Petr I, vysekaiushchii statuiu Rossii', in *Kul'tura i iskusstvo Rossii XVIII veka. Novye materialy i issledovaniia* (L, 1981), 35.

Bibliography

The Bibliography is a selective listing of primary sources and secondary literature on Peter the Great and the Petrine era. It does not include all works cited in the notes or works of a general nature consulted during the writing of this book. Major sources are listed in full in the Abbreviations.

Ageeva, O. G., 'Assamblei petrovskogo vremeni v russkoi dorevoliutsionnoi istoriografii', in *Istoriograficheskie i istoricheskie problemy russkoi kul'tury* (M, 1983), 47–66.

——, 'Kul'tovye pamiatniki Moskvy i Peterburga Petrovskogo vremeni', in *Problemy russkoi khudozhestvennoi kul'tury XVIII veka. Tesizy dokladov* (M, 1991), 21–3.

——, *Obshchestvennaia i kul'turnaia zhizn' Peterburga I chetverti XVIII v.* (M, 1991).

——, 'Severnaia voina i iskusstvo graviury v Rossii petrovskogo vremeni', in *Russkaia kul'tura v usloviiakh inozemnykh nashestvii i voin X–nach. XX vv*, pt 2 (M, 1990), 151–78.

Al'bom 200-letnego iubileia Imperatora Petra Velikogo, 1672–1872 (SPb., 1872).

Alekseeva, M. A., *Feierverki i illiuminatsii v grafike XVIII veka. Katalog vystavki* (L, 1978).

——, *Graviura petrovskogo vremeni* (L, 1990).

——, 'Graviury "khoromnogo stroeniia" pervoi chetverti XVIII veka: sotsiologicheskii mif i sotsial'naia real'nost'', in *Problemy russkoi khudozhestvennoi kul'tury XVIII veka* (M, 1991), 53–5.

——, 'Zhanr konkliuzii v russkom iskusstve kontsa XVII–nachala XVIII v.', in T. V. Alekseeva, ed., *Russkoe iskusstvo barokko* (M, 1977), 7–29.

——, comp., *Aleksei Fedorovich Zubov. Katalog vystavki* (L, 1988).

Alexander, J. T., *Bubonic Plague in Early Modern Russia: Public Health and Urban Disaster* (Baltimore, 1980).

——, 'Comparing Two Greats: Peter I and Catherine II', in *WOR*, 43–50.

——, 'Medical Developments in Petrine Russia', *CASS*, 8 (1974), 198–222.

Altbauer, D., 'The Diplomats of Peter the Great', *JGO*, 28 (1980), 1–16.

Anderson, M. S., *Europe in the Eighteenth Century*, 3rd edn. (London, 1987).

——, *Peter the Great* (London, 1978), 2nd edn (London, 1995).

——, 'Peter the Great: Imperial Revolutionary?', in A. G. Dickens, ed., *The Courts of Europe: Politics, Patronage and Royalty, 1400–1800* (London, 1977), 263–82.

Androsov, S. O., 'Ivan Nikitin i Ioann Gotfrid Tannauer. Neizdannye dokumenty', *Voprosy iskusstvoznaniia*, 10 (1997), 510–15.

————, 'O portrete Petra I raboty Ivana Nikitina iz Ekaterininskogo dvortsa-muzeia', in *Kuchumovskie chteniia. Sbornik materialov nauchnoi konferentsii, posviashchennoi pamiati A. M. Kuchumova (1913–1994)*, (M, 1995), 9–14.

————, 'Petr I v Venetsii', *VI*, 1995, no. 3, 129–35.

Anisimov, E. V., *Gosudarstvennye preobrazovaniia i samoderzhavie Petra Velikogo v pervoi chetverti XVIII veka* (SPb., 1997).

————, 'The Imperial Heritage of Peter the Great in the Foreign Policy of his Early Successors', in H. Ragsdale, ed., *Imperial Russian Foreign Policy* (Cambridge, 1993), 21–35.

————, 'Otets otechestva', *Zvezda*, 1989, no.11, 101–18.

————, 'Petr Velikii: rozhdenie imperii', *VI*, 1989, no. 7, 3–21.

————, *Podatnaia reforma Petra I* (L, 1982).

————, 'Progress through Violence from Peter the Great to Lenin and Stalin', *Russian History*, 17 (1990), 409–18.

————, *The Reforms of Peter the Great. Progress through Coercion*, trans. J. Alexander (New York, 1993).

————, 'Remarks on the Fiscal Policy of Russian Absolutism during the First Quarter of the Eighteenth Century', *Soviet Studies in History*, 28 (1989), 10–32.

————, *Rossiia bez Petra* (SPb., 1994).

————. 'Sotsial'nye effekty podatnoi politiki russkogo absoliutizma v pervoi chetverti XVIII veka', in *Nauka i kul'tura Rossii XVIII v. Sbornik statei* (L, 1984), 188–200.

————, *Vremia petrovskikh reform* (L, 1989).

————, ed., *Petr Velikii. Vospominaniia. Dnevnikovye zapisi. Anekdoty* (SPb., 1993).

Aristov, N. 'Pervonachal'noe obrazovanie Petra Velikogo', *Russkii arkhiv*, 13/8 (1875), 470–88.

Arkhipov, N. I., and Raskin, A. G., *Bartolomeo Karlo Rastrelli* (L&M, 1964).

Arkhiv kniazia F. A. Kurakina, 10 vols (SPb., 1890–1903).

Arkhiv pravitel'stvuiushchago senata. T. I. Opis' imennym vysochaishim ukazam i poveleniiam tsarstvovaniia imp. Petra Velikogo 1704–1725 (SPb., 1872).

Artamonov, V. A., *Rossiia i Rech' Pospolitaia posle Poltavskoi pobedy (1709–1714)* (M, 1990).

Avrich, P., *Russian Rebels 1600–1800* (New York, 1972).

Babkin, A., 'Pis'ma Frantsa i Petra Lefortov o "Velikom posol'stve" ', *VI*, 1976, no. 4, 120–32.

Baehr, S., 'From History to National Myth: *Translatio imperii* in 18th-Century Russia', *RR*, 37 (1978), 1–13.

————, *The Paradise Myth in Eighteenth-Century Russia* (Stanford, Calif., 1991).

Bagger, H., *Reformy Petra Velikogo* (M, 1985).

————, 'The Role of the Baltic in Russian Foreign Policy 1721–1773', in H. Ragsdale, ed., *Imperial Russian Foreign Policy* (Cambridge, 1993), 36–55.

Baklanova, N. A., ed., 'Tetradi startsa Avraamiia', *Istoricheskii arkhiv*, 7 (1951), 143–55.

————, 'Velikoe posol'stvo za granitsei v 1697–1698 gg', in A. I. Andreev, ed., *Petr Velikii. Sbornik statei* (M&L, 1947), 47–8.

Banks, J., *A New History of the Life and Reign of Czar Peter the Great, Emperor of All Russia, and Father of his Country* (London, 1740).

Baron, S. H., 'Henri Lavie and the Failed Campaign to Expand Franco-Russian Commercial Relations (1712–1723)', *Forschungen zur osteuropäischen Geschichte*, 50 (1995), 29–50.

————, 'Shipbuilding and Seafaring in 16th-Century Russia', in D. C. Waugh, ed., *Essays in Honor of A. A. Zimin* (Columbus, Oh., 1983), 102–29.

Barsov, E. V., 'Novye razyskaniia o pervom periode russkogo teatra', *Chteniia*, 1882, bk 3, 8–10.

Bassewitz, H-F. de, 'Eclaircissemens, sur plusieurs faits, relatifs au regne de Pierre le Grand, extraits en l'an 1761 à la requisition d'un savant des papiers du feu Comte Henningue Frederic de Bassewitz, conseiller privé de L. M. Imperiales romaine et russienne, chevalier de St. André', *Magazin für die neue Historie und Geographie*, 9 (1775), 283–380.

————, 'Zapiski grafa Bassevicha, sluzhashchie k poiasneniiu nekotorykh sobytii iz vremeni tsarstvovaniia Petra Velikogo (1713–1725)', *Russkii arkhiv*, 3 (1865), 93–274.

Beliaev, N. D., 'Russkoe obshchestva pri Petre Velikom', *Den'* (1864), no. 2, pp. 3–6; no. 3, pp. 3–6.

————, 'Shtraf za russkoe plat'e pri Petre Velikom', *Chteniia*, 1899, bk 1, 1–6.

Beliaev, O., *Dukh Petra Velikogo* (SPb., 1798).

————, *Kabinet Petra Velikogo*, 3 vols (SPb., 1800).

Belov, M. I. ed., *Voprosy geografii petrovskogo vremeni. Sb. statei* (L, 1975).

Benson, S., 'The Role of Western Political Thought in Petrine Russia', *CASS*, 8 (1974), 254–73.

Berezovsky, N. Iu., et al., *Rossiiskii imperatorskii flot, 1696–1917. Voenno-istoricheskii spravochnik* (M, 1993).

Berkh, V. N., *Sobranie pisem imp. Petra I k raznym litsam*, vol. 1: 1704–15 (SPb., 1829); vol. 2: 1704–15 (replies) (SPb., 1829); vol. 3: 1716–24 (SPb., 1830); vol. 4: 1716–24 (replies) (SPb., 1830).

————, *Zhizneopisanie adm. I. M. Golovina* (SPb., 1825).

————, *Zhizneopisanie adm. K. I. Kriuisa* (SPb., 1825).

————, *Zhizneopisanie gen.- adm. F. M. Apraksina* (SPb., 1825).

————, 'Zhizneopisanie gen.-leit. V. I. Gennina', *Gornyi zhurnal*, 1826, bk 1, 51–129, bk 4, 83–132, bk 5, 87–149.

————, *Zhizneopisanie pervykh rossiiskikh admiralov* (SPb., 1831–3).

Beskrovny, L. G. 'Voennye shkoly v pervoi polovine XVIII v.', *IZ*, 42 (1953), 285–300.

Bespiatykh, Iu., ed., *Peterburg Petra I v inostrannykh opisaniiakh* (L, 1991).

Billington, J., *The Icon and the Axe* (New York, 1970).

Bissonnette, G., 'Peter the Great and the Church as an Educational Institution', in J. S. Curtiss, ed., *Essays in Russian and Soviet History in Honor of G. T. Robinson* (Leiden, 1963), 3–19.

————, 'Pufendorf and the Church Reform of Peter the Great' (Ph.D. thesis, Columbia University, 1962). .

————, 'The Church Reform of Peter the Great as a Problem of Soviet Historiography', *Etudes Slaves et Est-Européans*, 1 (1956–7), 146–57, 195–207.

Black, C. E., 'The Reforms of Peter the Great', in C. E. Black, ed., *Rewriting Russian History* (New York, 1962), 232–59

Black, J. L. *Citizens for the Fatherland. Education, Educators and Pedagogical Ideals in 18th-Century Russia* (Boulder, Colo., and New York, 1979).

Blamberg, M. O., 'The Publicists of Peter the Great' (Ph.D. thesis, Indiana University, 1974).

Blanc, S., 'The Economic Policy of Peter the Great' (1962), in repr. W. L. Blackwell, ed., *Russian Economic Development from Peter the Great to Stalin* (New York, 1974), 21–49.

Blanchard, I., 'Eighteenth-Century Russian Economic Growth: State Enterprise or Peasant Endeavour?', in *Studies in Economic and Social History: Discussion Papers*, nos 95–1 (University of Edinburgh, 1995).

Bobrova, E. I., comp., *Biblioteka Petra I. Ukazatel'-spravochnik* (L, 1978).

Bobylev, V. S., *Vneshniaia politika Rossii epokhi Petra I* (M, 1990).

Bochkarev, V. N., 'Dvorianstvo i krestianstvo pri Petre Velikom', *Tri veka*, 3 (M, 1912), 198–219.

Bogdanov, A. P., 'Silv'estr Medvedev', *VI*, 1988, no. 2, 84–98.

Bogdanov, G., *Istoricheskoe, geograficheskoe i topograficheskoe opisanie Sanktpeterburga, ot nachala zavedeniia ego s 1703 po 1751 god* (SPb., 1779).

Bogoiavlensky, S. K., *Moskovskii teatr pri tsariakh Aleksee i Petre* (M, 1914).

Bogoslovsky, M. M., *Byt i nravy russkogo dvorianstva v pervoi pol. XVIII v.* (SPb., 1918).

———, *Oblastnaia reforma Petra Velikogo. Provintsiia 1719–27* (M, 1902).

———, 'Petr I v Anglii v 1698', *Institut istorii. Moskva. Trudy*, vol. 1 (1926), 393–432.

———, *Petr I. Materialy dlia biografii*, 5 vols (M, 1940–8).

———, 'Petr Velikii (opyt kharakteristiki)', in *Tri veka*, vol. 3 (M, 1912), 15–33.

Bogotyrev, I. V., 'Petrovskie suda botovogo tipa', *Sudostroenie*, 1988, no. 6, 56–8.

Bolotova, G., *Letnii sad. Leningrad* (L, 1981).

Borisov, V., 'O brakosochitanii Petra Velikogo s Ekaterinoi Alekseevnoi', *Chteniia*, 1861, bk 3, 196–9.

Bozherianov, N., *Sankt-Peterburg v Petrovo vremia* (SPb., 1903).

Brown, P. B., 'Early Modern Russian Bureaucracy. The Evolution of the Chancellery System from Ivan III to Peter the Great, 1478–1717' (Ph.D. thesis, University of Chicago, 1978).

Brown, W. E. *A History of Eighteenth-Century Russian Literature* (Ann Arbor, 1980).

Bruce, P. H., *Memoirs of Peter Henry Bruce Esq. A Military Officer in the Service of Prussia, Russia and Great Britain* (London, 1782).

Bruyn, Cornelius de, *Travels into Muscovy, Persia, and Part of the East Indies; Containing an Accurate Description of what is most Remarkable in those Countries*, 2 vols (London, 1737).

———, *Voyages de Corneille le Brun par la Moscovie, en Perse, et aux Indes Orientales* (Amsterdam, 1718).

Buganov, V., *Petr Velikii; lichnost' i epokha* (M, 1990).

Bulgakovsky, D. G., *Domik Petra Velikogo i ego sviatynia v S. Peterburge* (SPb., 1891).

Bulygin, I. A., *Monastyrskie krest'iane Rossii v pervoi chet. XVIII v.* (M, 1977).

Burke, P., *Popular Culture in Early Modern Europe* (London, 1978/88).

Bushkovitch, P., 'Aristocratic Faction and the Opposition to Peter the Great: The 1690s', *Forschungen zur osteuropäischen Geschichte*, 50 (1995), 80–120.

Buslaev, F., 'Drevne-russkaia boroda', in *Drevne-russkaia literatura i iskusstvo*, vol. 2 (SPb., 1861), 216–37.

Bychkov, A. F., 'O svad'be imp. Petra Velikogo s Ekaterinoi Alekseevnoi', *Drevniaia i Novaia Rossiia*, 3 (1877), 323–4.

———, ed., *Pis'ma Petra Velikogo, khraniashchiesia v imp. Publ. biblioteke* (SPb., 1872).

Bykova, T. A., and Gurevich, M. M., *Opisanie izdanii, napechatannykh kirillitsei (1689-ianvar' 1725)* (M, 1958).

———, eds, *Opisanie izdanii grazhdanskoi pechati. 1708–ianv. 1725 gg. Dopolnenie i prilozheniia* (L, 1972).

Castle, Terry, *Masquerade and Civilization: The Carnivalesque in Eighteenth-Century English Culture and Fiction* (Stanford, Calif., 1986).

Chaev, N. S., *Bulavinskoe vosstanie (1707–1708 gg.)* (M, 1935).

Chechot, I. D., 'Korabl' i flot v portretakh Petra I. Ritoricheskaia kul'tura i osobennosti estetiki russkogo korablia pervoi chetverti XVIII veka', in *Otechestvennoe i zarubezhnoe iskusstvo XVIII veka* (L, 1986), 54–82.

Cherniavsky, M., 'The Old Believers and the New Religion', *SR,* 25 (1966), 1–39.

———, *Tsar and People: Studies in Russian Myths* (New York, 1961).

Chernov, A. V., 'Astrakhanskoe vosstanie 1705–1706 gg.', *IZ,* 64 (1959), 186–216.

———, *Gosudarstvennye uchrezhdeniia Rossii v XVIII v.* (M, 1960).

Chernyshev, G. P., 'Zapiski', *Russkaia starina,* 5/6 (1872), 791–802.

Chernysheva, A. V., 'K voprosu o sushchestvovanii "uchenoi druzhiny"', *Vestnik Moskovskogo universiteta. Seriia 7. Filosofiia,* 1989, no. 6, 40–3.

Clay, J. E., 'God's People in the Early 18th Century. The Uglich Affair of 1717', *CMRS,* 26 (1985), 69–124.

Clements, B., ed., *Russia's Women. Accommodation, Resistance, Transformation* (Berkeley, 1991).

Cracraft, J., *The Church Reform of Peter the Great* (London, 1971).

———, 'Did Feofan Prokopovich Really Write *Pravda Voli Monarshei?*', *SR,* 40 (1981), 173–93.

———, 'Feofan Prokopovich', in Garrard, 75–105.

———, 'Opposition to Peter the Great', in *Imperial Russia 1700–1917. State. Society. Opposition. Essays in Honor of Marc Raeff* (De Kalb, Ill., 1988), 22–36.

———, *The Petrine Revolution in Russian Architecture* (Chicago, 1988).

———, *The Petrine Revolution in Russian Imagery* (Chicago, 1997).

———, 'Some Dreams of Peter the Great', *CASS,* 8 (1974), 173–97.

———, 'The Tercentenary of Peter the Great in Russia', *CASS,* 8 (1974), 319–26.

———, ed., *For God and Peter the Great. The Works of Thomas Consett, 1723–1729* (Boulder, Colo., 1982).

Cross, A. G. 'The Bung College or British Monastery in Petrine Russia', *SGECRN,* 12 (1984), 4–14.

———, *'By the Banks of the Neva'. Chapters from the Lives and Careers of the British in Eighteenth-Century Russia* (Cambridge, 1996).

———, *'By the Banks of the Thames'. Russians in 18th-Century Britain* (Cambridge, 1980).

———, 'Petrus Britannicus': The Image of Peter the Great in 18th-Century Britain', in *WOR,* 3–10.

———, *The Russian Theme in English Literature from the Sixteenth Century to 1980: An Introductory Survey and a Bibliography* (Oxford, 1985).

———, e.d. *Russia in the Reign of Peter the Great. Old and New Perspectives* (Cambridge, 1998).

Crummey, R. O., *Aristocrats and Servitors: The Boyar Elite in Russia, 1613–1689* (Princeton, 1983).

———, *The Old Believers and the World of Antichrist. The Vyg Community and the Russian State 1694–1855* (Madison, 1970).

Danilov, M. V., *Zapiski Artillerii Maiora Mikhaila Vasil'evicha Danilova, napisannye im v 1771* (M, 1842).

Davies, N., *God's Playground. A History of Poland,* vol. 1 (Oxford, 1981).

Deane, J., *History of the Russian Fleet during the Reign of Peter the Great* (London, 1899).

Degtiarev, A., and Lavrov, A., 'Baloven' bezrodnyi? Arkhivy raskryvaiut tainu Aleksandra Menshikova', *Nedelia*, 31 (1991), 11.

Delo o pozhitkakh gosudaryni Natalii Alekseevny (M, 1914).

Dolgorukov, P., *Mémoires*, vol. 1 (Geneva, 1867).

Dolgova, S., 'Knigoliub ili knigochei?', *Nedelia*, 26 (1983), 14.

————, 'O biblioteke A. D. Menshikova', in *Russkie biblioteki i ikh chitateli* (L, 1983), 87–104.

Dolskaya, O., 'From Titov to Teplov: The Origins of the Russian Art Song', in *WOR*, 197–213.

Donnelly, A., 'Peter the Great and Central Asia', *CS P*, 17 (1975), 202–18.

Dopolneniia k tomu III dvortsovykh razriadov (SPb., 1854).

Duffy, C. *Russia's Way to the West: The Origins and Nature of Russian Military Power* (London, 1981).

Efimov, S. V., 'Evdokiia Lopukhina—posledniaia russkaia tsaritsa XVII veka', in *Srednevekovaia Rus'. Sbornik nauchnykh statei para. 65-letiiu so dnia rozhdeniia professora R. G. Skrynnikova* (SPb., 1995), 136–65.

————, ed., *Avtografy Petra Velikogo: katalog* (SPb., 1995).

Eigentliche Beschreibung der an der Spitz des Ost-See neuerbauteten Russischen Residenz Stadt St. Petersburg (Frankfurt & Leipzig, 1718).

Elagin, S., *Materialy dlia istorii russkogo flota* (SPb., 1866).

Englund, P., *The Battle of Poltava. The Birth of the Russian Empire* (London, 1992).

Epifanov, P. P., 'Voinskii ustav Petra Velikogo', in A. I. Andreev, ed., *Petr Velikii. Sbornik statei* (M&L, 1947), 167–213.

Eroshkin, N. P., *Istoriia gos. uchrezhdenii dorevoliutsionnoi Rossii* (M, 1983).

Esipov, G. V., *Liudi starogo veka* (SPb., 1860).

————, *Raskol'nich'i dela XVIII stoletiia* , 2 vols (SPb., 1861).

————, *Tsaritsa Evdokiia Feodorovna* (M, 1862).

————, 'Zhizneopisanie kniazia A. D. Menshikova', *Russkii arkhiv*, 1875, no.7, 233–47.

Evangulova, O. S., 'Portret petrovskogo vremeni i problemy skhodstva', *Vestnik MGU. Seriia 8. Istoriia*, 1979, no. 5, 69–82.

————, 'K probleme stilia v iskusstve petrovskogo vremeni', *Vestnik MGU. Seriia 8. Istoriia*, 1974, no. 3, 67–84.

Exacter Relation von der . . . neu erbauten Festung und Stadt St. Petersburg . . . von H.G. (Leipzig, 1713).

Farrell, D. E., 'Some Early Russian Woodcuts in the Context of the Schism', in *WOR*, 185–96.

Feigina, S. A., *Alandskii kongress. Vneshniaia politika Rossii v kontse severnoi voiny* (M, 1959).

Flerovskaia, M. A., 'Navigatskaia shkola', *VI*, 1973, no. 10, 215–19.

Flier, M., 'Breaking the Code: The Image of the Tsar in the Muscovite Palm Sunday Ritual', in M. Flier, and D. Rowland, eds, *Medieval Russian Culture*, vol. 2 (Berkeley & London, 1994), 213–42.

Freeze, G. L., *The Russian Levites: Parish Clergy in the Eighteenth Century* (Cambridge, Mass., 1977).

Fuller, W. C., *Strategy and Power in Russia 1600–1914* (New York, 1992).

Gasiorowska, X., *The Image of Peter the Great in Russian Fiction* (Madison, 1979).

Gavrishchik, V. V., *Voennye reformy Petra I v otechestvennoi istoriografii (1917–1991) gg.*, diss. abstract (M, 1993).

Gerasimova, Iu. U., 'Aria dlia Petra Velikogo', *Nedelia*, 1966, no. 16, 5.

———, 'Vospominaniia Filippo Balatri. Novyi inostrannyi istochnik po istorii Petrovskoi Rossii (1698–1701)', *Zapiski otdela rukopisei*, 27 (1965), 164–90.

Ger'e, V., 'Kronprintsessa Sharlotta, nevestka Petra Velikogo. 1707–1715, po eia neizdannym pis'mam', *Vestnik Evropy*, 3/5 (1872), 19–62.

———, *Sbornik pisem memorialov Leibnitsa, otnosiashchikhsia k Rossii i Petru Velikomu* (SPb., 1873).

Gerschenkron, A., 'Russian Mercantilism', in *Europe in the Russian Mirror* (Cambridge, 1970), 69–96.

Gilchrist, M. M., 'Aleksei Petrovich and Afrosin'ia Fedorovna', *Slavonica*, 1 (1994), 47–66, and 2 (1995/6), 61–4.

Ginsburg, S. M. 'Peter Shafiroff – Jewish Adviser to Peter the Great', *Judaism*, 22 (1973), 409–17.

Glebov, P., 'Izvestie o pervykh voennykh shkolakh, uchrezhdennykh v tsarstvovanii Petra Velikogo', *Otechestvennye zapiski*, 44 (1846),

Golikov, I. I., *Anekdoty, kasaiushchiesia do gosudaria imperatora Petra Velikogo*, in E. Anisimov, ed., *Petr Velikii. Vospominaniia. Dnevnikovye zapisi. Anekdoty* (SPb., 1993).

———, *Deianiia Petra Velikogo, mudrogo preobrazitelia Rossii, sobraniiye iz dostovernykh istochnikov i raspolozhennye po godam*, 12 vols (M, 1788–9).

———, *Dopolneniia k deianiam Petra Velikogo*, 18 vols (M, 1790–7); 2nd ed., 15 vols (M, 1837–43).

Golikova, N. B., *Astrakhanskoe vosstanie 1705–6* (M, 1975).

———, *Politicheskie protsessy pri Petre I* (M, 1957).

Golombievsky, A. A., *Sotrudniki Petra Velikogo* (M, 1903).

Golovin, V. V., 'Zapiski bednoi i suetnoi zhizni chelovecheskoi', in *Rodoslovnaia Golovinykh vladel'tsev sela Novospaskogo* (M, 1847), 44–57.

Gordin, Ia., 'Delo tsarevicha Alekseia ili tiazhba o tsene reform', *Zvezda*, 1991, no. 11, 120–43.

Gordon, P., Original of diary, in Rossiiskii Gosudarstvennyi Voenno-Istoricheskii Arkhiv, f. 846, op. 15. ed. khr. 1–7.

———, *Passages from the Diary of General Patrick Gordon of Auchleuchries, A.D. 1635–A.D. 1699* (Aberdeen, 1859).

———, *Tagebuch des Generals Patrick Gordon, während seiner Kriegsdienste unter den Schweden und Polen vom Jahre 1655 bis 1661, und seines Aufenthaltes in Russland vom Jahre 1661 bis 1699*, ed. M. A. Obolenski and M. C. Posselt, 3 vols (M&Leipzig, 1849).

Gorlé, F., 'Les Sanctions en droit pénal russe sous Pierre le Grand', *Slavica Gandensia*, 13 (1986), 355–61.

———, 'Quelques Aspects du droit pénal russe sous Pierre le Grand', *Slavica Gandensia*, 12 (1985), 99–105.

Grabar', I, ed., *Istoriia russkogo iskusstva*, vol. 5 (M, 1960).

Gradova, B. A. 'Rukopisnye memuary petrovskogo vremeni', in *Issledovanie pamiatnikov pismennoi kul'tury v sobraniiakh i arkhivakh otdela rukopisei* (L, 1987).

Grebeniuk, V. P., 'Publichnye zrelishcha petrovskogo vremeni i ikh sviaz' s teatrom', in *Novye cherty v russkoi literature i iskusstve (XVII-nach. XVIII v.)* (M, 1976), 32–50.

Haigh, B. 'Design for a Medical Service: Peter the Great's Admiralty Regulations (1722)', *Medical History*, 19 (1975), 129–46.

Hans, N., 'The Moscow School of Mathematics and Navigation (1701)', *SEER*, 29 (1951), 532–6.

Hartley, J., 'England Enjoys the "Spectacle of a Northern Barbarian". The Reception of Peter I and Alexander I in England', in *WOR*, 11–18.

Hatton, R., *Charles XII of Sweden* (London, 1968).

Hellie, R., 'Material Culture and Identity in Late Medieval and Early Modern Russia' (unpub. seminar paper, UCLA, Mar. 1994).

———, 'The Petrine Army: Continuity, Change, Impact', *CASS*, 8 (1974), 237–53.

———, *Slavery in Russia, 1450–1725* (Chicago, 1982).

Herd, G., 'General Patrick Gordon of Auchleuchries – a Scot in Seventeenth-Century Russian Service' (Ph.D thesis, Aberdeen, 1994).

Hittle, J. M., *The Service City. State and Townsmen in Russia, 1600–1800* (Cambridge, Mass., 1979).

Hughes, L. A. J., ' "Ambitious and Daring above her Sex": Tsarevna Sophia Alekseevna (1657–1704) in Foreigners' Accounts', *Oxford Slavonic Papers*, 21 (1988), 65–89.

———, 'Between Two Worlds: Tsarevna Natal'ia Alekseevna and the "Emancipation" of Petrine Women', in *WOR*, 29–36.

———, 'Did Peter the Great Abolish the Palm Sunday Ceremony?', *SGECRN*, 24 (1996), 62–5.

———, 'German Specialists in Petrine Russia', in R. Bartlett and K. Schönwälder, eds, *The German Lands and Eastern Europe. Essays in their Historical, Political and Cultural Relations* (forthcoming).

———, 'The Moscow Armoury and Innovations in 17th-Century Muscovite Art', *CASS*, 13 (1979), 204–23.

———, 'A Note on the Children of Peter the Great', *SGECRN*, 21 (1993), 10–16.

———, 'Peter den store – ett karaktärsporträtt', *Historisk Tidskrift för Finland*, 81 (1996), 378–408.

———, 'Peter the Great and the Fall of Communism', *Irish Slavonic Studies*, 17 (1996), 1–18.

———, 'Peter the Great's Two Weddings: Changing Images of Women in a Transitional Age', in R. Marsh, ed., *Women in Russia and Ukraine*, (Cambridge, 1996), 31–44.

———, 'Russia in 1689. Court Politics in Foy de la Neuville's *Relation curieuse et nouvelle de Moscovie*', in L. Hughes, ed., *New Perspectives on Muscovite History. Selected Papers from the Fourth World Congress for Soviet and East European Studies, Harrogate 1990* (London, 1993), 177–87.

———, 'Russia's First Architectural Books: A Chapter in Peter the Great's Cultural Revolution', in C. Cooke, ed., *Russian Avant-Garde Art and Architecture* (London, 1983), 4–13.

———, 'Sofia Alekseevna and the Moscow Rebellion of 1682', *SEER*, 63 (1985), 518–39.

———, 'Sophia, "Autocrat of all the Russias": Titles, Ritual and Eulogy in the Regency of Sophia Alekseevna (1682–89)', *CSP*, 28 (1986), 266–86.

———, *Sophia Regent of Russia 1657–1704* (New Haven, 1990).

———, 'Strel'tsy', *MERSH*, 37 (1984), 205–10.

———, 'V. T. Postnikov's 1687 Mission to London', *SEER*, 68 (1990), 447–60.

Iakovlev, A. A. 'Karmannyi zhurnal Iakovleva', *Otechestvennye zapiski*, 20/54 (1824), 74–91; 23/63 (1824), 85–102.

Iasiukov, M., ' "Nel'zia dolgo khodit' mezhdu razvalinami". Rasskaz o tom, kak Petr I reformiroval rossiiskuiu armiiu', *Armiia*, 1992, nos 11/12, 70–2.

Il'ina, T. V., and Rimskaia-Korsakova, S. V., *Andrei Matveev* (M, 1984).

Indova, E. I., *Dvortsovoe khoziaistivo v Rossii. Pervaia polovina XVIII v.* (M, 1964).

Istomin, K., *Kniga liubvi znak v chesten brak* (facs.) (M, 1989).

Istoriia Akademii Nauk, vol. 1 (M&L, 1958).

Iunosti chestnoe zertsalo (SPb., 1717).

'Iz perepiski Petra I i Ekateriny I so svoimi docher'mi', in *Pamiatniki novoi russkoi istorii*, vol. 1 (SPb., 1871), 37–82.

Jensen, C. R., 'Music for the Tsar: A Preliminary Study of the Music of the Muscovite Court Theatre', *Musical Quarterly*, 79/2 (1995), 368–401.

Jones, R. E., 'Opening a Window on the South: Russia and the Black Sea 1695–1792', in *WOR*, 123–9.

Kabuzan, V. M., *Izmeneniia v razmeshchenii naseleniia Rossii v XVIII–pervoi pol. XIX v.* (M, 1971).

Kafengauz, B. B., 'Voprosy istoriografii epokhi Petra Velikogo', *Istoricheskii zhurnal*, 9 (1944), 24–42.

———, and Pavlenko, N. I., eds, *Ocherki istorii SSSR. Period feodalizma. Rossiia v pervoi chetverti XVIII v.* (M, 1954).

Kaganov, G., 'As in the Ship of Peter', *SR*, 50 (1991), 754–67.

Kahan, A., 'Continuity in Economic Activity and Policy during the Post-Petrine Period in Russia,' *Journal of Economic History*, 25 (1965), 61–85.

———, 'Observations on Petrine Foreign Trade', *CASS* 8 (1974), 222–36.

———, *The Plow, the Hammer and the Knout. An Economic History of Eighteenth-Century Russia* (Chicago, 1985).

Kalach, V., ed., *Tri veka*, vol. 3 (SPb., 1912).

Kaliazina, N. V., *Arkhitekturnaia grafika Rossii. Pervaia pol. XVIII veka. Sobranie Ermitazha* (L, 1981).

———, 'Materialy dlia ikonografii A. D. Menshikova (prizhiznennye portrety)', in G. I. Komelova, ed., *Kul'tura i iskusstvo petrovskogo vremeni* (L, 1977), 70–87.

———, Dorofeeva, L. P. and Mikhailov, G. V., *Dvorets Menshikova* (M, 1986).

———, and Saverkina, I. V., 'Zhivopisnoe sobranie A. D. Menshikova', in *Russkaia kul'tura pervoi chetverti XVIII veka. Dvorets Menshikova* (SPb., 1992), 54–61.

Kamensky, A. B. *Arkhivnoe delo v Rossii XVIII veka: Istoriko-kul'turnyi aspekt* (M, 1991).

Kaminski, A., *Republic vs Autocracy. Poland-Lithuania and Russia 1686–1697* (Cambridge, Mass., 1993).

Karlinsky, S., *Russian Drama from its Beginnings to the Age of Pushkin* (Berkeley, 1985).

Karnovich, E. P., 'Assamblei pri Petre Velikom', in *Istoricheskie rasskazy i bytovye ocherki* (SPb., 1884), 238–50.

Kartina zhizni i voennykh deianii rossiisko-imperatorskogo generalissima kniazia A.D. Menshikova (M, 1809).

Kartsov, A., *Istoriia leib-gvardii Semenovskogo polka, 1685–1852*, vol. 1 (SPb., 1852).

Keep, J., *Soldiers of the Tsar. Army and Society in Russia 1462–1874* (Oxford, 1985).

Kelpsh, A. E., 'Rubles of Peter the Great', *Numismatist*, 62 (Mar. 1949), 161–74.

Kennett, V. and Kennett, E., *The Palaces of Leningrad* (London, 1973).

Kepsu, S., *Pietari ennen Pietaria. Nevansuun vaiheita ennen Pietarin kaupungin perustamista* (Helsinki, 1995).

Khodarkovsky, M., *Where Two Worlds Met. The Russian State and the Kalmyk Nomads, 1600–1772* (Ithaca, NY & London, 1992).

Kirby, D., *Northern Europe in the Early Modern Period. The Baltic World 1492–1772* (London, 1990).

Kirilov, I. K., *Tsvetushchee sostoianie Vserossiiskogo gosudarstva* (M, 1977).

Kivelson, V., *Autocracy in the Provinces. The Muscovite Gentry and Political Culture in the Seventeenth Century* (Stanford, Calif. 1996).

Kizevetter, A. A., *Posadskaia obshchina v Rossii XVIII st.* (M, 1903).

———, *Russkoe obshchestvo v XVIII st.* (M, 1904).

Kleimola, A., ' "In Accordance with the Holy Apostles": Muscovite Dowries and Women's Property Rights', *RR*, 51 (1992), 204–29.

Klibanov, A. A., *Narodnaia sotsial'naia utopiia v Rossii* (M, 1977).

Kliuchevsky, V. O., *Kurs russkoi istorii*, 2nd edn, vol. 4 (M, 1923).

Klochkov, M., *Naselenie Rossii pri Petre Velikom po perepisiam togo vremeni. I. 1678–1721* (SPb., 1911).

Kniazhetskaia, E. A., 'Nauchnye sviazi Rossii i Frantsii pri Petre I', *VI*, (1981) no. 5, 91–100.

Kniga Marsova, ili voinskikh del (SPb., 1713/66).

Kommissarenko, A. I., 'Russkii absoliutizm i dukhovenstvo v usloviiakh podgotovki i provedeniia sekuliarizatsionnoi reformy XVIII v.', in *Pravoslavnaia tserkov' v istorii Rossii* (M, 1991), 117–48.

Kopanev, N. A., *Frantsuzskaia kniga i russkaia kul'tura v seredine XVIII v.* (L, 1988).

———, 'Petr I — perevodchik', *XVIII vek.*, 16 (1989), 180–3.

Kopii ego ts. vel. ukazov, publikovannykh ot 1714 po nyneshnii 1719 (SPb., 1719).

Kopii vsekh ego tsar. vel. ukazov, publikovannykh ot 1714 marta 17 dnia po nyneshnii 1718. Spb. 1718, vol. 1 (SPb., 1739), vol. 2 (SPb., 1780).

Kornilovich, A. O., *Nravy russkikh pri Petre Velikom* (SPb., 1901).

Korsakov, D. A., *Iz zhizni russkikh deiatelei XVIII veka* (Kazan', 1981).

Korshunova, T. T., *Kostium v Rossii XVIII–nachala XX veka* (L, 1979).

Kostium v Rossii pervoi chet. XVIII v. Kratkii putevoditel' po vystavke (L, 1984).

Kostomarov, N. I., 'Ekaterina Alekseevna, pervaia russkaia imperatritsa', *Drevniaia i novaia Rossiia*, 2 (1872), 129–70.

———, *Mazepa* (M, 1992).

Kovalevsky, P., 'Petr Velikii i ego genii', *Dialog*, 1992, nos 2, 4–5, 8–10, 11–14, 15–18.

Kovrigina, V. A., *Inozemnoe naselenie Moskvy kontsa XVII-pervoi chet. XVIII vv.* (M, 1991).

———, 'Remeslenniki Moskovskoi Nemetskoi Slobody v kontse XVII–pervoi chet. XVIII veka', *Russkii gorod*, 9 (1990), 182–201.

Kozlov, O. F., 'Delo tsarevicha Alekseia', *VI*, 1969, no. 9, 86–92.

———, 'Reforma tserkvi Petra I i otkliki na nee v russkom obshchestve v pervoi polovine XVIII veka', *Vestnik MGU (Istoriia)*, 5 (1968), 86–92.

Kozlova, N. V., *Pobegi krest'ian v pervoi treti XVIII veka* (M, 1983).

Kozyrev, A. V., *Kul'turnye reformy Petra I* (Stavropol, 1948).

Kratkii putevoditel' po otdelu istorii russkoi kul'tury, vol. 1 (L, 1950).

Krekshin, P., 'Kratkoe opisanie blazhenykh del velikogo gosudaria, imperatora Petra Velikogo, Samoderzhtsa Vserossiiskogo', in N. Sakharov, ed., *Zapiski russkikh liudei* (SPb., 1841), 1–128.

Kroll, R., *Andreas Schlüter und der Sommerpalast Peters I. Forschungen und Berichte* (Berlin, 1976).

Krotov, P. A., 'Russkaia zhenshchina Petrovskoi epokhi: A. S. Mordvitsova i ee pis'ma k synu', in *Rossiiskie zhenshchiny i evropeiskaia kul'tura. Tezisy dokladov II nauchnoi konferentsii* (SPb., 1994), 51–2.

Kukushkina, E. D., 'Tekst i izobrazhenie v konkliuzii Petrovskogo vremeni (na primere portreta tsarevny Natalii Alekseevny)', *XVIII vek*, 15 (1986), 21–36.

Kul'tura i iskusstvo petrovskogo vremeni, ed. G. I. Komelova (L, 1977).

Kvadri, V. V., *Svita Petra Velikogo* (SPb., 1902).

Lakhtin, M., *Materialy k istorii meditsiny v Rossii* (M, 1907).

Lanshchikov, A., 'Imperator-bol'shevik', *Rodina*, 3 (1992), 86–92.

Lapteva, T. A., 'Dokumenty o vnutrennei politike Rossii nach. XVIII v. v fonde "Kabinet Petra I i ego prodolzhenie"', *Sovetskie arkhivy*, 6 (1986), 35–9.

———, 'Ob "arape Petra Velikogo"', *Istoricheskii arkhiv*, 1 (1992), 182–8.

Lastovskii, M., *Materialy dlia istorii inzhenernogo iskusstva Rossii.*, vol. 2 (SPb., 1861).

Lebedev, V. I., *Bulavinskoe vosstanie 1704–1708* (M, 1934).

Lebedeva, I. N., 'Biblioteka tsarevny Natal'i Alekseevny', in V. P. Leonov, ed., *Kniga v Rossii: Vek Prosveshcheniia* (L, 1990), 109–10.

———, 'Leib-medik Petra I Robert Areskin i ego biblioteka', in *Russkie biblioteki i ikh chitateli* (L, 1983), 98–105.

LeDonne, J. P., *Absolutism and Ruling Class. The Formation of the Russian Political Order 1700–1825* (Oxford, 1991).

Lentin, A., trans. and ed., *Peter the Great: His Law on the Imperial Succession. The Official Commentary* (Oxford, 1996).

Lettres du comte Algarotti sur la Russie (London & Paris, 1769).

Lewitter, L. R., 'The Apocryphal Testament of Peter the Great' *Polish Review*, 6/3 (1966), 27–44.

———, 'Peter the Great and the Modern World', in P. Dukes, ed., *Russia and Europe* (London, 1991), 92–107.

———, 'Peter the Great's Attitude towards Religion', in R. Bartlett, ed., *Russia and the World of the Eighteenth Century* (Columbus, Oh., 1988), 62–77.

———, 'The Russo–Polish Treaty of 1686 and its Implications', *Polish Review*, 9 (1964), no. 3, 5–29; no. 4, 21–37.

———, 'Russia, Poland and the Baltic, 1697–1721', *Historical Journal*, 2 (1968), 3–34.

Librovich, S., 'Zhenskii krug Petra Velikogo', *Smena*, 6 (1993), 80–97.

Liria, duc de, *Mémoires du duc de Lihria et de Berwick* (Paris, 1788).

———, 'Pis'ma o Rossii v Ispaniiu', in *Osmnadtsatyi vek*, vol. 2 (M, 1869), 6–198.

———, 'Zapiski diuka Liriiskogo i Bervikskogo vo vremia prebyvaniia ego pri Imperatorskom Rossiiskom dvore', *Russkii arkhiv*, 1909, bk I, pt 3, 377–442.

Lotman, Iu. M., *Besedy o russkoi kul'ture. Byt i traditsii russkogo dvorianstva (XVIII–nach. XIX veka)* (SPb., 1994).

———, 'The Poetics of Everyday Behaviour in Russian Eighteenth-Century Culture', in A. Shukman, ed., *The Semiotics of Russian Culture* (Ann Arbor, 1984), 231–56.

———, and Uspensky, B. A., 'Echoes of the Notion of "Moscow the Third Rome" in Peter the Great's Ideology', in A. Shukman, ed., *The Semiotics of Russian Culture* (Ann Arbor, 1984), 53–67.

Lubok, The Russian Folk Pictures. 17th to 18th Century (L, 1984).

Luppov, S. P., *Kniga v Rossii v pervoi chetverti XVIII v.* (L, 1973).

———, *Kniga v Rossii XVII veka* (L, 1970).

Lushin, A., 'Nizhegorodskie samozvantsy', *Rossiia molodaia*, 1991, no. 7, 72–5.

McKay, D., and Scott, H. M., *The Rise of the Great Powers, 1648–1815* (London, 1983).

Mackiv, T., *English Reports on Mazepa 1687–1709* (New York, Munich & Toronto, 1983).

Madariaga, I. de. 'Penal Policy in the Age of Catherine II', in L. Berlinguer and F. Colao, eds, *La "Leopoldina". Criminalità e Giustizia Criminale nelle Riforme del Settecento Europeo* (Milan, 1990), 2: 497–537.

————, 'Portrait of an Eighteenth-Century Russian Statesman: Prince Dmitry Mikhaylovich Golitsyn', *SEER*, 62 (1984), 36–60.

————, 'The Russian Nobility in the Seventeenth and Eighteenth Centuries', in H. M. Scott, ed., *The European Nobilities 1600–1800: Eastern Europe* (London, 1995), 223–73.

————, 'The Staging of Power', *Government and Opposition*, 31 (1996), 228–40.

————, 'Tsar into Emperor: The Title of Peter the Great', in R. Oresko et al., eds, *Royalty and Republican Sovereignty in Early Modern Europe* (Cambridge, 1996), 351–81.

Maier, A. L., 'O starom zimnem dvortse i palate v koei skonchalsia gos. imperator Petr Velikii', *Vestnik Evropy*, 3/5 (1872), 1–18.

Maikov, T. S., 'Petr I i "Gistoriia Sveiskoi voiny"', in *RPR*, 103–32.

Maikov, V. V., *Postupki i zabavi imp. Petra Velikogo (Zapis' sovremennika)* (M, 1895).

Makarov, V. V., *Russkaia svetskaia graviura I chet. XVIII veka. Annotirovannyi svodnyei katalog* (L, 1973).

Malinin, S., 'Ten' Leforta', *Moskovskii zhurnal*, 1991, no. 2, 64–70.

Malinovsky, K. V., 'Zapiska Iakoba Shtelina o Prutskom pokhode Petra I', *Russkaia literatura*, 2 (1982), 163–8.

'Maloizvestnyi istochnik po istorii severnoi voiny [Daniel Krman]', *VI*, 1976, no. 12, 93–111.

Man'kov, A., 'Pro"ekt Ulozheniia rossiiskogo gosudarstva 1720–25 gg.', in S. L. Peshtich et al., eds, *Problemy istorii feodal'noi Rossii* (L, 1971), 157–67.

Marker, G., *Publishing, Printing, and the Origins of Intellectual Life in Russia, 1700–1800* (Princeton, 1985).

Martin, J., *Medieval Russia 980–1584* (Cambridge, 1995).

Maslovsky, D. O., *Zapiski po istorii voennogo iskusstva v Rossii* (SPb., 1891).

Massie, R. K., *Peter the Great. His Life and World* (London, 1981).

Materialy dlia istorii Akademii nauk, vols 1 and 4 (SPb., 1885).

Materialy dlia istorii russkogo flota, vols 1–4 (SPb., 1865–7), 5 (1875), 6 (1877).

Materialy voenno-uchenago arkhiva glavnogo shtaba, vol. 1 (SPb., 1871).

Matley, I. M. 'Defence Manufactures of St Petersburg 1703-1730', *Geographical Review*, 71(1981), 411–26.

Matsulensko, S. A., 'Voennye reformy Petra I', *Voenno-istorisheskii zhurnal*, 1988, no. 5, 83–7.

Matveev, V. Iu., 'K istorii vozniknoveniia i razvitiia siuzheta "Petr I, vysekaiushchii statuiu Rossii"', in *Kul'tura i iskusstvo Rossii XVIII veka. Novye materialy i issledovaniia* (L, 1981), 26–43.

————, 'Raznykh zhudozhestv mastera', in *Nauka i kul'tura Rossii XVIII veka. Sbornik statei* (L, 1984), 144–77.

————, and Tarasova, E. A., *Bartolomeo Karlo Rastrelli (1675–1744). K 300 letiiu s dnia rozhdeniia. Katalog vremennoi vystavki* (L, 1975).

Medushevsky, A. N., *Utverzhdenie absoliutizma v Rossii* (M, 1994).

————, 'Petrovskaia reforma gosudarstvennogo apparata', in F. Shelov-Kovediaev, ed.,

Reformy vtoroi poloriny XVII–XX v.: podgotovka, provedenie, rezul'taty (M, 1989), 64–83.

——, 'Reformy Petra Velikogo v sravnitel'no-istoricheskoi perspektive', *Vestnik vysshei shkoly*, 1990, no. 2, 79–88; no. 3, 65–72.

Meehan-Waters, B., *Autocracy and Aristocracy. The Russian Service Elite of 1730* (New Brunswick, NJ, 1982).

Mémoires du règne de Pierre le Grand, par le baron Iwan Nestesuranoy 4 vols (Amsterdam, 1729–37).

Mémoires secrets pour servir à l'histoire de la cour de Russie, sous les règnes de Pierre-le-Grand et de Catherine Ire. Rédigés et publiés pour la première fois, d'aprés les manuscrits originaux du Sieur de Villebois (Paris, 1853).

Merguerian, B. J., 'Political Ideas in Russia during the Reign of Peter the Great', (Ph.D. thesis, Harvard, 1971).

Mezen, S. A., 'Osveshchenie deiatel'nosti Petra I s pozitsii konservativnogo dvorianstva. (M. M. Shcherbatova)', *Istoriograficheskii sbornik*, 13 (1987), 40–60.

Mezhov, V. I., *Iubilei Petra Velikogo. Bibliograficheskii ukazatel'* (SPb., 1881).

Mikhailov, G. V. 'Graviura A. Zubova. Svad'ba Petra I. Real'nost' i vymysl', *Panorama iskusstv*, 2 (1988), 20–55.

Mikhnevich, V. O., *Russkaia zhenshchina XVIII stoletiia. Istoricheskie etiudy* (M, 1895/1991).

Miliukov, P. N., *Gosudarstvennoe khoziaistvo Rossii v pervoi chet. XVIII st. i reforma Petra Velikogo* (SPb., 1905).

——, *Ocherki po istorii russkoi kul'tury*, pt 3 (SPb., 1903).

——, 'Petr I Alekseevich Velikii', in *Entsiklopedicheskii slovar'*, vol. 23 (1898), 487–95.

Minzloff, R., *Pierre le Grand dans la littérature étrangère* (SPb., 1872).

Mironov, B. N., *Russkii gorod v 1740–1860e gody* (L, 1990).

Mirskii, M. B. 'Doktor Robert Erskin—pervyi rossiiskii arkhiatr', *Otechestvennaia istoriia*, 2 (1995), 135–45.

Moiseenko, E. Iu., comp., *Kostium v Rossii pervoi chetverti XVIII v.* (L, 1984).

——, 'Plat'e rubezha XVII i XVIII vekov iz "Garderoba Petra I" ', in *Kul'tura i iskusstvo Rossii XVIII veka. Novye materialy i issledovaniia. Sbornik statei* (L, 1981), 58–73.

Moiseeva, G., comp., *Russkie povesti pervoi treti XVIII veka* (M&L, 1965).

——, *Zapiski i vospominaniia russkikh zhenshchin XVIII-pervoi pol. XIX v.* (M, 1990).

Moleva, N. M., ' "Persony" vseshuteishego sobora', *VI*, 1974, no. 10, 206–11.

—— and Beliutin, E. M., *Zhivopisnykh del mastera. Kantseliariia ot stroeniia i russkaia zhivopis' pervoi poloviny XVIII veka* (M, 1965).

Monas, S. 'Anton Divier and the Police of St Petersburg', in M. Halle, ed., *For Roman Jakobson: Essays on the Occasion of his Sixtieth Birthday* (The Hague, 1956), 361–6.

Moon, D., 'Reassessing Russian Serfdom', *European History Quarterly*, 48 (1996), 483–526.

Morozov, P. O., 'Russkii teatr pri Petre Velikom', in *Ezhegodnik imperatorskikh teatrov. 1893-1894* (SPb., 1894), bk 1, 52–80.

Mottray, A. de la, *Travels through Europe, Asia and into Part of Africa* (London, 1723).

——, *Voyages en Anglois et en Francois en diverses provinces et places de la Prusse ducale et royale, de la Russie, de la Pologne etc.* (The Hague, London & Dublin, 1732).

Mozgovaia, E. B., 'Obraz Petra I v tvorchestve Karlo Bartolomeo Rastrelli', in *Problemy razvitiia russkogo iskusstva*, vol. 18 (L, 1985), 33–40.

————, 'Obraz Petra I–imperatora v proizvedeniiakh tvorchestva Bartolomeo Karlo Rastrelli', in *Monarkhiia i narodovlastie v kul'ture prosveshcheniia* (M, 1995), 3–16.

————, 'Sintez iskusstv v triumfakh pervoi chetverti XVIII veka', in *Problemy sinteza iskusstv i arkhitektury*, 21 (L, 1985), 58–67.

Münnich, B. C., 'Ocherk daiushchii predstavlenie ob obraze pravleniia Rossiiskoi Imperii', in *Bezvremen'e i vremenshchik. Vospominaniia ob epokhe dvortsovykh perevorotov 1720e–1760s gody* (L, 1991), 26–78.

Murzanova, M. N., 'Kniga Marsa—pervaia kniga grazhdanskoi pechati, napechatan-naia v Peterburge', *Trudy Biblioteki Akademii Nauk SSSR*, 1 (1948).

Nauka i kul'tura Rossii XVIII v. (L, 1984).

Nekrasov, G. A., *Russko-shvedskie otnosheniia i politika velikikh derzhav v 1721–26 gg.* (M, 1964).

Nelipovich, S. G., 'Pozitsiia B. Kh. fon Miunnikha v diskussii 1725 goda o sokrashchenii armii i voennogo biudzheta Rossii', *Voenno-istoricheskii zhurnal*, 1990, no. 8, 3–7.

Nemiro, O. V., 'Dekorativno-oformitel'skoe iskusstvo i prazdnichnyi Peterburg pervoi poloviny XVIII v.', in *Otechestvennoe i zarubezhnoe iskusstvo XVIII veka* (L, 1986), 82–94.

Nepotrebnyi syn. Delo Tsarevicha Alekseia Petrovicha (SPb., 1996).

Neuville, F. de la, *A Curious and New Account of Muscovy in the Year 1689*, ed. L. Hughes (London, 1994).

Neverov, O., ' "His Majesty's Cabinet" and Peter I's Kunstkammer', in O. Impey and A. McGregor, eds, *The Origins of Museums. The Cabinet of Curiosities in 16th–17th-Century Europe* (Oxford, 1985), 54–61.

Nichik, N. M., *Feofan Prokopovich* (M, 1977).

Nichols, R. L., and Stavrou, T. G., eds, *Russian Orthodoxy under the Old Regime* (Minneapolis, 1978).

Nikiforov, L. A., 'Rossiia v sisteme evropeiskikh derzhav v pervoi chetverti XVIII v.', in *RPR*, 9–39.

Nosovich, I. 'Vsep'ianeishii sobor uchrezhdennyi Petra Velikogo', *Russkaia starina*, 2/12 (1874), 734–9.

Novikov, N., 'Sozdanie voenno-morskogo flota v Rossii pri Petre I', *Partiino-politich-eskaia rabota v VMF*, 1941, no. 7, 40–7.

————, ed., *Boevaia letopis' russkogo flota* (M, 1948).

Obshchestvo i gosudarstvo feodal'noi Rossii. Sb. statei . . . L'va Vl. Cherepnina (M, 1975).

Obshchii arkhiv Ministerstva imp. dvora: vol. 1: Opisanie del i bumag; vol. 2: Spiski i vypiski iz arkhivnikh bumag (SPb., 1888).

Okenfuss, M., 'The Jesuit Origins of Petrine Education', in Garrard, 106–30.

————, 'Popular Educational Tracts in Enlightenment Russia', *CASS*, 14 (1980), 307–26.

————, 'Russian Students in Europe in the Age of Peter the Great', in Garrard, 131–45.

————, ed. and trans., *The Travel Diary of Peter Tolstoy* (DeKalb, Ill., 1987).

Olart, N. N., *Petr I i zhenshchiny* (Stavropol, 1990).

Olearius, A., *The Travels of Olearius in Seventeenth-Century Russia*, ed. and trans. S. Baron (Stanford, Calif., 1967).

Oliva, L. J., ed., *Peter the Great. Great Lives Observed* (Englewood Cliffs, NJ, 1970).

Opisanie dokumentov i del, khraniashchikhsia v arkhive sviateishego prav. Sinoda, vol. 1 (SPb., 1868), vol. 2 (1878), vol. 3 (1878), vol. 4 (1880).

Opisanie koronatsii e.v. Ekateriny Alekseevny (SPb., 1724; M, 1725).

Opisanie poriadka derzhannogo pri progrebenii blazhennyia vysokoslavnyia i vernodostoineishiia pamiati vsepresvetleishago derzhavneishago Petra Velikago (Spb., 1725; M, 1726).

'Opisannoe samovidtsem torzhestvo, proiskhodivshee v S-Peterburge 22 okt. 1721 goda', *Syn otechestva*, 1849, bk 2, 1–4.

Osmnadtsatyi vek. Istoricheskii sbornik izdannyi P. Bartenevym, 4 vols (M, 1869).

Ovchinnikov, P. V., 'Krushenie "poluderzhavnogo vlastelina"', *VI*, 1970, no. 9, 87–104.

Ovchinnikova, E. S., *Portret v russkom iskusstve XVII veka* (M, 1955).

Paaskoski, J., 'Noble Land-holding and Serfdom in Old Finland', in *WOR*, 83–90.

Pamiatniki diplomaticheskikh snoshenii drevnei Rossii s derzhavami inostrannymi, 10 vols (SPb., 1851–71).

Pamiatniki russkogo zakonodatel'stva XVIII stoletiia (SPb., 1907).

Panchenko, A. M., 'Nachalo petrovskoi reformy: ideinaia podelka', in *XVIII vek*, 16 (1989), 5–16.

Pavlenko, N. I., *Aleksandr Danilovich Menshikov* (M, 1981).

——, 'Petr I (K izucheniiu sotsial'no-politicheskikh vzgliadov)', in *RPR*, 40–102.

——, *Petr Velikii* (M, 1990).

——, *Poluderzhavnyi vlastelin* (M, 1991).

——, *Ptentsy gnezda petrova* (M, 1989).

——, *Razvitie metallurgichekoi promyshlennosti Rossii v pervoi pol. XVIII v.* (M, 1953).

——, 'Strasti u trona. Ekaterina I', *Rodina*, 1993, no. 10, 106–12.

——, 'V zashchitu Petra Velikogo', *Politicheskoe obrazovanie*, 1989, no. 15, 92–5.

—— and Artamanov, V., *27 iunia 1709 g.* (M, 1989).

Pavlov-Sil'vansky, N., *Proekty reform v zapiskakh sovremennikov Petra Velikogo* (SPb., 1897).

Pekarsky, P. P., *Istoriia Imp. Akademii Nauk*, 2 vols (SPb., 1870–3).

——, *Nauka i literatura v Rossii pri Petre Velikom*, 2 vols (M, 1862).

——, *Peterburgskaia starina* (SPb., 1860).

Pereladov, K., 'Konchina avgusteishego kolodnika', *Rodina*, 1994, no. 9, 39–42.

Perepiska i bumagi B.P. Sheremeteva i drugie bumagi (*SIRIO*, 20).

Perkowski, J., 'Peter the Great—A Catalogue of Coins and Medals in the Smithsonian Collection', *Numismatist*, 95 (1982), 1188–1204.

Perrie, M., *Pretenders and Popular Monarchism in Early Modern Russia. The False Tsars of the Time of Troubles* (Cambridge, 1995).

Perry, J., *The State of Russia* (1716), (London, 1967).

P'esy shkol'nykh teatrov Moskvy. Ranniaia russkaia dramaturgiia (M, 1974).

P'esy stolichnykh i provintsial'nykh teatrov pervoi poloviny XVIII v., ed. A. S. Eleonskaia, (M, 1975).

'Peterburg v 1720 g. Zapiski poliaka-ochevidtsa', *Russkaia starina*, 35(1879), 263–89.

Peter de Grote en Holland (Amsterdam, 1996), Amsterdams Historisch Museum.

Peterson, C., *Peter the Great's Administrative and Judicial Reforms* (Stockholm, 1979).

Petr Velikii, ego polkovodtsy i ministry (M, 1848).

Petr Velikii. Sbornik statei, ed. A. I. Andreev (M&L, 1947).

Petrov, P. N., 'Korennoe izmenenie russkogo byta pri Petre Velikom', *Severnoe siianie*, 2/78 (1863), 390–412, 431–52.

——, 'Tsesarevna Anna Petrovna', in M. Mikhailov, ed., *Sbornik istoricheskikh materialov i dokumentov otnosiashchikh k novoi Russkoi istorii XVIII i XIX veka* (SPb., 1873), 83–123.

Petrovskii sbornik, izdannyi "Russkoiu Starinoiu" 30 maia 1872 (SPb., 1972).

Petschauer, P., 'In Search of Competent Aides: Heinrich von Huyssen and Peter the Great', *JGO*, 24 (1978), 481–502.

———, 'The Philosopher and the Reformer: Tsar Peter I, G. W. Leibnit and the College System', *CASS*, 13 (1979), 473–87.

Phillips, E. J., *The Founding of Russia's Navy. Peter the Great and the Azov Fleet 1688-1714* (Westport, Conn., 1995).

Pipes, R., *Russia under the Old Regime* (London, 1974).

———, ed., *Karamzin's Memoir on Ancient and Modern Russia* (Cambridge, Mass., 1959).

'Pis'ma generala-anshefa I. I. Buturlina', *Russkaia starina*, 1878, no. 10, 161–86; 1879, no. 5, 151–8.

Pis'ma i doneseniia iezuitov o Rossii (SPb., 1904; repr. 1965).

Pis'ma i ukazy E. I. V. G. I Petra Velikogo, pisannye k Naumu Akimovichu Siniavinu (SPb., 1786).

Pis'ma Petra Velikogo B. P. Sheremetevu (M, 1774).

'Pis'ma Petra I I.I. Buturlinu', *Severnyi arkhiv*, 1823, parts 5, 6 and 7.

'Pis'ma ... Ia. F. Dolgorukomy', *Chteniia*, 1904, kn. 4.

Pis'ma russkikh gosudarei i drugikh osob tsarskogo semeistva, vol. 1 (Peter and Catherine) (M, 1861); vol. 2 (Anna Ivanovna) (M, 1862); vol. 3 (Alexis; Evdokia Fedorovna, etc.) (M, 1862); vol. 4 (Praskovia Fedorovna and daughters) (M, 1861).

Pis'ma tsarevicha Alekseia Petrovicha, k ego roditeliu gosudariu Petru Velikomu, gosudaryne Ekaterine Alekseevne i kabinet-sekretariu Makarovu (Odessa, 1849).

Platonov, S. F., 'Iz bytovoi istorii Petrovskoi epokhi', *Izvestiia AN SSSR*, 8 (1926).

———, *Petr Velikii. Lichnost' i deiatel'nost'* (Paris, 1927).

Pliukhanova, M. B., 'Istoriia iunosti Petra I u Krekshina', *Uchenye zapiski TGU*, 513 (1981), 17–39.

Pod"iapol'skaia, E. P., 'Ob istorii i nauchnom znachenii izdanii "Pis'ma i bumagi imperatora Petra Velikogo"', in *Arkheograficheskii ezhegodnik za 1972* (M, 1974), 56–70.

Pogodin, N., 'Petr Pervyi: Pervye gody edinoderzhaviia, 1689–1694', *Russkii arkhiv*, 1879, 1: 5–57.

———, *Semnadtsat' pervykh let v zhizni imp. Petra Velikogo 1672–1689* (M, 1875).

Poltava. K 250-letiu Poltavskogo srazheniia (M, 1959).

Portnov, A., 'Byl li Lomonosov vnebrachnym synom Petra I?', *Trud*, 65 (13 Apr. 1995).

Portret Petrovskogo vremeni. Katalog vystavki (L, 1974).

Potter, C., 'The Russian Church and the Politics of Reform in the Second Half of the Seventeenth Century' (Ph.D. thesis, Yale, 1993).

'Pravila Petra Velikogo dlia lits, priezhaiushchikh v Pitergofskii dvorets', *Russkii arkhiv*, 1907, 2: 615.

The Prerogative of Primogeniture ... Written on the Occasion of the Czar of Muscovy's Reasons in his Late Manifesto for the Disinheritance of his Eldest Son, from the Succession to the Crown (London, 1718).

Pridvornaia zhizn': 1613–1913. Koronatsii, feierverki, dvortsy (SPb., 1913).

Prokopovich, F., *Istoriia imp. Petra Velikogo ot rozhdeniia ego do Poltavskoi batalii* (SPb., 1773), 2nd edn (M, 1788).

———, *Kratkaia povest' o smerti Petra Velikogo Imperatora i Samoderzhtsa Vserossiiskogo* (SPb., 1831).

———, 'Sermon on Royal Authority and Honour' (1718), in M. Raeff, ed., *Russian Intellectual History. An Anthology* (New York, 1966) 13–20.

———, *Sochineniia*, ed. I. P. Eremin (M&L, 1961).

Punin, A. L., 'Petr I i Kristofer Ren. K. voprosu o stilevykh istokakh petrovskogo barokko', in *Iskusstvo arkhitektury. Sbornik nauchnykh statei* (SPb., 1995), 34–41.

Rabinovich, M. D., *Polki petrovskoi armii 1698–1725* (M, 1977).

Raeff, M., ed., *Peter the Great Changes Russia* (Lexington, Ky, 1972).

Rasmussen, K., 'Catherine II and the Image of Peter I', *SR*, 37 (1978), 57–69.

Repin, N. N., *Problemy istoricheskoi demografii SSSR*, vol. 2 (Tomsk, 1982).

———, *Promyshlennost' i torgovlia v Rossii XVII-XVIII vv.* (M, 1983).

'Reskripty i ukazy Petra I k lifliandskim general-gubernatoram: Polonskomu, kn. Golitsynu i kn. Repninu', in *Osmnadtsatyi vek. Istoricheskii sbornik izdannyi P. Bartenevym*, vol. 4 (M, 1869).

Riasanovsky, N., *The Image of Peter the Great in Russian History and Thought* (Oxford, 1985).

Rieber, A. J., 'Politics and Technology in Eighteenth-Century Russia', *Science in Context*, 8 (1995), 341–68.

Roetter, J. H., 'Russian Attitudes towards Peter the Great and his Reforms between 1725 and 1910' (unpub. Ph.D. thesis, University of Wisconsin, 1951).

Rogger, H., *National Consciousness in Eighteenth-Century Russia* (Cambridge, Mass., 1960).

Rothstein, A., *Peter the Great and Marlborough. Politics and Diplomacy in Converging Wars* (Basingstoke, 1986).

Runkevich, S. G., *Uchrezhdenie i pervonachalnoe ustroistvo sviateishago pravitel'stvuiushchego sinoda (1721–1725) gg.* (SPb., 1900).

Russian Catechism Composed and Published by Order of the Czar, The, trans. J. T. Philipps (London, 1723).

Russkaia dramaturgiia poslednei chetverti XVII i nachala XVIII v., ed. O. A. Derzhavina (M, 1972).

Russkaia kul'tura VI-XVIII v. Ocherk-putevoditel' (L, 1983).

Russkaia kul'tura petrovskogo vremeni. Putevoditel' po zalam gos. Ermitakzha (L, 1967).

Ryan, W., 'Navigation and the Modernization of Russia', in R. Bartlett and J. Hartley, eds, *Russia in the Age of Enlightenment: Essays for Isabel de Madariaga* (London, 1990), 75–105.

———, 'Peter I's English Yacht', *Mariner's Mirror*, 69/1 (1983), 65–87.

———, 'Scientific Instruments in Russia from the Middle Ages to Peter the Great', *Annals of Science*, 48 (1991), 367–84.

Rylov, I., and Sobolin, B., *Monety Rossii i SSSR, Katalog. 1700–1993* (M, 1994).

Salm'an, G. Ia, 'Morskoi ustav 1720 g.—Pervyi svod zakonov russkogo flota', *IZ*, 53 (1955), 310–22.

Sarantola-Weiss, M., 'Peter the Great's First Boat, "Grandfather of the Russian Navy"', in *WOR*, 37–42.

Savel'eva, E. A., 'Biblioteka Ia. V. Briusa v sobranii BAN SSSR', in *Russkie biblioteki i ikh chitateli* (L, 1983), 123–34.

Saverkina, I. V., 'Orkestr i khor A. D. Menshikova', *Pamiatniki kul'tury*, 1989 (1990), 232–43.

Sbornik biografii kavelergardov, ed. S. Pangulizdeva, vol. 1: *1724–62* (SPb., 1901).

Sbornik Mukhanova, 2nd edn. (SPb., 1866).

Sbornik voenno-istoricheskikh materialov, 16 vols (SPb., 1892–1904)).

Schuyler, E., *Peter the Great*, 2 vols (New York, 1884).

Scott, R. C., *Quakers in Russia* (London, 1964).

Sederberg, G., 'Zametki o religii i nravakh russkogo naroda 1709–1718', *Chteniia*, 1873, bk 2.

Sedov, P. V., 'Reforma sluzhilogo plat'ia pri Fedore Alekseeviche', in *Tezisy*, 77–83.

Semenova, L. N., 'Inostrannye mastera v Peterburge v pervoi treti XVIII v.', in *Nauka i kul'tura Rossii XVIII v. Sbornik statei* (L, 1984), 201–24.

———, 'Obshchestvennye razvlecheniia v Rossii v pervoi polovine XVIII v.', in *Staryi Peterburg* (L, 1982), 147–63.

———, *Ocherki istorii byta i kulturnoi zhizni Rossii. Pervaia polovina XVIII v.* (L, 1982).

———, *Rabochie Peterburga v pervoi pol. XVIII v.* (L, 1974).

Semevsky, M. I., 'Elizaveta Petrovna do vosshestviia svoego na prestol', *Russkoe slovo*, 2 (1859), 209–78.

———, *Slovo i delo, 1700–1725. Ocherki i rasskazy iz russkoi istorii XVIII veka* (SPb., 1884).

———, 'Ts. Evdokiia Fed. Lopukhina', *Russkii vestnik*, 1859, no. 9.

———, *Tsaritsa Katerina Alekseevna, Anna i Villem Mons 1692–1724* (SPb., 1884).

———, *Tsaritsa Praskov'ia 1664–1724* (M, 1989).

Serov, D., 'Pervonachal'noe nakoplenie kapitala: tainy imperii kniazia Menshikova', *Russkaia Aziia*, 41/11 (1994), 3.

———, 'Rossiiskaia mafiia: nachalo puti', *Russkaia Aziia*, 38/8 (1994), 14.

———, *Stepennaia kniga redaktsii Ivana Iur'eva (1716–1718 gg.)*, dissertation abstract (L, 1991).

———, 'Zametka o biografii P. P. Shafirova', *SGECRN*, 21 (1993), 57–63.

———, 'Zhitie statskogo sovetnika Mikhaila Abramova' (typescript).

Shafirov, P., *A Discourse Concerning the Just Causes of the War between Sweden and Russia: 1700–1721*, with an introduction by W. E. Butler (Dobbs Ferry, NY, 1973).

Shapiro, A. L., 'O fundamental'nom izdanii dokumentov "Pis'ma i bumagi Petra Velikogo"', *Istoriia SSSR*, 1968, no. 1, 231–3.

Sharaia, N. M., *Voskovaia persona* (L, 1963).

Sharandak, N. P., *Russkaia portretnaia zhivopis' petrovskogo vremeni* (L, 1987).

Sharymov, A., 'Byl li Petr I osnovatelem Sankt-Peterburga?', *Avrora*, 1992, nos 7/8, 106–65.

Shaw, D., 'Geographical Practice and its Significance in Peter the Great's Russia', *Journal of Historical Geography*, 22 (1996), 160–76.

Shcherbatov, M. M., *Istoriia imperatora Petra Velikogo ot rozhdeniia ego do Poltavskoi batalii* (SPb., 1773).

———, *On the Corruption of Morals in Russia*, ed. and trans. A. Lentin (Cambridge, 1969).

———, 'Petition of the City of Moscow on Being Relegated to Oblivion', in M. Raeff, ed., *Russian Intellectual History: An Anthology* (New York, 1966), 49–60.

Shchukinskii sbornik, vol. 8 (M, 1909), vol. 9 (M, 1910).

Sheremetev, B. P., *Perepiska* (SPb., 1750).

———, *Zapiski puteshestviia generala feldmarshala ... grafa B. P. Sheremeteva v evropeiskie gosudarstva* (M, 1773).

Shitsgal, A. G., ed., *Grazhdanskii shrift pervoi chetverti XVIII veka 1708–1725* (M, 1981).

Shmurlo, E., 'Petr Velikii v istoricheskoi literature: istoriko-bibliograficheskii obzor', *ZhMNP*, 22 (1889), 57–121, 305–75.

——, *Petr Velikii v otsenke sovremennikov i potomstva* (SPb., 1912).

Shubinsky, S. N., *Letnii sad i letnie peterburgskie uveseleniia pri Petre Velikom* (SPb., 1864).

'Shutki i potekhi Petra Velikogo. Vsep'ianeishii sobor', *Russkaia starina*, 5/6 (June 1872), 845–92.

Shutoi, V. E., *Bor'ba narodnykh mass protiv nashestviia armii Karla XII 1700–1709* (M, 1958).

Shvorina, T., *Voennye artikuly Petra I* (M, 1940).

Simonov, R. A., 'Kogda rodilsia Petr I?', *Vspomogatel'nye istoricheski distsipliny*, 21 (1990), 158–69.

Sindalovsky, N. A., *Legendy i mify Sankt-Peterburga* (SPb., 1994).

Sivkov, K. V., 'Petr-pisatel'', in *Tri veka*, vol. 3 (M, 1917), 34–57.

Smirnov, N. A., *Zapadnoe vlianie na russkii iazyk v petrovskuiu epokhu* (SPb., 1910).

Sobranie sobstvennoruchnykh pisem Petra V-ogo k Apraksinu, 2 vols (M, 1811).

Soloviev, S.M. *History of Russia*, vol. 25: *Rebellion and Reform. Fedor and Sophia 1682–1689*, trans. L. Hughes (Gulf Breeze, Fla., 1989).

——, *Istoriia Rossii s drevneishikh vremen*, bk 7 (M, 1962).

Spassky, I. G., *The Russian Monetary System* (Amsterdam, 1967).

——, and Shchukina, E., *Medals and Coins of the Age of Peter the Great* (L, 1974).

Spunde, A. P., 'Ocherk ekonomicheskoi istorii russkoi burzhuazii', *Nauka i zhizn'*, 1988, no. 1, 79–82.

Stählin, J., *Originalanekdoten von Peter dem Grossen* (Leipzig, 1785/1988).

Staniukovich, T. V., *Kunstkamera Peterburgskoi Akademii nauk* (M&L, 1953).

Stasov, V. V., *Gallereia Petra Velikogo v imp. Publichnoi biblioteke* (SPb., 1903).

Stevens, C. B., *Soldiers on the Steppe. Army Reform and Social Change in Early Modern Russia* (De Kalb, Ill., 1995).

Strahlenberg, F. J., *Das Nord- und Östliche Theil von Europea un Asia* (Stockholm, 1730).

——, *Zapiski kapitana Filippa Ioganna Stralenberga ob istorii i geografii Rossiiskoi imperii Petra Velikogo*, trans. and ed. Iu. Bespiatykh et al., 2 vols (M&L, 1985).

S-tskii, A., 'Russkaia preobrazovannaia zhenshchina v epokhu Petra Velikogo', *Russkii mir*, 1859, nos. 29–32, 663–4, 675–6, 686–8, 696–700.

Subtelny, O., 'Mazepa, Peter I, and the Question of Treason', *Harvard Ukrainian Studies*, 2 (1978), 158–84.

Suknovalov, A. E., 'Pervaia v Rossii voenno-morskaia shkola', *IZ*, 42 (1953), 301–6.

Sumner. B., *Peter the Great and the Emergence of Russia* (London, 1958).

——, *Peter the Great and the Ottoman Empire* (Oxford, 1949).

'Sviatki pri Petre I', *Vsemirnaia illiustratsiia*, 7/157 (1872), 7–10.

Syromiatnikov, B. I., *"Reguliarnoe" gosudarstvo Petra I i ego ideologiia* (M&L, 1943).

Tarlovskaia, V. R., 'Iz istorii gorodskoi reformy v Rossii kontsa XVII–nach. XVIII v.', in *Gosudarstvennye uchrezhdeniia Rossii XVI–XVIII vv* (M, 1991), 98–118.

Tel'pukhovsky, B. S., *Severnaia voina* (M, 1946).

Tikhonov, Iu. A.,*Pomeshchich'i krest'iane v Rossii. Feodol'naia renta v XVII—nachiale XVIII v.* (M, 1974).

Titova, L., 'Iz istorii teatral'noi zhizni v epokhu Petra I', *Sovetskoe slavianovedenie*, 1972, no. 5, 53–9.

Torke, H. J. 'Crime and Punishment in the Pre-Petrine Civil Service', in E. Mendelsohn and M. Shatz, eds, *Imperial Russia 1700–1917. State. Society. Opposition. Essays in Honor of Marc Raeff* (De Kalb, Ill., 1988), 5–21.

Toshchev, A. I., 'Petrovskie "Vedomosti" kak tip izdaniia', *XVIII vek*, 16 (1989), 184–99.

Treasures of the Czars from the State Museums of the Moscow Kremlin. Presented by Florida International Museum St Petersburg (London, 1995).

Trediakovsky, V. K., *Izbrannye proizvedeniia* (M&L, 1963).

Troitsky, S. M., 'Iz istorii sozdaniia Tabeli o rangakh', *Istoriia SSSR*, (1974), no. 1, 98–111.

Trudy imp. Russkogo voenno-istoricheskogo obshchestva, vols 1–4 (SPb., 1909).

Tryal of the Czarewitz Alexis Petrowitz, who was Condemn'd at Petersbourg, on the 25th of June, 1718, The (London, 1725).

'Tsarevich Aleksei Petrovich po svidetel'stvam vnov' otkrytim', *Chteniia*, 1861, bk 3, 34.

'Tsaritsa Ekaterina Alekseevna, supruga Petra Velikogo v 1707–1713 gg.', *Russkaia starina*, 28/8 (1880), 758–66.

Ulanov, V., 'Oppozitsiia Petru Velikomu', in *Tri veka* (M, 1912), 63–86.

Ul'ianov, N. I., 'Petrovskie reformy (K voprosu o meste Petra I v otechestvennoi istorii'), *Sanktpeterburgskaia panorama*, 5 (1992), 3–4, 16–18; also in V. Shechkarev, ed., *Otkliki: sbornik statei pamiati N.I. Ul'ianova (1904–1985)* (New Haven, 1986), 9–28.

Urness, C., 'Rybakov on the Delisle Map of 1706', in L. Hughes, ed., *New Perspectives on Muscovite History. Selected Papers from the Fourth World Congress for Soviet and East European Studies, Harrogate 1990* (London, 1993), 24–34.

Uspensky, B. A., 'Historia sub specie Semioticae', in H. K. Baran, ed., *Semiotics and Structuralism. Readings from the Soviet Union* (New York, 1976), 64–75.

———, 'Tsar and Pretender: *Samozvancestvo* or Royal Imposture in Russia as a Cultural-Historical Phenomenon', in Ju. Lotman and B. A. Uspensky, eds, *The Semiotics of Russian Culture* (Ann Arbor, 1984), 269–71.

Ustrialov, N., *Istoriia tsarstvovaniia Petra Velikogo*, 6 vols (SPb., 1858–69).

———, *Lefort i potekhi Petra Velikogo* (SPb., 1851).

Varlamova, N. A., 'Tserkovnaia reforma Petra I v rabotakh sovetskikh istorikov', in *Problemy izucheniia i prepodavaniia istoriografii istorii SSSR v vysshei skole* (Syktyvkar, 1989), 127–31.

Vasil'chikov, A. A., 'O novom portrete Petra Velikogo', *Drevniaia i novaia Rossiia*, 3 (1877) 325–6.

———, *O portretakh Petra Velikogo. Issledovaniia* (M, 1872).

Vasil'ev, A. A., 'O sostave russkoi i shvedskoi armii v Poltavskom srazhenii', *Voenno-istoricheskii zhurnal*, 1989, no. 7, 59–67.

Vasil'ev, V. I., *Starinnye feierverki v Rossii (XVII–perv. ch. XVIII v.)* (L, 1960).

Vasil'ev, V. N., 'Sochinenie A. K. Nartova "Teatrum makhinarium" (K istorii peter-burgskoi tokarni Petra I)', *Trudy Gosudarstvennogo Ermitazha*, 3 (1959), 70–8.

Vasil'eva, L., 'Zhenskaia revoliutsiia Petra Velikogo', *Nauka i religiia*, 1997, no. 1, 4–11; no. 2, 16–21; no. 3, 10–15.

Vedomosti vremeni Petra Velikogo, vol. 1: *1703–1707* (M, 1903); vol. 2: *1708–1719* (M, 1906).

Verkhovskoy, P. V., *Uchrezhdenie Dukhovnoi Kollegii i Dukhovnyi reglament*, 2 vols (Rostov/Don, 1916).

Vernadsky, G., *A Source Book for Russian History*, vol. 2 (New Haven, 1972).

Veselago, F. F., 'Dedushka russkogo flota', *Russkaia starina*, 4 (1871), 463–82.

Viktorov, A., *Opisanie zapisnykh knig i bumag starinnykh dvortsovykh prikazov, 1613–1725*, 2 vols (M, 1883).

Vil'bua, F., 'Rasskazy o rossiiskom dvore [XVIII v.]', *VI*, 1 (1992), 139–55.

Vilinbakhov, G. V., 'K istorii uchrezhdeniia ordena Andreia Pervozvannogo', in *Kul'tura i iskusstvo petrovskogo vremeni* (L, 1977), 144–8.

———, 'Otrazhenie idei absoliutizma v simvolike Petrovskikh znamen', in *Kul'tura i iskusstvo Rossii XVIII veka. Novye materialy i issledovaniia. Sbornik statei* (L, 1981), 7–25.

———, *Russkoe iskusstvo epokhi barokko (Katalog)* (L, 1984).

Vockerodt, J. G., *Rossiia pri Petre Velikom po rukopisnomu izvestiiu Ioanna Gottgil'fa Fokkerodta* (SPb., 1874).

Vodarsky, Ia. E., *Dvorianskoe zemlevladenie v Rossii v XVII–pervoi pol. XIX vv.* (M, 1988).

———, *Naselenie Rossii v kontse XVII–nach. XVIII veka* (M, 1977).

———, 'Petr I', *VI*, 1993, no. 6, 59–78.

Voennye ustavy Petra Velikogo (M, 1946).

Vossler, K., ' "Russische Zustände am Ende des 17. Jahrhunderts" nach dem Zeugnis eines italienischen Sängers', *Arkhiv für Slavische Philologie*, 39 (1925), 150–8.

Vozgrin, V. E., *Istoricheskie sud'by krymskikh tatar* (M, 1992).

———, *Rossiia i evropeiskie strany v gody Severnoi voiny* (L, 1986).

Vucinich, A., *Science in Russian Culture. A History to 1860* (London, 1963).

Warner, R., 'The Kožuchovo Campaign of 1694', *JGO*, 13/4 (1965), 487–96.

Whitworth, C., *An Account of Russia as it was in the Year 1710. Rossiia v nachale XVIII veka. Sochineniia Ch. Uitvorta* (M&L, 1988).

Widmer, E., *The Russian Ecclesiastical Mission in Peking during the Eighteenth Century* (Cambridge, Mass., 1976).

Wirtschafter, E. K., *Structures of Society. Imperial Russia's 'People of Various Ranks'* (De Kalb, Ill., 1995).

Wittram, R., *Peter I. Czar und Kaiser*, 2 vols (Göttingen, 1964).

Wortman, R., *The Development of a Russian Legal Consciousness* (Chicago, 1976).

———, 'Peter the Great and Court Procedure', *CASS*, 8 (1974), 303–11.

———, *Scenarios of Power, Myth and Ceremony in Russian Monarchy*, vol. 1 (Princeton, 1995).

Zakharov, V. N., 'Denezhnyi kredit zapadnoevropeiskikh kuptsov Rossii v pervoi chet. XVIII v. i ego rol' v razvitii russkoi torgovli', *Russkii gorod*, 9 (1990), 165–81.

Zaozerskaia, E. I., *Manufaktura pri Petre I* (M&L, 1947).

———, *Razvitie legkoi promyshlennosti* (M, 1953).

Zaozersky, A. I., 'Fel'dmarshal Sheremetev i pravitel'stvennaia sreda Petrovskogo vremeni', in *RPR*, 172–98.

'Zapiski diuka Liiriskogo u Berikovskogo', in *Russkii arkhiv*, (1909), no. 1, 377–442.

Zapiski Iakoba Shtelina ob iziashchnykh iskusstvakh v Rossii, ed. K. V. Malinovsky, 2 vols (M, 1990).

Zapiski Ivana Ivanovicha Nepliueva (1693–1773) (SPb., 1893).

'Zapiski o vazhneishikh vnutrennikh proisshestviiakh i uchrezhdeniiakh v Rossii s 1707 po 1712 god', *Severnyi arkhhiv*, 20/5 (1826), 3–38.

Zapisnaia knizhka liubopytnykh zamechanii Velikoi osoby, stranstvovavshei pod imeni dvorianina Rossiiskogo posol'stva v 1697 i 1698 gg. (SPb., 1788).

Zernova, A. S., *Svodnyi katalog russkoi knigi kirillovskoi pechati XVIII veka* (M, 1968).

Zharkova, I. M., 'Zhivopisets petrovskogo vremeni Iogann Genrikh Vedekind', in *Soobshcheniia Gosudarstvennoi Tret'iakovskoi Galerei. Drevnerusskoe iskusstvo. Iskusstvo XVIII–pervoi poloviny XIX veka* (M, 1995), 64–78.

Zheliabuzhsky, I. A., 'Zapiski', in A. B. Bogdanov, ed., *Rossiia pri tsarevne Sof'e i Petre I* (M, 1990), 201–327.

Zhivov, V. M., 'Azbuchnaia reforma Petra I kak semioticheskoe preobrazovanie', *Uchenye zapiski Tartuskogo gos. universiteta*, 720 (1986), 55–66.

———, 'Kul'turnye reformy v sisteme preobrazovaniia Petra I' in *Iz istorii russkoi kul'tury. Tom III (XVII–nachalo XVIII veka)* (M, 1996), 528–83.

———, and Uspensky, B. A., 'Tsar' i Bog: Semioticheskie aspekty sakralizatsii monarkha v Rossii', in B. A. Uspensky, ed., *Iazyki kul'tury i problemy perevodimosti* (M, 1987), 47–154.

Zhurnal ili podennaia zapiska Blazhennyia i vechnodostoinnyia pamiati gos. imp. Petra Velikago s 1698 goda, dazhe do zakliuchenia neishtatskogo mira, 2 vols (SPb., 1770–2).

Index

Key references (e.g. biographical data) are listed at the beginning of entries. Towns and rivers are included selectively, e.g., when they are the sites of battles and sieges. Selected thematic references only are made to Moscow, St Petersburg and Peter himself.

INDEX